AMERICA'S GREATEST PLACES TO WORK WITH A LAW DEGREE

AND HOW TO MAKE THE MOST OF ANY JOB, NO MATTER WHERE IT IS!

By Kimm Alayne Walton, J.D.

HARCOURT BRACE LEGAL & PROFESSIONAL PUBLICATIONS, INC.
Editorial Offices: 111 West Jackson, 7th Floor, Chicago, IL 60604
Regional Offices: Chicago, Dallas, Los Angeles, New York, Washington, D.C.

Distributed by:
HARCOURT BRACE AND COMPANY
6277 Sea Harbor Drive, Orlando, FL 32887-6777
Phone: 1-800-787-8717
Fax: 1-800-433-6303

Requests for permission to make copies of any part of the work should be mailed to: Customer Service, Harcourt Brace Legal & Professional Publications, Inc., 6277 Sea Harbor Drive, Orlando, FL 32887-6777.

Printed in the United States of America.

Reprint Permissions:

Chapter 3:

- Profiles of Peter J. Carton and Sean Johnson, from "Beyond L.A. Law," published by Harcourt Brace. Reprinted with permission.

- Profiles of Glenn Gulino and Jack Ford, from "Alternative Careers for Lawyers," by Hillary Mantis. Reprinted with permission.

Chapter 12:

- Chart of federal courts and overall structure of "Judicial Clerkship" section, reprinted with permission from Yale Law School.

HARCOURT BRACE
Legal & Professional Publications, Inc

Harcourt Brace Legal & Professional Publications offers a variety of products and services for professionals, including Gilbert Law Summaries, Legalines, Bar/Bri Bar Review, and Conviser Duffy CPA Review. For a complete listing of products and services visit Harcourt Brace on the Web at www.gilbertlaw.com, or contact: Harcourt Brace Legal & Professional Publications, Inc., 111 West Jackson, 7th Floor, Chicago, IL 60604. Phone: 1-800-782-1272. Fax: 1-312-360-1842.

"Strike while the iron is."

The message my friend Leslie once found in a fortune cookie.

Dedication

*This book is dedicated to my extraordinary father,
Dr. Alan Walton. He is not only the smartest person and
best card player I've ever known, but he had the incredible
restraint to express only support and encouragement
when, as a freshly-minted law school graduate, I told him:
"Dad, I'm not going to work for that firm in New York.
I think I want to be a writer."
Thank you for helping to make my life so wonderful, Dad.
I love you.*

Acknowledgements

Like the old Cecil B. de Mille movies, this is a book that features a cast of thousands—from people who offered their expertise on who great employers *are*, to all of the people *at* those wonderful employers who took the time to share what makes their jobs so terrific.

You should know right off the bat that I don't personally *know* anything, but fortunately a bunch of really smart people have been exceptionally generous in sharing their expertise with *me*, so I could put it into this book for *you*. First among these are the many wonderful law school administrators around the country who put me onto the employers who appear in this book, and who also supplied all kinds of wonderful advice about how to make the most of any job you have. They are all incredible people, devoting their professional lives to helping other people—law students—make their dreams come true. If you go to a law school where any of them work, and you like this book—seek them out, shake their hand, and thank them. They *deserve* it!

Lucy Allard, Seattle University School of Law
Laurie Allbright, University of Colorado School of Law
Carol Allemeier, Pepperdine University School of Law
Elizabeth Armour, Boston University School of Law
Drusilla Bakert, University of Kentucky College of Law
Sarah Joan Bales, Loyola University Chicago School of Law
Diane Ballou, University of Connecticut School of Law
William Barrett, Jr., Wake Forest University School of Law
Pat Bass, Mercer University School of Law
Anthony Bastone, University of Colorado School of Law
Laurie Beck, Brooklyn Law School
Gerald Beechum, University of Missouri at Columbia School of Law
Amy Berenson, UCLA College of Law
Mary Birmingham, University of Arizona School of Law
Elaine Bourne, Dickinson Law School at the Pennsylvania State University
Kathleen Brady, Fordham University School of Law
Carolyn Bregman, Emory University School of Law
Mark Brickson, University of North Dakota School of Law
Collins Byrd, University of Minnesota Law School
Nancy Carver, George Washington University School of Law
James Castro-Blanco, St. John's University School of Law
Camille Chin-Kee-Fatt, Brooklyn Law School
Stephanie Rever Chu, Chicago-Kent College of Law
Catherine Comeaux, University of Texas School of Law

Marci Cox, Miami University School of Law
Donna Daugherty, University of Texas School of Law
Bernice Davenport, Thomas M. Cooley Law School
Elizabeth Davis, Northwestern University Lewis & Clark College of
   Law
John DeRosa, Brooklyn Law School
Michael Doty, Vanderbilt University School of Law
Eric Eden, Western New England College of Law
Alexandra Epsilanty, Syracuse University School of Law
Brian Ferrell, Creighton University School of Law
Neal Fillmore, DePaul University School of Law
Kristin Flierl, Tulane University School of Law
Norma Gaier, St. Mary's University School of Law
Jose Bahamonde Gonzalez, University of Maryland School of Law
Steven Hargrove, Emory University School of Law
Louis Helmuth, California Western School of Law
Suzanne Alexander Holmes, University of Colorado School of Law
Skip Horne, University of Texas School of Law
Kitty Cooney Hoye, Notre Dame University School of Law
Annette Jones, University of Texas School of Law
Laura Share Kalin, Harvard Law School
Valerie Kapilow, Northeastern University School of Law
Robert Kaplan, William & Mary College of Law
Joan King, Brooklyn Law School
Beth Kirch, University of Georgia School of Law
Cheryl Kitchen, Ohio Northern University School of Law
Audrey Koscielniak, SUNY School of Law at Buffalo
Joyce Laher, Hamline University School of Law
Laura Rowe Lane, George Washington University School of Law
Lisa Lesage, Northwestern University Lewis & Clark College of Law
Merv Loya, University of Oregon School of Law
Sarah Madden, formerly of Northern Kentucky University School of Law
Karen Maheu, Detroit College of Law at Michigan State University
Pam Malone, Vanderbilt University School of Law
Hillary Mantis, Fordham Law School
Meredith McQuiad, University of Minnesota Law School
Chris Miller, University of Pittsburgh School of Law
Terri Mische, University of Minnesota Law School
Suzanne Mitchell, The University of Chicago, The Law School
Mary Obrzut, Northern Illinois University College of Law
Pam Occhipinti, Loyola University School of Law
Jacqueline Ortega, University of San Francisco School of Law
Susan Palmer, Washington & Lee University School of Law
Gail Peshel, Valparaiso University School of Law
Janet Griffin Pittman, Regent University Law School

Gloria Pyszka, Stanford University School of Law
Jeanette Rader, Sanford University Cumberland School of Law
Susan Richey, Franklin Pierce Law Center
Mary Karen Rogers, Suffolk University Law School
Joann Rothery, University of Tennessee College of Law
Gina Rowsam, Oklahoma City University School of Law
Gina Sauer, William Mitchell College of Law
Ann Skalaski, University of Florida College of Law
Susan Spalter, Quinnipiac College of Law
Jane Steckbeck, University of Oregon School of Law
Mary Brennan Stich, St. Mary's University School of Law
Debra Strauss, Yale Law School
Suzanne Thorpe, University of Minnesota Law School
Fred Thrasher, William & Mary College of Law
Kelly Townes, Indiana University School of Law
Marilyn Tucker, Georgetown University Law Center
Caroline Vinyl, Syracuse University School of Law
Anne Stark Walker, University of Denver College of Law
Deidre Washington, St. Thomas University Law School
Susan Kalb Weinberg, University of Michigan School of Law
Barbara Weinzierl, Case Western Reserve University School of Law
Wendy Werner, St. Louis University School of Law
James Whitters III, Suffolk University Law School
Joyce Whittington, University of Mississippi School of Law
Rebekah Woods, Regent University Law School

On top of these named sources, there were many law school administrators, as well as people at government agencies, corporations, public interest employers, and people in a whole slew of other positions who spoke with me on condition of anonymity. You know who you are, and I thank you.

A special thank you goes to the incomparable Susan Gainen of the University of Minnesota Law School, who dragged herself from a sickbed to contribute everything on the law school administration jobs you find in Chapter 12.

I would also like to thank the Career Services Offices at Quinnipiac Law School and St. Mary's School of Law for letting me use their libraries—and Xerox like crazy.

I must also thank the following people who made special contributions to this book:

Chris Raistrick   Jill E. Burtis
Jane Reinhardt   Chip Lipscomb
Rich Colangelo   Ellen Titlebaum
Jack Swarbrick   Douglas Kmiec
Michael McCartney   Laura Brewer

Valerie Cohen
Marcia Goodman
David James
Paula Vickers
George Jameson
Richard Garrett
Adam Epstein

Tracy Smith
Rachel Zelkind
Theresa Murray Hughes
Abel Montez
Frank Kara
Linda Aaker

No book I write would be possible without my brother Keir's encouragement and insights. I get all the credit for the books I write, but most of them are Keir's idea. I'm pretty sure this one was as well. Keirbo—without you I'm nothing.

Much of the reason you can hold this book in your hot little hands is the hard work of Stephanie Kartofels of Harcourt Brace, who came onto the scene very late and was the magician midwife for this monster project. You are a miracle worker Stephanie. I would also like to thank Norah Faigen and Cathy Szillage of Harcourt Brace, who are eternally cheerful when dealing with a sometimes whiny Kimmbo. Speaking of Harcourt, I would like to thank "the man", Richard Conviser, who has not only been behind this project from its inception, but who took the news that his former law firm wouldn't be in the book with such good grace.

Thank you also to Rosemary Kocis of Oxford Bioscience Partners, who faithfully collected all of the faxes from employers. *Hundreds* of faxes. And in the same vein, thank you to Tom, Jack, and George of the Greens Farms Post Office, who collected box after box of material from employers for me, without a single complaint. You often read about disgruntled post office employees, and I am happy that the three I see all the time are the most gruntled post officers imaginable.

On a personal note, I would like to thank my wonderful fiancé, Henry, who stoically tolerated our townhouse looking like an explosion in a paper factory as I worked on this book. I love you Lambchop. I would also like to thank my nieces, Emily and Hailey Walton, and the mom who is doing such an incredible job raising them to be wonderful human beings, my sister-in-law Ellie Walton. Whenever I get too wrapped up in grown up-type problems—like book deadlines—Em and Hailey remind me of what's really important. And by the way, Hailey, *you're* the tooty-face.

And I would especially like to thank the many thousands of law school students and graduates who have come to my seminars at law schools around the country, and who write to me, as the Job Goddess, sharing anecdotes and dreams with me. You make every single day of my professional life a joy. I fervently hope this book will help you make your dreams come true. You deserve it.

KIMM ALAYNE WALTON
WILTON, CONNECTICUT

Disclaimer

This is the section that makes lawyers at publishing houses very happy—the part where I tell you about anything that would suggest bias when it comes to the employers who appear in this book.

I found all of the employers via objective third party sources - namely, law school administrators. No employer appearing in this book paid to be included. (A couple of employers not appearing here *did* call and sort of subtly offer me bribes to include them, but I didn't take the bait. It wasn't like they offered me very much of anything, anyway.)

The most that employers in the book got was the opportunity to review what I wrote about them in order to correct any factual inaccuracies. Some of them proposed editorial changes which I mostly didn't make. I don't take direction well. That's why I was fired from every job I ever had, and what sort of forced me to become a writer.

The only two legal employers I've ever worked for are not included in this book. The first, a small firm I clerked for after my first year in law school, is too small to be included here, and that's a shame because they were terrific. The second is a large firm I clerked for after second year. They certainly fit the size criteria for firms in this book, but they were miserable schmucks and fortunately for my integrity, they got uniformly bad reviews from everybody I talked to. Really. And I'm not going to tell you who they are. Suffice it to say that on the last day of my summer clerkship they told me, "Kimm, some people just aren't good enough." It took me several years to be able to say, authoritatively: I guess some firms aren't either.

On the other hand, there are several employers in this book with whom I interviewed as a law student, but they didn't make me an offer. *They* don't even know who they are, so obviously— no hard feelings.

I am not represented by any law firm in this book. My lawyer is Joe Meuser, a very nice man in Bridgeport, Connecticut. Whenever I want advice, I go visit Joe, he cracks open a couple of beers for us, and then he says, "So what's the problem?" He's not in this book because he works alone.

When it comes to my publisher, Harcourt Brace, you need to know that they own Bar/Bri, and Bar/Bri *is* in this book. Again, Bar/Bri was recommended to me by law school administrators—in fact, most of them didn't realize when they recommended Bar/Bri that it was owned by Harcourt. So that's legit, too.

And I think that's just about it.

TABLE OF CONTENTS

America's Greatest Places To Work With A Law Degree . . . And How To Make The Most Of Any Job, No Matter Where It Is!

Dedication iv
Acknowledgments v
Disclaimer ix
Fast-Find Index—All Employers Listed Alphabetically xix

CHAPTER 1

How Employers Made It Into *America's Greatest Places*—And Why There Are Great Employers Who *Aren't* In It! 1

CHAPTER 2

The Sometimes Surprising Traits That Great Employers Share . . . And Insider Tips for Smoking Out Whether the Employer You're Considering Will Make You Happy. 11

The Nineteen Qualities That Count 13

Danger, Will Robinson! Factors to Watch Out For 24

Doing Your Own Sleuthing: How Do You Smoke Out Employers
Who Will Make You Happy? 28

CHAPTER 3

Ultimate Dream Jobs: The Glamorous Sports, Entertainment, International, and Headline-Making Employers That Most Law Students Only Dream About. 37

Sᴘᴏʀᴛs 40

What's Out There? Traditional and Non-Traditional Careers in Sports 41

Breaking Into the Sports Industry 44

Sports Guru Jack Swarbrick's "Do's" and "Don'ts" ....

Great Internships That Get Your Foot in the Door · · · · · · · · · · 48

The U.S. Olympic Committee · 49

Names, Addresses and Phone Numbers of Professional Sports Teams in
Football, Basketball, Baseball and Hockey · · · · · · · · · · · · · · · 49

Exceptionally Useful Associations, Conferences, Web Sites and Books · · · · · · · 59

What It's Like to Work in Sports: A Profile of Peter J. Carton, Jr.,
Director of Southeast Asia, Australia, and New Zealand
Operations for Major League Baseball International · · · · · · · · · · · · 61

Sports Employers Receiving Rave Reviews · 63

Profile of a Great Sports Employer: The National Football League · · · · · · · · · · 64

Entertainment · 67

What You Need to Know to Break In · 67

Profile of a Great Entertainment Employer: The Walt Disney Company · · · · · 69

What It's Like to be a Talent Agent: A Profile of Glenn Gulino,
an Agent With The William Morris Agency. · · · · · · · · · · · · · · · · · 75

Glenn Gulino's Advice for Lawyers Interested in the
Entertainment Industry · 77

What It's Like To Be A Television Personality: A Profile of
Former Litigator Jack Ford, NBC News Chief Legal
Correspondent and Co-Anchor of *Today, Weekend Edition* · · · · · · · 77

What It's Like to Work at MTV: A Profile of Sean A. Joell Johnson,
Counsel for Law and Business Affairs at MTV · · · · · · · · · · · · 80

Great Internships That Get Your Foot in the Door in the
Entertainment Industry · 82

The Academy of Motion Picture Arts and Sciences · · · · · · · · · · · · · 83

MCA/Universal · 83

National Public Radio · 84

Entertainment Employers Who Received Rave Reviews · · · · · · · · · · · · 85

International · 86

What You Need to Know to Break In · 86

The U.S. Foreign Service · 87

The Central East European Law Initiative · · · · · · · · · · · · · · · · · · 90

**Beer! Toys! Great In-House Counsel Jobs At
Companies In Sexy Industries** · · · · · · · · · · · · · · · · · · · 94

Mattel · 95

Anheuser Busch · 98

Jobs In Paradise · 100

Clerking for the Supreme Court of Hawaii · · · · · · · · · · · · · · · · · · 100

Visiting Professorships in Malibu, at Pepperdine Law School · · · · · · · · · · 103

To Boldly Go Where No Lawyer Has Gone Before · · · · · · · · · · 106

Intellectual Property at NASA 106

THE PLUMMIEST OF PLUM JUDICIAL CLERKSHIPS 109

Clerking for the United States Supreme Court 109

CHAPTER 4

The #1 All-Around Best Legal Employer in America—
The United States Department of Justice 115

CHAPTER 5

The Law Firms. 143

How to Read Profiles 145

Profiles for Firms With 15 to 1200+ attorneys 147

CHAPTER 6

How to Find Great Firms Too Small to Be Included in This Book. 677

What Kinds of Small Firms *Are* There? 680

What It's Like to Work at a Small Firm 681

How Small Firms Do Their Hiring 683

What Small Firms Look for in People They Hire 684

How to Find Small Firms—More Importantly, How to
Find *Good* Small Firms! 686

How to Get Around the "One to Three Years of Experience"
That Many Small Firms Ask for in Job Ads 690

A Snapshot of Small-Firm Life: Brett & Daugert,
Bellingham, Washington 691

CHAPTER 7

Where the Bucks Are: Where to Work When What You're After
is Money, Money, Money. (Pssst: You Might Even Enjoy It.) 697

CHAPTER 8

The Corporations. 709

Dear Job Goddess: I'd Like to Be In-House Counsel 711

What You Ought to Know About Being in a Corporation's
Legal Department, Including Things People Like
About Working for Companies 714

The Experience Corporations Seek for In-House Counsel Jobs—
It May Not Be What You Think! 715

Corporate Jobs Your Law Degree Can Help You Get,
Outside of the Legal Department—And Get a Grip on
What You Bring to the Table! · 717
Doing Your Own Research on Companies: Useful Resources
at Your Fingertips · 721
The Corporations Receiving Rave Reviews: Profiles · · · · · · · · · · · · · · · · 722

CHAPTER 9

The Crusaders! Great Public Interest Jobs. · · · · · · · 765
Introduction · 767
Helpful Web Sites · 769
Fourteen Ways to Break Into Public Interest Law · · · · · · · · · · · · 770
Public Interest Employers Receiving Rave Reviews:
Nationwide Organizations—Public Defenders,
Legal Services, Legal Aid · 772
Trade Unions · 785
Public Interest Organizations in One (or Just a Few) Cities · · · · · · · · · 791

CHAPTER 10

Great Government Jobs—Federal, State, and Local. · · · · · · · · · 817
FEDERAL AGENCIES · 819
Twelve Things You Need to Know About Working for the
Federal Government (Including Web Sites, Starting Salaries,
and Application Information) · · · · · · · · · · · · · · · · · · 819
A Salacious Little Tidbit About Government Web Pages · · · 822
The Agencies Receiving Rave Reviews · · · · · · · · · · · 822
STATE GOVERNMENT · · · · · · · · · · · · · · · · · 874
State Attorney Generals' Offices (Including Contact
Information and Web Sites for All Fifty States) · · · · · · · · · · 874
Writing Legislation for States · · · · · · · · · · · · · · · · 885
LOCAL GOVERNMENT · · · · · · · · · · · · · · · · · 889
City Attorneys' Offices, Featuring the San Diego City Attorney's Office · · · · · 889

CHAPTER 11

Prosecutors (Federal and Local). · · · · · · · · · · · · · 899
Federal Prosecutors—The U.S. Attorneys Office · · · · · · · · · · · · 901
District Attorney's and State's Attorney's Offices · · · · · · · · · · · 904

CHAPTER 12

Great Alternative Careers You Probably Haven't Thought About. 913

JUDICIAL CLERKSHIPS AND RELATED COURT JOBS 915

The Spinal Tap *'But This List Goes to Eleven'* Set of
Great Reasons to Consider a Judicial Clerkship 916

Common Misconceptions About Judicial Clerkships . . .
Like *'My Grades Aren't Good enough'* 919

Early Preparation—How to Use Law School to Set
Yourself Up for a Judicial Clerkship
(Including Summer Internships and Externships) 920

What's Out There? The Tons & Tons of Courts that
Employ Judicial Clerks 923

The Clerkship Experience: The Nuts and Bolts of What You Do as a
Clerk in Various Different Kinds of Courts 924

Other Court-Related Jobs (Including Staff Attorneys) 926

A Gold Mine of Frequently-Overlooked Clerkship Opportunities 926

Court and Federal Agencies 927

Categories of Judges 928

How to Get Judicial Clerkships 930

Judicial Clerkship Checklist 930

Choosing a Court and a Judge (Including Courts and Judges
Who Are Known as United States Supreme Court Feeders) 931

Cover Letters, Resumes, Transcripts, Writing Samples,
Letters of Recommendation, Interviewing, Following Up,
Handling Offers and Acceptances, and How to Try Again
if at First You Don't Succeed! 942

Research Sources 943

Hard Copy Sources 943

Lexis/Nexis & Westlaw 944

Web Sites 945

THE INTERNET 946

TRADE ASSOCIATIONS (IN BOTH LAWYER AND
NON-TRADITIONAL ROLES) 948

Law School & College Administration Jobs 953

College and University Attorneys 954

Director of Career Services 956

Dean of Students 958

Director of International Programs 959

Director of Judicial Affairs 960

Director of Public Interest Programs In (or Near) a Law School 961

Public Interest Counselor 962

Athletic Department Compliance Offices 964

Director of Admissions 966

Alumni Relations 968

Director of Student Legal Services 969

LAW LIBRARIANSHIPS 971

Dear Job Goddess: How Do I turn a Little Computer Knowledge
and law Degree into Big Bucks?... 971

CHAPTER 13

Handling Debt: How to Take on Your Dream Job When Your Student Loans Make You Think That You Can't Afford It. 975

Do's and Don'ts When It Comes to Law School Debt 978

Three Common Programs for Lowering (or Temporarily
Eliminating Your Student Loan Payments) 979

Helpful Web Sites 980

"*Idealism and Dreams of Saving the World Will Get You so Far,
but Realistically,* You Must Also Eat While Saving the World!"—
Repayment Options: The Experiences of Chris Raistrick,
Who Took a $25,000 Public Interest Job With $90,000 in
Law School Debt—And Made it Work! 980

Ways to Avoid Student Loan Debt in the First Place—Including
My *Phenomenal* 'Mystery Ingredient' Barbecued Chicken 986

How to Save Money Once You're Out of School 989

CHAPTER 14

"Hair on Fire" Days—How to Make the Most of *Any* Job, No Matter *Where* It Is. 991

The 1,640-Hour Interview: The 26 Secrets Every Summer Clerk
Should Know After You Graduate: The 130 "Do's" and "Don'ts" That
Distinguish New Lawyers Headed for the Top 994

Sticks & Stones May Break Your Bones & Words at Work Can Kill You 1076

Upping the Ante: How to Make Thousands More Than You
Thought You Would 1077

CHAPTER 15

Other Books to Read. 1081

CHAPTER 16

How to Get Your Two Cents Into the Next Edition of This Book. 1085

APPENDIX 1

All of the Web Sites Mentioned in This Book. 1089

APPENDIX 2

Geographic Index of Law Firms, Public Interest Employers, and Corporations, by State. 1109

Index—Listing of All Employers by Type (e.g., Law Firms, Government, etc.) . . . 1139

All Employers Listed Alphabetically

All Employers By State 1111
All Employers by Type 1139

The Academy of Motion Picture Arts & Sciences 83
Advantage International 63
Akin, Gump, Strauss, Hauer & Feld, L.L.P.—San Antonio 147
Akin, Gump, Strauss, Hauer & Feld, L.L.P.—Washington D.C. 153
Alston & Bird—Atlanta, GA 581
American Airlines (AMR Corporation) 722
American Civil Liberties Union 783
American Judicature Society 791
Anheuser-Busch Companies, Inc. 98
Arent Fox Kinter Plotkin & Kahn 583
Arms Control Association 792
Armstrong Allen Prewitt Gentry Johnston & Holmes, P.L.L.C. 585
Arnold & Porter 162
Baker & Botts, L.L.P. 170
Baker & Daniels 178
Baker Donelson Bearman & Caldwell, P.C. 586
Baker & Hostetler LLP 185
Balch & Bingham, LLP 588
Bamberger, Foreman, Oswald & Hahn 590
Bar/Bri Bar Review 723
Barnes & Thornburg 191
Bass, Berry & Sims, PLC 591
Beckman, Lawson, Sandler, Snyder & Federoff 593
Best, Best & Krieger L.L.P. 594
Bickerstaff, Heath, Smiley, Pollan, Kever & McDaniel 596
Bingham, Summers, Welsh & Spilman 598
Boult, Cummings, Conners & Berry 599
Brett & Daugert, L.L.P. 692
Brown, Todd & Heyburn PLLC 199
Burns, Doane, Swecker & Mathis, LLP 601

Burns, White & Hickton 208
Carlton, Fields, Ward, Emmanuel, Smith & Cutler, P.A. 214
Carrington, Coleman, Sloman & Blumenthal, L.L.P. 224
CEELI (The American Bar Association Central and
Eastern European Law Initiative) 90
Center for International Environmental Law 793
Central Intelligence Agency 822
Clemens & Spencer 602
The Coca-Cola Company 726
Cohen, Weiss and Simon 603
Columbia/HCA Healthcare Corporation 727
Comptroller of the Currency 828
Consumers Union 794
Cooley Godward L.L.P. 232
Cors & Bassett 604
Cowles & Thompson 236
Cox & Smith, Inc. 605
Crowley, Haughey, Hanson, Toole & Dietrich, PLLP 607
Davis, Polk & Wardwell 243
Davis Wright Tremaine L.L.P. 246
Deloitte & Touche Consulting 706
Department of the Interior 848
Department of State—Office of the Legal Advisor 872
Dinsmore & Shohl, L.L.P. 609
DNA—Legal Services 795
Dominick, Fletcher, Yielding, Wood & Lloyd 611
Dorsey & Whitney, L.L.P. 612
Earthjustice Legal Defense Fund (formerly the Sierra Club) 796
Employment Law Center 798
Environmental Protection Agency 837
Equal Employment Opportunity Commission 834
ESPN (In-House Counsel and Broadcast Headquarters) 63
Federal Bureau of Investigation 839
Federal Communications Commission 843
Federal Defender Program (Chicago) 777
Federal Express (a subsidiary of FDX Corporation) 728
Federal Mediation & Conciliation Service 844
Federal Trade Commission 846
Fish & Richardson P.C. 253
Fliesler Dubb Meyer & Lovejoy 614
Florida Public Service Commission 799

Folger Levin & Kahn LLP 259
Ford Motor Company 729
Foster, Swift, Collins & Smith, P.C. 616
Fowler, White, Gillen, Boggs, Villareal and Banker, P.A. 264
Frost & Jacobs LLP 271
Gardner, Carton & Douglas 276
General Motors Corporation 729
Gentry, Locke, Rakes & Moore 618
Gibson, Dunn & Crutcher, L.L.P. 619
G.L.A.D. (Gay & Lesbian Advocates & Defenders) 801
Goulston & Storrs, P.C. 284
Gray Cary Ware & Freidenrich 621
Gray, Plant, Mooty, Mooty & Bennett, P.A. 292
HBO 85
Heller, Ehrman, White & McAuliffe 623
Hill, Ward & Henderson, P.A. 302
Hillis Clark Martin & Peterson, P.S. 309
Hodgson, Russ, Andrews, Woods & Goodyear, L.L.P. 625
Hoeppner, Wagner & Evans 627
Hogan & Hartson 628
Honeywell, Inc. 731
Host Marriott Corporation 733
Human Rights Watch 802
International Human Rights Law Group 803
Jackson & Kelly 315
Jenkens & Gilchrist, P.C. 322
Jenner & Block 630
Jolley, Urga, Wirth & Woodbury 327
Jones, Day, Reavis & Pogue 332
Jones Vargas 341
Kirkland & Ellis 632
Kirkpatrick & Lockhart L.L.P. 346
Klinedinst, Fliehman & McKillop 353
Kraft Foods (a subsidiary of Phillip Morris) 734
Latham & Watkins—Los Angeles 360
Latham & Watkins—San Diego 367
Latham & Watkins—San Francisco 374
Latham & Watkins—Washington, D.C. 382
LeClair Ryan, P.C. 634
Legal Assistance Foundation of Chicago 806
Lexis-Nexis 735

Lincoln National Corporation · 737
Long Aldridge & Norman L.L.P. · 388
Loomis, Ewert, Parsley, Davis & Gotting, P.C. · · · · · · · · · · · · · 635
Lord, Bissell & Brook · 395
Major League Baseball · 63
Maniei, Herod, Hollanbaugh & Smith, P.C. · · · · · · · · · · · · · · · · · 636
Markowitz, Herbold, Glade & Mehlhaf, PC · · · · · · · · · · · · · · · · · · 401
Masuda, Funai, Eifert & Mitchell · 637
Mattel, Inc. · 95
MCA/Universal · 83
McAndrews, Held & Malloy, Ltd. · 406
McDonald, Hopkins, Burke & Haber Co., LPA · · · · · · · · · · · · · · 412
McDonald's Corporation · 738
McKinsey & Company · 702
Mette, Evans & Woodside P.C. · 638
MGM–United Artists · 85
Microsoft Corporation · 740
Millisor & Nobil Co., LPA · 418
Minnesota Advocates for Human Rights · · · · · · · · · · · · · · · · · · · 809
Moore Ingram Johnson & Steele, L.L.P. · · · · · · · · · · · · · · · · · · · 421
Morrison & Foerster L.L.P.—Irvine · 430
Morrison & Foerster L.L.P.—Los Angeles · · · · · · · · · · · · · · · · · · 433
Morrison & Foerster L.L.P.—New York · 436
Morrison & Foerster L.L.P.—Palo Alto · 442
Morrison & Foerster L.L.P.—San Francisco · · · · · · · · · · · · · · · · · 427
Morrison & Foerster L.L.P.—Washington, D.C. · · · · · · · · · · · · · · 439
Motorola · 741
MTV · 85
NAACP Legal Defense and Education Fund · · · · · · · · · · · · · · · · · · 810
The National Aeronautics & Space Administration (NASA) · · · · · 106
National Basketball Association (NBA) · 52
National Collegiate Athletic Association (NCAA) · · · · · · · · · · · · · 63
National Football League (NFL) · 64
National Hockey League (NHL) · 54
National Labor Relations Board · 860
National Park Service (part of the Department of the Interior) · · 849
National Public Radio · 84
The Nature Conservancy · 811
Nelson Mullins Riley & Scarborough, L.L.P. · · · · · · · · · · · · · · · · · 640
Niles, Hansen & Davies, Ltd. · 642
Norfolk Southern Corporation · 744

O'Connor, Cavanagh, Anderson, Killingworth & Beshears 643
Office of the San Diego City Attorney 890
O'Melveny & Myers 645
Overseas Private Investment Corporation 861
Paramount Pictures 85
Parker, Hudson, Rainer & Dobbs LLP 445
Partners HealthCare System, Inc. 745
Perkins Coie L.L.P.—Los Angeles 467
Perkins Coie L.L.P.—Portland 457
Perkins Coie L.L.P.—Seattle 451
Perkins Coie L.L.P.—Washington, D.C. 462
Pretzel & Stouffer 647
Proskauer Rose LLP 470
Procter & Gamble 747
Public Counsel Law Center 812
Qualcomm 753
Railroad Retirement Board 864
Rendigs, Fry, Kiely & Dennis 648
Robinson, Bradshaw & Hinson, P.A. 649
Sachnoff & Weaver 651
Securities & Exchange Commission 865
Shell Oil Company 755
Shook, Hardy & Bacon L.L.P. 478
Shumaker, Loop & Kendrick, LLP 486
Sidley & Austin 491
Snell & Wilmer L.L.P. 501
The Solicitor's Office (part of the Department of the Interior) 850
State Attorney General's Offices, listed by state 874
Steel Hector & Davis, L.L.P. 652
Steptoe & Johnson 510
Stewart & Irwin, P.C. 654
Stites & Harbison 518
Stradley, Ronon, Stevens & Young, L.L.P. 655
Strasburger & Price, L.L.P. 527
Sugarman, Rogers, Barshak & Cohen, P.C. 657
Supreme Court of Hawaii 100
Sutherland, Asbill & Brennan, L.L.P. 658
Tonkon, Torp L.L.P. 660
Troutman Sanders 662
Tyco International Limited 755
United Airlines 756

United Mine Workers of America · 785
United Parcel Services · 756
United Services Automobile Association · · · · · · · · · · · · · · · · · · 757
United States Foreign Service · 87
United States Olympic Committee · 49
United States Supreme Court · 109
United States Air Force Judge Advocate General's Corps · · · · · · 859
United States Army Judge Advocate General's Corps · · · · · · · · · 853
United States Department of Justice · 123
United States Navy Judge Advocate General's Corps · · · · · · · · · 859
Visiting Professorship at Pepperdine Law School · · · · · · · · · · · 103
Vinson & Elkins L.L.P. · 664
Vogel, Kelly, Knutson, Weir, Bye & Hunke, Ltd. · · · · · · · · · · · 666
Waller Lansden Dortch & Davis, P.L.L.C. · · · · · · · · · · · · · · · · 533
Walt Disney Company · 70
Ward & Smith, P.A. · 541
Warner Norcross & Judd, L.L.P. · 667
Watkins & Eager P.L.L.C. · 548
Webb, Carlock, Copeland, Semler & Stair, L.L.P. · · · · · · · · · · · 669
Weil, Gotshal & Manges, L.L.P. · 670
Wharton, Aldhizer & Weaver, PLC. · 553
Wiggin & Dana · 672
The Williams Companies · 758
Wilmer, Cutler & Pickering · 674
Winston & Strawn · 557
Women's Advocacy Project · 813
Workman, Nydegger & Seeley, P.C. · 676
Writers Guild of America, west · 788
Wyatt, Tarrant & Combs—Louisville · 560
Wyatt, Tarrant & Combs—Memphis · 574
Wyatt, Tarrant & Combs—Nashville (downtown) · · · · · · · · · · · 569

How Employers Made It Into *America's Greatest Places*

*—And Why There Are
Great Employers Who Aren't In It!*

Sixty-five years from now, it'll all be over. In the meantime, you might as well make the most of it and live as happily as you possibly can. I hope this book will help you do exactly that.

The fact is, whether you're just thinking about going to law school, you're a law student now, or you've already embarked on your career, there's an incredible job with your name on it, just waiting for you.

It may be that you think you don't have the grades to get a great job. Or that no one, single job can give you the variety or excitement that you want. Or that all the legal jobs that are meaningful pay diddly. Or maybe you think that all law firms are the same, that all large firms are sweat-shops, or that all jobs that pay a bunch will make you miserable. Or maybe you're sure that there's a great job out there somewhere but there's no way for you to find it.

No matter what you think, I've got great news for you. No matter what *you're* like, or what *you* like, you'll find a great job in this book. This country is just *full* of amazing jobs, no matter what it is that's important to you. If you want to make a load of money, there *are* large firms that belie the "sweatshop" image, and there are non-traditional jobs, *great* jobs, where you'll bring home buckets of cash. If you want nine-to-five hours (or less), there are terrific jobs that let you do exactly that. If you want to save the world, there are incredible public interest opportunities just wait-ing for you. If you'd rather work in a company, or for a trade union, or for a school or for the government…if you want to travel, or work in enter-tainment or sports or you want to work for headline-makers, I've researched all of those opportunities for you. This book will tell you where those jobs are, what they are, and how to get them.

On top of that, I'll show you how to smoke out whether the employer you're looking at is one that you'll like. We'll talk about how to take a job you really want even if you think your law school debt means you can't afford to. I'll give you insider tips from employers themselves on making the most of your job, no matter where you decide to work.

And more than anything else, I'll prove to you that you can take your law degree and have a *great* life, doing work you truly enjoy. You *deserve* it!

But to start with, we're going to do something a little more mundane than all of that. We're going to talk about how it is that all of these employers got into this book in the first place. My hunch is that you're thinking something like this: "You've got *some nerve*"—or some other word you'd use instead of 'nerve'—"claiming that *you* know the greatest places to work!"

I don't blame you for being skeptical. And frankly, the places listed in this book *aren't* the greatest places to work. Or more accurately, they aren't the *only* great places to work. It's not a matter of inclusio exclusio blah blah blah—you know, the Latin saying from law school that roughly states that the fact that some things are included means that everything else is excluded. Nothing could be further from the truth. A more accurate title might have been "Some of the Greatest Places to Work with a Law Degree," but that's not exactly memorable, is it?

Anyway, just do me a favor and holster your guns for a while as I tell you how I went about finding the employers included in this book. When I'm done, I think you'll agree that it was a pretty good system after all. And I'll even tell you what kinds of employers fell through the cracks—because no matter how much I'd love to include *every* great employer in a book like this, they aren't all here. And finally, I'll tell you how to make your own nominations for the next edition of this book. So if you're really mad that an employer you think is wonderful doesn't appear in here, it's not a permanent situation. They might very well appear the next time around.

In a nutshell, here's what I did. I contacted law school administrators all over the country, and I asked them this question: "Where are your happy graduates?" I actually asked them in more detail than *that*, but let's start here.

First of all—why law school administrators? I figured they'd be more objective than any other source. I've had lots of experience working with law school administrators, both because they were the sources for my last book, *Guerrilla Tactics For Getting The Legal Job Of Your Dreams*, and they're also the ones I turn to for much of the expert advice for my column, *Dear Job Goddess*, which appears in law school newspapers nation-wide. The administrators I've worked with have always struck me with their integrity, and they talk to law school students and graduates all of the time—they're incredibly plugged into the legal community—so they're more knowledgeable than anybody about great employers.

I also chose law school administrators because I wasn't too psyched about my other options. One obvious one would be to survey law school graduates and say, "Are you happy?" Yikes! Not only would that be a monumental task (and the people who would respond would probably have an ax to grind), but let's face it—when you're actually working for somebody, you're hardly going to be an objective source about whether or not they're a great employer. I counted out employers themselves for the same reason. Can you imagine? Asking employers, "Hey! Are your junior lawyers happy?" Suffice it to say that the Miss America competition got rid of the Miss Congeniality contest when, a few years ago, 49 of the contestants voted for themselves. Enough said.

The other obvious option would be to rely on published sources. That is, to look at the original research of other writers, and glom onto that. The problem there is that I *really* wanted to unearth new veins of great employers, whole categories of jobs that law students and law school graduates don't often even *think* about. So I dismissed the idea of published sources, as well.

So that's how I wound up with law school administrators. Beyond the "Where are your happy graduates?" question, I gave them some parameters, and those parameters tell you exactly who made it into this book.

THE SURVEY PARAMETERS

1. Employers with more than 20 law school graduates.

There's a very simple reason for this. For a start, employers with fewer than 20 law school grads probably don't hire law school types on a regular basis, and so there would be a huge frustration factor in reading all about great employers who hire once a millennium. What that means is that most of the employers appearing in this book do hire routinely, so that if you're game to give them a try, you've got a fighting chance.

Of course, if you glance through this book you'll find I wasn't exactly religious about following this "20 or more" rule. The big exceptions are public interest organizations and corporations. Many, many corporations have fewer than 20 in-house lawyers (although when you count law school graduates in management, most corporations *do* meet the 20-count minimum). And many public interest organizations have many fewer than 20 lawyers. But if I had firmly imposed the "one score" minimum on these two types of employers, there would be *virtually none* in this book, and I thought that would be a terrible disservice to you, since there are many great public interest and corporate employers.

The 20-person floor by and large means that many, many wonderful law firms aren't in this book, even though I'm sure you'd truly enjoy working for one of them. In fact, many lawyers think that the *only* firm worth working for is a small law firm, and it's true that there are lots of things about small firms that almost every law student—certainly me, when I was a law student—tends to overlook, traits that help make an employer wonderful. But it wasn't feasible to profile tons and tons of tiny law firms. Instead, what I've done to remedy this is to give you advice about how you go about finding small law firms, how you find really *good* ones to work for, and how you encourage them to hire you. You'll find the small firm information in Chapter 6.

2. *Employers that law school graduates generally enjoy working for.*

The operative word here is "generally." As I explained to law school administrators when I surveyed them, "There's no place where everybody in the history of the organization has enjoyed themselves. And by the same token, for even the most evil, Simon Legree-ful employer, *somebody* is happy."

Instead, what I wanted were employers who *overall* are regarded as treating their junior-ish law school graduates well. And I told administrators that this impression could come from any objective source, typically alums or the administrator's own observations as part of the legal community.

You don't have to think too long to figure out who slipped through the cracks *here*. For a start, an employer with happy employees who keep their mouths shut is one that I'd love to include, but I wouldn't have heard about them from any of my sources. Ideally these employers will no longer be anonymous for the second edition of this book, and if you know employers like this, check out Chapter 16 for guidance on contacting me with your recommendations!

Another flaw with the "generally happy" requirement is that employers aren't static. *People* are the key ingredient in any happy workplace, and that means that as personnel change, the work atmosphere evolves and the enjoyable nature of the office follows suit.

I'll give you an example. One of the firms featured in this book was greatly relieved to find that their reputation had improved, and they knew exactly when things started looking up. As the recruiting administrator told me, "Until eight years ago, we had a partner here who was just a tyrant. Associates and support staff left in droves. *Nobody* could work for this s.o.b. The things he did were just unthinkable. One day, he was having a lunch meeting with some clients in our conference room, and he instructed his assistant to order sandwiches. He told her, 'and make sure there is *no mayonnaise* on mine.' Well, of course, the deli made a mistake, and there was mayonnaise on his sandwich. He buzzed his assistant from the conference, on speaker phone, in front of all of the clients, and told her, 'There's mayonnaise on my sandwich.' She apologized for the deli's mistake and said she'd get him another sandwich right away. He said, 'No, you won't. You're going to come in here and scrape off this mayonnaise.'" As the recruiting coordinator recounted it, the assistant did the right thing—she calmly picked up her purse, went out to lunch, and never came back. However, the recruiting coordinator added, "If it had been *me* that he said that to, I would have responded, 'You're going to want to hang on to that mayonnaise, because if I have to come into that conference room, you're going to need all the lubrication you can get!'"

Shortly after that, the other partners voted this jerk out of the partnership, even though he was one of the firm's biggest rainmakers. They relied on the old saw that it's a lot easier to find good lawyers than it is to find good help. Since then, she told me, "The clouds have parted, and this is a great place to work. I'm glad to hear that everybody views us that way."

The moral of the story? Today's wonderful employer could be tomorrow's sweatshop—and vice versa.

Another possibility—and hopefully a much more remote one—is that the wrong people at an employer are the blabbermouths. In other words, it's possible that no matter how diligently I researched, a bad employer sneaked into this book. I don't think it happened, based on all of the people I talked to. And I also took the prophylactic step of asking around, once I had a basic list of employers, to see if any of the employers on my list had major negatives. I actually eliminated 10% of my original list this way, and I believe I removed anybody who shouldn't have been included.

This doesn't mean that you'll never talk to a single person at any of these employers who isn't happy. If you have the one bad supervisor at a law firm or company or government agency or public interest organization, you're not going to be happy even if everybody else is euphoric. If you've got to work on a case you don't believe in, you're just not going to enjoy it. And if you didn't anticipate the working hours or the sacrifice of autonomy or the emotional toll of your work before you started, it doesn't matter how wonderful it is to other people—you're not going to like it. By way of example, one lawyer I knew a few years ago was working at a law firm in Washington, D.C. that he truly enjoyed. Then, one day, in walked Ferdinand Marcos, the Philippine leader widely suspected of plundering his country's coffers. It turns out that Marcos was going to be represented in the U.S. by my friend's firm. He told me, "The moment I looked at him, I looked into his eyes, I just said to myself, 'I can't work for a place that would represent a guy like this. I just can't.'" And so he left.

So while I've worked my butt off finding great places for you to work (actually I *haven't*. I still have a butt, so I can't recommend writing books as a weight-loss method), you're not absolved from reading Chapter 2, and taking responsibility for figuring out what will make *you* happy.

3. *Employers who are enjoyable to work for from a junior-ish perspective.*

I specifically asked law school administrators for employers who are enjoyable for people with fewer than five or so years of experience after law school. Why is that? Frankly I figured that if you hang around for 10 or 20 years with an outfit, you probably like it because you're either the grand poobah or pretty close to it.

Having said that, a good number of jobs in this book are not ones you can get straight after law school graduations. Many terrific employers, including the most terrific one of all, the Department of Justice, prefer (and sometimes even require) a couple of years of experience under your belt before you work for them. Most corporate in-house counsel's departments are this way, although a few (like Procter & Gamble) take new law school graduates.

If you are still in school and despair at the idea of not getting your dream job on graduation, read about these employers anyway—you'll learn the kinds of things you ought to do right after graduation that will pave the way to your dream job, a couple of years from now.

4. *Employers for whom a law degree is necessary or useful.*

Law school administrators told me about a ton of people who are happy doing things *completely* unrelated to law. People who do voice-overs for television commercials, or design wedding cakes, or run coffee shops, or my old friend Will Shortz, a former editor of *Games* magazine who is now the New York Times' crossword puzzle editor.

The fact is, having a law degree doesn't stop you from being a lion-tamer. However, in the hopes of putting out a book shorter than the Manhattan Yellow Pages, I had to put a limitation on the scope of jobs I'd include, and the "necessary or useful" boundary made sense.

Having said that, all of the wonderful people who do things that are completely unrelated to law sounded so fascinating to me that I'll be including some of them in my next book—the second edition of *Guerrilla Tactics For Getting The Legal Job Of Your Dreams.* Keep an eye out for that one, if you're interested in reading about people who pursue jobs *way off* the beaten path!

WHO DIDN'T MAKE IT IN—AND WHY

I've already mentioned how *some* wonderful employers didn't make it in. They were too small, or I just didn't hear anything about them, good or bad. There is another category of great employer who didn't make it this time around, and that's employers who *would* have been included except that I heard about them too late. Publishing is a world of deadlines, and that's why God created second editions. By way of a sneak preview, three employers who will be in "Son of America's Greatest Places" include the law firms Powell Goldstein in Atlanta, Miller Cassidy in Washington D.C., and at least one company—Nabisco.

There are also, of course, employers about whom I heard actively awful things. In fact, while I was researching this book, I kept an "evil twin" file of employers which must be *hideous* black holes of Calcutta in which to work.

Offices where partners, in fits of pique, are known to throw furniture through office windows—on the 20th floor. Firms where an associate takes a few hours off because his wife is in labor, and when it turns out to be false labor, he finds those hours docked from his next paycheck.

Sweatshops where a supervisor, concerned about the well-being of a new associate who'd been putting in spirit-breaking seven-day weeks for month after month, took her to dinner, stated his concern, and asked what he could do, and when she sobbed, "I need a day off, just *one day*," he shrugged, and said, "I'm afraid that's not possible."

A book based on the stories I collected would certainly be morbidly fascinating, but it's not *this* book, and I'm not telling who those employers are! This book is designed to show you what makes employers great to work for. It's designed to answer the question, "Hey, Kimmbo, what should I do? Where should I work?" And that's what it does!

HOW TO CONTRIBUTE TO THE SECOND EDITION OF THIS BOOK

If you build up a righteous head of steam because I've neglected to include an employer (or a type of job) you think really should appear in this book, by all means contact me and let me know, so that they're in the running for the next edition.

For complete information on contacting me, take a look at Chapter 16. I'd love to hear from you!

The Sometimes Surprising Traits That Great Employers Share

. . . And Insider Tips for Smoking Out Whether The Employer You're Considering Will Make You Happy.

Simply put, the greatest employer in the world is the one where you enjoy working the most. It doesn't matter if everybody else hates the place or thinks you're nuts for liking it. Your own perception is all that counts.

Having said that, and having spoken with hundreds and hundreds of young law school graduates all over the country, I've found that the same factors come up again and again when people talk about why they like what they do. I think you're going to be surprised at what they had to say; I certainly was.

It's important to remember as you look through these qualities that no one employer will have *every* quality you like. Happiness in your work is largely a matter of compromise, understanding which qualities are expendable and which aren't. You know yourself and what's important to you better than anyone else ever could; you alone know what you're willing to surrender to enjoy your work as much as possible.

The Nineteen Qualities That Count:

1. *The employer in general matches or beats your idea of what work would be like.*

Expectations are *everything*. From hours to pay to responsibility to interesting work to office atmosphere, the more realistic your expectations, the better off you are. I found that all of the associates at the large firms that actually made it into this book said that they had expected the horror stories they'd heard to be true—frequent all-nighters, meaningless chimp work, stuffy offices, Torquemada-esque partners—and were pleasantly surprised when the truth was far better than their dire predictions.

The best way to be realistic (other than reading this book, of course) is to think *very carefully* about what's important to you and what you are willing to sacrifice to get it. This book is full of *great* employers. It doesn't contain *any* "perfect" employers. If you insist on making a great deal of money right away, you will typically not have a lot of autonomy and you will work very long hours. If you want to go directly into a glamorous field, like entertainment or sports, you can give up the idea of making very much, if any, money at the start. The more autonomy you want, the less security you generally have. Would you realistically not mind foregoing a paycheck for a few weeks or months—and does your lifestyle permit that? Or would that make you crazy? Do you like the idea of a leisurely pace, or do you want a constant adrenaline rush from your work? Do you want to develop a niche for yourself, or do you want a great deal of variety? What constituency do you want to work with—other lawyers? Or other people in a corporate in-house counsel's office? Or customers? Or indigents? Or celebrities? Realize that for great employers, your work is *not* your life, and you've got the right—and the obligation—to have outside interests to round out your life in ways your work cannot. The less pressure you put on your employer, the happier you are likely to be.

2.   *Your work is intellectually challenging.*

The ABA conducted a study a few years ago, and found from surveying young lawyers all over the country that the number one factor in determining job satisfaction was intellectual challenge. This is consistent with "flow theory," which says that people are happiest when their mental faculties are pushed to the limit.

Presumably you went to law school in the first place with the idea in mind that you'd get more stimulation from your work than you would if you worked, say—at the Northbound tollbooth. You'll be delighted to find that for every novice lawyer I interviewed for this book, it was very difficult for them to describe a typical day, and on top of that, the projects they work on present a novel challenge on a *very* regular basis. Almost every satisfied lawyer will tell you that what they like about their work is "solving puzzles"—and that's true all the way from helping to set precedent on a national level (*e.g.,* clerking for the United States Supreme Court), to trying to settle disputes between individual people.

3.   *The hours are livable—or at least better than you thought they'd be.*

Notice that I didn't say the hours are *short.* I get letters to my *Dear Job Goddess* column all the time, with the same, very reasonable lament: "Am I crazy to think that I can work 9 to 5 after law school?" No, you're not. But if you insist on working 9 a.m. to 5 p.m.—or less—you're going to *greatly* restrict your possible employer pool. By and large, state attorneys' generals offices, court administration jobs, state's attorney and district attorney's ("D.A.") offices, law librarianships, banks, and corporate in-house counsels' offices tend to offer the shortest hours. Some private firms offer part-time work to entering associates, but beware: Part-time *can* mean 30 to 35 hours to a private firm, or what would be full-time to clerical help, so make sure you're on the same page vis-a-vis your meaning of part-time if you go after a job like that.

You may be surprised that I didn't include federal agencies and small firms in the "shorter hours" category. That's because there's no general rule to be drawn from them. For instance, attorneys at the Securities and Exchange Commission ("SEC") just love their work, but find they often have to work late. The Department of Justice ("DOJ")—an employer *so* wonderful it has its very own chapter in this book—sometimes requires long hours, and many DOJ jobs involve travel, and even if you enjoy travelling, you could also view it as 24-hour work days, because you can't do anything at home with friends or family when you're on the road.

Small firms can also require long hours, because they are subject to the same vicissitudes of the private practice of law as any other firm. If anything, it's *specialties* that determine hours more than the size of the firm you're looking at. If you are a small firm associates and you're working on a trial, you'll be burning the midnight oil. If you're in M&A and have a deal ready to close, you'll be pulling down some serious night work. Whereas if you do wills, trusts, estate planning kinds of things, you'll find your work isn't so time-sensitive and so it requires fewer long days, no matter how large a firm you work for.

If you want to minimize your workday, you also want to pay attention to a very important non-work factor: where do you plan to live? You'll notice that an awful lot of employers in this book aren't in big cities. One thing that many young lawyers cite as benefits of their job is a five-to-15 minute commute. If you work in a large city, like New York or Chicago or Los Angeles, it's easy to spend an hour and a half each way commuting. That's three hours a day, and if you spent two and a half hours fewer in travel for each weekday, that adds up to 625 hours a year. That's the difference between very livable hours and a sweatshop in most people's minds, and if you're concerned about hours, it's something for you to heed.

Another "hours factor" to take into account is that you'll find that even if you put in tremendous hours at the start of your career in private practice, those tend to diminish naturally over the first couple of years. Why? Because of what so many young lawyers have described to me as the "steep learning curve" in law. At the beginning of your career, it just takes you a lot longer to bang out briefs or memos or motions or whatever just because you haven't done them very much before. So even if you take a job with long hours at the start, take heart—as you get better at doing what you do, it will take less of your time.

In the section later in this chapter about "Insider Tips for Smoking Out Whether the Employer You're Considering Will Make You Happy," I'll tell you ways to determine if any particular employer requires hours that suit you. But for right now I want to tell you a couple of facets to hours that are more important than how many of them you strictly work:

a. Do you have control over scheduling the hours you work?

Most new law school graduates find that being able to control their own schedules is more important than how many hours they put in. Having to make an appearance at the office at any given time is called "face time"—is your face at the office? "Face time" is a serious negative. At least one law firm (obviously not one in this book!) has a senior partner who comes in on Sunday mornings to check the associates' mailboxes, to see which of them showed up on Saturday. If they've got no mail, they were in. Ones who still have mail in their boxes are dressed down on Monday morning. That's the worst kind of face time—shame on any employer who plays games like that! Great employers don't. And not being required to put in "face time" is part of what junior associates mean when they talk about "being treated like a professional."

b. Are your partners or supervisors sympathetic when you do have to put in long hours?

Great employers may sometimes require long hours, but when they *do*, they're not happy about it. This can come across in a number of ways. Partners or supervisors might stay and work with you side by side. One law firm associates I talked to said when he expected to put in an all-nighter to cover a 10-item checklist, his supervising partner tore the list in half, and said, "Which half do you want?" Other associates reported supervisors who call in frequently to check on them when they're working late to see how they're doing, and who apologize for requiring late hours.

Another way to show concern is to give you unexpected time off after a grueling project. One associate at Jones Day (yes, Jones Day) told me that during a tough early year in her career, at Thanksgiving her supervising attorney told her she'd been working too hard, and told her to "Take the rest of the year off." He meant it. And she did. Great employers frequently tell junior lawyers to get lost after a time-consuming project. Again—it shows the hours aren't considered de rigeur. Many private employers offer extra-hours bonuses (see more on this below, under "warnings"). For unexpectedly hard hours, some employers go even further and give junior lawyers gift certificates or lavish dinners out. And here again, associates take this as reflecting the employer's attitude that "We want you to have a life, and we're sorry when work gets in the way of that."

c. You can avoid keeping track of your hours.

"Billable hours" are the bane of the existence of junior associates at private firms. It's not unusual to have to keep track of time in private firms in increments as small as six minutes (that is, tenths of hours). If you don't think this is a chore, try doing it for a couple of days, right now. It's a *pain*. And it's a pain that governmental lawyers, corporate lawyers, public interest lawyers, law school administrators, judicial clerks—in fact, almost everybody in this book *other* than junior associates at private firms—don't have to tolerate. For lawyers who escape from private practice into corporations or the government, not having to keep track of billables (along with not having to generate business) is one of the major assets of their new work life.

So that's what you really need to know about hours. By and large, you can't avoid long hours in private practice, at least not all the time. Susan Kalb Weinberg, the wonderful Career Services Director at the University of Michigan's law school, says "That makes law no different than any *other* profession. Doctors, engineers, you name it— being a professional means putting in hours." And one associate at a mid-size firm told me perfectly bluntly: "If all I wanted was regular hours, I would have been a garbage man."

4. You get little tokens of appreciation from your employer.

One particularly insightful junior lawyer told me something you'll appreciate: "The key to a great job is in the details—the kinds of things law students don't pay attention to at all. But when you're working, you find these things aren't really details at all."

What kinds of things are we talking about here? A pat on the back for work well done. At one law firm, the managing partner himself makes up little hand-made signs that he posts on the door of any associate who's done a good job, for instance in successfully arguing a motion, so that everyone in the firm will be aware of the achievement and stop by with congratulations. A day off after a grueling project fits the bill also. As does a free pizza party for the few people who actually straggle into the office during a blizzard. I know these sound corny, but they *count*—otherwise why would so many people make a point of telling me about these acts of kindness? If anything, "simple pleasures" mean more than lavish formal functions - they're that important to job satisfaction.

5. You feel that your work is meaningful.

People who like their work need to feel as though it *means* something. Junior attorneys at the Department of Justice say that there's no feeling in the world like standing up to introduce themselves in court, and saying: " . . . and I represent the United States of America." *Damn*—it's a *thrill*! People in public interest find that the meaningfulness of their work is its most obvious virtue. You'll hear them say "Without me, these people would be *lost*." People at companies feel they're helping the company achieve its goals, and they *like* the company. Associates who like their private firms feel they're helping the clients achieve what they want, that their contribution is making a difference. Judicial clerks believe they're helping to make the right decision.

The antithesis of this is "make-work," and the place you'll find the most of that is in very large law firms. If you're performing constant research on memos to file, or working on a teeny piece of a brief for a client you don't know on a project whose breadth you don't understand, you're not going to find your work very meaningful. And you'll dread doing it.

6. *You feel like you're a significant part of the picture.*

I've talked with associates at some law firms—clearly not ones in this book!—who describe their lives as "Sitting in a cubicle in the firm library working on an injunction, Subpart B, then you hand it over to someone else in the next cubicle to work on Subpart C." They'll talk about people in litigation departments who haven't seen the inside of a courtroom in their whole 10-year careers. They'll talk about "Partners who have 150 files, and they'll hand out little dribs and drabs of those files, little brief-writing projects, then reel them back in and huddle over the files. You're totally in the dark. It's terrible."

As those comments suggest, feeling as though you are a significant part of the whole goes a long way toward making you like your job. Now if you work on huge projects—be they class action suits as either a prosecutor or judicial clerk or as a lawyer—or antitrust cases, or product liability litigation, or other similar behemoths—you're going to be, *technically*, a very little fish. A guppy. But your employer's *attitude* determines how you'll feel. Great employers will clue you in as to how your work fits into the big picture. As so many people tell me, "They tell me exactly *why* I'm doing what I'm doing." That's what makes you feel important—not your technical slice of the pie.

Great employers also tend to clue you in to how the organization as a whole is doing. Obviously that's pretty easy for public companies like Honeywell or Microsoft, meaningless for government agencies, and for some private employers, they are so small that you can't help but know everything that's in the works. But for all the rest, people tend to enjoy being part of "the loop"—being routinely updated on the financial progress of the organization. Some law firms even have monthly print-outs saying everyone's hours, the billings of the firm, compensation paid to every partner, and the like. While this isn't a *necessary* ingredient of a great work place, people say they appreciate being apprised of information like this. And interestingly enough, I've never noted even a trace of resentment over seeing older lawyers making a bundle compared to novices—presumably junior lawyers at great employers enjoy what they're doing now, assume that their day will come, and feel that seeing the books provides them with an incentive, not a source of sour grapes.

7. *The compensation system suits you, whether it's lock-step
    or "eat-what-you-kill."*

I'm not talking about the *size* of your paycheck here—I cover that in the
"warnings" section later in this chapter. And frankly for many of the
employers in this book—corporations, government agencies, public
interest employers, in fact almost all of the non-law firm employers—
what you get is by and large what you get. For law firms, however, there
are two basic models for the way you're paid: Does everybody get the
same pay for the same work? Or do you get a cut of the business you
bring in, which is called an "eat-what-you-kill" system?

The very vast majority of large law firms consider "rainmaking" a non-
issue for junior associates. They don't expect you to bring in business for
your first few years, and it would be kind of weird if you did. As one large
firm associate told me, "If you're in litigation you can't really bring in
clients, because you can't anticipate those cases. And for corporate—what
am I going to do at the age of 28? Bring in AT&T?" But even so, *some* large
firms aren't that way, especially for newer, smaller, more "entrepreneurial"
offices of large firms—like Baker & Hostetler's Columbus office, where
business development is a significant focus for younger associates, with
training programs and mentoring to get them on the rainmaking track.
(That's what "entrepreneurial" is a code word for, by the way—when a
firm says it's entrepreneurial, it means that it wants you to be looking to
the community for ways to bring in more business.) And at Davis Wright
and Tremaine in Portland, an associate made partner in *three years* in part
by being a fabulous rainmaker. Those kinds of outliers aside, most large
firms expect you to spend your first few years learning your craft before
you have to worry about harpooning clients.

As a rule of thumb, the smaller the firm, the larger rainmaking will
loom in your early career. That's not sleazy, oleaginous, used-car salesman
stuff—most lawyers get business through involvement in the community,
with nonprofits and civic boards and things like that. If you're outgoing,
you like talking to people and think you'd be good at it, a place where
those skills can turn to bucks in your pocket is something you should be
aware of, and that's likely to occur in a smaller rather than a larger firm.

Incidentally, there's a practical reason why this is so. As one associate
from a huge firm (not in this book) told me, "Our real estate practice is so
huge that you *can't* bring in business, because it's going to be hard for you
to find anything that doesn't conflict out"—meaning that the firm can't
take the work because of current or former client conflicts.

So if you're the retiring type, with few connections, a place without an
emphasis on generating business will likely suit you. That's true of almost
every employer except for smaller private law firms. If you're gregarious or
well-connected in the community—an "eat-what-you-kill" is one that you
might find more emotionally, not to mention financially, rewarding.

Other factors also figure into compensation systems—like profit-sharing, bonuses for excess billable hours, contributions to the organization's administration, or pro bono hours that are sometimes billable. Before you accept an offer, ask the questions you need to ask to see if the compensation system suits *you*.

8.   *There are no artificial deadlines.*

People at great employers don't get jerked around on deadlines. In corporations, the person who needs the advice really needs it *now*, because they're going to take action depending on what you say. You're a judicial clerk and your judge needs your work *now* to incorporate it into his or her opinion. You're an assistant state's attorney and D.A. or assistant state's attorney and you've got cases needing immediate dispositions. In a private firm, your corporate client wants to make an acquisition or your litigation client is facing a court date imposed by a judge. They key to all of these situations is that they involve *real* deadlines. Those are deadlines that happy novice lawyers don't mind, and those are the kinds of deadlines you find at great employers.

At not-so-great employers, people talk about supervisors whose attitude is, "I paid my dues, and so will *you*." I've heard stories about partners who drop meaningless research projects on associates' desks on Friday afternoon at 4:30 p.m. with a 9 a.m. Monday deadline—knowing that will mean all weekend at the office, for no reason other than some kind of professional hazing ritual. Or others who demand work by Monday morning and then don't even look at the fruits of the associate's labor before Thursday—and never intended to look at it sooner. *That* doesn't lead to happy, motivated underlings.

9.   *You feel your employer respects and cares about you personally.*

If you enjoy your work, it's likely that you feel as though the people you work with would pitch in and help out if you've got a sick kid or a wedding anniversary celebration or some other personal obligation. Or there'll be a maternity wardrobe that gets passed around to any pregnant woman at the office. Or your higher-ups, like the managing partner or director of the firm or general counsel, stops by sometimes just to say "hi" and see how you're doing.

The novice lawyers I talked to indicated through a thousand different anecdotes how important it is for them not to feel like "profit-generating robots," and that their employers take the time—and effort—to treat them as a "whole person."

10.   *You know where you stand, all the time.*

What I'm talking about here is feedback, and interestingly enough, it's not formal feedback that means so much to junior lawyers. Almost every organization has some kind of routine formal feedback, typically annual sit-downs with superiors. Those obviously *aren't a negative*. But the feedback that is handed out for happy junior lawyers goes beyond that. You hear about virtually constant informal feedback at great employers. Junior lawyers will say things like, "I always know where I stand." An open give-and-take between you and your supervisor gives you this kind of feedback. Junior lawyers will talk about having everything they write marked up, and how supervisors will sit down and say "This is how I would have handled that" or "Next time, try offering this" or "I saw a lawyer do this when he had the same kind of issue you're dealing with now." If this sounds to you like constant criticism, it's not—it's the kind of polishing that takes a new lawyer and makes them into a *great* lawyer, and that's how junior lawyers take it.

Formal reviews themselves are not created equal. At great employers, formal reviews frequently have elements that set them apart from the ordinary. For instance, some employers require that every superior contributing to a junior lawyer's review must include their name with their review. Junior lawyers like this approach because it makes them feel as though "It's not the whole world who feels a certain way about you; if you know who it is, you know for a start that because their cover is blown they'll try and be constructive. And also, you can put what they say into context, knowing what your involvement with them was." Formal reviews at great employers are also frequently greatly enhanced by including the reviewee's input. Many junior lawyers told me about their ability to have input into their own reviews, to give their side of any project which they feel might otherwise reflect badly on them. Some even get to review their superiors—anonymously, of course! That's a kind of 'reverse feedback' that's greatly appreciated.

11.   *You have superiors to whom you can freely ask questions—typically, mentors.*

Great employers make sure that the questions you have can be readily—and happily—answered. There are several ways of accomplishing this. Mentoring is one route, and it is becoming more and more common and junior lawyers who have it, like it. Typically, great employers will match you up with an older employee—at law firms, it'll be a senior associate or a partner—to whom you can go with any kind of question. There's a lot that goes into making the transition from school to work, and having a workplace confidante makes a tremendous difference in smoothing out the bumps.

With or without mentors, an open door policy is something fledgling lawyers like. It's nice to be able to feel as though the people you work with will answer your questions, no matter how silly those questions are, and regardless of whether those people are in your "chain of command."

12. **Your supervisors readily share their expertise with you.**

There are many, many employers whose top echelons are filled with amazing people. But that doesn't matter to you if you don't get to interact with them. At great employers, you typically have the opportunity to absorb all kinds of advice and job skills from phenomenal lawyers, just by being able to work with them. This is called "elbow learning" (i.e., you're learning at the elbow of experts). For some employers, this means working side-by-side with experts; sometimes it means tagging along and being able to observe experts at work; and other times it means having experts give you tips and advice on the projects you're doing.

13. **You get lots of early responsibility.**

A great advantage of most government jobs, prosecutor positions, public interest jobs, and small firm associateships is that you get to hit the ground running. You get lots of responsibility, very early on. As the ads of Hillis Clark, a small-ish Seattle firm featured in this book, say: "You always get our A Team because we don't have a B Team." Feeling as though your work has a real impact on someone else from an early point in your career creates an adrenaline rush very little else can match.

14. **You enjoy the company of the people with whom you spend the most time.**

When I first started researching employers for this book, I would ask junior lawyers: "Tell me what you like most about what you do." I quickly had to revise this approach, because nine times out of 10 the answer would be, "The people."

It sounds rather obvious, but liking the people you spend most of your workday with is vital. And that doesn't necessarily mean your colleagues, although in corporations and law firms that's frequently true. If you're a judicial clerk, you better like the judge. If you're a judicial administrator, you better like *all* (or at least many) of the judges and clerks. But if you do public interest work, you'll spend most of your time with the constituency you serve; if you are an assistant state's attorney or assistant D.A., you're going to spend most of your time with the public, in the form of suspects, witnesses and victims. You've got to *like* those people in order to like your work; junior lawyers almost always cite the people they work with *over* the work they do as being the most significant element in determining whether they like what they do.

15. **Your employer is "family-friendly."**

If you're single, this might not be so important to you. But an employer's family-friendliness says a lot about how the employer feels toward people in general, and so it might be more important than you think—it shows a respect toward your life outside of work. And it certainly *will* be important if you plan to have a family in the future, whether you're a man or a woman. As many a young male lawyer told me, "You know, we want to spend time with our kids, too; it's not just a women's issue."

Many, many people have resoundingly told me that the best way to be family-friendly is to have livable hours. As I've often heard, any employer can talk the talk when it comes to being family-friendly, but it takes a selfless employer to walk the walk.

An employer who's family-friendly will see that you're covered if you want to go see your kid in the school play on Thursday morning. And include families in organization activities, like picnics and parties, zoo trips, Santa visits, and the like. In some organizations, senior lawyers will even have "candy drawers"—meaning desk drawers filled with candy, not licorice underwear—for any visiting kiddies. These kinds of things indicate a humane attitude that benefits everyone at work, not just people with children.

16.   *You get direct contact with your constituency.*

In firms, that means client contact. In public interest and for prosecutors, there's contact with "clients" almost immediately. And in corporations, your sole function is to have contact with your only client.

It's law firms where client contact is an issue. Great employers tend to introduce you to clients early on. The idea that many of them state is, "We want the clients to be comfortable with you." Even if that just means tagging along to client meetings or sitting in on client conference calls or even being cc'd on client correspondence, contact with the final recipient of your services is something that is likely to add to your enjoyment.

17.   *The support staff is happy.*

When I first started hearing this from people, I thought it was kind of silly. After all, if you're a professional, who cares if your secretary is happy? I've since learned that *you* should care, because if your support staff is happy, you're likely to be, as well. For one thing, if the most senior person in the organization is on first-name terms with the administrative help, they're going to treat you with at least that much respect. And when you're faced with a time crunch or a question about the way the office runs or any one of a million minor and major dilemmas, the support staff can be your best friend. They can make your job vastly easier and make you more efficient, and that's worth *a lot*. At some great employers, the support staff has been around forever. They know more about how to do your job than you do, and that's a valuable asset.

18.   *You feel that whatever you're doing now is helping to set you up for whatever you want to do next.*

Did you know that the average person has seven different careers in their lifetime? Your first job out of law school, no matter how happy it makes you, is unlikely to be your last (although I spoke with *plenty* of lifers at different employers in this book, which is hardly surprising!). Happy law school graduates tend to feel that the experience they're getting now will be valuable to them down the road. For instance, Justice Department attorneys know that with the prestige of the Department behind them, as well as tons of hands-on experience very early on, they're set no matter whether they want to go to a corporation, law firm, law school, or virtually anywhere else after the DOJ. And judicial clerks, who typically work for only a year or two as a clerk, face a similarly rosy future. The same is true of many, many terrific junior employers, where junior lawyers feel like they're "casting their bread upon the water" with their first jobs: they don't know *exactly* where their careers will take them, but they know they're building an excellent foundation now.

19.   *The city where you live gives you a chance to contribute to the community in a meaningful way.*

Many happy law school graduates take part in civic activities not because they *have* to, but because they *like* a sense of making a difference in the place where they live and work. And that draws many, many people to smaller cities and towns. As Jack Swarbrick, a sports lawyer you'll get to know well in Chapter 3 on "Ultimate Dream Jobs," says, "If you can live anywhere, live in San Francisco. It's beautiful. But the consequence of living in a city like that is that everyone is from somewhere else. There is a definite link between happiness and places that value community higher. Being able to get involved in the community is a big reason people move out of large cities."

Danger, Will Robinson! Factors to Watch Out For . . .

It's *very easy, too easy, dangerously* too easy to put the emphasis on the wrong factors when you're deciding what to do next. The last thing you want is to get into a job and only then have a "V-8" moment, when you smack your forehead and say, "Dang!"—or whatever word you'd replace that with—"Why didn't I think about *this* before now?" There are five principal areas that call for caution. They are:

1. *Money.*

I'm not going to pretend that money isn't important. If you've got a walloping big loan debt to pay back, it can be very important. (In fact, the idea of loan debt is so big that I've got a separate chapter about handling it—Chapter 12.) But what I'm talking about here is to make the kinds of mistakes I see people making all the time.

a. *Assuming that the employer that pays the most is the "best."*

This is very dangerous! I usually see it come about when a third year student is considering different large firms in the same city, and, figuring "they're all alike," takes the one that pays the most. There *are* differences between firms, but the differences typically aren't large in terms of pay—because large firms are all competing for the same tiny pool of law students, they *have* to pay about the same. If you choose solely on the basis of money, you may find yourself at a horrible sweatshop where, for $40 less per week, you could have been very happy.

b. *Assuming that certain kinds of jobs don't pay enough, and eliminating entire categories from consideration on that basis.*

You probably think that public interest jobs and government positions couldn't possibly compete with private firms—right? It's a mistake to make broad generalizations when it comes to pay. For instance, while public interest jobs *do* typically pay less than private firms, the Federal Defender Program starts you off better than many private firms. And for government jobs—did you know that Assistant State's Attorneys in Connecticut start at more than $50,000 a year? *Moral:* Don't count out *any* individual employer on money grounds without doing a little bit of digging first, to find out what they actually pay.

c. *Looking at a job that pays less than you like to start, and not examining the kinds of raises you can expect.*

When I was in law school I never would have bothered to look past starting salaries when it came to comparing jobs monetarily. That's a *big* mistake, and here's why: many jobs start with lower pay, but ratchet up very, very quickly. At the Department of Justice, for instance, it's not uncommon to find your salary goosed up to more than $80,000 by your fourth year.

d. Not taking into account cost of living differences between cities when comparing salaries.

Where you live will have more impact on the quality of your life than the amount of money you make. If you travel around the country, you quickly realize that $200,000 buys something very different in Roanoke than it does in San Francisco. If you like the idea of owning a home or driving a nice car or you have a family to support (or you'd like to start one), starting your career in a not-so-large city can cut the amount of money you need by half.

e. Don't equate money with happiness.

I realize how hackneyed that sounds, but as Madeline Kahn said in *Blazing Saddles*, "It's twue! It's twue!" If you take a job that starts at $80,000 a year because you figure there's no way to be unhappy with that kind of money flowing in, you couldn't be more wrong. If you don't have any time of your own in which to spend it, it doesn't matter how much you make. And if you hate your job, you'll find yourself resenting the money. It will turn to ashes in your hands. You'll feel like a whore, selling yourself for money. And in a sense if all you get out of your job is the money, you *are* a whore. You will find what so many people have told me—money doesn't make a difference unless it reflects payment for something you enjoy doing. Remember that when you feel you might be swayed by that American Express Platinum Card!

2. Bonuses.

This is somewhat related to money, but I separated it because from what I've heard, bonuses can be a real snake pit. Of course, there *are* valid bonuses. Many private employers offer bonuses based on a variety of factors, including tangibles like profit sharing, and intangibles like how well you're progressing with your career, the amount of responsibility you're taking on, and similar benchmarks.

But not all bonuses are like that. Here's what you have to watch out for: bonuses that are either unattainable, or result in an hourly salary that makes them a waste of your time.

The unattainability can be particularly hard to smoke out, but here's what you want to do. If a large part of your interest in a particular job stems from the bonus they're offering you, *with your offer in hand* (and not before), talk with some of the junior people there and ask them specifics about the bonus system. Have they actually gotten a bonus? How many people get the bonus? Are the criteria likely to change once you get there? If you ask for specifics, you'll quickly uncover a bonus that's really a scam.

Bonuses based on excess hours can sound good, but when you work them out on an hourly basis, they are sometimes laughable. One associate told me about a bonus based on working 400 extra billable hours per year. The bonus was $2,000. Standing alone, $2,000 sounds pretty good—it's enough for a decent vacation, right? But when you work it out on an hourly basis, you understand why the associates at this particular law firm call it the "Taco Bell" bonus. You'd be much better off taking those same hours and spending them tutoring law students or people taking the bar exam—or, come to think of it, actually *working* at Taco Bell!

3. *Prestige.*

Prestige is a funny thing. We *all* like the idea of telling people what we do, and having them respond with a drop-jawed "Wow!" And let's face it, if you get a job with anybody I list in the "Dream Jobs" chapter—like Disney, or ESPN, or the NFL, or Anheuser-Busch, or the Foreign Service—that's how people will react. If you work for any of the biggest law firms in the country, at the very least your stock will rise in the eyes of other lawyers and law students, because if large law firms aren't anything else, they *are* very prestigious.

But here's the problem. Prestige means nothing when you're actually doing the work. It doesn't matter if the firm does cutting-edge, *Wall Street Journal* kinds of cases, if you don't get to work on any of them. If you're a research drone, it doesn't really matter what anybody else in the office gets to do. You're miserable.

You will find that the thrill of prestige doesn't have much lasting impact. It's like new love—it's exciting, but after a while you better like shopping for curtains together, because what counts is your day-to-day life, and how enjoyable you find it. It's true that some wonderful employers combine both. All of the employers in the chapter on "Ultimate Dream Jobs" are like that. The Department of Justice, the #1 best place to work for law school graduates, is *definitely* like that. And the well-known law firms in the law firm chapter are, as well. So it's possible to combine prestige with enjoyable work. Otherwise, don't sacrifice a job you'd otherwise love just because you feel as though it will be greeted with a "ho-hum" at cocktail parties. Instead, come up with words to describe what you do in such a way that you make it sound as interesting and fun as it really is. When I introduce myself at parties and people ask me what I do, if I said "I'm a writer," well, that's somewhat interesting. But if I say, "I'm the Job Goddess," that's sure to start a conversation. Instead of saying "I'm a lawyer," say "I help people do this," or

"I work on these kinds of projects," and talk about what you like. That's really much more accurate, anyway!

4. **Perspectives from senior lawyers.**

This is not to suggest that everybody who's been out of school for thirty years doesn't have a valid opinion, but when it comes to determining whether you're going to like *the beginning* of your career with any organization, the thoughts of someone who started their career *before you were born* are about as valid as your recollection of what it's like to be a sixth grader. The rough edges are worn smooth by the intervening years, and in any case, it's a different world now than it was then. This isn't to say that you don't have anything to learn from older lawyers; they're full of extremely valuable advice. But when it comes to understanding what it must be like to be you—no. Look to more junior people for their perceptions if you want an accurate picture.

5. **"Teamwork."**

I am very suspicious when I hear employers stress "teamwork" over and over again. It's not that teamwork is necessarily a bad thing; it's not. But it depends what's meant by teamwork. If teamwork means that you don't get to be the prima donna, that's to be expected when you're starting your career working for somebody else. If it means chipping in when someone else has a deadline or a crisis knowing that they would, or have, done the same for you, that's fine, too. In fact, that's part of what makes a pleasant working environment so pleasant.

But if "teamwork" means that you get to subvert yourself so that your supervisors can take credit for your work, if it means being a "good soldier" by putting in 15-hour days in the library for months on end for the "good of the team"—that's not so good. Just below, when I talk about the questions to ask when you're interviewing with an employer, you'll see how to determine whether "teamwork" at any given employer is a good or a bad thing.

Doing Your Own Sleuthing: How Do You Smoke Out Employers Who Will Make You Happy?

As I mention frequently in this book, there are many terrific employers you won't read about here. And conversely, not every job in this book would make you happy, because different features appeal to different people. That makes it crucial that you do some of your own sleuthing. How? There are two ways: research you can do ahead of time, and when you interview *at your potential employer's office,* questions to ask and things to observe.

RESEARCH

Let's talk about the research first. There are two kinds of things you're looking for: narrative insights into what the employer is like, and statistics. I'll give you your sources in a moment, but first I'll tell you the three statistics that you'll want to look at if it's a private law firm you're considering joining. (As you'll see, these statistics aren't relevant for governmental, public interest, or corporate employers.)

i. **Check out the partner to associate ratio.** While it's impossible to generalize perfectly, if the partner to associate ratio is low—for instance, 1:2 or less—that typically means that the associates are not "highly leveraged," and that you won't likely be weeded out. If the ratio is very high, it *generally* means that the partners expect for many of the associates to leave before partnership—either voluntarily or not.

ii. **Look at the number of summer clerks eligible for offers vs. offers made.** If there are many more summer clerks eligible than offers made *on a routine basis,* that means that the firm is using the summer program as a weeding-out process, and there's going to be a lot of competition between summer associates. That's not a happy state of affairs if you're in a summer program like that, and it's not a terribly nice thing for law firms to do.

iii. **Look at the retention rate.** I've probably referred elsewhere in this book to firms that bleed new associates, losing up to 90% of their associates within the first two years. *Nobody* goes to a large firm expecting to stay less than two years; most people are willing to give a firm a try for two years with the idea in mind that they will then leave and do something they really want to do. For great employers, people stay longer than they'd anticipated. There isn't a problem with retention. In fact, some firms find themselves having to rent more offices to accommodate the people who've decided to stay; it's not unusual for great employers to retain most, if not all, of their associates for several years. Of course people are *always* going to leave for some reason—because they're a trailing spouse, or a simply unbeatable offer from somewhere else—but the fact that most people stick around is a good sign.

So those are the three statistics you particularly want to note if you're looking at a law firm. No matter what kind of employer you're researching, you have four principle sources of research.

1. Your Career Services Office.

If you've read my book *Guerrilla Tactics For Getting The Legal Job Of Your Dreams*, you know what a fan I am of career services people. They really do dedicate their lives to helping you get what you want, and if you've never talked to your Career Services Director, you're missing out on a tremendous—and free!—resource.

If you ask your Career Services Director about a particular employer, you'll frequently find that (s)he knows somebody who's worked there, and can either put you on to that person directly, or recount what (s)he's heard about the employer. Either way, your Career Services/Director is a clearing house of information that you shouldn't overlook. (They'll also be able to put you on to printed materials, like firm brochures and copies of articles about different employers, since most Career Services Office keep voluminous files of these kinds of things.)

2. Firm and company brochures and web pages.

These are excellent resources for doing "hard research"—namely, finding out where employers are, what they do, how many people they have, and the like. Lots of them have great links to other web pages, and some fascinating history (the Kraft web page, for instance, gives you the history of Jell-O, and the Shell Oil home page answers a question that's probably plagued you forever:"What is gasoline?"). Web pages also gives you very practical nuts and bolts information about job openings and job descriptions. But when it comes to determining personality, brochures and web pages have to be analyzed carefully for useful tidbits, because most firm brochures and web pages are actually pitched toward clients and customers, not you, the job-seeker. You'll find lots of lofty talk about "high-quality work," "a collegial atmosphere," "responsive personnel," blah blah blah.

You have to scratch the surface to find information that reveals a lot about the personality of the place. For instance, some law firms have brochures that list the lawyers' hobbies. It doesn't sound like much, but the fact that they make a point of letting you know something about them personally suggests that they'll care about you personally, as well. And sometimes brochures and web sites can reveal an organization's sense of humor, and that again is a plus. So even though you can expect to wade through a lot of boilerplate, it's worth taking a look at brochures and web sites.

3. Surveys in The American Lawyer, profiles in The National Law Journal, and the book The Insider's Guide To Law Firms.

Yes, *American Lawyer* and *The Insider's Guide* are controversial, but heck, so is this book. The controversy stems from the fact that it's just not feasible to get feedback from *everybody* in an organization, and even if you could, every single person in the world has an agenda, and so they may or may not be great sources. So to some extent we all face the "reliable source" issue.

Having said all that, *I* like *American Lawyer* and *The Insider's Guide. The Insider's Guide,* in case you aren't familiar with it, is a very chatty, detailed look at the country's largest firms in the biggest cities, and if that's where you're focusing your search, *The Insider's Guide* is a great resource. *American Lawyer* runs a survey periodically reflecting the views of mid-level associates at large-ish firms around the country. (The most recent national winner, Long Aldridge in Atlanta, is profiled in this book.) And every year *American Lawyer* runs a "Summer Associate" survey of the country's largest firms, based on feedback from summer associates. This again is great fun reading, but a word of caution: they don't call them "summer partners" for nothing, you know. It's easy for a terrible firm to put on a happy face for summer associates, and I can name you several where the permanent associates will be the first to admit that their summer associates are deliberately kept in the dark. So if you're relying on the summer associate survey for information on a permanent job, take the results with a grain of salt.

Finally, the *National Law Journal* ("*NLJ*") runs periodic profiles of legal employers. They ran one relatively recently on Jenkens & Gilchrist, for instance, and that firm is profiled in this book. You'll find that *NLJ* profiles are frequently photocopied by Career Services Offices, and you can find them there. Or you can visit the *NLJ* web site, at ljx.com, and find some legal employer information there. (And while you're visiting ljx.com, be sure to click on the *Job Goddess* icon, so you can read that charming and delightful job search column that's coincidentally written by yours truly!)

4.   *Any members of the legal community that you happen to know.*

If you are fortunate enough to know lawyers and/or judges in the city where you intend to work, by all means tell them where you're interviewing and ask what they've heard about the employer. If you follow the advice I often give in the *Job Goddess* column and you do a judicial clerkship, your judge (and your judge's colleagues) are an excellent resource, as well. It's amazing how an employer's reputation flies around the legal community, and those kinds of insights can save you from choosing a bad employer—and guide you toward a great one.

INTERVIEWING — AND OBSERVING

I'm not talking here about standard interview techniques—I cover all of that in excruciating detail in *Guerrilla Tactics For Getting The Legal Job Of Your Dreams,* and this book is plenty long enough without reinventing the wheel!

In *Guerrilla Tactics*, my focus is on how to get the employer to want you. Here, I'm going to talk instead about how to determine, via the interview and your own observations, whether or not the employer will make you happy. That's a very different kettle of fish. Let's see how you go about identifying employers that will make you happy, when you go to interview with them:

1. *Questions you can ask in any interview, even before you have an offer:*

If you are interviewing with a junior-ish person—someone who is within four years of starting with the organization—ask questions like this: How do you like your job? What do you like about it? What kinds of things did you look for when you were talking to employers? Is your job what you expected it to be? How is it different? What would you change about it if you could? What do you wish you'd known before you started?

What I want you to do when you ask these questions is twofold. First of all, *watch the interviewer very carefully as you ask the questions, especially "How do you like your job?"* Many interviewers are fairly glib and will be able to summon an answer quickly, but they probably *won't* be able to control their immediate facial reaction, and that can be very telling. If the interviewer winces slightly, or pauses, when asked about how much (s)he likes his/her job, that's not a good sign!

The second thing you want to do is to pay attention to the answers, identifying particularly whether the interviewer looked for the kinds of things you're looking for, and likes the kind of things you like. If livable hours are important to you and the interviewer mentions the fact that she gets to spend a lot of time with her family, then you've smoked out the hours issue without ever having to ask about it! Some interviewers are caught so unawares by this "how do you like your job" question that they are more honest than they want to be. One law student told me a hilarious story about interviewing on-campus with a utility company. She followed the *Guerrilla Tactics* advice and asked the interviewer how he liked his job, and she said that "He looked at me like a deer frozen in headlights. He stuttered, and said, "Actually, now that you ask, I *hate* it. It's tedious. I'm not sure why I'm still here." Well, thank you Mr. Ambassador from the utility, for a start! Can you *imagine* a more useful question, in terms of determining what kind of an employer that particular utility is? I can't!

2. *Things to observe—and questions to ask—at call-back interviews in the employer's office:*

When you visit an employer's office, you can find out a whole bunch of useful information *without ever asking even one question.* Don't under-value your powers of observation! When you are walking around an employer's digs, they'll be telling you how collegial they are, what a great atmosphere they have, how they aren't a sweatshop, how they want you to have a life, how family-friendly they are. Your eyes will go a long way toward telling you whether or not they're coming clean. What should you look for? Consider the following:

a. Look and see whether the support staff looks happy.

I can't count the number of people who stress the importance of support staff. If you walk by the desks of secretaries, paralegals, researchers, if they all look happy, there's a good chance it's a good place to work. Why? For one thing, if the support staff is happy and treated well, it's likely that management's attitude is a magnanimous one toward you, as well. And secondly, a happy support staff is more efficient and more helpful. When you start your job, you'll quickly find that you really don't know much. But the support staff does, and if they're contented, they'll help you out in a million ways you couldn't have anticipated in school.

You can also watch to see whether or not you're introduced to support staffers as you're shown around the office. If you are, it's just more evidence that they are treated with respect, and you can expect to be, as well.

b. Look to see whether office doors are primarily open or closed.

Open communication between senior and junior people is a key element of enjoyment for most new lawyers. You often hear people talk about an "open door" policy. This is one policy with a physical manifestation. As you walk around, look to see if people's doors actually are open. Take into account that if someone is working on a project where they can't be disturbed, they're going to have their door closed no matter how friendly an environment it is. But if the office doors are by and large open, that's a good sign.

c. Is there laughter in the hallways?

Everybody will tell you how collegial a place they work in. But if as you walk around you see a lot of long faces, they've got an interesting definition of "collegial." Great employers tend to have happy offices, and that means that people will feel free to stop in the hallways and chat—and laugh. If you notice this going on, you won't have to ask whether they're collegial or not. You've already seen it for yourself.

d. See how they refer to each other.

What you're looking for here is "Bart Simpson" or "Buffy Vampireslayer", as opposed to "Mr. Simpson" or "Miss Vampireslayer." Junior lawyers at great employers often talk about everybody being on first name terms. If they do this off-hand as they show you around, that's a good sign. You may also want to glance at nameplates on offices. Some junior lawyers say that the fact that their nameplates say "Bart Simpson" as opposed to "Mr. Simpson" is an indication of non-stuffiness that appeals to virtually everybody.

e. Notice what kinds of things decorate the offices.

Many employers will tell you how family-friendly they are, and how they value the private lives of their employees. You can see if they're true to their words by looking at what decorates their offices. At stuffy employers, you're likely to see wood-framed diplomas. At more relaxed employers, you'll see family photos, artwork by kids, sometimes little desk toys. If families really matter to them, those kinds of little touches are likely to be all over the place. You can tell what's important to people by looking at what surrounds them at work, and the extent to which your personality will be allowed to flourish as well.

f. Look for little keys to the hours you'll be expected to work.

It goes without saying that if you see cots in some junior lawyers' offices, they aren't there to accommodate afternoon naps. They're there for all-nighters, and you proceed at your own risk!

8. Questions to ask, to flush out hours and early responsibility.

If you want to find out about the hours you'll be expected to work and the kinds of projects you'll get, there are plenty of ways to accomplish this without asking straight out.

For hours, let's see what your options are. One thing you can do is to ask whether or not people at the office socialize during the week. If they work late, the answer will probably reveal that: "Oh, no, by the time we get out, we just want to get home," or "Sure, we get together for Happy Hours twice a week at the local watering hole." Also listen for indirect indications that you're expected to work late. For instance, if an employer talks about "closing the offices early on Fridays so we can have an in-house Happy Hour at 5:30," that suggests that they consider 5:30 p.m. "early"—and would otherwise expect you to be there somewhat later on Friday nights.

Another way to determine hours requires a bit more work, but if it's something that worries you, it's worth it. Find a reason to stop by the employer's offices at 6:30 or 7 p.m. during the week, either to drop off a writing sample or an article you think might interest some-one you've spoken with from there. If there are a lot of lights still on, and they tell you that they regularly quit work at 6 p.m., either it's a very unusual night or—what's more likely—6 p.m. is a goal they don't often meet. You can similarly call a junior associate with a question at 6:30 or 7 at night, at the office. If they're there to answer your question, you may want to casually ask what they're working on—if it's nothing out of the ordinary, then they're expected to be there at that time, and you may well be expected to do the same.

There are questions you can ask that will help you determine *exactly* what kind of projects you can expect to get early in your career. As one large firm associate explained to me, "You need to ask young associates, 'What are you working on today?' and not 'How many depositions have you taken?' or 'What have you gotten to do?' Ask them, *right now,* what they are working on. Ask them, 'When I walk out of here, what are you going to be doing?'" As other associates have told me, "Everybody is going to try to get you 'windshield time' somehow"—that is, time outside of the office—but it's what you do on a *regular* basis that determines how much you'll enjoy the job. *Every* new lawyer does a certain modicum of mundane work (well, *almost* all of them). You can't totally avoid it. But asking what your interviewer is going to go back to the moment you leave is a great way to smoke that out.

3.   *Questions you can ask once you have an offer:*

As I hammered home in *Guerrilla Tactics For Getting The Legal Job Of Your Dreams,* before you have an offer, you can't ask questions that scream, "What's in it for me?" Once you have an offer under your belt—and if you follow the advice in *Guerrilla Tactics,* of course you *will* have one—then all bets are off. You can ask virtually any question that concerns you. You can:

• Ask about the pay.

• Ask about the bonus schedule, and how bonuses are determined.

• Ask about how much business (if any) you are expected to bring in (if you're interviewing with a law firm), when you're supposed to start generating business, and what kind of training there is associated with that.

• Ask about the benefits, and ask junior lawyers which benefits are important to them. For instance, if you're going to be working in a large city and you plan to drive to work, "free parking" can mean an extra several hundred dollars in your pocket every month.

• Ask junior lawyers who they go to with questions—in other words, do they have a mentor program? Or are informal mentors easily found?

• Ask how closely junior lawyers work with supervisors. Most junior lawyers prefer "elbow learning," that is, working with and observing more experienced people. While formal training programs can be elaborate and a lot of fun, they won't make up for "the real thing."

- Ask how junior lawyers' issues are addressed by management. Is management responsive to what associates have to say, and how does that come across? Do managers ask junior lawyers informally what's on their minds, are there formal meetings, and do they take action on what junior lawyers suggest or do they blow them off?

- Ask whether junior lawyers have worked with anybody difficult and how those kinds of problems are addressed.

- Ask how many women at the office have small children, and how the organization handles family issues, if those kinds of things matter to you.

- Talk with as many junior lawyers as you can, to get a good feel for whether you'll get along with your colleagues. In other words—I'm ending this chapter the way I started it, by ensuring that you're going in with your eyes open. You know what to expect, and the employer is in line with your expectations. If you do *that*, I *promise* you'll be happy with what you choose!

Ultimate Dream Jobs

*The Glamorous Sports, Entertainment,
International, and Headline-Making Employers
That Most Law Students Only Dream About.*

All of the jobs in this book are great, in some way, otherwise I wouldn't have included them. But for the jobs in this chapter? Ah—there's something extra special about them. These are the jobs I call "the droolables"— they've got that certain je ne sais quoi that makes people say, "No way! How did you get that job?"

I won't pretend that these jobs are easy to come by. For one thing, there aren't many of them. In-house counsel's jobs at companies in sexy industries, or for government agencies like NASA, are few and far between. For another, the requirements can be pretty hairy. The Foreign Service exam is notoriously grueling. If you're going to be a clerk for a Supreme Court Justice, you'd better have *stratospheric* paper credentials. If you're going to be a sports or talent agent, your paper credentials don't matter, but you'd better have brass cajones—and two sets of them.

And if you want to start out making pots of money, don't even think about getting your feet wet in the sports or entertainment industries, where starting out in the mailroom—in terms of responsibility *and* pay— isn't far from the truth.

Beyond that, getting many of these jobs is a matter of being in the right place at the right time. For many of the people I've profiled in this chapter, luck very much tapped them on the shoulder. This idea of luck playing a major role in our lives is awfully difficult to accept, isn't it? We don't like to leave things to chance; we prefer to be masters of our destiny. But luck has played a role in many, many great successes throughout history. I could tell you a million stories along these lines, and you probably have heard many of them already, so I'll just tell you this one. You may not have known that the first person to fly from New York to Paris wasn't supposed to be Charles Lindbergh—the likely history-maker was supposed to be a famous World War I flying ace named Rene Fonck. He had a plane specially built for the crossing, and in honor of the historic occasion, he had it magnificently fitted out with mahogany and red Spanish leather, all kinds of exotic navigational equipment, and he and his three crewmen planned to take many gifts with them as well as a vacuum-packed six-course meal to eat as a celebration dinner when they landed in Paris. The plane, as kitted out, was almost 50% heavier than it should have been, and as Fonck tried to take off from New York, the landing gear buckled, the plane started breaking up and it tore through a fence at the end of the runway, and burst into flames, killing two of the crewmen. The accident made all of the newsreels all over the country, and one of the people who saw the newsreel was a young mail pilot—Charles Lindbergh. He hadn't previously given a thought to crossing the Atlantic, but seeing that newsreel changed his life. No newsreel—no "Lucky Lindy."

Of course, while a *particular* job might be a matter of luck, having a career in an industry you dream about isn't. There are things you can do to improve your chances substantially. Strategically-chosen internships are just one option. Leaping at opportunities that give you a chance to rub elbows with people who can help you (like volunteering at NCAA meets, parking cars at the Sundance Film Festival), outside of your day-to-day responsibilities—*even if that means giving up nights and weekends*—is another. But the fact is, with so few "ultimate dream" jobs and so many wannabes, there are no guarantees.

Does all of that depress you? It shouldn't. A philosophy you might consider is the one espoused by the character Esther Plotkin, in the old version of *The Star Is Born*, when she was asked why, out of the millions of girls in America, she thought she'd get to be a movie star. "Well," she said, "They've got to pick *somebody*." And I'd say to you—*someone's* got to do the jobs in this chapter. Maybe—just maybe—someday it will be you!

Sports

If the very thought of sports makes you weak at the knees—well, you probably shouldn't be a professional athlete. But thankfully, no matter what your knees are like, there are a million things you *can* do in the sports industry with your law degree, both traditional and nontraditional. What I'm going to do here is to take you *briefly* through a bunch of different options, give you some expert tips for breaking into the sports field, profile a sports lawyer and a great employer and give you the names of specific sports employers who've received rave reviews across the country. I've also given you some helpful sports publications, web sites and books to take a look at, because while the information here will give you a start, it just skims the surface of the sports possibilities open to you. If you want to go into sports, you'll want to turn over every stone, and check out those resources. What this section *will* do is get you started. After that, keep an open mind and be as creative as possible—and hopefully what you'll read here will help you do just that.

WHAT'S OUT THERE? TRADITIONAL AND NONTRADITIONAL CAREERS IN SPORTS.

Before we get into anything more specific, I want to spend a minute talking about exactly what the heck the sports industry *is*, at its core. And to do this I'm going to share with you the wisdom of the wonderful Jack Swarbrick. He is not only a partner at Baker & Daniels in Indianapolis—one of the best law firms in the country to work for, which is why it's profiled in Chapter 4—but he also runs J.B. Sports, which provides marketing and management services to the sports industry. You'll see a list of Jack's "Do's and Don'ts" for breaking into the sports industry a little further on in this section, but for right now, I'll give you his handy thumbnail breakdown of all of sports, as it relates to law school graduates. You have:

- Intellectual Property (in the form of what's known as 'soft' IP, namely, trademarks and copyrights);

- Broadcasting rights;

- Event identities;

- Unique antitrust issues;

    and

- Traditional business associations issues (as in forming franchises, forming and negotiating agreements, and creating new event properties).

   As you'll see, virtually everything else we talk about in this section will involve one or more of these areas.

A.   *Traditional sports lawyering jobs.*

Let's start by talking about traditional lawyering activities that happen to involve sports. You've got three basic possibilities (remember, I'll give you tips on breaking into these areas later on in this section):

- Working for a firm that does sports law, representing athletes, team, leagues, and other related entities.

- Working for a team or a league as in-house counsel.

- Working for an entity that sponsors, or invests in, sports. Jack Swarbrick feels that this is the area that will experience the biggest growth in sports, and what he's talking about is this: "The Coca-Colas, the McDonalds, the John Hancocks of the world, these are companies that have investments in sports, and they need to protect those investments. These kinds of organizations need people to work on agreements and protect the marks associated with sports sponsorships." (For breaking into corporations—both in-house counsel's offices and nontraditional jobs on the business side—check out Chapter 8.)

B. *Nontraditional sports careers.*

Remember, I'm limiting the scope of careers to things where your law degree will be necessary or useful. There isn't anything that stops you from being a professional beach volleyball player with your law degree, but if you're that good at beach volleyball, why waste your time in law school?

Also, keep in mind that many of these jobs are ones to shoot for down the road, if ever. You're just not going to start your career as General Manager of the New York Yankees—but for a rookie league team, the position of General Manager is a much more distinct possibility in the near term. Be willing to work for a team doing *anything*, sometimes for very little pay, and take it from there.

With that little disclaimer out of the way, let's look at some nontraditional sports careers that law school graduates enjoy. (For a much more in-depth description of these kinds of jobs, check out the excellent book *The 50 Coolest Jobs In Sports*, by David Fischer):

1. Jobs aligned with specific sports teams, including General Manager, Business Manager, Director of Minor League Operations, Marketing Director, or Traveling Secretary.

2. Sports agenting/marketing.

3. Director of a sports complex/stadium operations/sports event coordinating.

Since these kinds of jobs probably aren't as familiar to you as traditional sports-oriented jobs, let's talk a little bit about what each one of these careers involves.

JOBS ALIGNED WITH PARTICULAR TEAMS

TEAM GENERAL MANAGER

What it is: Every professional sports team, in every professional sport (football, baseball, basketball, soccer, hockey) has a general manager. You're the sports equivalent of the president of a company, in that you handle the team's day-to-day activities, and you hire and fire people, among other duties. Depending on how large an organization you're talking about, you might also handle the team's publicity and marketing. You are also responsible for helping to put together a winning team, and so you have to stay up-to-date on your sport and who the prospects are. You also help negotiate salaries. In the smaller, lower-division teams, you might go by the title of "Business Manager" or, in baseball, "Director of Minor League Operations."

BUSINESS MANAGER FOR A PROFESSIONAL SPORTS TEAM

What it is: All professional sports teams in every sport (baseball, football, basketball, hockey, soccer) have a business manager. In this role, as the name suggests, you handle the business of the team. You solicit bids for any goods and services the team needs, help handle contracts, and deal with problems confronting the team and any of its members. You may also have to work with the stadium that hosts your team. You have to keep track of all of the bills associated with the team, and keep accurate records. You also work closely with the traveling secretary who handles the team's travel needs, helping to plan hotels, transportation, and everything associated with travel. As all of this suggests, the job is one with lots of varied responsibility.

MARKETING DIRECTOR FOR A PROFESSIONAL SPORTS TEAM

What it is: You handle every aspect of marketing the team and its players. You create and implement marketing campaigns, create new markets, and handle licensing for the team's name and logo. Your duties may stretch from handling giveaways and contests at the stadium itself, to developing and handling personal appearances and press interviews for the athletes.

For bigger, higher-level teams, there are assistant marketing directors, and you typically move into the marketing director's role from the assistant position. For lower-level teams, you'd probably also have public relations duties, which would mean preparing brochures, newsletters, press releases, and handling trade shows.

Because any kind of marketing position requires a lot of writing, accentuate your writing skills!

TRAVELING SECRETARY FOR A PROFESSIONAL SPORTS TEAM.

What it is: This doesn't involve the traditional secretarial roles like taking dictation. Instead, you handle all of the travel arrangements for the team, including chartering planes and buses and negotiating deals with hotels and restaurants. You handle operational details on the road and make sure that all of the athletes and other people associated with the team have their basic needs met. You also handle crises and problems that crop up on the road.

SPORTS AGENTING/MARKETING AND DIRECTOR OF A SPORTS COMPLEX/STADIUM OPERATIONS/SPORTS EVENT COORDINATING

What it is: If you've seen Jerry Maguire—and if you're interested in sports law, you probably *have*—you know about sports agenting. In fact, many people think *only* of sports agents when they think about sports lawyers, although as Jack Swarbrick points out, "There are many, many facets to the sports industry and its needs for traditional legal services. Representing athletes is a very small part of it."

Sports agenting is a tremendously cutthroat business, involving convincing young athletes to let you represent them, and then getting those athletes (and sometimes coaches and other sports-related personalities) the best possible deal with their team and companies who want them to endorse products and services. Some agents also act as financial advisers, helping athletes handle their investments. As some sports agents have told me, "I spend all day on the phone, looking for deals, making deals, closing deals. If you don't 'give great phone,' this is not the business for you."

Here's the scoop on sports event coordinating. Events like the Olympics, the Kentucky Derby, the U.S. Open, and every other major sports event don't just happen—they are carefully planned. And the people who do that careful planning are sports event coordinators. In this role you either work for a facility, like a resort or stadium or arena, or you work for (or as) a sports promoter who handles different events at different locations.

If you work for a particular facility, you might be a director of a sports complex or director of stadium operations (or any one of a myriad of people who work with them). You work with others (like public relations, marketing people, security) to figure out what kinds of preparations will be necessary. You may have to handle the media and set up related events like press conferences and cocktail parties or meals, and you may have to handle transportation and accommodation for athletes, officials, and other visitors. In addition, you have the preparations peculiar to each sport or event—for instance, track events will require special equipment, timers, and the like. And you will always have to troubleshoot problems that are sure to arise.

Sports marketing has a variety of meanings, but all of them revolve around one activity: selling. For instance, when you represent an athlete and you analyze that athlete's appeal and then try and encourage sponsors to have your athlete hawk their products, that's sports marketing. And it's also selling. Jack Swarbrick points out that sports marketing "involves many things that athlete clients will ask their lawyers for beyond representing them in negotiating a contract, like packaging a sports event for presentation to a network."

BREAKING INTO THE SPORTS INDUSTRY

You already know that sports is competitive. That's the bad news. But as I've said before and I'll say many times again, *somebody* has to get those jobs. But *how?* The whole subject of job search is one that I cover in excruciating detail in my book *Guerrilla Tactics For Getting The Legal Job Of Your Dreams*, and yes, that's a blatant pitch for you to buy *that* book. But the fact is that when you're talking about a glamorous industry like sports, there are certain unique steps that make sense. What I'll do here is to outline a few of those. To start with, I'll give you some advice from Jack Swarbrick, which many, many people have echoed:

Jack Swarbrick's "DO'S" and "DON'TS" for breaking into sports.

DO look broadly at the sports industry. "Sports isn't just being an agent." There are *many* administrative jobs (as I outlined above and profile below), and if you love sports, you'll find that not only will you enjoy those jobs, but you'll find that your law degree is a real plus!

DO "become a good lawyer first." Jack Swarbrick feels that you need good writing skills, good negotiating skills, you know how to draft agreements and solve problems.

DO "go where the industry has a presence." For entertainment, that's Los Angeles or New York, and for sports, that means a sports-oriented city or "a firm that does sports."

DON'T rely on Martindale-Hubbell for firms that say they practice sports law, since those listings tend to include "everyone who has ever had any involvement in sports," as opposed to a vigorous, growing practice now. Instead, "Talk to someone with an honest-to-God sports practice, and find out who's doing what through them. Or search Martindale-Hubbell, or Lexis or Westlaw, for litigation matters involving sports." Sports-oriented publications (I've listed several below, in the publications section) would also help. And I can tell you that at least three of the firms in this book have substantial sports law practices. They are Waller Lansden in Nashville, Proskauer Rose in New York City, and Jack Swarbrick's own firm, Baker & Daniels in Indianapolis.

DO be flexible. Jack Swarbrick laughs that "90% of law careers are shaped completely by accident!" He got his own start in sports as a labor and litigation lawyer at Baker & Daniels in Indianapolis, representing traditional clients, Midwestern manufacturers. He had no ambition for sports law. However, one day the managing partner stopped him in a hallway and said, "Do you have any time? Call this guy. He's got a problem." The managing partner handed him a slip of paper, and the 'guy' turned out to be involved with U.S.A. Gymnastics, which had just relocated to Indianapolis. When Swarbrick called him, he explained that they had a 14-year-old girl, a gymnast, and her hometown in Texas wanted to sell bumper stickers to help pay for her training. They were worried about whether selling the bumper stickers would harm her eligibility. Swarbrick researched it, found that the bumper sticker sales wouldn't fly, and he set up systems to preserve her eligibility. That 14-year-old girl turned out to be Mary Lou Retton. Swarbrick says that "After that, other people in other sports started calling me." As he advises, "Just follow your career wherever it goes. Don't ever say, 'I don't do that,' because you don't know where it might lead."

DO network. I know what a hideous word that is, but it's important to meet as many people as you can. Attend conferences and seminars (I'll give you some organizations and conferences in just a little while), but realize that it takes determination to get to the people you want to meet. In their own habitats, "established presences have elaborate defense mechanisms," because they get contacted "all the time."

DO volunteer. "If you live in New York City, work your normal workweek as a lawyer and then volunteer at Madison Square Garden." Others have told me that you can volunteer while you're still in school, even if you're not in a big sports mecca. For instance, for intramural teams you can organize the fields, the insurance, the schedule and the referees. And of course you can volunteer for sports agents, teams, and leagues, as well.

DO recognize that when it comes to sports agenting, "No kid who can't read a freshman literature book is going to take a new law school graduate as their agent, unless they were college roommates." If you want to be an agent, there's nothing stopping you from volunteering for one during school, and then joining a firm as a sports lawyer and moving into agenting from there. Alternatively, you can volunteer for a sports agent, but "In order for them to take you on permanently, you'll have to have a unique skill. For most agents, that means either a financial skill that they can sell—for instance, you have a CPA—or you have relationships, you know athletes."

DO be a good writer. "If you can't write clearly, you can't think clearly." A lot of sports work involves writing proposals, brochures, and other "plain language" literature. Notice that you don't need Law Review to prove your writing skills—you can write for sports-oriented newsletters and other publications.

DO be technologically sophisticated. "It's important to know how to manage and manipulate databases."

DO show that you're creative. Much of what goes on in sports-related careers doesn't have precedent, there aren't applicable case laws or statutes. Jack Swarbrick looks for people who show creativity "in virtually anything. For instance, maybe it wasn't so easy for you to get to law school in the first place—maybe you didn't have the money, maybe you had other obligations that made it difficult. Overcoming obstacles like that requires creativity."

DON'T bother with sports-related job fairs. "If you look at what's going on at these, it's all sellers and no buyers. They tend to be a waste of time."

Do's and Don'ts in general . . .

You can't beat Jack Swarbrick's advice—but you can supplement it. Other great tips to jolly along your sports career include . . .

DO *whatever it takes to get your foot in the door.* You couldn't learn from a better role model than Dave Dombrowski, general manager of the Florida Marlins. You know how he got his start? While he was in college, he interviewed the Chicago White Sox general manager while researching a paper on the general manager's role in baseball—who suggested that he job hunt at baseball's winter meetings in Honolulu. Dombrowski went there, and at the meetings he snagged a job interview with the White Sox. Dombrowski said he'd do "anything" to work for them—move cartons, shovel sidewalks, type, anything at all. He started, at $8,000 a year (!), as an administrative assistant in the White Sox minor league and scouting department, doing everything from filing, to making travel arrangements for spring training, to operating the scoreboard to chauffeuring around the team's owner, Bill Veeck. Within a year he moved up to assistant director of player development, and two years later, he was director of player development. Then, at the age of 26, he became assistant general manager. By 1990 he was general manager of the Montreal Expos, and in 1993 he joined the Marlins. What does all of this tell you? It doesn't matter where you *start.* It only matters where you *wind up.*

DO check your ego at the door. The people you contact in the sports industry are not only very busy but also *very* put upon. It's not the career for you if your feelings are easily hurt when a phone call or letter goes unanswered.

DON'T give up when you don't get a response. Follow up time and time again. "Not now" does mean "not ever." Remember that especially for sports agents and people like them, their jobs require a great deal of self-confidence and assertiveness, and if you want to work with them, you're going to require the same skills *getting* the job as you would in *performing* the job.

DO keep records of your contacts, and follow up with people you meet at conferences, seminars, and every other networking opportunity.

DO write as much as you can for sports-oriented publications (I've listed some below), or take advantage of *any* writing opportunity to write about a sports-oriented theme (remember Dave Dombrowski and his research paper on the role of general managers in baseball). You'll not only give yourself writing experience, proof of your writing skills, and a great resume item, but you'll have something to send to people *other* than your resume—something that will actually *help them!*

DO keep in mind that you only get what you want through mutually beneficial relationships. Every person you contact in the sports industry knows what they can do for *you*—what can you do for *them?* Often that means that you have to work for free (or very little) to start out, while you develop a marketable skill. The chief operating officer of the New Jersey Nets, in a recent radio interview, was asked how to get ahead in a professional sports team, and his advice was, "Be willing to do *anything*." The old "up from the mail room" story *works* in professional sports.

GREAT INTERNSHIPS THAT GET YOUR FOOT IN THE DOOR

Everybody I talked to in any sports capacity agreed that internships are an excellent way to break into the industry. There are *tons* and *tons* of internships; Jack Swarbrick's J.B. Sports in Indianapolis always has law student interns. There are many others. For instance, you'll find internships with:

- Professional sports leagues (like the NFL, NBA, MLB, NHL)—you'll find their web sites a little later on in this chapter

- Teams (both major and minor league)—I've provided you with the names and addresses for professional sports teams in football, baseball, hockey and basketball in the next section

- College athletic departments in Division I or Division II schools

- The NCAA

- Corporations that sponsor leagues, teams and athletes

- News organizations that report on sports

- Sports marketing agencies

- Sports agents

On top of that, you can intern in any number of areas—operations management, recruiting, marketing, and law. For many more interning opportunities, check out the publications, web sites and books I recommend under "Exceptionally Useful Associations, Conferences, Web Sites and Books" in just a couple of pages.

To get information on specific internships, write to the human resources or personnel director at any sports organization that interests you—I've included the names of some on-line and hard copy references below—and ask when and how to apply. You'll find that there's a tremendous advantage when it comes to digging up opportunities most people will never realize exist if you're a living, breathing person in the office, instead of existing solely as a mailed-in resume!

Another internship to consider is one featured in Princeton Review's excellent book *The Princeton Review's Guide to America's Top Internships*—the U.S. Olympic Committee ("USOC"). Here are more details about this particular internship:

United States Olympic Committee

Coordinator of Educational Programs
One Olympic Plaza • Colorado Springs, CO 80909-5760
Phone: 719-632-5551, ext. 2597 • Fax: 719-578-4817

Details on the Internship:

The internships last approximately 13 weeks in the summer, and 15 weeks in the fall and 21 weeks in the spring (if you're willing to take a semester off). The pay is paltry—$45 a week—but you get room and board. The internships take place mostly at the USOC's facility in Colorado Springs, but there are a few openings in Lake Placid, New York, and San Diego, California—all of them gorgeous spots.

The USOC is divided into 17 divisions, including Broadcasting, Accounting, Journalism, Computer Science, Sports Administration, International Relations, and Marketing/Fundraising. The USOC also houses the national governing bodies of 15 sports associations. Obviously, your duties as an intern vary greatly depending on the division, and different divisions require different skills (for instance, the International Relations division requires fluency in French or Spanish, and the Journalism division requires six recent writing samples). All internships require familiarity with computers.

To apply: Deadlines are June 1 for the fall semester, February 15 for the summer term, and October 1 for the spring semester. For more information, or for a Student Intern Program Application, contact the USOC.

*Incidentally, while internships get universal rave reviews, I've heard mixed reviews of Sports Law Administration master's degrees. Some people actually break into sports as a result of these programs (as in the case of Peter Carton, who is profiled just below), because of the contacts if not for the specific skills you learn. Others believe that they aren't tremendously useful, and that if you just have to spend another year or two in school, you're better off with an all-purpose business degree, like an MBA, since you can always use the business administration skills you learn there in a sports context.

NAMES, ADDRESSES AND PHONE NUMBERS OF PROFESSIONAL SPORTS TEAMS IN FOOTBALL, BASEBALL, BASKETBALL AND HOCKEY

Remember these three bits of standard advice when you contact any sports team, either looking for internships or permanent jobs:

1. Don't ever write a letter to "personnel director" or any other job title. Instead, call ahead and find out the name of the person you ought to contact.

2. Be willing to take any job to break in, and then move up from there by making friends with, and impressing, everybody there.

3. Be *very* nice to receptionists and whoever answers the phone. They can frequently persuade your "quarry" to interview you by saying nice things about you to that person.

NFL Football Teams

Arizona Cardinals
8701 S. Hardy Drive
Tempe, AZ 85284
602-379-0101
www.azcardinals.com/

Atlanta Falcons
One Falcon Place
Suwanee, GA 30024-2198
770-945-1111
www.atlantafalcons.com/

Baltimore Ravens
11001 Owings Mills Blvd.
Owings Mills, MD 21117
410-654-6200
www.nfl.com/ravens/

Buffalo Bills
One Bills Drive
Orchard Park, NY 14127-2296
716-648-1800
www.buffalobills.com

Carolina Panthers
800 South Mint Street
Charlotte, NC 28202
704-358-7000
www.nfl.com/panthers

Chicago Bears
1000 Football Drive
Lake Forest, IL 60045
847-295-6600
www.nfl.com/bears

Cincinnati Bengals
One Bengals Drive
Cincinnati, OH 45204
513-621-3550
www.nfl.com/bengals

Cleveland Browns
(beginning in 1999)
80 First Avenue
Berea, OH 44017
440-891-5000
www.clevelandbrowns.com/

Dallas Cowboys
One Cowboys Parkway
Irving, TX 75063
972-556-9900
www.dallascowboys.com/

Denver Broncos
13655 Broncos Parkway
Englewood, CO 80112
303-649-9000
www.denverbroncos.com/

Detroit Lions
1200 Featherstone Road
Pontiac, Michigan 48342
248-335-4131
http://detroitlions.com/

Green Bay Packers
1265 Lombardi Avenue
Green Bay, WI 54304
920-496-5700
www.packers.com

Indianapolis Colts
7001 W. 56th Street
Indianapolis, IN 462534
317-297-2658
www.colts.com

Jacksonville Jaguars
One ALLTEL Stadium Place
Jacksonville, FL 32202
904-633-6000
www.jaguarsnfl.com/

Kansas City Chiefs
One Arrowhead Drive
Kansas City, Missouri 64129
816-924-9300
www.kcchiefs.com/

Miami Dolphins
7500 S.W. 30th Street
Davie, FL 33314
954-452-7000
http://dolphinsendzone.com/

Minnesota Vikings
9520 Viking Drive
Eden Prairie, Minnesota 55344
612-828-6500
www.nfl.com/vikings/

New England Patriots
60 Washington Street
Foxboro, MA 02035
508-543-8200
www.patriots.com/

New Orleans Saints
5800 Airline Highway
Metairie, LA 70003
504-733-0255
www.nfl.com/saints/

New York Giants
Giants Stadium
East Rutherford, NJ 07073
201-935-8111
www.nfl.com/giants

New York Jets
1000 Fulton Avenue
Hempstead, NY 11550
516-560-8100
www.nfl.com/jets

Oakland Raiders
1220 Harbor Bay Parkway
Alameda, CA 94502
510-864-5000
www.raiders.com/

Philadelphia Eagles
3501 South Broad Street
Philadelphia, PA 19148-5201
215-463-2500
www.eaglesnet.com

Pittsburgh Steelers
300 Stadium Circle
Pittsburgh, PA 15212
412-323-0300
http://pittsburghsteelers.com/

Tampa Bay Buccaneers
One Buccaneer Place
Tampa, FL 33607
813-870-2700
800-282-0683
www.nfl.com/buccaneers/

Tennessee Oilers
Baptist Sports Park
7640 Highway 70 South
Nashville, Tennessee 37221
615-673-1500
www.nfl.com/oilers/

Washington Redskins
Redskin Park
P.O. Box 17247
Washington, D.C. 20041
703-478-8900
www.nfl.com/redskins/

St. Louis Rams
One Rams Way
St. Louis, MO 63045
Phone: 314-982-7267
www.stlouisrams.com/montage.html

San Diego Chargers
Qualcomm Stadium
San Diego, CA 92160
619-874-4500
www.nfl.com/chargers/

San Francisco 49ers
4949 Centennial Boulevard
Santa Clara, CA 95054
408-562-4949
www.sf49ers.com/

Seattle Seahawks
11220 N.E. 53rd Street
Kirkland, WA 98033
206-827-9777
www.seahawks.com/

National Basketball Association Teams

Atlanta Hawks
One CNN Center
Suite 405, South Tower
Atlanta, GA 30303
404-827-3800
www.nba.com/hawks/

Boston Celtics
151 Merrimac Street
Boston, MA 02114
617-523-6050
www.nba.com/celtics/

Charlotte Hornets
100 Hive Drive
Charlotte, NC 28217
704-357-0252
www.nba.com/hornets/

Chicago Bulls
1901 W. Madison Street
Chicago, IL 60612
312-455-4000
www.nba.com/bulls/

Cleveland Cavaliers
1 Center Court
Cleveland, OH 44115
216-420-2000
www.nba.com/cavs/

Dallas Mavericks
Reunion Arena
777 Sports Street
Dallas, TX 75207
214-748-1808
www.nba.com/mavericks/

Denver Nuggets
McNichols Sports Arena
1635 Clay Street
Denver, CO 80204
303-893-6700
www.nba.com/nuggets/

Detroit Pistons
The Palace of Auburn Hills
Two Championship Drive
Auburn Hills, MI 48326
810-377-0100
www.nba.com/pistons/

Golden State Warriors
Oakland Coliseum Arena
7000 Coliseum Way
Oakland, CA 94621
510-638-6300
www.nba.com/warriors/

Houston Rockets
Ten Greenway Plaza
Suite 400
Houston, TX 77046
713-627-3865
www.nba.com/rockets/

Indiana Pacers
300 E. Market Street
Indianapolis, IN 46204
317-263-2100
ww.nba.com/pacers/

Los Angeles Clippers
Los Angeles Memorial Sports Arena
3939 S. Figueroa St.
Los Angeles, CA 90037
213-745-0400
www.nba.com/clippers/

Los Angeles Lakers
Great Western Forum
3900 W. Manchester Blvd.
Inglewood, CA 90306
310-419-3100
www.nba.com/lakers/

Miami Heat
The Miami Arena
Miami, FL 33136-4102
305-577-4328
www.nba.com/heat/

Milwaukee Bucks
Bradley Center
1001 N. Fourth St.
Milwaukee, WI 53203
414-227-0500
www.nba.com/bucks/

Minnesota Timberwolves
Target Center
600 First Avenue North
Minneapolis, MN 55403
612-673-1600
www.nba.com/timberwolves/

New Jersey Nets
405 Murray Hill Parkway
East Rutherford, NJ 07073
201-935-8888
www.nba.com/nets/

New York Knicks
Madison Square Garden
Two Pennsylvania Plaza
New York, NY 10121
212-465-6000
www.nba.com/knicks/

Orlando Magic
One Magic Place
Orlando Arena
Orlando, FL 32801
407-649-3200
www.nba.com/magic/

Philadelphia 76ers
Veterans Stadium
P.O. Box 25040
Philadelphia, PA 19147
215-339-7600
www.nba.com/sixers/

Phoenix Suns
201 East Jefferson
Phoenix, AZ 85004
602-379-7900
www.nba.com/suns

Portland Trail Blazers
700 N.E. Multnomah Street
Suite 600
Portland, OR 97232
503-234-9291
www.nba.com/blazers/

Sacramento Kings
One Sports Parkway
Sacramento, CA 95834
916-928-0000
www.nba.com/kings/

San Antonio Spurs
Alamodome
100 Montana Street
San Antonio, TX 78203
210-554-7700
www.nba.com/spurs/

Seattle Supersonics
190 Queen Anne Avenue North,
    Suite 200
Seattle, WA 98109
206-281-5800
www.nba.com/sonics

Toronto Raptors
20 Bay Street, #1702
Toronto, Ontario, Canada M5J 2N8
416-214-2255
www.nba.com/raptors/

Utah Jazz
Delta Center
301 West South Temple
Salt Lake City, UT 84101
801-325-2500
www.nba.com/jazz/

Vancouver Grizzlies
Third Floor
780 Beatty Street
Vancouver, British Columbia,
    Canada V6B 2M1
604-681-2226
www.nba.com/grizzlies/

Washington Wizards
601 F. Street, N.W.
Washington, D.C. 20004
202-661-5000
www.nba.com/wizards

National Hockey League Teams

Mighty Ducks of Anaheim
2695 E. Katella Ave.
Anaheim, CA 92803
714-704-2700
www.mightyducks.com

Atlanta Thrashers
1 CNN Center
12 South Tower
Atlanta, GA 30303
404-584-7825
www.atlantathrashers.com

Boston Bruins
150 Causeway Street
Boston, MA 02114
617-227-3206
www.bostonbruins.com

Buffalo Sabres
1 Seymour Knox, III Plaza
Buffalo, NY 14203-3096
716-856-7300
www.sabres.com

Calgary Flames
P.O. Box 1540, Station M
Calgary, Alberta, Canada T2P 3B9
403-261-0475
www.calgaryflames.com

Carolina Hurricanes
5000 Aerial Center, Suite 100
Morrisville, NC 27560
919-467-7825
www.caneshockey.com

Chicago Blackhawks
1901 W. Madison St.
Chicago, IL 60612
312-455-7000
www.chicagoblackhawks.com

Colorado Avalanche
1635 Clay Street
Denver, CO 80204
303-893-3865
www.coloradoavalanche.com/

Columbus Blue Jackets
150 E. Wilson Bridge Road
Suite 235
Worthington, OH 43084
614-540-4625
www.columbusbluejackets.com

Dallas Stars
Dr. Pepper StarCenter
211 Cowboys Parkway
Irving, TX 75063
214-712-2890
www.dallasstars.com

Detroit Red Wings
600 Civic Center Drive
Detroit, MI 48226
313-396-7544
www.detroitredwings.com

Edmonton Oilers
11230 110th Street
Edmonton, Alberta, Canada T5G
    3GB
403-414-4000
www.edmontonoilers.com/

Florida Panthers
National Car Rental Center
2555 N.W. 137th Way
Sunrise, FL 33323
954-768-1900
www.flpanthers.com/

Los Angeles Kings
3900 W. Manchester Blvd.
Inglewood, CA 90305
310-419-3160
www.lakings.com

Minnesota Wild
444 Cedar Street, Suite 2000
St. Paul, MN 55101
No phone calls, please.
www.wild.com/

Montreal Canadiens
1260 Delagauche Tiere
Montreal, Quebec, Canada H3B 5E8
514-932-2582
www.canadiens.com/francais.index.cgm
    (in french); or
www.canadiens.com/english
    (in english)

Nashville Predators
501 Broadway
Nashville, TN 37203
615-770-2300
www.nash-nhl.com/

New Jersey Devils
Continental Airlines Arena
50 Route 120 North
East Rutherford, NJ 07073
201-935-6050
www.newjerseydevils.com

New York Islanders
1255 Hempstead Turnpike
Uniondale, NY 11553-1200
516-794-4100
www.xice.com/

New York Rangers
2 Penn Plaza, 14th Floor
New York, NY 10121
212-465-6485
www.newyorkrangers.com/

Ottawa Senators
1000 Promenade Palladium Drive
Kanata, Ontario, Canada K2V 1A4
613-599-0250
www.ottawasenators.com/

Philadelphia Flyers
3601 S. Broad Street
Philadelphia, PA 19148
215-465-4500
www.nhl.com/teams/phi/index.htm

Phoenix Coyotes
Cellular One Ice Den
9375 E. Bell Road
Scottsdale, AZ 85260
602-473-5600
www.nhlcoyotes.com

Pittsburgh Penguins
Gate No. 9
Civic Arena
Pittsburgh, PA 15219
412-642-1300
www.pittsburghpenguins.com/

St. Louis Blues
1401 Clark Avenue
St. Louis, MO 63103
314-622-2500
www.stlouisblues.com/

San Jose Sharks
525 W. Santa Clara Street
San Jose, CA 95113
408-287-7070
www.sj-sharks.com

Tampa Bay Lightning
401 Channelside Drive
Tampa, FL 33602
813-229-2658
www.tampabaylightning.com

Toronto Maple Leafs
60 Carlton Street
Toronto, Ontario, Canada M5B 1L1
416-977-1641
www.torontomapleleafs.com

Vancouver Canucks
800 Griffith Way
Vancouver, British Columbia,
    Canada V6B 6G1
604-899-4600
www.orcabay.com/canucks

Washington Capitals
601 F. Street, N.W.
Washington, D.C. 20004
202-628-3200
www.washingtoncaps.com

Major League Baseball Teams

(For other information and other web sites, visit
www.majorleaguebaseball.com)

Anaheim Angels
2000 Gene Autry Way
Anaheim, CA 92806
714-940-2000
www.angelsbaseball.com

Arizona Diamondbacks
P.O. Box 2095
Phoenix, AZ 85001
602-426-6500
www.azdiamondbacks.com

Atlanta Braves
P.O. Box 4064
Atlanta, GA 30302
404-522-7630
www.atlantabraves.com

Baltimore Orioles
Send resumes c/o Martena
    Clinton
Oriole Park at Camden Yards
333 W. Camden St.
Baltimore, MD 21201
410-685-9800
www.theorioles.com

Boston Red Sox
4 Yawkey Way
Fenway Park
Boston, MA 02215-3496
617-267-9440
www.redsox.com

Chicago Cubs
1060 W. Addison St.
Chicago, IL 60613
773-404-2827
www.cubs.com

Chicago White Sox
Comiskey Park
333 W. 35th St.
Chicago, IL 60616
312-674-1000
www.chisox.com

Cincinnati Reds
100 Cinergy Field
Cincinnati, OH 45202
513-421-4510
www.cincinnatireds.com

Cleveland Indians
Jacobs Field
2401 Ontario Street
Cleveland, OH 44115
216-420-4200
www.indians.com

Colorado Rockies
2001 Lake Street
Denver, CO 80205-2000
303-292-0200
www.coloradorockies.com

Detroit Tigers
2121 Trumbull
Detroit, MI 48216
313-962-4000
www.detroittigers.com

Florida Marlins
2267 N.W. 199th St.
Miami, FL 33056
305-626-7400
www.flamarlins.com

Houston Astros
P.O. Box 288
Houston, TX 77001
713-799-9500
www.astros.com

Kansas City Royals
P.O. Box 419969
Kansas City, MO 64141
816-921-8000
www.kcroyals.com

Los Angeles Dodgers
1000 Elysian Park Ave.
Los Angeles, CA 90012
213-224-1500
www.dodgers.com

Milwaukee Brewers
P.O. Box 3099
Milwaukee, WI 53201
414-933-4114
www.milwaukeebrewers.com

Minnesota Twins
34 Kirby Puckett Place
Minneapolis, MN 55415
612-375-1366
www.wcco.com/sports/twins

Montreal Expos
4549 Pierre-De-Coubertin Parkway
Montreal, Quebec, Canada H1V 3P2
514-253-3434
www.montrealexpos.com

New York Mets
Shea Stadium
126th and Roosevelt Avenues
Flushing, NY 11368
718-507-6387
www.nymets.com

New York Yankees
Yankee Stadium
Bronx, NY 10451
718-293-4300
www.yankees.com

Oakland Athletics
7677 Oakport St., 2nd floor
Oakland, CA 94621
510-638-4900
www.oaklandathletics.com

Philadelphia Phillies
3501 S. Broad Street
Philadelphia, PA 19148
215-463-6000
www.phillies.com

Pittsburgh Pirates
600 Stadium Circle
Pittsburgh, PA 15212
412-323-5000
www.pirateball.com

St. Louis Cardinals
250 Stadium Plaza
St. Louis, MO 63102
314-421-3060
www.stlcardinals.com

San Diego Padres
P.O. Box 122000
San Diego, CA 92112
619-283-4494
www.padres.org

San Francisco Giants
3Com Park
San Francisco, CA 94124
415-468-3700
www.sfgiants.com

Seattle Mariners
P.O. Box 4100
Seattle, WA 98104
206-346-4000
www.mariners.org

Tampa Bay Devil Rays
One Tropicana Drive
St. Petersburg, FL 33705
813-825-3137
www.devilray.com

Texas Rangers
The Ballpark in Arlington
1000 Ballpark Way
Arlington, TX 76011
817-273-5222
www.texasrangers.com

Toronto Blue Jays
1 Bluejays Way, Suite 3200
Toronto, Ontario, Canada M5V 1J1
416-341-1000
www.bluejays.ca

EXCEPTIONALLY USEFUL ASSOCIATIONS, CONFERENCES, WEB SITES AND BOOKS

These resources come courtesy of my friend Chip Lipscomb, who is just starting what I'm confident will be a brilliant career in sports law. Chip has a tremendous database of resources related to sports careers, and here are some of the highlights from that treasure chest:

Conferences

• The American Bar Association runs the "Forum on the Entertainment and Sports Industries" at least once a year. It attracts some "very high-profile speakers," making it a worthwhile event to attend (or better yet, volunteer for). For information, contact:

The American Bar Association
Forum on the Entertainment and Sports Industries
MS 11
750 North Lake Shore Drive
Chicago, Illinois 60611
Phone: 312-988-5666
Fax: 312-988-5677
Web site: abanet.org/forums/entsports/home.html

• The Institute for Sports Advancement also runs conferences once a year, called the "Sports Summit," covering issues like "broadcasting, player representation, college athletics, facility management, and event marketing." You can get more information about the conference by contacting the Institute, care of:

E.J. Krause & Associates
6550 Rockspring drive
Suite 500
Bethesda, MD 20817
Phone: 301-493-5500
Web site: ejkrause.com/sports/

Publications

- Sportsguide of Princeton, NJ, publishes the "Sports Market Place" annually. It lists teams, associations, publications, broadcasters, promoters, suppliers—really every sports resource you could want. It is also indexed by product, brand name, executive, and geographic area,

- The Sports Lawyers Association puts out a worthwhile bimonthly newsletter called "The Sports Lawyer." To contact them:

The Sports Lawyers Association
11250 Roger Bacon Drive, Suite 8
Reston, VA 20190
Phone: 703-437-4377
Fax: 703-435-4390
E-mail: sla@sportslaw.org
Web site: sportslaw.org/sla/

- The Institute for Sports Advancement publishes the "Sports Business Directory." The name is self-explanatory. (You can reach the institute at the address/web site listed above.)

- Fitness Information Technology publishes the "Sports Marketing Quarterly." Guess how often it comes out. You can reach them at:

Sports Marketing Quarterly
Fitness Information Technology
P.O. Box 4425
University Avenue
Morgantown, WV 26504
Phone: 304-599-3482 or 800-477-4348
E-mail: FIT@acess.mountain.net

- The Sports Business Daily gives you a daily insight on sponsorships, advertising, sports governing bodies, franchises, stadiums, and legal issues. You can contact them at:

Sports Business Daily
12 South Main Street, Suite 401
South Norwalk, CT 06854
Phone: 203-838-0800
E-mail: thedaily@sportsbizdaily.com

Websites

All of the major sports leagues have their own web sites, with full information about teams, league news, and the like, and the addresses are fairly predictable. They are:

The NFL: NFL.com
The NBA: nba.com
Major League Baseball: majorleaguebaseball.com
The NCAA: ncaa.org

Books

These are all excellent resources, and will tell you *much* more about the specific duties of different kinds of sports jobs, give you more profiles, and in general flesh-out everything I've told you here.

The 50 Coolest Jobs In Sports, written by David Fischer, published by Arco.

How to Get a Job in Sports: The Guide to Finding the Right Sports Career, written by John Taylor, published by Macmillan.

Career Opportunities in the Sports Industry, written by Shelly Field, published by Facts on File.

How to Get a Job in Sports, by Dale Ratermann & Mike Mullen, published by Masters Press.

WHAT'S IT LIKE TO WORK IN SPORTS

A Profile of Peter J. Carton, Jr., Director of Southeast Asia, Australia, and New Zealand Operations for Major League Baseball International

(This profile is condensed from the book *Beyond L.A. Law,* a collection of profiles of people doing interesting things with their law degrees.)

Peter Carton manages Major League Baseball's broadcast rights, licensing, marketing, sponsorship, special events, and game development in Southeast Asia, Australia, and New Zealand (sometimes called "Australasia"). Interestingly enough, Peter's lifelong interest in sports didn't involve baseball. In school, he started out playing soccer, and then became a nationally-ranked tennis player while attending undergrad school at Catholic University in Washington, D.C. During college, Peter says that "I knew I wasn't going to make a living playing professional tennis, yet I was anxious to keep up my contacts with sports." He adds that "People were asking me, 'what are you going to do when you graduate?'

My family role models pointed toward the law, yet my heart was also in sports."

During college, he wound up interning at PROSERV—a major sports marketing group in Washington, D.C.—by contacting an alum who had a colleague at PROSERV. He loved the dynamic atmosphere at PROSERV, and that internship made him realize that a career combining sports and law was very feasible—and exciting. "I looked around and realized that a lot of the major people in the organization were lawyers," says Peter, "and that the importance of good analytic and communication skills that I knew law school gives you as a foundation cannot be underestimated."

As a senior, Peter faced a dilemma that was both wonderful and excruciating. He was accepted to law school, and he also received an offer from PROSERV to come on board full-time after graduation, with a promise that his first assignment would be traveling to Georgia to live with the entertainer Kenny Rogers and his family while preparing for an upcoming made-for-television sports/rock all-star competition. The timing, work loads and geography involved made it a one-or-the-other proposition. He opted for law school, attending Seton Hall in New Jersey. While there, he served as the first Editor-in-Chief of the *Journal of Sports Law,* published a sports law-related article, and coordinated the Sports Law Symposium. Through these activities "I was constantly meeting sport law attorneys who had similar backgrounds to my own," says Peter. During his two law school summers, he studied international business law at Cambridge and clerked for a law firm in New Jersey. After law school, he found that nailing a permanent position at the entry level in a sport-law-related field was "very frustrating. All sport law positions are highly competitive and no structure is in place to hire right out of law school. I felt either overqualified for non-law-related positions within sport or underqualified for law-related ones. I felt I had tried so hard and achieved a great deal but couldn't lock onto that first right position."

He decided to pursue a masters in sports management through the University of Massachusetts in Amherst. He was recruited out of that program by Paul Archey of Major League Baseball International (Archey himself was also an alum of University of Massachusetts's sports management program). Peter first served as a consultant and then as Director of Major League Baseball International's Australia Operations in Sydney, Australia.

Peter, his wife, Susan, and their daughter, Mackenzie, still live in Sydney, where, as director of operations for the Australasia region, Peter established the office, and is responsible for handling all Major League Baseball activities. He controls all licensing, marketing, sponsorships, special events, and negotiations and sales of broadcast rights in the region. He recently conducted the "Bo Jackson Australia Tour" with Nike, and he has also established a primary school baseball teaching program. Peter describes the Australian sports fan as "just as passionate" as the American sports fan. He enjoys representing the U.S. national pastime and the league's interests abroad. He equally enjoys returning to the States to see family and colleagues, attending sports events, and, of course, playing some tennis. Today Peter is where he dreamed he would be, when, as a child, when he told himself, "This is where I want to be in life—surrounded by the thrill of professional sports . . . I feel very lucky."

SPORTS EMPLOYERS WHO RECEIVED RAVE REVIEWS IN MY SURVEYS

As in every other chapter in this book, law school administrators reported that they have happy graduates at a number of sports employers. Those employers include:

Agents

Advantage International, Inc.
1751 Pinnacle Drive
McLean, VA 22102-3833
Phone: 703-905-3300

League-Related Organizations

Major League Baseball International
1301 Avenue of the Americas
New York, NY 10019-6022
Phone: 212-350-8300

The NCAA
6201 College Boulevard
Overland Park, Kansas 66211-2422
Phone: 913-339-1906
Web site: ncaa.org

*Note that the NCAA is an association of more than 1,200 institutions—mostly schools—and their web site lists all of the schools who take part in any of the sports the NCAA covers, everything from Football to Water Polo. (The word on the street is that the easiest way to break into the NCAA is to start out on the college side, at a school with a prominent sports program, working on NCAA compliance from that angle, and then making the lateral move (or "lateraling") into the NCAA.)

Television Sports

ESPN (in-house counsel office)
605 3rd Avenue
New York, NY 10158
Phone: 212-916-9200

ESPN (broadcast headquarters)
ESPN Plaza
Bristol, CT 06010
Phone: 203-585-2000

PROFILE OF A GREAT SPORTS EMPLOYER: THE NATIONAL FOOTBALL LEAGUE

The NFL is a fantastic place to work, and it's got a ton of law-related jobs. Here's a snapshot of exactly what they do.

The National Football League

(including NFL Films, NFL Properties, Inc., and NFL Management Council)
280 Park Avenue • New York, NY 10017
Phone: 212-450-2000 (for Films, 609-722-6779)
Fax: 212-681-7599 (for the NFL); 212-681-7599
(for NFL Properties); 212-681-7590 (for Management Council);
212-681-7584 (for NFL Enterprises). • Web site: NFL.com

COMPONENTS:

The NFL itself, comprising the league's overall administration.

The word on the street is that "It's great for strategic planning, finance, management decisions, really having a hand in everything the NFL does."

NFL Properties: It is considered the "jewel of the sports marketing industry." It handles the licensing, marketing, and publishing for the 31 clubs in the NFL. Among other functions, it licenses merchandise with team insignias; brings sponsors together with league-sanctioned programs; creates special events like "The NFL Experience"; develops and produces television specials; produces game programs and books; and safeguards club trademarks and ensures quality control.

The word on the street is that "You can work with the teams in their marketing endeavors, approving the use of various logos by league, team, or athletic sponsor, or work as a member of the front team and go to a city and work to get illegal merchandise off the streets."

NFL Enterprises: It is the division responsible for enhancing fan enjoyment of the game through innovative programming and distribution. Its components include NFL Interactive (handling the NFL's web site at NFL.com), NFL SUNDAY TICKET (which allows home satellite dish owners and restaurant and bar patrons to watch up to 13 live regional telecasts), and NFL Films (winner of 69 Emmy Awards, the Films division produces over 150 hours of original programming each season, to be distributed across broadcast and cable networks, syndication, and home video).

The word on the street about NFL Films is "talk about an awesome job! You get to combine a love of football with the excitement of entertainment, putting together things like highlight films and those special edition videos sold through Sports Illustrated."

MANAGEMENT:

Commissioner: Paul Tagliabue
NFL President: Neil Austrian
NFL Enterprises President: Ron Bernard
NFL Films President: Steve Sabol
NFL Properties President: Sara Levinson
Executive Vice President and Chairman, NFL Management Council: Harold Henderson

Personnel Directors:

NFL: John Buzzeo (Senior Director of Administration & Human Resources), phone: 212-450-2000
NFL Properties: James McCloskey (Senior Director of Administration), phone: 212-450-2000
NFL Films: Barry Wolper (Vice President— Finance and Administration), phone: 609-778-1600

General Counsel:

NFL: Jeffrey Pash (Harvard Law)
NFL Properties: Gary Gertzog (NYU Law)
NFL Management Council: Dennis Curran (Boston College Law)

HISTORY AT A GLANCE . . .

The NFL is the number one professional sports league in the United States. Sports fans consistently rank NFL football as their favorite sport. Twenty-seven of the 39 top-rated sports events of all time are NFL games, and the Super Bowl is televised in over 175 countries to audiences numbering in the hundreds of millions. Through its affiliates, NFL Enterprises, NFL Films and NFL Properties, the NFL reaches millions more with satellite television programming and Emmy-winning video productions. NFL Properties, the world's number-one sports marketing company, sets the standard in the sale of licensed merchandise, has developed more corporate sponsorship relationships than any other league, and produces more special events for its business partners than any other league.

The NFL was formed in 1920, when a group of businessmen, led by George Halas of the legendary Chicago Bears, met in a Hupmobile showroom. Halas and his colleagues had no idea then what their fledgling sports venture would grow into. Over the succeeding decades, the NFL was well behind both baseball and college football in popularity. It was not until 1958, when the Baltimore Colts defeated the New York Giants in a dramatic overtime game to win the League championship, that people throughout the country took notice.

The NFL's modern era began in 1960, when a young commissioner, Pete Rozelle, took over for the late Bert Bell. In short order, Commissioner Rozelle developed a plan to guarantee that all NFL games would be shown on free television, which continues to this day and is unique to the NFL. He oversaw a merger between the NFL and the rival American Football League, which led to the Super Bowl and further expansion of the League into new cities. Under his leadership, the NFL became America's number-one sport.

In 1989, Paul Tagliabue succeeded Pete Rozelle as Commissioner. Under Commissioner Tagliabue, the NFL has continued its growth, with new teams in the Carolinas, Jacksonville, and starting in 1999, Cleveland. In addition, the League's strength as a television product has resulted in a nearly five-fold increase in television revenues in the past decade. Commissioner Tagliabue has also brought long-term labor peace to the League, with a collective bargaining agreement now slated to run until 2004.

NUMBER OF LAW SCHOOL GRADUATES EMPLOYED . . .

There are 16 law school graduates in the in-house counsel's office; and 4 others (the Commissioner, the Chairman of the Management Council, the VP of Player and Employee Development).

While most of the NFL's lawyers work full-time, the associate council for Litigation and Operations works four days a week to accommodate child care obligations.

WHO GETS HIRED?

Permanent: Most lawyers with the NFL are lateral hires; the NFL "seldom if ever" hires new law school graduates. Typical hires have 4 to 10 years of experience. Laterals have come in with litigation, corporate transactions, labor law and intellectual property law experience. Helpful backgrounds include: (i) private law firms; (ii) other sports leagues; and (iii) government experience.

Summer Clerkships: The management council hires summer clerks; write to the NFL (at the address above) for application information. Individual teams hire interns and entry-level front-office personnel; contact each club for more information. (You'll find the names and addresses above, under "Conferences, Websites, Names & Addresses.")

Entertainment

Virtually everything I just told you about sports careers goes for entertainment as well. In fact, sports superagent David Falk (a lawyer himself, by the way) says that sports and entertainment are quickly merging. As a result, if you want to break into the entertainment field, you'd be well advised to read everything in the immediately preceding sports section. And you need to remember that:

1. All positions as in-house counsel for large entertainment companies go to laterals. You're best off going to a firm that has a vigorous entertainment practice, and moving over to an in-house counsel's job from there.

2. Entertainment law firms tend to be small, and tend to differ from other law firms in several important respects. First of all, entertainment law firms—meaning ones that focus exclusively on entertainment—tend to be small. The largest ones have no more than 30 attorneys, and a 10-person entertainment firm is considered large (both Polygram and MCA have more in-house lawyers than the largest entertainment firms). Associates can expect to start at between $65,000 and $85,000, and as a partner you can make $350,000 and up. Note that entertainment firms bill by the value of the transaction to the client, not by the hour. Entertainment firms also tend to be different in that their clients rarely dispute fees; since the fees are based on the value of the transaction and lawyers are *bringing* piles of money to the table. More good news with entertainment law firms is that they tend to hire few laterals; they prefer to hire younger people and train them. The partnership track also tends to be different. In small entertainment firms, there may only be two partners, but top associates may make $500,000, so partnership is not as relevant as it would be at a large firm where partnership determines pay.

3. If you want to go to an entertainment law firm, start early. Don't wait until your third year to send out resumes. Try for a clerkship after first year. And don't try to impress them with your knowledge of the entertainment business, because many entertainment lawyers are amused by the misconceptions of law students. Instead, stress that you are going to work your butt off to be the best clerk they've ever had. As many an entertainment lawyer says, "It's not about hanging out with stars. It's hard work! The first time you meet a star, that's great. After two years after traveling forty-eight weeks a year, you're tired."

4. Attend all of the law-related entertainment functions that you can, and buttonhole the speakers—they expect it. For instance, the ABA

Entertainment & Sports Law Section puts on seminars periodically; keep your eye on your Career Services Office's bulletin board, or call the ABA, or look in entertainment industry publications (Variety, Billboard, and the like) to see what's going on. You can't afford to be shy!

5. Helpful backgrounds include business (an MBA doesn't hurt) and/or accounting, with a great facility in English. It's important to be able to communicate well and be understood. As is true for athletes, performers may have a high intellectual level but they won't typically be well-educated, and so being an entertainment lawyer means communicating with people who have brains but not necessarily the academic background to go along with it. Because entertainers can make huge amounts of money, there are important decisions to be made relating to that wealth, and entertainment lawyers have to be able to explain that business to them.

6. By way of understanding your constituency, if you intend to be an agent or an entertainment lawyer representing entertainers, be aware of what you'll be dealing with. You will be on call every hour of every day. If your client gets arrested, you've got to bail them out, or figure out a way to get that done if they're on the other side of the world. You see what it is really like to be a star— namely, being under constant pressure to outdo that last success. That kind of pressure sometimes leads to, let's say, unattractive behavior, and sometimes involvement in drugs and alcohol (by your clients, not you). You, the lawyer, become psychiatrist as well as lawyer, and have to deal with important issues for which you are unlikely to have any formal training.

7. The nontraditional jobs in film, like being a studio executive, are ones where a law degree is extremely useful. People in the industry tell me that the typical way you break into these positions is to work as the lawyer for studios first, where you get to see how deals are done and to facilitate those deals, and then it's a relatively small jump to actually being in a production role yourself.

8. You break into agenting positions either by: (i) working your way up from the mail room—yes, it still works; (ii) Interning (I discuss that in more detail immediately below); (iii) bringing in clients; or (iv) bringing in deals. I'm going to briefly tell you the tale of two law students, and you decide for yourself who's going to make it as an agent. When I was presenting the *Guerrilla Tactics* job search seminar at a law school in Florida about six months ago, a student came up to me after the seminar and said, "Tell me what you think about what I'm doing." She went on to explain that she wants to be

an agent representing music groups after law school. And in the meantime, she goes to nightclubs for "new talent" night every weekend (not a bad way to spend your free time!), and when she sees promising groups, she introduces herself to them and says, "I'm not a lawyer yet, so I can't represent you right now. But you don't have any money, so you can't afford a lawyer anyway. In the meantime, when you get gigs, why don't we just talk about it informally, and I'll give you some friendly advice, you can use it if you want or ignore it. But by the time I get out of school, maybe you'll like me enough and trust me enough to represent you for real." The other student I want to tell you about was in New York. She was *very* angry, *very* frustrated, and after my seminar she came up to me and said, "I've talked to everybody I can talk to, and the best thing I've been offered is as a receptionist at a record company. A *receptionist!* And I've got a *law degree!*" I was about to congratulate her when I realized she was insulted by this, and I told her about the woman in Florida. She huffily responded, "I'm not going to do *that.* I want to be *trained.*" Needless to say—if you are relying on somebody taking you under their wing and tutoring you, entertainment isn't the field to pursue. It might happen, but it's extremely unlikely. Assertiveness *pays.* Creativity *pays.* If you *do* want to break in gently, you should consider . . .

9. Don't forget about internships. I've listed some below. In addition to the ones I've listed, many record companies have internships, and you'll find those concentrated primarily in New York, Los Angeles, and Nashville. You'll also find that booking agencies, like William Morris (I've included a profile of a William Morris agent, Glenn Gulino, below), ICM, CAA, as well as management companies, film companies, and concert promoters all hire interns, and every entertainment attorney I've talked to agrees that internships are the fastest way to get into the entertainment industry. As is true for sports, there are tons of great internships available. They don't pay much, if anything, but it's a great—and fun—way to get your feet wet.

10. A useful web source for finding entertainment employers is "Pollstar." It is a monthly directory which lists all record companies, all booking agencies, all management companies.

What I'm going to do here is to profile a great entertainment employer— Disney!—as well as profiling a talent agent, Glenn Gulino, an on-air personality, Jack Ford, and a lawyer for MTV, Sean Joell Johnson. I'll also tell you about some great internships, and some entertainment employers who, along with Disney, get rave reviews as great places to work.

The Walt Disney Company

Corporate Headquarters
500 South Buena Vista Street • Burbank, California 91521
Phone: 818-560-1000

WHAT DO THEY DO?

Disney is a family entertainment company, spanning movies, TV, theater, animation, books, retail outlets, theme parks and resorts, and broadcasting, with revenues of almost $23 billion per year.

DIVISIONS:

Creative Content:

Walt Disney Studios (including Theatrical Films, Miramax, Home Entertainment, Network TV Production, Hollywood Records, Mammoth Records, Stage Plays)
  Television Production/Distribution (TV Network Productions, Domestic Distribution, International Distribution)
  Consumer Products (including Merchandise Licensing, The Disney Store, Walt Disney Records, Disney Publishing, Walt Disney Art Classics, Disney Direct Marketing, Disney Interactive, and Disney Online)
  Fairchild Publications
  Televentures

Broadcasting:

Cable Network & International (including ESPN and the Disney Channel)
  ABC Broadcast Network
  TV Stations
  Radio Network
  Radio Stations

Theme Parks & Resorts:

Walt Disney Attractions (including Disneyland Resort, Walt Disney World Resort, Disney Vacation Club, Disney Cruise Line, Tokyo Disneyland)
  Walt Disney Imagineering
  Anaheim Sports (including The Mighty Ducks of Anaheim and The Anaheim Angels)
  Disney Regional Entertainment (including Club Disney, DisneyQuest, The ESPN Zone)

HISTORY AT A GLANCE . . .

It will come as an enormous surprise to you, no doubt, to learn that the Walt Disney Company was founded by Walt Disney and his brother, Roy, in 1923, as "The Disney Brothers Studio." Much of Disney's intervening history reads like the answers to Trivial Pursuit questions. Mickey Mouse debuted in 1928 in the cartoon *Steamboat Willie*. The first feature-length animated film emerged in 1937—*Snow White and the Seven Dwarfs*. Since then, Disney has expanded into theme parks (Disneyland, the Magic Kingdom, Tokyo Disneyland and Disneyland Paris), live action films, network and cable television stations, and many other businesses.

WHO'S WHO . . .

Chairman and Chief Executive Officer: Michael D. Eisner
Senior Executive Vice President and Chief of Corporate Operations, General Counsel: Sanford M. Litvack (LL.B., Georgetown)
President, ABC, Inc.: Robert A. Iger
President, Disney Consumer Products: Anne E. Osberg
President, Walt Disney Imagineering: Kenneth P. Wong
President, Disneyland Paris: Gilles Pelisson
Chairman, The Walt Disney Studios: Joseph E. Roth
Chairman, Walt Disney Motion Pictures Group: Richard W. Cook
President, Walt Disney Feature Animation: Peter Schneider
President, Walt Disney Attractions: Judson C. Green

WHAT IT'S LIKE TO WORK THERE . . .

What do you think of when you hear the word "Disney"? Animated movies like *Snow White* or *The Lion King*? Disneyland? The Disney Channel? Or do you start humming M-I-C . . . K-E-Y . . . the fact is, when you talk about entertainment, the "Company That Mickey Built" has a paw in just about everything you can imagine. From movies to theme parks to cable television to the recently-acquired ABC Television Network to sports teams like the Anaheim Mighty Ducks hockey team. That creates a vibrant, exciting environment for people lucky enough to be Disney lawyers—like Valerie Cohen, Senior Vice President and Assistant General Counsel for the parent company, The Walt Disney Company.

Valerie talks about her job with all of the charm and enthusiasm you'd expect from someone who—well—you might say has had Tinkerbell sprinkle her career with magic dust. Valerie raves that "The diversity of subject matter here is great! There are the obvious businesses like the movies and theme parks and television, but then there are things like our real estate development business, which designs and builds resorts." And she finds that "The people here are every bit as interesting as you'd imagine they would be. Working not just with lawyers gives you great variety. Creative people are *very* interesting to work with." She also likes the fact that contrary to the common image of lawyers, "We're not the ones who just say 'no' to projects. Sometimes we have to, but more of the time we say 'how to' rather than 'no.' We *enjoy* that. I feel like I'm far more of a help than a hindrance to getting projects done."

With Disney's wide variety of businesses, "We have as many different specialties as there are in law," Valerie says. Of course there is lots of intellectual property, for all of Disney's copyright and trademark and licensing issues. There are lawyers who handle standard transactional work, like contracts and financing. There are environmental lawyers and real estate lawyers and labor lawyers. A relatively new specialty at the company is information systems. And there are litigators—Valerie herself is one of those.

The dozens of lawyers at Disney are broken down in a bunch of different ways. In each of the businesses units, there will be one to three lawyers. For instance, there are a couple of lawyers in the feature animation business unit. There are many at Walt Disney World. There are some at ABC, and there's one at the Disney Channel. And then there are more lawyers, like Valerie, who are "corporate" lawyers and work for the parent company. They do projects for the parent company and the subsidiaries. "For instance, if there's litigation involving feature animation, even though there's a lawyer in that business unit, we'll handle that case."

Projects come into the litigation department from a variety of sources. Sometimes they come down from Disney's general counsel, Sandy Litvak. And of course, the litigators get called upon whenever a lawsuit is filed against Disney. But Valerie finds that "more than 50% of my time is spent counseling other people in the company. They'll say, 'We're doing this deal. How do we avoid problems?' I enjoy that *very* much." She also finds that lawyers in the business units will call when they need help structuring agreements, and also that "as you get to know people on the business side, they'll call you directly with questions."

Valerie's journey to Disney didn't involve wishing upon a star. She clerked for the Supreme Court of New Jersey after graduating from Harvard in 1981, and then became a litigation associate at the firm Donovan Leisure in New York. As is true of so many lawyers in dream jobs, Valerie made her initial career choices not so much as part of a deliberate plan to wind up at Disney, but by going on a hunch that proved to be spectacularly right for her. For instance, she chose litigation as a specialty because "Frankly, it was litigation or corporations, and I thought transactional work would be boring. Not that I knew what it was like—I'm not sure anybody knows what work is like before they actually do it!" As a fourth year associate she moved over to Dewey Ballantine in New York, where she made partner in 1989. She landed her job at Disney in 1991 "by backing into it," making the jump with Sanford Litvak, another Dewey Ballantine partner, when he was named General Counsel of Disney. "I like to tell people that they just hired Sandy to get me!" she laughs.

Of course, not *every* lawyer at Disney follows Valerie's path to the door. You probably won't find it hard to believe that when there are job openings at Disney, "We don't use headhunters—we don't *have* to," laughs Valerie. Disney gets many, many resumes. "If the resumes look interesting, we hang onto them. We'll write to people and tell them we want to consider them." Disney hires all of its in-house lawyers as laterals. Valerie says that what they look for on resumes is "A good law school, and good firm experience. We don't usually get resumes from other companies, but if we did get them we'd consider them." She says that it helps to have "Three to four years of experience, at least. Twelve to thirteen is too high, because you'd be coming in a too high a level. The ideal is probably a senior-ish associate." In terms of background, "It's great when we get resumes showing experience in areas we cover, like copyrights or intellectual property in general. For somebody with a background exclusively in criminal defense or product liability or antitrust, those just aren't things we see very much. It won't help us."

Valerie says that Disney doesn't hire entry-level lawyers because "We just don't have the luxury that law firms have for training new people. We don't have the staff for it. When you join Disney, you're immediately bombarded with questions. You get a *lot* of work. I can't imagine that new law school graduates could handle it, not because of ability but just because you need the experience. *I* couldn't have done it straight out of law school!"

While Disney is a phenomenal place to work, it's not a 10-to-4 lifestyle. As Valerie says, "We work very hard. Not as many hours as in a firm maybe, and not as many weekends, but we work long days." Valerie herself routinely works from 8:30 or 9 until 7 at night, "sometimes later," and those hours are relatively common in the corporate group. Valerie points out that "Great law jobs are *hardworking* law jobs. I don't know anyone with a great job who doesn't work hard. The responsibility you have demands it. Nobody *makes* you put in the time. You see the need yourself, and you do the work."

She also advises lawyers looking to work at Disney that "We're lawyers *first*. We don't think of ourselves as 'entertainment lawyers'—our business just happens to be in a sexy context. When people come to us looking for a job as a lawyer, they'll think it's helpful to have done films in college or to have worked in a production company. I'll interview people who will say, 'Oh, I love entertainment, I love the movies.' Actually, a love of the entertainment business is suspicious. It makes you think they want to do *entertainment*, not what we're doing. We're *lawyers*."

Of course, the flipside of that is that, as is true of every large company, there are a lot of law school graduates on the business side of Disney. As

Valerie explains it, "Virtually all of the business affairs people are lawyers. They negotiate deals with talent, they handle movie location agreements, rights acquisitions deals, those kinds of things. They aren't technically lawyers, but almost all of them have J.D.'s. There's only one person over there that I can think of who *doesn't* have a J.D., and she knows as much about law as any lawyer." It's not at all unusual for lawyers to make the jump into the business side, and many of Disney's senior executives got their feet wet as lawyers, first. Valerie points out that "One of the nice things about Disney is that if you *want* to jump into a business context, you *can*," although that "happens more with transactional people than with litigators."

Valerie said that while there aren't any entry-level positions for lawyers, and no summer internships, "there *are* summer internships available in the studios, and law students could do those."

Although Disney doesn't hire new law school graduates, you can't blame people for trying! There are, after all, the kinds of benefits you'd get from working as in-house counsel at many companies—there's no need to generate new clients, for instance, and no time sheets. And there's the ability to see how a business really works, which is *especially* fascinating when that business is entertainment in so many different forms. Valerie also appreciates "the real college campus environment here. It's not a button-down kind of place. Everyone's on a first name basis. If you call Michael Eisner's office, it's 'Michael Eisner,' not 'Mr. Eisner.'"

And of course there's the magic that is uniquely Disney. If you work for a wire company you might have a job you really like, but you're never going to walk into McDonald's, buy a Happy Meal for your kid, look at the free toy and say to yourself, "Yep, that's ours." It's a kind of magic that, well, you'd expect from the company that created the Magic Kingdom.

The lawyers' offices are on the studio lot in Burbank, and the building where Valerie works is adorned with the Seven Dwarfs! Perks include "Good employee discounts for all of the Disney parks and stores and catalogs. *Many* people take advantage of those." When Disney is "opening a new movie or a new Disney TV station, they'll do events on the lot with all of the characters." From time to time the lawyers get to go to screenings of Disney movies before they're released, and sometimes they even visit the sets where Disney films are being made. That's obviously a blast, "although it's not every day—just once in a while!" says Valerie. And then there are the films that are routinely being shot on the Disney lot. The new movie *Armageddon* was shot there, and the television show *Home Improvement* is filmed there. With so many entertainment projects going on, "You're going to see stars come and go. You can't avoid it."

All in all, Valerie enthuses, "I love being a lawyer. I love helping people figure things out. I *love* it here!"

Who *wouldn't*?

WHAT IT'S LIKE TO BE A TALENT AGENT

A Profile of Glenn Gulino, an agent with the William Morris Agency.

(As with the Jack Ford profile that follows this one, this profile comes from my friend Hillary Mantis's wonderful book, *Alternative Careers For Lawyers,* which I *strongly* encourage you to read.)

Glenn Gulino does not look like a typical lawyer. He breezes into our interview with his sunglasses on, dressed in a black Hugo Boss suit with black and white polka dot suspenders, radiating energy and charisma. It is August, and he has just returned from the Cannes Film Festival. Indeed, Glenn is not a lawyer any more—he is now an agent with William Morris, the oldest and most prestigious talent agency in the world.

The road to William Morris was not, as many lawyers might think, an easy one. Glenn started to work on making entertainment-related contacts back in high school when he was in a band and hung out with musicians. After deciding that he would rather represent rock stars than try to become one, Glenn attended Boston College Law School. While there, he started the Arts, Entertainment and Sports Law Society. He also started to network with other entertainment lawyers by attending entertainment law symposia and conferences. Right away, Glenn caught on to the credo of the entertainment world: "it's not what you know, but who you know," and became a master at networking.

While in law school he was also able to do an externship with an entertainment law firm in Boston that represented the musical group New Kids on the Block. They offered Glenn a job but, needing to make some money, he went with a larger law firm instead. He became an associate in the corporate public finance department at Mudge, Rose, Guthrie, Alexander and Ferdon for two years before joining LeBoeuf, Lamb in New York. He sensed right away that it wasn't for him and started to look for an entertainment law job.

"I would go to California on assignment, and take extra days to attend things at the Century City Bar Association and the Beverly Hills Bar Association. I went to everything," he remembers. Glenn was quite savvy about the keys to networking—asking people for advice, information, and referrals—but not directly for a job. "I was looking to get out of this drudgery, but I knew enough not to ask, 'Can you give me a job?'"

"The day I came to New York in 1989,"—the year he graduated from law school—"I joined every entertainment organization imaginable," he said. He also started attending entertainment law section meetings at the New York State Bar, and the American Bar Association. He learned a lot by reading the entertainment trades—*Billboard, Variety,* the *Hollywood Reporter*—on a regular basis. He knew that it would take immense social skills, time, and hard work to break into the industry. "It takes a lot of phone calls and a lot of energy."

In 1993 he decided to quit his six figure salary job at LeBoeuf cold turkey. "My heart is in the entertainment business," he told the partners. "A lot of my friends were surprised I had the guts to do it." He had saved some money from LeBoeuf, and once again headed west to L.A., where he started cold-calling agents in the Hollywood Creative Directory. Glenn thought he might like to be an agent because of his interpersonal skills, and because, unlike law, it is a "proactive, not reactive" career.

One of the agencies he cold-called back in New York City, Fifi Oscard, said to "come right over," and hired him for a $180-a-week, low-level position—obviously a pretty substantial pay cut from his days at LeBoeuf! A few months later, that job led to an interview for a job in the mailroom at the William Morris Agency.

He had to meet with seven agents just to get a starting position at the bottom of the barrel. "Barry Diller started in the mailroom there, David Geffen started there," he said. Like most jobs in the entertainment industry, in order to move up you have to pay your dues. William Morris has a five-year training program for people who want to become agents, but the equivalent of being a first-year associate there was to work in the mailroom and run scripts around town for agents.

"It was the winter of '93, and I was in snow up to my ankles doing errands," Glenn remembers. He was thirty at the time. His starting salary was $300 a week, better than at Fifi Oscard, but a far cry from his salary as a lawyer. The usual path was to become "king or queen of the mailroom," then become a floater who temped for different agents. Eventually, if things worked out, you could become an assistant to a particular agent in a particular department of interest, like Motion Pictures or Music. Then, after some time training, you would get promoted to a full agent. Two years into the five-year training program, Glenn made agent.

He advanced more quickly in part because of a controversial article featuring him entitled: "Michael Ovitz Michael Ovitz Michael Ovitz: The Mogul Wannabes at the William Morris Agency Must First Have to Wannabe in the Mailroom" in *The New York Times*, which was also picked up by international papers and appeared all over the world. Although Glenn had no idea he would be the centerpiece of the article (the reporter had interviewed a dozen people), he apparently represented a unique slant, a former lawyer working in the mailroom. It received a mixed reaction, internally, but after it appeared, everybody at the agency knew who he was.

When Glenn became a full agent, he was able to represent clients of the William Morris Agency, which is analogous to making partner at a law firm, at least from the status angle, if not financially. He was assigned to a new division, Licensing and Merchandising. He now primarily works on projects involving signature lines for celebrities—for example, if a celebrity wanted to start his own clothing line, Glenn would help put the deal together.

Glenn's new career uses his legal skills nicely: It involves business skills, interpreting contractual agreements, intellectual property rights, research skills, as well as gathering information on different companies and studying their annual reports. Good negotiation skills are also paramount. Although he has been an agent for a relatively short time, so far it is a good fit for Glenn.

It is a tough job in terms of dealing with clients, just as it is for lawyers. "We are a buffer to the client," Glenn said. "We are dealing with people's feelings and we need to be as careful as possible." Although he is making considerably less than he would have had he remained at the firm, the potential to make money as an agent is much greater in the long run. For example, an agent could make a piece of the overall business he brings into the company.

"Agents are creative in a non-linear way," he said. "Lawyers are always reactive—fixing problems. It's very refreshing to do something proactive instead." But there are negatives as well. "While lawyers are respected for their intellect, agents sometimes rule by fear. It can be a 'swimming with sharks' environment." Like almost everything in the entertainment world, the competition is fierce.

For now, he is grateful for the experience of working for William Morris, which worldwide has 200+ agents, and a lot of clout. "I am very fortunate to be able to learn from them," he said. He plans to remain an agent there and continue to work his way up, networking all the way.

Glenn Gulino's advice for lawyers interested in the entertainment industry:

- Networking pays off!

- When you are networking, give others a chance to tell their story. Ask for advice and names of more contacts to network with. But *never* ask for a job!

- Do your research. Read all of the trade papers (like *Billboard, Variety,* and *Hollywood Reporter*) on a regular basis.

- Be patient! Breaking into the entertainment industry takes time.

- Determine what it is that you like about the entertainment industry. If you like the process, for instance, consider producing films.

- You have to have a sincere interest in the business and a strong work ethic to succeed. In a business full of $%*@(#&!!, character and sincerity are key!

WHAT IT'S LIKE TO BE A TELEVISION PERSONALITY

A Profile of Former Litigator Jack Ford, NBC News Chief Legal Correspondent and co-Anchor of Today, Weekend Edition.

Jack Ford sits in his office in NBC's Rockefeller Center, surrounded by his awards (both television and legal—he was a lawyer for eighteen years), books and tapes for *Today Show* segments, and framed pictures of his family. His is a life that most lawyers would envy—and many aspire to.

But, as he cautions the many lawyers who write to him, the transition from lawyer to NBC anchor doesn't happen overnight. "Don't say to your-self, 'I'm going to quit practicing law tomorrow and the next day I'm going to start sending resumes to networks saying I'd like to anchor one of your shows,'" he advises. "The meteoric rise doesn't happen as meteori-cally as people think it does."

Jack's own progression happened gradually. After graduating from Yale, he attended Fordham University School of Law, graduating in 1975. He appeared several times on the quiz show *Jeopardy* during law school in order to help pay his tuition. He started his legal career as an Assistant Prosecutor in Monmouth County, New Jersey. Later, he became an accomplished trial attorney in New Jersey, arguing the successful defense of New Jersey's first death penalty case in 1983.

It was during this time that an unplanned "lucky break" launched Jack's television career. The death penalty case garnered a lot of media attention, and when it was over, Jack was asked to do a lot of television interviews. One of them was with CBS anchor Jim Jenson. After the inter-view, Jenson, impressed with Jack's on-air personality, asked him if he would be interested in an interview with the news director to become CBS's legal commentator. He got the job. "I literally stumbled into televi-sion," he said. "I never had any plans to get into it."

He was on the air once or twice a week and continued to maintain his full-time law practice for many years. He viewed television at the time as an adjunct to his legal career, rather than a new field. "It helped me, quite candidly, with juries. You would be picking a jury and they'd raise their hand and say, 'I know Mr. Ford; I don't know him personally, but I saw him on television.'"

His broadcast career flourished at the same time as his legal career. Jack received an Emmy award in 1989. He also started moderating Fred Friendly's highly-regarded series on PBS and was asked by Steven Brill in 1991 to become an anchor on a brand new network, Court TV. Jack anchored Court TV on a part-time basis, and was approached by NBC soon thereafter to become their legal commentator, starting on the *Today Show.*

"At that point, I was juggling a number of things . . . I was starting to realize it might be too many balls in the air. It may be time to make a choice." He decided to go with NBC on a full-time basis and to give up his law practice.

His timing could not have been better. Within months of his arrival, the O.J. Simpson case came to trial. Jack was suddenly on the air every day, reporting on the case from New York and California. It put him directly in the spotlight, and, like many others involved in the case, boosted his celebrity status. Midway through the Simpson trial, NBC offered him a chance to anchor the *Today Show,* the "best job in television," according to Jack.

Between the *Today Show* and the Simpson trial he was working a seven-day week and gaining tons of exposure on the air. "My *mother* said she was getting sick of seeing me everyday," he laughed. After the Simpson trial, Jack settled into a regular position with NBC, working on various shows, including anchoring the weekend *Today Show,* and working on stories for *Dateline, MSNBC,* the *Nightly News,* and other shows. He has now established himself as both a legal expert and a general news anchor watched by millions of viewers every week.

His advice to lawyers who want to get into television? Many lawyers' biggest mistake is to underestimate the amount of time Jack, and others like him, needed to achieve national prominence. He emphasizes that it's not likely that anyone would go from never having done any television to anchoring the *Today Show,* as some lawyers who write to Jack would like to believe.

"I always say to people, here is what you should do—find yourself a *starting niche.* With the introduction of cable television there are all sorts of channels around that have their own sort of local news or talk shows."

The second step, according to Jack, is to establish yourself as an expert in some area of the law. For Jack, it was criminal law. "And then, you have to really sell yourself to a cable network or a local station as somebody who could provide some expertise." Eventually, you build up a body of work and are sometimes able to move up to bigger networks.

Jack illustrates his point by telling people "about my friend Katie Couric, because people think all of a sudden she just appeared as a major star on the *Today Show.* In reality, Katie started 10 years before she ever got on the *Today Show* answering phones in a little station in Washington, D.C. . . . and whenever she could, she would tape a little segment of herself and put it on a demo reel . . . and ultimately got her shot at the networks."

Other colleagues who are lawyers have made the transition through networks like Court TV and CNN as legal commentators. "There are a lot of people who have done it, but the formula has always been the same. They establish themselves *first* in the practice of law as being talented in some area; they then use that talent and expertise and recognition to get them on the air as commentators and analysts."

Although Jack sometimes still misses trying cases, he does not miss his life as a lawyer. His lament about how the practice changed in the 1980s is common among lawyers. "I think it was a profession, and now it is a business. That's very unfortunate."

A big plus of his new career is that he is still involved in law and legal issues without having to deal with the daily grind of practicing. Television also fulfills his love as a trial attorney of being in the spotlight. 'Instead of being in the spotlight in the courtroom with 12 jurors, every time you're on the air you have five, six, seven million people watching." The same intense, focused zone of concentration Jack experienced and relished while interviewing witnesses at trial is replicated when he is doing live interviews on television.

Finally, as busy as his days are now, they have a definite beginning, middle, and end, unlike his days as a litigator. "At some point my day is over, [and] when it's over, it's over. I'm home with my family and I'm not returning a million calls from clients and not juggling the next day's witness list. The boundaries are frenetic, but there are boundaries."

Jack's transition was in some respects a product of luck and good timing. The use of legal experts on television as commentators had started at about the time he was spotted by Jim Jenson. He had already done quite a bit of television by the time Court TV went on the air. The O.J. Simpson trial started shortly after he joined NBC on a full-time basis. It doesn't hurt that Jack also has the all-American good looks and natural comfort in the spotlight that television requires.

But he also worked very hard for a very long time to get to where he is now. Jack essentially worked at two careers on an almost full-time basis for many years before choosing television. Like many lawyers who have moved into another career, his transition out of the law was very gradual, but ultimately very successful.

WHAT IT'S LIKE TO WORK AT MTV

A Profile of Sean A. Joell Johnson, Counsel for Law and Business Affairs at MTV

Sean Johnson looks out at the Hudson River from his office window at MTV, where he is Counsel for Law and Business Affairs. He is involved in all aspects of negotiating and drafting agreements related to MTV programming—series, specials, news, sports, music—including talent, production-related, and programming acquisition agreements, licensing and intellectual property, general corporate transactional matters, and day-to-day legal production issues. When Sean travels, he takes his laptop, cell phone, and modem for e-mail. Needless to say, it's a job that keeps him very busy. "It's a lot of work and a lot of responsibility," he says. "MTV maintains a growing, fast, hectic pace. It is not structured like a normal corporation."

In addition to Sean, the Legal Department at MTV consists of four other attorneys, four paralegals, and a number of assistants. Each attorney specializes in an area, and Sean characterizes all of them as "exceptional." Sean handles shows out of development and deals with venue and production. He also works on a great number of copyright issues.

How does an attorney arrive at MTV? Sean worked for Black Entertainment Television ("BET") at a time when they were working with MTV on the Urban Aid Project—a major R&B benefit concert. Originally,

BET and MTV were to co-produce the concert. As other issues developed, BET's role changed from coproducing the concert to licensing it. Sean dealt with the matter effectively and professionally, and several months later he received a call requesting that he come interview at MTV for an open position.

What Sean likes best about lawyering is solving the puzzle, putting the pieces together, especially when working with producers. He also enjoys working collectively on creative teams to provide legal advice. "I see the big picture," he says. That is one of his many contributions to a creative team. He also maintains an incredible amount of autonomy, balanced with a dose of team work. He handles the basic legal portion of his job on his own and brings in various parties, creative or business, on given issues. While enjoying this autonomy, Sean notes that everyone at MTV works together. "You can't be an island here. You won't survive."

When Sean entered law school, he had no idea he'd wind up at MTV, and he had no intention whatsoever of working in New York City. A native Californian, his friends still find it hard to believe he is in New York City or even on the East Coast. However, he realizes that he has to be in a major city to work in entertainment law, and, if that means a stint in New York City, that's all right with him.

While MTV and New York weren't in his plans, when he started law school at George Washington, Sean *did* know that he wanted to work in entertainment. After graduating from the University of Southern California, he spent one year as a business manager at a performing arts theater. He enjoyed his job, but he wanted to do more and to make more money. He consulted a mentor for advice, and that mentor suggested law school. He got his law degree from The George Washington University Law School, spending his summers at Paramount Pictures Motion Picture Group and Motown Records.

Networking has been the key to Sean's success. He enjoys meeting people, and he is good at it. Even more significantly, he likes to listen to people. "Everybody has something to say, whether you agree with what they are saying or not," he comments. "People love to talk about themselves and give advice." To illustrate, Sean tells a story about going to lunch with one of his mentors, a film producer in Los Angeles who spent the entire lunch talking about himself. Sean just kept nodding his head and saying, "Yes, I see, uh-huh." As Sean tells it, the producer walked away thinking, "That was a great lunch." Sean laughs at the end of the story but adds that luck is where opportunity meets preparation.

He ought to know. A big part of his networking success is his persistence. When trying to obtain a summer job at Motown Records during law school, he sent his resume and then called every couple of weeks from about February through April until he got an interview. He developed a rapport with the assistant answering the phone, and she encouraged the contact person to give Sean a chance. He was different from the other callers—he sounded like a very nice guy, she said. For this job, like every other job he's ever nailed down, Sean laid the ground work first. When he was working at BET, he sent Christmas cards to the people at MTV he had worked with on the benefit concert. He received a call the next month to interview. "Always keep in contact," Sean says.

Networking and persistence don't pay off without hard work, however, a concept made clear to Sean when he worked at Paramount Pictures during the summer after his first year of law school. "It makes you humble," he said, "and I was happy to have the opportunity." At Paramount, someone told Sean that the best thing he could do was to make himself indispensable—to be "the one they call." With hard work, says Sean, this can happen in any work setting. "Even when you network," he notes, "You have to prove yourself."

As far as law school grades are concerned, Sean never thought they predicted how well he would perform as an attorney. He believes in the practical over the theoretical and adds, "I know lots of people doing very well with middle-of-the-road grades." Two of Sean's extracurricular activities at law school were being SBA President and Director of the Small Business Clinic. These activities helped him learn how to deal with people, and, he says, "They were a source of great personal growth." In the Small Business Clinic, he dealt with clients and the legal aspects of starting a business. As SBA President, he dealt with law students, who, he admits, were "a tough bunch."

None of Sean's fabulous jobs came easily. At the end of his first year of law school he still had no summer job and wasn't sure he'd get the Paramount job until he finally got the call for an interview. At graduation a number of opportunities fell through. It was not until two months after taking the bar that he received a call from BET. During those months, Sean traveled and worked at temporary jobs while he waited for a position at BET to open up. He adds, "I wasn't even sure that MTV was going to come through." But it did.

Sean credits his mentors for being an invaluable resource over the years. "I could name at least five mentors from high school to college to places where I worked," he says. He adds that he "needs the opinions of educated people to help make the right decisions."

Sean has always lived by the motto *carpe diem*—"seize the day"—and it flashes across his computer as his screen saver. His other motto, which he says keeps him grounded, is "Be ashamed to die until you've achieved some victory for humanity."

GREAT INTERNSHIPS THAT GET YOUR FOOT IN THE DOOR IN THE ENTERTAINMENT INDUSTRY

As with Sports, internships are a *great* way to get your start in Entertainment. There are lots and lots of them. The following three are from the terrific Princeton Review book, *The Princeton Review's Guide to America's Top Internships.*

The Academy of Motion Picture Arts & Sciences

Student Internship Program
5220 Lankershim Boulevard
North Hollywood, CA 91601
Phone: 818-754-2830

WHAT DOES IT DO?

It's the largest organization representing the U.S. television industry. It awards the Emmys, holds filmmaking contests, and sponsors industry-wide meetings, among other functions.

INTERNSHIP INFORMATION . . .

There are internships in 24 categories: Agency, Animation, Art Direction, Business Affairs, Broadcast Promotions, Casting, Children's Programming, Cinematography, Commercials, Development, Entertainment News, Episodic Series, Editing, Movies for TV, Music, Network Programming Management, Production Management, Public Relations, Sound, TV Directing (multicamera and single-camera), TV Scriptwriting, Syndication, and Postproduction.

Duration: 8 week summer program; pay is approximately $2,000 to 2,400 for the entire program.
Due date for applications: March 31.
Number of interns: 28
Who's eligible: Undergraduate and graduate students.

FOR MORE INFORMATION . . .

Check out The Princeton Review's Guide to America's Top Internships for a bird's-eye view of what the internships are like. Visit the Academy's web site at emmys.org or write to them.

MCA/Universal

Intership Program
100 Universal City Plaza
Universal City, CA 91608
Phone: 818-777-1000

WHAT DOES IT DO?

It's part of the mega-giant MCA, Inc. entertainment empire. MCA/Universal has several divisions, including Universal Pictures, MCA

Television, MCA Records, MCA Home Video, and Universal Studios. As an intern at MCA/Universal, you work for any one of the divisions in the areas of production, publicity, casting, legal, finance, and marketing.

INTERNSHIP INFORMATION . . .

Duration: 12 to 15 weeks in the summer, fall, or spring (part-time internships are available). Most positions are volunteer, although some positions pay between $5 to 9 per hour.

Due date for applications: No set date; you can apply any time. It helps to have an applicable background (*e.g.,* a finance undergrad for finance positions), and to demonstrate a commitment to the entertainment industry.

Who's eligible: Graduate students, as well as college juniors and seniors.

FOR MORE INFORMATION . . .

Check out *The Princeton Review's Guide to America's Top Internships,* for a more complete description of the internships, and/or contact the company directly.

National Public Radio

Internship Coordinator
635 Massachusetts Avenue, N.W.
Washington, D.C. 20001-3753
Phone: 202-414-2909

WHAT DOES IT DO?

All kinds of interesting, intellectual, and quirky—and all ad-free!—radio programming, including *All Things Considered, Morning Edition,* and *Car Talk.*

INTERNSHIP INFORMATION . . .

Departments: You can intern in one of NPR's departments—like News, Cultural Programming, Promotion and Public Affairs, Development, Human Resources, Audience Research, Legal, Training, Marketing, Engineering and Operations, or Audio Engineering, or with one of its programs, like *All Things Considered.*

Duties: They differ depending on your particular assignment, but include everything from fact-checking to editing tape to arranging interviews for show hosts.

Where: Washington, D.C.

Duration: 8 to 12 weeks, in summer, fall, or winter/spring. Available part-time or full-time. Pay is $5 per hour.

Due date for applications: For summer, March 30; for fall, August 15; for winter/spring, December 15.

Number of interns: Between 20 and 30.

Who's eligible: Graduate students as well as college juniors or seniors.

FOR MORE INFORMATION . . .

Check out *The Princeton Review's Guide to America's Top Internships* for a complete description of what the internships are like, or contact NGR directly.

ENTERTAINMENT EMPLOYERS WHO RECEIVED RAVE REVIEWS IN MY SURVEYS

According to law school administrators around the country, the following entertainment entities employ some very happy law school graduates:

HBO
1100 Avenue of the Americas
New York, NY 10036
Phone: 212-512-1000
Web site: hbo.com

MTV
1515 Broadway
New York, NY 10036
Phone: 212-258-8000
Web site: mtv.com

Universal Pictures
100 Universal City Plaza
Universal City, CA 91608
Web site: universalstudios.com
(They have three in-house lawyers)

MGM-United Artists
2500 Broadway Street
Santa Monica, CA 90404
Web site: mgmua.com

Paramount Pictures Corp.
5555 Melrose Ave
Hollywood, CA 90038
Web site: paramount.com

International

I get an awful lot of letters to my *Dear Job Goddess* column at the *National Law Journal* that fit one of these profiles: lawyers in other countries wanting to work in America, and law students in America wanting to work abroad. I don't know the extent to which there's a bit of "the grass is always greener" going on here, but I *do* know this: unlike medicine, law is something that differs from country to country, and so your American law degree isn't tremendously versatile overseas. A lot of international work actually involves working in the United States with domestic clients who want to do deals overseas, or with foreign governments or private clients who want to accomplish something here in America. For instance, mergers and acquisitions, joint ventures, foreign project finance, and a lot of international trade work would fit this description, where you'll typically be working domestically, in conjunction with local counsel in some other country. That's probably not what you think of when you think about international work—you think about travel. At least, that's what *most* of the people I hear from, think about!

But don't fret, *cheri*. There is hope, if you are intent on going abroad. There are a few fruitful avenues to explore:

1. Apply for jobs with companies that have branches in the foreign country where you want to relocate, and aim for one of two likely possibilities: either in a division that researches business opportunities abroad, or in the in-house counsel's office, handling international affairs. (Note that this is a job that generally goes to laterals, not new graduates, although I profile a former law student, J.T. Mann, who wound up abroad by weaseling his way into an American company with foreign branches in my *Guerrilla Tactics For Getting The Legal Job Of Your Dreams* book; it's Appendix B of Chapter 4.)

2. Go on a Summer Abroad program, but *focus on one that offers you a law-related internship in the foreign country, not just classes.* The Syracuse University Law School Summer Program is one that comes to mind. I've talked with many law students who have used the internship as a springboard for making contacts and nailing down a permanent job.

3. Go to work for a law firm with an office in the foreign country where you'd like to work, but as part of your research, check Martindale-

Hubbell, Westlaw or Lexis-Nexis for the backgrounds of the lawyers in the foreign offices. Many law firms hire local lawyers for their foreign offices rather than exporting Americans. Also keep in mind that foreign assignments don't typically go to new associates; you usually need a couple of years under your belt before you're eligible for a foreign tour.

4. Attend every international conference that comes anywhere near your city. Keep your eye on your local newspaper, and check bulletin boards and your Career Services Office at school (or visit the local law school if you've already graduated). I can tell you many wonderful stories about the opportunities these kinds of events create, but I'll limit myself to two that I learned from a couple of very industrious law students in different parts of the country. One is a student going to law school in Florida, who read about a conference for the Organization of American States that was going to take place in her city. She volunteered to help at the conference, and by doing so, she met a U.S. Senator, volunteered at his office, through that job met other people, and wound up with a truly plum summer clerkship—at the U.S. Embassy in Barbados. Wow! Another is a law student in New York City, particularly interested in doing work with South Africa. He also kept his eye on the newspaper and read about a conference involving trade with South Africa. He attended the conference, and noticed after the keynote speech that the speaker was standing alone for a moment. The student went and introduced himself, said what an inspiration the speech had been, stated his interest in working in South Africa and solicited the speaker's advice in accomplishing his goal. The speaker graciously wrote down a couple of names for him to contact in the South African government. When I asked the student who this particularly helpful speaker was, he shrugged and said, "Nelson Mandela." *Moral:* Get out there and show the world your wonderful face!

SPECIFIC EMPLOYERS RECEIVING RAVE REVIEWS:

United States Foreign Service

(part of the State Department)
Recruitment Division U.S. Department of State
P.O. Box 9317 • Arlington, VA 22219-0317
Phone: 703-875-7490
Web site: www.state.gov/index.html

Working for the Foreign Service is an amazing, incredible, and exciting life. In fact, a former U.S. Ambassador to Australia commented a few years ago that most law students who *think* they want to go into international law *really* want to work for the Foreign Service—it's everything you dream about when you think of international work. It's glamorous, it's interesting—and it's somewhere else. And if you're still in law school, good news—there are a growing number of internships available, both domestically and abroad.

There are literally thousands of people who work for the U.S. Foreign Service, at over 230 embassies and consulates in more than 140 countries.

While there are *some* civil service positions with the State Department, most people at the State Department are U.S. Foreign Service Officers, who are called "FSO's."

FSOs work at embassies abroad and in Washington at the State Department. Obviously, with the new countries created by the breakup of the former Soviet Union and other new countries—like Uzbekistan, Georgia, and the like—there are a bunch of new embassies, and a corresponding number of new jobs.

In each embassy, there are several principal types of jobs: Foreign Service administrative officers, consular officers, economic officers, political officers, information and cultural affairs officers, and commercial officers. (There is *tons* of information about what each of these jobs entails at the Foreign Service's web site. I've given the web address, above—and I *strongly* encourage you to visit to find out more!)

Let's take a look at what each of the different kinds of officers do. Foreign Service administrative officers are, as the name implies, the ones who manage operations of foreign posts. They administer foreign national personnel systems, assure secure and reliable communications, oversee financial operations, contract for security services and real estate, and handle other essential services.

Then there are the consular officers, who handle a smorgasbord of responsibilities, from handling passports and issuing visas, to assisting American citizens in distress. They also help coordinate the visits of U.S. officials, international conferences, and meetings. As these duties suggest, consular officers need a variety of skills, from being a good and intuitive "people person" to being able to exercise common sense and cultural sensitivity.

Economic officers handle not only traditional economic analysis, but may do everything from negotiating international civil aviation, trade policy, fishing rights and multilateral lending policies, pursue agreements in scientific, environmental and technological cooperation, or defend the interests and rights of U.S. businesses.

Political officers focus on political developments wherever they are posted, taking a particular interest in anything of direct relevance to American interests. In doing so they develop and maintain contacts with government ministries, political parties, labor unions, student groups, and social and cultural leaders. They assess how much support there is for U.S. policies, advocate policy consistent with U.S. interests, and try to maximize cooperation among governments.

Information officers typically act as official embassy spokesperson and arrange briefings, interviews, press conferences and other media events.

Cultural affairs officers administer educational exchange programs, and coordinate U.S. cultural and sports presentations.

And finally, commercial officers have a fascinating job, combining the skills of an analyst, the resilience of a broker, and the creativity of an entrepreneur. They identify overseas networking opportunities for American exporters and investors, conduct market research for American products, and organize trade promotion events.

HOW TO GET IN . . .

OK—this isn't the easiest job in the world to get, but then, *none* of the jobs in this chapter are. About 25,000 people a year take the first step in joining the Service, which is to take the Foreign Service written exam, and 200 people eventually get in.

The application process is long and grueling. It can take well over a year to get a job. You start by applying to take the Foreign Service written exam, and while the deadline for applying varies from year to year, it's usually in the late summer or early fall. The exam is given once a year. (Check the web site, or call the Foreign Service, for information about deadlines and exam dates.)

Anyone who's taken the exam will tell you that it's a killer, but then, *some* people pass, so it's not impossible. There's a multiple choice section, as well as an essay to write. The multiple choice section (which is subject to change at any time) is likely to contain three sections: job-related knowledge, English expression and usage, and a non-cognitive component. (The Foreign Service has a Study Guide for the exam, which you can order when you register to take the exam.) You find out by mail if you've passed, and an interview is set up for you. An interviewing panel travels the country, and you interview with them when they come to a place near you. Alternatively you can go to D.C. and interview there.

The interview lasts all day and includes personal interviews, group exercises, and a written administrative "in-basket" test. You are given a ranking in all the functional areas based on your performance. It helps to be knowledgeable about U.S. and world history, economics, and culture (and incidentally, it helps to know a foreign language, and the more exotic, the better). You also have to get a medical and security clearance.

Assuming you pass all of those hurdles, you get an offer. In theory, you don't have any say over where you go and what you do when you're an FSO. However, as with virtually everything, it pays to be political. If you develop a good "corridor reputation," you'll be able to lobby for the post-ings, and positions, that you want.

Incidentally, it's OK if you don't make it into the Foreign Service the first time around—the average incoming age is thirty, and many people are now entering at older ages (the oldest you can be when you enter is 59).

By the way—the starting salary for the Foreign Service is approxi-mately between $30,000 to $50,000, depending on education, relevant work experience and foreign language skills.

INTERNSHIPS WITH THE FOREIGN SERVICE

A *great* way to get your feet wet with the Foreign Service is through an internship. While many of these internships take place in Washington, D.C., there are more and more opening up at various embassies and con-sulates overseas, at the U.N. in New York, and at several locations in the U.S. with the Office of Foreign Missions. While duties vary, interns typi-cally do things like research, report writing, correspondence, information systems, analysis of international issues, and assistance in cases related to domestic and international law.

Here's what you need to know about the internships:

• They're typically unpaid.

• You need to be an American citizen.

• You need to be a part-time or full-time student, and you must be returning to school immediately after the internship.

For more information, contact the Foreign Service at the address listed above.

The American Bar Association Central and Eastern European Law Initiative ("CEELI")

740 15th St., N.W. • Washington, DC 20005-1022
Phone: 202-662-1950 or 1-800-98CEELI • Fax: 202-662-1597
Web site: abanet.org/ceeli

CEELI IN A NUTSHELL . . .

CEELI is a public service project of the ABA, primarily funded by the U.S. Agency for International Development, designed to advance the rule of law in the world by supporting legal reform in Central and Eastern Europe and the New Independent States ("NIS") of the former Soviet Union. In the words of CEELI attorney Gary Marek, "CEELI liaisons are posted in 23 countries to help build the legal infrastructure that is indispensable to strong, self-supporting, democratic free-market systems. CEELI liaisons focus their activities in four major areas: judicial, legal education, and legal profession reform, and legislative assistance. Since a strong and independent judiciary is the cornerstone of a society devoted to the rule of law, CEELI liaisons have assisted in the creation of judicial training centers, judicial associations, and judicial continuing education programs . . . To strengthen the legal profession at its foundation, liaisons also help develop legal education programs. One example is the creation of clinical education programs to provide practical training to law students. Finally, CEELI provides an array of services to assist in the process of legislative reform. American and Western European legal experts assess draft legislation from the region to encourage the enactment of laws reflecting democratic and free market principles. Also, liaisons provide training to host countries' parliaments and work to educate them on the necessity for certain types of legislation."

WHO'S WHO . . .

Executive Director: Mark S. Ellis, Executive Director
Chairman, CEELI Executive Board: Homer E. Moyer, Jr.
Director of Liaison and Legal Specialist Department: Kamala H. Mohammed (phone: 202-662-1984, e-mail: ceeli@abanet.org).

WHERE DO THEY WORK?

CEELI has Liaisons and Legal Specialists working in Tirana, Albania; Yerevan, Armenia; Minsk, Belarus; Sarajevo and Banja Luka, Bosnia Herzegovina; Sofia, Bulgaria; Zagreb and Vukovar, Croatia; Tbilisi, Georgia; Budapest, Hungary; Almaty, Akmola, and Shymkent, Kazakhstan; Bishkek, Kyrgyzstan; Riga, Latvia; Vilnius, Lithuania; Skopje, Macedonia; Chisinau, Moldova; Bucharest, Romania; Moscow, Irkutsk, and Rostov, Russia; Belgrade, Serbia; Bratislava, Slovakia; Dushanbe, Tajikistan; Kiev, Ukraine; and Tashkent, Uzbekistan.

WHAT DO THEY DO?

Since 1990, more than 4,000 lawyers, judges, and professors have traveled abroad with CEELI. There are two principal kinds of international jobs with CEELI: "liaisons" and "legal specialists". CEELI liaisons (positions lasting a year or more) and legal specialists (6-week to 1-year positions). There are currently 45 liaisons, 8 associate liaisons, and 8 legal specialists serving abroad. There are 17 lawyers who work for CEELI in Washington, D.C.

The liaison positions require 3 to 5 years of legal experience. You have to have a J.D. or LL.M. from a U.S. law school, you must have passed the bar, and they prefer people with foreign languages and international experience. Liaisons work closely with members of the host country's legal community and government representatives, and activities have included projects like founding commercial law centers in Poland, Bulgaria, and Lithuania; developing judicial training centers in Bulgaria, Estonia, and Latvia; establishing law libraries in Belarus, Estonia, and Poland; and creating environmental public advocacy centers in the Ukraine and Armenia. (Some longer-term positions require U.S. citizenship, but not all of them.)

The associate liaison positions are for people with foreign language skills but limited legal experience. The position requires, beyond competency in foreign languages, a J.D. or LL.M. from a U.S. law school, membership in a U.S. bar, and preferably two years of legal experience or international experience.

The legal specialist positions are for lawyers who provide expertise on specific projects or for a limited period of time, from six weeks to one year. Projects legal specialists have worked on include training judges and prosecutors, improving court administration, promoting criminal law reform, and developing bar associations.

CEELI also offers volunteer internships to first year through recent law school grads at its Washington, D.C. headquarters. All of the internships are part-time during the school year. Interns provide legal research support to CEELI liaisons and legal specialists overseas. Their projects include drafting assessment reports of pending legislation from the region, assisting with implementing special projects like developing law libraries, and researching and drafting white papers on various aspects of legal reform.

CEELI also has projects available in other cities through its Legal Assessments and Concept Papers Program, but since the focus here is exciting foreign assignments, I'll leave you to visit the CEELI home page to learn more about its domestic programs!

BUCKS AND TRANSPORTATION . . .

You don't do a CEELI project for the money! CEELI provides quarterly payments for renting furnished apartments, as well as a living allowance. Depending on the country, the living allowance currently ranges from $850 to $1,500 a month for meals and incidentals, and $400 to $1,700 for rent. (You should realize that money goes a long way in the countries CEELI services.) You also get transportation to and from overseas assignments, reasonable medical coverage, business expenses, local language tutors, and if you serve for at least a year, you typically get a public service deferment of any student loans you owe.

HOW TO APPLY . . .

Call or send for CEELI's application materials at the main address and phone number listed above, or visit CEELI's web site, at abanet.org/ceeli. Once you apply, your application is kept in a database and every time a position becomes available, the database is searched and you will be considered. Getting a job with CEELI may involve telephone and personal interviews, as well as reference and background checks. (For the interview, it pays to exhibit the personality traits they look for—a high level of energy and initiative, and strong interpersonal skills.) When your expertise and interests match a current need, you'll be contacted. Your application remains active until you notify CEELI that you don't want to be considered, or they've tried to contact you several times without luck.

WHAT IT'S LIKE TO WORK THERE . . .

If you want to see the world and have a hand in projects that will help change the world, then you should *definitely* look at CEELI. The scope of CEELI projects in the last few years is mind-boggling. From training judges in Moldova and establishing legal education programs in Armenia to creating bar associations in Croatia and a million other building blocks of law in a democracy, CEELI lawyers help put together the kinds of institutions and practices that we take for granted here at home. As one CEELI alum commented, "There's no question it's the highlight of my legal career."

When you look at the kinds of places where CEELI liaisons and legal specialists work, you probably haven't heard of most of them—and can't spell most of the ones you *do* recognize! As Gary Marek, a current Liaison in Bucharest, Romania, comments, "'Where?!' is without a doubt the first and most frequently-asked question when I broke the news to my family, friends and colleagues that I was planning to move to Bucharest, Romania." After five years as an Assistant State's Attorney in Illinois, Marek stumbled upon a CEELI brochure at a local law school, and found himself several months later in Bucharest. Within a week of arriving, he had met the General Director of the Ministry of Justice and "many other very powerful and influential Romanian citizens." His primary assignments turned into developing a bar association (!) and helping to reform legal education in Romania. As he marvels, "Many of the concepts and ideas that we are promoting here—CLE, law clinics for the indigent, the ability to borrow money, ethics codes—are things that I have become accustomed to and, at times, even taken for granted. To be able to share those experiences and concepts with a less-fortunate and receptive citizenry is very rewarding."

Patricia Noonan, who spent three months in Bulgaria as a legal specialist, was assigned to work on judicial reform in Varna, Bulgaria, a small town on the Black Sea which "the Soviets had used as a vacation getaway." She couldn't have been assigned to a place more foreign to her home in

Oregon; in Varna, she stayed in a "lovely apartment on the top floor of a building with a balcony facing south and a view of the Black Sea," sharing her digs with "a Russian, who was to continue to occupy the apartment during the first week of my stay. In deference to propriety, my landlady slept on the couch between our two bedrooms. Her 12-year-old son joined her when he got the flu, and their extended family and friends from the building continued to flow through. Bulgarian, Russian and French were the languages of choice, with only occasional English being spoken!"

Terry Ann Rogers, a legal aid lawyer, took a year off to volunteer for CEELI in Kyrgyzstan, "a mountainous ex-Soviet republic bordered by China on the east and approximately 200 miles north of Pakistan." She found that her "expense account as a pro bono attorney was $1,100 a month, which was more than enough to live on. It even covered a housekeeper who cooked, cleaned, marketed and did laundry!" Her project, to develop "the first and only public law library in Kyrgyzstan," involved her attempts to bring together two local organizations, an independent, voluntary bar association, and the National Library of the Republic. Each of them wanted to open the library by themselves, but financially weren't able to do so. Rogers' goal was to "help the two sides work together, plan a completely new library department, raise funding, and open the library," all in approximately nine months! The project brought her into contact with all kinds of local dignitaries, including the Chief Justice of the Constitutional Court, the Minister of Justice, and many others. Ultimately, the library opened on time, with funds provided primarily by the United Nations High Commission for Refugees. For the library's opening, Rogers "stayed in the President's compound. At the compound we were treated to 'terrorist hospitality.' In one day we were wined and dined with five complete meals in five different settings!" As Secretary of State Madeline Albright said to CEELI participants in her comments at a CEELI luncheon a couple of years ago, "You have helped draft constitutions, train judges, establish commercial law, and get fledgling criminal justice systems off the ground . . . you have tapped into a project that really matters, that is fulfilling for you, truly helpful for others, and important to your country."

Beer! Toys! Great In-House Counsel Jobs At Companies In Sexy Industries

There are *many* wonderful companies to work for. You'll find a couple of dozen of them in Chapter 8, which talks about great corporate employers.

In that chapter, I also spend a few pages talking about the different kinds of jobs your law degree can help you get in large companies, outside of the in-house counsel's office. You shouldn't consider a corporate job *anywhere* without reading that chapter first. But what I want to do here is to focus on a couple of companies in industries that make them glamorous—beer and toys—and on top of that, they're companies that were strongly recommended to me by law school administrators. When you hear what lawyers from these companies have to say about their jobs, you'll understand why!

Mattel, Inc.

333 Continental Boulevard • El Segundo, California 90245
Phone: 310-252-2000

Toys on every desk—and half-day Fridays!

OTHER OFFICES:

Fisher-Price, Inc., 636 Girard Avenue, East Aurora, New York 14052
Mattel Mt. Laurel, 6000 Midlantic Drive, Mt. Laurel, New Jersey 08054

WHAT DO THEY DO?

If the name "Barbie" doesn't ring a bell with you, well—welcome to Planet Earth. To put it more formally, Mattel is the worldwide leader in the design, manufacture and marketing of children's toys. In 1997, revenues were approximately $4.8 billion. With headquarters in El Segundo, California, Mattel has offices and facilities in 36 countries, and sells its products in more than 150 nations throughout the world.

WHO'S WHO . . .

Chairman of the Board and Chief Executive Officer: Jill E. Barad
Senior Vice President-Human Resources:
Alan Kaye, phone: 310-252-6345, e-mail: kayealan@Mattel.com
General Counsel: Ned Mansour (J.D., University of San Diego '73)

NUMBER OF LAW SCHOOL GRADUATES EMPLOYED . . .

There are 13 within the General Counsel's office in the three locations listed above. Several other lawyers are employed outside the department and throughout the company.

WHO GETS HIRED . . .

The company only hires laterally. The years of experience and preferred backgrounds vary with the particular position being filled. The company's lawyers are mostly full-time, although there is one part-time attorney in intellectual property.

HISTORY AT A GLANCE . . .

Mattel was founded by Ruth and Elliot Handler, two remarkable people. In 1945, they started their business in a garage, with three pieces of shop equipment purchased from Sears on installment. The first Mattel product was picture frames, but Elliot soon developed a side business in doll house furniture made from picture frame scraps. Sales were $100,000 in 1945, the company's first full year, and earnings were $30,000.

From the beginning, Ruth had the vision for the Barbie doll, a $2 billion business today that remains the best-selling toy of all time, and Elliot's numerous creations include Hot Wheels and the sound mechanism used in See 'N Say products, both of which remain strong brands to this day. Ruth and Elliot's complementary strengths in product development, marketing, and management made them perhaps the most effective husband and wife partnership in the history of American business. And it made Mattel—by the end of its second decade—the world's largest toy company. Ruth and Elliot had an early partner named Harold Matson. He went by the nickname of "Matt," and that nickname—combined with the first two letters of Elliot's name—spelled "Mattel," a name that is now known all around the world.

Matson left the business after a short time, and the company's original focus on doll house furniture led the company into an emphasis on toys. The Uke-A-Doodle, a child-size ukelele, was the first in a line of musical toys. Then, a hand-crank, patented music box gave Mattel its first 'staple' business. Versions of this product carried the company through the 50s and 60s, and were included in the Mattel line as recently as the late 1980s.

Ruth and Elliot nearly bet the whole company when they agreed to pay $500,000 for 52 weeks of advertising on the new "Mickey Mouse Club" Show in the 1950s. Never before had toys been advertised on national television or on a year-round basis. It worked! Letters and calls flooded in, and retailers begged for more merchandise. The advertising was directed to kids, and the kids began asking their parents for what they saw on TV. They haven't stopped asking since.

The product introduction with the biggest impact in the company's history came in 1959. That was the year that Barbie was introduced. The idea had come to Ruth Handler in the early 1950's while watching her daughter—whose nickname was Barbie—play with cut-out adult paper dolls. Ruth believed there would be a market for a three-dimensional doll through which little girls could act out their dreams of growing up. But it wasn't until the later 1950's that she was able to convince others in the company to give her idea a try. The doll was introduced in 1959 at the New York Toy Fair.

WHAT IT'S LIKE TO WORK THERE . . .

It's easy to get excited about Mattel when you hear the comments of the lawyers who work there. One comments that "Working for the world's largest toy company has its advantages. Every day, we are surrounded by adults who spend all of their time thinking about toys. We never have to explain to anyone who was a child or has a child what Mattel does! Our own kids love to come visit us at work. There are toys in everyone's office and throughout the facilities." Another adds that the benefits at Mattel are unbeatable. "While we have all the normal benefits you would expect from a company of Mattel's size, we also have full-time casual dress, an on-site health and fitness center and on-site child care, a company toy store, and two weeks vacation at Christmas." And yet another in-house lawyer says that "Our department is very lean. Every attorney is on the front lines with their clients in the company every day. As a result, the experience we get and the knowledge we develop about the company are fantastic. On the other hand, we work hard. To the extent there are any anymore, this is not a cushy in-house job."

Jill Burtis, who is Mattel's Senior Counsel and manages a substantial portion of the company's litigation, summarizes what makes it so great to work at Mattel:

"As far as I'm concerned, being in-house counsel at Mattel is the ultimate dream job for a lawyer. Two years ago, after a six-year stint as a billable hours machine at a private law firm, I decided to get a life and go in-house. When I visited Mattel for my initial job interview, I noted two sand volleyball courts, a basketball court and a large grassy area shaped like the Mattel logo as I crossed the pedestrian bridge to the headquarters building. I was getting a good feeling about Mattel! In the lobby I was greeted by a life-sized Barbie doll dressed in a pink evening gown. 'Oh, this looks like fun,' I thought.

"During my interview, I learned that Mattel has a state-of-the-art employee fitness center, and on-site infant and day care. I later learned Mattel even has a "lactation room" for use by nursing mothers. No wonder that *Fortune Magazine* and *Working Mother Magazine* list Mattel as one of the 'Top 100' companies to work for!

"When I learned that Mattel's headquarters closes every Friday at 1 p.m., I said 'Sign me up!'" (One of the other in-house lawyers comments that on hearing about the half-day Fridays during an initial interview, "I almost fell out of my chair.") "Since that day, things have only gotten better. The company went to 'casual dress' five days a week. (The law department participated in a 'casual dress' fashion show which followed the announcement of this new policy . . . we did a zippy little dance number using our brief cases as props.) My office is filled with toys, as is everyone's office from the CEO on down. The Mattel Foundation, responsible for Mattel's charitable gifts and programs, helped me get a position on the advisory board of a major nonprofit organization. Mattel stock, which I purchase through the employee 401K plan, has increased by leaps and bounds. And to top it all, my job is fun and interesting—I deal with employment, products liability, intellectual property, environmental and a myriad of other issues, sometimes all in the same day!

In all, "It's a wonderful life!(. . . and it's without time sheets!)"

★   ★   ★   ★   ★

Anheuser-Busch Companies, Inc.

One Busch Place • St. Louis, Missouri 63118
Phone: 314-577-2000 • Fax: 314-577-2900

Great work—and free beer!

WHAT DO THEY DO?

You probably know about the beer thing. Anheuser-Busch is the world's leading brewer, and it makes the world's most popular beer, Budweiser, as well as numerous other brands. As well, the company runs theme parks, including Busch Gardens, Sea World, and Sesame Place.

WHO'S WHO . . .

Chairman of the Board and President: August A. Busch III
Vice President-Corporate Human Resources: William L. Rammes
Group Vice President and General Counsel: Stephen K. Lambright

NUMBER OF LAW SCHOOL GRADUATES EMPLOYED . . .

There are 50 within the Legal Department, including three who handle international matters exclusively for Anheuser-Busch International; and numerous law school graduates in other management positions throughout the company.

WHO GETS HIRED . . .

The Legal Department only hires laterally, and most of the lawyers in other capacities with the company are either hired from other employers (*e.g.*, other companies, law firms, the government) or make the jump from the Legal Department.

WHAT IT'S LIKE TO WORK THERE . . .

Let's get one thing out of the way right off the bat. Yes, you get free beer—two cases a month. That may be enough to convince you that Anheuser-Busch is the greatest employer in the world. But if it's *not,* there are plenty of other benefits that give Anheuser-Busch a "great overall atmosphere," according to Mike McCartney, associate general counsel.

For one thing, there's the "tremendous variety of work. Glamorous work includes dealing with entertainment and sports contracts and sophisticated joint ventures. It's all interesting, and it's all different. However, everyone also has to deal in the day-to-day issues for our clients." The Legal Department has 47 lawyers, divided into eight sections: corporate and commercial, labor, employment, employee benefits, litigation, intellectual property, and marketing and distribution. While each department has a specialty, "you coordinate with other sections. For example, if you are working on a big deal, all eight sections could actually be involved." On top of that, there are three lawyers who focus exclusively on doing international work for Anheuser-Busch International.

According to Mike, "You're dealing with people throughout the business all the time. Often they call you directly for advice. For instance, you might get a call from someone in the company saying 'We want to have someone sponsor this brand—can you draft an agreement?' or they'll want to buy a business."

Because Anheuser-Busch's business is worldwide, there can be a lot of travel involved with the work. Mike McCartney routinely travels to places most of us dream about. But in a sentiment that many business travelers echo, he says, "It sounds more glamorous than it is! When you travel on business, you fly overnight, you have meetings, and you get very familiar with the insides of conference rooms. You do get to stay in great hotels, you eat nice meals, but you're there for a reason—you don't get much chance to be a tourist!"

Outside of the Legal Department, there are opportunities in the company, either for lawyers lateraling in from other companies, firms, or the government, as well as for lawyers who jump out of the Legal Department. As is true in all kinds of corporations, "If you're going to do something other than the law, you've got to convince them that you can add value."

Mike's own background included four years as an associate at St. Louis's Lewis, Rice, and Fingersh, followed by two years in the in-house counsel's office at McDonnell Douglas. He got into Anheuser-Busch by "hearing from friends who worked there that the position was open." He found that "changing industries isn't that tough. The legal issues aren't really different. Asset sales, buying goods, selling goods— the issues are the same whether you're talking about airplane parts or beer, believe it or not." He did say, however, that "international issues are much different than domestic ones. You have to deal with multilateral treaties, international letters of credit, international arbitration rules, and labor laws that are different.

All in all he characterizes Anheuser-Busch as "a great place to work. We're treated well." On top of the interesting, varied work and livable hours, they have excellent benefits." And then there's the beer. Mike laughs, "You know, with everything that makes this a great place to work, the only thing people are going to remember is the free beer!"

Well . . . free admission to Sea World isn't *nothing.*

Jobs In Paradise

Everybody has their own definition of paradise. Not meaning to wax sentimental, but mine is to be around people I love. You can pick yours. But there are places that I think we'd all agree are outrageously attractive. As it turns out, throughout this book you'll find employers in all kinds of beautiful places—in Seattle and San Francisco, two of your more pulchritudinous American cities—and virtually everywhere else in the country as well.

How to pick a couple of "jobs in paradise," then, out of the many, many candidates? Well, I chose the two here because they are unique, in that they aren't law firms, they aren't companies, and I'll bet you'd never think of them if I didn't tell you about them. Oh, and yes—they're incredibly wonderful jobs, and to borrow a line from the immortal Eubie Blake, when you buy the chicken, you get the coop—a gorgeous workplace.

CLERKING FOR THE SUPREME COURT OF HAWAII

Ho, hum. It's time to go to work.

If it's wintertime, it will be a chilly 70 degrees outside. As you approach the "office," the beautiful Iolani Palace is across the street—the royal residence of the old Hawaiian monarchy, with its picture-perfect grounds. Directly in front of your building is a statue of King Kamehameha V, surrounded by towering torch ginger plants, with their spectacular red flowers. But of course, you vaguely recognized the statue even before you came to work here, because it's the opening shot of the old TV show "Hawaii 5-0." Your building itself is a treasure, having been built by Kamehameha V in 1874, and lovingly maintained today.

Yes, it's just the beginning of another day at your job as a judicial clerk for the Supreme Court of Hawaii. Laura Brewer, a '96 grad of the Indiana University School of Law at Bloomington, has had this enviable position for the last year and a half. She laughs as she says that "I can't believe my luck in winding up here. I knew that I wanted to get out of Indiana—I wanted warm, I wanted mountains, I wanted water, and that's not Indiana. I sent out reams of resumes to judges all over the Southwest. When I thought about Hawaii, I thought I'd never get it, but why not give it a try anyway?" And try she did.

As is true of many state supreme courts, in Hawaii you apply to each justice individually (see Chapter 12 for a whole ton more about judicial clerkships). The Hawaiian Supreme Court has five justices who have a total of 11 clerks, each of whom serves for two years. Laura got an interview with Chief Justice Levinson, and she laughs that "I've never had to prepare so hard for an interview in my life! He lets you know that he wants you to read all of his published opinions before you interview with him, and he wants you to be able to discuss them. You have to prepare a statement about yourself and discuss formative experiences." Add to that the usual writing samples, and you've got a formidable process. But Laura says that "He's an excellent person to work for. He genuinely wants to hear your ideas. I feel very lucky to be working for him." (Of course, it doesn't hurt to have the kinds of credentials that state supreme court justices like to see—law review or moot court, for proof of writing skills. Laura herself was on Law Review at Indiana.)

A typical day at the courthouse starts at 7:45 a.m., when the court opens, although Laura gets in by 7 a.m. "because I'm an early riser." (No kidding. I interviewed her from my home in Connecticut at 11 in the morning, *my* time. There's a six hour time difference. And I didn't wake her up when I called!) Most of the clerks get in around 7:30 a.m., although "we don't punch a time clock by any means." They spend most of their days researching and writing, and interacting with the justices they work for. "There's a different amount of contact depending on the justice, but most of them are *very* accessible." There's an hour for lunch, and then the court closes at 4:30 p.m., although "most clerks stay over, because as soon as the court closes things quiet down and it's easier to get work done." Most clerks leave for the day between 5:15 and 6 p.m.

Laura finds that clerking in Hawaii is unique because "the court faces unique legal problems. For one thing, the legal history is very different than anywhere else. Before Hawaii became a state, it was a territory, and it was a monarchy until 1893. For the old law, for instance the old property law, all of the deeds are in Hawaiian. So there are some interesting twists in property law." And because of Hawaii's short history of statehood, "There are many things for which there is little precedent. For instance, Hawaiian corporate law is kind of a joke. We're always looking to Delaware. In many cases our work is very interesting because we're developing areas where many other states have a long, firm foundation." On top of that, "The general climate is fairly liberal. Both the state and the court are very liberal on social issues. There's no knee-jerk reaction here to doing things a certain way because they've always been done that way." Laura agrees that the fact that the Hawaiian Supreme Court was the first state supreme court to address same-sex marriages shows that "The court won't just throw out concepts based on the idea that 'we've never done that before.'"

She finds that living in Hawaii is "intriguing" because "It's clearly going through a transition. Of course tourism is still huge. But agriculture is changing. Pineapple is still here, but sugar is gone, and a lot of the agriculture is going to third world countries. Hawaii is trying to develop sustainable industries other than tourism. For instance, telecommunications is getting big, in part because Hawaii is so uniquely situated between the U.S. and Asia. There's a strong perception here that the industry could grow dramatically."

Another big difference between working on the mainland and working in Hawaii is that you probably wouldn't be tempted to learn Hawaiian in any other state, while Laura takes Hawaiian language classes every Tuesday at lunch time. She likes it because "It's a very symbolic language, very poetic. They have little words put together into big ones that are developed visually. For instance, the word for 'eyelids' combines the word for 'eye' and the word for 'petals.' You find pretty quickly that you can look at the big long Hawaiian words and pick them apart, and figure out what they mean." However she admits that "It's not much help with my work at the court. Everything we get is translated first, because it's always in *somebody's* best interests to translate documents before they get to us!"

When it comes to living in Hawaii on a clerk's wages, Laura says that "Housing in Hawaii isn't nearly as steep as it used to be. It's true that our houses and apartments are small by Midwestern standards, but no one needs bigger space—who the heck stays inside in *Hawaii?*" Laura likes Hawaii so much that she intends to stay on after her clerkship. She finds that "Most people who do judicial clerkships in general see them as an extension of their education, an opportunity to hone their writing skills. Some of the clerks intend to stay in Hawaii, and others don't want to. If you have huge student loans, the pay overall on the mainland will be better. And actually what some clerks intend to do is to go back to the mainland, work for a few years to pay off their student loans, and then come back." She finds that by way of background "The University of Hawaii is a predictable feeder for the court—about half of the clerks come from there. The other half come from all over." There are also five summer clerkships, and while there's no requirement that students come from the University of Hawaii, "the clerkships aren't paid, so the students tend to be local. It's tough to survive without any money, unless you're living with your parents or you're a trust fund baby!"

It's no surprise to find that Laura is "very happy here. When I told everybody in Indiana that I was going to do this clerkship, some of them thought I'd lost my mind. But then, anytime you try something new, some people will raise their eyebrows! Everybody else—well, it's *Hawaii*. You know you really belong here when you stop wearing shorts and T-shirts when it gets down to 70 degrees, and you pull out your sweats and jackets! The work is interesting, the people are great, and Hawaii is wonderful. I definitely feel like a fish *in* water."

VISITING PROFESSORSHIPS IN MALIBU, AT PEPPERDINE LAW SCHOOL

The Straus Distinguished Visiting Professorship ("DVP") at Pepperdine is currently Doug Kmiec, who normally teaches at Notre Dame. He explains the charms of the visiting professorship better than anybody else ever could, but he admits that the job entails a certain ribbing from other professors—"My colleagues at Notre Dame call the Straus chair the 'beach chair,'" he laughs.

From the way he describes it, there's a lot about his job to make people green with envy. For a start, "Physically, Malibu is a beautiful place—although not every day!" As the nightly news has documented, "El Nino storms have wrought havoc on the area—the storms come in and the hills come down with it." However, Pepperdine Law School itself is "about 1,000 acres on the side of a gentle slope of the Santa Monica Mountains, facing—on most days!—a bright, blue Pacific Ocean. It's laid out compatibly with the landscape, the stucco buildings and Spanish tile roofs blending in with the hillside. It's a very harmonious setting."

Aside from the beautiful setting, Doug finds that "as a teacher, Pepperdine provides a different kind of beauty." For a start, "I've found the students here are earnest, dedicated, and very teachable. Because Pepperdine is private it's very expensive, and I've found that students match their financial commitment to the school with an intellectual commitment. And the students tend to come from loving, responsible families who want them to succeed. On top of that, Pepperdine is a religiously-affiliated school—it's broadly Christian—in the middle of a pluralistic, diverse city.

We have a significant number of students here who are religious—Hindus, Muslims, Jews—and while they don't share the same views, they take a level of spirituality as significant in their lives. And you find that *any* faith commitment tends to make people less 'self- centered' and more 'other-regarding.' Frankly the profession *needs* more people like my students!"

Doug also finds that a factor impacting life at Pepperdine that "isn't obvious to tourists" is that "behind those hills, facing away from the Pacific, is a California prison. Many Pepperdine students volunteer at the prison. While many schools have legal clinics, the goal here isn't quite the same. What the students try and do is figure out tangible ways the young men in the prison can be reintegrated into the community without rejoining the gangs that got them in trouble in the first place. They try to help them reconstruct jobs, create new networks of friends, learn a new vocabulary—in other words, take an interest in them that maybe nobody has ever taken before." Doug says that "What the students are doing many times is just reflecting on the blessings in their own lives."

Doug says that when it comes to the actual teaching experience at Pepperdine, "The focus of what we do is *teaching*. The Carnegie Commission just did a study on major undergraduate research universities, and found that they don't really educate students. They create wonderful atmospheres for highly-paid faculty members, who get to attend conferences and write books in solitude. They do some nice things but there's no real focus on passing knowledge to the next generation. The same thing happens at many law schools. Sad to say, to many law professors, students are a tiny name on a seating chart, with an entire semester judged on one exam." Doug points out that the upshot of this is "a world of make believe when it comes to writing letters of recommendations. What can you really know about a student based on that kind of exposure?"

Instead, at Pepperdine, "The system forces you to be a better teacher. In every case, there must be at least a mid-term and a final, instead of just a final exam. And they have an Exam Standards Committee, which is comprised of professors who review all professors' exams, and ask questions like, 'Is this exam clear? Is it even-handed? Is it comprehensive?' They really take the time and the effort to make sure that each professor winds up with a body of information about students." Doug feels that "You feel more like a teacher here, and less of a showman. You are more of a senior colleague for people who want serious direction." And that means that "when a student asks me for a letter of recommendation to a judge, for instance, I don't have to think twice about who they are—you know their goals, their analytical and writing ability, and you can give an honest assessment of them to employers. It's just so much more enjoyable because it's more personal and less anonymous."

The relationship between the school and the students is strengthened even more by its annual "Family Day," when the parents of the law students are invited to school, to go to classes with their children. As Doug laughs, "Lawyer parents don't hesitate to participate!"

While a warm, collegial atmosphere and an excellent teaching experience are tremendous benefits of being a visiting professor at Pepperdine, I'd be lying to you if I told you that that's what led me to include this particular job in this particular chapter. Instead, it's because I'd heard that the visiting professorship comes with an unbelievable perk—a beach house in Malibu. When I asked Doug about it, he laughed and said, "Yes, it's true. And it's not just any beach house, either. It's something of a landmark. It's one of the earliest beach houses in the area. A woman named Birdie Bettingen owned it. She had apparently made her money in oil in Beverly Hills, something like a TV family you may be familiar with. Birdie went on to own a number of things, including the Beverly Hills Hotel." If you've ever seen that hotel, you know that it's memorable for being bright pink with a black roof. Doug says that, "Like the hotel, the cottage is indeed bright pink with a black roof!" Happily for future generations of Straus DVPs, the cottage made it through El Nino intact, "Although we lost the back steps, and students helped to sandbag the cottage. Water at one point reached the door's edge." Doug points out that "It's all part of the drama of living in Malibu. Fires in the hills, mud slides, 10-to-15-foot waves—it's part of the excitement."

When it comes to nailing down this particular dream job, there's no application process. Instead, "you have to be invited by the dean." Doug himself has been invited twice. In the mid 1980's, then-dean Ron Phillips and Doug had "met at various law school events, and he invited me to visit Pepperdine." Shortly after that invitation, President Reagan asked Doug to take a prestigious position at the Department of Justice (see Chapter 4—this guy just goes from one dream job to another!). Ten years later, while teaching at Notre Dame, Doug got the call from Pepperdine again, and this time he jumped.

His advice to others who would like the Straus DVP? "First, dedicate yourself to teaching. Second, it wouldn't hurt to be a person who felt a religious faith of any kind meshed with professional growth. Third, be the kind of faculty member who isn't pretentious. If you're going to fit in at Pepperdine, you can't be unapproachable, you can't be haughty! It pays to be a good colleague, to be comfortable with yourself and what you have to contribute." And based on his own experience, he agrees that it doesn't hurt to gussy up to the dean of Pepperdine when you run into each other at law school functions!

He summarizes the Pepperdine experience by saying that "the great joy of being here is that the work doesn't seem like work, although you *do* work hard. It's not like Doonesbury. We don't sit and wait for the surf to come up. I'm here early. We put in a full day. But if a dream job is where your work is a calling, this is a place where you feel called to it almost every day. You're tired when the day is over not because your work was mindless or repetitive, but because you did something good, and lots of it."

To Boldly Go Where No Lawyer Has Gone Before . . .

INTELLECTUAL PROPERTY AT NASA

The National Aeronautics & Space Administration

Office of the General Counsel
400 Maryland Avenue, S.W. • Washington, D.C. 20546

WHAT DOES IT DO?

NASA, established in 1958, does research and development related to—and here's a real surprise—space.

NASA's legal work is handled by lawyers at several locations: the headquarters in Washington, D.C. (where the Office of General Counsel is), as well as at field offices at places like the Goddard Space Center (in Maryland), Johnson Space Center (in Houston), Langley Research Center (in Virginia), Lewis Research Center (in Cleveland), Marshall Space Flight Center (in Alabama), and Kennedy Space Center (in Florida). The headquarters' Office of General Counsel, in Washington, D.C., has about 20 lawyers, in four specialties: general law (5 lawyers), intellectual property (5 lawyers), contracts (5 lawyers), and commercial (4 lawyers).

While the other areas are nothing to shake a stick at—NASA work is pretty exciting no matter how you cut it—our focus here is on the intellectual property ("IP") section. IP attorneys for NASA do everything you'd expect from an IP attorney. They handle patents, copyrights, trademarks, and trade secrets, create and prosecute patent applications, license NASA technology, handle patent and copyright infringements, and the like. The difference between the work at the field centers and at headquarters is that the field offices prepare and file patents on behalf of NASA, and do the patent prosecutions for scientists and engineers. At headquarters, there are more policy people and program managers.

HOW TO APPLY . . .

Openings are *very* rare, and they generally (although not always) go to laterals. Everybody at headquarters is a minimum of a GS-13 in terms of rank, which would put them at least two to three years out of law school (entry level is GS-11).

For "hard" intellectual property (*i.e.*, patents), you need patent experience, and for that you need a technical background, as you probably already know. You need to be a member of a state bar and you must have passed the patent bar as well.

All of the attorneys current working in IP at NASA headquarters have government experience (although government experience isn't mandatory; patent counsel at some of the field offices come from the private sector). Two headquarters IP attorneys started at the Patent & Trademark Office, one came from the Department of Energy, another from the Department of the Army, and the other from the Navy.

To apply for NASA jobs, you send in government form SF-171 directly to the Chief Counsel at either NASA in Washington, D.C. (address above) or the field office where you're interested in working. (You'll find the addresses at NASA's web site, NASA.gov.)

WHAT IT'S LIKE TO WORK THERE . . .

Intellectual property is an inherently exciting specialty, no matter *where* it's practiced. But when you add the aspect of "space" to it, you've got something that's got to be an exceptional job. And it's that combination that IP lawyers at NASA work with every day. They do everything from preparing and prosecuting patents for NASA-created technology, to licensing NASA patents, to defending NASA against IP claims, to protecting the NASA logo and insignia. As with every job, some of what they do is routine, but some of it is *out there*—and some of it is not what you'd expect at all!

For instance, whenever you see movies involving space—like *Apollo 13,* or *Contact,* or *Deep Impact,* or *Armageddon*—you know that lawyers come into the picture *somewhere.* You know that lawyers help put movie deals together, drafting agreements at the very least. What you may *not* know is that there are lawyers at NASA who review movie scripts to see how the NASA logo and insignia are used, and to offer their advice about any space vehicles that are used. For older gadgets, like vintage moon rovers, the movie makers use replicas with the NASA logo. For space shuttles, they typically take off the NASA logo. And for future-oriented space vehicles, NASA works with them on how those ought to look.

The NASA image also comes into play in advertising, and creates some interesting issues for NASA lawyers. Under Section 310 of the Space Act, nobody can use the name NASA so as to convey an association or endorsement that doesn't exist. So for instance, if you see an ad for a barbecue grill that shows astronauts on the space shuttle using the grill, that would violate the Space Act, since it impliedly conveys an endorsement, while if the same ad didn't show astronauts but simply said "There are 30 of our barbecue grills at NASA," that would pass muster because it's just a statement of fact.

Section 310 of the Space Act also comes into play with Internet domain names. As you may have already noticed, NASA's home page is at "NASA.gov," instead of "NASA.com." You may think that's strange, because if you were surfing the Internet and punched in names at random to find NASA's web site, the first one you'd probably try would be "NASA.com." As it turns out, somebody very early on took all of the obvious government abbreviations, and created porn sites for them. So for instance you might have some kid innocently looking for stuff about the space program, and they try "NASA.com," and boom! They're at a porn site. Predictably enough, the porn provider refused to change the web site name, and that's where Section 310 of the Space Act became useful, stopping that site name from being used, since it obviously conveys an association or endorsement.

When it comes to actual patent filings for NASA technology, much of that kind of work is done by patent lawyers at NASA's research facilities, like the Johnson Space Center in Texas or the Kennedy Space Center in Florida. Since that's where the scientists and engineers are—the ones who create the inventions that require the patents; that's where the lawyers are, too. The work at NASA's headquarters in Washington involves other kinds of functions. For instance, one of the lawyers handles more of NASA's licensing work, one handles Space Act agreements, another works with issues involving the logo and insignia and any claims filed against NASA for IP claims, and yet another handles patent and solicitation activities with the Patent & Trademark Office (which involves coordinating patents that are filed by the "field" lawyers).

As you might expect, some of the work NASA intellectual property lawyers get to do involves handling people who approach NASA with inventions and suggestions for the space program. While there might be a million ways to improve a space station design, NASA lawyers say that people don't realize that for every pound you add to a payload, it adds $10,000 to $20,000 to the price of sending that payload into space. So suggestions like "send up this experiment" or "put this on the space shuttle" requires a lot more jockeying than people realize!

The patents that inventors present to NASA are all reviewed by the lawyers, and they find that 99 times out of a 100 the patent in question is relatively low-tech. That's because by the time an inventor approaches NASA, that same person has probably already visited big companies like

Boeing and Lockheed and haven't gotten them to bite. NASA lawyers laugh when they point out that NASA is the *very* leading edge of technology—it *has* to be! So if a major NASA contractor isn't interested in a technology, the Space Agency itself likely won't be, either. Instead, NASA most often sees people's inventions after those people have been very handsomely paid by a big company, and the technology is part of a contract proposal from that company.

The NASA lawyers also have to handle situations where people sue the agency, claiming it has violated a patent. Fortunately for NASA, and unfortunately for the claimants, patent infringement claims against NASA are very different from private patent infringement claims in one very important respect: you can't get an injunction against NASA. You can't shut down the space program with a patent claim!

As you might imagine, there are a mountain of NASA patents that are available for licensing by private businesses, and that creates work for the NASA lawyers. Currently, those patents number over three thousand. They're described in a monthly NASA publication called "Tech Briefs," which describes all kinds of innovative stuff that NASA is doing. (Note to NASA wannabes: it doesn't hurt to keep up with "Tech Briefs." You can find it at any technical library.)

Predictably enough, NASA lawyers love what they do. The industry they work in is part of every child's dreams. And no matter how long they work for the Space Agency, the bloom is never off the rose. When you ask them about their work, they'll tell you, "Being at NASA—I'm honored to do it."

The Plummiest of Plum Judicial Clerkships . . .

CLERKING FOR THE UNITED STATES SUPREME COURT

The Supreme Court of the United States

Washington, D.C. 20543 • Phone: 202-479-3000

NUTS AND BOLTS ON CLERKSHIPS

Personnel director: Cyril A. Donnelly
Phone: 202-479-3000
Length of clerkship: One term, which is about twelve months.
Salary: GS-12 equivalent (mid $40's)

WHAT DO THEY LOOK FOR?

Most Supreme Court clerks have clerked elsewhere for a year, and *usually* for a U.S. Circuit judge. In addition to that—and this will come as no surprise to you—Supreme Court clerks tend to be leading graduates of top tier schools, like Harvard, Yale, Stanford, Boalt Hall, Columbia, NYU, Michigan, and the rest of the "usual suspects."

NON-CLERKSHIP (AND JUSTICE) SUPREME COURT POSITIONS FILLED BY LAW SCHOOL GRADUATES . . .

If you want the United States Supreme Court to be your business address, you don't *have* to be a Supreme Court Justice or a clerk for one of the Justices. Many jobs at the Supreme Court have to be filled by law school graduates, including the Clerk of Court, the Librarian, the Reporter of Decisions, the Counsel, and their top deputies. As it turns out, the Administrative Assistant to the Chief Justice and the Marshal of the Court are both law school graduates, although they don't have to be. All of these positions are filled by people with experience in their fields, although three positions—Counsel, Staff Counsel, and Applications Attorney— may be filled by younger, less experienced people. In addition, there are law students who work for the Supreme Court during the day and attending classes at night; for instance, one of the people currently in the Public Information Office fits this description.

SUMMER JOBS . . .

Both the Legal Office and the Reporter of Decisions hire first-year law students during the summer. The pay is about $12 an hour. (For information on these positions, write to personnel director Cyril Donnelly, at the address above.)

HOW TO APPLY . . .

There are major hoops to jump through for a Supreme Court clerkship, and even with the most sterling possible credentials, it's *still* a long shot.

For a start, I can't stress strongly enough that you've got to have *24-karat gold paper credentials* in order to clerk for the Supreme Court. Of the 75 Supreme Court clerks for a recent two-year period, fewer than a half dozen were from law schools outside the top ten. On top of that virtually all Supreme Court clerks do a federal appellate clerkship first. (Lightning does strike once in a *great* while, and you find a Supreme Court clerk from a less-than-distinguished school. For instance, a recent Supreme Court clerk had been a Justice's law student many years before. But that appears to happen *very* infrequently and require *extraordinary* circumstances.)

Assuming you've got the "credentials jack" that it takes to even be considered, you write to the particular Justice for whom you wish to clerk. There's no limit to the number of Justices you can write to; the more the merrier. Along with your cover letter you send your resume, references, and a law school transcript.

Most Justices hire their clerks about a year in advance.

WHAT IT'S LIKE TO WORK THERE . . .

In a chapter full of incredible jobs, there's something about clerking for the Supreme Court that, well, stands out even in this remarkable crowd. It's a combination of so many things. One is the fact that there are so few clerkships—only thirty-four a year. Even if you graduate from a top-tier law school, the odds are still significantly *against* snaring a clerkship with the Supreme Court. And it's fleeting—the clerkships only last for a year. Then there's the history aspect. You work on cases that carry a *very* big stick in American jurisprudence, the *biggest,* and you routinely rub elbows with people who are history makers themselves.

But maybe the true "gee whiz" nature of the job is more than that. I remember being struck by a line I once read in an interview with a recent Academy Award winner, who said that what struck him particularly about winning was that for the rest of his life, he would always be introduced as "Oscar winner . . . " When you talk about jobs you can get within a couple of years of law school graduation, and you limit it to jobs that *everybody* will respect, *forever,* you've narrowed the field down to just about one: Clerking for the United States Supreme Court. No matter what happens to you, for the rest of your life, you'll always have that one, tremendous quill in your cap.

Needless to say, entering this profile with that kind of perspective, the last thing I wanted to do was talk with a Supreme Court clerk who would say, "Actually, it's not all that special." I'm not sure *who,* of sound mind and body, would be blasé about a Supreme Court clerkship, but I can tell you that Rick Garnett isn't one of them! Rick clerked last year for Chief Justice William Rehnquist, and the way he describes his clerkship is *exactly* the way you'd want it to be. He laughs when he says that "You never really get over the thrill of it! I would drive by the Supreme Court building and look at it and say, 'Geez, that's my *office.*' You never lose that feeling."

As a high school student in Alaska, Rick read the book "The Brethren," where he first learned about Supreme Court clerkships. He thought, "That would be a cool job." He went on to Duke University and then spent a year as a paralegal at a law firm in Phoenix, where he heard more stories about life as a Supreme Court clerk from some of the partners who'd clerked for the Court themselves. After graduating from Yale Law School, he clerked for Eighth Circuit Chief Judge Richard Arnold in Little Rock, Arkansas. He said that when he applied for a Supreme Court clerkship, "I didn't honestly think I'd get it." He didn't hear anything from the court for the six months after he applied, and then he got a call from the Chief Justice's secretary, saying that "He'd like you to come in and interview." Rick says he thought to himself, 'Yeah, right, *sure* he does.' But that didn't stop him from hopping on a plane to Washington a few days later.

He says that from first glance, Chief Justice Rehnquist "wasn't at all what I expected." For a start, the Chief Justice came walking out to meet Rick in a sport coat. "It's a surprise, when all you're used to doing is seeing the Justices in their robes." Rick recounts that "He showed me around the chambers, and we chatted for about 15 minutes." They talked about Arizona, having that background in common ("I think that's why I got the job," laughs Rick), and that was about it. He says that "I wouldn't say that's the typical interview. All of the Justices are different. Some interview you for hours. They have complex hypotheticals, that kind of thing. Some will have their current clerks grill you on tough questions. The Chief Justice's attitude is that he knows your credentials, he knows what you can do, he's interviewing you to see if he likes you. He doesn't have a political litmus test."

After the interview, "I left, and the following week, I got a call from his secretary. She said, 'The Chief Justice would like you to work for him.'" Rick says he responded, "Hot *damn!*" and she laughed and said, "Does that mean yes?"

Of course, it did!

He found in clerking for the Supreme Court that the Justices can be very different from the way they seem in their writings and the way they're portrayed in the media. Rick says that "Chief Justice Rehnquist is very stern on the bench, but he's a very nice man in person. He's a *great* guy. You'll always have people who will disagree with some of the opinions any Justice writes, but people all love Rehnquist personally." He cites Justice Clarence Thomas as another example of a person who is "very quiet in public, but in real life he is very funny, very talkative. You'd walk down the halls and find him swapping football talk with Justice Stevens. He's very personable."

Rick typically worked 10-to-12-hour days as a clerk for Chief Justice Rehnquist, "which isn't as long as some of the other clerks." The Chief Justice has a "very efficient system" for streamlining work, but "different Justices have different styles. For some of them, they'll spend more time talking back and forth with their clerks during the day. Others will have long, elaborate meetings. The Chief Justice has regular meetings where he'll check the status of his clerks, discuss who's doing what, and that's it." Clerks "often talk about cases together, and there's a dining room just for the Supreme Court clerks, where people will sit around and discuss cases—or sometimes shout about them! You get advice from other clerks, you learn from them, there is lots of cooperation. But ultimately you are responsible to, and must be loyal to, your own Justice."

The hours can be *very* long, depending on the Justice you're working for. Some clerks work sixteen hour days, and some are there seven days a week. It's not uncommon for clerks to have a workday that stretches from eight in the morning until one a.m. A Supreme Court clerkship isn't, by *any* stretch of the imagination, the job for you if you expect a nine-to-five workday!

Rick says that one of the factors that makes the long hours livable is that "You are working on a great variety of cases, and you can move between them. You might be working on an opinion on one case, a memo for another case that's coming up on writ of cert, and sometimes you'll be working on a last-minute appeal for an execution that's supposed to take place that night." The mention of executions gets Rick talking about "the worst aspect of the job," which is that "There are often last-minute appeals in capital cases, and they are very emotionally draining and difficult, especially for those of us who don't like the death penalty."

While situations like that are inherently disturbing and dramatic, Rick says that "Most of the portrayals of what the Supreme Court is like in books and movies are totally wrong." He says that one exception is the John Grisham book "The Chamber," which "didn't really say much about the Supreme Court" but it was "very accurate in describing death-penalty procedure in the federal courts, at least in the way it portrayed capital cases being bounced from court to court." He says that the reason for much of the inaccuracy in the media is that "What really goes on is a lot of late-night reading. You don't ever read about that or see it in the movies because that's just not sexy."

He adds that one book that paints an accurate picture of life as a Supreme Court clerk—at least, the way it was a couple of decades ago—is the Chief Justice's own book, "The Supreme Court: How It Was, How It Is." (The book was published in 1988 and is now out of print, but you can find it in just about any library.) As Rick says, "He spends about 30 pages talking about his experience as a Supreme Court clerk. He had fun with it, and he clearly wants his clerks to have the same quality experience."

Working for the Chief Justice is certainly not a case of all work, no play. For one thing, there's the weekly game of doubles that the Chief Justice plays with his three clerks. Rick says that "There's a myth that you have to be a good tennis player to clerk for the Chief Justice. In fact, he'll say, 'Would you be willing to play tennis with me?' You don't have to be a tennis player. You just have to be willing to whack a ball around with him." But if you *are* a good tennis player, and you're playing against the Chief Justice, you don't have to let him win! Rick laughs as he explains that "When I first started clerking for the Chief Justice, his partner was another clerk who was a really good tennis player. They would consistently beat us 6-0, 6-0. He didn't like that—he wanted to play with a worse player to balance it out. So he got me. And we lost a lot of the time, and he was fine with that."

All in all, Rick still marvels when he looks back on his year as a Supreme Court clerk. He says, "The moment you get that call, your life *changes*. Those Justices, they change *everything*. So many doors open for you. Teaching, law firms, you name it." He adds that, "They don't have to hire you. Some people are more surprised to get in than others. I was *totally* surprised. I felt, I still feel, that there are 500 people who could do the same thing as you. They don't owe you anything." He reflects that "I had a *great* year. The cases were interesting and challenging. I would do it again in a minute. And best of all was sitting around talking with the Chief Justice. He's been there for 25 years. He's got story after story about these famous cases, these famous Justices he's worked with, people like Brennan and Marshall and Black. It's amazing. I'm so grateful for the experience."

CHAPTER 4

The #1 All-Around Best Legal Employer In America

—The United States Department of Justice.

You've probably heard the classic oxymoron "I'm from the government, and I'm here to help you." Well, if it's the Department of Justice that's paying you a visit, and they're here to offer you a job—they are here to help you. It's a phenomenal place to work. To put it bluntly: The DOJ rocks!

When you write a book like this, you *know* that everybody's going to have the same question: "So who's the best?" I get that question every day. The only way for me to answer is to say that the employer who gets the most rave reviews is *far and away* the Department of Justice. When I was interviewing law school administrators for the names of great employers, I started thinking of the DOJ as the "of course" employer. That's because no matter who else they recommended, they'd add, "And *of course*, the DOJ." And what's even more remarkable is that I have *never heard a negative word about working for the DOJ*. Not one! And I've talked to an awful lot of people, both current and former DOJ employees. The Attorney General herself often says that when she travels throughout the country, she is often approached by attorneys who tell her, "I worked at the DOJ, and I just want to tell you how much I loved that experience. There has been nothing like it—before or since." When you see what novice DOJ lawyers have to say about their work at the end of this chapter, you'll catch a sense of the excitement, the sheer gratification they get from being at the DOJ!

In this chapter I'm going to tell you everything you need to know to convince you that the DOJ really is terrific. (Incidentally, two components of the DOJ—the FBI and the U.S. Attorneys' Offices—aren't included here. Not that those are not great places to work, they *are*— it's just that you'll find them elsewhere in this book. The FBI is with other federal agencies in Chapter 10, and the U.S. Attorneys' Offices are with other prosecutors in Chapter 11.) What I'll start out with is a list of "The Top Ten Reasons You'll Love the DOJ." I've culled these from a variety of sources, and you'll see them reflected in the profiles at the end of this chapter. Then I'll tell you some common misconceptions about the DOJ. After that, I'll give you a general overview of how the DOJ is set up, and give you the nuts and bolts of how Justice is organized and how to get in. And finally, I'll let the DOJ attorneys speak for themselves, and tell you how wonderful their jobs are. I think you'll come away with an understanding of exactly why it is that the DOJ is such a great place to work!

THE TOP TEN REASONS YOU'LL LOVE THE DOJ

1. You'll get responsibility, right away, that you simply can't get any-where else. One of the attorneys profiled at the end of this chapter compared working at the DOJ to "walking on a tightrope—with a huge safety net." As another DOJ attorney said, "You get thrown into stuff you wouldn't get privately, no way. This is not the place where you do research memos for the first three or four years!" DOJ attor-neys frequently report taking depositions, arguing motions in court, second-chairing trials, handling litigation strategy, conducting dis-covery, handling settlements, a whole raft of varied responsibilities—within six months of joining the Department.

2. " . . . and I represent the United States of America." That's how you introduce yourself in court. Sends chills down your spine, doesn't it? Every new DOJ attorney finds that experience awe-inspiring.

3. You get amazing support and feedback from your supervisors. A DOJ lawyer in the Environment and Natural Resources Division said that "Responsibility is thrown into your lap from the moment you step through the door, but you aren't left to sink. There is always someone who is willing to throw you a life vest and help you swim the difficult stroke." Another added that "Even though you do important work right away, you don't worry about mistakes getting out the door. Everything goes through several sets of eyes to make sure that doesn't happen." Novice DOJ lawyers routinely rave about everybody's will-ingness to share advice, experience, notes—whatever you need to help you out, it's there for you.

4. You get to work on issues that are frequently in the news. A few examples of the many recent or current high-profile cases include the Microsoft antitrust case, defense of Megan's Law, tobacco litiga-tion, health care fraud, the Oklahoma City Bombing case, the Unabomber, "Operation Chameleon" (prosecuting international live reptile smuggling rings—part of a $10 billion annual black market), protecting the Chesapeake Bay, and "Operation Senior Sentinel," involving the consensual tape-recording of fraudulent telemarketer solicitations by senior citizens recruited through the American Association of Retired Persons, as well as active-duty and retired federal agents. Senior Sentinel alone has resulted in federal charges being brought against more than 1,000 fraudulent telemar-keters. In fact, there's hardly a newscast that goes by without the DOJ being mentioned. As one junior DOJ lawyer raved, "It's excit-ing, interesting, cutting edge. I was extremely apprehensive as to what was in store for me when I came here, but what I've found is a whole package—phenomenal work, excellent collegiality, learning

from people I couldn't respect more—that I will likely never again experience."

5. The fact that you don't have to worry about making partner makes for a very friendly work environment. DOJ attorneys rave about the lack of competitiveness they enjoy—they truly feel that they are one team, working for one client. This creates a kind of "one for all, all for one" feeling that's hard to beat.

6. *No billable hours.* Any attorney in private practice will tell you that a substantial drawback to their work is the necessity of keeping track of their time, in tiny increments. With only one client—the United States Government—there's no necessity to keep track of time for billing purposes when you work for the DOJ. And as any non-firm lawyer will tell you, that's a *tremendous* benefit.

7. No business development pressure. In private practice, it's enormously likely that as you move up the ladder, there will be increasing pressure on you to bring in business. In small firms, that pressure comes even more quickly. While some people don't mind it, others actually wind up leaving private practice to avoid it. That's not an issue with the DOJ, where you never have to schmooze *anybody* for business.

8. Better hours than a lot of jobs. While it's difficult to make generalizations like this—and there *are* times when you have to work late at the DOJ, and on top of that, you may be the kind of person who just feels comfortable spreading their work out over a longer day—DOJ lawyers *tend* to work shorter, more normal hours than their analogs in private practice, *especially* early in their careers. As one DOJ lawyer pointed out, "I was in private practice and just joined the DOJ a few weeks ago. There was a federal holiday last week, and for the first time 'holiday' meant I had a day off, rather than being just a day I get to wear jeans to work!"

9. Amazing job prospects if and when you leave the DOJ. *Everybody* knows that DOJ lawyers get excellent experience right away, and on top of that, it's very prestigious. That puts you in an outstanding position to pursue anything else you want—in a firm, in business, in academia, in government, anywhere. For instance, many corporate lawyers tell me that it's *more* valuable to get DOJ litigation experience than it is to work for a large law firm, if you want to litigate in-house.

10. You develop a great wealth of "war stories" to tell your friends (respecting confidentiality where necessary, of course). Everybody at the DOJ can regale you with terrific tales; you'll find some of them in the DOJ's lawyers' reflections on their work at the end of this chapter. I'll whet your appetite with just one story, from Gail K. Johnson, a trial attorney, and wonderful raconteur, with the Torts Branch in the Civil Division:

"Being a lawyer at Justice sometimes puts you in the position of being a seemingly out-numbered and overwhelmed David facing a towering and powerful Goliath. In fact, one of my favorite aspects of working for the Department of Justice is toughing it out against bigger—and allegedly better—opposing counsel. A particular story perfectly illustrates this. When I was a 'baby attorney' a few years ago, I had a case where the United States was the plaintiff, and we were suing a prominent New England hospital to recover several million dollars in damages. The United States had been successfully sued by the estate of a former patient of the hospital for alleged medical malpractice years earlier and had paid out over $5 million in a judgment. Years later, the United States brought suit against the hospital, alleging that its medical care caused the injuries to the patient; thus, it should reimburse the government. At first glance, the case looked like an ordinary case for 'contribution' of a co-tortfeasor. However, as the facts unfolded, the case looked more like a Hollywood screenplay for a medical thriller.

"When I was first assigned to the case, I had a difficult time determining facts to support the United States' theory of negligence by the hospital. I spoke to the attorney who had handled the initial litigation, and she suggested that I call the husband of the now-deceased patient for background information. Fortunately, the husband had no ill will against the United States and was willing to discuss the case with me. This is what he told me.

"It turns out that nurses of the hospital had been assigned to provide 24-hour care for his wife who was respirator-dependent. She had been a recipient of a government-approved vaccine and was suffering from its adverse effects. Her respirator had an alarm system which would sound if it became clogged or disconnected. During the course of one of the nursing shifts, the respirator became disconnected. Unfortunately, the alarm had been "disarmed" by someone, because it was irritating and highly-sensitive, which caused it to produce numerous false alarms. No one came to the rescue of his poor wife when she became disconnected, and she suffered extensive brain damage. The husband visited his wife every day at the hospital. When he arrived the morning after the disconnect, he was told by an Italian nurse what had happened. Her story was markedly different from the 'official' story told by the hospital. As I later discovered, this nurse was so upset about the events that had occurred on the prior shift, she wrote about it in her nursing notes. The husband said: 'If you can find that little Italian nurse, you can find out what really happened to my wife!' I thumbed through the nursing notes and called off every Italian-sounding name that I could find. When I got to one of the last names, he said, 'Bingo! That's the one.' I thanked him for his cooperation, hung up the phone, and began a nationwide search for the nurse.

"Weeks later, I located her through, believe it or not, the phone book. (No need to call the FBI when I am on a case!) I called and left her a message to call me either at home or at the office. A few days later as I sat in my bed, in my pajamas, working on the case file, my phone rang. I picked it up and heard on the other end, 'Hello, I believe that you've been looking for me.' It was the nurse. She proceeded to tell me about the events surrounding the disconnect of the respirator, how the *hospital* had tried to cover it up, and that she was willing to come forward to tell the truth even at the expense of her career. I thanked her profusely and knew from that point on that our case was on a roll. The truth would prevail, even against a cadre of high-priced defense lawyers.

"Later discovery not only corroborated the husband's and nurse's stories, but revealed that the hospital had removed incriminating nurses' and doctors' notes from the records and that the hospital's high-priced lawyers from a well-regarded firm had tried to intimidate the nurse who was providing the evidence of the hospital's negligence. To make a long story short, on the fourth day of the jury trial (and my second one), and after the testimony of the nurse, the Court called a recess to talk to both sides. Having read the 'writing on the wall,' the hospital paid the United States $1 million to settle the case. After a year of handling a case considered a loser by many, the United States walked away victorious. I still have copies of that check in my file. Score one for the folks in the 'white hats'!"

COMMON MISCONCEPTIONS ABOUT THE DOJ

1.   It can't compete with the money you get from large firms.

Not true, and not fair, either. As one DOJ lawyer said, "When I added my salary, benefits, and the hours I work, and compared it to the same package in private practice, I found that I made *more* per hour at the DOJ than I did when I worked for a law firm." It *is* true that the starting salary at the DOJ is somewhat lower than many large firms (although it's pretty competitive with firms outside of the largest cities), but there are two things you have to take into account: The promotion schedule gets you into real money pretty quickly, and federal benefits are nothing to sneeze at.

First, salary. If you go to the DOJ straight out of law school, you have to enter under the Honor Program. You start at the GS-11 salary level, which is currently about $40,000 in D.C. (note that the Federal Government pay scale is locality based—there are 30 different pay scales, depending on the region of the country. Many areas of the country are paid at a higher rate than the D.C. area, like San Francisco, where a GS-11 status pays $41,024 to start.). And if you're coming out of a judicial clerkship or graduate degree program, you'll start higher—a one-year judicial clerkship or master's in law starts you at GS-12, which is about $47,000, and a two-year clerkship can start you at GS-13, which is about $56,000. So the starting salary isn't exactly chicken feed. But it's the promotion schedule that ought to really catch your attention. If you do well, in many DOJ offices it's possible to be promoted from the entry level GS-11 salary to GS-15—which is almost $80,000—in less than four years.

On top of strict salary figures, you can't compare government and private jobs without taking into account the federal benefits package (which is true for every federal employer, including all of the ones in this book). Here are the highlights of the benefit program: The Federal Employees' Retirement System ("FERS") includes a basic government pension and social security coverage. FERS also features an optional thrift plan that allows employees to contribute up to 10% of pay, tax-free until retirement, with the government matching contributions up to 5%. Health insurance is available for a wide variety of plans, with the government paying a portion of the cost. Group life insurance is also available. Annual leave is accrued this way: first 3 years of government service, 13 days a year; 3 to 15 years, 20 days a year; and after 15 years, 26 days a year. Thirteen days a year of sick leave are accrued. Two statutes—the Family and Medical Leave Act ("FMLA"), and the Federal Employees Family Friendly Leave Act ("FEFFLA") provide leave options for federal employees who need to deal with a medical crisis for themselves or close relatives, a death in the family, or the birth or adoption of a child.

2.   *You can't get in without great grades.*

Entry-level lawyers get into the DOJ through the Honor Program, and it's aptly named—it's an honor to be in it, because it's not easy. It's true that you need pretty stellar paper credentials to jump into the DOJ coming straight out of school; they rarely reach below the top-third of a law school class. But if your grades aren't great, don't give up. There are many ways to skin the DOJ cat. In fact, about three-quarters of the attorneys DOJ hires are laterals—they *don't* come in through the Honor Program.

One thing you can do is to try for the Honor Program after doing judicial clerkships first. Say, do a judicial clerkship for a year (if your grades aren't your strong suit, opt for a state court, which isn't as competitive as federal courts), and then go to a higher court (or move into the federal courts) for another year. The DOJ sends an application form for the Honor Program to every federal judge in the country, inviting their clerks to apply.

Another way to get into the DOJ with less-than-blue-chip law school credentials is to get out and work at a private firm for a couple of years, in the specialty you'd like to practice with the DOJ. As the DOJ itself suggests, the work experience that will be helpful varies widely depending on the office, but for many offices, obviously litigation experience helps, and in others, experience in the office's practice area (environmental, tax, or antitrust, for example)—either instead of or in addition to litigation experience—is the helpful ingredient.

One lawyer I talked with who took this route into the DOJ said that he *never* would have qualified for the Honor Program with his law school performance, but once he'd worked at a firm and gotten excellent references there, he was very marketable. "They want people with a solid, hands-on knowledge of a specialty. I worked at an environmental law boutique before I came to the DOJ, and once I worked at the DOJ, I realized that I was really doing the same kind of thing from a different angle. In private practice, I had worked with clients on complying with environmental laws. At the DOJ, I handled compliance issues, as well."

3.   *In everything you do, you're always the unmitigated "good guy."*

Many DOJ lawyers have said the same thing: Yes, you *are* doing important work, and you *believe* in it, and it's incredibly gratifying. But it can frequently involve line-drawing that's not so clear-cut. One DOJ lawyer told me about an experience several years ago, working problems involving the Love Canal—remember, that's the upstate New York town that had to be evacuated because of underground hazardous waste. The Federal Government decided that residents within a certain perimeter would receive governmental compensation, and people outside of that line wouldn't be eligible. The lawyer told me, "You knew that there was a possibility that there were some ramifications of this hazardous waste *outside* of the line that was drawn, and you felt terrible about it. But at the same time, you knew that a line had to be drawn *somewhere*—you couldn't have people in Montana claiming they'd been harmed by Love Canal. When you work for the DOJ, you're arguing the government's position, and you get behind it just as you would for any private client." So while "doing the right thing" is a *huge* motivation for most DOJ lawyers—and justifiably so!—don't assume that issues will always be crystal clear. One DOJ lawyer said that during her interview with the DOJ, the interviewer asked her, "If you look at positions on issues in black and white, where do you put DOJ's stance?" She responded, "Shades of gray," and the interviewer smiled. It's great work—but don't be naïve about it!

★   ★   ★   ★   ★

United States Department of Justice

Office of Attorney Personnel Management • 950 Pennsylvania Avenue, N.W.
Room 3525, Main Building • Washington, DC 20530-0001
Phone: 202-514-3396 (voice-mail number providing
information on all legal hiring programs, 24 hours a day)
Web site: www.usdoj.gov

NUTS AND BOLTS ABOUT THE DEPARTMENT OF JUSTICE

By the way, *all* of the information in the rest of this chapter came courtesy of Paula Vickers, the Associate Director of the Office of Attorney Personnel Management, who worked *feverishly* to get me all of the information I requested from all kinds of sources. If you are inspired by this chapter and decide to go for the DOJ (good choice!) and you are lucky enough to wind up working there, stop by Paula's office and thank her. She deserves it!

Attorney Personnel Director: Linda A. Cinciotta
How many attorneys work there: Approximately 9,200. Of those, about
    half are in Washington, D.C., and the other half are *mostly* in the 94
    U.S. Attorneys' Offices.
Total women: Approximately 37%
Total minorities: Approximately 15%
Total disabled: Approximately 2%

WHAT DOES THE DOJ DO?

Established in 1789, the Office of the Attorney General (which later became the Department of Justice) has been accurately described as the largest law office in the world. The DOJ's major client is the executive branch of the federal government and all its agencies. The Attorney General is the federal government's chief legal officer. The Department, comprised of approximately 108,700 persons throughout the world, performs many law enforcement functions, in addition to providing legal services to the government. A primary responsibility of the DOJ is to represent the United States in court; thus, the DOJ is aptly billed as "The Nation's Litigator." Attorneys in the general counsel offices of other federal departments and agencies perform the day-to-day legal duties of the government. However, since most of those other departments and agencies do not have their own litigating authority, when they are involved in or are contemplating litigation, they generally turn the matter over to the DOJ and become the DOJ's client.

While the DOJ performs an enormous variety of functions, in a nutshell these include: providing legal advice to the President, representing the executive branch in court, investigating federal crimes, enforcing federal laws, operating federal prisons, and providing law enforcement assistance to states and local communities.

STRUCTURE:

(This is a *very* brief summary of the complete description of the DOJ that's in its "Legal Activities" book, which you can find at every law school career services office in the country. (I strongly encourage you to get your hands on that book—it's terrific.) Also, you can visit the web site, www.usdoj.gov, for more details.)

The Department has 35 components, and they are clustered under four broad categories:

1.   Litigation Divisions and Offices

This is where you'll find more than 80% of the DOJ's attorneys—and the most job opportunities, as well. The Divisions and Offices here include the Civil Rights Division, the Civil Division, the Antitrust Division, the Criminal Division, the Environment and Natural Resources Division, the Tax Division, and the U.S. Attorneys' Offices (U.S. Attorneys' Offices are profiled in Chapter 11).

Each of these Divisions is broken down into sections. (For very complete descriptions of each section, look at the DOJ's *Legal Activities* book. I know I keep yammering on about that book, but it's required reading if you want to work for the DOJ.) Anyway—about those sections—most of the names are self-explanatory. For instance, Antitrust is broken into the Office of Operations, Appellate Section, Civil Task Force, Computers and Finance Section, Foreign Commerce Section, Health Care Task Force, Legal Policy Section, Litigation I (criminal price-fixing and bid-rigging investigations and cases), Litigation II and the Merger Task Force (with a focus on merger enforcement), Telecommunications Task Force, Transportation, Energy and Agriculture Section, and field offices (in Atlanta, Chicago, Cleveland, Dallas, New York, Philadelphia, and San Francisco, which handle local and regional criminal investigations and prosecutions within their geographic areas, as well as nationwide matters arising in part within those areas).

The Civil Division is broken down into the Commercial Litigation Branch, Federal Programs Branch, Torts Branch, Office of Immigration Litigation, Office of Consumer Litigation, and Appellate Staff.

The Civil Rights Division consists of an Appellate Section, Coordination and Review Section, Criminal Section, Disability Rights Section, Educational Opportunities Section, Employment Litigation Section, Housing and Civil Enforcement Section, Office of Special Counsel for Immigration Related Unfair Employment Practices, Special Litigation Section, and Voting Section.

In the Criminal Division, you'll find the Office of Professional Development and Training (which basically trains judges and prosecutors abroad), Executive Office for the Organized Crime Drug Enforcement Task Force, Appellate Section, Child Exploitation and Obscenity Section, Fraud Section, Computer Crime and Intellectual Property Section, Internal Security Section, Asset Forfeiture and Money Laundering Section, Narcotic and Dangerous Drug Section, Organized Crime and Racketeering Section, Public Integrity Section, Office of Enforcement

Operations, Office of International Affairs, Office of Policy and Legislation, Office of Special Investigations (which investigates Nazi-sponsored acts before and during World War II, whose perpetrators subsequently entered the U.S.), and the Terrorism and Violent Crimes Section.

The Environment and Natural Resources Division is home to the Environmental Crimes Section, Environmental Enforcement Section, Environmental Defense Section, Wildlife and Marine Resources Section, General Litigation Section, Indian Resources Section, Land Acquisition Section, Policy, Legislation and Special Litigation Section, and Appellate Section.

In the Tax Division, you'll find the Appellate Section, as well as Criminal Enforcement Sections and Civil Trial Sections, among others.

2.　Management Offices

These consist of the Justice Management Division, Office of the Inspector General, Office of Legislative Affairs, Office of Professional Responsibility, and the Office of Public Affairs. These Offices employ a relatively small number of attorneys.

3.　Legal and Policy Offices

Among others, these include the Immigration and Naturalization Service, the Executive Office for Immigration Review, and the U.S. Trustees' Offices, which are the legal and policy offices which actively recruit and hire large numbers of attorneys.

4.　Investigatory and Law Enforcement Offices

These include the Bureau of Prisons, which has expanded considerably in recent years and is the largest employer of attorneys within the investigatory and law enforcement offices. (Note that the FBI is also considered an investigatory and law enforcement office, and it hires lots of attorneys, but I talk about that separately in Chapter 10, along with other government agencies.)

If you break down the number of attorneys at the DOJ by substantive practice area, here's how it shakes out, approximately: Antitrust (4.1%); Civil (7.9%); Civil Rights (3.1%); Criminal (5.0%); Environmental (4.8%); Immigration (11.5%); Tax (4.2%); Bureau of Prisons (1.4%); U.S. Trustees, Bankruptcy (2.5%); U.S. Attorneys' Offices, variety of both civil and criminal substantive areas (55.5%).

ENTRY LEVEL . . .

The way to get into the DOJ as a new law school graduate (or coming directly out of a judicial clerkship or graduate law degree program) is through the "Attorney General's Honor Program." Every year, the Department hires approximately 150 entry-level attorneys this way. Here's some information on the Honor Program.

Choosing an organization: There are 10 organizations, representing 10 different practice areas that typically participate in the Honor Program. They are the six litigating divisions (antitrust, civil, civil rights, criminal, environment and natural resources, and tax), the Federal Bureau of Prisons, the Executive Office for Immigration Review, the Immigration and Naturalization Service and the Executive Office for U.S. Trustees. Applicants designate two of the 10 participating organizations on the application, and their applications are considered by the two selected.

Honor Program attorneys are hired for specific organizations and discuss their section assignments within the division/office before they come on board (there is no place to indicate a section preference on the application form). Preferences for specific section assignments are honored, when possible. Since they choose the practice area, it is rare that any Honor Program attorney makes a division change.

Interviews: Each November, the Department interviews applicants for both the Honor Program and the Summer Law Intern Program (this is discussed below) at 13 host law schools that serve as regional interview sites nationwide, as well as Washington, D.C. Interviews take place in one law school in each of the regional locations, where all students and judicial law clerks from that geographical area are interviewed. (While many of the host schools are the same from year to year, there are always *some* changes. Having said that, city locations of the 13 regional interview sites, in addition to Washington D.C., *typically* include Ann Arbor, MI; Atlanta, GA; Austin, TX; Boston, MA; Chicago, IL; Denver, CO; Los Angeles, CA; Miami, FL; New York, NY; Philadelphia, PA; San Francisco, CA; Spokane, WA (which rotates every other year with Tacoma, WA); and St. Paul, MN. Complete interviewing information is available in the DOJ's application booklets, and your career services office would also have interview location information for you.)

Contacting DOJ directly: The DOJ actively solicits and receives Honor Program applications from every accredited law school in the country. Last year's Honor Program admittees represent 80 different law schools.

Note that there is a *strict* deadline for receipt of applications for the Honor Program—there are *no exceptions* for late applications. The receipt deadline is in late September—check with the DOJ (at 202- 514-3396 or on the Internet at www.usdoj.gov) for the precise date.

The DOJ points out that while the application booklets look lengthy, the application is deceptively short and simple to complete. Most of the application booklet is actually background information about the hiring process, interviews, etc. The actual application is a one-pager (two sides)—basically a checklist form which takes about 15 to 20 minutes to complete. A resume and transcript—and not even an official transcript at this point—complete the application package. As the DOJ's Office of Attorney Personnel Management says, "We promise that this is the *easiest,* most user-friendly government application form you will ever complete!"

Hours: The basic DOJ workweek is 40 hours, but attorneys frequently work longer hours as their caseloads and individual styles warrant. Also, approximately 3% of DOJ lawyers work part-time. Typically, they are highly-valued attorneys who had worked full-time at the DOJ for a number of years before becoming part-timers. Part-time work is rarely, if ever, available at entry level.

Starting salary: Approximately $39,000 if hired right out of law school (*but see above—under "Common Misconceptions About DOJ"—for a better picture of how much you can expect to make at Justice*).

The kinds of credentials that will help you break into the DOJ: Moot Court experience; law journal writing experience or articles written in the substantive area of the office; clinical experience (working with clients); relevant courses; volunteer and other employment experience. The DOJ looks at the "whole picture" of the person—searching for good, well-rounded applicants. Although the name of the program—the Attorney General's Honor Program—implies that applicants must have a certain class rank to be considered—there is no grade cut-off threshold for consideration. However, the reality is that the vast majority of those hired under the Honor Program are in at least the top one-third of their class. It is extremely rare for the DOJ to hire Honor Program applicants ranked below the top half of their class, regardless of their other credentials. Judicial law clerkships are particularly valued by the litigating divisions. At least one-third of the Honor Program hires each year are judicial law clerks.

Location: Note that the majority of Honor Program attorneys work in Washington, D.C. The organizations participating in the Honor Program that hire attorneys for positions both in and outside the Washington, D.C. area are: the Antitrust Division, the Executive Office for Immigration Review, the Immigration and Naturalization Service, the Federal Bureau of Prisons, and the Executive Office for U.S. Trustees. Of the six litigating divisions (Antitrust, Civil, Civil Rights, Criminal, Environment and Natural Resources and Tax), only the Antitrust Division hires Honor Program attorneys for Washington, D.C. and its seven field offices. All other litigating divisions noted above hire Honor Program attorneys for Washington, D.C. only. The "Legal Activities" book mentioned throughout this profile has a directory of all the DOJ field office locations that employ attorneys.

Travel: As a novice attorney, you are very likely to travel to conduct investigations or litigate, depending on your practice area and caseload.

Career Path: There's no typical career path at the DOJ. Many attorneys come to the DOJ planning to spend their careers with the Department, and they do—top management throughout the DOJ includes many of these "lifers." Others come to the DOJ planning to obtain the world's best litigating experience for four or five years, and then move on to private practice or academia. Still others are "refugees" from private practice, many of them leaving lucrative law firm partnerships to start new careers as DOJ attorneys. As the DOJ says, "It's a wide mix that works well."

LATERALS . . .

The Department employs approximately 9,200 attorneys, of whom about 75% were hired as experienced laterals. The number of attorneys hired varies each year depending on turnover. In the past, the Department has hired approximately 500 to 1,200 experienced attorneys each year. The type of substantive experience that's valuable varies widely, depending on the office. As I explained earlier in this chapter, for many offices litigation experience obviously helps, since the DOJ does so much litigation work. For others, experience in the office's practice area (*e.g.*, environmental, antitrust), instead of or along with litigation experience, is the helpful ingredient.

To find openings at the DOJ and other attorney career information, check out the DOJ web site, which lists many job announcements: www.usdoj.gov.

SUMMER PROGRAMS . . .

Summer internships with the DOJ are *awesome*. Interns rave about the important work they do, the interesting assignments, the fast pace of the work, the open-door environment—they just *love* it. And you will, too! There are two kinds of summer internships with the DOJ: paid and unpaid.

Paid internships:

The DOJ runs the compensated Summer Law Intern Program ("SLIP") for second-year law students. Third-year students who will serve in a judicial clerkship or full-time graduate law program immediately post-J.D. are also eligible for the SLIP. First year students ("1Ls") are not eligible for the SLIP, but they *can* volunteer (see below).

Number of summer associates under the SLIP program: This year, there were 146.

Salary: Most summer interns are 2Ls and are hired at the GS-7 level, which pays approximately $510 per week (in D.C.; it varies around the country). 3L SLIP hires are at the GS-11 level—about $755 per week.

Location: Most Summer Law Interns spend the summer in Washington, D.C. Only the Antitrust Division and the Executive Office for Immigration Review routinely hire summer interns for positions outside of Washington (take a look at the DOJ *Legal Activities* book for office locations).

How to apply: The deadline for receipt of SLIP applications is in late September each year. This is a *strict* receipt deadline—don't miss it! You can find the applications in your law school career services office in August each year, or on-line at the DOJ's web site (www.usdoj.gov).

For the summer internship program, you apply to particular divisions in the same way as applicants to the Attorney General's Honor Program (see above for details).

Volunteers:

The DOJ has many legal volunteer opportunities in Washington, D.C. and throughout the country—over 1,900 student volunteer internships during the course of a year! You can apply by sending your resume to the hiring contacts for the offices in which you're interested. Hiring contact names, mailing addresses and telephone numbers are in the *Legal Activities* book (the book is in every law school career services office, and on the DOJ web page at www.usdoj.gov). Check the "Other Law Student Programs" section of the *Legal Activities* book for detailed information on how to apply through Washington, D.C. or local offices.

WHAT IT'S LIKE TO WORK THERE—DOJ LAWYERS TALK ABOUT THEIR WORK:

Lisa Lynne Russell, Environment and Natural Resources Division, Environmental Defense Section, Entered the DOJ via the Attorney General's Honor Program, September 1996

"My division is divided into smaller sections. My section consists of about 60 attorneys and 30 support staff. Within a few weeks of starting work, everyone had stopped by to introduce themselves and welcome me to the section.

"I have compared working here to walking on a tightrope—with a huge safety net. New attorneys are given tremendous responsibility as soon as they walk in the door. It is not at all unusual to take depositions and argue motions within the first six months of joining the Division. While exhilarating and educational, the experience can be overwhelming or intimidating. That is where the safety net comes in. Nearly all the attorneys and managers are happy to take the time to talk about their experiences as a new attorney and share their outlines, briefs, and war stories. There is never a time that I cannot pick up the phone to call for advice—no matter what time zone I happen to be in. Our managers and senior attorneys are extremely accessible. I ask questions constantly, and there is no one whom I would not approach for help.

"Competition is not a factor in our workplace—collaboration is. In our section there is a constant flow of information requests and responses over e-mail, and briefs and research are shared by all. We all work for the same client, and no one is vying for partnership. The cooperative environment enables us to work together to provide the best representation for our client.

"Our Division has great social activities to meet people outside of your section. We have Division 'potlucks' in the Great Hall, a golf tournament, and host a huge Earth Day celebration for the entire Department. Where else do you get to talk to the Attorney General with your arms submerged in an ice cold mini-wetland?

"Working here is a continuing educational experience. Although our section litigates primarily under four statutes, my cases have involved any number of situations. I have learned about gold mining in Alaska, nuclear power units for submarines, silver mining during World War II, agricultural fungicides, wetlands, and reclaiming scrap metals from almost anything. Every case provides the opportunity to learn more about the law as well as history, science, industry, and economics.

"I am one of the few people I know who can honestly say that I have the one job I always wanted. When I started law school, I had envisioned the type of work I wanted to do as well as the environment in which I wanted to work. When a professor suggested to me that the Environment Division would be a good place for me to work, he could not have been closer to the mark. After my summer internship in 1994, I realized that the Division and I were a perfect fit. After working as a trial attorney for a year and a half, I can happily report to my professor, and everyone else, that I have the job of my dreams."

Anthony S. Barkow, Civil Division, Office of Consumer Litigation, Entered the DOJ through the Attorney General's Honor Program in September 1996

"From the start, I've worked on interesting cases. They include civil affirmative, defensive litigation, and criminal investigations. One of the most interesting was a continuing and complex white-collar criminal investigation into the conduct of a colorful figure who a major newspaper described as a 'former nightclub hypnotist . . . who once was married briefly to [a late, famous Hollywood actress].'

"My initial responsibility on this case involved coordinating the continuing investigation and preparing the case for trial. In that role, I spoke regularly to the case agent, asking her to interview witnesses and gather additional facts that I viewed as necessary to prove the government's case. After eight months of investigation, I wrote the charging documents and filed them in federal district court. And, at the same time I was working on this investigation, I was working on other investigations and on civil litigation. On all these cases, I was given front-line responsibility; for example, although skilled and experienced supervisors are always available to give advice and direction, I was regularly on the telephone with senior partners at law firms; I was making front-line strategic and litigation decisions in my cases; I was taking and defending depositions; and I was writing and arguing dispositive motions.

"After filing the charges in district court, I conducted all pre-trial plea negotiations, prepared all the papers that were filed with the court, and appeared on behalf of the government at all pre-trial conferences. The case, however, was not resolved, and it proceeded to trial.

"I was amazed by the amount of responsibility my office entrusted to me, particularly given that I had only been out of my judicial clerkship about a year when the case went to trial. I was the lead attorney at the trial, and an attorney from the Federal Trade Commission with years of experience as a state prosecutor was my co-counsel. The trial lasted almost two weeks and involved testimony from 18 government witnesses and the introduction of 143 government exhibits. I conducted the direct examinations of the primary government witnesses and of other, sub-sidiary witnesses; wrote all the pleadings filed with the court; delivered the government's closing argument and rebuttal closing argument; and made all the legal arguments to the court during pre-trial, trial, and post-trial sessions, including sentencing. As far as I know, the experience and responsibility I receive at the Department, and in particular that I received during this trial, exceeds that of virtually all of my law school classmates.

"The jury convicted the defendant of 10 counts of 'criminal contempt' for violating a 1991 injunction order entered by a federal judge. The case involved a large-scale fraud, in which the defendant, using over 10 male and female aliases, operated two 'vocational training programs' through which he defrauded thousands of consumers by falsely promising high salaries to graduates and failing to include disclosures in advertising that the judge had ordered be made. As I argued to the jury, the defendant preyed on people who were seeking to improve their lot in life by gaining skills that would enable them to make more money, but the 'training' they received from the defendant was worthless.

"The defendant failed to appear for the final day of trial, which led the court to issue a bench warrant for his arrest. I wrote the sentencing papers for the government and argued the government's position at sentencing. The court sentenced the defendant to 5 years and 7 months in prison, 3 years of supervised release, and required him to pay restitution to some of his victims. The defendant remains a fugitive and is being sought by the U.S. Marshals Service.

"The tremendous opportunity I had for early responsibility reflects the culture here at the Department and in the Office of Consumer Litigation: attorneys are assigned to cases, take the cases as far as the case goes, and do the work required of the case—large and small—rather than handing off the interesting work to a senior attorney.

"One of the best parts of the trial, aside from the tremendous opportunity to do such significant work on a complex case, was the reception I received upon returning to the office. I'll never forget the greeting my supervisor gave me when I walked in the day I returned to the office. His congratulations and the camaraderie shown when virtually all the other attorneys in the office stopped by to offer congratulations and hear stories—which happens every time someone here conducts a trial—were reminders that the people who work at the Department of Justice feel like part of a team, doing good work on behalf of the people of the United States. It's a great feeling, and I get a thrill—and feel awed—every time I introduce myself in court, appearing 'on behalf of the United States.'"

Michael J. Desmond, Tax Division, Civil Trial Section, Entered the DOJ through the Attorney General's Honor Program, October 1995

"One of the main reasons I accepted a trial attorney position with the Justice Department's Tax Division was my understanding that I would be given immediate responsibility over my own docket of cases. I had heard this same promise of 'early responsibility' in a number of firm interviews as well, so when I started with the Tax Division I wasn't totally prepared for what would come my way. On day one, I was shown my desk, given a stack of new cases and told, 'This is your docket; go to it!' Not only was this my first day with the Tax Division, it was also my first day as a practicing attorney, and the task of litigating a dozen cases on behalf of the United States was a little intimidating. Although the Tax Division has a process for reviewing all of my pleadings and correspondence, there is no partner telling me what must be done in a case, or even an associate suggesting what should be done.

"As a new attorney without any practical experience in litigation, I had only a vague idea of what I should be doing to litigate a case. Thinking to myself, 'I remember studying something about starting a case with discovery . . . ,' I soon found that, while I did have responsibility over my own docket of cases, I was working with a group of 30 experienced trial attorneys who, along with three supervising attorneys, were all more than willing to spend an unlimited amount of time helping me figure out what I should be doing. These attorneys are always willing to share their insight about how they would handle issues, ranging from practical advice on how to get a complaint served, through discussions about how to use document summaries in cross-examination at trial. In addition, the supervising attorneys are always a great source of feedback on any issue raised in a case, providing an excellent sounding board for arguments I think should be raised in a brief or positions that might be taken in a case. This network of training and support has proven to be one of the best parts of my job—giving me not only practical insight from experienced attorneys, but also a real sense of comradeship.

"After more than two years with the Tax Division, I have almost 40 active cases assigned to me that I generally have a free hand to litigate in any way I feel appropriate. This includes everything from initiating settlement discussions with opposing counsel; deciding whether, when and how to do discovery; filing dispositive motions; and, even trying the case. Moreover, while I don't have any independent ability to settle a case, my input is significant; I alone usually deal with opposing counsel, appear at settlement conferences, and make recommendations on settlement to my section chief. In my two years with the Tax Division, the process of working with my supervisors on settling dozens of cases has itself been a great learning experience, highlighting the strengths and weaknesses in a case and allowing me to see how the case can be handled to address them.

"I've also been able to work with other trial attorneys on several large cases, being given total responsibility for major aspects of that litigation. Within six months of starting with the Tax Division, I volunteered to help several other attorneys working on a $200 million tax claim in a bankruptcy case. I thought I would be the 'junior' attorney on the case; I soon learned that wouldn't be the case. In the Tax Division, if you are ready and able to work the case, it's yours! I was soon traveling the country, reviewing rooms full of documents, meeting with IRS agents, and taking expert depositions trying to determine the tax consequences of some incredibly complicated international financial transactions. Since I was relatively new to the job and didn't have as many commitments to other cases, I was able to devote a lot of time to the case and soon found myself heading up the government's defense of one of the major issues raised in the case. At some point during the middle of deposing the opposing side's expert witness, I realized that I had a better understanding of the issue than he did—a real confidence booster!—as we were moving quickly toward a scheduled three-week trial. In the end, the week before trial I spent some late nights working with the other attorneys on the case to hammer out a settlement agreement. Being able to play that kind of a role in the case less than two years out of law school was amazing. While it was more than a little trying at the time, that kind of experience quickly made me feel like a seasoned litigator.

"Working with other attorneys on cases, making court appearances several times a month, and constantly talking with the IRS, opposing counsel and other attorneys in the section about my cases, I have obtained a great deal of experience in just a short time on the job. Most of my friends from law school who went to work for large firms are just now making their first appearances in court. In two years with the Tax Division, I've made dozens of court appearances, taken more than 30 depositions, co-chaired two jury trials and just last week was I preparing for my first solo jury trial, in a case that I spent a year and a half developing. That case settled the day before trial, but it was an incomparable learning experience to take it that far.

"After a few years on the job, the rewards for having prime responsibility for handling a docket of several dozen cases have become apparent. I have the opportunity to move cases along as I see appropriate, learn from my mistakes, and take the credit for getting a good result. The Tax Division has also provided me with a unique opportunity to travel the country, become familiar with my California docket, and work directly with the 'client' to develop my cases. One of the unexpected benefits of working with the Tax Division has been the opportunity to work with IRS people out in the field. When a case ends up in litigation, it's usually after someone has put a lot of time and effort into it. When I get the case, there's always a great sense of appreciation for the time and effort I put in. In one case, I spent a week doing depositions on a case that a Revenue Officer had been working on for several years. When the depositions eventually led to a favorable ruling on a summary judgment motion, the appreciation expressed by the Revenue Officer for my work gave me an enormous sense of satisfaction.

"In terms of time commitment, litigating cases for the Tax Division has got to be just as demanding as any job in the private sector, particularly when you factor in the frequent travel that is a part of the job. While the compensation may not always compare, it's more than made up for by the incomparable level of responsibility I've been given and the satisfaction that comes with that responsibility. While litigating a docket of 40-plus active federal tax cases can be demanding, those demands come from the cases themselves and from the personal commitment each attorney makes to them. No partner is ever going to make you work all weekend to get ready for a trial or a round of depositions, but your own personal commitment to the case will. Somehow that makes a Saturday afternoon at the office seem a lot easier to handle. It also leads to a supportive and informal work environment, where most of the learning comes not from any formalized training or from following the directions of senior attorneys, but from simply pulling up a chair in the office next door and, over a cup of coffee, throwing out ideas about how to handle a case."

Nicole M. Healy, Criminal Division, Fraud Section, Entered the DOJ through the Attorney General's Honor Program, September 1991

"From the beginning of my tenure with the Criminal Division, I have been given significant responsibility. During my first year at the DOJ, I spent six months at the U.S. Attorney's Office in the Eastern District of Virginia, where I worked on a major case involving a murder and racketeering conspiracy in which a motorcycle gang attempted to kill members of a rival gang. Although I was the third lawyer on the case, I was given the opportunity to write most of the motions and briefs for the two 1992 trials, which involved a number of issues of first impression in the Fourth Circuit.

"Since coming to the Fraud Section in November 1992, I have had substantial responsibility for investigating and prosecuting violations of statutes, including the Foreign Corrupt Practices Act (which prohibits the bribery of foreign officials by U.S. persons and companies to gain a business advantage), mail and wire fraud, fraud against the government, and money laundering. In 1997, I was part of the team that negotiated a \$35 million criminal plea and civil settlement for defrauding the government against a commodities exporter, Arab Finagrain Agri-Business Trading, Inc.—the largest criminal/civil recovery in any of the cases arising out of the Banca Nazionale del Lavoro investigation. In 1996, I participated in obtaining a \$25 million plea and civil settlement against the American Eurocopter Corporation, which pleaded guilty to illegally paying sales commissions and submitting false documentation to the Department of Defense in connection with the sales of U.S. government financed military helicopters to the government of Israel.

"Travel is a big part of the experience of a Fraud Section attorney. Our cases are spread out across the country, and we frequently travel to meet with agents, witnesses and counsel, as well as to appear before grand juries and in court. Because my practice has focused on transnational white collar crime, I have also traveled to Europe, the Middle East and Latin America. I have participated in symposia and meetings with law enforcement agencies in the United Kingdom, France and Hungary and was a member of the U.S. government team that negotiated the Inter-American Convention Against Corruption, which was signed in Caracas, Venezuela in March 1996.

"One of the best things about working at the DOJ, and particularly in the Fraud Section, is that the attorneys—from the most experienced to the newest law school graduates—consider themselves to be members of a team. Attorneys are always willing to share materials, give advice and help one another on projects. In addition, the Fraud Section's management welcomes and encourages input from all the attorneys on a variety of issues. I regularly participate on indictment review committees, which are staffed by senior and junior attorneys, each of whom votes on whether to indict the case, generally after a spirited debate. I have also sat on hiring committees for permanent attorneys and interns, where the opinions of each attorney are given consideration.

"Although we work very hard, the section's attorneys and management try to balance the requirements of our work with our personal lives. Many of the attorneys have young children, and parents take time off to attend a field trip, or a parent-teacher conference. In addition, although the ratio of women to men in the legal profession, and particularly in law enforcement and litigation, may be low—I often attend meetings where I am the only woman present, or one of very few—the section makes an effort to attract women, and the number of women attorneys is high (in fact, the chief is a woman). And, although at times I have experienced both blatant and subtle discrimination from defense counsel, I have never experienced any form of discrimination from my DOJ colleagues."

Scott B. Murray, Antitrust Division, Telecommunications Task Force, Entered the DOJ through the Attorney General's Honor Program, October 1995

"The Antitrust Division is a great place to work for all of the reasons you look for in a prospective employer—wonderful people to work with, important and complex matters to work on, and the feeling that the work of the Division is a benefit to a great many people.

"For a start, the Antitrust Division is full of lawyers, all at various stages of their careers, who are able to lend a helping hand on both work-related and career-related questions. My section, the Telecommunications Task Force, has attorneys who worked on the case that led to the break-up of AT&T, attorneys who would be junior partners at large firms, and attorneys my own age who are two to four years out of law school. The benefit of being surrounded by attorneys with a variety of experience is that you can go into any office and have your questions answered from a historical perspective, from a current perspective, and from a future perspective. You can not only discuss the genesis of an issue, but also the current ramifications of the issue and pragmatic assessments of the future ramifications of the issue.

"Almost every attorney is willing to discuss such matters in detail and to help their colleagues grow as attorneys. Whether it is because no one is competing against one another to become a partner, or simply because the Division attracts compassionate and caring people, there is never an air of unhealthy competition at the office. Most people are more than willing to help another attorney without regard for whether they get the credit or not. This is true of staff attorneys and the Chiefs and Assistant Chiefs of each section, as well as the attorneys in management positions in the front office. Even highly-regarded attorneys in other sections often take the time to help nurture new attorneys. An attorney in the Appellate Section who has been with the Division for over a decade has often taken the initiative to contact me about ways in which I can work on interesting matters or become a more integral part of my section. She has given me direct, yet helpful, criticism of my work, and provided me with pointers to help me correct areas of weakness. In a similar vein, I have been contacted by attorneys from other sections who think that I might be a good candidate for certain opportunities within the Division. Knowing that other attorneys are looking out for my best interests, without my asking for such treatment, is a feeling that I don't think many new lawyers could get anywhere else.

"There is a feeling at the Division that we are all on the same team, working for the same common interest. Many of the attorneys have already worked in the private sector, have seen the results of a highly competitive work atmosphere, and try to create exactly the opposite atmosphere at the Division. To have a group of such talented attorneys, not trying to beat each other out for partner positions, but instead focused on practicing the law in its finest manner, has created a wonderful learning atmosphere.

"In addition, the Division is full of fun, good-natured individuals. For years, many people would get dressed up in elaborate costumes for Halloween, each year trying to top their outfit from the previous year. In addition, some attorneys would videotape spoofs of other attorneys to show at the annual Christmas parties. The new attorneys are encouraged to carry on the tradition. The ability to laugh at oneself is a highly-regarded trait at the Division. At the going away party for an attorney who recently left for another job, his colleagues showed the videotapes that he had made in previous years. Not only was it wonderful to see how people had changed over the years, but it was refreshing to see that attorneys who were in supervisory positions were willing to participate in the spoofs and have a laugh.

"The Division has a softball team that competes in the Senate League, and recently created a Division-wide basketball league. Not only are all welcome to play, but you get the chance to meet the attorneys and paralegals from other sections and even the front office attorneys. Indeed, the Assistant Attorney General for Antitrust is on the roster! It's in these settings that you learn a lot about the other cases the Division is handling and the issues that are confronting other attorneys. From these events, I have been able to establish friendships with staff members from other sections whom I can contact when I am facing similar issues. In addition, by seeing your supervisors in non-work related situations, you can build the interpersonal relationships necessary to feel more comfortable approaching those individuals in work-related situations. Most sections have one or two individuals who push everyone to go out after work or engage in section-wide activities. One of the most fun things to do is to challenge another section to a competition, most often some sporting event. It really brings a section together and helps the Division stay in contact. My section chief asked me to lead one of our weekly staff meetings, and since the basketball league was just about to start, I took a few minutes to introduce our team to the section in style—dimmed lights, flashlights, and Chicago Bulls' theme music! I only heard good comments about my little skit, and it just might go down in Section lore.

"When it comes to the work I do at the DOJ, it is wonderful to have a job where, on three to five mornings of each week, there is an article in the newspaper about a transaction or issue that my section is handling or will handle in the future. The Telecommunications Act of 1996 has led to an abundance of work for my section, and the cases not only involve vast sums of money, but also will have an impact on how the nation will communicate in the future. Large corporations, federal and state authorities, and consumer groups all have strongly held opinions about how the antitrust laws should be applied to a quickly changing industry. But the best thing about working for the Antitrust Division is that we always know that we are working for the just result. This does not mean that the Division's position will always win, or even that our position will ultimately be proven correct; it simply means our goal—protecting competition—is always a just pursuit.

"When I walk across the Great Seal in the Main Justice Building, or when I look at the pictures of past Assistant Attorneys General for Antitrust in the Assistant Attorney General's conference room, I am constantly buoyed by the thought that for close to 100 years, my predecessors, and now my contemporaries, have had one goal—to protect competition in American industries for the benefit of the American people. No matter how each generation of antitrust enforcers has chosen to implement that goal, the goal has always been the same. I think it is because of that noble goal, that Division attorneys attempt to practice law with the highest degree of honor, integrity, and compassion. At a time when the public perception of lawyers seems to be growing worse on a daily basis, I think the Division's employees represent what is best about the legal profession. I have seen Division attorneys voice their displeasure at what they perceive to be poor lawyering or unethical lawyering. Not only do experienced Division attorneys highlight such actions, but they also take the time to explain what a good attorney would have done.

"New attorneys are also given the opportunity to grow at their own pace at the Division. I have found that the more work you ask for, and successfully complete, the more work you are assigned. Exuberance and a willingness to work hard are well-rewarded. My supervisors not only ask me whether I am happy with my workload, but also approach other staff attorneys to verify that my morale is not suffering. The fact that my supervisors realize that a new attorney might not feel completely comfortable expressing such a concern to them—and take the extra step to find out whether the attorney is expressing such thoughts to other staff members—is a source of comfort to me. Not only is my well-being of concern to my supervisors, but they actively seek feedback to make sure I am challenged by my workload and responsibilities.

"In addition, new attorneys are often given quality assignments much more quickly than they would receive them in private practice. Within six months of joining the Division, I was conducting six depositions over a two-week period in a Section 1 investigation. I second-chaired a number of depositions, but then was given the opportunity to conduct my own depositions. The lead attorney on the case, and the attorney I was partnered with—both of whom had over 10 years of litigation experience—spent a substantial amount of time preparing me for the depositions and critiquing my performance. Being given such early responsibility made me feel that I was a trusted and valuable member of the section and was a great boost to my morale at an early stage of my development. In addition, due to the help of the other attorneys, I was able to see an improvement in each successive deposition.

"In addition, given the number of parties and third-parties involved in our cases, new attorneys are often on the phone, and in meetings, with senior partners and corporate General Counsels who have much more experience and expertise. New attorneys at the Division quickly learn how to handle the nervousness that comes from being in such situations and how to act in an appropriate manner. During a merger investigation, I called a General Counsel's office to inform the company that the Division would soon be sending a third-party Civil Investigative Demand to the company. During the course of the conversation, the other attorney asked me a couple of questions that were clearly attempts to find out where the Division's investigation was and whether the Division might file to block the merger. Having been in so many meetings with such counsel and having listened to so many other similar phone conversations, I almost laughed while I deflected his questions. After the conversation ended, I reflected on how much my confidence has grown in just two and a half years with the Division.

"I was also asked to participate in the Division's hiring process this year. After only two years with the Division, I was giving presentations at area law schools to interested students, reviewing resumes of potential summer interns and new attorneys in the Division, conducting interviews, and preparing detailed interview reports for the Hiring Committee. One of the members of the Hiring Committee, a very experienced attorney within the Division, even sent me an e-mail thanking me for the thoroughness of my reports. Through this experience, I really felt that I had a hand in continuing the tradition of excellence at the Division. Although I did not have the final hiring authority, I truly felt that my role was an integral part of the hiring process."

Juliette Nicole Kayyem, Civil Rights Division, Office of the Assistant Attorney General for Civil Rights, (she started her DOJ career with the Educational Opportunities Section), Entered the DOJ via the Attorney General's Honor Program, October 1995

"I began work at the Department of Justice only a few months after law school. I had already spent a summer in the Educational Opportunities Section and was excited about returning. When I began in October, I had not heard about my Bar results, so I assumed that I would have a few weeks' reprieve to get acquainted with the job. I was wrong.

"A major trial in an urban school desegregation case was set for January. At the time, there was only one senior attorney assigned to the case. I was picked to assist him. In the government, especially in litigation departments where the court deadlines are so quick and the needs so urgent, there is definitely a work ethic of sink or swim. The presumption is always that you can do the work, and so long as you can, the work keeps coming. Two days after I had been admitted to the Bar, I was taking depositions for discovery, finishing the pre-trial brief and preparing for the three-week trial. While there is always someone to turn to for advice, or to answer a question, I never had the feeling that I was waiting around for the 'good' work. I never wrote a memo for the 'filing cabinet,' never sat around just to watch what it was like to be a lawyer.

"The travel is also an exciting part of the job. If you can stand to be in motels a lot of the time, then this job is for you. Spending time talking to people, getting a sense of their concerns, is pretty amazing, especially if you have only spent time on the two coasts. As a representative of the United States, it is often thought that you do not have clients that you represent. That is not exactly true. There is a sense in the work we do that the United States is a real client; maybe not a person or someone who pays legal fees, but by spending time in a community and getting to know the people who are harmed by some discriminatory action, you do feel like there is an important interest you are representing.

"The Department of Justice bills itself as the largest law firm in the country. That *is* true, but somewhat misleading. Within any given office, there isn't much hierarchy. As a new attorney, your point or opinion is given as much weight as any other. You feel like your opinion counts. The Civil Rights Division has plenty of ambitious, novice attorneys who are fun, love their work, and care about important issues.

"After two years in litigation, I was asked to join the Office of the Assistant Attorney for Civil Rights. At that time, the nominee, Bill Lann Lee, was in the midst of his confirmation hearing, which would later turn out to be controversial. I was asked to help in the confirmation, but also to help in the work of the 'front office,' that is, making sure that the work of the Division got done, was well expressed, and that the other parts of the Division understood why we were doing what we were doing.

"I have no doubt that working here is not only an amazing opportunity, but also the best decision in my work life. To go to work each day feeling like what you do is not only effective, but important, makes me grateful that I went to law school. Civil rights work can be frustrating, no doubt, but it is also rewarding, and working for the government gives you opportunities and freedoms that you don't often find in the private sector."

CHAPTER 5

The Law Firms.

I realize that "Well—duh" would be a reasonable reaction to a subsection title like this, because the profiles are pretty self-explanatory. But they do merit a bit of explanation, and that's what you'll get here. (Note that I haven't mentioned every section that appears in every profile—I think you'll be able to figure out everything else for yourself.)

The office information at the beginning of each profile

As you'll see, each listing has state and city listings. If the firm's main office is listed, it's included first, and if several offices of the same firm are profiled, the main office is the first one that appears. Note that in many cases I've included the words "main office"; in others, the firm in question asked that no office be designated as its main office. It's a Three Musketeers, 'one-for-all-and-all-for-one' philosophy as far as I can tell; they don't want to ruffle feathers in what would otherwise be called branch offices.

The reason I've included branch offices of firms is that either I heard great things about the branch offices as well, or didn't hear anything bad about them. Based on all of the interviews I've conducted, for any firm the largest office is the one you're likely to enjoy the least, because of autonomy and bureaucracy issues. If the firm creates a good environment for junior associates in its largest office, odds are that its branch offices follow suit. And that's why I've included them.

You can't make that same assumption if it's a branch office that got recommended. That happened in a few cases. For profiles where you find that the only office listed is followed by a mention of where the firm's main office is, that means that I specifically heard recommendations for the office in question, and either heard nothing—or worse—about the main office.

Number of attorneys in the firm

I've included as much information as I could get about women, minorities, and disabled attorneys. For firms that don't include these listings, it doesn't necessarily suggest any lack of diversity. Instead, especially for the "disabled" category, some firms just don't keep track of personnel to the level of detail I sought.

Hours and bucks

There are a couple of things to make note of here. One is the starting salary plus typical bonus. I've created four categories that apply throughout the book: $ means under $35,000 to start; $$ means $35-50,000; $$$ means $50-65,000; and $$$$ means over $65,000 to start. If a firm is known for being particularly generous, I've noted that as well. The reason for these categories instead of strict dollar amounts is this: If you're looking at two employers of basically the same size in the same area, they're going to pay about the same amount, whether they call it a straight salary; or salary plus stipend; or salary plus stipend, bonus, profit sharing, whatever. They *have* to pay just about the same in order to be competitive. Furthermore, it's way too easy to focus on money to the exclusion of every other factor. My heart has been broken any number of times, hearing law students choose an employer based on what they perceive as a $2,000 difference in pay—going to someone I know is a sweatshop, and foregoing an employer I know they'd love. All for 40 lousy bucks a week, *before* tax. Your life is worth more than that. And so I like to think I've done you a favor by giving you a general idea of what people pay, without nailing it down more specifically than that.

You'll also notice that for some law firms, there is the statement "no minimum billable hours requirement." Read the firm's "What it's like to work there" section before you draw any conclusions about the lack of a minimum; being 'strongly encouraged' to work 1,900 hours has just the same effect on your lifestyle as a minimum billable requirement.

Pro bono

Firms vary greatly in their approach to pro bono. For some, serious pro bono involvement is looked upon with great favor. For others, it's not meaningful at all. You can *generally* tell how seriously a firm takes its pro bono obligations by whether or not it counts pro bono hours as billables, and I've included that information wherever possible.

I think you can figure out everything else by yourself.

Akin, Gump, Strauss, Hauer & Feld, L.L.P.—San Antonio

300 Convent Street, Suite 1500 • San Antonio, TX 78205
Phone: 210-281-7000 • Fax: 210-224-2035 • Web site: akingump.com

OFFICES

Washington, D.C. (main office)*; Austin, Dallas, Houston, Texas; Los Angeles, California; New York City, New York; Philadelphia, Pennsylvania

"When I interviewed here, one of the people I interviewed with told me this: 'I could tell you this is an incredible firm—and it is. I could tell you about the great pay, the prestigious clients, and the high-profile cases we get. But as a new associate, here's what you really need to know: we don't eat our young.'"

HIGHLIGHTS

- Over 675 lawyers, domestic and internationally—10TH largest firm in the country, with main office in Washington, D.C. San Antonio office is the largest firm in the city.
- A burgeoning international practice, with offices and/or clients in Asia, Europe, Latin America, and South Africa.
- Pro bono hours are treated as billables.

NUTS AND BOLTS

Managing partners:

Cecil Schenker, W. Thomas Weir

Hiring partners:

Michael C. Elrod, phone: 210-281-7231, melrod@akingump.com

Recruiting coordinator:

Ann Jacobson, phone: 210-281-7181, ajacobson@akingump.com

Number of attorneys in firm:

680 (258 partners)

WHOLE FIRM:

Women partners (65), minority partners (18)

SAN ANTONIO OFFICE:

Total attorneys (75), total partners (23), women partners (2), minority partners (2), total associates (45), women associates (19), minority associates (3), total of counsel (4), women of counsel (2)

OTHER OFFICES:

(* represents an office profiled elsewhere in this book)
Austin (55), Dallas (129), Houston (57), Los Angeles (22), New York (73), Philadelphia (6), Washington* (258), Brussels (17), London (5), Moscow (8)

Years to make partner:

Approximately 8

WHAT DO THEY DO?

Primary specialties (more than 5% of practice):

Corporate and Securities (16), Intellectual Property (3), Labor and Employment (10), Litigation (31), Public Finance (4), Public Law and Policy (1), Real Estate (5), Tax (2).

New associates are assigned to a practice area and a supervisor. All of their projects come through the supervisor.

WHO DO THEY REPRESENT?

Vast array of domestic and international clients, including American Airlines, America Online, Atlantic Richfield, Lukoil (Russia's largest oil company), Samsung, AT&T, Volkswagen, Archer Daniels Midland, USAA, Hartford Life Insurance Company, Clear Channel Communications, H.E.B. Grocery, Taco Cabana and House of Blues.

WHERE NEW ASSOCIATES COME FROM . . .

Akin Gump routinely interviews on campus at the following law schools: University of Texas and St. Mary's. The firm also hires from law schools where it doesn't interview on campus.

HOURS AND BUCKS . . .

Average billable hours for first year associates: 1,850. There is no minimum billable hour requirement, but associates who bill 2,000 hours (including client *and* pro bono hours) are eligible for a bonus.

Part-time work is available for associates, including entry level on a case-by-case basis.

The firm routinely hires contract associates; to date no contract associate has become a regular associate.

Typical first year associate salary for San Antonio, including typical bonus: $$$$ (over $65,000)

SUMMER PROGRAM . . .

Last year, there were 11 summer associates, 8 of which were eligible for offers, and all 8 did receive them.

Weekly pay: $1,200 last year

Our summer program is geared for 2Ls.

Deadline for applying for summer clerkships: No strict deadline, but hiring decisions are usually made by December

PRO BONO . . .

Akin Gump strongly encourages pro bono participation. Pro bono hours are considered billables. Associates have been involved in pro bono projects including criminal appointments, representing charitable organizations, and representing indigents in civil matters. There are no upper and lower limits concerning the amount of time an associate dedicates to pro bono work.

HISTORY AT A GLANCE . . .

The firm as a whole is very young. It was founded in 1945 by Robert S. Strauss and Richard A. Gump, in Dallas. Strauss later became Chairman of the Democratic National Committee, Special Trade Representative under President Carter, and U.S. Ambassador to the Russian Federation. The San Antonio office merged with Akin Gump in 1984.

WHAT IT'S LIKE TO WORK THERE . . .

"This is one place where you're not a filing and research grunt."

Associates rave about the quality of projects that they get, right from the start. One associate commented that "you expect to push paper for 4 to 5 years at a big firm, and that just doesn't happen here." A litigation associate said, "I've got friends at other firms who are just research grunts. They don't expect any real responsibility until their fourth year. It couldn't be more different here. You do deals and depositions right away. I did four depositions in my first year. That's just unheard of at a large firm." A corporate associate added, "Client contact here is the rule, not the exception."

The firm prides itself on the way it trains junior associates. Young associates take part in seminars and workshops year-round, honing their skills on a 'learning by doing' basis in areas like deposition and trial skills, ethics, pro bono matters, legal writing, and oral advocacy. Individual practice groups enhance this with specialty-specific training programs, staffed by not only firm attorneys but by outside consultants as well.

Akin Gump puts an emphasis on solving client problems on a multi-office basis. For example, the firm's Washington office recently drafted an energy policy for an Asian nation, while lawyers in Texas worked on helping arrange joint ventures for the country to help provide equipment to implement the policy.

Not only does responsibility come early, but so does the quality of the work associates get. One associate raved about his experience as a first year associate, when he got to be "one of three attorneys working on an international class action suit. I knew I wanted to do international work, but never dreamed I'd get the chance so early in my career." Regardless of specialty, associates compliment the firm for keeping them intellectually stimulated. "You get a wide variety of projects here. They don't pigeon-hole you."

The trend toward early responsibility is unlikely to trail off anytime soon, due to the office's burgeoning business. "Akin Gump's San Antonio office is growing like mad," said one associate. "The work is just streaming in."

As a burgeoning practice might suggest, the hours at Akin Gump can be long. Associates typically work about a 10-hour day. Early birds who come in at 7 a.m. don't "feel odd" leaving at 5 p.m., while those who show up at 8 a.m. will routinely stay until 8 p.m. or longer. While it's not considered unusual to work an evening or Saturday, "It's not every day, and it's not face time. You only come in if you have a deadline." One associate reported that if you show up for weekend work and you don't have a deadline, "You'll get razzed. People will say, 'so who are you kissing up to?'" Another associate commented that "It's so open here, everybody knows what you're doing. The important thing is just getting your work done." A corporate associate noted that "I'm having a great time and doing the work I want, and I'm learning something new every day. It's very rewarding, and for me that outweighs the hours." Another associate agreed, saying that "We do put in overtime, but we take pride in what we do, and enjoy doing it right. That's what counts." Another associate added, "We aren't in the dark. We know we are helping to build something for the future."

*"Coming from another large firm, I was just blown
away by how friendly this place is."*

It's impossible to talk with anybody at Akin Gump's San Antonio office without being charmed by how much they truly like working together. Laterals from other firms—who are in a position to compare—often talk of being "blown away by the atmosphere. I'm always telling other associates, 'You don't know how good you have it. This is a different world.'" Another lateral described the office as "positive, alive."

This camaraderie extends from lawyers to support staff, an important factor in creating the office's genial work environment. One support staffer commented that "Everybody here is on a first-name basis. They consider everybody important." Associates talk of "everybody's door" always being open. "There's just great banter among the secretaries, paralegals, lawyers. There's no real hierarchy, just a really warm atmosphere." A litigation associate talked of being able to ask questions of everybody, including being able to poke your head in litigation partner Barry Chasnoff's office, even to ask a simple question like "What's the deadline for filing a summary judgment?"

Another associate commented, "I've always been struck by how partners *genuinely* like to help. Everybody is accessible. Everybody from the mail boy to senior partners call the managing partner, Cecil Schenker, just 'Cecil.'"

"People here are always ready with a helping hand."

The sense of camaraderie at Akin Gump is especially evident when a colleague needs help, whether it's professional or personal. One staffer told of a "Huge project that came into the office, totally unexpected. The lawyers who got it were absolutely swamped, and everybody else was busy. It looked like there was no way they were going to make their deadline. But one of the other lawyers in the office used the in-house e-mail to say, 'These guys need help. Let's help out!' There was overwhelming support, and the project got done on time. That kind of thing happens all the time."

The firm's caring nature toward its people is shown particularly vividly through a touching story. An attorney at the office was diagnosed with leukemia. As one associate told it, "As he got worse, it was soon determined that he needed a bone-marrow transplant. The office rallied together and held a blood drive for him. Everyone, including partners, associates, and staff, volunteered to donate blood."

"People bring in their kids if day care doesn't work out."

The firm's caring nature toward its lawyers shows in its sociability and family-friendliness. Lawyers at the office get together for all kinds of social events, both structured and unstructured. One associate is a former military pilot who owns his own single engine airplane. "During the summer, he'll often fly two or three law clerks to breakfast or lunch at a nearby town, and give them an aerial view of San Antonio." When there's a wedding or anniversary party for anybody at the office, "Everybody from the office goes." Golf, softball, basketball, cycling, running, rock concerts, art exhibits, the symphony, hunting and fishing are some of the hobbies that Akin Gump lawyers routinely take part in, while those who are "solitary types" don't feel the pressure to take part. "They're certainly not penalized for it."

One associate noted the "Good mix of married and single people here." Summer clerks are invited to attorneys' houses and get to know their families, not just the attorneys themselves. And when anybody has day care problems, "They just bring the kids to the office. The firm recognizes that you just don't always have control over these things." Another pointed out that "It's a common saying around here that 'no amount of money is worth time.' They know how important families are."

"This is just a great place to live."

Associates love living in San Antonio, even for those who initially thought they had no interest in the city. "I clerked at another firm in another city, but it just took me a few weeks here to fall in love with the place." One associate summed it up by saying, "I live 10 minutes from the office, in a great neighborhood with great schools. I'd say it costs much less to live here than to live in other Texas cities even, and Texas isn't expensive." Another associate commented that "We have a running joke with other offices in the firm. When they call San Antonio, they always start out by saying, 'I hear the traffic's really bad there.' Bad traffic just doesn't exist."

One associate summed up Akin Gump's appeal perfectly by saying, "All you've got are the people you work with, the work you get, where you live, and what you get paid. Akin Gump is the top in every respect. The pedigree of the firm and being able to live and work in San Antonio—I'm positive it just can't be beat."

Akin, Gump, Strauss, Hauer & Feld, L.L.P.—Washington, D.C.

1333 New Hampshire Avenue, N.W. Suite 400 • Washington, D.C. 20036
Phone: 202-887-4000 • Fax: 202-887-4288 • Web site: akingump.com

OFFICES

Washington, D.C. (main office); Austin, Dallas, Houston, San Antonio*, Texas; Los Angeles, California; New York City, New York; Philadelphia, Pennsylvania

"The atmosphere here is totally unique, especially for a top-flight firm. It's a very social, outgoing place to work."

HIGHLIGHTS

- Over 675 attorneys domestically and internationally, 10TH largest firm in the country. Washington is the firm's largest office.
- Explosive growth in D.C.—Washington office has grown from 2 lawyers to 250 in just over 25 years.
- Pro bono hours are considered billables.
- No minimum billable hour requirement.
- Partners Robert Strauss and Vernon Jordan are listed in "America's 100 Most Influential Lawyers" by the *National Law Journal.*
- In-house back-up day care for employees whose normal day care plans break down unexpectedly.
- One of the top 10 law firms ranked by gross revenues in *The Legal Times.*

NUTS AND BOLTS

Managing partner:

R. Bruce McLean (firm-wide chairman)

Hiring partner:

Dennis M. Race, phone: 202-887-4028, e-mail: drace@akingump.com

Recruiting coordinator:

Mary G. Beal, phone: 202-887-4181, e-mail: mbeal@akingump.com

Number of attorneys in firm:

675 (258 partners, 384 associates)

WHOLE FIRM:

Women partners (65), minority partners (18)

WASHINGTON OFFICE:

Total partners (103), total associates (136), women partners (16), women associates (57), minority partners (6), minority associates (17)

OTHER OFFICES:

(* represents an office profiled elsewhere in this book)
Austin (55), Dallas (129), Houston (57), Los Angeles (22), New York (73), Philadelphia (6), San Antonio* (73), Brussels (17), London (5), Moscow (8)

Years to make partner:

Approximately 8

WHAT DO THEY DO?

Primary specialties (more than 5% of practice) in D.C.:

Litigation (67), Labor (45), Public Law & Policy (29), International (20), Corporate (21), Energy (11), Food & Drug (10), Healthcare (9), Tax (9), Real estate (8), Environmental (6), Communications (4), Bankruptcy (6).

For a detailed run-down on the activities of each section, visit Akin Gump's homepage, at akingump.com.

New associates are assigned to a practice group, almost always of their choice. All projects come through the practice group's "point person." There is no rotation between departments but it is possible to switch specialties.

WHO DO THEY REPRESENT?

Vast array of domestic and international clients as befitting one of the country's largest and most profitable law firms, including American Airlines, America Online, Atlantic Richfield, Lukoil (Russia's largest oil company), Samsung, AT&T, Volkswagen, Archer Daniels Midland, Food Lion, Starbucks, Campbell Soup, American Express, Boeing, Exxon, Time Warner, and General Electric.

WHERE NEW ASSOCIATES COME FROM . . .

Akin Gump routinely interviews on campus at the following law schools: American, Boalt Hall, Catholic, Columbia, Duke, Emory, George Washington, Georgetown, Harvard, Hastings, Michigan, NYU, Northwestern, Penn, Stanford, Texas, Virginia and Yale. Associates and summer associates are also hired from law schools where Akin Gump doesn't conduct on-campus interviewing.

HOURS AND BUCKS . . .

Associates work an average of 1,880 hours per year. There is no minimum billable hours requirement.

Part-time work is available for associates, both continuing and entry level, on a case-by-case basis; 7 attorneys in the D.C. office currently work part-time (including one associate recently elected to the D.C. City Council). Akin Gump does not routinely hire contract associates in the D.C. office.

Typical first year associate salary, including typical bonus: $$$$ (over $65,000). The firm is known for its generous financial package.

SUMMER PROGRAM . . .

Last year there were 28 summer associates, 27 of whom received offers.

Weekly pay: $1,400 last year.

1Ls are not hired for the summer program in the D.C. office.

There is no strict deadline for applications, but hiring decisions are usually made by December 1.

PRO BONO . . .

Akin Gump strongly encourages pro bono participation; in 1997 alone, 235 of the firm's legal staff logged more than 20,000 hours handling approximately 160 pro bono matters. Approximately 3 to 5% of the firm's work is pro bono. Pro bono hours are considered billables. Associates have been involved in a variety of projects including criminal appointments, representing charitable organizations, and representing indigents in civil matters. There are no upper and lower limits concerning the amount of time an associate dedicates to pro bono work.

In the Washington office, pro bono work in 1997 included adoption referral cases as well as work with the Greater Washington Exploratory Committee, an organization seeking to bring the 2012 Olympics to D.C. Washington associates also have initiated a tutorial program for homeless children, called "Project Northstar." The Washington office has adopted a local elementary school and supports it with the time and service of volunteers from the office. Other civic activities lawyers take part in include Gifts for the Homeless; Race for the Cure; American Heart Association Lawyers Have a Heart 10K Race; United Way Campaign; Red Cross Blood Drive.

HISTORY AT A GLANCE . . .

The firm as a whole is very young. It was founded in 1945 by Robert S. Strauss and Richard A. Gump, in Dallas. Strauss later became Chairman of the Democratic National Committee, Special Trade Representative under President Carter, and U.S. Ambassador to the Russian Federation.

Stars at the Washington office include Strauss as well as Vernon Jordan, civil rights leader and presidential confidant (both Strauss and Jordan have made the *National Law Journal's* list of the 100 most influential lawyers in America); Sylvia de Leon, lobbyist; Sukhan Kim, lawyer for South Korean interests; Michael 'Mad Dog' Madigan, chief counsel for the Senate Governmental Affairs Committee probe of 1996 campaign finance violations; David Catania, first openly gay member of Washington, D.C.'s City Council; John Dowd, litigator, best known for his investigation of Pete Rose; Joel Jankowsky, head of the firm's legislative practice and listed in the *Washingtonian's* Top 10 Lobbyists. Four partners were named in the *National Law Journal's* "Who's Who of Employment/Labor Lawyers" last year: Ron Johnson, Don Livingston, George Salem, and Richard Wyatt.

WHAT IT'S LIKE TO WORK THERE . . .

When you see a letterhead filled with the names of some of the country's most influential movers and shakers—Vernon Jordan, Robert Strauss—the last thing you expect to hear from associates is how much fun it is to work in Akin Gump's Washington office. Of course, associates like the training, the early responsibility and the interesting projects they get—more about all of that in a minute—but the word "fun" is the one that comes out over and over again when you talk with "the Gump's" associates.

One associate told a story that reflects both the camaraderie among colleagues as well as the exciting work junior associates get. "I recently took a trip to Korea with two of the partners in my section and an outside consultant. We were originally staying in Seoul at the Ritz and commuting each day to a small town where the client was. Well, after a week of battling two-hour traffic on either side of the commute, we decided to forsake the comfort of the Ritz for closer digs. Our client, being a gracious host, offered us rooms in the company "dorms" where many of the company's employees stay. Unfortunately, there were only two apartments available, each with a suite of three rooms. Since I was the only woman in our group, I was given my own separate apartment, even though I was by far the most junior member of the team. The three men shared the other apartment. Since they were so cramped, I offered to share my apartment, but they refused, ostensibly on grounds that for their generation, even platonic co-habitation with a female would be inappropriate. Well, that's what they *said*. I later found out the real reason. When I visited my dorm-mates on the first night, I felt like I was back in college! These grown men had frozen pizza boxes, uneaten cereal, and empty beer cans everywhere. It became clear to me that they let me have my own apartment, not because of a sense of decorum or chivalry, but because they wanted an all-guy sleep-over! They were not what you would expect stuffy, middle-aged lawyers to be. They were really fun to hang out with and made the trip very memorable."

Other associates chime in with their own raves about the firm's unique atmosphere. "There's no doubt that this place is, well, quirky. Social gaffes that would sink you at any other firm are accepted here. For instance, one of the summer clerks challenged a litigation partner to a chugging contest in a local bar. It got pretty raucous. Not only wasn't this frowned upon, but the guy wound up getting an offer." As that story illustrates, "They really mean it when they say they recruit for personality," according to one junior associate. Another associate pointed out that "Everybody who visits for the first time comments on how they get a sense of the genuine friendliness here when they walk through the halls."

In fact, the lawyers at Akin Gump enjoy each other's company so much that they form many friends among their co-workers. One associate enthused that "There aren't many firms where you would want to hang out with your co-workers on the weekend or grab a beer with a partner. Many of my friends at other firms lament about how boring or unsociable the people are at their firms. Not so here. I feel incredibly lucky." Another associate added that "Before I started working here, I would not have imagined wanting or actually having dozens of work colleagues at my wedding, or spending so much of my free time with people from work."

While you start to get the feeling that an 'Animal House' mentality pervades the offices, it doesn't. As one junior associate pointed out, "The lawyers here are by and large very outgoing, very interesting people, and it makes for an interesting workplace. However, reserved people fit in as well. About a third of the junior associates, up to three years with the firm, have families, so their priorities are different. If you are married or your focus is on your family, and you don't want to socialize outside of work, that's OK, too. But you'll enjoy it while you're here."

"You get tons of responsibility and client contact right away."

One of the factors that contributes to that enjoyment is the amount of responsibility the associates at Akin Gump get very early on. The firm has a lean staffing policy on projects, eschewing multiple levels of responsibility, which gives even the most junior associates lots of chances to appear in court, take depositions, and maintain client contact. One associate raved that "In my first six months with the firm, I've worked one-on-one with in-house counsel of Fortune 100 companies." Another new associate pointed out that "One of the best aspects of working here is feeling like an important part of the team. Even as a first year on my first case, I was never kept out of the loop. Partners and senior associates on the case keep you apprised of what's going on, and you sit in on conference calls and meetings with clients. They actually encourage me to establish contact and take on responsibility. And they definitely make you feel as though they appreciate your effort. When we reached a favorable settlement for one of our clients, the partner in charge of the project took us all out to celebrate, and made a point of thanking us for our hard work."

Many associates are very taken with the high-profile nature of their clients. As one said, "As a first year associate, I'm already developing a specialty in high tech communications systems. I've got clients that you read about in the newspapers all the time. And I get constant contact with those clients. It's not only interesting, but that kind of contact helps you to know exactly *why* you're doing what you're doing." Another pointed out that "All the associates here have at least one high-profile project. Some are working on campaign fundraising investigations. Others work on the defense case for Fife Symington, the former Governor of Arizona who was charged with fraud. The list goes on and on."

The responsibility they get and the interesting nature of the projects makes junior associates at Akin Gump feel that "The firm really respects me and values what I do." One satisfied associate commented that "I appreciate the confidence the firm has in me, even as a new associate."

As you might expect from an office that attracts outgoing people, "It pays you to 'find your own level', and seek out work you find interesting." Another associate bluntly stated, "Wallflowers do not succeed at Akin Gump."

"There's a lot of crossover work between departments, and a strong 'Washington' flavor to all of the work we get."

The firm is divided into departments, but it's a mistake to think that the departments operate totally independently. As one associate pointed out, "Almost everything in every department has a public policy aspect, and in Washington, you *want* that." The firm prides itself on its ability to come up with innovative solutions to client problems, instead of meting out "the same old traditional arguments." This interdisciplinary approach has lured some well-known clients. Food Lion—the grocery store chain that successfully sued ABC for its unflattering "Prime Time Live" coverage—came to Akin Gump because, in the words of general counsel R. William McCanless, "Akin Gump had . . . a solid labor practice that understood corporate campaigns, but they were broad enough" to handle all of Food Lion's litigation.

Unlike some large firms, Akin Gump does not rotate new associates through each department. Instead, "At the end of your summer, you get 'debriefed' and they ask you for your two choices of departments. If you want labor or litigation, the two largest departments, no problem—they take and need the most people." However, it's very rare for anybody to be put in a department they didn't ask for—many associates had never heard of it happening even once. That's largely because the "Firm is incredibly busy, globally." Perhaps because of the lack of rotation "junior associates can switch departments," and this happens without repercussion.

"The hours can be long, but it's all driven by the clients' own deadlines."

The price new associates pay for interesting work and an enjoyable atmosphere is sometimes long hours. As the firm itself admits, "Stress and long days are not unusual." One associate said that "The hours can be long, but by 7:30 at night most people are gone, and frankly that's better than I expected. I know other firms in town where the offices are pretty full at 9 at night." It's not unusual to be at work on a weekend at least once a month, "Either because of deadlines or because of being lazy during the week." One partner pointed out that "A lot of times junior associates feel compelled to work late or on weekends because they waste time during the regular work day, or don't work efficiently yet."

Any resentment over long hours is dampened among associates by the feeling that the late hours aren't due to any artificial deadlines, but "because of client needs." They say that "When partners say they need stuff by a certain time, they really need it by that time. If they want something on their desk by 9 a.m. Monday, they won't wait until Wednesday afternoon to look at it." And when it comes to weekend work, the associates uniformly feel it's not a matter of face time. As one commented, "There are no kudos for showing up on a Saturday if you don't have a deadline to meet."

"The firm runs its own day-care center."

Long hours would seem to convey a lack of family-friendliness, but Akin Gump ameliorates the problem of work-vs.-family in several important respects. For instance, it runs a day-care center, providing back-up care for any employee—lawyer or support staffer—whose routine child care arrangements break down. The center is staffed by a director and 12 trained childcare providers, and it's not a matter of simple in-house babysitting. Children up to the age of 10 get to go on field trips, to the zoo and to museums. And the service is clearly a godsend, in a routine year caring for upward of 200 children on over a thousand visits. The firm also has a holiday party for the children of firm members, and a family picnic in the summer.

"The social activities here reflect the firm's light-hearted atmosphere."

Social activities help foster camaraderie among the lawyers, and between the lawyers and support staff. There are monthly associate breakfasts, periodic firm and section meetings, dinners, informal parties, a holiday dinner-dance, and the slate of summer social events you'd expect of a firm with a large summer associate program.

One associate told of "The legal assistant holiday luncheon, where each legal assistant, all 60 of them, invites their favorite attorney as their guest. Part of the entertainment is attorneys who have any talent performing. For example, a partner who fancies himself a magician puts on a magic show. Another associate and I performed a medley of songs that poked fun at the firm and spoofed life as a legal assistant. I don't know of many firms who encourage this kind of light-hearted atmosphere or who can laugh at themselves."

Other social activities include a weekly basketball league, summer soft-ball league, a fall flag-football league, annual golf tournament, an annual bowling party, an annual trip to see the Orioles play, and for the more highbrow, an annual "Shakespeare in the Park" event. One associate pointed out that "A number of people I work with are close friends, and they'd be my friends whether we worked together or not." That kind of warmth has associates routinely getting together for Friday happy hours at neighborhood bars and for dinner parties.

The firm's caring nature comes out both in its attitude toward its own people, and toward the community. One associate recounted that "My wife had a baby last year, in the middle of a large initial public offering I was working on. The corporate section covered me so I could take two weeks off, and were very supportive."

"Akin Gump puts its money where its mouth is with pro bono projects."

With members like Robert Strauss and Vernon Jordan, with their noteworthy contributions to American political and civic life, you'd expect a strong pro bono commitment from Akin Gump. Pro bono work is managed and supervised full-time by a senior attorney, and pro bono hours are treated as billable hours. In 1997, pro bono work included work with the Greater Washington Exploratory Committee, an organization looking to bring the Olympics to Washington in 2012. Associates have also initiated a tutorial program for homeless children in the area, and the firm has adopted a Washington, D.C. elementary school and supports it with the time and service of many volunteers from the firm. While "billing 8 or 9 hours a day on client work doesn't leave a lot of time for community projects," one associate told of the rewards of working with the homeless children tutorial project and vol-unteering at the elementary school. "Doing both projects gave me the chance to meet other Akin Gump lawyers and employees from all differ-ent sections of the firm who participate in the programs. Akin Gump really 'puts its money where its mouth is' by encouraging attorney par-ticipation and allowing attorneys to bill the time they spend working on pro bono projects like these."

"One of the things that drew me to Akin Gump was its training program. It's been so good it surpassed even my high expectations."

Akin Gump puts a priority on training, reflected even in its summer associate program. For the past 10 years, the firm has run a litigation training program for all summer associates, even those with no interest in going into litigation. As one junior associate pointed out, "Even if you're not going to be litigator, it's important as a lawyer to be able to think quickly on your feet, and the summer training program does just that."

The training program consists of an afternoon each week, devoted to 'learning by doing' experiences. The topics cover everything from initial client meetings and interviews, to drafting responses, discovery requests, arguing motions, deposing and defending witnesses in depositions (complete with court reporters and transcripts), settlement negotiations which include estimating the values of claims for settlement and dealing with clients who don't want to settle, trial preparation including direct and cross-examination, making objections, prepping witnesses, and actually trying actions to a judge. The firm's legal assistants act as clients and witnesses in the cases, and the sessions themselves are taught by senior associates, partners and outside consultants.

This training program earns raves from summer associates. One enthused, "I felt like a litigator for the first time." Another said, "I really enjoyed taking depositions and the trial . . . it made me feel like a 'real' lawyer. It also took a lot of the fear and anticipation out of these things because they aren't so mysterious and foreign anymore."

This emphasis on training continues for permanent associates. The firm recently created a full-time position of Attorney Development Coordinator to focus on improving its orientation, mentoring and performance valuation programs and expanding its already-ambitious professional development program. The firm routinely gives seminars on a range of topics from research to writing to ethics and beyond. In addition to traditional litigation skills programs or workshops, there are training sessions involving labor law and corporate transactions, as well as informal sessions on time management, public speaking and the like. One associate remarked that the devotion to training is so pervasive that "You feel as though you're being trained on a day-to-day basis. You get comments on what you've done, and it's not just a matter of marked-up memos. Instead, partners and senior associates will ask you if you understand the changes they've made, and if you agree with them. It's like every project is a learning experience. It's very respectful, as well as being educational."

One of the office's junior associates worked there as a legal assistant while she was still in law school. She summed up "the Gump" experience: "In law school I didn't think I wanted to practice law in the traditional sense, and certainly not in a law firm. However, my experience here was so rewarding, professionally and personally, that it changed my mind. The work I've done and the people I work with are exceptional. I can honestly say I don't think I would want to work in any other law firm."

Arnold & Porter

555 12ᵀᴴ Street, N.W. • Washington, D.C. 20004
Phone: 202-942-5000 • Fax: 202-942-5999

OFFICES

Washington, D.C. (main office); New York City, New York; Denver, Colorado; Los Angeles, California; London, England

"We do really sexy law. For a lot of the things we do, there are no precedents—it's incredibly intellectually challenging."

HIGHLIGHTS

- With 463 lawyers, 54ᵀᴴ largest firm in the country.
- Only law firm in the country offering full-time in-house day care.
- Pronounced dedication to pro bono work, with a distinguished history of high-profile pro bono cases. Pro bono hours are treated as billables.
- No minimum billable hours requirement.
- Voted one of the 100 best places to work by *Working Woman* magazine (only one of two law firms so honored).
- Consistently ranked as one of the top 20 merger and acquisition practices nationwide.

NUTS AND BOLTS

Managing partner:

James J. Sandman, Esq.

Hiring partner:

Claire E. Reade, Esq.

Recruiting coordinator:

Ms. Taylor C. Kell, phone: 202-942-5059, e-mail: Taylor_Kell@aporter.com

Number of attorneys in firm:

463 (203 partners)

TOTAL FIRM:

Partners (203), associates (260), women partners (28), women associates (97), minority partners (9), minority associates (33), disabled partners (1), disabled associates (2), of counsel (14), special counsel (19)

WASHINGTON OFFICE:

Total attorneys (318), partners (141),associates (177), women partners (21), women associates (63), minority partners (6), minority associates (22), disabled partners (1), disabled associates (1), of counsel (7), special counsel (16)

OTHER OFFICES:

(* represents an office profiled elsewhere in this book)
New York (64); Denver (22); Los Angeles (47); London, England (12)

Years to make partner:

7 to 9

WHAT DO THEY DO?

Primary specialties (more than 5% of practice):

General litigation, including international trade, appellate, white collar, product liability, antitrust; Corporate & Securities (including international transactions); Banking; Trusts & Estates; Benefits; Environmental; Bankruptcy; Government Contracts; Public Policy; Legislation; Telecommunications; Intellectual Property; Real Estate; Food, Drug & Medical Devices.

The firm is not formally departmentalized; associates are assigned to practice groups but occasionally switch groups.

WHO DO THEY REPRESENT?

Multinational corporations and banking institutions (including Xerox, General Electric, PNC Bank Corp.), regional companies, start-up enterprises in virtually every major industry, foreign governments literally from A (Argentina) to Z (Zambia), federal and state agencies (including the U.S. Navy), municipalities, universities and other nonprofit organizations (including the National Women's Law Center), and individuals as well as significant pro bono matters.

WHERE NEW ASSOCIATES COME FROM . . .

Arnold & Porter routinely conducts on-campus interviews at the following law schools: Chicago, Columbia, Cornell, Duke, George Washington,

Georgetown, Harvard, Howard, Indiana-Bloomington, Iowa, Maryland, Michigan, Minnesota, NYU, North Carolina-Chapel Hill, Pennsylvania, Stanford, Texas, Vanderbilt, Virginia, Washington & Lee, William & Mary, Yale. The firm does hire routinely from law schools where it doesn't conduct on-campus interviews.

HOURS AND BUCKS . . .

Associates work an average of 2,396 hours, of which average billables are 1,958. There is no minimum billable requirement.

Part-time work is available to both ongoing and entry-level associates.

Typical first year associate salary, including typical bonus: $$$$ (over $65,000). The firm is known for its particularly generous financial package.

SUMMER PROGRAM . . .

In 1998, there were 32 summer associates, all of whom received offers.

Weekly pay: $1,500 in 1998

1Ls are not hired for the summer program in the D.C. office (they are hired on a case-by-case basis in the firm's LA, NY and Denver offices).

PRO BONO . . .

The firm encourages all of its attorneys to spend up to 15% of their time on pro bono matters, with pro bono hours being treated as billables. Its strong history of pro bono service extends back to its defense of government employees and leading academics during the McCarthy era, its work in the landmark Supreme Court decision Gideon v. Wainwright, and its representation of miners in the Buffalo Creek mining disaster.

Currently A&P lawyers take part in a wide variety of pro bono projects, including representing death row inmates in habeas corpus proceedings; housing discrimination; filing amicus curiae briefs on behalf of the National Women's Law Center in the gender discrimination suit involving the Virginia Military Institute; representing various international human rights organizations and numerous nonprofit organizations, including the Children's Defense Fund, Gifts for the Homeless, and several international arts organizations.

HISTORY AT A GLANCE . . .

Arnold & Porter was founded shortly after World War II as Arnold, Fortas & Porter. The "Arnold" was Thurman Arnold, a former academician and U.S. Appeals Court Judge. The "Fortas" was Abe Fortas, later a Supreme Court Justice. And "Porter," Paul Porter, was a former FCC Chairman.

The firm was a trail-blazer from the start, not just for its high-profile and controversial pro bono work, but also for its attitude toward women.

From its very beginning it hired female attorneys, when very few law firms did so. As early as the 1960's, A&P allowed women to work part-time, in an era when most other law firms were just abandoning regular weekend hours. In fact, in 1974, a part-time female attorney made partner— Brooksley Born, who is today the chair of the Commodity Futures Trading Commission.

Today, the firm is something of a "revolving door" with senior government positions. A number of Arnold & Porter attorneys have held senior positions in the White House and in government agencies including the State Department, Justice Department, the Federal Reserve Board, the Federal Trade Commission, the Federal Communications Commission, the Department of the Treasury, the Central Intelligence Agency, and the Securities and Exchange Commission.

WHAT IT'S LIKE TO WORK THERE . . .

When you talk with associates at Arnold & Porter, you're immediately struck by the fact that they consider the work they do, and the people they work with, utterly unique.

The tone of the office is greatly influenced by the managing partner, Jim Sandman. One associate raved, "He's just an incredible man. He respects people. When you start here, he makes a point of spending time with you to get to know you. Anytime anyone in the firm has a family illness, any big event, he's right there. He's a truly caring man." Another chimed in, "We all consider him our friend," and another added, "He's on a first-name basis with *everyone*." An associate told a tragic story of a new associate who was killed in a plane crash. "Jim Sandman handled all of the arrangements for the family, and had people at the firm handle everything. After it happened, none of the other junior associates could bring themselves to do any work. Partners picked up all of the work, even doing document reviews for the distraught associates." One associate pointed out that this level of caring creates a 'touchy-feely' environment, where "The firm does just about everything it can to address issues, big and small. We always joke around that if you complain, you'll find yourself on a committee to address whatever it is you complained about!"

"Strong personalities"

The firm clearly attracts and respects strong personalities. One associate pointed out that "There is a wide variety of people here. They appreciate differences. There's no fraternity or sorority feel to the place. It pays to be self-assured, outspoken, because there's nobody meek or wishy-washy. They're all very strong-willed people." Another agreed, saying, "We all speak our minds here. It makes for an especially dynamic and interesting environment." As one associate recounted, "This is a place that respects your individuality. You can tell from the people they hire that it's the quality of your work that counts, not the kind of person you are. I mean, everybody here is kind, and ethical, but they're all *different*. When I interviewed here, I interviewed with a guy who was a complete freak. He shook when he talked, and he babbled. I figured, 'If he can make it here, I can, too.'"

This respect for individuality leads to a kind of casualness unusual in a large firm. One associate said that "I don't wear shoes in the office. I can come in at noon and work late. There's no face time and blue suit b.s. here." Another associate said that, "I've gone fishing with one of the senior partners who used to be general counsel for the CIA. He's a fascinating guy, with great stories to tell. For instance, he's got this rug in his office that is really crappy. He tells about how when he was in government, there was a strict rule about not accepting gifts over a certain dollar value. He says that when he was on a trip abroad, an 'unnamed dignitary' gave him this rug. He was very proud of it, but figured that he'd have to give it up when he got home because of the rules against accepting valuable gifts. Well, he said that when he got back to Washington, the government people who review gifts took one look at the rug, and said disdainfully, 'Oh, you can keep *that*.'"

The sense of camaraderie between lawyers leads to a we're-in-this-together attitude. One associate said that "Lawyers are always helping each other out in a pinch. You do it for them because you know they'd do it for you. There's no dog-eat-dog world here."

"Early responsibility and great projects"

The firm encourages associates to take on responsibility quickly. One associate said, "There's no sense of hierarchy here. You get treated with respect and you get as much responsibility as you can handle." Junior associates often get projects like preparing and examining witnesses, taking depositions, drafting agreements, preparing disclosure statements, pleadings, motions and briefs, attending client meetings, and participating in negotiations and settlement conferences. An associate recalled that "My first project was to write a brief. Not a memo to a partner to incorporate into a brief, but the whole damn brief! The first day I was here, I was on the phone with a client. And my experience isn't unusual." Another associate raved that "What I've *never* done says a lot more than what I've *done*. I've never spent a day in the library, or done a file memo. I've never done busy work. Everything I do has a purpose with a client's benefit in mind."

The firm backs up its junior associates with first-rate training. Informally, associates work with a variety of senior attorneys with different approaches, to help them learn a broad range of skills. Formally, the firm gives new associates rigorous instruction on legal research and writing. It presents a series of programs and seminars to strengthen their research and writing skills, as well as to learn new skills like oral advocacy, conducting depositions, drafting contracts, and negotiating. Partners in each specialty conduct seminars on various areas of the practice. And the firm maintains a video and print library of all kinds of continuing legal education materials.

The trade-off for high caliber work and excellent training is hours that can be long. As one associate pointed out, "I actually thought the hours would be worse than they are, from the stories I'd heard. But the fact remains that if you have an expectation of getting home every night at six o'clock, you're setting yourself up for disappointment." Typically, associates come in pretty late—by 9:30 or 10 a.m. or so—and leave by 7:30 or 8 at night. However, this isn't routine; one associate pointed out that "there are weeks when I'll leave at 4 o'clock every day. It all depends on what the clients need." When it comes to weekends, "If you show up people will look at you and wonder what's wrong with you that you can't get your stuff done during the week." However, "Weekend work ebbs and flows. You might work every weekend for a month, and then none at all for two months." One associate pointed out that "You have to put the hours in perspective. I love what I do. The partners respect my work. My work is valuable. I'm no cog in a wheel. They'll sit me down and say, 'Here's what we're doing, and why.' You don't think about the hours when you're treated that way."

"Relaxed firm structure"

The firm has resisted the idea of departmentalization; historically, it "disliked the idea of putting people in little boxes." However, as one associate pointed out, "It's the nature of modern practice that clients want specialties, they want experts. The nature of the beast is changing and the firm is changing along with it." This actually benefits associates, as one pointed out that "even though the firm likes a loosy-goosy feel, as it's grown it's gotten more formal with size. And that helps us, because it means the work is more evenly distributed."

The firm has different practice groups. Most attorneys are attached to one practice group, but a number work in two areas. As one associate pointed out, "You can work in different departments if you want, and it's easy to change departments." Another added that "You get to choose which department you want. Virtually everybody gets their first choice."

Within each practice group, there is an assignment partner, and the bigger departments have more than one. While the assignments flow in theory through that one partner, one associate said that, "There's no working for one supervisor here. It definitely pays to take responsibility for yourself. If you want other or different kinds of projects, you go and bug the assigning partner for them. Sometimes you get more than you bargained for!"

The firm's respect for its associates is reflected by associates' participation in managing the firm. The firm is largely run by committees of attorneys. Associates serve along with partners on a number of committees, including the ones that run hiring, the summer associate program, and the pro bono program. There is also an associate member on the management committee, who has input on associate issues. And associates provide feedback to the partners they work for through periodic confidential evaluations. One associate pointed out that "Associates here definitely feel they have a big say in management. Being on all of the committees helps, as does the fact that many of the partners are homegrown. There aren't many laterals. It makes you feel closer to them, not as though the firm is divided into 'haves' and 'have-nots.'"

"Strong dedication to pro bono work"

As one associate pointed out, "This place has a sterling reputation for pro bono work." Another added that "You don't have to do it, and some people don't. But other people do tons of it, so it balances out. Nobody is ever told they've done too much." Another told that "If you're working on a death penalty case, that's going to take two months, and you can't do anything else while you're doing that. That's respected. If you have a pro bono deadline, it's treated the same as any other deadline. Partners won't tell you, 'Oh, that's weekend stuff.'"

The pro bono program is run by a social worker. One associate explained that "You tell her what you want, and she finds it. For instance, you can choose a substantive area, like employment law. Or a kind of experience, like 'I want a trial,—she'll find it for you. Or an ideological bent, say, you want to help people with AIDS, she'll find you the work." Another associate added that "If you want to stand out, a great way to do that is to get involved with pro bono. The firm really supports and recognizes it."

"A friendly—and family-friendly—office"

Arnold & Porter is legendarily understanding of family matters. As one associate pointed out, "The firm has infant high chairs in the cafeteria to make it easier for parents and children to eat together." On top of that, it's the only firm in the country with a full-time on-site day care center. The Children's Center can hold up to 38 children on a full-time basis, and it also provides free back-up child care when any lawyer or staff member's child care arrangements falls through. This kind of family-friendliness comes at a price—the firm spends $100,000 a year on the center.

The firm's friendliness is also reflected in its 'Garden Room' tradition. As the firm points out, "The 'Garden Room' is an A & P tradition going back to the days when the firm offices were in townhouses with an actual garden room. It started when Abe Fortas used to invite all of the lawyers into his office at five o'clock for a scotch, so they could discuss the business of the firm. Today there's no 'garden', but we still have the Garden Room. It is a combination bar/living room on the top floor of our building, which gives the lawyers a place to gather and relax. Every evening snacks and drinks are available. It's like a happy hour between six and eight, and there is a core group of 'garden room regulars.' On Fridays they add pizza to the mix, and they attract a big crowd."

Although one associate pointed out that "All of my friends work here," there's no pressure to socialize with colleagues. One associate pointed out that "You know the married people have their families to think about," although another pointed out that "There's a lot of socializing among the attorneys, both married and single, gay and straight, partners and associates." While the firm has the usual variety of activities focusing on the summer program, including a cruise on the Potomac, many smaller groups of attorneys participate in extracurriculars on their own initiative. Some tutor inner city elementary school students, others are involved in politics, and they take part in various sports together, be it running, basketball, tennis, golf, or softball.

All in all, as one associate pointed out, "Working here is so much better than I ever thought work could be."

Baker & Botts, L.L.P.

2001 Ross Avenue • Dallas, TX 75201
Phone: 214-953-6500 • Fax: 214-953-6503 • Web site: bakerbotts.com

OFFICES

Dallas (Houston-based firm), Texas

"With a firm as old as this one, there's the perception that it must be a stodgy, dusty old museum full of ancient partners. That couldn't be further from the truth—it's young, energetic and entrepreneurial."

HIGHLIGHTS

- 29TH largest firm in the country.
- Strong intellectual property practice, with the largest intellectual property section of any general practice firm in the world.
- Cutting-edge computerized offices, with all amenities—including time-keeping, e-mail, Internet—at every desk.
- Strong dedication to pro bono work; pro bono hours are considered billables, and the firm recently received a "Superior Service Award" from the Dallas Bar Association in recognition of the pro bono work done this past year.

NUTS AND BOLTS

Managing partner:
    Jack L. Kinzie, Partner-In-Charge (Dallas office)

Hiring partner:
    Timothy S. Durst, phone: 214-953-6542, e-mail: tim_durst@bakerbotts.com

Recruiting coordinator:
    Stacy Moore, phone: 214-953-6536, e-mail: stacy_moore@bakerbotts.com

Number of attorneys in firm:

495 (186 partners)

WHOLE FIRM:

Women partners (21), women associates (124), minority partners (4), minority associates (26), disabled partners (0), disabled associates (0)

DALLAS OFFICE:

Total attorneys (118), partners (32), associates (63), of counsel (2), special counsel (3), women partners (7), women associates (25), minority partners (0), minority associates (8), disabled partners (0), disabled associates (0)

OTHER OFFICES:

(* represents an office profiled elsewhere in this book)
Houston, Texas (main office) (215); Austin, Texas (also recommended) (38); Washington, D.C. (58); New York, NY (63); Moscow (2); London (1)

Years to make partner:

8 years

WHAT DO THEY DO?

Primary specialties (more than 5% of practice) in Dallas:

Trial (47), Intellectual Property (29), Corporate (17), Real Estate (6), Bankruptcy (4), ERISA (4), Tax (3), Government Contracts (1), General Assignment (1).

There is a general assignment program that gives new associates one year in which to claim a department, and once in a department, associates rarely switch specialties.

WHO DO THEY REPRESENT?

The firm does substantial work for a growing number and wide range of Dallas-based clients, including Electronic Data Systems Corporation, Centex Corporation, NationsBank, Texas Instruments, Dr. Pepper/Seven-Up, GTE, Marcus Communications, and Mesa Inc. The firm also represents numerous Fortune 500 corporations, including Arco, Novartis, Upjohn, Merck, and many national investment banking firms.

WHERE NEW ASSOCIATES COME FROM . . .

Baker & Botts interviews on campus at the following 14 law schools: Chicago, Columbia, Cornell, Duke, Georgetown, Minnesota, Harvard,

Michigan, Pennsylvania, Southern Methodist University, Stanford, Texas, Virginia, and Yale. The firm also hires from law schools where it doesn't do on-campus interviewing, and encourages students to write. The firm occasionally hires contract attorneys, some of whom have been hired as permanent associates.

HOURS AND BUCKS . . .

Associates work an average of 2,100 hours a year, with average billable hours of 1,902. There is no minimum billable hour requirement.

Part-time work is available to both ongoing and entry-level associates on a case-by-case basis.

Typical first year associate salary, including typical bonus: $$$$ (over $65,000)

SUMMER PROGRAM . . .

In 1997, there were 27 summer associates; 24 of 26 2Ls received permanent offers, the one 1L was given an offer to return. In 1998, all summer associates were given offers.

Weekly pay: $1500

1Ls are typically not hired for the summer program, but exceptions are occasionally made; the 1L from last summer's program was from SMU. There is no specific deadline for the firm's summer program; however, most hiring decisions for the summer program are made by December 1 (the firm emphasizes that exceptions are occasionally made to this deadline).

PRO BONO . . .

The firm strongly advocates pro bono work; not only is credit given for pro bono hours, but the firm recently received a "Superior Service Award" from the Dallas Bar Association in recognition of the pro bono work done this past year.

Participation in the pro bono program is voluntary; there are no minimum/maximum expectations in relation to hours spent on pro bono work. Some of the pro bono projects the Dallas office has been involved in include: The AIDS Legal Clinic, Attorneys Serving The Community, Dallas Tenants Association, Dispute Mediation Center, Lawyers Against Domestic Violence (handling cases and manning a hotline), East and South Dallas Legal Clinics, Partners in Education (the firm has 'adopted' a local elementary school), Dallas CASA (benefiting abused and neglected children), RISD Invention Center (doing patent work for young inventors).

HISTORY AT A GLANCE . . .

The firm was founded in 1840. Over the many years it has existed, the nature of its business has evolved to keep up with the times. At the turn of the century, much of its business came from the railroads. In the 1940s and 1950s, it was the big oil companies. Today, the firm's growth is largely in technology.

The Dallas office opened in 1985 with 10 lawyers, and has since then grown to 107 lawyers.

WHAT IT'S LIKE TO WORK THERE . . .

As one associate pointed out, "You can tell this is a good place to work by the fact that virtually nobody leaves. I'm fairly typical, and I get two or three calls a week from head hunters, so it's not that the opportunities to leave aren't there. It's just that nobody takes advantage of them."

"Great training and early responsibility"

Baker & Botts' training gets raves, but it's not the traditional kind of training. As with most large firms, there's the usual slate of seminars, CLE's and retreats; one associate said that "Each section has a retreat every year. It's technically work-oriented, but it turns out to be golf, cigars, and sprinkled in here and there there's a little CLE."

Instead, the training that impresses associates comes through the firm's unique and innovative mentoring system. As an associate recounted, "There was a guy who just took an offer from Baker over another firm that was offering him an extra $15,000, to start. He said it was the training here that made the difference." The way the training works is that the day you walk in, you get assigned to a mentor. One associate explained that "The mentor keeps up with what's going on with you on a day-to-day basis. Do you have enough work? Or too much? Are you getting the right mix of projects? The firm feels like the most important thing in your early years is to get all the skills you need, and the only way you can do that is to get a variety of tasks. Your mentor makes sure that you're getting that kind of variety." Mentors are also useful in taking care of otherwise sticky political situations at the office. "Your mentor runs interference for you if necessary. Like a partner looks like they're giving you too much work. The mentor will go to the partner, and say, 'Look, we've got to make sure he's not overloaded.' It's a great way to handle times that might otherwise be uncomfortable." The mentoring program results in "Everybody getting to do sexy stuff. There's a real diversity of work," according to one associate. "Nobody is pigeonholed. You don't have somebody just doing a certain narrow type of litigation, for instance. In litigation, you have litigation—that's it. In corporate, you've got deal makers, that's it. You'll work with one partner on something, and then with another on something else entirely."

Fast-track mentoring allows new associates to take on responsibility right away. As one associate described it, "We get outstanding client contact. It's actually unbelievable. I was going out from my first day here with the partners, and within a month I was going out to clients on my own." Another said that, "Partners will tell you, 'Get in your car and go to the client and get to know them.'" This arrangement winds up benefiting the firm as well as new associates. As one associate explained, "One of the reasons we get client contact so early is that the nature of our clients is changing. The fact is, some of the older partners don't know how to talk shop with our young clients. You'll have people saying, 'What if they want to talk about the Internet?' New associates aren't the slightest bit intimidated by new technology. And that's great, because it means more client contact."

Another associate applauded the firm's diverse clients. "It's not just your big institutional clients, the kind you'd expect with a very old, very respected law firm. Because our IP practice is growing so fast, you get these guys coming in, they've got a lab in their garage, that's where they spend all their time, cooking up stuff. And they come in here, they've got big shoes and bad coats, and they're holding a shoe box real close to them, saying, 'I've got something and I've got to talk to a lawyer.' It makes the office really interesting."

The hours, as you might expect from a large firm, can be long. While some associates are early risers and get in around 7 a.m., most show at the office between 8:30 and 9 a.m. If you're an early type, you're typically out by 6 p.m., but the later arrivers naturally stay somewhat later. One associate said that people are in "sometimes" on evenings and weekends, "but not if you don't have litigation." Another associate pointed out that "Outside of litigation, you have control over your docket. Patent prosecution, things like that just don't spill over into weekends. But litigation is different; people freak because of court deadlines, or the big bucks involved." Another pointed out that "On weekends there won't be many people in the office, and it's predictable who *will* be there—it's whoever has litigation pending." Another pointed out that "Even in litigation you've got two attitudes. If you have the attitude that you're in the office on a Saturday morning, and it's 'Poor me,' you won't last. Or you can look at it that you like everybody there, you're in casual clothes, you're in there to help your colleagues, and on top of that you *know* your clients. They're your own client, not somebody that only some partner way above you knows. You *know* them, and what you need to do for them. There's a tremendous amount of job satisfaction from that." Another associate chimed in that "You get a lot out of the work, otherwise you wouldn't be there on a weekend working."

Another associate pointed out that because the firm is highly-computerized, it's not necessary to stay at the office to get work done. "I have small children, and it's important for me to be at home for dinner, and to tuck them in to bed. If I have any more work to do left over from the day, as soon as they're asleep I can do my work via e-mail. A lot of associates do that, more and more all the time in fact."

"You're an important part of the firm from the time you get here."

Although the firm is run by an executive committee at the top of big-time partners, one associate pointed out that "The firm isn't really that much into committees. There aren't a lot of them. If you express an interest in anything, like information systems, or pro bono, or recruiting, there's a partner in charge of it, you go to them, state your interest, and boom—you're involved." An associate said that "I wanted to get involved in recruiting, and next thing I know, I'm reviewing resumes, talking to people, making decisions."

One associate pointed out that "The associates really get involved in the summer associate committee, but that committee actually handles much more than summer associate issues—it also recruits permanent associates." Even associates not on the summer associate committee have a heavy role in recruiting. "Even if you're new, you'll be asked, 'What did you think of this guy? Or this woman? When people interview here, everyone they interview with, from partners to brand-new associates, fills out a form, with possibilities like 'definitely hire,' 'probably hire,' all the way down to 'do not hire.' If anybody, even if it's a new associate, fills in 'do not hire,' that interviewee probably won't get an offer. It really makes you feel like your opinion is important." Another associate pointed out that "If you want to maintain morale, a person who doesn't fit in can cause so much damage. There's no room in an office like this for someone who isn't going to feel comfortable in a collegial atmosphere. People who are into 'me me me' won't fit in. Iconoclasts, contrarians, this isn't their place. But if you're the person who is willing to jump in and help out your colleagues, knowing they'd do the same for you, you'll love it here."

"The firm holds out open arms and takes different flavors"

It's obvious that the people at Baker & Botts' Dallas office enjoy working together. One associate said that, "I've got friends in all different sections. We do deals together, form friendships, and those friendships stay when the project is over." Another pointed out that "This is not the place where you say 'hi' when you come in and you don't talk to anybody else until you leave at the end of the day."

Others commented out that people socialize outside of work, not just with each other but with families. And there is a definite tendency to hire people with lives outside of their work. One associate advised that "The firm likes 'citizens.' You can't be out for yourself. If you're interviewing and you talk about Dallas, getting involved in the community, teaching classes downtown maybe, that's a huge plus. You can't just do your work and go home." Nonetheless, the firm "doesn't consider it a negative if you don't 'hang out.' The firm is old-fashioned in the sense that it still has the traditional values of advocacy, and so it values effectiveness more than anything, even more than business development." This is reflected in the firm's compensation plan, which doesn't financially reward business development, even for partners. As one associate said, "This is not a place where you eat what you kill." Another summed it up by saying, "What the firm wants are people who aren't just their work. It embraces multi-dimensional lives."

The firm's attitude toward the lives of its attorneys is reflected in many comments by associates. As one said, "When it comes down to brass tacks, your family comes first, and the firm supports that." Another added that "When anybody here has a personal problem, before they know it there'll be five people at their office door, offering to help." One associate recounted a situation recently when his wife was nine months pregnant. He had a bunch of big deals going on, and the combination of the two made him nervous about juggling his responsibilities. The partner in charge of his section called him and said, "Listen, take the time you need. You work in a large firm for a reason: to have people to back you up. You're not a firm of one. There are people to cover for you, and I'll find them for you."

The firm's caring nature extends to the community. It has a pro bono partner, and staffs a legal services clinic, mans the phones, and helps with divorces, as one associate pointed out, "The typical stuff." But the firm gets involved in some community activities that are out of the ordinary. For instance, it supports the Julius Dorsey School, a local elementary school. The firm takes responsibility for all kinds of programs, all the way down to simple things like having attorneys go to the school and read stories to the children. The children come out to the firm once a year and put on a Christmas show. As one associate said, "It's too easy to sit in big old expensive offices doing work for big old rich clients. Seeing this show, these kids . . . it choked me up."

The IP section also supports a fascinating project called the "Invention Convention," which has IP lawyers going and doing 'invention talks' at schools, from elementary to high school. The attorneys "encourage kids to invent their own things." Those inventions are entered into contests between schools, and the firm sends attorneys to judge inventions. The winner gets a "Most Patentable Invention" award, and the kid gets invited to the firm's offices where the firm's attorneys write a patent application for the invention, something that would normally cost upwards of eight thousand dollars. As one associate pointed out, "This program is so fantastic. Kids have actually gotten patents from it. In the last couple of years, one kid invented a 'net of lights,' you've probably seen it. Instead of strings of Christmas lights, it's a net of lights that you just drape over a tree. Another winner was a kid who invented what was essentially a paint can with ice in it and a container inside of that. What you would do is fill the bucket with ice, put ice cream mix in the inside container, and strap it to the back of your bike. This kid invented a way that when you pedal, the motion of the back wheel churns the mix and you make ice cream!"

On top of community activities, attorneys regularly socialize outside the office. One said that, "We have spontaneous golf outings. If you've just closed a big deal or finished a big project, it's nothing to blow out of the office in the afternoon and go to the golf course." Another said that, "We love Mexican food here. People at the office go and do Mexican at least once a week." One favorite haunt is Metita's, which is a "great salsa experience."

All in all, one associate summed up Baker & Botts by saying, "There are students who say, 'There's no place I can go for the sophistication I want, and still have a life outside of the office.' If you want sophisticated work at a firm that values your life outside as well, I'd say, 'Baker & Botts is waiting for you!'"

★   ★   ★   ★   ★

Baker & Daniels

300 North Meridian Street, Suite 2700 • Indianapolis, IN 46204
Phone: 317-237-0300 • Fax: 317-237-1000 • E-mail: bakerd.com
Web site: bakerdaniels.com

OFFICES

Indianapolis (main office), Fort Wayne, South Bend, Elkhart, Indiana;
Washington, D.C.

*"I interviewed with firms who told me straight out, 'Don't come
here, don't be a lawyer.' That's sad, and it's so different from Baker
& Daniels. Everybody here seems genuinely happy to be a lawyer."*

HIGHLIGHTS

- 143RD largest law firm in the country.
- Voted one of the best overall summer associate programs in the country in last year's *American Lawyer* survey.
- Recently certified by the Chinese government as one of only 20 U.S. law firms licensed to open offices in China.

NUTS AND BOLTS

Managing partner:

David K. Herzog (Indianapolis office)
Brian K. Burke (Firm)

Hiring partner:

Indianapolis office:
Alan L. McLaughlin, phone: 317-237-1279, e-mail:almclaug@bakerd.com
Firm:
John W. Purcell, phone: 317-237-1324, e-mail: jwpurcel@bakerd.com

Recruiting coordinator:

Jacqueline Kost, phone: 317-237-1105, e-mail: jkkost@bakerd.com

Number of attorneys in firm:

216 (123 partners)

WHOLE FIRM:

Women attorneys (50), minority attorneys (8)

INDIANAPOLIS OFFICE:

Total attorneys (142), total partners (88), total associates (65), women attorneys (41), minority attorneys (5)

OTHER OFFICES:

(* represents an office profiled elsewhere in this book)
Fort Wayne, IN (37); South Bend, IN (19); Elkhart IN (4); Washington, D.C. (3)

Years to make partner:

8 ¹/₂

WHAT DO THEY DO?

Primary specialties (more than 5% of practice):

Litigation (52 attorneys in firm, 30 in Indianapolis); Business Planning/Corporate Finance (42 attorneys in firm, 24 in Indianapolis); Employment Relations/Employee Benefits (42 attorneys in firm, 32 in Indianapolis); Intellectual Property (17 attorneys in firm, 5 in Indianapolis); Commercial, Financial & Bankruptcy Services (16 attorneys in firm, 12 in Indianapolis); Real Estate Law (16 attorneys in firm, 11 in Indianapolis); Individual/Family Services, Estate & Probate (16 attorneys in firm, 9 in Indianapolis); Insurance (13 attorneys in firm, 12 in Indianapolis); Environmental Law (10 attorneys, all in Indianapolis); and Municipal Law/Tax-Exempt Finance (14 attorneys in firm, 9 in Indianapolis).

The firm is departmentalized. It encourages new associates to identify the specialty they'd prefer, and the firm tries to match those preferences. Associates can and do switch specialties.

Each associate has a partner supervisor, who works closely with the associate to plan and coordinate the associate's professional development. The process for assigning work to associates varies from team to team, but typically the supervisor plays a role in monitoring the quantity and quality of the workload.

WHO DO THEY REPRESENT?

A broad range of clients including Eli Lilly and Company, Indianapolis Water Company, Bank One, Anthem, United Airlines, and Conseco.

WHERE NEW ASSOCIATES COME FROM . . .

The firm routinely interviews on campus at the following law schools: Duke, Illinois, Indiana/Bloomington, Indiana/Indianapolis, Michigan, Notre Dame, and Vanderbilt.

The firm routinely hires from schools where it doesn't conduct on-campus interviews.

HOURS AND BUCKS . . .

Typical first year associate salary, including typical bonus: $$$ ($50-65,000).

Associates work an average of 2,025 hours per year, including billable and non-billable time. Of those, the minimum billable hours requirement is 1,850.

Part-time work is available to ongoing associates; the firm currently has 13 attorneys working reduced-hours schedules.

The firm does not routinely hire contract associates.

SUMMER PROGRAM . . .

Summer associate program last year: 10 summer associates, of whom 9 received offers (and all 9 accepted).

Weekly pay: $1,000 last year

1Ls are routinely hired for the summer program. Last year's 1Ls came from Michigan, Chicago, and NYU; this year's 1Ls are from Harvard, Northwestern, Vanderbilt and Yale.

The 2L deadline for applying for the summer program is mid-September; the 1L deadline is late December.

PRO BONO . . .

The firm strongly encourages its lawyers to participate in pro bono work; the decision to do so is left up to personal choice, with most lawyers taking part. There is no formal expectation regarding the amount of time associates dedicate to pro bono work, and pro bono hours are not counted as billables. Nonetheless, the firm's significant involvement in pro bono was recognized by the Indiana Bar Foundation a couple of years ago with its *Pro Bono Publico* Award.

B&D's lawyers are involved in virtually all of the civic and not-for-profit public betterment organizations in Central Indiana. The firm helped launch Project PEACE, a statewide program that teaches peaceful dispute resolution techniques to elementary school students. Several of its attorneys continue to volunteer their time for the program. Through the Lawyers' Network for Children, B&D attorneys volunteer their time to represent children in abuse and neglect proceedings. Through COLAP

(Community Organization Legal Assistance Project), the firm helps neighborhoods with legal challenges involving abandoned houses, unsafe property and drug problems.

HISTORY AT A GLANCE . . .

A credible history of Indiana could be written by tracing the achievements of Baker & Daniels' lawyers and clients. The clients have included several of the state's oldest and best-known enterprises, as well as cities and towns throughout the state. The lawyers have included former members of the U.S. House of Representatives and Senate, as well as the Indiana legislature. One of the firm's founders was elected vice president of the United States, and three Baker & Daniels lawyers have served as governors of Indiana, including Evan Bayh, who joined the firm in 1997.

WHAT IT'S LIKE TO WORK THERE . . .

When it comes to caring about people, Baker & Daniels is one place where they walk the walk, as this story illustrates: a few years ago a new associate was having trouble with his work. He couldn't concentrate, and wasn't efficient. It got to the point where he sought medical help. After explaining to the doctor that he hadn't had any time off since starting law school four years previously, the doctor said that all he needed was some rest and relaxation. As a new associate, he was justifiably reluctant to ask for time off. However, when he told his supervisor about what the doctor had said, the firm actually encouraged him to take the time necessary to feel better.

This concern for lawyers as individuals encompasses every attorney at Baker & Daniels. As one associate describes it, "The firm recognizes that each person is an asset . . . one way it shows this is to be supportive when attorneys are struggling with problems outside the office."

Associates find that the firm's caring nature is reflected in its attitude about other aspects of their personal lives. One associate recounted that "Last year, I spent a substantial amount of time establishing a new church. I wasn't even close to my billable goal. My supervising attorney knew it, everybody at the firm knew it, but I got nothing but support from the firm. It's the kind of thing that makes you loyal to your firm. You can't put a dollar value on support like that."

Another associate dedicates substantial time to pro bono work, as a member of the board of directors of the Neighborhood Development Corporation, through which he has "initiated some creative inner-city projects." He approached the firm for support "and got it, both in the form of donations of money and time." With pro bono in general, associates feel that "There's a general recognition that it's important," but "There's more pressure to be productive with your time, either meeting prospective clients or billing. It's just a function of the economics of the legal profession." Even so, attorneys have taken on pro bono work to the extent that the firm was recently given the *Pro Bono Publico* Award by the Indiana Bar Foundation.

A great reputation in the legal community

A point of justifiable pride for lawyers at Baker & Daniels is the word "on the street" that the firm is a great place to work. One young associate says that, "When I interviewed with the firm, I was talking to other lawyers as well. I got the impression that it was highly respected for the way the firm treats its people. And it's not as though lawyers are shy when they don't like their jobs. I interviewed with firms who told me straight out, 'Don't come here, don't be a lawyer.' That's sad, and it's so different from Baker & Daniels. Everybody here seems genuinely happy to be a lawyer."

"You get as much responsibility as an associate as you seek out and can handle."

New associates get to choose their specialty, and by and large they get their first choice. As one associate points out, "Of the two or three people I know who didn't start out in what they wanted, they moved into it very quickly." Perhaps more importantly, the firm is conscious of the importance of a personality match. Each associate is assigned to a supervisor, and if the "personalities aren't right," the firm is flexible about moving associates to a different supervisor. Depending on the specialty, "Your work may come through your supervising attorney or not." For instance, associates in employment or corporate find that it's 'open season'—any attorney in the department can give them work.

When it comes to responsibility, a junior associate said, "You get lots of client contact early on here, but you aren't left out on a limb. I get to be the point person on lots of projects, but I get a lot of guidance." Another associate commented that "A lot of my friends have to struggle with their peers to get credit for work, or to get work at all. We just don't have any of that here." Another added that "When you talk about interesting projects, take your pick! There's so much that's interesting going on here all the time." Of course, there's going to be time dedicated to things that aren't exciting. "It's driven by practice areas. For instance, if you start out in tax-exempt organizations, you've got to spend some time with the tax code because you simply have to know it to serve your clients. You're going to get the work you want, but you have to do the prep work, as well." In some teams, like the insurance team, "New associates will be out meeting clients, at high-level meetings, doing that kind of thing." But there is enough going on to keep the associates pumped on what the firm is up to.

For instance, the firm just got a license to open an office in China. "That whole initiative was started and to a large extent rests on the shoulders of an associate." Along the way to opening that office, "Some associates were involved in an arbitration case in Europe that led to a multi-million dollar award for our client." Another associate added that "We represent large hospitals, and a lot of that work is handled primarily by associates." And this year, one senior associate "handled a huge insolvency in Kentucky, one of the five biggest insolvencies ever, anywhere. He started handling it himself as a fourth-year associate. It was hectic and scary, but he did it, and got help from the partners whenever he needed it." One associate summed up by saying that, "The responsibility you get here depends entirely on how much you want, how much you take on." That isn't to say that there's pressure to take on huge projects, but if you *do*, you're rewarded. One associate explained that "There is lock-step compensation here. You know that there are bonuses for associates who go way above and beyond, for instance by handling some huge cases or working huge hours, but those bonuses aren't announced. You just know it's there."

While "huge hours" are rewarded, they aren't demanded. Most people come in by 8:30 a.m. and leave around 5:30 p.m., but "You have to sometimes work more in order to make billables," and it's not uncommon for associates to work long enough to bill 8 to 10 hours a day. "You can work late here if you want, or you can work from home if you want to get something done at night—the firm is hooked up by e-mail to everybody's house, so it's possible to work without physically being here if you don't want to." Most people don't show on weekends and "There's no face time." People who do come in on weekends "Tend to come in by 9 a.m. on Saturday or even earlier, so they can get done and get out by noon." One associate pointed out that "If you show up on a weekend you'll often see some of the older partners here, and that's just because they've grown up always working weekends." When you see associates in on weekends it's inevitably because "They've got a research project or brief due or generally want to get unburied."

The firm coaches associates into the business of law by running a "stepped series" where associates are divided into three groups: first and second year associates in one group, three to five year associates in another, and six to eight year associates in the third. They learn rainmaking skills by "being taken through a series of different scenarios to help them start thinking about business development, handling referrals, billing problems." These programs take place on a monthly basis and "Accentuate the firm's interest in opening your eyes to the economics of law."

The firm also trains associates with different kinds of programs. Starting with the summer program and continuing for permanent associates, the firm "dedicates time for internal half-day or full-day sessions on different topics, like negotiating, or ethics. For instance, for the negotiating sessions, all associates from all of the offices come in, break into teams, and are given different fact patterns. Each side gets a different set of facts, and you negotiate a settlement." The firm also has "monthly attorney lunches where you'll hear one of the firm's attorneys talk about what's going on in his or her practice area, or about business opportunities." It "keeps you plugged into what's going on outside of your own practice area."

"There's something special about the kind of people who come here."

The work, the training, the reputation of the firm—nothing matters if you don't like the people you work with. That doesn't happen at Baker & Daniels, where "Many people's social life consists entirely of people from work." One associate recounted that "I was unusual in that I spent a year working here before I even started law school. I was what you'd call a 'nobody.' But people here didn't make me feel that way. I know from personal experience that they are down-to-earth and friendly. There's no hierarchy of secretaries, paralegals, associates, and on up." Another pointed out that "Nobody here is a stuffed shirt; nobody puts on airs," and another added that "People here are just *nicer*. It's a Midwestern thing." Another chimed in that "Nobody here hangs their Ivy League law degrees on their wall, even though they have them. You wouldn't think of hanging out your credentials. The kind of people that sort of showing off matters to just aren't here."

One associate shared that "Every summer, some summer associates will say, 'I've interviewed at lots of firms—there's something different, something special about the kind of person who comes here.' It's hard to put into words. You can't institutionalize certain values or world views, but the core values of the firm, we all believe in them. If all you want is money, you're going to go to Chicago or New York. That isn't to say we don't make a good living; we make a *very* good living. But we foster an environment that recognizes the difficult balances people have to make—a good lawyer and a good husband or wife or mother or father."

To sum it up, one associate describes Baker & Daniels as "a very supportive environment. Most of my friends are at big firms. They get home at 10 at night, and they are just not happy. It's such a contrast here. The people are friendly, supportive, and considerate. We get to do very high-quality work in a congenial environment."

Baker & Hostetler LLP

Capitol Square, Suite 2100 • 65 East State Street • Columbus, OH 43215-4260
Phone: 614-228-1541 • Fax: 614-462-2616

OFFICES

Columbus, Cleveland, Cincinnati, Ohio; Beverly Hills, Long Beach, Los
Angeles, California; Denver, Colorado; Washington D.C.; Orlando,
Florida; Houston, Texas

*"This is a very entrepreneurial office . . . they keep you informed on
where the firm is going, and they are dedicated to establishing you
as an important member not only of the office culture but the community, as well."*

HIGHLIGHTS

• Columbus office of Cleveland-based firm, 39TH largest in the country.

NUTS AND BOLTS

Managing partner:

George W. Hairston

Hiring partner:

Ronald G. Linville, phone: 614-462-2647,
e-mail: linville@baker-hostetler.com

Recruiting coordinator:

Jeanie M. Fulton, phone: 614-462-4703,
e-mail: jfulton@baker-hostetler.com

Number of attorneys in firm:

493 (281 partners)

WHOLE FIRM:

Total partners (281), total associates (212), total women partners (38), total minority partners (3)

COLUMBUS OFFICE:

Total attorneys (71), partners (48), associates (23), women attorneys (10), minority attorneys (3)

OTHER OFFICES:

(* represents an office profiled elsewhere in this book)
Cincinnati, OH (6); Cleveland, OH (159); Denver, CO (37); Houston, TX (43); Beverly Hills, CA (13); Long Beach, CA (7); Los Angeles, CA (41); Orlando, FL (44); Washington, D.C. (69)

Years to make partner:

7 1/2 to 9 years

WHAT DO THEY DO?

Primary specialties (more than 5% of practice):

Business; Employment Law & Employee Benefits; Litigation; Tax & Personal Planning. Some attorneys are not assigned to a particular practice group.

WHO DO THEY REPRESENT?

The firm as a whole represents a vast array of clients, including many in the hospitality industry, newspapers, major league baseball clubs and other professional sports teams, heavy manufacturing industries, and many others. Specific clients include Boeing, Emery Worldwide, Miller Brewing, Ford Motor Company, Shell Chemical Company, American Dental Partners, Inc., and the Miller Brewing Company.

The Columbus office represents clients including financial institutions, insurance companies, health care providers, motor carriers, retailers, individual entrepreneurs, trade associations and developers. Columbus clients include the Central Benefits Mutual Insurance Company, The Galbreath Company, Grant Medical Center, Red Roof Inns, Big Bear Stores Company, Cardinal Health, Inc., and the Central Ohio Transit Authority.

WHERE NEW ASSOCIATES COME FROM . . .

The firm's Columbus office interviews on campus at the following law schools: Capital University, Case Western Reserve, Columbia, Howard, Indiana-Bloomington, University of Michigan, University of North

Carolina, Notre Dame, Ohio State, and Vanderbilt. The firm also coordinates recruiting efforts among the different offices, to maximize its on-campus interviewing potential. The firm frequently hires from law schools where it doesn't conduct on-campus interviews.

HOURS AND BUCKS . . .

Average billable hours for first year associates: 1,900

There is no minimum billable requirement.

Part-time work is available to ongoing associates on a case-by-case basis; the need for part-time has not occurred yet at the entry level, and the firm points out that part-time work usually occurs more often among senior level associates and/or partners. The firm does not routinely hire contract associates.

Typical first year salary, including typical bonus: $$$$ (over $65,000)

SUMMER PROGRAM . . .

In 1998, there were 10 summer associates, all of whom were eligible to receive offers.

Weekly pay: $1,300

1Ls are routinely hired for the summer associate program. Last year there were 2 1Ls in the summer associate program, both from Ohio State University. The 1999 class will have 8 2Ls and 3 or 4 1Ls.

PRO BONO . . .

The Columbus office attorneys engage in pro bono work on an individual basis; there are no firm guidelines on hours. Instead, it depends on the individual and the project. Some cases come in that become pro bono cases, like representing prisoners in civil rights matters.

The firm's attorneys routinely take part in a variety of civic projects, including the Columbus Zoo, the Columbus Museum of Art, the Columbus Light Opera, Junior Achievement, YMCA/YWCA, Children's Hospital.

HISTORY AT A GLANCE . . .

Baker & Hostetler was founded in 1916 by Newton D. Baker, Joseph C. Hostetler and Thomas L. Sidlo, all former Cleveland City Council members. Baker was the best known, and exceptionally well-respected, with Justice Oliver Wendell Holmes calling him "the outstanding lawyer of his generation," and Woodrow Wilson saying of him that he had a mind like "chain lightning." Hostetler established the firm's continuing involvement in sports law by acting as counselor to the American League.

Since then, the firm has grown to almost 500 lawyers, with a number of high-profile partners, including counselors to U.S. Presidents, former U.S. congressmen, a former Chairman of the National Labor Relations Board, and previous director of the FTC's Bureau of Competition.

WHAT IT'S LIKE TO WORK THERE . . .

When you hear words like "entrepreneurial" and "laid-back attitude" and "new kid on the block," you probably don't think of one of the biggest law firms in the country. But those are the kinds of things associates talk about at Baker & Hostetler's Columbus office.

Working in one of the offices of a huge firm is the classic "big firm benefits, small firm feel" situation, and Baker's Columbus office epitomizes why associates like it so much. They rave about the fact that as a relatively new player in Columbus, "They tend to be more entrepreneurial." The ramifications of that include a unique training program called the 'practice development program,' where the associates routinely meet in small groups with partners to talk about networking and product development ideas. As one associate explains it, "There's no pressure—it's more of partners sharing what they did, and do, to expand the business. It makes you feel like part of the practice; you hear how they generate business, and you know they are devoted to helping you become part of the community." Another associate added that, "They keep you informed on the direction the firm is going. They are dedicated, as a firm, to helping establish you as an important person in the city." This kind of focus leads to associates being rewarded for bringing in new business, and also means that, "The firm highly encourages client-development-based activities." It also means that community involvement that is "high profile" tends to focus on business development and client relationships. Pro bono activities, by contrast, tend to be the result of individual initiative.

"Significant early responsibility."

Junior associates find that the office size leads to "lean staffing. You get more responsibility early on—and not just on substantive work, but on things like client entertainment, and managing cases and clients." One third-year litigation associate talked of trying seven lawsuits since joining the firm. Another associate pointed out that "With the combination of lean staffing and a diverse client mix—big companies and individuals and small companies—associates get significant responsibility early on."

The hours can be long, but not by large firm standards. Most attorneys get to the office between 8 and 8:30 a.m., with some arriving as early as 7, others as late as 9:30. Most leave by 6:30 p.m., and "On average you come in maybe one or two weekends a month, for one day of the weekend." Even when hours are long associates don't "resent it because you understand the importance of a deadline. It is very, very rare for me to feel as though anyone has imposed weekend work on me. Normally weekend time comes up when I want to start next week fresh, or get a start on something early, or because I want a three-day weekend next weekend." Another associate added that, "You're treated as a professional. There's not a lot of face time. They're not very into that."

"Diverse work."

As a new associate in Columbus, you're unassigned at first. As one associate explained "All of the practice group coordinators try to give new associates work with different partners, and expose you to different subgroups." Coordinators tend to "guard and protect your workload." This 'unassigned' period "Typically lasts a year, but it can stretch to two or three. Typically by then people have figured out their niche." The office has several practice groups, with the business group being perceived by associates as having the highest profile, but "We're all pretty busy."

Once in a department, "It's open season—any partner can give you work." However, "Most associates feel comfortable turning down work if they're overloaded." Getting interesting work is the reward for assertiveness. "If you see a new client sheet, a new case come in, you feel very comfortable approaching the billing partner and asking to help out."

The office helps junior associates sharpen their professional skills with not only "the normal seminars and conferences" but also with a "Mock trial program which uses a NITA format. They rent a mock courtroom, rent a retired judge, and we associates try a case. Partners and senior level associates watch, and the summer associates are second chairs for the trials." First and second year associates take part in the program, which takes place once a year.

"A caring, kid-friendly, family-oriented office."

Associates rave about the environment at Baker's Columbus office. One associate pointed out that "Everybody here feels comfortable approaching managing partners, hiring partners, senior partners." The offices are arranged to foster this kind of camaraderie, in that "Everybody is mixed up together. Management doesn't have its own floor. Everybody is together, group chairs, associates, everybody." One associate pointed out that "Of course we like money and prestige, but we don't make money at any cost. We're into quality of life." That caring nature comes across when anyone in the office suffers a personal setback. One associate who'd recently borne a personal tragedy said that "The firm was very concerned about me, and told me over and over, 'Take whatever time you need.' They were incredibly understanding. When I came back, they would ask, 'Are you sure you don't need more time?' I was very pleasantly surprised by their attitude. They were great about it."

When it comes to socializing, lawyers, secretaries and paralegals "routinely" get together outside of the offices. On top of the "regular slate of summer stuff" the firm has a few more unusual social activities. One is the office's involvement in "Operation Feed," a local charity. For two weeks a year, there are "auctions, pie in the eye of a partner's face, a chili cook-off, a talent show. You can pay for 'celebrity waiters,' where you can have partners serve you." Many of these activities take place during the day for that one week, "So not much work gets done that last week." Associates also appreciate the fact that "Partners take associates along to do lots of client entertainment. The partners don't keep client entertainment activities for themselves."

Associates also note that "The environment at the firm is very conducive to families," which is a benefit, especially since "Columbus itself is very family-oriented." Another associate adds that, "Lots of people here have kids. Many partners and senior associates coach soccer and baseball." One of the female partners takes off every Friday to be with her family, proving that "You don't physically have to be in the office. They treat you as a professional—you don't have to be sitting there for them to respect you."

The combination of interesting work, a family-friendly environment and a "laid-back attitude" led one associate to sum up, "When people leave here, it's because they're going into business or government or something like that. Nobody goes to another law firm from here, because this place has everything you'd want from a firm."

Barnes & Thornburg

11 South Meridian Street • Indianapolis, IN 46204
Phone: 317-236-1313 • Fax: 317-231-7433 • Web site: btlaw.com

OFFICES

Indianapolis (main office), Fort Wayne, South Bend, Elkhart, Indiana; Chicago, Illinois; Washington, D.C.

"We have the best of both worlds. When we work on cases with associates at New York firms, they are amazed at the kind of exposure we get early on . . . At the same time, the firm doesn't take itself too seriously. A velvet Elvis portrait mysteriously turned up in a prominent display area of a newly-redecorated part of the office— and it stayed there for the rest of the week."

HIGHLIGHTS

- 126TH largest firm in the country.
- In the American Lawyer Midlevel Associates Survey, ranked 13TH nationally. Outstanding marks in interest level of work, training and guidance, and tied for 1ST in the country on likelihood of staying at the firm another two years.
- The firm has 37 lawyers who are listed in *The Best Lawyers in America.*

NUTS AND BOLTS

Managing partner:

Alan A. Levin

Hiring partners:

Peter J. Rusthoven, phone: 317-231-7299, e-mail: prusthov@btlaw.com
Mark D. Boveri, phone: 219-237-1119, e-mail: mboveri@btlaw.com

Recruiting coordinator:

LaNell D. Black, phone: 317-231-7435, e-mail: lblack@btlaw.com

Number of attorneys in firm:

272 (113 partners)

TOTAL FIRM:

Partners (113), associates (116), women partners (13), women associates (42), minority partners (1), minority associates (9), disabled partners (0), disabled associates (0), minority of counsel (2)

THIS OFFICE:

Total attorneys (152), partners (64), associates (69), women partners (9), women associates (24), minority partners (1), minority associates (5), disabled partners (0), disabled associates (0), minority of counsel (2)

OTHER OFFICES:

(* represents an office profiled elsewhere in this book)
Fort Wayne, IN (35); South Bend, IN (48); Elkhart, IN (12); Chicago, IL (18); Washington, D.C. (8)

Years to make partner:

8 $^1/_2$

WHAT DO THEY DO?

Primary specialties (more than 5% of practice):

Business, Tax & Real Estate (72); Creditors' Rights (17); Environmental Law (12); Government Services & Finance (13); Intellectual Property & Trade Regulation (40); Labor & Employment Law (42); Litigation (68); Public Utilities & Transportation (9).

The firm is departmentalized. Attorneys may choose up to three departments. Young associates can, and do, switch specialties.

WHO DO THEY REPRESENT?

The firm represents a variety of clients domestically and internationally, including Arvin Industries, Hillenbrand Industries, Eli Lilly & Company, Bristol-Myers/Mead Johnson, Ameritech, Purdue Research Foundation, and numerous Japanese corporations. (For a more complete client rundown, visit the firm's home page at btlaw.com.)

The firm has handled a number of high-profile Midwestern cases in the last few years. It represented Toyota Motor Corporation in opening its new truck manufacturing facility in southern Indiana—a plant that involves an investment of $1.2 billion and will employ 2,300 workers. It was involved in the Joint Medical Products versus DePuy case, a patent infringement case for hip prostheses that resulted in over $600 million plus attorneys' fees. It has helped more Indiana companies go public than any other law firm in this decade. And it has represented major news media organizations—including The Associated Press, The Hearst Corporation, Fox Broadcasting, and many others, in defamation and other First Amendment cases.

Internationally, the firm has represented the Republic of Bosnia and Herzegovina in arbitration mandated by the Dayton Peace Accords, to determine control of Brcko. And it represents the Mercantile Companies in financing a new hotel in Bosnia and other projects both domestically and in the Balkans.

WHERE NEW ASSOCIATES COME FROM . . .

B & T routinely interviews on campus at the following law schools: Chicago, Duke, Georgetown, Harvard, Howard, IU-Bloomington, IU-Indianapolis, Michigan, Northwestern, Notre Dame, Ohio State, Valparaiso, and Vanderbilt. The firm also hires students and graduates from schools where it doesn't conduct on-campus interviews.

HOURS AND BUCKS . . .

Associates spend an average of 2,200 hours at the office, with average billable hours between 1,800 and 1,900. The minimum billable hours requirement is 1,800.

Part-time work is available to ongoing associates, on a case-by-case basis. B & T routinely hires contract associates, some of whom have become partnership-track associates.

Typical first year associate salary, including typical bonus: $$$$ (Over $65,000)

SUMMER PROGRAM . . .

Last year, there were 22 summer associates, 20 of whom received offers.

Weekly pay $1,100 for 2Ls, $1,000 for 1Ls, $1,150 for 3Ls.

1Ls are hired for the summer program; last year, 1Ls came from Harvard, Notre Dame, and IU-Bloomington.

The deadline for applying for the summer clerkship program is November 1 for 2Ls, and January 15 for 1Ls.

PRO BONO . . .

B & T lawyers represent a variety of clients which the attorneys select themselves. Pro bono hours are counted as billables for both evaluation and compensation purposes. There is no set number of minimum/maximum pro bono hours required/expected of associates.

Some of the pro bono projects associates have been involved in include serving as deputy prosecuting attorneys, representing not-for-profit organizations, and staffing "Legal Lines," an Indianapolis Bar Association-sponsored legal advice hot-line.

HISTORY AT A GLANCE . . .

The firm was formed as the result of a merger in 1982 between one of the largest Indianapolis firms (from which the "Barnes" name comes) and a South Bend/Elkhart firm (which supplied the "Thornburg), which was the largest law firm in the state outside of Indianapolis. Both firms had long and proud traditions, spanning many decades, and well-established practices and client bases. After a merger later that year with one of Indiana's oldest patent boutiques, the firm became one of the first full-service firms in the country. The Washington, D.C. office also opened that year.

In 1986 the firm opened its Fort Wayne office, merged with two other firms in 1987, and in 1994, the firm opened its newest office in Chicago.

WHAT IT'S LIKE TO WORK THERE . . .

Whenever you talk with **anybody** at a great employer and ask them what they like about their work, the first reason will typically be: "the people." It's one thing to say that, but it's entirely something else to put meaning to those words. But when you talk with associates at B&T, you hear story after story that paints a vivid picture of just how much these people truly enjoy working together. One associate recounts a time "last spring when the partners went to Florida for their annual partners' retreat. We strung a net down the middle of one of the partners' new, and extremely large, desks, and held a ping-pong tournament." The associate laughed that "The prizes for the winners were selected from that same partner's collection of 'plastic'," the little Plexiglas cubes that celebrate a company's initial public offering. "We took Polaroids of the event and mailed them to the partners' retreat, along with a "Status of the Firm" report which detailed our behavior—and encouraged them to stay away on an extended vacation!" The partners took it in stride, as you'd expect from a place where, when "they redecorated one of the floors the firm is on, there was a prominent display area left vacant. One day, someone placed a velvet Elvis portrait there. And it stayed there for the rest of the week."

As stories like these suggest, "The partners here don't take themselves too seriously. At a firm picnic talent show, the chair of the Professional Responsibility Committee and his wife did a musical rendition of Bobby McFarrin's 'Wizard of Oz.' They alternated parts, with him playing the female parts and his wife the male parts, to raucous applause."

"We routinely get complimented by our New York and Chicago counterparts for the talent at this firm."

One associate raves that "The caliber of people here is incredible." The firm leverages the talent of its junior associates by giving them a lot of responsibility early on. As one labor and employment associate tells it, "I have taken a number of plaintiffs' depositions, deposed experts, participated heavily in out-of-state trials, bargained a union contract, handled critical union representation elections, and assumed primary responsibility for a number of key client relationships. To put it another way, I've had the opportunity at an early stage to routinely do things that many labor and employment *partners* do only on an infrequent basis." Another adds that "As a brand new associate, I had to make numerous trips to the Cayman Islands in connection with a premises liability case we were defending in Indiana"—not the kind of travel you might otherwise expect from an Indiana-based law firm!

Associates get assignments "informally, from many people." One associate explains that "rather than being told what type of projects you're going to handle and what direction your practice will take, you get the chance to make those determinations yourself." Another associate agrees, saying that, "They give you a lot of latitude in devising your own destiny." A junior associate describes his career path so far, saying that, "When I initially expressed an interest only in discrimination litigation, I got that in ample supply. Then I wanted ERISA litigation, and got an ERISA case. I then wanted to shift gears and focus more on client counseling and new client development. My department fully supported me and put me in situations where I could reach those goals. Most recently when I wanted more traditional labor experience, union-related issues, the balance of my practice shifted dramatically within a short period of time, so that traditional labor issues now comprise about half of my practice." As this suggests, B&T associates find that "It pays to take the time to become close to senior and mid-level partners here, and they're very approachable. You're not going to get the projects you want the most if you sit back and distance yourself from the partners. You're definitely rewarded for seeking out the work you want, and asking for it."

As this kind of experience suggests, "Training here is mostly informal. You work on projects with a variety of people, and you learn from all of them." Another associate adds that "I'd describe the training here as 'learning by fire, with feedback whenever you need it.' You get lots of work on your own, and tons of client contact." None of this is to say that junior associates are left to sink or swim. Rather, "You have a supervising attorney there for 'wise tutelage' when you need it." B&T associates prefer it this way, saying that "Sitting in on conference calls and client meetings is more helpful than any seminar." This kind of experience leads to situations where "when we work on cases with associates at New York firms, they are amazed at the kind of exposure we get early on. Working here, I get to learn a great deal about many fascinating client businesses, contribute to how well those businesses operate—and still save time for five weeks of vacation time every year!"

"There's never a need to put in 'face time,' and you can truly work flexible hours."

B&T associates report that while the minimum billable hours requirement is 1,800, "They really go for 1,850, and that's reasonable." There's an "unwritten rule that 1,850 is what you need to get a bonus. And if you're between 1,900 and 2,000 billable hours, you're in good shape. There are no 'New York' hours expected from anybody here." As one associate puts it, "Sometimes you work better under stress, but not *too* much stress!"

As is true in any law firm, "Deadlines on big deals, and trials, mean big hours. But those big hours are pretty rare," although "we do get our share." Associates with young children say that it's possible to "work no long late hours or weekend hours," and even when they do have to work longer hours than they'd like, "You tell yourself that you have the power to relax on a different day. It's 'If I get through this, I can relax when I want to.' And you always know that the long hours are strictly temporary."

While there is no pressure to bring in business as a new associate or to put in long hours, associates sense that "The firm is moving toward rewards for excess billables, bringing in business, those kinds of things. For the last two years, they've adopted a philosophy that 'productivity is rewarded.'" As one associate hastens to point out, the firm "is more impressed with your ability to manage cases cost-effectively, to be a terrific client custodian, than billing long hours."

While the billables requirements are very livable, associates say that "It pays to invest in your career here by performing committee work and writing or lecturing for the profession, whether in the bar association or otherwise." One associate says that, "They encourage you to get involved in the community, to bring in clients. The impetus in your early years is on training, but bringing in clients is a fact of life, and associates are rewarded if they do it." While that is a natural result of community involvement, associates also take part in what B&T calls its 'elevator trade.' As one associate explains it, "You sometimes get clients out of the blue. Apparently, clients used to come up in the elevator, and that's where 'elevator trade' got its name. Now one or two associates staff the 'elevator trade' calls on a rotating basis. You're taught to open a file, and how to interview clients. It's actually very interesting."

When it comes to community involvement, "There's more credence given to legal work that supplements your skills. It's encouraged on two levels. They want you to do things that improve your skills, for instance advocating for a displaced poor tenant. It not only helps that person but gets you court experience, as well." On another level "being out in the community

helps you make contacts that down the road help you develop business."
Traditional pro bono work "Isn't a high priority. If you do it, you'll definitely
get credit for it, and if it helps make you a better lawyer at the same time, it's
definitely encouraged—as long as you make your billables."

"The partners actively get you involved in different parts of the practice, like recruiting and personnel."

Associates are generally impressed with the receptiveness and openness
of the partners. The associates formally meet on a quarterly basis with the
firm's management committee, and there are also departmental meetings,
where "We let partners know what we'd like." Associates report that "The
partners have been receptive to a certain degree," and one associate adds
that, "The partners are especially receptive when we say we need additional
associates or paralegals when our workloads get heavy." Associates feel that
"the partners are getting more open with associates. There used to be a mystique here about the partnership, but they disclose more and more about
the business to us, and we like that." The firm has made an "active effort to
get associates involved in recruiting and personnel," and that in some
departments "associates get a near-dispositive voice in hiring decisions."

"The firm is very supportive of families."

Associates say that "The firm philosophy is 'family first and friendship
among colleagues' as a recipe for long-term professional success." They
point to the fact that "Three of the female partners have grammar-school
aged children. They made partner with small kids. That says all you need
to know about the firm being supportive of having families." Associates
also say that, "Many of the younger lawyers have young kids." For those
young parents "The firm has been flexible with part-time arrangements.
You can tell that they recognize the importance of being home with kids."
One associate says that "The firm obviously appreciates talent, and it does
what it can to keep its talented young female attorneys. And that means
being flexible with family time." Family life at B&T is given a big boost
from the firm's Midwestern setting, since "From a quality of life and cost
of living perspective, it's definitely worth it to be here."

Associates adore the social life at B&T. Apart from "A formal Holiday
Party, which everybody enjoys; Pub Crawls; various wine and beer tasting
parties," and other formal firm events, many attorneys get together informally. As one associate tells it, "A lot of my friends at other firms talk
about the need to keep their work and social lives separate. I'm grateful to
be at a firm where that doesn't have to be the case."

Associates talk about activities like playing softball and basketball with
large groups of colleagues on a weekly basis. Many of the young married
associates get together routinely, with their spouses, for big get-togethers,
including annual pumpkin carving contests, Halloween hayrides, Super
Bowl parties, New Year's Eve parties, and birthday parties. One associate

talks about being in a 'gourmet club' with four colleagues and their spouses. One group of five associates "travel the country every summer, checking out a new baseball stadium." Others talk about being in Bible-study with a couple of colleagues, or hitting the local streams for fly fishing with fellow lawyers. An associate says that, "social outings here know no boundaries. They include partners and associates, people a lot older and younger than each other, and people from all different departments."

An associate says that "Something happens here all the time to remind you that the firm is always thinking of ways to support the camaraderie at the office. For instance, during the NCAA Men's Basketball Tournament, the firm set up a large-screen projection TV in the largest conference room and set up refreshments, so we could all enjoy the game during the day." To sum it up, one associate says that, "At this firm, you can have a good life—because you're *encouraged* to have one."

Brown, Todd & Heyburn PLLC

400 West Market Street, 32ND Floor • Louisville, Kentucky 40202-3363
Phone: 502-589-5400 • Fax: 502-581-1087 • E-mail: info@lou.bth-pllc.com
Web site: bth-pllc.com

OFFICES

Louisville (largest office), Lexington, Covington, Kentucky; New Albany, Indiana; Nashville, Tennessee

"Even though the firm is big by Kentucky standards, and the practice is thriving, it's a friendly place . . . You think nothing of sticking your head out of the door of your office and yelling down the hallway for something. I've visited other firms where you'd hear a pin drop."

HIGHLIGHTS

• Largest law firm in Kentucky; 233RD largest firm in the country.

NUTS AND BOLTS

Managing partner:

C. Edward Glasscock

Hiring partner:

James A. Giesel, phone: 502-568-0307, e-mail: JamesG@lou.bth-pllc.com

Recruiting coordinator:

Amy L. Patterson, phone: 502-589-5400 x545,
e-mail: Amy@lou.bth-pllc.com

Number of attorneys in firm:

160 (78 partners)

TOTAL FIRM:

Partners (78), associates (82), women partners (8), women associates (33), minority partners (0), minority associates (2), disabled partners (0)

THIS OFFICE:

Total attorneys (110), partners (59), associates (51), women attorneys (33), minority attorneys (2)

OTHER OFFICES:

(* represents an office profiled elsewhere in this book)
Lexington, KY (31); Covington, KY (4); New Albany, IN (6)

Years to make partner:

Associates are considered for promotion to "income member" status with full voting rights after 6 $1/2$ years with the firm. Income members may then be considered for promotion to full equity/capital member status after two more years. (For lateral hires, consideration for membership is negotiable.)

WHAT DO THEY DO?

Primary specialties (more than 5% of practice):

The firm is divided into the following practice groups: Litigation (96 attorneys in firm); Corporate and Business Law (45 attorneys in firm); Real Estate (12 attorneys in firm); Estate Planning/Administration (7 attorneys in firm).

Specifically, the firm handles all kinds of clients and cases involving business acquisitions, handling catastrophic losses (like the Oklahoma City bombing), commercial finance, employee benefits practice, environmental law, equine law, health care, insurance litigation, tax, international law, labor and employment, national counsel practice (serving as 'national counsel' for various large manufacturers and their insurers on complex, potentially large exposure matters), product liability, public finance, and real estate.

On occasion, associates have moved from one practice group to another.

WHO DO THEY REPRESENT?

A broad variety of clients, including Alcan Aluminum; Alliant Health System, Inc.; American Commercial Lines; American Cyanamid Co.; American Horse Shows Assn., Inc.; Brown & Williamson Tobacco Corporation; The Budd Co.; Colt Industries, Inc.; Commercial Union Assurance Companies; Cosmos Broadcasting Corporation; DMI Furniture, Inc.; Dow Chemical Co.; E. I. DuPont de Nemours and Company; Electric Insurance Co.; The Firestone Tire & Rubber Co.; General Electric Company; GTE Products; Grays Knob Coal Co.; Hillerich & Bradsby Co.; Ichikoh Manufacturing, Inc.; ICI Americas Inc.; J.J.B. Hilliard, W.L. Lyons,

Inc.; FoodService Purchasing Cooperative, Inc.; Liberty Mutual Insurance Company of Boston; Louisville Gas & Electric Co.; Marathon Oil Company; McGraw Cellular Communications, Inc.; McGraw Edison Corp.; Monsanto Co.; Northwestern Mutual Life Insurance Company; The Ohio Casualty Insurance Group; Thoroughbred Owners and Breeders Assn.; United Mercantile Agencies, Inc.; UPS, Inc.; Westinghouse Electric Corp.

WHERE NEW ASSOCIATES COME FROM . . .

Brown, Todd routinely interviews on campus at the following law schools: University of Kentucky; University of Louisville; University of Cincinnati; Northern Kentucky University; University of Virginia; William & Mary; Washington & Lee; Vanderbilt University; Indiana University-Bloomington. Associates and summer associates are also hired from law schools where Brown, Todd doesn't conduct on-campus interviews.

HOURS AND BUCKS . . .

Minimum billable hours for first year associates: 1,800

Several attorneys currently work on a part-time basis, but none of them started with the firm that way; new associates should expect to start out working full-time. Brown, Todd does hire contract attorneys, some of whom have become full associates.

Typical first year associate salary: $$$ ($50-65,000)

SUMMER PROGRAM . . .

Last year, there were 14 summer associates, 10 of whom were 2Ls. Of those 10, 8 received permanent offers.

Weekly pay: $1,000 last year

1Ls are routinely hired for the summer program. Last year's 1L summer interns came from Harvard University, the University of Louisville, University of Cincinnati, and University of Texas.

PRO BONO . . .

Attorneys are encouraged to take part in pro bono work. Organizations benefiting from Brown, Todd pro bono services include the Legal Aid Society, Wills Clinic for the Elderly, HIV/AIDS Legal Project, and the Volunteer Lawyer Program.

HISTORY AT A GLANCE . . .

Brown, Todd & Heyburn was founded in 1972 when three well-established Louisville law firms merged, with a total of 20 attorneys. In 1984 the firm merged with Park & Sullivan in Lexington, Kentucky.

Over the years the firm has been involved in many high-profile cases, including the Beverly Hills Supper Club Litigation; law suits arising from the Oklahoma City bombing; and the nationwide breast implant litigation.

WHAT IT'S LIKE TO WORK THERE . . .

Perhaps the best compliment you can pay to Brown, Todd & Heyburn is to say that while it earns rave reviews now, the perception among current associates is that until several years ago, associates didn't enjoy themselves, and didn't stay around very long. However, "It's as though the partners looked up a few years ago and thought, 'wait a minute. We want our associates to be the foundation for the future. We *want* this to be a pleasant place to work. We've got to turn this around.'"

And they did that—spectacularly well. One junior associate commented that "From the way we get treated now, it's hard to believe this was *ever* anything but a great place to work. People just don't leave anymore."

"We get unbelievable projects here."

While "large firm associates are always going to get some research, some document reviews," Brown, Todd associates rave about the "unbelievable projects" they get. For instance, the firm represented the fertilizer company that was sued as a result of the Oklahoma City bombing. While a fertilizer company wouldn't offhand seem to be a great client, listen to what associates got to do: "There were 10 or 12 associates on the team who handled that case, and we traveled all over the world—Scotland, Africa, England, Australia, Mexico—we went anywhere the Europe-based company had outlets to interview personnel and take a look at documents. We spent three or four weeks in each of the cities we visited. It was absolutely fantastic." As one associate said, "The partners here make a point of not hogging travel for themselves, as they do at a lot of firms where my friends work."

Associates also appreciate that "the partners make a point of including you" in important parts of projects. They feel they are on the "fast track" to professional development, being included in all parts of the representation from client contact, to strategy sessions, to depositions, negotiations, and court appearances. "As a second-year associate I worked on some breast implant litigation, where we defended a foam supplier. The partner handling the case brought me in to sit at the defense table, and when he got up he started out by telling the judge that he wanted to take a moment to thank me and the other two associates for our hard work on the case. Being appreciated like that really makes the job more interesting and fun."

Another associate talked about assisting a litigation partner in preparing for a critical deposition in a multimillion-dollar/multidistrict lawsuit. The associate had only been practicing for six months at the time. The associate appreciated the "solid feedback on all of my suggestions" and the fact that the partner "took the time to explain the strategy for approaching the deposition, and handling other aspects of complex cases." When it came time to conduct the deposition, the partner had the associate come with him for the deposition itself, which took place in Santa Barbara, California. "He wanted me to see the fruits of my labor firsthand." When the deposition resumed the following week, "The partner asked me to spend another couple of weeks in Santa Barbara to protect the client's position." The associate raved that "I got a chance to see a lot of highly-qualified lawyers work. It was a tremendous experience."

Another associate adds that "Laterals who come here always comment that they get to talk with clients more here than they do at other places. They always say, 'You're much more a part of it here.' The firm is really good at letting you take cases and run with them, all the time with somebody there to keep an eye on you. But you're making the decisions. If you say, 'I need this expert witness,' the partners will tell you, 'If you think you need it, do it.'"

Associates find that with their early responsibility much of the training they get is a "learning by doing" experience. As one associate commented, "They've had a couple of record-breaking years here business-wise, and that means you're going to learn on the run." That doesn't mean that professional development is overlooked; there are formal in-house training programs, but perhaps more importantly the firm has a mentor system, under which each new associate gets a checklist of things they should do during their first two years with the firm. "The mentor makes sure you get a taste of everything." One litigation associate explained that "In litigation, the items on the list would include prepping a summary judgment, or arguing a motion in court." The mentor also fills the important role of acting as a "go-between" in otherwise awkward situations. "If a partner assigns you something confusing, you can go to your mentor and ask, 'What exactly am I supposed to do here?' This is really useful because the mentor doesn't fill out an evaluation for you, so you get to ask questions freely, without worrying how it will affect your evaluations."

There is also a MADD Committee, which stands for "Members on Associate Development." (Well, almost.) They give seminars every three months, on a Saturday morning, at the office. "We get a free lunch, and it's interactive." For instance, one Saturday might focus on depositions, and associates will get a chance to take and defend mock depositions. Associates enthuse that "It's great—it's fashioned after NITA."

On an informal basis, one associate pointed out that "There are always e-mails flying around, saying 'Has anybody done this?' or 'Does anybody know about this judge?' People are incredibly helpful. You'll always get e-mails back with 'Here's how to do that,' or 'Yeah, I had the same judge, here's what she wants.'"

Associates love the "$3,000 CLE account" they get every two years. "It's great, because you can use it to do CLE anywhere you want." One associate reported that "I used mine for a CLE program in New Orleans. I spent three days there. The program was great, and of course it doesn't hurt to stay in a nice place and eat at great restaurants while you're earning CLE credits, courtesy of the firm."

"The firm doesn't fool you with hours."

Associates appreciate the fact that the firm is truthful when it gives them billable-hours requirements. "They expect 1,800 hours in billables," explains one associate, "And they mean it. The goals are realistic. At 1,900 hours, you're a shining star, and 2,000 might get you a bonus."

As one associate points out, "You pay the price for interesting work. People are sometimes here until eleven or midnight." That's not the norm, however. Lawyers typically get to the office between 8:30 and 9 a.m., and most leave by 6:45 p.m. Everybody is in at least one weekend a month, in the form of a Saturday morning. "Most of the time it's to check mail, straighten up. But if you've got a trial coming or a deal closing, you'll be there every weekend until the project is done."

Associates don't resent the hours at least partly because of the attitude of the partners. "The partners come in with you most of the time. You're here, they're here. There's none of this 'I'm going golfing, you prepare the speech.' They're willing to spend time away from home too, so you feel like you're all in it together." On top of that, "There is very little feeling that any project is worthless. You know it's beneficial in this case. And you know the client. You've probably just talked to the client and said, 'We'll get it done and overnight mail it to you.'" Another added that, "There are no false deadlines here."

Associates respect the fact that the firm is honest with summer associates, as well. "As a summer associate, you get to see people working until 6:45 p.m. There's no hustling summer associates out at five o'clock so that they think everybody leaves then. If there are softball games at six, you know that some people are going back to get work done after the game."

"You control your own destiny here."

After the first three years, associates may be evaluated by the Membership Selection Committee, which rates them on qualities including ability to generate business, hours billed, and the like. As one associate pointed out, "What this system means is that when you start bringing in business, it can only help you." Another pointed out that "You can control your own destiny. Whether you work long hours or bring in business, you choose the way you want to contribute." Associates feel that "This kind of flexibility helps you if you're not from the city or just a couple of years out of law school, because it's unlikely you'll be able to generate much business in that situation, and the firm doesn't expect you to."

As part of its demonstrated commitment to business development, the firm has a popular and unusual program: it gives each associate a generous client development account to entertain current and potential clients. It works like this: "If you have a buddy who might be vice president of a potential client in five years, you can take him or her out to dinner on the firm. The firm recognizes that that's where new business comes from." Another associate added that "It's what the partners do, and it's nice to be viewed as a potential future partner this way."

"The associate liaison partner makes sure associates have a voice in issues that concern them."

While there is an associate on each of several important committees, like the recruiting committee and the practice committee, associates feel that their real say comes through the associate liaison partner. Associates say that, "If you have thoughts about anything, the associate liaison partner is your funnel to the partners. You know your issue will be brought up, and you know the liaison is very trustworthy." A big issue the last couple of years was raises, the feeling among associates being that, "Now that the firm is being recognized as a national firm, we should be paid accordingly." They went to the associate liaison partner with this concern, and sure enough, they got a raise that made them all *very* happy. "When he says he's going to bring up an issue for you, he does. And there are no comebacks. Having him bring things up means you get your say without any worries." That's not to say that the partners aren't responsive to the well-being of associates; they are. As one associate points out, "There are a lot of very level-headed partners here who rein in anyone who's a jerk. Anyone who tried to mistreat associates—well, I wouldn't want to be them. The other partners wouldn't tolerate it."

"Many lawyers have pro bono cases."

While the firm has several lawyers who are on the city's pro bono committee, "Many lawyers in the firm have at least one pro bono case." The tax department does some tax work pro bono, but the main focus of the firm's pro bono work is consumer protection. For instance "There was a scam with car dealerships who were repossessing poor people's cars after they didn't make the first payment, reselling the cars for nothing, and suing these people for the difference. These guys thought, 'they're not in a position to do anything about it.' Then all of a sudden they get a letter from Brown, Todd, with all of those names on the letterhead, and their attitude changed immediately."

Although the pro bono hours aren't billables, each associate gets a report on a monthly basis showing "What you did during the month. In

Kentucky, you need to spend at least 25 hours per year on pro bono." One associate pointed out that "Nobody ever says, 'Don't do that pro bono case; work on this instead.' I had an 80-hour pro bono trial, and got nothing but support from the firm when I did it."

"On any given day, half a dozen people will ask you if you want to grab lunch."

Even though "The firm is big by Kentucky standards," associates report that "It's a friendly place where the day-to-day pressures of a thriving practice doesn't stop anybody from taking the time to rehash their kid's performance in the school play, or the previous night's basketball results." (This is the home of the University of Kentucky, after all.) Another associate adds that, "There's a more open atmosphere here. You think nothing of sticking your head out of the door of your office and yelling down the hallway for something. I've visited other firms where you'd hear a pin drop."

The firm encourages friendships with "Friday afternoon cocktail parties at the office" once every few months, where all of the lawyers and support staff socialize as a group. "When schedules and weather allow it—and sometimes when they don't—it's not unusual for some of us to sneak away for an afternoon on the golf course or to go to Churchill Downs or Keeneland Race Tracks."

Associates also view the firm's location as "a major incentive." One associate noted that "I'm not from here, but I learned to love it in a hurry. There are many cultural things, and sports—like Kentucky basketball!" Another associate raved about "The city's beautiful parks, where the firm has fielded many softball teams." Even more importantly, one associate pointed out that "The work we get is the same quality and as interesting as any you'd find in any big cities. That's because the firm can offer the same high-level work at lower prices, which attracts clients from around the country and around the world."

Being in a more "laid-back" city also means that, "You can live in a great place, near the office. I can't tell you how much it means not to spend two hours a day commuting." Another associate adds that "There are so many people here from all over the country, you always have people who are experiencing the city for the first time. The firm isn't a 'closed community.' All doors are open. People will come in, you'll talk about family and sports. And when you've got work to do and you have to close your door, people respect that too."

"The firm makes a point of being family-friendly."

As one associate said, "This is one firm where your work doesn't get in the way of you having a life outside of the office, raising a family." Brown, Todd lawyers "Get together with each other's families" outside of the office. "We routinely socialize on weekends." Associates also point out that for people who want to limit their hours to spend more time with their families "The firm doesn't encourage part-time work per se, but people *do* work part-time."

One associate whose wife was pregnant realized that he had a trial scheduled for the week his baby is due. As he told it, "The firm said, 'Pass the work off to somebody else as the date gets closer.'" He went on, "Firms where my friends work would just say, 'Too bad.' The attitude here is, 'We have a lot of talent. They'll help you when you need it, and when *they* need time off, you'll take over some other case for them.' They make you feel as though they really care about you when they do things like that."

Burns, White & Hickton

2400 Fifth Avenue Place • 120 Fifth Avenue • Pittsburgh, Pennsylvania 15222-3001
Phone: 412-394-2500 • Fax: 412-281-1352 • Web site: bwhllc.com

OFFICES

Pittsburgh (main office), Pennsylvania; Wheeling, West Virginia; San Francisco, California

"It's a very young firm, very interested in new technology and new ideas . . . the members have been able to convey the message that this is a firm without boundaries or limits. It's wonderful!"

HIGHLIGHTS

- 16TH largest law firm in Pittsburgh.
- First big city law firm to be headed by a woman; one-third of the firm's attorneys are female.
- Nationally recognized leader in alternative dispute resolution techniques.
- One of the first Pittsburgh firms to install computer networks allowing clients to track the firm's performance and the status of cases.
- Received "Pro Bono Firm Of The Year" award for Allegheny County two years ago.

NUTS AND BOLTS

Managing partner:

Lisa Pupo Lenihan

Number of attorneys in firm:

45 (17 partners)

WHOLE FIRM:

Women attorneys (17), minority attorneys (0), disabled attorneys (0)

PITTSBURGH OFFICE:

Partners (15), associates (25), women (15)

NUMBER OF ATTORNEYS IN OTHER OFFICES:

Wheeling, WV (4); San Francisco, CA (1)

Years to make partner:

7 to 10

WHAT DO THEY DO?

Toxic Torts (6); Commercial Litigation (5); FELA Law (12); Professional Liability Litigation (7); Employment & Labor (5).

The firm is departmentalized. New associates get into their department through a combination of assignment and choice. Junior associates can, and do, switch specialties. Associates get assignments primarily from any of the attorneys in their department.

WHO DO THEY REPRESENT?

The firm represents clients in the transportation industry, communications industry, architects, insurance companies, medical practices, as well as various large and small companies.

WHERE NEW ASSOCIATES COME FROM . . .

The firm routinely interviews on campus at the following law schools: The University of Pittsburgh and Duquesne University. The firm also hires from law schools where it doesn't interview on campus.

HOURS AND BUCKS . . .

Associates work an average of 1,800 to 2,200 hours per year. There is no minimum billable hours requirement.

Part-time work is available to both ongoing and entry-level associates. The firm does not hire contract associates.

Typical first year associate salary, including typical bonus: $$ ($35-50,000).

SUMMER PROGRAM . . .

Last year, there were 4 summer associates, 1 of whom received an offer.

The weekly pay for the summer program varies.

1Ls are routinely hired for the summer program; last year, the 1Ls came from the University of Pittsburgh and Duquesne.

The deadline for applying for summer clerkships is November.

PRO BONO . . .

The firm encourages associates to do pro bono work, but doesn't require it. All pro bono hours are treated as billables. The firm's lawyers participate in a variety of pro bono projects, including Neighborhood Legal Services, where they represent a number of clients each month, particularly victims of abuse.

HISTORY AT A GLANCE . . .

The firm was founded in 1987 by five attorneys who broke away from the firm Dickie, McCarney & Chilcote. Since then it has grown rapidly, and intends to continue doing so. The firm is maintains a very young, vibrant practice; the managing partner, Lisa Pupo Lenihan, is only 39.

WHAT IT'S LIKE TO WORK THERE . . .

Think about traditional law firms. Got the picture in your mind? Well, when you think about Burns, White & Hickton, you can throw everything you *thought* you knew out the window. It's an unusual, groundbreaking firm, best exemplified by the fact that it's got a woman as managing partner. While that in itself is unusual among mid-sized firms, it's even more incredible when you learn that this particular managing partner, Lisa Lenihan, is a young mother with three children under the age of seven; on paper works part-time—although as one associate points out, "Frankly, it's full-time. It would *have* to be, running a firm with aggressive growth plans like this one has. She works at home all the time."

The firm's up-to-date attitude is reflected in the office environment, which is "very young. It's nice to work in an office where the oldest person, until last year, was 50—now they hired a slightly older lateral, but it's still very youthful." That means that, "They don't buck technology or new ideas. If you tell them about something new, for instance a computerized research tool that gets the answer quicker, they recognize that it's better for the client and they'll let you get it, on the spot."

The firm's youthfulness also creates a situation where "Everyone is addressed by their first name." One associate added that, "The partners are very approachable. It's not 'Mr. This' or 'Ms. That,' it's 'Mike' or 'Dave' or 'Lisa.'" Another associate pointed out that "It is very common for partners and associates to kid around with one another." "Practical jokes, particularly by the partners, are legendary and, at times, brutal!"

The firm fosters a "dynamic and creative" culture with a number of formal and informal practices. On a monthly basis, the firm opens "the bar" in its main conference room, and "partners, associates and staff have drinks and socialize, telling war stories from the previous month." It also doesn't hurt that "The firm has a sauna and exercise room open for everybody's use."

One associate raved about the firm's "support and respect" for associates' specific skills. "'Thank you,' 'Great job,' 'I really appreciate your help with this' are the kinds of phrases you hear frequently in this office." Another pointed out that "There are associates here who started to work for the firm way back when they graduated from high school, before they even went to college, let alone law school. One of the current partners started working here as a law clerk. The fact that they've stayed makes the best statement I can think of about what a great place this is to be."

"Many of the attorneys travel a lot."

The firm "primarily specializes in defense litigation," and since "the firm is national counsel for many clients, there are cases throughout the country." Depositions, hearings, those kinds of client issues require travel. As one associate pointed out, "If your case is in California or North Dakota or Ohio, you have to be there." Another explained that "Some junior associates are out of town two to three weeks every month. Some don't leave at all." This isn't a problem because "The firm doesn't blindside you. They only hire for particular positions, so when you interview here you know at the outset how much travel time your particular job will require." That means that "obviously if you've got family obligations or a special needs person at home, you're not going to take the job that requires lots of travel."

"You get your own cases from the day you come here."

Although associates are hired for specific roles "Once you're in the firm, your position can change." It's not unusual to start with the firm as a law clerk and become a permanent associate. One associate pointed out that "You can switch departments and positions, and sometimes it's not your choice." But the effect of that is minimized by the fact that "The firm gives new associates a lot of responsibility," and "It's a great place to learn about a whole lot of different areas." New associates get "immediate client contact and significant responsibility very early on in their careers," at least partially because all new associates get their own cases right off the bat. "Some are small, for instance, an arbitration," but nonetheless "You get a *lot* of autonomy." While that might suggest it's easy to be overwhelmed, "If you feel you're sinking, you tell the partners. They'll help you any way they can. Every door is open, and that's important in an environment where you get so much responsibility, *fast*." One associate raved that "The first year I was here, I argued before the Supreme Court of Pennsylvania. I couldn't have done that *anywhere* else."

The availability of partners for help and advice is important, because "There isn't really any formal training. We're so busy that there's very little time to show *why* things are done—you just *do* it." The firm does encourage associates to "Expand professionally. They pay for all CLEs, any books, anything that furthers your career—let them know about it, and they're behind you." The firm encourages associates to take other states' bar exams, and "They give you paid time off to study and then pay all the fees for you to take the exam."

An informal feeling of "We're all in it together" keeps associates feeling comfortably challenged. One senior associate keeps files of briefs and research resources; other associates go to her when they have to write motions or create other documents. It's "not official," but "there's no cutthroat atmosphere, no back-stabbing here. There's a feeling that there's no point in reinventing the wheel if somebody in the office has already done some of what you're trying to do." On top of that, there is "all kinds of informal advice that you get from everybody here," ranging from major issues to the "little touches like the quirks of various judges. If you're going before a certain judge for the first time, someone might tap you on the shoulder and tell you that for this particular judge, in the courtroom you shouldn't hang your coat over the rail, you should put it on your chair, because the judge doesn't like coats piled on the rail. Little things like that make your life a lot easier." In addition, the associates hold a monthly lunch meeting called the 'sidebar,' where "We do departmental updates, and sometimes partners do presentations, sometimes demonstrations of different techniques, and sometimes it's not anything to do with the law. We spent two sessions learning yoga."

"All of the partners have young kids."

Managing partner Lisa Lenihan isn't the only partner with young children. All of the partners have young families, and that results in an environment where "There's no clock-punching for attorneys; you come and go as you please, as long as your work is done."

That doesn't mean hours are necessarily short; as one associate points out, "You *do* have to spend time here." Most people are in by 8 a.m. and most leave by 5:30 p.m., but "Most people come in one day of the weekend to keep their hours up." Although there is no billable requirement, "If you've got a court date, you'll have a longer day," and even without a court date "There's definite pressure to get your billables up." The lack of a minimum billables figure is responsible for the policy that "Pro bono hours aren't technically viewed as billables," however, "They do recognize that you're working when you do pro bono work." Much of the pro bono work in the firm is in the form of "quick fixes" because the firm's attorneys travel so much. For the last Monday of every month, two lawyers from the office hear four cases each for Neighborhood Legal Services. "It's done on a rotating basis, two different lawyers every month." While the associates' perception is that the firm historically wasn't very pro bono oriented, "Its attitude warmed up considerably after we were named Pro Bono Firm of the Year in 1996 for Allegheny County." Now, attorneys in the firm can either take part in the Neighborhood Legal Services project "Or you can bring in your own pro bono projects and get them approved."

"Lawyers, paralegals, and staff all socialize regularly."

Although the firm is growing rapidly—200% in the last five years alone—it makes an effort to maintain a "small firm feel." There are annual events like a day watching a Pirates baseball game, which everybody in the firm attends. The firm also regularly supports groups of lawyers who want to take part in charity events, like running races. The monthly happy hours in the firm's bar is another routine—and much appreciated—event.

Informally, the firm is organized so that smaller groups of lawyers can get together. The floor that houses that firm is divided into quads, and each quad regularly has parties of its own. "People will just casually ask around, 'What day is good for you?' and when they've set a date, they'll tell everybody 'Bring a covered dish.'" And whenever "People are getting married or celebrating an anniversary or they've had a new baby, we'll get together and get them a cake and chip in for a present."

Some of the members of the firm recently bought a building on Pittsburgh's North Shore, where all of the new development in Pittsburgh is going, including its new sports stadiums. The firm is moving to the new building department by department, as existing tenants' leases expire and they leave. While "It will take a few years to move the entire firm into the new building," the firm sponsors bi-weekly lunches for both Pittsburgh offices (the firm is split into two buildings) to keep its attorneys and staff in touch. Also, "because there isn't great public transportation to the new office, the firm bought a van and shuttles people and files back and forth," to minimize any inconvenience to lawyers and staff. Despite the minor inconveniences "The new building was a great move for the firm. The North Shore is where all the excitement in the city is going to be for many years to come."

"New ideas are encouraged here."

As you'd expect from a firm with "aggressive growth plans," new ideas are "encouraged and examined for potential, no matter who they come from." As one associate explained, "It was only 11 years ago that the five founding partners, all of them very young, started the firm based on their own ideas. They realized it didn't take them 20 years of practicing law to formulate those new ideas, and so they're always responsive to ideas that come from young people here." It might be a point of law brought to them by a law clerk, or a way to streamline a process that a paralegal dreams up, or even a different kind of client or practice area that a junior associate would like to explore. As one associate explains it, "It's just a wonderful firm! The members have been able to convey the message that this is a firm without boundaries or limits."

Carlton, Fields, Ward, Emmanuel, Smith & Cutler, P.A.

One Harbour Place • 777 S. Harbour Island Blvd. • Tampa, FL 33602-5799
Phone: 813-223-7000 • Fax: 813-229-4133 • Web site: carltonfields.com

OFFICES

Tampa (main office), Miami, West Palm Beach, St. Petersburg, Orlando, Tallahassee, Pensacola, Florida

*"At the end of the day, do you like your work, your people, your life—more importantly, do you **have** a life? I **do**. I'm really happy here."*

HIGHLIGHTS

- 222ND largest firm in the country.
- Pronounced dedication to pro bono work; pro bono hours are considered billables (up to 50). The firm received the National Public Service Award from the ABA's Business Law Section in recognition of its significant pro bono legal services to the poor.
- The firm has represented 62 of the Fortune 100 companies.
- The firm received the Making Strides 'Striders' Cup' award last year, for generosity to cancer charities.

NUTS AND BOLTS

Managing partner:

Thomas A. Snow

Hiring partner:

Luis Prats, phone: 813-223-7000, e-mail: lprat@carltonfields.com

Recruiting coordinator:

Elizabeth Bergen Zabak, phone: 813-223-7000, e-mail: ezaba@carltonfields.com

Number of attorneys in firm:

172 (108 partners)

WHOLE FIRM:

Women partners (19), women associates (24), minority partners (8), minority associates (9), disabled partners (0), disabled associates (0)

TAMPA OFFICE:

Total attorneys (80), total partners (51), total associates (29), women partners (8), women associates (13), minority partners (2), minority associates (2), disabled partners (0), disabled associates (0)

OTHER OFFICES:

(* represents an office profiled elsewhere in this book)
Miami, FL (33); West Palm Beach, FL (18); St. Petersburg, FL (12); Orlando, FL (13); Tallahassee, FL (10); Pensacola, FL (6)

Years to make partner:

7

WHAT DO THEY DO?

Primary specialties (more than 5% of practice):

Litigation, Antitrust, Appellate (54); Real Estate, Environmental, Land Use (23); Product Liability, Medical Malpractice (20); Commercial, Bankruptcy, Creditors Rights (18); Tax, Corporate, Probate, Securities, Bond (18); Construction (15); Banking, Finance, Business (12); Employment (8); Intellectual Property (7); Administrative (3); Insurance (2).

Note that the numbers exceed the firm attorney total because attorneys practice in more than one area. Associates rank the departments they want to join at the end of their summer associateships (or before they join the firm as permanent associates if they don't summer clerk there). Associates "virtually always" get their first choice.

WHO DO THEY REPRESENT?

The firm is "business-oriented," and along with numerous banks, hospitals, insurance companies, and many Florida city, county, and other governmental bodies, Carlton Fields represents the following clients: Allegheny

Health, Armour Pharmaceutical Company, AT&T Wireless Services, The Bank of New York; BASF Corporation, Blue Cross & Blue Shield, Burger King Corp., Canadian Imperial Bank of Commerce, CF Industries, Chase Manhattan Bank, Chrysler Capital, Cigna Companies, The Coca-Cola Company, Columbia HCA Healthcare, Commercial Credit, Dow Chemical, Dowelanco, EDS, E. I. DuPont de Nemours & Co., Exxon Company, USA, FDIC, First Union National Bank of Florida, Florida Power Corporation, Ford Motor Company, GD Searle & Company, Healthmark Corporation, Heitman Retail Properties, Honda North America, Inc., John Hancock Mutual Life, Lawyers Title Insurance, Miller Brewing Company, Inc., NationsBank, Owens Corning Fiberglass Corporation, Philip Morris Corporation, Pirelli Tire Corporation, Prudential Insurance, Reliance Insurance, Republic Bank, R. J. Reynolds Tobacco Company, The Rouse Company, SmithKline Beecham Laboratories, Snapper Power Equipment, Sofamore Danek Group, Inc., The Southland Corporation, Time Warner Communications, Uniroyal Goodrich Tire Company, Westinghouse, Zeneca Agricultural Products, Inc.

WHERE NEW ASSOCIATES COME FROM . . .

Carlton Fields routinely interviews on campus at the following law schools: Duke, UVA, Vanderbilt, University of Florida, Florida State University, University of Miami, and Stetson University. Associates and summer associates are also hired from law schools where Carlton Fields doesn't conduct on-campus interviewing; Carlton Fields lawyers are alumni of over 50 different law schools.

HOURS AND BUCKS . . .

Last year, first year associates worked an average of 1,940 billable hours. They contributed an average of 2,275 hours for billable and quality non-billable time to the firm (quality non-billable hours include observation and training time, recruiting, marketing, civic and bar activities, community activities, firm administrative activities, pro bono activities over 50 hours, and other professional development activities).

1ST and 2ND year associates have a minimum billable requirement of 1,900 hours/year.

3RD through 5TH year associates have a minimum billable requirement of 1,850 hours/year.

6TH through 8TH year associates have a minimum billable requirement of 1,800 hours/year.

Part-time work is available to continuing associates; currently, 10 associates work on what Carlton Fields terms an 'alternative work schedule.' The firm's policy is that entry-level associates joining the firm from law school or judicial clerkships must work for two years before they are eligible for an alternative work schedule. Lateral hires may be considered for an alternative work schedule immediately. Carlton Fields hires contract associates, some of whom have been hired as permanent associates.

Typical first year associate salary, including typical bonus: $$$ ($50-65,000) in Tampa, Orlando, St. Petersburg, and Tallahassee; $$$$ (Over $65,000) in Miami and West Palm Beach.

SUMMER PROGRAM . . .

In 1998, there were 11 summer associates, all of whom received offers.

Weekly pay: $950 in Tampa, Orlando, and St. Petersburg; $1,200 in Miami and West Palm Beach.

1Ls are eligible for summer clerkships; in recent summers, 1Ls have come from Vanderbilt, Harvard, Stanford, Duke, UVA and the University of Florida. There is no strict deadline for applying to the summer associate program.

PRO BONO . . .

Carlton Fields has been committed to public service since its founding, and the firm is one of only three in Florida to accept the ABA Law Firm Pro Bono Challenge, which requires a contribution of time equal to 3% of the Firm's total billable hours to pro bono work. In 1997, this amounted to more than 7,350 hours of pro bono services to the poor and charitable organizations. In fact, the firm has recently agreed to sponsor the National Association for Public Interest Law's Partner Fellowship Program. For the next two years, the fellow will be working on the Child Victim Rapid Response School Program.

Associates receive billable hour credit for 50 pro bono hours.

The firm contributes professional services to numerous nonprofit groups such as museums, housing programs, community assistance programs, legal aid associations, and other corporations providing free legal services to the poor. In recent years, it has also undertaken a major commitment in the representation of three Florida death penalty inmates in post-conviction collateral proceedings. Currently the firm is handling two death-appeal matters.

HISTORY AT A GLANCE . . .

The firm was founded in 1901 in Tampa by Giddings E. Mabry. He was joined three years later by his father, Milton H. Mabry, a former lieutenant governor of Florida, who also served as Chief Justice of the Supreme Court of Florida. A few years later Doyle E. Carlton (later Governor of Florida) joined them, as well as O.K. Reaves, who served in the Florida

Legislature and as a Circuit Judge. The firm name included Mabry, Reaves & Carlton for over 40 years.

WHAT IT'S LIKE TO WORK THERE . . .

The first thing you notice when you talk to associates at Carlton Fields is how much they genuinely like each other. "People here are down-to-earth and sincere." One associate said that "This might sound silly, but you can tell what kind of firm this is even by the name plates on the offices. There's no 'Mr. Smith' or 'Ms. Smith,' there are names, just first and last names." And in attorney offices "The thing I noticed the most when I interviewed here is that in every office, people have pictures of their families on the wall, spouses and kids. I interviewed with all of the big Florida firms, and that's not true in other firms."

One associate recounts that "The thing that brought me here was the fact that individual values and individual flexibility really mean some-thing." Another adds that "I like the diversity—you have a wide range of people and personalities. There isn't a mold you're expected to follow."

An associate raved that "The people here are all so *different*. There's one guy, a total Republican, wears Mr. Rogers cardigan sweaters. Then there's a woman, she's been practicing 10 or 12 years, she's part-time, has two kids, she's a Democrat, she likes to work out. That's what we talked about when I interviewed with her—working out! Then you have the two founders, Smith and Cutler, and they're in their 70's and 80's, and they're here every day." This kind of diversity results in an atmosphere where *everybody* feels comfortable. As one associate reports, "For the last few years, everybody who has gotten an offer from the summer program has joined the firm. It's virtually always that way. The only time people don't come back, it's because there's something like a family reason that takes them to another state. Otherwise, they love it. We all do."

"The firm has a culture of pulling together for a fallen comrade."

As you'd expect in a place where the people care for each other, they're there when anybody "is ill or having a rough time for one reason or another." One associate tells the story of "A second year associate who was diagnosed with breast cancer and required major surgery. From the day she was released from the hospital and for several weeks after that, someone—clerks, secretaries, paralegals, lawyers—prepared dinner and delivered it to her home. For the six months' of chemotherapy after that, moral support, offers to clean her house, drive her to treatments, do her shopping, things like that were endless." A year later, the associate had a relapse and required a bone marrow transplant and radiation. As she her-self describes it, "Carlton Fields' compassion again manifested itself in incredible ways." Before the bone marrow transplant, she couldn't go to the office for fear of infection, so the firm gave her a complete computer system interfaced with the office. When she sent an e-mail to the office saying that she 'might' need blood and platelet transfusions, 80 offers of donations came her way. She says that above everything else, the calls, visits, and literally hundreds of cards from people at the firm were instrumental in her efforts to maintain a positive attitude about her treatments. As she points out, "Others have received the same kind of support from the firm and its people who care, give and keep on giving." This kind of caring extends to everyone in the firm. The firm's coordinator of client services, who's been with the firm for 22 years, recently became extremely ill and had to go on disability. As one associate described it, "The care and concern of people from the firm was so outflowing that her husband had to ask us not to call and leave messages on his answering service, because the sheer numbers were overwhelming!" At the suggestion of one of the shareholders, the firm produced a video of almost all of the employees in the Tampa office, sitting at their desks, extending a greeting to her. She was, needless to say, "overwhelmed with joy" at the thoughtfulness of her colleagues at the firm, lawyers and staff alike.

The firm's compassionate nature extends to its attitude toward pro bono work. As one associate explains, "The firm is very dedicated to pro bono. The projects are a combination of what you want to bring in and what the firm does. Normally, projects come to two shareholders and they e-mail out to everybody what the projects are, and if you want to do one of them, you respond." Alternatively "You can get pro bono from community organizations you're involved with, for instance, a nonprofit that needs representation. You bring it in and get it approved." The first 50 hours of pro bono are considered billables and the rest are considered "Nonbillable quality hours, which are considered for bonuses." Excelling on a pro bono project greatly impresses the supervising attorneys. "One associate made a huge impression on his supervisor by setting up elder care programs for the county. He completed the manual from scratch while billing beaucoup hours and then went out and got volunteers to staff the meeting with the use of his manual." As one associate pointed out, "The whole idea is that they want you to get out of the office, because they believe that a quality lawyer is well-rounded, not just a craftsman."

The firm's concern for the community is also reflected in its participation in all kinds of local events. For instance, it fields teams in the annual 5K and 15K Gasparilla Distance Classic, the Run for Justice sponsored by the Hillsborough County Bar Association, and other road races. Firm lawyers also participate annually in the American Cancer Society's "Strides Against Cancer," as well as "Paint Your Heart Out," "Hands On Tampa," and a number of functions for children, the arts, and numerous health-related charities in each of the cities where the firm has offices.

"What brought me here was that people I respect who are already lawyers said that Carlton Fields has some of the best lawyers in Florida."

Associates are drawn to Carlton Fields because of its "stellar" reputation. "Even the firm resume, on paper, it's fantastic—the lawyers are incredible." "I wanted to come here to work on cutting-edge legal issues, and that's just what I've done."

Associates wind up in their specialties by "letting the firm know what you want during your summer clerkship. As you develop interests in different areas, you let them know and they'll get you assignments in those areas." "For your exit interview, you tell them your preferences." For people who don't know what they want, or join the firm without going through the summer clerkship program, "You rank the departments you think you want. The hiring committee matches you and you join the firm in that department. I've never heard of anybody not getting what they wanted."

Associates get projects from "everybody in your practice group," although "as you move on, you can specialize with one partner, or stay in an 'open season' mode. Some practice groups are always that way. For instance, litigation associates work with everyone in the group, and so does construction." No matter who approaches associates with projects "they will normally coordinate it with your supervising attorney. That's a huge help because a project may be more involved than you thought it would be, just because you don't have the experience to judge. For instance, you might think a project will only take an hour or two, but there may be follow-up that will take weeks. Your supervising attorney will save you from situations like that."

One junior associate raved that "I'm never in the library. They ask me when I go there, 'Wow—what are *you* doing here?'," While 'library time' varies depending on the specialty, and "Litigation associates do more research," they "still get to go to hearings. They can be frustrated since it's easy for clients to cancel and reschedule. You'll get psyched up for something and then find that it's been rescheduled. But that's not the firm's fault. The firm makes every effort to get you talking to clients and observing a lot." Some transactional associates find themselves "On the ground floor of every project. I'm in every meeting from the very first one with a new client. I know they're not technically my client, but I feel like they are, because I'm included in everything."

Predictably enough, the hours associates work "can be long" depending on the project they're involved with, and whether or not they're 'morning people' or 'night owls.' "Some people are here at 7 a.m. For instance, one partner takes his son to school in the morning, and comes straight to the office from there. That happens to bring him here at 7 a.m." The office typically comes to life around 8 to 8:30 a.m. At night, people typically leave around 7 p.m. But "work hours are driven by deals. It depends what's going on." One associate says that "If I'm in the middle of a big deal, I might come in at 5 a.m.—for instance, a client is going to sign a deal that day—and not leave until 2 the next morning. Once in a great while the hours will go off the scale like that. But normally, you're out by 7 at night."

When it comes to weekends, again "It depends on deals. It's not standard. On average, associates spend one or two weekends here a month, maybe a couple of hours each day. But then there'll be months where you don't come in on weekends at all." And "Department heads make sure that you're not under- or over-loaded with work."

With hours that can be long, associates say that, "You respect the people you work with. You like them. They're smart, they're good to work with and learn from. Many of the partners are great teachers. You'll get lots of samples with your assignments, and they'll tell you to ask any questions you have. You get lots of feedback. They'll tell you, 'you did this great, here's what you can improve'—but more importantly than that they want to make sure you understand *why* everything is done. You're not a robot. They're making you into a great lawyer. So you don't mind the hours."

"The new mentoring program makes sure you're where you're supposed to be in your professional development."

The firm trains its associates through a combination of department meetings and a new mentoring program. The department meetings "differ in how often they take place; for some departments, it's once a week. For others, once a month. Different partners will talk about what they do, so that you understand the full extent of the practice and you can better serve your clients. You learn about what's new in the practice area. Usually it's a lunch thing, for an hour and a half."

Associates rave about the new mentoring program, instituted last year at the firm. "The whole system itself was in response to looking at what the associates needed." Each associate gets "two mentors—one partner and one senior associate." The mentors are responsible not only for the associate's legal development "but also your social development into the city where your office is, which is important since most people aren't from Florida originally." When it comes to substantive skills, "You and your mentors come up with an 'action plan'—you have goals that will be different depending on your practice area. For instance, in litigation, after six months, it might be that you'll have done a certain number of hearings, taken or defended a deposition. It's a barometer of where you should be. The idea is to make sure that once you're a shareholder, you've got all the skills you need." The social aspect of the mentoring "makes sure that you're plugged into the city. Of course the firm buys a lot of tables at a lot of events, but the mentoring is more than that." One associate raved that "My mentor has given me tickets to a 'Final Four' game. I get tickets to hockey games, things like that." While there is a strong business development flavor to the socialization, "That's only part of it—they want you to love the city. And eventually you get involved in bar functions, committees, that kind of thing." The pervasive feeling created by the mentoring program is that "the focus at the early stage of your career is professional development. They want you to be a great lawyer."

Associates pointed out that the mentoring program is helpful in "developing you so that you *can* bring in business. It's just that the firm believes you have to be a great lawyer *first*." The firm's combination of lock-step compensation and a bonus system for business development reflect this attitude. "You don't feel any pressure to bring in business, but you get rewarded if you do. And the mentoring program makes you feel as though you *can*. By the time you're a fourth or fifth year associate, the focus starts to shift and they expect you to get more into client development, meeting people, getting involved in the community with an eye toward business. But by then, they've been preparing you all along."

"You feel plugged into what's going on with the firm."

The firm has several committees, and associates are on all of them except the "obvious ones, like the Executive Committee and the Shareholder Compensation Committee." As one associate explained, "Tom Snow is the firm CEO, and he meets with associates a lot, every three months or so. He tells you what the firm is doing, and gets feedback from you. He wants to know what the firm has to work on." Another associate added that, "If you don't feel comfortable talking in front of everyone, you can let him know otherwise, drop him a note or go through your supervising attorney or one of the firm administrators."

One indication of the firm's responsiveness to associates came last year, with a compensation task force. "The firm wanted to revamp associate compensation and timing aspects of the job. They formed a compensation task force, with six people on it, half of them associates." One associate explains that "even if you weren't on the committee, they wanted your input. The task force went on for six or seven months, and they came out with a resolution which is exactly what the associates had asked for." Another associate commented that "I was really impressed that the firm listened to us and implemented what we wanted." One associate laughingly added that, "this is one firm where nobody gets penalized for complaining. God knows people were very vocal during the compensation task force meetings, and there weren't any comebacks."

"They're really creative with social events."

Associates rave about the firm's in-office happy hours, which occur weekly during the summer and monthly during the rest of the year in Tampa. "They do theme happy hours. For instance, there's been a Hawaiian one, where they decorated with shells. They've done Caribbean, Spanish, Mardi Gras. All of them are catered. It's a great chance to meet the lawyers you don't normally work with."

Apart from the usual raft of summer associate events, the firm has firm retreats where all spouses and administrative staff are included. Each office holds holiday dinners and various holiday parties for attorneys and staff. "Tampa has a holiday lunch, where lawyers do skits spoofing firm events during the year." There's a firm-wide New Attorney Orientation including a dinner and wine tasting, "A great place to test your alcohol tolerance in front of your new colleagues."

The firm has a basketball team in the City of Tampa Attorney Basketball League "which, incidentally, is looking for a few good ringers." The Miami and Tampa offices also participate in the City Attorney Softball League. And as you'd expect with people who so enjoy working with each other, attorneys regularly get together socially outside of work for "dinner, drinks, golfing, fishing, all kinds of social activities."

As one associate summed it up, "At the end of the day, do you like your work, your people, your life—more importantly, do you *have* a life? I *do*. I'm really happy here."

Carrington, Coleman, Sloman & Blumenthal, L.L.P.

200 Crescent Court, Suite 1500 • Dallas, TX 75201
Phone: 214-855-3000 • Fax: 214-855-1333 • E-mail: Recruit@CCSB.com
Web site: CCSB.com

OFFICES

Dallas, Texas

"Carrington, Coleman has been entirely too well kept a secret—I could easily talk for hours without running out of praises to sing."

HIGHLIGHTS

- No billable hour requirements; compensation and advancement don't depend on reaching billable targets.
- Very little bureaucracy, with no requirement that attorneys specialize; those who want to specialize can, but nobody is required to confine themselves to a narrow practice area.
- Has been named one of the 10 best litigation firms in the United States in a survey published in *International Corporate Law*.
- Backed down the FDIC in a bank closure for the first time ever, and obtained payment in full of shareholders' equity claims.
- Awarded the W. Frank Newton Award by the State Bar of Texas, recognizing the firm's dedication to providing legal services to the poor.
- Named Law Firm of the Year by the Dallas Bar Association and Legal Services of North Texas.

NUTS AND BOLTS

Managing partner:

Fletcher Yarbrough

Hiring partner:

Jane Makela, phone: 214-855-3536, e-mail: Recruit@CCSB.com

Recruiting coordinator:

Kim Liptak, phone: 214-855-3536, e-mail: Recruit@CCSB.com

Number of attorneys in firm:

78 (44 partners)

Total partners (44), total associates (32), women partners (6), women associates (20), minority partners (1), minority associates (5), disabled partners (1), disabled associates (0)

Years to make partner:

8

WHAT DO THEY DO?

Primary specialties (more than 5% of practice):

The firm is not departmentalized or otherwise rigidly structured by substantive area; instead, the firm encourages flexibility, allowing lawyers to participate in a variety of areas as needed and interested. Somewhat more than half of the lawyers spend most of their time trying lawsuits, and the rest work on a wide variety of transactional practices.

Lawyers who wish to specialize, do so. Others continue to do a variety of different types of work throughout their careers.

"Litigation" Practice Areas (Appellate, Malpractice, Products Liability, Securities, General)

"Transactional" Practice Areas (Real Estate & Lending, Corporate, Estate Planning, Tax)

Practice Areas that combine litigation and transactional work: Antitrust, Corporate Reorganization & Bankruptcy, Intellectual Property, Technology, Healthcare, Employment, Environmental.

WHO DO THEY REPRESENT?

A broad variety of clients in complex litigation and transactional matters in Dallas and nationally, including some of the state's largest banks, as well as multinational businesses from New York, Atlanta, Los Angeles, and San Francisco. The firm's clients include Goldman Sachs & Co., The Coca-Cola Company, Prudential Securities, Home Savings of America FSB, The Bank of Nova Scotia, Compass Bank, J. C. Penney Co., John Deere Company, The Glidden Company, Tetra Pak, Dresser Industries, Electronic Data Systems, OXY Oil and Gas, and Eastman Kodak Company.

WHERE NEW ASSOCIATES COME FROM . . .

Carrington Coleman routinely interviews on campus at the following law schools: Baylor, Columbia, Cornell, Duke, Harvard, NYU, SMU, Stanford, University of California at Berkeley, University of Chicago, University of Houston, University of Texas, Vanderbilt, and Virginia. The firm does hire from schools where it doesn't conduct on-campus interviews; it solicits resumes from many schools and welcomes other write-in candidates.

HOURS AND BUCKS . . .

Typical hours worked by first year associates: approximately 2,000 to 2,100 (which includes non-billables).

The firm does not have a minimum billable work requirement; it dislikes the idea of 'looking over each other's shoulders.' Instead, an associate's supervising partner is responsible for ensuring that the associate has an appropriate workload, and the associate's billable hours are not disseminated to any other lawyers in the firm.

Part-time work is available to ongoing associates; not at entry level. The firm periodically hires contract associates to help with special matters or projects, and they typically stay for a limited time period.

Typical first year associate salary, including typical bonus: $$$$ (over $65,000). The firm is known for its generous financial package. New associates coming from judicial clerkships receive a $10,000 starting bonus.

SUMMER PROGRAM . . .

Last year, there were 19 summer associates, 14 of whom received offers.

Weekly pay: $1,300 per week

The firm does hire 1Ls; this year's 1Ls came from the Harvard, the University of Michigan, the University of Texas, and SMU.

Deadline for applying for the summer program: November 15 for second years, February 1 for first years.

PRO BONO . . .

The firm strongly encourages all of its lawyers to take part in pro bono projects, and was named "Pro Bono Firm of the Year" in 1995 by the Dallas Bar Association. Just as the firm doesn't prescribe minimum billable hours, it doesn't have a set number of hours for pro bono work.

The firm has received several awards for its pro bono work, which extends to a wide range of individuals and community organizations, including the South Dallas Legal Clinic, the Dallas Legal Hospice, Lawyers Against Domestic Violence, the Center for Nonprofit Management, various local and national charities.

HISTORY AT A GLANCE . . .

The firm was founded in 1970 with 12 lawyers, has grown over the years to 78 lawyers at the firm's single office in Dallas.

Stars in the office include Jim Coleman, a "lawyer's lawyer" presented with the first ever American Inns Of Court Award in 1996, given to the lawyer in the Fifth Circuit (comprising Texas, Louisiana, and Mississippi) who best exemplifies the ideals of integrity, ethics, and professionalism. Coleman was also named "Trial Lawyer of the Year" in 1995 by the Dallas Bar Association.

WHAT IT'S LIKE TO WORK THERE . . .

If you read a lot of law firm brochures, you quickly begin to think you could just cut the name out of any one of them, glue it to another, and nobody would ever be able to tell the difference. Well—if the firm you're talking about is Carrington Coleman, you quickly realize that you're talking about a place that doesn't take itself too seriously. All of the attorney biographies spend as much time talking about hobbies as they do on academic and professional achievements. And these are *interesting* people. The Senior Partner, James Coleman, talks about his country place in Oklahoma, which he calls his 'laughing place,' and about his hobbies of sky diving and canoeing. Another partner talks about designing and building his own weekend home in East Texas. Another refurbished and runs a '57 Chevy. Another owns thoroughbred racehorses. There are lawyers who collect model trains, play "mediocre" golf, share their daughters' "uncertainty about careers and romance." There are Room Dads for fourth graders, a lawyer who plays Latin percussion for a popular local pop/funk dance band called 'Professor D and the Playschool,' and on and on and on. And there's even a section called "Miscellaneous Self-Serving Statements."

Associates say that this 'hoot of a firm resume' perfectly reflects the atmosphere in which they work. One associate commented that "By the time I was two hours into my interview day, I realized that I had already *laughed* more with this firm than with all the firms I had interviewed with over the past two years . . . I accepted the firm's offer on the spot." Another added that "I am more proud to be associated with this firm with every passing year and I do not believe I have ever met anyone, in any job, who loves their job more than I do." An associate pointed out that "Everybody here is on a first name basis. The first week I started, one of the senior partners came into my office, sat down, and just started b.s.'ing with me. Based on what I'd seen of other firms, it was the last thing I expected."

Many associates appreciate their lot even more when they talk with associates from other firms. One associate recounted a situation where "We were defending an extremely complicated lawsuit brought here in

Texas against a major New York investment banking firm. We were working closely with the well-known New York firm that represented them. At one point four of us and several lawyers from the New York firm conducted a week-long review of documents at a corporate office in Florida. While we were all out having dinner and relaxing one night, one of the New York firm's associates pulled me aside and said, 'Wow! The partners in your firm really *like* you guys!' It made me wonder what the culture at their office must be like."

This enjoyment of the firm atmosphere is coupled with respect for the different personalities that make up the firm. As one associate explained, "This place takes all kinds of personalities. Some are loud. Others are meek. Some you'd never dream of using bad language around, while others can swear a blue streak on occasion. They're all respected for their work, and that's all that counts." There's Barbara Lynn, a litigation partner who is chair elect of the ABA's Litigation Section. One associate raved that "She's a tremendous lawyer, a real star, very intimidating, incredibly smart. But she has a real life, too. She never misses one of her kid's soccer games." Another associate mentioned Tyler Baker, "a partner we call 'Mr. Resume,' because he's everything there could be on a resume—a Rhodes Scholar, clerk for a Supreme Court Justice, you name it. A tremendous intellect. But you'd never know it from talking to him because like everybody here, no one is very high on themselves."

Associates also feel that if they are ever "in a bind, somebody is there to pick up the slack. My impression from friends who are young associates at other firms is that they often feel isolated, with no one to help them out." One associate commented that when he first started with the firm, he asked a partner, "What if I make a mistake? They told me, 'It's not you against the world. If you make a mistake, the firm circles the wagons to help out and figure out a solution.' I thought, this is where I want to be. I feel incredibly privileged to work here." As that suggests, the firm cares for its lawyers on a personal level. One associate recounted her first Thanksgiving at the firm, when she was far away from her family. "One of the firm's partners opened her home to me and my friend. I was incredibly touched by that."

"Whatever you want to do, whatever you want to learn, the firm backs you up."

Of course, it wouldn't matter how much associates liked the people they work with if they didn't enjoy their work. But they *do*. As one associate said, "There's tons of work here. The firm is growing like crazy—intellectual property, litigation, commercial, transactional, it's all going nuts. If you want the work, you'll get it, no matter what it is." Another chimed in that "After I'd been here for three days, I wrote the jury instructions for a patent infringement case. I read all I could about it, bounced questions off my supervisor, and did it. They're always telling you, 'Just do your best, I'll review it, you'll improve it.'"

The assignment system at the firm is a combination of mentor and open assignment systems. Each associate works principally but not exclusively with a 'supervising partner.' In the beginning, most of the associate's work comes from that partner. But within a year or so associates work on projects with other lawyers, sometimes in conjunction with the supervising partner and sometimes not. As one associate described it, "I started out wanting intellectual property, and that's what I did for my first year. After that, they told me I was going to work with another partner, and they gave me a supervising partner who does more antitrust work. With this kind of system, you wind up working with partners throughout the firm, getting a smattering of everything. They do ask you what you want, but they also look at you and figure out the skills that you need. The firm tries to make you better-experienced; they try to get you projects that will make you a better-rounded lawyer." Another associate added that "We get some document reviews. Everybody does, you can't avoid it as a new associate, anywhere. But even when you do, even if it's not that interesting, you at least feel like you're working on an important case."

With the firm's loose assignment system, it pays to take the initiative. As one associate describes it, "If I hear about a case that's coming into the office and it sounds interesting, I'll go to that partner's door and knock, and ask, 'Do you need help?' Or you'll see office e-mails coming around, with people asking for help on cases. If you respond to those e-mails, you work on that project."

The firm also applauds steps associates take for their own development. One associate said, "Everything I've wanted to do, they've let me do. For instance, I wanted to go to seminars in other cities. I've never been told 'no'—if you can substantiate it because you will learn some new skills, the firm will back you on it." Another told a fascinating story about his first year at the firm. "It turns out that a guy from my college, a guy I didn't know, wound up playing for the Dallas Mavericks, the basketball team here. I dropped him a note basically mentioning I was from the same school, and shortly after that I ran into him on the street, totally by accident. We wound up chatting, and ultimately he suggested that maybe I could be his agent. When I told this to the firm, they sent me to New York to get my certification as a player's agent, and sent me to the East Coast to talk to this player's father, and even sent me around talking to other players. It was a substantial outlay of cash for the firm, with no promise of a return. I couldn't believe they'd give me that kind of latitude as a new associate. I would have expected them to say, 'You're a first year associate. You can't do that.' Instead, they had full confidence in me. And it gave me full confidence in them in return."

This 'help yourself' attitude extends to pro bono work, as well. One associate told that "When I was in law school, my son was born with a disease called GBS, which is actually the most frequent infectious disease killer of infants in this country. He turned out to be fine, but I naturally took a great interest in the disease. I researched it from a legal stand-point and wrote a paper about it. When I came here, the firm defends a lot of hospitals, and I figured they wouldn't be interested in what I'd written about. But when I showed it to people here, they encouraged me to publish the paper, and I took on the GBS Society as a pro bono client—all with the firm's encouragement."

"The hours are sometimes long, but there's no billable pressure at all."

Associates at Carrington Coleman point out that "When they say there's no billable hours requirement, they mean it." That doesn't, of course, mean that associates don't work hard; they do. It's typical for associates to work 10-hour days, with most associates coming to work by 8 a.m. and leaving by 7 p.m., with an hour for lunch. Some early risers come in early in the morning in order to leave by 5 and spend time with their families, and "The firm is very accommodating that way." One associate pointed out that "Of course if you're getting ready for trial, that can mean 12 to 14 hour days for four weeks at a time. It's all based on workload. But ordinarily, if you organize your time well, you can avoid long hours." Another added that, "I came here because people told me about the great quality of life, and that's been borne out in my experience."

The lack of a billable hours requirement has a number of benefits. For one thing, it gives associates a chance at hands-on training, which they very much enjoy. As one associate explained it, "There's minimal sitting down and teaching us the basics here. They have all the usual training sessions and seminars, but the more important idea is that you learn by doing. You learn the law by actually touching it. My first year here I was supposed to draft a complaint for a declaratory judgment. I had absolutely no idea how to do it—I learned it from ground zero, by researching it and asking lots of questions. It took me 10 days longer to do that than a partner would have taken, and none of my time was billed to the client. But the philosophy of the firm is that by taking that time now I know how to do this, and I won't have to ask questions anymore. I learned to do it right by not having billable hours pressure. That really gives you the extra time to learn things the right way." Another associate applauded the fact that "Everybody here is a stud, or stud-ette, at what they do. They're incredibly smart, very good lawyers. I feel like I improve my skills just by working with them."

Another associate added that "The size of the clients here, most of them are very large, means that we're not so restricted in how much time we can spend to find the right answers for them. I can turn over every stone if I want to, because our clients don't want thumbnail sketches of what we think they ought to do—they want complete answers. That means I don't have to worry about spending an extra 20 minutes doing electronic research. It sounds trivial, but it winds up being a big benefit. Whether it's taking the time to look up something on the computer or bounce ideas off a partner without fear of intruding, it's very rewarding."

"There's no hierarchy socially here—no dividing
line between partners and associates."

The lawyers at Carrington Coleman pride themselves on socializing 'up and down the ladder.' As one associate commented, "We're treated as people, not associates." Predictably enough, lawyers with families tend to socialize with other lawyers with families—"We have a firm maternity wardrobe that has circulated among us for years"—and those who are single socialize a lot together. Whether married or single, "If you want to go play golf, you'll always find someone who's willing to do that."

The firm puts on the usual slate of summer events, giving lawyers and their families a chance to get to know the summer associates. The firm fields 'spirited and occasionally talented' softball, basketball and flag football teams that play in local bar leagues. Every year, a group of lawyers takes a long weekend to make an annual pilgrimage in which they cram as many major and minor league baseball games as humanly possible. Lawyers get together for all kinds of informal pursuits like running in races, fly fishing in Montana, parties in lawyers' homes, and a couple of years ago, a few of the lawyers from the office went up to Alaska for a dog sled trip. As the "interests" lines for the lawyers in the firm's brochure indicate, "It doesn't matter how you like to spend your free time—if it's alone, that's OK. But no matter what you like, there's somebody else at the firm who's into the same thing."

As one associate at Carrington Coleman sighed, "Every day, I say to myself, 'Damn, I came to the right firm!'"

★ ★ ★ ★ ★

Cooley Godward L.L.P.

5 Palo Alto Square • 3000 El Camino Real • Palo Alto, CA 94303-2155
Phone: 650-843-5000 • Fax: 650-857-0663 • E-mail: webmaster@cooley.com
Web site: cooley.com

OFFICES

Palo Alto (main office), San Francisco, San Diego, Menlo Park, California;
Denver, Boulder, Colorado

*"At Cooley it's possible to have a life outside the office and still do a
very high quality of work . . . choosing it is a 'no-brainer.'"*

HIGHLIGHTS

- 68TH largest firm in the country; grew from a biotech boutique to a high tech specialist.
- Consistently ranked at the top of Bay Area firms in the *American Lawyer's* midlevel associate survey.
- Strong dedication to pro bono; pro bono hours are treated as billables.
- In the last few years, the firm has organized or reorganized more than 125 venture capital or buyout funds with subscribed capital of more than $4.5 billion.
- The firm's San Diego office has been called the city's "Hottest information technology and life sciences specialty firm" by the press.

NUTS AND BOLTS

Managing partner:

Lee F. Benton

Recruiting partner:

Martin L. Lagod, phone: 650-843-5000, e-mail: lagodml@cooley.com

Recruiting coordinator:

Olga M. Kearns, phone: 800-861-6889, e-mail: kearnsom@cooley.com

Number of attorneys in firm:

378 (113 partners)

WHOLE FIRM:

Women partners (18), women associates (131), minority partners (4), minority associates (55), disabled partners (0), disabled associates (1)

PALO ALTO OFFICE:

Total partners (55), total associates (144), women partners (11), women associates (71), minority partners (4), minority associates (23), disabled partners (0), disabled associates (1)

OTHER OFFICES:

(* represents an office profiled elsewhere in this book)
Please note that all offices of Cooley Godward received excellent reviews.

San Francisco: 104 (35 partners, 46 women, 22 minorities); San Diego: 38 (14 partners, 11 women, 4 minorities); Menlo Park: 12 (4 partners, 4 women, 1 minority); Boulder, CO: 20 (3 partners, 6 women, 1 minority); Denver, CO: 5 (2 partners, 1 minority)

Years to make partner:

6 to 8

WHAT DO THEY DO?

Primary specialties (more than 5% of practice) for the entire firm:

Corporate & Securities (122), Business & Regulatory Litigation (71), Information Technology/Licensing Healthcare (42), Technology Litigation/ Trademark Patent (52), Credit Finance/Creditors Rights/Bankruptcy (16), Employment/Labor/Immigration (24), Real Estate/Environmental (12), Tax/Compensation & Benefits/Estate Planning (24), Venture Capital (12), Mergers & Acquisitions (9).

The firm is departmentalized. Work is assigned differently depending on whether the associate is in a business or litigation department. In both cases, attorneys are divided into small working groups so that "people feel like they're not one of a sea of associates."

For the business department, work is assigned to associates through the team leader, as well as attorneys in other teams. The associate's team leader monitors those assignments. Associates are encouraged to let their team leaders know if they are particularly interested in a certain area, since there is a fair amount of flexibility in the assignment process. In addition to being given specific assignments, associates are assigned to a number of client teams. Work assignments come from other attorneys on the client teams as well as through the team leader. The team leader also monitors these assignments. The idea behind this system is to give associates an opportunity to work with a number of attorneys, and provide consistent contact with the firm's business clients and their work, while still allowing the team leader the chance to manage the overall workload and see that the associates have the opportunity to work on a variety of subjects with a variety of people, but not become overloaded.

For litigation, there are nine practice groups, and each office also maintains a general assignment pool comprised of associates with two years or less experience. All associates with more than two years' experience are expected to choose one or two practice groups.

Assignments for junior associates are normally made within each practice group. The Office Head for Litigation Management in each office (or a partner with that responsibility) makes assignments out of each office's general assignment pool.

Junior associates can, and do, switch specialties.

WHO DO THEY REPRESENT?

Clients include Sun Microsystems, Qualcomm, Amgen, Silicon Storage Technology, PETsMART, SunGard Data Systems, URS Corporation, ACC Consumer Finance, Elexsys International, Arris Pharmaceuticals, Gene Logic, Metabolex, Quantum Corp., SABRE Group.

WHERE NEW ASSOCIATES COME FROM . . .

The firm routinely interviews on campus at the following law schools: Boalt Hall, Chicago, Colorado, Columbia, UC Davis, Denver, Duke, Harvard, Hastings, Michigan, Northwestern, NYU, San Diego, Santa Clara, Stanford, UCLA, University of San Francisco, UVA, and Washington. The firm also routinely hires associates and summer associates from schools where it doesn't conduct on-campus interviews.

HOURS AND BUCKS . . .

On average, first year associates spend 2,479 hours at the office, of which the minimum billable hourly requirement is 1,900. The minimum billable hours requirement was instituted only a couple of years ago; the firm's intent is "not to use the requirement as a club to bludgeon people with."

Attorneys are allowed to work part-time, but not at entry level. The firm sometimes hires contract associates, and contract associates have become full time associates.

Typical first year salary, including typical bonus: $$$$ (Over $65,000)
(The firm is known for its very generous financial package.)

SUMMER PROGRAM . . .

Last year, there were 44 summer associates.

Weekly pay: $1,500

1Ls are routinely hired for the firm's summer program. Last year, the firm's 1Ls came from Santa Clara University (the firm hires 1Ls through the Bar Association Minority Student Program).

The firm's deadline for applying for the summer program is February through March.

PRO BONO . . .

The firm strongly encourages pro bono work. Pro bono hours are treated as billable hours. The firm staffs as an on-going basis the San Francisco Legal Aid Clinic Services Project; any matters that require continuing attention are then assigned to attorneys in the firm. The firm also staffs an intake session of the East Palo Alto Community Law Project every 10 weeks. In Southern California, pro bono projects are conducted on an ad hoc basis. Lawyers are also actively involved in other outside legal activities, ranging from the EarthJustice Legal Defense Fund to the U.S. Marine Corps, that may produce continuing projects. Lawyers who have projects of their own are encouraged to submit them to the Pro Bono Committee.

HISTORY AT A GLANCE . . .

Cooley Godward was founded in 1920 as Cooley & Crowley, in San Francisco.

In 1980, Cooley was one of the first San Francisco firms to establish an office in Silicon Valley, focusing primarily on high technology companies in the information technology and life sciences fields, as well as other high growth "emerging" industries, such as health care and specialty retail industries. By early 1998, this Palo Alto office had grown from four attorneys to 198.

The Menlo Park office opened in 1988, to capitalize on the burgeoning venture capital industry in the area.

In January 1992, the firm opened its San Diego office. And in September of 1993, the Boulder office opened to be near technology companies on Colorado's Front Range. The most recent office to open, in November 1994, is in Denver, which focuses on litigation.

Cowles & Thompson

901 Main Street, Suite 4000 • Dallas, TX 75202-3793
Phone: 214-672-2000 • Fax: 214-672-2020

OFFICES

Dallas (main office), Tyler, McKinney, Texas

*"There have been several times when I've met attorneys who say
that they know I'll be fair and honest with them, because I'm from
Cowles & Thompson. That makes me incredibly proud."*

HIGHLIGHTS

- Principally a trial and litigation firm; has one of the largest medical malpractice defense sections in Texas.
- Ranked as best law firm in Dallas for associate training in a recent issue of *Texas Lawyer.*
- Founding shareholder Jim Cowles named one of the top 12 lawyers in Dallas in 1996 by *D Magazine.*

NUTS AND BOLTS

Executive Committee:

William D. Cobb, Jr., Mark A. Stinnett, and David R. Woodward

Hiring partner:

John M. Pease, phone: 214-672-2145, e-mail: jmpease@ctpclaw.com

Recruiting coordinator:

Martha Notestine, phone: 214-672-2227, e-mail: mcnotes@ctpclaw.com

Number of attorneys in firm:

105 (51 shareholders)

DALLAS OFFICE:

Total attorneys (88), total shareholders (40), total associates (48)

OTHER OFFICES:

(* represents an office profiled elsewhere in this book)
Tyler, Texas (14); McKinney, Texas (4)

Years to make shareholder:

7

WHAT DO THEY DO?

Primary specialties (more than 5% of practice):

General Litigation, Business Litigation, Estate Planning & Trusts, Medical
Malpractice Litigation, Appellate, Corporate, Employment, Oil & Gas,
Healthcare Law, Insurance Coverage, Legal & other Professional Liability,
Public & Municipal Law.

The firm is departmentalized, although many lawyers work in more
than one discipline (*e.g.*, Medical Malpractice and General Litigation).
Each new associate is assigned a junior and a senior supervisor, through
whom their work flows. Young associates can, and do, switch specialties.

WHO DO THEY REPRESENT?

A vast array of diverse clients, including aviation (including Beech
Aircraft); Corporations (including Coca-Cola, Marathon Oil, ORYX
Energy, Payless Cashways, The Southland Corporation, Southwestern Bell
Telephone, Vingcard, and many others); banking (including NationsBank
of Texas, PMC Capital); many cities and towns; and transportation
(including Southern Pacific, Caliber Systems, Dallas Area Rapid Transit,
FEE Transportation Services, Fleetline, John Deere, and Viking Freight
Systems); many insurance companies (including State Farm Insurance,
Allstate Insurance, Blue Cross & Blue Shield of Texas, among many others),
claims management companies (including Alexsis, Crawford & Co., GAB
Business Services, Gallagher and Bassett, General Star Management, Lobo
Claims Management, and Risk Enterprise Management); medical malprac-
tice and professional liability companies (including CAN Insurance, Harris
Methodist Hospital, Kemper National P & Co Companies, UT
Southwestern Medical Center, and many others); health care companies
(including the Baylor College of Dentistry, Baylor Health Care Systems,
BloodCare, Irving Healthcare System, and St. Paul Medical Center).

WHERE NEW ASSOCIATES COME FROM . . .

The firm routinely does on-campus interviewing at the following law
schools: University of Texas, Baylor University, Texas Tech, SMU, and the

University of Houston. The firm hires from schools where it doesn't do on-campus interviewing.

HOURS AND BUCKS . . .

First year associates typically spend 2,250 (or 9 hours a day) at the firm.

Minimum billable hours requirement for first year associates: 1,800.

Part-time work is available to continuing and entry-level associates on a case-by-case basis. The firm occasionally hires contract associates, of whom some have become permanent associates.

Typical first year associate salary, including typical bonus: $$$ ($50-65,000)

SUMMER PROGRAM . . .

Last summer, there were 12 summer associates, 10 of whom received offers (and all 10 accepted).

Weekly pay: $1,150 last summer

1Ls are generally not hired for the summer program, although exceptions have been made over the years.

There is no particular deadline for summer clerkships, though early fall applicants are definitely preferred.

PRO BONO . . .

The firm encourages pro bono work, but it is considered optional. The firm staffs the North Texas Legal Services Clinic twice each year. For 10 consecutive years, the firm has received awards and recognition for pro bono contributions of its attorneys and staff, and many attorneys have received individual awards for outstanding pro bono service.

Associates have been involved in various projects. Some of the firm's lawyers serve on the U.S. District Court, North District of Texas, Dallas Division's Criminal Justice Act Volunteer Attorney Panel and accept appointments to defend indigent criminals.

HISTORY AT A GLANCE . . .

The firm was founded in 1978 by six lawyers, and has grown since then to number more than 100 attorneys in four offices in Texas.

The star of the Dallas office is Jim Cowles, a founding shareholder, who was named as one of Dallas' top twelve lawyers by *D Magazine.*

WHAT IT'S LIKE TO WORK THERE . . .

You're interviewing with prominent law firms all over Texas. You're not wild about what you find, thinking that some of the firms you visit are overly formal, even patronizing. Then you come to one particular firm, and as you're led through the offices, you are introduced to every employee, lawyer or not. You come to a guy kneeling on the carpet, scrubbing up a coffee stain. You are introduced to the carpet cleaner, who turns out to be . . . founding partner Jim Cowles, one of the most respected lawyers in Texas.

Welcome to Cowles & Thompson.

The lawyer who recounted this story said that "It convinced me more than anything else to accept C&T's offer. It showed me a down-to-earth, get-things-done atmosphere that's persisted ever since."

The 'down to earth' sense is reflected in the firm's dress code of 'casual Fridays' throughout the year, and casual dress all summer long (within the bounds of good taste—no bathing suits!). And the opportunity to 'get things done' starts almost as soon as you walk through the door. One associate said that, "I tried my first lawsuit two months after I was licensed. It wasn't a big lawsuit by objective standards, I guess, but it was important to me and of course to my clients. The firm let me handle the case completely, with senior attorneys there whenever I needed advice. After we won, Jim Cowles and many of the other lawyers and staffers stopped by to congratulate me on the win. It was nice to know that the firm supports us irrespective of the size of the cases we're handling." Other associates talk of getting the chance to "carry their own briefcase" very soon after joining C&T. Many try their first lawsuits, argue their first hearings, take their first depositions only days—and in some cases hours—after they start. One associate comments that "Although the senior attorneys are supportive and always available if I need guidance, I've gotten a tremendous amount of autonomy and responsibility for managing cases assigned to me. From day one, I've been treated as an attorney, not a trainee." As one associate tells it, "This is a great place to get experience in a broad range of areas early in your career. It's not the kind of place where you're going to be spending your time researching obscure points of law. While some of my friends are stuck in the library at other places, I've tried all kinds of cases. I even defended a guy on a claim arising when his 450-pound pet lion, Dexter, attacked a visitor. I guess you could say I was thrown to the lions early!"

Junior associates at C&T feel comfortable handling their own cases largely because of the firm's well-respected training program. In a recent issue of *Texas Lawyer,* the firm was ranked best in Dallas in associate training. As one associate told the magazine, "This firm does an excellent job of training its associates, involving them in firm decisions, and treating them as pros. I have worked for one of the 'national' firms, where there is an 'us' and 'them' relationship between associates and partners."

The training program includes seminars on trial practice, and a mock trial program for mid-level associates. Aside from formal training, the firm jollies junior associates along by giving them progressively more responsibility on cases. With a low partner-to-associate ratio, associates feel as though the firm "treats us as though we're all going to be future shareholders. You don't get the feeling you're going to be 'weeded out' along the way."

While there is more assurance that they will make partner, along the way C&T associates have to deal with the reality that they don't earn as much as multi-hundred lawyer national firms. The firm is candid with new associates that because of the size of the firm and the nature of the practice that while the pay is handsome by any objective measure, if what they want is to make top dollar they're at the wrong place. As one associate says, "There's always going to be somebody who resents that they're not making as much as somebody at another, bigger firm. Once in a great while you'll hear somebody whine that they shouldn't have to work as hard as associates at some other firms because they aren't making the same money. The fact is, you know that ultimately you're going to do well here because you've got such a better chance of being a shareholder than you do anywhere else. You have to believe that the money issue works itself out over a very few years, and according to everything I've seen, it does."

"The camaraderie here is rare."

Associates at C&T rave that "many of my fellow associates have become great friends." At weddings, it's not unusual for most of the bridesmaids or groomsmen to be colleagues from C&T. And lawyers tend to like the atmosphere so much that they stay on instead of jumping ship—a recent survey of Dallas firms showed C&T near the top in retaining associates. As one associate pointed out, "At this firm it doesn't matter if you're young or not-so-young, a man or a woman, tall or short, Republican or Democrat, married or single, a native Texan or an adopted Texan or someone who's rejected Texas citizenship altogether, you're part of the team here." Another pointed out that "It's obvious even to the summer clerks that we like to work together. Last year, all of the clerks had also clerked for other firms, but every one who got an offer from us accepted it."

The firm fosters a friendly atmosphere in a variety of formal and not-so-formal ways. On the formal side there is the ritual involving bar results. As one associate tells it, "Every year, there's some mystery about when the Texas bar results will come out, because it's never the same day. When we get word from the courthouse that the results are about to be released, the staff orders cakes and balloons and champagne, and they pull out the business cards that have been printed out months before for the new associates who took the bar exam. When the results are announced, our managing partner, Jim Cowles, administers the oath and gives them their business cards." The associate added, "It sounds kind of corny, but for a lot of us it's our favorite time of year."

The firm similarly celebrates successes by any of the lawyers. As one associate explained, "With over a hundred lawyers, we can't really have an

'L.A. Law' type meeting every week to discuss all of our cases and announce our victories. But the firm thinks it's important to pat us on the back when we do well, and they have a unique way of showing it. Whenever you win a trial or an appeal, Jim Cowles makes a handmade sign that says either "GTL," for Great Trial Lawyer, or "GAL," for Great Appellate Lawyer, and he puts the sign on the victorious lawyer's door. Winning a trial or an appeal all by itself is a great experience, but that's magnified when everybody who walks by sees the sign and stops in to congratulate you! Believe me, when you get one of those signs, it's one of your most treasured mementos."

The firm's caring nature comes to the forefront when anyone at C&T runs into trouble. Last Christmas, a support staffer's mother lost everything she owned in a house fire. The firm rallied with donations of food, furniture, clothes and money. A few years before, when another employee's house was destroyed in a tornado, the firm again stepped up to the plate with money, clothing, and food, and one employee even donated a place for the family to live until the home could be rebuilt. And when a well-liked legal assistant in the office was diagnosed with terminal cancer, the firm responded by raising several thousand dollars to send her and her husband on the first-class cruise they had always dreamed of.

In the community, beyond pro bono cases, every summer the firm takes part in a local project called "People Helping People." As one associate explains it, "We go out with scrapers, brushes, paint, hammers, all kinds of home improvement stuff, and spent a day painting and working on a needy Dallas resident's house. It's not what you'd call typical summer clerk 'entertainment,' but we always include the summer clerks, and everybody gives the project high marks. It makes you feel good to help the community."

C&T takes advantage of almost any excuse to hold a party. There are, of course, the usual summer activities, including ranch outings, and attorney-clerk softball games for which the firm prints T-shirts and invites all of the families of the lawyers. The firm also has its own choir, consisting of lawyers and staffers, who start practicing every November for an annual "spectacular" at the firm's Christmas party. The firm is particularly proud of its luxury suite at the Ballpark at Arlington, where the Texas Rangers play. As one associate describes it, "It's pretty wild. The managing partner, Hardy Thompson, designed it, and it's got stuff like 'baseball' glass-top tables and a giant baseball glove beanbag." When the firm isn't using the suite to entertain clients, it gives tickets to the associates and staffers on a first-come, first-served basis. There are also firm softball, flag football, and basketball teams, and on top of that, there are lawyers who get together to go to the theater, or play golf or tennis or go back-packing. In short, they're a tremendously social lot, with an extracurricular activity to suit just about everybody. As one associate recounts, "It doesn't matter what you want to do, there'll be people from the office there to support you. We had an associate last year who ran in her first marathon. She was greeted at several mile markers, and of course at the finish line, by numerous screaming fans from the office."

All in all, comments one associate, "Whenever you see surveys of law firms, you always see Cowles & Thompson in the very top ranks when they're talking about how contented associates are. That says it all, to me."

Davis, Polk & Wardwell

450 Lexington Avenue • New York, NY 10017
Phone: 212-450-4000 • Fax: 212-450-4800 • Web site: dpw.com

OFFICES

New York City (main office), New York; Washington, D.C.

HIGHLIGHTS

- 32ND largest firm in the country.
- Broadest, most extensive international business practice of any law firm in the country.
- Strong dedication to pro bono work.
- Ranked first among 25 major New York firms in minority hiring, according to a survey in *The New York Law Journal* in April 1997.
- Marked dedication to diversity—the firm's 515 attorneys include 212 women and 106 members of minority groups.

WORD ON THE STREET . . .

"They're good at generating loyalty. Their partners are 'home grown.'"
"They tend to hire only new associates—no laterals."
"They have a unique loan repayment program."

NUTS AND BOLTS

Managing partner:

Francis J. Morison

Hiring partner:

Gail A. Flesher, phone: 212-450-4469, e-mail: flesher@dpw.com

Legal staff and recruiting admistrator:

Bonnie Hurry, phone: 212-450-4143, e-mail: hurry@dpw.com

Number of attorneys in firm:

544 (123 partners)

WHOLE FIRM:

Partners (123), women partners (22), minority partners (6)

NEW YORK OFFICE:

Partners (109), associates (348), women partners (21), minority partners (5)

OTHER OFFICES:

(* represents an office profiled elsewhere in this book)
Washington, D.C. (3); London (33); Paris (3); Frankfurt (5); Tokyo (5); Hong Kong (17)

Years to make partner:

Approximately 7

WHAT DO THEY DO?

Primary specialties (more than 5% of practice):

Corporate (354), Litigation (129), Taxation (45), Trusts & Estates (10), General (6).

New associates may either join a particular department (if they know what they want to do), or remain unassigned for a year, doing projects for different departments until they choose which one they want to join.

WHO DO THEY REPRESENT?

The firm represents companies worldwide.

WHERE NEW ASSOCIATES COME FROM . . .

Davis Polk routinely interviews on campus at the following law schools: Boalt Hall, Boston College, Boston University, Brooklyn, Chicago, Columbia, Cornell, Duke, Fordham, Georgetown, Harvard, Howard, Michigan, NYU, Northwestern, Pennsylvania, Pittsburgh, Rutgers, St. John's, Stanford, Texas, Tulane, Vanderbilt, Virginia, and Yale.

The firm also routinely hires associates and summer associates from schools where it doesn't interview on campus.

HOURS AND BUCKS . . .

There is no minimum billable hours requirement.

Part-time work is available to ongoing associates. The firm does not routinely hire contract associates.

Typical first year associate salary, including typical bonus: $$$$ (Over $65,000). The firm is known for its particularly generous financial package.

SUMMER PROGRAM . . .

Last year, there were 85 summer associates, all of whom received offers.
Weekly pay last year: $1,925
The firm does not hire 1Ls for its summer program.

PRO BONO . . .

Associates are encouraged to pursue the kind of voluntary pro bono commitment they find rewarding. Pro bono work is considered Firm work, of equal stature to regular matters, and is generally conducted in the Firm's name. Pro bono time is included as part of attorney time on Firm matters, and both regular performance evaluations and partner selection take into account work on pro bono matters. The Firm employs a full-time Pro Bono Coordinator who serves as a liaison to the City's pro bono community and works with individual lawyers to match their interests with the needs of public service organizations.

As a reflection of the Firm's approach to pro bono, the associates work on a wide variety of projects, including: housing, employment, education, welfare, arts law, criminal defense and appeals, domestic violence, and civil rights. The Firm's current pro bono docket includes class action litigation challenging certain aspects of the City's workfare policies, representation of tenants groups in building-wide litigation, extensive political asylum and immigration work, including a challenge to the expedited removal provisions of the new immigration law, and representation of battered women seeking divorces. The Firm's corporate lawyers undertake pro bono work focused primarily on community development, providing real estate, financing, and tax advice to projects that produce affordable housing and assist in the development of small businesses.

There is no requirement that lawyers perform pro bono service, nor is there any upper limit on the amount of time they may dedicate to approved projects. Last year, on average, associates devoted 64.5 hours to pro bono.

HISTORY AT A GLANCE . . .

The firm was founded almost 150 years ago. Over the years it has developed a reputation for complex business and financial transactions, and has also been involved in headline-making litigation.

Davis Wright Tremaine L.L.P.

1300 S. W. Fifth Avenue, Suite 2300 • Portland, Oregon 97201
Phone: 503-241-2300 • Fax: 503-778-5299 • E-mail: lesliedustin@dwt.com
Web site: dwt.com

OFFICES

Portland (Seattle-based firm), Oregon

*"There's no question that the firm expects you to be a darn good
lawyer, but it also expects that that's not **all** you'll be. From what
I've seen an attitude like that attracts a breadth of skill and interest
that benefits not only us but our clients as well."*

HIGHLIGHTS

- Portland office of a Seattle-based firm, the 99TH largest firm in the
  country.
- Serious dedication to pro bono work; pro bono hours are considered
  billables.

NUTS AND BOLTS

Managing partner:

   Rodney E. Lewis, Jr. is the Partner-in-Charge

Hiring partner:

   Thomas S. Hillier, phone: 503-241-2300, e-mail: tomhillier@dwt.com

Recruiting coordinator:

   Leslie J. Dustin, phone: 503-778-5243, e-mail: lesliedustin@dwt.com

Number of attorneys in firm:

   313 (182 partners)

WHOLE FIRM:

Women partners (26), women associates (77), minority partners (9), minority associates (15), disabled partners (0), disabled associates (0)

PORTLAND OFFICE:

Total attorneys (77), total partners (45), total associates (29), women partners (5), women associates (13), minority partners (2), minority associates (4), disabled partners (0), disabled associates (0), of counsel (3)

OTHER OFFICES:

(* represents an office profiled elsewhere in this book)
Anchorage, Alaska (10); Bellevue, Washington (20); Boise, Idaho (4); Charlotte, North Carolina (4); Honolulu, Hawaii (4); Los Angeles, California (18); Richland, Washington (1); San Francisco, California (20); Seattle, Washington (143); Washington, D.C. (8); Shanghai, China (2)

Years to make partner:

Between 6 and 7

WHAT DO THEY DO?

Primary specialties (more than 5% of practice):

The firm is not strictly departmentalized; instead, it has practice groups in which lawyers specialize. The firm doesn't assign associates to practice groups; partners can work with any associate and associates can request work from any partner. As associates decide which practice areas they like and where there is enough work, they begin to specialize and work more within the practice group. Associates can also develop their own practices.

Current practice groups include Antitrust; Banking/Finance; Bankruptcy/Creditors' Rights; Business/Corporate; Communications/Media; Consumer Products; Education; Employee Benefits; Employment/ Labor; Energy/Regulatory; Entertainment/Sports; Environmental/ Natural Resources; Food/Agriculture; Government Relations; Healthcare; Hospitality; Intellectual Property; International; Litigation; Mergers & Acquisitions; Municipal Finance; Real Estate/Land Use/ Construction; Securities; Tax/Trusts & Estates; Technology; Telecommunications; Transportation.

WHO DO THEY REPRESENT?

A broad variety of clients, including AT&T; Bank of America; Blockbuster Video; Costco; Crabble Huson Group; Komatsu Silicon America; NBC; Oregon Television (Oregno's 12/KPTV); Saguro; Smurfit Newsprint;

Software AG; Sony; Toshiba; Tri-Met; Tristar Pictures; United of Omaha Life Insurance; Vernonia School District; Viacom.

WHERE NEW ASSOCIATES COME FROM . . .

DWT routinely interviews on campus at the following law schools: University of Oregon, Northwestern School of Law at Lewis & Clark College, Willamette, University of Washington, the University of Michigan.

Other offices of DWT interview regularly at Stanford, Boalt Hall, Northwestern, Chicago, Seattle University, Yale, Harvard, Columbia, NYU, Georgetown, and UVA.

The firm plans to add several other Midwestern, eastern, and California schools in this and coming years.

In addition to on-campus interviews, DWT hires from schools where it does not interview on campus.

HOURS AND BUCKS . . .

First year associates typically spend between 2,250 to 2,500 hours at the office; 1,700 hours is the minimum billable hour requirement.

The firm does have part-time attorneys, and part-time work is available at entry level on a case-by-case basis. The Portland office currently has one part-time associate and two part-time partners, and one part-time associate made partner last year. The firm does not routinely hire contract associates.

Attorneys are encouraged to take a three-month sabbatical after their fifth year as partner.

Typical first year associate salary, including typical bonus: $$$ ($50-65,000)

SUMMER PROGRAM . . .

Last year, there were four 2Ls, three of whom received offers.

Weekly pay: $1,100

1Ls are hired for the summer program periodically, most recently from the University of Oregon and Harvard.

Deadline for applying for summer program: October 1 for 2Ls, and January 1 for 1Ls (March 1 for the Oregon state Bar Affirmative Action First Year Honors Program).

PRO BONO . . .

DWT is involved in a tremendous number of community activities, reflecting its philosophy that to be of service to its clients it must be aware of the concerns and needs of its neighbors and friends in the community. The firm has a "pro bono hours bank" whereby attorneys may receive billable hour credit for pro bono work. The pro bono bank for DWT's Portland office includes approximately 4,350 a year.

Associates get to choose their own pro bono clients, provided the client is approved through regular file opening/conflict checking procedures. Examples of recent and/or current associate pro bono work projects include providing legal services to Open Adoption and Family Services, St. Andrews Legal Clinic, and low income people with tax disputes. The firm is general counsel to Oregon Water Trust on a pro bono basis. The firm also represents pro bono Community Action Organization (a nonprofit organization that serves low income people); Planned Parenthood of the Columbia/Willamette Valley against anti-choice activists; elderly indigent citizens with a variety of legal issues; Gales Creek Camp Foundation (a camp for diabetic children); and the Oregon chapter of the National Multiple Sclerosis Society. It has represented a college student who was being stalked by a man who worked on campus and has recently accepted an ABA pro bono case to represent a man convicted of murder and sentenced to death in Nevada in state and federal post-conviction proceedings.

Some other pro bono clients include the Greater Portland Chapter of the Susan G. Komen Foundation, Pacific Crest Outward Bound, the Boys and Girls Clubs of the Portland Metropolitan Area, Springleaf Chinese School, Chinese Friendship Association of Portland, Japanese Immersion Education Foundation, and Mercy Corporation International.

HISTORY AT A GLANCE . . .

In 1985, the firms of Ragen, Roberts, O'Scannlain, Robertson & Neill (founded in 1976) and Black, Tremaine, Lankton, Krieger & Schmeer (founded in 1911) merged. Each of these small firms (20 to 25 attorneys) had a friendly, family-like environment, which the new firm of Ragen, Tremaine, Krieger, Schmeer & Neill made great efforts to maintain.

In 1990, Ragen, Tremaine—at that point numbering 55 attorneys—merged with Davis, Wright & Jones (a firm founded in 1908, with 138 attorneys, with offices in various Washington cities, as well as Anchorage and D.C.) to form Davis Wright Tremaine. The merger gave DWT's Portland office the best of both worlds—all of the advantages of a large, regional firm, while still maintaining a small-medium firm atmosphere.

WHAT IT'S LIKE TO WORK THERE . . .

You're in law school. You're ambitious. You spend your summer clerkship at a large firm, and you start dreaming about how to get ahead there. You look at ways to bring in clients, and you actually go out and get clients while you're still a summer associate. You work hard. When you come back as a permanent associate after graduation, you figure when the time comes, you'll be a partner.

At Davis Wright, don't blink. It might only take you three years to make it to partner. In fact, it already happened—a DWT associate just made partner just three years out of law school!

While not every associate is going to have a track record like that—in fact, we may be looking at the only third year associate at any large firm in the entire *country* to make partner—Davis Wright definitely rewards initiative, on every level, with bonuses for bringing in business and working extra hours, and great work for associates who go after it. As one associate said, "There's no point in coming here if you're the kind of person who wants to sit in your office and wait for work. It pays to get out and talk to people about what they're doing, about what you can do to help out." Another associate advised that "It's important to be able to 'multitask'—you've got to be able to take on more than one or a few assignments at once."

One associate explained that "You get assignments from all kinds of people. You do bits of everything. You'll get calls from partners and senior associates, saying what they've got and asking if you can help out." This associate acknowledged that "Getting work from all directions sometimes makes it hard to regulate your workload, especially when you're new—you want to say 'yes' to everybody and everything. But the fact is that people are really receptive to being put off. If they get a 'no' from a couple of junior associates, they'll just go to the head of a practice area to informally see how busy other people are." And if you want to try a different practice area, "If the firm needs attorneys in what you want to do, they'll set up travel so you can meet people who do what you want to do in the firm's other offices. I've heard about associates spending sometimes weeks or months with specialists in other offices so they can develop expertise in a particular practice area."

The point behind this kind of exposure to different kinds of projects and multiple personalities is to get new associates feeling like a part of the firm as quickly as possible. The firm makes a point of hiring "future partners, not 'profit centers.'" New associates get two mentors—a senior associate and a partner—to help usher them into the practice. They also formally learn right away how to bring in business, both through writing proposals and, if they're comfortable with it, through community activities like speaking to local groups or writing articles.

New associates immediately find themselves learning the ropes by actually working on projects with teams of more experienced lawyers in the firm. One second year associate raved about working directly with a very high profile public charity. Another associate, who had been with the firm only a month, talked about dealing one-on-one with the general counsel for a Fortune 100 company, and also representing a NASDAQ client on a small matter before the FDIC. The associate commented that "It wasn't a big deal in the overall scheme of things, but it wasn't bad for somebody who's only been a lawyer for a month, especially in light of what some of my law school classmates have been doing."

While associates get a lot of exposure to different projects, they aren't hung out to dry. As one associate explained, "All of the offices of the firm in all different states are hooked up via e-mail. You get the sense that you've got 300 lawyers to rely on even though they're not in your office. You can just get on e-mail, and say, 'Has anybody ever come across this weird situation?' And you'll get an answer back, maybe from somebody you've never actually met in person." Another explained that "I can go to anybody here, I can walk into the managing partner's office with what I think might be a silly question, and he'll say, 'Well, here's my experience with it.' You can literally toss ideas around with anybody here without feeling uncomfortable."

"Compared to all of the other firms where I interviewed, this place is pretty relaxed."

You'd think that a firm that so highly prizes initiative would have a "chew 'em up, spit 'em out" attitude toward junior associates. That's not the case with Davis Wright. For one thing, the hours are livable—or at least they become that way very quickly. As one junior associate described it, "As a first year associate you tend to work longer hours, but that's not so much because the firm is working you to death but because of the normal new associate fears, like the idea that you're going to commit malpractice. What that translates into is that it takes you an hour to write a letter that says 'Enclosed are your documents.' But that goes away in a hurry. The senior associates here keep an eye on new associates to make sure they're not working too much. They'll tell you that it's not expected, and even more than that, that it'll wear you out, especially if they find out you're coming in on weekends."

One associate pointed out that most people come in around 8:30 or 9 a.m, and are gone by 5 or 5:30 p.m. She explained that "There's a definite attitude here of 'I like to get my work done and get out.'" People with childcare concerns can get in at 7 a.m. and leave correspondingly earlier. On top of that, there are part-time attorneys, both associates and partners. One associate explained her experience: "The firm is very flexible toward leaves. At the end of my first year, I took an extended parental leave. I came back on a part-time basis so that I could not only spend time with my child, but also so I could get involved in the arts and other community activities I'd been wanting to spend time on. When I had my second child, I took another extended parental leave, and I'm still working part-time." She continued, "There's no question that the firm expects you to be a darn good lawyer, but it also expects that that's not *all* you'll be. From what I've seen an attitude like that attracts a breadth of skill and interest that benefits not only us but our clients as well."

The firm's attitude toward encouraging its attorneys to be well-rounded extends to the kind of people it likes to attract. It prefers law students and graduates with "real world experience, rather than being educated in a vacuum." The firm says that, "Associates who don't have work experience seem less able to identify with clients. They are more likely to think that their task is to answer an academic question, when what the client really wants is specific advice. With prior work experience it's easier for associates to catch on quickly to what it means to be an advocate for clients." The backgrounds of Davis Wright's lawyers reflect this philosophy. One associate has 15 years' experience as a journalist. There are former CEO's, former nurses, a Ph.D. in neurophysiology. There are former teachers, pastors, engineers, bankers, military officers—the list goes on and on. As one associate explained it, "When I interviewed here, it was very important to me to feel comfortable where I work. What I like about DWT is that there is lots of room here for different kinds of people. Some people here go camping together, some people run together every day at lunch, some have never eaten a vegetable in their lives and they go to Happy Hour together every night. Whatever you want to do, there's somebody here who's like you." On top of this casual socializing, the firm hosts all kinds of social events, including an annual retreat at the Black Butte Ranch near Sisters, Oregon, for all the lawyers in the office. Mixed in with a little bit of CLE are all kinds of games—foosball, ping-pong, poker, as well as dancing and a golf tournament. (At the end of the golf tournament, there is an unsportsmanlike conduct award handed out, which is named after a partner whose club somehow ended up in a lake during a past tournament.)

Once new associates get to Davis Wright, they find a firm that is "Responsive to associate concerns," according to one junior associate. "There is an associate's committee, and they make a point of coming around and asking if you have any issues. If you have a question about bonuses, or anything really, you can bring it up." Another associate added that, "The firm is very responsive to associate concerns. There's a great amount of accountability to the associates. For instance, there's a real sharing of numbers here, from the top down. They tell us on a monthly basis how the firm is doing in terms of profits, things like that. You feel like you're really part of the team." The firm further fosters this team feeling by weeding out anybody who has a hierarchical approach to an office. As one associate explained, "They don't just pay lip service to 'getting along' or this whole 'team' business. I heard that they actually turned away a potential lateral hire who had a $1 million book of business just because he'd had a history of mistreating the associates and staff who worked for him." Another associate said that, "They make a real effort here to erase any 'us and them' distinctions between partners and associates, and lawyers and staff. It's just inappropriate to treat staff poorly here. There might be a dinosaur or two among the partners who refuse to learn to type, but that's very much not the norm. It's not the kind of place where you'll ever hear anybody yelling at their secretary."

One Davis Wright lawyer summed up the firm by saying, "We pride ourselves in doing excellent legal work without taking ourselves too seriously. As one of our partners says, 'If it isn't fun, it isn't worth doing.'"

Fish & Richardson P.C.

225 Franklin Street • Boston, MA 02110-2804
Phone: 617-542-5070 • Fax: 617-542-8906 • Web site: fr.com

OFFICES

Boston, Massachusetts; La Jolla, Menlo Park, California; New York City, New York; Minneapolis, Minnesota; Washington, D.C.

"I feel like a lawyer now, instead of a person who pushes paper."

HIGHLIGHTS

- Third largest intellectual property and technology firm in the country, with one of the largest biotechnology practices in America.
- Uses cutting-edge computer technology, including filing the first ever CD-ROM brief in hypertext markup (the language used on web sites), in a patent infringement case in the U.S. Court of Appeals for the Federal Circuit.
- A fully-equipped mock courtroom set up to mimic in detail the Federal Circuit Court in Washington, D.C., where patent cases are heard—equipped with four hidden video cameras which focus on the judges, witnesses, jurors and attorneys. Gives lawyers a chance to watch simultaneously the facial expressions on all courtroom participants, hone their arguments and prepare witnesses.
- As one of the oldest patent firms in America, has represented many historic clients, including Alexander Graham Bell.
- Voted 'best large law firm website' in the legal web challenge in 1997.

NUTS AND BOLTS

Managing partner:

Robert E. Hillman

Hiring partner:

Wayne E. Willenberg

Recruiting coordinator:

Jill E. McDonald; phone: 619-678-4369; e-mail: jmcdonald@fr.com

Number of attorneys in firm:

148 (59 principals)

TOTAL FIRM:

Partners (59), associates (81), women partners (8), women associates (20), minority partners (2), minority associates (7), disabled partners (0), disabled associates (0), of counsel (8)

THIS OFFICE:

Total attorneys (65), partners (29), associates (33), women partners (3), women associates (4), minority partners (1), minority associates (2), disabled partners (0), disabled associates (0), of counsel (3)

OTHER OFFICES:

(* represents an office profiled elsewhere in this book):
La Jolla, CA (17); Menlo Park, CA (24); New York, NY (17); Minneapolis, MN (13); Washington, D.C. (12)

Years to make partner:

8

WHAT DO THEY DO?

Primary specialties (more than 5% of practice):

Intellectual property and technology law—100% of practice.

The practice is divided into four broad groups: litigation; prosecution; trademark & copyright; and regulatory.

WHO DO THEY REPRESENT?

The company has a variety of high-profile and interesting clients, more than a thousand all together, from small companies to research institutions to Fortune 50 corporations, including Bose, Steinway, Dyonics, Ben & Jerry's Homemade, Adobe Systems, Concept Design Electronics and Manufacturing, PPG Industries, 3M, Nordica, Braun, Lotus Development, and Keds.

(The firm has a very cool "patent and trademark gallery" on its homepage, at fr.com/working/about/f_patentgallery.html)

WHERE NEW ASSOCIATES COME FROM . . .

F&R routinely conducts on-campus interviews at the following law schools: Berkeley, Boston College, Boston University, Columbia, Duke,

George Washington, Georgetown, Harvard, Iowa, New York University, Santa Clara, Stanford, Michigan, Minnesota, USC, Texas, UVA, Wisconsin, Houston, William Mitchell, and Yale. The firm does hire associates and summer associates from schools where it doesn't do on-campus interviewing.

HOURS AND BUCKS . . .

Billable hour goal for first year associates: 2,000 hours

Part-time work is available on a case-by-case basis, for both continuing and entry level associates. The firm does not routinely hire contract associates.

Typical first year associate salary, including typical bonus: $$$$ (over $65,000).

SUMMER PROGRAM . . .

Summer associate program: Last summer, there were 21 summer associates, 19 of whom received offers.

Weekly pay: $1,730

The firm periodically hires 1Ls for its summer program; there was one 1L in the program last summer.

There is no deadline for the summer program, but the firm recommends that 2Ls apply by October 1, and for 1Ls the suggested date is January 15.

PRO BONO . . .

The firm approves pro bono work on a case-by-case basis. The attorneys have provided pro bono representation in a number of intellectual property and non-intellectual property areas, consistent with attorneys' personal interests and legal expertise.

HISTORY AT A GLANCE . . .

Fish & Richardson is one of the oldest law firms in this book, and has one of the most fascinating histories. It was founded in 1878 by Frederick Perry Fish as the law firm of Wadleigh & Fish, in Boston. One of its biggest cases was to successfully defend American Bell Telephone and Alexander Graham Bell's patent on the telephone against a challenge. In the years thereafter the firm prosecuted and litigated many of the fundamental patents of an industrialized America, representing inventors like the Wright Brothers. Fish became one of the most highly respected lawyers in the country; by 1920 his reputation reached such stratospheric proportions that clients literally formed lines in the reception room to see him. By the time he died in 1930, it was said that he had represented one side or the other in almost all the great patent cases between 1890 and 1930.

The firm stayed relatively small through the 1980's; in 1987, the firm had 25 attorneys. Since then, it has grown eightfold and opened several new offices nationwide, until today it has 164 lawyers.

WHAT IT'S LIKE TO WORK THERE . . .

When you look at Fish & Richardson, you realize why intellectual property is an increasingly popular specialty. The firm does projects that are inherently interesting and sexy. Its lawyers have created the patents for all kinds of familiar gadgets, from the highly-publicized Bose Acoustic Waveguide Loudspeaker System, to man-made ivory for Steinway piano keys, to trademarking logos like Ben & Jerry's familiar ice cream label. And Fish & Richardson's patent litigation is no less interesting. It has been lead counsel for 3M for a patent infringement suit involving 'Post-It' notes. It has represented Keds to enforce the company's familiar "Blue Label" logo against infringement. It has protected Nordica in litigation involving ski boot patents . . . the list goes on and on. As one associate enthuses, "We have a cutting-edge practice. It's fast-moving, dynamic and challenging. Many of the cases we work on involve issues that have little or no precedent."

The firm reflects its practice with fascinating innovations of its own. It recently filed the first ever hypertext appellate brief, "the most significant innovation in recent appellate practice." With multimedia tools, the firm's appellate group can prepare briefs either on compact disc or post them on an Internet site. The first of these briefs let the firm pack the equivalent of 20,000 pages of documents, including the appellate brief, the case record, evidence, depositions and the transcript of the lower court proceedings, all cross-referenced, so that at the touch of a computer key, the appellate judge could instantly view any other document referred to throughout the brief. As one associate points out, the hypertext brief "went from drawing board to final cut on the compact disc in less than a month." Another associate added that, "The firm fosters the kind of environment that welcomes innovation. We don't practice law by formula."

"This is one of the few IP firms where you can do both prosecution and litigation."

The firm is divided into four broad practice groups. Regulatory, which handles food and drug technology regulation; litigation; prosecution; and trademark & copyright. Associates appreciate that in each of the groups, they can do both "prosecution and litigation. You don't have to choose." One associate pointed out that "If you do litigation, you take depositions and appear in court shortly after you join the firm." Patent prosecutors get to "Meet with inventors and begin preparing patent applications as soon as we get here." The firm has an "informal assignment structure" that gives associates the ability to decide "with whom and on which assignments they will work." Associates are encouraged to "solicit work from any attorney," in any of F&R's seven offices nationwide.

Associates rave that the firm's "entrepreneurial atmosphere" gives them a chance to work on projects that particularly interest them, and to get a diversity of experience "right from the start." They are not, however, left out on a limb. As one associate points out, "You get hand-holding if you need it; if you don't, you don't. You get as much responsibility as you can handle. It's not at all unusual to meet with clients your first year here."

"Many of the attorneys have technical degrees."

As you'd expect from a firm with an exclusively high-tech focus, "It helps to have a technical background." While "you don't need a technical background for trademark or litigation," more than a third of the firm's lawyers have advanced degrees in engineering, science or math. It creates the kind of intellectual environment that leads associates to say that "I am always learning from everyone around me."

The non-attorney staff at the firm is also unique. To help with increasingly complex issues involving patents and licensing, the firm employs dozens of scientists from academia and industry, in everything from biology to chemistry, electrical engineering and physics. One associate points out that "No matter what you need to know, there's *somebody* here who has the answer, no matter how esoteric it is."

"Most people get along very well here."

Doing cutting-edge IP work might suggest that F&R houses a bunch of isolated techno-geeks. That's not the case. One associate recounted that "I used to work for a New York City firm that was, frankly, stuffy and oppressive. I guess some of that must have rubbed off on me, because when I interviewed here, one of the partners asked me a question that amounted to: 'Has anyone ever suggested to you that you have an ego problem?'" The associate, "totally taken aback" by this question, said that, "Nobody at the dozen or so other law firms where I interviewed would ever have dared to ask such a question. They all basically fit the formal, stuffy, repressed mold that I had left behind." The associate added that, "When I came here I finally felt like I found a place where people can be themselves and be judged on their merits, not appearances. Everything I've found since I've been here has confirmed that original impression."

Other associates add that "The partners here are not nearly as abrasive as the partners at other firms," and that "Because each of the firm's offices are not outrageously large, we all get the benefit of a large firm but maintain the culture of a smaller firm."

One large firm hallmark that does exist is that "the hours are long," but as one associate points out, "It's worth it to get to do the kind of work we do. It's so interesting and challenging that you don't mind the hours."

The firm is "not big on formal social events." Instead, "much of the socializing here is informal. Going to the movies, dinner, get-togethers at someone's house, attending sporting events together—we tend to do the 'come-along-if-you-can' kinds of events."

One associate sums it up by saying, "This firm has given me exactly what I want. Fascinating work, lots of responsibility. I really feel like a lawyer now, instead of a person who pushes paper."

Folger Levin & Kahn LLP

275 Battery Street, 23RD Floor • San Francisco, California 94111
Phone: 415-986-2800 • Fax: 415-986-2827

OFFICES

San Francisco (main office), Los Angeles, California

"Even if you are the most junior person on the totem pole, the partners trust you and have tremendous faith in you. I have to laugh when people ask if you get client contact and responsibility early on here!"

HIGHLIGHTS

- Extraordinary associate participation in firm management; the firm's two most important committees are staffed and chaired by associates, with only one partner on each committee.
- Strong dedication to pro bono; pro bono hours are considered billables.
- The firm's three founding partners are called in the press "Three of the most dynamic lawyers and rainmakers in the state."
- Partner John Levin was named by the *San Francisco Daily Journal* as one of the Bay Area's 20 most powerful lawyers.

NUTS AND BOLTS

Managing partner:
John P. Levin

Recruiting committee chair:
Karen J. Petrulakis, phone: 415-986-2800

Recruiting coordinator:
Leslie A. Williams, phone: 415-986-2800

Number of attorneys in firm:

53 (25 partners)

WHOLE FIRM:

Women attorneys (23), minority attorneys (4)

SAN FRANCISCO OFFICE:

Partners (21), associates (24), women attorneys (23), minority attorneys (4)

OTHER OFFICES:

Los Angeles, CA (8)

Years to make partner:

7 to 8

WHAT DO THEY DO?

The firm has a broadly-based commercial practice, covering both litigation and transactional work. Its litigation practice focuses primarily on real estate, labor, environmental, antitrust, corporate and commercial disputes. Its business practice includes corporate and tax planning, commercial transactions, mergers & acquisitions, securities regulation, real property matters, intellectual property licensing, finance, estate planning & probate.

The firm is departmentalized into two broad groups—litigators and transactional attorneys. The firm has a "work committee" that meets regularly to discuss associate work assignments. On larger matters, attorneys typically form teams consisting of a partner, one or more associates and legal assistants. Business and litigation attorneys often work together in the counseling and managing of disputes prior to litigation. While the firm stresses training and supervision of new associates, an associate often has principal responsibility in a number of matters. In a relatively short time, each new associate works with a number of different attorneys in the firm on a variety of projects.

WHO DO THEY REPRESENT?

The firm's clients include national and multi-national corporations, local businesses, entrepreneurial ventures, individuals and public service organizations. They conduct business in a wide variety of industries including manufacturing, hospitality, financial services, aerospace, high technology, professional services, real estate, retailing, communications and entertainment.

Clients include Bally Total Fitness, The British Land Company, The Chase Manhattan Bank, Citibank, Coca-Cola, Coopers & Lybrand, Creative

Labs, The Daimler-Benz Group, Dell Computer, The Deutsch Company, Eastman Kodak, Fairchild Aircraft, Ford Motor, Four Seasons Hotels, The Gap, Goodwill Industries, Hilton Hotels, Kenetech Corporation, KITS-FM, KQED, Lyon's Restaurants, Macrovision Corporation, Post-Newsweek Cable, Philips Electronics North America, Prudential Insurance, the San Francisco Opera, and Westin Hotels and Resorts.

WHERE NEW ASSOCIATES COME FROM . . .

The firm routinely conducts on-campus interviews at the following law schools: Stanford, Boalt Hall, Hastings, University of San Francisco, USC, and UCLA.

The firm also routinely hires from schools where it doesn't interview on campus.

HOURS AND BUCKS . . .

The firm does not have a minimum billable hour requirement.

Part-time work is available to both continuing and entry-level associates.

The firm hires contract attorneys from time to time; to date, none have become permanent associates.

Typical first year associate salary, including bonus: $$$$ (Over $65,000) (The firm is known for its exceptionally generous financial package.)

SUMMER PROGRAM . . .

Last year, there were 6 summer associates in San Francisco and 2 in Los Angeles, all of whom received offers. This summer, the firm has hired 7 summer associates in San Francisco and 5 in Los Angeles.

Weekly pay: $1,350 last year

1Ls are routinely hired for the summer program.

There is no specific deadline for the summer program. Second and third year students typically send resumes from mid-August through October, and 1Ls send resumes from December 1 through March 1.

PRO BONO . . .

The firm has a strong commitment to pro bono work, and actively encourages individual associates to participate in pro bono projects. Pro bono hours are treated as billables.

The firm has handled pro bono matters including consumer transactions, landlord-tenant disputes, homeless advocacy cases, an AIDS discrimination suit, business planning and counseling for nonprofits, protecting the proprietary rights of artists and a death penalty appeal, among many others.

HISTORY AT A GLANCE . . .

The firm was founded in 1978 by Peter Folger and John Levin. Michael Kahn joined the firm the following year. Although it has grown to become what *California Law Business* calls "one of California's premier powerhouses," it had a humble start; when they first opened their office, they had few clients and even joked about adding a 'No Waiting' note to their letterhead.

That rapidly changed, and in the years since, the firm has grown to almost 60 lawyers, and developed a fantastic reputation among both clients and associates. Stars at the office include Michael Kahn, chief litigator, Levin, and Folger, whom *California Law Business* calls "Three of the most dynamic lawyers and rainmakers in the state." Former U.S. Circuit Court Judge William Norris joined the firm in 1997.

WHAT IT'S LIKE TO WORK THERE . . .

It's hard to imagine a firm that is more beloved by its clients than Folger Levin. Mark Litow, formerly chief counsel for one of Folger Levin's clients, Edison Brothers (and currently with another client, Enterprise Rent-A-Car), has been quoted in the press as saying that, "If all lawyers conducted themselves like those at Folger Levin, you wouldn't see the kind of criticism of lawyers that has become all too common." Another client, Edward Firestone, formerly of General Electric, enthuses, "They will go to the ends of the earth for you. The bottom line is that they get results in an ethical, honest, straightforward way. They are just a remarkable conglomeration of people."

Wow.

As you might intimate from comments like those, associates at Folger Levin are as enamored with the firm as its clients are. They rave about the firm's "close-knit culture" and that "everyone here is really committed to everyone else's success. You go out and do battle all day, and you come home to the place where people are really pulling for you. Everybody is really happy here. It doesn't hurt that they pay at the very top of the market."

New associates are immediately struck by the down-to-earth nature of the partners; everybody, even the most senior partners, is on first name terms. Said one associate, "When Peter Folger is called 'Mr. Folger' by someone new in the office, he will look around for his father."

Part of what creates a tight workplace is the policy that all clients are clients of the firm, not of any particular partner. Without a 'you-eat-what-you-kill' philosophy, "You don't have the political battles that are waged at other firms."

As a mid-size firm, much of the training associates get is a "learning by doing" approach. The firm's "rigorous training and support" comes in the form of "pairing new associates with senior lawyers, sometimes even the firm's founders" to learn practice skills and exactly what makes the firm tick. With this system new associates not only learn to be great lawyers themselves but also enjoy a "halo effect" from the senior lawyers' reputations, which "couldn't be better" in California.

While the senior partners are greatly respected in the legal community, they don't hog client contact. As one associate pointed out, "Associates get tons of client contact, sometimes in their first few weeks here." One junior associate recounted that "As a summer associate, Michael Kahn, the head of the firm's litigation department, asked me to research a complex issue of lender liability for one of our clients, which was a major company. Mike actually brought the president of the company to my office and asked me to explain what I'd found in my research." The associate adds that, "Even if you are the most junior person on the totem pole, which I was at the time, Mike trusts you and has tremendous faith in you. All of the partners do. I have to laugh when people ask if you get client contact and responsibility early on here!"

Fowler, White, Gillen, Boggs, Villareal and Banker, P.A.

501 E. Kennedy Blvd., Suite 1700 • Tampa, Florida 33602
Phone: 813-228-7411 • Fax: 813-229-8313

OFFICES

Tampa (main office), St. Petersburg, Clearwater, Fort Myers, Tallahassee, Florida

"This is one place where you're not a robot. It's fun and casual with great people, a family-friendly workplace, hands-on experience, and early responsibility working on great cases . . . associates are not just billable hour numbers here."

HIGHLIGHTS

- 238TH largest firm in the country.
- One of Florida's oldest and most successful law firms, with over 150 attorneys in five Florida offices.
- The firm received the 1995 Florida Supreme Court's Chief Justice's Law Firm Commendation Award.
- Founding partner Cody Fowler was an early civil rights activist, leading one of the first Biracial Committees in America, started in 1959.

NUTS AND BOLTS

Managing partner:

E. Jackson Boggs, President

Hiring partner:

Bradley E. Powers, phone: 813-228-7411

Recruiting coordinator:

Amy M. Polonsky, phone: 813-228-7411, e-mail:
polonsky@fowlerwhite.com

Number of attorneys in firm:

152 (78 partners)

TOTAL FIRM:

Partners (78), associates (74), women partners (9), women associates (21), minority partners (5), minority associates (5)

THIS OFFICE:

Total attorneys (117)

OTHER OFFICES:

(* represents an office profiled elsewhere in this book)
St. Petersburg, FL (16), Clearwater (8), Ft. Myers (6), Tallahassee (5)

Years to make partner:

7

WHAT DO THEY DO?

Primary specialties (more than 5% of practice):

Insurance Defense (44), Business Litigation (30), Corporate Securities/Tax (16), Environmental/Regulated Industries (13), Workers' Comp (10), Coverage Litigation (9), Products Liability (7), Appellate (6), Admiralty (5), Real Estate (5), Labor (5), International/Immigration (2).

The firm is departmentalized. Young associates can switch specialties, but they rarely do.

Offers are extended by department, so that associates know what they will do before they start. There is no formal rotation during the summer program, but summer associates are given the opportunity to sample all of the firm's practice areas. As the summer progresses, the summer associates focus on the area(s) they would like to work for. At the end of the summer, the various departments make offers and the summer associates choose which offer to accept.

WHO DO THEY REPRESENT?

Fortune 500 companies, small business and individuals located throughout Florida, the nation and the world.

WHERE NEW ASSOCIATES COME FROM . . .

Fowler, White interviews on campus at the following law schools: University of Florida, Florida State, Stetson, Virginia, Duke, North

Carolina, and Vanderbilt. Fowler, White hires associates and summer associates from schools it doesn't interview on campus.

HOURS AND BUCKS . . .

Average first year associate hours worked: 2,100
Minimum annual billable hour requirement: 1,800
Part time work is available to continuing and entry-level associates on a case-by-case basis.
Typical first year salary, including typical first year bonus: $$$ ($50-65,000)

SUMMER PROGRAM . . .

Last year, there were 11 summer associates, all of whom received offers.
Weekly pay: $900 last year
1Ls are sometimes hired for the summer program; decisions are made on an annual basis.
There is no strict deadline for applying for the summer program, but the firm does try to complete all summer recruiting by Thanksgiving.

PRO BONO . . .

The firm requires all associates to work 20 hours annually at the Courthouse Assistance Project. Project attorneys assist low income pro se litigants in completing forms for divorces, landlord/tenant and small claims matters. In addition to work at the Project, associates are encouraged to volunteer for other projects of interest to them, which includes guardian ad litem, teen court and Bay area Legal Services volunteer programs. Fowler, White received the 1995 Florida Supreme Court's Chief Justice's Law Firm Commendation Award as well as a nomination for the ABA Pro Bono Publico Award for its commitment to the Courthouse Assistance Project in Tampa.

HISTORY AT A GLANCE . . .

Cody Fowler and Morris White founded Fowler White in 1943. Fowler served as President of the American Bar Association.
Since then, Fowler, White has grown to be one of Florida's largest law firms, with over 150 lawyers. The *National Law Journal* lists Fowler White as one of the nation's leading law firms and Martindale-Hubbell has given Fowler, White its highest rating (AV).

WHAT IT'S LIKE TO WORK THERE . . .

Junior associates at Fowler, White feel that the firm gives them a world of opportunity. As one junior associate enthuses, "From the day you're sworn in, you might do a deposition, go to a hearing. If you do research for a memo on a motion to dismiss, or you help write a summary judgment motion, you go to court and argue it." An admiralty associate adds that, "As a summer associate, I did research relating to some multi-million dollar litigation. A few months after I came here as a permanent associate, the same litigation was scheduled for trial, and I got to second chair the case." The associate marvels, "I don't think I would have had the same amount of responsibility or been able to gain more experience anywhere else." Another first year associate tells of the "great cases" that come in, and other associates point out that "You get your own files fast" and "You're expected to make decisions right away." While this creates some pressure, "It sure expedites the learning curve." Another adds that, "You get lots of responsibility. The older lawyers give us younger lawyers a lot of trust." And one associate says succinctly that, "With the work they give you here, you feel like a real lawyer, not a dork."

"On the whole the partners are extremely *helpful; they've always got time to give you advice."*

When associates join Fowler, White, they enter the firm as a member of a particular department, since offers are extended department by department. While all of the departments are bustling and the firm in general is "very busy," associates point out that the firm is getting "tons of big insurance defense cases."

Once with the firm, as one associate explains, "You are largely allied with one partner, who is your mentor, and you get most of your work through that person." But when it comes to interesting projects, "You talk to different partners, and you find the ones you want to do projects for." "You can seek out assignments from other partners you like. So for instance if you want to cover depositions or hearings, you can get hands-on experience from other lawyers." As one junior business litigator points out, "My department doesn't overstaff cases like some large firms, so the younger associates don't spend all of their time in the library. Oftentimes, although I am the junior lawyer on a case, I am the person with much of the client contact."

This "hands-on" approach is the one the firm favors for training its associates. "There's a lot of 'learning by doing' here. Some of the partners are known for teaching, and they love to be informal mentors. One of the partners, for instance, used to be a professor, and he loves to help." Another associate adds that "Much of the help is by word of mouth," and yet another says that, "Some partners are more hands-on than others. But on the whole they are *extremely* helpful, and will take the time to explain things to you whenever you ask." When it comes to formal training, associates appreciate the fact that "Department heads will pay for any CLEs you want, anything that will help hone your skills."

"You definitely put in the hours, but there's no billables pressure as a junior associate."

Things get going at the Fowler, White offices around 8:30 on weekday mornings. "If you're in at 7:30 or so, you're alone." The office tends to empty around 6 at night, but "younger associates stay until between 6 to 7 p.m." All of that is thrown out the window when there's a big deal pending, or a trial is going on, when you'll be "Working weekends as well." However, on a routine basis, "Some people come in on weekends, if they have a high case volume" but "There's no face time" and "There are some partners who like their associates to be in when they themselves are in, but not many." In general, "Partners don't tell associates they have to come in on weekends. Associates who *do* come in, it's typically for two or three hours on Saturday morning."

Associates say that while there are rarely late nights "There's a lot of work, and the norm is busy, 50-hour weeks." One points out that "It's the nature of the practice. You can't get out of it" and another adds that, "Your hours are driven by the business. If a motion is due on Monday, you'll be in on Saturday and Sunday to do a great job. It's personal, a pride-driven thing."

The focus for junior associates is "First and foremost" on "learning the skills that will make you a great lawyer." As one associate explains it, "They'd rather have you take four hours to do something and bill one of those hours to the client, just so that you learn it well." There is "not a big emphasis" on billables your first year, but that becomes more noticeable— "more so in years two, three and four." Another associate adds that, "One of the most refreshing aspects of working here is the lack of a strong emphasis on billable hours and fees collected as a first year associate. The firm is more concerned with the professional development of new lawyers than its 'bottom line.' That means 'hands-on' experience like taking depositions, attending hearings and trials, and being involved in significant client contact. Overall, this provides the firm's lawyers with the opportunity to be well-rounded and highly competent, at an early age."

Associates find that when it comes to bringing in business "The firm is so well-established that there's no pressure to bring in business, but if you do, it's rewarded." Associates get a salary plus a bonus based on 'production.' There is a bonus for hours billed over a set amount, and a bonus for "money collected on clients you bring in. That bonus kicks in from day one."

"Nobody has to die or leave for you to make partner."

Associates applaud the firm for making them feel as though "If you do the job well, and you bill the time, you know you'll make partner when it's your turn. And it's not one of these two-tier situations. There's a one-tier track. Every partner is an equity partner." There's "no ambiguous performance evaluation. It's not a personality thing. They make a point of letting you know how you're doing." There are formal evaluations once a year, put together by the associate evaluation committee. But more importantly there is "informal feedback as well, on a project-by-project basis."

Associates participate in firm management on some of the firm's "many" committees, including the marketing committee and the summer clerkship committee, where "Associates are heavily involved. We pretty much exclusively get to supervise summer clerks." When associates have any issues with the firm, they can "informally talk with their supervisors about any issues. It goes up through the chain of command that way, normally," but "you can talk to any other partners you feel comfortable with." However, issues don't arise often because "Associates here are a pretty contented bunch. You can always nitpick. You can always make more money, for instance, but the compensation here is top-flight, and you don't hear any real complaints about anything, really."

"It's a fun place to work."

Associates routinely talk about how much they like their colleagues, and how much they enjoy working with them. "There's no barrier in communication between partners and associates." One litigation associate reports that "This is an unusual big firm in that it's a very close-knit group. People are laid back. It's the opposite of being stuck in the library for two years." An associate in the regulated industries department says that, "We have a tradition in the department that whenever an exceptional professional or personal event occurs in the life of one of the attorneys or staff members, we host a champagne party for the honoree. Since I've been here there have been *many* flowing champagne glasses! We've celebrated everything from engagements and birthdays to prestigious appointments and hard-fought victorious hearings." The associate added that, "Even though the firm is large, we make a point of celebrating each other's successes."

One associate tells how "They're not above practical jokes here. There's one story that's passed down about getting a local judge and a local attorney to help out playing a joke on an associate here who was, well, let's say, overly confident. They made this associate think that there was a case that overruled a case he'd depended on in his argument, and then they watched in great amusement as he pretended to be familiar with this 'fake case' and said, 'I can distinguish that case.'" Much to everyone's relief "When they told him he'd been set up, he laughed as loud as anybody."

When it comes to social events, the firm has a number of firm-wide annual events, including big holiday parties, and the biannual firm retreat, "usually at a very nice resort like the Vinoy in St. Pete, or the Longboat Key Club in Sarasota." The retreat is "A flat out good time. The firm spares no expense—golf, tennis, meals, everything is taken care of for the three days we're there." Beyond that, "Every department has its own parties. Those are a lot more common than the formal firm-wide events." Informally, "The young single associates get together" and "many people at the firm socialize with colleagues," although "Many people are married, and they spend their free time with their families" and "There's no pressure to socialize." Some partners spring for tickets to Tampa sporting events for groups of associates, and one associate talked of just having returned from Colorado, where a department head owns a condo, and he routinely invites partners and associates to join him for a ski vacation there.

As you'd expect from a large firm, with the summer associate program there are "tons of parties, and three or four big firm-wide events." And speaking of the summer program, associates volunteer that Fowler, White's summer program "must be the best one in the country. The purpose of it is to show you the quality, not the quantity of work that you can expect—and to let the partners get to know you." One associate explains that "They suggest that you bill 25 hours a week during the summer. That means one or two projects a week, and you work hard on them. But the rest of the time, you go to mediations, hearings, and trials, and get to know the senior partners to see who your personality meshes with, what kind of work you want to do." Associates say that "They look for associates with a good sense of humor and the potential to handle real-life situations," and that "It's not the firm for one-dimensional, pure researchers." Associates add that "They never hire more summer clerks than permanent positions available. If they bring you in, they really expect you to make it as an associate, and they *want* you to."

To sum it up, one associate describes Fowler, White as "A firm where you can come in and get great work. It's not good if you're not ready to handle responsibility, if you just want to research and write. They don't want robots here. It's a great place for ambitious people, who want to do interesting things. For that kind of person, it's the best place in the world to work."

Frost & Jacobs LLP

2500 PNC Center • 201 East Fifth Street • Cincinnati, OH 45202
Phone: 513-651-6800 • Fax: 513-651-6981 • Web site: www.frojac.com

OFFICES

Cincinnati (main office), Middletown, Columbus, Ohio; Lexington, Kentucky

"You'd be hard pressed to find associates at any other firm our size who have had the work experience we get . . . you're more competent, and confident, as you develop your career, and ultimately you feel like you're a better lawyer."

HIGHLIGHTS

- The firm is dedicated to making sure attorneys have the 'latest and greatest' technology available to them, with all kinds of computer tools. The firm employs a nine-person Information Systems Staff to keep everything running smoothly and train attorneys in the use of the most up-to-date tools.
- The firm's Intellectual Property Department recently voted #2 Intellectual Property firm in the Midwest by "Lawyers On Lawyers In America."
- Represented Federated Department Stores and Allied Stores Corporation in their successful chapter 11 bankruptcies in the early 1990s, the largest retail bankruptcies ever filed in the country.

NUTS AND BOLTS

Managing partner:

William H. Hawkins, Chairman of Executive Committee

Hiring partner:

Mina Jones Jefferson, phone: 513-651-6104, e-mail: MJefferson@frojac.com

Recruiting coordinator:

Karen Laymance, phone: 513-651-6875, e-mail: Klaymance@frojac.com

Number of attorneys in firm:

167 (76 partners)

TOTAL FIRM:

Partners (76), associates (60), women partners (9), women associates (29), minority partners (1), minority associates (1), disabled partners (0), disabled associates (0), of counsel (15), women of counsel (5), senior attorneys (6), women senior attorneys (1), staff attorneys (10), women staff attorneys (8)

THIS OFFICE:

Total attorneys (139), partners (68), associates (50), women partners (8), minority partners (1), minority associates (1), disabled partners (0), disabled associates (0), of counsel (10), women of counsel (4), senior attorneys (4), women senior attorneys (1), staff attorneys (7), women staff attorneys (6)

OTHER OFFICES:

(* represents an office profiled elsewhere in this book)
Middletown, Ohio (5); Columbus, Ohio (10); Lexington, Kentucky (13)

Years to make partner:

7

WHAT DO THEY DO?

Primary specialties (more than 5% of practice):

Litigation (50); Commercial, Real Estate, Bankruptcy (32); Labor, ERISA, Immigration, Worker's Comp (23); Corporate, Securities (19); Intellectual Property (14); Tax, Estate, Family, Probate, Wills, Trusts (11); Health (7); Environmental (5).

WHO DO THEY REPRESENT?

Clients include AK Steel, Inc.; Cincinnati Bell, Inc.; Cincinnati Milacron, Inc.; Commonwealth of Kentucky; Federated Department Stores, Inc.; LensCrafters, Inc.; Mercantile Stores Co., Inc.; Mercy Health Systems; PNC Bank, National Association.

WHERE NEW ASSOCIATES COME FROM . . .

F&J routinely interviews on campus at the following law schools: Case Western Reserve, Chase College of Law, Dayton, Duke, Franklin Pierce

Law Center, George Washington, Georgetown, Northwestern, Notre Dame, Ohio State, Chicago, Cincinnati, Kentucky, Michigan, Pittsburgh, Virginia, and Vanderbilt. F&J routinely hires associates and summer associates from schools where it doesn't interview on campus.

HOURS AND BUCKS . . .

Typical hours spent at the office by first year associates: 2,200
   Minimum billable hours requirement: 1,800
   Part-time work is available to continuing and entry-level associates on a case-by-case basis, depending on the needs of the department in question. F&J does not typically hire contract associates.
   Typical first year salary including typical first year bonus: $$$ ($50-65,000)

SUMMER PROGRAM . . .

Last year, there were 17 summer associates, 14 of whom received offers.
   Weekly pay: $1,100
   1Ls are routinely hired for the summer program; last year, there were 5 1Ls, and they were from the University of Cincinnati, University of Illinois, University of Kentucky, and Duke.
   The deadline for applying to F&J's summer program is January 15TH.

PRO BONO . . .

F&J encourages pro bono activities in a variety of ways. First, it actively supports, with both financial and professional resources, a local program called "Volunteer Lawyers For The Poor" which provides legal aid service to clients referred by a variety of community service organizations. Assignments include appearance in court and counseling clients on landlord-tenant, consumer law, domestic relations, uninsured motorist, and similar issues.
   Second, F&J accepts special appointments from the U.S. District Court for representation of prisoners filing civil rights actions. These lawsuits generally result not only in full jury trials in the U.S. District Court but often appeals to the Sixth Circuit Court of Appeals.
   Third, F&J accepts appointments by the U.S. Court of Appeals for the Sixth Circuit in prisoner habeas corpus proceedings, which include both preparing briefs and arguing cases in the Court of Appeals.

HISTORY AT A GLANCE . . .

The firm was founded by Henry Frost and Carl Jacobs in 1919.

WHAT IT'S LIKE TO WORK THERE . . .

In law school, it's easy to get the impression that when you go to a large firm, you'll spend the first couple of years in the library (if you do transactional work) or reviewing documents (if you go into litigation). One of the things that associates love at Frost & Jacobs is that that's what they **don't** do. As one associate raves, "You get almost immediate client contact on sophisticated business matters." Associates point out that the firm is structured so that they don't spend "months in the library" or "work week after week on very narrow issues in a matter." Instead, they feel that the firm gets them "interacting with clients, and taking responsibility, right away. In this firm, you quickly learn how to understand client needs and give practical advice, because you understand what it is the clients are trying to accomplish." The firm accomplishes this with a very lean staffing philosophy; as one associate explains it, "We don't 'lawyer up' on client matters. Most things, including court cases, are staffed by only one or two attorneys." The associate points out that "That gives us almost immediate contact with mid- to high-level managers and executives at our clients, and the chance to work on challenging assignments."

This 'learning by doing' approach works for Frost & Jacobs associates because "Partners and senior associates make themselves available to junior associates for any kind of advice we need," says one associate. "It can be something substantive, or even something practical, the 'how do I fill out a time sheet?' kinds of questions."

"You get a hand in firm management as an associate."

As is true of most firms, the firm is managed by an executive committee, chaired by the firm's managing partner, William Hawkins. Until a few years ago, associates had little say in the firm's business. However, associates recount that "The associates made a proposal to the partnership to add associate members to several of the firm's managing committees several years ago. The partners agreed." Today, associates say that, "when we talk, the firm listens," especially when it comes to "hiring decisions." One associate points out that "Often candidates think that only the partner comments matter. Wrong! Everyone has to work with new hires, and all of our opinions count."

"We really enjoy each other's company."

Associates at Frost & Jacobs point out that because "Law is a demanding profession, it's important to enjoy and respect your colleagues. We're all on first name terms here, except for a few semi-retired partners." One associate says that "While there's always going to be competition to excel, there's no competition among us that would create a mean-spirited environment—and that's not something that's very common in a very competitive legal world."

Associates say that they regularly go to lunch with partners, and that "The entire firm has been sighted bowling together." Firm attorneys regularly play together in Cincinnati's golf, basketball, and softball leagues. Not everything the associates do socially involves the partners, though; the associates have their own annual golf outing, and there is an "end-of-summer bash for the summer associates—no partners allowed!"

Some departments regularly schedule happy hours for "all members of the department, from partners and associates to paralegals and staff." There is also an annual Holiday Party in December, where "groups of associates and partners put on satirical skits lampooning the firm and notable happenings of the past year." One associate tells of a particularly memorable Halloween: "Last October, one of the senior partners—a highly respected partner who's been with the firm for 22 years—announced that we would have a lunch and 'Costume Parade' to celebrate Halloween." In return for a free lunch, all of the associates had to "Wear ridiculous hats and parade around the office," which, predictably enough, was "a riot."

As one associate sums it up, "We enjoy the people we work with here. I really feel as though I work in a place where we support each other, professionally and personally."

Gardner, Carton & Douglas

321 North Clark Street, Suite 3400 • Chicago, IL 60610
Phone: 312-644-3000 • Fax: 312-644-3381
E-Mail: GCDLAWCHGO@GCD.COM • Web site: gcd.com

OFFICES

Chicago (main office), Illinois; Washington, D.C.

"This is the best of all worlds, as law firms go . . . a great balance between top-quality legal work, reasonable hours, and fun, personable people, with a very low 'jerk' factor."

HIGHLIGHTS

- 138TH largest firm in the country.
- Health care practice recognized by *National Law Journal, Illinois Legal Times,* and the *Chicago Lawyer* as being among the finest in the nation.
- One of the largest employee benefits practices of any U.S. law firm.
- Pro bono hours are counted as billables (up to 50).
- Associates given billable credit for up to 50 hours training time in each of their first two years.

NUTS AND BOLTS

Managing partner:

James D. Parsons

Hiring partner:

Wendy Freyer, phone: 312-245-8473, e-mail: wfreyer@gcd.com

Recruiting coordinator:

Lisa A. Costa, phone: 312-245-8748, email: lcosta@gcd.com
Joanne M. DeSanctis, phone: 312-245-8529, e-mail: jdesanctis@gcd.com

Number of attorneys in firm:

232 (126 partners)

TOTAL FIRM:

Partners (119), associates (99), women partners (24), women associates (50), minority partners (5), minority associates (15), disabled partners (0), disabled associates (0), of counsel (12), openly gay partners (3), openly gay associates (0)

THIS OFFICE:

Total attorneys (197), partners (103), associates (85), women partners (19), women associates (43), minority partners (5), minority associates (13), disabled partners (0), disabled associates (0), of counsel (11), openly gay partners (2), openly gay associates (0)

OTHER OFFICES:

(* represents an office profiled elsewhere in this book)
Washington, D.C. (38 attorneys); Member of the World Law Group

Years to make partner:

7 to 10

WHAT DO THEY DO?

Primary specialties (more than 5% of practice):

Corporate & International (57), Litigation & Labor (56), Employee Benefits (18), Environmental (12), Health (14), Trusts & Estates (5), Real Estate (7), Intellectual Property (15), Bankruptcy & Creditor's Rights (5), Tax (6).

The firm is departmentalized. Young associates can, and do, switch specialties. New associates state their practice area preferences before they start work, and most of the time they get their first choice.

WHO DO THEY REPRESENT?

Diverse client base, including major U.S. and overseas manufacturing and service companies; universities; commercial and investment banks and other financial service institutions; insurance companies; hospitals and other health care providers; public utilities; broadcasters; common carriers; private communications users; municipalities; advanced technology businesses; and individuals.

WHERE NEW ASSOCIATES COME FROM . . .

The firm interviews on campus at the following law schools: Chicago, Duke, Northwestern, Michigan, Harvard, Georgetown, Illinois, Loyola/Chicago, Notre Dame, DePaul, Chicago-Kent College of Law, NYU, UVA, and Washington University. The firm hires routinely from schools where it doesn't conduct on-campus interviews.

HOURS AND BUCKS . . .

Average associate hours worked: 2,152; Minimum billable hours: 1,950
    Part-time work is available to continuing associates, but generally not at entry level. The firm does not routinely hire contract associates.
    Typical first year salary: $$$$ (Over $65,000)

SUMMER PROGRAM . . .

Last year, there were 17 summer associates, 16 of whom received offers.
    Weekly pay: $1,730 last year
    1Ls are routinely hired for the summer associate program; last year's 1Ls came from the University of Chicago, Columbia, NYU, and Harvard. There is no deadline for the summer program.

PRO BONO . . .

The firm encourages pro bono work and community involvement, and up to 50 hours of approved pro bono work per year is counted as billable time.
    Volunteers from the firm staff a community legal clinic, and participants in that program are eligible for up to 75 hours of pro bono work to be counted as billable time. Associates have spent significantly greater time on a broad variety of pro bono matters.
    The firm hands out an annual "pro bono attorney of the year" award to recognize outstanding pro bono contributions.

HISTORY AT A GLANCE . . .

Founded in Chicago in 1910.

WHAT IT'S LIKE TO WORK THERE . . .

If you ask anyone at any great employer what stands out about where they work, they'll inevitably tell you "the people." When you ask associates at GarCar that same question, they tell you exactly what makes the people at the firm so special. For instance, one associate tells that "I don't have to rush around before a vacation trying to find people to cover my deals. They show up at my door before I'm leaving asking how they can help me. It makes me happy to work with a group of people that I not only like but who also support me." Another adds that "Everyone works together to make the job easier. This is an easy place to make life-long friends," and another associate agrees, "Most people here consider everyone not only their colleagues, but friends as well."
    Associates feel that the partners have made a serious effort to give them an environment they enjoy. One associate says that "The firm's

management has obviously worked hard to preserve and foster a firm culture that holds respect for everyone first and foremost. This actually makes it easier to provide excellent legal service to our clients, because egos and attitudes don't make being a young lawyer more challenging than it already is." One element of that culture is making sure that associates feel appreciated. As one associate tells it, "People here are willing to give credit where credit is deserved. There is not a single person trying to steal the limelight from you. In one case I am currently working on, we had some big successes early on, right up to the Illinois Supreme Court. A partner from another department, who is also involved in the case, sent a memo out to the entire firm letting them know what we did. All four of us, three associates and one partner, were named in the memo and everyone around the firm was congratulating us when it came out. We were even invited to the closing dinner by the clients, who were thrilled with what we had done. It was a really great feeling."

As the firm grows—there are currently almost 200 lawyers in the Chicago office alone—maintaining this kind of environment takes a little more creativity, but the firm still accomplishes it. For instance, in the rapidly-expanding employee benefits department, associates started an official 'fun committee' last year. The committee has set up a number of department outings, in addition to establishing profiles for each of the attorneys in the department. As one associate in the department describes it, "At each of our regular department meetings, one of us hands out our official 'profile' for others to read. Rather than containing the kinds of things you expect—academic/professional credentials, that kind of thing—the profile contains the answers to question like 'What is your favorite book? Favorite movie?' 'What is your favorite childhood memory?' and best of all, each person is asked to attach a baby photo and high school photo of themselves. We get a kick out of seeing these old photos and learning about each other on a more personal level—and it really makes working together a lot of fun!"

Associates appreciate the firm's philosophy of respect for staff members. After all, it makes your job a lot easier if you know that the staffers you depend on for so many things, every day, are happy with what *they* do. One associate says that "A tangible indication of the respect for staff members here is that all of the buzzers were taken off of secretaries' phones because the management felt that buzzing your secretary was too demeaning and impersonal." Another associate adds that "There are many friendships between attorneys and staff. Many times I have had to shut my door due to the noise coming from the secretaries' desks near my office, which tend to be the gathering point for conversations between attorneys and secretaries. I'm not complaining; it's good to hear that people here take the time to enjoy themselves at work." GarCar even has an award for staffers, named after one of the secretaries. As one associate tells it, "We have a secretary named Lucy Allen who has worked here for over 50 years.

And this wasn't even her first job! She's almost 82. Instead of encouraging her to retire, the firm supports her desire to keep working, although she is the only employee without a personal computer. Several years ago the firm established the Lucy Allen Award, given quarterly to an administrative support staffer who goes 'above and beyond.'"

"If you take the initiative, there is a world of opportunity at GarCar."

Associates uniformly rave about the quality of the work they get, right from the start. One brand-new associate in the health care department told that "I've been here for only four months, but I've already worked on some complex legal transactions, I've had client contact, I've attended conferences, I've met regularly with the colleagues in my department to exchange information and ideas, and I've been encouraged to continue to meet and work with other professionals in my field. In this department, young attorneys can pursue assignments on complex deals from the first day of work. Client contact is immediate. My experience is a stark contrast from the experiences of my colleagues in corporate departments at other firms who have mundane tasks and little, if any, client contact."

A litigation associate agrees, saying that, "This is one of the only 'big' firms where young, even first year, associates are allowed, and even encouraged, to take on significant responsibility. Unlike most large law firms, at Gardner Carton you won't spend all your time in the library doing research for a memo, and then hand that memo over to another attorney who gets to write the brief. You help write the brief yourself. You go to court on motions and status calls. Sometimes you get to make an opening statement, direct- or cross-examine a witness during a trial. You get to take depositions and write and answer discovery requests, communicate with clients, and generally do those things that upper level associates at the other big firms do." A second year litigation associate was similarly thrilled with getting to argue a high-profile case with significant media coverage in the district court.

Associates uniformly find that the firm supports them in pursuing activities that expand their legal and professional skills, even if that means leaving the office for a while. For instance, a second year associate in the international group spent three months in Hamburg, Germany at a German law firm interacting with German counsel and a German-based firm client. A third year associate served 11 months as the Deputy General Counsel for the Chicago Democratic National Convention Committee. A fourth year associate spent three months on loan to the in-house legal department for a major banking client.

GarCar rewards associates for thinking 'outside the box' about the concerns of the firm. One associate tells of how he "had worked at a management consulting firm, and learned about 'intellectual capital' and how it can be a great asset to a firm. I once mentioned this to the firm's vice chairman, and she was very open to hearing more about it. I offered to invite someone from my old consulting firm to speak with her and the firm's chairman about the concept. She was very receptive. Within weeks, I was having lunch with one of my old colleagues, the firm's chairman and vice chairman, discussing these concepts." The associate marveled that, "I have never worked in a place where a relatively new member of the firm could approach top management with ideas on how to run their firm. They really take seriously everybody's contribution." As one associate tells it, "If you take the initiative, there's a world of opportunity at GarCar. The partners will allow you to take responsibility and handle matters and tasks normally reserved for senior associates and partners."

As the level of responsibility given to junior lawyers implies, much of the training at Gardner Carton is 'on-the-job.' The firm's lean staffing policies lead to tons of hands-on training—and happy clients, which leads to even more good work. One happy client wrote a letter to the editor of *American Lawyer,* citing how his company had beaten the FTC in a merger case using GarCar, which got the entire job done for less than $1.2 million and with only five attorneys. The client compared this in his letter to the Staples and Office Depot merger problems with the FTC, in which Staples spent $13 million in legal fees, had 70 attorneys on the case—and lost.

The firm has regular departmental meetings to give lawyers a chance to catch up on what everybody in the department is doing. "We have a lunch meeting twice a month where we talk about what's going on in the industry we cover. We each talk about what we're working on, and an associate presents information on an issue he or she has been researching." The firm also encourages junior associates to attend conferences—one four-month associate in the health law department tells of having the opportunity to attend two national health law conferences so far—but the most valuable professional development associates get comes from "The senior attorneys and staff, who are always willing to help out and spend their precious time during the day to assist you. They'll give you advice if you need it, teach you how to do things, and even talk about personal issues."

"The hours aren't as outrageous as those at some other large firms."

Junior associates sometimes put in late nights, but stress that "We have the time to do the activities that we like to do outside of the firm because most attorneys here keep the concept of work in perspective—it's a significant part of your life, but it should never *be* your life. By keeping things in perspective, many people here do a variety of activities outside of work, including playing on sports teams, working out regularly, going on family vacations, hosting dinner functions, serving on boards, participating in charities, taking music lessons. This isn't to say that lawyers at other firms don't do these things. But it *is* to say that the healthy balance of work and play that the firm offers means that attorneys here have the opportunity to get involved in a number of activities, rather than just selecting one or two."

One associate points out that "Like all large firms, there have been and will be late nights, but it's how the attorneys respond to these late nights that sets the firm apart. Because many of us like each other, when we have late nights we are with people whose company we enjoy. That makes even the longest nights bearable." Another echoes that sentiment with "You don't have to spend an incredible amount of your waking hours here, and when you *do*, you don't mind it quite so much because you have a lot of really terrific people to work with."

Another associate explains that when "huge hours" are required, they're appreciated. "One night I was here by myself until 2:15 in the morning. The partner I was working for felt awful about it, but the client needed it; they had a filing deadline the next day. Because the partner had a dinner and a board meeting to attend she had to leave the office, but she called frequently to make sure I was doing okay. She even told me to leave if I felt I was at a standstill. The next day we filed at 4:15 p.m. The partner told me that with my work taken care of, I should leave. A couple of other lawyers stopped by during that day and asked me how I was doing. This partner had obviously mentioned to them that I had spent the night there." The associate continued, "It showed me that even though we sometimes have to work late nights, the partners here don't take it for granted that we are sacrificing part of our personal life—not to mention sleep!—to make sure the work gets done." Another associate comments that "It's not as if staying late at the office is looked upon as the norm, and we should come to think of it as part of our daily lives. Instead, when we *do* have projects that make our days and weeks extremely busy, the partners appreciate what we're doing. They try and reinstate the balance that the firm epitomizes by pushing us out the door when the work allows it." As one associate explains it, "The partners here are genuinely concerned about the associates, and everyone at the firm, being happy. A positive attitude seems to exist throughout the firm. The hours expected of us, particularly when we're fairly new, just aren't as outrageous as other big firms I've heard about." Another adds, "Partners have gone out of their way to make sure that I meet clients, understand the background of the work I'm doing, and that I am having a good time doing it. That puts the hours in perspective."

"The people here respect your life outside of work."

Associates at GarCar routinely tell about incidents showing that the firm makes an effort to accommodate their personal lives. One associate tells of putting in many hours on a particular deal, "And when I thought the deal would be over, I had made plans to go out of town to see my family. A development at the last minute meant we had to make changes to our documents for the deal. The partner I was working with insisted that I keep my vacation plans, and he made the necessary changes himself." Another associate says that "It was my anniversary, and I was in the middle of a closing from hell. The supervising partner knew I had dinner plans and offered to finish up so I could get out of the office and keep my plans."

Another associate adds that, "While of course the client's interests are first and foremost, the partners I have worked with understand that I have interests and obligations outside the firm. They do all they can to ensure I don't sacrifice those. This translates into situations like the time a partner stayed an extra hour so that I could catch my ride home for Christmas, and another associate offered to have a confirmation sent to her so that I could catch a flight." The associate said that, "These kinds of things always confirm for me that we are a team. These attorneys take extra steps to help me, both because they're the kind of people this firm attracts, and also because they know that I would do the same for them if the situations were reversed."

"Much of the socializing here goes on outside of firm-sponsored events."

As you'd expect of a large firm, GarCar hosts all kinds of social events. There are holiday parties, an annual beach volleyball tournament for attorneys and staff, monthly Friday happy hours at the firm, an annual all-lawyer black-tie 'prom' at various cultural locales, a country western square dance, and a Halloween masquerade at Planet Hollywood. Summer associate activities include a bowling party at "probably one of the few bowling alleys left in the country that has human pin setters." The litigation partners sponsor an annual golf tournament, and the firm sponsors basketball and softball teams that compete in the law firm leagues, and it also typically sponsors teams to compete in various 10K races.

Nonetheless, as you'd expect from attorneys who enjoy each other's company, much of the socializing among lawyers at GarCar is informal. As one associate tells it, "It's not at all unusual for us to get together with our significant others, have dinner parties, and go out on weekends together."

As one associate sums it up, "We have blue chip clients. We are involved in front-page *Wall Street Journal* deals, and landmark litigation. But most important of all, we lead fulfilling, well-rounded lives."

Goulston & Storrs, P.C.

400 Atlantic Avenue • Boston, MA 02110-3333
Phone: 617-482-1776 • Fax: 617-574-4112

OFFICES

Boston, Massachusetts

"When they hire you as an associate, they intend for you to stay with the firm and ultimately make partner. The partners here are truly interested in our professional development, and they back that up with an open-door policy and every formal and informal opportunity to learn. It makes for a very interesting and challenging work environment."

HIGHLIGHTS

- Pro bono hours are counted as billables.
- Voted #1 firm in the United States at which to practice law by *The American Lawyer*'s mid-level and summer associate 1998 survey.

NUTS AND BOLTS

Managing partner:

Michael J. Haroz and Douglas M. Husid

Hiring partner:

Steven R. Astrove, phone: 617-482-1776, e-mail: sastrove@goulstorrs.com

Recruiting director:

Nancy E. Needle, phone: 617-574-6447, e-mail: nneedle@goulstorrs.com

Number of attorneys in firm:

135 (74 partners)

Total partners (74), total associates (61), women partners (14), women associates (26), minority partners (1), minority associates (3)

Years to make partner:

7 1/2

WHAT DO THEY DO?

Primary specialties (more than 5% of practice):

Corporate/Business/Securities (33), Finance (28), Real Estate (53), Litigation (21), Healthcare (12), Environmental (15), Tax (10), Pro Bono (56), Bankruptcy (9), Trusts & Estates (9).

The firm is team-oriented and its practice areas are broadly defined. Many attorneys have experience in more than one practice area. Junior associates can switch specialties.

WHO DO THEY REPRESENT?

Current and recent clients: Banking and financial institutions, including Bank Boston, State Street Bank and Trust Company, Citizens Bank, Mellon, Fleet Bank, US Trust, Key Bank, Chase Manhattan, Met Life, Prudential, Travellers, and Nomura.

Corporate and Healthcare clients including Tweeter, joan & david, CB Whittier, Avegis Zildjian Company, Eclypsis, Photo Electron, Malden Mills, Doubletree, Ann & Hope, Joan Fabrics, Harvard Pilgrim Health Care, Beth Israel Hospital, Pastene, General Cinemas, Viacom, Bowthorpe, TLC, Nexabit Networks, Inc., King Cannon, Inc., Massachusetts Hospital Association, Massachusetts Extended Care Federation, Mass Dental Society, Mass Medical Society, Beth Israel-Deaconess Medical Center, Partners Health Care, ADS Group, and Integrated Health Services.

General Real Estate clients including Avalon Bay, New England Development, The Beacon Companies, Boston Properties, Hewlett Packard, Boston Redevelopment Authority, Northland Investment Corporation, Samuels & Associates, Manley-Berenson, S.R. Weiner Co., The Druker Company, Stop & Shop Supermarkets, Jordans Furniture, General Cinema, Rockefeller Center, The Ice Palace in Tampa, Rowes Wharf in Boston, Ritz Carlton Condominiums, Boston/Fleet Center.

Retailers including J Crew, Speedo, NEXT, BJ's, Lids, Barnes & Noble, Rockefeller Center, Learningsmith, Walmart, Hoyts Cinemas, Loews Theatres, Toys 'R' Us, The Limited, The Disney Store, and Ghurka.

And litigation clients including the Gardner Museum, Coretta Scott King, Massachusetts Bay Transit Authority, Beacon Construction, Rockwell International, Malden Mills, Cincinnati Milicron, Arvin Industries, Morison-Knudson Corporation, and Met Life Insurance.

WHERE NEW ASSOCIATES COME FROM . . .

The firm routinely interviews on campus at the following law schools: Boston College, Boston University, Chicago, Columbia, Georgetown, Harvard, Michigan, Northeastern, NYU, and Yale. The firm also hires routinely from schools where it doesn't interview on campus.

HOURS AND BUCKS . . .

First year associates typically spend 1,850 to 2,000 hours at the office. The firm does not have a minimum billable hours requirement.

The firm allows part-time work. Currently, the firm has 14 part-time attorneys, six partners and eight associates. The firm routinely hires contract associates, and contract associates have become full-time associates. In fact, one recently became a partner.

Typical first year salary, including typical bonus: $$$$ (Over $65,000)

SUMMER PROGRAM . . .

Last year, there were 15 summer associates, all of whom received offers.

Weekly pay: $1,600 last year

1Ls are routinely hired for the summer program. Last year's 1Ls came from Harvard and Georgetown.

Deadline for applying for summer program: For 2Ls and 3Ls: December 1; for 1Ls, February 1.

PRO BONO . . .

The firm is strongly committed to pro bono work by both partners and associates. Pro bono work is considered billable time and part of an associate's workload.

G&S has had a historic commitment to pro bono which dates back to at least its early involvement in the famous Sacco and Vanzetti case, when the firm was involved in its defense. In March, 1998, the American Bar Association Section on Business Law awarded G&S its National Public Service Award for the firm's commitment to providing services to the poor in a business context. The American Bar Association also awarded the firm its Pro Bono Publico award a few years ago, and in its commendation, the ABA noted that the naming of G&S represented only the second time in history that an entire law firm, as opposed to an individual attorney, had been so honored. As such, the firm has been cited across the nation as a model for firm-wide commitment to and accomplishment in pro bono work. In 1995, the Boston Bar Association awarded one of the firm's co-managing partners the Thurgood Marshall Award for his commitment to pro bono work.

Current and recent projects include legal assistance to two public housing tenant organizations in connection with rehabilitating housing developments; representing Nuestra Comunidad Development Corporation, a Hispanic community development corporation; representing Coretta Scott King in a widely-publicized suit against Boston University regarding certain papers of hers and the late Dr. Martin Luther King, Jr.; representing Oxfam America, the worldwide relief organization; and many others.

Founded at the turn of the century. The firm grew slowly until 1975, when it had 15 lawyers. Since then, it has grown to over a hundred lawyers.

When you talk with associates at G&S, you immediately notice that they appreciate the efforts the partners make to provide them with interesting, varied work, right from the start. As one associate points out, "The practice teams are based around clients, not legal specialties. So if you're a corporate lawyer, you might work on a bank financing, stock option plans, trademark work, and an IPO for a single corporate client." Another associate raves about getting a "tremendous variety of work. From patent litigation, to employment discrimination, to environmental litigation, representing a charter school, and health care litigation." A real estate associate adds that, "The variety of transactions I get is very rewarding. The firm refers out all of the routine real estate work, like title searches, so we get to focus on representing lenders and borrowers, landlords and tenants, buyers and sellers. All of the associates get the opportunity to wear all different hats throughout the day." Better yet, "Many of the sophisticated projects we get don't fit into established molds. We often have to develop novel strategies concerning zoning and other land use rules and regulations because there just isn't any precedent." Another real estate associate adds that, "We often have to come up with a fresh approach to resolve environmental problems. Many times we get cases specifically to handle complicated issues in this area. It makes the work tremendously exciting."

One of the firm's more recent projects made headlines around the country. "A couple of years ago, a terrible fire destroyed the factory of one of our clients, Malden Mills," explains one junior associate. "Thousands of people were thrown out of work, but the owner, Aaron Feuerstein, vowed to rebuild the factory and to keep on paying everyone who'd been left jobless by the fire. The story made news around the world. Some associates here worked on every aspect of the company's effort to rebuild. The corporate, financial, real estate, construction, insurance, litigation, tax, legislative issues, you name it. Everything was done and the entire factory was rebuilt in 15 months. Needless to say, it was an incredibly rewarding project."

As these stories suggest, "The firm makes an effort to involve us in entire transactions, not just isolated assignments," says one associate. "They get us working directly with clients, both so that the clients will accept us and also to give us experience in client relations." Another associate adds that "Partners consistently emphasize their commitment to helping junior associates develop our practices, and it's not just talk. We get to attend meetings and hearings that, according to my friends at other firms, they don't get a chance to attend."

The firm also encourages associates to pursue professional interests that fall outside the firm's current practice. As one associate raves, "Once I let the firm know that I was interested in an area outside of our traditional practice, they encouraged me to attend training programs and volunteer for programs that gave me experience in that area." The associate went on, "Based on what I know of law firms, it's unusual for a firm to be so receptive to very junior associates' interests. I expected them to insist that I work exclusively in areas where the firm needs me the most. They haven't done that at all."

This interest in expanding junior associates' horizons extends to the firm's attitude about training, both formal and informal. Formally, the firm pays for outside training programs, and "spends an enormous amount of time developing and conducting" regular in-house programs featuring both experienced partners and outside speakers to deliver seminars on a variety of topics, "all geared toward improving the quality of lawyering at G&S." The firm also "allows associates to attend almost any legal education seminar, conference, or class we believe will help our careers," says one associate.

The firm also ensures that associates get a variety of experiences by giving each new associate a supervisor from the firm's Associate Development Committee. The supervisor "monitors the associate's work assignments to make sure the associate gets exposed to different aspects of the firm's practice," and also to see that "each associate gets appropriate increases in responsibility, so we don't get stuck in a rut."

On an informal basis, one associate says that, "Senior partners here make a point of being accessible to young associates. They're always ready to offer advice, give pointers, explain strategies. They make us feel as though they're interested in our professional development, not just our billable hours."

Of course, the firm *is* interested in associates' billable hours, and even though the firm doesn't have a formal billable hours requirement, "the needs of the clients often mean long hours." However, associates feel that the partners are sensitive to the time they put in at the office. As one associate explained, "I have had a partner ask me whether a particular project could be completed on a given day without my working on the weekend. When I said 'no,' she changed the due date to ensure that I didn't have to come in on Saturday or Sunday." This sensitivity to time is reflected in the fact that the firm doesn't give hours-based bonuses. "There's a difference between being committed to quality lawyering, and pure hours generation," says one associate. "G&S is definitely interested in you giving great service, but they're not at all inhuman about it. When I'd been here a couple of years working very long hours, each of the partners I had worked with made a point of visiting me and warning me about the risk of burnout. One statement I particularly remember was 'This is not a sprint.'"

Another associate recounts a situation where "one of the managing partners noticed that I was stressed. He approached me and asked why. I told him I was extremely busy and he pressed me about what was on my plate. The upshot was that he drafted a credit agreement for me. Not many managing partners at other firms—if any!—would have had that attitude. From what my friends say about other places, there's a lot of 'dues to pay' attitude. Not here." Another associate agrees, saying "The partners are genuinely concerned, and address those concerns, when associates seem flat out or struggling with their work loads."

Partners' willingness to chip in when associates are overburdened is a recurring theme at G&S. One associate talks about how "During my third month of practice with G&S, the most senior partner in the litigation department spent almost an hour one night helping me figure out the answer to a question on a case that wasn't even his." Ultimately, what makes the hours most bearable is that the partners don't take it for granted. As one associate explains, "I have had many partners thank me for the time and effort I put into my work. Although it doesn't sound like much, having someone mention that they appreciate the work you are doing is surprisingly uplifting."

"There's no competition among the associates here. The feeling is, if you're an excellent attorney, when it's your turn you'll make partner."

Associates at G&S often point out that because of the very low partner-to-associate ratio, the feeling is that the firm never hires an associate expecting to weed them out a few years down the road. As one associate says, "People here really want it to work out for new associates." This attitude results in an environment where "I feel comfortable with everybody here." Another points out that "The lawyers here are genuinely proud of the work they do for their clients, but because everybody views it as an accomplishment of the institution rather than any one individual, it doesn't translate into huge personal egos. We are all proud of our colleagues and we regularly promote each other." This one-for-all attitude is borne out in a story from one associate: "Last August, a major deal came along suddenly and the closing schedule crossed the vacation times of the attorneys most closely involved. Others jumped in, learned the job and covered the transaction for the vacationing attorneys. People do these things for each other here, without complaint, because we all realize that we need to look out not only for the firm's business but also for each other's quality of life." Another associate tells of being "a young associate working on a closing in Bermuda. The senior partner made me promise to miss my Friday evening plane so I'd be forced to stay in Bermuda for the weekend. And then he added, 'By the way, make sure your wife makes the trip with you, and make sure she misses the same plane.'"

Another associate raves that "What's remarkable about the people here is their dimensionality. We have a tax lawyer who used to be a carpenter, a number of lawyers who were formerly Peace Corps volunteers or Legal Services attorneys, several lawyers who were formerly in government or politics, and several who are singers or musicians." As this kind of diversity suggests, "The people here aren't all the same, and they're not all close friends," says one associate, "But the thing that binds us is that we all have the same basic values. I remember something that happened here a couple of years ago. The IRS threatened to revoke the tax-exempt status of a pro bono client of the firm—an internationally-known famine relief organization with a distinctly left-of-center image. No one here was more outraged than a senior partner whose views, though eclectic, would never be left of anything. The values people have in common here cut across conventional categories." These values include the philosophy that "When everyone gets up from the table after the deal is made, everyone should leave feeling that they were respected and not beaten up."

"The firm makes an effort to balance professional commitments with family."

Associates praise the firm for allowing them to work reduced hours to accommodate family matters. This is true not only for female lawyers, but also for men; one associate tells that the firm is "more than flexible" with fathers. Another associate says that while the firm is sensitive to family issues, "Everybody here realizes that your absence necessarily means that other attorneys will carry an increased burden." That creates an atmosphere where "The attorneys respect each other's outside commitments but don't take advantage of the freedom that arises from the firm's willingness to be flexible."

"G&S puts a premium on assuring the happiness of its people."

Associates rave about the "general camaraderie around the firm" and the "affable work environment," and the little touches that make them feel cared for. Associates talk of "the great chef in the kitchen," "free cookies," "Friday treats," "weekly cocktail hours," and in non-food and drink categories, there are "Skybox tickets for sporting events for all of the professional sports teams here." The firm also has various annual outings and receptions, golfing events, museum events, and a firm-sponsored softball team. And informally, attorneys regularly socialize with cocktail parties at the homes of various partners.

Associates also enjoy the firm's setting. While Boston itself is a hard city not to like, G&S has a particularly charming location. It's in the Atlantic Building, a rehabilitated turn-of-the-century building on the waterfront. The building has a preserved brick and archway design, a spacious sundeck and "spectacular views of the harbor," in all creating a "splendid physical environment." The building is next to Rowes Wharf, a mixed-use development with restaurants and shops, a health club and European spa and many other amenities available to G&S attorneys.

One associate sums it up by saying that, "This is a very affable work environment. Moreover, the senior partners seem very aware and committed to maintaining the atmosphere. Often I am asked how things are going, what could be done to improve the work environment, questions like that. From what my friends at other firms say, this kind of communication between partners and associates is unusual and most welcome. G&S is genuinely concerned about us."

Gray, Plant, Mooty, Mooty & Bennett, P.A.

3400 City Center • 33 South Sixth Street • Minneapolis, MN 55402-3796
Phone: 612-343-2800 • Fax: 612-333-0066
E-mail: gpm@gpmlaw.com • Web site: gpmlaw.com

OFFICES

Minneapolis (only office), Minnesota

"GPM has been described in a newspaper article as 'a haven for people who want a life outside of work,' and while that's true, as an associate I would describe the firm as a haven for people who enjoy being treated and respected as individuals. In a variety of ways, GPM consistently fosters and encourages individual development. Associates are given relative freedom and control over their careers."

HIGHLIGHTS

- Very low billable hour requirement among large firms, at only 1,680 annually.
- Highest percentage of women partners of any Minneapolis law firm, with 17%.
- Two years ago, the Minnesota Women Lawyers awarded GPM its Leadership Award, given annually to a legal employer who 'exemplifies support of women in the workplace.' This was the first time the award had been presented to a large law firm. Factors considered were GPM's percentage of women partners and department and committee leaders, flexible work arrangements and child care leaves, and institutionalized equality programs, including the firm's Gender Awareness Taskforce and Diversity Committee.
- The firm has a Diversity Committee, designed to increase the diversity of GPM attorneys and staff, and to make people of all cultures and backgrounds feel accepted and challenged in their work at the firm.

NUTS AND BOLTS

Managing partner:

Michael R. Cunningham, phone: 612-343-2847,
e-mail: Michael.Cunningham@gpmlaw.com

Hiring partner:

Brian B. Schnell, phone: 612-343-2982,
e-mail: Brian.Schnell@gpmlaw.com

Recruiting manager:

Linda M. Spotts, phone: 612-343-2946, e-mail: Linda.Spotts@gpmlaw.com

Number of attorneys in firm:

123 (66 partners)

Total partners (66), total associates (44), total other attorneys (13), women partners (11), women associates (18), women other attorneys (3), partners of color (1), associates of color (7), openly GLBT partners (1), openly GLBT associates (3), disabled partners (7), disabled associates (1), disabled other attorneys (2)

Years to make partner:

7 to 9. Newly-hired associates with prior experience or judicial clerkships are frequently given credit toward partnership.

WHAT DO THEY DO?

Primary specialties (more than 5% of practice):

The firm is divided into twelvel practice groups:

Business (9); Business Litigation (20); Business Tax (4); Corporate Finance & Entrepreneurial Services (18); Employee Benefits & Executive Compensation (8); Employment Law (10); Financial & Estate Planning (11); Franchise & Product Distribution (13); Government Relations & Regulated Industries (9); Health, Human Services & Nonprofit Organizations (9); Products Liability & General Litigation (5); Real Estate Law (7).

Associates can, and do, switch specialties.

WHO DO THEY REPRESENT?

Significant clients include Allstate Insurance; ARKLA, Inc.; ARMCO, Inc.; Banker's Systems, Inc.; Barr Engineering Co.; Bridgestone/Firestone; Bureau of Engraving, Inc.; Cargill, Inc.; Carlson Travel Network Associates, Inc.; Carmichael-Lynch Advertising; Cendant Corporation; Children's Health Care; China National Aero-Technology Import & Export Corporation; Chronimed, Inc.; Ellerbe, Inc.; Fine Associates; Ford Motor Credit Company; General Motors Corp.; Grow

Biz International; Honeywell, Inc.; International Dairy Queen, Inc.; IPSCO Inc.; Lawson Software; Lutheran Brotherhood; MCI; Medtronic, Inc.; Minneapolis Community Development Agency; Minnesota Vikings Football Club, Inc.; National Car Rental; Norwest Bank Minnesota, N.A.; Opus Corporation; OUR OWN Hardware Co.; R. J. Reynolds Tobacco Co.; REM, Inc.; Radisson Hotels; Resource Bank & Trust; Riverway Co.; Novartis Nutrition Corp.; Sears; St. Olaf College; Taylor Corporation; Teacher's Insurance & Annuity Association of America; The Goodyear Tire & Rubber Co.; Travelers Express Co., Inc.; TSI Inc.; University of Minnesota Foundation; Whirlpool Corp.; Ziegler, Inc.

WHERE NEW ASSOCIATES COME FROM . . .

GPM routinely interviews on campus at the following law schools: University of Chicago, Chicago-Kent/ITT, Georgetown, Hamline, Harvard, University of Iowa, University of Minnesota, University of Michigan, Northwestern, Notre Dame, William Mitchell, and the University of Wisconsin. GPM does hire from schools where it does not perform on-campus interviews, and encourages write-in applications. "We read and respond to every application."

HOURS AND BUCKS . . .

Junior associates routinely spend about 2,070 hours at the firm on an annual basis, of which 1,748 are billable hours. The minimum billable hours requirement is 1,680.

Part-time work is available on a case-by-case basis to both continuing and entry level associates. The firm routinely hires contract associates, although none recently have become permanent associates.

Typical first year salary, including typical bonus: $$$$ (Over $ 65,000)

SUMMER PROGRAM . . .

In 1998, there were 13 2L summer associates, 10 of whom received offers.
Weekly pay: $1,200
The firm does not routinely hire 1Ls for the program.
Interested candidates are encouraged to apply for summer clerkships by mid to late September.

Summer associate projects come from a centralized pool of available projects, allowing GPM to accommodate, whenever possible, a summer associate's particular interests. Projects typically include drafting pleadings, contracts and other corporate documents, legal research and preparation of correspondence, memoranda and briefs. A special effort is made to give summer associates opportunities to observe depositions, motion hearings, trials, negotiations, and closings.

PRO BONO . . .

GPM has accepted the "ABA Pro Bono Challenge" goal of 3% of total billable hours expended on pro bono matters. There is no minimum or maximum number of hours for pro bono work, but the firm credits up to 50 hours of pro bono work toward associates' minimum billable hour requirement.

The firm has a committee responsible for coordinating its pro bono efforts. The committee actively encourages the firm's attorneys to volunteer for pro bono work. A newsletter is published "somewhat regularly" which spotlights various pro bono matters in which the firm's attorneys are involved. The committee annually presents awards at the firm's winter party to attorneys and paralegals who have recorded a significant number of pro bono hours for the year.

HISTORY AT A GLANCE . . .

The firm was founded in 1866. It is the oldest continuing law firm in Minneapolis.

WHAT IT'S LIKE TO WORK THERE . . .

It would be impossible for a firm to make it into this book without offering interesting work and an intellectual challenge, and of course GPM associates talk about that. "The firm works hard to make sure that we get a mixture of cases and experiences. We get a diverse caseload that makes the work really enjoyable." But that's not the thing that stands out the most when you talk with GPM associates. Instead, you feel that what stands out for them, for lack of a better word, is the entire GPM experience. Simply put, it's a place with a *bucketful* of personality.

You kind of know what to expect of GPM when you see its ads, which are hilarious. One, for instance, has a plain page with one statement in the middle: "We've earned enough trust to fill the Grand Canyon.*" When you look to the asterisked information at the bottom of the page, you see this: "Please note that while this statement does, in spirit, reflect our clients' satisfaction with their legal counsel, it should be considered hyperbole and thus not legally binding, as defined by Mile Long Hot Dog Co. v. State of California: 'A claim made of such exaggerated, fantastic nature that a reasonable person would not interpret it in a literal manner.'" Another ad says, in the middle of the page: "We're on your case like argyle on a sock.*" The asterisked footnote here says: "The extent to which argyle is 'on' a sock varies widely from sock to sock. Such inconsistencies as pattern, fiber content, prolonged use, and the foot type of the wearer make a direct comparison nearly impossible. The above statement is an estimate, intended solely as a guide to the caliber of our legal representation."

These kinds of ads perfectly reflect the atmosphere at the firm. Associates tell story after story that show what a friendly, warm—and diverse—workplace they enjoy. As one associate tells it, "GPM is a place where a variety of personality types are allowed to thrive. There is no one image or model of what a GPM attorney should be. I found this out from the day I first interviewed with the firm, when one of the partners did on-campus interviews at my school. Of course I wore a suit and tie to the interview, although I did fancy myself a bit daring with my choice of an olive-colored, double-breasted suit. Right away, I liked the female principal who interviewed me. She was casual and witty. But I was even more impressed with what happened after the interview. Later that same day, I ran into her in the hall. But by this time, I had ditched the suit and was wearing my typical law school attire: a ratty T-shirt, denim cut-offs, sandals, and an earring (which I had taken off for the interview). She just smiled and commented that I looked 'a little different' than the last time she saw me. When I did my call-backs, I was just as impressed with everybody here as I had been with my original interviewer. I knew GPM was the place. And as for that earring—I no longer wear it, although two of our male attorneys do!" The firm's diversity is encouraged via a formal Diversity Committee, which "has done a number of things to make the firm stand out." As one associate explains it, "The committee's goals are to increase the diversity of the workforce at GPM through recruiting, retaining, and mentoring attorneys, paralegals, administrators and support staff of diverse backgrounds. The idea is to create a firm culture so that people of all cultures and backgrounds will feel accepted and challenged in the work they do."

According to GPM's associates, this effort at diversity has proven wildly successful—and popular. One associate echoes the fact that "What's so attractive about GPM is the diversity of its lawyers. Many law firms seem to hire people who fit a particular mold. If there is a GPM 'mold,' however, it is simply that the people who work here are friendly. Beyond that, there is an incredible variety of tastes, talents, interests and personalities. We have theater lovers and Green Bay Packers fans, a motorcycle enthusiast, an intrepid sailor who recently made a solo journey across the Atlantic, musicians and marathon runners, a knitting (yes, knitting) group, a kayaker, an avid photographer whose office is always strewn with photographs, and an amateur chef who, in a massive undertaking, makes gourmet soup for the whole office once a year." As the associate points out, "Lawyers here maintain their vitality because they maintain active lives outside of work. At GPM, having a life outside the office is something the firm highly values, and encourages."

Many associates at GPM rave that they love the firm because of the wildly different kinds of people they get to work with. One associate tells of "two very different social events that I attended within the same month this past summer. Between them, they say a lot not just about the diversity of the firm, but its inclusive nature. The first was a theatrical event. One of the partners here is a board member of a small and struggling local theater company. Knowing that I enjoy theater, she sent me a flyer for an upcoming production called 'Kalevala: Dream of the Salmon Maiden.'" The associate laughs, "A rather unusual play, as you might guess from the title! When I expressed an interest in going, she congratulated me on my fearlessness and invited me to go out with her after the play, along with the director and some of the cast members. I spent a very enjoyable—if somewhat mystifying—theatrical evening, followed afterwards by dinner, martinis and much hilarity at a nearby restaurant." The associate goes on, "On a slightly more mainstream note, later that same month I played golf with some of the other associates. This particular golf excursion was unusual because it was organized specifically to conquer my vociferous dislike of the game. I'm still not sure about golf, but I did have a fabulous time—at least in part because the other associates encouraged me to excel by wagering clubhouse hot dogs on whether I would sink a particular putt!"

This kind of joviality creates an environment with "An overall lack of competition between associates. With very few exceptions, I don't see a lot of people comparing themselves to their colleagues, or trying to 'one-up' each other," says one associate. Another adds, "Every member of the team at GPM is respected. Unusually large egos just are not well tolerated."

"We aren't just 'worker bees' here."

GPM associates feel "respected" by the firm both in the way that they are trained and in their participation in management, principally through the firm's Attorney Personnel Committee. The firm is managed by an elected Board of Directors, consisting of seven principals, and the board is supported by several management committees. However, the Attorney Personnel Committee is "key," and as one associate explains it, "GPM's Attorney Personnel Committee consists of almost equal numbers of principals and associates. What's amazing is that the associates are allowed to vote on most associate hiring matters, and associate votes are equal to principal votes. When I was invited to join the committee as a second-year associate, I didn't fully realize how unique the invitation was." Now the associate says that, "It's a great opportunity to represent the interests of associates and shape GPM's future in a meaningful way."

For training, as with many large firms, GPM has "in-house seminars, mock trials, and continuing legal education programs." In addition, the firm recently started participating in a program that partners with the Minneapolis City Attorney's office. Under the program, for three-month periods litigation associates from GPM work at the City Attorney's office, "prosecuting misdemeanors and gross misdemeanors and handling traffic court matters on behalf of the city." As one associate says, "It's a great way to get stand-up courtroom experience early in your career."

Associates rave about GPM's formal mentoring program, through which each associate is assigned a senior attorney to act as a guide early on. As one associate points out, "The mentor program is vigorously supported." The mentor program helps stop associates from being overworked, since assignments come about through an 'open season' plan, where senior associates and principals approach junior associates for help on cases. Associates point out that "Almost always, associates are asked if they can help with a new case, rather than being assigned without regard to the associate's interests." Another adds that "More often than not, e-mails are sent to the associate group saying 'Does anyone have time to cite-check a brief for me' or 'does anyone have time to help me with a document production,' things like that. You get the feeling that people here are genuinely committed to providing a quality result, rather than just furthering themselves." Associates also point to "the abundance of good role models and teachers here. There's a distinct absence of excess ego. And on top of that, most people have a great sense of humor even when the going gets tough. Given the general level of stress that is inherent in legal work, this adds up to the GPM environment being as good as it gets for a new attorney." One associate adds that, "There is a general sense of informality here that makes young associates feel very comfortable knocking on the doors of senior partners for advice and guidance."

One of the elements that minimizes stress at GPM is that everybody recognizes that new associates will make mistakes, and that while the firm "consistently provides outstanding client service and quality work product," mistakes happen and that the firm feels that it's still important to treat the erring associate as a professional. As one associate tells it, "About six months after I started at GPM, I was working on a research project when I happened upon a statutory provision that was relevant to a different project I had worked on, for a different client, about two months earlier. My heart sank and my palms started to sweat when I realized that I hadn't referenced this particular statute in my earlier memo. I went to the attorney I'd worked for on the earlier project. She and I together went to a senior partner who was the client contact. The three of us reviewed my earlier work, assessed the relevance of the added provision, and decided how to communicate this additional information to the client. Throughout the process, they didn't praise me for bringing the issue forward, but they didn't chastise me, either. They dealt with the whole issue very matter-of-factly. The whole incident told me that my conduct, and theirs, was the norm at GPM."

While associates are assigned to a department (typically of their choice) when they join the firm, they can subsequently switch, and the associates feel that the firm goes out of its way to accommodate their professional desires. As one associate says, "GPM has been described in a newspaper article as 'a haven for people who want a life outside of work,' and while that's true, as an associate I would describe the firm as a haven for people who enjoy being treated and respected as individuals. In a variety of ways, GPM consistently fosters and encourages individual development. Associates are given relative freedom and control over their careers." Another associate recounts that "After I had been practicing here for about a year and a half, I realized that I was not all that happy with the work I was doing. Not knowing what to do, I talked with the head of the Attorney Personnel Committee and the head of my department, who encouraged me to think about what aspects of my practice I enjoyed, and who told me that the firm would do its best to accommodate my desires. I had worked in three related but different areas of the law, and realized that I really enjoyed only one of the three areas of practice. Although we were not sure if the one area of practice could sustain me full time, we reconfigured my practice, and it has now grown to the point where we have hired other associates to work with me and the partners in the area!"

> *"When an associate is overworked, the firm takes*
> *affirmative action to relieve the burden."*

Associates rave that "The firm supports associates with varying work styles. While the minimum billable hours requirement is reasonable—and accurate—associates who do exceed the requirements are normally rewarded handsomely with a corresponding bonus." Despite bonuses that are in part hours-based, GPM associates uniformly feel that the firm is sensitive to their lives outside of work. As one associate recalls, "When I was looking for a lateral change in law firms, I generally had heard that GPM did excellent work and across the board, the lawyers were excellent. However, the tenet that was repeated often internally—but not necessarily known in the marketplace—was that GPM wanted its lawyers to have a balanced life. In essence, that happy lawyers make better quality lawyers." The associate continued, "Since I've been here I've found that the firm really means it, especially in this market-driven business. It would be so easy to require higher billable hours, but the firm doesn't do it. It's not that the lawyers don't work hard. I think they do, and generally everyone is willing to put in the extra time when it's needed. And that includes partners. But I feel as though the senior attorneys ask for my time instead of demanding it. That level of respect is rare, and it builds loyalty among associates."

One associate tells of "a Saturday phone call I received at home. I am working on a file with two partners who, from a hierarchy standpoint, qualify as top of the letterhead, corner office. One of them knows that I attend French classes every Saturday morning from nine to noon. When I got home from French one Saturday recently, there was a message on our answering machine from these two partners, both of whom were working Saturday morning. They said that they were preparing for a Saturday afternoon meeting with the client, and they had a few clarification questions about some of the work I was doing. The message was, 'We know you are probably at French, but if you get home before one o'clock, could you give one of us a call?'" The associate, amazed, notes that "Either could have requested that I come to work Saturday morning. Either one could have been peeved that I wasn't available. Either could have asked that I come in as soon as I got home. Instead, even with 130 lawyers here, they knew enough about me to know that I was at my French class, and with no pressure, said 'call if you get in.'" The associate continues, "Of course I reached them, and answered their questions, and I was delighted to! At least for me, respect nurtures loyalty."

This sense of caring extends to the community. There's a strong dedication to pro bono work—the firm has a committee responsible for coordinating pro bono projects, and pro bono hours are counted as billables, up to 50. Beyond that "The attorneys here feel a commitment to the community that's reflected in active volunteer lives," says one associate. "It's this sense that we have a duty to give back to the community because we are fortunate people that truly makes GPM a unique place to work."

"This place is the antithesis of 'stodgy'."

As you've probably already gathered, associates at GPM love the fact that they work with people they genuinely enjoy. One associate says that, "There are no artificial barriers between partners and the rest of the firm. Partners and associates work, interact and socialize in an atmosphere of mutual respect. I feel lucky to be here."

While the firm sponsors the normal variety of social events, the attorneys bring an extra fillip of imagination to those events. "There's a summer party every year at a local country club where we spend the day boating, playing tennis, golfing, and wining and dining at night." There's also a winter all-firm dinner/dance party, and a casual summer all-firm family picnic. "Associates help plan all of the events and they are encouraged to bring their own personal touch to the selection of events." One of the most popular social events of the summer program is a miniature golf team competition between partners and associates. Attorneys drive go-karts, do battle on bumper boats and play video games. As one associate describes it, "Even the senior attorneys let go and have fun."

As one associate tells it, "In the 'I guess they're not so stodgy' category, every fall the attorneys go to a resort in northern Minnesota for two days and nights at a firm 'seminar.' Although we have a few hours a day in organized sessions, we spend most of our time getting to know each other in more informal circumstances. Last year at the firm seminar, the associates planned the entertainment on the first night and invited everyone to the ballroom for the 'Gray Plant Mooty Aloha Lounge.' Karaoke and Blue Hawaiian drinks were the order of the evening, which started off with a bang when a second-year associate and the third most senior member of our firm, decked out in Hawaiian skirts, leis, and shaking maracas, belted out 'I'm So Excited' by Donna Summer. The evening turned into morning as everyone sang and danced and generally let down their hair." The associate laughingly added, "You just feel a little closer to all of the attorneys you work with when you've done the conga line to 'Shout' at one in the morning with them."

Another associate talks about the firm's annual winter party, to which all attorneys, support staff and their guests are invited. "For the past several years, various groups of employees have provided the entertainment. One year, one of the associates, who had been a band teacher before law school, directed a musical ensemble. They called the group 'Music In Limine,' practiced over lunch hour and included about 15 GPM employees. There was the senior corner-office partner playing drums, the secretary on saxophone, the word-processing operator on violin and a variety of others with musical talent." Another associate adds that, "The following year we wondered what could possibly be as good as Music In Limine. So what we did was to form a choir called 'The Promissory Notes.' They performed three jazz pieces at the party, and again we saw a whole new side of our co-workers. People talk about those kinds of things all year." Another associate recounts a winter party experience. He "secretively put together a little song I planned to sing at the party. At the right moment after dinner, I strolled onto the stage and took my place at the makeshift office—basically, a desk chair and a phone—that had been assembled for me. I then began to sing my version of the song 'If I Were A Rich Man' from the musical 'Fiddler on the Roof,' which I had re-titled 'If I were A Partner.' Fortunately for me, I had been right about the firm's collective sense of humor, and I still have my job! I received a standing ovation for my performance and still have co-workers who smile when they see me in the hall. We work hard at GPM and do good legal work. But it's also nice to know that we can laugh at ourselves."

As one associate sums up the GPM experience, "You can pick the largest, flashiest firm that will impress all of your friends, or you can choose a firm where you'll want to continue to practice until you leave the practice of law. If you take the large, flashy route, you'll be paid large sums of money, be one of a horde of new associates at a firm, bill more hours in a year than you could imagine, and not have a great chance of making partner. If you go to GPM, you have the opportunity to work with some of the best attorneys in the city in one of the most envied working environments. Although GPM consistently provides outstanding client service and quality legal work product, it doesn't take itself too seriously. You'll be treated with respect from your first day; your opinions are valued and your comments are listened to. You'll have the opportunity to learn and to take on as much responsibility as you feel comfortable with. You'll feel valued."

Hill, Ward & Henderson, P.A.

101 East Kennedy Boulevard, Suite 3700 • Tampa, Florida 33602
Phone: 813-221-3900 • Fax: 813-221-2900

OFFICES

Tampa, Florida

*"We've got a unique set of circumstances. The firm is small enough
so that you get an incredible amount of meaningful work as a new
associate; you'll have 15 cases popping left and right. But it's also
big enough to have the resources to handle complex matters for
multinational clients, and we have a lot of those."*

NUTS AND BOLTS

Managing partner:

Benjamin H. Hill, III

Hiring partner:

Douglas P. McClurg, phone: 813-221-3900

Recruiting coordinator:

Stephen B. Straske II, phone: 813-221-3900, e-mail: sstraske@hwhlaw.com

Number of attorneys in the firm:

45, Partners (called shareholders)(26), women shareholders (3), women
associates (9), minority shareholders (1)

Years to make partner:

7

WHAT DO THEY DO?

The firm's primary specialties are commercial litigation, products liability and malpractice (especially legal) defense litigation, bankruptcy and creditors rights, real estate transactions and finance, business law and corporate transactions, tax, and estate planning and probate.

The firm is loosely compartmentalized into practice groups including general civil litigation, creditors rights and bankruptcy, real estate development and finance, land use and environmental practice, and business and tax law.

New associates are assigned to practice groups based on the firm's needs and their own preferences. They are assigned projects from any attorney in the practice group and, over time, will develop legal specialties and often work principally with one or two shareholders (partners). Junior associates occasionally switch specialties, and many are involved in projects which allow them to cross specialties.

WHO DO THEY REPRESENT?

The firm has a long list of clients, including numerous financial institutions, automobile manufacturers and dealers, insurance companies, legal and accounting practices, architectural firms, advertising firms, engineering firms, real estate developers and contractors, agricultural and mining concerns, healthcare providers, and a professional football team.

WHERE NEW ASSOCIATES COME FROM . . .

The firm routinely interviews on campus at the following law schools: Florida, Florida State, Georgetown, Virginia, and Duke. The firm occasionally hires from schools where it doesn't conduct on-campus interviews.

HOURS AND BUCKS . . .

Associates bill on average approximately 2,000 to 2,100 hours per year; there is no minimum billable hours requirement.

Part-time work is generally not available. The firm does not presently hire contract associates.

Typical first year salary, including typical bonus: $$$ ($50-65,000)

SUMMER PROGRAM . . .

Last year, there were 2 summer associates; both received offers to return.

Weekly pay: $950 last year.

1Ls are sometimes hired for the summer program.

PRO BONO . . .

All of the firm's lawyers provide pro bono legal services of some kind. The firm requires that all attorneys take part in pro bono, but since the firm doesn't have a billable hour requirement, the hours aren't considered billable. Instead, the firm takes note that the attorneys have taken part in pro bono activities.

HISTORY AT A GLANCE . . .

The firm was founded in 1986, principally by successful partners at the leading Tampa law firms of the time. The firm has grown from seven lawyers at that time to 41 lawyers today.

WHAT IT'S LIKE TO WORK THERE . . .

When you talk with associates at Hill, Ward and Henderson, you get the feeling that the firm is tremendously influenced by the personality of its managing partner, Ben Hill. "He's not just well-known as one of the best lawyers in America, but he's an extraordinary person. He's got a genuine concern and affection for everyone here. The first time he sees you every day, he asks about your family and mentions anything big that's going on in your life." The story one junior associate tells illustrates this perfectly.

"My wife was going to give birth to twin girls. One of my projects at the firm was a case that was due to come to trial around the time the twins were going to be born. The partner in charge of that case went to Ben Hill and said, 'I really need all of this associate's time. His other work has to be shifted to other associates.' Hill's immediate response was, 'He's got two babies coming.' I went to Hill myself and assured him that, while of course I was going to be in the delivery room when my babies were born, my wife understood the fact that I had a trial coming and I wouldn't have as much time with the babies as I would want. But Hill told me, 'I know something you don't know. When those babies come, they're going to take up more time than you think they will, and it's important for you to spend time with them.' He assured me, 'Trust me on this. When your babies are born your perspective will be different than it is now, and you'll need the time with them, even though you don't realize it now.' He reassured me that he wasn't dissatisfied with my work, and he told the partner on my case to pull in extra help on it." The associate continues, "Of course, he turned out to be right. I did need the time, and I got it." The firm clearly "doesn't just care about you professionally—they take a personal interest in you, too."

That isn't to say that the associates don't work hard; they do. They typically come in at around 8 or 8:30 in the morning, and stay until anywhere between 6 and 7 at night. On weekends, "It's routine to spend a

quarter of your weekend here, either a morning or an afternoon."
However, associates don't resent the hours because "There's lots of flexibility. You have a fair amount of control over what you're doing, a lot of
autonomy. The time you put in here isn't face time. You're not a clone in
the library." Furthermore, "You don't get the feeling anybody is riding on
your coattails. When you get in in the morning, one of the name partners
will be here already. And when you leave at night, there'll be a name partner still here. They're not loafing off on the strength of your work."
Another associate adds that "When you get to do fact discovery all over
the country, argue motions, take depositions, you're willing to put in the
time to get work like that. The fact is that if you do your work, nobody
says anything to you about your hours."

Associates report that when it comes to hours, "There's no minimum
billables requirement, and they mean it." They feel that that's because
"There's so much work coming in here that it goes for the asking; you
don't have to keep yourself busy."

"The quality of the work you get, the discretion and the autonomy, is unmatched."

Associates rave that "There's no three years in the library when you get
here." One reports that "I had to be sworn in by my secretary, who was a
notary public, to handle a garnishment proceeding the next day," and
another adds that "Within a week of being sworn in, I was handling hearings, taking depositions and interacting frequently with clients. This is not
a place where they hide associates away." Other junior associates talk of
taking and defending depositions both locally and elsewhere in the country, arguing motions, and helping prepare cases for trial.

Associates believe that the firm's work philosophy best befits go-getters.
"If you like assignments passed out to you, this isn't the best place. We
don't have the staff to put six lawyers on cases and break things down into
discrete assignments. You need to carve your own trail, and fall flat on
your face sometimes. They expect it. You need to be a self-starter. If you're
not that way, you'll be more comfortable somewhere else. At this firm,
you'll have 15 cases popping left and right. It's very exciting." An associate
in the bankruptcy department adds that, "Because of the firm's size and
philosophies, you learn by being involved in the day-to-day handling of
cases. As a new associate at HWH I've had the chance to work alongside
some of the most well-respected and talented lawyers in Florida. Every
one of our senior attorneys is willing to teach and pass on expertise,
knowledge and techniques." Other attorneys similarly rave about the "caliber of the attorneys here" and how you learn "just from being around
them." One lateral hire from a large New York firm applauds the firm's
"extremely sophisticated and challenging practice" and the firm's shareholders' "willingness to oversee and guide junior and senior associates
through complicated transactions and litigation projects," and feels that

"the degree of concern for the professional development of the junior associates here is very satisfying."

Assignments flow differently in the different departments and practice groups. While associates "nominally have a mentor," that doesn't determine the source of assignments. For instance, one associate shares that "The firm represents Chrysler nationwide, and a team in the litigation department exclusively handles Chrysler. On that team, that's what you do, exclusively." In bankruptcy, another litigation-affiliated department, "You get work only from bankruptcy partners." However, in other departments the work tends to come from "any and every source," but "They keep an eye on your workload and make sure you aren't overloaded."

"The firm only hires associates it thinks will become shareholders."

Associates report that the firm is "top heavy" with partners; "you aren't leveraged very much at all." That contributes to an understanding that "If there's a problem with your partnership potential, they let you know about it before your fifth year. If you make it to five or six years, you can expect to become a shareholder at seven years."

The firm lets associates know how they're doing both formally and informally. "You get an annual, formal review with your supervisor, and on top of that, Ben Hill himself meets with every associate at the end of every year." Associates say that the firm has a "holistic" picture of each associate's contribution to the firm, and that the firm's explicit philosophy is that "it tries to be fair to everyone," and fairness is defined as "recognizing contributions and compensating accordingly." That results in a policy of giving associates a cut of the business they bring in, as well as having "no fixed criteria" for bonuses. "There's no '1,800 hours gets you this bonus' or '2,000 gets you that bonus' here." Instead, "You get credit for contributions that don't reflect on billable hours. It's very much part of the firm's small-firm mindset. For instance, the firm wants you to be involved in the community, they expect you to do pro bono, and those kinds of things reflect in your compensation, because they strongly believe in giving back to the community." Although there is no "lock step" compensation, this doesn't give rise to competition between associates because "Ben Hill sits down with you and discusses your contributions to the firm, and when he does that, he asks you to respect the privacy of the decision about compensation," and "everybody does that. The fact is that we are well compensated and we get good benefits, so there's nothing to complain about."

On a day-to-day basis "You work so closely with partners that you get an on-going dose of feedback." One associate reports that "It's rare that a case will be staffed so that there are lawyers between you and the partner. You get one-on-one interaction with partners on cases every day. So you know how you're doing all the time."

Associates also feel connected with what's going on in the firm because "Everybody here has direct access to everyone else." While the firm has committees to handle various functions, it's "still possible to speak personally with any partner about anything that's on your mind," and "If you feel strongly about something, Ben Hill will hear you out no matter what it is." There are monthly associate training lunches which provide for more compartmentalized decisions, and at those meetings "They'll say things like, 'The personnel committee is considering doing this' or 'The compensation committee is considering this action,' and then they'll say, 'What do *you* think?'" Regardless of formal input, however, associates believe that "The best way to accomplish things here is definitely to speak directly with whichever partner can do something about it."

"It's a strong mindset of the firm to give back to the profession, to give back to the community."

Associates report that the Florida Bar's aspirational standards for pro bono work—50 hours per attorney per year—are taken by the firm as "mandatory." One associate says that, "You're expected to put in the 50 hours a year," and that "the pro bono work typically comes in informally, but there is never any shortage of it." While pro bono hours aren't considered billables, "It's time that's recorded and it's considered in your evaluation at the end of the year."

The firm is very supportive of the bar and community involvement and expects attorneys to serve in "meaningful capacities" on activities like bar boards and projects, as well as writing or editing articles for bar publications. The firm also encourages quasi-pro bono functions in the form of teaching days at schools, "Like a mock trial for the Three Bears at elementary schools. Those are fun." Attorneys also sit on boards of "almost every civic organization you can think of," including charitable, political, environmental, historic preservation, youth sports, and drug intervention programs.

The firm's commitment to the community, legal and otherwise, sometimes opens up interesting opportunities for associates. One associate recounts how "When I had been here for six months, a federal judicial clerkship opened up because a federal judge here in Florida had a clerk leave unexpectedly. I had a buddy who was the judge's other clerk, and he called and told me about the vacancy, and told me I should apply for it. I wanted to, but I also realized that I had a commitment to the firm, and I loved what I was doing. So I talked to Ben Hill one night, and said I only wanted to do the 18-month clerkship if I had the firm's blessing to take a leave of absence. I knew it wouldn't be easy on the firm, because *everybody* pulls hard on the oars here; they couldn't lose even one junior associate and not feel it." The associate goes on, "I felt like they'd invested six months in 'drying my ears' professionally, and here I was wanting to leave for 18 months. But Ben Hill recognized it as a great opportunity not just for me, but for the firm to give something back to the profession. He talked to the other shareholders and they agreed that I could take a leave of absence and, on top of that, he called the judge and gave me a 20-minute, glowing review. I'm sure that's why the judge took me. I did the clerkship for 18 months, and then was welcomed back to the firm with open arms." The associate marvels, "That showed me more than anything that this is a firm that treats you as an individual, and is truly interested in your well-being—and they're willing to make sacrifices for what they view as the good of the profession."

"It's a classy and caring place to work."

Associates say that "The firm is flexible with family things," and that many of the women attorneys have small children. "The firm lets you work from home. We're all hooked up to the office. That's particularly helpful for mothers," although "It's easier to work from home in corporate than in litigation," just because of the nature of the work.

The fact that "most of the people here have young families" means that "There aren't many Happy Hours that we hit together at local bars, although a few younger single associates do that." One associate suggests that, "If somebody is straight out of school, 25 years old and single, and has it in mind that coming to a firm will mean hanging out with cool guys from the office and hitting the bars on weekends, we're just not big enough to have a big incoming class like that." But there is a "good amount of collegiality here" and "There are dinner parties, things like that, and a lot of the parents get together and take their kids to the park." The associates are "pretty athletic" and routinely "play softball together." Much friendly banter at the office revolves around "college sports" since the firm's three largest feeder schools—Duke, Florida, and Virginia—are sports-oriented schools. One associate—clearly not a Duke grad!—laughingly said that "the Duke people here are beyond obnoxious with their basketball," but "We all have fun comparing our schools' athletic triumphs."

Even for the non-sports oriented, HWH is a "caring and classy" place to work. "Many of the attorneys, both partners and associates, eat lunch together regularly," and "when any female attorney or spouse is pregnant, someone will invariably host a baby shower." The firm also keeps a friendly atmosphere by "including not just attorneys but spouses as well in all kinds of firm functions, like the annual firm retreat, the Christmas party, and the summer party." As one associate says, "I had heard before I came here that this place was remarkable for the friendliness of its people, and that's absolutely true."

Hillis Clark Martin & Peterson, P.S.

500 Galland Building • 1221 Second Avenue • Seattle, WA 98101
Phone: 206-623-1745 • Fax: 206-623-7789 • E-mail: info@hcmp.com
Web site: hcmp.com

OFFICES

Seattle, Washington

"The people here are good mentors. They're light-hearted and fun—there's definitely no 'hazing' behavior here . . . they're truly interested in seeing you become a great lawyer."

HIGHLIGHTS

- HCMP prides itself on being a "high-quality smaller firm," with 34 attorneys.
- HCMP was the first firm in Seattle to institute a mandatory sabbatical program for lawyers and staff.

NUTS AND BOLTS

Managing partner:

Louis D. Peterson

Hiring partner:

Michael R. Scott, phone: 206-623-1745, e-mail: mrs@hcmp.com

Recruiting coordinator:

Eileen J. Kraabel, phone: 206-623-1745, e-mail: ejk@hcmp.com

Number of attorneys in firm:

34 (22 partners)

Women partners (5), women associates (4), minority partners (0), minority associates (1), disabled partners (0), disabled associates (0)

Years to make partner:

8

WHAT DO THEY DO?

Primary specialties (more than 5% of practice):

The firm is not formally departmentalized; it is informally organized into three practice groups: Land Use/Zoning/Environmental (12), Litigation (12), Business/Real Estate (10).

Lawyers have switched specialties in the firm; however, because the firm often takes an interdisciplinary approach to matters (e.g., active teamwork between a litigator and a land use lawyer on land use litigation), lawyers must be "generalists with specialties."

New lawyers are placed in practice groups based on their interests and HCMP's needs, and the firm encourages lawyers in their early years of practice to venture from that 'home base' into other practice groups within the firm.

Each new lawyer works with a supervising lawyer. Projects are assigned by the supervising lawyer as well as other lawyers in the firm. The supervising lawyer monitors and coordinates the associate's work load, and serves as a resource for the new lawyer as (s)he settles into practicing law.

WHO DO THEY REPRESENT?

Weyerhaeuser; Mitsubishi; University of Washington; Horizon Air; Port of Seattle; Merrill Lynch Pierce Fenner & Smith; Smith Barney; Continental Savings Bank; Seattle Coffee Company (holding company for Seattle's Best Coffee and Torrefazione Italia); Magic Mouse Toys.

WHERE NEW ASSOCIATES COME FROM . . .

The firm routinely interviews on campus at the following law schools: University of Washington; Stanford; Boalt Hall; Harvard; and Virginia. The firm also regularly hires from schools where it doesn't conduct on-campus interviews.

HOURS AND BUCKS . . .

On average, first year associates spend 2,000 hours at the office.

All attorneys, associates and partners, have a 1,750 billable hour "budget"—it's neither a maximum nor a minimum, and reflects reasonable expectations and historical reality.

The firm does not routinely allow lawyers to work part-time. It does accommodate special circumstances, and has occasionally allowed attorneys to work part-time on a case-by-case basis. The firm does not routinely hire contract associates.

Typical first-year salary, including typical first-year bonus: $$$ ($50-65,000)

SUMMER PROGRAM . . .

Last year, there were 3 summer associates. Two are going to be federal judicial clerks, and so were ineligible for offers; the third received and accepted an offer.

Weekly pay: $1,000 last year

The firm only hires 1Ls through the Puget Sound Minority Clerkship Program.

The firm typically completes its interviewing for summer associates in mid-November.

PRO BONO . . .

The firm encourages and supports pro bono work. While attorneys don't receive billable credit for pro bono hours, the budgeted target of 1,750 billable hours per attorney is designed to allow attorneys significant time to participate in pro bono and civic activities.

A number of associates are involved in legal work for low income clients referred to the firm by the "No Fee Panel" of the King County Bar Association. Other associates take on projects as cooperating attorneys for the ACLU, or get directly involved with pro bono projects for other non-profit entities.

HISTORY AT A GLANCE . . .

Founded in 1971. The firm has been involved in a large number of high-profile cases and major business deals, from billion-dollar class action suits to large mergers.

WHAT IT'S LIKE TO WORK THERE . . .

Hillis Clark is one law firm that proves that while law is a serious business, practicing it can be enjoyable—and even *fun*. You can tell a lot about the firm personality from its ads. One of them reads, "With a firm our size you always get the 'A' team because we don't have a 'B' team."

Associates confirm the light-hearted nature of the firm. One associate says, "I can tell you a story that sums up this firm. There were two third year associates, they're going out to try a case, and they're all dressed up, they've got their briefcases and their rain gear, they're all dressed for battle and ready to go. As they're leaving the office, the word processing person sees them, and says, 'Look, there go Dumb and Dumber!'" As that story suggests, "People here have a sense of humor about themselves. You can give people a hard time, write funny, biting e-mails, and they like it." That self-deprecating humor encompasses even the most senior partners at the firm. As one associate tells it, "One of our founding partners, Geordie Martin, is an inveterate bow tie wearer. On his fiftieth birthday, several staff members and lawyers brought in an assortment of bow ties, and I mean some real classics, from people's attics and from thrift stores. That day everybody at the firm, lawyers and staff, men and women, wore a bow tie."

"The people here are great mentors."

HCMP associates appreciate that the principals are "into training, they're light-hearted and fun. There's no 'hazing' behavior here." Another adds that "This is an amazing place—even though it's small, everybody here is really smart, really impressive."

When associates join the firm, they are assigned a supervising attorney, but they say that "work never really comes in through your supervising attorney. If you're overloaded, you tell the partner who's offering you work to go and talk to the one you're working for now. Or you tell your supervising attorney. Either way, there are no comebacks—they genuinely appreciate honesty."

Associates talk about the "incredible variety" of work they get. One junior associate says that "I've worked on *tons* of different things. As a young associate you get your own, smaller cases. Right now, I'm representing a family in a landslide case. And in another recent case I represented a guy who sold his dating service to an enormous nationwide outfit, in return for a five-year employment contract. They canned him before the five years was up, and we got his business back for him." Another associate talked of "getting your own individual clients early on, and getting to work as part of a team on big projects." As that associate pointed out, "It's a great way to be a great lawyer—do your own stuff, and work under the tutelage of others as well." One associate, who joined the firm as a lateral from a large firm in town, said that, "I'll never forget my first day at HCMP, when my supervising partner came in and talked to me for over an hour about a project. I was overwhelmed that she took the time to give me the background and strategy of the project, although I've since found that that's the norm here. Although the partners at my previous firm were good lawyers, no one there ever took more than a couple of minutes to assign projects. The difference between the two firms was not so apparent to me when I was interviewing at HCMP, but today it is like night and day."

"They include you in decision-making right from the start."

Associates rave that "The firm expects every associate who comes here to become a principal," and that the firm encourages them to "take part in decision-making early on through service on firm committees, and open communication about firm business." Associates are members of most of the firm's committees, including the Business Development Committee, the Hiring Committee, and the Special Events Committee, but one associate notes that "The truth of the matter is that there is very little bureaucracy here. There just isn't a lot of management to have input *into*. They *do* things rather than create committees to do them." Associates also rave that "The firm is very responsive to associates, the management committee in particular." One associate says that when there were big raises at Seattle firms last year, the associates mentioned it informally to members of the management committee "and they gave us a raise right away to bring us into line with the other firms in town."

"They're more interested in seeing you become a great lawyer than seeing you bill a ton of hours."

The perception among junior associates is that "The firm is interested in how you're doing overall, and rewarding you accordingly. You get the feeling that there's no lock-step compensation. They'll look at things like, how do you deal with clients? How do you take on responsibility? How thorough are you? How do you treat the staff? Do you meet your deadlines? They want to see you progress as a lawyer." Pro bono is considered "big but not huge." Instead, "Most of the attorneys do *something*, and there's some pro bono going on year round, but it doesn't have a high profile at the office." Similarly, associates say that, "There's no bonus for bringing in business for the first several years. They're truly interested in seeing you become a great lawyer, before there's any pressure on you to bring in clients."

Associates say that the firm's billable target of 1,750 hours "really is the target. They're happy if you hit it." One associate says that, "It's not the kind of place where an extra 250 hours gets you a $2,000 bonus. It's not worth it!" As that billable goal suggests, the midnight oil doesn't burn very much at HCMP. Attorneys tend to get in around 8:30 in the morning. If you get in by 7:45, "you're the first one there." The office empties out around six at night. Associates put in the "*very* occasional weekend. Most of the time, nobody's in the office on weekends at all."

These "very reasonable hours" are supplemented by an "unusually generous parental leave program." Associates say that "While many of the junior associates are single, it's a family-type firm. People bring their kids to work, and they leave early for Indian Guides." On top of that, "The firm has events for families, picnics and that kind of thing." A huge plus is that "the firm gives full benefits for families. You don't need to pay anything toward the benefits."

The firm's interest in its people is accentuated by its sabbatical program, which gives attorneys a six-month sabbatical every six years after they become principals. The sabbatical program also gives sabbaticals to staff members who've been with the firm for 10 years, and as one associate points out, "You can tell the firm really respects the staff. It's a family that stays and stays. My secretary has been here for over 17 years. People stay forever because they're treated so well." Sabbaticals, which are viewed as "part of the culture of the firm," are "mandatory—everybody eligible takes them." The sabbaticals are with full pay, and staff members get an additional stipend so that they can "travel or do something else out of the ordinary while on sabbatical." Associates say that, "The sabbatical program helps foster a team approach to clients. With different partners on sabbatical at different times, we wouldn't be able to serve clients effectively if the clients weren't considered clients of the whole firm, instead of a particular principal."

"We've got a 'social club' where we swap stories every Friday."

One associate tells of the firm's 'social club,' saying that "While having a social club may sound snobby and might conjure up images of male partners wearing tweed jackets, standing around a room sipping whiskey and chatting about duck hunting, that's not our social club at all! Our social club is an open gathering of staff and attorneys who meet at a local bar every Friday after work. The 'social club' gives us a chance to decompress after a busy week, and enjoy each other's company for a few hours before everybody takes off for the weekend." The associate says that, "While the 'members' of the social club change from week to week, the group always has a healthy mix of both attorneys and staff. The 'club' represents the most positive aspects of our firm—a mutual respect among attorneys and staff, and a genuine enjoyment of the people we work with." Another associate adds that, "Whenever an attorney has something big on the horizon, like an argument in court or an appearance before a regulatory agency, everybody in the office knows about it. People will stop by that attorney's office and ask if they can help out, or just offer encouraging words. When the attorney comes back from the 'big event,' we'll all gather around to ask how it went. We are typically entertained by a re-enactment of the highlights." The associate often smiles at "the sound of 'high fives' echoing through the halls, and says, "This firm is so supportive. I just love it."

Jackson & Kelly

1600 Laidley Tower • 500 Lee Street, East • Charleston, WV 25301
Phone: 304-340-1000 • Fax: 304-340-1130 • E-mail: info@jacksonkelly.com
Web site: jacksonkelly.com

OFFICES

Charleston (main office), Fairmont, Martinsburg, Morgantown, New Martinsville, Parkersburg, Wheeling, West Virginia; Denver, Colorado; Lexington, Kentucky; Washington, D.C.

"There's no 'caste system' between partners and associates here . . . you get excellent, meaty work early on . . . it's not at all rare to routinely find yourself playing golf with partners—and you don't even feel like you have to lose!"

HIGHLIGHTS

- Largest law firm in West Virginia.
- The West Virginia College of Law recently honored J&K as Pro Bono Firm of the Year for its significant contributions to pro bono projects.
- West Virginia member of *Lex Mundi*.

NUTS AND BOLTS

Managing partner:

John L. McClaugherty, phone: 304-340-1349, e-mail: jmcclaugherty@jacksonkelly.com

Hiring partner:

Robert G. McLusky, phone: 304-340-1381, e-mail: rmclusky@jacksonkelly.com

Recruiting coordinator:

Robert G. McLusky, phone: 304-340-1381, e-mail: rmclusky@jacksonkelly.com

Number of attorneys in firm:

140 (89 partners)

TOTAL FIRM:

Partners (89), associates (51), women partners (17), women associates (24), minority partners (1), minority associates (0), disabled partners (0), disabled associates (0)

THIS OFFICE:

Total attorneys (86)

OTHER OFFICES:

(* represents an office profiled elsewhere in this book)
Fairmont, West Virginia (3); Martinsburg, West Virginia (4); Morgantown, West Virginia (11); New Martinsville, West Virginia (4); Parkersburg, West Virginia (1); Wheeling, West Virginia (3); Denver, Colorado (6); Lexington, Kentucky (15); Washington, D.C. (7)

Years to make partner:

6 to 7 years; less if the attorney in question has legal experience prior to joining the firm.

WHAT DO THEY DO?

Primary specialties (more than 5% of practice):

The attorney figures represent assigning each attorney to only one practice area, although in real life many J&K attorneys practice in more than one area:

Banking (5); Bankruptcy (4); Intellectual Property (4); Legislative Affairs (4); Mergers, Acquisitions & Transactions (3); Public Finance (2); Regulated Industries (including health law) (8); Real Estate (8); Environmental (9); Family Law (3); Federal Black Lung (5); Government Contracts (2); Labor & Employment (11); Litigation (34); Natural Resources (8); Safety & Health (mine and occupational) (7); Taxes, Estates & Trusts (8); Workers' Compensation (15).

Associates generally are assigned to a practice group after they consult with practice area managers. Once they're in a practice group, they generally remain there—although there have been occasions when the needs of the firm and the associate's desire or willingness to change match up.

Associates typically get projects from partners in the associate's practice group. From time to time there are opportunities to participate in matters outside the associate's developing area of expertise.

WHO DO THEY REPRESENT?

Clients include individuals, partnerships, business and industrial corporations, insurance companies, financial institutions, public utilities, trade associations, professional associations, media, trusts, and other public and private entities.

WHERE NEW ASSOCIATES COME FROM . . .

J&K routinely interviews on campus at the following law schools: West Virginia, Dayton, Kentucky, Washington & Lee, Richmond, William & Mary, and Virginia. The firm also routinely hires students from schools where they don't conduct on-campus interviews.

HOURS AND BUCKS . . .

First year associates typically spend 2,000 hours at the office, with a billable hours goal of 1,900.

Part-time work is available to continuing and entry-level associates. The firm routinely hires contract associates, and contract associates have become permanent associates.

Typical first year salary, including typical bonus: $$$ ($50-65,000)

SUMMER PROGRAM . . .

J&K typically has six summer associates in the Charleston, WV office, and two to four additional summer associates located in other offices. A majority of the summer associates typically receive offers.

Monthly pay: $3,400 for 2Ls, $3,200 for 1Ls.

The firm routinely hires 1Ls for its summer program.

While there are no specific deadlines for the summer clerkship programs, the firm likes to make offers to 2Ls by December 1, and 1Ls by February 1.

PRO BONO . . .

Attorneys are encouraged to participate in pro bono efforts. The firm leaves the number of hours committed to pro bono activities to the discretion of each associate, and the pro bono hours worked are not counted as billable hours.

J&K's involvement with pro bono projects has been across the board, ranging from representing individuals charged with serious crimes, to staffing pro bono telephone call-in lines, to representing victims of domestic violence.

The West Virginia College of Law recently honored J&K as Pro Bono Firm of the Year for its significant contributions to pro bono projects.

HISTORY AT A GLANCE . . .

J&K is West Virginia's oldest and largest law firm. What started in 1822, when Benjamin H. Smith entered into the practice of law in Charleston, evolved into a firm involved in the affairs of the Commonwealth of Virginia and the events leading to the formation of West Virginia, to the First Constitutional Convention and early sessions of the West Virginia legislature, and has since grown to a full-service law firm with some 140 attorneys.

Smith was appointed a U.S. District Attorney by Abraham Lincoln, and served with distinction during the Civil War. Another early partner, James H. Brown, entered the practice of law in 1842, and was elected in 1863 as a Justice on the first Supreme Court of Appeals of West Virginia. The firm Brown subsequently founded with his son, Brown & Brown, was one of several predecessor and parent firms which, together with successors to Smith's beginnings as a solo practitioner, resulted in the present Jackson & Kelly. From the early years to 1956, the firm's name changed several times to incorporate the identities of partners and for more than 50 of those years was Brown, Jackson & Knight. In 1956, the firm became known as Jackson, Kelly, Holt & O'Farrell, and in 1988 the name was shortened to Jackson & Kelly.

The firm has had a number of illustrious lawyers, including judges, and a former governor of West Virginia. The firm has 20 lawyers included in the current edition of *The Best Lawyers In America,* more than any other firm in West Virginia.

WHAT IT'S LIKE TO WORK THERE . . .

Associates at J&K will tell you that "This is a place that is really and truly made up of people who treat each other like partners. There's no 'eat what you kill' mentality here. Everybody relies on everybody else." That kind of atmosphere results in a place where "there is no rigid 'caste system' between partners and associates, which is what my friends tell me exists at a lot of other firms." One third-year associate laughs that "I routinely play golf with partners in the firm, and I don't even feel like I have to lose! Admittedly, if I win, I can't shout something like, 'So who's the boss now, little man?'—but I've never really had the desire to do that, anyway." Another associate tells of the time when, "As a third year associate, the annual associate reviews were about to take place. One of the partners I worked for had just bought a brand new car. As I left the parking lot one night, I backed my car smack into his new car, leaving a huge dent in the bumper. I walked very slowly back into the building, visions of unemployment dancing in my head!" The associate recounts that "After I found him and somehow managed to stumble through a less-than-coherent explanation of what had happened, his first concern was whether I was hurt. He then calmly went down to the parking lot to survey the damage. He never raised his voice or expressed any anger at all, much to my relief." The associate adds that, "He even gave me a good associate review later that week, without one mention of my driving abilities!"

"You find your niche here by working with different people."

J&K associates say that "Working here is very much a 'learning by doing' experience," and "every partner has a different idea of what 'training' means." They add that "We work with very smart people" and they impress on you that "this is a business. There aren't a lot of hokey programs, formal things designed to train you." Instead, "You get lots of assignments coming in from different partners." On the rare occasions when a single partner dominates a junior associate's time, "The firm considers that a disservice to the associate. The idea is to expose you to lots of different styles." Associates applaud the fact that "It's not long before you're doing depositions, and within a year you're traveling alone. It takes a lot less time to do meaty things than it would elsewhere." Associates determine for themselves if "they've got the right amount of work." They also have the "head of the department watching workloads, but it's pretty rare to see an associate actually report that they're too busy."

When it comes to client contact, it "depends on the clients. With bond work, you need contact with cities, and you get that early. With corporate clients, you wouldn't see clients early on as much," but "it's not a problem here. People don't complain for lack of client contact."

"We have time for our families."

Associates find that "hard workers here bill 2,200 hours or so; it's much less than a big city, where you hear that 3,000 hours are considered a lot of billables." One associate adds that, "There is no pressure to bill hours," the sense at the firm being that "there's really only so much hard work you can do in a day. We're as productive as anybody anywhere, but they make sure you know that they don't want you to pad your hours or put in lesser-quality time." One associate agrees, stating that "You've got to believe that if you're working 15 or 16 hour days on a routine basis, your client is getting cheated."

The J&K offices tend to fill up between 7:30 and 8 in the morning in litigation, and the litigators tend to stream out around 5:30 at night. In business, the day runs from 8:45 or so and stops buzzing around 6:30. For weekends, the feeling is that "we value our weekends." One associate says that, "you're only here if you have a ton of stuff to do, and that happens a good bit—maybe every third or fourth Saturday or Sunday for a half day." Associates say that "if you have a deal closing or a trial going on, people will be here on weekends, but otherwise it's very quiet." There is "no face time on weekends—there are no partners here to see you."

When associates do work long hours, their attitude is that "It's part of the job. There's a lot of jobs that don't require hours at all, but it's nice being a big fish in the small pond of Charleston." Speaking of Charleston, associates describe it as "a nice little city in a big valley. It has enough tall buildings to make you feel like you're 'someplace.' You don't feel gypped out of a big city practice. You aren't in a pine-paneled office on the first floor of a department store, the way some lawyers are." Instead, "we're in a big, glass building with beautiful views." Others rave that it's a "beautiful, well-kept city. If you like hiking, skiing, kayaking, it's a great area." One associate notes that "I could make twice as much money in a big city, but I couldn't do what I'm doing, and I *like* doing what I'm doing."

Associates also point out that "The firm is pretty family friendly, because they don't encourage you to be here when you don't have to be."

When it comes to compensation, associates are "completely lock step" for the first couple of years, but then "in kind of an unofficial way, in the third year the firm starts to break people out according to merit," although "there's a lot of secrecy over who bills what. You never know whose raise is more than the next person's." Associates do know that "Billing 2,200 hours definitely counts," but there's "no emphasis on bringing in business. They make you feel as though they have lots of partners for that. You get the sense that the partners feel our time isn't best spent that way."

Associates get involved in the firm through the Associate and Staff Attorney Committee, which meets every two months, "since there's not enough to talk about once a month." That committee raises any associate issues with partners. While partners are "pretty responsive," there's "not a lot of need for responsiveness—it's not as though people are burning down their doors with questions and issues." Instead, "They make you feel like when the firm does well, you do well, and vice versa—we're all in it together." On the whole there "just aren't a lot of problems that need to be fixed around here."

"The firm is really into community service."

J&K is heavily community-involved, on a variety of levels. On a personal level, associates "regularly take sabbaticals" for things like "working with the state legislature, as a lobbyist." The firm's attitude is basically that "if it's good for future business development, you can do it. And it's interesting, too."

The firm has a close association with a local elementary school, Piedmont Elementary, which has a substantial population of underprivileged children. Some of the firm's lawyers "read to the children once a week," including the firm's managing partner, John McClaugherty. The firm also supports the sixth grade's annual trip and funds school events. The firm is also heavily involved in teaching Junior Achievement classes during the school year, and many of the lawyers volunteer time for the United Way, Red Cross, YMCA and YWCA, Hospice Care, and the West Virginia Symphony, as well as other organizations. One associate pointed out that "You're encouraged to get involved in community activities, and you find that many of the partners run them." Associates find that "community work is pushed more than traditional pro bono work." Pro bono hours aren't billable, and "it's not too visible at the firm," although the firm has won pro bono prizes for the efforts of individual attorneys. Says one associate, "People do pro bono on their own. It's the schools and non-profits that get most of the focus, and the firm does an awful lot of that."

"It's easy to put together an informal 'firm function' here."

While "you can keep to yourself outside of work if you want to," and "not everybody looks to the firm for friends," associates rave that "The greatest thing about working here is how quickly you can put together a simple, informal 'firm function.' It's easy to get a foursome of associates or partners together on a sunny afternoon for a golf outing. It's never a problem to get eight or 10 people together for an Alley Cats game" (the Alley Cats are the local minor league baseball team). "There's always someone looking for a 'happy hour' group on Friday afternoon." Other associates talk about the firm's softball team, pointing out that "Most people don't know that we won the city league championship last year. The team is comprised of lawyers and staff. It was an exciting season, because after a mediocre run we rallied in the tournament and defeated another local law firm for the championship." The associate added that "It was not only a great chance to spend time with my co-workers, but it's pretty nice to have bragging rights in the legal community."

"When I was sick, people at work brought me Elvis movies to watch."

Associates tell stories about how the firm takes a personal interest in their well-being. One associate says that "I once became seriously ill and had to be off work for almost three weeks. When I was recuperating, I got flowers, cards and daily telephone calls from people at the office. Everyone wanted me to know that I was missed, and to find out if there was anything they could do for my family or me. The staff even pitched in and bought me a collection of my favorite Elvis movies to watch while I recuperated." The associate continued that "Because my absence had been so sudden and unexpected, I was dreading the stacks of work I knew would be waiting for me when I returned to work. However, when I could finally go back to the office, I found that all of my work was up to date. Everyone in the department had pitched in, working overtime and weekends, to get my work done in addition to their own." The associate marveled that "They told me they were afraid I would wear myself out trying to catch up. This caring and supportive atmosphere is what makes J&K a great place to work."

Jenkens & Gilchrist, P.C.

1445 Ross Avenue, Suite 3200 • Dallas, TX 75202
Phone: 214-855-4500 • Fax: 214-855-4300 • Web site: jenkens.com

OFFICES

Dallas (main office), Austin, Houston, San Antonio, Texas; Los Angeles, California; Washington, D.C.; Chicago, Illinois

"Jenkens has a tradition of letting associates bite off whatever they can chew. You get to work on 'real deals' early on, in a setting that has a reputation of being the most comfortable environment in Dallas."

NUTS AND BOLTS

Managing partner:

David Laney

Hiring partner:

Charles R. Gibbs, phone: 214-855-4500, e-mail: Cgibbs@jenkens.com

Recruiting manager:

Caren Ulrich, phone: 214-855-4659, e-mail: Culrich@jenkens.com

Number of attorneys in firm:

401 (161 partners)

TOTAL FIRM:

Partners (161), associates (214), women partners (21), women associates (84), minority partners (6), minority associates (20), disabled partners (1), disabled associates (0)

THIS OFFICE:

Total attorneys (233), partners (96), associates (120), women partners (12), women associates (45), minority partners (1), minority associates (13), disabled partners (1), disabled associates (0)

OTHER OFFICES:

(* represents an office profiled elsewhere in this book)
Austin (40); Houston (40); Los Angeles (16); San Antonio (46);
Washington, D.C. (21); Chicago (5)

Years to make partner:

7 1/2 to 9

WHAT DO THEY DO?

Primary specialties (more than 5% of practice):

Litigation (43), Real Estate (28), Corporate/Securities (3), Financial
Services (11), Bankruptcy (12), Labor (4), Intellectual Property (40),
Health Law (4), Tax/Estate Planning (9).

WHO DO THEY REPRESENT?

J&G represents a wide range of businesses, from entrepreneurs to public
companies, as well as individuals. Clients include real estate, banking,
health care, telecommunications, professional sports, securities brokerage,
energy, publishing, entertainment, and computer technology concerns.

WHERE NEW ASSOCIATES COME FROM . . .

J&G routinely interviews on campus at the following law schools: Cornell,
St. Mary's, Texas, Georgetown, Harvard, Texas Tech, Vanderbilt, Duke,
North Carolina, NYU, Columbia, Harvard, Penn, South Carolina, Notre
Dame, Baylor, Wake Forest, UCLA, Michigan, Virginia, Tulane, Arkansas,
SMU, Northwestern, Chicago, Houston, Boalt Hall, LSU, and Stanford.
The firm also routinely hires associates and summer associates from
schools where it doesn't conduct on-campus interviews.

HOURS AND BUCKS . . .

On average, associates spend 1,950 hours at work.

Part-time work is available to ongoing associates; typically not at entry
level.

The firm does not routinely hire contract associates.

Typical first year associate salary, including typical bonus: $$$$ (Over
$65,000). The firm is known for its generous financial package.

SUMMER PROGRAM . . .

Last year, firm-wide, there were 99 summer associates, 93 of whom were
2Ls. 70 permanent offers were made; there were 6 offers to the 1Ls to
return in the summer of 1999.

Weekly pay: $1,350 last year

1Ls are routinely hired for the summer program; last year's 1Ls came from Stanford and University of Texas.

PRO BONO . . .

The firm encourages, but doesn't require, attorneys to abide by the state's 50-hour annual pro bono contribution. The attorneys at J&G are involved in pro bono projects representing nonprofit organizations as well as individuals. One recent beneficiary of the firm's pro bono efforts is Volunteer Legal Services of Central Texas, for which J&G attorneys are representing poor and disabled children who are threatened with a cutoff of Social Security benefits.

HISTORY AT A GLANCE . . .

The firm was founded in 1951 in Dallas.

WHAT IT'S LIKE TO WORK THERE . . .

Associates say that when you visit a firm as big as Jenkens & Gilchrist, you expect to see hallowed halls, a hushed atmosphere, wood-paneled offices with oak-framed law degrees on the walls. In fact, "You can tell a lot about what this place is like by taking a peek in the offices. There are tacked-on pictures of children gracing the walls. There are frivolous little goodies on desks. The head of the corporate group does have his diploma on his wall—it's mimeographed and hung up with a piece of tape, next to a drawing of the Ninja Turtles that his kid drew." As you might imagine, "There's an ability here to hang loose, to have fun." There's even an in-house rock band called "Aisle Nine," consisting of a partner and two associates. As one associate reports, "When I was looking at law firms, J&G had the reputation as having the most comfortable environment in Dallas. That put it at the top of my list, and it's turned out to be exactly right."

"You feel like you'll stay because you're part of a family."

J&G associates rave that they "have a say in what's going on." They feel that the partners are "pretty open" with how the firm is doing. "We have a good feel for the strategic plan of the firm," and while it is "a major force in the Southwest, it's got very aggressive growth plans."

One associate reports that "Jenkens stands head and shoulders above other firms when it comes to associate participation. We have a heavy say in the recruiting program, for instance. Some sections even have second year associates running the summer associate program." Associates also keep their finger on the firm's pulse through the Associates committee. Every class has one representative on the committee, "And the board listens to their concerns." The committee addresses issues of "compensation, 401Ks, anything the associates are concerned about." Associates report that "The board is *very* responsive. Last year, there was grumbling that other firms were making more money. Two associates drafted a memo, and sent it to the board. Two days later we got a raise."

"They let you bite off what you can chew."

When associates come to J&G, in "some sections" they are assigned official mentors, whereas "in others it's an unofficial mentoring system." Even without formal mentors associates find that "There is a very open-door policy here—you can confide in shareholders, and ask any question, 'How do I draft this form?' 'What's the rule on this regulation?' without feeling stupid for asking." One associate comments that "The learning curve is steep. You learn by doing everyday things, from putting together stock option plans, to drafting pleadings, that kind of thing." Another adds that, "This is definitely a place where you learn by doing. Jenkens has a tradition of letting associates bite of whatever they can chew—you do it but you have a safety net of senior associates and shareholders for strategy, and you get feedback before things go out."

Associates get a variety of projects because "You're open to getting assignments from anybody in your group. You're not designated to one person. You work with a series of shareholders that way." The shareholders in each practice section typically meet once a week to discuss what they are doing and what the associates in the section are working on. "They look at the hours the associates put in the month before, and they mete out the work that way." And associates say that when there's a project they want to work on, "You *can* pitch for new deals, new cases, but much of the time you're too busy doing what you're doing to notice what's coming in."

The hours shareholders are looking at tend to be long. Associates report that people generally get to work between 8:30 and 9 a.m., and leave between 7 and 7:30 p.m., "with some stragglers there until 10 or midnight, but that's not the same people all the time." Furthermore "You can leave at 6:30 p.m. if you want—it's not frowned upon. That works for people with families. There's no 'face time' necessary."

When it comes to Saturdays and Sundays, associates say that "It's pretty rare to lose a weekend," and "Generally nobody is here on weekends. Every few weekends you may put in five or six hours, but it's not a regular thing."

One ramification of long hours is that pro bono tends to take a back seat. "The business often means stepping back from it." Nonetheless, the firm has a shareholder who encourages associates and shareholders to do pro bono, and that shareholder e-mails available projects to everybody in the firm. "The firm encourages it, but junior associates are so busy that it's not a priority."

Associates handle the long hours by adopting a philosophy that "If you want to make a name for yourself, you work harder. To make yourself understand the law and what's going on, how the business works, that takes hours." Furthermore, "The business is cyclical—you may be very busy right now, the corporate groups are *real* busy, but that ebbs and flows. It's the nature of the business." And on top of that, "There's a bonus for excess hours."

Associates rave that "Jenkens has a very high base salary," reflecting the firm's refusal to have any Texas firm pay associates more than Jenkens does. And while there is pressure to put in hours, there is no pressure on junior associates to bring in business. "The firm recognizes that it's hard for young associates to bring in clients, especially since the firm is weeding out the smaller clients and focusing on blue chips." Associates say that, "Junior associates bring in snippets of small clients here and there, but business development isn't pushed on junior associates." Instead, it's not until associates get to their fifth year or so that "it's time to think about stepping out and developing a reputation, bringing in business."

The payoff for long hours is "very sophisticated work." Associates report that "This is not a place where you get put behind a desk. You get to work on deals that you read about in the paper, and your Saturdays and Sundays are still your own." One associate says that, "When I came here, it was important to me to be in a place where you could do 'real deals,' sophisticated work on big projects, but not a mill or a New York-style sweatshop. I got what I expected." Others report that "Usually everyone has good work—nobody feels they're pigeonholed. Everyone has at least one glamorous, exciting client."

"We all have fun, we enjoy each other at work."

The firm caters a lunch every Friday for attorneys, which "gives you a chance to talk to people in different sections. Everybody takes advantage of that." There's also a firm-sponsored happy hour every Friday for attorneys and staff, but associates find that "it's more utilized by the staff, since the attorneys want to blow out of the office on Fridays." And as you'd expect from a large firm with a well-entrenched summer program, "There are tons of social events during the summer" as well as a well-attended holiday party.

The extent to which the attorneys socialize with each other outside of work "depends on the practice group. Some have friends at the firm, others want to stay with family and friends outside the firm. There's no pressure to socialize. We all have fun and enjoy each other's company while we're here."

One associate sums up life at J&G by saying that, "The culture here combines three elements you don't often find together. You get to work on real deals as a very junior associate. You also have a life, you get to enjoy your free time. And you get trained by some of the best attorneys, anywhere."

Jolley, Urga, Wirth & Woodbury

3800 Howard Hughes Parkway, Sixteenth Floor • Las Vegas, NV 89109
Phone: 702-699-7500 • Fax: 702-699-7555

OFFICES

Las Vegas, Boulder City, Nevada

"You're at the forefront of major lawsuits and corporate transactions from the very beginning . . . but the partners aren't above practical jokes. When I showed up with my hair cut a little shorter than usual, one of the partners added the words 'Private First Class' to my office nameplate. It took a couple of days to figure out why everyone in the office was saluting me when they passed me in the halls."

HIGHLIGHTS

• Pro bono hours are counted as billables.

NUTS AND BOLTS

Managing partner:

William R. Urga

Hiring partner:

Roger A. Wirth

Number of attorneys in firm:

16 (7 partners)

TOTAL FIRM:

Partners (7), associates (8), women partners (2), women associates (2), disabled partners (1), disabled associates (0)

OTHER OFFICES:

(* represents an office profiled elsewhere in this book)
Boulder City, Nevada (1)

Years to make partner:

5 to 7

WHAT DO THEY DO?

Primary specialties (more than 5% of practice):

(Note that some attorneys have more than one specialty)
Bankruptcy, Creditor's Rights (3); Construction (3); Transactions,
Business Organization (4); Family Law (2); Employment (2); Litigation
(6); Product Liability, Tort (3).

The firm is not departmentalized, although attorneys tend to gravitate
to certain areas of emphasis. New associates wind up in their specialties
through exposure to various areas of the practice during their first to third
years with the firm, and tending to emphasize one or two areas where they
feel comfortable and do well. In other words—they handle a case in a certain area, acquire a little expertise, then handle another case, and soon
they are the "go-to" person in that area.

Young associates receive projects through a modified "open season"
approach. They receive assignments directly from partners, but there is a
weekly meeting at Wednesday noon among the young associates and two
young partners, where they discuss their case loads and are given nuts and
bolts one-hour training sessions.

WHO DO THEY REPRESENT?

National and local clients, including Wells Fargo Bank, Nevada State
Bank, Chicago Title Insurance Company, Citicorp National Services Inc.,
Fidelity National Title, TICOR, American Nevada Corporation, Melvin
Simon & Associates, Continental National Bank, General Motors, General
Motors Acceptance Corp., Ford Motor Credit, Owens-Corning Fiberglas,
Prudential Securities, Lincoln Property, Circus Circus Casinos, Metmor
Financial, Western Pipeline Construction Company, Southwest Gas,
Independence Mining, and Aid Association for Lutherans.

WHERE NEW ASSOCIATES COME FROM . . .

The firm occasionally does on-campus interviewing at law schools.
However, the firm hasn't found on-campus recruiting as efficient as in-
office recruiting of people who are sufficiently interested in Las Vegas that
they will travel to the firm to seek out an interview.

HOURS AND BUCKS . . .

On average, first year associates spend between 2,100 to 2,200 hours at the
office.

Of those hours, there is a minimum billable hour requirement of 1,900 hours.

Part-time work is permitted for ongoing associates. The firm does not routinely hire contract associates.

Typical first year salary, including typical bonus: $$$ ($50-65,000)

SUMMER PROGRAM . . .

Last year, there were two 2Ls, both of whom received offers.

Weekly pay: $850 last year

The firm occasionally hires 1Ls for its summer program; this year's 1L came from the University of Virginia.

The deadline for applying for the summer associate program as a 2L is October 1, although earlier applicants have an advantage. The deadline for 1Ls is flexible.

PRO BONO . . .

Associates are encouraged, but not required, to do pro bono work. Pro bono hours are counted as billable hours. Typically, associates are involved in family law pro bono matters, but occasionally they do other types of projects such as real estate transactions or disputes.

There are no specific minimum/maximum hours associates may spend on pro bono projects.

HISTORY AT A GLANCE . . .

The firm began in 1974 with partners Gardner Jolley (one-time president of the Nevada Bar Association) and William Urga. Roger Wirth joined in 1977, and Bruce Woodbury in 1984. Former associates have since become partners, with the firm currently numbering 7 partners and 8 associates.

WHAT IT'S LIKE TO WORK THERE . . .

When you mention Jolley, Urga to lawyers in Las Vegas, you invariably get a response like "Now, that's a great firm to work for." And when you talk to associates, they confirm that impression. With only 15 attorneys, they get "tons of opportunity in large cases from the very beginning." And just as importantly, they enjoy the people they work with.

Associates tell story after story about what makes their work environment so enviable. One tells how "Even our most senior attorneys aren't above practical jokes. For instance, I recently cut my hair a little shorter than usual. One of the senior partners had the words 'Private First Class' added to my nameplate. It took me a couple of days to figure out why everyone in the office was saluting me when they passed me in the hallways!"

The relatively small size of the firm—at 15 attorneys, it's one of the smallest law firms in this book—breeds a kind of family atmosphere that associates particularly enjoy. They tell how all of the attorneys get together every Friday morning to have coffee and to discuss "new and interesting issues" that have come up during the week. Every Friday afternoon, "The whole firm is invited into the large conference room for a beer." One associate recounts that "I've had friends from other firms see the conference room on Friday afternoons and ask what the occasion was. They were all shocked to learn that it was just a normal Friday afternoon at the office." And once a month, the firm has an afternoon birthday party, complete with cakes and pies, to celebrate all of the attorney and staff birthdays that month.

"Associates are at the very forefront of major lawsuits and corporate transactions from the very beginning."

Associates rave about the amount of responsibility they get at Jolley, Urga. "This is the firm to go to if you are interested in the opportunity to have significant opportunities in large cases from the very beginning," says one. "Associates here are at the very forefront of major lawsuits and corporate transactions from the very beginning. This is not the place to come to if you feel you need to research and write briefs to 'get your feet wet' the first few years."

Junior associates get assignments through a modified 'open season' approach. They receive assignments directly from the various partners in a variety of specialties at first, and then as they get some expertise they tend to gravitate toward some specialties more than others.

The firm's training, above and beyond the "learn by doing" approach, focuses on a one-hour training session every Wednesday, when "all associates get together with two young partners to discuss the cases they're working on," and learn about the nuts and bolts of the practice. One lateral applauds the Wednesday training sessions, saying that "I had been practicing for a year and a half before I came to JUWW. Rather than assuming that I knew the skills needed for good lawyering, the firm invited me to participate in the training program. It's perfect for new associates, as well as us laterals unlearning bad habits."

The firm also has a monthly partner-associate luncheon where they discuss "the latest developments from the Nevada Supreme Court, or a specific area of law." The associates play an active role in these luncheons, where they can, if they want to, "summarize the latest Supreme Court cases, or make a presentation concerning an area of law interesting to them."

Beyond the formal training and information sharing sessions, associates find that "When it comes to open door policy, this firm has it. Anytime, I can ask a partner a question concerning a case, or ethics, or the law in general. You will not be turned away because they are too busy . . . even though they truly are."

This open-door policy, combined with the firm's small size, dispenses with much of the bureaucracy you find in larger organizations. Associates say that "Once a month when the partners begin their partners meeting at

4 o'clock, the associates leave and have an out-of-the-office 'associates meeting' for the rest of the day, at a local pub." As one associate laughs, "Needless to say, the associates' meetings tend to last much longer than the partners' meetings!"

"One of the partners has a gas-powered margarita machine."

The firm's warm, friendly nature helps overcome the fact that "Working in Las Vegas is, well, different," according to one associate. "No one actually seems to be a native, and I'm no exception. When I moved here, the entire firm seemed to go out of its way to make me feel comfortable."

The firm has a whole raft of outside-the-office activities that the associates enjoy. There's the JUWW hiking club, formed by two partners who do quite a bit of hiking and camping. Associates report that "although we pride ourselves on being in shape, we were truly humbled by our seniors after a breathtaking—literally and figuratively—hike up Angel Point in Zion National Park."

As that suggests, many of the firm's extracurriculars are very active. There's the firm-sponsored attorney-and-staff co-ed sand volleyball team, which takes part in a local league. "Our team is named the 'Sand Sharks.' Some of the team members can get—well, rather competitive, but the goal is definitely to have fun." Others add that the "volleyball league is great. No one talks about work. Everybody is there to have a good time. And as an added bonus, those games create numerous great stories to bring back to the office."

There's also a yearly firm seminar on the shores of Lake Mead, organized by the firm's "Lake Mead Summer Seminar Committee." As one associate tells it, "Although intellectually challenging, the seminar allows ample time to swim, water ski, jet ski, and (most importantly) drink margaritas made with the help of a partner's gas-powered margarita machine." (That margarita machine shows up, quite naturally, in a lot of JUWW associate stories.)

Other annual events include a "klutz of the year" contest and awards banquet, where "All attorneys and staff are encouraged to turn in anonymous reports of 'klutzy' moves made by others, which are tallied and evaluated for presentation at the banquet." And the firm even manages to put a unique spin on its Christmas party. As one associate tells it, "I'll never forget my first Christmas party with the firm. We had a white elephant exchange, where you swap gifts consisting of things other people have given you, which you can't stand. I became the proud owner of a cream and orange buffalo, which now proudly sits in my office as a constant reminder of the first gift I got as an attorney—from a partner, no less!"

As one associate puts it, "This is a firm that goes out of its way to make sure not just that your work is challenging, but that you enjoy yourself, as well. I love it here."

Jones, Day, Reavis & Pogue

2300 Trammell Crow Center • 2001 Ross Avenue • Dallas, TX 75201-2958
Phone: 214-220-3939 • Fax: 214-969-5100 • E-mail: counsel@jonesday.com
Web site: jonesday.com

OFFICES

Dallas (Cleveland-based firm), Texas

*"This place isn't what anybody expects when they hear 'Jones, Day.' .
Sure, there are the front-page cases, the prestigious clients, and
intellectually challenging work. But there are plenty of people at
other firms who work longer hours than we do, and when it comes
to an informal atmosphere—this is not a get-a-sandwich, close-
your-door, eat-at-your-desk kind of place, not at all."*

HIGHLIGHTS

- Dallas office of the 2ND largest firm in the country.
- Strong dedication to pro bono work; firm-approved pro bono work is countable as billable hours.
- Very generous maternity leave policy, with a six month allowance (three months paid, three months unpaid).
- During the last year, the firm represented the issuers or underwriters in securities offerings totaling more than $10 billion.
- The firm has the largest single real estate and construction practice of any U.S. law firm.
- Ranked 14TH in *PC Week's* "Fast-Track 500," a list of the most technologically innovative companies in the country.
- Considered by some scholars to have "the largest and most effective litigation capability in the world."

NUTS AND BOLTS

Regional managing partner:

Francis P. Hubach, Jr.

Hiring partner:

James P. Karen, phone: 214-969-5027, e-mail: jpkaren@jonesday.com

Recruiting coordinator:

Nancy Steele Carey, phone: 214-969-4885, e-mail: nsteelecarey@jonesday.com

Number of attorneys in firm:

1,239 (422 partners)

TOTAL FIRM:

Partners (422), associates (688), women partners (57), women associates (298), minority partners (11), minority associates (90), of counsel (33), counsel (48), senior staff attorneys (4), staff attorneys (44)

THIS OFFICE:

Total attorneys (147), partners (49), associates (87), women partners (8), women associates (45), minority partners (1), minority associates (6)

OTHER OFFICES:

(* represents an office profiled elsewhere in this book)
Cleveland (230); Washington, D.C. (187); Chicago (118); New York City (112); Atlanta (100); Los Angeles (102); Columbus (64); Pittsburgh (43); Paris, France (35); Frankfurt, Germany (27); London, England (20); Taipei, Taiwan (12); Brussels, Belgium (12); Irvine, California (8); Hong Kong (7); New Delhi(Pathak & Associates, an associate of Jones, Day) (5); Riyadh, Saudi Arabia (4); Geneva, Switzerland (3); Tokyo, Japan (3)

Years to make partner:

9 1/2

WHAT DO THEY DO?

Primary specialties (more than 5% of practice) in Dallas:

Business Practice (53), Government Regulation (1), Litigation (65), Tax (10).

The firm is departmentalized, and young associates do sometimes switch specialties. New associates don't go to a practice group; rather, they go to the 'new associates group,' of which all first-year associates are members. For their first year, they are encouraged to work with various practice areas to see what they like the most. After that first year, the associate chooses the practice group (s)he wants.

WHO DO THEY REPRESENT?

As one of the world's largest law firms, Jones, Day has a predictably vast and diverse client base. Jones, Day serves approximately half of America's

500 largest companies, and regularly furnishes legal services to a substantial number of major multinational companies with headquarters abroad. In addition, the Firm represents a broad range of smaller businesses, individuals, estates, and trusts as well as embassies, religious institutions, and universities.

[For a partial list of clients, visit Jones, Day's home page at jonesday.com]

WHERE NEW ASSOCIATES COME FROM . . .

The firm as a whole routinely interviews on campus at—now, take a deep breath—the following law schools: Akron, American University, Boalt Hall, Boston University, Cardozo, Catholic, Chicago, Chicago-Kent, Cincinnati, Cleveland Marshall, Columbia, Cornell, Case Western Reserve, Dickinson, Duke, Duquesne, Emory, Fordham, George Mason, George Washington, Georgetown, Georgia, Georgia State, Harvard, Houston, Illinois, Iowa, Loyola of Chicago, Loyola/Los Angeles, Michigan, Minnesota, Nebraska, Northwestern, Notre Dame, NYU, Ohio Northern, Ohio State, Pennsylvania, Pepperdine, Pittsburgh, SMU, Stanford, Texas, Texas Tech, Toledo, UC Davis, Hastings, UCLA, USC, Vanderbilt, UVA, Washington & Lee, Wisconsin, and Yale.

While it is hard to believe that there *are* any law schools where the firm doesn't interview, there are—and the firm does periodically hire associates and summer associates from schools where it doesn't interview on campus.

HOURS AND BUCKS . . .

First year associates typically spend 2,100 hours at the office, and while there is no minimum billable hours requirement, average annual associate billable hours amount to 1,900.

Part-time work is available to both continuing and new associates. Jones, Day periodically hires contract associates, and while it's not common, some have become permanent associates.

Typical first year salary including typical bonus: $$$$ (Over $65,000)—Jones, Day is noted in the press for its very generous financial and benefits package.

SUMMER PROGRAM . . .

Last year, there were 25 summer associates, 23 of whom received offers
   Weekly pay: $1,500 last year
   1Ls are routinely hired for the summer program; last year's 1Ls came from Harvard, Texas, and Virginia.
   The deadline for applying for summer clerkships is November 30TH for 2Ls, and February 28TH for 1Ls.

PRO BONO . . .

The firm strongly encourages associates to take part in pro bono matters, with all firm-approved pro bono work countable as billable hours. The attorneys participate in a broad range of pro bono matters, per their individual interests; pro bono projects include Legal Services of North Texas and the Dallas Volunteer Attorney Program. The office staffs legal clinics several times during the year, and takes on as clients people attorneys see at the clinic.

HISTORY AT A GLANCE . . .

The firm was founded in 1893 in Cleveland. It grew steadily over the ensuing decades, having 62 lawyers in the mid-'60's—considered large at the time. Between 1985 and 1990, the firm grew from 350 lawyers to over 1,200. The firm has bounced back remarkably after a rough stretch ending in the early 1990's, when it paid a $51 million fine to the Resolution Trust Corporation to settle claims (which the Firm vehemently denied) relating to the savings and loan scandal. It had also been perceived by the legal community as growing too quickly in the 1980's, the impression being that it had sacrificed quality as a result. (The firm had merged with or gobbled up law firms around the country, as well as hiring individual partners laterally. *American Lawyer* reports that during the 1980's, partners would gather over drinks and joke that Jones, Day was the best 800-lawyer firm in the country—too bad it had 1,200 lawyers.)

The Dallas office was opened in 1980 and has grown steadily to over 140 lawyers practicing in a variety of areas. The office's clients include companies based in Texas as well as throughout the United States. As of 1999, the office is located in new offices in the brand new International Center in downtown Dallas.

Stars include managing partner Patrick McCartan, widely considered one of the best trial lawyers in the country. His victories include winning a reversal of a $100 million judgment against Firestone Tire & Rubber Company, defending candidate Ronald Reagan's right to $29.4 million in federal election funds, and triumphing for General Motors in injury and death cases that claimed design flaws in the old Chevy Corvair. Jones Day lawyers have come from high government and business positions, and have gone on from Jones, Day to become judges, senators, presidential advisers and U.S. Supreme Court justices—including Antonin Scalia, who was a Jones, Day associate from 1960 to 1967.

WHAT IT'S LIKE TO WORK THERE . . .

If you've spent any time at all looking through this book—or even reading the cover—you know that the sole criterion connecting all of the employers in here is that people are happy working for them. And if you're like a lot of people, "happy" and "Jones, Day" aren't words you'd expect to see in the same sentence. Prestige, big bucks, high-profile cases, and Jones, Day, yes. But happy? *Happy?* In fact, when I was interviewing law school administrators for employers to profile in this book, I frequently heard raves about Jones, Day's Dallas office. In fact, after a while, whenever a law school administrator would haltingly say, "I know you're going to have a hard time believing this one, but—I could interrupt and say, "Don't tell me—Jones, Day Dallas."

So here it is. Jones, Day, Dallas. And if all you know about Jones, Day is the nasty nickname "Jones, Day, Evenings, and Weekends," you're in for a *very* pleasant surprise—because people really enjoy working here. From the fantastic resources, to the livable hours, to the outstanding work, to the informal atmosphere, to the excellent pay—"It's just a great place to work," according to associates.

Associates rave about "the friendly atmosphere," where "People rarely work with their doors closed, and everyone is on a first-name basis." Associates feel "very appreciated." They report that "Partners often go out of their way to recognize a job well done. For example, after winning a trial, one partner flew an associate and his wife to Las Vegas to thank the associate for his hard work on the case." Another partner "sent balloons and candy to her team of associates after settling a major case." One associate says that "It sounds hokey, but those little things mean a lot. Sometimes they'll hand out poems, and umbrellas. Last year, it was engraved mugs with our names on them. It seems silly but it really is nice to be appreciated."

"There's always somebody to talk to, no matter what's on your mind."

New associates at Jones, Day Dallas aren't assigned to a particular department. Instead, they join the "New Associates Group," and as part of that group, they are encouraged to work in various practice areas, the philosophy being that "it's very difficult, if not impossible, for graduating law students to know which practice area they'll like the most." After a year of 'experimenting,' each associate then chooses the practice area (s)he wants to join. As associates report, "This program lets you see for yourself the day-to-day practice in different areas before you make a decision."

Associates are also assigned to mentors to ease their transition into the firm. There's a distinct sense that "There are many partners who were here when the office was small, and they're concerned about mentoring young associates, and keeping a one-on-one environment." This results in a pattern of "routine feedback and strategies from all of the lawyers."

Associates report that "From your supervising partner on down to you, there'll typically be somebody in that food chain that you click with." That's the person you can go to "If you want to ask 'how do I do a motion?' or 'how do I handle this situation?' There's never a reason to go to a person who'll be reviewing you if you don't feel comfortable asking them any particular question." Associates also say that, "It pays to make friends with older associates so that you understand how different people like things done. You can find out what fonts they like used on their memos, how to format briefs for them—there are always senior associates who'll be very willing to give you outlines, examples of briefs to see how different partners like arguments structured. And they'll even tell you how to word it if you're busy and you have to turn down work."

While that kind of informal advice is irreplaceable, Jones, Day has a formal training program you'd expect from one of the biggest law firms in the world. There are extensive in-house training programs, monthly departmental lunches where "they bring in a CLE, or we just interact," and once a year there is an associates-only retreat in some warm climate—typically Florida, California, or Mexico—which is designed for training purposes, "but with an eye toward social events, as well."

Associates also say that, "The resources here are second to none." The firm's communications and computer systems are integrated worldwide. Any lawyer in any office can access a host of database resources, including external legal and business research services, client databases, and a whole host of internal databases. On top of that, associates report that "The library here can get you anything you need, at any time. The infrastructure in place here makes things happen. You only have to strategize—you don't have to sweat the details, or how things will get done." Associates rave that "with over 1,200 attorneys around the world, there's an incredible network of experience and knowledge you can draw on." In fact, the *Wall Street Journal* wrote that, "Few law firms have gone as far as Jones, Day in combining advanced technology with advanced office design. The firm's intent is not only to streamline operations but also to unify its work force, all the while sending a message to clients that it is efficient, high-tech and flexible."

"You can structure your workload and level of responsibility any way you want."

Associates say that Jones, Day Dallas is "remarkably flexible" when it comes to giving them the experience they want. As one associate tells it, "You can be a tiny part of a big case, if that's your personality. If you like coordinating things, working on a team, larger cases are fun, seeing how things are juggled." If you prefer to call more of the shots, "You can do smaller cases, not the multi-million dollar ones, and there'll be just you and one other person. You'll get to advocate more, take depositions." And the partners are very willing to accommodate associates who want a combination of experiences. "You can go to the partner in charge of your section and say, 'I want to have client contact and handle my own cases or my own deals, with someone to lean on for questions, and balance that with bigger high-profile cases,' and they'll make it happen for you." As this suggests, "This is an office where it pays to be assertive, it pays to be outgoing. You say, 'This is the practice I want—help me get there' and you get what you want."

When it comes to assignments, "There are two partners in charge of workflow for all associates in each department." Every week, each associate talks about what they're doing with those partners, "you anticipate your open time, and you ask for stuff." As an alternative, "if you've formed a good relationship with a senior associate or a partner with an interesting case you hear about through the grapevine or at one of the firm lunches, you go and ask to help out. They're very responsive to that kind of approach." And when you are overloaded, "You just say no, even to big cases. They don't take it badly. There's plenty of interesting work to go around, and plenty of people to do it."

Associates rave that "the legal matters we handle are on the breaking edge, the kind of things you see reported in the *Wall Street Journal.*" Associates report that they are "actively involved in high-profile, complex matters and we get significant responsibility." The stories are endless: a third year litigation associate argued and won an employment discrimination suit before the Tenth Circuit. A fourth year corporate associate helped negotiate a merger agreement, and drafted the public filings for a $700 million+ acquisition. A second year associate recently participated in a jury trial in federal court, and he got to examine the client's key witness and argue motions and jury instructions. And then there's the international work, which junior associates often get to do. One second year associate said that "You definitely get the chance to do great international stuff, although less in this office than in Los Angeles or New York or D.C." The international work "depends on the stage of the case, and the nature of the client. For instance, there was a product liability case involving Korea and Costa Rica my first year, and I got to travel a lot for that." Associates say that "If you want to travel, you keep an ear to the grapevine for international opportunities, go to the partner in charge, and you get to work in the other country." However, "The firm doesn't make you travel. If the travel is too much, you tell them, 'My family is suffering, I need a change,' and they'll reallocate the work to accommodate you."

"My friends don't want to believe it, but people at other firms work a lot later than we do."

If you think that working at a huge firm means sweatshop hours, you're not thinking of Jones, Day Dallas. In fact, quite the opposite. "The partners are genuinely concerned if they see you burning out," says one junior associate. "When I was a first year associate, I was working on a big case and I was at 2,000 for the year—and that was before Thanksgiving. The head of my department took me aside, and said, 'Listen, you've done enough—take the rest of the year off.' A whole month! And so that's what I did."

Associates report that the offices typically fill up between 8:30 and 9 in the morning, and empty out between 6 and 7p.m. On weekends, you only come in if you "have something due, a deadline. There's no face time. Frank Hubach (the managing partner) isn't roaming the halls. He doesn't care at all about weekend time." Another associate reports that "No one tells you that you *have* to work on anything. They *ask* you if you want to work on it—it's a sign of respect."

Associates like the fact that "There's a good balance here. If you work dead-out for a week on a summary judgment motion, you can go shopping for three hours Monday afternoon. There's no punching a time clock. It's worth putting in the time now for flexibility at the other end, when you're working under deadline. There are no negative repercussions for whatever hours you work. As long as your work gets done, no one cares how you structure your life."

The firm also has "some women attorneys who work part-time," in order to spend time with their small children. There are "guys who've taken time to spend with their newborns, two or three weeks at a time." Associates rave about the firm's "exceptionally generous maternity leave policy, six months all together—three months paid, and three months unpaid." New mothers don't feel pressure to come back any sooner; "People take their full allotted time." The feeling is that "They're much better with maternity issues than most other firms."

When it comes to compensation, associates report that it's "lock step—there aren't any bonuses at all for the first couple of years." After that, "As you take things on, as you start taking charge of cases, as you step up to the plate and make the move from writing memos to running cases and deals, thinking ahead, they reward you. We're fortunate because our pay is excellent. We don't need an eat-what-you-kill environment." As you'd expect from a firm with huge, blue-chip clients, "There's no pressure to bring in business as an associate. You do your work, you help other associates, you proofread for them, you get stuff out, and they help you."

"Associates are encouraged to participate in firm activities."

Jones, Day as a whole has a famously centralized management structure, with a single managing partner, Patrick McCartan, in the firm's Cleveland headquarters. One magazine quoted one of the partners as joking that "We have a system of one man, one vote. And the one man is the managing partner." McCartan decides who makes partner, where and when to open new offices, who heads practice groups, which laterals are pulled in, and how the profit pie gets sliced.

However, from the perspective of junior associates, "those aren't the kinds of decisions that really matter to us." The firm is very bureaucratic—"there are tons of committees"—and "associates get input into many of those." For instance, a "big governing committee" is the Recruiting Committee, which is composed of both partners and associates, with associates being "heavily depended on" in the recruiting process. Associates run the summer program, with the recruiting committee making the final "hire/not hire decision."

Associates get to mentor the summer associates, and "that's great experience, because you decide how to get them exposed to different kinds of work, different out-of-office experiences."

> *"It's not a get-a-sandwich, close-your-door,*
> *eat-at-your-desk kind of place."*

Associates report that "camaraderie in the office is high" and that there is a lot of socializing. There's the huge raft of summer events focused on the summer associate program, of course. There are "lots of sports teams," including a co-ed softball, men's softball, basketball, and volleyball teams. Both "formal and informal" social events are frequent, including favorites like the annual clam bake, a black tie dinner dance "complete with tuxedos and ice sculptures," holiday parties, casino parties, and golf tournaments.

Associates say that, "it's common to get e-mails from people looking for someone to join them on the patio for a beer." Practice groups regularly do happy hours together, but "There isn't pressure to take part. People with kids will do more PTA stuff, pick up Joey from soccer practice, so they're not going to be at so many happy hours." To bring families into the fold, the firm has a number of regular events, including Easter egg hunts at the Dallas Zoo, where they hire a children's entertainer for attorney and staff kids. As one associate says, "It's things like that that go back to the idea that little things mean a lot."

All in all, associates at Jones, Day Dallas say that "When you think about your firm, ask yourself: Do you feel good? Do they take an interest in you and help you along? Will they nurture you? I couldn't put my finger on it, but people here will help you develop as a lawyer. I wouldn't go anyplace else to do what I do."

Jones Vargas

3773 Howard Hughes Parkway, Third Floor South • Las Vegas, NV 89109
Phone: 702-734-2220 • Fax: 702-737-7705 • Web site: jonesvargas.com

OFFICES

Las Vegas, Reno, Nevada

"For a lot of what we do, there aren't a lot of treatises, a lot of 'how to' manuals. What you've got here are people with years of knowledge that they're more than willing to share with you. It makes a big difference!"

HIGHLIGHTS

- State-of-the-art computer systems.
- Very low lawyer and staff turnover.

NUTS AND BOLTS

Managing partner:

Gary R. Goodheart, phone: 702-862-3330, e-mail: grg@jonesvargas.com

Hiring partner:

Richard F. Jost, phone: 702-862-3383, e-mail: rfj@jonesvargas.com

Recruiting coordinator:

Tom J. Christensen, phone: 702-734-2220, e-mail: tjc@jonesvargas.com

Number of attorneys in firm:

48 (24 partners)

TOTAL FIRM:

Partners (24), associates (24), women partners (3), women associates (9), minority partners (1), minority associates (0), disabled partners (0), disabled associates (0)

LAS VEGAS OFFICE:

Total attorneys (34), partners (18), associates (16), women partners (2), women associates (5), minority partners (1), minority associates (0), disabled partners (0), disabled associates (0)

RENO OFFICE:

Total attorneys (14), partners (6), associates (8), women partners (1), women associates (4), minority partners (0), minority associates (0), disabled partners (0), disabled associates (0)

OTHER OFFICES:

(* represents an office profiled elsewhere in this book)
Reno (12)

Years to make partner:

7 to 9

WHAT DO THEY DO?

Primary specialties (more than 5% of practice):

Litigation, including bankruptcy and domestic relations (30); Real Estate (10); Administrative, including government relations and gaming (12); Estate Planning and Probate (5); Municipal Finance (3); General Business and Commercial, including corporate, partnership, limited liability company, tax, securities and banking (9); Healthcare (3); Natural Resources, including water, mining and environmental (4).

The firm is departmentalized only to the extent that people working in litigation and litigation-related practices are grouped together and have periodic meetings, as do the lawyers in transactional specialties. Associates do move between litigation and transactional practices and many associates do both. Associates generally practice in those areas in which they have a particular interest although on occasion associates do receive assignments in other areas, as the workload dictates.

Generally, associates working in particular areas of practice receive work from the partners practicing in those areas directly, although in the litigation practice there is a supervisor who is responsible for redistributing litigation work as necessary.

WHO DO THEY REPRESENT?

A range of individuals and small businesses to large corporations and institutions, local, national and foreign, including various state and local bond issuers, hotel-casinos, contractors, and nonprofit organizations. Clients include Aetna Casualty & Surety, American Society of Composers, Authors & Publishers, Atlantic Richfield Corporation, C.N.A. Insurance,

Chase Manhattan Bank, Coca-Cola, Eastman Kodak, Greyhound Lines, Harrah's Entertainment, Montgomery Ward, Mount Grant General Hospital, Owens-Corning Fiberglas, Santa Fe Hotel & Casino, Sears, Roebuck & Co., Shearson Lehman Brothers, Transamerica Insurance Service, United Parcel Service, and Unocal.

WHERE NEW ASSOCIATES COME FROM . . .

The firm doesn't do on-campus interviewing; it gets new summer and permanent clerks by way of law students contacting the firm.

HOURS AND BUCKS . . .

On average, first year associates spend between 2,200 and 2,300 hours at the office; of those, the average first year associate bills 1,850 to 1,900 hours, and the minimum expectation is 1,800 billable hours.

Attorneys are allowed to work part-time, but none currently do so. The firm does not routinely hire contract associates.

Typical first year associate salary including typical bonus: $$$ ($50-65,000)

SUMMER PROGRAM . . .

Last year, there were 4 summer associates, 3 of whom received offers.

Weekly pay: $825 last year

1Ls are occasionally hired for the summer program; this year's 1L is from Columbia University.

There is no deadline for applying for summer clerkships, but the firm generally fills its clerkship program by the end of January.

PRO BONO . . .

The firm encourages pro bono work. While pro bono hours are not counted as billables, salary and bonuses are determined on the basis of a number of factors, and pro bono projects as well as similar community activities are figured into those calculations.

Pro bono projects undertaken by firm lawyers include the United Way, Catholic Community Services, HELP of Southern Nevada, Boys and Girls Clubs, the Nature Conservancy, North Las Vegas Neighborhood Housing Services.

HISTORY AT A GLANCE . . .

The firm is the result of a December 1997 merger between Jones, Jones, Close & Brown and Vargas & Bartlett. Although each firm was young by East

Coast standards—as the firm points out, "nobody in the letterhead of either firm died before the Civil War"—by West Coast and more particularly by Nevada standards, the firm is the result of a merger between the oldest firm in Southern Nevada and one of the oldest firms in Northern Nevada.

Partner Cliff Jones is a former Lieutenant Governor of Nevada. Partner Herb Jones is a former President of the Nevada State Bar, and a major player in the growth of the gaming industry in Southern Nevada. One of the founding partners, Morley Griswold, was Governor of Nevada in the 1930's.

WHAT IT'S LIKE TO WORK THERE . . .

When it comes to attitudes about Las Vegas, there are only two kinds of people: those who love it, and those who wouldn't touch the city with a very long stick. If you're the latter, welcome to the club—some of Jones Vargas' associates felt that way, too. At least, they did before they joined the firm, and found—much to their surprise—that they really liked it.

As one associate says, "Most people don't dream about living in Las Vegas. I sure didn't. The first time I came here, I thought, 'What a pit.' It was windy and dusty. But I really liked the people at the firm, and when I looked for a place to live, I found that there's a really nice city here, once you get away from the Strip." Others report that "I like it here, more than I ever thought I would. I don't see myself leaving," and "I like having lunch at the casinos. It's fun and exciting." Associates also love the "firm dinners once a month, at a fine restaurant in town. Everybody at the firm gets a chance to hang out together. It's totally not stuffy."

At Jones Vargas, associates rave that "The lawyers here are more than willing to discuss a case, a strategy, or even a personal issue most any time." One associate comments that "I used to work for a bigger firm, and it's *very* different here. There's an 'open door' policy—*nothing* is stupid. If you want to ask something, they encourage you to ask it."

That's important to associates, since "We get lots of responsibility early on," and "For a lot of what we do, there aren't a lot of treatises, a lot of 'how to' manuals. What you've got here is a group of people with years of knowledge that they're willing to share with you. It makes a big difference—it creates a first-class experience that teaches you how to deliver first-class legal services."

Associates find that while "you can't be a lawyer without having a foundation of *some* research, doing some things you'd consider mundane," the partners make "a real effort to give you feedback on everything you do. They'll sit down with you and show you what revisions they make to your work, and why." Associates appreciate that, because "There's no getting around the fact that law is a business with a steep learning curve." Associates find that there is a lot of flexibility with practice areas; they can specialize in a litigation or transactional area, but the "workload sometimes dictates that you will get projects in other areas."

While you'd expect a Las Vegas-based firm to do lots of casino work, that's not the lion's share of what goes on at Jones Vargas. The sense is that casinos have their own in-house counsel and divide up their work for outside counsel between different firms. "We do some gaming, some zoning and land use" for casinos, and "some big loan transactions," but "it's not most of the firm's business. The client base is very diverse." The casino work associates *do* get to do is "unique. For instance, it's hard to foreclose on and then operate gaming property if you're not licensed. There are issues with casinos that you just don't find with any other kind of work."

The firm strongly encourages community involvement, "particularly state bar activities." Associates say that "if you don't do litigation, it's hard to do traditional pro bono work, representing indigents" and that "not a lot of people do pro bono, it's very much an individual thing here."

"They treat you like a partner."

Associates say that formally, the firm is managed by "committees of partners," including the management committee, which consists of four partners. However, associates feel that "There's a lot of casual input from associates. You can talk to any partner about any issue, you can express your concerns to anyone." There's a sense that "the management committee is *very* responsive." Associates believe that part of that responsiveness springs from the fact that "They treat you like a future partner here. Some firms mouth that, but they'll make casual, joking comments here, like 'I guess I'll be stuck with you for the next 15 years.' And in reviews, they talk with you about building a book of business. You know from things like that that they're looking at you as a future member of the business." However, the firm "doesn't formally train you on business development issues; it's too small for that," and the belief with junior associates is that "you need knowledge and experience before you build a book of business. They appreciate that." Before associates are in a position to bring in business, "Pay is lock-step with years of experience, although they have flexibility to reward you for things like community service and pro bono work."

Associates report that "they are expected to work hard," but the hours are livable. The offices fill up between 8:30 and 9 in the morning, and tend to empty out around 6. The associates say that the firm is family-oriented and "as flexible as they can be when it comes to working around family commitments." There are some people in the office on weekends—"It tends to always be the same ones"—but associates feel that the only consideration is "Are you getting your work done? If you can do that during the week, you don't come in on the weekend." Associates say that "Billables are the bottom line, but you respect that. The partners treat you as equals."

All in all, associates at Jones Vargas feel that "As simplistic as it sounds, this is a nice environment, with easygoing people who get along with everybody, and an open door policy. If you don't have an attitude, if you're a hard worker, you'll get along here."

Kirkpatrick & Lockhart L.L.P.

Payne Shoemaker Building • 240 North Third Street • Harrisburg, PA 17101-1507
Phone: 717-231-4500 • Fax: 717-231-4501
E-mail: info@kl.com • Web site: kl.com

OFFICES

Harrisburg (Pittsburgh-based firm), Pennsylvania

"This is a place where assertiveness and entrepreneurialism get you somewhere. 'I want to work with you on that' are words that get you a long way here. I've gotten opportunities that I didn't expect to get."

HIGHLIGHTS

- The 23-attorney office of a Pittsburgh-based firm, the 36TH largest in the country.
- All six offices are connected on a single computerized network, allowing concurrent work across offices on any project, and electronic access to the data base of the firm's collective work product.
- A very well recognized insurance coverage practice, whose litigation efforts are routinely mentioned in the national press.

NUTS AND BOLTS

Managing partner:

Peter J. Kalis, Chair of Firmwide Management Committee
For the Harrisburg office:
Andrew H. Cline, Administrative Partner of Harrisburg Office,
phone: 717-231-4500, e-mail: clineah@kl.com

Hiring partner:

Joel R. Burcat, Recruiting Chair, phone: 717-231-4500, e-mail:
burcatjr@kl.com

Recruiting coordinator:

Jaime M. Zellers, phone: 717-231-5848, e-mail: Zellerjm@kl.com

Number of attorneys in firm:

480 (184 partners)

TOTAL FIRM:

Partners (184), associates (296), women partners (24)

THIS OFFICE:

Total attorneys (23), partners (9), associates (14), women partners (1), women associates (6)

OTHER OFFICES:

(* represents an office profiled elsewhere in this book)
Pittsburgh, PA (215); Boston, MA (34); Miami, FL (22); New York, NY (29); Washington, D.C. (121)

Years to make partner:

8

WHAT DO THEY DO?

Primary specialties (more than 5% of practice) in the Harrisburg office:

Environmental (30%), Commercial and Constitutional Litigation (20%), Administrative (10%), Construction & Government Contracts (10%), Legislation (10%), Health Care (10%), Public Utilities (10%).

The Harrisburg office is not departmentalized. New associates start work on an informal rotation program lasting roughly 24 months. The idea is to get associates acquainted with different substantive areas of the law and gain perspectives on how different disciplines come together to solve legal problems, and also to work directly with as many of the office's attorneys as possible so they can observe, study, and learn from different styles of practice.

WHO DO THEY REPRESENT?

Clients include corporations in the Fortune 50 and small business enterprises, families and individuals, colleges and schools, health care organizations and hospitals, governmental agencies and nonprofit foundations.

WHERE NEW ASSOCIATES COME FROM . . .

The Harrisburg office conducts on-campus interviews at several law schools; consult the firm's web page at kl.com for a rundown of those campus visits.

HOURS AND BUCKS . . .

First year associates typically spend approximately 2,030 to 2,200 hours at the office, of which 1,850 to 2,050 are billable. There is no minimum billable requirement.

The firm does not routinely hire contract associates.

First year associate salary, including typical first year bonus: $$$$ (Over $65,000)

SUMMER PROGRAM . . .

Last year, there were three summer associates, and all received (and accepted) offers.

Weekly pay: $1,346 last year

While 1Ls are occasionally hired for the summer program, 2Ls are strongly preferred.

There is no strict deadline for the summer program, but for applications received after October 15, it may be difficult to arrange an interview.

PRO BONO . . .

The firm encourages its attorneys to engage in pro bono representation of individuals and organizations. Attorneys in the Harrisburg office are involved in both organized and individual pro bono efforts. At the organizational level, attorneys participate in the Dauphin County Bar Association pro bono program, which handles the overflow cases from Central Pennsylvania Legal Services. Participating attorneys agree to take two assignments during each two-year cycle of the program. Harrisburg office attorneys also participate in the Federal Bar Association's court-appointed counsel panel. Members of the panel have agreed to accept court appointments in civil rights cases where indigent plaintiffs would otherwise be unrepresented.

At the individual level, Harrisburg office attorneys have undertaken numerous cases for clients of limited means. They have also devoted time to numerous charitable, civic, and educational organizations.

HISTORY AT A GLANCE . . .

The firm was founded in Pittsburgh in 1946 by seven lawyers. The founding partners were originally associated with another Pittsburgh firm, but left in the early 1940s to enter military service. Returning at the end of World War II, they decided to establish a small general practice firm of their own. They began practice in 1946 under the name Kirkpatrick, Pomeroy, Lockhart & Johnson.

Offices in Washington, D.C., Harrisburg, Miami, Boston and New York followed. The Harrisburg office opened in 1987, both to strengthen the firm's regulatory practice in Pennsylvania's capital, and to expand the firm's general practice in a steadily growing area of Pennsylvania. Having started with three partners, the office now has more than 20 lawyers, and continues to grow. The Harrisburg office now has both a regional and national practice, representing a variety of clients with cases and facilities across the country.

The firm as a whole, with more than 400 lawyers, has grown into one of the largest firms in the country.

K&L lawyers have served in local and state offices, in federal and state judiciaries, as Attorney General of the United States, and in both houses of the U.S. Congress.

WHAT IT'S LIKE TO WORK THERE . . .

The Harrisburg office of Kirkpatrick & Lockhart is a perfect example of the principle that a smaller office of a huge firm gives you the best of all possible worlds: you have the resources of a huge firm, and the atmosphere of a small one. On the 'resources' side, associates at K&L in Harrisburg find that "There are tie-ins among all six of the firm's offices, e-mail, full document exchange—it gives you access to a vast pool of knowledge and experience." Because the offices are so connected, "It's very easy to work with partners in other offices—it happens all the time. It's kind of like having one firm that just happens to have its feet planted in different places."

The 'small firm' feel, with only 22 attorneys, gives Harrisburg lawyers a chance to do the kinds of things a larger office couldn't accommodate. For instance, "Every Monday morning, we have an 'L.A. Law' type meeting. Everybody talks about what they're doing for the week, any new cases that have come in, and they'll say, 'Here's the issue,' and we'll bat around ideas for how to handle it." One associate comments that "I get the sense from other large firms that you pay your dues, in the library, doing other people's research. You do some of that here, but you get good work from the very beginning."

"Lots of the training here comes from 'elbow learning'."

Associates at K&L Harrisburg report that "on the one hand, we get formal training like CLE's, in-house training seminars and conferences, formal things like that," but more important to them is the "Less-formal mentoring. A lot of what we learn here is through 'elbow learning'—that is, learning at the elbow of an experienced attorney. This office is great for that. It's very common for associates as they move up to hook up with senior attorneys with whom they have a particular rapport."

The Harrisburg office is "not heavily structured. It's part of the firm culture. They don't want to restrict people's independence." One associate reports that "No one parcels out work for associates here. You work for anyone who needs it. They call you." And another adds that

"Over time, you wind up allying with the two or three partners whose work and work styles mesh best with your personality and what you want to do."

Associates rave that "Partners here make a point of giving you suggestions that go beyond the project. They're into teaching. They'll sit down and say, 'To be more persuasive, this brief needs this' or 'Here's what I'm thinking' or 'When you argue it you might try this.' That kind of feedback is a huge benefit of working here."

"There's a great variety of work here."

Associates compliment the office's "extremely varied practice," with a strong litigation focus; "It's largely a litigation shop, with very few strictly transactional lawyers."

Much of the work that comes into the office is the result of either the expertise of Harrisburg's partners, or its location in Pennsylvania's capital city. Associates report that "One focus of the practice is administrative. There's a lot of work with state courts, and this office is well-positioned with that." The firm "also does a lot of political work, representing various legislative actors—largely Republicans." That's not surprising, since two-term Pennsylvania Governor Thornburgh is of-counsel to the firm's D.C. office. "Despite the Republican work, a lot of attorneys here have a Democratic bend on their resumes. It's not an issue."

Associates also say that a lot of work comes in because of the partners' focus; for instance, "Two of the founding partners in Harrisburg, Krill and Weston, are well-known environmental lawyers, they're nationally recognized. So we're representing a lead party in a California Superfund case, which you wouldn't see in other firms here."

Associates find that they get "extraordinary opportunities at early moments of our careers here." One associate with only five months' experience under his belt actively second-chaired a 10-day civil RICO jury trial. Another associate told of "appearing in federal district court in Atlanta, chairing a preliminary injunction hearing, two months after I got here." Associates uniformly say that, "It's a real mistake to think that you get lower-quality work or that you're less visible away from the main office. The number one principle here is that we're fully integrated—we get very interesting, very visible projects in Harrisburg."

"We get vigorous, exciting work, and it demands a lot of hours."

The offices at K&L Harrisburg tend to fill up around 8:30 a.m. and typically empty out between 6 and 6:30 p.m. Associates say that weekends at the office "depend on the flow of work." If you've got a "high class" problem, "you'll be in on weekends, but there are relatively few weekends of eight hours each day." More importantly, "There's no face time on weekends. It all depends on what's on your plate." When their work does require long hours, associates don't resent it because "the hours are part

of the deal. It's like a contract, in a way—'I'll offer you X and you'll do Y.'
It's vigorous, exciting work, and it demands hours." On top of that, "The
partners treat us well, and we get to do cutting-edge stuff," and "the partners are there, too, when you're there—you're in it together." Associates
also recognize that "Because we're a litigation shop, our schedules are
ruled by the courts. It's not as though the firm is imposing anything on
you." The hours associates put in at the office are allayed by the fact that
"There's no spending hours a day in traffic jams—Harrisburg isn't big
enough for that." Speaking of Harrisburg, associates point out that it's
not exactly in the middle of nowhere. "We're within an hour of a bunch
of attractions, and two to three hours from Baltimore, Philadelphia,
Washington, and New York City, so if you want to, you can get away for
the weekend very easily."

"They want you to know that you're not just a 'revenue generating unit.'"

When it comes to compensation, associates feel that "the philosophy of
the firm, within certain guidelines, is that they want associates to know
what's going on in the firm." There is an annual retreat for all of the firm's
attorneys at a resort in Virginia, and while there, "they have various sessions, including a business session. They get up and have a slide show,
'here's income,' 'here's median compensation,' that kind of thing. They
want you to know that you're not just a 'revenue generating unit.'"

Associates report that the firm pays three kinds of bonuses. There are
firm-wide bonuses that are the same for all associates in the firm. There is
an office bonus, which reflects a combination of the productivity of your
particular office, "and there's a bonus for the merit of your work."
Associates say that, "If you bring in business, they'll take that into
account." The firm trains associates in how to generate business, "but they
don't pressure you to do it until you're approaching partnership." Anyway,
"At the Harrisburg office, your most prominent clients are the other
offices of the firm. If you're going to promote at all as an associate, it pays
to get to know other lawyers in the firm."

Associates find that "We don't get an overwhelming voice in management," but they don't find that terribly bothersome. "The partners insti-
gated a raise for associates with no input from us at all, a couple of years
ago. We did well to start with, but they wanted to make our salaries even
more competitive." One associate laughingly says that, "For a job with no
heavy lifting, I'm getting paid really well." Associates do take part in the
recruiting committee, and they are consulted in an organized format for
input into the Associates Committee, which is exclusively comprised of
partners. However, associates feel that "because the office is flexible and
individualistic in the way it's structured, that kind of encourages associates to say what's on their mind to senior attorneys."

Outside of work, associates consider many of their colleagues friends,
and "we get together once in a while." While the office "isn't hugely social,"

there are a number of office events that draw attorneys, including the county bar association's volleyball league, the annual firm-wide softball game at Three Rivers Stadium in Pittsburgh, and a particular favorite, the "Watering Hole of the Month." That involves "going to a local tavern and eating lots of grease and drinking beer, which we do whenever someone's cholesterol count is down a quart." In all, the office "has room for different kinds of personalities." As one associate says, "I'm not a cocktail-party schmoozer. At those kinds of functions, I do a great imitation of wallpaper." But "it's a place where you don't have to be a schmoozer. What they appreciate are assertiveness and entrepreneurialism, and they reward you when you show that."

Klinedinst, Fliehman & McKillop

501 West Broadway, Suite 600 • San Diego, CA 92101
Phone: 619-239-8131 • Fax: 619-238-8707 • E-mail: mail@kfmlaw.com
Web site: http://www.kfmlaw.com

OFFICES

San Diego (main office), Orange County, Los Angeles

"This is a young and exciting place to work. It's growing quickly, and it's fun to be a part of that growth. It's the kind of place where you can explore new practice areas and have a hand in expanding the firm. That's a great feeling."

NUTS AND BOLTS

Managing shareholder:

John Klinedinst

Hiring attorney:

Arthur S. Moreau, phone: 619-239-8131, e-mail: ART@KFMLAW.COM

Recruiting coordinator:

Crystal Garcia, phone: 619-239-8131, e-mail: CMG@KFMLAW.COM

Number of attorneys in firm:

29 (7 partners)

TOTAL FIRM:

Partners (7), associates (22), women partners (0), women associates (10), minority partners (0), minority associates (0), disabled partners (0), disabled associates (0)

THIS OFFICE:

Total attorneys (29), partners (7), associates (18), women partners (0), women associates (10), minority partners (0), minority associates (0), disabled partners (0), disabled associates (0)

OTHER OFFICES:

(* represents an office profiled elsewhere in this book)
Orange County, CA; Los Angeles, CA

Years to make partner:

5 to 7

WHAT DO THEY DO?

Primary specialties (more than 5% of practice):

Appellate (3), Banking (5); Business Litigation (8); Employment
Litigation & Counseling (5); Environmental (4); Nursing & Mental Health
(3); Premises Liability (4); Product Liability (4); Professional Liability
Defense (6); Real Estate/Construction Litigation & Transactions (6).

The firm is not formally departmentalized. The areas of practice
include Employment Litigation & Counseling, Environmental, Business
Litigation, Real Estate/Construction Litigation and Transactions,
Intellectual Property, Professional Liability Defense, Insurance Defense,
Nursing & Mental Health, and Products Liability.

WHO DO THEY REPRESENT?

A broad range of clients, including American International Group, Centex
Corporation, Circuit City, CNA Insurance, Coca-Cola, Fireman's Fund
Insurance, Freddie Mac, GTE, General Motors, Home Savings of America,
Hometown Buffet, In-N-Out Burger, National Steel and Shipbuilding,
Navy Federal Credit Union, San Diego Padres, and Westinghouse.

WHERE NEW ASSOCIATES COME FROM . . .

The firm routinely interviews on campus at the following law schools:
Boston College, Boston University, Columbia, NYU, Georgetown, UVA,
Washington & Lee, William & Mary, Vanderbilt, Emory, Northwestern,
Michigan, Colorado, Arizona, University of Washington, Harvard,
Stanford, U.C. Berkeley, UCLA, USC, Pepperdine, Loyola/Los Angeles,
and San Diego.

The firm routinely hires associates and summer associates from
schools where it doesn't conduct on-campus interviews.

HOURS AND BUCKS . . .

First year associates spend on average 2,100 hours at the office; the minimum billable hour requirement is 1,850.

Attorneys are not allowed to work part-time, and the firm does not
routinely hire contract associates.

Typical first year salary including typical bonus: $$$$ (Over $65,000)

SUMMER PROGRAM . . .

Last year, there were 4 summer associates, 3 of whom got offers.
Weekly pay: $1,000 last year
1Ls are not hired for the summer program.
Deadline for applying for the summer program: September 1

PRO BONO . . .

The firm actively encourages, but does not require, its attorneys to do pro bono work. Pro bono hours are not counted on billable hours, and attorneys are allowed to do a reasonable amount of pro bono work as long as it doesn't negatively impact their annual billables requirements.

Pro bono projects are usually done by attorneys to broaden their experiences in areas or causes in which they have a particular interest. Typical pro bono projects have included real estate, contract disputes and administrative law.

HISTORY AT A GLANCE . . .

Over the last five years, the firm has doubled in size.

WHAT IT'S LIKE TO WORK THERE . . .

Associates at Klinedinst talk about the "excitement" of being in a firm that is "small but expanding rapidly, with the goal of becoming the pre-eminent litigation-based firm in Southern California." For junior associates, this translates into an atmosphere where "You're part of the common vision the partners have for the future of the firm. They want all of us to have a role in making that vision a reality. They make you feel as though you have a stake in the organization as a whole, not just occupancy of an office space and a chair in the library."

Associates tell all kinds of stories about the rewards of taking the initiative at the firm. There's the partner who, "As an associate, found that there was no employment law practice here at all, and that's what he wanted to do. He forged that specialty for himself, and now there are four or five lawyers who do it." And they tell of another lawyer who, as an associate, "got involved in improving the firm, and went directly to the partners with his ideas. They applaud that kind of thing here. They expect you to take the initiative. And that guy himself is a partner now." As one associate comments, "If you make the partners aware of what you want, they respond. You can make this experience what you want it to be. All of the opportunity is here for you."

"You get a significant amount of responsibility and independence."

The firm is not formally departmentalized. When new associates come in, they are assigned to "one supervising attorney, and get work from other attorneys through that supervisor. If you want different kinds of projects, your supervising attorneys will suggest to other partners that you are available." Associates find that "It pays to ask people what they're doing, and also to pay attention to your e-mails, because people are always sending e-mails saying what they're doing and asking if people are interested in helping out." There's a sense that "If you're interested in pursuing something, they encourage you to do that." There is also no problem with crossing specialties, and "It's possible to focus on several areas. The firm monitors what your experiences are, and if you want variety, you get it. If you want to focus on something, you can do that, too; for instance, if you want transactional, they'll put you there and that's what you'll do."

Associates report that while they get lots of responsibility and independence, partners and senior associates supervise their work, and "You have a mentor for any questions or problems that you have." Associates applaud their supervising attorneys for "meeting with them frequently to discuss strategies on different cases." There is also a monthly training session, an "in-house seminar kind of thing" where either a senior attorney or outside expert will give a talk on a particular area of litigation practice. "At the seminars, we'll have a topic like defending depositions. While they're normally presented by one person, others throw in suggestions and experiences, and that's really helpful." While the seminars are litigation-based, "by and large everyone here does *some* litigation, so most attorneys go to the sessions."

Associates rave that "You're not stuck in the library, you don't just do lots of research here. You get to do real client stuff." There is also a lot of client contact, due to the fact that "The partners aren't protective of their clients. There are some places where partners won't let you speak to clients as a young associate. Here, they *want* you to talk with the clients so that the clients feel comfortable working with you. You get very early exposure, and you're rewarded for taking the initiative." Not surprisingly, the firm looks for "more than just strong paper credentials. They want associates with entrepreneurial flare, people who can think quickly on their feet." It is routine for first year associates to conduct initial client interviews and develop strategies for handling their cases. They get to decide what information they need to obtain through discovery, and the best ways to obtain it. They take the depositions, propound the written discovery requests, and subpoena any business records they believe are necessary. They prepare and argue dispositive motions and represent clients in settlement conferences. And they negotiate settlements with opposing counsel and, if necessary, take cases to trial.

Associates talk on and on about their extraordinary first years with Klinedinst. One associate talks of her first year of practice, when "I was given a business tort case to defend. I attended most of the depositions and hearings, and I was responsible for the day-to-day handling of the case. As it approached trial, the supervising partner and I discussed our respective roles. I was eager to get the trial exposure, but at the same time I was a little reluctant given my inexperience. The partner asked me if I wanted to take lead on the trial while he sat second chair. Because we only had authority for one attorney to attend the trial, he offered to write off his time." The associate marvels, "Nothing could say more to me about the commitment the partners here have to our personal growth as attorneys."

Another associate talks about coming to Klinedinst "three years ago as a second year lateral. When I interviewed with one of the main partners, he told me, 'the only constraints on your professional growth here are the ones you impose on yourself.' Boy, did that turn out to be true. In the last three years, I've handled four jury trials, four binding arbitrations, and now I'm the point of contact with general counsel of several large restaurant chains."

One very junior associate tells of how, "Two weeks after I received my bar number, a partner walked into my office, dropped a file on my desk, and told me to call the client and introduce myself and let him know that I was working with the partner, and would be handling the case. I developed the discovery plan and handled all of the discovery myself. I checked in with the partner once a week and discussed our position before any significant meetings took place. I represented the client in mediation and settled the matter after approximately eight months." The associate shakes his head, saying, "A lot of my friends from law school are still writing research memoranda!" As these experiences suggest, "By the time you're a third or fourth year associate here, you're typically the lead attorney on complicated litigation matters with hundreds of thousands or even millions of dollars at stake."

"They don't care who's putting in the hours, as long as you get your work done."

Associate at Klinedinst find that huge responsibility doesn't translate into sweatshop hours. The offices typically fill up between 7:45 a.m. and 8:15 a.m. in the morning, and most people are gone by 6 p.m. The feeling is that "We're here for clients, and those are the hours when they'll need us." The office is "not too busy on weekends. You typically come in when you're brand new here, just because you're on a high learning curve, and it takes you more time to get things done. As you get more efficient, you work less in the office and spend more time out of the office and with business development. Most attorneys try to take weekends off as a regular practice, and only come in if they have a deadline or otherwise need to catch up." One associate agrees that "Weekend time here is not expected.

They expect you to get your work done and take whatever hours are necessary to accomplish that. If you can do that between 8 a.m. and 7 p.m. you're fine." The associate adds that "I have classmates from school who work really late, and I just don't. This place isn't concerned with putting in the hours for hours' sake. They're more concerned with you putting high-quality work into those hours."

Associates report that "much of the evaluation here is self-evaluation." The firm gives bonuses, and extra hours are a factor in determining bonuses, but "no more than any other contribution to the firm, like involvement in firm administration, or committees, or bringing in business, and how the firm is doing in general." When it comes to business development, "The firm makes you feel like part of the business from the very beginning. At the annual retreat the firm looks at where it wants to go in the next year as well as its long-term goals, and encourages you to do some planning of your own. Partners are very open with plans and suggestions." The firm "encourages you to get out and meet people in the community," through things like bar association dinners, or political fundraisers. The firm sends e-mails to the associates to let them know the kinds of community events that are going on, and sends out applications for profession-oriented activities like "Inns of Court." The partners' openness doesn't end with their plans for the business; associates say that "The partners are very easy to talk to" and "There's no fear of going to the partners here. They listen to associates. When we agitated for new computers, for instance, we got them."

"It's a young, friendly, outgoing place."

An aggressive business stance doesn't translate into a cutthroat atmosphere at the Klinedinst offices. Instead, associates rave about "The classic small firm atmosphere. It's *very* friendly. When you start here, every attorney comes in to meet you, everybody offers to help." Other associates add that, "It's a very young firm. There's nobody over 50 here. They're all very outgoing." One associate talks of starting at the firm just one week before the annual retreat. "I was kind of scared. I was driving down to this resort in Mexico with the head partner, and I thought, 'I've got to make a good impression or I'm dead.' But everybody could not have made me feel more comfortable. They all wanted to eat meals with me, buy me drinks, dance—it was great."

Associates say that, "There is no formal hierarchy at the firm. All of the lawyers, all of the staff are on a first-name basis." And when it comes to family friendliness, associates report that "Important family matters always take priority over work. Attorneys and staff regularly manipulate their schedules to accommodate school award assemblies, recitals, child care emergencies and sick children." When a project requires weekend work, "You'll often find kids and dogs in the 'war room' in front of the television watching Saturday morning cartoons, while Mom or Dad finishes up some last-minute work." Many of the attorneys have small children, and when "one lawyer here recently had a baby, the firm really helped with time off and managing her cases while she was out." Associates say that overall "Nobody here complains that the firm prevents them from spending time with their family."

Social events at the firm include a firm-sponsored outing for the first night baseball game in June to watch the San Diego Padres, "one of our clients." As one associate tells it, "We arrive early and tailgate, setting up barbecues and having a picnic before the game starts. Family, friends and clients are invited, and what's better, the seats are pretty good!" The summer also brings a series of Wednesday-afternoon yacht races called the 'Beer Can' series, sponsored by the local yacht club. "One of the partners who sails a lot will take off around 3:30 p.m., taking two or three associates or summer clerks out with him to race around the buoys in San Diego Bay, followed by a visit to the post-race party." And on a monthly basis, "We close the office doors at 5:30 p.m. on Friday and have a happy hour. It's a great opportunity to catch up with each other on a personal basis." Associates add that "Even when events like these aren't 'formally' organized, a lot of attorneys and staff often socialize together." As associates point out, "This isn't just a place that's dedicated to great legal work. They want you to have a great life, as well."

Latham & Watkins—Los Angeles

633 West Fifth Street, Suite 4000 • Los Angeles, CA 90071-2007
Phone: 213-485-1234 • Fax: 213-891-8763 • Web site: lw.com

OFFICES

Los Angeles (main office), Orange County, San Diego*, San Francisco*, Silicon Valley, California; Chicago, Illinois; Newark, New Jersey; New York City, New York; Washington, D.C.*

"People think that you go to a large firm, put in a couple of years, and then leave. When I started, with that image in mind, I never thought I'd stay. But now I can't imagine leaving. It's so challenging and stimulating. I just love it!"

HIGHLIGHTS

- 4TH largest firm in the country, with over 800 lawyers.
- Pronounced dedication to pro bono work; pro bono hours are counted as billables. In one recent year, the firm logged over 30,000 pro bono hours and contributed almost $6,000,000 in legal time to pro bono projects.
- New associates don't have to commit to a specialty for their first two years at the firm.
- Uniquely democratic management style—associates play a significant role in running the firm.
- Routinely ranks among top 10 firms nationwide in *American Lawyer* corporate scorecard table for corporate finance transactional work, including mergers and acquisitions, financing projects, stock offerings, and real estate investment trusts. In a recent 6-month period, corporate transactional work firm-wide resulted in more than $20 billion in mergers and acquisitions and $13 billion in public and private financings.
- Leads California law firms in profits per partner.

NUTS AND BOLTS

Managing partner:

Robert A Long, Los Angeles office

Robert M. Dell, National (San Francisco office)

Hiring partner:

Hank A. Flagel, Los Angeles office
Roger S. Goldman, National (Washington, D.C. office)

Recruiting coordinator:

Kathy Yaffe, Los Angeles office, e-mail: kathy.yaffe@lw.com
Debra Perry Clarkson, National (San Diego office)

Number of attorneys in firm:

838 (292 partners)

WHOLE FIRM:

Women partners (41), women associates (201), minority partners (12), minority associates (75), disabled partners (1), disabled associates (2)

LOS ANGELES OFFICE:

Total attorneys (224), total partners (83), total associates (130), women partners (17), women associates (54), minority partners (6), minority associates (31), disabled partners (1), disabled associates (0), of counsel (11)

OTHER OFFICES:

(* represents an office profiled elsewhere in this book)
Chicago (83); Newark (13); New York (160); Orange County (61); San Diego* (71); San Francisco* (72); Silicon Valley (12); Washington, D.C.* (113); Hong Kong (3); London (14); Moscow (8); Tokyo (3); Singapore (1)

Years to make partner:

8

WHAT DO THEY DO?

Primary specialties (more than 5% of practice):

Corporate (includes Corporate Finance Practice, General Company Representation, Mergers and Acquisitions/Leveraged Buy-Out Practice, Health Care Industry, and Entertainment, Sports & Media)

Environmental (includes Enforcement and Litigation, Rulemaking and Legislation, Permitting and Compliance, Transactional Advice, and Land Use Practice)

Finance and Real Estate (includes Project Finance, Electric Utility Deregulation, Real Estate, Bankruptcy and Insolvency, Infrastructure Finance, Structured Finance, and Banking)

Litigation (includes Litigation Support and Technology, Appellate, White Collar Government Investigation and Corporate Governance, Bankruptcy/Creditors' Rights, Employment, Government Contracts, Securities and Corporate Control Litigation Group, Intellectual Property, Product Liability and Product Safety, Antitrust and Trade Regulation, Professional Liability, Health Care)

Tax (includes General Income Tax Practice, Transactional Practice, International Tax Practice, Personal Legal Services and Benefits and Compensation Practice)

New associates are unassigned for the first two years of practice, and have an opportunity to obtain broad exposure to the firm's practice areas. Associates do not rotate through departments on a fixed schedule; rather, they select a mix of work from their areas of interest, thus "putting them in the driver's seat" with their careers from the outset.

WHO DO THEY REPRESENT?

Latham's client list reads like a Who's Who in American business, with a wide variety of small, dynamic businesses as well as many Fortune 500 companies. For a more complete list than can be included here, visit Latham's web site at http://www.lw.com. Some famous name clients include Amgen; Bear, Stearns & Co.; Cedars-Sinai Medical Center; DIRECTV; Donaldson, Lufkin & Jenrette Securities Corporation; DreamWorks SKG; E! Entertainment Television; Harrah's Entertainment; Hilton Hotels; Hughes Communications; Kohlberg Kravis Roberts; Nestlé USA; Nintendo of America; Safeway; Smith Barney; and the United States Soccer Federation.

WHERE NEW ASSOCIATES COME FROM . . .

Latham routinely interviews on campus at the following law schools: Boalt Hall, Boston College, Boston University, Brigham Young, Chicago, Columbia, Cornell, Duke, Emory, Fordham, George Washington, Georgetown, Harvard, Hastings, Howard, Illinois, Iowa, Kansas, Michigan, Minnesota, Northwestern, North Carolina, Notre Dame, NYU, Pennsylvania, Pepperdine, San Diego, Stanford, Texas, Davis, UCLA, USC, Vanderbilt, Washington, Virginia, William & Mary, Wisconsin, and Yale. Associates and summer associates are also hired from law schools where Latham doesn't conduct on-campus interviewing.

HOURS AND BUCKS . . .

Minimum billable hour requirement for first year associates: 1,900
Part-time work available for associates, but not at entry level

Typical first year associate salary, including typical bonus: $$$$ (over $65,000); Latham is often noted in the press for its particularly generous financial package.

SUMMER PROGRAM . . .

In 1997, there were 32 summer associates, 30 of whom received offers.
Weekly pay: $1,500
There are no 1L summer associates in the Los Angeles office.
Deadline for applying for summer clerkships: December 1

PRO BONO . . .

Latham strongly encourages its attorneys to do pro bono work. Pro bono hours are considered billables. Pro bono work is routinely done for the Alliance for Children's Rights, the Asian American Legal Defense and Education Fund, Chrysalis (a homeless assistance agency), the Committee for the Prevention of Child Abuse, the Legal Assistance Foundations, the Lawyers Committee for Civil Rights, Phoenix House, Strategies Against Gang Environments, and the West Hollywood Community Housing Corporation. The firm also represents indigent individuals, and cases have included numerous federal *habeas* proceedings, state criminal matters, death penalty cases, and representing individual victims of domestic violence and AIDS patients.

HISTORY AT A GLANCE

Latham was founded in Los Angeles in 1934 by Dana Latham and Paul Watkins, focusing primarily on tax. It wasn't until the last couple of decades that the firm experienced spectacular growth, from 40 attorneys in 1969 to over 800 today. With an aggressive marketing effort under managing partner Robert Dell, Latham recovered from setbacks in the early '90s (largely attributable to the collapse of a major client, New York junk bond dealer Drexel Burnham Lambert), to become one of the most profitable and highly-respected law firms in the country.

Today Latham's Los Angeles office has a number of local headline makers, including partner Edith Perez, a president of the Los Angeles Police Commission; partner Barry Sanders, who helped lead the "Rebuild L.A." campaign after the riots in 1992; partner George Mihlsten, voted by *Buzz* magazine as one of the top 10 power brokers in Los Angeles; and partner Alan Rothenberg, president of the U.S. Soccer Federation and chairman of Major League Soccer.

If you've spent any time glancing through the employers profiled in this book, you've noticed that very few large firms made the cut. Why not? Well, it's tough to combine great pay, prestigious clients, and exciting work, while still avoiding a reputation as a "sweatshop."

Fortunately for Latham & Watkins' associates, Latham does exactly that. It is not only one of the country's premier law firms, but it lives up to its image as a "young, ambitious" place to work. As one associate put it, "People think that you go to a large firm, put in a couple of years, and then leave. When I started, with that image in mind, I never thought I'd stay. But now I can't imagine leaving. It's so challenging and stimulating. I just love it!"

"You're a 'free agent' for two years when you get here."

At Latham, new associates aren't assigned to a particular department for two years. Interestingly enough, the firm actually prefers it if associates don't have a stated preference; instead, associates are encouraged to work with a variety of partners, on all different kinds of projects. These projects come out of a book which is called—appropriately enough—"the book." As one associate described it, "The book has every project at the firm. You state a preference, and then the person in charge of that project will give you a call." Latham expects associates to take advantage of the book to try out a variety of projects, and once you state an interest in a project, you'll "usually" get it. Not all associate projects come out of the book. Once associates are assigned to a department, they *are* allowed to take on projects directly from senior associates or partners, which puts a premium on getting to know senior associates and partners with whom you'd like to work. But as one associate put it, "The book gives you an 'out'—it stops any one partner from hogging your time."

The fact that new associates take projects from various departments doesn't stop them from getting work they enjoy. As one associate said, "From Day One I've never been bored. I'm constantly learning new things." One associate, for example, talked of second chairing a jury trial as a second year associate.

With a practice that cuts across so many specialties, and clients with varying needs, one associate noted that "it pays to be flexible" with your time. Most associates work from 8:30 in the morning until 6:30 p.m. or so, although "Your hours totally depend on the needs of the matter you're working on." While some associates come in on weekends, "It's not necessary to come in just for 'face time.'" One associate said that it's perfectly acceptable to work from home if you have something to finish on a weekend, and another pointed out that, "I've sometimes worked from home during the week. The only important thing here is to do what it takes to make the client happy."

When long hours are necessary, associates stress that "It's important to understand what drives deals. Nobody here sets false deadlines. You do whatever you have to do for the clients, realizing that they're driven by circumstances, too." One associate said that "Being unassigned to a department for your first two years here gives you a chance to see which practice groups will accommodate your time commitments. For instance, helping to form partnerships or joint ventures is work that is typically not so time sensitive. But in mergers and acquisitions, there's so much at stake—jobs, credibility, money—every minute of every day counts. It's exciting but demanding, and you have to appreciate that so that you don't resent the hours it sometimes requires."

"You get a voice in firm management as an associate."

Latham has a management style that associates rave about, and for good reason: associates have input in virtually all management decisions at the firm on the same basis as partners. As one associate commented, "It's excellent management experience." Here's how the system works. There are eight firm-wide management committees, with associates frequently outnumbering partner members. Each committee has a different responsibility; for instance, one of the biggest committees handles recruiting matters. Others handle issues like associate performance evaluations, compensation levels, bonuses, business development opportunities, pro bono activities, and even recommendations for admission to the partnership. One associate commented, "They described the management style when I interviewed here, and it works just the way they told me it would."

This cooperative management style goes beyond formal committees. As one associate explained it, "There is a major emphasis on critiques here. You get to see the practical effects of your actions on deals and on the people you work with, and you get to see how others impact you." Associates even get an opportunity to critique their supervisors, reflecting the philosophy that "both sides have something at stake." Happily for associates, these supervisor critiques are anonymous! A performance evaluation committee processes the critiques and conglomerates them so that it's not obvious who gave any particular criticism. These supervisor critiques are taken seriously, especially for "Senior associates, who have their admission to the partnership to worry about."

The firm is particularly committed to aggressively seeking out new business opportunities. One associate pointed out that since the demise of Drexel Burnham Lambert, the New York junk bond dealer which was one of the firm's biggest clients, in the early 1990's, the firm has become "very sensitive to changes in the market." Managing partner Robert Dell has been credited with shrugging off the old "internal navel-staring" philosophy at Latham with an approach that one young associate describes as "dynamic and forward-looking. The firm is constantly asking, what are growth areas? It is very pro-active in developing business, which makes me feel good about my future here."

"The managing partner played a practical joke
on another new associate and me!"

Latham prides itself on its friendly work environment. One associate raved about the "open, fun, humorous" people at the firm. Latham attorneys routinely go to concerts, weekenders, restaurants, and sporting events together. One group of associates gets together Saturday mornings to play basketball, and the firm has a softball team. The firm also hosts Friday cocktail hours after work, as well as ice cream socials and coffee breaks to encourage partners and associates to get together.

The firm also has a management meeting one weekend every year in March, typically in Palm Springs or a resort in Arizona, and all attorneys attend. There's also a yearly weekend in Lake Arrowhead for summer associates and firm attorneys.

In spite of the firm's aggressive social schedule, there's no penålty for not taking part in firm social activities; one highly-regarded associate noted that many people "go their own way" after work, and that's not frowned upon. And at the office, the firm prides itself on an open-door policy that encourages interaction between associates and partners. As one associate said, "We're very close. There's a great sense of teamwork here. Compared to what you'd expect from a large firm, I've found it surprisingly enjoyable to work at Latham."

Latham & Watkins—San Diego

701 B Street, Suite 2100 • San Diego, California 92101-8197
Phone: 619-236-1234 • Fax: 619-696-7419
E-mail: michelle.carne@lw.com • Web site: lw.com

OFFICES

Los Angeles (main office)*, Orange County, San Diego, San Francisco*,
Silicon Valley, California; Chicago, Illinois; Newark, New Jersey; New York
City, New York; Washington, D.C.*

*"Based on their credentials, everyone here could have been at any
firm in any city. The fact that they chose Latham San Diego means
that they want to do top notch legal work but also maintain a low-
key lifestyle . . . the people here are infamous for being frank, casual
and fun. In few other large law firms would a summer associate feel
comfortable playing a joke on a corner-office partner—and living
to tell about it."*

HIGHLIGHTS

- 4TH largest firm in the country, with over 800 lawyers.
- Pronounced dedication to pro bono work; pro bono hours are counted
  as billables. In one recent year, the firm logged over 30,000 pro bono
  hours and contributed almost $6,000,000 in legal time to pro bono pro-
  jects.
- New associates don't have to commit to a specialty for their first two
  years at the firm.
- Uniquely democratic management style—associates play a significant
  role in running the firm.
- Routinely ranks among top 10 firms nationwide in *American Lawyer*
  corporate scorecard table for corporate finance transactional work,
  including mergers and acquisitions, financing projects, stock offerings,
  and real estate investment trusts. In a recent 6-month period, corporate
  transactional work firm-wide resulted in more than $20 billion in merg-
  ers and acquisitions and $13 billion in public and private financings.

- $5,000,000 in legal time to pro bono projects.
- Leads California law firms in profits per partner.

NUTS AND BOLTS

Managing partner:

Donald P. Newell, San Diego office
Robert M. Dell, National (San Francisco office)

Hiring partner:

Donna Jones, San Diego office
Roger S. Goldman, National (Washington, D.C. office)

Recruiting coordinator:

Michelle Carne, San Diego office (e-mail: michelle.carne@lw.com)
Debra Perry Clarkson, National (San Diego office)

Number of attorneys in firm:

838 (292 partners)

WHOLE FIRM:

Women partners (41), women associates (201), minority partners (12), minority associates (75), disabled partners (1), disabled associates (2)

SAN DIEGO OFFICE:

Total attorneys (71), total partners (28), total associates (40), women partners (4), women associates (15), minority partners (0), minority associates (4), disabled partners (0), disabled associates (1), of counsel (3)

OTHER OFFICES:

(* represents an office profiled elsewhere in this book)
Chicago (83); Los Angeles* (224); Newark (13); New York (160); Orange County (61); San Francisco* (72); Silicon Valley (12); Washington D.C.* (113); Hong Kong (3); London (14); Moscow (8); Tokyo (3); Singapore (1)

Years to make partner:

8

WHAT DO THEY DO?

Primary specialties (more than 5% of practice):

Corporate (includes Corporate Finance Practice, General Company Representation, Mergers and Acquisitions/Leveraged Buy-Out Practice, Health Care Industry, and Entertainment, Sports & Media)

Environmental (includes Enforcement and Litigation, Rulemaking and Legislation, Permitting and Compliance, Transactional Advice, and Land Use Practice)

Finance and Real Estate (includes Project Finance, Electric Utility Deregulation, Real Estate, Bankruptcy and Insolvency, Infrastructure Finance, Structured Finance, and Banking)

Litigation (includes Litigation Support and Technology, Appellate, White Collar Government Investigation and Corporate Governance, Bankruptcy/Creditors' Rights, Employment, Government Contracts, Securities and Corporate Control Litigation Group, Intellectual Property, Product Liability and Product Safety, Antitrust and Trade Regulation, Professional Liability, Health Care)

Tax (includes General Income Tax Practice, Transactional Practice, International Tax Practice, Personal Legal Services and Benefits and Compensation Practice)

New associates are unassigned for the first two years of practice, rotating through all of the departments before settling into a specialty. Associates do not rotate through departments on a fixed schedule, but instead select a mix of work from their areas of interest, thus allowing each associate to shape his/her career from the outset.

WHO DO THEY REPRESENT?

Latham's client list reads like a Who's Who in American business, with a wide variety of small, dynamic businesses as well as many Fortune 500 companies. For a more complete list than can be included here, visit Latham's web site at http://www.lw.com. Some famous name clients include Amgen; Bear, Stearns & Co.; Cedars-Sinai Medical Center; DIRECTV; Donaldson, Lufkin & Jenrette Securities Corporation; DreamWorks SKG; E! Entertainment Television; Harrah's Entertainment; Hilton Hotels; Hughes Communications; Kohlberg Kravis Roberts; Nestlé USA; Nintendo of America; Safeway; Smith Barney; and the United States Soccer Federation.

WHERE NEW ASSOCIATES COME FROM . . .

Latham routinely interviews on campus at the following law schools: Boalt Hall, Boston College, Boston University, Brigham Young, Chicago, Columbia, Cornell, Duke, Emory, Fordham, George Washington, Georgetown, Harvard, Hastings, Howard, Illinois, Iowa, Kansas, Michigan, Minnesota, Northwestern, North Carolina, Notre Dame, NYU, Pennsylvania, Pepperdine, San Diego, Stanford, Texas, Davis, UCLA, USC, Vanderbilt, Washington, Virginia, William & Mary, Wisconsin, and Yale. Associates and summer associates are also hired from law schools where Latham doesn't conduct on-campus interviewing.

HOURS AND BUCKS . . .

Minimum billable hour requirement for first year associates: 1,900

Part-time work is available for associates, but not at the entry level. The firm does not routinely hire contract associates.

Typical first year associate salary, including typical bonus: $$$$ (over $65,000); Latham is often noted in the press for its particularly generous financial package.

SUMMER PROGRAM . . .

Last year, there were 14 summer associates; all 14 received offers.

Weekly pay: $1,500

1Ls are hired for the summer program on a "very limited basis."

Deadline for applying for summer clerkships: December 1

Latham's San Diego office has done particularly well in the *American Lawyer* summer associate survey, with clerks praising the office's high level of feedback, importance of work, and interest level of work.

PRO BONO . . .

Latham strongly encourages its attorneys to do pro bono work. Pro bono hours are considered billables. As a firm, in a recent year Latham & Watkins logged over 30,000 pro bono hours and contributed well over $6,000,000 in legal time. Examples of pro bono projects include the Alliance for Children's Rights, Chrysalis Homeless Assistance Agency, Asian American Legal Defense/Education Fund, and Humane Society of the United States.

HISTORY AT A GLANCE . . .

Latham was founded in Los Angeles in 1934 by Dana Latham and Paul Watkins, focusing primarily on tax. It wasn't until the last couple of decades that the firm experienced spectacular growth, from 40 attorneys in 1969 to over 800 today. With an aggressive marketing effort under managing partner Robert Dell, Latham recovered from setbacks in the early '90s (largely attributable to the collapse of a major client, New York junk bond dealer Drexel Burnham Lambert), to become one of the most profitable and highly-respected law firms in the country.

The San Diego office opened in 1980, with four attorneys. It has grown since then to over 70 attorneys, making it one of the largest law firms in San Diego.

WHAT IT'S LIKE TO WORK AT LATHAM . . .

Please read the firm's Los Angeles profile first! It will give you a feel for what it's like to work at Latham in general. Here are thoughts specifically from Latham's associates in San Diego:

When you hear what Latham's San Diego associates have to say, you quickly realize that they feel they've found the best of all possible worlds: great work in a wonderful city with people they truly enjoy.

As you would expect with one of the country's premier law firms, associates are blown away by the scope of the projects they work on. As one junior environmental associate said, "In the last year, I have represented a utility selling over a billion dollars worth of power generation assets in Southern California, an investment bank underwriting over four billion dollars in debt for developing a new casino in Las Vegas, and a former manufacturing facility defending a claim brought by the federal government alleging over a billion dollars in natural resources damages." Another associate raved that, "Our client base is uniquely diverse and sophisticated, from the famous San Diego Chicken, to local real estate developers, to regional utilities, to national manufacturing companies, to international banks to the governments of developing countries."

Many associates pointed out that the firm's 'one-firm approach' made them feel particularly connected with lawyers in other Latham offices. Several pointed out that even as junior associates they had worked with lawyers in every one of Latham's offices. One associate commented that, "With e-mail and Latham's own Intranet page, I can draw on the expertise of Latham lawyers in any office in this country and abroad. It's an amazing feeling to work with lawyers in all of the offices and on projects all over the country and the world." Another associate commented that, "The size of this office, with 70 attorneys, is ideal. It is large enough to provide a varied practice and all of the resources you'd expect of a large firm, while at the same time being small enough to let you get to know everybody in the office."

As with associates in Latham's other offices, San Diego associates point out that they work long hours. However, the supportive nature of the San Diego partners, along with a generous bonus pool, helps put those hours in perspective. As one junior associate pointed out, "I was assigned to be the only associate on a high-profile litigation for one of the office's most important clients. While I loved the early responsibility the case provided, that by itself would not have been worth the sacrifice that the intense briefing schedule would have required. What *did* make it worth it was that rather than simply passing the workload onto me without a thought to my schedule, the partner in charge of the project would do the work herself when she saw that my schedule was full. It was important to me that she made an effort to make sure that I wasn't overloaded, and that she was willing to get 'down in the trenches' with me, working side-by-side with me during several late nights, rather than taking the attitude that she had 'paid her dues' and that it would be all right to leave the all-nighters to me to struggle through alone." Another associate added that, "While occasional late nights are unfortunately still a part of life at this firm, we all know that our efforts are appreciated and rewarded." Another pointed out that, "Our compensation includes a profit-sharing component, and it gives the associates a stake in how the firm does. We are generously rewarded when we contribute to the firm throughout the year. You think about that when you have to work late." On top of that, because the firm did so well last year, the partners decided to give all of the associates an additional $5,000 bonus in December, with the stated purpose of rewarding them for their hard work. As one associate pointed out, "It was unexpected but very much appreciated."

Latham's San Diego associates uniformly rave about the city. If you've been to San Diego, you understand how they feel; if not, well, there's no question that it's one of the most desirable cities in the country. As one associate summed it up, "I live four blocks from the beach, eight blocks from the bay, and 10 minutes from work, in the best climate in the world. Enough said."

Of course, it doesn't matter how wonderful your city is or how compelling your work is if you don't like the people you work with. That's definitely *not* the case at Latham San Diego. Associates talked about how "The people here are infamous for being frank, casual and fun. In few other large law firms would a summer associate feel comfortable playing a joke on a corner-office partner and living to tell about it." Others told stories that exemplified a "work hard, play hard" spirit. There are tales of one lawyer dyeing his hair six different colors to help his team win a contest at a firm social event, and another doing an award-winning Elvis impersonation in front of a crowd of his colleagues. One associate commented that, "It's true that the attorneys in the office take their work very seriously. But at the same time, they are not only fun to be around, but they are warm and considerate of others. On several occasions attorneys have opened their homes to newly-hired associates so that the associate can have a place to stay in town while house-hunting."

People at the office routinely socialize together. On top of the usual raft of summer associate events, there's the annual firm-wide business meeting at a Southwestern resort, which mixes in business meetings with a liberal dose of spa packages, golf, hot air balloon rides, and the like. On an informal basis, different groups of attorneys plan ski trips together, celebrate birthdays together, and gather for weekly happy hours. Often attorneys will get together on an impromptu basis to go see the latest movie, or take advantage of San Diego's gorgeous climate and beachfront to go surfing, ocean kayaking, sport fishing, or rollerblading. Also, whenever an attorney is having a baby or getting married, other attorneys in the office plan a co-ed baby and/or wedding shower in which virtually everybody at the office participates.

The firm also provides nice touches like breakfast for everyone every Monday, and special events throughout the year in addition to the typical holiday parties. For instance, the firm brings in coffee carts and hosts pie or cake and ice cream celebrations on a regular basis. And to mark the anniversary of the San Diego office's opening, there's a Mexican-themed party complete with a mariachi band.

As one associate enthused, "This place is simply the best. Everybody here, based on their credentials, could have been at any firm in any city in the country. The fact that they chose Latham San Diego means that they wanted to do top notch legal work in a place where they can maintain a more low-key lifestyle than you could find in other cities and at other large firms. The premium that everybody here places on lifestyle, combined with the caliber of work we do, makes Latham San Diego unique."

Latham & Watkins—San Francisco

505 Montgomery Street, Suite 1900 • San Francisco, CA 94111-2586
Phone: 415-391-0600 • Fax: 415-395-8095 • Web site: lw.com

OFFICES

Los Angeles (main office)*, Orange County, San Diego*, San Francisco, Silicon Valley, California; Chicago, Illinois; Newark, New Jersey; New York City, New York; Washington, D.C.*

"At Latham San Francisco, you get to live in the most desirable city in the country, have the most sophisticated and interesting work, practice law with really great colleagues and on top of that, be compensated very generously. I'd never make any comments about another firm, but I don't see how anything could top this."

HIGHLIGHTS

- 4TH largest firm in the country, with over 800 lawyers.
- Pronounced dedication to pro bono work; pro bono hours are counted as billables. In one recent year, the firm logged over 30,000 pro bono hours and contributed almost $6,000,000 in legal time to pro bono projects.
- New associates don't have to commit to a specialty for their first two years at the firm.
- Uniquely democratic management style—associates play a significant role in running the firm.
- Routinely ranks among top 10 firms nationwide in *American Lawyer* corporate scorecard table for corporate finance transactional work, including mergers and acquisitions, financing projects, stock offerings, and real estate investment trusts. In a recent 6-month period, corporate transactional work firm-wide resulted in more than $20 billion in mergers and acquisitions and $13 billion in public and private financings.
- $5,000,000 in legal time to pro bono projects.
- Leads California law firms in profits per partner.

NUTS AND BOLTS

Managing partner:

> J. Thomas Rosch, San Francisco office
> Robert M. Dell, National (San Francisco office)

Hiring partner:

> Richard B. Ulmer, San Francisco office
> Mary Rose Alexander, National (Washington, D.C. office)

Recruiting coordinator:

> Suzanne M. Kane, San Francisco office (Suzanne.kane@lw.com)
> Debra Perry Clarkson, National (San Diego office)

Number of attorneys in firm:

> 838 (292 partners)

WHOLE FIRM:

> Women partners (41), women associates (201), minority partners (12), minority associates (75), disabled partners (1), disabled associates (2)

SAN FRANCISCO OFFICE:

> Total attorneys (72), total partners (18), total associates (49), women partners (2), women associates (25), minority partners (0), minority associates (13), disabled partners (0), disabled associates (0), of counsel (5)

OTHER OFFICES:

> (* represents an office profiled elsewhere in this book)
> Chicago (83); Los Angeles* (224); Newark (13); New York (160); Orange County (61); San Diego* (71); Silicon Valley (12); Washington, D.C.* (113); Hong Kong (3); London (14); Moscow (8); Tokyo (3); Singapore (1)

Years to make partner:

> 8

WHAT DO THEY DO?

Primary specialties (more than 5% of practice):

> **Corporate** (includes Corporate Finance Practice, General Company Representation, Mergers and Acquisitions/Leveraged Buy-Out Practice, Health Care Industry, and Entertainment, Sports & Media)

Environmental (includes Enforcement and Litigation, Rulemaking and Legislation, Permitting and Compliance, Transactional Advice, and Land Use Practice)

Finance and Real Estate (includes Project Finance, Electric Utility Deregulation, Real Estate, Bankruptcy and Insolvency, Infrastructure Finance, Structured Finance, and Banking)

Litigation (includes Litigation Support and Technology, Appellate, White Collar Government Investigation and Corporate Governance, Bankruptcy/Creditors' Rights, Employment, Government Contracts, Securities and Corporate Control Litigation Group, Intellectual Property, Product Liability and Product Safety, Antitrust and Trade Regulation, Professional Liability, Health Care)

Tax (includes General Income Tax Practice, Transactional Practice, International Tax Practice, Personal Legal Services and Benefits and Compensation Practice)

New associates are unassigned for the first two years of practice, having an opportunity to obtain broad exposure to the firm's practice areas. During that two years, associates do not rotate through departments on a fixed schedule; rather, they select a mix of work from their areas of interest, thus enabling each associate to shape his/her career from the outset.

WHO DO THEY REPRESENT?

Latham's client list reads like a Who's Who in American business, with a wide variety of small, dynamic businesses as well as many Fortune 500 companies. For a more complete list than can be included here, visit Latham's web site at http://www.lw.com. Some famous name clients include Amgen; Bear, Stearns & Co.; Cedars-Sinai Medical Center; DIRECTV; Donaldson, Lufkin & Jenrette Securities Corporation; DreamWorks SKG; E! Entertainment Television; Harrah's Entertainment; Hilton Hotels; Hughes Communications; Kohlberg Kravis Roberts; Nestlé USA; Nintendo of America; Safeway; Smith Barney; and the United States Soccer Federation.

WHERE NEW ASSOCIATES COME FROM . . .

Latham routinely interviews on campus at the following law schools: Boalt Hall, Boston College, Boston University, Brigham Young, Chicago, Columbia, Cornell, Duke, Emory, Fordham, George Washington, Georgetown, Harvard, Hastings, Howard, Illinois, Iowa, Kansas, Michigan, Minnesota, Northwestern, North Carolina, Notre Dame, NYU, Pennsylvania, Pepperdine, San Diego, Stanford, Texas, Davis, UCLA, USC, Vanderbilt, Washington, Virginia, William & Mary, Wisconsin, and Yale.

Associates and summer associates are also hired from law schools where
Latham doesn't conduct on-campus interviewing.

HOURS AND BUCKS . . .

Minimum billable hour requirement for first year associates: 1,900
    Part-time work available for associates, both continuing and entry-
level. Latham does not routinely hire contract associates.
    Typical first year associate salary, including typical bonus: $$$$ (over
$65,000); Latham is often noted in the press for its particularly generous
financial package.

SUMMER PROGRAM . . .

Last year, there were 15 summer associates, 13 of whom received offers.
    Weekly pay: $1,500
    1Ls are hired for the summer program on a very limited basis.
    2L/3L deadline for applying for summer clerkships: December 1.
    Latham San Francisco does particularly well in the *American Lawyer*
summer associate survey; last year, Latham's associates ranked their work
"the most interesting" and the "best work in the Bay Area," placing the
firm first in the category.

PRO BONO . . .

Latham strongly encourages its attorneys to do pro bono work. Pro bono
hours are considered billables. Examples of projects include Alliance for
Children's Rights, Chrysalis Homeless Assistance Agency, Asian American
Legal Defense/Education Fund and the Humane Society of the United
States. The San Francisco office was 1996 BASF Pro Bono "Firm of the
Year."

HISTORY AT A GLANCE . . .

Latham was founded in Los Angeles in 1934 by Dana Latham and Paul
Watkins, focusing primarily on tax. It wasn't until the last couple of
decades that the firm experienced spectacular growth, from 40 attorneys
in 1969 to over 800 today. With an aggressive marketing effort under
managing partner Robert Dell, Latham recovered from setbacks in the
early '90s (largely attributable to the collapse of a major client, New York
junk bond dealer Drexel Burnham Lambert), to become one of the most
profitable and highly-respected law firms in the country.
    The San Francisco office opened in 1990 to expand the firm's strong
base in California and complement its broad, multi-national practice.
Stars in the San Francisco office include widely respected anti-trust maven

J. Thomas Rosch, high-profile health-care specialist Jerry Peters, and professional liability specialist Peter Wald.

WHAT IT'S LIKE TO WORK AT LATHAM . . .

Please read the firm's Los Angeles profile first! It will give you a feel for what it's like to work at Latham in general. Here are thoughts specifically from Latham's associates in San Francisco:

Every law student knows the routine with large firms, right? Go there, work your butt off for a year or two, hate every minute of it, and then leave and do what you really want.

That's clearly not the case at Latham. As one associate pointed out, "The fourth year associates move into larger offices in the new year. That created a real problem this year, because the entire 4TH year class was still here, in its entirety. They don't have enough of the right sized offices to go around!"

"You don't feel like you're at a 'branch office'—it's a one-firm firm."

Why is that? You have all of the reasons that Latham's Los Angeles associates love the firm. On top of that, San Francisco associates don't feel like they're 'out of the loop' because they're not at the firm's main office. As one associate pointed out, "Students often wonder if they'll have the same resources, the same opportunities, the same visibility and ability to build a network in the firm if they aren't in the L.A. office. From what I've found, Latham doesn't operate in a traditional head office/branch office sense. It's very much a 'one-firm firm.'" There are several elements that contribute to this feeling. For a start, as one associate offers, "The L.A. office doesn't control decision-making or the firm's purse strings. All of the strategic and policy decision-making is done on a firm-wide basis. People from every office participate in every firm committee. It's just that those decisions are carried out so that they make sense in whatever local market you're in." Another associate adds that, "You feel like you're part of one firm because it's common to work with other attorneys in other offices. For instance, on a daily basis I might speak with a supervisor in New York, an associate providing help in Los Angeles, an antitrust specialist here in San Francisco, and an employee benefits partner in Orange County. It gives you a great opportunity to learn from experts in a whole variety of specialties."

This kind of cross-staffing is possible because of the firm's huge investment in technology. Firm-wide e-mail, document management software, and intranet and Internet capabilities make all kinds of communication between offices the norm. As one associate pointed out that, "If I'm looking for precedent for a stock purchase agreement, I can get a Latham form from the intranet, use the Internet to pull precedent from the SEC web site, send an e-mail to attorneys throughout this office or the entire firm, and I can use document management software to search through thousands of Latham documents."

Associates also love Latham San Francisco's excellent support staff. One associate was recently heavily recruited by another firm, and one of the reasons he wouldn't leave Latham was that "Our support staff is unmatched." He said that, "It means a lot to have the best staff in the Bay Area. Every attorney here respects that."

"Our 'unassigned' system gives you a lot of variety, working with a lot of different people."

As they do at all of Latham's offices, San Francisco associates rave about the firm's unassigned program; that means that first and second year associates aren't assigned to a particular department. Instead, "You have an opportunity to try all types of work," according to one associate. "From what I hear from my friends at other firms, too many firms try to impose their needs and ideas onto junior attorneys. Latham really wants us to find our talent. I get to work with several different partners throughout the year. Not one of them 'owns' me." Another associate added that, "In every department, we get the most sophisticated and interesting work in the market."

The size of the office is another benefit to associates. One commented that, "There are over 70 attorneys here now, and the firm intends to keep it that way. It's not huge, but you still get an assortment of practices in all of the firm's specialties."

"You know that they care about your opinion, even though you're only a junior associate."

Associates at all of Latham's offices have great things to say about the firm's management style, since associates get what they perceive as a real say in firm affairs. As one associate pointed out, "Many firms make grand claims about their management structure, but there are really amazing examples at L&W in San Francisco. Our Associates Committee occupies a central place in our management structure. It's got truly far-reaching responsibilities and influence. It does things like work allocation for unassigned associates, career development, evaluations and reviews, recommendations for partnership, compensation, and really everything that affects all of the associates." The committee comprises equal numbers of associates and partners in all of the firm's domestic offices. In San Francisco, a second year associate was assigned to the committee and has served on it for two years, along with a partner in the office. One associate pointed out that, "It's amazing to a lot of lawyers in other firms, and to students outside of Latham as well, that such a junior associate would be an important player in such major firm responsibilities and management.

We don't think that much about it because we're used to that kind of thing. What *does* impress me is that he's not just some silent junior associate who is a lame duck on the committee. He's had major say in some of the most sweeping changes in associate policies. In fact we joke that his title is Office Managing Associate!"

Another associate complimented the fact that heavy associate involvement in managing the firm gives associates "Access to information about the firm's direction, strategic plans and financial performance. Latham is very unusual in how open it is, and how much it encourages dialogue, about firm policies. They really make us feel like valuable team members, not fungible commodities."

The interest in associate opinions even extends to summer associates. One associate told of how "The firm-wide managing partner, Bob Dell, spent a very long lunch with our San Francisco summer associates. It's something he does every year. I think the summer associates probably think he's there to 'check them out,' but he's not. He wants to get a perspective on the future of the legal market. It's just him and the summer clerks, and he encourages them to speak up. He asks them lots of questions. Some of them you'd expect, about what they're looking for in a firm, what they're looking for in the future, how they like their experience at Latham so far. But according to what some of the summer associates have told me, he also asks them questions like 'What do your friends say about law firms? What do they want? What do they say about Latham?' He wants frank opinions and honest answers. From everything I've seen, Bob is truly interested in what qualities of Latham are successful for recruiting great students, and what areas we should work to improve." The associate went on to point out that, "Frankly I'm not sure how much he *could* improve. It is just plain fun to work here!"

"They make you feel as though they care about the well-being of all of the associates."

Associates tell story after story about how Latham San Francisco values them as people. One associate said that, "It's a matter of pride that the firm offers domestic partner benefits, but it really goes much further than that. In San Francisco, we have several summer associates who received permanent offers which they accepted, went back to school for their third year, and became involved in serious relationships that changed their minds about wanting to be in San Francisco when they graduated." At least two of the summer associates felt comfortable calling the firm and explaining that they'd be happier staying in New York for their first year out of law school, so that they could be with their significant others—one who was finishing school, and another who was doing a clerkship. The associate continued that, "They both still wanted to be in San Francisco long-term, but in the short-term their personal relationships were a priority. The firm made an offer to each of them to spend their first year in

New York and then transfer to the San Francisco office the next year." Of course the associate added that, "This isn't the kind of thing the firm encourages, but at the same time the firm feels as though it makes a commitment to its associates." As one partner concurs, "We have the best attorneys in the country, working for the best clients in the world, and we want to attract the best students, and we want them to be happy."

Part of what contributes to associate contentment is the fact that "Attorneys, managers and staff really work together, but really like each other, too!" according to one associate. "We plan lots of social activities together, both in and out of the office. This summer, for instance, our office administrator retired after several years with the firm. She was very much responsible for establishing the warm atmosphere in the office, with little touches like passing out candy to everybody in the office on Friday afternoons, and passing around oranges to everyone when a cold epidemic hit the office, all kinds of things like that. When she left, the firm threw a party for her fit for a king. Many attorneys and staff got up and spoke about their experiences with her and how she touched them personally and professionally. It seemed normal to us, but our summer associates were really surprised by the emotional reaction."

Another associate added that, "The most distinct quality of the San Francisco office is that we don't have many purely attorney social events because we really enjoy social events with the whole office. We have lots of parties that have become part of the firm tradition. For instance, the first Friday of the month is 'Birthday Cake at 4 p.m.' where we sing—or try to sing, depending on talent—Happy Birthday. We have a pumpkin carving contest at Halloween. We have a holiday cookie party. And we have brown-bag lunches open to everyone where we learn about somebody's outside interest. It's been everything from craft classes to how to buy a house to cooking tips to Internet ideas."

The firm of course hosts a whole variety of summer associate functions and holiday parties, but also has a number of other social events. For instance, there's an out-of-office attorney get-together once a month, like a dinner, or a party, or a trip to the theater. The office's women attorneys hold a firm-sponsored event every other month. The firm just started an all-office community service program, on top of the firm's formal charity participation in programs like the United Way. And for the sporting types, the firm fields teams in different sports, including softball, "which has lost every game this year!"

As one associate summed it up, "When people lateral in here, they've heard that the culture is unique, but every day they find occurrences that back that up. Everybody here believes in the environment we've created and we all work hard to maintain it."

Latham & Watkins—Washington, D.C.

1001 Pennsylvania Avenue, N.W., Suite 1300 • Washington, D.C. 20004-2505
Phone: 202-637-2200 • Fax: 202-637-2201 • Web site: lw.com

OFFICES

Los Angeles (main office)*, Orange County, San Diego*, San Francisco*, Silicon Valley, California; Chicago, Illinois; Newark, New Jersey; New York City, New York; Washington, D.C.

*"It doesn't matter if you want to do deals, try cases, provide strategic advice, or help make public policy. You can do **anything** here."*

HIGHLIGHTS

- 4TH largest firm in the country, with over 800 lawyers.
- Pronounced dedication to pro bono work; pro bono hours are counted as billables. In one recent year, the firm logged over 30,000 pro bono hours and contributed almost $6,000,000 in legal time to pro bono projects.
- New associates don't have to commit to a specialty for their first two years at the firm.
- Uniquely democratic management style—associates play a significant role in running the firm.
- Routinely ranks among top 10 firms nationwide in *American Lawyer* corporate scorecard table for corporate finance transactional work, including mergers and acquisitions, financing projects, stock offerings, and real estate investment trusts. In a recent 6-month period, corporate transactional work firm-wide resulted in more than $20 billion in mergers and acquisitions and $13 billion in public and private financings.
- $5,000,000 in legal time to pro bono projects.

NUTS AND BOLTS

Managing partner:

Mark E. Newell, Washington, D.C.
Robert M. Dell, National (San Francisco office)

Hiring partner:

Leonard A. Zax, Washington, D.C.
Roger S. Goldman, National (Washington, D.C. office)

Recruiting coordinator:

Laurel E. Barnes, Washington, D.C. (e-mail: laurel.barnes@lw.com)
Debra Perry Clarkson, National (San Diego office)

Number of attorneys in firm:

838 (292 partners)

WHOLE FIRM:

Women partners (41), women associates (201), minority partners (12), minority associates (75), disabled partners (1), disabled associates (2)

WASHINGTON, D.C. OFFICE:

Total attorneys (133), partners (41), associates (66), women partners (4), women associates (24), minority partners (2), minority associates (10), disabled partners (0), disabled associates (0), of counsel (9)

OTHER OFFICES:

(* represents an office profiled elsewhere in this book)
Chicago (83); Los Angeles* (224); Newark (13); New York (160); Orange County (61); San Diego* (71); San Francisco* (72); Silicon Valley (12); Hong Kong (3); London (14); Moscow (8); Tokyo (3); Singapore (1)

Years to make partner:

8

WHAT DO THEY DO?

Primary specialties (more than 5% of practice):

Corporate (includes Corporate Finance Practice, General Company Representation, Mergers and Acquisitions/Leveraged Buy-Out Practice, Health Care Industry, and Entertainment, Sports & Media)
   Environmental (includes Enforcement and Litigation, Rulemaking and Legislation, Permitting and Compliance, Transactional Advice, and Land Use Practice)
   Finance and Real Estate (includes Project Finance, Electric Utility Deregulation, Real Estate, Bankruptcy and Insolvency, Infrastructure Finance, Structured Finance, and Banking)
   Litigation (includes Litigation Support and Technology, Appellate, White Collar Government Investigation and Corporate Governance, Bankruptcy/Creditors' Rights, Employment, Government Contracts,

Securities and Corporate Control Litigation Group, Intellectual Property, Product Liability and Product Safety, Antitrust and Trade Regulation, Professional Liability, Health Care)

Tax (includes General Income Tax Practice, Transactional Practice, International Tax Practice, Personal Legal Services and Benefits and Compensation Practice)

New associates are unassigned for the first two years of practice, and have an opportunity to obtain broad exposure to the firm's practice areas. Associates do not rotate through departments on a fixed schedule; rather, they select a mix of work from their areas of interest, thus "putting them in the driver's seat" with their careers from the outset.

WHO DO THEY REPRESENT?

Latham's client list reads like a Who's Who in American business, with a wide variety of small, dynamic businesses as well as many Fortune 500 companies. For a more complete list than can be included here, visit Latham's web site at http://www.lw.com. Some famous name clients include Amgen; Bear, Stearns & Co.; Cedars-Sinai Medical Center; DIRECTV; Donaldson, Lufkin & Jenrette Securities Corporation; DreamWorks SKG; E! Entertainment Television; Harrah's Entertainment; Hilton Hotels; Hughes Communications; Kohlberg Kravis Roberts; Nestlé USA; Nintendo of America; Safeway; Smith Barney; and the United States Soccer Federation.

WHERE NEW ASSOCIATES COME FROM . . .

Latham routinely interviews on campus at the following law schools: Boalt Hall, Boston College, Boston University, Brigham Young, Chicago, Columbia, Cornell, Duke, Emory, Fordham, George Washington, Georgetown, Harvard, Hastings, Howard, Illinois, Iowa, Kansas, Michigan, Minnesota, Northwestern, North Carolina, Notre Dame, NYU, Pennsylvania, Pepperdine, San Diego, Stanford, Texas, Davis, UCLA, USC, Vanderbilt, Washington, Virginia, William & Mary, Wisconsin, and Yale. Associates and summer associates are also hired from law schools where Latham doesn't conduct on-campus interviewing.

HOURS AND BUCKS . . .

Minimum billable hour requirement for first year associates: 1,900

Part-time work available for associates, but not at entry level. Latham does not routinely hire contract associates.

Typical first year associate salary, including typical bonus: $$$$ (over $65,000); Latham is often noted in the press for its particularly generous financial package.

SUMMER PROGRAM . . .

Last year, there were 17 summer associates, all of whom received offers.
   Weekly pay: $1,500
   1Ls hired in the D.C. office only on a very limited basis.
   2L/3L deadline for applying for summer clerkships: December 1

PRO BONO . . .

Latham strongly encourages its attorneys to do pro bono work. Pro bono
hours are considered billables. Examples of projects include Alliance for
Children's Rights, Chrysalis Homeless Assistance Agency, Asian American
Legal Defense/Education Fund, the Humane Society of the U.S., Opera
America (a nonprofit organization promoting the growth and expansion
of opera through a catalog-based distributorship of opera CDs and
videos), and the Learning Disabilities Association of America.

HISTORY AT A GLANCE

Latham was founded in Los Angeles in 1934 by Dana Latham and Paul
Watkins, focusing primarily on tax. It wasn't until the last couple of
decades that the firm experienced spectacular growth, from 40 attorneys
in 1969 to over 800 today. With an aggressive marketing effort under
managing partner Robert Dell, Latham recovered from setbacks in the
early '90s (largely attributable to the collapse of a major client, New York
junk bond dealer Drexel Burnham Lambert), to become one of the most
profitable and highly-respected law firms in the country.
   The Washington office opened in 1978 with 7 lawyers, and has since
become a full-service practice with over 105 lawyers. The Washington
office has strong domestic and international practices in a host of areas,
including trial and appellate litigation, government contracts, communications, corporate finance, mergers & acquisitions, real estate, environmental, energy and project finance, tax, and government relations. Many
of Latham's Washington attorneys have served in federal government
positions and are active in public affairs and politics.

WHAT IT'S LIKE TO WORK AT LATHAM . . .

*Please read the firm's Los Angeles profile first! It will give you a feel for what
it's like to work at Latham in general. Here are thoughts specifically from
Latham's associates in Washington, D.C.:*
   If you like the idea of working on cases that you read about in the
papers, you couldn't do better than Latham Washington. When you look
at major cases in the 1990's, Latham's Washington office has played a central role in many of them—from Hilton's well-publicized efforts to

acquire ITT, to defending Columbia HCA in the government investigation and the securities and consumer class actions related to it, to the merger of Evergreen Media and Chancellor Broadcasting creating the second largest broadcast company in the country, to representing America Online in numerous lawsuits—including its efforts to halt 'spammers' who foul up the Internet with junk messages—to working with the Environmental Protection Agency in developing new approaches to managing environmental risks.

But it wouldn't matter how good the work is if Latham didn't have the features you see in the Los Angeles office's profile—the strong associate participation in management, the ability to remain unassigned to a department for the first two years with the firm, the smart, friendly and interesting lawyers the firm attracts. Associates in D.C. rave about the "challenging, cutting-edge" work they get, the "ability to work with a broad range of clients and supervisors" before selecting a department, and the "top-notch" client base. And because of the firm's "very lean, flexible staffing policies" you get to work on "challenging work across a broad range of practice areas." As one associate pointed out, "It doesn't matter if you want to do deals, try cases, provide strategic advice, or help make public policy. You can do *anything* here."

The experience of one D.C. associate fleshes out Latham's commitment to include associates in firm management. As a member of the Associates Committee, he got to participate in some of the most important decisions in the firm—including recommendations for partnership and associate compensation. The associate commented that, "Latham means it when they say that they engage associates in all aspects of firm life. You really feel as though they value and trust associates."

Another associate pointed out how the firm's caring nature came out before she even joined the firm. Her resume showed a strong interest in environmental law, and on her call-back interview she wasn't scheduled to meet with anybody at the firm doing environmental work. When one of her morning interviewers noticed this, he immediately had her schedule rearranged to talk to two lawyers in the environmental department, including Bob Sussman, the head of the department. The associate said that, "Even though Bob was extremely busy that day, he made time to meet with me. He showed a real interest in me as a person, and not just in my credentials." She found that after joining the firm, every day has just "given me more evidence that this is the right place for me."

As is true for every Latham office, the firm lavishes its lawyers with social events. There's the annual meeting for all partners and associates, including the ones from the foreign offices. That meeting usually takes place at a resort in the Southwest, where business meetings are liberally interspersed with sports and opportunities to socialize and meet in person many of the lawyers from other offices (although associates feel as though they already know their colleagues from other cities, since the firm frequently cross-staffs projects, and the lawyers communicate via e-mail and the firm's intranet). There are the summer associate social activities that you'd expect from a top-flight firm. As one associate points out, "It's the informal socializing that really stands out here. One partner in the Communications Group sponsors weekly basketball games, for instance. And lawyers here often get together with spouses and children. It's the kind of place where you make friends in the office, and carry those friendships over into your personal life."

Long Aldridge & Norman L.L.P.

303 Peachtree Street, Suite 5300 • Atlanta, GA 30308
Phone: 404-527-4000 • Fax: 404-527-4198 • Web site: lanlaw.com

OFFICES

Atlanta (main office), Georgia; Washington, D.C.

"I guess every law firm has a certain level of camaraderie, but here it goes beyond the first-name basis, no-jacket-required-in-the-hallway, open-door-policy kinds of things. It's hard to explain, but we get along so well that it's sometimes like a Seinfeld episode around here. We once had a spirited discussion about which candy was better—cherry sours or candy corn. We at least all agreed that circus peanuts are not really food at all."

HIGHLIGHTS

- Recently ranked first overall in the country in *American Lawyer*'s mid-level associate survey.
- Are currently representing Big Rivers Electric Corporation, one of the five largest bankruptcy matters pending in the U.S.
- Public Finance section has served as bond counsel to state and local governments in 45 of the 50 states, and has advised on more than 500 financings with an aggregate principal amount of some $19.2 billion.

NUTS AND BOLTS

Managing partner:

Clay Long, Chairman of the Board of Directors

Hiring partner:

Mark Kaufman, phone: 404-527-4120, e-mail: mkaufman@lanlaw.com

Recruiting coordinator:

Jennifer Queen, phone: 404-527-4139, e-mail: jqueen@lanlaw.com

Number of attorneys in firm:

167 (74 partners)

TOTAL FIRM:

Partners (74), associates (91), senior counsel (2), women partners (9), women associates (36), minority partners (2), minority associates (4), disabled partners (0), disabled associates (0)

THIS OFFICE:

Total attorneys (147), partners (65), associates (70), women partners (8), women associates (29), minority partners (1), minority associates (5), disabled partners (0), disabled associates (0), of counsel (10), women of counsel (5), senior attorneys (2)

OTHER OFFICES:

(* represents an office profiled elsewhere in this book)
Washington, D. C. (20)
The firm also has a correspondent relationship with a Paris-based law firm, Lacourte Balas & Associates

Years to make partner:

8

WHAT DO THEY DO?

Primary specialties (more than 5% of practice):

Commercial Litigation (38); Real Estate (20); Bankruptcy and Creditors' Rights (13); Energy (12); Healthcare (8); Mergers & Acquisitions (24); Administrative/Regulatory/Government Law (12); Securities/Public Finance (15); Tax & Employee Benefits/Trusts & Estates (10); Environmental (4).

The firm is departmentalized for work assignments and supervisory purposes, though often services are delivered through cross-team efforts. The firm typically hires from its summer program, and at the end of the summer the summer associates are asked to rank their preferences for permanent team assignments. The Firm's strong preference is to match every summer associate with the team for which (s)he is interested in working, though this isn't always possible. Occasionally, associates request a change in practice areas, and the firm fully cooperates, subject to its available needs, in accommodating a requested change.

WHO DO THEY REPRESENT?

Clients include the boxer Evander Holyfield, Newt Gingrich, many large national investment banks, Big Rivers Electric Corporation, Atlanta Gas Light Company, BlueCross & BlueShield of Georgia, WorldCom, Cablecasting.

WHERE NEW ASSOCIATES COME FROM . . .

The firm routinely interviews on campus at the following law schools: Columbia, Duke, Emory, Florida, Georgetown, Georgia, Georgia State, Harvard, Mercer, Michigan, NYU, North Carolina, Texas, Vanderbilt, Virginia, and William and Mary. The firm does hire associates and summer associates from schools where it doesn't interview on campus.

HOURS AND BUCKS . . .

On average, first year associates spend 2,200 hours at the office. There is no minimum billable hourly requirement; however, the average target for annual associate billable hours is 1,900.

The firm allows continuing associates to work part-time on a case-by-case basis. Part-time work is not available to new associates. The firm occasionally hires contract attorneys.

Typical first year associate salary including typical bonus: $$$$ (Over $65,000)

SUMMER PROGRAM . . .

In the summer of 1998, there were 2 3Ls with judicial clerkships and both received offers; there were 12 2Ls, 10 received offers; and there were 8 1Ls, and 7 received offers to return for their 2L summer.

Weekly pay: $1,200 for post-third year students, $1,100 for 2Ls, and $1,000 for 1Ls.

Last year's 1Ls came from Harvard, Virginia, North Carolina, Georgia, Duke and Emory.

The deadline for applying for summer clerkships is November 15 for 2Ls and 3Ls, and January 15 for 1Ls.

PRO BONO . . .

The firm has a well-organized pro bono practice under the leadership of Deborah Ebel. Ebel practiced with the Atlanta Legal Aid Society for 10 years and was formerly lead counsel in Atlanta for the Mariel Cuban litigation. She is immediate past President of the Board of Directors of the Atlanta Volunteer Lawyer's Foundation.

Along with the Atlanta Volunteer Lawyer's Foundation, LA&N associates routinely participate in the Saturday Morning Lawyer's Program organized by the Atlanta Legal Aid Society, and pioneered the award-winning Guardian Ad Litem Project, under which attorneys and paralegals at the firm, with the help of support staff, act as guardians ad litem in child custody cases.

The firm has no fixed rules regarding pro bono requirements. The firm encourages attorneys to participate in their communications with legal organizations and pro bono projects.

HISTORY AT A GLANCE . . .

The Firm was founded in 1974 by four Atlanta lawyers, three of whom (Clay Long, Bill Stevens and John Aldridge) are senior partners today. In its first 10 years, the Firm grew to 51 lawyers and today is a full-service firm with 140 lawyers in offices in Atlanta and Washington, D.C.

In 1986, Al Norman and several other partners joined the firm, and the firm changed its name to Long Aldridge & Norman. The D.C. office opened in 1994 and added an Energy practice.

Roughly 60% of the firm's growth has been generated by lawyers joining the firm after law school or a judicial clerkship; the other 40% are lateral hires.

Firm stars include Clay Long, listed in *The Best Lawyers In America* both as one of the best corporate lawyers and one of the best real estate lawyers in Georgia, Litigation head Jim Thomas, who represents Evander Holyfield, and John Aldridge, a highly respected Financial Restructuring specialist. The firm is a formidable political player, boasting many current and former politicians among its ranks. There is Gordon Giffin, recently appointed Ambassador to Canada; Steve Labovitz, former Chief of Staff to Atlanta Mayor Bill Campbell; Keith Mason, former Deputy Assistant for Intergovernmental Affairs to President Clinton, serving as the President's chief liaison with the nation's governors; and Buddy Darden and Jim Lightfoot, both former U.S. Congressmen.

WHAT IT'S LIKE TO WORK THERE . . .

When you put together a book like this, you've really got one of two choices. You can rely on other published sources and go by what *they* say are great employers. Or you can do original research, and ignore published sources—which, as you already know, is what I did. But when a law firm is voted the best law firm in the country in *American Lawyer*'s survey of midlevel associates—as Long Aldridge was—you can bet I held my breath, hoping against hope that the law school administrators I polled would say it's a terrific place to work. No surprise here—they did. And from what associates at Long Aldridge say—it is a *fabulous* place to work.

You notice immediately that the partners show exceptional sensitivity to the associates. For instance, one associate recounts that "After only a few months with the firm, my team got clobbered with a very large project, and we had only a few days to tackle a mountain of research. During a meeting, a partner and I made a list of at least 10 issues that needed to be researched that night. I looked at the list, took a deep breath, and prepared to pull my first 'all-nighter' at the firm. But instead, the partner took the list, tore it in half, and asked whether I wanted the top half or the bottom half. We both headed up to the library and worked together until we were both finished." The associate marveled, "The best part of the experience for me was that it was obvious that it had never occurred to him to leave me, a junior associate, to handle the research alone. I felt like a respected member of the team, instead of the low man on the totem pole."

Another associate tells of going on an "out of town client meeting with the partner who is the head of our team. He had been scheduled to go for several weeks, but it was decided only a few days before the meeting that I should be there also. The only seats remaining on the flight at that point were in first class, and the partner's previously-booked seat was in coach. The partner told me to take the seat in first class, and he sat in coach."

Other associates rave about the firm's "progressive values," some partners' practice of "handing out bottles of champagne at Christmas," and the "modest, down-to-earth" nature of the lawyers. Not that the firm lacks its share of characters—they're there. For instance, litigation head Jim Thomas, a karate expert and former kickboxer, once fought a boxing match with one of firm client Evander Holyfield's boxing partners. And as one associate says, "I guess every office has a level of camaraderie, and we do, too. But here it goes beyond the first-name basis, no-jacket-required-in-the-hallway, open-door-policy kinds of things. It's hard to explain, but we get along so well that it's sometimes like a Seinfeld episode around here. We once had a spirited discussion about which candy was better—cherry sours or candy corn. We at least all agreed that circus peanuts are not really food at all."

"It really matters to the partners that nobody 'falls through the cracks' here."

Associates at Long Aldridge rave about the partners' concern for "our training and development. It really matters to them that nobody falls through the cracks." What the firm has is a 'subteam' system. A partner is in charge of each subteam, and "that partner makes sure that partners in other subteams don't demand work from you without asking permission from your subteam head, first. That way they make sure you aren't too loaded down with work." Other associates report that, "The subteam system makes you feel like there's a buffer against unreasonable demands on your time." When associates do have the time, they frequently work on projects outside of their subteam, and in so doing wind up working with a variety of partners. If they decide to change practice areas, it's not a problem. One associate reports that, "I know several associates who decided that their practice area wasn't what they hoped it would be, and thought a change was in order. Rather than just shop resumes to other firms, they went to firm management, explained the problem, and the firm moved heaven and earth to find the right fit for them within the firm." The associate says that, "Just knowing that you aren't 'stuck' does a great deal for the morale around here."

Associates learn mostly by working with "the great lawyers we've got here, people who are not just excellent practitioners but worldly-wise as well," and appreciate that when they run into difficulties, the partners go to bat for them. One associate recalls when "A senior attorney at another firm wrongfully accused me of making a mistake. Without even telling me about it, my partner called that lawyer and demanded that the lawyer apologize to me. He did."

"We work really hard, but in return we get fantastic work."

Long Aldridge associates feel that, "We aren't coddled. If you're a wallflower, you won't succeed here. We are very hardworking." But in return "Young associates are asked to do a wide range of challenging and interesting work, and we legitimately feel like valuable members of the firm." One associate reports that, "As a summer associate, I had expressed an interest in a specialty that the firm didn't engage in. However, both as a summer and first-year associate, the firm let me try to develop this practice area, and supported me by paying for trips to various domestic and European cities. As a result, within six months of joining the firm, I was being permitted to manage new relationships with some of the world's largest financial businesses."

One associate's experience particularly illuminates the kind of trust and responsibility the firm gives its newest members. As the associate tells it, "About six weeks after I started, a long-standing client of the firm called us and said that he wanted to sell a division of his business. He had already negotiated the primary business terms of the deal, but none of the legal issues related to the transaction had been dealt with nor had the documents necessary to complete the transaction been drafted. We were called in to help him make the deal happen, and the closing was scheduled for six days after we were contacted. The only two M&A attorneys assigned to work on the deal were the second year partner with whom I work most of the time, Briggs Tobin, and me. In the midst of what was to be an extremely busy week, Briggs became ill and completely lost his voice."

The associate continues, "For two days, while Briggs was home sick and almost completely unable to talk, I was put into the role of coordinating the deal on our end. Obviously, I had a lot of help from other more specialized attorneys within the firm and Briggs at home, and most of the actual document drafting was taken care of by others. However, the responsibility for making sure that things continued to happen—questions getting answered, information getting to the right people, coordinating the effort among other lawyers within the firm, keeping our client informed, and keeping Briggs informed—was left to me. In one day, I spoke to our client, his company's chief financial officer, his company's president, the general counsel of the other party to the deal, and the other side's attorneys, one of whom was a senior partner at a large Houston law firm. In the end, Briggs got healthy again, the deal closed as scheduled, just six days after we were asked to help, and our client had the result he wanted. Just six weeks into my career, I felt I had played an important role in closing a deal and making one of our clients very happy."

The associate adds, "It was somewhat overwhelming, considering my lack of real experience. But it was also extremely exciting and rewarding. Certainly, the confidence that Briggs and others had in me to handle the situation bolstered my own confidence to do the job and says a lot about the firm. I wasn't hired to lay low for a few years under piles of documents, but to add value to the services we provide, help our clients accomplish their goals, and help more senior attorneys help our clients." The associate concludes that, "I think it is rare to find a big firm that trusts its young associates so much and, in my opinion, it is that level of trust that creates the environment that makes this a special place to work."

"The firm knows the value of family."

Associates point out that, "the partners here really set the tone when it comes to balancing family and your professional life." Many of the partners have children, and "they keep regular, and reasonable hours, for the stated purpose of being able to get home to their children." As one associate points out, "When my parents are coming into town, I don't even have to ask permission to leave early to meet them—it's just expected." As another associate sums up the Long Aldridge experience, "When you decide to work for a large corporate law firm, you know you're going to work hard. Working hard is pretty universal, but feeling good about the kind of work you're doing, unfortunately for many of my classmates and colleagues at other firms, is *not* so universal. That kind of positive feeling is the norm at Long Aldridge—and it's one of the reasons that the people who work here feel so lucky to be here."

Lord, Bissell & Brook

115 South LaSalle St. • Chicago, IL 60603
Phone: 312-443-0700 • Fax: 312-443-0336

OFFICES

Chicago (main office), Rockford, Illinois; Atlanta, Georgia; Los Angeles, California; New York City, New York

"I may be a junior associate, but I have an incredible amount of autonomy here. I have power over my files and a lot of responsibility. I'm no tiny cog in a big wheel. Sure, there are times when I'd rather be home lounging around on the couch, but I'm proud of the fact that the decisions I make affect a lot of people."

HIGHLIGHTS

- The country's 87TH largest law firm.
- The firm has state-of-the-art interactive video training technology to hone the trial and negotiation skills of firm attorneys.
- Extensive electronic databases for all kinds of work-product and research services, and linked to every office via e-mail.
- Was awarded the Chicago Volunteer Legal Services "Law Firm Of The Year," recognizing the firm's commitment to public service.

NUTS AND BOLTS

Managing partner:

John Gurley

Hiring partner:

Mark Goodman, phone: 312-443-0409, e-mail: mgoodman@lordbissell.com

Recruiting coordinator:

Kerry Jahnsen, phone: 312-443-0455, e-mail: kjahnsen@lordbissell.com

Number of attorneys in firm:

328 (156 partners)

TOTAL FIRM:

Partners (156), associates (157), women partners (24), women associates (74), minority partners (3), minority associates (11), disabled partners (2), disabled associates (0)

THIS OFFICE:

Total attorneys (272), partners (136), associates (130), women partners (22), women associates (60), minority partners (3), minority associates (6), disabled partners (2), disabled associates (0)

OTHER OFFICES: ·

(* represents an office profiled elsewhere in this book)
Atlanta (25); Los Angeles (28); New York City (4); Rockford, Illinois (4)

Years to make partner:

6 for income partners; 9 to 10 for capital partners

WHAT DO THEY DO?

Primary specialties (more than 5% of practice):

Business litigation, including antitrust, commercial contract disputes and consumer class action defense (54); Insurance litigation, including environmental, insurance contract analysis and disputes, and specialty representation of London insurers in U.S. litigation (76); Corporate, including corporate mergers and acquisitions, securities, corporate finance and tax, health care and sub-specialty group of 20 attorneys focused on corporate representation of regulated financial services companies like insurers, banks and finance companies (63); Medical litigation (32); Products Liability (15); Real Estate (16).

The firm consults with new associates to determine their interests, and, taking into account practice area needs, the new associate is assigned to a practice area. The new associate also gets a "reporting partner" in that practice area, to monitor his/her professional progress. Associates can, and do, switch specialties, due either to their changing interests or the firm's expansion into new areas.

WHO DO THEY REPRESENT?

A vast array of clients, including Lloyd's of London and Rank Industries.

WHERE NEW ASSOCIATES COME FROM . . .

Lord Bissell interviews on campus at the following law schools: Boston University, Chicago, DePaul, Georgetown, George Washington, Harvard, Illinois, Indiana, Iowa, Chicago Kent, Loyola/Chicago, John Marshall, Michigan, Notre Dame, Northwestern, Washington U./St. Louis, Wisconsin. The firm routinely hires associates and summer associates from schools where it doesn't conduct on-campus interviews.

HOURS AND BUCKS . . .

Minimum billable hour requirement for all lawyers: 1,900, which includes pro bono, recruiting, and business development.

Part-time work is available to continuing associates, not entry-level associates. The firm does not typically hire contract associates.

Typical first year salary, including typical bonus: $$$$ (Over $65,000). The firm is known for its particularly generous financial package.

SUMMER PROGRAM . . .

Last year, there were 14 summer associates, 12 of whom received offers.

Weekly pay: $1,700 this year in Chicago

1Ls are routinely hired for the summer program. Last year's 1Ls came from Michigan, Chicago, Harvard and Northwestern.

There is no deadline for 2Ls for applying to the summer program; for 1Ls, the deadline is December 15.

PRO BONO . . .

The firm encourages pro bono, sponsors programs, and gives billable credit for pro bono hours. Among other projects, attorneys staff a walk-in legal clinic and volunteer at the Chicago Committee for Civil Rights under the law. The firm was recently named Pro Bono Advocates firm of the year two years running (Pro Bono Advocates is an organization whose volunteer lawyers obtain protective orders for battered spouses).

HISTORY AT A GLANCE . . .

The firm was founded in Chicago in 1914 when John S. Lord opened his Chicago law office. The firm has grown steadily over time, and today has more than 300 lawyers.

Incidentally, by way of historical sidelight—the "Bissell" apparently isn't related to the vacuum cleaner folks, although associates report that "'Brook' wasn't hurt by the fact that he was Lord's son-in-law."

When you talk with associates at LB&B, you get the feeling that they find big firm practice refreshingly different than what they expected. For instance, associates report that "The diversity of the kinds of people here is a real plus," and "I'm much happier here than most of my friends at other big firms." One associate laughingly said that, "The people here are very smart, very skilled—and the best thing about them is that I don't see them at the office for 3,000 hours a year!" Other associates report that "My friends don't seem to have the goofy things going on that we do here. We can make fun of each other, we really enjoy it." And associates point out that, "It's a mistake to think that because this is a big firm, grades are the be-all and end-all. They aren't. Nasty, uncommunicative people just won't get in here, no matter how good they look on paper. The firm looks beyond resumes to find people who are motivated and friendly, believing they'll not only be better lawyers, but they'll fit in here, as well."

"The lawyers here are very receptive to tossing ideas around."

While the firm has all of the training bells and whistles you'd expect from a large firm—including in-house CLEs on a wide range of topics, state-of-the-art interactive video training technology, as well as a comprehensive orientation program—what associates rave about is the "informal training you get from senior associates." Associates point out that, "We get great feedback—you get marked-up copies of what you write, and you get to discuss it." Others point out that "They are very receptive to tossing ideas around." Associates also appreciate the fact that "The firm will pay for you to go to outside CLEs, seminars—anything that will help improve your skills, they'll foot the bill."

When associates join the firm, they join a particular practice group— typically their first choice. In that group, the associate will be assigned to a partner, and for many associates "all of your work comes from that partner and associates under that partner." The firm closely monitors new associates to prevent them from getting "too specialized." "If they see that happening, they'll assign you to a partner who does something else for six months, so you don't get pigeon-holed." Associates report that, "While there was some resistance to this reassignment idea at first, people generally feel as though it gives them good exposure."

Associates find that they get a "decent amount of hands-on experience" early on. They suggest that "Self-starters are *definitely* happy here" and that "It pays to shoot the breeze with senior associates, to find out what's going on in the office. When you hear something you like, you push for responsibility, and they give it to you."

Whether in transactional or litigation practice groups, associates tell story after story about getting a lot of responsibility in exciting projects. Litigation associates rave that "We are a great choice for students who want to be trial lawyers. We get a tremendous amount and diversity of litigation work." New litigation associates "enter into direct client relationships early in our careers. We take depositions, draft and argue motions, prep witnesses for trial, and communicate directly with clients regarding case handling and strategy." Over a recent four-year period, associates report that the firm's medical malpractice lawyers tried almost a hundred cases to verdict, "and associates participated as first or second chair in virtually all of those cases." Associates also tell of a recent environmental coverage suit, which was settled after six years of litigation. The litigation, "involving one of the country's largest companies, involved many years of chemical disposal practices at more than 200 hazardous waste sites in approximately 30 states. Associates working on the case did everything from taking depositions around the country, preparing and presenting clients for deposition, preparing and arguing motions, and preparing witnesses for trial."

On the transactional side, "new associates handle initial filings, prepare and negotiate all kinds of documents, from prospectuses to purchase contracts to loan agreements, conduct due diligence reviews on securities offerings, and participate in closings."

When it comes to hours, junior associates report that "While people here have to work very hard" to succeed, "This is no sweatshop." The firm's 1,900-hour billable hour target "is something that people are expected to meet, although a good chunk of people don't." Associates say that "If you beat that 1,900 target, you are doing really well."

LB&B's offices fill up around 8:30 to 9 in the morning, and start emptying out around 6 to 6:30 p.m., but "that varies for international work, to reflect whatever country it is that you work with." Weekends "vary." The general sense is that "we try not to come in on weekends. There can be anywhere from one to a dozen attorneys from any department in on a weekend, depending on the case or project they're working on and the lifestyle they want. You can do long hours on weekdays or a day on weekends when you've got a lot on your plate," and "You can work from home if you want." When associates do have to put in long days, they feel that "it's very interesting work, and you feel a loyalty to the firm." One associate points out that "They pay you wonderfully, and when you've got to work late to complete something, you feel you owe it to them, and to the clients." Associates find "For the first few years they have you focus on your work," although "Mid-level associates get seminars on business development."

For pro bono work, pro bono hours are counted as billables. One partner acts as pro bono coordinator. The firm is heavily involved with Pro Bono Advocates, which represents battered women, and associates who work with that program say "It's wonderful." On top of that, "We staff a clinic at a church on the South Side, and give general legal advice to indigents on all topics—real estate, taxes, you name it." Lawyers "also bring in their own pro bono work," but in general "Not everybody does it. The emphasis isn't that great on pro bono work. They don't hugely push non-billable hours."

"We play each other in holiday skits, and enjoy ribbing each other."

LB&B is clearly a place where it pays to know how to tease, and be teased. Many formal and informal firm events, including holiday parties, involve "skits, and they are merciless. We play each other and generally enjoy ribbing each other." In some departmental holiday parties there is "often a 'roast' of the partners by the associates, and vice versa."

For sporting types, the firm has "two golf outings a year," and "since there are only a handful of true low handicap golfers in the firm, these are an opportunity for everyone to embarrass themselves equally." The firm also has softball and basketball teams that play in Chicago lawyer leagues, and "some lawyers have organized a more recreational softball team that plays in a Saturday league." For people who prefer to watch sports instead of play them, "Every year some departments go to a Cubs game. It's a great chance to have fun—and drink beer." The firm also sponsors regular monthly cocktail parties in the office on the first Friday of every month, as well as quarterly dinners for attorneys and paralegals in a downtown restaurant or club. Informally "Practice groups often go out, and most have their own holiday parties as well."

All in all, associates feel that "Lord, Bissell isn't the place for people who just want money and power. But if you want challenging work, financial rewards *and* a full life outside of work, it's the perfect place."

Markowitz, Herbold, Glade & Mehlhaf, PC

1211 S. W. Fifth Avenue • Portland, OR 97204-3730
Phone: 503-295-3085 • Fax: 503-323-9105

OFFICES

Portland, Oregon

"When you look at the partners here, you can see that the firm values diversity in every sense of the word—professional talent and skills, personality, minority status, you name it . . . the fact that the firm has a full-time researcher as a partner, well-respected and valued by everybody, says tons about the firm's recognition and value of diversity."

HIGHLIGHTS

• Half of the partners are women, as are seven of the firm's eight associates.

NUTS AND BOLTS

Managing partner:

Peter H. Glade, e-mail: peter@mhgmlaw.com

Hiring partner:

Barrie J. Herbold, phone: 503-295-3085, e-mail: barrie@mhgmlaw.com

Number of attorneys in firm:

18 (10 partners)

Total partners in firm (10), total associates in firm (7), women partners (5), women associates (6), minority partners (1), minority associates (1)

Years to make partner:

Generally 4 to 6

WHAT DO THEY DO?

Primary specialties (more than 5% of practice):

Business and employment litigation is the firm's only specialty. Associates get work through 'open season' from any partner in the firm, but "we try to be reasonable!"

WHO DO THEY REPRESENT?

Portland General Electric Company (now Enron), May Department Stores, the State of Oregon, Matsushita Electronic Materials, Hollywood Entertainment Corp., Equifax, and dozens of local businesses and business people, including numerous law firms within the state of Oregon.

WHERE NEW ASSOCIATES COME FROM . . .

The firm doesn't interview on campus; new associates come to them mostly by word-of-mouth, sending resumes, or on referral from others lawyers and judges.

HOURS AND BUCKS . . .

Junior associates typically bill 1,800 hours per year, but the firm does not have a minimum billable hours requirement.

The firm does not have part-time associates right now, but it would consider job-sharing (that is, two attorneys each working part-time for the equivalent of one full-time attorney). The firm has hired contract associates, and they have not only gone on to become full-time associates, but partners as well.

Typical first year salary plus typical bonus: $$ ($35-50,000)

SUMMER PROGRAM . . .

The firm does not have a summer program.

PRO BONO . . .

Associates are welcome to take part in pro bono activities of their choosing. Since the firm doesn't strictly count billable hours, it is "hard to say" if pro bono counts, although it does count in the firm's incentive overtime program.

The associates have been active in a volunteer program to provide services to seniors, in the ACLU, have prepared amicus briefs on important social issues, and have participated in many bar activities, including as disciplinary counsel for the bar and as a member of the Gender Fairness Task Force, which was charged by the bar to study the existence of sex discrimination in the legal profession and in the courts.

HISTORY AT A GLANCE . . .

The firm was founded in 1983 by David B. Markowitz and Barrie J. Herbold as a small litigation firm. Both Markowitz and Herbold left a large Portland firm (now called Lane Powell). Markowitz brought in the business while Herbold managed the firm. The firm grew fairly rapidly to 10 lawyers, then remained at that size until about two years ago when they began adding associates. One partner came in laterally in 1989; the rest of the partners have been "home grown," starting with the firm as associates. The firm as currently constituted is unusual in that half the partners are women, as are the majority of associates.

David Markowitz is considered one of the best business trial lawyers in the state. He lectures nationally on the subject of deposition practice. Barrie Herbold has recently received the Oregon Women Lawyers Association annual award in recognition of her efforts to promote the interests of women in the law.

WHAT IT'S LIKE TO WORK THERE . . .

You know that MHGM is a special firm when you hear that its reputation in Portland is for "First-class people" and that "It's a great place, especially for women." Interestingly enough, when you listen to associates at MHGM, the word that comes to mind immediately is: harmony. The firm seems to provide a harmonious environment in every way, with "Appearances and social graces" being "important to the partners and the firm." Associates rave about the firm's "Beautiful offices with real art," the fact that "people dress well," and that they "participate in the niceties of life," in every way. Associates applaud the firm's "warmth and inclusiveness," with one associate commenting, "I have never felt that my status as a single parent is viewed by the shareholders as a 'problem' or 'disadvantage' or something to overcome."

As one associate says, "This place is so much different than firms I've worked at before. Every firm talks about being a healthy, team-oriented place, but I've found that's often more of a wish than a reality." At MHGM "Everybody is treated with respect. The partners appreciate the positive attributes we all bring to the firm." And from what MHGM associates say these attributes couldn't be more different. As one associate says, "When you look at the partners here, you can see that the firm values diversity in every sense of the word—professional talent and skills, personality, minority status, you name it." The firm even has one partner, Chris Herrick, who is a full-time researcher—quite a switch from the usual image of a golf-playing rainmaker! As one associate points out, "That Chris Herrick could be a full partner, well-respected and valued by everybody, says tons about the firm's recognition and value of diversity." The associate marvels that, "It makes me feel like someday they may also accept me for all of my talents and idiosyncrasies!" Another adds that, "Associates here don't need to conform to a cookie-cutter ideal in order to be successful and make partner."

"We don't participate in 'Rambo litigation.'"

Associates appreciate that "We are encouraged to treat everyone, including opposing counsel, politely and with respect. We don't participate in 'Rambo litigation.' The partners teach us how to win cases while also winning friends among our opponents." Associates add that they "enjoy working with lawyers who are very good and very successful without falling into step with some of the demeaning stereotypes of lawyers as overzealous advocates," and that "This attitude increases the likelihood that we'll be treated respectfully in return."

The prevailing feeling among associates is that "The shareholders clearly want us to succeed" and offer "constructive, positive reinforcement and as much support as they can to make it easy and pleasant to perform well." One associate, with the firm for only a month so far, enthuses that "Already it's obvious that this firm is great for a number of reasons. Not only is the work exciting and interesting, but every lawyer here performs at such a high level that it pushes me to do my absolute best as well."

The work associates get all involves the firm's sole specialty, business and employment litigation. Associates say that, "The work we do is fascinating, especially the complex commercial litigation." They appreciate learning at the elbows of partners who "are an amazing group. They are evenly split men and women, and they represent different talents, skills and personalities." Associates say that, "When you consider the body of skills required to be a truly outstanding lawyer, you find that every partner here has something, or many somethings, that make him or her fit that description."

When it comes to hours, the firm doesn't have any "exhausting billable goals" or "distracting intra-office competition." Instead, associates say that "the shareholders have been extraordinarily devoted to fostering a work environment that encourages you to do your best, while still recognizing that you have a life outside of work." One associate, a single mother, says she went to law school at night and only made it through because of the "example of the partners here, who showed that you can practice litigation at a very high degree of excellence and sophistication without burning out."

The firm's humane approach to practicing law is also reflected in its social activities. As one associate commented, "Our holiday party, summer picnic, and firm retreat include all employees, not just the lawyers. On top of that, they hold all of these functions during business hours and close down the office." The firm's parties get rave reviews from associates, who say that "Many people in the local legal community tell us, even in writing, that we give the best parties!" One associate says that, "The food and wine are top quality. No Costco quiches here! Everybody gets dressed up. The offices pass the 'white glove' test. We put our best face forward, and as a result invitations to our parties are much sought-after. And by the way—everybody has a wonderful time!" All in all, associates say that with MHGM, "The partners' efforts don't go unnoticed. We all work harder, and better, as a result of being treated with respect and appreciation."

McAndrews, Held & Malloy, Ltd.

500 W. Madison, 34TH Floor • Chicago, IL 60661
Phone: 312-707-8889 • Fax: 312-707-9155 • Web site: mhmhome.com

OFFICES

Chicago, Illinois

*"My law school professors warned me that practicing law would
be boring. Doing patent litigation for MH&M is anything but
that—it's been so much more interesting and exciting than I
expected! I was working on a case for a statuary company, where
another statuary company had copied their animals. We had all of
these stone frogs, toads, squirrels, rabbits sitting around the office.
I'd be taking a deposition, with a gnome sitting there on the table,
asking the witness for similarities between the gnome and a frog.
It was great fun."*

HIGHLIGHTS

• Intellectual property boutique that has experienced spectacular growth
in the last four years.

NUTS AND BOLTS

Managing partner:

George P. McAndrews, e-mail: georgem@mhmlaw.com

Hiring partner:

John J. Held, e-mail: johnh@mhmlaw.com

Recruiting coordinator:

Michael Carson, e-mail: michaelc@mhmlaw.com

Number of attorneys in firm:

66 (31 partners)

Total partners (31), total associates (35), women partners (5), women associates (10), minority partners (7), minority associates (11), disabled partners (0), disabled associates (0)

Years to make partner:

5

WHAT DO THEY DO?

Primary specialties (more than 5% of practice):

The firm's sole specialty is Intellectual Property. 90% of the firm's work is litigation-oriented, while the rest involves patent prosecution, copyright and licensing issues.

WHO DO THEY REPRESENT?

The firm primarily concentrates on litigating patent lawsuits. It has represented litigants in such diverse technology as satellites, medical devices, bar-coders, appliances, paper machines, disposable diapers, sports equipment, truck structures, cellular telephony, chemical formulations, printing equipment, and many others.

WHERE NEW ASSOCIATES COME FROM . . .

The firm does not routinely interview on law school campuses. Rather, the firm asks the law schools to have interested law students contact the firm directly. In recent years, most of the firm's associates have come to the firm from its summer clerk program. Others come through job fairs. Applicants are asked to visit the firm and meet with as many of its attorneys—both associates and partners—as possible.

HOURS AND BUCKS . . .

Associate work an average of 2,300 hours per year. The minimum billable hours requirement is 2,000 hours per year.

Part-time work is available both to continuing and entry-level associates. The firm does not routinely hire contract associates.

Typical first year associate salary, including typical bonus: $$$$ (Over $65,000). The firm is known for its particularly generous financial package.

SUMMER PROGRAM . . .

Last year, there were 18 summer associates, all of whom received offers.
Weekly pay: $1,730 last year.

1Ls are routinely hired for the summer program. Last year's 1Ls came from Chicago, Chicago-Kent, Loyola/Chicago, Rutgers, Arizona State, Boston College, Harvard, John Marshall, and Michigan.

PRO BONO . . .

The firm encourages its lawyers to perform pro bono work. There are no minimum pro bono hours requirements, and pro bono hours do not count as billables.

HISTORY AT A GLANCE . . .

The firm was founded in 1988, when six lawyers left what had been Allegretti, Newitt, Witcoff and McAndrews in Chicago. The six were George P. McAndrews, John J. Held, Timothy J. Malloy, Lawrence M. Jarvis, Gregory J. Vogler and Robert C. Ryan.

WHAT IT'S LIKE TO WORK THERE . . .

When I was interviewing law school administrators, learning about the employers who ought to be included in this book, I heard an incredible story about McAndrews, Held: "They had a guy who had a two-year judicial clerkship, and everybody knows how wonderful *those* are. He gave up the second year of the clerkship to get back to the firm, he likes it so much there."

You don't have to spend much time talking to lawyers at MH&M to figure out what it was that made that judicial clerk such a rabid devotee. Associates rave that "People are really happy here," "The quality of life is really good," and "The lawyers here are very funny, just great to work with." It's a place where "there's a very casual atmosphere, every day," and, according to one associate, "The partners are incredible with families. My little girls all love George McAndrews"—the managing partner—"They run to him like he's their grandfather."

One standout feature of the firm is its diversity of personalities, which you wouldn't necessarily expect from a firm where almost all of the lawyers have either an undergraduate or graduate degree in science or engineering. Some associates affectionately refer to themselves as "Double-geeks—engineers *and* lawyers." Associates say that, "There are two different kinds of people who will be happy here, two totally different standards. Of course you've got a few of your studious types, the techno-nerds, the ones who like to hole up and write patents for 30 hours at a time. There's room for them here." But "On the other hand, you have lots of very outgoing people, the kind who will be comfortable taking a deposition"—which is fortunate since 90% of the firm's business involves litigation. As managing partner George McAndrews said in an interview with *Chicago Lawyer,* MH&M is the kind of place where lawyers who are also engineers and scientists can be comfortable, since the firm belies "the cobra-mongoose college history where the 'Arts and Letters' or business students derisively referred to engineers and science majors as 'nerds.'"

The firm's outstanding atmosphere stems from its recruiting philosophy. It makes a point of looking for people who have "more than a technical paper under their belt. *Everybody* here has that. That's not what makes people stand out." One associate speaks enthusiastically about "A candidate I interviewed who had flown Top Gun jets in the Navy! We love that kind of stuff. We look for interesting life experiences that people can weave in, other than jobs and papers they've written."

"The senior partners have a wealth of knowledge and experience and really seem to enjoy sharing it with you."

Much of the training at MH&M is a matter of "'learning by example' with the guidance of more senior attorneys," although the firm "also holds weekly CLE discussions over lunch." Those CLEs, however, aren't confined to lectures about evidence and procedure from local law professors. They have been far-ranging, including "stress management workshops, recent developments in patent law, and even a golf workshop!"

The firm makes a point of giving junior associates responsibility early on. They are assigned to "practice teams," with most of their work flowing from their supervising partner. Lawyers report that you often find "first year associates taking depositions, doing presentations to clients, arguing motions, and writing appeal briefs." One junior associate commented that on smaller cases, "We get substantial responsibility in our second year," and another said that "it's not unusual to do depositions within a few months of starting here."

Associates rave about the quality of the work they get. One associate commented that "The work is much more interesting and exciting than I expected when I was in law school. I had a law school professor who said that he talked to graduates who complain that they're bored. That's definitely not the case here. There's lots of variety, and it's academically very challenging." Associates say that "Doors are always open here. The partners are always available to help if you've got questions."

Interestingly enough, it's not the big, headline-making cases that associates consider the most fun, although they recognize that cases like that are the firm's "bread and butter." Instead, "The fun cases are the copyright and trademark cases." One junior associate recalled working on a case for a statuary company—the kind of company that makes lawn dwarfs and that kind of thing—"where another statuary company had copied their animals." The associate laughs that "We had all of these stone frogs, toads, squirrels, rabbits sitting around the office. I'd be taking a deposition, with a gnome sitting there on the table, asking the witness for similarities between the gnome and a frog. It was great fun."

"The senior partner has a playpen in his office!"

MH&M is a "paradox" when it comes to family-friendliness. The lawyers all agree that the firm is very family-friendly, and every article that's appeared in local media backs that up. That would suggest that the lawyers put in light schedules, but that's not the case. Associates report that "It's a dichotomy. In terms of hours, it's a sweatshop. The culture is to work very long hours. But at the same time, they are interested in our families, and they really mean it."

The offices tend to fill up around 9 in the morning, with "a few people who come in at 8." Any weeknight "you might find yourself at the office until 10 p.m.," although "the evenings and weekends depend on cases— one or two practice teams at a time will have to work long hours." Associates say that "There might be 10 or 20 people in the office on the weekends," although "if you have nothing to do, you leave, no one cares, they're not watching over your shoulder." Despite the long hours, associates say that, "It's worth it to get the kind of responsibility I get in my cases. You don't mind prepping a motion if you draft it, too, and argue it in court, and I get to do that. I get to be on the front line, doing depositions, taking witnesses in front of a jury." That kind of responsibility "makes the work worthwhile," and it doesn't hurt that "We are very well paid. They are good about keeping us in line with the salaries at the big firms in town."

One of the ways the firm maintains a family-friendly atmosphere while expecting long hours is that "the firm bends over backwards to accommodate pregnant attorneys and attorneys with young children." One female attorney recalls telling George McAndrews that, "my difficult pregnancy would require ongoing testing that would reduce the amount of time I could be in the office. He told me to take whatever time I needed, that having a healthy baby was more important than anything else."

The firm recently instituted a policy that allows women attorneys with small children to work part-time. In fact, the firm is notoriously protective of the interests of its women attorneys. As one lawyer tells it, "Several years ago, an older client gave not-so-subtle hints that he would prefer not to have female associates assigned to his work. The firm responded by refunding all the fees he had paid, returning his files and suggesting that he would be happier being represented by some other firm." This attitude "has not been isolated. The firm is well-known for its understanding, support and equal treatment of female attorneys."

The firm's offices are incredibly kid-friendly, with a common observation that "it's not uncommon to see young children in the office." Lawyers report that "Half of the artwork in the firm are drawings made by the children of attorneys and staff." One lawyer shares that "The senior partners not only say 'hi' to my children, they call my children into their offices and the kids get to choose a treat from their treat drawers." Lawyers also comment that "No one was surprised when a crib showed up in a senior partner's office and remained there, often with a baby of one of the associates having sitter problems."

The firm's interest in the welfare of children goes beyond the children of its employees. For the last four years, members of the firm have been involved in acting as "Secret Santas," answering letters to Santa written by underprivileged children in and around Chicago. "No letter that's received by the firm goes unanswered. If we get more letters than we have people from the firm who can participate in the program, the firm provides gifts to all remaining families."

*"The people here are great to be around,
at the office and outside of work, as well."*

Associates say that "We socialize together a lot. We'll have poker games, things like that." They say that "Attorneys will routinely get together on weekends with families and kids, and the single ones will routinely go out together every couple of weeks."

The firm itself sponsors picnics, golf, basketball and football outings, and formal parties for the whole firm. In addition, the firm provides weekly breakfasts, as well as "spontaneous free lunches, as well as ice cream and cake parties to celebrate court victories, birthdays, and any other events that come up!" The firm also "encourages, if not sponsors, outings to sporting events, like Bulls, Cubs, or White Sox games, for all of the employees." Associates also like the firm's "annual Christmas party at Sears Tower," although they appreciate even more "the McAndrews philosophy of giving you money instead of perks."

All in all, associates feel that "Everything here is structured like a family, with George McAndrews as the patriarch. He gives us the philosophy of taking care of each other and the staff, and working hard. He talks about the 400 people who depend on our paychecks—all of our families. He cares about us, and he gets involved in the work we do. This is just a great place to work."

McDonald, Hopkins, Burke & Haber Co., L.P.A.

2100 Bank One Center • 600 Superior Avenue, East • Cleveland, OH 44114-2653
Phone: 216-348-5400 • Fax: 216-348-5474 • Web site: mhbh.com

OFFICES

Cleveland, Ohio

"As a very junior associate, you have some control over what will ideally be your firm. They want your input and your suggestions. And they want you to be excited about what you do . . . it's a very open and friendly place. If you're just 'Mr. Lawyer' you won't fit the firm personality."

HIGHLIGHTS

- One of Ohio's 20 largest law firms.
- Former associates include the son of Ohio Senator George Voinovich.

NUTS AND BOLTS

Managing partner:

Thomas W. Keen, President

Hiring partner:

Shawn M. Riley, phone: 216-348-5773, e-mail: smr@mhbh.com

Recruiting coordinator:

Pamela A. Chesnik, phone: 216-348-5728, e-mail: pac@mhbh.com

Number of attorneys in firm:

61 (38 partners)

Years to make partner:

7 to 10

WHAT DO THEY DO?

Primary specialties (more than 5% of practice):

Business law (including labor, worker's comp, employment litigation, and employment practices counseling), tax and employee benefits, health law, estate planning and probate, and litigation.

Associates can, and do, switch specialties.

WHO DO THEY REPRESENT?

Clients include local, regional, and national business corporations; health care entities; financial institutions; insurance companies and agencies; governmental authorities; nonprofit corporations, including tax-exempt entities; universities; professionals including physicians, accountants, lawyers, athletes; estates, guardianships, and trusts; general and limited partnerships, and individuals.

WHERE NEW ASSOCIATES COME FROM . . .

The firm routinely interviews on campus at the following law schools: Cleveland Marshall, Case Western Reserve, Ohio State, Georgetown, Boston University, Boston College, Michigan, George Washington. The firm also hires associates and summer associates from schools where it doesn't interview on campus.

HOURS AND BUCKS . . .

First year associates spend an average of 2,200 hours at the office, of which 1,800 is the minimum yearly billable hour requirement.

The firm allows part-time work on a case-by-case basis. The firm does not routinely hire contract associates.

Typical first year salary, including typical bonus: $$$$ (Over $65,000)

SUMMER PROGRAM . . .

Last year, there were 7 summer associates.

Monthly pay: $5,000 for 2Ls, $4,500 for 1Ls

Last year's 1Ls came from Georgetown and Boston College.

The deadline for applying for the firm's summer program is January 31ST.

PRO BONO . . .

The firm anticipates that the 400-hour difference between yearly hours and billables is to be used for pro bono and any other non-billable work.

HISTORY AT A GLANCE . . .

The current firm is the result of a 1990 merger between McDonald, Hopkins & Hardy, and Burke, Haber & Berick.

Today, several of the firm's estate planning lawyers are listed in *Best Lawyers in America.*

WHAT IT'S LIKE TO WORK THERE . . .

Associates at McDonald, Hopkins applaud their "very impromptu environment," a "low-key, personal firm" where "If you're just 'Mr. Lawyer,' you won't fit the firm personality." Associates talk about the firm's "*very* open door policy—you can ask questions of anyone here. Even the president of the firm. They're happy to help." Their sense is that "Everybody works hard to get the job done, but we don't have the stress of working around the clock."

"The size of the firm is a positive. It's big enough to have complex stuff, small enough not to leave you bored."

Before associates join the firm, they choose a specialty, and "By and large you get your first choice." Each department "avoids a rigid, hierarchical structure" with a "work teams" approach. Each "work team" consists of a partner, associates, paralegals and secretaries. However, associates say that "Anyone in your department can give you assignments," they don't just get projects from their work team leader. In fact, the perception among associates is that the way to get great assignments is to "Go to shareholders in your department who do something you want to do and tell them 'I'd like to try this kind of project,' and they give it to you." Another way to find out about incoming projects is through monthly committee meetings. The committees each essentially cover a different specialty; for instance, in the business department, there are two different committees, one for real estate and commercial law, and one for employment law. Each attorney in the firm is a member of "about two" committees of their choosing. Associates say that "You can go to any committee meetings you want and learn about what they're doing, to see if there are projects you want to get in on," and the meetings are also good for "updates in the law, or standard concepts you need to be reminded about." The committee meetings give associates a chance to hear "people talk about what's coming in, and you pipe up and volunteer." Even without committee meetings,

"You quickly find out who does what, so that you can position yourself for the work you want."

When it comes to picking up lawyering skills, the sense among associates is that rather than formal training, the firm stresses a "baptism by fire. It's, 'Let's throw you into transactions and cases and you'll pick up skills and concepts.'" Associates find this exciting because "It's not a matter of sink or swim, not at all. They don't expect you to run documents without questions." As one associate laughingly explains, "When you receive assignments as a new associate, you don't even know the questions to ask! They know and expect you to stumble a bit, to not know exactly what you're doing at first. They're there to help."

Part of that helping comes from mentors. Every associate gets their own mentor, and associates find that "The mentors are a great source of solid advice, about everything to do with the firm."

Associates say that they get "quite a bit" of feedback. "Unless it's a rush project, they walk you through everything you do, giving you comments on it." As one associate explains it, "They're interested in you becoming a better attorney by sharing with you what you could have done better. It's refreshing." On top of informal project-by-project feedback, associates find that "some non-charge projects lend themselves to training. For instance, document assembly software—if you can put together documents, you can understand transactions and how documents work together."

"The firm president's philosophy is to make you a manager from Day One."

Associates rave about the amount of responsibility they get at McDonald, Hopkins, right from the start. The firm's approach is to give new associates rapid exposure to clients as a means of developing their professional skills. Associates report that "The amount of responsibility you get as a new associate here is a real standout." One associate says that "I've got lots of friends from school who are in everything from two-person offices all the way to huge national firms, and neither of those extremes gives them what I get here. We get a good degree of responsibility but we also get supervision. You don't just get library research in business or document reviews in litigation," you get "real work."

Associates also like the fact that "You have some control over what will ideally be your firm." They report that "The firm president's philosophy is to make you into a manager from Day One. You have input and suggestions from Day One. You can talk to the firm president directly about anything that's on your mind." Associates find that they have a "remarkable amount of information about how the firm is doing," through annual firm retreats as well as extensive monthly financials revealing the firm's well-being.

Associates have a voice in firm management through serving on firm committees, although "We're not burdened with committees, teams, that kind of thing." They appreciate not just formal involvement in the firm, but also the fact that they are informally consulted on a variety of issues. For instance, when it comes to technology changes, associates say that "We're force-fed Lexis and Westlaw in school, while more senior attorneys get that kind of technology second-hand. They don't have time to play with new 'toys.'" Associates find that "If a few associates say, 'We should really have this or that software,' they look into it, get us involved with a review of competing products, and take it from there."

The firm also makes associates feel like valuable members of the organization by placing a "pretty strong emphasis" on business development. Associates say that "there's no expectation that you'll do it in your first or second year, but there is an emphasis on things calculated to bring in business in future," like "knowing local bankers, so that four years from now, when they hand out loan documents, you're in a position to take them." The firm feels that "Associates might not get business now, but it's important to train us how to bring in clients later on." Associates find that their mentors are an "excellent source of guidance for becoming a complete lawyer—you can ask them what to do to be on pace for developing business, what activities to be involved in the community, and they'll tell you." Associates find that they like the business development emphasis because "It preps you for being a partner. It's laying the groundwork." They also appreciate that in their early years "The emphasis is on you becoming a good attorney, and business generation is a part of that. But the firm teaches you that if you aren't good, no one you know will want to send you business. So they make sure you hone your skills, first."

When it comes to working hours, associates report that they "routinely work 60-hour weeks." The offices tend to fill up between 8:30 and 9 in the morning, although "there are some early risers who come in at 7, and leave early." At night, the offices typically clear out between 6 and 7 p.m. With weekends, "We work more Saturdays than not," although "No one *expects* you to be in on Saturdays." Instead, "You're generally there for something that needs to be done on Monday. It's all driven by client deadlines." And "The partners are in as much as you are on weekends. There are no Friday afternoon assignments due Monday, while they go off and play golf."

Associates don't resent the hours they put in because "You enjoy the work, so the hours don't seem so long," and besides, "If there's ever a time you're going to put in the hours, it's when you're a new associate." Associates say that "Being in a firm like this gives you exposure to the broad spectrum of legal issues. You get a bird's-eye view of the community. That's very rewarding." They also point out that the 1,800 billable hours requirement is a "real goal." They add that "If you work long hours and bill in excess of that, you get a bonus." To accommodate families, the firm "works out a plan for the women attorneys who are pregnant, and everybody's fine with that." The plan typically involves part-time work for a while after the lawyer has a baby, and "That part-time can stretch on." In general, associates feel that the firm is "accommodating with lawyers with small children. You don't hear complaints about it."

"It's just fun *here."*

Associates enthuse that "People are happy here. They work hard, but the firm views work as just one part of your life. They send the message that if you're happy in life, you'll be a better lawyer." When it comes to extracurriculars, among the McDonald, Hopkins lawyers there is "Lots of involvement in lawyers' league sports." Many associates take part in those, "especially softball." There is also "Basketball, as well as golf outings."

For lawyers who aren't so sporty, there's still the opportunity to socialize at quarterly firm happy hours, as well as informal happy hours at local watering holes. There are holiday parties, and on an informal basis, celebrations like baby showers for pregnant attorneys and support staff. And, of course, there are "lots of summer associate gatherings," which associates enjoy. And speaking of the summer program, associates respect the fact that "The firm hires summer associates strictly based on the spaces they have to fill permanently next year. As a summer associate here, the job is yours to lose. There's no competition among summer associates," and that contributes to a convivial summer atmosphere. Life at the firm also isn't hurt by the fact that "Cleveland isn't what it used to be, when it was the butt of all of those 'mistake on the lake' jokes. You've got everything here—a world-class symphony orchestra, beautifully rebuilt theaters, the Rock & Roll Hall of Fame, Jacobs Field, the Flats, where all of the great nightclubs are." As one associate says, "This is a great place. I'm excited when I get in, and I'm still fired up when I leave. It's a reflection on the work I get to do, where I get to do it, and the people I work with."

Millisor & Nobil Co., LPA

9150 South Hills Boulevard, Suite 300 • Cleveland, Ohio 44147-3599
Phone: 440-838-8800 • Fax: 440-838-8805 • E-mail: laborlaw@millisor.com

OFFICES

Cleveland (main office), Downtown Cleveland, Columbus, Canton, Ohio

*"It's a very open, friendly place. I've worked at law firms where
everybody called each other 'Mr. this' and 'Ms. that.' There's none of
that here."*

HIGHLIGHTS

• Labor and employment law boutique.

NUTS AND BOLTS

Managing partner:

Kenneth R. Millisor

Hiring partner:

Sue Marie Douglas, phone: 440-838-8800, e-mail: sdouglas@millisor.com

Number of attorneys in firm:

31 (23 partners)

WHOLE FIRM:

Women attorneys (9), minority attorneys (3)

CLEVELAND OFFICE:

Attorneys (23), partners (16), women attorneys (7), minority
attorneys (2)

OTHER OFFICES:

Downtown Cleveland (3), Columbus, OH (3), Canton, OH (3)

Years to make partner:

> There is no set number of years, but an associates must be at least 5 years out of law school.

WHAT DO THEY DO?

The firm is exclusively a management-side labor and employment law firm.

WHERE NEW ASSOCIATES COME FROM . . .

The firm routinely interviews on campus at the following law schools: Case Western Reserve and Ohio State. The firm also hires from schools where it doesn't interview on campus.

HOURS AND BUCKS . . .

First year associates typically work 2,200 hours per year, of which the minimum billable hours requirement is 1,800.

Part-time work is available to both ongoing and entry-level associates. The firm does not routinely hire contract associates.

SUMMER PROGRAM . . .

Last year, there were two summer associates, one 2L (who received an offer) and one 1L.

Weekly pay: $1,000 last year

1Ls are routinely hired for the summer program; last year's 1L came from Cleveland Marshall.

The deadline for applying for summer clerkships is September 30TH.

PRO BONO . . .

The firm encourages pro bono involvement. Pro bono hours are not treated as billables.

WHAT IT'S LIKE TO WORK THERE . . .

Associates rave that Millisor has an environment where "Everybody gets along," and that it's "a very friendly place." One associate reported that "Before I came here I clerked at a law firm where everybody called each other 'Mr. this' or 'Ms. that.' We don't have any of that here." And one feature associates definitely appreciate is "the fully-stocked cafeteria!"

The firm, which exclusively does management-side labor law, is separated into three departments. There's Labor, which handles "traditional union issues." Labor and Employment does litigation. And Worker's Comp handles benefits and human resources matters. The firm's small size means that associates get a variety of assignments from different partners, although "They are great about giving you assignments in things you'd like to try. You need to ask for it. You can always talk to the head of your department. They're very approachable."

As you'd expect from a small-ish firm, with 29 attorneys, associates get lots of responsibility, very fast. Associates say that it's not at all unusual to have a partner say, "Watch me depose this expert, and then next time I'll watch you." One associate talked about "Arguing two appellate court cases, drafting all of the briefs—I did everything but oral arguments in an Ohio Supreme Court case. The partner told me, 'Here's the case, handle it and ask me any questions if you have them.'" This 'here's-a-case-go-do-it' attitude is typical of the firm, although "You aren't left out on a limb." The firm assigns each associate a mentor, where "you can go with issues, balancing the workload, really any problem that you have."

The firm does "a little bit of in-house training." For instance, the litigation department has regular weekly or bi-weekly meetings where the attorneys discuss recent cases and new issues, and the same goes for worker's comp. Associates also learn about new developments in "memos from partners, which get forwarded to us informally."

Associates report that the firm's 1,800 hour billable hour target is "What they really expect." There's an appreciation for the firm's "flexibility about the amount of time you spend in the office." One associate wanted to go to a part-time schedule, and the firm accommodated her. "As long as you bill your hours, the firm doesn't care where you are—you can be at home if you want." Any work that has to be finished up at home is made easier with "Home computers that are hooked up to the office, to Lexis/Nexis." The firm doesn't put pressure on associates' non-billable time. Associates report that involvement in pro bono is "an individual issue," and "there really isn't much of it here, not because the people don't care about it, but because expertise with labor and employment issues isn't helpful with pro bono clients."

Associates find that when it comes to bringing in business, "It's definitely something they like to see you do," but "They don't push you. They let you figure out business generation on your own." The firm provides several avenues for business development, including giving associates a business development fund, encouraging them to take advantage of speaking engagements, helping them take part in community organizations, and providing them with mentors. All in all, associates applaud Millisor for its "flexibility and willingness to work with us as individuals. It's the kind of place where as soon as you show you can handle more, you get it."

Moore Ingram Johnson
& Steele, L.L.P.

192 Anderson Street • P. O. Box 3305 • Marietta, GA 30060
Phone: 770-429-1499 • Fax: 770-429-8631 • E-mail: MIJS@MIJS.COM

OFFICES

Marietta, Georgia

*"The best thing about this place is that you have the nest. If you fall
out of it, they pick you up. When you start out, you make stupid
mistakes, but nobody browbeats you—they know you'll stumble as
a new associate, and they know you'll learn and do it perfectly next
time. I'm just tickled to be here."*

NUTS AND BOLTS

Managing partner:
John H. Moore

Hiring partner:
G. Phillip Beggs

Recruiting coordinator:
G. Phillip Beggs

Number of attorneys in firm:
33 (9 partners)

Partners (9), women partners (1), associates (24), women associates (6)

Years to make partner:
8 $^1/_2$

WHAT DO THEY DO?

Primary specialties (more than 5% of practice):

Litigation (17), Corporate/Tax (7), Real Estate (6), Domestic (3).

Associates are normally hired into their specialties. As much as possible, the firm tries to hire from its second year law clerks, who have had an opportunity to rotate through the various departments of the firm and determine what they want to do.

Associates can switch specialties if the firm has a need in another area and the associate has skills that would be of benefit in that area.

WHERE NEW ASSOCIATES COME FROM . . .

The firm routinely interviews on campus at the following law schools: Mercer, Georgia, and Georgia State. The firm also routinely hires associates and summer associates from schools where it doesn't interview on campus.

HOURS AND BUCKS . . .

Minimum billable hours for associates are 1,900; the average billable hours for most first year associates is approximately 2,100, but the firm's formula for calculating this total is somewhat unique: associates are given credit for a 'billable hour' whether or not the hour is billed to the client, as long as the work is performed on a billable file. This means that associates are not penalized concerning billables as long as the work is written down. The firm does allow part-time work, but not at entry level. The firm does not routinely hire contract associates.

Typical first year salary, including typical bonus: $$ ($35-50,000)

SUMMER PROGRAM . . .

Last year, there were 4 summer clerks, 3 of whom received offers.

Weekly pay: $750 last year.

The firm routinely hires 1Ls for its summer program.

PRO BONO . . .

The firm firmly favors pro bono work, with all time spent on pro bono cases being credited as billable time. The firm encourages all attorneys to become members of the Cobb Justice Foundation, which the local bar association uses to provide pro bono legal assistance to the community. As a member of the Cobb Justice Foundation, each member agrees to make a monetary contribution, or agrees to accept 2 pro bono cases per year in their specialty. These cases are screened by the Foundation to determine need and are then referred to the attorney.

HISTORY AT A GLANCE . . .

The firm was founded on January 1, 1984 when John H. Moore left another local firm and opened his own practice. Within 3 years the firm had grown to 10 attorneys, and has steadily grown to its current level of 33 attorneys.

Partners John Moore and Robert Ingram have both been presidents of the Cobb County Bar Association (Ingram is the current president).

WHAT IT'S LIKE TO WORK THERE . . .

When you talk with associates at Moore Ingram, you are immediately struck by how they feel they're working at a warm, caring, nurturing place. Associates will tell you how "It's not a pressure-packed place." "It's young. Everybody is very approachable." "It's a family. They treat you like part of a family." "It's growing very quickly, so there are lots of young associates. You can commiserate with them if you stumble. If you say, 'What the hell did I do?' there are lots of ears to hear you. And you help others." As one associate explained it, "I'll have interviewees tell me, 'I don't want to get lost in the shuffle.' That doesn't happen here. You work in very small teams, and the doors of partners are always open."

"It's a great place if you like the idea of having a coach."

Associates rave about the support that they get from the partners. They explain that in each of the firm's three practice groups—Litigation, Workers Comp, and Contract Liability—each associate works with "four people or so." The firm "makes an effort to limit the number of sources from which a junior associate receives assignments," and "at the very least, junior associates have a primary source of supervision by either a partner or a senior associate."

Associates say that they get lots of mentoring from their supervising partners. "They are phenomenally accessible at any time." One associate laughingly tells how "Sometimes you'll see three or four associates standing outside a partner's door, waiting to ask a question. Anything you want to know, the partners are happy to answer."

Associates also talk about their "comfort zone" and "safety net" which comes from the feedback they get. "When you draft letters, propound discovery, they tell you what you did wrong and right," and "Since the partners are young, there's no generational disparity. You're getting help from people you can identify with."

Associates describe the firm as "up and coming" and talk about the perception that work is coming in "like crazy." Associates say that "We get all kinds of clients, insurance companies mostly, doing personal injury defense work," but the firm is "very diverse, and getting all kinds of clients all the time, from big companies to start-ups, and the projects are all over the board—product liability defense, employment discrimination defense, workers comp defense, lots of road construction stuff, zoning, real estate, lots of estate planning. There's lots of variety." Associates rave about the fact that "If you research a motion, or anything else you're in on the end product." One associate recalled how "The first day I was here, I sat in on a motion for abuse of litigation, then I got to research that issue." The firm even has new associates handling their own cases very early in their careers, in the form of "small things, traffic court civil stuff. You handle those right away under the review of a senior partner. You ask for strategy, and then you go and do it. You ask things like, 'Are these the right interrogatories?' and you get feedback at every step. You handle it, and they review it." Associates uniformly feel "There's no better way to learn to be a lawyer than by actually handling real things, yourself, with excellent backup." Associates also appreciate the fact that "The partners don't cut us out of client development. We often go to lunch or dinner or golf with prospective clients. They make you feel like part of the team."

Associates find that their principal contribution to helping run the firm come through recruiting. Associates do the "initial screening of new recruits," and at the "annual recruiting session, they bring in the interviewees, and the associates and partners all have input on who comes in. Of course the partners have the final say, but they ask us for what we think, and they take that into account. They're very sensitive that we're going to be working with new people, and so they let us help pick them out."

On administrative matters associates find the partners "very responsive," in everything from the right to "hire your own secretary" to issues involving how the office is run. One associate tells of how the associates wanted changes made in the way filing was done. "The partners asked the secretaries to submit a solution, and then we all met together to resolve it. They pay attention to things that concern us, even small things."

"There are seven newlyweds among the associates."

Associates comment that Moore Ingram is "a very family-friendly place." While several of the junior associates are single, some are married, and many of the married lawyers have children. Two female associates with small children reworked clients among other attorneys "and they cut their workload in half." Associates say that "because many of the partners have young children themselves, they understand the pressures." There is a prevailing sense that "If you ever have a sick kid with a fever, any kind of family emergency, people will help you out so that you can go," and that "Everybody is good about it, nobody abuses anyone else's good nature. But they definitely recognize that kids have needs, that you have a life outside of work."

One associate told a story that particularly highlights the firm's understanding attitude toward families. "After having only been at work for two weeks following a maternity leave, my babysitter quit suddenly. I had no contingency plan for childcare, so I thought I had no choice but to resign because it quickly became apparent that childcare was going to be a continuing problem for me." The associate continues that "I didn't think it would be fair to ask the firm to wait for me to find a new sitter, and be burdened with an undependable employee in the meantime. However, when I spoke with my supervising partner about resigning, he talked me out of quitting and assured me that the partners expected these occasional snags. As a result, I worked from home when I could until I found a new babysitter. Once I had childcare again, I returned to work with an even greater affection and loyalty to the firm."

"They don't tell you to do anything, they ask you. It's a respect thing."

Associates say that the Moore Ingram offices fill up between 8 and 8:30 in the morning, and tend to empty out between 6 and 6:30 at night. There are "not many people in on weekends," although the feeling is that "If I've got work to do, I come in and do it. If it means three or four hours on a weekend, I do it. If I don't have anything left to do at the end of Friday, fine—I'll leave then and come in on Monday." Associates applaud a firm attitude towards hours, reflected in the advice to first year associates of the two partners who head the litigation department, Robert Ingram and Bill Johnson: "We don't want you in on weekends. You've got so much going on during the week that you need your weekends free as a first year associate." Associates say that "if they do need you on weekends, they ask you, they don't *tell* you. It's a respect thing."

Associates report that when they *do* have to work long hours, because of a trial or a very involved case, the firm has a "cool deal" for showing its appreciation. "If there's a month where you have to bill 200 hours, you get a $100 gift certificate to a restaurant, or a play, or something like that— you never know what it's going to be." Associates point out that "It's not designed to turn the firm into a sweatshop—it's kind of a 'thank you' when the project you're working on demands long hours."

When it comes to bringing in business, associates say that, "If you bring in clients, it's part of the consideration for your bonus. The attitude is definitely that 'It's good for the firm so ultimately it's good for you.'"

"It's great relaxing in social settings with my colleagues."

The firm makes a point of creating a social environment that the associates consider "cool." One associate applauded the firm's "sports-oriented nature. There are softball and basketball teams, co-ed teams. It's fun."

Along with holiday parties and formal social events, the partners are very sensitive to knowing when the circumstances call for an impromptu party. As one associate tells it, "We recently moved into newly-remodeled offices. During that first week, our new, upgraded computer system spent more time 'down' than 'up,' and coupled with the frustrations you always have when you move, it was a week from hell. On that Friday morning, I noticed there was a universal inter-office voice mail in my mailbox. It turns out that the partners had decided to close the firm at noon and take everyone, attorneys and support staff, to Dave & Busters, a super-duper arcade/restaurant here in Marietta. The firm picked up the entire tab and we all spent the afternoon eating everything in sight, and taking our computer and moving frustrations out on various 3-D interactive racing games."

"The firm is very involved in the community."

Associates report that the firm is "very open to pro bono work," and that it's got a broad definition of pro bono. "You can bring in your own family work, that's considered pro bono as well." For traditional pro bono projects, "You can bring in cases on your own initiative, or get assigned by the court. The firm will almost always let you do it, unless there's just no merit to the case at all." Associates say that the firm "actively goes out and gets pro bono work as an issue of community involvement. They're big on that."

"The firm will stick its neck out for new associates."

The thing that stands out most to associates is that they feel as though they are part of the Moore Ingram family, from day one. As one associate tells it, "I'm tickled as can be. I'm having a great time here. They treat you like part of a family." One associate recounts his first day at Moore Ingram, which perfectly highlights why it is that the firm is so beloved. "On my very first day working as a brand new associate, I became aware of a conflict that existed between me and a long-standing client of the firm. My heart sank. The partners could have taken the easy road, and either withdrawn my offer or put it off until the conflict passed. They didn't do either one. Instead, they explained the conflict to the client, and risked that relationship in order to let me start work right away. I thought it was remarkable that the firm would stick its neck out for a brand new associate, who had yet to bill a single hour, when they were confronted with the possibility of ruining the relationship with the client in order to keep me." The associate marvels, "Not only did the conflict resolve itself with the client's approval, but the firm earned my respect immediately by sticking up for the 'new guy' when it would have been so easy not to. I've since found that this is the kind of support the partners here give us every day."

Morrison & Foerster L.L.P.—San Francisco

425 Market Street • San Francisco, CA 94105
Phone: 415-268-7000 • Fax: 415-268-7522 • Web site: mofo.com

OFFICES

San Francisco (main office), Los Angeles*, Irvine*, Palo Alto*, Walnut Creek, California; New York City*, New York; Washington, D.C.*; Denver, Colorado

HIGHLIGHTS

- Undoubtedly the most decorated law firm in America when it comes to 'great place to work' accolades. Among others: Morrison & Foerster is the only law firm to appear in the best-selling book *The 100 Best Companies To Work For*, as well as *Forbes Magazine*'s 1998 "100 Best Companies To Work For In America" survey, and 1997's *Working Mother Magazine* workplace award. The firm won the 1993 Catalyst Award from 'Catalyst,' a nonprofit women's rights organization recognizing the firm's initiatives in supporting the advancement of women in the law.
- 19TH largest firm in the country.
- The firm prides itself on its diversity; *Forbes Magazine* describes it as "a magnet for women and minorities." Many women, minority and gay and lesbian lawyers have held, or currently hold, important management positions within the firm.
- Offers health insurance and other benefits to same-sex partners.
- 22% of partners and 45% of associates are women.
- Strong commitment to cutting-edge computer technology.
- Exceptional associate participation in the firm; apart from participation in many firm committees, associates routinely evaluate partners on a confidential basis concerning partners' training and associate development abilities. Associates receive detailed information on the firm's financial performance on an annual basis.
- Strong dedication to pro bono work. Pro bono hours are treated as billable hours.

NUTS AND BOLTS

Managing partner:

Stephen Dunham, Chairman

Hiring partner:

Craig B. Etlin (San Francisco office)

Recruiting coordinator:

Susie Elitzky in San Francisco, phone: 415-268-7409, e-mail:
sfattyrecruit@mofo.com

Number of attorneys in firm:

600+ (220 partners)

TOTAL FIRM:

Partners (220), associates (400+)

THIS OFFICE:

Total attorneys (243), partners (79), associates (134), women partners
(16), women associates (61), minority partners (7), minority associates
(41), disabled partners (0), disabled associates (1)

OTHER OFFICES:

(* represents an office profiled elsewhere in this book)
Los Angeles, CA* (97); Irvine, CA* (44); New York* (66); Washington,
D.C.* (60); Palo Alto, CA* (87); Denver, CO (17); Walnut Creek, CA (13);
Tokyo, Japan (17); Hong Kong (6)

Years to make partner:

6 to 9 years

WHAT DO THEY DO?

Primary specialties (more than 5% of practice) in the San Francisco office:

Corporate Finance, including Securities and Venture Capital (22);
Finance, including Lending, and Bank Regulation (12); Intellectual
Property and Patent (15); International (8); Labor & Employment Law
(10); Land Use, Environmental & Energy (11); Litigation (122); Real
Estate (10); Tax and Estates (18).

The firm is divided into four departments: Business, Labor, Litigation,
and Tax. Associates do not rotate between departments, but often work in
more than one practice area within a department and occasionally switch
between departments and even between offices.

WHERE NEW ASSOCIATES COME FROM . . .

The firm routinely interviews on campus at the following law schools:
Boalt Hall, Chicago, Columbia, Cornell, UC Davis, Harvard, Hastings,

Howard, Michigan, NYU, Northwestern, Santa Clara, Stanford, UCLA, and Yale. The firm also hires routinely from schools where it doesn't interview on campus.

HOURS AND BUCKS . . .

Minimum billable hours requirement: 1,850, plus an additional contribution of 450 non-billable hours in the form of activities like practice development, recruiting, participation on firm committees, continuing legal education, writing projects, the summer associate program and training.

Part-time work is available to continuing attorneys; not at entry level. Currently, the San Francisco office has 2 part-time associates and 4 part-time partners.

Typical first year salary, including typical bonus: $$$$ (Over $65,000). Morrison & Foerster is known for its particularly generous financial package.

SUMMER PROGRAM . . .

Last year, there were 40 summer associates, 37 of whom received offers.
The San Francisco office doesn't hire 1Ls for its summer program.

PRO BONO . . .

The firm is strongly dedicated to pro bono work. Pro bono hours are treated as billable hours. Projects span the full range of public interest work, from staffing legal services clinics and counseling over 150 non-profit organizations, to handling high-impact litigation. The greatest efforts have been focused on children in poverty and school education issues, civil rights and civil liberties cases, international human rights and political asylum, environmental matters, access to justice, issues of housing and homelessness, and AIDS-related work. The firm handles referrals of both civil and criminal matters from local courts, bar associations and legal services panels.

In addition, the firm runs the Morrison & Foerster Foundation, a non-profit charitable organization that serves charities in the communities where its offices are located. The firm also matches charitable contributions of its employees.

HISTORY AT A GLANCE . . .

The firm was founded in San Francisco in 1883.
Stars include Carla Oakley, litigation partner, and Peter Williams, corporate and intellectual property partner, both of whom were cited by *California Law Business* as 2 of the "20 under 40" most likely to succeed.

Morrison & Foerster L.L.P.—Irvine

19900 MacArthur Boulevard, 12TH Floor • Irvine, California 92612-2445
Phone: 949-251-7500 • Web site: mofo.com

OFFICES

San Francisco (main office)*, Los Angeles*, Irvine, Palo Alto*, Walnut Creek, California; New York City*, New York; Washington, D.C.*; Denver, Colorado

HIGHLIGHTS

- Undoubtedly the most decorated law firm in America when it comes to 'great place to work' accolades. Among others: Morrison & Foerster is the only law firm to appear in the best-selling book *The 100 Best Companies To Work For*, as well as *Forbes Magazine*'s 1998 "100 Best Companies To Work For In America" survey, and 1997's *Working Mother Magazine* workplace award. The firm won the 1993 Catalyst Award from 'Catalyst,' a nonprofit women's rights organization recognizing the firm's initiatives in supporting the advancement of women in the law.
- 19TH largest firm in the country.
- The firm prides itself on its diversity; *Forbes Magazine* describes it as "a magnet for women and minorities." Many women, minority and gay and lesbian lawyers have held, or currently hold, important management positions within the firm.
- Offers health insurance and other benefits to same-sex partners.
- 22% of partners and 45% of associates are women.
- Strong commitment to cutting-edge computer technology.
- Exceptional associate participation in the firm; apart from participation in many firm committees, associates routinely evaluate partners on a confidential basis concerning partners' training and associate development abilities. Associates receive detailed information on the firm's financial performance on an annual basis.
- Strong dedication to pro bono work. Pro bono hours are treated as billable hours.

NUTS AND BOLTS

Managing partner:

Stephen Dunham, Chairman

Hiring partner:

Robert A. Naeve (Irvine office)

Recruiting coordinator:

Janel Ozar, phone: 949-251-7500, e-mail: ocattyrecruit@mofo.com

Number of attorneys in firm:

590 (220 partners)

TOTAL FIRM:

Partners (220), associates (370)

THIS OFFICE:

Total attorneys (46), partners (17), of counsel (7), associates (22), women partners (5), women associates (9), minority partners (1), minority associates (5), disabled partners (0), disabled associates (0)

OTHER OFFICES:

(* represents an office profiled elsewhere in this book)
San Francisco* (243); Palo Alto* (87); Washington, D.C.* (60); New York* (66); Los Angeles* (97); Denver, CO (17); Walnut Creek, CA (13); Tokyo, Japan (17); Hong Kong (6)

Years to make partner:

6 to 9

WHAT DO THEY DO?

Primary specialties (more than 5% of practice) in the Irvine office:

Corporate (7), Real Estate (5), Tax (3), Litigation (17), Labor (5), Land Use/Environmental (1), Financial Transactions (3), Project Finance (3).

The firm is divided into four departments: Business, Labor, Litigation, and Tax. Associates do not rotate between departments, but often work in more than one practice area within a department and occasionally switch between departments and even between offices.

WHERE NEW ASSOCIATES COME FROM . . .

The Irvine office routinely interviews on campus at the following law schools: Arizona, Arizona State, Boalt Hall, Brigham Young, Chicago, Columbia, Cornell, Davis, Georgetown, Harvard, Hastings, Howard,

Loyola/LA, Michigan, NYU, Notre Dame, USC, UCLA, and Yale. The firm also routinely hires from schools where it doesn't interview on campus.

HOURS AND BUCKS . . .

Minimum billable hours requirement: 1,850, plus an additional contribution of 450 non-billable hours in the form of activities like practice development, recruiting, participation on firm committees, continuing legal education, writing projects, the summer associate program and training.

Part-time work is available, both to ongoing associates and new associates, on a case-by-case basis.

Typical first year associate salary, including typical bonus: $$$$ (Over $65,000). Morrison & Foerster is known for its generous financial package.

SUMMER PROGRAM . . .

In 1998, there were 6 summer associates, 5 of whom received offers.
Weekly pay: $1,500 last year
1Ls are routinely hired for the summer program.

PRO BONO . . .

The firm strongly encourages pro bono work. All pro bono hours are treated as billable hours. Projects span the full range of public interest work, from staffing legal services clinics and counseling over 150 non-profit organizations, to handling high-impact litigation. The greatest efforts have been focused on children in poverty and school education issues, civil rights and civil liberties cases, international human rights and political asylum, environmental matters, access to justice, issues of housing and homelessness, and AIDS-related work. The firm handles referrals of both civil and criminal matters from local courts, bar associations and legal services panels.

In addition, the firm runs the Morrison & Foerster Foundation, a non-profit charitable organization that serves charities in the communities where its offices are located. The firm also matches charitable contributions of its employees.

HISTORY AT A GLANCE . . .

The firm as a whole was founded in San Francisco in 1883.

Morrison & Foerster
L.L.P.—Los Angeles

555 West 5TH Street, Suite 3500 • Los Angeles, CA 90013-1024
Phone: 213-892-5233 • Web site: mofo.com

OFFICES

Los Angeles, San Francisco (main office)*, Irvine*, Palo Alto*, Walnut Creek,
California; New York City*, New York; Washington, D.C.*; Denver, Colorado

HIGHLIGHTS

- Undoubtedly the most decorated law firm in America when it comes to 'great place to work' accolades. Among others: Morrison & Foerster is the only law firm to appear in the best-selling book *The 100 Best Companies To Work For*, as well as *Forbes Magazine*'s 1998 "100 Best Companies To Work For In America" survey, and 1997's *Working Mother Magazine* workplace award. The firm won the 1993 Catalyst Award from 'Catalyst,' a nonprofit women's rights organization recognizing the firm's initiatives in supporting the advancement of women in the law.
- 19TH largest firm in the country.
- The firm prides itself on its diversity; *Forbes Magazine* describes it as "a magnet for women and minorities." Many women, minority and gay and lesbian lawyers have held, or currently hold, important management positions within the firm.
- Offers health insurance and other benefits to same-sex partners.
- 22% of partners and 45% of associates are women.
- Strong commitment to cutting-edge computer technology.
- Exceptional associate participation in the firm; apart from participation in many firm committees, associates routinely evaluate partners on a confidential basis concerning partners' training and associate development abilities. Associates receive detailed information on the firm's financial performance on an annual basis.
- Strong dedication to pro bono work. Pro bono hours are treated as billable hours.

NUTS AND BOLTS

Managing partner:

Stephen Dunham, Chairman

Hiring partner:

Janie F. Schulman (Los Angeles office)

Recruiting coordinator:

Jannette M. Lyon in Los Angeles, phone: 213-892-5233, e-mail: laattyrecruit@Morrison & Foerster.com

Number of attorneys in firm:

590 (220 partners)

TOTAL FIRM:

Partners (220), associates (370)

THIS OFFICE:

Total attorneys (97), partners (35), associates (48), women partners (10), women associates (20), minority partners (0), minority associates (13), disabled partners (0), disabled associates (0)

OTHER OFFICES:

(* represents an office profiled elsewhere in this book)
San Francisco* (243); Palo Alto* (87); Washington, D.C.* (60); New York* (66); Irvine* (44); Denver, CO (17); Walnut Creek, CA (13); Tokyo, Japan (17); Hong Kong (6)

Years to make partner:

6 to 9

WHAT DO THEY DO?

Primary specialties (more than 5% of practice):

Commercial Litigation (46); Intellectual Property (5); Bankruptcy (3); Corporate Finance (15); Financial Services (2); Financial Transactions (14); Real Estate (6); Land Use/Environmental (3); Energy (2); Employment Law & Labor (10).

The firm is divided into four departments: Business, Labor, Litigation, and Tax. Associates do not rotate between departments, but often work in more than one practice area within a department and occasionally switch between departments and even between offices.

WHO DO THEY REPRESENT?

Clients range from Fortune 500 corporations and global conglomerates to emerging high-tech companies and individuals with sophisticated legal problems.

WHERE NEW ASSOCIATES COME FROM . . .

The Los Angeles office interviews on campus at the following law schools: Boalt Hall, Chicago, Columbia, Cornell, Georgetown, Harvard, Hastings,

Howard, Loyola/LA, Michigan, Minnesota, NYU, Northwestern, Pepperdine, USC, Stanford, UCLA, and Yale. The office also hires from schools where it doesn't interview on campus.

HOURS AND BUCKS . . .

Minimum billable hours requirement: 1,850, plus an additional contribution of 450 non-billable hours in the form of activities like practice development, recruiting, participation on firm committees, continuing legal education, writing projects, the summer associate program and training. Part-time work is available to ongoing associates on a case-by-case basis. Part-time work is not available to new associates.

Typical first year associate salary, including typical bonus: $$$$ (Over $65,000). Morrison & Foerster is known for its generous financial package.

SUMMER PROGRAM . . .

Last year, there were 13 summer associates, 12 of whom got offers.
Weekly pay: $1,300 last year.
1Ls are routinely hired for the summer program.

PRO BONO . . .

The firm strongly encourages pro bono work. All pro bono hours are treated as billable hours. Projects span the full range of public interest work, from staffing legal services clinics and counseling over 150 non-profit organizations, to handling high-impact litigation. The greatest efforts have been focused on children in poverty and school education issues, civil rights and civil liberties cases, international human rights and political asylum, environmental matters, access to justice, issues of housing and homelessness, and AIDS-related work. The firm handles referrals of both civil and criminal matters from local courts, bar associations and legal services panels.

In addition, the firm runs the Morrison & Foerster Foundation, a non-profit charitable organization that serves charities in the communities where its offices are located. The firm also matches charitable contributions of its employees.

HISTORY AT A GLANCE . . .

The firm as a whole was founded in San Francisco in 1883. The Los Angeles office opened in 1974.

Stars in the L.A. office include Donna Zenor, cited by *California Law Business* as one of the top rainmakers in California.

Morrison & Foerster L.L.P.—New York

1290 Avenue of the Americas • New York, NY 10104
Phone: 212-468-8096 • Web site: www.mofo.com

OFFICES

Los Angeles*, San Francisco (main office)*, Irvine*, Palo Alto*, Walnut Creek, California; New York City*, New York; Washington, D.C.*; Denver, Colorado

HIGHLIGHTS

- Undoubtedly the most decorated law firm in America when it comes to 'great place to work' accolades. Among others: Morrison & Foerster is the only law firm to appear in the best-selling book *The 100 Best Companies To Work For*, as well as *Forbes Magazine*'s 1998 "100 Best Companies To Work For In America" survey, and 1997's *Working Mother Magazine* workplace award. The firm won the 1993 Catalyst Award from 'Catalyst,' a nonprofit women's rights organization recognizing the firm's initiatives in supporting the advancement of women in the law.
- 19TH largest firm in the country.
- The firm prides itself on its diversity; *Forbes Magazine* describes it as "a magnet for women and minorities." Many women, minority and gay and lesbian lawyers have held, or currently hold, important management positions within the firm.
- Offers health insurance and other benefits to same-sex partners.
- 22% of partners and 45% of associates are women.
- Strong commitment to cutting-edge computer technology.
- Exceptional associate participation in the firm; apart from participation in many firm committees, associates routinely evaluate partners on a confidential basis concerning partners' training and associate development abilities. Associates receive detailed information on the firm's financial performance on an annual basis.
- Strong dedication to pro bono work. Pro bono hours are treated as billable hours.

NUTS AND BOLTS

Managing partner:

Stephen Dunham, Chairman

Hiring partner:

James E. Hough (New York office)

Recruiting coordinator:

Kristan Lassiter in New York, phone: 212-468-8096,
e-mail: klassiter@mofo.com

Number of attorneys in firm:

590 (220 partners)

TOTAL FIRM:

Partners (220), associates (370)

THIS OFFICE:

Total attorneys (88), partners (31), associates (56), women partners (5),
women associates (23), minority partners (1), minority associates (8), disabled partners (0), disabled associates (0)

OTHER OFFICES:

(* represents an office profiled elsewhere in this book)
San Francisco* (243); Palo Alto* (87); Washington, D.C.* (60); Irvine*
(44); Los Angeles* (97); Denver, CO (17); Walnut Creek, CA (13); Tokyo,
Japan (17); Hong Kong (6)

Years to make partner:

6 to 9

WHAT DO THEY DO?

Primary specialties (more than 5% of practice):

Litigation (30); Business & Intellectual Property (42); Real Estate (6); Tax
(9); Corporate (37); Finance (10).

The firm is divided into four departments: Business, Labor, Litigation,
and Tax. Associates do not rotate between departments, but often work in
more than one practice area within a department and occasionally switch
between departments and even between offices.

WHERE NEW ASSOCIATES COME FROM . . .

The firm routinely interviews on campus at the following law schools:
Columbia, Cornell, Fordham, Harvard, Michigan, NYU, and Stanford.
The firm also hires from schools where it doesn't conduct on-campus
interviews.

HOURS AND BUCKS . . .

Minimum billable hours requirement: 1,850, plus an additional contribution of 450 non-billable hours in the form of activities like practice development, recruiting, participation on firm committees, continuing legal education, writing projects, the summer associate program and training.

Part-time work is available to ongoing associates on a case-by-case basis.

Typical first year associate salary, including typical bonus: $$$$ (Over $65,000). Morrison & Foerster is known for its generous financial package.

SUMMER PROGRAM . . .

Last year, there were 7 summer associates, all of whom received offers.

Weekly pay: $1,750 last year

1Ls are sometimes hired for the summer program.

The deadline for applications for the summer program is December 1.

PRO BONO . . .

The firm strongly encourages pro bono work. All pro bono hours are treated as billable hours. Projects span the full range of public interest work, from staffing legal services clinics and counseling over 150 non-profit organizations, to handling high-impact litigation. The greatest efforts have been focused on children in poverty and school education issues, civil rights and civil liberties cases, international human rights and political asylum, environmental matters, access to justice, issues of housing and homelessness, and AIDS-related work. The firm handles referrals of both civil and criminal matters from local courts, bar associations and legal services panels.

In addition, the firm runs the Morrison & Foerster Foundation, a non-profit charitable organization that serves charities in the communities where its offices are located. The firm also matches charitable contributions of its employees.

HISTORY AT A GLANCE . . .

The firm as a whole was founded in San Francisco in 1883.

Morrison & Foerster L.L.P.—
Washington, D.C.

2000 Pennsylvania Avenue, Suite 5500 • Washington, D.C. 20006
Phone: 202-887-1500 • Web site: mofo.com

OFFICES

Los Angeles*, San Francisco (main office)*, Irvine*, Palo Alto*, Walnut Creek, California; New York City*, New York; Washington, D.C.; Denver, Colorado

HIGHLIGHTS

- Undoubtedly the most decorated law firm in America when it comes to 'great place to work' accolades. Among others: Morrison & Foerster is the only law firm to appear in the best-selling book *The 100 Best Companies To Work For*, as well as *Forbes Magazine*'s 1998 "100 Best Companies To Work For In America" survey, and 1997's *Working Mother Magazine* workplace award. The firm won the 1993 Catalyst Award from 'Catalyst,' a nonprofit women's rights organization recognizing the firm's initiatives in supporting the advancement of women in the law.
- 19TH largest firm in the country.
- The firm prides itself on its diversity; *Forbes Magazine* describes it as "a magnet for women and minorities." Many women, minority and gay and lesbian lawyers have held, or currently hold, important management positions within the firm.
- Offers health insurance and other benefits to same-sex partners.
- 22% of partners and 45% of associates are women.
- Strong commitment to cutting-edge computer technology.
- Exceptional associate participation in the firm; apart from participation in many firm committees, associates routinely evaluate partners on a confidential basis concerning partners' training and associate development abilities. Associates receive detailed information on the firm's financial performance on an annual basis.
- Strong dedication to pro bono work. Pro bono hours are treated as billable hours.

NUTS AND BOLTS

Managing partner:

Stephen Dunham, Chairman

Hiring attorney:

Cristina Chou Pauze (Washington, D.C. office)

Recruiting coordinator:

Daniel Conway in Washington, D.C., phone: 202-887-1596,
e-mail: dconway@mofo.com

Number of attorneys in firm:

590 (220 partners)

TOTAL FIRM:

Partners (220), associates (370)

THIS OFFICE:

Total attorneys (63), partners (17), associates (29), women partners (3),
women associates (21), minority partners (2), minority associates (9), disabled partners (0), disabled associates (0)

OTHER OFFICES:

(* represents an office profiled elsewhere in this book)
San Francisco* (243); Palo Alto* (87); New York* (66); Irvine* (44); Los
Angeles* (97); Denver, CO (17); Walnut Creek, CA (13); Tokyo, Japan
(17); Hong Kong (6)

Years to make partner:

6 to 9

WHAT DO THEY DO?

Primary specialties (more than 5% of practice):

Corporate Finance, including Securities & Venture Capital (10);
Finance—Lending, Bank Regulatory (7); Intellectual Property & Patent
(10); Business (8); Litigation (17); Communications (7); Land Use,
Environmental, and Energy (3); Tax (1).

The firm is divided into four departments: Business, Labor, Litigation,
and Tax. Associates do not rotate between departments, but often work in
more than one practice area within a department and occasionally switch
between departments and even between offices.

WHERE NEW ASSOCIATES COME FROM . . .

The Washington, D.C. office interviews routinely at the following law
schools: George Washington, Georgetown, Harvard, Howard, and

Virginia. The firm also hires from schools where it doesn't conduct on-campus interviews.

HOURS AND BUCKS . . .

Minimum billable hours requirement: 1,850, plus an additional contribution of 450 non-billable hours in the form of activities like practice development, recruiting, participation on firm committees, continuing legal education, writing projects, the summer associate program and training.

Part time work is available to ongoing associates on a case-by-case basis.

Typical first year associate salary, including typical bonus: $$$$ (Over $65,000). Morrison & Foerster is known for its generous financial package.

PRO BONO . . .

The firm strongly encourages pro bono work. All pro bono hours are treated as billable hours. Projects span the full range of public interest work, from staffing legal services clinics and counseling over 150 non-profit organizations, to handling high-impact litigation. The greatest efforts have been focused on children in poverty and school education issues, civil rights and civil liberties cases, international human rights and political asylum, environmental matters, access to justice, issues of housing and homelessness, and AIDS-related work. The firm handles referrals of both civil and criminal matters from local courts, bar associations and legal services panels.

In addition, the firm runs the Morrison & Foerster Foundation, a non-profit charitable organization that serves charities in the communities where its offices are located. The firm also matches charitable contributions of its employees.

HISTORY AT A GLANCE . . .

The firm as a whole was founded in San Francisco in 1883.

Morrison & Foerster L.L.P.—Palo Alto

755 Page Mill Road • Palo Alto, CA 94304-1018
Phone: 650-813-5600 • Web site: mofo.com

OFFICES

Los Angeles*, San Francisco (main office)*, Irvine*, Palo Alto, Walnut Creek, California; New York City*, New York; Washington, D.C.*; Denver, Colorado

HIGHLIGHTS

- Undoubtedly the most decorated law firm in America when it comes to 'great place to work' accolades. Among others: Morrison & Foerster is the only law firm to appear in the best-selling book *The 100 Best Companies To Work For*, as well as *Forbes Magazine*'s 1998 "100 Best Companies To Work For In America" survey, and 1997's *Working Mother Magazine* workplace award. The firm won the 1993 Catalyst Award from 'Catalyst,' a nonprofit women's rights organization recognizing the firm's initiatives in supporting the advancement of women in the law.
- 19TH largest firm in the country.
- The firm prides itself on its diversity; *Forbes Magazine* describes it as "a magnet for women and minorities." Many women, minority and gay and lesbian lawyers have held, or currently hold, important management positions within the firm.
- Offers health insurance and other benefits to same-sex partners.
- 22% of partners and 45% of associates are women.
- Strong commitment to cutting-edge computer technology.
- Exceptional associate participation in the firm; apart from participation in many firm committees, associates routinely evaluate partners on a confidential basis concerning partners' training and associate development abilities. Associates receive detailed information on the firm's financial performance on an annual basis.
- Strong dedication to pro bono work. Pro bono hours are treated as billable hours.

NUTS AND BOLTS

Managing partner:

Stephen Dunham, Chairman

Recruiting coordinator:

Gretchen D. Hug in Palo Alto, phone: 650-813-5600,
e-mail: paattyrecruit@mofo.com

Number of attorneys in firm:

590 (220 partners)

TOTAL FIRM:

Partners (220), associates (370)

THIS OFFICE:

Total attorneys (87), partners (26), associates (49), women partners (5),
women associates (25), minority partners (2), minority associates (9), disabled partners (0), disabled associates (0)

OTHER OFFICES:

(* represents an office profiled elsewhere in this book)
San Francisco* (243); Washington, D.C.* (60); New York* (66); Irvine*
(44); Los Angeles* (97); Denver, CO (17); Walnut Creek, CA (13); Tokyo,
Japan (17); Hong Kong (6)

Years to make partner:

6 to 9

WHAT DO THEY DO?

Primary specialties (more than 5% of practice):

Corporate (26); Patent (23); Litigation (20); Labor & Employment Law
(12); Environmental Law/Land Use (2); Real Estate (4); Tax (1).

The firm is divided into four departments: Business, Labor, Litigation,
and Tax. Associates do not rotate between departments, but often work in
more than one practice area within a department and occasionally switch
between departments and even between offices.

WHERE NEW ASSOCIATES COME FROM . . .

The Palo Alto office interviews on campus at the following law schools:
Boalt Hall, Chicago, Columbia, Cornell, UC/Davis, Harvard, Hastings,
Howard, Michigan, NYU, Northwestern, Santa Clara, Stanford, UCLA, and
Yale. The firm also hires from schools where it doesn't interview on campus.

HOURS AND BUCKS . . .

Minimum billable hours requirement: 1,850, plus an additional contribution of 450 non-billable hours in the form of activities like practice

development, recruiting, participation on firm committees, continuing legal education, writing projects, the summer associate program and training.

Part-time work is available to ongoing associates on a case-by-case basis.

Typical first year associate salary, including typical bonus: $$$$ (Over $65,000). Morrison & Foerster is known for its generous financial package.

SUMMER PROGRAM . . .

Last year, there were 15 summer associates, all of whom received offers.
Weekly pay: $1,500
1Ls are not hired for the Palo Alto office's summer program.

PRO BONO . . .

The firm strongly encourages pro bono work. All pro bono hours are treated as billable hours. Projects span the full range of public interest work, from staffing legal services clinics and counseling over 150 non-profit organizations, to handling high-impact litigation. The greatest efforts have been focused on children in poverty and school education issues, civil rights and civil liberties cases, international human rights and political asylum, environmental matters, access to justice, issues of housing and homelessness, and AIDS-related work. The firm handles referrals of both civil and criminal matters from local courts, bar associations and legal services panels.

In addition, the firm runs the Morrison & Foerster Foundation, a non-profit charitable organization that serves charities in the communities where its offices are located. The firm also matches charitable contributions of its employees.

HISTORY AT A GLANCE . . .

The firm as a whole was founded in San Francisco in 1883.

Parker, Hudson, Rainer & Dobbs LLP

1500 Marquis Two Tower • 285 Peachtree Center Avenue, N.E. • Atlanta, GA 30303
Phone: 404-523-5300 • Fax: 404-522-8409

OFFICES

Atlanta (main office), Georgia; Tallahassee, Florida

"The key thing at PHR&D is opportunity. Because there are fewer people, there's much less politics. The opportunities to create your own practice are greater. If you like the idea of developing a business, it's a great place to be."

NUTS AND BOLTS

Managing partner:

Paul L. Hudson, Jr.

Hiring partner:

Marbury Rainer, phone: 404-523-5300, e-mail: mrainer@phrd.com

Recruiting coordinator:

Christie A. Rogers, phone: 404-523-5300, e-mail: carogers@phrd.com

Number of attorneys in firm:

38 (20 partners)

TOTAL FIRM:

Partners (20), associates (18), women partners (1), women associates (7), minority partners (1), minority associates (0), disabled partners (0), disabled associates (0)

THIS OFFICE:

Total attorneys (36), partners (19), associates (17), women partners (1), women associates (6), minority partners (1), minority associates (0), disabled partners (0), disabled associates (0)

OTHER OFFICES:

(* represents an office profiled elsewhere in this book)
Tallahassee, Florida (2)

Years to make partner:

8 ½

WHAT DO THEY DO?

Primary specialties (more than 5% of practice):

Commercial Finance (8), Health (14), Real Estate (5), Bankruptcy (3), Litigation (8).

New associates get to choose which department they want to join. In terms of work assignments, it's open season within the department—any attorney can assign a new associate projects. Associates do not as a rule switch specialties, but it has been done.

WHO DO THEY REPRESENT?

Clients are involved in a wide range of businesses, including telecommunications, lending, credit card processing, commercial real estate, computer software development and distribution, management consulting services, healthcare, and retail securities brokerage. They include AT&T Wireless PCS, Inc.; Baptist Health Care of Pensacola; Barclays Bank, PLC; Borders, Inc.; Capital Business Credit; The Cleveland Clinic; First Data Corporation; The First National Bank of Boston; Fleet Bank, N.A.; Fults Realty Corporation; Galaxy Health Alliance; Georgia Alliance of Community Hospitals; Lehman Brothers Inc.; Merrill Lynch; NationsBank; Planet Music, Inc.; Promina Health System, Inc.; Prudential Securities; Sarasota Memorial Hospital; Transamerica Business Credit; Travelers Insurance; Wachovia Bank of Georgia; and WellStar Health System, Inc.

WHERE NEW ASSOCIATES COME FROM . . .

The firm routinely interviews on campus at the following law schools: Emory, Vanderbilt, Georgia, and Wake Forest. The firm routinely hires associates and summer associates from schools where it doesn't conduct on-campus interviews.

HOURS AND BUCKS . . .

On average, first year associates spend 2,113 hours at the office. There is no minimum billable hour requirement, but the average billable hours for first year associates is 1,817.

The firm does allow attorneys to work part-time. It has never had an entry-level part-time attorney, but "never say never"—the firm is willing to consider it.

The firm has hired contract associates over the last couple of years to supplement the permanent attorneys in areas that have grown more rapidly than anticipated, and thus have not been covered by the firm's law school recruiting program. Thus far, none of the contract attorneys has been hired as a regular, full-fledged associate, but the firm anticipates that this may change soon.

Typical first year associate salary, including typical bonus: $$$$ (over $65,000)

SUMMER PROGRAM . . .

Last year, there were 5 summer associates; all 5 received offers.

Weekly pay is $1,385

1Ls are generally not hired for the summer program.

There is no deadline for the summer program, but it is usually filled by the end of October.

PRO BONO . . .

The firm encourages associates to do pro bono work. Pro bono hours are not counted as billables, but they are considered in the overall evaluation of associates.

Associates are involved in the Atlanta Bar Association Saturday Lawyers Program, do pro bono work on death penalty cases, and numerous other pro bono projects for charitable organizations.

HISTORY AT A GLANCE . . .

The firm began in Atlanta in 1981, with 2 lawyers who left King & Spalding. It has grown since then to almost 40 lawyers, and opened a second office, in Tallahassee, Florida.

WHAT IT'S LIKE TO WORK THERE . . .

Associates at PHR&D make you think that the firm must be a very busy, very happy place to work. As one associate explains it, "I spent two years at a large firm before I came here, and the environment is very different. I know everybody. It's a very young crowd, and that makes things a lot of fun." In that spirit of fun, one associate tells that "During my first year as an associate, another lawyer in the firm nominated me as Valentine's King for a Valentine's dating game sponsored by a local radio station. I competed in the dating game, wearing a crown, in front of over 200 people—including a whole bunch of people from the office of course. The firm now has a three-year tradition of nominating a Valentine's King or Queen for the contest."

Associates also applaud the firm's "family atmosphere. I don't think there's a great gulf between the lawyers and 'OTA'—'other than attorneys,' as staff members were called at my previous firm—and this leads to a closeness in the firm." There's a corresponding closeness between partners and associates. One associate says that, "Each year one of the named partners enters a team in a charity golf tournament sponsored by one of our clients. The partner asked me to be on his team as a first year associate, and I've played on his team both years since then."

"There's nobody here between you and the senior partner who heads your practice group. There aren't layers of people to wade through."

Associates cite the relatively small size of the firm as an asset, since it gets them early responsibility, lots of routine contact with partners, and an informal structure that isn't burdened with lots of committees.

The firm is divided into distinct practice groups. "Many of the partners are from larger firms, and they brought their practices with them." New associates get to choose the department they want to join—Commercial Finance, Health, Real Estate, Bankruptcy, or Litigation—and in those departments, they are assigned to a practice group. These practice groups consist of four or five people, and associates "can get assignments from the senior partner or junior partner in the group, but that's it. Other practice groups don't approach you directly." If other practice groups need help, they'll approach "the partner you work for and ask if you can help. So each partner in each group keeps close tabs on you, to make sure you aren't overloaded." When it comes to switching specialties, "It doesn't happen often, but it's been done."

Associates find that most of the training is "on the job, with someone to watch over you." Occasionally there is formal training, but "not much of it. There are a few internal seminars." This leads to a level of responsibility early on that junior associates really like. One associate tells of how, "As a less-than-four-month associate, I argued my first discovery motion, without anybody else there from the firm. I received a lot of support from everyone on my team in preparing—and lots of congratulations when I returned with our motion granted."

As for firm structure, associates say that "Paul Hudson reigns over everything except recruiting," and that that's a system that works well for the firm. "He's very approachable. If you have any problem or any suggestion or anything you think ought to change, you can go to him directly, or to Marbury Rainer, or to the head of your practice group. The fact is, the firm is financially successful, and it runs fine without a lot of committees." Associates report that, "Paul Hudson gets input from a lot of people informally," and he knows whom to approach for different kinds of issues. "For computers and technology-oriented things, he gets input from the tech-oriented partners and associates."

The Recruiting Committee is the area where associates have the most input. It has 11 members, with six partners and five associates. Associates also have the task of handling the summer entertainment program, "and that's just a lot of fun."

Associates find that much of their development comes from the heavy emphasis on "what your business will look like as a partner." They say that, "No associate believes they don't have a chance of making partner—everybody *does*." As a result, associates rave about the "Excellent long-term opportunities here." While there is no "eat-what-you-kill mentality for associates—if you bring in business, you get a year-end bonus for it," associates recognize that "as partners, how well you do depends in part on the business you bring in, and so that's in the back of your mind." One of the real assets of PHR&D in the minds of associates is that "Because it's a smaller firm and therefore has a smaller client base than a huge firm does, you won't be 'conflicted out' of nearly as many cases as you would be at a huge firm. That gives you great opportunities to build your own practice when you become a partner, and it makes you excited about your prospects in the meantime."

"We put in some long hours."

Associates say that the offices fill up between 8:15 and 8:45 a.m., and tend to empty out between 6:15 and 6:45 p.m., although "if you want to avoid weekends you put in long weekdays." As a result, on weekends, "Some of the people work them, and some don't." However, "there's no face time on weekends." As one associate jokes, "With such a small shop, you might not time your 'face time' right—there'd be no guarantee that the person you'd want to have seeing your face would be in when you're in!"

Associates say that the hours "aren't motivated by billables"—there's no minimum billable hours requirement—but by "how hot your area is. It's a cyclical thing." For instance, "when real estate is hot, the real estate lawyers are going to be working long hours. It's the nature of the business." When they do work long hours, the associates don't resent it because "If you didn't want to put in the hours, you could work at a bank. You wouldn't make the money, either. If you want to do better, you work more, and you know that. And because you know it, you don't have anything to complain about."

Associates also say that regardless of the hours they put in, they feel in control of their work. As one associate explains it, "Everybody is family around here. If they can't find me, that's OK. They're very understanding, and ready to pick up the ball for you when you need it."

The focus of non-billables hours includes "some community service. Many of the lawyers do something in the community, pro bono or not.

For instance, lots of people do Habitat for Humanity." When it comes to traditional pro bono work, "A few people do a lot of it, but it's more of an individual thing. The firm doesn't promote it. It's not a firm-wide point of emphasis, at least not to the extent community service in general is."

The firm has a "strong focus on families," with about half of the lawyers having small children. Associates say that "as a profession, law is a tough place for women to 'do it all,'" but that the firm has been understanding with "notching down the hours of women attorneys with small children," and it has regular social events for employees' children, including a Santa Party and an Easter Picnic.

Other regular social events include an annual golf tournament during the summer, and a Christmas party, where "the highlight of the evening is a performance by the Parker, Hudson Band—a group of six attorneys who play together only for the Christmas Party. It's a great way to get everybody on the floor dancing." Associates report that "The stuff the firm puts on is great. We have a really good time together at firm outings." That applies to informal get-togethers, too. "People are very friendly here. They get together a lot," particularly the single associates.

All in all, associates say that, "The key thing at PHR&D is opportunity. Because there are fewer people, there's much less politics. The opportunities to create your own practice are greater. If you like the idea of developing a business, it's a great place to be."

Perkins Coie L.L.P.— Seattle

1201 Third Avenue, 48TH Floor • Seattle, Washington 98101-3099
Phone: 206-583-8888 • Fax: 206-583-8500 • Web site: perkinscoie.com

OFFICES

Seattle (main office), Bellevue, Olympia, Spokane, Washington; Anchorage, Alaska; Denver, Colorado; Los Angeles*, California; Portland*, Oregon; Washington, D.C.*, Hong Kong, Taipei

"You get excellent experience here that you can use to go anywhere with your career, if that's what you want. But it's not such a pressure cooker that you'll be miserable while you're here. We aren't cutthroat competitors with each other; we routinely pitch in and help each other out. You get to work with an outstanding, diverse group of smart, dedicated lawyers. And if you want to stay for the long haul, the firm is well-managed, profitable, and busy."

HIGHLIGHTS

- The largest law firm in the Pacific Northwest, and the 69TH largest firm in the country.
- Perkins was one of the first in the country to hire female attorneys, hiring its first woman associate in 1920.
- The firm runs the Perkins Coie Community Service Fellowship; each year, between two and four associates work full-time for community organizations in the arts, human services, education, health care and indigent legal services.
- In the 1990s, the firm has been involved with 100 public offerings, and completed transactions and cases in more than 50 countries.
- The firm keeps on the cutting edge of technology, with fast computers and innovative uses of technology in a variety of client service matters.

NUTS AND BOLTS

Managing partner:

Robert E. Giles, phone: 206-583-8536, e-mail: giler@perkinscoie.com

Hiring partner:

William L. Green, phone: 206-583-8888, e-mail: greew@perkinscoie.com

Recruiting coordinator:

Laura Spies, Manager of Lawyer Personnel,
phone: 206-583-8888; e-mail: spiel@perkinscoie.com

Number of attorneys in firm:

412 (182 partners)

TOTAL FIRM:

Partners (182), associates (186), women partners (25), women associates (73), minority partners (2), minority associates (25), disabled partners (1), disabled associates (0), of counsel (49)

THIS OFFICE:

Total attorneys (248), partners (108), associates (116), women partners (17), women associates (48), minority partners (2), minority associates (18), disabled partners (1), disabled associates (0), of counsel (24)

OTHER OFFICES:

(* represents an office profiled elsewhere in this book)
Please note: The Seattle/Bellevue offices are counted together, which is why Bellevue does not appear separately here.
Anchorage, Alaska (13); Denver, Colorado (10); Hong Kong (2); Los Angeles, California* (25); Olympia, Washington (3); Portland, Oregon* (39); Spokane, Washington (3); Taipei, Taiwan (20); Washington, D.C.* (38)

Years to make partner:

7

WHAT DO THEY DO?

Primary specialties (more than 5% of practice) in Seattle/Bellevue:

General Litigation (76), Labor/Employment (38), Real Estate (4), Technology Business (16), Energy (8), Business (15), Commercial Transaction (19), Corporate/SEC (34), Land Use/ENR (13), Personal Planning (6), Product Liability (21), Tax (9)

The firm is departmentalized, and associates often move between departments.

WHO DO THEY REPRESENT?

A huge variety of clients, including nearly 100 Fortune 500 companies, in Aviation (including AlliedSignal, Delta Air Lines, Beech Aircraft, Boeing, and Northwest Airlines); Chemical and Pharmaceutical Industries (including Monsanto); Consumer Products (including Arctic Alaska Fisheries, Denny's, Egghead Software, Sears Roebuck, SmithKline Beecham Consumer Brands, and Winchell's Donut Houses); Entertainment (including the American Society of Composers, Artists and Performers, the Baseball Club of Seattle, MCA, and Westin International Asia); Environmental/Natural Resources (including American Ecology, Browning-Ferris Industries, and General Electric); Financial Services (including Bank of Montreal, the Bank of Tokyo, U.S. Eximbank, and Wells Fargo Bank); Forest and Paper Products (including Cavenham Forest Industries, James River Corporation, and Weyerhaeuser); Gas and Coal (including British Petroleum); Heavy Manufacturing (including B.F. Goodrich and General Motors); High Technology (including Amazon.com, NCR, IBM, and Nintendo); Insurance (including Lloyd's of London); Investment Banking (including Alex Brown & Sons, Hambrecht & Quist, and Smith Barney); Life Sciences (including Immunex Corporation, Owens-Corning Fiberglas); State and Local Governments (including the city of Spokane, the Seattle School District, and the State of Texas); Telecommunications (including AT&T, US West); Utilities (including OESI Power Corporation and Puget Sound Energy); and Venture Capitalists (including Battery Ventures and U.S. Venture Partners).

WHERE NEW ASSOCIATES COME FROM . . .

The firm routinely interviews on campus at the following schools: Columbia, NYU, University of Washington, Georgetown, Howard, Chicago, Seattle University, Northwestern University, University of Michigan, Harvard, UVA, Duke, Boalt Hall, Stanford, Hastings, Yale and the University of Pennsylvania. The firm does hire associates and summer associates from firms where it doesn't conduct on-campus interviews.

HOURS AND BUCKS . . .

First year associates have a minimum billable hour requirement of 1,800 hours.

Attorneys are allowed to work part-time, but not at entry level. Contract attorneys are routinely hired to work on projects, and contract attorneys have become full-time associates.

Typical first-year salary, including typical bonus: $$$$ (Over $65,000), at the "top end" of the Seattle market.

SUMMER PROGRAM . . .

Last year, there were 18 summer associates (12 2Ls, 2 3L [a judicial clerkship candidate], 4 1Ls); 14 offers of full-time employment were made.

Weekly pay: $1,100 last year; $1,350 for 1999

The Perkins Coie Student Fellowship is offered to up to two 1Ls at the University of Washington and Seattle University. The firm also conducts a 1L summer-job outreach program to enhance diversity within the firm.

Deadlines for summer program: Late Fall (offers are completed by December 1).

PRO BONO . . .

The firm encourages pro bono work, and up to 100 hours of pro bono time is considered billable (for productivity and performance bonuses) as long as the minimum billable hours requirement of 1,800 is met. The firm's lawyers are involved in both large and small pro bono cases, including death penalty cases; First Amendment, strip search, privacy, religious activities and other constitutional law cases for the ACLU and others; Fair Housing Act class action litigation; Child placement cases for guardian ad litem programs; Representation of political refugees seeking asylum; Estate planning services for people with AIDS; and representation of indigents through local legal services corporations and bar associations.

The firm also runs the Perkins Coie Community Service Fellowship, which each year donates the full-time services of between two and four associates to work full-time for six months, at full pay, on behalf of community organizations in the arts, human services, education, health care, and indigent legal services.

HISTORY AT A GLANCE . . .

The firm was founded in 1912 by George Donworth, a federal district court judge, and Elmer Todd, the U.S. Attorney for the Western District of Washington. They quickly attracted major clients, and others that would grow to become major clients—including a little start-up "aero" company, which is today the Boeing Company.

Around 1920, the firm hired its first female associate, Lady Willie Forbus, at a time when virtually no other firm hired women as lawyers.

The firm grew steadily over the years, both through mergers and hires, growing today into the largest firm in the Pacific Northwest.

WHAT IT'S LIKE TO WORK THERE . . .

When you talk to associates at Perkins Coie, it strikes you immediately that there isn't one profile of a Perkins Coie lawyer. They cut across a broad spectrum of interests and backgrounds. As one associate describes it, "Perkins is a large, corporate firm—a potentially chilling description!—

but what makes it wonderful is the extraordinarily eclectic group of people who work here." Another adds that, "There's a niche here for almost every qualified lawyer, no matter what your personal or professional interests are." Sure, there are the former U.S. Supreme Court clerks, but there's also "a lawyer who had a Top 40 hit once." There's an art historian, an ex-minor league baseball player, and "a bicycling aficionado who pedaled from Seattle to Key West." Associates rave about the "almost incongruous balance" of political ideologies and visions of the law among their colleagues. As one associate sums it up, "If you're looking for uniformity and one 'firm perspective,' then Perkins is not the place."

"As a young lawyer at Perkins, you're given all the responsibility and opportunity you can handle."

Rather than locking its junior associates in the library, Perkins' philosophy is to give young lawyers lots of responsibility, which associates say, "creates a lot of interesting opportunities." One second-year associate talked of being involved in a large arbitration, where he got to handle several depositions and witnesses, as well as "dismantling an opposing expert." A third year associate talked about arguing a case before the Washington Supreme Court. Perkins associates say that, "Partners go out of their way to set up plum assignments for us, and then prepare us so that we can handle them." Associates find that a healthy dose of responsibility doesn't mean they'll be left out on a limb. As one associate explains it, "Early in my career, I was on the receiving end of a diatribe by a federal judge about something I did that I thought was perfectly proper. I didn't know how my supervising partner would react. When I told him about it, he explored the facts and reassured me that the judge's remarks wouldn't be a problem." As the associate says, "It meant a lot to me that I wasn't going to be hung out to dry, that the partner was behind me," and the associate laughingly adds, "Of course, it didn't hurt that the appeals court ultimately found that the judge was wrong!"

On top of informal project-by-project advice, associates take part in a two-year training program when they join Perkins. The training program consists of periodic seminars in areas of general interest, like professional responsibility and legal research, as well as specialized training in either business or litigation, depending on what the associate's interests are. The specialized training for business associates exposes them to a series of specific topics like business financing, licensing and leasing transactions, environmental law, bankruptcy, and legal opinions. Litigation associates cover basic elements of litigation practice, from pleadings, discovery, alternative dispute resolution and depositions, to trial preparation and oral arguments. Perkins has a mock courtroom where associates refine their courtroom skills and learn to prepare witnesses to testify at trial.

In addition to the seminars, each of the practice groups holds periodic meetings to cover new developments, and generally keep all the lawyers up-to-date on what everybody else in the group is doing.

Associates point out that "You control your destiny here," and that means there's a premium placed on "keeping your eyes open and seeing who you'd like to work with, what you'd like to do."

Associates report that pro bono has a "very high profile," at the firm, and one of the ways to get noticed is to shine on pro bono projects. For instance, two associates established contact with a homeless shelter and set up a "sort of cleaning-house of pro bono projects, everything from basic family law to tax oddities." Another associate commented on being involved in "a large, seemingly Kafka-esque commercial litigation, and at the same time challenging the constitutionality of denying a cancer patient marijuana for medicinal use." As the associate commented, "The firm values and encourages both the big lawsuit and the pro bono case."

"The firm does a terrific job of responding to people and being willing to change, in areas important to associates."

Most of the associates' involvement in managing the firm comes through participation in committees. Associates participate in the Hiring, Summer Associate, Governmental Affairs, Legal Assistant, and Women & Minority Lawyers Committees. In addition, there is an Associate Committee, comprised (not surprisingly) mostly of associates, "which advises firm management on issues of particular interest and concern to us."

Associates find that the social activities at the firm reflect the diversity of the people there. As one associate comments, "Perkins is a place where people have whole lives. They're not defined simply as lawyers." Of course, there is the usual panoply of summer activities, and associates have a heavy hand in organizing the summer social program. On top of that, practice groups and offices have periodic retreats, and the firm as a whole occasionally has an all-lawyer retreat. "Last year, for example, each lawyer and guest was flown to Beaver Creek, Colorado, for three days of meetings, socializing, and recreational activities."

Back home, the Seattle and Bellevue offices are so close that they participate in all firm activities together. The firm sponsors teams in a variety of sports, like softball, running, and skiing, "at different levels of seriousness." Informally, "groups of lawyers with like interests often get together for activities like hiking, climbing, kayaking, and volleyball," and "we regularly visit each others' houses for dinners and parties." The firm's Seattle location is another huge plus, with associates finding it "an exciting, attractive city, everything you'd dream it would be."

All in all, an associate summarizes the Perkins experience by saying, "You get excellent experience here that you can use to go anywhere with your career, if that's what you want. But it's not such a pressure cooker that you'll be miserable while you're here. We aren't cutthroat competitors with each other; we routinely pitch in and help each other out. You get to work with an outstanding, diverse group of smart, dedicated lawyers. And if you want to stay for the long haul, the firm is well-managed, profitable, and busy."

Perkins Coie L.L.P.—Portland

1211 Southwest Fifth Avenue, Suite 1500 • Portland, Oregon 97204-3715
Phone: 503-727-2000 • Fax: 503-727-2222 • Web site: perkinscoie.com

OFFICES

Seattle (main office)*, Bellevue, Olympia, Spokane, Washington; Anchorage, Alaska; Denver, Colorado; Los Angeles*, California; Portland, Oregon; Washington, D.C.*

"Where else could you (i) represent the world's most famous killer whale, with a partner who took a month off last summer to work with Habitat for Humanity to build a house for an underprivileged family? (ii) Represent major corporations in litigation with a partner who was picked to clerk for a Supreme Court justice and was in the original MTV house band? And (iii) prepare a public offering with a lawyer who owns a house right out of Architectural Design and drives a Harley to work?"

HIGHLIGHTS

- The largest law firm in the Pacific Northwest, and the 69TH largest firm in the country.
- Perkins was one of the first in the country to hire female attorneys, hiring its first woman associate in 1920.
- In the 1990s, the firm has been involved with 85 public offerings, and completed transactions and cases in more than 50 countries.
- The firm keeps on the cutting edge of technology, with fast computers and innovative uses of technology in a variety of client service matters.

NUTS AND BOLTS

Managing partner:

Roy W. Tucker

Hiring partner:

Robert L. Aldisert

Recruiting coordinator:

Ann Carroll, phone: 503-727-2034

Number of attorneys in firm:

371 (182 partners)

TOTAL FIRM:

Partners (182), associates (186), women partners (25), minority partners (2), minority associates (25), disabled partners (1), disabled associates (0)

THIS OFFICE:

Total attorneys (39), partners (19), associates (18), women partners (2), minority partners (0), disabled partners (0), disabled associates (0).

OTHER OFFICES:

(* represents an office profiled elsewhere in this book)
Anchorage, Alaska (11); Denver, Colorado (5); Hong Kong (3); London (1); Los Angeles, California* (22); Olympia, Washington (37); Seattle and Bellevue, Washington* (239); Spokane, Washington (5); Taipei, Taiwan (13); Washington, D.C.* (35)

Years to make partner:

7

WHAT DO THEY DO?

Primary specialties (more than 5% of practice) in Portland:

Environmental (2), Real Estate (4), General Business (13), Litigation/Labor (19), Commercial Law & Bankruptcy (2).

The firm is departmentalized, and young associates can, and do, switch specialties.

WHO DO THEY REPRESENT?

An enormous variety of clients, including Act III Theaters; Advanced Laboratory Systems; American Physician Network; Boeing; Boise Cascade; Calbag Metals; Cavenham Forest Industries, Division of Hanson Natural Resources; Columbia Colstor; Consolidated Freightways; Cummins Northwest; CYCOMM; Dain Bosworth; Endeavor Capital; Evergreen International Aviation; EVI Corporation;

General Motors; City of Gresham; Hertz Corporation; Interactive Systems; Interconnectix; IBM; Kentrox Industries; King Broadcasting; Louisiana Pacific; Microtek International; Molecular Probes; Morrow Snowboards; Northwest Magnetic Imaging Center; Northwest Natural Gas; NNW; OESI Power; Oregon Art Institute; Oregon International Air Freight; Pacific Generation Company; PacifiCorp Financial Services; Portland Radio; Rogue Wave Software; Ross Stores; Russell Development; SARIF; SHE America; Shaw, Glasgow & Co; Summit Information Systems; Switchlink Systems; Synthetech; Truax Harris Energy Company; Viking Star Shipping; Waggener Edstrom; WTD Industries; Yoshida's; and ZIBA Design.

WHERE NEW ASSOCIATES COME FROM . . .

The Portland office regularly interviews on campus at the following law schools: Lewis & Clark, Oregon, Willamette, Boalt Hall, Stanford, and Hastings. The firm routinely hires from schools where it doesn't do on-campus interviews.

HOURS AND BUCKS . . .

Minimum billable hours requirement: 1,800 hours/year

Attorneys are allowed to work part-time, but not at entry level. The firm routinely hires contract associates on a project-by-project basis, and contract associates have become full-time associates.

Typical first-year associate salary, including typical bonus: $$$$ (Over $65,000)

SUMMER PROGRAM . . .

The Portland office started its summer associate program last year. It had 4 summer associates, two 2Ls and two 1Ls. Both 2Ls received an offer.

Weekly pay: $1,100 last year

1Ls will not be routinely hired for the summer program.

PRO BONO . . .

The firm encourages pro bono work. Associates receive credit for up to 100 hours of pro bono time per year for productivity and performance bonus purposes, provided they meet the minimum billable hour requirement of 1,800 hours. The firm's lawyers are involved in both large and small pro bono cases, including death penalty cases; First Amendment, strip search, privacy, religious activities and other consti-tutional law cases for the ACLU and others; Fair Housing Act class action litigation; child placement cases for guardian ad litem programs; representation of political refugees seeking asylum; estate planning services for people with AIDS; and representation of indigents through local legal services corporations and bar associations.

HISTORY AT A GLANCE . . .

The firm was founded in 1912 by George Donworth, a federal district court judge, and Elmer Todd, the U.S. Attorney for the Western District of Washington. They quickly attracted major clients, and others that would grow to become major clients—including a little start-up "aero" company, which is today the Boeing Company.

Around 1920, the firm hired its first female associate, Lady Willie Forbus, at a time when virtually no other firm hired women as lawyers.

The firm grew steadily over the years, both through mergers and hires, growing today into the largest firm in the Pacific Northwest.

WHAT IT'S LIKE TO WORK THERE . . .

Please read the firm's Seattle profile first! It will give you a feel for what it's like to work at Perkins in general, including descriptions of typical projects, management involvement, and training. Here are thoughts specifically from Perkins' associates in Portland:

Associates at Perkins' Portland office rave about their "very interesting and varied work." As one points out, "The things we do cover the whole business law spectrum, both in transactional and litigation work." As is true of all of Perkins' offices, associates rave about the firm's "top clients from all fields" and the opportunity to work with "talented lawyers from all corners." One associate marvels, "Where else could you (i) represent the world's most famous killer whale, with a partner who took a month off last summer to work with Habitat for Humanity to build a house for an underprivileged family? (ii) Represent major corporations in litigation with a partner who was picked to clerk for a Supreme Court justice and was in the original MTV house band? And (iii) prepare a public offering with a lawyer who owns a house right out of *Architectural Design* and drives a Harley to work?"

On top of their fascinating work in a "friendly and good-humored" environment, associates love their surroundings. "Portland is an incredibly livable city. You're 75 miles from both the Pacific Ocean and the Cascade Range. You can surf, ski, wine taste, backpack or rock climb, within an hour of leaving the office." Lawyers in the Portland office take advantage of their spectacular surroundings at every opportunity, frequently enjoying each other's company for "kayaking in the San Juan Islands in the summer, beach retreats, hiking, and rafting." As well, a few of the partners have their own retreats that they open up to their colleagues. The head of the litigation department has a river cabin, where he entertains firm lawyers for fly-fishing outings. And two of the corporate partners have a mountain home, where lawyers from the office go to ski. In addition, there are "wine-tasting parties at the home of the partner with the extensive wine cellar," as well as "All kinds of summer associate based activities," and informally, "beers after work, electric guitar jam sessions, NBA games." Lawyers with small children frequently get their kids together for "play dates." Associates also rave about the office's "Holiday party skit, where all the partners are skewered for their particular mannerisms or memorable moments—all in bad fun!"

As all of this suggests, one of the highlights of the Portland office is the "camaraderie of everybody here." As one associate explains it, "We have on average one or two unofficial birthday celebrations a week, where many of us with gather informally in the hall and celebrate somebody's birthday, with great food—compliments of the firm." There is also a group of lawyers, legal assistants and secretaries who meet for their monthly unofficial "Suds-Com" meeting on the first Friday of the month. "The committee's mission is irreverence, and the meetings take place at any one of Portland's many microbreweries."

Excellent work, great fun, beautiful surroundings, and interesting characters for colleagues. As one associate sums it up, "At this office, there's a well-developed sense of being the best in town—but we're not arrogant or uptight."

Perkins Coie L.L.P.—
Washington, D.C.

607 Fourteenth Street, N.W., Suite 800 • Washington, D.C. 20005-2011
Phone: 202-628-6600 • Fax: 202-434-1690 • Web Site: perkinscoie.com

OFFICES

Seattle (main office)*, Bellevue, Olympia, Spokane, Washington; Anchorage, Alaska; Denver, Colorado; Los Angeles*, California; Portland*, Oregon; Washington, D.C.

"We don't suffer for being the branch office of a big firm . . . We have high profile political law cases, to mega-mergers in the aircraft industry, to ground-breaking telecommunications matters, to a natural resources practice that is unmatched on the East Coast . . . on top of that, the firm gives us the privacy and ability to have lives of our own. They're actually apologetic when your outside life is disrupted because of work."

HIGHLIGHTS

- The D.C. office of the largest law firm in the Pacific Northwest, and the 69TH largest firm in the country.
- Perkins was one of the first in the country to hire female attorneys, hiring its first woman associate in 1920.
- In the 1990s, the firm has been involved with 100 public offerings, and completed transactions and cases in more than 50 countries.
- The firm keeps on the cutting edge of technology, with fast computers and innovative uses of technology in a variety of client service matters.

NUTS AND BOLTS

Managing partner:

Robert F. Bauer

Hiring partner:

Judith L. Corley, phone: 202-628-6600, e-mail: corlj@perkinscoie.com

Number of attorneys in firm:

371 (182 partners)

TOTAL FIRM:

Partners (182), associates (186), women partners (25), women associates (73), minority partners (2), minority associates (25), disabled partners (1), disabled associates (0), of counsel (49)

THIS OFFICE:

Total attorneys (38), partners (17), associates (13), women partners (3), women associates (5), minority partners (1), minority associates (2), disabled partners (0), disabled associates (0), of counsel (8), women of counsel (5)

OTHER OFFICES:

(* represents an office profiled elsewhere in this book)
Anchorage, Alaska (11); Denver, Colorado (5); Hong Kong (3); London, England (1); Los Angeles, California* (22); Olympia, Washington (2); Portland, Oregon* (37); Seattle, Washington* (239); Spokane, Washington (5); Taipei, Taiwan (13)

Years to make partner:

8

WHAT DO THEY DO?

Primary specialties (more than 5% of practice):

Corporate (7), Political Law (6), Environmental/Natural Resources (7), International (3), Litigation (12).

The firm is divided into practice areas. New associates are generally not assigned to a particular practice area, but instead are encouraged to work in a variety of practice groups before narrowing their focus.

WHO DO THEY REPRESENT?

An enormous variety of clients, including Act III Theaters; Advanced Laboratory Systems; American Physician Network; Boise Cascade; Calbag Metals; Cavenham Forest Industries, Democratic Congressional and Senatorial Campaign Committees, Division of Hanson Natural Resources; Columbia Colstor; Consolidated Freightways; Cummins Northwest;

CYCOMM; Dain Bosworth; EMILY's List; Endeavor Capital; Evergreen International Aviation; EVI Corporation; General Motors; City of Gresham; Hertz Corporation; Interactive Systems; Interconnectix; IBM; Kentrox Industries; King Broadcasting; Louisiana Pacific; Microtek International; Molecular Probes; Morrow Snowboards; Northwest Magnetic Imaging Center; Northwest Natural Gas; NNW; OESI Power; Oregon Art Institute; Oregon International Air Freight; Pacific Generation Company; PacifiCorp Financial Services; Portland Radio; Rogue Wave Software; Ross Stores; Russell Development; SARIF; SHE America; Shaw, Glasgow & Co; Summit Information Systems; Switchlink Systems; Synthetech; Truax Harris Energy Company; Viking Star Shipping; Waggener Edstrom; WTD Industries; Yoshida's; and ZIBA Design.

WHERE NEW ASSOCIATES COME FROM . . .

The Washington office routinely interviews on campus at the following law schools: Harvard, Yale, UVA, Georgetown, Duke, and George Washington. The office also hires associates and summer associates from schools where it doesn't interview on campus.

HOURS AND BUCKS . . .

Target annual billable hours: 1,800

Attorneys are allowed to work part-time; although no entry-level associate has ever worked part-time, "It's possible." The firm has hired contract associates, but not routinely. Contract associates have become full-time associates.

Typical first year salary, including typical bonus: $$$$ (Over $65,000). Perkins Coie D.C. is known for its particularly generous financial package.

SUMMER PROGRAM . . .

Last year, there were 3 summer associates, all 2Ls. One of the 2Ls will go to a judicial clerkship next year, and the other two were given offers. Offers were given to 3 prior 1L summer associates. Last year's summer associates came from Georgetown, Duke and William & Mary.

PRO BONO . . .

The firm encourages pro bono work, and up to 100 hours of pro bono hours count for productivity and performance bonuses as long as the associate otherwise meets the 1,800 annual billable hours target.

HISTORY AT A GLANCE . . .

The firm was founded in 1912 by George Donworth, a federal district court judge, and Elmer Todd, the U.S. Attorney for the Western District of

Washington. They quickly attracted major clients, and others that would grow to become major clients—including a little start-up "aero" company, which is today the Boeing Company.

Around 1920, the firm hired its first female associate, Lady Willie Forbus, at a time when virtually no other firm hired women as lawyers.

The firm grew steadily over the years, both through mergers and hires, growing today into the largest firm in the Pacific Northwest.

The Washington office opened in 1979.

WHAT IT'S LIKE TO WORK THERE . . .

Please read the firm's Seattle profile first! It will give you a feel for what it's like to work at Perkins in general, including descriptions of typical projects, management involvement, and training. Here are thoughts specifically from Perkins' associates in Washington:

Perkins' Washington associates rave about the fact that even though they're a long way from the firm's main office in Seattle, "We have an incredibly diverse practice for a small branch office of a large firm." One associate talked about having a strong interest in trademark law when he joined the D.C. office, but that "the D.C. office didn't handle many trademark projects." Partners in D.C. encouraged him to contact the head of the firm's Intellectual Property group in Seattle, and get some assignments sent to D.C. The firm also "encouraged me to spend some time in Seattle working with the department head and her entire group, so that the group would feel comfortable sending more work to me in D.C." The associate comments, "That worked out great. The firm really went out of its way to accommodate my interest in trademarks, and I get requests to work on trademark matters from Seattle on a regular basis." As that experience suggests, "D.C. is very flexible with work and departmental assignments, and they try very hard to match associates with whatever their particular interests are, even if the firm's other offices have to be drawn in to accomplish that."

Associates particularly like the fact that the D.C. office's practice ranges from "high-profile political law cases, to mega-mergers in the aircraft industry, to ground-breaking telecommunications matters, to a natural resources practice that is unmatched on the East Coast." As one associate comments, "Perkins Coie D.C. illustrates that you don't need to be in a large, impersonal office to work on top-notch cases for sophisticated clients." There are the monthly attorney lunches "Where our entire office can fit around a large conference room table, while many firms with practice areas as diverse and similar in caliber can't even fit one practice group into a conference room, let alone the whole office."

"Everyone looks after one another here."

Perkins Coie D.C. associates talk about the "pleasant and personal interaction among attorneys and staff," and the fact that "the D.C. office makes substantial efforts to ensure that the entire office, and not just attorneys, works well as a unit." Part of this harmonious atmosphere is reflected in the many stories associates tell about social life at the office, both during the workday and outside of business hours. One associate tells of how "my practice group had three separate celebrations for me passing the bar—and not just lunches, either"—no 'six or nine McNuggets?' outfit, that Perkins Coie. Some junior associates tell about spending "a significant amount of time outside of work with colleagues," including "boating, trips to Martha's Vineyard, dinners, lunches, and social gatherings on a regular basis." Also, there are the summer associate activities you'd expect from a large firm, including "Attending baseball games, concerts, and other events like that."

Associates find that they have the time to dedicate to extracurriculars because of the firm's "humane billable hours expectations." As one associate explained it, "The firm recently dropped its production bonus award hour level from 1950 to 1800, while most firms continue to raise their productivity expectations and the hours you have to work to get a bonus." An associate says that, "If you work 2,100 hours at Perkins Coie, you can expect a substantial bonus. The firm feels as though billing 2,100 hours is a sacrifice, not an expectation." The associate adds that, "At a lot of the firms in town where my friends work, associates are *expected* to bill 2,100 hours."

Associates feel that the firm's realistic billable-hours quotient "translates into a more healthy recognition of outside interests, whether that's civic activities, family, or just getting away from the office." Associates applaud the office's "part-time policy, which people actually use. They're encouraged to use it, unlike a lot of places that pay lip service to part-time work but then discourage people from doing it. Part-time attorneys aren't penalized for working part-time."

When it comes to weekends and late hours, "Nobody here expects you to put in 'face time.' If your work is done, you're free to walk out the door without anybody questioning you or looking at the clock." Associates say that, "We're lucky because Perkins gives us the privacy and ability to have lives of our own. They're actually apologetic when your outside life is disrupted because of work!"

Perkins Coie L.L.P.—Los Angeles

1999 Avenue of the Stars, 9TH Floor • Los Angeles, CA 90067
Phone: 310-788-9900 • Fax: 310-788-3399 • Web site: perkinscoie.com

OFFICES

Seattle (main office)*, Bellevue, Olympia, Spokane, Washington; Anchorage, Alaska; Denver, Colorado; Los Angeles, California; Portland*, Oregon; Washington, D.C.*

HIGHLIGHTS

- The Los Angeles office of the largest law firm in the Pacific Northwest, and the 69TH largest firm in the country.
- Perkins was one of the first in the country to hire female attorneys, hiring its first woman associate in 1920.
- In the 1990s, the firm has been involved with 85 public offerings, and completed transactions and cases in more than 50 countries.
- The firm keeps on the cutting edge of technology, with fast computers and innovative uses of technology in a variety of client service matters.

NUTS AND BOLTS

Managing partner:

Bruce E. Sherman

Hiring partner:

Mark E. Birnbaum, phone: 310-788-3228, e-mail: birnm@perkinscoie.com

Recruiting coordinator:

Becky A. McClure, phone: 310-788-3279, e-mail: mcclb@perkinscoie.com

Number of attorneys in firm:

371 (182 partners)

TOTAL FIRM:

Partners (182), associates (186), women partners (25), women associates (73), minority partners (2), minority associates (25), disabled partners (1), disabled associates (0), of counsel (49)

THIS OFFICE:

Total attorneys (27), partners (11), associates (16), women partners (0), women associates (3), minority partners (1), minority associates (4), disabled partners (0), disabled associates (0), of counsel (1)

OTHER OFFICES:

(* represents an office profiled elsewhere in this book)
Anchorage, Alaska (11); Denver, Colorado (5); Hong Kong (3); London, England (1); Seattle, Washington* (239); Olympia, Washington (2); Portland, Oregon* (37); Spokane, Washington (5); Taipei, Taiwan (13); Washington, D.C.* (35)

Years to make partner:

7

WHAT DO THEY DO?

Primary specialties (more than 5% of practice) in Los Angeles:

Civil Litigation (12), Real Estate (4), Bankruptcy (3), Business (2)
The office is departmentalized. New associates are unassigned originally, but when they choose a specialty, they rarely switch to another specialty.

WHO DO THEY REPRESENT?

A vast variety of clients, including ACL Holdings; Alaska Airlines; Becton Dickinson; Boeing; Bugle Boy; Egghead; Elsinore Aerospace; Fujisawa U.S.A.; W.R. Grace & Co.; Gucci America; Human Monoclonals International; International Paper; Key Bank; Landmark Theatre; MCA; Northwest Airlines; Northwest Natural Gas Company; Penguin's Frozen Yogurt, Inc.; Tiger Shark Golf; US WEST; Weyerhaeuser; and Zausner Foods.

WHERE NEW ASSOCIATES COME FROM . . .

The L.A. office routinely interviews on campus at the following law schools: UCLA, Loyola/Los Angeles, USC, Boalt Hall, Stanford, and Hastings. The L.A. office routinely hires from schools where it doesn't do on-campus interviewing.

HOURS AND BUCKS . . .

First year associates typically spend 1,900 hours at the office, of which 1,800 hours are the minimum billable hourly requirement.

Attorneys are allowed to work part-time, but not at entry level. The L.A. office does not routinely hire contract associates.

Typical first year salary, including typical bonus: $$$$ (Over $65,000). The firm is known for its generous financial package.

SUMMER PROGRAM . . .

Last year, there were 2 summer associates, both of whom got offers.
Weekly pay: $1,538 last year
The L.A. office occasionally hires 1Ls for its summer program.

PRO BONO . . .

The firm encourages pro bono work. Up to 100 hours of pro bono time count towards productivity and performance bonuses, as long as the associate has met the 1,800-hour billable hours requirement.

Pro bono projects at the L.A. office include homeless assistance, guardian ad litem work, and indigent representation.

HISTORY AT A GLANCE . . .

The firm was founded in 1912 by George Donworth, a federal district court judge, and Elmer Todd, the U.S. Attorney for the Western District of Washington. They quickly attracted major clients, and others that would grow to become major clients—including a little start-up "aero" company, which is today the Boeing Company.

Around 1920, the firm hired its first female associate, Lady Willie Forbus, at a time when virtually no other firm hired women as lawyers.

The firm grew steadily over the years, both through mergers and hires, growing today into the largest firm in the Pacific Northwest.

The Los Angeles office opened in 1988.

WHAT IT'S LIKE TO WORK THERE . . .

Please read the firm's Seattle, Portland, and Washington profiles. That will give you a feel for what it's like to work at Perkins in general, including descriptions of typical projects, management involvement, training, and the firm culture.

Proskauer Rose LLP

1585 Broadway • New York, NY 10036-8299
Phone: 212-969-3000 • Fax: 212-969-2900 • Web site: proskauer.com

OFFICES

New York City (main office), New York; Los Angeles, California; Washington, D.C.; Boca Raton, Florida; Clifton, New Jersey

*"We're getting ready to file a reply brief. We got the other side's papers, and when I looked them over I was shocked at how sloppy they were, all the way down to silly things like misspellings. Something like that wouldn't even make it to a **partner** here, let alone get out of the office. It makes me proud thinking that nothing less than top quality work goes out with Proskauer's name on it. It sounds corny, but they're going to make me great here. They'll make my legal education pay off. I love watching great attorneys at work—and the fact that they're giving me the opportunity to be like them, someday."*

HIGHLIGHTS

- 37TH largest law firm in the country.
- A renowned litigation practice, known in the press as a "warrior in the courtroom."
- The firm is strongly committed to pro bono work. Up to 125 hours of pro bono work count towards each associate's minimum billable hours requirement.

NUTS AND BOLTS

Managing partner:

Stanley Komaroff

Hiring partner:

Ira Akselrad, phone: 212-969-3880, e-mail: iakselrad@proskauer.com

Recruiting coordinator:

Catherine McDermott, phone: 212-969-5061

Number of attorneys in firm:

471 (131 partners)

TOTAL FIRM:

Partners (131), associates and senior counsel (340), women partners (12), women associates (120), minority partners (3), minority associates (37)

THIS OFFICE:

Total attorneys (360), partners (99), associates (261), women partners (9), women associates (92), minority partners (2), minority associates (30)

OTHER OFFICES:

(* represents an office profiled elsewhere in this book)
Los Angeles, CA (44); Washington, D.C. (32); Boca Raton, FL (28); Clifton, NJ (3); Paris, France (4)

Years to make partner:

8 to 10

WHAT DO THEY DO?

Primary specialties (more than 5% of practice):

Corporate/Securities (116) and Litigation/ADR (147)—Corporate and Litigation also include Banking, Bankruptcy, Environmental, Health, Insurance, Intellectual Property, and International; Labor/Employment (113); Personal Planning (13); Real Estate (34); Taxation (19); Unassigned (29).

The firm is departmentalized. Offers are made departmentally, so new associates join the firm in a particular department. Associates can switch departments, according to their desires and each department's needs.

WHO DO THEY REPRESENT?

An enormous variety of clients domestically and abroad, including Celebrity Cruise Lines, Cray Research, Del Monte Foods, Price Communications, Henry Schein, Inc., Charterhouse Group International, J. P. Morgan Capital, the National Hockey League, the National Basketball

Association, Donna Karan International, Banco de Colombia, Citibank International plc, Wilshire Credit Corporation, Spin Magazine, NBC, Time, Inc., Metropolitan Opera, U.S. Soccer Federation, Lucas Film, Ltd., Air India, BellSouth, Bristol-Myers Squibb, Columbia University, Club Med, Daily News, The Hearst Corporation, Madison Square Garden, McDonalds, McKinsey & Co., Prentice-Hall, Inc., USA Networks, Warner Brothers, Bell Atlantic, TWA, Simon & Schuster, and The New York Times.

WHERE NEW ASSOCIATES COME FROM . . .

The firm routinely interviews on campus at the following law schools: Harvard, Yale, Columbia, NYU, Stanford, Boalt Hall, Michigan, Cornell, Chicago, Pennsylvania, Georgetown, UVA, Duke, Northwestern, UCLA, Fordham, and Brooklyn. The firm also hires from schools where it doesn't do on-campus interviews.

HOURS AND BUCKS . . .

First year associates spend at least 1,900 hours at the office. The minimum billable hourly requirement is 2,000 for associates in general.

Attorneys are allowed to work part-time, but part-time work is not available at entry level. The firm occasionally hires contract associates, and some contract associates have become full-time associates.

Typical first year salary, including typical bonus: $$$$ (Over $65,000). The firm is known for its generous financial package, competitive with other large New York firms.

SUMMER PROGRAM . . .

Last year, there were 33 summer associates, all of whom received offers.

Weekly pay: $1,750 last year

1Ls are routinely hired for the summer program. Last year's 1Ls came from Harvard, Yale, Columbia, Chicago, Cornell, UVA, and New York Law School.

PRO BONO . . .

The firm is strongly committed to pro bono work. Up to 125 hours of pro bono work count towards each associate's minimum billable hours requirement.

The firm's pro bono program is coordinated by a committee comprised of four partners. They communicate pro bono opportunities to all attorneys, coordinate the staffing of each project undertaken, and supervise the pro bono matters. Associates may also engage in pro bono activities of their own choice (subject to conflict procedures and firm policies).

The firm maintains ongoing referral relationships with many organizations, and its pro bono docket is extremely varied, being designed to provide Proskauer attorneys with valuable experience in diverse areas of the law. Projects encompass litigation, both individual and broad-scale, corporate, labor and tax advice to community groups and other not-for-profit organizations, immigration and political asylum representation, and personal planning assistance to people who need wills, divorces, guardianships and living wills.

The firm's pro bono docket includes matters like habeas corpus representation of a prisoner on Florida's death row; preparing an amicus brief for NOW Legal Defense and Education Fund in Edwards v. City of Santa Barbara, regarding the constitutionality of "buffer-zone" legislation that seeks to protect abortion clinics; representing five disabled permanent resident aliens as co-plaintiffs with the City of New York, in a constitutional challenge to the Welfare Reform Act; participating as a Charter Member of Project Life, involving matrimonial representation of battered women; representing indigent criminal defendants on their appeals; and assisting HIV-Positive patients in a large New York hospital with respect to guardianship proceedings and the preparation of living wills.

HISTORY AT A GLANCE . . .

The firm has many well-recognized attorneys; in fact, it's known as the 'home of bar presidents.' Stars include Edward Brodsky, litigator, current president of the American College of Trial Lawyers. Michael Cardozo, current president of the New York Bar Association. Bettina Plevan, labor and employment specialist, president of the Federal Bar Council. Ronald Rauchberg, head of the litigation unit, spearheading the firm's leading role in alternative dispute resolution. Stanley Komaroff, Chair of the firm, with a burgeoning French clientele.

WHAT IT'S LIKE TO WORK THERE . . .

Quick! Come up with a mental picture of what it's like to work at a big, New York-based law firm, and what do you see? Cots in associates' offices, for quick naps during those regular all-nighters? Years spent on document reviews, or stuck in a cubicle in the library slaving away on a make-work document that no client will ever see? Spending much of your productive work life on subsection b to Roman Numeral II of a memo to file, and passing it on to the associate in the next cubicle to work on subsection c? Getting a year or two under your belt—time with no life outside of the office, and God knows no enjoyment—so that you can do what you really want?

Hold that thought. And then forget about it. Because you're not talking about Proskauer Rose. Yes, there are the stresses of high-quality work in a Type-A city, but associates rave that "No one is around watching what color shirt you wear or what you put on the walls of your office. The attorneys care about you, both as a professional and as a person." One associate comments that "Not only do they tolerate me, but the attitude here is that if you do good work, you can be yourself. You can be a freak if you want. That's great! It's a very tolerant place. It's great for many, many people. Some are openly gay, and everybody is comfortable with that," and "You wouldn't believe the respect we get." And one very junior associate says that "A lot of people talk about how life at law firms changes after the summer program, but I find that we still hang out and do fun stuff even though we're not getting 'credit' for it. The other day six or seven of us ran off to catch a movie because one of the people in the group was in a bad mood."

"You can seek out the work you want directly from partners who do what you want to do."

When associates join the firm, they enter a particular department, and in the largest departments there is a non-practicing "assigning attorney" who does all of the assignments for associates. In addition, associates each have an "associate advisor," "a mid-level associate whom you can ask *anything*." They also get a reviewing attorney, who is a partner or senior counsel. "They review everything you do and let you know about your progress, and if you get to know them, they are also an excellent mentor."

By way of training, associates say that, "It's both formal and informal." The formal training is "practice-specific," the "general young attorney kind of stuff, like how to file papers, how to do a deal, mergers, those kinds of things. You have those sessions for the first six months, every three weeks." Each associate also gets an annual training allowance of $1,000, to be used for attending seminars and other training opportunities. And associates get an annual 125-hour 'associate training time' allowance, which is "time that may be spent observing or participating in an activity that provides 'hands-on' experience, like attending a deposition or client meeting. The associate's time counts toward the associate's 2,000 hour billables goal, but it isn't charged to the client."

Informally, "You do everything from tagging along to a deposition or an oral argument, to going over drafts of your stuff with a partner or senior associate, and changing things and having them tell you why." Associates say that "they encourage you to ask questions, and it's easy to find people who are open to that."

When it comes to being overworked, associates say that, "The assignment people make sure you aren't overloaded, but you have to speak up to avoid it. They'll offload projects for you if there's too much on your plate." In spite of the formal assignment system, associates say that, "You can seek out work you want directly from partners who do what you want to do." One associate sums up the Proskauer approach to assignments by saying that "There are two things you have to know about Proskauer. One is that they expect you to be vocal about what you want to do. And the other is that if you *are* vocal, they'll go out of their way to get you what you want."

> *"The opportunities are so great here, I would have come here even if I thought I'd be miserable—but that's not the case at all."*

Associates rave about the firm's "sexy, diverse clients" and the interesting projects they get to do. "You often hear that the work at large law firms is fungible and the associates are, too. But given the mix of large and small clients at Proskauer, neither cliché is true here." As one mid-level associate put it, "Since I started at Proskauer, I've been given the opportunity to work on a very wide variety of issues for both small and large clients. It's really given me a chance to explore different options for my career focus." In the firm's brochure, junior associates share stories of being closely involved in projects like initial public offerings, acquisitions, and venture capital investments. They uniformly talk about being "engaged at all levels of the transaction and not only being involved in a 'small piece' of the deal." Rather than being a drone in the library while the partners get all of the contact with clients, junior associates often say that they get to talk to clients directly, with supervision by senior associates and partners.

When it comes to handling clients, associates also get an annual business development allowance, "which we can use for entertaining clients" and other business development opportunities. "They don't expect you to bring in business in your first few years. With the caliber of clients we have, it wouldn't make sense to expect us to do that, and so we get paid set salaries, albeit very high ones! But it's nice to know that they're thinking about your business development potential, even as an associate."

> *"The hours are pretty flexible."'*

Great opportunities and interesting projects can mean long hours at Proskauer. The offices tend to fill up between 9 and 9:30 a.m., although "There *are* early birds, and then there are some people who come in later than that, and some partners come in at 10:30. It's flexible. As long as you don't have meetings, you can come in pretty much any time in the morning."

At night, associates' perceptions are that "The offices get quiet around 7 p.m." although "It's cyclical, and some departments are just known for staying later than others." Personal planning, for instance, "tends to be one of the earlier departments to clear out." In litigation, "It varies, depending on deadlines. The night before a brief is due, you're going to be late. Two weeks before papers are due, you're going to put in the late hours."

For weekends, "If you'd rather leave at 6:30 p.m. Friday and come in for a couple of hours on the weekend, you can—it's a choice." Associates say that "You easily have stretches without working any weekends," and "the weekend work is not typical, on a regular basis. It totally depends on what's going on." One associate said that "On the one occasion that required me to stay through the night, the partner I was working with stayed to help me, when he could easily have gone home and checked with me in the morning."

Associates don't resent the hours they put in for several reasons. For one thing, it's "what you expect. You condition yourself to it." But more importantly, "I enjoy my work, and on weekends when I'm there with other people, I enjoy watching people who can teach me. When you get here, you know nothing." And "from a service perspective, our clients pay a lot, and they deserve great service. If that means weekend work once in a while, that's what it means. They expect their money to win cases, and that means we do everything we can to deliver." Associates echo the fact that "The firm gives us a big dose of the 'appreciating the client' message, and it gets through. What hits home even more than that is that the partners teach it by example."

The hours are ameliorated by the firm's attitudes about counting learning experience and pro bono activities in the 2,000-hour expectation. Associates say that "The firm wants to get away from competitive hours, they don't want people falling over themselves for projects at certain times of year to chase up their billables." The 2,000 hours includes the 125 hours of observation 'training time,' for which associates get credit but clients aren't billed. Associates can also spend 125 hours on pro bono projects, and have that count toward their billable hours. Associates say that "Everybody here does pro bono," and it can be everything from traditional pro bono, representing indigents, to "mentoring high school students in moot court-type activities." They say that "We get lots of e-mail about pro bono projects, and you can also bring in your own." The sense is that "pro bono has a very high profile at the office—you definitely get kudos for it."

"There are pictures of kids all over the place."

The firm's caring nature comes across both in formal and informal ways. Formally, the firm has an ombudsman program, which involves "special partners. You can go to them any time in complete confidentiality on any issue. The firm tells us that 'it doesn't matter whether it would be something like a personality conflict all the way to an issue as serious as sexual harassment, if it ever happened, they'd be the ones to talk to,' and people really trust them." Informally, "It's an easy place to develop a support network," which is important because "In an office this big there are always going to be some people you work with better than others, some people who rub you the wrong way, and there are always people who've been there before and are willing to lend a sympathetic ear and solid advice."

Associates say that as to family friendliness, "Many female lawyer have kids. There are pictures of kids all over the place." They say that "Some women work part-time and flex-time to accommodate their families," and that that's something that is a "Big concern for younger women." Female junior associates say that, "Two female partners sat down with all of the first year women, to listen to the kinds of issues on our minds. They're interested in what we have to say, and they listen to our concerns." In fact, associates say that in general, the partners "will hear you out on anything." Every department at Proskauer has its own committees, and "The only committee without associates is the Executive Committee. But people on that committee are on others as well, and you get to meet them that way. They'll listen to anything you have to say." Associates have a particularly notable say in recruiting. "We interview everyone and all of our evaluations are taken seriously. The partners tell us, 'These will be your colleagues,' and they give us a corresponding say in who those colleagues will be."

Associates also have a large role in the summer program, where there are "many, many organized events." On top of the summer associate social calendar, the firm has a "variety of sports teams it sponsors in the lawyers' leagues," and "Each October, the new associates and their guests, as well as many of the other attorneys, go away for a weekend retreat to help acclimate them to life at the firm." Informally, there are "softball games, bowling, billiards, cocktail parties and movies." One associate sums up the Proskauer experience by saying, "I would be *nowhere* else!"

Shook, Hardy & Bacon L.L.P.

One Kansas City Place • 1200 Main Street • Kansas City, Missouri 64105-2118
Phone: 816-474-6550 • Fax: 916-474-6550

OFFICES

Kansas City (main office), Missouri; Overland Park, Kansas; Houston, Texas; Washington, D.C.

"Great clients, great lawyers, great causes, and great cases are what make this a great firm. But when you peel away the sophistication and the complex legal issues, what matters for associates is that everything you need to make your job easier is here. An amazing library, great access to on-line resources, great support—paralegals, analysts, library staff, partners whose doors are constantly open to guide you—everything I work on is top quality, and that's a great feeling."

HIGHLIGHTS

- Largest law firm in Kansas City, and 63RD largest firm in the United States.
- Enormous and widely-respect product liability defense practice, including several decades of successful tobacco defense work.
- No minimum billable hours requirement.
- A growing international practice, with new (and planned) offices in London, Buenos Aires, Melbourne, and Geneva.
- Fourteen of the firm's lawyers are listed in *The Best Lawyers in America*.

NUTS AND BOLTS

Managing partner:
Patrick McLarney

Hiring partner:

John W. Simpson, phone: 816-474-6550

Recruiting coordinator:

Laura M. Spies, phone: 816-474-6550, e-mail: lspies@shb.com

Number of attorneys in firm:

350 (113 partners)

TOTAL FIRM:

Partners (113), associates (237), women partners (17), minority partners (11), disabled partners (1)

THIS OFFICE:

Total attorneys (274), partners (89), associates (185), women partners (12), minority partners (8), disabled partners (1)

OTHER OFFICES:

(* represents an office profiled elsewhere in this book)
Overland Park, KS (31); Houston, TX (21); Washington, D.C (13); London, England (8); Zurich, Switzerland (1); Geneva, Switzerland (1); Melbourne, Australia (1)

Years to make partner:

7

WHAT DO THEY DO?

Primary specialties (more than 5% of practice) for the entire firm:

Products Liability Litigation (230); Corporate Finance & Banking (21); Commercial Litigation (27); Intellectual Property (23); Labor & Employment (14); Health Care (7); Tax (12); Energy Law (5); Real Estate/Estate Planning (6).

The firm is departmentalized. Young associates can, and do, switch specialties.

WHO DO THEY REPRESENT?

Representative clients include AFG Industries, Applebee's International, Big Twelve Athletic Conference, BioTechnica Corporation, Brown & Williamson Tobacco, Ciba-Geigy Corporation, Citibank N.A., Dodson Insurance Group, Elf Atochem North America, Eli Lilly, Ford Motor Company, G.D. Searle & Company, GTE Products, Hoechst Marion

Roussel, Johnson & Johnson, Kansas City Royals Baseball Corporation, Mark Twain Banks, Missouri Pacific Railroad Company, Norfolk Southern Corporation, PepsiCo, Pharmacia & Upjohn, Phillip Morris, Phillips Petroleum, Safeco Insurance, Schering-Plough Corporation, Sears Roebuck & Co., Southwestern Bell Mobile Systems, Texaco, The Clorox Company, Travelers Insurance, and the Union Pacific Railroad.

WHERE NEW ASSOCIATES COME FROM . . .

The firm routinely interviews on campus at the following law schools: Baylor, Creighton, Duke, Emory, George Washington, Georgetown, Harvard, Northwestern, Notre Dame, St. Louis University, South Texas, Tulane, Houston, Iowa, Kansas, Michigan, Minnesota, Missouri-Columbia, Missouri-Kansas City, Nebraska, North Carolina, Oklahoma, Texas, Tulsa, Virginia, Vanderbilt, Washburn, Washington University, Yale. The firm routinely hires associates and summer associates from schools where it doesn't interview on campus.

HOURS AND BUCKS . . .

First year associates are at the office for an average of 2,225 hours per year. There is no minimum billable hourly requirement.

Attorneys are allowed to work part-time on a case-by-case basis, and part-time work is available at entry level. The firm only very occasionally hires contract associates.

Typical first year salary, including typical bonus: $$$$ (Over $65,000)

SUMMER PROGRAM . . .

Last year, there were 27 summer associates. Of the 23 eligible for offers, all received offers, and 22 accepted (the other 4 associates were deferred pending judicial clerkships).

Weekly pay: $1,150 last year

1Ls are not hired for the summer program.

PRO BONO . . .

The firm strongly encourages associates to do pro bono work. Associates have taken part over the years in a wide variety of pro bono cases, from the day-to-day juvenile appointment or prisoners' rights litigation, to trial and ultimately oral argument in the first "right to die" case ever heard by the U.S. Supreme Court, the Nancy Cruzan case.

The firm has a full-time pro bono lawyer, who tries to give all new associates a case for which they will be solely responsible.

HISTORY AT A GLANCE . . .

The firm traces its roots to Kansas City in 1889, when Frank P. Sebree began a partnership with William A. Alderson under the name Alderson and Sebree. Early leaders other than Sebree and Alderson included Samuel Sebree, Edgar Shook, David Hardy, and Charles Bacon, all of whom were civic, political and business leaders.

The firm's success in the ensuing decades has focused mostly on its product liability defense work, much of it relating to tobacco litigation. However, Shook, Hardy's story doesn't begin and end with tobacco; it has also defended many other headline-making cases, defending products like Agent Orange, DES, the Dalkon Shield, the Copper 7 IUD, and Halcion. It also won millions of dollars in damages for the victims of the Kansas City Hyatt Hotel collapse. Today, it continues its reputation as a high-stakes class action litigator by handling more than 20 class action cases nationwide, including the controversial Desert Storm Syndrome litigation.

It has been successful in areas outside of product liability litigation, as well. For instance, it handled the public stock offering of Interstate Bakeries in 1989, the fifth largest public offering in history.

In the 1990's, the firm has seen explosive growth, from 150 lawyers in 1990 to well over 300 today.

In 1997 the firm merged with the intellectual property firm of Kokjer, Kircher, Bowman & Johnson, to create one of the largest intellectual property groups in the Midwest.

Firm stars include Harvey Kaplan, who has tried more than five years' worth of Dalkon Shield cases without a loss; William Colby, who won the famous Nancy Cruzan right-to-die case. And Gary Long, who has handled many successful tobacco cases for a variety of tobacco companies.

WHAT IT'S LIKE TO WORK THERE . . .

When you talk about Shook, Hardy, you're talking about a firm that's been involved in many of the most controversial, high-profile cases in the country. The Cruzan right-to-die case. Dalkon Shield. And of course, tons of tobacco litigation. While that kind of work creates an intellectually challenging environment, it doesn't make for a dog-eat-dog attitude at the Shook, Hardy offices. Associates say that, "Despite the high stakes national and international scope of our complex litigation and corporate work, this place is brimming with people who are down to earth, who are appreciative and thoughtful of one another, and who know how to have fun."

Associates rave that "It's a first-name kind of place, where performance is more important than appearance or prissy protocol," and "They accept diversity, and even idiosyncrasies, as far as personal styles." Associates say that, "You can tell what a great place this is to work by testing it. Don't just talk to the lawyers. Look around at all the staff, from the messengers and the file clerks to the secretaries and analysts. They look and act like they enjoy working for the firm, and that's the best indication that it's a pretty good place for lawyers, as well. Other places may start off paying you more money, but no place will give you more rewards." As one associate sums it up, "When I meet people who work at other places, it only makes me realize how great we have it here."

"They bend over backwards to make sure we get what we need."

When people interview with the firm, "You interview for a particular section, and you get offered jobs by particular sections, not the firm as a whole," although "once you're here, you can switch specialties." Summer clerks rank the sections they want to join "and always get one of their top three sections. If you ranked Tobacco #1 and Labor #2 and you wind up in labor, and then you say, 'I really want Tobacco,' they'll do what they can to get you in."

The structure of the departments, which are called sections, varies with the size of the section. "In smaller sections, like Intellectual Property, there aren't teams. The section itself is a team. You work on every kind of assignment. You get your own cases early, and you follow them through." For bigger sections, like Tobacco, "They are divided into teams. In Tobacco, for instance, there's a class action team, and if you're on that team, you'll only get assignments from lawyers on the team. And then you'll have teams that are case-specific." Regardless of the type of team associates are in, they find that "Once you're on a case, you really follow it through. You get to learn about each stage of the trial," and "We get lots of feedback on everything we do." In addition, there are partner/mentors for each associate, and there are associate meetings, and section meetings, typically once a month, "where you keep up with new developments in the law—and which some sections follow up with a happy hour."

In spite of what seems to be a fairly formal assignment structure, associates find that "There's a real emphasis on getting a variety of assignments, getting us exposed to various things." While "all associates initially spend some time in the library," associates rave about the firm's "completely open door policy. You can go to any partner, ask questions, seek advice, seek interesting work. You can say, 'I've been to one deposition, I'd like to see more'—no problem, you'll see more. You tell them what you need, and you know they'll make an effort for you." Other associates add that, "We are treated with incredible respect. The firm takes a huge interesting in teaching us, helping us develop our professional skills. They bend over backwards to make sure we get what we need." One associate told about how "After I'd been here three weeks, I got an assignment from one partner, who mentioned that another partner might be a good resource for the project. I left a message for that partner, introducing myself and asking for help. Next thing I knew, I had three voice mails with advice on handling the assignment. He didn't even know me, and he still took the time to give me tips to help me. It's typical. They take such pride in helping associates develop."

Associates say that, "They take you to depositions to show you how those work. They treat it as a learning experience." One associate told of a "seven week trial I just took part in. It was amazing. It was the first trial of its kind ever, a second-hand smoke case." It's "very exciting to work on national issues in the comfort of the Midwest."

"The work we get is controversial and interesting."

To say that the work Shook, Hardy does is controversial is something of an understatement. While it has small sections that handle other kinds of work, its bread-and-butter is product liability defense work—and primarily for tobacco companies. Associates uniformly rave that "The work we get is controversial and interesting. It is exciting, cutting-edge law. It couldn't be more intellectually fascinating." But they admit bluntly that, "If tobacco defense is something you're uncomfortable with, clearly you can't work here." The sense is that "There are two philosophies about tobacco. One is, 'how can you do that?' The other is, 'people have a right to choose, and to take responsibility for themselves.' If you work here, you believe the latter." Associates also point out that "When it comes to getting criticized for what you do, we're hardly alone. A lot of lawyers get that. Public defenders get asked how they can represent criminals. The criticism is also there in insurance defense, white collar criminal defense, any product liability work." And they add that "It's much more than just a matter of 'everybody deserving representation,' the idea that you learn in law school."

The tobacco flavor to the firm's business "isn't something they hide from interviewees." Associates say that, "When you interview with the firm, they ask to make sure you're comfortable, to make sure you can handle situations where you're put on the spot, because they're going to come up." Associates who do on-campus interviewing for the firm say that they are "surprised when people don't ask about it. Tobacco cases are controversial, interesting, front-page stuff. When students *don't* ask, it makes you think, 'Do you even know what we do?'"

Of immense importance to Shook, Hardy associates is that "the quality of the work we do—I'm so proud of it." One associate talked of getting back from a trial "where I read the pleadings from elsewhere, and it made me appreciate what we do, the way they train us, that much more. Everything we do is the highest possible quality. We produce the absolute best work product, and that's very refreshing."

"The emphasis on quality of life is unmatched."

Associate say that "There's no minimum billable hours requirement here, and they *mean* it." They report that "There is no discussion of hours. None. Every month you get a printout of everybody's hours, so you know what everybody is doing. You get two associate evaluations every year, and they never bring up hours. It's just not an issue." One associate added that "If anything, they tell you, 'Take time off. You'll burn out.'" An associate talks about "A two-month trial I worked on. When you work on a trial, you're going to put in some long hours, and they'll tell you to take a few weeks off afterwards. When I got back from the trial, the next week I billed six hours—and they encouraged me to take another week off!" As that suggests, "We don't have a set vacation policy. They tell you to 'take it when you need it.' They are *very* flexible."

With so little emphasis on hours, predictably enough "There are no bonuses for excess hours. Everyone gets a bonus based on a percentage of their salary for the year." Raises are based on merit, "based on your associate evaluations." The "partners you worked with for the last six months give you written evaluations, you meet with them to discuss it, and raises are based on those evaluations." Associates are given scores of 1 to 5 on various aspects of their performance, and "The more 5's you have, the better a raise you get." The firm evaluates associates based on "Written skills, interaction with clients, the way you handle projects in general," but "Because you're getting constant feedback, all the time, you really know how you're doing." There's a pervading feeling that "The partners view us as their future partners. There's no weeding out. You get the sense that nothing would make them happier than if every associate stayed, and every associate made partner."

Associates' participation in management typically isn't formal. There are committees, and "associates are on a few of those." Instead, "You can take an interest in any particular aspect of the firm, and you can get involved in that. If you express what you want, you get it." For instance, "with recruiting, you can interview as much as you want." With the summer program, "If you want to supervise summer associates, you tell them, and you get to do it." In general, associates find that "You have to be vocal, and let your wishes and desires be known. Nobody reads your mind." They report that "You can go directly to the partner in charge of anything. You don't have to wait for formal committee meetings, or go through 'channels.' They're so approachable."

"It's very important to the firm that associates have an outside life."

Associates say that Shook, Hardy has "very Midwestern values." They look for "friendly, well-rounded people." Associates point out that "So many of the lawyers have kids. One partner coaches his son's little league games." Many of the associates and "tons of the partners have small children. One female partner has three small children, another has two small kids, and one of the female partners is a single mother." As the family-focus suggests, "The hours here are flexible. Nobody's watching you come in and leave. If you've got a kid in a school play, you're not going to be here, and nobody expects—or *wants*—you to miss that."

As that family-friendliness suggests, "We try hard to strip away the B.S." The firm's social activities reflect that attitude. Every fall, the firm has what it calls the "Annual Retreat for the Contemplation of Law and Justice." Associates explain that "That's a purposefully high-sounding name for a weekend of very little work and lots of fun."

During the summer, there are a predictably high number of social events designed to help summer associates and lawyers get to know each other. "We have a series of small 'dinner at the partners' parties. Those range from sit-down catered events, to back-yard burger cookouts where we bring our families." Associates remember one particularly memorable summer event, when "A large group of summer associates were late for a dinner party, to the concern of the hosting partners. The concern wasn't alleviated when it became known that the reason was that 15 of the summer associates had arranged an activity of their own—a one-day course in skydiving—and *all* of them had made the jump!"

Informally, associates say "Pick your sport or activity, and there's probably a group of us who do it together on a regular basis." There's a firm basketball team that plays "generally poorly" in the lawyers' league. There's a co-ed softball team, and the "usual groups of golfers, fishers, and boaters," and "there's a bunch, including some of the retired partners, who find a monthly gathering for small stakes—two-bit ante poker—is a good cover for an old-fashioned gossip session."

Associates uniformly like Kansas City. One associate says that "I'd never lived anywhere but on the coasts, never been anywhere near the Midwest before I came to Shook, Hardy. I didn't know what to expect but this is truly a wonderful city. New associates can own a home. I could never have done that in L.A.! There are great neighborhoods, a very low cost of living." Others enthuse that the city "has a lot to offer. Diverse entertainment, plays, theater, art galleries, museums, a wonderful zoo." Downtown, where the firm's luxurious offices are, "is dead at night, but there are neighborhoods within 30 blocks of the office that have lots of bars and restaurants, we sometimes go to Happy Hours there. And the firm itself sponsors a lot of Happy Hours. What the town lacks, the firm makes up for."

One associate sums up what it's like to work at Shook, Hardy in saying that "Great clients, great lawyers, great causes, and great cases are what make this a great firm. But when you peel away the sophistication and the complex legal issues, what matters for associates is that everything you need to make your job easier is here. An amazing library, great access to on-line resources, great support—paralegals, analysts, library staff, partners whose doors are constantly open to guide you—everything I work on is top quality, and that's a great feeling."

Shumaker, Loop & Kendrick, LLP

1000 Jackson • Toledo, Ohio 43624
Phone: 419-241-9000 • Fax: 419-241-6894

OFFICES

Toledo (main office), Ohio; Tampa, Florida; Charlotte, North Carolina

"I came here from a huge, big-city law firm, where I had started in a class of 30 associates. At the end of two years, I was the 17TH person to leave. I worked awful hours, with stuffy, rude people. I suffered, and I had no life. OK, I took a pay cut to come here, but I couldn't care less. Now I'm happy, I do great work, I love the people I work with, I put in reasonable hours—and most important of all, I still have my family!"

HIGHLIGHTS

• Largest law firm in northwestern Ohio.

NUTS AND BOLTS

Managing partner:
David F. Waterman

Hiring partner:
Mary Ellen Pisanelli

Recruiting coordinator:
Julie Stillberger, phone: 419-321-1240, e-mail: jstillbe@slk-law.com

Number of attorneys in firm:
129 (84 partners)

TOTAL FIRM:

Partners (84), associates (38), women partners (14), women associates (10), minority partners (2), minority associates (2), of counsel (2), staff attorneys (3)

TOLEDO OFFICE:

Total partners (61), total associates (16), women partners (11), women associates (5), minority partners (2), minority associates (1)

OTHER OFFICES:

Tampa, FL (37); Charlotte, NC (9); Columbus, OH (3)

Years to make partner:

7

WHAT DO THEY DO?

Corporate; Real Estate; Environmental; Litigation; Trusts & Estates, Employment Law; Employee Benefits/ERISA/Compensation; Health Law.

WHERE NEW ASSOCIATES COME FROM . . .

The firm's Toledo office routinely interviews on campus at the following law schools: Case Western, Chicago, Duke, George Washington, Georgetown, Michigan, Northwestern, Ohio State, Toledo, Vanderbilt, and Virginia. The firm also hires from schools where it doesn't interview on campus.

HOURS AND BUCKS . . .

Associates work an average of 2,078, of which average billables are 1,854. Associates have a billable goal of 1,800 hours per year.

Part-time work is available to continuing associates on a case-by-case basis; it is not available at entry level. The firm does not routinely hire contract associates.

Typical first year salary, including bonus: $$$ ($50-65,000)

SUMMER PROGRAM . . .

Last year, there were 4 summer associates, 3 of whom received offers.

Weekly pay: $965 last year; estimated to be $1,000 to $1,110 for summer 1999.

1Ls are routinely hired for the summer program.

PRO BONO . . .

The firm encourages its attorneys to participate in pro bono work. Pro bono hours are not treated as billables. Pro bono projects undertaken by firm attorneys include the U.S. District Court Volunteer Appointments program, and the Citizens Dispute Settlement Program.

HISTORY AT A GLANCE . . .

The firm was founded in 1925.

WHAT IT'S LIKE TO WORK THERE . . .

When you talk with associates at Shumaker, Loop, you find a bunch of people who are contented in every way. They like the responsibility they get, the people they work with, and their opportunities at the firm.

When you start with Shumaker, Loop, "You pick the department you want, and nine times out of 10, there's a match. If there's not, and you want to change, you can." Associates say that, "You get a great mixture of assignments." There's no formal assignment system. Instead, "Generally people just walk in and say, 'Got a second to talk?' and they sit down and tell you what they've got. If you're too busy, you say, 'I'm jammed,' and they'll let others know that it's hands off for a while, until your load lightens up." On top of that, "Your department head monitors your work flow. He knows if you're light or busy, and protects you if you're too busy."

Associates rave that "because of the way the cases are staffed, you get lots of responsibility." There is usually one partner and one associate on a project, "and that's it." The rule is that "You get brought in from the get-go on a case. By your third or fourth year, you get your own cases, it's your baby, sink or swim."

"Our lives don't consist of billable hours."

Associates say that, "When people get out of law school, they worry about how their life is going to consist of billable hours. Here, we work hard—we bill in the 1,700 to 1,900 hour range. But if you don't make the 1,800-hour target, you don't get heat for it. The partners are great about looking at a five-year range, not any particular year. There's no heat on hours."

The Shumaker, Loop offices "start to fill up around 8, and most people are in by 9 a.m." At night, "Most people are gone between 5:30 and 6:15 p.m.," but "If you're working on a deal or a trial, you'll work around the clock." On weekends, "You're not expected to be at work," although "for weekends, on average, associates will spend one or two Saturday mornings at the office in a month, between 10 a.m. and noon, at the office."

Associates don't mind the occasional long hours because "If you're working late or on weekends, the partner is there, too. You're not a slave so he can play golf. He's right there, working with you." On top of that, "We don't have a long commute to worry about. Everybody lives within 10 or

15 minutes of the office, and that gives you a lot more time of your own. You don't suck up hours and hours every week with a long commute." And on top of that, associates respect the fact that "We get paid top dollar for this part of the country, and the dollar goes a long way here. Most of us buy a home our first year with the firm."

Speaking of pay, associates say that the pay is pretty much lock-step, with "increases ranging from 4.5% to 6.5%." At the end of the year, there is a bonus based on firm productivity, and "everybody gets that, across the board," as long as the firm meets its budget. Associates say that "officially, billable hours have nothing to do with the increase you get. It's much more a matter of your progress as a lawyer, client development skills, your commitment to the firm." There's a bonus program that's "unofficial, in that if you bill over 2,000 hours you will be considered for a bonus, $3,000 to $6,000 or so." But "they don't make a huge deal about it because they want you to bill efficiently. That's more important than your strict billable hours, because nobody wants you to pad your hours just to get a bonus. You have to defend the hours you bill. They're very serious about the idea that if you can't justify the hours you bill, it's like stealing from the client."

Associates appreciate the fact that they know early on how they're progressing toward partnership. They say that, "After your third year, you know if you're going to make it. You get voted on every six months by the partners." Even though "It's a confidential vote, it's no secret that if you keep your nose clean and do good work, you'll be partner. Even without a client base, you'll get in. One of the best things about this firm is that the partnership potential is great." It doesn't hurt that the firm is "top-heavy," with many more partners than associates. Associates feel that not only does that increase their partnership potential—there's not an associate percentage to be weeded out—but it means that "partners bill time and collect money rather than just delegating work. They work *with* you."

Before they make partner, associates find that "the firm is great about clueing us in to what's going on." After every partnership meeting, twice a year, there is an associate meeting, where "they call us all in and tell us, in great detail, what was said at the partner meeting. And they have a person from the management committee and the professional development committee, the one that's in charge of associates, and the chief operations officer all talk to us." In general associates feel "*very* free to speak our minds. We're encouraged to speak up. The partners are very responsive," although if the issue is a big one, associate sometimes find that the response "can be a bit slow." A couple of years ago, associates wanted to revamp their pay scale, and the partnership responded by instituting big raises and percentage raises instead of dollar amounts, and introducing merit-based bonuses. "That took several months to accomplish, but to the partners' credit, they paid attention to what we wanted, and gave it to us."

Associates find that there is not much pressure on their non-billable time in the form of pro bono work. Associates say that, "Mostly litigation people do pro bono. Any that you do is at your own initiative." It's not considered a high profile item at the office, the attitude being that "Fine if you do it, fine if you don't."

The firm *does* encourage community activities. One popular one is a program called "Leadership Toledo." It consists of a series of monthly sessions for a year, and while the tuition is $2,000, "the firm pays for it." Associates explain that "Lots of banks, businesses, and other large institutions formed it to promote leadership. They do different presentations on things like charitable boards, the diversity of the community, touring historical sights. The idea is to create community leaders by getting you very familiar with every aspect of the city." In addition, the firm "passes around lists of boards that lawyers in the firm belong to, and you're encouraged to talk to them about it. They also encourage church involvement, those kinds of things," so the "visibility of the firm in the community is pretty high. We've got people doing lots of high visibility activities."

"We get together a lot outside of the office."

Associates say that "We socialize a lot together." There are summer events when the summer associates are around, including "the summer softball team. Either you're on the team, or you're invited to the games." One of the formal events the firm takes part in is unusual. "The Toledo Junior Bar Association, an under-40 crowd, has a satirical show every year. A partner from the firm directs it. It's gone on for 66 years. It makes fun of local politicians and judges." Associates say that, "It's a pretty elaborate show. They hire a professional band. The firm encourages us to take part in it, and usually five or six associates do. The rest of us are in the audience, which is pretty large—they normally draw a crowd of around 1,000 people."

Informally, "There's a crew that goes to Happy Hour on Fridays after work. Many people have parties all the time." In fact, "A lot of people *only* socialize with people from the firm. Some don't, but many do."

Associates say that when it comes to family-friendliness, "Many female lawyers have small children," and one commented that "I can only think offhand of one or two women here who *don't* have kids." The firm is very flexible with family obligations. "They don't care if you're in the office, as long as you get your work done. You are free to come and go as you please."

As one associate explains it, "The normal concerns that associates have, we don't have them. We don't live for billable hours. We get top-drawer pay and lots of responsibility. And we know that if we put in the time and do good work, we'll make partner. It's a good life."

Sidley & Austin

One First National Plaza • Chicago, Illinois 60603
Phone: 312-853-7000 • Fax: 312-853-7036
E-mail: info@sidley.com • Web site: sidley.com

OFFICES

Chicago, Illinois; Los Angeles, California; New York City, New York; Dallas, Texas; Washington, D.C.

"One standout quality of this firm is that you can enjoy life outside the office as an associate here . . . the partners will tell you that 'in order to be an effective lawyer, you've got to have a life away from work, as well,' and they mean it . . . I was so sure that when I joined a large firm, I'd sign away my life. That's not the case at all! I'm here at 7:30 in the morning, but that's because I'm an early riser. If you blew up the building then, I'm the only one you'd get!"

HIGHLIGHTS

- Largest law firm in Chicago, and 4TH largest in America.
- Some women have made partner while working part-time and raising children. Widely cited for being very flexible with part-time work for attorneys.
- Frequently recognized as one of the country's leading representatives of corporate and financial clients.
- Ranked 6TH nationwide in last year's *National Law Journal* survey of "Who Represents Corporate America," naming the outside law firms used most frequently by the nation's 250 largest industrial and service corporations.
- Recently cited as having the best web site among the nation's 250 largest law firms in a review by Red Street Consulting, a Boston-based Internet consulting and writing firm.
- The firm has a Public Interest Law Initiative program, in which new associates work on pro bono projects the summer they graduate while getting full pay from the firm.

NUTS AND BOLTS

Managing partner:

R. Eden Martin (Management Committee Chairman)

Hiring partner:

John G. Levi (Firmwide Chairman)
D. Cameron Findlay (Chicago Chairman)

Recruiting coordinator:

Claudia M. Reilly, phone: 312-853-7714, e-mail: creilly@sidley.com

Number of attorneys in firm:

889 (447 partners)

TOTAL FIRM:

Partners (447), associates (442), women partners (71), minority associates (82)

THIS OFFICE:

Total attorneys (438), partners (234), associates (204), women partners (34), minority associates (34)

OTHER OFFICES:

(* represents an office profiled elsewhere in this book)
Los Angeles (114); New York (114); Dallas (29); London (47); Singapore (5); Tokyo (1); Washington, D.C. (140); Hong Kong (1)

Years to make partner:

8 to 9

WHAT DO THEY DO?

Primary specialties (more than 5% of practice) in the Chicago office:

Commercial, Financing and Banking Transactions (33); Commodities and Financial Transactions and Litigation (19); Corporate and Securities (68); Corporate Reorganization and Bankruptcy (12); Employee Benefits (16); Employment and Labor Law (17); Environmental Law (17); Estate Planning, Trusts and Estates (15); Federal and State Taxation (19); Intellectual Property and Marketing (17); Litigation (149); Real Estate (31).

The Chicago office is divided into 19 practice groups. These groups change from time to time, depending on changes in the firm's practice, and a significant number of lawyers have also switched to different practice groups at different points in their careers.

In a few instances litigation associates have started at the firm without a group assignment, and moved into a group later on. Most lawyers spend a significant part of their time working with lawyers from practice groups other than their own.

WHO DO THEY REPRESENT?

Representative clients include the American Bar Association, American Medical Association, American Suzuki Motor, Aon Corporation, Armour Pharmaceuticals, Arthur Anderson LLP, AT&T, Bank of America, Baxter International, Borden, Canadian Pacific Limited, CITGO Petroleum Corporation, Citicorp, ComEd/Unicom, Commerce Clearing House, DEKALB Genetics, Deloitte & Touche LLP, First Data Corporation, First National Bank of Chicago, G. D. Searle & Co., General Electric, Household International, IMC Global, Kimberly-Clark, KPMG Peat Marwick LLP, Maytag, Merrill Lynch Pierce Fenner & Smith, NationsBank, Norfolk Southern, Northwestern, Premark International, R. R. Donnelley & Sons, Smith & Nephew plc, Starwood Lodging Trust, Stone Container, Telephone & Data Systems, Tribune Company, True North Communications, Union Carbide, United States Cellular, Whitman Corporation, Zenith Electronics.

WHERE NEW ASSOCIATES COME FROM . . .

The firm routinely interviews on campus at the following law schools: UC Berkeley, Chicago-Kent/IIT, Chicago, Columbia, DePaul, Duke, Georgetown, Harvard, Howard, Illinois, Indiana/Bloomington, Iowa, John Marshall, Loyola/Chicago, Michigan, Minnesota, NYU, Northwestern, Pennsylvania, Stanford, Vanderbilt, Virginia, Wisconsin, and Yale. The firm routinely hires from schools where it doesn't conduct on-campus interviews.

HOURS AND BUCKS . . .

First year associates average approximately 2,200 hours a year at the office, including training, pro bono, office administration, recruiting, and other non-billable work.

Associates average approximately 1,950 billable hours a year. Although there's technically no "minimum requirement," as a practical matter the firm expects associates' billable hours to be at least 1800 hours per year.

Part-time work is an optional component of the firm's parental leave policy; beyond that, part-time work is available on a case-by-case basis. Part-time work is available to new associates, including one associate who started this year. The firm generally does not hire contract associates.

Typical first year salary, including typical bonus: $$$$ (Over $65,000). The firm is known for its very generous financial package.

SUMMER PROGRAM . . .

Last year, there were 68 summer associates, 67 of whom received offers.
    Weekly pay: $1,400 last year
The firm does hire a few 1Ls for its summer program; they generally come from Chicago, Harvard, Northwestern, Michigan and Yale, sometimes from Duke, Stanford, and Illinois, and occasionally from other schools as well.

PRO BONO . . .

The firm has an extensive pro bono program. In most circumstances the firm expects associates' billable hours to be at least 1,800 per year excluding pro bono projects and other non-billable work. Beyond that, pro bono hours are treated the same as billable hours for purposes of bonus determinations and evaluations of associates' performance. Associates are encouraged to spend 50 hours a year on pro bono projects.

Most pro bono projects are based on individual attorneys' interests and concerns. It involves providing counseling to community organizations and not-for-profit corporations, death penalty appeals, ACLU cases, cases for Chicago Volunteer Legal Services, and cases for the Lawyers' Committee for Civil Rights Under The Law. The firm participates in programs sponsored by the U.S. Court of Appeals, the Illinois Appellate and Supreme Courts, and the Criminal and Juvenile Courts in Cook County. The firm also operates a neighborhood legal clinic in the Uptown neighborhood.

The firm also participates in the Public Interest Law Initiative program, which offers a Graduate Summer Fellowship program in Chicago, providing new lawyers with experience and training in legal institutions serving the public interest. As a participant in the program, the firm offers a few of its new associates (on a first-come, first-served basis) the opportunity to work at the participating public interest agency of their choice during the summer. Fellows work for 5 part-time weeks before the bar examination and 5 full-time weeks after the examination, and are paid a full-time salary for 12 weeks by the firm.

HISTORY AT A GLANCE . . .

The firm was founded in 1866.

WHAT IT'S LIKE TO WORK THERE . . .

When you look at a firm the size of Sidley & Austin, your first reaction is that it must be a horrible place to work. Aren't *all* large law firms miserable?

In the case of Sidley & Austin, the answer is a resounding "no." It's a "warm, caring" place with "fascinating work," in large-firm clothing. As one associate says, "It's easy for me to do recruiting stuff for the firm, to go and talk to law students, because there are nothing but good things to say about it." Another comments that "When I was looking for a firm to join, it was important to me to be at a place where you could have a life outside of work. Everything I heard about S&A said this was that kind of place, and since I've been here, I've seen for myself that everything I heard was true." Another adds that "It was obvious to me as a summer associate, talking with my friends at other firms and seeing how the junior associates here felt about the firm, that there was a marked difference between S&A and everybody else." The prevailing feeling is that "Not only is this firm professionally and financially rewarding, everybody here thinks it's important that we like each other, that we have a good time practicing law together, that by helping each other we all benefit in the long run, and that we can have lives outside the office. Well, most of the time, anyway!"

"They reward initiative—you get the work you want, with the people you want to work with."

Associates say that the firm is structured around narrowly-defined practice groups. For instance, in litigation, there is a complex and emergency litigation group, "general litigation" which is the largest litigation group, as well as products liability, patents and antitrust, and so on. "As a summer associate, at the end of the summer, they ask you for your preferences. It's not a draft, by any means. There's a committee on assignments. You tell them what you want, you give them your top three choices, and they try to match up everybody as best they can." Associates report that "Nobody doesn't get one of their top three choices, and it's rare to go lower than first or second. And once you're in your group, if you're not happy, you can switch." One associate tells a story of ranking labor as her first choice, general litigation second, and securities litigation third, coming out of the summer program. She got securities litigation. But a month before she came to the firm, a labor lawyer left, and the firm called her and said, "There's an opening in labor after all, and you should take it if you still want it." Associates feel that "It makes you really proud that the firm is more concerned about your own welfare than its convenience." One associate says that, "They really do look out for associates' happiness. If you wanted to look at it purely economically, you could, in that it wouldn't be in their best interest to have associates leave after two years because they were miserable."

The firm has an extensive training program, for both litigation and transactional associates. In litigation, most first year associates go to a 14-week litigation skills training program that starts in January of their first year with the firm. It consists of "weekly seminars, an hour and a half every Wednesday, where partners give you everything from preparing motions, to cross-examination, to direct examination, to appellate issues, everything." Then "in May they give you a trial practice exam, and in June, the program culminates with a mock trial." Associates find that "the program isn't burdensome in the first three months," but "preparing for the mock trial is more work." The firm considers the program "legal services to the firm. It's mandatory. And it's viewed as legitimate work. You can do it during the day, at the office." For transactional associates, there's the "Corporate College," which is intensive training along the same lines but with a corporate focus.

In each practice group, "There is a supervising partner, and they tend to be very protective of their associates." One associate says that "The head of my group is an incredible person, really a father figure. A lot of them are like that." In addition to practice group heads, each associate has a "Non-work assignment mentor, for any questions and issues that you have."

While associates' assignments technically come from their practice group, they say that, "The practice groups are very loosely structured. It's easy to get work outside of your group. No one looks cross-eyed at you if you go for a project in another specialty." Associates say that "You can go to people you want to work with, and ask for work. They reward initiative. It's easy to keep your plate full with work from people you know and like. There are always going to be people you like less, but everybody here *does* get work they like." Other associates comment that "There are a few difficult people here. That's going to be true anywhere you've got this many people. But there are so many different kinds of people, and most of them are so pleasant to work with, that you overlook the ones you aren't so fond of."

Associates rave about the fact that "There's a basic respect for associates here. You never feel like anyone *gives* you things—people *ask* you if you can work on something for them. That's a big difference, at least in the way you feel about what you do. I have a friend who works at another, huge firm, who makes more money than I do, but earns every lousy penny of it. He'll have partners drop stuff on his desk Friday afternoon, and just say 'Do this by Monday,' and walk out. That would never happen here." Associates say that "Sometimes partners will come in and say to you, 'Do you have any time?' and at first, you're nervous to say 'no.' But I've never had a negative reaction to turning down work. No one gives you grief. They treat you like a professional." One associate recounts that "If you're busy on another case, partners help you. I actually had a partner offer to do research on a motion, and said to me 'come help out when you can.'"

Associates say that the feedback they get "varies from project to project." It can be everything "from hearing 'Good job,' the very basics," to "what happens more of the time, which is to go back and forth, with reviews of different drafts of things you write. Some partners give you ideas for other arguments to make, they're very conceptual. They'll tell you what you need to do to form better arguments." One associate observes that "They don't go through your stuff line by line, but you're never left hanging on how people feel about your work, either. You always know where you stand."

When it comes to the work they get to do, S&A associates feel that "We do the most interesting, sophisticated work in the country." They frequently find themselves "dealing directly in litigation and transactions with much more senior lawyers from other major law firms, as co-counsel or opposing counsel." Associates find that they "get cases that are just you and a partner—you can get in at the beginning, and be in on them going forward." They say that if you want more responsibility, "if you decide you want to do depositions, you ask the head of your group, and other partners, and you'll get the work. You'll get to watch depositions being taken and defended, and then you'll get to take part. There's no question that you can get the exposure you want here. Where you want involvement in the bigger picture, you get it."

Associates say that "You only get a tiny piece of a big case for either an emergency, or for things you don't like too much so you don't *want* to be heavily involved in them," or "if you are part of a practice group that only has enormous cases, like antitrust. Junior associates just can't have a substantive role in that kind of work, but it's not because the firm doesn't want you to have it—it's inherent in those kinds of cases." Even when associates do have to do document reviews, "You don't get much. You can usually go to your supervisor and see if that kind of work can be spread around, so everybody does a bit of it. With so many people, there are always ways to make the workload even," but "the fact is that document reviews happen." One associate notes that "I had to spend two months at a client's place once, on an antitrust case. *Somebody's* got to do them. But it doesn't happen on a routine basis that you'll get document reviews. It balances out. They make an effort to make sure that it balances out for you, because they know it's an issue. If you're unhappy, you let them know, and they do something about it." One associate laughingly says that "Hard as it is to believe, some people actually *like* doing document productions, although most of us would consider that kind of person—you know—a freak." But on a more serious note, "They won't change anything without you asking, and it's not like you have to make a formal complaint to get more of the work you want. You just ask for it."

"The 'Care & Feeding of Associates' Committee makes sure your plate is balanced."

Associates say that partners are "incredibly responsive" to associate issues. One of the principal means of accomplishing this is the "Committee on Assignments and Compensation for Associates," which S&A lawyers affectionately call the "Care and Feeding" Committee. As one associate tells it, "whenever there's an issue with pay or hours, the Care &

Feeding Committee is right there. One of the other big firms in Chicago bumped associate starting salaries by a few thousand dollars, and as soon as the Care & Feeding Committee found out about it, they took steps the next day to make sure we got a raise, as well."

There are also "a bunch of other committees, a management committee for the big decisions, an executive committee, those kinds of things." The feeling among associates that an important conduit to firm management is "The senior associate liaison in each group, between associates and partners. If you've got something you want to suggest but you don't want to attach your name to it, you just tell the senior associate liaison, and that person will present your concerns to the partners anonymously."

"The firm is incredibly successful at retaining and promoting women."

One of the most visible ways that the firm has responded to the needs of the associates is through its extraordinary, and widely-publicized, family-friendly policies. The *Illinois Legal Times* wrote an article about S&A's "success in retaining and promoting women," and said that "Part of the reason stems from the firm's flexible policy regarding part-time work. While the need to take care of elderly parents is one reason some lawyers go part time, the option is mainly chosen by women at the firm who are parents and want to play more of a role in child-rearing. Associates or partners giving birth or adopting a child may take up to three months of short-term disability, followed by an optional four months of unpaid time off. After that leave of absence, the lawyer is offered up to five months of part-time work. After that five months, the lawyer either returns to work full-time, or a flex-time schedule is negotiated on an individual basis." The article cited the fact that "since the executive committee implemented the part-time policy" about 12 years ago, "dozens of lawyers have taken advantage of it," and "one woman has even made partner working part-time."

The firm's former chairman, Robert D. McLean, was quoted in the article as saying that, "Truly talented lawyers are very rare. It's in the firm's best interest to keep such lawyers by offering options that satisfy their dual obligations to their families and their professions." One associate told the *Times* that "The attitudes of everyone at the firm foster the growth of women lawyers. It's important that when people at the office see someone's light off three days in a row, they don't say, 'Oh, she's off with her kids.' That's damaging. I don't see it happening here. It's hard for people to make cutting remarks when someone can reply, 'Wait a second, what are you talking about? She's home working, reviewing some material for me. I know because I'm going to talk to her later and she's going to give me her comments."

"I get here at 7:30 in the morning, but if you blew up the building then, I'm the only one you'd get."

When you ask S&A about the hours they work, you'll hear that "One standout quality of this firm is that you can enjoy life outside the office as an associate here." One associate said that, "I was so sure that when I joined a large firm, I'd sign away my life. That's not the case at all!" Associates say that hours typically run about 160 to 190 billables a month, with a couple of "200-hour months thrown in here and there," because "When you're a lawyer, particularly if you're a litigator, your schedule is not your own. Courts, and other parties, impose limits on you whenever they can, and that means you can't always control your schedule as you'd like to."

Associates hasten to point out that "When you count your hours at the office, that time includes the 'important box'—billables, pro bono, legal services to the firm like recruiting and writing articles." They say that "If you've got 160 or 170 hours in a month, nobody is going to question you about your hours. That's a 10-hour day at the office, maybe a day or two on the weekend per month," but generally "It's empty on weekends" and "there are months and months where you won't be in the weekends at all." One associate characterizes the hours he works by saying that "The best way I can say it is that work fills my days, not my nights and weekends." Another adds that "My wife goes with me on recruiting dinners, and she loves that, because she can honestly rave about the hours. It's a rare night when we don't eat dinner together, a rare weekend when we break plans because of my work." Another associate adds that, "When we work relatively long hours it's either because we want to, or because client needs require it. It's not because of any institutionally-imposed pressure for more billable hours."

One associate shares a telling story: "One partner taught me an important lesson about hours. He told me about a client who works typical New York lawyer hours, on a regular basis. This client left a Saturday afternoon message for the partner, nothing urgent, and when I asked the partner why he didn't call back that same day, the partner smiled and said 'he knew he wouldn't see me here.' He added, 'The longer you're here, it'll roll off your back.' What he meant was, if it's an emergency, when the work demands it, of course you do whatever the client needs, because the clients are the whole reason we're here. But on a regular basis, no, you're not going to return routine business calls on Saturday afternoons. The partners impart the philosophy that to be an effective lawyer, you have to have a life outside the office." The partners back up that philosophy by being willing to pitch in when associates need it. One associate had plans with his wife for their anniversary dinner, and he said, "I turned down writing a motion because of that. My reviews didn't even mention it. They tell you, 'This is a big firm—there are other places for work to flow.' And they mean it."

Associates get reviews twice a year, with "The fall review being geared to compensation and bonus. That's your chance to voice concerns. Someone from Care & Feeding visits you first, so you have a chance to talk about any problems, any frame of reference for your review."

When it comes to salary, associates are paid "in lock-step for your first three raises, which covers your first four years with the firm." There's a "small bonus for billing over 2,100 hours," but "there are other, non-bill-able-hour ways to get bonuses," to recognize special contributions to the firm. Associates say that these bonuses "aren't really something you expect. You do things for the firm out of loyalty. But it's nice that they recognize your efforts."

Business generation at the firm "isn't an issue for junior associates, there's no training in it." Associates feel that it's "more of an issue on the transactional side, but even then, not for junior associates." For litigation, "it's institutional, big clients like AT&T, and you can't go after that kind of thing as a junior associate," and that "for some of the partners it's not even that big a thing. There are a good number of partners who don't bring in business at all. So as an associate you certainly don't feel any pressure that way."

"There are all kinds of social activities here."

As you'd expect from one of the country's largest law firms, S&A has a healthy number of firm-sponsored social events. There's an annual holiday party for all office personnel in Chicago every December. The firm frequently has a picnic for all lawyers, staff and their families in July, a lawyer's sports outing in late summer, and a formal dinner dance sometime during the year. The Firm Functions Committee arranges other social and cultural functions for smaller groups throughout the year, and predictably, "Many of the lawyers participate in the events that go along with the summer program, and there are a lot of those."

Sportswise, "The Chicago office fields teams in the Chicago Bar Association leagues for football"—the S&A team has been in seven championship games and won four championships in the last eight years—"softball, basketball, and volleyball," and it also frequently sponsors teams in various "corporate challenge" races. Those teams all consist of partners, associates and staff. As well, a fair number of attorneys participate together in other sports, particularly golf and tennis, on a more informal basis.

"They mean it when they say they care."

One associate sums up the humane nature of S&A with this story: "I was working on a brief, and I had a deadline breathing down my neck—we had to get something out FedEx, that night, by 7:45 p.m. My wife called at 4:30, saying that her car had broken down in a bad neighborhood. She had called a tow truck, but I was nervous anyway. I wanted to go and wait with her. The senior associate I was working for said, 'print off the relevant cases, and go.' Anybody here could tell you stories like that. The firm knows that some things are more important than work, and they mean it when they say they care."

Snell & Wilmer L.L.P.

One Arizona Center • Phoenix, Arizona 85004-0001
Phone: 602-382-6000 • Fax: 602-382-6070 • Web site: swlaw.com

OFFICES

Phoenix (main office), Tucson, Arizona; Irvine, California; Salt Lake City, Utah

"A partner and several associates were recently working on a high-profile case for the Fiesta Bowl. It got a lot of media coverage, and in one newspaper article, the partner's appearance in court was likened to Douglas Neidermeyer, the ROTC guy in the movie 'Animal House.' One of the third year associates saw the article, and immediately sent the Neidermeyer comment on e-mail to everybody at the firm . . . There's a lot of kidding between partners and associates here. There is easy interaction. Very few people take themselves seriously—the rest of us wouldn't let them get away with it."

HIGHLIGHTS

• Ranked #1 law firm in a recent *Arizona Business Magazine* opinion survey of the state's 15 largest publicly-held corporations.

NUTS AND BOLTS

Managing partner:
John J. Bouma, Chairman

Hiring partner:

> Joel P. Hoxie, phone: 602-382-6264, e-mail: hoxiej@swlaw.com

Recruiting coordinator:

> Bonnie J. Lang, Director of Attorney Recruitment & Development,
> phone: 602-382-6014, e-mail: langb@swlaw.com

Number of attorneys in firm:

> 273 (135 partners)

TOTAL FIRM:

> Partners (135), associates (138), women partners (20), minority partners
> (6)

THIS OFFICE:

> Total attorneys (177), partners (87), associates (90), women partners (14),
> minority partners (4)

OTHER OFFICES:

> (* represents an office profiled elsewhere in this book)
> Tucson, AZ (29); Irvine, CA (39); Salt Lake City, UT (28)

Years to make partner:

> Associates are first considered for partner at 6 $^1/_2$ years of practice. The
> firm does not have an "up-or-out" policy, and discusses an associate's
> partnership opportunities during the associate's annual evaluations.

WHAT DO THEY DO?

Primary specialties (more than 5% of practice):

> Commercial Litigation (41), Business & Finance (38), Product Liability
> Litigation (34), Real Estate & Commercial Finance (26), Employment and
> Labor Law (22), Tax, ERISA and Estate Planning (22), Bankruptcy (18),
> Environmental (14), Intellectual Property (13).
>
> The firm is departmentalized. Permanent associates are typically
> hired into a particular department. Junior associates can, and do, switch
> specialties.

WHO DO THEY REPRESENT?

> The firm has more than 10,000 clients, ranging from large, publicly-traded
> corporations to emerging enterprises to individuals. The firm's largest
> clients include Arizona Public Service Company, Tucson Airport Authority,

Bank One Arizona, Honeywell, Del Webb, Intel, General Motors, Toyota Motor, Ford Motor, Mercury Marine, and Household International.

WHERE NEW ASSOCIATES COME FROM . . .

The firm routinely interviews on campus at the following law schools: Arizona State, Arizona, BYU, Utah, Iowa, Kansas, Michigan, Northwestern, Notre Dame, Georgetown, Duke, Vanderbilt, UCLA, UC Davis, Hastings, Loyola/LA, and Stanford. The firm routinely hires associates and summer associates from schools where it doesn't interview on campus.

HOURS AND BUCKS . . .

On average, first year associates spend 1,900 hours in the office. The firm does not have a minimum billable-hours requirement.

Part-time work is available to ongoing associates, not entry-level ones. The firm does not routinely hire contract associates.

Typical first year salary in this office: The firm's starting salary is competitive with firms in each of the markets where it has offices.

SUMMER PROGRAM . . .

Last year, there were 28 summer associates, 27 of whom received offers. Weekly pay: Between $1,100 and $1,650 depending on the city.

1Ls are hired from time to time and in different offices. Last year, the only 1L in the summer program was in the Tucson office. That 1L was from the University of Arizona.

There is no set deadline for the summer program, although 2Ls are typically hired in the fall prior to the summer program, and 1Ls are typically hired in the spring semester.

PRO BONO . . .

The firm strongly encourages all of its attorneys to dedicate 50 hours per year to pro bono matters. Pro bono hours are considered billables. Associates develop a variety of community-wide projects, including offering assistance to homeless people, those with AIDS, and victims of domestic violence. Firm-wide pro bono projects include the Volunteer Lawyer Program, the Community Housing Partnership, the Arizona Senior Citizen Law Project, the VLP Tenant's Rights Clinic, the HIV Legal Support Clinic, the Juvenile Justice Project, the ASU Homeless Legal Assistance Program, and the representation of an individual currently on death row.

Consistently year after year, the firm, as well as individual attorneys, is recognized for its pro bono activities at the local, state and national levels. A sampling of those awards are: Maricopa County Volunteer Lawyers Program Award, American Bar Association National Public Service Award, State Bar of California President's Pro Bono Service Award, The Public Law Center of Orange County Firm of the Year Award, and Pima County Bar Association Outstanding Pro Bono Firm of the Year Award.

HISTORY AT A GLANCE . . .

The firm was founded in 1938, when Frank Snell, a corporate lawyer with a thriving practice (he had handled the merger of Safeway Stores and a prominent Arizona grocery store chain called Pay 'N' Take It), joined forces with the man local judges had told him was "the best trial lawyer in Phoenix," Mark Wilmer.

The firm opened its Tucson office in October 1988, the Irvine, California office in 1989, and Salt Lake City in 1991.

WHAT IT'S LIKE TO WORK THERE . . .

There are a lot of ways to determine whether associates at a law firm are happy. One is to look at the complaints they have. At really hideous places to work, the beefs are huge—slave-driving hours, abusive partners, tedious, Sisyphian projects, a permanent space in an airless library complete with shackles at every cubicle. Do you know what associates complain about at Snell & Wilmer? Parking, and casual day.

Yes. Parking. And casual day.

As one associate explains it, "Every year, the associates meet with senior management in a gripe session. People are *very* blunt. The big issue now is casual day—we don't have casual Fridays, even though it seems as though every other law firm in the Universe *does*." The other gripe is that "A smaller firm in our same building pays for parking, and here, the associates still pay for it themselves."

The associate pauses for a minute, and says, "Of course, two years ago, the gripe was a high medical co-payment, and the partners were very responsive to that. They slashed what associates had to pay. They listened." The associate pauses again, and after thinking about the impact of his words, says, "Hmm. Parking is the downside of working here." Laughing, he adds, "*That* is really not a big deal!"

And that says a lot about how much there is to *like* about Snell & Wilmer.

Some associates talk about the fact that "There is a lot of laughter in the halls," and others cite the firm's "Open door attitude. You can always walk down the hall and get advice." Others rave about the way the firm gives them "the flexibility to create your own style, in every way. Client development, community involvement, you do what's most comfortable for you." One associate talks about "playing in a band on weekends, in local coffeehouses," and says that "The firm not only allows me to maintain my individuality, but insists on it." And still others talk about the partners' ability to laugh at themselves. "A partner and several associates were recently working on a high-profile case for the Fiesta Bowl. It got a lot of media coverage, and in one newspaper article, the partner's appearance in court was likened to Douglas Neidermeyer, the ROTC guy in the movie *Animal House*. One of the third year associates saw the article, and immediately sent the Neidermeyer comment on e-mail to everybody at the firm." As that story suggests, "There's a lot of kidding between partners and associates here. There is easy interaction. Very few people take themselves seriously—the rest of us wouldn't let them get away with it." This is reflected in the firm's annual retreat, where "the firm features videos and skits from associates and/or offices. These skits and videos parody the firm and various attorneys. The most recent video was titled 'Phoenix Pulp Fiction.'"

"This place has an unusually good method for managing work flow."

There are a couple of different means of joining departments at Snell & Wilmer. "Some groups go and try to recruit from the summer associate pool, like bankruptcy—they're expanding rapidly, and they go after summer associates." For other groups, "You're hired into a particular department." If you go into litigation, rather than joining a particular practice group, "you are in a pool for a year before you commit, sometimes a few months more or less." During that time, "There are three assigning attorneys and senior associates. Work flows through them." Associates like this approach because there is "no 'sheer terror' of working for one partner who burns out associates. As with every large firm, there are some partners who are more difficult to work for than others, and the pool concept has people keeping an eye on you so that you don't work for a more difficult partner exclusively. They do a great job of balancing your projects," and they also "keep tabs on your hours so that you're not billing a million hours!" The firm also keeps hours down with its "partner/mentor program. There's somebody who's always watching your hours, making sure you don't burn out." Associates tell of one associate who "put in too much time, and after three months of that they were told to slow down."

The training associates get varies by department, although they uniformly say that "The best training you can get is from having partners with open doors, who are willing to answer your questions, and we have that." Associates find that the firm is both "strong and efficient" with training. In litigation, the in-house training program is "pretty good," and goes on for the first six months associates are with the firm. After that, "it's just too tough to give in-house training that takes into account everybody's different levels of experience. There's no point in you spending time at a seminar on discovery if you've already done it." Instead, the firm encourages junior associates to go to "CLEs to help you progress in your field." That way "you can tailor your training to what you're doing. The projects people work on here are just too diverse to do very much in-house." On the transactional side, "There's more hands-on experience early on," although there are still some CLEs that transactional associates go to. Transactional associates say that "The frustrating thing about law school is that you have no idea of what it is to be a transactional lawyer. It's doing deals. The firm gives us an excellent opportunity to actually *do* deals, and that's the best way to learn about them."

Associates rave about the fact that the firm "gives you big firm experience, in the sense of outstanding, big clients who use us for national work, not just local representation, without the downsides of traditional large firms." They say that, "we get early responsibility in major cases and transactions." One associate comments that "Everybody says the thing they like most about where they work is 'the people,' and even though the people are great here, for me the work is what comes first to my mind: the type and quality of work, the size, its high profile and the fact that what we get to do is important, not redundant. You get into client meetings right from the start. You're not working on some discrete issue."

Associates appreciate the firm's "interesting management philosophy, which is structured and not structured at the same time." There are no "weekly memos saying 'Here's new policy X.' In fact, there are very few paper policies at all." The firm is "very destructured, so that groups manage their own practice, and so do individual lawyers, with great support. The staff is excellent, and there's full technology support, with Internet access as well as a firm intranet. But still, there's just not a lot of structure, and that gives us all great flexibility."

"The firm is family-friendly in the most important ways."

Associates say that the firm is very "family-friendly," and while many applaud "the corner office partner who gets into a Santa suit at Christmas, and does the 'Santa thing' for all of the attorneys' and staffs' kids," others say, "You know what makes this firm truly family-friendly? The fact that they encourage you to work from home if you have to. They've made this tremendous investment in technology, so we can dial-up the office from home, and work from there if we want. The best way for a firm to be family-friendly is to let that family see your face, and this firm does that."

This flexibility and "no face-time" policy goes a long way toward making up for the "lack of an official part-time program, although there are women who work reduced hours." As one associate says, "Many people work an hour or two after the kids go to sleep, just by logging onto their computers from home." The general sense is that "the partners' philosophy is that even they themselves may be very busy, but they'll be gone in the afternoon because their kid is the tooth in the school play." Associates say that, "If you get the work done, you can get out of here at noon if you want. You can come in at 11, to spend time with your kids if that's what you want. There's never a thought of 'leave your light on when you leave.' Nobody has to play those kinds of games here."

Typically, associates say that the offices fill up around 8:30 in the morning, and most people are gone by 6 p.m., with those hours being aided by the ability to work from home. When it comes to weekends, "You don't do it if you can avoid it. And most people who work on weekends do it from home." At the office, associates estimate that on any given weekend "There'll be 10 or 20% of the lawyers in the office, sometimes for a half day on Saturday. It's not empty on weekends, but there's no 'face time' either." When long hours are required, it's a matter of "trials or deals with deadlines," and associates recognize that "business is cyclical. Sometimes you'll be very busy, and sometimes you won't. And other things impact your hours as well, for instance when a group is understaffed."

Associates say that although the firm doesn't have a minimum billable hours requirement, "There's pressure to bill hours, and you expect that. It's not a charity." As a first year, "the goal is 1,850, although that's just a strong suggestion, not a mandate. There's no '1850-or-you're-out' mentality, not by any stretch." Associates say that "the partners recognize that you could be stuck in a significant pro bono case, and since those are only billable to 50 hours a year, you could be doing some work that the firm considers really valuable, you just can't bill it. They understand that." And sometimes "You'll be in a group that will be slow business-wise compared to other groups, and you won't make billables." All in all "You're evaluated as a first year associate at six months and at the one year point, and the partners recognize at both of those points that it's not your fault if you didn't meet the hours goal."

After the first year, "The billable goal seems to get more group-specific. You're looking more at 2,000 billables as a goal, 1,950 if you don't count pro bono," although associates say that "the 2,000 hour goal is one that few junior associates actually meet, and it's not something we get hammered about."

Associates say that when they do have to put in long hours, they don't mind because "The work we get to do is often more than interesting—it's ground-breaking." Also, "partners and senior associates are there working with you. You're not alone. It's not like you're there, by yourself, doing some massive document production. They mix it up." In fact, the firm takes active steps to *avoid* burdening junior associates with major document production projects, even though "complex litigation *does* get massive document stuff. What they do is to have document clerks and paralegals pick up that kind of work, so it doesn't bog down the associates."

When it comes to compensation, associates rave that "The firm is very conscious of paying what they have to pay to get what they consider great associates. They're up-to-the-minute with pay issues." When it comes to determining raises, associates say that, "the firm has an interesting solution to the potential in-fighting problem of not paying associates on a lock-step basis. You get your first bonus at the end of three months here, and that's pretty nominal. At the end of one full year with the firm, you get a *real* bonus. After that, *nobody* talks about pay!" Bonuses are determined by a compensation committee with input from the partners, and the bonuses reflect "a combination of community participation, billables, quality of work, write-off rate, just about everything that goes into making you the lawyer they want you to be." There is a sense among associates that "the firm is moving toward focusing more on business generation," but that doesn't figure into the mix for junior associates. Associates say that "As a first year, you won't bring in business, and they don't expect you to." They do mention that "the firm has skyboxes at the Cardinals, Suns, and Diamondback facilities, and encourages us to use them. It's a great training ground for honing business development skills—that is, entertaining clients!"

The associates all agree that "community participation is definitely encouraged." They rave that "The firm has a really high profile in the community. It gives you instant credibility. There's no question that the firm leads the pack with community involvement." Some comment that "The firm has a master list of what people from the firm do in the community, professional organizations and everything. The senior people will help junior people get in on what they want. The feeling is that lawyers shouldn't just be lawyers." There's a feeling that "all you have to do is say, 'Hey, I want to get involved with the Phoenix Symphony,' and they'll get you into it." One associate adds that "It doesn't matter what your community interest is, the firm will be supportive of your involvement. The firm philosophy is that community involvement makes the attorneys more well-rounded, more satisfied, and more interesting to work with."

As associates progress toward partnership, there's a sense that "If you're working well, you get in. In some groups, there are more partners than associates, and you'd think there'd be a concern about whether there's room for *more* partners. But we don't have any leverage ratio concerns. If you're bringing in business when it's time for them to consider you for partnership, you're making it easier for them to vote you in. But by that time they've been coaching you for years on the kinds of community involvement that generate business." As one associate says, "The big difference between working here in Phoenix instead of LA or New York isn't something that's going to change your life in a lot of ways. Yes, you'll get the same quality work and the same great clients while working fewer hours, but you haven't hit the jackpot. The major thing to focus on is that here, most associates make partner—and that's a *big* difference."

"The firm is very big on pro bono."

One associate marvels that "The local bar used to give the firm awards for its pro bono work, but after a while, they stopped. The firm does so much pro bono work all the time that there wasn't any point in continuing to hand out the awards!" Associates get 50 hours per year billable credit for their pro bono work, "but unofficially you can probably get more." Associates report that "the firm is really serious about getting you pro bono work that's different from what you do at the office. For instance you'll have a utility lawyer do domestic violence work pro bono. Well, that's not going to help that person's practice at all, because we don't do domestic work. But they encourage it anyway." The firm's flexibility on billable hours is at least in part a reflection of its dedication to pro bono work, because associates who work on big, time-consuming pro bono cases are "encouraged to do that, and not to worry about billables."

One associate talks about his pro bono work involving domestic disputes, talking about "one case where a young woman was referred to me in what was becoming a very dangerous situation. Her estranged husband had kidnapped her children. This woman spoke little English and knew nothing about her rights. In a struggle that lasted for nine months, I found the children, forced the husband to release them, and won full custody for the mother." As the associate says, "My pro bono work is a way of balancing the intellectual challenge of my practice with the basic human desire that I think everybody has—to help people in need. The impact my work has on the lives of my clients is no match for the impact it has on mine."

Steptoe & Johnson

Bank One Center • P. O. Box 2190 • Clarksburg, WV 26302-2190
Phone: 304-624-8000 • Fax: 304-624-8183 • Web site: steptoelaw.com

OFFICES

Clarksburg, Charleston, Morgantown, Martinsburg, Wheeling, Parkersburg, West Virginia

*"General firm philosophies trickle down to us from senior partners, but the way those philosophies get molded is in junior partners' and associates' hands. They don't say 'We're doing this. Do it!' They say, 'This is what we want to do. How can you contribute?' They make you feel important. They **want** to talk about firm life. They'll say, 'We're glad you're here. You're the future of the firm. Take pride in what you're doing.' They treat you as though you'll be around for a while."*

NUTS AND BOLTS

Managing partner:

Robert M. Steptoe, Jr. (Bob), phone: 304-624-8142,
e-mail: steptoerm@steptoe-johnson.com

Hiring partner:

W. Henry Lawrence, IV (Hank), phone: 304-624-8186,
e-mail: lawrenwh@steptoe-johnson.com

Recruiting coordinator:

Carey Swiger, phone: 304-624-8351,
e-mail: SwigerCW@Steptoe-Johnson.com

Number of attorneys in firm:

113 (55 partners)

TOTAL FIRM:

Partners (55), associates (58)

THIS OFFICE:

Total attorneys (47), partners (26), associates (21)

OTHER OFFICES:

(* represents an office profiled elsewhere in this book)
Charleston, WV (35); Morgantown, WV (14); Martinsburg, WV (8);
Wheeling, WV (5); Parkersburg, WV (4)

Years to make partner:

6 1/2 years for first consideration.

WHAT DO THEY DO?

Primary specialties (more than 5% of practice) for total firm:

Business (44); Labor & Employment (23); Litigation (46).
    The firm is departmentalized, and junior associates can—and do—
switch specialties.

WHO DO THEY REPRESENT?

Banking, manufacturing, extraction, publishing, health care, resort, and
government entities throughout West Virginia.

WHERE NEW ASSOCIATES COME FROM . . .

The firm routinely interviews on campus at the following law schools:
West Virginia, William & Mary, Washington & Lee, Richmond, Kentucky,
and Virginia. The firm also hires associates and summer associates from
schools where it doesn't conduct on-campus interviews.

HOURS AND BUCKS . . .

On average, first year associates spend 2,100 hours at the office, of which
1,800 hours are the minimum billable requirement.
    Part-time work is available to both continuing and entry-level associates.
    The firm routinely hires contract associates, some of whom have
become full-time associates.

Typical first year salary, including typical bonus: $$ ($35-50,000)

SUMMER PROGRAM . . .

Last year, there were 17 summer associates (six 2Ls and 11 1Ls); offers were made to 13 of them.

Weekly pay last year: $667 for 2Ls, $555 for 1Ls.

1Ls are routinely hired for the summer program; last year's 1Ls came from West Virginia University, William & Mary, Widener, and Maryland.

PRO BONO . . .

Associates are encouraged to become involved in the community in many ways, and pro bono work is one forum for meeting the firm's expectation on community activity. The firm doesn't have guidelines on how many hours associates should dedicate to pro bono work, but rather evaluates projects on an ad hoc basis. Pro bono hours are not counted as billable hours.

Some of the pro bono projects associates have been involved in include the West Virginia State Bar Pro Bono Referral Project; legal work for non-profit corporations, United Way Agencies, and humane societies.

HISTORY AT A GLANCE . . .

The firm was founded in Clarksburg, West Virginia in 1913, by Philip Steptoe and Louis Johnson. The firm grew and opened new offices over the ensuing decades. In 1980, the firm divided into two separate law firms, in West Virginia and Washington, D.C., each continuing its practice under the name Steptoe & Johnson.

In 1990, the firm merged its practice with Avey & Steptoe of Martinsburg, and in 1995, it merged with Ruley & Everett of Parkersburg, expanding the firm's practice to the western part of the state.

Over the years, the firm has had a number of well-known lawyers, including co-founder Louis A. Johnson, Secretary of Defense under President Truman. Among current lawyers, Robert Steptoe, Jr., Patrick Deem, and Herbert Underwood are listed in *Best Lawyers in America.*

WHAT IT'S LIKE TO WORK THERE . . .

When you're talking about Steptoe & Johnson, the most important thing to get out of the way right from the start is that this probably isn't the Steptoe & Johnson you think you've heard of, the one in Washington, D.C. They *were* the same firm until 1980, but then they split into two totally different firms. And the Steptoe & Johnson we're talking about here is the one in West Virginia. As one associate laughingly says, "I do a lot of law school interviewing, and a red flag comes up whenever a student says, 'I realize you have an office in Washington.'" Others add that, "It was just a matter of time before word got out that there's a well-kept secret in West Virginia, and it's this firm."

"It's an incredibly closely-knit office."

New associates join the firm in one of its three departments— Litigation, Labor & Employment, or Business. Associates coming out of the firm's summer program "have had a really good exposure to everything. You express an interest in a department, and you'll generally mesh with a partner there." Typically, new associates "Stay in one department, and see one or two practice areas and choose one of those," but "You *can* see more if you want, before you settle into a practice group." One associate recounts that "I got a chance to see all different things when I came in." Each practice group has "between four and 10 lawyers, with a partner as a chair of the group."

Each associate has a mentor in his or her practice group, and "Normally your mentor funnels you much of your work," but "you *can* get calls from other lawyers in the department, they can all give you assignments." Associates feel that "We're such a close-knit office, other lawyers just call you and ask if you have the time to help them. It's not very formal, and it doesn't have to be." However, associates find themselves "specializing kind of naturally. Once you're working in an area, and the practice group head likes you, you can't help but get streamlined in. It just happens."

When it comes to soliciting projects, associates say that, "it pays to make a conscious effort to seek out the work you want." One associate says that, "If you hear of interesting work, you can offer to help the partner in charge." This even applies to items in the news, which haven't even generated lawsuits yet. As one associate tells it, "West Virginia football is one rung below God in importance in this state! Miami beat WVU a couple of years ago, in the last second. A riot broke out, and a fan threw a garbage can on a Miami coach on the way out. I heard about that in the news, and I went to talk to the head of the litigation department, and said, 'If we get that case, I'd like to work on it.' He said, 'Sure.' There's a very open door policy that way."

Associates rave about the quality of work they get. One junior associate says that, "My very first project was an expert witness issue involving Evidence Rule 702. I got to go to trial two days later and hear the motion argued." Another says that "I've taken countless depositions, done minor trials, I have bigger ones on the horizon, and obviously they might settle, but if they don't, I'm looking forward to that experience as well." Associates say that "You name it, I've gotten to do it. There's lots of client contact," and "You get great experience as a junior associate. As soon as you show the wherewithal to stand on your own, they turn you loose."

As that suggests, S&J associates say that "Much of the training here is 'hands on'—it's the pioneer method. You learn by doing." That's not to say, however, that associates feel as though they're pushed out of the nest; they uniformly applaud the support they get. "Normally you go to your mentor first with any questions, but you can go to just about anybody here and ask questions. I've never experienced *anybody* who had anything but time to talk, and if they're swamped, they'll say, 'Come back at six so we can talk.'" One associate adds that "Time flies by, but they make the time to explain things—they'll stay at the office after they're finished with their own work to help you out, if that's what you need."

Associates say that they also get valuable advice through "Friday morning formal meetings, which are a tradition here. People sit around and talk about what they're doing. Others will toss out advice. You say, 'I've got a case in this county,' and someone will say, 'Don't even be one minute late, or the judge will fine you.'" And the firm's new computer network, with internal and external e-mail, "has revolutionized communication in the firm. You'll send something out, like 'Has anyone ever dealt with this expert? Should we use him?' and you'll get 20 e-mails back, 'He's crazy' or 'He's great' or 'He's this or that.'"

Feedback is a strong point at the firm. Associates say that, "They will almost always sit down and talk strategy with you, they tell you why you're doing what you're doing." And associates find that when they draft a document, "like a motion for summary judgment or a support memo, it comes back marked up, then they'll tell you why they made the changes." Overall, "It's really good feedback."

On a broader basis, associates find that the firm helps along their professional progress by way of "associate planning forms," which each lawyer has to fill out every January. "That form forces you to identify your strengths and weakness, and steps you'll take to improve your weaknesses." Most associates view it as "valuable, introspective time. It forces you to recognize trends, and what you need to improve. It's a useful tool." One associate adds that "The following year, they'll ask you, 'For your weaknesses last year, what did you do to improve them?'" The associate laughs that "They're not going to be happy if your answer is, 'I said 10 Hail Marys'!"

"They treat you as though you're going to be around for a while."

Associates say that, "If you want to get involved in marketing the firm, there are plenty of opportunities. The firm does a lot of marketing-oriented activities. For instance, there's the national Employment Law Newsletter, and we contribute articles for West Virginia every month." "The firm does marketing seminars fairly frequently; in the Spring and Fall, they'll have them every week or two. We get people to come in and listen, like human resources people for labor and employment seminars.

Those are very well received." Associates say that "We can be very involved in marketing, if we want to be," although "there are a few associates who just want to practice law, and that's fine, too."

Associates observe that "There are more and more associates on firm committees, all except for the Executive Committee," which consists of five partners. They feel as though "We are listened to well. The partners actually solicit associate feedback and comments. The managing partners will ask associate opinions on marketing, the direction of the firm, lots of things like that." Associates report that "General firm philosophies trickle down to us from senior partners, but the way those philosophies get molded is in junior partners' and associates' hands. They don't say 'We're doing this. Do it!' They say, 'This is what we want to do. How can you contribute?' They make you feel important. They *want* to talk about firm life. They'll say, 'We're glad you're here. You're the future of the firm. Take pride in what you're doing.' They treat you as though you'll be around for a while."

"Quality work sometimes means long hours, but we're very proud of what we do."

Associates say that "the firm has been growing very quickly the last five years or so," and that "it is very strong, and very busy." That translates into working hours that can be long. It's typical to work from 8:30 in the morning until 7 at night, and on weekends, "Sure, you *do* come in. There's no requirement for it, but many Saturday mornings are for catching up on paperwork." Associates report that "About half of the lawyers come in on weekends, and if you've got a big project, you're there." However, "Nobody expects you to be there on weekends. There's no face time. It's totally decided by your workload. You know what you have to do to maintain your 1,800 hours, or whatever higher level you set for yourself." When it comes to billables, associates say that, "If you want to do minimum billables, you can, that's fine." Furthermore, "The days get shorter as you adapt to the environment and get comfortable with what you're doing."

Associates find that they don't resent the long hours because "I enjoy what I'm doing." One associate says that, "I know people here work hard, but the trade-off is that you're well-respected in the community and in the state, and you feel privileged to practice here. That adds value to what you're doing, to your career, that can't be measured monetarily." Another adds that "You have to ask, can you go to bed at night and say that you're satisfied with your job? Yes, a lounge singer job looks good after you've put in a long day. But as you become a more proficient lawyer your hours get shorter, so you have that to think about."

Associates applaud the firm's summer program for "Not hiding how hard we work. The foremost philosophy here is 'doing quality work'— they want everything that leaves here to be top quality, and they don't hide the fact that that requires hard work, and that sometimes means long hours. But we're so proud of what we do, it's worth it."

Associates are reviewed each February and July, with the July review being "the monetary review—bonuses or raises come up then." For the first year, associates get "a lock-step raise." After the first year, bonuses and raises are merit based, and merit "means many things. Hours count. So do contributions to the firm internally, so that if you spent a lot of time updating the firm's practice manual, you improved the firm and that will be taken into account. And your contribution to the bottom line. And any marketing you did, any recruiting; if you go to schools and do interviewing, that's noticed." They "really take into account your contribution as a whole, your growth as a lawyer and a potential future member of the firm."

"It's a very social place."

Associates say that the big formal event at the firm is its annual three-day retreat at a spa resort, at either the Greenbrier in West Virginia, the Homestead Resort in Virginia, or the Nemacolin Resort in Pennsylvania, where "we get to bring guests, and that's great. There are some business meetings, but the general flavor of the weekend is to get out and enjoy ourselves." The rest of the year, "there's more informal kinds of things." The Charleston office has teams in the lawyers' leagues there, and in all of the offices "We play all kinds of sports informally," and "there's not a weekend that goes by without someone poking their head in your office and saying, 'We're having people over. Can you stop by?'" The firm also has a "Turkey Bowl," which is becoming a tradition. "It's an aggressive touch football game on Thanksgiving morning—all attorneys in the firm, as well as family members and friends, are welcome to play."

When it comes to families, "Women attorneys almost all have small children, although some of the younger ones don't." The general perception is that "The firm has had a lot of success with women balancing kids and practice. You get the feeling that the firm has a general understanding that the family comes first." Associates say that, "Women have gone part-time when they've wanted to. And what's really excellent to see is that they're still considered important, contributing members of the firm. It's worked out well." The firm's family-friendliness is also reflected in "The family outings during the summer—they put on cookouts, those kinds of events, and we bring our whole families."

Associates like their Clarksburg surroundings, saying that, "Clarksburg is a 'larger city,' at least by West Virginia standards. There are about 40,000 people here. It rose up out of the coal industry, manufacturing, railroads, those kinds of industries. Today it's an ethnically diverse place—there are people from every background, Eastern European, Mediterranean, and a strong African-American population." Even more importantly, "The firm reflects the city—the folks here are as nice as anybody anywhere," and "if you really need a dose of a big city once in a while, you hop on Route 79 going north, and in an hour and a half you're in Pittsburgh." Associates add that, "It's unusual for a West Virginia firm to be headquartered in Clarksburg. Most of them have main offices in Charleston. It's refreshingly different in the sense that you don't get mired down with a bunch of other main offices. You're with the mother ship."

"They look at 'whole people', not just grades."

One associate recounts that "This firm was my first and only interview in law school. I had talked to people about it, I had researched everything I could, I had xeroxed the firm brochure and committed it to memory. I interviewed with the firm as a first year, when all I had were my first semester grades—and they weren't Law Review quality. I thought, 'I've got no shot, but I might as well go at least for the practice interviewing.' I did, and it was clear that while I was explaining away my grades, they didn't care. As it turns out, my grades shot up after first semester, but I'll never forget the fact that they were willing to look at me as a 'whole person.' That's the kind of people they are." Another associate adds, "Look at the basic questions, and that's all that counts. Am I happy? Yes! Do I see myself sticking around? Yes! Nothing else matters."

Stites & Harbison

400 West Market Street, Suite 1800 • Louisville, Kentucky 40202-3352
Phone: 502-587-3400 • Fax: 502-587-6391

OFFICES

Louisville (main office), Lexington, Frankfort, Hyden, Kentucky; Jeffersonville, Indiana; Washington, D.C.

*"People at all levels of the firm can laugh at themselves, and do it for a good cause. Every year the firm sets up a 'dunking booth' for the local United Way campaign. The managing partner is joined by several other firm 'notables' to get soaked for the cause, at a dollar a shot . . . needless to say, people who have been particularly 'popular' during the course of the year wind up raising a **lot** of money for the cause!"*

NUTS AND BOLTS

Managing partner:

T. Kennedy Helm, III

Hiring partners:

Brian A. Cromer, phone: 502-681-0440, e-mail: bcromer@stites.com
Gregory P. Parsons, phone: 606-226-2300, e-mail: gparsons@stites.com

Recruiting coordinator:

Laura L. Cassaro, phone: 502-681-0532, e-mail: lcassaro@stites.com

Number of attorneys in firm:

138 (73 partners)

TOTAL FIRM:

Partners (73), associates (61), women partners (18), women associates (26), minority partners (0), minority associates (2)

THIS OFFICE:

Total attorneys (72), partners (37), associates (35), women partners (6), women associates (16), minority partners (0), minority associates (2)

OTHER OFFICES:

(* represents an office profiled elsewhere in this book)
Lexington, Kentucky (50); Frankfort, Kentucky (6); Hyden, Kentucky (1); Jeffersonville, Indiana (4); Washington, D.C. (1)

Years to make partner:

7

WHAT DO THEY DO?

Primary specialties (more than 5% of practice):

Business Litigation (24), Products Liability (11), Trial Practice (13), Construction Law (11), Creditors' Rights/Bankruptcy (4), Employment (5), Medical Defense (8), Health Care (8), Environmental (6), Tax Group (9), Real Estate (13), Corporate & Banking Services (24), Personal Services (9).

The firm is departmentalized. Junior associates can, and do, switch specialties.

WHO DO THEY REPRESENT?

Clients include Aetna Life & Casualty, Alcan Aluminum, Alexander & Alexander, Allstate Insurance, Ambrake, American Brands, American Electric Power Service Corp., American Medical Systems, Amoco, ARCO Metals, Astra Pharmaceuticals, Bank of Louisville & Trust Co., Bethlehem Steel, Blount, Blue Cross & Blue Shield of Kentucky, Caldwell Tanks, Carman Industries, Chrysler Financial, CIBA-GEIGY, Connecticut Mutual Life Insurance, Darby Dan Farm, D.D. Williamson & Co., Eastman Kodak, Emerson Electric, European Breeders Fund, Fashion Shops of Kentucky, Fetter Printing, Ford Equipment Leasing, General Dynamics, Glenmore Distilleries, Goodyear Tire & Rubber, Greyhound Travel Services, Griffin & Co., Hazelet & Erdol, Heilig-Meyers, Hyatt, Illinois Central Railroad, James River, John Deere Insurance, Kentucky Medical Assn., KFC Corporation, Kentucky Medical Insurance, Lawyers Mutual Insurance Company of Kentucky, LG&E, Liberty National Bank & Trust Company of Louisville, London International, Louisville Presbyterian Theological Seminary, L.M. Berry & Co., Manufacturers Hanover Trust, Manville, Marine Office of America, Martin Marietta, MEDMARC New England Mutual Life Insurance, National City Bank, Kentucky, New York Life Insurance, North American Van Lines, Northwestern Mutual Life Insurance, Optical Radiation, Owens-Illinois,

Panhandle Eastern, Peabody Coal, Pepsi-Cola General Bottlers, Pfizer, Physio-Control Corp., Pittsburg & Midway Coal Mining, Playtex Family Products, Pyramid Mining, Regional Airport Authority of Louisville & Jefferson, Steel Technologies, Stock Yards Bank & Trust, Struck Construction, Sullivan & Cozart, Coca-Cola, Upjohn, U-Haul, US Aviation Underwriters, United States Fidelity & Guaranty Co., University of Louisville, Utica Mutual Insurance, Volkswagen of America, and Whayne Supply Co.

WHERE NEW ASSOCIATES COME FROM . . .

The firm routinely interviews on campus at the following law schools: Louisville, Kentucky, Washington & Lee, Indiana/Bloomington, and Vanderbilt.

The firm also routinely hires associates and summer associates from schools where it doesn't interview on campus.

HOURS AND BUCKS . . .

There is a minimum billable hour requirement of 1,900 hours/year.

Part-time work is available, but only to continuing associates, not entry-level. The firm sometimes hires contract associates, and contract associates have become full-time associates.

Typical first year salary, including typical bonus: $$$ ($50-65,000)

SUMMER PROGRAM . . .

There were 9 summer associates last year in all of the firm's offices (five 2Ls and four 1Ls). Four 2Ls received offers.

Weekly pay: $1,000 this year.

The firm routinely hires 1Ls for its summer program; last year's 1Ls came from Kentucky, Vanderbilt, and George Washington.

PRO BONO . . .

The firm expects associates to contribute 50 hours to pro bono projects. Some of the projects associates have been involved in include Habitat for Humanity, Home of the Innocents, Legal Aid Society, Metro United Way, and J.B. Speed Art Museum. Associates also assist at many homes for the elderly and speak at schools throughout the community.

HISTORY AT A GLANCE . . .

The firm traces its origins in Louisville to 1832, when it was founded by former circuit court judge Henry Pirtle and joined later by James Speed, Abraham Lincoln's future Attorney General.

Over the last decade, the firm has grown steadily to its current 137-attorney practice. Current partners include a former Lieutenant Governor and Attorney General of Kentucky, and a past president of the Kentucky Bar Association.

WHAT IT'S LIKE TO WORK THERE . . .

"It's a wonderful firm!" is a common statement from associates at Stites & Harbison. "There's so much to like here. The work is really challenging." "They let you develop at your own pace." "There's a great open door policy. It's very laid back." "People genuinely like each other." One associate reflects that "It's nice to pursue your career surrounded by friends. The firm exemplifies the notion that practicing law can, and should, be fun!"

Associates applaud the fact that "People at all levels of the firm can laugh at themselves, and do it for a good cause. Every year the firm sets up a 'dunking booth' for the local United Way campaign. The managing partner is joined by several other firm 'notables' to get soaked for the cause, at a dollar a shot. As you might imagine, those who are dunked are typically attired in unique and flattering fashions—no navy blue suits here." One associate laughs that "The people who have been particularly 'popular' during the course of the year wind up raising a *lot* of money for the cause!"

"They make sure you get a variety of experience, not all research."

Associates characterize the firm as "loosely departmentalized," into three broad categories—real estate, corporate, and litigation, and those departments are further split into sections. "You basically have your department as a home base." Associates say that, "You sometimes hear rumors that the firm used to be stronger in litigation than corporate, but the fact is that it's not true—the corporate section is great and it's growing quickly."

As a new associate, "technically everybody goes through your section head to give you assignments. It's like your parents—they make sure you get a variety of experience, not all research. They also make sure you aren't working too many hours. If you're working way over 155 billable hours in a month, or way under it, the section head will look into it."

Associates say that initiative is rewarded, and that "You go out and solicit projects until you find the people you want to work for exclusively, then you seek more stuff from them." One associate adds that, "You can go to different partners for variety. You don't have to find your niche if you don't want to."

Junior associates say that they get to do "a bunch." They are "encouraged to solicit different-sized cases from partners. They want you to get your nose out there and do smaller cases." The nature of the responsibility associates get varies from department to department. "On the transactional side, you can have incredible responsibility early on. Your client contact will depend on how comfortable you feel in client situations. But they do a lot of due diligence, and junior associates get to travel a lot for that." Tax associates talk about appearing before the board of tax appeals very early on. And for litigators, "Smaller cases, like slip and falls, give you the trial experience."

Associates point out that "We do get some big, complex cases in here, and you're just not going to be able to handle those yourself. No first year associate is going to be able to do a merger," but "even for very large cases, they give you a feel for the very big picture. You don't work on a tiny piece of it without knowing what's going on." One associate talked about working on a case as a first year associate with seven other lawyers from the firm. "I could be told a small piece, but I was always told why I was doing what I was doing, and how it fit in." The associate laughingly added that, "As a brand new associate, there are cases where you just don't *want* to know more than a little bit. I worked on an insurance company insolvency that's taken up the time of 12 partners for going on six years here. I did some research on that, but believe me, there wasn't any way I wanted to actually get to know the entire insurance code just to do that one project!"

For some of the firm's big cases, "There are going to be big document reviews. If you're new and you're in litigation, and you do something like a class action, you're going to do document production." One junior associate talked about having just completed a seven-week document production; "The upside is that it's great client contact. And the firm makes an effort to mix it up for you if you get a project like that, to make sure you don't get a bunch of them in a row." Other associates add that "Document production is a rite of passage—all young attorneys do some of it, some research. But the thing that's important is that the firm hires legions of paralegals to do the bulk of it, and as a junior associate you're allowed to manage the paralegals as well." It doesn't hurt that "When we do have big document reviews, in a product liability class action or big commercial litigation cases, *everyone* gets pulled in, including corporate associates, and the firm brings in pizza." The firm obviously does a good job of making sure nobody gets saddled with an undue amount of mundane work, because "The firm has an incredibly strong retention rate," and "People don't complain. It's really a wonderful place to work."

Associates are trained both formally and informally at Stites. Formally, "There are weekly lunch meetings for each section where one of the section attorneys gives a presentation. There is a big variety of things that are presented. You might hear about a new development in the law, or you might hear about the Kentucky Opera soliciting you, or you'll hear about a case in the news." Associates are also part of "training teams," which consist of two partners and two associates "who all do the same kind of work." "You'll discuss a practice issue, like in litigation it might be interrogatories. Then it's an open forum, and you can bring up anything you'd like to brainstorm. You might say, 'I'm trying to structure a settlement with parties from different countries,' and people will give you suggestions on how to handle it. It's very useful." Associates also get to tag along to trials so they can watch and see what happens, and the firm "encourages you to do pro bono projects that will get you good experience, things that will polish your professional skills." Most importantly, associates rave about the "very open door" policy at the firm, saying that "You get a lot of informal training from senior associates here. There's a culture of helping junior associates. You can go to them and say, 'I know this is a really stupid question, but . . .' and they'll tell you anything you want to know. They're incredibly great."

Associates say that the feedback they get on projects "varies from partner to partner." Partners "will all mark your documents. They'll go through drafts with you for your first couple of years, until you feel comfortable with what you're doing, and then they'll say, 'Just do it.'" Associates report that "Some attorneys will sit and plan strategy with you. It's not billable time for them, but they enjoy it. Other partners will give you a few minutes. But if you need help on a document, senior associates will always read stuff for you. You can ask, 'Is this what this is supposed to look like?' and they'll help you."

"The firm is very responsive on the whole."

Associates say that, "The firm's responsiveness changes as the managing partner changes, and that happens every four years." They say that "right now the firm is very responsive, on the whole." The feeling is that "They know what we think, they hear us out. There's never any retaliation for speaking our minds," although "We don't always get everything we want. Nobody does, anywhere."

One example of the firm's concern for its associates was a change in the evaluation system that took place a couple of years ago. It used to be that evaluations included blind comments from partners. "Since you didn't know who was saying what, there was no way to defend yourself. You didn't know if it was one project that was the problem, or a whole series of them." Needless to say, associates weren't too happy with that system, and the firm changed it. "Now there are no blind comments on evaluations. Since they know you are going to know who they are, they make an effort to give you constructive feedback. It was a great thing to do. It really helped us out, and it's just one more example of how they have their eyes open to issues that affect us."

"You're a grown-up here. You don't come in on weekends unless you've got work to do."

The Stites offices tend to fill up between 8:45 and 9:15 in the morning, and empty out between 5:30 and 6 p.m., although "the firm is on three separate floors, and each floor has its own culture." The 18th floor, which houses the corporate lawyers, "starts early." Regular litigation, on the 19th floor, "comes in later, stays later, they routinely have pizza delivered." Commercial litigation is "kind of in the middle." On a more individual basis, associates find that "You adapt your hours to the hours your partner works. If they're in early, you are; if they're late, you have to be. Some parts don't come in until 9:30, and if you're a late riser, that's great for you."

On weekends, "people are in for three hours on the weekend, depending on the case or project. If you're busy, you do the three hours on Saturday." If you have a huge out-of-town document production, "You'll have a big, 250-hour month, but then the next month, it'll be 108 hours."

Associates don't resent it when they have to put in long hours because "You'll take the time off when you want it." Others add that, "You love the work you're doing, the responsibility they give you, the client contact you're getting, so you put it in perspective." One associate appreciates that "You're a grown-up here, You don't come in on weekends unless you've got work to do. There's no face-time here. At some firms, where my friends work, there's this attitude that 'You need to be here just so they see you—do your mail, whatever, just be here.' That's not the case with us. You get to handle your own schedule. I appreciate the respect they give me, that I get to make my own decisions." Another associate adds that, "This is a fun place to work. It's not a sweatshop."

Compensation at the firm means "no bonuses for the first two years, because they want you to focus on being a great lawyer, not working for bonuses. They want you to do training, attend trials, write articles, and just be a good attorney in general, without any billable pressure." After two years "All kinds of things go into determining your raises and bonuses. The hours you bill count, but that's just a piece of it. You know you should make your 1,850 hours. But from there, they look at: how do you reflect the firm in the community? Do you manage junior associates? Do you manage cases? You get 'responsibility credit' to reflect your management contributions," and the responsibility credit "is a kind of a 'no hassle factor' for partners. They want to see you pick up management duties, they like to see you progress like that, and they reward you for it." Associates say that, "The bonuses for hours won't make you stay an extra five hours a day. They've got more of a 'whole lawyer' approach. It's not going to help your career here if you work long hours and just go home." By way of example, one new associate took the initiative to create "Project 2000" for the firm, "which involved researching and analyzing the potential effects of the new millenium on the firm's existing technology and software, and then presenting suggested solutions to the firm." That presentation got the associate plenty of kudos.

Associates say that, "The firm wants us to get out into the community. Community involvement is a big thing here." In addition, associates join partners for client dinners "to get our feet wet in business development."

And associates get an "entertainment budget, so we can entertain clients ourselves." The firm also pays for female associates to belong to the Women's Executive Golf League, because "They recognize that Louisville is an old-boy kind of city, and they do things to help out. That's where organizations like the Golf League come in."

Associates find that when it comes to pro bono, "There's a lot of it but you don't have to do it if you don't want to," and "the firm views community involvement in other organizations on a par with pro bono work." One of the partners does a lot for Habitat for Humanity, the organization that helps the underprivileged build homes of their own, "and many associates have followed his lead in doing that." Some firm associates do pro bono work through the bar. The sense is that "You're encouraged to do it, but you better also be working." Associates feel that "pro bono is particularly useful in your first and second year, because it's a good learning experience," while after that, "The firm makes a big deal of it, but there's a sense that it's possible to do too much of it." Associates suggest that "They give out a prize every year to an associate for pro bono work, but it would be a mistake to think you can come here and just do pro bono. 1,400 hours of billables won't outweigh a ton of pro bono. The firm has to look at you working some of your own hours, too, and then the firm will give somewhat with the billables requirement." But the bottom line is "You still have to work."

"It's a friendly, social kind of place."

Associates say that, "There's a lot of laughter here. That's one of the great things about working at Stites." They find that "the amount of socializing associates do is sort of cyclical, in that the senior associates are very social, the mid-level associates tend to go their own way a little more, and the very junior associates are all *very* social." It's "Not at all unusual to have all of your classmates go to your wedding," and associates say that, "All of the junior women associates hang out, go out together on Thursdays."

As for partner and associate socializing, associates say that "Some of the partners are very comfortable partying with associates," while others "are happy doing lunch with you." One associate pointed out that "There are some *very* senior people who show up at social events, at lunches, and they will tell you interesting stories about how much law has changed over the years. They're fun!"

Formal events "focus around the summer program and Christmas time." Every January, the firm has a "prom" for all of the attorneys from all of the firm's offices, "which gives you a chance to see the people from other offices that you don't normally get to see." During the summer "Everybody parties with the summer associates," and "Everyone is invited to play on the firm softball team, and if you can't play, you're encouraged to come out and cheer the team on." Many associates also play golf, tennis, and go bicycling together.

When it comes to family-friendliness, associates say that, "It's something the firm is conscious of, especially since they've hired more women than men recently." They say that "Many of the women attorneys have small children," and that the firm "works with them to come up with a schedule they can live with." The policy is that "You can work part-time for two years after you have children, which is around 30 hours a week." The sense is that "There's a 'mommy step-down' but it doesn't hurt you to cut back. The part-time women in litigation still try cases." Some of the women with children "come in early, and leave at 4:45 to be with their kids." The firm is also flexible with fathers. "There's a new father with a baby, and he makes his own hours."

"They're always willing to help."

Associates uniformly applaud the firm for providing a supportive atmosphere. "People here are always willing to help one another, and that goes a long way toward making this such a great place to work. Whether it's a project at work, or a situation in their personal life, it doesn't matter. I have seen attorneys roll up their sleeves and make copies alongside a staff person and stay until the project is complete. I have seen employees volunteer to go the extra mile when a project is coming down to the wire. It doesn't matter which practice area they are in, it just matters that the product is excellent and completed on time." Associates also point out that "Something that nobody from the outside would notice is that we've had the same staff members for years and years and years here. There are 67 staff members who have been with the firm for at least 10 years. That makes them incredibly knowledgeable about how the firm works, and if you're a new associate that's a godsend. It makes you infinitely more productive."

Associates feel that the firm cares about them as people, not just employees. One associate recounts how "My father was ill, and I was working but not knowing when I would be called away without any notice. When I got the call, I got up and left my desk, with my work left out on it. While I was gone, other people came in and picked up my work, and did it for me. They took care of *everything!*" Another associate adds, "When someone asks for help, the call is always answered. Many times people say, 'I don't need to be acknowledged in any way, I just want to do what I can to help.' The outpouring of support in difficult situations makes everyone here realize they're part of a very special place."

Strasburger & Price, L.L.P.

901 Main Street, Suite 4300 • Dallas, Texas 75202
Phone: 214-651-4300 • Fax: 214-651-4330 • Web site: strasburger.com

OFFICES

Dallas (main office), Austin, Houston, Texas

"Strasburger & Price is all about good work, good people, high pay, and you won't have to work as much as any of your friends . . . walk the halls at 6 p.m., it's a ghost town. Come in Sunday, and the air conditioning isn't even on—and we're talking about Texas, remember!"

HIGHLIGHTS

- 136TH largest firm in the country.

NUTS AND BOLTS

Hiring partners:

D. Randall Montgomery, phone: 214-651-4538,
e-mail: montgome@strasburger.com
Richard L. Smith, Jr., phone: 214-651-4698,
e-mail: smithr@strasburger.com

Recruiting coordinator:

Denise B. Thompson, phone: 214-651-4502,
e-mail: recruit@strasburger.com

Number of attorneys in firm:

190 (106 partners)

TOTAL FIRM:

Partners (106), associates (82), women partners (13), women associates (39), minority partners (2), minority associates (5), disabled partners (0), disabled associates (0)

THIS OFFICE:

Total attorneys (166), partners (97), associates (69), women partners (11), women associates (34), minority partners (2), minority associates (4), disabled partners (0), disabled associates (0)

OTHER OFFICES:

(* represents an office profiled elsewhere in this book)
Austin, TX (12); Houston, TX (13); Mexico City, Mexico (1)

Years to make partner:

7 ¹/₂

WHAT DO THEY DO?

Primary specialties (more than 5% of practice):

General Litigation/Labor & Employment; Business; Litigation/Environmental; Product Liability; Health; Taxes & Estates/ERISA; International; Intellectual Property; Corporate/Real Estate.

The firm is departmentalized. Junior associates can, and do, switch specialties.

WHO DO THEY REPRESENT?

Major clients include Bristol-Myers Squibb; Columbia/HCA Health Care Corporation; Dallas/Fort Worth Airport; DDB Needham Dallas; Dell Computer; General Motors; IBM; Maguire/Thomas Partners; Mobil Land Development; NationsBank of Texas; Nissan Diesel Motor Company; Rolex Watch U.S.A.; Schepps and Oak Farms Dairies; The Southland Corporation; Texas Commerce Bank.

WHERE NEW ASSOCIATES COME FROM . . .

The firm routinely interviews on campus at the following law schools: Baylor, Duke, Emory, Georgetown, Harvard, Houston, Michigan, SMU, Texas Tech, Texas, Vanderbilt, UVA.

The firm routinely hires from schools where it doesn't conduct on-campus interviews.

HOURS AND BUCKS . . .

First year associates typically spend 1,985 hours at the office; 1,800 hours is the minimum billable hours goal.

The firm allows part-time work by continuing associates; no part-time work at entry level. The firm does not routinely hire contract associates.

Typical first year salary, including typical bonus $$$$ (Over $65,000)

SUMMER PROGRAM . . .

Last year, there were 17 summer associates, 14 of whom received offers.
Weekly pay this year: $1,275 (for 2Ls) and $1,150 (for 1Ls)

The firm sometimes hires 1Ls for its summer program; last year, it had
1L summer associates from the University of Texas and Columbia.

PRO BONO . . .

The firm does not have a policy on pro bono work, although associates are
encouraged to participate. The firm hosts the South Dallas Legal Clinic
and the Travis County Legal Aid Center.

HISTORY AT A GLANCE . . .

The firm was founded in 1939 by Texans Henry Strasburger and Hobert
Price, law school classmates who came to Dallas after graduating from the
University of Texas. Henry Strasburger was a colorful courtroom lawyer.
Hobert Price was also remarkable for his photographic memory that
turned many court decisions in his favor with his impressive ability to
instantly cite case precedents supporting his position. Together,
Strasburger and Price created a charismatic combination.

Through the ensuing years, the firm grew from seven lawyers to almost
200, with four Texas offices and one in Mexico City. Four of the firm's
members have served as presidents of the Dallas Bar Association.

WHAT IT'S LIKE TO WORK THERE . . .

When you listen to associates at S&P, you can't help but wonder at the
sheer *humanity* of the place. As one associate enthuses, "They mean it
when they talk about 'quality of life' here. It's not just lip service." Another
adds that, "The firm makes you feel like it has a commitment to you as a
person, not just a pawn for more power. That overall attitude comes
across in a million ways, the training, the hours, the interesting work,
everything."

One associate shares that "There is very little competition here, and no
one wants to see someone else fail. Everyone benefits by helping each
other out, and due credit and true appreciation are easy to come by!" The
associate illustrates this point with a story: "There was a deposition in
Port Arthur, Texas, and I was going to fly there from here in Dallas. On the
way to the airport, I had car trouble. I called a cab, but missed my plane by
about three minutes. I called someone from our Houston office, who
agreed to help out and cover the deposition, on a moment's notice—even
though he had deadlines of his own to deal with." Another associate adds
that, "When I was trying to leave for vacation, and had an emergency
hearing, someone covered it for me so that I could leave. And another

time, when I was running up against a court-ordered deadline to get doc-uments produced, I was able to recruit several willing volunteers to help me meet my deadline." The associate continues that "The volunteers haven't always been associates, either. And they haven't always been 'lower on the totem pole.' Part of what makes S&P a nice place to work is that this 'teamwork' model of practicing law is in the firm culture. Partners, associates, everybody follows it."

"The caliber of attorneys here, I'd put against anyone in the country."

S&P associates rave about the quality of the work they get—and the quality of the people they get that work *from.*

When associates join the firm, "for the first several months, you're assigned projects. After that, you don't get projects so much as being assigned to cases themselves, and you'll have cases with several partners. You only get work from partners here, not associates." Associates report that "It fluctuates depending on need, but some people work for two or three partners because that's what they want to do."

Associates find that "You can go to partners with interesting stuff in other sections, and just say to them, 'You're doing neat stuff, I want to work with you,' and you get the variety of work you want that way." Associates find out about new work coming into the firm in a couple of different ways. "Different practice groups meet every month or so, to talk about business development and the cases that are coming in." However, "It pays to have lunch with people, to keep up with what's going on, and keep your ear to the ground for interesting projects that way."

Early responsibility is a way of life at S&P. Associates say that, "The partners made a personal commitment to our lives, and not just the memos we can write. They want us to be well-rounded. They give you early case-handling experience, your own cases, your own dockets. You get a mix of your own small cases, where you learn by fire, and at the same time being a team member on bigger cases with partners." One associate tells of "starting here in October. I did my first opening statement at a trial the very next month." As that indicates, "They make a serious effort to get people responsibility, to get people involved."

Associates feel that they can handle early responsibility both because of the support and feedback they get, and the firm's formal training programs. By way of formal training, S&P has its own 'training academy,' which includes mock trials and videotaped cross-examination. Associates say that, "They show you everything—how to do opening statements, examine wit-nesses, everything. It meets twice a week for the first year you're with the firm, even if you're a lateral. It's taught by partners, and they tailor it to show you what works for you personally. There's nothing cookie-cutter about it. They videotape you, and sit with you one-on-one to discuss it."

When it comes to feedback, associates say that "It's constant, both for-mal and informal." Formally, "you get a review every six months, so you can see how you're doing." Associates find their informal feedback tremendously valuable. "For every deposition, every summary judgment motion you write, they'll tell you, 'Think about doing it this way,' or 'Try this,' 'I like this,' 'Here's a strategy,' 'I'd do it this way, but this seems to work for you.' They turn everything you write into a valuable learning experience."

Associates are also trained to develop business. "They encourage junior associates to go out and seek business, to bring in clients." Associates go to seminars and business development activities "as first year associates," where "they tell you what you can and can't do." Associates report that "Business development isn't a 'priority' for junior associates, but they do encourage you to get involved, and they show you how to do it."

Associates have a voice in firm management through the Associates Committee, which has a representative from each year. "For issues like salaries, the Associates Committee talks to the partners formally." For more individualized issues, associates find that "an informal 'Look, I need to talk to you' works fine. The doors are always open, partners will always hear us out."

"We're not a sweatshop."

Associates say that the offices fill up between 8 and 8:30 a.m. in the morning, and clear out between 5:30 and 6 p.m. "If you walk the halls at 6 p.m., it's a ghost town." On weekends, "The air conditioning is only on for 3 1/2 hours on Saturday morning. That tells you how much they expect you in on weekends!" Associates report that "Out of 165 attorneys, maybe 10 will show up on Saturday mornings. The same eight are always there, and then two other people on a rotating basis," although "With a trial or a big deal, all bets are off, and you put in the hours."

Associates uniformly feel that "The billable hours requirement is very reasonable. They expect you to bill about 155 hours a month on average. You're a 'high biller' at 165." The sense is that "There's no pressure to work more, but if you do, you get more responsibility. If you don't want to work more hours, you can do great work, just less of it." In a nutshell, "They mean it when they say that families count. They don't want you living here."

For pro bono work, the feeling is that "There's no push from partners to do it, but it's very respected. You still have to make your hours, do your work, but there's no disfavor toward pro bono work." Pro bono hours "aren't treated as billable time, but they still count as nonbillables on the same level as business development activities, recruiting, those kinds of things. What happens is that partners see that you're putting in the hours, and it counts as a contribution to the firm, which means that it counts for bonuses," although "nothing counts as much as handling client matters."

"It's a very social place, but you aren't branded if you don't socialize."

Associates report that socially, "It depends on how much you want the firm to be your family. The socializing is there if you want it. Some of my best friends are here. But you can be private, too, if you want. You won't be branded if you don't socialize."

Formally, the firm hosts events each year for all of the attorneys, including a firm retreat and a formal dinner dance called the "Prom." Associates report doing "all kinds of things together. Mostly happy hours, sporting events, concerts. People play on softball teams, football teams, do 'fun runs,' and work on charity events together. Really, anything you do with your friends, you do with your colleagues."

The firm also hosts a "family outing to Six Flags, or to the race track, for attorneys, staff and families." Speaking of families, associates laughingly say that "There's a saying here that if you're not married when you get here, you *will* be within two years," and more importantly, "everyone here is married to their first spouse." Associates agree that "The firm is very family-friendly," and "They want you to have a happy family—they don't want you to be a worker bee."

The firm has "several female partners who work part-time, so they can be with their kids; the firm came up with a unique pay structure to handle part-time work." Associates also report that "They expect you to bail out of the office for school plays." One associate says that "The guy next door to me just had a baby, and he's here for maybe three hours a day. The schedule is flexible," and "The firm makes it easy to work from home, because you can just log-on to your computer and get access to the office that way."

One associate sums up what makes S&P such a great place for associates: "Different firms utilize associates in different ways. A lot of firms will bring you in for three or four or five years, use you, and then spit you out. That's fine, as long as you know what you're getting into. But a lot of the time it's not obvious. Every single firm is telling you the exact same thing—'You're going to get a lot of experience here. We're not a sweatshop. We want you to have a life.' I know; I heard them. But what you need to do is talk with young associates. A 10-year partner can tell you what he thinks associate life is like, but he doesn't know. Ask the young associates, 'What are you working on today?' not 'What have you gotten to do?' Ask them, right now, what they are working on then. Ask them, 'When I walk out of here, what are you going to be doing?' At S&P, we are handling cases. We aren't working for senior associates on a research project. We're calling clients, negotiating settlements, preparing for hearings and mediations and depositions, and, yes, sometimes trials. There are so many factors for you to look at. I think the most important question to ask yourself is, 'What is my life going to be like for the next five years?' You have to look at people whose shoes you want to be in. Are they happy? Are they getting the type of work you would want? Are they becoming better lawyers? At S&P, the answer is 'yes.' It's a great firm, and a *particularly* great place to be an associate."

Waller Lansden Dortch & Davis, P.L.L.C.

511 Union Street, Suite 2100 • Nashville, Tennessee 37219
Phone: 615-244-6380 • Fax: 615-244-6804

OFFICES

Nashville (main office), Columbia, Tennessee

"This is a place where you aren't chained to a chair. You don't punch a clock. There was a woman who was interviewing here as a two-year lateral. She had great grades, a federal clerkship, a great resume in every way. She said, 'I know there are many places with a sophisticated practice, but I need a place that knows what it is to have kids.' I told her, 'I'd like you to ask the head of our litigation group about that, but he's home with his 8-year-old kid, who's sick.'"

HIGHLIGHTS

- One of the largest law firms in Tennessee and the Southeast.
- Nationally-recognized health care practice.
- Has appeared in *The American Lawyer* "Client's Choice" selection of the favorite law firms of in-house lawyers at 400 corporations across the country.
- Several firm attorneys are listed in *The Best Lawyers in America*.

NUTS AND BOLTS

Managing partner:

Ames Davis

Hiring partner:

David E. Lemke, phone: 615-252-2455, e-mail: dlemke@wallerlaw.com

Recruiting coordinator:

    Sue S. Hunter, phone: 615-252-2487, e-mail: sh@wallerlaw.com

Number of attorneys in firm:

    115 (51 partners)

TOTAL FIRM:

    Partners (51), associates (59), women partners (6), women associates (25), minority partners (2), minority associates (0), of counsel (5)

THIS OFFICE:

    Total attorneys (112), partners (50), associates (58), women partners (6), women associates (25), minority partners (2), minority associates (0)

OTHER OFFICES:

    (* represents an office profiled elsewhere in this book)
    Columbia, Tennessee (3)

Years to make partner:

    7

WHAT DO THEY DO?

Primary specialties (more than 5% of practice):

    Practice areas include Bankruptcy, Restructuring and Creditors' Rights; Business Organizations; Commercial Lending & Debt Financing; Corporate Finance & Securities; Employee Benefits, Executive & Stock Compensation, ERISA; Environmental; Government Relations; Healthcare; Immigration; Intellectual Property; Labor & Employment; Litigation; Mergers & Acquisitions; Real Estate; Relocating & Expanding Businesses; Tax; Trusts & Estates; and White Collar Criminal Defense.

WHO DO THEY REPRESENT?

    A vast variety of clients, including one of the largest for-profit healthcare companies in the world, and a number of healthcare companies with regional and national operations; two of the South's largest investment banking firms; two of the country's major automobile manufacturers; several regional banks; several nationally recognized manufacturing companies; and a National League Football Team. The clients include Healthcare Realty Trust, PhyCor, PMT Services, A+ Network, Healthwise of America, General Motors/Saturn Corporation, BancorpSouth, Bayou Steel, Columbia/HCA Healthcare, El Paso Energy, First American National Bank, Illinois Central Railroad, Landfill Solutions, Nissan Motor

Manufacturing, Olin Corporation, Rayovac, Rockwell International, Tenneco Packaging, many towns and cities, American Airlines, Bridgestone/Firestone, EMI Christian Music Group, Wackenhut, the Tennessee Oilers, and Union Carbide.

WHERE NEW ASSOCIATES COME FROM . . .

The firm interviews routinely on the following law school campuses: Vanderbilt, Tennessee, UVA, Washington & Lee, and Alabama. The firm also routinely hires from schools where it doesn't conduct on-campus interviews.

HOURS AND BUCKS . . .

First year associates typically spend an average of 1,850 hours at the office. There is no minimum billable hour requirement, but rather an objective of 1,800 billable hours per year. Practice group heads generally monitor associate workloads for too few or too many hours and make adjustments where called for.

The firm does allow part-time work for attorneys; it is handled on a case-by-case basis, and is not historically allowed at entry level. The firm does not routinely hire contract associates.

Typical first-year salary, including typical bonus: $$$ ($50-65,000)

SUMMER PROGRAM . . .

Last year, there were 11 summer associates, 10 of whom received offers.
    Weekly pay: $950 last year
    The firm does not routinely hire 1Ls for its summer program
    There is no deadline for the summer program, but practically speaking it's wise to apply before October 15TH .

PRO BONO . . .

The firm encourages all attorneys to participate in local bar association pro bono activities and to serve on boards of nonprofit agencies. There is no firm policy requiring numbers of hours dedicated to pro bono work; the decision to do pro bono is left up to individual attorneys.

Associates have taken part in a variety of pro bono projects, including domestic, criminal, juvenile, guardian ad litem, and unemployment compensation projects, among others.

HISTORY AT A GLANCE . . .

The firm was founded in Nashville in 1905 as Pitts & McConnico. Firm has grown 40% in last two years.

Associates say that you can tell how great it is to work at Waller Lansden just by walking around the office. "People laugh and carry on in the hallways. Everybody is on a first-name basis, all the way from our housekeeper to our managing partner." "When I interviewed here, I was impressed at the number of attorneys who have boom boxes in their offices. It told me a lot about the relaxed atmosphere and individuality of the lawyers here." "They've got a different vision of how a law firm is supposed to look. The architecture isn't stuffy. No wood paneling, no green felt on the tables. It's a light, bright place to work." "There's a kind of youthful energy here that you don't find anywhere else. It's a young place. The head of the litigation group and the head of the corporate group—the two largest groups here—they're both in their mid-to-late thirties."

> *"The place is really open to your level of curiosity and involvement and growing your own practice."*

When new associates join Waller Lansden, they join one of three departments—either dispute resolution, real estate, or business transactions. Within those departments are subgroups; for instance, there's the labor and employment subgroup, the environmental subgroup, the health care subgroup. "You can join one of those subgroups, or stay broad-based and grow from there." Associates find that "If you summer clerk here, you sit down toward the end of the summer with the head of the department you want to join, and tell them what you want to do. They're very open to hearing what you want. You wind up in the right place through some magic mix of self-direction and firm need."

From the beginning of their careers at Waller Lansden, associates find that "there are different approaches to giving assignments from group to group. There's no formal mentoring system. You can try to get experience from everyone. You can solicit assignments from people. The heads of the different practice groups are responsive. If you say, 'I'm interested in X,' when it comes up, you'll get X."

Associates learn about new projects coming into the firm through the firm's daily, computerized newsletter, as well as monthly group meetings. However, associates feel that "It's even better to develop good, informal relationships with partners you want to work with." It's also possible to "ask for more work with certain clients. The place is really open to your level of curiosity and involvement, and growing your own practice."

Associates find that the training is "mostly informal." "Of course the firm pays for CLEs and you're self-directed with those." If associates want to brush up their skills, they go to CLEs on their own initiative. The sense is that "the firm's training philosophy is learning by doing, with supervision from partners. "The first time I took a plaintiff's deposition, the senior partner watched and coached—'Here's how you build a point, here's where you get out.'" Associates say that, "They constantly tell you how to improve, when to play your cards in negotiation, that kind of thing. The idea is that you need to do these things to learn them. You can take a deposition, or play like you are, and they think you learn by actually doing, not by playing."

Associates say that this philosophy is reflected in the firm's recruiting, where "they tell you that they hire partners. They ask in recruiting: Does this person have the potential to be a partner? The expectation is that *everyone* they hire will eventually be a member of the firm. So they look at whether or not the recruit could be left alone in a room with a client. Whether they grasp the business and personal issues of representing people. Whether they can get organized. Whether they can accept responsibility. They really expect you to hit the ground running, and they look for the kind of person with the intelligence, motivation, and maturity to handle that."

"Management channels are incredibly open."

Associates rave about the openness of the partners. One reason for this may be that "Because the partners are by and large very young, age differences and cultural differences are not factors between the partners and associates." Associates find that "Everybody, up to and including the managing partner, is very approachable. You can walk in and talk to the managing partner any time. He's very open and gracious."

The firm is managed by a three-person Executive Committee, which has final say on management issues. Associates find that members of the Executive Committee make a special effort to solicit associate input. "It's 'management by walking around.'" "A couple of days ago, one member of the Executive Committee walked into my office and sat down, and asked 'How are you?' He was just strolling the halls. We talked about church, sports, business, novels, everything. That kind of spirit is something they maintain here." In addition to informal conversations, "There are quarterly associate meetings where our concerns are addressed. The Executive Committee comes to those meetings. They show us all of the financial data—partner compensation, margins, clients, associate expenses, everything. They keep everyone informed on exactly how we're doing." Before those meetings, questions are gathered from associates and presented anonymously at the meeting, "So you know they're not going to take notes on you." In addition to the quarterly meetings, the firm recently started an associates committee, "to increase the give and take between partners and associates even more, to put more associate concerns on management's plate."

Associates say that while they get reviewed formally on an annual basis, they also have the chance to review the partners—anonymously, of course! "The partners really pay attention to the results of those evaluations. They listen to us."

"They are too busy to keep substantive work bottled up at the partner level."

Associates say that "The firm makes an effort to get interesting work to everyone." Associates talk about being able to defend and conduct depositions all over the country, to argue motions in court, to handle mediation, to talk directly with clients from a very early stage of their careers. Associates say that the firm is even open to their suggestions about new practice areas to develop. One associate tells of how "When I came here four years ago, I told the head of the litigation group that I wanted to develop a health-care litigation practice. They didn't have much business litigation. The partner invited me to help develop it."

The sense among associates is that "You can tell how quickly they want to progress by the way they market the firm. They can tell clients totally truthfully that 'We've got great lawyers who happen to be associates. You'll get the same caliber work for much less than big city firm prices.' It's a calculated business decision to get the work to younger associates in the best interests of the clients. It means that they coach you into being the best lawyer you can be as quickly as possible, and that means great opportunities for junior associates."

"The firm makes an effort to keep the hours reasonable."

The Waller Lansden offices typically fill up between 8:15 and 8:45 in the morning, and clear out between 5:45 and 6:15 p.m., although "if you're working on a big deal or a trial, those hours are out the window." On weekends, there is "no face time. You might spend one weekend morning a month here. Most people don't come in on weekends at all, and only one of the partners makes it a habit to come in on Saturdays." One associate tells of staying late to wander the halls one night "just to see who was still here. Nobody was. The same thing in the morning. If you come in at 7 a.m., you'll be here by yourself."

One associate tells of an incredibly crushing day when "at 2 a.m. on Monday, seven of us were actually working at the office. We were stunned." It turns out there were three corporate lawyers working on a deal the client needed the next day. An appellate brief was due the next day, as was a summary judgment motion, and that accounted for the other three attorneys. "It was so unusual, we couldn't believe it. Late nights here are *definitely* not the norm."

What counts for raises and bonuses are not just billable and firm hours, but also "more of the intangibles—the quality of your work, the way you deal with clients." For the first two years, the compensation is lock-step. By the third year as an associate "you move into a 'band'— there's a range of pay for third to seventh year associates, and starting in your third year, you're eligible for bonuses. All partners in your group have input on your raises and bonuses." Associates also find that there is "credit for bringing in clients," but the credit they get isn't a "huge motivator," and associates comment that "It doesn't matter anyway because you don't have to bring in clients in order to receive bonuses and raises." Associates applaud the firm overall for recognizing that "You have good years and bad years, and sometimes that's out of your control. On the other hand, it *is* a business, and they expect you to contribute in return for everything you get."

Associates find that "the firm takes a 'broad view' of public service," and as such it makes pro bono a matter of each lawyer's choice. "Many lawyers participate in things like pro bono referral services. They don't dodge it at all." However, along with "just representing indigent clients," associates "can serve on the board of different projects. And not just blue-ribbon, black-tie things. They don't care if you generate business through your community involvement or not." One associate talked about spending one night a month at a shelter, doing pro bono work, and in return for that "the firm gives me 'community service hour' credit, just as they would for a business development lunch. It counts, and that's good." Associates find that "Everybody here develops their own community service, and you're encouraged to, as well. They review what you're doing to make sure that it's within the firm's expertise, but that's it."

"It's very family-friendly, there are kids everywhere."

Many of the women attorneys at Waller Lansden have small children, "And they're always hiring people with little kids. One of the summer associates this summer had twins, and there's a new woman lawyer who has three small children." Associates say that the family-friendliness at the firm is a trickle-down from senior management, "some of whom have elementary school-aged children themselves." One associate told of "a woman who was interviewing here as a two-year lateral. She had great grades, a federal clerkship, a great resume in every way. She said, 'I know there are many places with a sophisticated practice, but I need a place that knows what it is to have kids.' I told her, 'I'd like you to ask the head of our litigation group about that, but he's home with his 8-year-old kid, who's sick.'"

Associates find that "Nobody ever says, 'Where are you going?' if you leave the office. If someone looks for you in the middle afternoon and you're leaving the office, and you say 'I have an uncle in the hospital,' the immediate response will be 'This can wait. How is he?'" The prevailing feeling is that "The presumption is that you're a professional, and you'll take care of your work professionally."

When it comes to socializing, associates say that, "It varies. Everybody has a good time while they're working during the day." After that, "some people socialize after hours," while others "are young marrieds with young kids, so they're not going to do a lot of happy hours." The sense is that "The corporate group has more younger, single folks," so that, as one associate laughingly says, "they tend to go 'wilding in packs' more often." However, "People socialize a lot around the summer program. It's actually a great excuse to socialize among ourselves, not just to meet the summer folks." There is also "Golf, hunting, fishing, football games—both college games at the University of Tennessee or Vanderbilt, and professional games at the Oilers, a firm client—as well as firm softball games, dinner clubs, wine clubs, book clubs, you name it." Associates report "a lot of informal socializing, dinner at people's houses, that kind of thing." While associates say that they have "lots of friends at the office" there are always going to be "some people with whom you only have an office relationship, and that's fine."

Formally, in addition to summer associate activities, the firm holds a dinner dance every year, as well as a "staff holiday party, which is planned by the associates who've joined the firm within the last year." Associates say that, "a Waller tradition is that this group puts together a video in which the more senior attorneys are lampooned. *Nobody* is immune to the new associates' roast!"

Associates find that the firm's location is an asset, because "Nashville has a nice mix. You can club hop if you want, or have six people over for dinner. We've all got houses with yards—the cost of living here means you can have those kinds of things, fast." Associates say that, "Whether or not you'll be happy here depends in part on what attracts you to Nashville. Some people see Nashville as comfortable, slow, Southern. If you like that about Nashville, this isn't the place for you. They say that in the old days this firm had a reputation as being very stuffy, very 'old Nashville,' but that perception is at least 10 years out of date." One associate says that "What I see here is amazing potential, big changes, a newness culturally, new ideas brought by people moving here, from artists to entrepreneurs. This firm is uniquely in touch with everything new in Nashville. When organizations come here—like Saturn, the car company, or the Tennessee Oilers—they pick us to represent them. It's not only one of the largest firms in town, but it's *'the one'*—you can *tell* it's on the move. We match the growing, changing aspects of the city. The old idea was that you had to go to the 'right' schools. It was a closely-bred legal community. Now we have people from all over. It makes living and working here exciting. The level of excitement here is palpable. What's in the newspaper, who's doing what in the city—those are our clients. With Waller Lansden, you're part of the vanguard of things that are changing in Nashville."

Ward & Smith, P.A.

1001 College Court • New Bern, NC 28562
Phone: 252-633-1000 • Fax: 252-636-2121

OFFICES

New Bern, Greenville, Raleigh, Wilmington, North Carolina

"We're in a fairly small town, but when people from anywhere in North Carolina ask you where you work, and you say 'Ward & Smith,' it means something. There's respect and prestige that goes with it. If you want to be a big fish in a small barrel, this is the place you want to be. And it doesn't hurt that it's a beautiful place—we're right on a river and 40 minutes from the ocean. It's a wonderful lifestyle."

HIGHLIGHTS

- Eight of the firm's attorneys are listed in *The Best Lawyers in America.*
- The firm is consistently listed in the top 25 law firms in North Carolina; the largest law firm in the state east of Raleigh.

NUTS AND BOLTS

Managing partner:

J. Troy Smith, Jr.

Hiring partner:

J. Troy Smith, Jr., phone: 252-633-1000,
e-mail: jts@wardandsmith.com

Recruiting coordinator:

Donna H. Meadows, phone: 252-633-1000,
e-mail: dhm@wardandsmith.com

Number of attorneys in firm:

60 (36 partners)

TOTAL FIRM:

Partners (36), associates (24), women partners (6), disabled partners (1)

THIS OFFICE:

Total attorneys (33), partners (21), associates (12), women partners (2), disabled partners (0)

OTHER OFFICES:

(* represents an office profiled elsewhere in this book)
Greenville, NC (14); Raleigh, NC (1); Wilmington, NC (12)

Years to make partner:

5 to 7

WHAT DO THEY DO?

Primary specialties (more than 5% of practice) for the entire firm:

Business (16), Creditors' Rights (4), Employment and Government Contracts (10), Environmental (2), Financial Institutions—Securities (3), Litigation (19), Personal Injury (4), Real Property (6), Tax (4), Trusts & Estates (9).

The firm is departmentalized. Junior associates give the firm their top choices of departments, and the firm does its best to choose from that list, taking the workload of each department into account. Associates do not rotate through departments, but junior associates generally do work with other departments as well as their own. And junior associates can, and do, switch departments sometimes.

WHO DO THEY REPRESENT?

Clients include First-Citizens Bank & Trust Company, Smithfield Foods, Weyerhaeuser, State of North Carolina, Hatteras Yachts, Fountain Powerboats, North Carolina Global Transpark, Dixon Marketing Associates, N.C. State Fireman's Association, Duke University, Eckerd's, North Carolina Symphony, and Hannaford Brothers Company.

WHERE NEW ASSOCIATES COME FROM . . .

The firm routinely interviews on campus at the following law schools: North Carolina, UVA, Wake Forest, William & Mary, and Campbell.

The firm routinely hires associates and summer associates from schools where it doesn't interview on campus.

HOURS AND BUCKS . . .

The firm does not have any set hours for any attorney, including associates, and no minimum billable hour requirements.

Attorneys are allowed to work part-time—both continuing and entry-level associates. The firm routinely hires contract associates. None have yet become full-time associates.

Typical first year associate salary, including typical bonus: $$$ ($50-65,000)

SUMMER PROGRAM . . .

Last year, there were 5 summer associates, 4 of whom received offers.

Weekly pay: $950 last year.

The firm does not routinely hire 1Ls for its summer program.

The firm normally requires applications for its summer program by mid-October.

PRO BONO . . .

The firm does not have a formal pro bono policy, but the attorneys routinely perform pro bono services.

Since the firm doesn't have a billable hour requirement, it doesn't count pro bono hours as billable hours.

HISTORY AT A GLANCE . . .

D.L. "Libby" Ward started the firm in 1895, in New Bern. Between the mid-1980's and early 1990's, the firm opened its other three offices in North Carolina, in Greenville, Raleigh, and Wilmington.

Today, the firm has eight lawyers listed in *The Best Lawyers In America*. Among notable members are David Ward, and Hugh Overholt, Judge Advocate General of the U.S. Army in the late 1980's.

WHAT IT'S LIKE TO WORK THERE . . .

When I was originally interviewing law school administrators, looking for employers who ought to appear in this book, Ward & Smith got a memorable recommendation from one of the administrators I talked to. "There's this law firm in this very small town, it's just the most gorgeous place. Even though it's not in a big city, everybody knows the firm. They do incredible work, and they're a great group of people." The administrator's voice dropped: "To tell you the truth, *I'd* love to work there." Everything else I heard about the firm from outsiders confirmed that original recommendation, and associates at the firm back it up, as well. One associate said that "When I was looking at law firms, I heard that W&S was in the big leagues, that it recruited the best attorneys, that it was a force to be reckoned with."

"You get your feet wet, very fast."

When associates join the firm, they get an intensive two-week training session which "exposes you to every section of the firm. You see videos, you learn billing techniques, benefits, using on-line research, the file room, everything."

Associates "join a particular department right from the start, like litigation, or banking, or tax." In that department, each associate gets a partner/mentor, "and all of your work comes through that person, to make sure you're not getting in too deep. They monitor you and help you as you need it." Associates find that "you can seek out particular projects to develop your own expertise in something. They welcome that." Another associate echoes that sentiment, saying "This is a place where you can carve a niche out for yourself, if you want to."

When it comes to responsibility, "You get all the responsibility you can handle. You get your feet wet very fast. I did my first deposition by myself shortly after joining the firm." Associates say that, "Usually, as a junior associate, you're writing letters for other people's signatures, so they'll correct your stuff. As soon as you're ready, they'll turn you loose on clients, because they *want* clients to know you—you're sending stuff and copying the other lawyer before you know it." As that suggests, much of the training at W&S is "learning by doing." As one litigation associate explains it, "Normally you see a deposition, you see one of the partners argue a motion. Then you do one with a partner supervising to ensure you can handle it. Then you do one on your own."

For formal feedback, there's an associate evaluation committee that provides twice-yearly chances for associates to see how they're doing. The committee "consists of three partners. They solicit written evaluations of you from all of the partners, and meet with each partner individually to let the partner address any associate issues. Then the committee meets with you and your supervisor. If you had a problem, you can go to anyone in the committee. They really do want to see you succeed." The sense is that, "With any work issue, you know where you stand, all the time."

"You're told when you come here that they want to make you partner."

Associates at W&S rave that "They don't bring you here for leverage. They expressly tell you that they want to practice with you for the rest of their careers." As that hiring philosophy suggests, associates are made to feel that their opinions count and that their concerns are important to the firm. Administratively, the firm "doesn't burden you. They leave you more time to practice law, very little time worrying about administrative stuff."

By way of addressing associate concerns on a formal basis, the firm has "meetings with all attorneys four times a year." On top of that, associates rave that "the managing partner comes in every year to talk to you and tell you your raise, and he says, 'My door is always open—come in whenever you need something addressed.' He's the hardest working person here, but he's never too busy to hear you out." Other associates echo that, saying that "Even the named partners of the firm don't screen calls. They are incredibly accessible, and very supportive in dealing with us associates."

"We have a tremendous reputation for quality work, and the price for that is that we work really hard."

The W&S offices fill up between 8 and 8:30 in the morning, although some early risers are in at 7:30. Evenings "vary greatly. Attorneys start to leave around 5:45 to 6:15 p.m., although there's a second word processing staff who works from 3:30 in the afternoon until midnight, so the office is never *totally* empty. Some attorneys stay until 7:30 p.m., some eat dinner and come back." Associates say that, "People regulate their own time. Some people dash out to McDonald's, some take a two-hour lunch—although that's not too common." On weekends, "It's rare to be in for more than an hour on weekends. Some people stop in for their mail on Saturday morning, and that's it. The majority of lawyers don't regularly work on weekends, although some do. That's just because that's how they regulate their own time." Associates point out that "Some people who have family concerns actually find that it's easier to work odd hours, to work nights and weekends, and the office is very flexible that way."

Associates don't mind long hours when they occur because "No one tells you what hours to work. It's on you. You'd never have anybody telling you the hours to put in, but the work determines that. People here generally have a strong work ethic, although people have different stamina, and the firm appreciates that. You do the work you're given, and you can leave when it's done. If you want to ask for more, you can, but you're not penalized if you don't." Associates say that the bottom line is that "You're not questioned about where you're going when you leave the office. Just let them know you'll be in, and get your work done." As one associate puts it, "People sometimes don't equate hard work with a high quality of life, but that's what we have here."

When it comes to compensation, junior associates say that their pay is lock-step. "You know nothing about other people's salaries, so there's no need to feel competitive. Partners tell you that they felt they were paid commensurate with contemporaries at other desirable places to work, and that's how you're being paid, as well." Associates say that "You don't get bonuses as an associate, but if you start doing the things that make you look like you're on track to be partner, you'll get raises in your salary to reflect that. If you do extra hours, do community stuff, bring in business." For associates, "You're rewarded for it, but no more than you would be for serving on a firm committee and spending all day on that. Firm management contributions, training paralegals or other attorneys, that's taken as seriously as bringing in business."

The sense about pro bono at the firm is that "It's totally up to you how you look at it. You're not penalized if you don't do it." In fact, "Most people here don't do traditional pro bono, but people do an awful lot of things like serving on the board of the United Way." Almost everybody at the firm is involved with nonprofit community organizations to whom they provide free legal advice, "and that's where most of the community involvement comes in, not as much representing indigents."

"People understand family obligations, and they're willing to step in and help out."

Associates uniformly say that the firm makes an effort to accommodate families. There are two women partners who have small children, one of whom "went part-time as an associate. When she was in her second pregnancy, she needed bed rest at the seven-month mark. She wanted to keep working, so the firm set up phone lines and sent a runner back and forth to her at home. They did everything they could to keep her in the loop even though she had to be at home." The other partner "was actually hired as a part-time lawyer."

The importance of family is reflected in the way the firm handles new recruits. "They devote an entire weekend to the recruits, to provide a more complete perspective on living here, as well as giving them a chance to get to know the different personalities in the firm." As one associate points out, "Having dinner at an attorney's house rather than in a restaurant provides a pretty good insight into the lifestyle and personalities of the people here." Associates add that "They want to see how new recruits interact, they want to know you and your family. They're really asking themselves not just would they like to work with you, but would they want you as a friend, as a neighbor? It's important here."

Socially, associates say that "With four offices, we're considered a large firm in North Carolina—but it doesn't feel like a large firm. They make an extra effort to make it feel like one cohesive unit." Formally, the firm has "a very intensive summer associate program. The idea is two activities during the week and one invitation on weekends, with multiple attorneys. On weeknights, there might be boating, or volleyball, or basketball." There is also "a firm picnic in the fall" and "a firm retreat one weekend every Spring, where spouses get to go as well. There's very little business. It's mostly social. There'll be a little talk about profit sharing, then a firm meeting, then a speaker on quality of life issues. Then there's a band, and dancing. And the Sunday is mostly free."

Informally, "Lots of people throughout the year go out and eat together. Several play sports together." And "on certain Fridays after work, a group of attorneys, both partners and associates, gather at a local watering hole to celebrate any good news that's come in during the week. Sometimes the 'good news' is just an everyday occurrence, but frankly we just like an excuse to get together outside of work!" All in all, associates say that, "There's a classic work-hard-play-hard attitude here. You take care of the business, but when you're done, it's time to enjoy yourself. And lots of times the people you enjoy spending time with are the people you work with." The camaraderie of the attorneys is further highlighted by hijinks at the office. "When one attorney's alma mater is playing another attorney's alma mater in football or basketball, it's commonplace to receive an e-mail, with cc's to all attorneys, from an attorney's computer proclaiming that the rival school is far superior." As one associate laughingly explains, "That usually means that the attorney foolishly stepped out of his or her office, giving an 'e-mail bandit' the chance to send out a rogue e-mail from that attorney's computer!"

"I could leave the office right now and touch the sand in 40 minutes."

Associates just love the firm's New Bern location. On the off chance you aren't familiar with New Bern—and if you aren't from nearby and you *are* familiar with it, you ought to go and try out for *Jeopardy*—here's the scoop: It's a town of 20,000 people, about 45 minutes from Greenville, with "many small communities nearby." As one associate tells it, "We live on a river, and we're close to the beach. Lots of the attorneys have boats on the Atlantic. That obviously leads to lots of opportunities to get together outside of work, and enjoy the water."

The sense among associates is that "If you're from a small town, it's a benefit, because you understand the lifestyle. Someone from New York City would be making a major lifestyle change to come here, and to tell the truth, for people who are used to the go-getter pace of a city like New York, we'd want them first to understand how different it is to live in a town like ours. There *are* people here who've lived in large cities, and they're happy. But more are from small towns."

More importantly, one associate says that "Yes, it's a small town, but when people from anywhere in North Carolina ask you where you work and you say 'Ward & Smith,' it means something. There's respect and prestige that goes with it. If you want to be a big fish in a small barrel, this is the place you want to be."

Watkins & Eager P.L.L.C.

400 East Capitol Street • Jackson, MS 39201
Phone: 601-948-6470 • Fax: 601-354-3623

OFFICES

Jackson, Mississippi

"This is a firm that recognizes that families are important and should come first. If your three-year-old is a butterfly in the preschool play on Friday morning, this is the firm that will do all it can to see that you are covered and that you are indeed the proud parent of the butterfly, in the front row of the school auditorium that morning . . . and they have a simply outstanding reputation in the legal community."

HIGHLIGHTS

- Best recognized for its litigation practice.
- A long-standing dedication to women's issues; one of the first law firms in the state to establish liberal part-time policies for women partners and associates.
- No minimum billable hours requirement.

NUTS AND BOLTS

Managing partner:
John L. Low, IV

Hiring partner:
Walter J. Brand, phone: 601-948-6470

Recruiting coordinator:
Meredith H. Dodson, phone: 601-948-6470

Number of attorneys in firm:

49 (37 partners)

Years to make partner:

7

WHAT DO THEY DO?

Primary specialties (more than 5% of practice):

Contract, Commercial and Business Litigation; Tort Litigation; Insurance; Banking; Labor and Employment; Corporate and Tax; Environmental Affairs; Real Estate; Governmental Practice; Alternative Dispute Resolution.

The firm is departmentalized. New associates get to choose which department they join. Associates can, and do, switch specialties.

WHO DO THEY REPRESENT?

Clients include banks, oil and gas producers, manufacturers, cable television operators, major manufacturers, major insurers, RTC, FDIC, and many others.

WHERE NEW ASSOCIATES COME FROM . . .

The firm routinely interviews on campus at the following law schools: Mississippi, Mississippi College, and Vanderbilt. The firm routinely hires associates and summer associates from schools where it doesn't interview on campus.

HOURS AND BUCKS . . .

There is no billable hour requirement.

Part-time work is available to associates, but not at entry level. The firm does not routinely hire contract associates.

Typical first year salary, including typical bonus: $$$ ($50-65,000)

SUMMER PROGRAM . . .

Last year, there were 6 summer associates, 3 of whom got offers.

The firm routinely hires 1Ls for its summer program; last year's 1Ls came from Vanderbilt, Mississippi College, and the University of Mississippi.

PRO BONO . . .

The firm encourages associates to take on as many pro bono projects as they can handle. Associates typically are involved in Chancery Court projects and domestic work for indigents. Partners and associates also regularly donate time to the local Community Stew Pot, serving lunch to the underprivileged.

HISTORY AT A GLANCE . . .

The firm was founded in 1895 by William H. Watkins, the twentieth lawyer at the Jackson bar. Watkins' career eventually spanned 64 years, during which he argued over 25 cases before the U.S. Supreme Court. Pat Eager joined Watkins in 1916 and practiced with the firm until his death in 1970. Eager was recognized as a premier trial lawyer throughout his career, with many honors and accolades.

For several decades the image of the firm was heavily influenced by two of Will Watkins' children. Elizabeth Watkins Hulen, a highly respected appellate advocate, was the first woman in Mississippi history to argue a case before the U.S. Supreme Court. Thomas H. Watkins earned a national reputation representing corporate and governmental clients.

Current stars in the firm include U.S. Senator Thad Cochran; Former Chief Judge of the 5TH Circuit, Charles Clark; and Elizabeth Hulen, first woman from Mississippi to argue before the U.S. Supreme Court.

WHAT IT'S LIKE TO WORK THERE . . .

If you've glanced through this book at all, you know that it's fairly unusual to see comments from my original interviews with law school administrators. When you see the heading "Word on the Street" for some employers, or a mention of an employer's reputation in the community, as often as not those comments are from law school administrators. By and large, those comments are pretty short; an isolated remark about a particular aspect of an employer, something junior associates really like.

But in the case of Watkins & Eager, I'm going to do something unique—I'm going to give you the initial review I got, from the first law school administrator to recommend Watkins & Eager. While I can tell you that everything I learned about the firm after this first review backed up what it said, I think you'll quickly understand why I wanted you to see it. It really says everything you need to read to understand what makes Watkins & Eager so special:

"When you asked for great places to work, one place immediately popped into my mind—the law firm of Watkins and Eager in Jackson . . . in the decades I've been in law school administration and had the opportunity to observe them, few people have ever left Watkins & Eager.

Lawyers there are happy, and even more importantly, they have happy families outside of the office. It's one thing for attorneys to like their job, but it's another for their family to be happy with that job. This is a firm that recognizes that families are important and should come first. If your three-year-old is a butterfly in the preschool play on Friday morning, this is the firm that will do all it can to see that you are covered, and that you are indeed the proud parent of the butterfly in the front row in the school auditorium that morning.

"There is no glass ceiling at this firm for women. In fact, this is one of the first firms in this state, as far as I know, that was setting precedent and making the rules as they went along, years ago. One of their associates made partner in eight years because she was on the 'mommy track' first. And this didn't just happen yesterday—this was years ago, when the timetable for many female law school grads went like this: graduate, take the bar, start the job, get married, get pregnant, go back to work and then quit, because the general consensus among most of the people in the business, who were men, was that you couldn't possibly be a good mother and a good attorney. This is the firm that has actively sought out women who had outstanding credentials but may have wanted to work only 20 hours a week—and, I might add, the firm was willing to pay, and has always paid, the pro rata same salary to those who worked part time, which was almost unheard of. The firm has always worked hard to be flexible, adjusting itself to the woman's needs. And it's not just a great firm for women—this is a firm where many of the men who are now partners waited until they were older to marry and to have families. Therefore, families and their children have always been important to them.

"On top of all of this, they have a simply outstanding reputation in the legal community."

Wow.

Although that review pretty much says it all, you find when you hear from associates at Watkins & Eager that they have stories to add, to show how much they enjoy their firm. They enjoy the responsibility they get and the extraordinary teachers they have among the firm's partners. They say that, "Everybody here is willing to share their expertise. When you've got to write something, there's always someone who has done something similar so that you don't have to totally reinvent the wheel." Others comment how "senior partners make each of us feel as though we are part of the team no matter how many years of practice or experience we have."

Associates rave about the fact that "You can choose what area you want to work in, and there's no limit to the number of times you can change your area of practice." They appreciate that "the firm doesn't overly commit to the nonsense of committees and meetings," but rather the firm lets them hone the skills that will make them great lawyers. As one associate says, "You know they expect you to be here for the long haul, and they treat you that way. They only hire people they feel will make partner. They are very careful analyzing who gets job offers at the beginning, so that the people who get offers will stay here for a long time."

No matter how much they like the work, associates at W&E harken back again and again to the family atmosphere they appreciate so much. They say that, "The sense of not-taking-yourself-too-seriously starts right at the top. The firm just celebrated its centennial a couple of years ago, and it involved some really big-name speakers, followed by a reception and dinner at the country club. It was great to see the partners get out on the dance floor and boogie!" Then there's the annual pig roast at one of the partners' farms, where "all of the attorneys bring their children and fish and play football, while many of the younger associates spend the previous night celebrating and preparing the main course." There's also an "annual golf tournament" and the "annual fried chicken dinner prepared by one of our housekeepers, with all donations from people at the firm going to her church."

Associates talk about "the firm lunchroom, where we catch up on current events, test our analytical and debating skills, and socialize. If you miss out on the lunchroom, you really feel like you have missed out!" One associate says that, "Even people who take clients to lunch or go out of the office to eat, come back into the kitchen to catch the final couple of minutes of lunchroom banter." In the spirit of 'little things mean a lot,' one associate says that "Many associates and clerks say that one of their favorite things about W&E is that the firm provides peanut butter and crackers, Cokes and coffee for everyone in the office. There is nothing like a peanut butter and cracker break at 4:30 to help you through those long evenings!"

All in all, associates find that "The people at W&E are like a family. Many of us have strong friendships that started at the office, and have grown to encompass our families and become important parts of our lives."

Wharton, Aldhizer & Weaver, P.L.C.

100 South Mason Street • P. O. Box 20028 • Harrisonburg, Virginia 22801-7528
Phone: 540-434-0316 • Fax: 540-434-5502 • E-mail: waw@wawlaw.com

OFFICES

Harrisonburg, Virginia

"We get all kinds of cases here, from defending farmers whose cows have been the cause of automobile accident—we call those 'cow in the road' cases—to successfully defending a Fortune 500 company from a takeover attempt . . . working here has given me the chance to develop strong friendships with the finest attorneys I've ever known, become active in a family-oriented community, and discover the thrill of fly fishing."

HIGHLIGHTS

- 26-attorney firm, evenly split between transactional work and litigation.

NUTS AND BOLTS

Managing partner:

There are three members of the Management Committee:
Douglas Guynn, William E. Shmidheiser III, Jeffrey Lenhart

Hiring partner:

G. Rodney Young, II, phone: 540-434-0316, e-mail: Hilton@Shentel.Net

Recruiting coordinator:

Cindy Holsinger, phone: 540-434-0316, e-mail: waw@wawlaw.com

Number of attorneys in firm:

26
Partners (23), associates (3), total women (4), total minorities (0)

Years to make partner:

5 to 6

WHAT DO THEY DO?

Primary specialties (more than 5% of practice):

(Note that the numbers exceed the number of attorneys in the firm, because some attorneys have more than one specialty.)

Banking, Bond, Public Finance (3); Corporate, Securities, Tax (3); Employment, Environmental, Labor, Workers' Comp (6); Defense Litigation, Malpractice, Medical (8); Business, ERISA, Employee Benefits (1); Education, Health, Municipal (4); Land Use, Real Estate, Zoning (1); Bankruptcy, Creditor Rights (1); Antitrust, Health Care, Intellectual Property (1); Estates, Trusts, Wills (1); School Law (3).

First year associates are given exposure to many of the firm's practice areas, and then the firm tries to fit the associate's interests with the firm's needs. Associates sometimes switch specialties.

WHO DO THEY REPRESENT?

Clients include large poultry and fruit processors; container manufacturing specialists; design printers; electronics/satellite specialists; tax-exempt organizations, such as health-care providers including hospitals and retirement communities; educational institutions, including numerous school boards as well as colleges, and county government.

WHERE NEW ASSOCIATES COME FROM . . .

The firm routinely interviews on campus at the following law schools: UVA, William & Mary, Washington & Lee, Richmond. The firm routinely hires from schools where it doesn't perform on-campus interviews.

HOURS AND BUCKS . . .

On average, first year associates spend 2,200 hours at the office, of which 1,600 to 1,800 is the billable hour goal, depending on the practice area. There is no minimum billable hours requirement.

Attorneys have been allowed to work part-time in exceptional cases, but part-time work is not currently available at entry level. The firm does not routinely hire contract associates.

Typical first year salary, including typical bonus: $$ ($35-50,000)

SUMMER PROGRAM . . .

Weekly pay: $750.
The firm does not routinely hire 1Ls for its summer program.

PRO BONO . . .

Associates are encouraged to do pro bono work. Pro bono hours are not counted as billable hours. Associates have been involved in a variety of pro bono projects, including landlord/tenant disputes, divorce, and contract disputes.

HISTORY AT A GLANCE . . .

Firm began in the 1840's.

WHAT IT'S LIKE TO WORK THERE . . .

Associates at WAW marvel at the "high level of professionalism" at the firm, the "integrity" of the attorneys, and the "incredible support" they get from the partners. One commented that "not too long ago, I attended a professionalism seminar that the state requires. While I was there, several attorneys who represent opposing parties sang WAW's praises, universally saying how much they respect the members of the firm. In fact, one of the firm's most formidable opponents remarked to me that 'a handshake is all I need from one of your colleagues to seal a deal.' It is truly a place where an attorney's word is his bond."

The level of responsibility offered to junior associates is exemplified in one female associate's experience: "After I had been here for a year and a half, doing municipal finance work, my supervising attorney left the firm. I was sure that all the work I had done in municipal finance was going to be wasted, because I didn't think there was any way the firm would let me continue to do municipal finance work myself. I only had 18 months of experience! But the firm basically told me, 'If you can continue the municipal finance practice, fine. If not, we'll match you up with something else.' With a lot of support, I *did* continue the municipal finance practice. I realize now, a few years later, the level of confidence the firm had in me as an associate, giving me primary responsibility for an important practice area! It was a *tremendous* opportunity for me to grow professionally as an attorney, and as a woman who assumed a leadership position in our firm early in my practice. This firm never heard of a 'glass ceiling'—I'm proof of that!"

Other associates recount similar experiences, applauding the firm's "sophisticated practice in a small-town environment," with one associate talking about how he "handled my own cases at trial and before the

Supreme Court of Virginia and the Fourth Circuit, shortly after I arrived here."

Associates find that the responsibility they get is matched by the friendly environment in which they get to work. They recall that, "The last time a bad snow storm hit our area, the firm threw a lunchtime pizza party for all the staff and attorneys who had somehow managed to struggle in that day." Others talk about getting together often outside of the office. "Groups of lawyers go jogging just about every day, rain or shine, snow or sleet." And when it comes to appreciating the importance of families, "It would be hard for them *not* to, because almost all of the attorneys have children. In fact, most of them have large families, and some of them have as many as eight or nine children!"

It also doesn't hurt to be practicing in a place that associates consider "lovely." Harrisonburg is a town of about 30,000, and "growing rapidly" (which isn't too surprising, what with eight- and nine-child families in the neighborhood!). It is about two hours from Washington, and as one associate commented, "My concerns about leaving behind an exciting big-city, big-firm practice quickly dissolved with the friendly atmosphere, sophisticated work and beautiful surroundings of the Shenandoah Valley." Another added that "If you think working in a small town is going to be boring, think again. We get all kinds of cases here, from defending farmers whose cows have been the cause of automobile accidents—we call those 'cow in the road' cases—to successfully defending a Fortune 500 company from a corporate takeover attempt. There's all kinds of interesting work to be done!"

Winston & Strawn

1400 L Street, N.W. • Washington, D.C. 20005-3502
Phone: 202-371-5700 • Fax: 202-371-5950 • Web site: winston.com

OFFICES

Washington, D.C. (Chicago-based firm)

HIGHLIGHTS

- Washington branch office of the 20TH largest law firm in the country.
- Strong dedication to pro bono work; pro bono hours are considered billables.
- Partner James R. Thompson, former governor of Illinois, listed in the *National Law Journal* as one of the country's 100 most influential lawyers.

NUTS AND BOLTS

Managing partner:

J. Michael McGarry, III (D.C. office)

Hiring partner:

Paul H. Hensel (Hiring chairman for all offices),
phone: 312-558-5600, e-mail: phensel@winston.com

Recruiting coordinator:

Victoria Rozanski (D.C. office),
phone: 202-371-5995, e-mail: Vrozansk@winston.com

Number of attorneys in firm:

550 (240 partners)

TOTAL FIRM:

Women partners (27), women associates (111), minority partners (11), minority associates (39)

WASHINGTON OFFICE:

Total attorneys (123), total partners (67), total associates (47), women partners (4), women associates (11), minority partners (2), minority associates (4)

OTHER OFFICES:

Chicago (main office) (335), New York (106), Paris (7), Geneva (5)

Years to make partner:

Approximately 8

WHAT DO THEY DO?

Almost a third of the firm's attorneys are litigators, and almost a quarter are corporate lawyers. Other specialties include employment relations, energy, environmental, international, and tax. The firm's corporate practice is based primarily in Chicago and New York; the Washington office is the center for its international, energy, and governmental relations and regulatory affairs practices.

The firm is departmentalized. Junior associates can, and do, switch specialties.

WHO DO THEY REPRESENT?

An enormous variety of clients both domestically and abroad, including governments and government entities, Fortune 500 companies, major commercial and financial institutions, as well as individuals and small to mid-sized companies.

Clients include Abbott Labs, American Brands, Ameritech, Argosy Gaming Company, Bankers Trust, Barr Labs, Caterpillar, CIGNA, Commonwealth Edison, Deutsche Bank AG, Euro Disney, FMC Corporation, The First National Bank of Chicago, Gateway 2000, Harris Trust and Savings Bank, Heller Financial, Household International, Interstate Brands, Jefferson Smurfit, Luxottica Group, Mitsubishi International, Monsanto, NationsBank, Nebraska Public Power, Northeast Utilities, Northern Trust Company, Northrup-Grumman, Pacific Gas & Electric, Philip Morris, The Prime Group, Salomon Brothers, Sanwa Business Credit, State Farm, Tenneco, Tennessee Valley Authority, and USA Waste Services.

WHERE NEW ASSOCIATES COME FROM . . .

The firm routinely interviews on campus at the following law schools: Boalt Hall, Boston University, Chicago, Columbia, Cornell, Duke, Fordham, George Washington, Georgetown, Harvard, Hastings, Hofstra, Illinois, Indiana/Bloomington, Iowa, Michigan, Minnesota, NYU, Northwestern, Notre Dame, Ohio State, Pennsylvania, Stanford, UCLA, Vanderbilt, Virginia, Wisconsin, and Yale.

The firm also hires from schools where it doesn't interview on campus.

HOURS AND BUCKS . . .

Associates work an average of 2,100 hours per year. Average billable hours are 1,800. There is no minimum billable hours requirement.

Part-time work is available to continuing associates; it is not available at entry level. The firm does not hire contract associates.

Typical first year associate salary, including typical bonus: $$$$ (Over $65,000). The firm is known for its very generous financial package.

SUMMER PROGRAM . . .

Last year, there were 12 summer associates; nine 2Ls and three 1Ls. Eight of the 2Ls received offers.

Weekly pay: $1,400 last year

1Ls are routinely hired for the summer program. Last year's 1Ls came from Stanford and Michigan.

PRO BONO . . .

The firm encourages associates to take part in pro bono. Pro bono hours are treated as billable hours. Attorneys from the firm routinely provide a variety of pro bono representation in the following areas: community economic development, criminal defense, First Amendment/free speech, contested guardianship matters, landlord/tenant, not-for-profit corporate organization, political asylum, post-conviction relief in death penalty cases, and public assistance.

HISTORY AT A GLANCE . . .

One of the country's oldest and largest law firms, Winston & Strawn was founded in 1853. Since the Civil War, the firm has attracted and produced some of the firm's most influential lawyers, and been involved in many ground-breaking and headline-making cases.

Founders Frederick H. Winston and Silas H. Strawn were important players in Chicago's emergence as a powerful business and financial center. Today the firm's partners include a number of leaders in the American legal community. Among them: four-term Illinois Governor James R. Thompson, ranked as one of the nation's 100 most influential lawyers by the *National Law Journal;* former Arkansas Congressman Beryl F. Anthony; Dan K. Webb, a former U.S. Attorney who prosecuted John Poindexter in the Iran-Contra trial; and former U.S. Secretary of Transportation James H. Burnley, IV.

The Washington office opened in 1990.

Wyatt, Tarrant & Combs—Louisville

Citizens Plaza • 500 West Jefferson Street • Louisville, KY 40202-2898
Phone: 502-589-5235 • Fax: 502-589-0309 • Web site: http://www.wyattfirm.com

OFFICES

Louisville (main office), Lexington, Frankfort, Kentucky; Memphis*,
Nashville (downtown)*, Nashville (Music Row),
Hendersonville, Kingsport, Tennessee; New Albany, Indiana

"The partners put a tremendous amount of faith in us. Everybody respects everybody else, and everybody supports and stands behind you. There was one early case when I got here, six months out of school, where the opposing counsel was a hothead. He accused me of violating a settlement agreement, and that wasn't true—but he talked about suing me. I was shaking like a wet chihuahua. I told the senior litigation partner about it, concerned that I had done something wrong without realizing it. The partner said, 'You did nothing wrong. You call him back and tell him, if he wants to sue you, he should sue me, too, and I'll pay the filing fee. In fact—I'll call him myself.'"

HIGHLIGHTS

- One of the largest and best-known firms in the southeastern U.S., and the 154TH largest firm in the country.
- The firm received the Silver Designation Award from the Business/Family Partnership, which recognizes area employers that have family-friendly workplace policies and practices and that strive to help their employees to balance work and family issues.
- Cutting-edge technology, including video conferencing, and a full-time management information staff, including trainers, to help the firm's lawyers keep up with new systems.
- The firm was recently chosen by DuPont as one of 34 law firms to represent its interests throughout the country. DuPont researched and

interviewed over 300 law firms nationwide, and chose the firm to represent it in Kentucky and Tennessee.

NUTS AND BOLTS

Managing partner:

Stewart E. Conner

Hiring partner:

Virginia H. Snell, phone: 502-562-7366

Recruiting coordinator:

Nina Lucille Stack, phone: 502-562-7140

Number of attorneys in firm:

229 (124 partners)

TOTAL FIRM:

Partners (124), associates (71), women partners (15), women associates (31), minority partners (2), minority associates (11), disabled partners (0), disabled associates (0), of counsel (33), women of counsel (5)

THIS OFFICE:

Total attorneys (102), partners (64), associates (23), women partners (10), women associates (14), minority partners (1), minority associates (6), disabled partners (0), disabled associates (0), of counsel (5), women of counsel (1)

OTHER OFFICES:

(* represents an office profiled elsewhere in this book)
Lexington, KY (14); Frankfort, KY (3); New Albany, IN (7); Memphis, TN* (34); Nashville (downtown), TN* (31); Nashville (Music Row), TN (4); Hendersonville, TN (3); Kingsport, TN (4)

Years to make partner:

7 to 8

WHAT DO THEY DO?

Primary specialties (more than 5% of practice):

BUSINESS LAW DEPARTMENT:

General Business Group, including financial institutions (55); Real Estate and Lending Group (42); Taxation Group (10); Estate Planning Group

(16); Employee Benefits Group (8); Public Finance Group (7); Health Care Group (9); Entertainment Practice Group (7); Intellectual Property & Technology Licensing Practice Group (6); Opinions and Standards Group (9).

LITIGATION DEPARTMENT:

Antitrust, Securities & RICO (20); Commercial Litigation, including Governmental Law and Construction (71); Mineral & Energy Group (19); Environmental Group (20); Communications Law (6); Labor & Employment Law (38); Tort and Insurance Practice (34); Bankruptcy/ Creditors' Rights (29).

Most attorneys are assigned to more than one practice group.

Associates may switch practice groups, but this happens infrequently since they usually are not assigned to a particular practice group until they have been with the firm for 2 to 3 years. By that time they usually find a niche. However, sometimes firm needs and associate preferences change, and in that case everybody works together to make the switch.

WHO DO THEY REPRESENT?

The firm has a vast array of clients, including Aetna, Allied Health System, AnnTaylor, Bank of Nashville, Baptist Healthcare System, Bellsouth Telecommunications, Churchill Downs Incorporated, E.I. du Pont de Nemours & Company, Ford Motor, General Electric, General Motors, Harrah's Entertainment, Merrill Lynch, Metropolitan Life Insurance, Nashville Songwriters Association International, Perdue Farms, Pfizer, Resolution Trust Corporation, Reynolds Metals, Schering-Plough, Joseph E. Seagram & Sons, Shoney's, Sunbeam, Union Planters, the University of Memphis, and Westvaco Corporation.

WHERE NEW ASSOCIATES COME FROM . . .

The firm routinely interviews on campus at the following law firms: Kentucky, Louisville, Vanderbilt, Tennessee, Memphis, Washington & Lee, Virginia, and William & Mary. The firm also routinely hires from schools where it doesn't interview on campus.

HOURS AND BUCKS . . .

Associates have a 1,900 billable hour target, with a minimum billable hour requirement of 1,800 hours.

The firm allows part-time work on a case-by-case basis, and it is available to entry level associates. The firm only occasionally hires contract associates. None have become full-time associates.

Typical first year salary, including typical bonus: $$$ ($50-65,000)

SUMMER PROGRAM . . .

Last year (for all offices), there were 17 summer clerks, 8 of whom were eligible for immediate offers; 7 received offers.

Weekly pay: $1,000 this year

1Ls are routinely hired for the summer program. Last year's 1Ls came from the University of Virginia and Washington University.

The firm generally recruits 2Ls between September and December 1, and 1Ls from December 1 to the end of February, although these deadlines may be extended as needed.

PRO BONO . . .

A designated partner in each office monitors pro bono projects. The firm requires 50 hours annually from each attorney during the first three years the associate spends with the firm. Pro bono hours are not considered billables.

Partner Robert Ewald recently received the Arthur von Briesen Award, named for the National Legal Aid & Defender Association's first president, which recognizes outstanding volunteer contributions in support of legal assistance to the poor.

HISTORY AT A GLANCE . . .

The firm traces its roots to the 1800's, and today is the product of the merger of several distinguished law firms throughout Kentucky, Southern Indiana, and Tennessee.

The firm has a long history of well-known partners. Members of the firm have served as Governor of Kentucky, Kentucky Supreme Court Justice, Attorney General of Tennessee, Mayor of Louisville and Lexington, Presidential Cabinet Member, and many more. They include Wilson Wyatt, who died in 1996 at the age of 91, who is considered the real patriarch of the firm. As former Mayor of Louisville, Lieutenant Governor of Kentucky, and U.S. Solicitor General, he set the stage for Wyatt's commitment to community service. He often quoted from the oath taken by Athenian youth that one is "to leave his city better than he found it." The quote is engraved in the statue of Mr. Wyatt that is prominently displayed at the firm's Louisville office.

WHAT IT'S LIKE TO WORK THERE . . .

When you talk with associates at Wyatt Tarrant, you notice right away how relieved they are that the firm is not at all what they expected from a large firm. "Everybody told me, 'Don't go to a large firm, you won't last, it's a slave den.' None of the horror stories of large firms turned out to be true here." Another associate adds that "I came here because I researched it and found it wasn't what everybody expects from a large firm. I wasn't going to put up with the kinds of bull you hear about large firms dishing out. I'm too old for that."

On the contrary, when associates join Wyatt Tarrant, they find a place that's "'Comfortably prestigious,' I'd call it. It's important to be at a firm everybody respects, but also to work with people you enjoy, doing work you like. I didn't have to sacrifice one for the other." Other associates echo that sentiment, saying that, "There's a certain level of admiration for this firm that puts it head and shoulders above the others. It's so respected."

Associates rave that "This is not a firm where lawyers stay closeted in offices, working alone, with little contact. It's an open environment where people freely discuss cases, and when you've got a problem, whether it's professional or personal, people immediately express their concern, and they're always offering to help out." One associate tells how "Last year, a number of associates at one of the offices were heavily recruited by another regional law firm that made every effort to convince them to leave. The associates stayed, every one of them. That tells you everything you need to know about the firm." And one associate added, "You're looking at a happy lawyer. I like what I do. I like who I work with. I can't imagine working anywhere else."

"There's an open door policy—you are never chastised for asking questions."

When associates join the firm, they don't join a particular practice group until they've been with the firm for two or three years, and by that time, they usually find a niche. In the meantime, junior associates get assignments either from senior associates or partners, "There's no associate manager who funnels assignments to us," although "There is generally one senior associate or lower-level partner who supervises you." One associate laughingly says that, "I was the summer associate coordinator for the Nashville office. It was supposed to work so that assignments went through me, to the summer associates. That worked for about an hour."

With an 'open season' assignment policy, associates find it valuable that "Partners and senior associates are sensitive to workloads. They'll come to your office, sit down and say, 'How does your work look? If you can't fit this in, I'll give it to someone else.' And they *want* you to be honest with them."

Associates say they get a broad base of experience, and that "the 'cross-pollination' between practice groups at the firm gives you exposure to lots of things. For instance, there might be an estate problem that touches on bankruptcy, or there's a suit against someone who dies, the estate law people will walk down the hall and chat with the appropriate lawyers. So you see all kinds of things."

Associates find that "because they hire you fully expecting that you'll one day be partner, they do everything they can to train you well and give you the feedback you need to help correct any problems that come up." On top of that, "the training isn't just about substantive things. They have ongoing 'people skills' training, because they recognize that those kinds of abilities can make the difference between conventional law firm product and truly excellent client service. They want us to be outstanding lawyers." While the formal evaluation and training they get is useful, associates most appreciate that "You hear things through the crucible of the partners' experience. The whole point of working with some of the best lawyers in the country is to soak up their wisdom, and they make it easy to do that. Everybody is incredibly easy to work with."

The training and feedback associates get is vital because "They give you huge responsibility right off the bat!" according to a Nashville associate. "I was almost worried they were putting too *much* faith in me. Within one month of getting here, they dropped a civil RICO case in my lap, on behalf of a huge company. In this little town one of the employees decided he'd get into the trucking business. At the company, he was the control person concerning who got to ship the company's stuff, and what do you know—a lot of that work went to his own little trucking business, at very inflated prices." A junior associate in Louisville talks about being involved with "First Amendment cases that have gone all the way up. I had a defamation case where I represented a newspaper with a $1 million verdict against them." Another associate talks of "doing all the work for a guy who's running for the U.S. Senate, all of the legal work for the campaign, all of the forms, issues of campaign contributions. It's really exciting."

Other associates add that "They'll give you a case as a junior associate, and say, 'You draft the complaint, fire it up, we'll stand behind you and give you the help you need, from this office and any other office as well.'" Associates say that, "In litigation, it's not unusual to be a 'pick and shovel' guy. We prepare complaints or answers, do the discovery, do the initial interviews with clients and witnesses, all under the supervision of a partner. We dig the ditches and lay the pipe for the cases." Transactional associates agree that "client contact isn't what you'd call a problem here!" And associates all recognize that "This is a firm where self-starters are rewarded. Nothing washes you out more quickly than not getting your transmission in gear right away." "There's a knock at large firms that you're going to spend five or six years in the library. It's just not true here. They give you all the responsibility you can handle." One associate laughs that "Working here is challenging in the best possible way. I enjoy coming to work. It's always interesting. It's the work I'd always hoped I'd be doing. It's a joy to come here and work every day. My wife makes fun of me because I'm the only person she knows who loves my job!"

"They view us as future partners."

The firm makes a point of involving associates in firm management. Associates are responsible for the summer program every year, and the firm's Professional Personnel Recruiting Committee has associate members who are actively involved in hiring in every office. As one associate says, "The firm makes a point of putting associates, and not just partners, on committees. It gives them a fresh perspective. Partners just don't know what's going on out there anymore sometimes!"

Associates say that, "Every year at the partnership retreat, one of the primary topics on the agenda concerns ways to maintain high associate morale. The discussions always plainly show the partners' recognition that we are the firm's future, and our success is vital to the firm's success." Associates applaud the fact that "Even informally, the partners are really easy to approach with anything that's on your mind. And they have incredible integrity. They say what they mean and they do what they say."

"We aren't worked to death by any means."

Associates at all of Wyatt Tarrant's offices make a point of mentioning the livable hours they work. Typically the offices fill up around 8:30 in the morning, and "if there isn't anything pressing" associates are out by 5:30. Associates say that "if there's something you need to do after that, you can take it home and work after the kids go to bed, if that's what you want to do." On weekends, "You can come in on Saturday morning. Some people always do that. But it's generally uncommon to see people here on weekends." Others comment that "If you go to the office on Saturday morning, it's quiet time and it's easy to catch up on things. But many people don't show up at all on weekends. There's no point on coming in to show your face, because nobody will be here to see it." One associate raves that "One of the best perks about this place is free time! The law business is becoming so intense in terms of time and pressure. This firm gives you the time to raise a family. Most people are married with kids—it's very family-friendly. It's a place where you can actually enjoy your 20s and 30s." Other associates point out that "You don't feel like there's attrition here, either from summer associates to permanent ones, or permanent associates to partner. If you work hard, you become partner. It makes your lifestyle better. There's no competitive atmosphere, this idea that 'He's staying 'til 7, I have to stay until 8.'"

When associates do have to work late because of pressing projects, they don't resent it because "Either it's something you could have gotten to during the day but didn't, and so you brought the late hours on yourself. Or you're working on a project you're really excited about. Either way, you don't mind it." Other associates add that, "Depending on what you do, you know it's going to take long hours. If you work in Wills and Trusts or

Estate Planning, those hours aren't as sensitive. You just won't work long hours. But if you're in litigation, you know from the get-go that it's going to sometimes mean long hours. It's not because of the firm, it's because you're not entirely in control of your calendar—it's ruled by docket clerks. It's the nature of the beast. There are going to be crazy hours sometimes. That's why it's so important to love what you do—and I do!"

"Law is a stressful business. It helps to work with
people you consider your friends."

On a formal basis, "Each office has a lot of events during the summer, for the summer program." Summertime is also an opportunity for an all-attorney event at each office. For instance, the Louisville office "held a picnic during the summer for everyone and their families at the Louisville Zoo, complete with food, games, and a look at all of the animals." Other offices hold golf tournaments, and "some offices have softball teams. There are often softball games between offices." The firm has an annual "day at the races" at Churchill Downs for everyone in all of the offices, where "we enjoy the races—not to mention the full buffet lunch!" Informally, "Some of the associates get together and play poker," and in the Nashville office, "People get together for music—of course. One guy here is also a songwriter, and we go to see him play." Associates say that "People are always getting together to do things outside of work. There are football and basketball games, going to Spring Training in Florida, houseboat outings, socializing at local clubs and pubs, or just hanging out at someone's house for dinner."

"There's a great lifestyle here."

Associates uniformly say that, "The cities where the firm has offices offer a desirable lifestyle that costs a lot less than larger cities." One associate in Louisville comments that "I've lived in Boston and D.C., but Louisville is great. I could buy a house quickly. There's very little traffic. But we do have culture—theater, orchestra, sports. The lifestyle adds so much to enjoying your work." One associate tells of how "My father was a stockbroker on the stock exchange, in New York. He got up at 5:15 in the morning to drive to work, and got home after 6:30 p.m. That's a pain in the neck, that commute! That's not what I wanted. I wanted a smaller city, where you wouldn't get lost—you could get to know the geography. I wanted something less high-pitched. And I found it."

Associates admit that, "There are some cultural differences between Yankees and Southerners, especially among the older lawyers" who can "slather 'good ole boy' all over you once in a while." But it's a mistake to think that the partners are all a single note. On the contrary, associates love the "Eclectic collection of personalities here." One associate says that "You're not punished for whatever you've done before, for having a life before law school. I had two kids, I went to school at night, and I fit right in here." One associate laughingly recalls "We had a Halloween costume party, and a senior partner showed up wearing a pink tu-tu. You'd think we'd have been surprised, but the comment most people made was, 'He really should have shaved his legs.' It's a place that accommodates quirky personalities."

"Despite being the largest firm in the region, Wyatt, Tarrant has an amazingly personal, supportive relationship with its employees."

Associates appreciate that "The firm takes a long-term view of its associates. It never has a large entry-level group, with the idea in mind that it would be impossible for the entire group to make partner. Instead, the firm really focuses on us as individuals and treats us as though we all have the potential to qualify for partnership when it's our turn." This philosophy results in "an excellent retention rate. People have lots of opportunities to go to other places. You get calls all the time. But nobody leaves." One associate tells of how "I used to work at a small firm, and I liked that atmosphere, but I didn't like the feeling of waiting for the next client. Here, we have the best of both worlds. A small office feel, but the resources of a large firm—particularly a phenomenal library—and a lot of bicep behind you!"

One associate tells of how "Last year, I was faced with the quite devastating loss of both parents within months of each other. The firm was at my side in all respects. The funeral home was literally dominated by co-workers from every level. I was given—actually encouraged to take—every accommodation in terms of time off. Associates and partners alike rushed in to keep up my cases. As pleased as I was from the firm's reaction, I wasn't at all surprised. It's simply the way things are done here. And, of course, this kind of support breeds loyalty. So when I was recently heavily recruited to leave Wyatt to go work with another firm, there was no decision. Our low associate turnover rate confirms that I'm not alone in my loyalty to this place."

Wyatt, Tarrant & Combs—Nashville (downtown)

1500 Nashville City Center • 511 Union Street • Nashville, TN 37219-1750
Phone: 615-244-0020 • Fax: 615-256-1726 • Web site: http://www.wyattfirm.com

OFFICES

Nashville (downtown), Nashville (Music Row), Memphis*,
Hendersonville, Kingsport, Tennessee; Louisville (main office)*,
Lexington, Frankfort, Kentucky; New Albany, Indiana

"The partners put a tremendous amount of faith in us. Everybody respects everybody else, and everybody supports and stands behind you. There was one early case when I got here, six months out of school, where the opposing counsel was a hothead. He accused me of violating a settlement agreement, and that wasn't true—but he talked about suing me. I was shaking like a wet chihuahua. I told the senior litigation partner about it, concerned that I had done something wrong without realizing it. The partner said, 'You did nothing wrong. You call him back and tell him, if he wants to sue you, he should sue me, too, and I'll pay the filing fee. In fact—I'll call him myself."

HIGHLIGHTS

- One of the largest and best-known firms in the southeastern U.S., and the 154TH largest firm in the country.
- The firm received the Silver Designation Award from the Business/ Family Partnership, which recognizes area employers that have family-friendly workplace policies and practices and that strive to help their employees to balance work and family issues.
- Cutting-edge technology, including video conferencing, and a full-time management information staff, including trainers, to help the firm's lawyers keep up with new systems.

- The firm was recently chosen by DuPont as one of 34 law firms to represent its interests throughout the country. DuPont researched and interviewed over 300 law firms nationwide, and chose the firm to represent it in Kentucky and Tennessee.

NUTS AND BOLTS

Managing partner:

Stewart E. Conner (at the Louisville office)

Hiring partner:

Virginia H. Snell (at the Louisville office), phone: 502-562-7366

Recruiting coordinator:

Nina Lucille Stack (at the Louisville office), phone: 502-562-7140

Number of attorneys in firm:

229 (124 partners)

TOTAL FIRM:

Partners (124), associates (71), women partners (15), women associates (31), minority partners (2), minority associates (11), disabled partners (0), disabled associates (0), of counsel (33), women of counsel (5)

THIS OFFICE:

Total attorneys (31), partners (13), associates (10), women partners (2), women associates (5), minority partners (0), minority associates (4), disabled partners (0), disabled associates (0), of counsel (9), women of counsel (2)

OTHER OFFICES:

Louisville, KY* (102); Lexington, KY (41); Frankfort, KY (3); New Albany, IN (7); Memphis, TN* (34); Nashville (Music Row), TN (4); Hendersonville, TN (3); Kingsport, TN (4)

Years to make partner

7 to 8

WHAT DO THEY DO?

Primary specialties (more than 5% of practice):

BUSINESS LAW DEPARTMENT:

General Business Group, including financial institutions (55); Real Estate and Lending Group (42); Taxation Group (10); Estate Planning Group (16); Employee Benefits Group (8); Public Finance Group (7); Health

Care Group (9); Entertainment Practice Group (7); Intellectual Property & Technology Licensing Practice Group (7); Opinions and Standards Group (9).

LITIGATION DEPARTMENT:

Antitrust, Securities & RICO (20); Commercial Litigation, including Governmental Law and Construction (71); Mineral & Energy Group (19); Environmental Group (20); Communications Law (6); Labor & Employment Law (38); Tort and Insurance Practice (34); Bankruptcy/ Creditors' Rights (29).

Most attorneys are assigned to more than one practice group.

Associates may switch practice groups, but this happens infrequently since they usually are not assigned to a particular practice group until they have been with the firm for 2 to 3 years. By that time they usually find a niche. However, sometimes firm needs and associate preferences change, and in that case everybody works together to make the switch.

WHO DO THEY REPRESENT?

The firm has a vast array of clients, including Aetna, Allied Health System, AnnTaylor, Bank of Nashville, Baptist Healthcare System, Bellsouth Telecommunications, Churchill Downs Incorporated, E.I. du Pont de Nemours & Company, Ford Motor, General Electric, General Motors, Harrah's Entertainment, Merrill Lynch, Metropolitan Life Insurance, Nashville Songwriters Association International, Perdue Farms, Pfizer, Resolution Trust Corporation, Reynolds Metals, Schering-Plough, Joseph E. Seagram & Sons, Shoney's, Sunbeam, Union Planters, the University of Memphis, and Westvaco Corporation.

Some representative Nashville clients are the American Society of Composers, Authors and Publishers, Bank of Nashville, Country Music Foundation, E.I. du Pont de Nemours and Company, Gospel Music Association, H.G. Hill Company, Intermedia Partners, Independent Southern Bancshares, Inc., Nashville Thermal Transfer Corporation, Shop at Home, Inc., Trans Financial, Inc.

WHERE NEW ASSOCIATES COME FROM . . .

The firm routinely interviews on campus at the following law firms: Kentucky, Louisville, Vanderbilt, Tennessee, Memphis, Washington & Lee, Virginia, and William & Mary. The firm also routinely hires from schools where it doesn't interview on-campus.

HOURS AND BUCKS . . .

Associates have a 1,900 billable hour target, with a minimum billable hour requirement of 1,800 hours.

The firm allows part-time work on a case-by-case basis, and it is available to entry-level associates. The firm only occasionally hires contract associates. None have become full-time associates.

Typical first year salary, including typical bonus: $$$ ($50-65,000)

SUMMER PROGRAM . . .

Last year (for all offices) there were 17 summer clerks, 8 of whom were eligible for immediate offers; 7 received offers.

Weekly pay: $1,000 this year

1Ls are routinely hired for the summer program. Last year's 1Ls came from the University of Virginia and Washington University.

The firm generally recruits 2Ls between September and December 1, and 1Ls from December 1 to the end of February, although these deadlines may be extended as needed.

PRO BONO . . .

A designated partner in each office monitors pro bono projects. The firm requires 50 hours annually from each attorney. Pro bono hours are not considered billables.

Charles W. Bone, the Partner-in-Charge of the Nashville offices, is a member of the Board of Directors of the Nashville Bar Association and in 1997 received the YMCA of Middle Tennessee's Strong Kids Award and was named the Volunteer of the Year by the YMCA's Community Action Project for his work as a member of the Capital Committee.

HISTORY AT A GLANCE . . .

The firm traces its roots to the 1800s, and today is the product of the merger of several distinguished law firms throughout Kentucky, Southern Indiana, and Tennessee.

The firm has a long history of well-known partners. Members of the firm have served as Governor of Kentucky, Kentucky Supreme Court Justice, Attorney General of Tennessee, Mayor of Louisville and Lexington, Presidential Cabinet Member, and many more. They include Wilson Wyatt, who died in 1996 at the age of 91, who is considered the real patriarch of the firm. As former Mayor of Louisville, Lieutenant Governor of Kentucky, and U.S. Solicitor General, he set the stage for Wyatt's commitment to community service. He often quoted from the oath taken by Athenian youth that one is "to leave his city better than he found it." The quote is engraved in the statue of Mr. Wyatt that is prominently displayed at the firm's Louisville office.

In 1989, the firm developed a strategic plan for growth and as a result, merged with the distinguished Nashville, Tennessee law firm of Gilbert &

Milom. The Nashville office opened in 1990. In 1994, the Nashville office continued its growth and added prominent attorney Charles W. Bone and a group of four lawyers to its ranks.

WHAT IT'S LIKE TO WORK THERE . . .

Please read the firm's Louisville profile for a complete picture of what it's like to work at Wyatt, Tarrant.

Wyatt, Tarrant & Combs—Memphis

6075 Poplar Avenue, Suite 650 • Memphis, TN 38119-4721
Phone: 901-537-1000 • Fax: 901-537-1010 • Web site: http://www.wyattfirm.com

OFFICES

Memphis, Nashville (downtown)*, Nashville (Music Row),
Hendersonville, Kingsport, Tennessee; Louisville (main office)*,
Lexington, Frankfort, Kentucky; New Albany, Indiana

*"The partners put a tremendous amount of faith in us. Everybody
respects everybody else, and everybody supports and stands behind
you. There was one early case when I got here, six months out of
school, where the opposing counsel was a hothead. He accused me of
violating a settlement agreement, and that wasn't true—but he talked
about suing me. I was shaking like a wet chihuahua. I told the senior
litigation partner about it, concerned that I had done something
wrong without realizing it. The partner said, 'You did nothing wrong.
You call him back and tell him, if he wants to sue you, he should sue
me, too, and I'll pay the filing fee. In fact—I'll call him myself.'"*

HIGHLIGHTS

- One of the largest and best-known firms in the southeastern U.S., and
  the 154TH largest firm in the country.
- The firm received the Silver Designation Award from the
  Business/Family Partnership, which recognizes area employers that have
  family-friendly workplace policies and practices and that strive to help
  their employees to balance work and family issues.
- Cutting-edge technology, including video conferencing, and a full-time
  management information staff, including trainers, to help the firm's
  lawyers keep up with new systems.
- The firm was recently chosen by DuPont as one of 34 law firms to represent its interests throughout the country. DuPont researched and
  interviewed over 300 law firms nationwide, and chose the firm to represent it in Kentucky and Tennessee.

NUTS AND BOLTS

Managing partner:

Stewart E. Conner (in the Louisville office)

Hiring partner:

Virginia H. Snell (in the Louisville office), phone: 502-562-7366

Recruiting coordinator:

Nina Lucille Stack (in the Louisville office), phone: 502-562-7140

Number of attorneys in firm:

229 (124 partners)

TOTAL FIRM:

Partners (124), associates (71), women partners (15), women associates (31), minority partners (2), minority associates (11), disabled partners (0), disabled associates (0), of counsel (33), women of counsel (5)

THIS OFFICE:

Total attorneys (33), partners (16), associates (11), women partners (2), women associates (5), minority partners (1), minority associates (1), disabled partners (0), disabled associates (0), of counsel (7), women of counsel (1)

OTHER OFFICES:

(* represents an office profiled elsewhere in this book)
Louisville, KY* (102); Lexington, KY (41); Frankfort, KY (3); New Albany, IN (7); Nashville (downtown), TN* (31); Nashville (Music Row), TN (4); Hendersonville, TN (3); Kingsport, TN (4)

Years to make partner:

7 to 8

WHAT DO THEY DO?

Primary specialties (more than 5% of practice):

BUSINESS LAW DEPARTMENT:

General Business Group, including financial institutions (55); Real Estate and Lending Group (42); Taxation Group (10); Estate Planning Group (16); Employee Benefits Group (8); Public Finance Group (7); Health Care Group (9); Entertainment Practice Group (7); Intellectual Property & Technology Licensing Practice Group (2); Opinions and Standards Group (9).

LITIGATION DEPARTMENT:

Antitrust, Securities & RICO (20); Commercial Litigation, including Governmental Law and Construction (71); Mineral & Energy Group (19); Environmental Group (20); Communications Law (6); Labor & Employment Law (38); Tort and Insurance Practice (34); Bankruptcy/ Creditors' Rights (29).

Most attorneys are assigned to more than one practice group.

Associates may switch specialties, but this happens infrequently since they usually are not assigned to a particular practice group until they have been with the firm for 2 to 3 years. By that time they usually find a niche. However, sometimes firm needs and associate preferences change, and in that case everybody works together to make the switch.

WHO DO THEY REPRESENT?

The firm has a vast array of clients, including Aetna, Allied Health System, AnnTaylor, Bank of Nashville, Baptist Healthcare System, Bellsouth Telecommunications, Churchill Downs Incorporated, E.I. du Pont de Nemours & Company, Ford Motor, General Electric, General Motors, Harrah's Entertainment, Merrill Lynch, Metropolitan Life Insurance, Nashville Songwriters Association International, Perdue Farms, Pfizer, Resolution Trust Corporation, Reynolds Metals, Schering-Plough, Joseph E. Seagram & Sons, Shoney's, Sunbeam, Union Planters, the University of Memphis, and Westvaco Corporation.

Clients of the Memphis office include Conwod Company, L.P., E.I. du Pont de Nemours and Company, Gwatney Chevrolet, Harrah's Entertainment, International Paper Company, RFS Hotel Investors, Inc., Smith & Nephew Richards, Inc., Storage USA, Inc., Thomas & Betts Corp., and Union Planters Corporation.

WHERE NEW ASSOCIATES COME FROM . . .

The firm routinely interviews on campus at the following law firms: Kentucky, Louisville, Vanderbilt, Tennessee, Memphis, Washington & Lee, Virginia, and William & Mary. The firm also routinely hires from schools where it doesn't interview on campus.

HOURS AND BUCKS . . .

Associates have a 1,900 billable hour target, with a minimum billable hour requirement of 1,800 hours.

The firm allows part-time work on a case-by-case basis, and it is available to entry level associates. The firm only occasionally hires contract associates. None have become full-time associates.

Typical first year salary, including typical bonus: $$$ ($50-65,000)

SUMMER PROGRAM . . .

Last year, there were 17 summer clerks, 8 of whom were eligible for immediate offers. 7 received offers.

Weekly pay: $1,000 last year

1Ls are routinely hired for the summer program. Last year's 1Ls came from the University of Virginia and Washington University.

The firm generally recruits 2Ls between September and December 1, and 1Ls from December 1 to the end of February, although these are not strict deadlines.

PRO BONO . . .

A designated partner in each office monitors pro bono projects. The firm requires 50 hours annually from each attorney. Pro bono hours are not considered billables.

Thomas R. Dyer, the Partner-In-Charge of the Memphis office, is a member of the Board of Advisors to the Memphis Area Chamber of Commerce, the Board of The Dixon Gallery & Gardens and the Board of the Tennessee Supreme Court Historical Society.

HISTORY AT A GLANCE . . .

The firm traces its roots to the 1800s, and today is the product of the merger of several distinguished law firms throughout Kentucky, Southern Indiana, and Tennessee.

The firm has a long history of well-known partners. Members of the firm have served as Governor of Kentucky, Kentucky Supreme Court Justice, Attorney General of Tennessee, Mayor of Louisville and Lexington, Presidential Cabinet Member, and many more. They include Wilson Wyatt, who died in 1996 at the age of 91, who is considered the real patriarch of the firm. As former Mayor of Louisville, Lieutenant Governor of Kentucky, and U.S. Solicitor General, he set the stage for Wyatt's commitment to community service. He often quoted from the oath taken by Athenian youth that one is "to leave his city better than he found it." The quote is engraved in the statue of Mr. Wyatt that is prominently displayed at the firm's Louisville office.

In 1995, the firm opened its Memphis office when it merged with the Memphis-based McDonnell Dyer.

WHAT IT'S LIKE TO WORK THERE . . .

Please read the firm's Louisville profile for a complete picture of what it's like to work at Wyatt, Tarrant.

More of Americas Greatest Law Firms to Work for . . .

Alston & Bird—Atlanta, GA

One Atlantic Center • 1201 West Peachtree Street • Atlanta, GA 30309-3424
Phone: 404-881-7000 • Fax: 404-881-7777 • Web site: alston.com

OFFICES

Atlanta (main office), Georgia; Charlotte, Raleigh, North Carolina; Washington, D.C.

HIGHLIGHTS

• 48TH largest law firm in the country.

NUTS AND BOLTS

Hiring partner:

Mark Rusche

Recruiting director:

Emily Shields, 404-881-7014

Recruiting coordinator:

Karen Castleman, 404-881-7013

Number of attorneys in firm:

403 (186 partners)

ATLANTA OFFICE:

344 attorneys

OTHER OFFICES:

Charlotte, NC (36); Washington, D.C. (14); Raleigh, NC (9)

Years to make partner:

7

WHAT DO THEY DO?

Specialties (ranked from most attorneys to least): Corporate/Finance/International, Litigation, Tax/Fiduciary/ERISA/Estate Planning, Real

Estate, Healthcare and Medical, Malpractice, Antitrust, Labor, Technology & Intellectual Property, Bankruptcy, Environmental.

WHERE NEW ASSOCIATES COME FROM . . .

The firm routinely interviews on-campus at the following law schools: Boalt Hall, Chicago, Columbia, Duke, Emory, Florida, George Washington, Georgetown, Georgia, Georgia State, Harvard, Howard, Michigan, NYU, North Carolina, Stanford, Texas, Vanderbilt, Virginia, Wake Forest, and Yale. The firm also hires from schools where it doesn't conduct on-campus interviews.

HOURS AND BUCKS . . .

Hours: Associates work on average 2,410 hours/year; the average billable hours are 1,926; the minimum billable hours requirement is 1,800. Part-time work is available to associates, but not at entry level.

Starting salary: $$$$ (over $65,000)

SUMMER PROGRAM . . .

30 summer associates last year, of whom 27 received offers.

Weekly pay: $1,000 last year.

1Ls are not hired for the summer program, except for one 1L hired each year through the Minority Clerkship Program sponsored by the Atlanta Bar Association.

Arent Fox Kintner Plotkin & Kahn

1050 Connecticut Avenue, N.W. • Washington, D.C. 20036-5339
Phone: 202-857-6000 • Fax: 202-857-6395 • Web site: arentfox.com

OFFICES:

Washington, D.C. (main office); New York City, New York

HIGHLIGHTS

- 125TH largest firm in the country; 12TH largest in Washington, D.C.
- Strong dedication to pro bono work; pro bono hours are counted as billables.

NUTS AND BOLTS

Recruiting manager:

Colleen Mattingly

Number of attorneys in firm:

254 (114 partners)

WASHINGTON OFFICE:

226 attorneys (104 partners)

OTHER OFFICES:

New York, NY (19); Budapest (7); Jeddah, Kingdom of Saudi Arabia (2)

Years to make partner:

8

WHAT DO THEY DO?

Specialties: The firm is divided into five departments: Litigation (including Bankruptcy, Construction Litigation, General Litigation, and White Collar Criminal Defense); Federal Practice (including Advertising and Trade Regulation, Agricultural Law, Antitrust and Trade Regulation, Communications, Cyberspace Law, Environmental, Food and Drug, Government Contracts, and Intellectual Property); General Business (including Bank and Financial Institutions, Corporate/Securities, Estate Planning and Probate, Land Use and Zoning, Real Estate, Sports and Entertainment, and Taxation); International (including Energy and Natural Resources, Government Relations, and International Group); and EEHI (Employment, ERISA, Health and Immigration).

New associates choose the practice area they want to join, and depending on firm needs, they may choose more than one.

WHO DO THEY REPRESENT?

The firm's clients include governments and government entities, agencies or state corporations of a number of countries, and international institutions including the World Bank, International Finance Corporation, and the Inter-American Development Bank.

WHERE NEW ASSOCIATES COME FROM . . .

The firm routinely interviews on-campus at the following law schools: Cornell, Duke, Fordham, George Washington, Georgetown, Harvard, Howard, Maryland, Michigan, NYU, Pennsylvania, and Virginia.

The firm also hires from schools where it doesn't interview on campus.

HOURS AND BUCKS . . .

Hours: Associates work between 1,700 and 2,200 hours per year, of which between 1,600 and 2,100 are average billable hours. Part-time work is available to both continuing and entry-level associates, on a case-by-case basis.

Starting salary: $$$$ (Over $65,000). The firm is noted for its generous financial package.

SUMMER PROGRAM . . .

Last year, 17 summer associates, 14 of whom received offers.

Weekly pay: $1,300

HISTORY AT A GLANCE . . .

The firm was founded in 1942. Many of the firm's lawyers have a distinguished background in government, including a former U.S. Senator, a former member of the House of Representatives, and many others.

Armstrong Allen Prewitt Gentry Johnston & Holmes, P.L.L.C.

Brinkley Plaza, Suite 700 • 80 Monroe Avenue • Memphis, TN 38103-2467
Phone: 901-523-8211 • Fax: 901-524-4936

OFFICES

Memphis, Tennessee; Little Rock, Arkansas; Jackson, Mississippi

NUTS AND BOLTS

Hiring partner:
David Thornton

Recruiting coordinator:
Annette McGee

Number of attorneys in firm:
55 (29 partners)

WHAT DO THEY DO?

Specialties: General civil practice, including Litigation, Antitrust and Trade Regulation, Administrative Agencies, Arbitration, Banking, Bankruptcy, Computer Law, Condemnation, Copyrights and Trademarks, Corporate, Commercial, Employee Benefits, Entertainment, Environmental, Estate Planning, Franchising, Health Care and Hospitals, Insurance, Labor and Employment, Media, Medical Malpractice, Defense, Mergers and Acquisitions, Municipal Finance, Personal Injury, Probate, Products Liability, Real Estate, Securities, Taxation, Workers' Compensation, and Zoning.

WHO DO THEY REPRESENT?

A regional practice, serving clients mainly in Tennessee, Arkansas, and Mississippi. Clients include numerous national and international corporations, local business and individuals.

Baker Donelson
Bearman & Caldwell, P.C.

20ᵀᴴ Floor, First Tennessee Building • 165 Madison • Memphis, Tennessee 38103
Phone: 901-526-2000 • Fax: 901-577-2303

OFFICES

Memphis (main office), Chattanooga, Knoxville, Huntsville, and Johnson City, Tennessee; Jackson, Mississippi; Washington, D.C.

NUTS AND BOLTS

Hiring partner:

Mark Rusche

Number of attorneys in firm:

207 (110 partners)

MEMPHIS OFFICE:

76 attorneys

OTHER OFFICES:

Nashville, TN (39); Chattanooga, TN (28); Jackson, MS (22); Knoxville, TN (18); Washington, D.C. (12); Johnson City, TN (10); Huntsville, TN (2)

Starting salary:

$$$ ($50-65,000)

WHAT DO THEY DO?

Specialties: The firm is divided into four departments: Bankgroup, Corporate and Securities, Litigation, and Tax. The practice areas include: Administrative, Antitrust, Arbitration/Alternative Dispute Resolution, Banking and Bank Regulatory, Corporate Work, Domestic Relations, Employee Benefits/ERISA, Employment and Labor, Environmental Matters, Estate Planning and Probate, Health Care, Intellectual Property, International, Litigation, Public Policy, Real Estate, Sports and Entertainment, Taxation, and Transportation.

HISTORY AT A GLANCE . . .

The firm was created when Heiskell, Donelson, Bearman, Adams, Williamson and Caldwell merged with Baker, Worthington, Crossley & Stansberry in 1994. The "Baker" is Howard Baker, former majority leader of the U.S. Senate.

Balch & Bingham, LLP

1710 Sixth Avenue North • P. O. Box 306 • Birmingham, Alabama 35201
Phone: 205-251-8100 • Fax: 205-226-8798 • Web site: www.balch.com

OFFICES

Birmingham (main office), Montgomery, Huntsville, Alabama;
Washington, D.C.

HIGHLIGHTS

• Second largest firm in Birmingham, Alabama

NUTS AND BOLTS

Hiring partner:

Jesse S. Vogtle, Jr.

Recruiting coordinator:

Suzanne McKinney

Number of attorneys in firm:

111 (64 partners)

BIRMINGHAM OFFICE:

83 attorneys

OTHER OFFICES:

Montgomery, AL (20), Huntsville, AL (4), Washington, D.C. (4)

Years to make partner:

6 1/2 years

WHAT DO THEY DO?

Specialties (ranked from most attorneys to least): Litigation; Utility,
Regulatory, and Legislative; Banking, Commercial, and Real Estate;
Corporate and Securities; Tax, Estates, and Public Finance; Environmental;
Labor and Employment; Bankruptcy.

WHO DO THEY REPRESENT?

A variety of clients, including Fortune 500 companies, as well as Alabama-based public and private companies.

WHERE NEW ASSOCIATES COME FROM . . .

The firm routinely interviews on-campus at the following schools: Alabama, Samford, Tulane, Emory, Texas, Harvard, Vanderbilt, Virginia, and Washington & Lee.

The firm also hires from schools where it doesn't conduct on-campus interviews.

HOURS AND BUCKS . . .

Hours: Associates work on average 2,000 per year; the average associate billable hours are 1,950. There is no minimum billable hours requirement.

While the firm does not have part-time lawyers, it does routinely hire staff attorneys, who work fewer hours than partnership-bound attorneys.

Starting salary: $$$ ($50-65,000)

SUMMER PROGRAM . . .

Last year, 15 summer associates, of whom 11 received offers.

Weekly pay: $950 for 2Ls, $850 for 1Ls.

Between 10 and 15 1Ls are routinely hired for the summer program.

HISTORY AT A GLANCE...

The firm was founded in 1922 in Birmingham by Judge William Logan Martin, former Attorney General of Alabama.

Bamberger, Foreman, Oswald & Hahn

708 Hulman Building • P.O. Box 657 • Evansville, Indiana 47704-0657
Phone: 812-425-1591 • Fax: 812-421-4936

OFFICES

Evansville, Indiana (only office)

HIGHLIGHTS:

- State-of-the-art computer system.

NUTS AND BOLTS

Hiring partner:

Thomas Bodkin

Number of attorneys in firm:

25 (10 partners)

WHAT DO THEY DO?

Specialties: General civil practice, covering the following practice areas: Corporate; Utility; Insurance; Negligence and Product Liability; Admiralty; Banking; Commercial; Real Estate; Oil, Gas, and Mining; Probate, Estate Planning, and Administration; Hospital and Medical; Bankruptcy and Business Reorganizations; Creditors Rights; Pension and Profit Sharing; Workers Compensation; Labor and Employment Discrimination Law; and Municipal Law.

WHO DO THEY REPRESENT?

Clients include banks, construction companies, hospitals and HMOs, insurance companies, cities, manufacturers, real estate developers, utilities, communications companies and television stations.

HISTORY AT A GLANCE . . .

The firm was founded in 1959 when four lawyers left an established Evansville firm.

Bass, Berry & Sims, PLC

2700 First American Center • Nashville, Tennessee 37238
Phone: 615-742-6200 • Fax: 615-742-2794

OFFICES

Nashville (main office), Knoxville, Tennessee

NUTS AND BOLTS

Hiring attorney:

Felix R. Dowsley, III

Recruiting administrator:

E. Diane Marshall

Number of attorneys in firm:

108 (63 partners)

NASHVILLE OFFICE:

102 attorneys

OTHER OFFICE:

Knoxville, TN (6)

Years to make partner:

7 1/2 years

WORD ON THE STREET . . .

"Many people consider it the #1 firm in Nashville."

WHAT DO THEY DO?

Specialties: (From most attorneys to fewest): Corporate/Securities; Litigation; Commercial: Banking/Bankruptcy/Public Finance/Real Estate; Tax: Employee Benefits/ERISA/Estates and Trusts; Labor/Employment; Health; Environmental.

WHERE NEW ASSOCIATES COME FROM . . .

The firm routinely interviews on campus at the following schools: Duke, Kentucky, North Carolina, Tennessee, Texas, Vanderbilt, Virginia, Washington & Lee. The firm also hires from schools where it doesn't conduct on-campus interviews.

HOURS AND BUCKS:

Hours: Associates work on average 1,900 per year; the average associate billable hours are 1,754. The minimum billable hours requirement is 1,700 hours.

Part-time work is allowed on a case-by-case basis to continuing associates; it is not available at entry-level.

Starting salary: $$$ ($50-65,000)

SUMMER PROGRAM . . .

Last year, there were 17 summer associates, of whom 15 received offers.
Weekly pay: $1,000.
1Ls are not hired for the summer program.

HISTORY AT A GLANCE . . .

Firm was founded in 1922 in Nashville, making it one of the oldest full-service law firms in the Southeast.

Beckman, Lawson, Sandler, Snyder & Federoff

800 Standard Federal Plaza • Fort Wayne, Indiana 46802
Phone: 219-422-0800 • Fax: 219-420-1013 • E-mail: BLSSF@fortwayne.infi.net

OFFICES

Fort Wayne (main office), Syracuse, Indiana

NUTS AND BOLTS

Hiring attorney:

James A. Federoff

Number of attorneys in firm:

30 (15 partners)

WHAT DO THEY DO?

Specialties: Corporate, Bankruptcy, Family, Real Estate, Planning and Zoning, Probate and Estate Planning, Administrative, Health and Hospital, Personal Injury, Environmental, Employment and Labor Law, and School Law.

Best, Best & Krieger L.L.P.

400 Mission Square • 3750 University Avenue
P.O. Box 1628 • Riverside, California 92501
Phone: 909-686-1450 • Fax: 909-686-3083 • Web site: bbklaw.com

OFFICES

Riverside (main office), Rancho Mirage, Ontario, San Diego, Victorville, California

HIGHLIGHTS

- Inland Southern California's largest law firm; one of the 50 largest firms in California.
- Most partners are "home grown"; 39 of the firm's 51 partners started with the firm as first year associates.
- Pro bono hours are counted as billables.

NUTS AND BOLTS

Recruiting administrator:

Patricia Benter

Number of attorneys in firm:

101 (51 partners)

RIVERSIDE OFFICE:

59 attorneys (29 partners)

OTHER OFFICES:

Rancho Mirage (20), Ontario (9), San Diego (10), Victorville (3)

Years to make partner:

7

WHAT DO THEY DO?

Specialties: Real Estate; Health Care; Labor Relations and Employment Law; Tax and Employee Benefits; Estate Planning, Probate, and Trust Administration; Toxics and Air Quality; Land Use Planning; Water Rights;

Public Finance, Mergers, and Acquisitions; Endangered Species; Native American Law; School Law; Transportation; Environmental Protection; Government; Bankruptcy; Corporate; Eminent Domain; Antitrust; and Business Litigation.

New associates are asigned to a specific department when they join the firm. The firm has a mentor program, consisting of a partner and senior associate mentor for each new associate.

WHERE NEW ASSOCIATES COME FROM . . .

The firm routinely interviews on-campus at the following law schools: Boalt Hall, Brigham Young, UC Davis, Hastings, Loyola/Los Angeles, McGeorge, USC, UCLA, and Utah.

The firm also hires from schools where it doesn't conduct on-campus interviews.

HOURS AND BUCKS . . .

Hours: Associates work an average of 2,236 hours per year; the average associate billable hours are 1,923, of which 1,850 is the minimum billable hours requirement.

Part-time work is not available.

Starting salary: $$$ ($50-65,000)

SUMMER PROGRAM . . .

Last year, 12 summer associates, of whom 7 received offers.

Weekly pay: $1,000.

1Ls are not hired for the summer program.

HISTORY AT A GLANCE . . .

The firm was founded in 1891.

Bickerstaff, Heath, Smiley, Pollan, Kever & McDaniel

1700 Frost Bank Plaza • 816 Congress Avenue • Austin, Texas 78701-2443
Phone: 512-472-8021 • Fax: 512-320-5638

OFFICES

Austin, Texas

NUTS AND BOLTS

Hiring attorney:

Greg Hudson

Recruiting coordinator:

Ivory Tate

Number of attorneys in firm:

38 (22 partners)

Years to make partner:

7

WORD ON THE STREET . . .

"Great people, great work environment." "It's very diverse." "They run the firm by consensus—everyone's input is important." "They are very involved in the community."

WHAT DO THEY DO?

Specialties: Litigation; Administrative; Environmental and Water; Municipal, Public Law, and Public Finance; Telecommunications; Real Estate, Business, and Contracts; Commercial Litigation and Banking; International; Education; Utilities.

WHERE NEW ASSOCIATES COME FROM . . .

The firm interviews on-campus at the University of Texas. It also hires from schools where it doesn't conduct on-campus interviews.

HOURS AND BUCKS . . .

Hours: Associates work on average 2,080 per year. The minimum billable hours requirement is 1,800 hours. Part-time work is available to continuing associates; it is not available at entry level.

Starting salary: $$$ ($50-65,000)

SUMMER PROGRAM . . .

Last year, there were 4 summer associates, of whom 2 received offers.

Weekly pay: $900.

1Ls are routinely hired for the summer program.

Bingham, Summers, Welsh & Spilman

10 West Market Street • 2700 Market Tower Building
Indianapolis, Indiana 26204-2982
Phone: 317-635-8900 • Fax: 317-236-9907 • E-mail: bsws@bsws.com

OFFICES

Indianapolis (main office), Bloomington, Indiana

NUTS AND BOLTS

Hiring attorney:

David Prechtel

Recruiting coordinator:

Barbara Bradt

Number of attorneys in firm:

80 (37 partners)

WHAT DO THEY DO?

Specialties: The firm is evenly split between litigation and transactional work. It is divided into the following practice groups: Administrative Law and Governmental Affairs, Appellate, Business Litigation, Business Services, Creditors Rights and Bankruptcy, Dispute Resolution, Employee Benefits, Environmental Practice, Estate Planning and Administration, Federal and State Tax, Financial Institutions, Health Care, International Law, Labor and Employment Law, Local Government Services, Plaintiff and Subrogation, Public Finance, and Real Estate and Construction.

Boult, Cummings, Conners & Berry

414 Union Street, Suite 1600 • P.O. Box 198062 • Nashville, Tennessee 37219
Phone: 615-252-3824 • Fax: 615-252-2380 • E-mail: bccb@bccb.com

OFFICES

Nashville, Tennessee

NUTS AND BOLTS

Managing partner:

Thomas Trent

Recruiting coordinator:

Barry Maddux

Number of attorneys in firm:

71 (43 partners)

NASHVILLE OFFICE:

71 attorneys

Years to make partner:

8

WHAT DO THEY DO?

Specialties: The firm is split into transactional and litigation practice areas, with about 60% of the firm's attorneys performing transactional work. The transactional specialties include Corporate, Securities, Health Care, Real Estate, Tax, ERISA, Environmental, Estate, Government Relations, Telecommunications, Commercial Finance, International, Trademark, and Sports Law. The litigation specialties include General Business, Insurance, Arbitration, Construction, Antitrust, Intellectual Property, Bankruptcy, Labor/Employment, and Products Liability.

WHO DO THEY REPRESENT?

Clients in all areas of business, government and finance throughout the Southeast and the United States.

WHERE NEW ASSOCIATES COME FROM . . .

The firm routinely interviews on campus at the following law schools: Duke, Florida, Georgetown, North Carolina, Tennessee, Vanderbilt, and Virginia. The firm also hires from schools where it doesn't conduct on-campus interviews.

HOURS AND BUCKS . . .

Hours: Associates work on average 1,977 per year; the minimum billable hours requirement is 1,800. Part-time work is available to continuing associates on a case-by-case basis; it is not available at entry level.
Starting salary: $$$ ($50-65,000)

SUMMER PROGRAM . . .

Last year, there were 7 summer associates, of whom 3 received offers.
Weekly pay: $1,000.
1Ls are occasionally hired for the summer program.

HISTORY AT A GLANCE . . .

The firm was founded in 1910.

Burns, Doane, Swecker & Mathis, LLP

1737 King Street, Suite 500 • Alexandria, Virginia 22314
Phone: 703-838-6620 • Fax: 703-838-2021 • Web site: burnsdoane.com

OFFICES

Alexandria (main office), Virginia; Menlo Park, California; Research Triangle Park, North Carolina

NUTS AND BOLTS

Hiring partner:

Matthew Schneider

Number of attorneys in firm:

88 (40 partners)

WHAT DO THEY DO?

Specialties: It is a full-service intellectual property law firm, representing clients throughout the world in the areas of Patents, Trademarks, Copyrights, Trade Secrets, Unfair Competition and Antitrust matters relating to Intellectual Property Law. The firm's areas of concentration include Intellectual Property litigation (Federal District Courts, Federal Appellate Courts, U.S. International Trade Commission, Federal Court of Claims and Alternative Dispute Resolution), Patent Procurement (biotechnology, chemical, designs, electrical/electronics, mechanical, metallurgy, plants), Patent Interference, Trademark Procurement, Trademark Oppositions and Cancellations, Licensing, Copyright Protection (including mask works), Computer Law, Trade Secrets and Foreign Filing Strategies.

HISTORY AT A GLANCE . . .

The firm was founded in 1936.

Clemens & Spencer

112 East Pecan Street, Suite 1500 • San Antonio, TX 78205
Phone: 210-227-7121 • Fax: 210-227-0732

OFFICES

San Antonio, Texas

NUTS AND BOLTS

Recruiting administrator:

Faye Craig

Number of attorneys in firm:

18 (14 partners)

WHAT DO THEY DO?

Specialties: Bankruptcy, Creditors Rights, Employment Relations, Financial Institution Liability, Health Care and Hospitals, Insurance, Labor, Mediation, Professional Liability, Products Liability, Real Estate, and School Law.

WHO DO THEY REPRESENT?

Their clients include Albertson's Inc., The Cessna Aircraft Company, Chrysler Credit, GMAC, John Hancock Mutual Life Insurance, Liberty Mutual Insurance, Met Life, Mobil Oil, Prudential, Shand Moran & Company, Southwestern Bell, Texas Farm Bureau Insurance, and the Texas Lawyers Insurance Exchange.

HISTORY AT A GLANCE . . .

The firm was founded in 1901.

Cohen, Weiss and Simon

330 West 42ND Street • New York, NY 10036-6976
Phone: 212-563-4100 • Fax: 212-695-5436
E-mail: 74403.2712@compuserve.com

OFFICES

New York City, New York

NUTS AND BOLTS

Hiring partner:

Committee consisting of Michael Abram, Babette Ceccotti, Ann O'Shea, and Earl Pfeffer.

Number of attorneys in firm:

38 (18 partners)

WORD ON THE STREET . . .

"It's a very laid-back office environment. They work hard, but they're very relaxed around each other." "Every day is 'casual day'—they're allowed to dress casually, unless they're meeting with clients." "They do a lot of work with unions and employees."

WHAT DO THEY DO?

Specialties: Labor, ERISA, Pension & Health Benefits, ESOPS & Corporate Restructurings, Bankruptcy, International Labor, Employment, Litigation (trial level, appellate, and administrative), Internal Union Governance, Health & Safety, Libel & Slander, RICO, Entertainment, Interest & Rights Arbitration, Mediation, and Alternative Dispute Resolution.

HISTORY AT A GLANCE . . .

The firm was founded in 1943.

Cors & Bassett

537 E. Pete Rose Way, Suite 400 • Cincinnati, OH 45202
Phone: 513-852-8200 • Fax: 513-852-8222

OFFICES

Cincinnati, Ohio (main office); Fort Wright, Kentucky

NUTS AND BOLTS

Hiring partner:

David L. Barth

Number of attorneys in firm:

41 (24 partners)

WORD ON THE STREET . . .

"You only ever hear great things about this firm."

WHAT DO THEY DO?

Specialties: Corporate, Securities, Environmental, Energy, Land Use Planning and Zoning, Labor Relations and Employment Law, Transportation, International, Taxation, Bankruptcy, Estate Planning, Probate, Domestic Relations, Products Liability, Negligence, Real Estate Law, and Construction Contract and Claims Litigation.

WHO DO THEY REPRESENT?

Their clients include Star Bank, Dravo Corporation, Keco Industries, City of Montgomery, Met Life, Northern Kentucky Industrial Park, Zonic Corporation, Commonwealth of Kentucky, Heritage Bank, OHM Remediation, Hillman Fasteuer, Towne Properties, Midwest Group of Funds, Dorman Products, Oldenberg Brewery, Pomeroy Computer Resources, Dualite, KDI Precision Products, Dugan & Meyers Construction.

HISTORY AT A GLANCE . . .

The firm was founded in 1929.

Cox & Smith, Inc.

112 East Pecan, Suite 1800 • San Antonio, TX 78205
Phone: 210-554-5500 • Fax: 210-226-8395

OFFICES

San Antonio, Texas

NUTS AND BOLTS

Hiring partner:

Steven Seidel

Recruiting administrator:

Amy Miller

Number of attorneys in firm:

66 (37 partners)

Years to make partner:

6 to 8

WHAT DO THEY DO?

Specialties (ranked from most attorneys to least): Litigation (including Antitrust, Bankruptcy, Environmental, Intellectual Property, Labor, Patent, and General Commercial Litigation); Corporate; Oil and Gas; Real Estate; and Tax and Estate Planning.

WHERE NEW ASSOCIATES COME FROM . . .

The firm routinely interviews on campus at the following law schools: Baylor, Houston, New York Law School, St. Mary's, Southern Methodist, and Texas. The firm also hires from schools where it doesn't conduct on-campus interviews.

HOURS AND BUCKS . . .

Hours: Associates work an average of 1,950 hours per year; the average associate billable hours are 1,710.

Starting salary: $$$$ (Over $65,000)

SUMMER PROGRAM . . .

Last year, there were 11 summer associates, 7 of whom received offers.
Weekly pay: $1,100
1Ls are hired for the summer program.

HISTORY AT A GLANCE . . .

Firm was founded in 1939. Originally, the firm focused primarily on oil
and gas, but as the firm has grown, its clientele and specialties diversified.

Crowley, Haughey, Hanson, Toole & Dietrich, PLLP

500 Transwestern II • 490 North 31ST Street
P.O. Box 2529 • Billings, Montana 59101
Phone: 406-252-3441 • Fax: 406-259-4159

OFFICES

Billings (main office), Helena, Kalispell, Montana; Williston, North Dakota

HIGHLIGHTS

• The largest law firm in Montana and surrounding states.

NUTS AND BOLTS

Hiring attorney:

Bruce Fredrickson

Number of attorneys in firm:

58 (44 partners)

WHAT DO THEY DO?

Specialties: The firm is divided into three departments: Commercial/Tax, Litigation, and Natural Resources. Specialties include Litigation, Insurance, Workers Compensation, Personal Injury, Products Liability, Malpractice, Bankruptcy, Financing Transactions, Administrative, Immigration, Antitrust, Banking, Corporate, Commercial, Real Estate, Public Utilities, Securities, Tax, Municipal and Tax Exempt Bonds, Entertainment, Health Care, Agricultural, Estate Planning, Probate, Pension & Profit Sharing, Natural Resources (including Oil and Gas), Mining, Environmental and Water Law, Employment Law, Indian Law and Intellectual Property.

WHO DO THEY REPRESENT?

A large number of insurance companies, as well as the First Interstate Bank of Commerce, GMAC, Noranda Minerals, Montana Power, MDV

Resources, Chevron, Farm Credit Bank, Northwestern Farm Credit Services, Pegasus Gold, Mid-Rivers Telephone Cooperative, RJ Reynolds, Norfolk Energy, UPS, Sinclair Oil, Deaconess Medical Center, Peabody Coal, Billings Clinic, John Deere, Decker Coal, Kennecott, Manufacturer's Hanover, GE, AT&T, General Mills, Holly Sugar, Western Sugar, Grace Petroleum, Arch Minerals, Turner Enterprises, Natural Gas Processing, and Yellowstone Banks.

HISTORY AT A GLANCE . . .

The firm was founded in 1895.

Dinsmore & Shohl, L.L.P.

1900 Chemed Center • 255 East Fifth Street • Cincinnati, Ohio 45202
Phone: 513-977-8200 • Fax: 513-977-8141 • Web site: dinshohl.com

OFFICES

Cincinnati (main office), Columbus, Dayton, Hamilton, Ohio; Covington, Louisville, Lexington, Kentucky

HIGHLIGHTS

• Largest firm in Cincinnati; 163RD largest firm in the country.

NUTS AND BOLTS

Managing partner:

Clifford A. Roe, Jr., Esq.

Hiring partner:

Gregory A. Harrison, Esquire, phone: 513-977-8314

Recruiting coordinator:

Patricia C. Ventress, phone: 513-977-8347,
e-mail: ventress!cinti02.dishohl.com

Number of attorneys in firm:

202 (90 partners)

CINCINNATI OFFICE:

157 attorneys (68 partners)

OTHER OFFICES:

Columbus, OH (11); Dayton, OH (4); Hamilton, OH (1); Covington, KY (3); Louisville, KY (18); Lexington, KY (8)

Years to make partner:

8 to 9 years

WHAT DO THEY DO?

Specialties: The firm is divided into the following departments (listed from most attorneys to fewest): Litigation, Intellectual Property, and

Insurance; Corporate, Business, and Tax; Medical; Labor and Employment Law; Workers' Compensation; Real Estate; Environmental; Employee Benefits; Bankruptcy; Estates and Trusts. Junior associates can, and do, switch specialties.

WHO DO THEY REPRESENT?

Clients include Procter & Gamble, the Archdiocese of Cincinnati, the Castellini Company, Chemed Corporation, Children's Hospital Medical Center, Dow Chemical, Dow Corning, Franciscan Hospitals, General Electric, General Motors, Kroger, Liberty Mutual Insurance, Rockwell International, Sears Roebuck, and the U.S. Playing Card Company.

WHERE NEW ASSOCIATES COME FROM . . .

The firm routinely interviews on-campus at the following law schools: Chicago-Kent/IIT, Chicago, Cincinnati, Dayton, Emory, George Washington, Harvard, Howard, Indiana at Bloomington, Kentucky, Louisville, Michigan, Northern Kentucky, Northwestern, Notre Dame, Ohio State, Toledo, Vanderbilt, Virginia, and William & Mary. The firm also hires from schools where it doesn't conduct on-campus interviews.

HOURS AND BUCKS . . .

Hours: Associates work on average 2,000 hours per year; the minimum billable hours requirement is 1,800. Part-time work is available to continuing associates on a case-by-case basis; it is not available at entry level. The firm does not routinely hire contract associates.

Starting salary: $$$ ($50-65,000)

SUMMER PROGRAM . . .

Last year, there were 9 summer associates, 7 of whom received offers.

Weekly pay: $1,100 (additional $1,000 for 2Ls who spend 10 weeks or more with the firm)

1Ls are routinely hired for the summer program. Last year's 1Ls came from the University of Dayton, the University of Kentucky, Chase, and Vanderbilt.

HISTORY AT A GLANCE . . .

The firm was founded in 1908. Over the years, attorneys with the firm have gone on to noteworthy roles in government, including Justice of the U.S. Supreme Court, Commissioner of the Internal Revenue Service, as well as state and municipal elected and appointed offices.

Dominick, Fletcher, Yeilding, Wood & Lloyd

2121 Highland Avenue • Birmingham, Alabama 35205
Phone: 205-939-0033

OFFICES

Birmingham, Alabama

NUTS AND BOLTS

Hiring partner:

Terry McElheny

Number of attorneys:

19 (16 partners)

WHAT DO THEY DO?

Specialties: Litigation, Real Estate, Probate, Corporate Law, Insurance, and Taxation.

WHO DO THEY REPRESENT?

Clients include corporations, insurance companies, health care providers, individuals and closely held businesses.

HISTORY AT A GLANCE . . .

The firm was founded in 1943.

Dorsey & Whitney, L.L.P.

220 South Sixth Street • Minneapolis, MN 55402
Phone: 612-340-2641 • Web site: dorseylaw.com

OFFICES

Minneapolis (main office), Rochester, Minnesota; New York City, New York; Denver, Colorado; Washington, D.C.; Des Moines, Iowa; Billings, Great Falls, Missoula, Montana; Costa Mesa, California; Fargo, North Dakota; Seattle, Washington; Salt Lake City, Utah

HIGHLIGHTS

• 38TH largest firm in the country; largest law firm in the Upper Midwest.

NUTS AND BOLTS

Hiring partner:

Joseph W. Hammell

Recruiting administrator:

Renee Jernell

Number of attorneys in firm:

450

MINNEAPOLIS OFFICE:

275 attorneys

OTHER OFFICES:

New York (45); Denver (26); Washington, D.C. (22); Des Moines, Iowa (11); Billings, Montana (8); Costa Mesa, California (7); Fargo, North Dakota (6); Rochester, MN (5); Great Falls, NY (4); Seattle, WA (3); Salt Lake City, UT (2); Missoula, MT (1); Brussels (8); London (4); Hong Kong (3)

Years to make partner:

7

WORD ON THE STREET . . .

"Many, many people there say the experience is just great." "Lots of female partners." "They address diversity issues very seriously."

WHAT DO THEY DO?

Specialties: The firm is divided into two broad practice groups: Trial and Administrative, and Business and Finance.

The Trial and Administrative Group includes the following specialties: Commercial, Commercial Lease, and Real Estate Tax Appeals; Construction; Employment; Environmental and Natural Resources; Financial Institutions Litigation; Franchise; Insurance; Intellectual Property; Labor; Products Liability; Securities; Technology and Intellectual Property Litigation; Trade Practices and Antitrust Counseling; White Collar and Compliance.

The Business and Finance Group includes the following specialties: Asian; Bankruptcy, Commercial, and Banking; Community/Business Banking; Corporate; Emerging Companies; Employee Benefits; Estate and Trust Litigation, Estate Planning and Administration; Financial Markets; Health; Hedge Funds; Indian and Gaming Law; Institutional and Corporate Trust; International; International Capital Markets; Latin American; Mergers and Acquisitions; Mutual Funds; Private Business Succession Planning; Private Companies; Project Finance; Public Companies; and Public Finance.

WHERE NEW ASSOCIATES COME FROM . . .

The firm routinely interviews on-campus at the following law schools: Boalt Hall, Chicago, Colorado, Columbia, Denver, Duke, Fordham, Franklin Pierce, George Mason, George Washington, Georgetown, Hamline, Harvard, Howard, Iowa, Michigan, Minnesota, NYU, Northwestern, Stanford, Virginia, William Mitchell, Wisconsin, and Yale.

HOURS AND BUCKS . . .

Starting salary: $$$ ($50-65,000)
Hours: Associates bill on average 1,786 hours per year.
Part-time work is available both to continuing and entry-level associates.

SUMMER PROGRAM . . .

Last year, there were 11 summer associates, 9 of whom received offers.
Weekly pay: $1,100
1Ls are routinely hired for the summer program.

HISTORY AT A GLANCE . . .

Firm was founded in 1912.

Fliesler Dubb Meyer & Lovejoy

Four Embarcadero Center, 4TH floor • San Francisco, California 94111
Phone: 415-362-3800 • Fax: 415-362-2928

OFFFICES

San Francisco (main office), Santa Clara, California

NUTS AND BOLTS

Recruiting administrator:

Betsy Glover

Number of attorneys in firm:

23 (10 partners)

SAN FRANCISCO OFFICE:

2 attorneys

OTHER OFFICE:

Santa Clara, CA (2 attorneys)

WHAT DO THEY DO?

Specialties: The firm specializes exclusively in intellectual property law.

WHO DO THEY REPRESENT?

The firm's clients range from start-up companies to multi-national corporations and cover a variety of technological fields, including computers, electronics, semiconductor chip technology, software, magnetic storage devices, telecommunications, physics, medical developments, and mechanics.

WHERE NEW ASSOCIATES COME FROM . . .

The firm routinely interviews on-campus at the following law schools: Boalt Hall, Hastings, San Francisco, and Santa Clara. It also hires from schools where it doesn't conduct on-campus interviews.

* Note that the firm also has a summer associate program.

HOURS . . .

Associates bill on average 1,750 hours per year, which is the suggested minimum billable hours requirement.

HISTORY AT A GLANCE . . .

The firm was founded in 1982.

Foster, Swift, Collins & Smith, P.C.

313 South Washington Square • Lansing, Michigan 48933-2193
Phone: 517-371-8100 • Fax: 517-371-8200 • Web site: fosterswift.com

OFFICES

Lansing (main office), Farmington Hills, Michigan

NUTS AND BOLTS

Director of professional recruiting:
Sharon M. Smith

Number of attorneys in firm:
69 (42 partners)

LANSING OFFICE:
63 attorneys

OTHER OFFICE:
6 attorneys

WHAT DO THEY DO?

Specialties: The firm is divided into four principal departments: Business and Tax; Government and Commerce; Litigation; and Labor and Employment Law.

WHERE NEW ASSOCIATES COME FROM . . .

The firm routinely interviews on campus at the following law schools: Illinois, Indiana/Bloomington, Indiana/Indianapolis, Iowa, Michigan, Minnesota, Notre Dame, Wayne State, Wisconsin. The firm also hires from schools where it doesn't conduct on-campus interviews.

HOURS AND BUCKS . . .

Hours: Associates work on average 1,900 hours a year, of which 1,850 are the minimum billable hourly requirement. Part-time work is available both to continuing and entry-level associates on a case-by-case basis.
Starting salary: $$$ ($50-65,000)

SUMMER PROGRAM . . .

Last year, there were 5 summer associates, of whom 4 received offers.
Weekly pay: $1,000 last year.
1Ls are sometimes hired for the summer program.

HISTORY AT A GLANCE . . .

The firm was founded in 1902.

Gentry, Locke, Rakes & Moore

10 Franklin Road, S. E. • P.O. Box 40013 • Roanoke, Virginia 24038-0013
Phone: 540-983-9300 • Fax: 540-983-9400 • E-mail: glrm@gentrylocke.com

OFFICES

Roanoke, Virginia

NUTS AND BOLTS

Hiring partner:
William Rakes

Number of attorneys in firm:
51 (27 partners)

WHAT DO THEY DO?

Specialties: Banking, Corporate, Environmental, Insurance, Tax, International, Public Contracts and Securities, Health Care.

Gibson, Dunn & Crutcher, L.L.P.

200 Park Avenue • New York, New York 10166-0193
Phone: 212-351-4000 • Fax: 212-351-4035 • Web site: gdclaw.com

OFFICES

New York (Los Angeles-based firm), New York

HIGHLIGHTS

- New York office of a Los Angeles-based firm; the firm is the 18TH largest in the country.
- The firm uses a "free market" system, by which associates are unassigned for their first two years with the firm. They get to pick and choose the practice areas they want to pursue, and then they select a department to join.
- Strong dedication to pro bono work. The firm recently ranked among the top firms nationwide in the *American Lawyer's 100 Pro Bono Survey*. Pro bono hours are counted as billables.

NUTS AND BOLTS

Hiring partner:

Steven R. Shoemate

Recruiting coordinator:

Stefani Berkenfeld

Number of attorneys in firm:

643 (105 in New York, of whom 30 are partners)

OTHER OFFICES:

Los Angeles (main office), CA; Washington, D.C.; Irvine, CA; Dallas, TX; Palo Alto, CA; Denver, CO; Century City, CA; San Francisco, CA; San Diego, CA; London; Paris; and Riyadh, Saudi Arabia .

WHAT DO THEY DO?

Specialties: The firm is divided into five basic departments: Litigation, Corporations, Labor, Real Estate, and Tax. Most of the lawyers in the New York office do Litigation or Corporate work. The departments include a number of specialized practice groups, including First Amendment, Bankruptcy and Reorganizations, Corporate Tax, Project Finance, Latin America, Intellectual Property, White Collar Crimes, Mergers and Acquisitions, and Securities.

WHERE NEW ASSOCIATES COME FROM . . .

The firm routinely interviews on campus at the following law schools: American, Arizona, Boalt Hall, Chicago, Columbia, Cornell, Davis, Duke, Emory, Fordham, Georgetown, Harvard, Hastings, Michigan, Minnesota, NYU, North Carolina, Northwestern, Pennsylvania, Stanford, Texas, UCLA, USC, Vanderbilt, Virginia, William & Mary, and Yale.

HOURS . . .

Associates bill an average of 1,967 hours per year.

SUMMER PROGRAM . . .

Last year, the New York office had 23 summer associates, 21 of whom received offers.
    Weekly pay: $1,750

HISTORY . . .

The New York office was opened in 1982 with 2 lawyers, and has since grown to more than 100 attorneys.

Gray Cary Ware & Freidenrich

401 B Street, Suite 1700 · San Diego, California 92101
Phone: 619-699-2700 · Fax: 619-236-1048 · Web site: gcwf.com

OFFICES

San Diego (main office), Palo Alto (main office), San Francisco, Austin, California

HIGHLIGHTS

- 103RD largest firm in the country. One of California's largest firms, with 273 lawyers in five offices.
- Dedication to pro bono work. Pro bono hours are treated as billables.

NUTS AND BOLTS

Hiring attorney:

James W. Huston

Recruiting director:

Roberta Shrimpton

Number of attorneys in firm:

270 (104 in San Diego, of whom 51 are partners)

MAIN OFFICE:

There are two—San Diego (104) and Palo Alto (115).

OTHER OFFICES:

San Diego/Golden Triangle, CA (30); Austin, TX; Tijuana, Mexico (4); Mexico City, Mexico

WHAT DO THEY DO?

Specialties: Business, Corporate, Securities, Litigation, Banking, Intellectual Property, Patent, Real Estate, Employment, Tax, Trusts and Estate Planning Services.

WHO DO THEY REPRESENT?

The firm specializes in representing emerging growth and high technology companies, particularly focusing on high-tech start-ups. Its clients range from brand-new companies to Fortune 500 corporations.

WHERE NEW ASSOCIATES COME FROM . . .

The firm routinely interviews on-campus at the following law schools: Boalt Hall, Boston College, Davis, Harvard, Hastings, Michigan, San Diego, USC, Stanford, UCLA, Virginia, and Tulane.

HOURS AND BUCKS . . .

Hours: Associates work an average of 2,100 hours; the average billable hours are 1,900, and the minimum billable hourly target is 1,850. Part-time work is available to both continuing and entry-level associates.

Starting salary: $$$$ (Over $65,000) The firm is noted for its generous financial package.

SUMMER PROGRAM . . .

San Diego office: Last year, there were 14 summer associates, of whom 11 received offers.

Weekly pay: $1,200

HISTORY AT A GLANCE . . .

The firm was created in 1994 through a merger of the Palo Alto firm Ware & Freidenrich and San Diego's Gray Cary Ames & Frye.

Heller, Ehrman, White & McAuliffe

333 Bush Street • San Francisco, California 94104
Phone: 415-772-6000 • Fax: 415-772-6268 • Web site: hewm.com

OFFICES

San Francisco (main office), Palo Alto, Los Angeles, California; Washington, D.C.; Anchorage, Alaska; Portland, Oregon; Seattle, Washington

HIGHLIGHTS

- 72ND largest law firm in the country.
- Ranked #1 in the Bay area in the *American Lawyer's* 1996 Midlevel Associate Survey.

NUTS AND BOLTS

Chairman:

Robert A. Rosenfeld

Recruiting manager, San Francisco:

Janet Sikirica

Number of attorneys in firm:

368 (168 in San Francisco, of whom 67 are partners)

SAN FRANCISCO OFFICE:

158 attorneys

OTHER OFFICES:

Seattle (70); Los Angeles (55); Palo Alto (74); Portland (3); Anchorage (4); Washington, D.C. (4); Hong Kong; Singapore.

Years to make partner:

7 ¹/₂

HOURS AND BUCKS . . .

Hours: In San Francisco, associates work an average of 2,324 hours per year, of which 1,810 are the average billable hours. The minimum billable hour requirement is 1,900.

Part-time work is available to continuing associates on a case-by-case basis; it is not available at entry level.

Starting salary: $$$$ (Over $65,000); the firm is known for its generous financial package)

WHAT DO THEY DO?

Specialties: The firm is divided into three major practice groups: Litigation (which includes General Litigation, Antitrust, Construction/ Real Estate, Financial Institutions, Insurance Coverage, Intellectual Property, Labor and Employment, Products/Substances, Professional Liability, and Securities); Environmental (which includes Litigation, Administrative Representation and Compliance Counseling in the Environmental and Energy areas); and the Business Group (including Bankruptcy, Finance, International, Life Sciences, Information Technology, Corporate Securities, Intellectual Property Licensing and Transactions, Finance, Real Estate, Tax, Bankruptcy, and Estates and Trusts).

New associates generally get to choose the practice group they want to join. First year associates are generally assigned to one or two partners who delegate work and supervise them.

WHERE NEW ASSOCIATES COME FROM . . .

The firm routinely interviews on campus at the following law schools: Boalt Hall, Chicago, Columbia, Harvard, Hastings, Howard, Michigan, NYU, Santa Clara, Stanford, UCLA, USC, and Yale.

The firm also hires from schools where it doesn't conduct on-campus interviews.

SUMMER PROGRAM . . .

Last year, there were 26 2L associates in San Francisco, 25 of whom received offers.

Weekly pay: $1,350 last year

1Ls are routinely hired for the summer program.

PRO BONO . . .

Pro bono work is encouraged and supported. The firm is committed to devoting a minimum of 5% of attorney time to pro bono work. Projects include homeless advocacy, legal services clinics, human rights, and political asylum, among others.

HISTORY AT A GLANCE . . .

The firm was founded in 1890 in San Francisco.

Hodgson, Russ, Andrews, Woods & Goodyear, L.L.P.

1800 One M & T Plaza • Buffalo, New York 14203
Phone: 716-856-4000 • Fax: 716-849-0349

OFFICES

Buffalo (main office), Albany, Gloversville, Rochester, New York City, New York; Boca Raton, Palm Beach, Florida

HIGHLIGHTS

• One of upstate New York's oldest and largest law firms.

NUTS AND BOLTS

Hiring attorney:

Kenneth P. Friedman

Recruiting coordinator:

Jane T. McAvoy

Number of attorneys in firm:

160 (121 in Buffalo, of whom 67 are partners)

BUFFALO OFFICE:

121 attorneys

OTHER OFFICES:

Albany, NY (12); Rochester, NY (8); New York, NY (5); Boca Raton, FL (14); Palm Beach, FL (2); Gloversville, NY (3); Toronto, Canada.

Years to make partner:

7 to 9 years

HOURS AND BUCKS . . .

Hours: Associates bill an average of 1,810 hours per year; the minimum billable hours requirement is 1,750. Part-time work is available to both continuing and entry-level associates on a case-by-case basis.

Starting salary: $$$ ($50-65,000)

WHAT DO THEY DO?

Specialties: Corporate Securities, Health, Immigration, Real Estate, Banking, Finance, Intellectual Property, Trademark, Patent, Litigation, Environmental, Insurance, Creditors Rights, Bankruptcy, Commercial, Estates and Trusts, Labor, Employment, Education, Taxation, Employee Benefits, and ERISA.

WHERE NEW ASSOCIATES COME FROM . . .

The firm routinely interviews on-campus at the following law schools: Albany, Cornell, George Washington, Georgetown, Michigan, SUNY at Buffalo, and Syracuse.

The firm also hires from schools where it doesn't conduct on-campus interviews.

SUMMER PROGRAM . . .

Last year, there were 7 2L summer associates in Buffalo, 5 of whom received offers.

Weekly pay: $1,100 last year.

1Ls are occasionally hired for the summer program.

Hoeppner, Wagner & Evans

103 East Lincolnway • P.O. Box 2357 • Valparaiso, Indiana 46383
Phone: 219-464-4961 • Fax: 219-465-0603 • E-mail: hwe@niia.net

OFFICES

Valparaiso (main office), Merrillville, Indiana

NUTS AND BOLTS . . .

Hiring partner:

William Satterlee

Number of attorneys in firm:

28 (15 partners)

WORD ON THE STREET . . .

"This place has tons of personality."

WHAT DO THEY DO?

Specialties: Litigation, Bankruptcy, Commercial and Banking, Corporate, Creditors' Rights, Probate and Estate Planning, Estate Administration, Financial Resources Planning, Insurance Defense, Municipal Bonds, Municipal and Zoning, Personal Injury, Products Liability, Professional Malpractice, Real Estate, Taxation, Workers Compensation, Labor and Employment Mediation.

WHO DO THEY REPRESENT?

Clients include manufacturers, insurance companies, boards of education, and cities and towns, among others.

HISTORY AT A GLANCE . . .

The firm was founded in 1976.

Hogan & Hartson

555 13TH Street, N.W. • Washington, DC 20004-1109
Phone: 202-637-5600 • Fax: 202-637-5910
E-mail: HHINFO@DC4.HHLAW.COM

OFFICES

Washington, D.C. (main office); Denver, Colorado Springs, Colorado; Baltimore, Bethesda, Maryland; Newport Beach, Los Angeles, California; McLean, Virginia

HIGHLIGHTS . . .

- 21ST largest law firm in the country.
- Strong dedication to pro bono; the firm has received numerous awards for its pro bono efforts.

NUTS AND BOLTS

Hiring partners:

Stephen J. Immelt & Michael C. Williams

Recruiting coordinator:

Ellen Swank

Number of attorneys in firm:

498 (228 partners)

WASHINGTON OFFICE:

338 attorneys

OTHER OFFICES:

Denver and Colorado Springs, CO (24); Baltimore and Bethesda, MD (33); Newport Beach and Los Angeles, CA (6); McLean, VA (35); Brussels (8); Budapest (3); Prague (7); Warsaw (22); Moscow (7); London (5); Paris (11).

Years to make partner:

8

WORD ON THE STREET . . .

"It's a very warm, caring place. A 'people' firm. You aren't fungible there."

WHAT DO THEY DO?

Specialties: The firm is divided into three broad practice areas: Commercial, Government Regulation and Litigation. Within those areas, specialties include Antitrust and Trade Regulation; Appellate and Supreme Court Practice; Communications; Corporate and Securities; Education; Election Law; Energy and Natural Resources; Environmental; Estate Planning and Administration; Financial Institutions and Transactions; Food, Drug, and Medical Devices; Franchising, Government Contracts; Health, Immigration; International Trade; Labor and Employment; Legislation; Litigation; Privatization; Public/Project Finance; Real Estate; Sports and Facilities; Tax; Technology Licensing and Intellectual Property, and Transportation.

WHERE NEW ASSOCIATES COME FROM . . .

The firm routinely interviews on-campus at the following law schools: American University, Baltimore, Boalt Hall, Catholic, Chicago, Colorado, Columbia, Denver, Duke, George Washington, Georgetown, Harvard, Howard, Maryland, Michigan, NYU, Northwestern, Pennsylvania, Stanford, Texas, Virginia, William & Mary, and Yale. The firm also hires from schools where it doesn't interview on-campus.

HOURS AND BUCKS . . .

Hours: Associates work an average of 2,100 hours per year; the minimum billable hourly requirement is 1,800 hours. Part-time work is available both to continuing and entry-level associates.

Starting salary: $$$$ (Over $65,000)

SUMMER PROGRAM . . .

Last year, there were 41 summer associates, all of whom received offers.

Weekly pay: $1,350 last year.

1Ls are not hired for the summer program.

HISTORY AT A GLANCE . . .

The firm was founded in 1904, and has grown since then into the largest major law firm in Washington, D.C. Many of the firm's lawyers have a distinguished background in government, including former U.S. Trade Representatives, a former U.S. Secretary of Agriculture, a former House Minority leader, two former Chairmen of the Republican National Committee, and a former outside General Counsel to the Democratic National Committee.

Jenner & Block

One IBM Plaza, 4330 N. Wabash, Suite 4300 • Chicago, Illinois 60601
Phone: 312-222-9350 • Fax: 312-527-0484

OFFICES

Chicago (main office), Lake Forest, Illinois; Washington, D.C.

HIGHLIGHTS

- 62ND largest law firm in the country.
- One of the country's leading litigation firms.
- Strong pro bono dedication; more than 5% of client hours are dedicated to billables.

NUTS AND BOLTS

Hiring attorney:

Gregory S. Gallopoulos

Recruiting coordinator:

Mindy Friedler

Number of attorneys in firm:

360 (294 in Chicago, of whom 160 are partners)

CHICAGO OFFICE:

94 attorneys

OTHER OFFICES:

Lake Forest, IL (11); Washington, D.C. (55)

Years to make partner:

7 1/2

WORD ON THE STREET . . .

"It's like a fraternity. People always feel like part of the Jenner & Block family even when they've gone on to do other things."

WHAT DO THEY DO?

Specialties: The firm is split evenly between litigation and transactional specialties. Litigators handle both civil and criminal cases. The transactional specialties involve Securities Offerings, Mergers and Acquisitions, General Corporate Counseling, Financing Transactions, Bankruptcy and Reorganization, Tax, Real Estate, Labor, Employment and ERISA, Environmental and Energy, and Intellectual Property Law. The firm also has a significant Trade Association, Government, and Health Care practice and serves the needs of individuals in its Estate Planning, Probate, and Family Law practices.

Associates are not asked to specialize in a single area; rather, they are given the opportunity to work on all different kinds of matters.

WHO DO THEY REPRESENT?

A wide variety of clients, including MCI, Hitachi, the City of Chicago, Tenneco, General Dynamics, Continental Grain, Illinois Tool Works, Teltrend, Gateway 2000, John B. Sanfilippo & Sons, Northfield Laboratories, and a number of REITs.

WHERE NEW ASSOCIATES COME FROM . . .

The firm routinely interviews on-campus at the following law schools: Boalt Hall, Chicago-Kent/IIT, Chicago, DePaul, Duke, Harvard, Illinois, Iowa, Loyola/Chicago, Michigan, North Carolina, Northwestern, Stanford, Wisconsin, and Yale.

The firm also hires from schools where it doesn't interview on-campus.

HOURS AND BUCKS . . .

Hours: The minimum billable hourly requirement is 1,900 hours. Part-time work is allowed for continuing associates; it is not available at entry level.

Starting salary: $$$$ (Over $65,000)

SUMMER PROGRAM . . .

Last year, there were 49 summer associates, 41 of whom received offers.

Weekly pay: $1,400 last year

1Ls are routinely hired for the summer program.

HISTORY AT A GLANCE . . .

The firm was founded in 1914. Over the years it has handled many headline-making cases, including representing MCI in its $1.8 billion antitrust verdict against AT&T, representing Hitachi against Motorola in one of the largest patent infringement cases in history, representing the City of Chicago in the litigation stemming from the flood of the city's underground tunnels, and representing the adoptive parents in the front-page "Baby Richard" custody case.

Kirkland & Ellis

200 East Randolph Drive • Chicago, IL 60601
Phone: 312-861-2000 • Fax: 312-861-2200 • Web site: kirkland.com

OFFICES

Chicago (main office), Illinois; Los Angeles, California; New York City, New York; Washington, D.C.

HIGHLIGHTS

- 27TH largest firm in the country.
- Ranked 4TH in the country in midlevel associate satisfaction in a recent *American Lawyer* survey.
- Strong dedication to pro bono work. Pro bono hours are treated as billables.
- Cutting-edge computer technology, including e-mail and voice mail systems linking the firm with over 1,000 clients domestically and internationally.
- Fortune 250 corporations ranked the firm as the second most frequently used law firm in a recent survey in *The National Law Journal.*

NUTS AND BOLTS

Hiring partner:

Helen E. Witt

Recruiting manager:

Nancy Berry

Number of attorneys in firm:

528

CHICAGO OFFICE:

323 attorneys (139 partners)

OTHER OFFICES:

Los Angeles, CA (36); New York, NY (68); Washington, D.C. (98); London (3).

Years to make partner:

6

WHAT DO THEY DO?

Specialties: Practice consists of sophisticated Corporate Transactions and Commercial Litigation matters including Antitrust, Bankruptcy, Commodities, Communications, Securities, Creditors' Rights, Employee Benefits, Environmental, Energy and Natural Resources, Estate Planning, Intellectual Property, Real Estate, Tax, and Venture Capital.

WHERE NEW ASSOCIATES COME FROM . . .

The firm routinely interviews on-campus at the following law schools: Akron, Boston University, Brigham Young, Chicago-Kent/IIT, Chicago, Columbia, DePaul, Georgetown, Harvard, Howard, Illinois, Indiana/Bloomington, Loyola/Chicago, Michigan, Minnesota, Northwestern, Ohio State, Stanford, Utah, Wisconsin, and Yale.

The firm also hires from schools where it doesn't conduct on-campus interviews.

HOURS AND BUCKS . . .

Hours: Associates work an average of 2,200 hours per year; the average associate billable hours are 2,000. Part-time work is available to continuing associates; it is not available at entry level.

Starting salary: $$$$ (Over $65,000)

SUMMER PROGRAM . . .

Last year, there were 38 summer associates, all of whom received offers.

Weekly pay: $1,400 last year.

1Ls are not hired for the summer program.

WHO DO THEY REPRESENT?

More than a thousand clients, including Fortune 100 companies like General Motors, Motorola, Amoco, Abbott Labs and Dow Chemical, to medium and small corporations, financial institutions and leveraged buy-out and venture capital firms.

HISTORY AT A GLANCE . . .

The firm was founded in 1908.

LeClair Ryan, P.C.

707 East Main Street, 11TH Floor • Richmond, Virginia 23219
Phone: 804-783-2003 • Fax: 804-783-2294 • E-mail: email@leclairryan.com

OFFICES

Richmond (main office), Henrico, Virginia

NUTS AND BOLTS

Hiring attorney:

Gary LeClair

Number of attorneys:

70 (42 officers [corporate equivalent of partners])

WHAT DO THEY DO?

Specialties: Corporate, Securities, Mergers and Acquisitions, Venture Capital, Administrative, Alcoholic Beverage Control, Appellate Practice, Banking, Bankruptcy and Creditors' Rights, Commercial Litigation, Employee Benefits, Employment, Entertainment, Environmental, Estate Planning, Health Care, Intellectual Property, International Business, Labor (Management), Legislative Representation, Medical Malpractice, Public Finance, Public Utilties, Real Estate, Securities, Tax, Patents, and Immigration.

HISTORY AT A GLANCE . . .

The firm was established in 1988.

Loomis, Ewert, Parsley, Davis & Gotting, P.C.

232 South Capitol Avenue, Suite 1000 • Lansing, Michigan 48933
Phone: 517-482-2400 • Fax: 517-482-0070

OFFICES

Lansing, Michigan

NUTS AND BOLTS

Hiring attorney:

Robert Wirtz

Number of attorneys:

23 (14 partners)

WHAT DO THEY DO?

Specialties: Administrative, Banking, Bankruptcy, Business, Commercial, Communications, Construction, Corporate, Employee Benefit Plans, Employment, Energy, Environmental, ERISA, Estate Planning, Family, International Trade, Labor, Litigation, Motor Carriers, Mining, Oil and Gas, Partnership and Professional Corporations, Personal Injury, Planning for the Elderly, Privatization and Project Finance, Probate, Public Utilities, Real Estate, Securities, Sports and Entertainment, Syndication, Taxation, and Zoning.

WHO DO THEY REPRESENT?

Their clients include Altman Development, American WaterWorks, Citizens Commercial & Savings Bank, City of Grand Ledge, Comerica Bank, Ford Motor, Marathon Oil, Michigan Capital Fund for Housing, Pan Canadian Petroleum, Petrostar Energy, Providence Hospital, TransCanada Pipelines, Wal-Mart Stores, and Wisconsin Electric Power.

Manier, Herod, Hollabaugh & Smith, P.C.

First Union Tower, Suite 2200 • 150 Fourth Avenue North
Nashville, TN 37219-2494
Phone: 615-244-0030 • Fax:615-242-4203

OFFICES

Nashville, Tennessee (main office)

NUTS AND BOLTS

Hiring attorney:

John Gillum

Number of attorneys:

39 (27 partners)

WORD ON THE STREET . . .

"It's a real litigator's firm. They're cowboys."

WHAT DO THEY DO?

Specialties: Corporate, Insurance, Commercial, Construction, Fidelity and Surety, State and Federal Taxation, Estate Planning, Probate, Employee Benefits, Real Estate, Lending, Litigation, Bankruptcy, Environmental, Health Care, Administrative, Employment, and Entertainment.

WHO DO THEY REPRESENT?

Their clients include Ray Bell Construction Company, First Union National Bank, Tennessee Roadbuilders, PNC Bank of Kentucky, Texaco, Abbott Labs, Ford Motor, the Chubb Group, the Hospital Alliance of Tennessee, USAA, C.N.A. Insurance, CIGNA Property & Casualty, Purity Dairies, and the Tennessee Restaurant Association.

HISTORY AT A GLANCE . . .

The firm was founded in 1914.

Masuda, Funai, Eifert & Mitchell

One East Wacker Drive, Suite 3200 • Chicago, IL 60601-2002
Phone: 312-245-7500 • Fax: 312-245-7467 • E-mail: lawfirm@masudafunai.com

OFFICES

Chicago (main office), Rolling Meadows, Illinois; Cincinnati, Ohio

NUTS AND BOLTS

Hiring partner:

Thomas McMenamin

WORD ON THE STREET . . .

"They have one outstanding firm." "Their atmosphere is unique because a large percentage of their clients is Japanese." "It's a less stressful environment than many firms."

WHAT DO THEY DO?

Specialties: The firm's emphasis is on international transactions. Practice areas include International Business, Corporations, Corporate Financing and Reorganizations, Mergers and Acquisitions, Joint Ventures, Real Estate, Environmental, Banking, Antitrust, Unfair Competition, Commercial Transactions, Employment and Labor Relations, Immigration, Technology Licensing, Intellectual Property, Corporate and Commercial Litigation.

HISTORY AT A GLANCE . . .

The firm was established in 1961.

Mette, Evans & Woodside P.C.

3401 North Front Street • P.O. Box 5950 • Harrisburg, Pennsylvania 17110-0950
Phone: 717-232-5000 • Fax: 717-236-1816
E-mail: MEW@Mette.com • Web site: mette.com

OFFICES

Harrisburg, Pennsylvania

HIGHLIGHTS

- One of the largest firms in central Pennsylvania.
- Fantastic web page, with all kinds of links to other law-related sites.

NUTS AND BOLTS

Hiring partner:

Lloyd Persun

Number of attorneys:

32 (21 partners)

WORD ON THE STREET . . .

"Almost everyone who works for the firm finds it a great place to work."

WHAT DO THEY DO?

Specialties: Business and Commercial Law, Commercial Litigation, Construction Law, Creditors' Rights and Bankruptcy, Employment Law and Benefit Programs, Environmental Law, Estate Planning, General Litigation, Health Care Law, Insurance Defense, Municipal Finance, Personal Injury, Public Utility, Telecommunications and Energy, Real Estate and Land Development, Taxation and Estate Law.

WHO DO THEY REPRESENT?

Their clients include Bell & Howell, Commerce Bank, Dauphin County, B.F. Goodrich, Great Central Insurance, MCI Telecommunications,

Pennsylvania Bar Trust Fund, Polaris Industries, Procter & Gamble Paper Products, Potomac Edison, Resorts U.S.A., Sentry Insurance, and Westinghouse Electric.

HISTORY AT A GLANCE...

The firm was founded in 1969.

Nelson Mullins Riley & Scarborough, L.L.P.

1330 Lady Street, 3RD Floor • Keenan Building • Columbia, South Carolina 29201
Phone: 803-799-2000 • Fax: 803-256-7500 • Web site: nmrs.com

OFFICES

Columbia (main office), Greenville, Charleston, Myrtle Beach, Florence, South Carolina; Atlanta, Georgia; Charlotte, North Carolina

HIGHLIGHTS:

- 173RD largest law firm in the country; largest law firm in South Carolina.
- Strong dedication to pro bono work; won the American Bar Association's *Pro Bono Publico* Award a few years ago.

NUTS AND BOLTS

Hiring attorney:

Christopher J. Daniels

Recruiting administrator:

Cristina Malseed

Number of attorneys:

202

COLUMBIA OFFICE:

91 attorneys (48 partners)

OTHER OFFICES:

Atlanta, GA (56); Greenville, SC (21); Charleston, SC (16); Myrtle Beach, SC (10); Lexington, SC (2); Charlotte, NC (6)

WHAT DO THEY DO?

Specialties: Complex commercial and business litigation, products liability defense, professional malpractice defense, unfair trade practices litigation, construction litigation, labor and employment litigation, healthcare, environmental, banking & commercial law, securities, commercial real estate, taxation, bankruptcy, and estate planning.

WHERE NEW ASSOCIATES COME FROM . . .

The firm routinely interviews on-campus at the following law schools: Duke, Emory, Florida, Georgia, Georgia State, Loyola/New Orleans, Mercer, North Carolina, South Carolina, Tulane, Vanderbilt, Virginia.

The firm also hires from schools where it doesn't interview on-campus.

HOURS AND BUCKS . . .

Hours: Associates bill on average 1,935 hours per year; the minimum billable hours requirement is 1,900. Part-time work is available to continuing associates; it is not available at entry level.

Starting salary: $$$ ($50-65,000) in South Carolina; $$$$ (Over $65,000) in North Carolina and Georgia

SUMMER PROGRAM . . .

Last year 18 2L and 14 1L summer associates; of the 2Ls, 13 received permanent offers.

Weekly pay: In South Carolina: $850 for 2Ls, $800 for 1Ls. In Georgia: $1,100 for both 2Ls and 1Ls.

1Ls are routinely hired for the summer program.

HISTORY AT A GLANCE . . .

The firm was founded in Columbia, South Carolina in 1897.

Nilles, Hansen & Davies, Ltd.

1800 Radisson Tower • P.O. Box 2626 • Fargo, North Dakota 58108
Phone: 701-237-5544 • Fax: 701-280-0762

OFFICES

Fargo (main office), Williston, North Dakota

NUTS AND BOLTS

Hiring attorney:

Greg Selbo

Number of attorneys in firm:

20 (19 partners)

WHAT DO THEY DO?

Specialties: Civil and Commercial Litigation, Insurance, Errors and Omissions Litigation, Tort, Products Liability, Personal Injury, Railroads, Construction Litigation, Appeals, Professional Liability, Business Law, Probate, Estate Planning, Real Estate, Commercial Law, Banking, Bankruptcy, and Employment Law and Workers Compensation.

WHO DO THEY REPRESENT?

Numerous insurers, as well as the Greater North Dakota Association, Amtrak, Luther Hospitals, the First Bank of North Dakota, and Builders' Supply Inc.

O'Connor, Cavanagh, Anderson, Killingworth & Beshears

1 East Camelback, Suite 1100 • Phoenix, Arizona 85012-1656
Phone: 602-263-2400 • Fax: 602-263-2900 • E-mail: firminfo@arizlaw.com

OFFICES

Phoenix (main office), Tucson, Sun City, Nogales, Arizona

NUTS AND BOLTS

Hiring attorney:

Henry L. Timmerman

Recruiting administrator:

Paulette A. Bateman

Number of attorneys in firm:

137

PHOENIX OFFICE:

114 attorneys (58 partners)

OTHER OFFICES:

Tucson, AZ (18); Sun City, AZ (2); Nogales, AZ (3)

Years to make partner:

5 to 7 years.

WHAT DO THEY DO?

Specialties: Commercial Litigation, Insurance Litigation, Real Estate, Malpractice Defense, Securities and Corporate, Tax and Estate Planning, Financial Services and Bankruptcy, Labor and Employment Law, Intellectual Property, Domestic Relations.

New associates choose which practice group they want to join, and can usually switch specialties later on.

WHO DO THEY REPRESENT . . .

Clients include Abbott Labs, ABCO Holdings, Allied Signal, American Southwest Financial Corporation, Arizona Physicians IPA, Avis Rent-A-Car, Bank of Hawaii, Bank of America, Black & Decker, Charles Schwab & Co., Chase Manhattan Bank, Chemical Waste Management Inc., City of Phoenix, Cyprus Amax Minerals, Dean Witter, Del Webb, Dillard's Department Stores, Dow Chemical, First National Bank of Arizona, Forty Niners Golf & Country Club, GMAC, Hilton Hotels, Johnson Wax, Marshal Foundation, Mobil Oil, Motorola, Prudential Life Insurance, Sears Roebuck, Shearson Lehman Brothers, Smith Barney, The Equitable, Home Depot, The Money Store, and University Medical Center Corporation.

WHERE NEW ASSOCIATES COME FROM . . .

The firm routinely interviews on-campus at the following law schools: Arizona, Arizona State, Hastings, Iowa, and Notre Dame. The firm also hires from schools where it doesn't interview on-campus.

HOURS AND BUCKS . . .

Hours: Associates work an average of 2,150 hours per year; the minimum billable hours requirement is 1,900 hours per year. Part-time work is available to both continuing and new associates on a case-by-case basis.
   Starting salary: $$$ ($50-65,000)

SUMMER PROGRAM . . .

Last year, there were 7 summer associates, of whom 6 received offers.
   Weekly pay: $950
   1Ls are not hired for the summer program.

HISTORY AT A GLANCE . . .

The firm was founded in 1959.

O'Melveny & Myers

Citicorp Center· • 153 East 53RD Street • New York, NY 10022-4611
Phone: 212-326-2000 • Fax: 212-326-2061

OFFICES

New York City (Los Angeles-based firm), New York

HIGHLIGHTS

- 17TH largest law firm in the country; New York office is the second largest in the firm.

NUTS AND BOLTS

Recruiting coordinator for New York:

Jeanie Flynn

Number of attorneys in firm:

575 (121 in New York)

LOS ANGELES OFFICE:

216 attorneys

OTHER OFFICES:

Century City, CA (51); Newport Beach, CA (58); San Francisco, CA (50); Washington, D.C. (65); London (4); Tokyo (1); Hong Kong (4); Singapore (4).

Years to make partner:

7 to 9.

WHAT DO THEY DO?

Specialties: Corporate (including Mergers and Acquisitions, Public and Private Securities Offerings for Issuers, Underwriters and Buy-Out Funds, Bank Financings, Entertainment and Media, International Transactions, Project Finance, and Securitization Transactions); Litigation (including Antitrust, Bankruptcy, Construction, Contracts, Insurance, Intellectual

Property, Product Liability, Real Estate, Environmental Liability, Securities and White-Collar Crime), Bankruptcy and Creditors' Rights; Labor; Real Estate; and Tax.

New associates generally may choose which practice areas they want to join, and they may choose more than one.

WHERE NEW ASSOCIATES COME FROM . . .

The firm interviews on-campus at the following law schools: Boalt Hall, Brooklyn, Chicago, Columbia, Cornell, Duke, Fordham, George Washington, Georgetown, Harvard, Michigan, NYU, Pennsylvania, Rutgers/Newark, USC, Stanford, Texas, UCLA, Virginia, and Yale. The firm also hires from schools where it doesn't interview on-campus.

HOURS AND BUCKS . . .

Hours: Associates bill an average of 1,889 hours per year. There is no minimum billable hours requirement. Part-time work is available to both continuing and entry-level associates.

Starting pay: $$$$ (Over $65,000; the firm is known for its generous financial package)

SUMMER PROGRAM . . .

Last year, there were 20 summer associates in New York, all of whom received offers.

Weekly pay: $1,600 last year.

1Ls are routinely hired for the summer program.

Pretzel & Stouffer

One South Wacker Drive, Suite 2500 • Chicago, Illinois 60606-4673
Phone: 312-346-1973 • Fax: 312-346-8242

OFFICES

Chicago, Illinois (only office)

NUTS AND BOLTS

Hiring attorney:

Brian T. Henry

Number of attorneys in firm:

67 (41 partners, 26 associates)

WHAT DO THEY DO?

Specialties: Insurance, Environmental, Commercial, Corporate, Antitrust, Probate, Tax, Real Estate, Employee Benefits, Surety, Fidelity, Construction, Family/Matrimonial, and Admiralty.

WHO DO THEY REPRESENT?

Their clients include A.H. Robins, Allstate Insurance, American National Can Company, Cigna Insurance, C.N.A., Employees Reinsurance Company, Fireman's Fund Insurance, Health Plans, Inc., Merck, Michelin Tire, Mobil Oil, National Ski Areas Association, Pepsi-Cola General Bottlers, Travelers Insurance, U.S. Aviation Underwriters, and Zenith Electronics.

HISTORY AT A GLANCE . . .

The firm was founded in 1946.

Rendigs, Fry, Kiely & Dennis

900 Fourth & Vine Tower • 5 West Fourth Street • Cincinnati, Ohio 45202
Phone: 513-381-9200 • Fax: 513-381-9206
E-mail: Rendigs@aol.com • Web site: rendigs.com

OFFICES

Cincinnati, Ohio (only office)

NUTS AND BOLTS

Hiring partner:

Carolyn Taggart

Number of attorneys in firm:

40 (25 partners)

WHAT DO THEY DO?

Specialties: Appeals; Commercial Law; Corporate Law; Civil Rights; Construction Litigation; Employment Relations and Litigation; Environmental Law; Estate and Personal Business Planning; Health Care Law; Insurance Coverage Law; Litigation/Trial Practice; Maritime Law; Professional Negligence/Malpractice; Negligence/Personal Injury; Pension; Product Liability Litigation; Real Estate; Taxation Law; Trusts, Wills, and Probate; Workers' Compensation; and Wrongful Death.

HISTORY AT A GLANCE . . .

The firm was founded in 1946.

Robinson, Bradshaw & Hinson, P.A.

101 North Tryon Street, Suite 1900 • Charlotte, North Carolina 28246
Phone: 704-377-2536 • Fax: 704-378-4000 • Web site: rbh.com

OFFICES

Charlotte (main office), North Carolina; Rock Hill, South Carolina

HIGHLIGHTS

- Hours are not measured for performance or bonuses—only to bill clients; the result is a very high retention rate among associates and partners.
- Founding partner Russell Robinson II wrote *Robinson on North Carolina Corporation Law,* which is known as the bible of business practice in the state.

NUTS AND BOLTS

Hiring attorney:

John R. Wester

Recruiting aoordinator:

Susan Floyd

Number of attorneys in firm:

92 attorneys (55 partners)

CHARLOTTE OFFICE:

87 attorneys

OTHER OFFICE:

Rock Hill, SC (5)

WORD ON THE STREET . . .

"They have an amazing management philosophy, one of a kind."

WHAT DO THEY DO?

Specialties: Corporate, Litigation, Real Estate, and Tax.

New associates are unassigned. Instead, they try projects in several departments for a year to 18 months, and then join a department based on their interests and the firm's needs.

WHO DO THEY REPRESENT?

Clients include public and closely-held corporations both domestically and in foreign markets, limited liability companies, limited and general partnerships, individuals, municipal, county and state agencies, public utilities, health care institutions, financial institutions, and tax-exempt organizations. Among others, the firm represents Bowles Hollowell Connor & Company, Carolinas Freight Corporation, The Charlotte-Mecklenburg Hospital Authority, Duke Energy Corporation, First Boston Bancorp, Goldman Sachs, Mecklenburg County, Mountain Air Cargo, Plastics Manufacturing Inc., Prudential Securities, Star Paper Tube, Stork Screens America, The Duke Endowment, Wachovia, and Washburn Graphics.

WHERE NEW ASSOCIATES COME FROM . . .

The firm routinely interviews on-campus at the following law schools: Columbia, Duke, Georgetown, Harvard, NYU, Michigan, North Carolina, Vanderbilt, Virginia, Wake Forest, Washington & Lee, and Yale. The firm also hires from schools where it doesn't conduct on-campus interviews.

HOURS AND BUCKS . . .

Hours: The firm doesn't monitor hours. Part-time work is available on a case-by-case basis.

Starting salary: $$$$ (Over $65,000)

SUMMER PROGRAM . . .

Last year, there were 21 summer associates, 13 2Ls (12 received offers) and eight 1Ls.

Weekly pay: $1,000 last year

The firm routinely hires 1Ls for its summer program.

HISTORY AT A GLANCE . . .

The firm was founded in 1960.

Sachnoff & Weaver

30 South Wacker Drive • Chicago, Illinois 60606
Phone: 312-207-1000 • Fax: 312-207-6400
E-mail: swltd@aol.com • Web site: sachnoff.com

OFFICES

Chicago, Illinois

NUTS AND BOLTS

Hiring attorney:

Marshall Seeder

Number of attorneys in firm:

97 (64 partners)

WORD ON THE STREET . . .

"It's a great place. People love it." "They tend to be a little more liberal place to work." "They are friendly to alternative lifestyles." "They are casual—they wear jeans to work, unless they're meeting with clients."

WHAT DO THEY DO?

Specialties: Litigation (representing everything from large corporations to government to small businesses) and Business (corporate, marketing and intellectual property, antitrust, securities, tax, financial services, real estate, environmental, employment, and employee benefits).

Steel Hector & Davis, L.L.P.

200 South Biscayne Blvd. • Miami, Florida 33131-2398
Phone: 305-577-7000 • Fax: 305-577-7001 • Web site: steelhector.com

OFFICES

Miami (main office), West Palm, Tallahassee, Key West, Florida

HIGHLIGHTS

- 217TH largest firm in the country.
- Strong dedication to pro bono work; in recent years, the firm has received numerous awards for its pro bono efforts, including the American Bar Association's *Pro Bono Publico* Award.

NUTS AND BOLTS

Hiring attorney:

Joseph Clock

Recruiting director:

Abbe Mald Bunt

Number of attorneys in firm:

151 attorneys (98 partners)

MIAMI OFFICE:

112 attorneys

OTHER OFFICES:

West Palm Beach (32), Tallahassee (7), Caracas, London, Sao Paulo, Rio de Janeiro

WORD ON THE STREET . . .

"It's a great firm—people really enjoy it." "It's an incredibly caring place. After Hurricane Andrew, they did tremendous things to help their people. They set up day care. And they set up what amounted to an in-house bank, with cash available to people who needed it to rebuild. There were no formal terms, just 'Pay us back whenever you can.' I've never heard of another firm doing anything like it."

WHAT DO THEY DO?

Specialties: Particularly well-known for its largest specialty, litigation. Other specialties include Corporate, Real Estate, Administrative, Government, Tax, Health Care, Banking, Creditors' Rights, Bankruptcy, Financial Services, Probate, and International.

WHO DO THEY REPRESENT?

Many public and private corporations, charitable foundations, governmental bodies, families and individuals. Its clients include ABC Inc., American Airlines, Citicorp, Dean Witter Reynolds, DuPont, Fannie Mae, Flo Sun, Florida Power & Light, John Hancock Mutual Life Insurance, Mitsubishi Motor Sales of America, Petroquimica de Venezuela, Samsung Electronics, United Technologies, Mass Mutual Life Insurance, the Equitable Companies, and the John D. and Catherine T. MacArthur Foundation.

WHERE NEW ASSOCIATES COME FROM . . .

The firm routinely interviews on-campus at the following law schools: Columbia, Duke, Florida, Florida State, Georgetown, Harvard, Miami, NYU, and Nova. The firm also hires from schools where it doesn't conduct on-campus interviews.

HOURS AND BUCKS . . .

Hours: Associates work an average of 2,100 hours per year, of which 1,900 is the average billable hours requirement. Part-time work is available to continuing associates; it is not available at entry-level.

Starting salary: $$$ ($50-65,000)

SUMMER PROGRAM . . .

Last year, there were 10 summer associates in Miami, all of whom received offers.

Weekly pay: $1,000 last year.

1Ls are routinely hired for the summer program.

Stewart & Irwin, P.C.

Two Market Square Center, Suite 1100
251 East Ohio Street • Indianapolis, IN 46204
Phone: 317-639-5454 • Fax: 317-632-1319 • E-mail: Stewart8@ix.netcom.com

OFFICES

Indianapolis, Indiana

NUTS AND BOLTS

Hiring partner:

Ronald C. Smith

Number of attorneys in firm:

31 (16 partners)

WORD ON THE STREET . . .

"They do lots of plaintiff's personal injury, family law, international, and medical malpractice. People like it a bunch."

WHAT DO THEY DO?

Specialties: Insurance, Administrative Law, Business, Taxation, Corporate, Probate, Estate Planning, Environmental, Trial and Appellate Practice, Bankruptcy and Creditors' Rights, International Law, and Gaming Law.

WHO DO THEY REPRESENT?

Their clients include ADT Security Systems, Automobile Dealers of Indiana, Carnival Hotels & Casinos, Casualty Insurance Company, C.N.A. Insurance, Coca-Cola Bottling, Crum & Forester, CVS Corporation, General Accident Insurance Company, Mid-American Equipment Retailers Association, Sentry Insurance, Wausau Insurance, and One Call Communications.

HISTORY AT A GLANCE . . .

The firm was founded in 1921.

Stradley, Ronon, Stevens & Young, L.L.P.

2600 One Commerce Square • Philadelphia, PA 19103-7098
Phone: 215-564-8000 • Fax: 215-564-8120 • Web site: stradley.com

OFFICES

Philadelphia (main office), Malvern, Pennsylvania; Wilmington, Delaware; Cherry Hill, New Jersey

NUTS AND BOLTS

Hiring attorney:

Stephen C. Baker

Professional programs coordinator:

Deidre M. Mullen, Esq.

Number of attorneys in firm:

134 attorneys

PHILADELPHIA OFFICE:

7 attorneys (63 partners)

OTHER OFFICES:

Malvern, PA (13); Wilmington, DE (3); Cherry Hill, NJ (1)

Years to make partner:

7 $^1/_2$ to 9 $^1/_2$

WHAT DO THEY DO?

The firm is divided into 13 practice areas, which are: ADR (Alternative Dispute Resolution, Mediation, and Business Disputes); Business Law; Charitable, Religious and Educational Institutions; Environmental Law; Estates; Finance Services and Business Reorganization; Insurance; Labor and Employment Law; Litigation; Real Estate; Securities; Tax; and Technology Law and Computers.

Each new associate is assigned to a department and to a mentor, who directly supervises the associate's workload and training.

WHERE NEW ASSOCIATES COME FROM . . .

The firm routinely interviews on-campus at the following law schools: Dickinson, Duke, Georgetown, Howard, Pennsylvania, Pittsburgh, Rutgers-Camden, Temple, and Villanova. The firm also hires from schools where it doesn't conduct on-campus interviews.

HOURS AND BUCKS . . .

Hours: Associates work an average of 1,950 hours per year. The average billable hours are 1,802, and the minimum billable hourly requirement is 1,800 hours.

Part-time work is available to continuing associates; it is not available at entry-level.

Starting salary: $$$ (50-65,000)

SUMMER PROGRAM . . .

Last year, there were 6 summer associates, all of whom received offers.

HISTORY AT A GLANCE . . .

The firm was founded in 1926.

Sugarman, Rogers,
Barshak & Cohen, P.C.

101 Merrimac Street • Boston, Massachusetts 02114-4731
Phone: 617-227-3030 • Fax: 617-523-4001 • E-mail: srbc@srbc.com

OFFICES

Boston, Massachusetts

NUTS AND BOLTS

Hiring attorney:

Kenneth Ernstoff

Number of attorneys in firm:

23 attorneys (14 partners)

WHAT DO THEY DO?

Specialties: Products Liability, Tort, Business, Professional Liability, Employment, Environmental, Insurance Coverage, Domestic Relations Litigation, Mediation and Arbitration.

HISTORY AT A GLANCE . . .

The firm was founded in 1929.

Sutherland, Asbill & Brennan, L.L.P.

999 Peachtree Street, N.E. • Atlanta, GA 30309-3996
Phone: 404-853-8000 • Fax: 404-853-8806 • Web site: sablaw.com

OFFICES

Atlanta, Georgia (main office); Washington, D.C.; New York City, New York; Austin, Texas

HIGHLIGHTS

- 128TH largest law firm in the United States.
- Fantastic web site, with links to many other legal resources.

NUTS AND BOLTS

Hiring partner:

Victor Haley

Director of recruitment and professional development:

Carter Hoyt

Number of attorneys in firm:

236

ATLANTA OFFICE:

128 attorneys (68 partners)

OTHER OFFICES:

Washington, D.C. (105); New York City (3); Austin, TX (1)

Years to make partner:

8

WHAT DO THEY DO?

Specialties: Tax, Litigation, Corporate and Securities, Banking and Finance, and Real Estate.

WHERE NEW ASSOCIATES COME FROM . . .

The firm routinely interviews on-campus at Chicago, Columbia, Cornell, Duke, Emory, Florida, Georgetown, Georgia, Georgia State, Harvard, Michigan, NYU, North Carolina, Notre Dame, Tennessee, Vanderbilt, Virginia, and Yale. The firm also hires from schools where it doesn't interview on-campus.

HOURS AND BUCKS . . .

Hours: Associates work on average 2,400 hours per year; of those, associates bill an average of 1,700 hours.

Part-time work is available to continuing associates; it is not available at entry level.

Starting salary: $$$$ (Over $65,000)

SUMMER PROGRAM . . .

Last year, there were 10 summer associates in Atlanta, all of whom received offers.

Weekly pay: $1,000 last year.

1Ls are routinely hired for the summer program.

HISTORY AT A GLANCE . . .

The firm was founded in 1924.

Tonkon, Torp L.L.P.

1600 Pioneer Tower • 888 S. W. Fifth Avenue • Portland, Oregon 97204-2099
Phone: 503-221-1440 • Fax: 503-274-8779

OFFICES

Portland, Oregon

HIGHLIGHTS . . .

- Strong dedication to pro bono work; pro bono hours count as billables.

NUTS AND BOLTS

Recruiting coordinator:
Kandi Stayer

Number of attorneys in firm:
50 attorneys (34 partners)

Years to make partner:
6 to 7

WHAT DO THEY DO?

Specialties: Business and Corporate (including Banking Securities); Litigation (including Bankruptcy, Creditors' Rights, Employment, and Labor); Real Estate; Land Use; Wills; Estates; Tax; and Trusts.

WHO DO THEY REPRESENT?

The firm represents banks and other financial institutions, growth companies in various technologies, timber companies, public utilities, newspaper and television companies, real estate investors, local, national and international manufacturers, venture capitalists, and underwriters, among others. Clients include Arthur Andersen, Columbia Distributing, Costco Wholesale Corporation, Deloitte & Touche, Gemstone Systems, Informedics, Inland Empire Paper, KOIN-TV, McDonald's, NIKE, Paulson Investment Company, Portland General, Ron Tonkin Dealerships,

Southwest Marine, Symbol Technologies, Timberline Software, Travelers Insurance, and United States Bakery.

WHERE NEW ASSOCIATES COME FROM . . .

The firm routinely interviews on-campus at the following law schools: Boalt Hall, Harvard, Hastings, Lewis & Clark, Michigan, Oregon, University of Washington, and Willamette. The firm also hires from schools where it doesn't conduct on-campus interviews.

HOURS AND BUCKS . . .

Hours: Associates work on average 1,888 hours per year; the average associate billable hours are 1,772. The minimum billable hours requirement is 1,700. Part-time work is available to continuing associates; it is not available at entry level.

Starting pay: $$$ ($50-65,000)

SUMMER PROGRAM . . .

Last year, there were 3 summer associates, all of whom received offers.

Weekly pay: $900 last year.

1Ls are routinely hired for the summer program.

HISTORY AT A GLANCE...

The firm was founded in 1975 with 11 lawyers.

Troutman Sanders

Nationsbank Plaza, Suite 5200 · 600 Peachtree Street, N.E. · Atlanta, GA 30308
Phone: 404-885-3000 · Fax: 404-885-3900

OFFICES

Atlanta, Georgia; Washington, D.C.; Hong Kong

HIGHLIGHTS

- 124TH largest law firm in the country.
- Recognized as one of the nation's best law firms for women.

NUTS AND BOLTS

Hiring attorney:

Stephen W. Riddell

Recruiting administrator:

Jodie Kapral (jodie.kapral@troutmansanders.com)

Number of attorneys in firm:

213 (95 partners)

Years to make partner:

7 1/2

WHAT DO THEY DO?

Specialties: The firm has four principal sections—Corporate, Litigation, Real Estate, and Public Law—with more than 25 interdisciplinary practice groups in a variety of areas, including International, Environmental Law, Banking, Tax, Mergers and Acquisitions, Securities, Intellectual Property, Labor Relations, Employee Benefits, Utilities, Bankruptcy and Legislation.

WHERE NEW ASSOCIATES COME FROM . . .

The firm routinely interviews on-campus at the following law schools: Duke, Emory, George Washington, Georgetown, Georgia, Georgia State,

Harvard, North Carolina, Texas, Tulane, Vanderbilt, and Virginia. The firm also hires from schools where it doesn't interview on-campus.

HOURS AND BUCKS . . .

Hours: Associates work an average of 2,103 hours per year, of which 1,800 are the average billable hours.

Part-time work is available to both ongoing and new associates on a case-by-case basis.

Starting salary: $$$$ (Over $65,000)

SUMMER PROGRAM . . .

Last year, there were 41 summer associates, of whom 22 2Ls were considered for permanent offers. Of those, 21 received offers.

Weekly pay: $1,100 last year

1Ls are routinely hired for the summer program.

Vinson & Elkins L.L.P.

1001 Fannin • 2300 First City Tower • Houston, Texas 77002-6760
Phone: 713-758-2222 • Fax: 713-758-2346
E-mail: info@velaw.com • Web site: vinson-elkins.com

OFFICES

Houston (main office), Austin, Dallas, Texas; Washington, D.C.

HIGHLIGHTS

- 22ND largest firm in the country.
- Strong dedication to pro bono work; pro bono hours are counted as billables.
- Cutting-edge computers; all offices are linked with voice and e-mail, and similar links exist with many of the firm's clients.

NUTS AND BOLTS

Hiring attorney:

Robert H. Scheck

Director of attorney employment:

Kelly Zenner

Number of attorneys in firm:

549

HOUSTON OFFICE:

346 attorneys (171 partners)

OTHER OFFICES:

Austin, TX (34); Dallas, TX (83); Washington, D.C. (65); London (6); Moscow (4); Singapore (6)

Years to make partner:

8

WHAT DO THEY DO?

Specialties: Core practice areas include Admiralty; Antitrust; Bankruptcy; Business Transactions; Capital Markets; Contracts; Eminent Domain; Employee Benefits (ERISA) and Executive Compensation; Energy and Electric Power Regulation; Environmental; Finance; Financial Institutions; Health Law; Intellectual Property; International Law; Labor; Litigation; Natural Resources, Oil, and Gas; Real Estate; Refining and Petro-Chemicals; Project Finance and Development; Public Policy; Securities; Taxation; Telecommunications; Trusts and Estates; and White-Collar Criminal Defense.

WHERE NEW ASSOCIATES COME FROM . . .

The firm routinely interviews on-campus at the following law schools: Baylor, Chicago, Columbia, Duke, Georgetown, Harvard, Houston, LSU, South Texas, SMU, Stanford, Texas, Tulane, Vanderbilt, Virginia, and Yale. The firm also hires from schools where it doesn't conduct on-campus interviews.

HOURS AND BUCKS . . .

Hours: Associates work an average of 2,318 hours per year, of which 2,026 are the average billable hours.

Part-time work is available to continuing associates; it is not available at entry-level.

Starting salary: $$$$ (Over $65,000). The firm is known for its very generous financial package.

SUMMER PROGRAM . . .

Last year, there were 45 2L summer associates, 41 of whom received offers.

Weekly pay: $1,350 last year.

1Ls are occasionally hired for the summer program.

HISTORY AT A GLANCE . . .

The firm was founded in 1917.

Vogel, Kelly, Knutson, Weir, Bye & Hunke, Ltd.

P.O. Box 1389 • Fargo, North Dakota 58107
Phone: 701-237-6983 • Fax: 701-237-0847
E-mail: vogellaw@linup.net • Web site: vogellaw.com

OFFICES

Fargo, North Dakota

HIGHLIGHTS:

- 12 of the firm's attorneys are listed in *The Best Attorneys In America*.
- One of the largest law firms in North Dakota and northern Minnesota.

NUTS AND BOLTS

Hiring partner:

Jane Voglewede

Number of attorneys in firm:

20 (18 partners)

WHAT DO THEY DO?

Specialties: The firm is divided into the following practice groups: Bankruptcy/Collections, Criminal Law, Plaintiffs, Business Organizations, Domestic Law, Products Liability, Construction, Estate Planning and Probate, Real Estate, Commercial Litigation, Health Law, Tort and Insurance Litigation, Commercial Transactions and Securities, Labor and Employment, Year 2000 Legal Services, and Malpractice Defense.

HISTORY AT A GLANCE . . .

The firm was founded in 1905.

Warner Norcross & Judd, L.L.P.

900 Old Kent Building • 111 Lyon Street, N.W.
Grand Rapids, Michigan 49503-2487
Phone: 616-752-2000 • Fax: 616-752-2500
E-mail: meriwecm@wnj.com • Web site: wnj.com

OFFICES

Grand Rapids (main office), Holland, Muskegon, Southfield, Michigan

HIGHLIGHTS

- 246TH largest firm in the country.
- 6TH largest firm in Michigan, and largest in Grand Rapids.

NUTS AND BOLTS

Hiring attorney:

Douglas A. Dozeman

Director of lawyer recruitment:

Cathleen M. Meriwether

Number of attorneys in firm:

157

GRAND RAPIDS OFFICE:

35 attorneys (76 partners)

OTHER OFFICES:

Holland, MI (5); Muskegon, MI (14); Southfield, MI (3)

Years to make partner:

7 1/2

WHAT DO THEY DO?

Specialties: Antitrust, Bankruptcy and Creditors' Rights, Banking and Finance, Civil Litigation, Computers and Technology, Condominiums, Corporate and Securities, Employee Benefits, Environmental, Franchising,

Health Care, Immigration, Intellectual Property, International, Labor & Employment, Mergers and Acquisitions, Oil and Gas, Patent, Trademark and Copyright, Pension and Profit Sharing, Product Liability, Real Estate, Taxation (corporate, partnership, and individual), Trusts and Estates, and White Collar Criminal Defense.

The firm is not departmentalized. Associates choose their own area of concentration after they have been with the firm for a year. Most of the firm's attorneys practice in several specialties and participate in two or more practice groups.

WHERE NEW ASSOCIATES COME FROM . . .

The firm routinely interviews on-campus at the following law schools: Chicago, Harvard, Illinois, Indiana/Bloomington, Michigan, Minnesota, Northwestern, Notre Dame, and Wayne State. The firm also hires from schools where it doesn't interview on-campus.

HOURS AND BUCKS . . .

Hours: Associates work an average of 1,823 hours per year; the average associate billable hours are 1,757. The minimum billable hours requirement is 1,750.

Starting salary: $$$ ($50-65,000)

SUMMER PROGRAM . . .

Last year, there were 14 summer associates, of whom 14 received offers.

Weekly pay: $1,000 last year

1Ls are routinely hired for the summer program.

Webb, Carlock, Copeland, Semler & Stair, L.L.P.

2600 Marquis Two Tower • 285 Peachtree Center Avenue
Atlanta, Georgia 30343-0887
Phone: 404-522-8220 • Fax: 404-523-2345

OFFICES

Atlanta, Georgia

NUTS AND BOLTS

Hiring partner:

David Cookson

Number of attorneys in firm:

40 (17 partners)

WHAT DO THEY DO?

Specialties: Torts, Negligence, Personal Injury, Wrongful Death, Products Liability, Motor Carrier and Transportation, Property and Casualty, General Insurance and Insurance Coverage, Legal and Medical Malpractice, Architects' and Engineers' Liability, Premises and General Liability, and Workers Compensation.

WHO DO THEY REPRESENT?

They represent a wide variety of clients, including many insurance companies, as well as Food Lion, Pizza Hut, Silver Dollar City, Six Flags Over Georgia, Sunbeam Outdoor Products, Wells Fargo Armored Service Corporation, and Yellow Freight Systems.

Weil, Gotshal & Manges, L.L.P.

700 Louisiana, Suite 1600 · Houston, Texas 77002
Phone: 713-546-5000 · Fax: 713-224-9511 · E-mail: postmaster@weil.com

OFFICES

Houston (New York-based firm), Texas

HIGHLIGHTS:

- New York branch office of the 16TH largest law firm in the country.
- No minimum billable hours requirement.
- Strong dedication to pro bono work; pro bono hours are treated as billables.

NUTS AND BOLTS

Hiring attorney:

Melanie Gray

Number of attorneys in firm:

549 (49 in Houston, of whom 13 are partners)

NEW YORK OFFICE:

360 attorneys

OTHER OFFICES:

Washington, D.C. (37); Miami, FL (17); Dallas, TX (45); Menlo Park, CA (25); London; Budapest; Warsaw; Brussels; Prague

Years to make partner:

7 1/3

WHAT DO THEY DO?

Specialties: Business Finance and Restructuring, Corporate, Litigation, Tax, Employment, Real Estate, and Intellectual Property.

WHERE NEW ASSOCIATES COME FROM . . .

The Houston office routinely interviews on-campus at the following law schools: Columbia, Houston, New York Law School, Texas, and Vanderbilt. The firm also hires from schools where it doesn't conduct on-campus interviews.

HOURS AND BUCKS . . .

Hours: There is no minimum billable hourly requirement. Part-time work is available to continuing associates on a case-by-case basis; it is not available at entry level.

Starting salary: $$$$ (Over $65,000)

SUMMER PROGRAM . . .

Last year, there were 6 summer associates in Houston, of whom 4 received offers.

Weekly pay: $1,425 last year.

1Ls are routinely hired for the summer program.

HISTORY AT A GLANCE . . .

The firm was founded in 1931, in New York. The Houston office opened in 1985.

Wiggin & Dana

One Century Tower • New Haven, Connecticut 06508-1832
Phone: 203-498-4400 • Fax: 203-782-2889

OFFICES

New Haven (main office), Hartford, Stamford, Connecticut

NUTS AND BOLTS

Hiring attorney:

Elizabeth J. Dunham

Number of attorneys in firm:

107 (46 partners)

NEW HAVEN OFFICE:

86 attorneys

OTHER OFFICES:

Hartford, CT (14); Stamford, CT (7)

Years to make partner:

7 to 8

WHAT DO THEY DO?

Specialties: Litigation, Corporate, Health Care, Intellectual Property, Labor, Employment and Benefits, Real Estate and Environmental, Trusts and Estates, Public Utility and Regulatory, Antitrust, Appellate.

Associates are not assigned for their first year; they receive assignments from many practice groups before they choose a particular area or specialty.

WHO DO THEY REPRESENT?

The firm is general counsel to more than 400 businesses, as well as more than half of the general hospitals in Connecticut, half of the state's private psychiatric hospitals, among other health care providers. Clients also include four colleges, several secondary schools, and many other charitable organizations. The firm also represents an electric utility and telecommunications company.

WHERE NEW ASSOCIATES COME FROM . . .

The firm routinely interviews on-campus at the following law schools: Boston College, Boston University, Connecticut, Cornell, Georgetown, Harvard, New York Law School, NYU, Pace, Pennsylvania, Quinnipiac, St. John's, Virginia, and Yale. The firm also hires from schools where it doesn't interview on-campus.

HOURS AND BUCKS . . .

Hours: Associates work an average of 2,182 hours per year; the average associate billable hours are 1,734. There is no minimum billable hours requirement.

Part-time work is available to continuing associates; it is not available at entry level.

Starting salary: $$$ ($50-65,000)

SUMMER PROGRAM . . .

Last year, there were 5 summer associates, 4 of whom received offers.

Weekly pay: $1,125

1Ls are routinely hired for the summer program.

Wilmer, Cutler & Pickering

2445 M Street, N.W. • Washington, DC 20037-1420
Phone: 202-663-6000 • Fax: 202-663-6363 • E-mail: Law@wilmer.com

OFFICES

New Haven (main office), Hartford, Stanford, Connecticut

HIGHLIGHTS

- 108TH largest law firm in the country.
- Strong dedication to pro bono work; pro bono hours are treated as billables, and pro bono represents about 10% of associate hours.
- No minimum billable hours requirement.
- Has a recently-inaugurated New Associate Working Group ("NAWG") which ensures that new associates get appropriate assignments, receive prompt feedback, are not over- or underworked, and have opportunities to develop strong working relationships with partners.

NUTS AND BOLTS

Hiring attorney:

David P. Donovan

Lawyer recruitment coordinator:

Cheryl B. Shigo

Number of attorneys in firm:

262

WASHINGTON OFFICE:

237 attorneys (87 partners)

OTHER OFFICES:

Baltimore, MD (5); Berlin (7); Brussels (8); London (5).

Years to make partner:

7 1/2

WHAT DO THEY DO?

Specialties: A focus on federal law, with matters involving Securities, General Litigation, Transportation, Antitrust, International Trade and Project Finance, Regulation of Banks and Other Financial Institutions, Product Safety, Insurance, Taxation, Regulation of Food and Drugs, Communications, Environmental Matters, Bankruptcy, Government Contracts, Corporate Transactions, Copyright, and Computer Law.

Associates have the choice of either specializing, or working with a large number of lawyers in a variety of practice areas.

WHERE NEW ASSOCIATES COME FROM . . .

The firm routinely interviews on-campus at the following law schools: American University, Boalt Hall, Chicago, Columbia, Cornell, Duke, George Washington, Georgetown, Harvard, Maryland, Michigan, NYU, Northwestern, Pennsylvania, Stanford, Texas, Virginia, and Yale. The firm also hires from schools where it doesn't conduct on-campus interviews.

HOURS AND BUCKS . . .

Hours: Associates work an average of 2,293 hours; average associate billable hours are 1,989 (which includes pro bono hours). There is no minimum billable hours requirement.

Part-time work is available to both continuing and new associates, on a case-by-case basis.

Starting salary: $$$$ (Over $65,000)

SUMMER PROGRAM . . .

Last year, there were 31 summer associates in Washington, of whom 30 received offers.

Weekly pay: $1,300 for 2Ls and $1,400 for post-3Ls last year.

1Ls are not hired for the summer program.

HISTORY AT A GLANCE . . .

The firm was founded in 1962, with 19 lawyers.

Workman, Nydegger & Seeley, P.C.

1000 Eagle Gate Tower • 60 East South Temple • Salt Lake City, Utah 84111
Phone: 801-533-9800 • Fax: 801-328-1707 • E-mail: info@wnspat.com

OFFICES

Salt Lake City, Utah

NUTS AND BOLTS

Hiring partner:

Michael Krieger

Number of attorneys in firm:

30

WHAT DO THEY DO?

Specialties: Patent, Trademark, Copyright, Trade Secrets, Unfair Competition, Licensing and Complex Litigation.

How to Find Great Firms Too Small to Be Included in This Book.

If you've already looked through Chapter 5 on Law Firms, you may have noticed that none of the firms there were small—under 20 lawyers or so. And if you've read the stuff in Chapter 1, you know why—I specifically looked for firms with more than 20 lawyers when I interviewed law school administrators. Why is that? It's not because I thought small firms couldn't be great places to work—they can be, as we're about to discuss. It's because I wanted to put together a book that you could actually lift, and if I included the hundreds of small firms who'd be recommended—well, this book would be much more of a monster than it already is. And on top of that, small firms don't hire regularly, and I thought that would be a little bit unfair to you—kind of like standing with your nose pressed up against the candy store window, gazing at the sweets, but the candy store's closed.

What I'm going to do in this chapter is to remedy that somewhat, by talking about small firms. There's no question that you can be *very* happy at a small firm. In fact, many lawyers think you can't be happy at any other kind of law firm! And the satisfaction issue aside, for most lawyers in private practice, small firms are where they end up. More than three-quarters of attorneys in private practice are with firms of fewer than 20 lawyers. So it's lucky that the small firm environment tends to be one that people enjoy!

Here's what we'll cover in this chapter. First of all, we're going to figure out the nature of the best—what kinds of small firms *are* there? Then we'll talk about what it's like to work at a small firm. After that, we'll spend a minute talking about how they hire and what they look for in people they hire. Then we'll talk about how to find them, and more importantly, how to find the *good* ones. After that, we'll talk about how you get around the niggly requirement that many small firm job ads mention: one to three years of experience. (We'll do that by way of one of my *Dear Job Goddess* columns. I know that's cheating, but I think you'll like it.) And finally, we'll take a look at a small firm—Brett & Daugert, in lovely Bellingham, Washington. It's not only a firm that got rave reviews, but I think it epitomizes everything that's good about working for a small firm.

What I'm *not* going to do here is talk a lot about cover letters, resumes, and interviews. The reason for that is that you're going to want to do all the things you do for every other kind of legal employer when you're talking to small firms—for instance, targeting cover letters, researching the firm before you interview, and highlighting relevant experience on your resume. And the reason I know all this is that I already wrote a bunch of pages about all of these topics in my fabulous book (really, I'm not the only one who thinks so) *Guerrilla Tactics For Getting The Legal Job Of Your Dreams.* It's at your Career Services Office if you want to take a look at it. The point is, I'm not going to reinvent the wheel here when it comes to letters, resumes, and interviews.

So, let's get started!

What Kinds of Small Firms Are There?

I could make the hoary comment about all small firms not being created equal but I won't put you through that. What's important to realize is that it's a mistake to lump "small firms" into one ball and assume they're all the same. They aren't. It's easy to think about small firms and have your mind turn to images in the movies, like William Hurt's sleazy law practice in *Body Heat.* I suppose we should all be thankful that small firms aren't like *that!* As a general matter, you can separate real life small firms into four categories:

1. *Small firms that are actually boutiques.* These are firms that focus on a particular specialty. For instance, the large firm Cooley Godward— which is in Chapter 5—started as a biotech boutique, focusing on the biotech industry. Most entertainment law firms are also boutiques— small shops with a very distinct focus. These firms tend to do very sophisticated, cutting-edge work in their specialty, they tend to have a national practice, and they are often spin-offs from larger firms.

The other three categories depend on geography. You have:

2. *Small firms in large cities.* These firms may be spin-offs from larger firms, and like boutiques, may have a national practice. Because of their location, they are plugged into the way large firms hire and tend to hire more formally than small firms in smaller cities and rural areas. So they may use headhunters, and they may advertise openings in the classified section of legal newspapers.

3. *Small firms in smaller cities.* These will tend to be general practice firms, handling the gamut of problems from real estate to family law to the issues small businesses face. The practice will tend to be regional.

4. *Small firms in rural areas.* Like small firms in smaller cities, you'll find a general practice in these firms, but they will tend to be even

broader. They'll do local government work, criminal work, real estate, family law, wills and trusts and everything else that walks in the door.

What It's Like to Work at a Small Firm

When it comes to work environment, size matters. The environment in a small firm is *necessarily* going to be different than in a larger organization. Among the differences:

1. *You'll have more autonomy.* Small firms don't have the personnel to fill several layers of management, so you have a lot more control over what you do. While some people feel more comfortable in the cocoon-like environment of a larger organization, most people like the idea of having more direct control over what they do. That's a tremendous plus of small firms.

2. *You'll get hands-on experience quickly.* Again, without a cadre of lawyers ahead of you on the food chain, you'll find yourself thrown into responsible situations—taking depositions, handling cases, dealing directly with clients—*much* sooner in a small firm, in fact in most cases, immediately. While that can be terrifying, it's exhilarating, too, and it makes you feel like a "real lawyer."

3. *The amount and quality of training you get is likely to depend on how the small firm was created.* If it was a spin-off from a large firm, it's likely that the partners will offer the kind of training that they experienced—that is, they'll put a priority on training. If *not*— that is, if the firm sprang fully-formed from the imagination of one or a few of the partners—training is a wild card. They might put a priority on it, and they might not.

4. *You'll probably be expected to bring in business fairly quickly, because typically with small firms, you "eat-what-you-kill."* It's hard to make a generalization like this, and while it will almost certainly be true for small firms in smaller cities and rural areas, it certainly wouldn't be accurate for boutiques. But as a rule at a small firm, mommy and daddy birds are going to stop putting worms in your beak more quickly than they would at a larger firm (and of course generating business isn't an issue at all for corporate, governmental, and public interest employers). If you're the kind of person who was involved in all kinds of activities in law school, if you're gregarious, if you're a

"joiner," and/or if you have strong ties to the community, the idea of rainmaking will probably not be intimidating. If you think rainmaking means sleazy, oleaginous schmoozing, a small firm might not be your ideal destination.

5. *You'll start out making less money.* Truth be told, the thing that attracts most law students to large firms isn't that they think they'll enjoy themselves—they just want to make the buckets of doubloons that come with the job. It's true that small firms tend to start you out making less money than you would at a large firm. *However,* it's a mistake to look at that starting pay as a benchmark of how you'll do financially. Some of the most highly-paid lawyers in America are at small firms, because depending on the clientele you attract, you can rocket up in salary very quickly.

6. *You'll be more of a generalist than a specialist,* **unless** *you go to work for a boutique.* The reason for this is that most small firms have general practices, and with relatively few lawyers, each lawyer has to wear more than one hat. You'll undoubtedly develop more of an expertise in some things than others, but you'd be making a mistake to confine yourself to a particular specialty if you're going to look at non-boutique small firms.

7. *You'll do more hands-on administrative work than you would at a large organization.* When you're at a large firm, you are supported by a battalion of word processors, librarians, supply room clerks, mail room clerks, copy people, you name it. Obviously a small firm isn't going to foot the bill for that kind of support, so you'll spend more time doing things like handling your own paperwork and figuring out how to get papers served. That's not necessarily a negative, but when you're trying to solve a legal problem, it can be a distraction.

8. *The hours you work will not fit any particular mold.* I know that there is a popular feeling that associates at large firm, kill themselves, whereas everybody else—government lawyers, corporate lawyers, public interest lawyers, and small firm lawyers—doesn't. That hasn't been what I've found. While small firms *tend* to have an interest in quality of life issues, there's no guarantee that any *particular* firm won't work you like a rented mule. So if what you dream of when you think about working for a small firm is a guaranteed 9 a.m. to 5 p.m. schedule, make sure—before you accept an offer—that that's actually the case.

9. *Every attorney in the firm has a significant impact on your environment.* That can be good (if you like everybody) and bad (if you don't). At a large firm, you can much more easily avoid difficult personalities than you can in a small shop.

How Small Firms Do Their Hiring

In a nutshell—not like large firms. That is, large firms tend to hire through on-campus interview programs. Small firms don't, for a couple of reasons. For one thing, sending lawyers around to law school campuses takes *people* and *time*—two things that small firms can't afford. I mean, if you've got a four-person shop, it hardly makes sense to have one of you spend significant time away from the office just to goose that total up to five, does it? A few small firms *do* go on campus to interview. As I discussed above, those tend to be the small firms in large cities, who will tend to mimic large firms in their hiring practice more so than other small firms. But by and large, you won't find them doing on-campus interviews.

Another wrinkle in small-firm hiring is that they don't hire on a regular basis. With large firms, they hire as regularly as salmon spawn. That is, when fall comes, prospective associates get interviewed and then offers are made before Christmas for positions that will be there the following summer. Not so for small firms, many of whom hire by the seat of the pants. As Mark Brickson, Career Services Director at the University of North Dakota School of Law says, "Some smaller firms advertise and basically interview all comers until they find the right person. Sometimes this can last for months. Other firms need somebody *right now!*" As this statement suggests, openings at small firms can open up any time, and if it's a small firm that you want, you've got to face the reality that many of them aren't timing their hires according to graduation and bar exam schedules.

Still other small firms are coaxed into believing that they need an extra pair of hands. As one small firm practitioner told me, "What students don't understand is that for a small firm, hiring a new associate is like a marriage. In fact, in some ways it's *more* than a marriage, because you spend more time with your colleagues than you do at home." And furthermore, "Taking on a new person is a big commitment in terms of making sure you have the work to keep them busy, and that you'll continue doing so into the future, and that you have the money to pay them. Small firms look very coldly at their expenses—rent, support staff, all kinds of overheads, and then determine if they can budget in a new person. It can be an agonizing decision."

You would not be the first person to get into a small firm by volunteering for them, by the way. It happens a lot, according to stories I hear from law students and new lawyers. I talked with a wonderful freshly-minted law school graduate in the Midwest who'd gotten a job with a *great* small firm, by walking in, telling them he'd heard outstanding things about them from other lawyers in the community (which he *had)* and that he was so interested in working for them that he'd be willing to volunteer for a month to prove his worth. The partner he talked with was so blown away by this that he took him on the spot. As it turns out, the other partner in the firm walked in, and when this second partner was introduced to the young man and heard that he was willing to volunteer for the firm, he responded, "*Volunteer?* We can't have him work for *nothing.*" So they worked out an hourly fee for the first month, and needless to say, he impressed them sufficiently in that month to convince them to hire him as a full-fledged associate.

Other than volunteering, there's offering to be a contract associate (that is, work for a set period of time or on a stated project), or offering to work part-time. The key is this: enter with the idea that you're going to make yourself indispensable, so that once you're there they won't be able to figure out how they ever lived without you. And then actually *make* yourself indispensable!

You also need to be aware that many small firms won't hire you until you've passed the bar exam, because they'll need you to go into court and sign off on pleadings. Unlike larger firms, they often don't have the luxury of keeping you in the office researching until the bar results come out. So it's entirely possible that you'll have to cool your heels until you get your bar results. In the meantime, search out potential employers as I outline below—with the awareness that as soon as you've passed the bar, people who weren't willing to hire you before will step up to the plate with offers.

What Small Firms Look for in People They Hire

Obviously this is going to differ from firm to firm to some extent. Small boutiques, for instance, often demand the same paper credentials as large firms—that is, blue-chip grades, Law Review, the whole nine yards. Most small firms, however, are not that way, and there *are* qualities and skills that small firms in general look for. To be more specific, here are the ducks you need to have in a row in order to get small firm jobs:

1. The most important element is the most elusive: that is, small firms want a "fit." That is, they want to make sure that they'll be comfortable with you, and you'll be comfortable with them. In a small office this is more important than it is for large firms. I've never talked to an associate at a large organization who got along with *everybody* there, but when you've got a lot of people, it's easy to avoid the jerks. When there are only 10 of you, one bad apple is 10% of the population. So when they think about hiring you, they'll look for all of the

qualities that would suggest a harmonious marriage: common sense, maturity, a like sense of values and sense of humor, a willingness to pitch in, enthusiasm, and a positive attitude. Put yourself in their shoes, and think about the kind of person you'd want to bring on board if you'd built yourself up a nice little business. This will give you a clear snapshot of the way you should come off in your dealings with them.

2.   Remember that as a rule, small firms are not as concerned with grades as large firms are. What they *do* want is a strong all-around set of skills. They look for people with excellent people skills and a strong work ethic. When they look at your transcript, they typically want to see what courses you've taken more than how you've done in those courses.

3.   Small firms want to know that you can hit the ground running. They probably will not have the resources or the interest in the long, formal training programs that large firms sometimes offer. Proof that you'll be able to pick up the ball in a hurry are things like clinical courses, moot court involvement, prior work experience (volunteer or paid, it's the same thing), and evidence of practical writing skills. These skills are all valuable to small firms.

4.   Especially for non-boutique firms, it is *critical* that you show a commitment to the locality (moving there obviously helps!). That's *always* important for private firms. No firm wants to hire and train you only to find that you really want to live somewhere else, and that you have no intention of putting down roots in the community, and drawing in business. (Since boutiques tend to be national in scope, the "local connection" in that sense is less important, but you've *still* got to prove you'd accept an offer if you got one, and you'd stay if you *did* accept.) In terms of your resume, if you're from the area, show your community involvement along with extracurricular activities at law school and in undergraduate school. Fundraising activities are particularly attractive, because it portends your bringing in new clients in the future. If you grew up in an area and went away to college and law school, include ties to the community on your resume (you may want to mention where you went to high school, to show your local connections, and in a catch-all section on your resume, you'd mention your connection to the community).

5.   For small litigation firms, the kinds of experience to highlight are obvious: moot court, mock trial, debate experience—*anything* that suggests you can think on your feet.

6.   Make sure that your resume includes technical skills. As Mark Brickson advises, "Those computer skills may be just what a small

firm with no computer expertise is looking for." You make yourself infinitely more valuable to them if they know you're a whiz with the computer.

7. Include on your resume as much about your law school activities as you reasonably can, and any other community activities (like charity work, bar association involvement). Why? As Mark Brickson says, "If you are expected to be a 'rainmaker,' your social skills and willingness to be part of the larger business community are important."

8. Unless you are aiming for a boutique—that is, a highly specialized small firm—then de-emphasize specialties on your resume. Remember, most small firms need people who are generalists, or are willing to wear more than one specialty hat. If you've got a resume that screams "Sports Law," for instance, and you're talking to a small firm in a rural town, your resume is going to say: "I can't get what I really want, Sports Law, and so I'm settling for working for you." If your resume is too narrowly-focused, and it's too late to change your law school focus (*e.g.*, you've graduated), hurry up and take some CLE's in a variety of subjects (you can find out about when and where they're offered from your Career Services Office, the local bar association, or a librarian at your law library)—and put those on your resume as "Supplemental Legal Education." The point here is this: *Nobody* wants to be a second choice. Be sure that your resume, and your answers to interview questions, will accentuate why you want to be *here* doing *this*.

How to Find Small Firms— More Importantly, How to Find *Good* Small Firms!

In theory, you can find small firms *everywhere*. Here are a few ideas which are all-encompassing—that is, they don't make quality judgments:

1. The Yellow Pages, under "Attorneys." Duh. I thought I'd start with the most obvious source first.

2. Contact the local bar association and ask for a list of law firms in the geographic area where you want to practice. You can also check with them and see if they list job openings; some bar associations do.

3. Check with a law school Career Services Office (or law library) in the geographic area where you want to practice, to see if they have directories that list attorneys. For instance, The Legal Directories Publishing Company (which operates out of Dallas) publishes a lot of state directories (as the name suggests, I guess). Another useful publisher is the Lawyers Diary and Manual in Newark, New Jersey, which publishes annual directories for several states. Different states will have other options; for instance, in California, there's the Parker Directory of California Attorneys. You get the idea here, I think.

4. As Mark Brickson suggests, obtain reciprocity with a law school in the geographic region you're interested in. They may have fresh listings that aren't found in the job bulletins they publish. (To get reciprocity, you have to go to your own Career Services Director and have them send a letter for you to the school whose listings you want to access.)

5. Try the Internet. For instance, the Martindale-Hubbell lawyer lists (http://lawyers.martindale.com/marhub) are good resources, as is the West Legal Directory (http://www.wld.com/). As Mark Brickson says, you can focus not only on geographic areas, but also on a legal area of practice. And contrary to popular belief, "It's not just big firms that list information on the Internet about their organizations, members, and representative clients. Some small firms do as well."

6. You can also use the Internet to access local newspapers for their classifieds. Many local newspapers are on-line; use a browser to find them. Mark Brickson points out that in North Dakota, for example, "You can get classifieds for the local papers in all of the major cities— Grand Forks, Fargo, Bismarck and Minot."

7. Read the classifieds in local newspapers (and legal newspapers, if there are any that cover the geographic area you're interested in). Many of these listings will ask for experienced attorneys, although a few will ask for entry-level people. Even for experienced attorneys, you've got a shot if you follow the advice below, under "How to get jobs that require one to three years of experience."

8. Check with the bar association in the area where you want to practice to see if there are any local Spring job fairs. Small firms sometimes make an appearance at these.

Now, have you noticed the connecting link with these options? There's no weeding out process—in other words, you're likely to get scads and scads of small firms from these sources, with no qualifiers to separate the wheat from the chaff. While having a ton of possibilities is not a bad thing, remember that I started this section by talking about how you find *good* small firms. That's an important consideration, because it's a mistake to make the primitive division that some people make: small-firm-good-big-firm-bad-ug. If you're working in a three-person office where the other two people are *bloody bollocky pig-dogs* (in the words of Edwina of *Absolutely Fabulous*), you're not going to be happy. While you should certainly keep your eyes and ears open to sniff out a loser of a firm during the interview process, there *are* methods for finding small firm employers that, in and of themselves, do the weeding out for you. These include:

1. Career Services Directors—either at your own school or, with reciprocity (get this from your own law school Career Services Office), at a school that's located in the area where you want to settle down. Have you noticed what a huge fan I am of career services people? They spend their entire working lives helping others, and in doing so, they are *tremendous* eyes and ears into the legal community. As Mark Brickson says, "We have well-established relationships with the small firms in our region," and in North Dakota, he finds that "We get unsolicited calls and faxes from firms in the Minnesota, Montana, North Dakota, South Dakota, and Wisconsin-area all the time regarding positions available, both full-time associate and part-time clerking opportunities." On top of that, Career Services Directors normally have heard all kinds of scuttlebutt about all kinds of employers, and often can help steer you toward sterling employers—and away from bad ones.

2. Through either your Career Services Director (*again* they're useful) or your alumni relations director, find the names of alumni practicing law in the place where you want to live. Contact those alums and solicit their advice about firms that you ought to consider. If possible, get together with them in person (invite them for a cup of coffee, and drink decaf, because you'll be drinking a *lot* of coffee!). The more they feel comfortable with you, the more open and helpful they are likely to be. If your law school doesn't have any alums where you want to live, go back to your undergrad career services/alumni relations and see if any of anyone from your college went on to practice law in that location.

3. Talk to *any* local contacts that you have. Lawyers and judges are the best. If you know people in the community, they'll have their own lawyers, and you can start with those lawyers if you don't know any directly. The key here is that you need people who'll be straight with you, and not just tell you good things about *everybody*. You want to know who does good work, and who's ethical and honorable. One young lawyer told me about his experience looking for work with a small firm. He talked with local lawyers for their suggestions, and when he mentioned one lawyer who he'd heard was nice, the word he got was that "He's a very nice guy, but he does terrible work." Invaluable information, needless to say.

4. Do a judicial clerkship in the geographic area where you want to find small firm work. If this seems like a silly intermediate step to you, well—*who you callin' silly?* Here's why this idea's been recommended to me so much: it gives you an enormous jump on permanent employment. For a start, you get to see lawyers in their natural habitat, the kind of work they do and what they're like, and judge for yourself who you'd like to work with and who you want to avoid. You also get the ear of your judge, who (in most cases) will take a paternal/maternal interest in your well being and share with you which small firms to pursue. On top of that, you get a great resume builder—*everybody* likes to see judicial clerkships. And if you're worried about grades, don't get hung up on them. Especially for lower state courts, grades are not the issue they are for the more prestigious federal court clerkships. You still need good writing skills, but you can prove that in a variety of ways (non-law-review journal experience, moot court, researching for a prof, independent writing projects, etc.) other than law review.

5. Do freelance projects for a few months, before tying yourself down to a particular employer. Many small firms have projects they need done, but don't feel the need to hire a "whole person" right now. I've known a number of people who've done freelance brief writing for a living, and it gives you a great insight into what it's like to work with a variety of lawyers. When job openings with them *do* open up, you'd be first in line because they're already familiar with you and the quality of your work. (Among other ways of promoting yourself, you could advertise for yourself in the classifieds, offering freelance services, or talk to people at the local bar association and ask for leads that way.)

6. You could do some legal temping. This isn't an option in every city, but in many it is, and again it's a good way to get hands-on experience at a number of different employers before you choose one.

7. Volunteer for the local bar association or volunteer to help out at CLE programs (or just attend those kinds of functions). Of course, if you volunteer, you don't have to worry as much about breaking the ice with strangers—you've got a *reason* to be there, and that gives you something to talk about. But if talking to strangers isn't a problem for you, you don't have to volunteer. By all means just go as an attendee, bite the bullet, and talk to as many people as you can. Don't sound desperate (even if you are)—you're not looking for a job, you're meeting people who may someday be your colleagues. Tell them that you're settling in the community and getting a feel for the local firms. Ask what they do, how they like it, and what they would do in your shoes. You know—*talk.*

How to Get Around the "One to Three Years of Experience" That Many Small Firms Ask for in Job Ads

If you've been looking through classified ads for small or medium firms, and you don't have any experience, it's probably been pretty frustrating. That's because almost all job ads are looking for people with a bit of experience under their belt. People ask me about getting around this problem all the time—and I've received many letters about it at the *National Law Journal*. So many, in fact, that I wrote a "Dear Job Goddess" column about this very issue. Here it is:

Dear Job Goddess,

I am very frustrated. I'm in my last year of law school, and it seems as though all of the ads I see are looking for somebody with one to three years of experience. Is there any way I can get one of these jobs anyway?

VS, Massachusetts

Dear VS,

There may well be, VS, and the Job Goddess congratulates you for contacting her instead of just throwing in the career towel.

From the outset you have to appreciate that what employers *advertise* for and what they will *accept* are often two very different things. Many employers have pointed out to the Job Goddess that when they write job ads, they are describing their "ideal" candidate. It is often the case, VJ, that that ideal candidate may not apply for the job, and so it will go to someone who—like you—does not have the exact credentials stated in the ad.

With that in mind, how do you improve your odds of being the lucky candidate? Lisa Lesage, Career Services Director at Lewis & Clark Law School (and herself an attorney for several years), gives you two steps to follow: one is researching what you've got, and the other is finding out all you can about the employer.

When you look at what you bring to the table, Lisa Lesage says that, "When attorneys say they want one to three years of experience, what they really want is someone who knows the ropes. Jobs you have during law school can easily give you that." She advises you to, "Look at all the law-related work you've done, no matter what it is, and disgorge a line or two on every single thing. Don't simply say that you 'researched issues' or 'drafted memoranda and motions.' Instead, be very specific. Say that you drafted a motion for summary judgment in a 1983 case concerning privilege. Or that you prepared a deposition for a Title 7 case involving sexual harassment." For non-legal jobs you've had, be similarly specific so that you can pull out the skills that you can transfer to the legal job you want. Lisa Lesage advises that, "If you managed a restaurant before law school, don't just leave it at that. How many people did you manage? Did you handle budgets, or scheduling, or any other activities that would be similar in any setting?" The important thing here is that you "shouldn't ever self-select out!"

What will this self-research do for you, VS? As Lisa Lesage says, "It will help give you fodder for a cover letter, and it will also help you overcome any interview objections. You will be able to say, 'I may have just graduated, but I've got the experience you're looking for.'"

The other task at hand for you, VS, is to research the employer. Most ads state whom the employer is; if you find ads that don't—in other words, it's a "blind ad"—you are not out of luck. Lisa Lesage says that "If the return address is a P.O. Box, and the employer is incorporated, the post office must tell you the name of the box holder. Once you know who the employer is, go to your Career Services Office at school and see if they've compiled data on the employer or if there are alums from your school who have worked there." Such an alum can be an enormous help, since they will not only be able to tell you about the employer and how you can position yourself to get a job there—but they may also be willing to walk your application over to the person who's doing the hiring, and perhaps even put in a good word for you. Needless to say, this is a great way to distinguish yourself from other people applying for the same job.

Of course, VS, you know that the Job Goddess prefers that you find your dream job by getting to know people, through school and law-related activities, rather than through job ads. But the fact remains that many people *do* find jobs they like through ads, and if you follow the advice here—why, VS, there's no reason why you can't as well.

Eternally yours,
The Job Goddess

A Snapshot of Small-Firm Life: Brett & Daugert, Bellingham, Washington

In choosing a small firm to profile here, I had many, many choices. Frankly, it's hard to find many large firms between Chicago and Seattle—they almost *all* have fewer than 10 lawyers, and many of them are wonderful employers—*lots* of them get excellent reviews. Heck, even in my own state—Connecticut—the vast majority of law firms are few-person-shops.

But instead of giving you reams and reams of names, I thought I'd focus on one particular firm. Not only is it a great place to work, but it's in a really interesting town—Bellingham, Washington. You probably don't know about Bellingham—I didn't. It's a tiny oceanfront town, about 90 miles north of Seattle. It's incredibly picturesque—nestled between the mountains and Bellingham Bay—but what makes it really stand out is that it's, well, quirky. At least, it's got some quirky features, and a fascinating bit of history. It seems that on an island in Bellingham Bay called Eliza Island, in the late 19th century, a Cruella deVille-ish businessman named James Wardner decided to start a business selling pelts of—you're not going to believe this—cats. Yes, *kitty cats*. Eewwwww! He called it the "Consolidated Black Cat Company," and he brought cats in by the freightcar-load, most of them stolen from homes in California. He labeled the pelts as seal or otter and sold them to furriers on the East coast, who made them into muffs or collars for unsuspecting Victorian women.

Fortunately this ghoulish business disappeared quickly. When the local equivalent of the Humane Society figured out what was going on, they rescued the cats from Eliza Island, and turned them loose in Fairhaven, a historic section of Bellingham. To this day there are feral cats roaming around Bellingham, a living reminder of a dark moment in the town's history. Some softhearted townspeople, to atone for the crimes, have built a kitty shantytown of mini-plywood houses in an empty lot, but the cats will have nothing to do with humans.

On top of that bit of historical eccentricity, Bellingham boasts a bed and breakfast called the Castle B&B, which used to be the very same James Wardner's mansion. As you might imagine, the decor is offbeat. In one turreted Sultan's room, the decoration consists of an almost life-size camel. One guestroom featured a bed whose headboard was fashioned from a coffin, until it freaked out one too many guests and got moved to the gift shop, where it hangs above a fireplace made of small skulls.

You gotta love this place.

★ ★ ★ ★ ★

Brett & Daugert, L.L.P.

300 North Commercial • P.O. Box 5008 • Bellingham, WA 98227
Phone: 360-733-0212 • Fax: 360-647-1902
E-mail: deanbrett@brettlaw.com • Web site: brettlaw@brettlaw.com

*"The term 'minimum billable hour requirement' does not compute.
It's the attitude here. Their view is that work is a vehicle for enjoying life. It's not a means to an end."*

HIGHLIGHTS

- With 9 attorneys, it is the largest law firm in Whatcom County, Washington.

NUTS AND BOLTS

Managing partner:

Larry Daugert, phone: 360-733-0212

Hiring partner:

Gabrielle G. Gallegos, phone: 360-733-0212, fax: 360-738-2341,
e-mail: Gallegos@brettlaw.com

Recruiting coordinator:

Dean Brett, phone: 360-733-0212, e-mail: deanbrett@brettlaw.com

Number of attorneys in firm:

9 (7 partners, 2 associates); 2 women and 1 minority member

Years to make partner:

5 to 7 years in practice, with a minimum of two years with the firm

WHAT DO THEY DO?

Primary specialties (more than 5% of practice):

Business, Litigation, Estate Planning, and Personal Injury.

The firm is not departmentalized; associates initially help all partners where help is needed, but then develop their own strengths, which as the firm points out, usually parallel their own interests.

WHERE NEW ASSOCIATES COME FROM . . .

The firm routinely does on-campus interviewing at Stanford Law School. The firm does hire from law schools where it doesn't interview on campus.

HOURS AND BUCKS . . .

Hours: Partners and associates both routinely work 8:30 a.m. to 5:00 p.m., Monday through Friday. The firm notes that "with the exception of trials and closing, we try to avoid working evenings and weekends. Life is too short." Minimum billable hours: "The term 'minimum billable hour requirement' does not compute."

Part-time work is available on a case-by-case basis. One Brett & Daugert attorney currently works one-quarter time so he can devote the rest of his time to teaching at Western Washington University and carving birds. Another attorney worked three-quarters time until she became a Judge on the Washington State Court of Appeals.

The firm does not hire contract associates.

Typical first year associate salary, including typical bonus: $$ ($35-50,000)

SUMMER PROGRAM . . .

The summer associate program is informal because the firm is so small. As the firm says, "We do not hire a summer associate every summer because we don't intend to expand fast enough to incorporate that type of growth."

PRO BONO . . .

Associates are encouraged but not required to do pro bono work. For example, one then-associate spent major portions of two years defending a local bookstore against an effort by the local prosecuting attorney to impose a prior restraint on the magazines it stocked. The defense of the pro bono case was by far the lawyer's largest client for those two years. The associate prevailed in the criminal action, then filed a 1983 action against the prosecutor which eventually led to a $1.3 million verdict against the county on behalf of the pro bono client. As the firm points out, "Needless to say, that associate is now a partner."

HISTORY AT A GLANCE . . .

Brett & Daugert was founded in 1972 by Dean Brett and Larry Daugert, two recent Stanford Law School graduates who did not want to follow anyone else's direction. As Daugert recalls, "When we were in our last year of law school, Dean had a carefully crafted vision of where he wanted to practice. He wanted to be in a small to medium-sized city on the west coast. He'd carefully scoped out the towns he was interested in. He'd come to the conclusion that Bellingham was one of his first choices, and he knew I was from Bellingham. We met for coffee one day at the student union and talked about it." As Brett told a local newspaper a couple of years ago, "I decided I didn't want to have Stanford Law School's chess champion opposing me in the courtroom. So I suggested that we hang out a shingle together." They each invested $119 and rented an office above a shop called Tony's Tea and Spice. Their "office" hadn't been used since the 1930's, and they cleaned it up, got used furniture, typewriters and books, and did indeed hang out their shingles.

Their quirky approach has lasted over the ensuing years, as they have routinely attracted "the best and brightest" to work with them in Bellingham.

Interesting historical sidelight: Brett represented the "Hillside Strangler" Kenneth Bianchi (as a court-appointed attorney) in 1979.

WHAT IT'S LIKE TO WORK THERE . . .

Bellingham is a place that most people have never heard of, but Brett & Daugert finds that it's not a hard sell convincing recruits that it's a great place to live. "A typical recruiting ploy is to mail a Landsat map—a satellite photograph from space—of the region that includes the San Juan Islands and lower British Columbia." With one recruit, co-founder Dean Brett picked up sandwiches and said, "Let's see how far we can go in 15 minutes." Brett took him to Heron Point, where he and his family were building a waterfront home, and said, "This is where I'm going to live, and it's only 15 minutes from where I work." Associates chime in that "It's great to live in an area with a little bit of environment left to save," and that "Bellingham is a great place to raise a family. It's possible to be active in the community in a way it would be difficult to be involved in Washington or New York." The partners and associates at the firm regularly hold leadership positions in bar and civic groups, from establishment organizations like The Watch Museum of History and Art, The Mount Baker Theater, and the Levy Committee of the Bellingham School District, all the way to the Bellingham Chapter of the American Civil Liberties Union, the Food Co-op, and the Watch Land Trust.

The livable environment in Bellingham is mirrored in the firm itself, where "There's no 'eat-what-you-kill' situation," according to one associate. "Nobody is tempted to take cases outside of his or her expertise just to rack up more hours. Instead, clients get referred to the firm specialist best able to handle a particular case. With the competition for cases and dollars removed, there's a lot more camaraderie—and the work hours are a lot shorter." Another contributing factor to the camaraderie in the office is the fact that "Partners divvy up profits equally, no matter who wins big judgments." And the casual atmosphere is borne out in what people wear to work. One associate recounted, in a newspaper interview, that she had spent $5,000 to $6,000 working at other firms, and found that since she joined Brett & Daugert, "I've spent about $200 on clothes. I wear pants a lot, which I never, ever, ever did before."

The firm's casual, laid-back attitude doesn't translate into a lackadaisical approach to their work, however. As co-founder Larry Daugert says,

"Our offices are very dynamic. We've very rarely sat on our laurels. We're always looking towards what happens next. It's not static. We argue forcefully. Sometimes, people who have sat in on our strategy meetings have been more than a little shaken by our arguments. Dean and I argue, we've done that for more than 25 years and we're not always kind to each other, but that aggressive approach works for us. Even when we argue, our mutual respect holds us together." This approach results in a stellar reputation in the legal community. Another lawyer in Bellingham told a local paper that "Brett & Daugert is a great group to work with—and a great group to work against."

New associates at Brett & Daugert find that the small size of the firm means they are encouraged to be generalists. For instance, a business law specialist at the firm will need to know something of real estate, employment, contracts, commercial law, corporate law, and the like. As a result, when the firm hires new associates, "We choose new lawyers the way some football teams draft athletes. We don't draft for a particular position; we draft the best athlete." One associate points out that, "People here get to pursue aspects of the law suited to what they like. That means the firm is a constantly changing entity." Dean Brett adds that, "We encourage people to develop their own specialties, and to a large extent it depends on what their personality traits are. Some people like working on things that are steady. For that kind of person, estate planning and probate is great. I just couldn't do it. I've got too much nervous energy and too much of me is looking for the thrill of victory and the agony of defeat. That's drawn me to litigation." He goes on, "Each of the lawyers here has their own strengths and weaknesses. The reason this firm works is that we recognize each of us has those strengths and weaknesses and we try to help each other in our weaknesses so that we can all maximize our strengths. I don't do any estate planning, but I am part of a firm that does because I can call on Bruce Smith. I can't do any real estate closings and transactions but we can have a full firm because Larry [Daugert] likes to do that. Larry and Bruce can have clients who need a jury trial lawyer and they can serve those clients because they can come to me. That mix of diverse interests is what has given us our success as a firm."

When he reflects on the kind of recruits Brett & Daugert looks for, Dean Brett says, "We don't hire lawyers. We hire *people*. We have to live with these people 40 hours a week. Although there are many more good people than good lawyers, not all good lawyers are good people. We look for people who are both: good lawyers *and* good people. That is, active, interesting, engaged people whose love of life outside the law makes sharing a law practice with them worthwhile." As one lawyer—who left a large Midwestern firm to go west and join Brett & Daugert—summed it up, "It is a choice between money and a life. Now I have a life."

Where the Bucks Are

*Where to Work When What You're After is Money
Money Money. (Pssst: You Might Even Enjoy It.)*

Hello. My name is Kimm Walton.

I wouldn't typically be introducing myself this far back in a book, but if my hunch is correct, you turned to this page first. Am I right? Well, I promise you, there's a bunch of great stuff in this book, things that (hopefully) will ultimately mean a lot more to you than money, but I'm not going to let you down. I promised I'd tell you where to make the most money, so I'll do exactly that.

For a start, I didn't mean to make this chapter sound so crass, but frankly you'd be surprised how many law students ask me, straight out: "All I want is money. Where should I work?" That question, *by itself,* is very easy to answer. The biggest bucks with a law degree typically go to:

1. Lawyers who represent drug dealers. You not only make a bundle, but you don't have to worry about the check clearing, because you're always paid in cash.

2. Plaintiff's personal injury lawyers. There's big money in them thar spills.

3. Associates at mega-firms in New York City. Starting pay tops $100,000 at press-time. By the time you read this, perhaps it will be double that.

4. Investment bankers. Gordon Gekko didn't do it for love, you know.

5. Management consultants.

Now, what do all of these jobs share? With the exception of management consulting—and I'm going to address that in just a little while—when I was doing my research, talking with all kinds of people, I didn't hear lots of raves about what enjoyable jobs they are. I'm not suggesting that I heard *bad* things either, but of all of the many, many people I interviewed for this book, none of these categories of big-bucks jobs—*except for management consulting*—come complete with high job-satisfaction ratings. People *do* tend to enjoy consulting, and so if you're after big money, that job combines the best of both worlds: a fabulous starting salary—heck, *summer associates* at McKinsey pull in more than two grand a week—and a lot of job satisfaction.

What are the problems with the other jobs? Well, there's nothing technically wrong with representing drug dealers or doing plaintiff's personal injury work, but it's certainly emotionally draining, to the point that a lot of people—*most* people—aren't suited to it. Working for huge New York City firms . . . you can't lump them all together, because some of them are a lot more pleasant than others (for instance, Proskauer Rose, which I profiled in Chapter 5 on law firms). But by and large, you don't hear a lot of happy stories coming from big firm associates in the Big Apple. In fact, associates at one renowned New York firm are known for their saying, "Thank God It's Friday—only two work days left." Many graduates of prestigious law schools view these firms as an "up-and-out" proposition—bite the bullet, go for a year or two, and then move on to what you *really* want to do.

That leaves investment banking. If you want to make *great big huge money* pretty fast—if the idea of a $100,000 salary and a $1 million bonus flips your switch—then don't waste your time practicing law. Be an investment banker! While most investment bankers are MBAs, some law school grads—especially ones with blue-chip credentials, and those with a business undergrad degree—*do* become investment bankers. (If it's *really* what you want, you'd be well advised to get an MBA to go with your J.D.)

What's it like? If you really want a detailed account of investment banking and how to break into it, take a look at a terrific book on the subject—Mariam Naficy's *The Fast Track* (it's published by Broadway Books)—which tells you everything you need to know about breaking into big-bucks finance-oriented fields. The book has a web site you can visit, at www.thefasttrack.com, if you want to know more. What I'm going to do here is just give you a quick peek at investment banking.

Starting from ground zero, here's what investment bankers do. They basically shift money around. They're matchmakers. Middlemen. The term "investment banking" actually encompasses a number of functions, the primary ones being raising capital and advising clients on mergers and acquisitions and other financial issues. The "raising capital" aspect involves what investment banks are best known for, which is acting as "underwriters." That is, they buy a client's stocks or bonds and resell them immediately to investors. However, the most glamorous investment banking specialty is mergers and acquisitions ("M&A") because of the complexity of the deals and the strategic thinking required. Investment banking also involves other functions, like advising clients on real estate transactions and strategies, but it's the underwriting and M&A work that's the best known.

If you go into investment banking with a graduate degree, you'll typically start as an "associate." To radically simplify your role, you'll usually find yourself doing things like acting as the daily contact with clients, helping create financial documents and presentations, working on day-to-day details of transactions, and checking the work of analysts (lower-level investment banking people, who themselves do a lot of research and number-crunching).

Of course, that's not what you want to know, is it? Here's the scoop on pay: As a first-year associate at a major investment bank, you'll likely clear more than $100,000 a year to start, and that's just salary. It doesn't include your bonus, which may equal or exceed your salary. Your pay rockets up quickly; within three to five years you can be promoted to vice president, where your salary (remember, that doesn't include that scrumptious bonus) will beat half a mil a year.

Now, with all of this going for it, why didn't I hear rave reviews about investment banking as a career? And believe me on this one, I *wanted* to. I'd *love* to be able to tell you that the job that pays the most is the one you'd like a bunch. But I can't, because for every other chapter in this book—as well as the management consulting jobs I describe below—I got lots of positive reviews from law school administrators. That isn't true of investment banking. It may well be that it's a job you, personally, would enjoy. But there are a couple of significant downsides you should take into account.

For a start, there are the back-breaking hours. Some of the jobs in this book that people just love also involve long hours, but there are long hours, and then there's investment banking. You can expect to put in 80-hour weeks as the norm, and 100-hour weeks at busy times. There are no such things as weekends. In *The Fast Track,* Marian Naficy recounts the experience of one analyst who told her that he bought 50 pairs of underwear because he had no time to do laundry. When he needed a fresh pair, he'd open a new package.

Another factor that augers against actually *enjoying* investment banking is more elusive. When I asked investment bankers how they liked their jobs, a look of discomfort would cross their faces before they answered with things like, "Well, it's 364 days of pain—and bonus day." I talked with venture capitalists who deal with investment bankers all of the time, and when I asked, "Are they happy?" they inevitably looked away, thought for a moment, and said, "Well—no." I interviewed the director of a real estate investment trust, who described the investment bankers he routinely works with as reminding him of "a hungry man at a buffet table. They keep eating and eating and eating but they can never get enough." Perhaps that strikes at the heart of the problem: When you have a job that is so heavily focused on money, and the people above you on the food chain are raking in *truly stupendous quantities of money,* there's no such thing as enough. You aren't *ever* truly succeeding because somebody else is always doing better than you are, and your success is totally measured by money, money, money. That is not a promising underpinning for a happy work environment.

Of course, many people go into investment banking the same way they go to large New York firms—with the intention of only staying a year or two, and then moving on to what they really want to do. There's nothing inherently wrong with that philosophy, but it doesn't have anything in common with the idea behind this book—to tell you about places where you'll enjoy working.

And *that* is a perfect segue into a big-bucks job that people *do* tend to enjoy, and that's ...

MANAGEMENT CONSULTING

What do you do as a management consultant? Well, essentially you go into big companies, as part of a team of other consultants, and offer advice on strategy and operations. Consulting has actually oozed out of those traditional confines into a number of different roles, but that strategic and operations advice is at its core.

By singling out management consulting as a big-bucks field that you're likely to enjoy, let's not pretend it doesn't have its downsides. You travel a lot, and I mean *a lot*—four days a week isn't unusual. And while travel is one of those things that sounds glamorous when you're not doing it, being on the road constantly can get old quickly. Another downside—at least, for most of us—is that you need outstanding credentials to break in, at least fresh out of school. (You can get in later on as a specialist in a particular industry, and if your grades ain't great, that's a route to consider.)

But then there are the benefits. For a start, most people consider the work fun. It's varied, because you're working with all different kinds of clients. It's intellectually challenging, because you're always solving problems. The people you work with are exceptionally sharp. When you're ready for a career move, you've got not only a whole Rolodex full of contacts, but you've got an excellent job under your belt, as well.

And of course the pay is fantastic, which is why it's in this chapter.

If you go in as an associate—which is where you start if you go into consulting straight out of law school—between your salary, bonus, and profit sharing, you're looking at well over a $100,000 a year, *to start,* and that doesn't include a signing bonus which may run into the tens of thousands of dollars. As I mentioned just a little while ago, McKinsey pays its *summer associates* $2,000 a week!

There are a number of large consulting firms, and you can find a rundown of them in the book *The Fast Track*. What I'm going to do here is to tell you about the two consulting firms that got the most rave reviews from law school administrators—McKinsey and Deloitte & Touche.

McKinsey & Company

55 East 52nd Street • New York, NY 10055
Phone: 212-446-7200 • Fax: 212-688-9521
E-mail: asus_recruit@mckinsey.com • Web site: www.mckinsey.com

MCKINSEY IN A NUTSHELL . . .

McKinsey & Company may be the best known and most prestigious management consultants in the world. Last year, McKinsey teams conducted over 2,000 engagements, from identifying global market opportunities for a new satellite service in India, to determining how a multinational consumer goods company in China could expand its distribution network, to helping a leading German industrial conglomerate restore its strengths as an innovator, to helping a Siberian fishing fleet form an alliance with a Scandinavian partner, to working on recruiting the Argentinean social security system, to many projects here in America, including exploring ways for the government to connect all public schools to the Internet.

As all of that suggests, McKinsey & Company advises senior management of the world's leading companies on issues of strategy, organization, and operations. McKinsey serves clients in a variety of industries, including automotive, banking, energy, health care, insurance, manufacturing, public utilities, retailing, telecommunications, and transportation, to name a few. Its practice also extends to the public sector, where McKinsey consultants assist government agencies, not-for-profit institutions, and community service groups. It provides free advice to some educational and nonprofit institutions, including the American Red Cross and Habitat for Humanity.

While much of McKinsey's work focuses on long-term strategy issues such as growth and diversification, it also helps clients improve short-term performance. Some examples include: turning around a decline in profits, developing market strategies, redesigning organizational structures and systems, cutting operational costs, and increasing productivity. It also does extensive work in major functional areas like finance, sales, manufacturing, distribution, and information technology.

Collectively, McKinsey's 4,500 consultants are citizens of 88 countries. It has 75 offices in 38 countries including developing countries in Asia, Latin America, and Eastern Europe. Although each office adapts to the cultural values and management practices of its country, all share a common philosophy, draw on a common base of experience and skills, and adhere to a common set of standards with respect to professional responsibility, quality of work, caliber of staff, and problem-solving approaches.

Incidentally, McKinsey was ranked as the #1 ideal company to work for by both U.S. and European business graduates in recent surveys conducted by the Stockholm-based media and communications company Universum.

WORD ON THE STREET . . .

"One of the great things about working at McKinsey is that the people you work with are incredibly bright and interesting."

"They have a particular writing style that forces you to think logically and arrange your thoughts clearly."

"Because it's so prestigious, you can go on from there to senior management in companies—really anything you want."

"You've got to like to travel. They travel like crazy. And you've got to be savvy dealing with people, because a lot of your job involves interviewing people—getting information from them."

NUTS AND BOLTS

Managing director:
Rajat Kumar Gupta

General counsel:
Virginia "Jean" L. Molino (J.D., New York University)

Personnel director:
Jerome C. Vascellaro, 212-446-8340

LOCATIONS . . .

Other than its New York headquarters, McKinsey has law school graduates working in the following North American locations:

Atlanta, Georgia; Boston, Massachusetts; Charlotte, North Carolina; Chicago, Illinois; Cleveland, Ohio; Dallas, Texas; Florham Park, New Jersey; Houston, Texas; Los Angeles, California; Minneapolis, Minnesota; Mexico City, Mexico; Montreal, Quebec, Canada; Palo Alto, California; San Francisco, California; Stamford, Connecticut; Toronto, Ontario, Canada; Washington, D.C.

McKinsey also has law school graduates working in the following foreign offices:

Beijing, China; Dusseldorf, Germany; Frankfurt, Germany; Johannesburg, South Africa; London, United Kingdom; Madrid, Spain; Munich, Germany; Oslo, Norway; Prague, Czech Republic; Sao Paulo, Brazil; Seoul, Korea; Sydney, Australia; Tokyo, Japan

Number of law school graduates employed by McKinsey: Around 170.

About 10 of the law school graduates work in McKinsey's in-house counsel's office, and the rest are consultants.

WHO GETS HIRED?

McKinsey hires laterals as well as new law school graduates and summer interns.

FOR NEW LAW SCHOOL GRADUATES . . .

McKinsey hires approximately 25 new law school graduates every year.

McKinsey interviews on campus at the following law schools: University of Chicago, Columbia, Harvard, Stanford, and Yale. In addition, McKinsey hires from schools where it doesn't interview on campus, via ads and unsolicited resumes.

How much they pay to start: $$$$ (Over $65,000—*way* over $65,000). McKinsey is recognized for its spectacularly generous financial package.

Career path: You start out as an associate, and within five to seven years you typically advance to principal (the equivalent of a junior partner). Advancement to director (the equivalent of a senior partner) is possible after another five to six years. If you choose not to stay with McKinsey, it's an excellent springboard into business. Many of the most successful executives at large companies are McKinsey alumni.

Hours: McKinsey consultants typically work a 60-hour week with an average of two nights per week away from home, although this varies greatly depending on the project you're working on. There's no getting around the considerable travel that the job requires, and if you don't want to travel, don't even consider McKinsey!

What they look for: McKinsey likes people with "an outstanding record of academic achievement, strong analytic and quantitative skills, demonstrated leadership, excellent communication skills, and comfort in a team environment. A motivation to learn and to have impact in solving difficult, practical problems is essential." Note that they really do want more than just good grades—they want to see leadership experience.

FOR LATERALS . . .

Although they don't say so in so many words, clearly the best way to get into McKinsey with a few years of experience is to gain experience in a particular industry, so that you can become a "specialized consultant."

FOR SUMMER ASSOCIATES . . .

McKinsey hires 2Ls as summer associates. They seek the same kinds of qualities in summer associates as they do for permanent hires.

What the summer associate program is like: You work for 10 to 12 weeks, participating as a full-fledged member of McKinsey's consulting teams, and you get coaching and feedback from fellow team members and other people in the office where you work. Most people who summer clerk for McKinsey get invited back after graduation.

Summer associates work in McKinsey's foreign offices, as well as its domestic offices. For a foreign assignment, you have to have language fluency and prior work experience in the location you request.

Summer associate salary: $8,500/month.

WHAT IT'S LIKE TO WORK AT MCKINSEY . . .

McKinsey's work is accomplished via the "engagement team," which is the key unit of McKinsey consulting. You can be either a generalist or a specialist. You get to choose which industry you want to work in, and you work with engagement teams in that industry.

Engagement teams typically consist of a director or principal (the equivalent of a partner), an engagement manager (which is an associate with several years of experience), and two or more associates and business analysts. The director or principal takes the lead in planning and conducting the assignment, maintains relationships with client management, and bears ultimate responsibility for quality. The engagement manager is responsible for the day-to-day work of the team and coaching team members.

Associates and business analysts play an active role in all aspects of projects: fact gathering, analysis, developing and communicating recommendations, and implementation. You nearly always get involved in presentations to, and discussions with, top management, and you are encouraged to raise issues and express your opinions.

The kinds of projects you get to work on are incredibly varied. McKinsey typically gets called on to solve problems involving strategy and organizations, including exploring new avenues of growth, capitalizing on opportunities for new products, seeking entry into foreign markets, and combining organizations following a merger. Increasingly McKinsey is being called on to help clients design and carry out new processes to make an existing strategy work. For instance, an airline that's committed to shifting its competitive strategy from cost to service will need to make drastic changes that will affect its organizational structure and day-to-day operations, including staffing, training, compensation, technology, purchasing, sales, departure and arrival procedures. In these kinds of situations, McKinsey consultants work with people at all levels of the client organization helping to implement changes, build consensus, and develop new institutional skills.

As you would expect, the atmosphere at McKinsey differs from office to office. However, belying its conservative, elitist image, McKinsey publicly welcomes gay and lesbian applicants, and in general it is viewed as a very collegial place, full of highly-motivated, razor-sharp people.

Deloitte & Touche Consulting

Ten Westport Road • Wilton, CT 06897
Phone: 203-761-3000 • Web site: www.dttus.com

DELOITTE & TOUCHE CONSULTING IN A NUTSHELL:

Deloitte & Touche Consulting is the 7th largest management consulting firm in the U.S., with approximately $1.3 billion in revenues last year, and 10,000 consultants.

Deloitte & Touche ranks #14 on the *Fortune Magazine* list of "The 100 Best Companies To Work For In America." Among other things, *Fortune* cites D&T's "Women's Initiative," a successful program to help women balance the needs of work and family.

OFFICES (OTHER THAN THE WILTON, CT HEADQUARTERS):

Atlanta, Austin, Boston, Chicago, Cincinnati, Cleveland, Dallas, Detroit, Houston, Kansas City, Los Angeles, Minneapolis, New York City, Parsipanny, Philadelphia, Pittsburgh, San Francisco, Seattle, Stamford, Washington, D.C., Toronto, Montreal, London, Brussels, Paris, Singapore, Hong Kong, Sydney, Aukland, and Johannesburg.

WHAT IT'S LIKE TO WORK THERE:

Deloitte & Touche is considered a "kinder, gentler" place to work, compared to many of its competitors. Being a friendly, laid-back person is a plus; being arrogant is a definite turn-off. Its recruiting materials state that, "We have none of the politics, back-stabbing, and cut-throat competition that make life miserable at other firms." Average workweeks for consultants are between 50 and 60 hours (although there is an occasional 70-hour week), with very little weekend work. D&T is particularly family-friendly, perhaps explained by the fact that a quarter of D&T partners are women.

D&T provides consulting services in eight areas: Business Process Reengineering, Strategy, Value Chain and Logistics, Client/Server Solutions, World-Class Financial Management, Change Management, Enterprise Resource Planning, and Reorganization Planning. You typically start as a generalist and work in any of those areas, working in engagement teams of from 10 to 15 consultants.

Most D&T hires are MBAs, although they do hire law school graduates. D&T is known for being more democratic in the schools it will hire from than most consulting firms.

The Corporations.

Dear Job Goddess:
I'd Like to Be In-House Counsel . . .

Dear Job Goddess,

I am halfway through law school and am just beginning to seriously look for a job. I have always wanted to work in a corporation's Legal Department, but it seems like they always want someone with several years of experience in practice. Is there any way around this?

KS, Kentucky

Dear KS,

The Job Goddess gets many letters like yours, KS, basically asking the same question: Is it possible to get to Heaven without dying first? In this instance, the Job Goddess is happy to tell you that the answer is yes.

Let's talk for a moment about the nature of the problem you face, KS. And in doing so let's say that you run the MiB Clothing Company, which specializes in exactly one style of black suit. You need to have some lawyers in-house. Who are you going to choose? Somebody who has some experience in legal practice, who may be able to foresee and quickly handle potential legal problems? Or somebody with a freshly minted law school diploma, all enthusiasm but lacking hands-on knowledge? Ah, you see the difficulty companies face and why it is that they typically require a few years' worth of "real law" under your belt before they'll hire you. But having said that, not *every* company fits that mold, and the Job Goddess being the Job Goddess, she can't let you down. Let's see how to overcome that little matter of practical experience.

There are two basic ways to skin the in-house counsel cat. One is to look for companies that are sufficiently large that can afford to have new lawyers cut their teeth there. Some even have internship programs—the corporate equivalent of a summer associateship. Your Career Services Office will have resources that tell you who these companies are. As an alternative, you can do a little footwork of your own and call the human resources departments at any large corporations that interest you and ask them directly if their Legal Department has such a program. Needless to say, companies that have internship programs will typically hire new full-time lawyers from those programs, and presumably when their interns don't work out, they will hire new graduates, as well.

Aside from internship programs, there *are* a few large companies that routinely hire new law school graduates for their in-house counsel departments. One that comes to the Job Goddess' mind is Procter & Gamble ("P&G"), which has a law department that rivals the size of many large firms, including a number of new law school graduates. (Coincidentally, P&G is supposed to be a wonderful place to work; so wonderful, in fact, that it will appear in the Job Goddess's upcoming book, *America's Greatest Places To Work With A Law Degree.*)

Another option is to go to the other end of the scale, to very small companies. As Mary Birmingham, Career Services Director at the University of Arizona School of Law points out, "Look for small companies that can't afford someone with huge experience!" She recounts a couple of stories about recent law school graduates who did exactly that. One of them went to a new technology company that wanted a law school graduate who was interested in helping to get the business off the ground. The other went to a construction company that needed someone to be able to interpret and negotiate contracts, as well as help out on the business end. As she says, "Think about what it takes to run a business! Every business needs somebody to negotiate contracts, watch out for potential liabilities, and be aware of insurance matters. As a small business person, a lawyer is your right hand."

Mary Birmingham also points out, KS, that you may want to look at corporations as more than a source of in-house counsel jobs. The Job Goddess knows of many companies that hire law school graduates not as lawyers, but in all sorts of other interesting capacities. For instance, many multinational companies hire law school graduates as contract negotiators. You aren't technically a 'lawyer,' but on the plus side, you certainly get to use your legal knowledge doing interesting work, and you frequently get to travel to all kinds of exotic places. And when it comes to opportunities to advance, as Mary Birmingham explains, "You can make *much* more money moving up the business side than the legal side of a corporation. Companies have only one general counsel, but there are *many* steps up the ladder on the business side that will outstrip others in the Legal Department." For information on these kinds of opportunities, Bill Barrett, Jr., Career Services Director at the Wake Forest University School of Law, has an ingenious idea. He suggests that you visit the undergrad or MBA school affiliated with your law school (or your own undergrad alma mater), talk to the career services people *there*, and find out which corporations come on campus to interview. He says that those same companies may be ones who are interested in J.D.'s for the business track as well.

In short, KS, there are many incredible opportunities open to you, doing exactly what you want to do: namely, start off in a corporate environment. Now that you know what they are, the Job Goddess encourages you to put your energy into finding—and pursuing—those opportunities!

Eternally yours,
The Job Goddess

Isn't it obnoxious when authors quote themselves? Well—*sorry.* But I thought that particular Job Goddess column of mine was a particularly appropriate way to open this chapter. (And if you *liked* it, you'll love my other new book, *The Best Of The Job Goddess,* which features my favorite Job Goddess columns. Actually, it features *all* of them.)

That said, down to business. As that opening *Job Goddess* column suggests, many law students regard corporate jobs as real plums. And there's a good reason for that. No billable hours, no need to generate business-qualities like that are attractive to many of us. Not only that, working in a corporation's Legal Department gives you an excellent jumping-off point for other kinds of corporate work that you also might enjoy (I'll give you some ideas in just a little bit). So the attraction to corporate work isn't at all unfounded. Incidentally, it's a lot more accessible than it seems. As you'll see in the profiles in this chapter, a fair number of companies, especially large ones, *do* hire new law school graduates. And many, many more routinely hire law students for paid summer internships. In fact, as a rule of thumb, I'd say that any corporation with more than 20 people in its Legal Department hires summer interns, and so if you want to do your own sleuthing, it doesn't hurt you to go after a summer job with almost any large-ish company.

What are we going to do in this chapter? For a start, as is true of the public interest chapter, I could have profiled a whole boxcar full of employers, but instead I've focused on those few companies who received the most rave reviews. By way of sweeping in everybody else, I've started this chapter with a lot of information you'll ideally find helpful and interesting no matter *which* corporation you want to work for. We'll start out by talking about what it's like, in general, to work in corporate Legal Departments. We'll go on to discuss the kinds of experience corporations seek for in-house counsel's jobs. Then we'll look at the kinds of jobs your law degree can get you *outside* of the Legal Department. Part of that is figuring out exactly the kinds of skills you absorb in the process of getting your law degree, so that you can make the "perfect pitch" to companies you want to work for. I'll tell you exactly what those skills are. After that, we'll talk about how to research *other* companies you might be interested in working for. And finally, we'll get to the profiles of companies I heard wonderful things about from law school administrators.

What I'm going to do here, before we talk about specific companies who came with great recommendations, is to go over a few things you need to know about corporate work. First, I'll tell you some of the things you ought to know about being in a corporation's Legal Department, including things people like about working for companies (especially vis-a-vis law firms). Second, well talk about the kinds of experience that will help you break into corporate Legal Departments; and third—and perhaps most importantly, *particularly* if you're interested in nontraditional stuff—we'll talk about jobs in corporations that you can get with your law degree, *outside* of the Legal Department.

As is true with all of the rest of the advice in this book, none of this advice is from *me,* by the way. Instead, when I talked with people at corporations I asked them all kinds of questions about their work, the options open to them with their law degree, and how to break in. That's what I'm passing along to you, here:

What You Ought to Know About Being in a Corporation's Legal Department, Including Things People Like About Working for Companies

"KS," my correspondent in the *Dear Job Goddess* column that started this chapter, isn't the only one who loves the idea of in-house work. There's a lot to like about it! Here's what corporate lawyers know:

1. Your hours are "normal" in a corporation's Legal Department. You'll typically work less than you would in a law firm, and rarely, if ever, will you work on weekends. But remember, you're still a professional, and that means that when the work demands it, you've got to put in the hours. In Chapter 3, when I talked about "Ultimate Dream Jobs," I told you about how working in Disney's Legal Department can routinely demand days that don't end until 7 p.m. And many corporate lawyers will talk about leaving at 6 or 6:30 p.m. What does this tell you? It's a mistake to *assume* that a corporate job means a 35-hour workweek!

2. There aren't billable hours in a corporate law department. The necessity of keeping track of time in small, sometimes six-minute increments, is a big downside of private practice. After all, you can't bill clients for time unless you keep track of it, right? In-house lawyers

don't have to do that, because they only have one client. And on top of that they don't have to sweat taking a little extra time to read documents or toss ideas around with colleagues.

3. There's no need to generate business. There's no such thing as "rainmaking" in a corporate law department! Soliciting business is something that makes many people's skin crawl, but it's a fact of life, especially as you move up the ladder at most law firms. Corporate work saves you from that.

4. Corporations face a wide range of legal issues, and that gives in-house lawyers a lot of variety in their work. You'll frequently find corporate law departments with people who specialize in a dozen different specialties—or more. (If you wonder what a corporate law department does, many Martindale Hubbell corporate entries will list lawyers' specialties.)

5. In-house lawyers spend a lot of time focusing on addressing issues *before* problems arise, rather than putting out fires once problems have occurred—which is frequently where law firms step in. In-house lawyers like this kind of strategizing.

6. In-house lawyers forge long-term relationships with their client. Instead of juggling clients, as many private practice lawyers have to do, they are intimately involved with just one client, the corporation, and the people who work for it.

7. When it comes to pay, you can typically do better in private practice than you will in a corporation's Legal Department. In fact, many general counsel's jobs are snapped up by former partners of law firms, who are willing to take a *substantial* cut in pay—like 50%—to take in-house jobs. *However,* with bonuses and stock options, in-house counsel jobs can be competitive with firms.

The Experience Corporations Seek For In-House Counsel Jobs— It May Not Be What You Think!

I've already told you that corporations usually hire laterals for in-house counsel jobs. While corporations are different—some do hire law school graduates, some have Legal Departments that are highly specialized, and so on—there are *some* generalizations that are safe to make:

1. Once you have an in-house job with one corporation, it's fairly easy to jump companies and industries. The legal issues tend to be similar, making the skills very transferable—and corporations consider an in-house background at another company a valuable asset.

2. There are many, many backgrounds that are useful for in-house work—you don't *have* to go to the biggest firm that will take you, planning to bale out in a couple of years.

3. If you start your career in private practice, you are most marketable to corporations 3 to 5 years out. In fact, many of the in-house lawyers I talked to pointed out that when you get to be a third-year associate, don't worry about getting a corporate job—headhunters will call *you*. There *are* companies that take people with more experience, and the big cheese in big corporate law departments, the general counsel, is frequently somebody who used to be a partner at a firm. So the 3 to 5 year span isn't engraved in stone. But the reason 3 to 5 years typically works is because you've got some experience under your belt, but you're still—to be perfectly crass—cheap. The longer you stay in private practice after that, the more likely you are to price yourself out of the market (unless you're willing to take a large pay cut). Not only that, but the hallmarks of successful senior partners—aggressive people with rain-making and bill-collecting skill—are *not* considered assets in corporation, which value teamwork and deference to authority.

4. Government experience is a plus, be it the U.S. Attorney's Office or industry-oriented agencies like the FTC, FCC, or many, many others. There tends to be substantial hands-on work with government jobs, as well as rapid management experience, both of which are assets for corporations.

5. If you want to do litigation in-house, you are better off getting your feet wet in a small-to medium-sized firm or as a prosecutor. Corporations want their in-house litigators to have courtroom and drafting skills. A background that quickly gives you lots of trial experience is a plus; sitting in a library researching issues for several years isn't.

6. For transactional work, a large firm is a better bet for breaking into in-house counsel's offices—in fact, they are the traditional launch pad for that kind of work.

7. Business management experience is a plus. So if you go into a nontraditional corporate job (see below), that can help you lateral into the in-house counsel's office, as well—although most people go the other way, lateraling from the corporate law department to the "business side."

Corporate Jobs Your Law Degree Can Help You Get, Outside of the Legal Department— And Getting a Grip on What You Bring to the Table!

Many, many people in law school yearn to get a nontraditional job with a company—at least, that's what the letters I get suggest! I'll tell you the kinds of jobs where a law degree is useful in just a minute, but first I want to mention a few important points to you.

1. Being on the "business side" can be more satisfying than lawyering, because as one corporate in-house lawyer confided to me, "There's a lot of fun stuff out there! Lawyers don't always get the glory. If your company does a deal and you, as the lawyer, do 90% of the negotiating, it's *still* the business guy who gets the credit. It's *fun* to be on the business side, where you can be more of a big-picture, strategy person."

2. *Nobody* wants to hire an unhappy lawyer. *All* of the corporate personnel people I've spoken with have chanted the same chorus: If you come to them with a law degree and say you want to do something other than practice law, you've got to come up with a credible explanation for that 600-pound gorilla in the room: namely, why did you spend three years getting a law degree if you don't want to be a lawyer? If you wanted to be in business (or marketing or finance), why didn't you get an MBA? Or a CPA? Depending on the position— and whatever your reason really is—you'd be well-advised to immerse yourself in whatever it is you *want* to do, at least informally. I go over exactly how to go after nontraditional jobs in my book *Guerrilla Tactics For Getting The Legal Job Of Your Dreams,* and there isn't the space here to go into detail. But in general, do things like researching trade publications in the area you want to enter so you can get familiar with the lingo and the issues in the field. Find out from trade associations about industry meetings where you can go and bend the ear of people who do what you want to do.

   In general, do what's necessary to show that your desire to do "whatever" is a *genuine interest,* and not just a desire to be a "not lawyer." By way of example, if what you want to do is to get into the training program at an advertising outfit like J. Walter Thompson, it would pay you to accentuate any experience you have in advertising and promotion. So for instance if you were your law school's champion fund-raiser, and you came up with interesting and innovative ways to get people to donate money, that would be a valuable, transferable skill, and show your sincere interest in the field of advertising. Work, volunteer, or interning experience might also help you make your case.

3. There are *oodles* of internships with corporations outside of the Legal Department. The Princeton Review puts out my favorite book of internships—*America's Top Internships*—but there are many more. Check your local bookstore or library or an on-line organization called "Real World Interns," which you can find at www.rwinterns.com. You'll find that many business-side internships are offered to college students rather than grad students, but even in those cases it's worth a stab seeing if they'll take you—you might be pleasantly surprised. Needless to say, these internships are an *excellent* springboard into a non-law department job with a corporation.

4. Realize going in that it helps to get a nontraditional job in a corporation by starting out in the Legal Department and making the jump from there, once you're working as a lawyer with the colleagues you'd like to work with as a business person.

5. Be aware of the skill set that *just having your law degree* will give you in the eyes of employers. While your own experience, extracurriculars, and other factors may give you *other* skills, let's talk about the basic ones. (This is a list that appeared in my book *Guerrilla Tactics For Getting The Legal Job Of Your Dreams*, and in *there* it was adapted from the excellent book *The Road Not Taken*, by Kathy Grant and my wonderful friend Wendy Werner):

    a. *Ability to analyze facts.* Problem-solving is the main skill you get from law school. You get it from reading and briefing cases, Moot Court, any journals that you work on, and exams. This is a particularly useful skill when it comes to identifying business problems and creating solutions.

    b. *Ability to work in teams or groups.* I've already told you how corporations aren't interested in the "bull in a china shop" mentality associated with aggressive law firm partners. Rather, if you've worked with other students in Moot Court, or in a trial skills program, or in a study group, then you've got the transferable skill of teamwork; that is, the ability to divide responsibilities and come up with a cohesive outcome. This is useful in any enterprise that is project-oriented.

c. *Ability to be a self-starter.* As a law student, most of what you do is independent study. Any work as a law clerk typically exposes you to working without supervision as well. Every employer appreciates employees who are self-starters.

d. *Risk awareness.* As a law student you learn to be aware of the potential risk involved in transactions, products, policies, and programs. As an employee, risk awareness is useful in alerting your employer to any risks they may be taking, and it is very useful in creating preventive policies, products, or programs.

e. *Counseling (including the ability to establish rapport, to listen, to reflect concerns back to clients, to empathize, and to problem solve).* If you've taken part in client counseling competitions, clinics, or classes that involve counseling clients, then you have these transferable skills. These skills are useful in almost any position involving client or coworker contact.

f. *Familiarity with legal terminology.* Going to law school gives you the ability to read and understand documents that are Greek to lay people—things like contracts, leases, and statutes. This skill is useful to employers in predicting the long-term impact legal documents may have on their organization. It also gives you the ability to communicate comfortably with people who work with legal matters.

g. *Knowledge of specific topics (like insurance, labor, health care, tax, criminal law, corporations).* Depending on your coursework, you've got a broad base of knowledge about a wide variety of areas. Especially if you can combine this knowledge with an undergraduate degree that specializes in a certain area (*e.g.,* patent law with an undergrad technical major, or construction law with an undergrad architecture major, or labor law with an undergrad industrial relations major), you are a potential employee with a lot of knowledge to offer an employer—and a strong background for learning more.

h. *Strong motivation and the skills associated with it (working under pressure, ability to complete projects, ability to juggle multiple responsibilities).* In law school, you respond to an enormous amount of pressure while balancing a heavy workload. As a law student, you have to meet strict deadlines and juggle multiple responsibilities. Also, as a law student you are perceived as having a history of success as well as the ability to complete projects. These skills are all highly prized by employers.

i. *Ability to think independently.* As a law student, you are encouraged to think independently about issues and problems, coming up with your own solutions to them. You are taught to go beyond looking for answers and instead to identify issues. For potential employers, this translates into creative thinking skills and an ability to see the whole picture.

j. *Ability to negotiate.* If you've taken part in clinics, seminars, or classes that focus on negotiation or any extracurriculars that require you to negotiate (for instance, as the business editor for a journal, or the head of your school's speakers bureau), then the ability to negotiate is a skill you bring to the table for potential employers. Your ability to negotiate will enable you to open the doors to new clients and new business, as well as to "close the deal."

k. *Ability to persuade.* Taking part in Moot Court, as well as brief writing in your legal writing program, and writing for a journal, gives you the ability to persuade. This is a useful skill for convincing clients, other managers, staff, or peers.

l. *Ability to prepare effectively.* Law school demands that you be always prepared so that you can respond quickly and accurately (or have strips of flesh metaphorically torn from your back by irate law professors). This is a useful skill to business which must react and respond to new information and industry changes to stay profitable.

m. *Ability to speak before an audience.* Responding to questions in class, as well as taking part in Moot Court and any extracurriculars that require public speaking, will give you a valuable skill for employers. Ease in front of an audience is an asset in presenting facts, information, or business proposals.

n. *Research skills.* Much of the work you do in law school focuses on research, as do many extracurriculars and law clerking jobs. Research skills are a valuable asset for many employers who must rely on employees to dig up accurate and comprehensive information for them.

o. *Writing ability.* Your exams, legal writing program, Moot Court, and any journal experience give you the ability to write in a clear and precise manner. This skill gives you the edge in business communications. Good writing skills are *always* in high demand.

6. OK! Now that you know what you've got—what *are* the other jobs in corporations that you might want to consider? They include:

a. Mergers and acquisitions. This is perhaps the perfect leap for lawyers to make since law is so intertwined with merger and acquisition deals.

    b. The risk management—insurance group. With an understanding of risks and how to avoid them, a law background is perfect for risk management-oriented work.

    c. If you have a finance or accounting background, corporate finance is an option, as is the treasurer's office or comptroller's office.

    d. Employee relations, labor relations, personnel administration.

    e. Consumer awareness. A law background helps you figure out what you can, and should, say.

    f. Lobbying, which is an especially fertile option for businesses in aerospace, liquor, and tobacco—but many, many other industries have lobbyists, as well.

    g. Regulatory Compliance (depending on the industry).

    h. The traffic department—depending on the industry you're in, this can involve supervising, organizing and analyzing transportation, and distribution and shipping procedures.

    i. Public relations. A law degree helps here because with a knowledge of securities laws, you know what you can and can't say to shareholders.

7. To find job openings in these nontraditional areas, don't forget Bill Barrett's advice from my *Job Goddess* column, above—check job boards at your local business school or see who's coming on campus to interview MBAs. There are also tons of web pages that advertise corporate openings, including among the best recognized America's Employers (at www.americasemployers.com), Career Path (www.careerpath.com), and CareerMosaic (www.careermosaic.com). Also, many company web pages feature job openings both in the Legal Department and on the business side. In other words—use every resource you can find!

Doing Your Own Research on Companies: Useful Resources at Your Fingertips

To find out about corporate Legal Departments—whether you want to go in as a lateral, a new graduate, or as a summer intern, for that matter—you've got a number of great resources at your fingertips. For a start, you can find out about most companies' Legal Departments from Martindale Hubbell on-line at http://www.lawyers.martindale.com/arhub, and click on "Corporations." (They're not *totally* reliable when it comes to listing the personnel in Legal Departments, but they're a great start). You can also check out different corporate web pages—virtually every company has one now. Either call the company to find its web page address, or use a browser, keying in the company's name. You'll find that many corporate web pages include a job hotline and tons of useful information. There are a bunch of other useful web resources; AOL, for instance, has capsule summaries of companies. Beyond using your computer, of course, check with your law school's Career Services Office for further information about any alumni who might be at the company in *any* capacity, so that you can contact them for more insight into the company. You could check with your undergrad alumni relations person for the same kinds of contacts. The point here is: There are a million companies out there, and finding out whether they've got opportunities for you is a lot easier than you think.

The Corporations Receiving Rave Reviews: Profiles

American Airlines (AMR Corporation)

4333 Amon Carter Blvd. • Dallas/Fort Worth Airport, TX 75261-9616
Phone: 817-963-1234 • Fax: 817-967-9641 • Web site: www.aa.com

AMERICAN AIRLINES IN A NUTSHELL . . .

A bit of history. American Airlines is the result of a conglomeration of more than 80 small companies in the 1920s. Two of the more notable of these were the Robertson Aircraft Company, a Missouri outfit that employed Charles Lindbergh on the first mail run in 1926. Another was Colonial Air Transport, which made the first passenger flights between Boston and New York. In 1930, a man named Charles Coburn formally merged these two and many, many others into the American Airways Company.

An interesting tidbit in American's history: in the late 1930s, there was a general public scare about airline safety. American addressed this by running print ads with the headline, "Afraid to Fly?" It talked about the statistical impossibility of dying in a plane crash, and was remarkable for its straightforward discussion of the issue. It read, in part, "People are afraid of things they do not know about . . . there is only one way to overcome the fear—and that is, to fly." That ad allayed public fears and boosted American's business.

Today, AMR consists of three separate divisions: The American Airlines Passenger Division, The Cargo Division, and AMR Eagle. The Passenger Division is the one you know about. It serves more than 160 destinations throughout the world. The company also has a Cargo Division, which is one of the world's largest scheduled air freight carriers. And there's also AMR Eagle, which consists of four regional airlines that operate as "American Eagle."

The company employs 110,000 people, and job listings are posted on American Airline's web site.

The in-house counsel's office consists of six attorneys, but as the 'Word on the Street' shows, you can take your law degree to other departments in the company.

WORD ON THE STREET . . .

"People stay there *forever.*"

"They have great benefits."

"The Legal Department hires mostly laterals, but the great thing with American is that they hire J.D.'s for areas other than the in-house counsel's department. For instance, the American Airlines magazine is edited by a J.D. And there is a J.D. in charge of negotiating purchasing and contracts for materials to support maintenance at one of their major facilities."

WHO'S WHO . . .

Chairman, President and CEO: Donald J. Carty
General Counsel: Anne H. McNamara (J.D., Cornell)

Bar/Bri Bar Review

111 West Jackson, 7TH Floor • Chicago, IL 60604
Phone: 800-621-0498 • Web site: www.barbri.com

BAR/BRI IN A NUTSHELL . . .

Unless you have managed to make it through law school without ever entering your law school building or reading any law-student-oriented publication, you know who Bar/Bri is—it's the largest bar review course provider in the country. It has prepared nearly 700,000 lawyers for bar exams over the last 30+ years, including many famous lawyers and even a Supreme Court Justice or two.

It is now owned by Harcourt General.

NUTS AND BOLTS . . .

Chairman, President and CEO: Richard J. Conviser
Personnel Director: Sherry Beattner, phone: 800-621-0498
Law school graduates employed by Bar/Bri: Approximately 80 (as attorneys)
Positions: Marketing and Sales.

WHO GETS HIRED . . .

Bar/Bri hires new law school graduates, laterals, and offers part-time work for law students during the school year.

For laterals, a background in sales is helpful.

For new law school graduates, Bar/Bri looks for personality and involvement in law school activities.

Starting salary: $$ ($30-50,000)

PART-TIME WORK . . .

For part-time work during the school year: Part-time workers provide administrative support and work on marketing projects.

For part-time work, positions are typically available in the cities where Bar/Bri maintains offices: New York, Boston, Los Angeles, San Francisco, Seattle, Philadelphia, Washington, D.C., Atlanta, Dallas, Houston, Tallahassee, Chicago, St. Louis, Tempe, Nashville, San Diego, Cleveland, Pittsburgh, Chapel Hill/Durham, Indianapolis, and New Orleans.

WHAT IT'S LIKE TO WORK THERE, IN THE WORDS OF BAR/BRI ATTORNEYS . . .

"Bar/Bri is a great company to work for, because as an attorney you get to interact with people a lot, *and* you get to keep a foot in the law as well. You're always up on how the law is changing. And because so many law school graduates take Bar/Bri, you get to know the legal community on a grassroots level. You meet new, interesting people every day.

"Obviously your primary functions involve running and promoting bar review programs. When you start out, the breadth of your responsibilities depends on how big a state you're in. Typically you cover the law schools in a state, maybe two or three, along with other attorneys. On top of other attorneys, you have a support staff to rely on for help.

If you like the idea of marketing, you'll love it, because it's fun marketing to a niche market, which is what law schools are. You get to be very creative in terms of coming up with new marketing programs and new products to keep your customers, law students, happy. You spend most of your time out of the office at law schools, meeting students and seeing what they need. Sometimes that means new outlines. Other times it will involve sponsoring law school activities. Bar/Bri as an organization very much believes in the credo 'invest in those who invest in you,' and it gives you a great opportunity to help out all kinds of worthwhile legal-education related causes. People don't realize it, but Bar/Bri donates tons of money to the ABA for scholarships.

"There's also a strong public relations aspect. You want to make sure that the administration and faculty at schools are happy. You get to know them and work with them. And then you get to entertain the professors who come to town to lecture. Because Bar/Bri believes that the best bar review lecturers are not just great scholars but also great entertainers, it's a lot of fun having dinner with the professors. Some of them are a stitch!

"When it comes to autonomy, Bar/Bri gives you *tremendous* freedom to do what you need to do. Every state is different, and they're very smart about relying on you to realize what makes your state unique. When they see trends developing, nobody in top management says 'This is what you're going to do.' Instead, they'll sit down with you and say, 'Let's talk about how to improve things.' And you've got an incredible amount of brain power in other states you can turn to for ideas. People share. If you're thinking of running a certain kind of program or promotion, you can talk to pretty much anybody in any other state for input, and they're very open. There are also periodically regional meetings where we get a chance to get together with attorneys from other nearby states; then every other year there is a big, country-wide three-day weekend in Florida, where you get to party with your colleagues from around the country. That's something *everybody* looks forward to.

"You find that you quickly get close to the people you work with, even though most of the contact you have with them might be over the phone. We're always flying around for important life events of other attorneys, like weddings.

"Like any job, this isn't the job for everybody. You have to be tremendously outgoing. If you're the kind of person who got involved in a lot of things in law school, if you took an interest in your school and your classmates, you're the type. Working at Bar/Bri is all about being good at working with people—and keeping your word. Sometimes the hours are long, but they're always enjoyable. The longest hours are in the busy seasons before the two bar exams, which would be May and June for the July bar, and January for the February bar. That's when you'll be enrolling students, getting materials shipped to locations, and making sure students have everything together. That tends to be where you get a lot of administrative work to do, but it's not so burdensome because it's very team-oriented. You always have people helping you with it.

"What people find when they work here is that it's a great background for many other different kinds of jobs. It really gives you a unique set of skills. Of course, many people go on to practice law, because working at Bar/Bri keeps you right up to date with everything in the law. But that's only one avenue. Because you come out with administrative, organizational, and sales skills, people do everything from consulting to corporate work, and not just as corporate counsel, but also in employee relations and other corporate positions.

"I just can't say enough about it. It's a great, great job."

*As I pointed out in the disclaimer section at the front of the book, Bar/Bri is owned by Harcourt Brace; coincidentally, they published this book. I know that suggests a kind of log-rolling, but Bar/Bri got recommended for this book on the same basis as every other employer—that is, I heard about it from law school administrators, none of whom—as far as I could discern—even realized that Harcourt owns Bar/Bri.

The Coca-Cola Company

One Coca-Cola Plaza • P.O. Drawer 1734 • Atlanta, Georgia 30313
Phone: 404-676-2121 • Fax: 404-676-7636 • Web site: www.coca-cola.com

COCA-COLA IN A NUTSHELL . . .

You *know* what Coke does—it's the world's #1 bottler of carbonated soft drinks, sparkling waters, juices and the like. Its sales exceed $18 billion annually. The company employs 33,000 people nationwide.

Coca-Cola got its start in 1886, when the original formula was cooked up by an Atlanta pharmacist named John S. Pemberton. His bookkeeper, Frank Robinson, named the drink after two ingredients: coca leaves (later cleansed of their narcotic qualities), and kola nuts. By 1891, druggist Asa Candler had bought the company for $2,300. By 1895, the soda fountain drink was available nationwide. The famous contoured bottle was designed in 1916 by the C.J. Root Glass Company.

Today, Coca-Cola has 80 lawyers in its three Legal Divisions: The Corporate Legal Department, Coca-Cola U.S.A. Legal, and its Tax Department. Coke has 56 more lawyers working at offices around the world (some of those lawyers are native born, but quite a few are

Americans). The foreign offices include Buenos Aires, Argentina; New South Wales, Australia; Vienna, Austria; Brussels, Belgium; Rio de Janeiro, Brazil; Toronto, Ontario, Canada; Santiago, Chile; San Jose, Costa Rica; London, England; Windsor, England; Signes, France; Essen, Germany; Hong Kong; Drogheda, Ireland; Bombay, India; Milan, Italy; Tokyo, Japan; Nairobi, Kenya; Mexico City, Mexico; Oslo, Norway; Manila, Philippines; Moscow, Russia; Johannesburg, South Africa; Madrid, Spain; Bangkok, Thailand; Istanbul, Turkey; and Venezuela.

While most of Coca-Cola's in-house lawyers are laterals, they have hired new law school graduates, as well.

WORD ON THE STREET . . .

"They are an excellent company to work for. By way of example, when they won a big lawsuit, they sent the in-house people around the world as a bonus."

WHO'S WHO . . .

Chairman and CEO: M. Douglas Ivester
General Counsel: Joseph Rhea Gladden, Jr.

Columbia/HCA
Healthcare Corporation

One Park Plaza • Nashville, TN 37203
Phone: 615-344-9551 • Fax: 615-320-2598
Web site: www.columbia.net/columbia/

COLUMBIA/HCA IN A NUTSHELL . . .

Columbia/HCA owns and operates more than 330 hospitals and other healthcare facilities in 36 states, England, and Switzerland. The company employs 240,000 people, and its annual revenues exceed $19 billion. It has approximately 33 lawyers, who work in four departments: operations (18 lawyers), labor (6 lawyers), litigation (6 lawyers), and corporate (3 lawyers). They don't hire law students as summer interns, and hire "mostly laterals" for their Legal Departments.

Columbia/HCA was founded by Dallas lawyer Richard Scott and Fort Worth financier Richard Rainwater in 1987, when they bought two El Paso Hospitals for $60 million.

"People are pleased as punch to be there."

Chairman and CEO: Thomas F. Frist, Jr., M.D.
Senior Vice President and General Counsel: Bob Waterman

Federal Express
(a subsidiary of FDX Corporation)

1980 Nonconnah Blvd. • Memphis, TN 38132
Phone: 901-395-3382 • Web site: www.fedex.com/us

FedEx is the world's largest express transportation company, with more than 2 million customers a day and 140,000 employees worldwide. FedEx has 65 in-house lawyers (including some hired at entry-level) at its Memphis headquarters. They do hire law students as summer interns.

FedEx was the inspiration of Fred Smith, who recognized in the late 1960s that the U.S. was becoming a service-oriented economy with a need for reliable, overnight delivery services. Then a student at Yale, Smith presented FedEx's business concept in a term paper. His grade on the paper was a "C," the professor skeptical of his concept. (Last year, FedEx's revenues exceeded $11 billion. The professor's revenues last year are not known.)

Between 1969 and 1971, with investors willing to put up $40 million and $8 million in family money as well as some bank financing, Smith started FedEx with $90 million, making it the largest start-up every funded by venture capital. Service started in 1973, and the company went public in 1978.

Today, FedEx ranks #18 on the *Fortune Magazine* list of "The 100 Best Companies To Work For In America." *Fortune* cites, among other things, a good profit-sharing plan and a no-layoff policy.

President and CEO: Theodore L. Weise
Senior Vice President and General Counsel: Karen Clayborne

Ford Motor Company

The American Road • Dearborn, MI 48121-1899
Phone: 313-322-3000 • Fax: 313-390-8929 • Web site: www.ford.com/us
(this web site has some *very* cool historical stuff. Check it out!);
www.ford.com/careercenter (job openings)

FORD IN A NUTSHELL . . .

You need hardly be reminded that it was the legendary Henry Ford who founded the Ford Motor Company. That happened in 1903, when the company had a munificent $28,000 in the bank and 10 employees. You *also* probably know that Henry Ford didn't invent the automobile, but what he *did* do was to perfect and exploit the use of standardized parts, assembly lines, and to introduce the Model T—a car that, at $850, was an affordable buy for average Americans. In 1920, 60% of all vehicles on the road were Fords. One of Henry Ford's oft-repeated quotes is his observation that people could have Model T's in any color they wanted, as long as it was black.

Today, with annual sales of more than $146 billion—a figure that exceeds the gross national products of many industrialized nations—Ford is the world's second-largest industrial corporation. It sells almost 7 million cars and commercial vehicles every year, and it has more than 370,000 employees (including about 120 in-house lawyers).

WHO'S WHO . . .

Chairman, President and CEO: Alexander Trotman
Vice President and General Counsel: John W. Martin, Jr. (J.D., DePaul)

General Motors Corporation

3044 West Grand Blvd. • Detroit, MI 48202
Phone: 313-556-5000 • Fax: 313-556-5108

I could have organized GM's profile in a conventional way, but I've got to admit that I couldn't top the way they presented their own information.

When I got this fax, I laughed out loud. I think it says everything you need to know about what makes GM such a great place to work!

"The practice of law at General Motors is incredibly dull and boring, really. Just a bunch of lazy, inefficient corporate types who have and want no challenges, work short hours, do low-level, routine work, take endless vacations and work for meager pay. Mediocre academic backgrounds. Not real lawyers. Never think deeply about serious complex problems. Farm out any interesting work.

There, now, did we get them all into a single paragraph? Or did we miss one or two of the incredibly inaccurate myths that you may have heard about the corporate practice in general, or ours in particular?

As in many things, the reality is very unlike the myth. The practice of law at General Motors is an exciting, dynamic challenge. The sophistication of our practice in virtually every field of the law is second to none.

GM employs about 200 lawyers worldwide. Most are at the GM headquarters in Detroit, but we do have lawyers in New York, Washington, and also Switzerland, France, Germany, and China. We practice in areas of specialization, like credit and insurance, environmental and energy, general commercial and government contracts, general litigation and appeals, marketing and trade regulation, overseas, personnel and labor relations, product litigation and regulation, and securities regulations and corporate law.

Naturally, we have a single client . . . the largest industrial corporation in the world. It has been at or near the top of the Fortune 500 list for years. It's global. GM sells vehicles in 150 countries and has plants or facilities in 47 countries. It employs about 608,000 men and women around the world. Last year its sales exceeded $177 billion.

Primarily, GM makes motor vehicles, but it has many facets. GM subsidiaries include GMAC Financial Services, one of the largest financial companies in the U.S., with total assets at the end of 1997 of $111 billion; Delphi Automotive, the world's largest supplier of automotive components and systems; and Hughes Electronics Corporation, one of the world's fastest-growing space and telecommunications companies.

Professional development is absolutely a part of GM's Legal Staff. Frequent feedback and a strong commitment to continuing legal education supplement the ultimate professional challenge: dealing with complex legal problems in a world of increasing regulation and litigiousness. Complex problems that must be addressed now, thoughtfully, correctly, and in the best interests of GM's many constituencies. They are challenges that present continual growth opportunities for each of us, younger and older, at every career stage.

Beginning lawyers are not required to rotate through practice areas or sit in a common pool for the first few years. We are too busy for that! An attorney begins in a practice area that is mutually satisfactory—one that seems consistent with the attorney's particular abilities and the needs of the office. That work may evolve into a professional specialty, but there is always the flexibility to move into some other area and continue to develop there.

In some litigation, attorneys in our office work with outside counsel as a part of the litigation team. We would not serve the client very well if we were to try to impose all of our views upon the talented outside counsel who represent GM, and it would be equally undesirable merely to relinquish representing the client to them. So we work as a professional team, and that approach works very well. The result? Lawyers in our office— including those just beginning—enjoy the incomparable advantage of working regularly with many of the finest trial counsel now in practice.

Of course if you would prefer the unique exhilaration of courtroom work, we offer that too, at both the trial and appellate level. In fact, one attorney recently helped create new law by successfully arguing a case before the U.S. Supreme Court.

We are, of course, an equal opportunity employer. In addition, we are an enthusiastic participant in the Minority Counsel Demonstration Program of the American Bar Association's Commission of Opportunities for Minorities in the Profession.

Salary is competitive with the best Midwestern firms but is only part of a total compensation package. Our attorneys have the incomparable GM employee benefit package, including outstanding medical and dental coverages, a retirement plan, life and health insurance plans, product discounts, matching savings programs, vacations (but not endless ones!), and free parking.

Relocation expenses incurred by newly hired attorneys, including the cost of trips to locate housing, moving costs, and related expenses; costs related to taking the Michigan State Bar examination, such as the cost of the review course, registration fee and accommodations; and annual Bar dues—they're all paid by GM.

Increases in compensation are a function of demonstrated ability, teamwork, judgment, and productivity. Consequently, rates of growth in compensation and responsibility often vary substantially among attorneys of the same graduating class, particularly after the early years of practice."

P.S.: They *do* have paid summer internships for law students and, interestingly enough, the internships are currently only available to 1Ls (not 2Ls).

★   ★   ★   ★   ★

Honeywell, Inc.

Honeywell Plaza • 2701 South Fourth Avenue • South Minneapolis, MN 55408
Phone: 612-951-1000 • E-mail: corp.honeywell.com
Web site: www.honeywell.com

HONEYWELL IN A NUTSHELL . . .

If you have ever rented a car (or are lucky enough to own one) with GPS technology, then you've got Honeywell to thank for an outrageously Jetson-like car gadget. In case you aren't familiar with it, GPS stands for "Global Positioning Satellite," and driving a car with GPS makes you feel like James Bond. You have a little screen near the dashboard, and when you punch in the address you want to go to, the gadget not only shows you the way but actually *talks to you.* "Turn left one hundred feet ahead. Proceed straight for two point four miles." In addition, you can ask for tourist attractions and the gadget will give you the address and guide you there. It's one of those things that seems as though it couldn't be as good as it sounds, but *it is!*

Of course, Honeywell does a *lot* more than make fascinating do-hickeys for cars. It is an $8 billion company, with almost 60,000 employees in 95 countries. It ranks number 195 on the *Fortune 500* list of the largest U.S. industrial and service companies. It is one of the world's leading manufacturers and marketers of control systems and components used in buildings, homes, industry, space and aviation. Among other things, Honeywell invented the thermostat. The company provides integrated systems that can control not only the air condition, heat, lights, and televisions in houses (TotalHome) but also entire industrial entities (TotalPlant). The company is also among world leaders in developing automation and control systems to conserve energy and boost productivity.

Honeywell got its start in 1885, when Al Butz patented the "Damper Flapper," which led to the building regulation equipment that Honeywell still produces. The Damper Flapper, in case you're curious, was a forerunner of the thermostat—it opened furnace vents automatically.

Butz formed the Butz Thermo-Electric Regulator Company to market the Damper Flapper, but sold the patent to William Sweatt, an investor, in 1893. Sweatt grew the company until 1927, when he merged it with a competitor, Mark Honeywell Heating Specialties Company. In 1964 the company adopted its present name.

NUTS AND BOLTS

Who's Who . . .

Chairman and CEO: Michael R. Bonsignore
General Counsel: Edward D. Grayson
(J.D., University of Iowa School of Law)
Personnel Director: Gary C. Schulke, phone: 612-951-2105,
E-mail: gary.schulke@corp.honeywell.com

In-House Counsel's Office . . .

Number of attorneys: 65

How they got in: Most of the lawyers in the in-house counsel's office came in laterally, with 3-5 years of experience in their particular discipline. Honeywell looks for lawyers either from other corporations or from law firms.

Honeywell sometimes (but not regularly) hires new law school graduates as patent lawyers (so if you're going to start your career there, you need a technical background).

Starting pay: $$$ ($50-65,000).

OTHER OFFICES . . .

Other domestic offices where law school graduates are employed:
Cupertino, California; Phoenix, Arizona; Clearwater, Florida; Albuquerque, New Mexico; and Freeport, Illinois.
Foreign offices where American law school graduates are employed:
Brussels, Belgium; Ontario, Canada; Offenbach, Germany; Bracknell, United Kingdom

SUMMER JOBS . . .

Honeywell does hire law students during the summers. You perform legal research, and your pay depends on your experience.

Host Marriott Corporation

10400 Fernwood Road • Bethesda, MD 20817
Phone: 301-380-9000 • Fax: 301-380-8957 • Web site: www.marriott.com

MARRIOTT IN A NUTSHELL . . .

Marriott is the world's leading hospitality company, with revenues exceeding $12 billion a year and more than 4,700 hotels serving over four million people every day. In addition to running hotels (Marriott, Courtyard, Fairfield Inns, Ritz-Carlton, and Residence Inns, among others), Marriott also owns timeshare resorts (Marriott Vacation Club International), senior living communities, and a food distribution business.

Marriott got its start when newlyweds John and Alice Marriott set out from their Mormon settlement in Utah to open a root beer stand in Washington, D.C. The root beer sold like gangbusters in the hot summer months, and to attract winter customers they borrowed recipes from a cook at the Mexican Embassy for goodies like tamales and tacos, and sold those. That little business became a chain called The Hot Shoppe, and the business expanded beyond that into airline catering, hospital food service, and in 1957, into hotels, with the first one opening in Arlington, Virginia, in 1957.

Today, Marriott is rated #27 in *Fortune Magazine's* list of "The 100 Best Companies To Work For In America." *Fortune* cites the company's "strong ethical tone," and its 24-hour hotline for questions from employees with family and personal problems.

Host Marriott is the smaller of two companies formed when the Marriott Corporation restructured early in the 1990's, renaming its property unit Host Marriott and creating a new company, Marriott International, from its hotel management division.

Host Marriott employs about 70 attorneys. Most of them are in the company's Bethesda, Maryland headquarters. Six of them work for Marriott Vacation Club International (address: Dept. 38/980.10, 14344 SR 535, Orlando, FL 32821, phone: 407-206-6400).

WORD ON THE STREET . . .

"They have lawyers in offices in both Bethesda and in Lakeland, Florida. They are *so* enthusiastic about their work." "People just *love* working there."

WHO'S WHO . . .

Chairman: Richard E. Marriott
Executive Vice President and General Counsel: Christopher G. Townsend
President and CEO: Terry Golden

★   ★   ★   ★   ★

Kraft Foods
(a subsidiary of Philip Morris)

Three Lakes Drive • Northfield, Illinois 60093
Phone: 847-646-2000 • Web site: www.kraftfoods.com
(This is a terrific web site. For instance, check out the Jell-O history page, at www.kraftfoods.com/jell-o/history/).

KRAFT IN A NUTSHELL . . .

Kraft is a subsidiary of the tobacco giant Philip Morris which has over $29 billion in sales and produces over 2,500 products. It is the country's largest food company.

Kraft got its start in the early 1900s when J.L. Kraft, a 29-year-old with a burning desire to make his mark in cheese, left his Fort Erie home to go to Chicago and pursue his dream. He had $65, and that gave him enough for a month's start in his business. He spent years trying to perfect a means of overcoming cheese's highly perishable nature. After years and years of failure, he finally perfected a blending and pasteurization method, and soon after that—in 1924—he introduced Velveeta. Other products soon joined the Kraft family, including Oscar Meyer hot dogs, Post cereals, Kool-Aid, Jell-O, Stove Top stuffing, Miracle Whip—and Cheez Whiz. Incidentally, there is some evidence that Cheez Whiz may be an effective cancer fighter: it contains a lot of CLA, a polyunsaturated fat which has been shown to ward of several different cancers in lab animals.

Other things you probably didn't know about Kraft: 99% of North Americans are Kraft Food consumers, and if you are (or were) a normal, healthy graduate student, Kraft Macaroni & Cheese was one of your four basic food groups. Every day, at least 100 million North American consumers eat at least one Kraft product. And one out of every 10 American cows supplies Kraft with the raw materials for its dairy products.

Kraft North America has 35 in-house lawyers, with 31 in the U.S. and another 4 in Canada. While they only hire laterals for in-house counsel positions, they *do* periodically hire law students as summer interns.

WORD ON THE STREET . . .

"They hire J.D.'s in a number of different areas, not just their Legal Department. Human relations, marketing, contract review, environmental work, labor relations, and handling ADA—Americans With Disabilities Act—issues."

WHO'S WHO . . .

President and CEO: Robert A. Eckert

Lexis-Nexis

9443 Springboro Pike • Miamisburg, OH 45342
Phone: 800-227-9597 • Fax: 937-865-6909 • Web site: www.lexis-nexis.com

LEXIS/NEXIS IN A NUTSHELL . . .

My hunch is that as a law student or law school graduate, you know what Lexis-Nexis does without my having to explain it to you. But anyway—

Lexis-Nexis is the world's leading supplier of enhanced information services and management tools in online, Internet, CD-ROM, and hardcopy formats for legal, news, and business professionals. It has more than 707,000 legal, government, and business customers in 60 countries. It employs almost 4,000 people throughout the United States, Canada, and Europe.

The company began as the Data Corporation in 1966 and was purchased by The Mead Corporation in 1968. More recently, it became a division of Reed Elsevier, Inc. in late 1994.

Lexis-Nexis pioneered the field of online research in 1973 with the release of the LEXIS service, the first commercial, full-text legal information service. The LEXIS unit is a leading provider of online legal research materials and information products to legal professionals, small and large law firms, sole practitioners, and law schools. The NEXIS service began in 1979, starting with news content as a companion to the LEXIS service. Since that time, NEXIS has grown to become the largest news and business online information service with not only news, but company, country, financial, demographic, market research, and industry reports.

WHO'S WHO . . .

Chairman: Nigel Stapleton
CEO: Hans Gieskes
General Counsel: Michael Jacobs (J.D., George Washington University School of Law and University of Louisville School of Law)
Senior Vice President of Human Resources: Larry Fultz

WHO GETS HIRED . . .

In-house counsel's office: Lexis-Nexis only hires laterals with 3 to 5 years of experience. Helpful backgrounds include Tax, Corporate, and General Law.

Other corporate positions: Experienced lawyers are also hired in capacities other than in-house counsel, including Marketing, Content Development, and Sales.

New law school graduates: Lexis-Nexis hires 5 to 10 new graduates every year as Customer Service Representatives and Customer Training Consultants. Starting salary: $ (Under $35,000). Part-time work is also available for content editors.

SUMMER INTERNS . . .

Lexis-Nexis hires law students for summer jobs as content editors. Typically, the summer jobs go to 2Ls, but occasionally 1Ls are hired as well.

PART-TIME STUDENT POSITIONS . . .

The Company also has part-time law student help during the school year as program coordinators and content editors and developers. Most of these jobs are at the Company's headquarters in Dayton, Ohio.

HOW TO APPLY . . .

Send a cover letter and resume to:
Lexis-Nexis
P.O. Box 933
Dayton, Ohio 45401
Fax: 513-865-7476
E-mail: www.lexis-nexis.com

Lincoln National Corporation

200 East Berry Street • Fort Wayne, Indiana 46802
Phone: 219-455-2000 • Fax: 219-455-1590 • Web site: www.lnc.com

LINCOLN NATIONAL IN A NUTSHELL . . .

Lincoln National Corporation ("LNC") is a leader in the financial services industry. It is a fast-growing investment manager, one of the country's leading providers of individual annuities, one of the world's largest life/health reinsurers, and an insurance provider for the small business market. It has $120 billion in assets under management and $5 billion in annual revenues, and more than 10,000 employees. Their in-house counsel's office has about 45 attorneys, all hired as laterals.

WORD ON THE STREET . . .

"They are top notch!"

WHO'S WHO . . .

Chairman and CEO: John Boscia
Executive Vice President and General Counsel: Jack D. Hunter

WHO GETS HIRED . . .

In-house counsel's office: The Law Division employs 44 attorneys, in both Fort Wayne, Indiana and Hartford, Connecticut. (Affiliates in other locations employ in-house counsel but they have independent reporting relationships within those affiliates.)

How they got in: Depending on position requirements, the Law Division employs both new grads and experienced lawyers.

Opportunities: The Law Division hires one or two lawyers every year.

Starting pay for new graduates: $$$ ($50-65,000). (Salaries for laterals: $$$$ (Over $65,000).)

SUMMER JOBS . . .

LNC sometimes hires summer interns in Fort Wayne, but that's the exception rather than the rule. The pay is "modest but fair" and both pay and assignments take into account the experience and accomplishments of the interns. "Long hours and good performance in a variety of tasks are the norm."

OTHER DIVISIONS . . .

Law school graduates are also employed elsewhere in the company, but "not for any purpose directly related to legal education."

McDonald's Corporation

McDonald's Plaza, Oak Brook, Illinois 60523
Phone: 630-623-5865 • E-Mail: mc.jobs@mcd.com
Web site: www.mcdonalds.com/ (This web site has it all, from coloring books to download for kids, to information for school projects, to career information, as well as fun facts about McDonald's.)

MCDONALD'S CORPORATION IN A NUTSHELL

Everyone, and I mean everyone, knows what a "Mickie D's" is, don't they? (Go ahead, you can sing the jingle—"Have you had your break today...") McDonald's is the largest and best-known global foodservice retailer. With over 23,000 restaurants in over 100 countries, that's not hard to believe. No matter what state or country you're in, when you see the golden arches, you know what you're getting—good food, as well as fast and friendly service.

How McDonald's got its start is the kind of story people love to hear—two brothers with a vision open a restaurant. The brothers were Richard (Dick) and Maurice (Mac) McDonald and their first restaurant was in San Bernardino, California—at 14th and E Street, to be exact.

McDonald's opened in 1940 as a car-hop, barbecue restaurant, but was eventually transformed into a self-service, drive-in restaurant in 1948. The idea took off and McDonald's was franchised; eight new drive-ins opened in the west. In 1955, the brothers granted exclusive rights to develop and franchise McDonald's drive-ins for the United States to Ray A. Kroc. The rest is history.

The one thing that people may not know about McDonald's is that, as company, McDonald's supports a wide range of civic and charitable organizations. In 1974, McDonald's Corporation and Fred Hill (of the Philadelphia Eagles) joined forces to create Ronald McDonald House. In case you haven't seen the ads on television, there are now 160 Ronald Houses globally where families of critically ill children can stay while the kids are being treated in hospitals that are far away from home. Ronald McDonald House Charities supports the House, as well as other non-profit organizations dedicated to the health and well-being of children everywhere.

McDonald's has built a strong reputation as a training organization, from creating first jobs for one in eight Americans to advanced management training for franchisees and global executives at Hamburger University campuses.

HIGHLIGHTS

- McDonald's serves 387 million customers—a day!
- McDonald's has more than 23,000 restaurants in over 100 countries.
- With more than 600,000 U.S. employees, McDonald's trains more young people than the U.S. Army.
- ComputerWorld Magazine 1997 recognized McDonald's as one of the top 100 places to work in information systems and as one of "the tops" in training.

NUTS AND BOLTS

President and CEO: Jack M. Greenberg, J.D.
Executive Vice President and Corporate General Counsel: Jeffrey B. Kindler, J.D.

Law school graduates employed: McDonald's employs over 100 attorneys, both in the United States and internationally, to practice law. Furthermore, some of the company's key managers hold law degrees, including Jack M. Greenberg, President and CEO; Stanley R. Stein, Executive Vice President of Human Resources and Labor Relations; and several line managers.

Areas of law practiced: antitrust, corporate, franchising, international, labor relations, litigation, marketing, personal injury, real estate, regulatory, and tax.

SUMMER PROGRAM

McDonald's Corporation does not have an established summer intern program for law students.

HOW TO APPLY

Contact:
McDonald's Corporation
Recruitment Services
Department #144, HOHR
McDonald's Plaza
Oak Brook, IL 60523

Microsoft Corporation

1 Microsoft Way • Redmond, WA 98052-6399
Phone: 425-882-8080 • Fax: 206-936-7329
Web site: I don't think they have one. Ha ha. It's www.microsoft.com

MICROSOFT IN A NUTSHELL . . .

Microsoft is the world's leading software provider, selling software to 180 million people, in 50 countries, speaking 150 languages. It employs over 20,000 people around the world.

Microsoft ranks #8 on the *Fortune* list of "The 100 Best Companies To Work For In America." *Fortune* cited Microsoft's "remarkably challenging atmosphere for the brainy," the fact that everyone who works for the company gets stock options, making many professionals who've worked for the company for more than six years into millionaires, and Microsoft's practice of having company picnics with a rodeo and five bands. Also—everybody is on first name terms with "Bill." And Microsoft was voted one of the top 10 ideal companies to work for in a recent survey of European business graduates.

Here are a few little tidbits about a fascinating company. Microsoft was founded in 1975 by 19-year-old Harvard dropout Bill Gates and high school friend Paul Allen. They launched "Micro-Soft" to sell a version of the programming language BASIC. They moved to Albuquerque and set up Microsoft in a hotel room to produce the program, which they designed for the first commercial microcomputer, the Altair. Although the Altair disappeared in 1979, Microsoft modified its BASIC program for other computers and the company kept growing. Microsoft's first big break came in 1980, when IBM chose it to write the operating system for

IBM's new PC. Rather than reinventing the wheel in the face of a huge project with a tight deadline, Microsoft bought the rights to an operating system called QDOS (which stood for "quick and dirty operating system") for $50,000, and renamed it the Microsoft Disk Operating System—or MS-DOS. That $50,000 purchase must rank as perhaps the most successful business purchase of all time. Another successful purchase would have been Microsoft stock when it first went public—at about $6 a share—in 1984. If you invested $10,000 in Microsoft stock then, today your investment would be worth $7,200,000.

Today, Microsoft employs about 50 lawyers in its Law and Corporate Affairs Department in Redmond, Washington. While some in-house lawyers are lateral hires, the Department has many attorneys it hired as new law school graduates. They also hire law students as summer interns.

Incidentally, it's worth visiting Microsoft's web site if for no other reason than it's got a sense of humor. For instance, in the section that talks about what it's like to work at Microsoft, they say: "Oh, you've heard the rumors. You have to give up your life. We've grown so big that you could never make a difference. It rains here. Okay, that's no rumor . . . Microsoft people are part brainiacs, part free-spirited individualists, and 100% passionate about technology. Here you're encouraged not only to speak what's on your mind, but also to do it. You'll find a place where anything can happen—and most often does."

WHO'S WHO . . .

Chairman and CEO: William H. Gates III
Senior Vice President, Law and Corporate Affairs and Secretary: William H. Newkom (J.D., Stanford)

Motorola, Inc.

1303 East Algonquin Road • Schaumburg, IL 60196
Phone: 847-576-5000 • Web site: www.mot.com

MOTOROLA IN A NUTSHELL . . .

Motorola is one of the world's leading providers of wireless communications, semiconductors and advanced electronic systems, components and services. Major equipment businesses include cellular telephone, two-way radio, paging and data communications, personal communications, automotive, defense and space electronics, and computers. Motorola semiconductors power communication devices, computers, and millions of other products.

Motorola maintains sales, service, and manufacturing facilities throughout the world, conducts business on six continents, and employs more than 150,000 people worldwide. Net sales last year were almost $30 billion.

Motorola is listed in *Fortune Magazine's* list of the 100 Best Companies to Work For In America. *Fortune* cites the fact that Motorola supports more child-care centers—nine—than any other U.S. company, and its no-layoff history.

The company was founded by Paul W. Galvin in 1928 as the Galvin Manufacturing Corporation. Its first product was a "Battery Eliminator" which allowed consumers to operate radios directly from household current instead of using batteries supplied with early models. In the early 1930s, the company successfully commercialized car radios under the brand name "Motorola." During this period, Motorola also established home radio and police radio departments, and began national advertising. The name of the company changed to Motorola, Inc. in 1947—a decade that also saw the company enter government work and open a research laboratory in Phoenix to explore solid state electronics. By the time of Paul Galvin's death in 1959, Motorola was a leader in military, space, and commercial communications, had built its first semiconductor production facility, and was a growing force in consumer electronics.

Under the leadership of Robert W. Galvin (Paul Galvin's son), Motorola expanded into international markets in the 1960s and began shifting its focus away from consumer electronics. The color television receiver business was sold in the mid-1970s, allowing Motorola to concentrate its energies on high-technology markets in commercial, industrial, and government fields. By the end of the 1980s, Motorola had become the premier worldwide supplier of cellular telephones and in the early 1990s received its first orders as the prime contractor for the IRIDIUM satellite-based, global personal communications system. And now, Christopher B. Galvin (Robert's son and Paul's grandson), is leading Motorola forward into the new millenium.

WORD ON THE STREET . . .

"They hire J.D.'s in other capacities. For instance, they have people who act as contract negotiators all over the world, and they only hire law school graduates for this. You might find yourself in Argentina, Hong Kong, or Japan."

"They also hire law school graduates in human resources, market research, and other departments as well."

NUTS AND BOLTS

Who's Who . . .

Chairman: Gary Tooker
Chief Executive Officer: Christopher Galvin
General Counsel: A. Peter Lawson (Columbia University School of Law)
Personnel Director: Glenn Gienko, phone: 847-576-5260,
e-mail: cper01@email.mot.com

In-House Counsel's Office . . .

Number of attorneys: 98 (some work in offices other than the Schaumberg headquarters)

How they got in: The in-house counsel's office exclusively hires laterals, with 6+ years of experience. Helpful backgrounds include commercial, litigation, and environmental work. The in-house counsel's office does not hire new law school graduates.

SUMMER INTERNS . . .

Motorola *does* hire law students as summer interns, working primarily on research projects. 1L interns receive $15/hour, and 2L interns receive $16/hour.

OFFICES . . .

Domestic: Motorola Land Mobile Products Sector, Litigation Section, Consumer Business Office, Messaging Information and Media Sector, Network Management Group, and Iridium are all in Schaumburg, IL; Motorola Litigation Section—Scottsdale, AZ; Motorola Cellular Infrastructure Group—Arlington Heights, IL; Motorola Cellular Subscriber Sector—Libertyville, IL; Motorola Cellular Subscriber Sector—Harvard, IL; Motorola Automotive Component, Computer & Energy Sector—Northbrook, IL and Tempe, AZ; Motorola SATCOM—Chandler, AZ; Motorola Semiconductor Products Sector—Phoenix, AZ and Austin, TX; Motorola Space & Systems Technology Group—Scottsdale, AZ; Motorola Government Relations Office—Washington, DC; Motorola Latin America Office—Ft. Lauderdale, FL; Motorola Messaging Systems Products Group—Boynton Beach, FL and Fort Worth, TX; Motorola Energy Products Division—Lawrenceville, GA; and Motorola Information Systems Group—Mansfield, MA.

International Offices: Motorola do Brasil Ltda—Sao Paulo, Brasil; Motorola Canada Limited— North York, Ontario, Canada; Motorola Electronics Ltd.—Beijing, People's Republic of China; Motorola Limited—Slough, Berkshire, England; Motorola—Paris, France; Motorola GmbH, Wiesbaden, Germany; Motorola Asia Limited , New Delhi, India;

Motorola Israel Limited, Tel-Aviv, Israel; Nippon Motorolan Limited, Tokyo, Japan; Motorola Russia, Moscow, Russia; Motorola, Singapore; Motorola, Inc., Geneva, Switzerland.

WHAT LAWYERS SAY ABOUT WORKING IN THE IN-HOUSE COUNSEL'S OFFICE . . .

"The size and diversity of the law department here puts a vast network of lawyers with distinct expertise at your fingertips. With almost a 100 attorneys around the world, you've got a group of people with diverse interests and experiences. The annual Global Attorney Staff Meeting, held in cities such as Phoenix, Aspen, and Vancouver, showcases that diversity and gives the attorneys an opportunity to get to know one another through a variety of professional and social events."

"When you think of lawyers do you think of athletes? Probably not. However, every year the Motorola Law Departments in the greater Phoenix area get together to engage in a friendly—yet competitive—series of sporting events, most of which are low impact to encourage participation by all! The annual Sport-A-Rama brings attorneys, paralegals, administrative assistants and other staff members together for a day of camaraderie and entertainment."

Norfolk Southern Corporation

Three Commercial Place • Norfolk, Virginia 23510-2191
Phone: 757-629-2600 • Job Information Hotline: 800-214-3609
Web site: www.nscorp.com

NORFOLK SOUTHERN IN A NUTSHELL . . .

Norfolk Southern got its start as the result of a 1982 merger between two major U.S. railroads: Norfolk & Western Railway Company ("N&W") and Southern Railway Company.

Today, Norfolk Southern is a holding company that owns a major freight railroad, Norfolk Southern Railway, and a natural resources company, Pocahontas Land Corporation. It employs almost 26,000 people.

The railway has lines extending over 14,400 miles of road in 20 states, primarily in the Southeast and Midwest, and the province of Ontario, Canada. Pocahontas Land manages more than 1.2 million acres of coal, natural gas, and timber resources in Alabama, Illinois, Kentucky, Tennessee, Virginia, and West Virginia.

There are approximately 35 lawyers in the company's Legal Department, most of them at its Norfolk, Virginia headquarters. They practice in a variety of specialties, including real estate, contracts, environmental, railroad personal injury, antitrust, transportation, election, regulatory, litigation/claims, OSHA, securities, public utility, Federal Employers' Liability Act defense, labor and employment, finance law, bankruptcy, employment discrimination, common carrier liability, insurance, administrative, and intellectual property. They also hire law students every summer as interns.

WORD ON THE STREET . . .

"They are a huge conglomerate, primarily a commercial railroad company. They have many, many divisions."

"One unique aspect to the is that their corporate law department hires entry-level people."

"It's got all of the benefits you expect from the prototypical corporate law department: Good pay, interesting work, they'll pay for your MBA, very good hours, and a great variety of assignments."

WHO'S WHO . . .

Chairman, President and CEO: David R. Goode
Executive Vice President—Law: James C. Bishop

★　　★　　★　　★　　★

Partners HealthCare System, Inc.

Office of the General Counsel • 50 Staniford Street, Suite 1000 • Boston, MA 02114
Phone: 617-726-8625 • Fax: 617-726-1665 • Web site: www.partners.org

PARTNERS HEALTHCARE IN A NUTSHELL . . .

Partners HealthCare System is the corporation overseeing the affiliation of Brigham and Women's Hospital, The Massachusetts General Hospital, and the North Shore Medical Center, all in Boston. Partners is developing an integrated health care delivery system throughout the region that offers patients a continuum of coordinated, high-quality care. The system includes primary care physicians and specialists, community hospitals, the two founding academic medical centers (Brigham and Women's Hospital and Massachusetts General), and other health-related entities. Partners and its affiliated corporations have combined annual revenues and assets of approximately $2.2 billion and $3.5 billion, respectively, and employ approximately 30,000 people.

The Office of General Counsel ("OCG") is a department of Partners. The OGC was created in 1995 when Partners consolidated the legal offices of the Massachusetts General Hospital and the Brigham and Women's Hospital. During the 1960s and 1970s, each legal office had developed into full-service practices that provided a range of counseling and advocacy services to their clients. The Partners Office of the General Counsel is responsible for all legal work arising from the activities of Partners and its affiliated corporations.

WORD ON THE STREET . . .

"They are a group of very dedicated, caring and hard working attorneys who care a great deal about Mass General, Brigham and Women's Hospital, and North Shore."

NUTS AND BOLTS

General Counsel:

Ernest M. Haddad

Number of attorneys in Office of the General Counsel:

20; total women (13)

HOW THE OFFICE OF THE GENERAL COUNSEL IS ORGANIZED . . .

The OGC staff work directly with management personnel, physicians, and others with primary decision-making responsibility for a whole range of issues. Like colleagues in a private law firm, they train, counsel, assist and collaborate with each other. After a period of general training, each staff member is expected to develop one or more areas of specialization that form a significant portion of his/her responsibilities. Members are assigned to one, and sometimes two, practice sections, although they often also practice in areas outside their assigned sections. The OGC practice sections are:

(i) System Operations, which includes general corporate, real estate, land use, finance, conflicts of interest, research and technology transfer;

(ii) Employment, Litigation, and Patient Care, which includes labor, compensation/benefits, malpractice, general liability, and patient accounts;

(iii) Professional Staff and Other Health Professionals, which includes credentialing, clinical consolidation, and clinical service agreements; and

(iv) Network Development, which includes mergers, acquisitions, affiliations and payor relations.

One senior OGC lawyer serves as the Section Head for each section, and is responsible for managing the legal services performed by staff members in that Section. One staff attorney also is designated as the Client Coordinator for each corporate entity within Partner. The Client Coordinator is responsible for ensuring that the OGC, directly or through use of outside counsel, meets the client's legal service needs. The OGC engages outside counsel to work on particular matters under its supervision when factors such as cost, capacity, or expertise makes special counsel more appropriate.

OGC work encompasses a whole variety of practice specialties, including antitrust, charitable giving, conflicts of interest, contract development and review, dispute resolution, benefits/ERISA, Financings, general corporate matters, hospital and physician payment matters, intellectual property, labor and employment, network development, patient care (including risk management), professional/medical staff matters, real estate, land use, environmental and construction matters, research and licensing activities, and tax and related regulation of charitable corporations.

HOW TO GET INTO THE OFFICE OF THE GENERAL COUNSEL . . .

The OGC hires 2 to 3 attorneys per year. It doesn't interview on campus at any law schools; instead, "attorneys come to us from referrals, letters and resumes, and civic activities." Most attorneys the OGC hires have at least a year or two of experience with a law firm before joining OGC.

Interested applicants find out about job openings via the Partner's web site (address above) and through law school placement offices.

Starting salaries vary depending on prior experience. Full-time attorneys with the OGC spend an average of 50 to 60 hours per week at the office. Five of the OGC's 20 attorneys currently work part-time.

Procter & Gamble

1 Procter & Gamble Plaza • Cincinnati, OH 45202
Web site: www.pg.com

PROCTER & GAMBLE IN A NUTSHELL . . .

Procter & Gamble ("P&G") is the worldwide leader in marketing consumer products, with sales of approximately $36 billion last year. It ranks 17TH on the *Fortune 500* list of major U.S. industrial and service corporations, and 9TH on *Fortune's* list of most admired companies. And the company was voted one of the top 10 ideal companies to work for in a recent survey of European business graduates.

P&G products can be found in more homes around the world than those of any other company. The Company manufactures and sells more than 300 brands to nearly five billion consumers in over 140 countries. These brands include Tide, Ariel, Crest, Pantene Pro-V, Always, Whisper, Pringles, Pampers, Oil of Olay, and Vicks. Based in Cincinnati, Ohio, P&G has on-the-ground operations in over 70 countries and employs 106,000 people world-wide.

P&G has won all kinds of recognition as a great place to work, including appearances in *Fortune Magazine*'s "100 Best Companies To Work For In America" and "World's Most Admired Companies" List. *Fortune* cites, among other things, P&G's groundbreaking profit-sharing plan, which is also one of the most generous in the country: the company contributes up to 25% of pay to employees' retirement fund.

William Procter and James Gamble founded the company in 1837 in Cincinnati, Ohio as a soap and candle company. Incidentally, both of them came to the business under tragic circumstances. William Procter owned a woolen goods shop in London. The shop was a success, but one night it was robbed of its entire inventory. Dispirited, Procter and his wife hied off to America for a new start. Sadly, Mrs. Procter died of cholera as they neared Cincinnati. Procter, heartbroken, stayed in Cincinnati, and opened a candle shop.

James Gamble came to America in 1819, the 16-year-old son of an Irish minister. They intended to settle in Chicago, but on a boat trip down the Ohio River, James became violently ill and the family went to shore in Cincinnati. The Gambles decided to stay in "Porkopolis"—as Cincinnati was known then—and started a successful business making beer, building ships, and trafficking in hogs. James worked for the family business.

Fate brought Procter and Gamble together, in that they married two sisters, Elizabeth Ann and Olivia Norris, in 1934. As new brothers-in-law, they opened a business buying animal fats. They were immensely respected businessmen, and by the Civil War, they had the largest business in town. Ironically the War proved their ticket to an immense national business. They shrewdly foresaw the war and bought tons of rosin at a dollar a barrel, realizing that when war broke out the price would multiply. And it did—it rose to $15 a barrel, and Procter & Gamble was on its way to lasting national prominence. Its business eventually branched into other areas— food products (1911), laundry products (1933), hair care products (1934), health care products (1943), paper products (1957), pharmaceuticals (1978), skin care products (1985), and cosmetics and fragrances (1989).

P&G has been responsible for many innovative technologies and product categories, including the first synthetic laundry detergent (Dreft, 1933), toothpaste with fluoride (Crest, 1955), the first disposable diaper (Pampers, 1961), the first 2-in-1 shampoo/conditioner (Pert Plus, 1986), and the first fat-free, calorie-free cooking oil that provides full taste (Olean, 1996). P&G's goals include doubling unit volume in 10 years, achieving share growth in the majority of its categories, and delivering total shareholder return that ranks P&G over time among the top third of its peer group. Most importantly, P&G's goal is to continue to provide products of superior quality and value to the world's consumers.

P&G has also grown strategically through acquisitions. Significant transactions include Norwich Eaton Pharmaceuticals (1982), Richardson-Vicks (1985), Noxell (1989), Max Factor (1991), and Tambrands (1997).

Incidentally, P&G's biggest early success—Ivory Soap, "the soap that floats"—was the product of an accident. In 1879, Ivory soap was a standard soap that wouldn't float. However, a worker left a stirring machine on too long, working air bubbles into the soap. The air bubbles made the soap float, and instead of throwing it out P&G turned the mistake into an asset. When it took off, all of the other P&G soap formulas were changed as well.

WORD ON THE STREET . . .

"They hire out-of-school for their patent and corporate office."

"I've never heard a bad thing about them. They leave at 5:30 p.m. They get assigned whole divisions. Unless it's very technical, they handle all of the legal work in-house. It's like having your own client. They make good money and get great benefits. They hire nationwide. People just glow about the work and the people there."

"They are great for families."

NUTS AND BOLTS

Chairman and CEO:

John E. Pepper

General Counsel:

James J. Johnson (J.D., Ohio State Law School)

U.S. Hiring Counsel:

Karl S. Steinmanis, phone: 513-983-4349, e-mail: steinmanis.ks@pg.com

For Patent Counsel:

Koos Rasser, phone: 513-634-6332, e-mail: rasser.jc@pg.com

In-House Counsel's Office . . .

North America: 92 lawyers (In the Cincinnati headquarters, as well as Baltimore, Maryland); Latin America: 26 lawyers; Asia/Pacific: 17 lawyers; Europe: 54 lawyers.

FOREIGN OFFICES WHERE GRADUATES OF AMERICAN LAW SCHOOLS ARE EMPLOYED . . .

P&G's legal organization is globally focused, to mirror the company's focus. It has legal offices in over 50 countries. At any given time, these offices may have lawyers that are citizens of that country, or lawyers that are citizens of another country, or both. The following list shows where U.S. lawyers are located today:

Kobe, Japan (Headquarters of P&G Asia—provides legal and patent counsel for Far East business);

Brussels, Belgium (Headquarters of P&G Europe—provides patent counsel for European business);

Egham, England (Headquarters of P&G UK—provides patent counsel for UK business);

Schwalbach (Headquarters of P&G Germany—provides patent counsel for German business);

Hong Kong, China (Headquarters of P&G China—provides legal counsel for China business);

Buenos Aires, Argentina (Headquarters of P&G Argentina—provides legal counsel for Argentina business);

Mexico City, Mexico (Headquarters of P&G Mexico—provides legal counsel for Mexico business).

HOW TO GET IN TO THE IN-HOUSE COUNSEL'S OFFICE . . .

You can get in as a lateral, a new law school graduate, or as a summer intern. For specific questions, contact Ms. Delores McHargue, Recruiting Secretary, collect, at 513-983-8691.

Laterals: P&G will consider candidates who are up to two years out of law school.

New graduates: P&G hires 13 to 14 law school graduates per year on a world-wide basis into its in-house counsel department. The practice includes the wide spectrum of business law needed to support the company, including corporate, securities, advertising, patents, labor and employment, food and drug, environmental, trademark, and commercial law.

P&G interviews on campus at the following law schools: Duke, Virginia, Vanderbilt, Michigan, Howard, Syracuse, Indiana, Kentucky, Cincinnati and Ohio State. The Company also recruits at job fairs, including the LL.M. Job Fair in New York city, the Loyola Patent Interview Program in Chicago, the Southeastern Law School Consortium Minority Job Fair in Atlanta, and the Hispanic Bar National Consortium Job Fair. In addition, P&G hires from law schools where it doesn't interview on campus—send them a letter and a resume!

What they look for: Excellent academics (top 20% of law school class, Law Review or similar experience, excellent undergraduate academics), significant leadership capabilities, and strengths in initiative and problem-solving skills. In addition, for Patent Counsel the Company looks for people with an undergrad degree in science or engineering and a demonstrated interest in patent law.

P&G is known for providing an employee-friendly environment, and consistent with that, it has very favorable provisions for work-family situations that allow for reduced work schedules.

The starting salary for law school graduates is $$$$ (Over $65,000).

SUMMER INTERNS . . .

P&G hires law students after their second year in law school. Summer associates get a broad legal view of the businesses the in-house counsel's office supports. These areas include advertising, trademarks, patents, employment, environmental, general corporate, litigation, and food and drug work. About 50% of the summer associate's time is focused on research and writing, and the other half is "windshield time"—that is, time spent out of the office attending trials, depositions, client meetings, and the like.

While the summer associates are based in Cincinnati, there are sometimes opportunities for international travel, depending on the work assignments summer associates receive. All summer associates travel domestically as their work requires.

As with permanent hires, P&G looks for top 20% grades, leadership capabilities, and related skills.

The summer associates are paid approximately $1,250 a week.

WHAT DO P&G LAWYERS DO?

Simply put—just about everything!

For one thing, P&G lawyers are involved directly in corporate acquisitions and other major negotiations. In the last several years acquisitions and divestitures totaled more than $3 billion. The Legal Department takes a leadership role on the due diligence and negotiating team, including developing strategy and structuring the transaction. Lawyers draft all documents, negotiate the terms, set up new corporate entities if appropriate, and make necessary federal and state filings.

The Legal Department is involved in contract negotiation and writing for many parts of the Company's business. It handles its own "corporate" practice, including filing of SEC reports, developing the Company's annual Proxy Statement, providing legal advice on officer and director responsibilities and liabilities, structuring internal corporate procedures, and participating directly in corporate financing efforts.

The Legal Department has a major international law practice, involving both participation in foreign investment efforts of P&G and, through Regional General Counsel, the supervision of the legal affairs of the Company's foreign subsidiaries. Some of this work is done in Cincinnati, although there are an additional 90 lawyers employed throughout the world at foreign subsidiaries.

There's also a significant labor/employment law practice. This includes all facets of employment law, including EEO (equal employment opportunities), OSHA, wrongful discharge, and a challenging Labor/NLRB practice—which includes representing the Company in arbitration and Labor Board proceedings. The Legal Department even has an entertainment law practice, since the Company is a large producer of television shows and commercials in the United States.

In the administrative law area, the Legal Department deals with all major federal agencies, doing everything from negotiating and litigating with the agencies to analyzing and commenting on proposed rules.

The Legal Department supervises all litigation involving the Company and its subsidiaries. This includes managing key strategic decisions and participating in trial as well as directly managing discovery and settlement negotiations. Further, there is unlimited opportunity for the legal advocacy many lawyers seek. This comes frequently in administrative hearings, negotiations with outside parties, and negotiations with the government.

P&G expects its attorneys to participate actively in preventing and solving business/legal problems. As attorneys become knowledgeable about P&G's business operations, they are expected to guide proposals so that business objectives can be met within appropriate legal limits. Attorneys frequently take a leadership role in managing business problems that have significant legal considerations.

WHAT LAWYERS SAY ABOUT WORKING FOR P&G . . .

"I have been impressed with the ownership and responsibility given to each new attorney. During my first month here, I immediately started handling direct disputes with our competitors, as well as making significant decisions on advertising, hundred million-dollar contracts, and internal corporate issues. My experience is not unusual. For example, one of my first tasks was to assist in the divestiture of some of our subsidiary corporate holdings in Europe. I was also given direct and sole responsibility over a rather contentious lawsuit with one of our competitors. The instructions I received for that lawsuit were: 'You handle this. If you need help, don't be afraid to ask. Otherwise, let us know how it turns out.' This is incredibly frightening to a new attorney, but exhilarating as well! My responsibilities continue to grow, but every one of my colleagues works with an open door, so I always have help if I need it."

"The thing that I enjoy most about working in the P&G Legal Division is the constant, direct interaction with clients. On a daily basis, I work closely with business people in developing product claims and advertising strategies and structuring acquisitions and divestitures. This broad participation not only enables me to learn more about my client's products, but it also makes me feel like part of the team in growing the overall business."

"The business people here are mostly MBAs from top-ranked programs, and dealing with them on a daily basis is very stimulating."

"The P&G Legal Division is a place where good judgment is one of the most important attributes, and lawyers here are encouraged to use their judgment and knowledge of the business, as well as their legal training, to arrive at creative solutions and issues. For example, one of my current projects involves the development of a product that will be marketed in about two years. I attend all of the product development meetings and counsel the technical and brand management people on what type of support is necessary to support such claims. In this process, as with most of the work I do here, the line between legal and business issues is very blurry. The exciting thing is that people don't care, and welcome and encourage business-related comments from me as well as specific legal advice."

"When I compare notes with my friends from law school, it only reinforces my belief that I made the right decision when I came to P&G's Legal Division. P&G has a reputation for making its people a priority and I have consistently received support and encouragement from my management. I have been given very exciting and diverse assignments since the beginning and my managers have always been careful to make sure that I get the credit for my work when the results come in. I have had the opportunity to directly build relationships with my clients, including executives and senior managers, and I can routinely work with them without having to 'clear everything with my boss' beforehand."

"Several years ago, while I was at work, I found out from my family that my father was seriously ill. I needed to leave right away and travel several hours so that I could see him. When I received the phone call, my mother was concerned that my father did not have a living will, so I offered to draft one right before I left. Several members of the support staff offered to divide up the typing, so that I could leave sooner. I will never forget their kindness."

"The level of work that P&G has entrusted to me is a real sign of belief in their employees. In three years, I have worked on several large lawsuits and acquisitions, with primary responsibility on some of those projects. I have had the opportunity to work on P&G's global business, which has provided me a terrific educational experience as well as some pretty interesting travel. In fact, while on a recent business trip to Japan, I was contacted by my management and asked to detour to Seoul to handle the legal negotiations for a Korean acquisition. P&G is such a large company with so many different types of business, there is always an opportunity and rarely a dull moment."

"Much of the work that even the most junior attorneys do is high profile. We see the advertising that we worked on (and changed the wording for!) while we're watching *Seinfeld* or reading *Time*. Many times, the transactions and cases we handle appear in the national news. We can also have a significant impact on the bottom line by challenging our competitors' misleading advertising, by negotiating a great contract, or by suing a company for copying one of our product's trade dress. It's definitely challenging and headline-making. The great thing about it is that we all support each other in that work. There's always someone to bat ideas around with, or someone who's worked on a similar issue and is willing to share their expertise."

Qualcomm

6455 Lusk Boulevard • San Diego, California 92121-3779
Phone: 619-587-1121 • Fax: 619-658-1121
Job Hotline: 619-658-JOBS • Web site: www.qualcomm.com

QUALCOMM IN A NUTSHELL . . .

Qualcomm is a leading supplier of digital wireless communications products and technologies, including two-way mobile satellite communication and tracking systems, code division multiple access technology, and other cutting-edge communications systems.

It was founded in 1985, and today employs almost 8,000 people.

Qualcomm employs a *bunch* of law school graduates who get to do a whole ton of interesting things. There are many law school graduates on the business side, in areas including marketing, international sales, and a variety of other departments. On top of that, Qualcomm has about 30 in-house lawyers. The lawyers report getting "a huge variety of work. You might come in with a law degree and find yourself doing strategic marketing for Russia and the Ukraine. The sky is the limit at this place!" The Legal Department itself has a number of different groups, including a large patent group, a core corporate group (which handles litigation), an infrastructure group (which handles international work), a phone section, a group for Omni Track (involving the trucking industry), and a section that focuses on satellites and satellite tracking. While the lawyers are typically specialized, people who work at Qualcomm say that it "pays to think broadly, because the company is growing so fast." For instance, an attorney who recently passed the Bar and started out doing tax work is now working on international contracts.

Qualcomm hires new law school graduates (both as in-house lawyers and on the business side), and it also employs law students as summer interns (particularly in litigation). For legal jobs, both permanent and summer, contact Elizabeth Lopez, the Human Resources recruiter focusing on lawyers. (You can reach her at the above-captioned address and phone, as well as via Qualcomm's web site.)

Shell Oil Company

One Shell Plaza • P.O. Box 2463 • Houston, TX 77252
Phone: 713-241-6161 • Fax: 713-241-4044 • Web site: www.shell.com
(This web site has some offbeat stuff, like the
answer to "What Is Gasoline?" and "The Story Of Oil.")

SHELL IN A NUTSHELL . . .

It was founded by the Royal Dutch/Shell Group in 1912, to take advantage of the breakup of the Standard Oil trust and the expanding auto industry. That year, it formed American Gasoline in Seattle and Roxanna Petroleum in Oklahoma. Refineries were established in New Orleans in 1916 and Wood River, Illinois, in 1918.

Today, Shell is one of the country's leading oil and natural gas producers. It manufactures, transports, and markets oil and chemical products. It employs about 21,000 people. Its Legal Department employs about 90 lawyers.

WORD ON THE STREET . . .

"Their corporate Legal Department, their summer program—it's all great."

Tyco International Limited

Tyco Park • Exeter, NH 03833
Phone: 603-778-9700 • Fax: 603-778-7700 • Web site: www.tycoint.com

TYCO IN A NUTSHELL . . .

Tyco got its start in the 1960s, when Arthur Rosenberg founded Tyco Laboratories. Tyco Labs conducted experimental research for the government and commercial sectors, and among other breakthroughs, it developed the first blue-light laser. Tyco has enjoyed explosive growth over the ensuing decades with a series of acquisitions, including Simplex Wire & Cable (undersea cables) in 1974, Grinnell Fire Protection Systems in 1975, Armin (a polyethylene producer) in 1979, and Ludlow (packaging materials) in 1981. The company changed its name from "Tyco Laboratories" to "Tyco International" in 1993, to reflect its growing international operations (it has a presence in more than 50 countries around the world).

Today, Tyco wears a number of hats. It's the world's largest manufacturer and installer of fire and safety systems, the largest provider of electronic security services in North America and the United Kingdom, and it has a strong presence in disposable medical products, packaging materials, flow control products, electrical and electronic components, and underwater telecommunications systems. It operates in more than 50 countries around the world and has annual revenues of $12 billion. It recently made a $3.2 billion purchase of Connecticut-based U.S. Surgical Corporation.

They have approximately 20 in-house lawyers between corporate and Tyco's various operating divisions. Tyco hires both new law school graduates, as well as law students for paid summer internships.

WORD ON THE STREET . . .

"It's a growing conglomerate. The Legal Department gets to do a lot of mergers and acquisitions work."

United Airlines

UAL Incorporated • P.O. Box 66100 • Chicago, IL 60666
Phone: 708-952-4000 • Fax: 708-952-4683 • Web site: www.ual.com
(This web site is somewhat difficult to negotiate, but if you're tenacious, you can download recipes from Silver Palate co-founder—and cooking genius—Sheila Lukins)

UAL IN A NUTSHELL . . .

Not exactly an entry in the museum of the hard to believe. UAL operates United Airlines. It employs almost 80,000 people. Its annual revenues exceed $16 billion.

United got its start in the 1930s as the result of a merger of several companies, including Boeing Airplane and Transport and Varney Air Lines, which is recognized as the country's first commercial air transport company. Over the years, United has been responsible for a number of firsts, including the first use of air-to-ground radio and the first appearance of stewardesses. (In fact, United's eight original stewardesses were all registered nurses and they were hired to help ease passengers' fear of flying.)

United has 40 in-house lawyers. Their only permanent hires are laterals, but they do have paid summer internships for law students.

Chairman and CEO: Gerald Greenwald
Vice President, Law and Corporate Secretary: Francesca Maher

United Parcel Service

55 Glenlake Parkway, N.E. • Atlanta, GA 30328
Phone: 404-828-6000 • Web site: www.ups.com

UNITED PARCEL SERVICE IN A NUTSHELL . . .

"Big Brown" is the world's largest package distribution company. It delivers almost 11.5 million packages and documents every day, and operates 2,400 facilities in over 200 companies. Its annual revenues exceed $22.4 billion and it employs 338,000 people.

UPS was founded in 1907, at a time when few American homes had telephones, so personal messages had to be delivered by hand—and luggage and packages had to be delivered privately, too, since the U.S. Postal Service didn't start delivering parcels until 1913. To help meet this need, an enterprising 19-year-old, James Casey, borrowed $100 from a friend and established the American Messenger Company in Seattle, Washington. Casey soon began delivering packages for retail stores and by 1918 three of Seattle's largest department stores used the service regularly. The business grew over the ensuing decades and in the 1950s—with retail store business on the wane because customers were carrying home their own packages rather than having them delivered—UPS expanded into delivering packages between all addresses, for any customer, private or commercial—and that service is available today around the world.

The company has 26 in-house lawyers. Seventeen are in the corporate Legal Department in Atlanta and there are another three in Louisville, four in Brussels, one in Singapore, and one in Miami. There are also a handful of lawyers working in areas like real estate. In addition, UPS has about 20 law school graduates working in various areas of the company.

UPS hires law students as paid interns between their second and third year of law school. As a rule, the company doesn't hire recent law school graduates who don't have UPS experience.

Chairman and CEO: James P. Kelly
General Counsel: Joseph R. Moderow (J.D., Western State Fullerton)

United Services Automobile Association

9800 Fredericksburg Road • San Antonio, TX 78288

UNITED SERVICES AUTOMOBILE ASSOCIATION ("USAA") IN A NUTSHELL . . .

USAA is an automobile and life insurance business with almost $7 billion in revenues and almost 16,000 employees. It ranks #39 on *Fortune Magazine's* list of "The 100 Best Companies to Work for In America." *Fortune* cites the company's five on-site child-care centers, its two fitness centers, and its sports facilities: it has areas for softball, soccer, tennis, and golf. In addition, *Fortune* reports that about 80% of USAA's employees enjoy a four-day workweek.

USAA has 147 lawyers in-house. They hire new law school graduates. In addition, they hire law students for paid summer internships.

WORD ON THE STREET:

"It has a large bank and insurance business, plus other services for retired military personnel. It has been opened up to others who've left military service."

"It has a 'little city' environment. They promote from within. It's a large, complex building. They have their own health center, their own nurse, their own travel agency."

"They have a Legal Department in San Antonio, their main office, as well as in other places, like Colorado."

"People love it because they can work a four day, 40-hour week."

"It's a great alternative to large law firms."

"Students go nuts over job openings there."

The Williams Companies

One Williams Center • Tulsa, Oklahoma 74172
Phone: 918-588-2000 • Fax: 918-588-2296 (Human Resources—Corporate Group)
918-588-4190 (Legal Department—Recruiting Committee)
Web site: www.twc.com

THE WILLIAMS COMPANIES IN A NUTSHELL . . .

Williams is a global leader in energy and communications. Through its subsidiaries, the company is the nation's largest-volume transporter of natural gas and provides a full range of traditional and leading-edge energy and communications services. Last year, revenues totaled almost $4.5 billion.

Williams traces its roots to 1908 with two brothers' construction projects in Fort Smith, Arkansas. Within a few years Miller and David Williams were building cross-country natural gas and petroleum pipelines. By the time the brothers relocated to Tulsa in 1919, they had a reputation for building a job on time and on budget.

For more than 60 years, the company did business as Williams Brothers. It adopted the name The Williams Companies in the 1970s, reflecting its diverse businesses, and shortened its name to just Williams in 1997.

In 1966, Williams conducted the largest cash transaction to that date, paying $287 million for the country's largest petroleum products pipeline (known as Great Lakes Pipe Line Company). The new company was called Williams Pipe Line and laid the cornerstone for the modern-era Williams companies.

The company began assembling its nationwide system of interstate natural gas pipelines in 1983 with the purchase of Northwest Energy Company, which had two interstate natural gas systems. These now operate as Northwest Pipeline and Williams Natural Gas. In 1992 Kern River Gas Transmission was built through a joint venture between Williams and Tenneco. Williams purchased Transco Energy Company in 1995, bringing Transco Gas Pipeline and Texas Gas Transmission into the company. This acquisition established Williams as the largest volume-transporter of natural gas in the United States. In 1997, Williams announced an agreement to acquire another large, Tulsa-based petroleum pipeline company, MAPCO.

One of the most innovative ideas in American business began in 1986 when Williams ran fiber-optic cable through decommissioned pipelines. This was the groundwork for WilTel, which became the nation's fourth-largest long-distance network. The network portion was sold in 1995, with Williams retaining a segment of the network. This became Vyvx, a broadcast-video transmission network and is an important part of today's Williams.

NUTS AND BOLTS

Chairman and CEO:
Keith E. Bailey

General Counsel:
William G. von Glahn (J.D., Washington University School of Law)

Personnel Director:

John Fischer, phone: 918-588-2088, e-mail: jfischer@wcp.twc.com

Law School Graduates Employed By Williams: Approximately 125, with 80 serving as in-house attorneys. Other than the Legal Department, most law school graduates are hired into senior management (11), business development (3), tax (2), facilities management (2), governmental and legislative affairs (2), or contract administration/negotiation (6).

For the legal lepartment: Williams hires laterals, new law school graduates, summer interns, and has part-time work for law students during the school year.

For lateral hires: Williams typically seeks to hire attorneys with fewer than five years of experience. Any contract or regulatory experience, especially in the energy and telecommunications industries is helpful, but the company doesn't require any particular type or amount of experience. Williams also has lawyers who work part-time on a contract basis.

For new law school graduates: While there's no such thing as an 'average' year, the company typically expects to hire 2 to 3 new lawyers per year—although this number can vary dramatically from year to year! Most new law school graduates are hired for legal positions and contract administration/negotiation positions.

Williams typically interviews on campus at the following law schools: Tulsa, Oklahoma, Arkansas, Kansas, Missouri, and Texas. The company often interviews and hires students from law schools other than those at which it conducts interviews, usually through unsolicited resumes. The company also frequently participates in minority job fairs and similar activities.

The company typically hires from the top 20% of a law school class—*however,* some allowances are made for students at top national law schools, as well as for students with relevant work experience, law review experience, judicial clerkships, graduate degrees, volunteer work, and foreign language skills.

The starting salary for law school graduates is $$ ($35-50,000) (Which, as the company points out, goes a long way in Tulsa!) Also, the company offers a fabulous benefits package, including various kinds of deferred compensation. The benefits package includes generous medical, dental, and visual coverages; a 401(k) plan with a 6% company match in Williams stock; a fully-funded pension plan; life and disability insurance; annual bonus plans for all employees; education assistance programs; and a charitable contribution matching program. After six years of experience (which puts you at the senior attorney level), you also become eligible for the executive stock option and bonus plans. Williams also has a generous vacation and leave policy. Employees start with two weeks of vacation per year, then it increases to three weeks after five years, four weeks after 10 years, and five weeks after 20 years—and that is in addition to the 10 paid company holidays every year.)

SUMMER INTERNS . . .

The company typically hires between 3 and 6 summer interns. The interns usually perform research projects, attend client and staff meetings, and attend administrative and/or judicial hearings.

Williams normally hires second year students for summer internships, but occasionally will hire first years. (Williams sponsors a minority fellowship at the University of Tulsa Law School, making the recipient eligible for an internship after his/her first year of law school.) The company looks for the same kinds of credentials in its summer interns as for its permanent hires.

Summer salaries are currently $750/week.

PART-TIME WORK DURING THE SCHOOL YEAR . . .

The company occasionally hires law students during the school year on a part-time basis for the Legal Department. They work in the same capacities as summer interns. They are most often hired for the Tulsa office, but the Houston, Salt Lake City, and Owensboro (KY) offices might also hire one or more part-time interns from time to time.

WHAT IT'S LIKE TO WORK AT WILLIAMS FROM LAWYERS WHO WORK THERE . . .

"Having graduated from law school only three years ago, I never imagined I would be involved in legal work of such size and scope as the work I've done here! Already I've taken the lead attorney role in drafting contracts ultimately worth millions of dollars, representing Williams' interests in negotiations with counsel from companies like AT&T, Staples, and South Street Bank. I am also an officer (Assistant Secretary) for a major telecommunications partnership project."

"You get an amazingly large amount of responsibility as a young lawyer here. For example, the very first thing I worked on after graduating from law school was a $10 million guaranty that was part of an even larger transaction. I was given sole responsibility for drafting the guaranty and I played a large role in negotiating its final form with the counter party. As far as perks are concerned, aside from a great benefits package, I think the occasional trips taken on a company jet is a treat!"

"From my experience here, I've found that one of the greatest opportunities available to young attorneys in our Legal Department is the high level of client contact and complexity of responsibilities. I've also found that when I am apprehensive about these challenges, a senior attorney is always willing to lend a hand or offer advice. The world-class support staff is also a great asset to the Legal Department."

"Every member of the Legal Department is given an opportunity to participate in managing the Department. The Department is run through committee structures, with some committees being permanent and others *ad hoc*. While nobody is required to serve on a committee, most of us do at least occasionally participate in the committees. The committees include ones that study technological options, recruiting new attorneys, best practices, legal ethics, and many other subjects."

"There's a lot to like about working here, but I think one of the most meaningful things to me, at this early point in my career, is that I am given opportunities to learn, develop, and grow as an attorney commensurate with the initiative I put into my job. For example, having come to Williams a little less than one year after I graduated from law school, I was from the very beginning allowed—in fact, encouraged—to participate in direct client contact. Furthermore, they've made me feel as though as I continue to learn and gain experience, I'll be entrusted with more and more responsibility. I have always wanted to work in an environment where I was certain that good work and effort would be rewarded. I've found that place at Williams."

"The Legal Department has the benefit of a vast wealth of knowledge and experience in the form of its more experienced and senior attorneys. I appreciate the fact that I have access to those senior attorneys at almost any time the need arises. Starting at the highest levels and continuing all the way down the organizational chart, there's a commitment to an open door policy. Whether it's from an attorney working within or outside my particular group, I have always been free to seek the advice and guidance of a more experienced attorney—and of equal importance, that valuable assistance has always been gladly given!"

"Within my first few months of working as an attorney, I was shipped off to be the company attorney on a major Kansas Corporation Commission hearing. The really nice thing is that you are the outside attorney's client— so they take special care to teach you the ropes!"

"The company has many alternatives for attorneys. Within the Legal Department there is a wide variety of work available, from regulated issues to energy marketing to telecommunications. Williams is at the forefront of so many developments in both energy and telecommunications that the excitement is contagious. As an attorney, you get to help form the legal basis for many of these exciting and interesting projects. Also, you get to be part of the team that puts these items together. Unlike outside attorneys who normally never hear from their client until the client experiences a problem, attorneys within Williams help the business people (i) stay out of trouble and (ii) come up with creative solutions to legal, and sometimes business, issues."

"As a new attorney, I've been impressed with how much responsibility I've been given. The first day on the job, I met my clients and was given full responsibility for them. The level of responsibility is beneficial to me because it forces me to learn, it's exciting, and it makes me more marketable even inside the company as I learn practical skills."

"The environment in Legal is upbeat. Most people seem to truly enjoy their jobs."

"Williams, as compared to the law firms for which I worked, has a very team-oriented atmosphere in the Legal Department. Although there are different levels of attorneys, I do not feel the sort of sharp distinction found in law firms between the slaving associates and the golf-playing, client-schmoozing partners. At Williams, no partner owns you—you work for the company."

"As a female, I find Williams very appealing since about 40%—by my rough calculation—of the attorneys in the Legal Department are female, while in the law firms I've worked for the female attorneys only comprised about 20 to 30% of the attorneys. In addition, Williams is very family-oriented."

"There are opportunities within Williams to leave the Legal Department for the business world. The training in the Legal Department and your knowledge of the corporation as a whole give you an excellent basis for the business side. I left the Legal Department after about a year, when an opportunity to help create the new business development department in the regulated pipelines unit. It was a difficult decision on whether to leave the Legal Department, but what I think is the most important thing is that I was given the chance to make a decision like this in the first place!"

"One thing that really impressed me shortly after I started working at Williams is something that demonstrates how family-friendly the company is. Each year at Christmas time, on top of the lavish Christmas parties that the Corporate Group—including Legal and each of the major operating subs—host, Williams hosts a Christmas party on a Saturday morning for children of employees. Williams rents out a huge ballroom at one of the downtown hotels and has many clowns, face-painting stations, balloon artists, cookies, punch, hot chocolate and other treats, gifts for each child, cookie decorating stations, various games and other activities, and, last but not least, a number of Santas—strategically placed in separate rooms so each child only sees one, and no one has to wait in line too long!"

"Williams, Legal combines a New York-quality practice with the 'livability' of Tulsa. No one in our region can top the sheer number and size of complex transactions we do routinely at Williams. But we are able to live in a beautiful, clean city with affordable housing, easy commutes, low crime rates, good public schools, quality health care, world-class performing and visual arts, and friendly people. Although our salaries look low compared to salaries at firms in major cities, our salaries go a long way in Tulsa and we can maintain very comfortable standards of living. Our benefits package, including bonuses and deferred compensation, is fabulous!"

"Williams seems to really take care of its employees. The programs Williams has, like employee recognition and profit sharing, mean a lot to me as a new attorney because they demonstrate that Williams values people like me. Also, I heard a story about Williams sending its company jet to fly an employee with a serious medical condition to a hospital in New York. I really do feel like the company would help out an employee any way it could, and I think that is really rare."

"I like being part of a team, working toward the realization of corporate goals, instead of just being a hired gun to the highest bidder. The work at Williams is often delegated down to my level more out of necessity than choice, but I enjoy all of the legal supervision I need while stretching my wings on some major projects."

"While my friends in law firms are counting billable hours, working on five-digit cases, and spending seven years in a law library making their managing partners look good, I am providing services to my own clients, working on six- and seven-digit deals, and gaining partner-quality experience negotiating with counsel from major firms and corporations."

"The amount of 'good' work is high, the variety is high, and the sophistication of the clients is high. And if compensation is your motivator, take a look at the increase in stock price over the last 10 years!"

"Williams has long pursued a policy of promoting from within. The Williams Legal Department has likewise followed this practice. Members of the department routinely fill management roles and junior lawyers are advanced over time to positions of ever-increasing responsibility."

"Williams frequently offers responsible positions in its business segments to lawyers who are willing to give up actively practicing law. Each year a handful of lawyers leave positions in the department for management opportunities in one of the client groups. These opportunities are extended to junior lawyers all the way up to senior managing lawyers. As such, that gives members of the Legal Department a much wider range of opportunities to pursue than if their careers were limited to advancing within the Legal Department itself."

"The client base at Williams has traditionally drawn on input from their legal staffs in formulating strategic plans. Lawyers are invited to participate in weekly staff meetings where tactical decisions are made, as well as strategic planning sessions which occur on two separate cycles throughout the year. In this way, lawyers in the department are able to see how the client intends to operate its business in the future, what other activities it plans to conduct, as well as to participate in both tactical and strategic debates. Frequently, clients have noted the very useful input they've received from the members of the legal staff at these sessions."

"Williams puts you in a position that requires you to sharpen your legal skill set. As you gain experience, you are asked to handle projects as a lead attorney, not as a second chair to outside counsel. Since there is no assurance that any company will continue to exist or that any job position within that company will continue to exist, the development of a marketable skill set is critically important. Williams lets you develop the skills to be employable and productive."

CHAPTER 9

The Crusaders!

Great Public Interest Jobs.

Crusaders! That's a lot of what we're talking about here. Before we get into talking about specific employers—or specific categories of employers—let's go over a few general points first.

The first order of business here is pretty obvious: to figure out what the heck Public Interest *is*, anyway. I've talked with a bunch of people and read more publications about this than you can imagine, and pinning down an exact definition of public interest is like nailing Jell-O to a wall. (For more about Jell-O, visit the Kraft home page, at www.kraft.com).

As a general matter you could call public interest the area that provides legal representation to people, groups, or interests that are historically underrepresented in our legal system. That's pretty broad, and it actually encompasses some jobs that appear in other chapters of this book, because it sweeps in attorneys who work for the judiciary and for the government, including the Justice Department, the FBI, CIA, EPA, and others. The government typically gets included because the very fact that it's *the government* means that it *must* be in the public interest. It would also include county and city attorneys (there's a profile of the San Diego City Attorney's Office in Chapter 12). And you'd also include prosecutor's jobs like District Attorney's and State's Attorneys, and again, those are in a separate chapter. But at least it gives you an idea of what public interest *is*.

Other than government lawyers, you can break public interest jobs into two general kinds of organizations: nonprofit groups (like Legal Aid, Earthjustice, and virtually every other employer in this chapter), and public interest law firms (of which are only two listed here—Public Counsel in Los Angeles and the Center for International Environmental Law in Washington). Different firms dedicate different amounts of time to public interest work. There are very few that focus *solely* on public interest cases, although obviously they do exist.

An issue that is central to the minds of *many* people interested in public interest is: money. Not *accumulating* it, but rather, being able to handle law school debt while accepting a public interest position, since these jobs, while *incredibly* emotionally fulfilling, typically don't pay well (there *are* exceptions; for instance, the Federal Defender Program pays pretty well, but *no* public interest employer will compete with the pay at big firms). There are a couple of things to keep in mind when it comes to the money issue. First of all, if you are hankering for a public interest career, *get thee to the Career Services Office.* There are all kinds of loan forgiveness programs, loan assistance programs, scholarships, fellowships, and the like, for people who take public interest jobs. Your law school is the best place to find out about them. On top of that, read Chapter 13 on handling law school debt. It has a lot of advice and introduces you to a truly remarkable young man named Chris Raistrick, who took a public interest job paying $25,000—with $100,000 in law school debt. He's making it work, and his story is both inspirational and instructive!

Finally, I need to tell you something about the employers who appear in this chapter. I told you at the beginning of the book that I was only going to include organizations that have more than 20 lawyers. If you glance through this chapter, you'll quickly come to the conclusion that I lied. I didn't. Well, I didn't *mean* to. The fact is, most public interest organizations don't have 20 lawyers, so if I followed that "20 lawyer" minimum, this would be a mighty puny chapter. But public interest organizations *do* have lots of internships, and if you want to break into public interest work, the way to do it is with an internship demonstrating your dedication to the whole field of public interest work. So I took few liberties with violating my 20-lawyer floor.

Another point I have to mention is that I could quite easily have filled an entire book *exclusively* with public interest employers. Because there's a lower profit motive than there is with many kinds of jobs, people who go into public interest work tend to be more dedicated to what they're doing, and dedicated people are more likely to be happy people. That's a broad generalization, but there's merit to it, and it means that while the employers I've highlighted here are the ones I heard the most about, I could have given you many, many more. It also tells you that if you like the idea of public interest work, it's *very* worth your while to check out *The Public Service Employer Directory*, or the NAPIL *Directory of Public Interest Legal Internships*, two *excellent* books that will give you leads to *tons* of public interest jobs. (Those books are both probably in your career services library; if not, check Chapter 15 for details on buying them.)

POPULAR MISCONCEPTIONS ABOUT PUBLIC INTEREST LAW:

It's not the place to go when you want to "find God." Many students are interested in public interest law, believing it's a calling. It's great to be drawn to work that you find emotionally fulfilling, but remember, it's *work*. When you tell a public interest interviewer that you're interested in the work they do because you seek spiritual and emotional fulfillment, you perhaps aren't showing the knowledge of the practicalities of the job that will convince them to hire you.

Public interest work and *pro bono* work are not the same thing. As I've just described, public interest work generally involves people, groups, or interests that have been underrepresented in our judicial system. *Pro bono* work is *volunteer* legal work that attorneys in *any* field do in an effort to serve the public interest. As Nova Southeastern's public interest law pamphlet explains it, "All *pro bono* work is done in the public interest, but not all public interest work is done *pro bono.*"

Public interest work isn't exclusively a "liberal" affair. It often involves areas you'd consider quite conservative, because it includes work done in the name of *causes,* be they traditional liberal issues or issues associated with the "Religious Right," or any cause in between.

Helpful Web Sites

www.napil.org

This is the home page of the National Association of Public Interest Law. You'll find lots of information about NAPIL's annual job fair in Washington (every October), and you'll also get links to other public interest sites.

www.nlada.org

This is the home page of the National Legal Aid & Defender Association. They comprise Public Defender and Legal Services offices, which generally provide free services in the civil arena.

www.essential.org

Here you'll find many nonprofit organizations around the country. Good if you're looking for a summer internship.

www.des.state.mn.us

You'll find law positions with Minnesota public interest agencies and governmental positions.

www.nonprofitjobs.org

As the address suggests, here you'll find jobs, both legal and non-law, with nonprofits. The site is searchable a number of ways—by employer name, salary, type of work, and geographically as well.

www.pbsa.org

The site of Pro Bono Students America, which hooks up law students with great public interest opportunities. I can't say enough good things about these people. (For more information, see 'Breaking into Public Interest,' below).

www.law.umich.edu/academic/opsp

You can use this site, courtesy of the University of Michigan Law School, to search for public interest jobs geographically, by practice area, and several other ways as well. There are also job listings.

Fourteen Ways to Break into Public Interest Law:

1. Keep your eye on relevant publications for openings in public interest law. Your Career Services Office should have most if not all of the following (this list was compiled by the Northeastern University School of Law):

   a. National and Federal Legal Employment Report (monthly). This is a listing of attorney and law-related positions with the U.S. government and other public and private employers in Washington, D.C., throughout the U.S. and abroad.

   b. Job Market Previews (monthly), published by the National Clearinghouse for Legal Services, Inc. It is a newsletter of positions available nationwide in legal services programs and public interest law.

   c. The NLADA Cornerstone (bimonthly), published by the National Legal Aid & Defender Association. It includes national listings of public defender and legal services positions.

   d. Opportunities in Public Affairs (bimonthly), by Brubach Publishing Company. It lists over 200 current jobs in government affairs, public relations, broadcasting, and publishing on Capitol Hill in nonprofit organizations, private firms, and federal agencies in the Washington, D.C. area.

   e. Opportunities in Public Interest Law (three times a year), published by ACCESS: Networking in the Public Interest. Public interest/service positions available nationally in government and nonprofit organizations, indexed by state and type of employer.

   f. The Public Interest Advocate (monthly). It is a newsletter with features and job listings of interest to law students with a public interest bent, career services staff, professors, and others.

   g. Public Interest Employment Service: Job Alert (biweekly), published by the Public Interest Clearinghouse. Job listings for attorneys and administrators, primarily in California.

2. Take public interest oriented courses in law school and get to know the professor who teaches those courses.

3. Ask at the Career Services Office to see if any professor is writing about a public interest topic; be a research assistant for that faculty member.

4. Write an article on a public interest topic and submit it for publication in a public interest publication.

5. Join the National Lawyers Guild, a national public interest organization. Check with career services for information.

6. Volunteer to work in the community on public interest projects that interest you. Best of all, volunteer to work for the organization with which you'd like to work after school—*many* people have broken into public interest law that way.

7. Do a Pro Bono Students America project. I am PBSA's biggest booster, and with good reason—doing a project for them is *great* experience, no matter *what* you want to go into. If you want to go into public interest work, they're even better. The way PBSA works is that you tap into PBSA's database of more than 2,000 employers around the country—mostly government and private public interest organizations. You can search by location, interest area, type of work, and your year in school. The minimum time requirement is 40 hours (read: a week of school vacation). The only catch is that your law school has to be signed up for PBSA. Many of them are, and more are signing up all the time. If your law school belongs to PBSA, you can access jobs at their web site: www.pbsa.org.

8. Serve on the board of directors of a community or nonprofit organization.

9. Participate in school organizations that involve public interest events (*e.g.*, bringing in speakers on public interest topics).

10. Go to relevant Career Fairs, most importantly the NAPIL (National Association of Public Interest Law) Career Fair, which takes place every fall in Washington, D.C.

11. Go to conferences where you can meet and talk with public interest lawyers. These include the Initiative for Public Interest Conference at Yale Law School (every fall), the National Lawyers Guild Convention (early fall), and the National Legal Aid and Defender Association's Conference (every December).

12. Go to every seminar and hear every public interest-related speaker you can. Talk with them afterwards, share your interest in public interest law, and ask for a business card.

13. Talk with your Career Services Office, find out names of alumni who have the kind of public interest jobs you'd like, and contact them for advice.

14. Consider a fellowship—that is, programs that fund either your salary at an existing public interest organization, or fund a new project of

your own creation. These fellowships typically cover a short-term after-graduation job, or a summer job. The best known of the first type—the kind that funds an existing public interest job—is the Skadden Fellowship. Every year, the law firm Skadden, Arps, Slate Meagher and Flom, in New York, funds 25 fellowships to work in all kinds of public interest organizations providing legal services to the poor. NAPIL, the National Association for Public Interest Law, also has a popular fellowship program called the Fellowships for Equal Justice. If you'd rather come up with your own idea for public interest work, consider the echoing green foundation Public Service Fellowship. You come up with your own proposal and "pitch" it to them. For more information on fellowships in general, check with career services at your school or visit the NAPIL home page at www.napil.org.

Public Interest Employers Receiving Rave Reviews:

NATIONWIDE ORGANIZATIONS—PUBLIC DEFENDERS, LEGAL SERVICES, LEGAL AID

I got dozens and dozens of recommendations on public defenders, Legal Services, and Legal Aid—so many in fact, that it's a safe bet to say that it's a great job nationwide.

First, a definition. While the terms "public defender," "legal services" and "legal aid" are used interchangeably, they're not identical. What they *do* have in common is that they all provide services to the poor. "Public defenders" is the popular term for lawyers paid for by the court system or some part of a government (federal or state), to fulfill the government's constitutional obligation to ensure that every criminal defendant who might be incarcerated for some duration gets legal representation.

Legal Services and Legal Aid are different from public defenders in the sense that they are privately funded. Legal Services offices are funded by the Legal Services Corporation (a semi-autonomous corporation funded by the federal government and governed by a board of directors appointed by the President). They serve the poor in the areas of family, landlord/tenant, welfare, social security issues, and public benefits and assistance law. Legal Aid does similar work but it is a charity, and it's funded like other charities—by philanthropic contributions. It's a nationwide entity with local chapters. The United Way is a big resource for Legal Aid chapters in many areas.

Legal Aid and public defender work often overlaps because in some places, the Legal Aid Society chapter has bid for, and gotten, the contract to receive assignments to represent accused people from criminal court judges. It's sort of an analog to an "output contract," in the sense that Legal Aid will take everyone referred (except where there's a conflict of interest and the court has to find someone else). The Legal Aid Society, on top of its public defender work, does civil cases in line with its own agenda, which is typically impact-litigation in the area of civil rights or poverty law.

WHAT'S GREAT ABOUT BEING A PUBLIC DEFENDER?

The Thoughts of Sarah Madden, Public Defender in Frankfort, Kentucky

Public Defenders ("PDs"), have often been called "the frontline of the Bill of Rights." They provide legal services for indigent clients. They are often overworked and underpaid. They don't have the luxury afforded to private attorneys of picking their own clients. Often, their clients are less than appealing. It's only with their great sense of advocacy and belief in the system that they are able to defend some of the people that they are ordered to represent.

With all of this in mind—why become a Public Defender? There are many different answers to this question. I've talked with lots of people who've become Public Defenders why they choose the work—and why they stay. There are three general factors that draw people to PD's offices in the first place:

1. *Experience.* This is the central reason many new attorneys are attracted to PD work. They like the idea of being thrust into court immediately—and they *will* be! They go straight from law school to trial experience. If what you want is to go to court *right away,* the PD's office is the place to be.

2. *Training.* PD's offices offer some of the best training in the nation.

3. *Criminal law practice.* If you want to concentrate on criminal law, it's tough to do so in private practice. O.J. Simpson cases are few and far between. The majority of criminals are indigent, with no money to pay for a lawyer. Most private criminal defense lawyers will have to take civil cases to help pay the bills. Not only can you focus exclusively on criminal work with the PD's office, but you can even specialize:

most PD's offices have different divisions, like a trial division, a post-trial division (appellate), and sometimes a juvenile division.

Once attorneys become Public Defenders, what makes them stay? Again, there are a few reasons:

1. *Making the difference.* One underlying theme present with attorneys who have been with PD offices for a while is that they feel they are making a difference—they're dealing directly with people whose lives they are impacting in a major way. It is this true commitment to the poor that sets them apart from others.

2. Cause work. Whether it's working with juveniles or on capital cases, some people live for causes. There's no better place to carry the torch than the PD's office.

3. Changing the law. One appellate attorney told me that if you stay long enough with the PD's office, you could actually see the law being restructured as a result of your work!

4. Not being alone. For some attorneys, the idea of a solo practice is terrible. They need to feel like part of a group; they like to be able to work down the hall and find somebody like-minded close by. PD offices offer that.

5. Being part of a large law firm. Believe it or not, PD's offices have this attraction! One PD in Kentucky said that he is part of the largest law firm in the Commonwealth.

6. Money. This is admittedly a small group, since the pay for PDs is not an allure for most people—it's lower than what you'd make in private practice, by a long shot. However, for people who would otherwise have hung out a shingle as private criminal defense lawyers, they sometimes join a PD's office intending to get some experience, but then find that they stay because the benefits and the lack of overhead make the money they do receive that much more attractive.

7. Pride. Public Defenders aren't known as "The Best Lawyers Money Can't Buy" for nothing!

How to Find Public Defender Jobs, and More Information About PD's Offices:

All states have some kind of PD office. To find out about employment opportunities with the PD office in a particular state, you have several options. You can contact the bar association in the state or contact the state personnel department in the capital city. You may also check the Directory of Legal Aid and Defender Offices in the United States and Territories. All law school Career Services Offices stock this *very helpful* book—or you can order it directly from NLADA, Attn: DMC Division, 1625 K Street, N.W., Suite 800, Washington, D.C. 20006.

You can also visit web sites. Here are a few to try:

www.nettally.com/fpda

This is the home page of the Florida Public Defender Association.

http://governor.state.co.us/gov_dir/pdef_dir/pd.htm

This is the home page of the Office of the Public Defender for the State of Colorado.

www.opd.state.md.us/

This is the home page for the Maryland Office of the Public Defender.

www.state.de.us/govern/agencies/pubdefen/indexpd.htm

This is the Delaware Office of the Public Defender.

www.sado.org

This is the Michigan State Appellate Defender Office.

http://advocate.pa.state.ky.us/index.htm

This is the home page of the Kentucky Department of Public Advocacy.

http://advocate.pa.state.ky.us/kpcdo.html

This is the home page of the Capital Post-Conviction unit with the Kentucky Department of Public Advocacy.

www.nlada.org

This is the home page of the National Legal Aid and Defender Association. They are made up of Public Defender and Legal Services offices.

www.webtest.state.oh/us/scripts/phonelagency/pub.asp

This is the home page of the State of Ohio's Public Defenders Office.

An Insider's View of Legal Services—The Thoughts of Jane Reinhardt, Senior Staff Attorney of the Mental Health Law Project at Nassau/Suffolk Law Services Committee, Inc., in New York.

Why do people do what I do? We feel like crusaders! There's plenty of opportunity for glory and accomplishment, if not wealth. The clients are very compelling. The working environment is comfortable and informal. Everyone is in political agreement. There has typically be a high proportion of novices, so no one worries about being correct and unfazed. There's no concern about getting paid or with only doing as much as the client can afford (although there *are* cost-benefit analyses so that the public money is not wasted).

A day in a legal services office is never typical. The attorney will have "intake" a couple of days a week, when new clients come in. Court dates inject variety into the schedule and, particularly when you carry a general caseload, you will be juggling responsibilities in many different courts.

Research and writing and conferring with colleagues take up the rest of your time. Other kinds of case-development, like phoning and letter writing, go on constantly. New attorneys spend a fair amount of time at training events and substantive-law programs to learn the ropes. If you concentrate on one area of the law, there is eventually less research and more productivity. However, having done this kind of work for many years, I still find a lot of the subject matter to be very complex and endlessly surprising, there is always new case law, and there are new statutes and new regulations to contend with almost constantly.

On top of the substance of the work, a big benefit of public interest law is that there is a lot of autonomy, because no matter what kind of public interest job you have, there's so much work and not enough staff to allow supervisors to be full-time supervisors. Responsibility comes early, because, historically, there has been high turnover in these programs. Soon, you find that you are the expert in a subject because people with experience have left your program, and there were never very many people doing your kind of work anyway!

Public interest work in general is a great career, if money's not too important to you. One effect of the rather low pay is that the industry is staffed disproportionately by partners, most often wives, in two-career marriages. This effect is intensified by the equal-opportunity-employment objective of all public interest employers.

Of course, there *are* downsides to litigating in a public interest office. For one thing, there isn't a lot of money or a lot of time for the most ambitious advocacy. Clients don't have much bargaining power, and they are under stresses that prevent them from following through on the plans we make with them. Criminal defense work and family-court defense work can be discouraging. If you look at other employment possibilities after having been in legal services work for a few years, you don't see much relevance in your experience to what you might find in the private sector. However, some public benefits are available to the middle class as well as the poor, and some poor people have property and family issues that arise for the middle class as well. You certainly don't learn much about corporations, tax, banking, or insurance in a public interest job. You *could* go into private practice with poverty law, however—taking class actions and other cases where attorneys' fees might be awarded by courts against government or private defendants. And you might also work for the government in other capacities.

But for many of us, the downsides don't outweigh the benefits—not by a long way. We hard-liners, of course, see public interest work as a career commitment. When we interview people who are looking for jobs with us, we try hard to identify people who aren't going to stick with it, and we avoid hiring them (although when the economy is humming and there are many competitors for law students, we sometimes find ourselves taking candidates who aren't ardent!)

When I hire lawyers, I'm interested in people who enjoy the study of law. There's a lot to learn and a need to keep learning and thinking imaginatively about the law. Clinic participation and extracurricular socially conscious activities are good credentials. Often, the more active a student is outside of school, the less competitive are his grades, so we look at the total picture in hiring. One successful approach to employment that many legal services attorneys have used is to volunteer at a legal services office for as long as it takes to win hearts there. My legal services office has hired many who first came to us as volunteers. Some of these people have taken the first legal practice jobs opening up in the legal services offices where they have been volunteering. For some, although bar-admitted, they've gotten in by snatching up a paralegal job, awaiting the first vacancy among staff attorneys.

One warning—"hours" is a sore point with me, and many public interest lawyers. I've actually interviewed people who said they were looking for public interest employment because they didn't want to work as long and hard as they would have to in private offices! The official hours *are* very conventional: 9 a.m. to 5 p.m., 5 days a week, and there are usually liberal holiday, vacation, personal leave, and sick leave policies. But there are times when it's necessary to work on weekends, and to work late. As you get more experienced, you normalize and separate your private and employment lives. You learn that courts generally work slowly, and that, if you have a real crunch, adjournments are possible. When I first started working in legal services, every social occasion involving at least two of us was an opportunity to talk shop. We were obsessed! Over time the obsession fades, but I've never stopped being fascinated by my work.

THE FEDERAL DEFENDER PROGRAM

There are lots of Federal Defender offices, all over the country—in fact, it's the federal equivalent of state Public Defender offices. While there are Federal Defender offices in major cities, and I've heard rave reviews about a number of them (including San Diego), here I'll profile just one office, in Chicago.

Federal Defender Program (Chicago)

55 E. Monroe Street, Suite 2800 • Chicago, IL 60603
Phone: 312-621-8300 • Fax: 312-621-8399

WHAT DO THEY DO?

The sole focus of the office is federal criminal law—they represent criminal defendants in the Northern District of Illinois who can't afford to retain counsel. The office, founded in 1965, was also designed to provide law school students with the opportunity to receive "internship" training in trial advocacy. The Executive Director, Terence F. MacCarthy, is a nationally-known lecturer on trial advocacy, having lectured in all 50 states and over a dozen foreign countries.

WORD ON THE STREET . . .

"It's like a law firm. They get *great* work."
"There's a lot of appellate writing."

NUTS AND BOLTS

Executive Director: Terence F. MacCarthy
How many people work there: 18; 9 are women and 6 are minorities

FULL-TIME POSITIONS . . .

They hire "when openings arise, when a lawyer leaves the office, or when a new position is created," although even when there are no current openings, "We accept resumes and applications."

The office doesn't routinely interview on campus, although it does occasionally visit Chicago law schools and a few out-of-state law schools. Ordinarily, interested applicants normally come to the Office through recommendations and resumes.

What they look for: "Commitment to the type of work we do and the type of clients we represent! Law Review and top 10% are helpful but not necessary. Alternative experience that demonstrates the commitment we are looking for would be most helpful. Those we consider are interviewed by all of the attorneys in the office, so what impresses would be difficult to define—although knowing something about the office and even more important and obvious, fully understanding the nature of the work we do are most important! People who simply want to be 'litigators,' wherever they do it, usually don't impress us."

HOURS AND BUCKS . . .

Hours: Typically 60 hours a week, arriving around 9 a.m. While the Office has allowed attorneys to work part-time, it has never hired a new attorney on a part-time basis.

When there *are* openings, the starting salary is $$ ($35-50,000).

SUMMER INTERNSHIPS . . .

The office has a summer intern program which employed nine interns last summer, one of whom will join the staff permanently.

Pay: $400/week.

The internship program is open to both 2Ls and 1Ls.

Last year's interns came from University College Dublin, Chicago-Kent College, South Texas, Michigan, NYU, Northwestern, University of California, Loyola, DePaul, and Northeastern.

The deadline for applying for summer clerkships is mid-January.

PART-TIME POSITIONS DURING LAW SCHOOL . . .

The Office employs 3 to 4 law students on a part-time basis during the school year. Some receive pay and others are work-study.

WHAT LAWYERS SAY ABOUT WORKING THERE . . .

"Representing indigent people is, in and of itself, quite rewarding. Add to the mixture the ability to match wits with—and, at times, overcome—the formidable forces of the U.S. Government, and one has a job which might be the envy of a John Grisham hero! When many a trial or sentencing is complete, I feel as though my law school experience was entirely worthwhile, and that I've undertaken a magical career."

"This may be one of the few law offices in the nation which allows the least-experienced attorney to undertake as much responsibility as (s)he desires. To be sure, there is always a level of supervision available to assist the novice attorney at every stage of a case. But the autonomy is remarkable! I know of no other office where a new attorney can assume the representation of individuals charged with federal felony offenses from the initial appearance stage through trial to plea and sentencing, and through the appeals process, to the United States Supreme Court, where necessary."

"Cases are never assigned or prioritized on the basis of seniority—there is no 'pecking order.' All cases are randomly assigned on the basis of 'duty days.' The assigned duty day attorney, regardless of experience level, is responsible for the legal care of that respective client until the case is complete."

"Frustrations *do* exist here. The process can be difficult. The road to successfully resolving a case is fraught with hazard. In an era of sentencing rules, minimum-mandatory sentences, and "three strikes" laws, it is easy to feel overwhelmed. Dealing on a day-to-day basis with lifetime-tenured judges can also be quite challenging. At this stage, the supportive atmosphere of the office takes over. After a particularly rough experience, it is comforting to know that others have had similar experiences. The therapeutic effect of discussing job frustrations with other highly-regarded attorneys in the office is invaluable. Despite the busy nature of the practice, it seems that no attorney here is ever too preoccupied to assist another with whatever problem or concern might be pressing at that moment."

"The only common law student misimpression about what I do arises out of stereotypical notions of what it takes to represent individuals charged with crimes. It takes some appreciation of the adversarial system to fully comprehend why a defense attorney represents someone she 'knows is guilty.' Experience is the best teacher in most instances, however. Most law students who spend time working within the Federal Defender Program quickly learn to appreciate notions of attorney-client confidentiality and prosecutorial burdens of proof. Perhaps those who don't go on to become prosecutors!"

"Every case is unique. Accordingly, each new case presents fresh challenges. Although trials aren't infrequent, Federal Defense Program attorneys spend a great deal of time in court—initial appearances, detention hearings, status hearings, change-of-plea hearings, sentencings, probation revocation hearings, evidentiary hearings on motions to suppress or disputed sentencing issues. Direct client contact is also frequent. In addition, research, writing, and investigation all play a part in case preparation. As in every profession, 'grunt work' often pays grand dividends. This isn't to suggest that life as a Federal Defender attorney is always grim and serious. Indeed, dire circumstances at times compel a need for comic relief, which quickly abates the more stressful aspects of the job. Humor and camaraderie go hand-in-hand, and this office is certainly no exception to the rule. Additionally, a bit of self-effacing humor aids greatly in the process of case negotiation or persuasive argument. When a case proceeds to trial, the tempo increases. During the week preceding trial, it seems as though every waking minute is consumed with trial preparation—continued investigation, additional discovery submissions, motions in limine, discussions concerning trial strategy and case theory. Although tiring, at the conclusion of a trial, no feeling could be more professionally exhilarating. To be able to say 'I did my very best'—this is the stuff upon which successful careers are sustained!"

"Relationships in appointed cases are unique and complex. Suffice it to say that the vast majority of clients I've represented are gracious and grateful for the help I've rendered. I am never offended, however, when a client for whom I've done good work does not keep in touch. I have come to understand that I represent an unpleasant chapter in that client's life. Like a therapist, I see my role as helping an individual through a difficult time so that individual might go on to lead a successful and fulfilling life. When my help is no longer needed, I want my client to continue on in life in a more positive vein. Some clients do not achieve that. The vast majority, however, do re-enter society as law-abiding, contributing citizens. If I have helped in that achievement, I am content. A client who wishes to forget that dark chapter in life demonstrates a natural human reaction to unpleasant circumstances. I support that completely. My reaction would likely be the same. By the same token, 'There but for the grace of God go I.' Every Federal Defender Program lawyer appears to maintain the pulse of human empathy within this practice. Under different circumstances, I could be the one in need of defense. It is only through the grace of God that I am the defender and not the defended. I try always to keep that thought somewhere in the files of my mind: *[A]ny man's death diminishes me, because I am involved in Mankind; and therefore never send to know for whom the bell tolls; it tolls for thee.* (John Donne, *Devotions).*"

"The biggest difference between our office and that of a large law firm is the independence we have in representing our clients and practicing law. Despite some supervision, our attorneys are allowed to litigate their cases as they see fit. We don't have to run to higher-ups every time any decision needs to be made in regard to the case. Of course, lawyers are always available for opinions if you need them. But in this office you are a lawyer, not an intern."

"There are two stories that jump to mind about what makes our office so wonderful. I once lost a trial in my fourth year here that for some crazy reason I was convinced we were going to win. I had unbiased eyewitness testimony and physical evidence that completely contradicted the law enforcement testimony. The penalties in the case were severe. I lost. My client was looking at a minimum sentence of 20 years and there was no doubt in my mind that he didn't do it. I was sitting in my office with the deputy director of our office talking about the verdict when I received a call from our receptionist. My client's wife and mother, who had missed the verdict when it came in, were here to see me to find out the jury's decision. I guess having to meet with his family and tell them the news was the last straw. As I walked out of my office, with my boss right behind me, I punched a wall in the hallway and put my fist right through it leaving a pretty good-sized hole. After realizing what I had just done—and in front of whom I had just done it!—I said to her, 'Wow, I'm sorry. I'll pay for that.' She looked at me and just asked if my hand was OK. She then told me to deal with my client's family and to then go take a walk. I did just that. When I returned from my walk, a painting had been hung over the hole in the wall. How could you not love this place? The second story is that I was diagnosed with a serious illness a few years ago. I was incapacitated for a while. This office was completely supportive in every way imaginable. From the top to the bottom, every person here helped me focus on one thing and that was getting healthy. There was never a hint that my illness caused any type of disruption to the office. The Federal Defender Program's unflinching support was one of the main reasons I was able to overcome this illness, get healthy, and resume my life and job. For that, I will be forever grateful."

"The Federal Defender Program is wonderful for a variety of reasons. First, the entire staff is extremely supportive We are a true family. There is nothing that we would not do for each other. I found it a real testament to the family atmosphere that everyone came to my wedding. I felt such support and love. The second reason is the work we do. It is rare to fully enjoy your work. We have the ability to enjoy what we do because everything we do is for the benefit of those who have never had anyone fight for them before. It is a rush knowing that what we do will help someone in need.

There is substance to our work that is lacking in most of the legal profession. And the third reason is the variety of work we do. There is no 'typical' day. We are courtroom lawyers, writing lawyers, trial lawyers, and appellate lawyers. We represent postal workers, bank robbers, kidnappers, businessmen, drug dealers, gang members, and preachers. We advocate, negotiate, and commiserate. There is a whole world of what we do such that it can never become boring or dull. We are not only lawyers—we are also social workers, friends, and supports. There is no other job that I would like. This job and this office are special. I'm grateful I've been given the opportunity to work here."

"From the minute I began work here, I felt an incredible amount of support from every lawyer here. Each person made clear—and really meant it—that there is no question too dumb, too small, or too obvious. This kind of support was invaluable to me as a new lawyer. Law school did not prepare me for the actual realities of daily work; most of what I have had to learn, therefore, has had to come from those with whom I work. From day one until now, I have an office full of colleagues who will sit down with me to discuss any question I might have, or offer insight into any particular issue.

"A lot of what we do is social work—everything from helping a client cope with what is happening to him or her and explaining how the system works and what he or she can expect, to arranging drug or mental health treatment, dealing with family members, and the like. Next comes legal research, writing, reviewing discovery and other documents, and investigation, closely followed by negotiation with prosecutors and working out plea agreements.

"My colleagues are incredible—dedicated, caring, supportive, hardworking, and committed to ideals of equality and fairness. The interesting thing is that I can say the same about many of my clients. As one colleague has aptly put it, 'There are a lot of really good honest people out there who make serious mistakes.' It is the work with my clients and the interactions with them that drive me forward."

"During my second year at the office, after I had tried my first case and had argued dozens of motions in court, I was waiting for a status at the courthouse when I ran into a classmate of mine who was at a big firm. She was nervous because it was her first court appearance. We chatted a bit and then her case was called. I almost fell off the bench when she went forward and stood next to the partner on the case. The only thing she said was her name. Needless to say, the partner argued the substance of the motion. I could not believe that she had gotten so little experience that this court appearance with a partner at her side seemed like a big deal."

"The Federal Defender Program offers a new lawyer tremendous responsibility and autonomy. Our lawyers are not handed some huge stack of cases and left to flounder. We are also not sent to some dark room to do research and review documents for a case in which we are never going to meet the client or see the inside of a courtroom. We are responsible for a manageable number of cases, which includes communicating with the client and the prosecutor, deciding the best strategy to pursue, filing and arguing appropriate motions and trying the case if necessary. The beauty of the office is that our lawyers provide a tremendous amount of support for each other. There are plenty of experienced and generous attorneys who will spend whatever amount of time is necessary to talk through a case. So while a young lawyer has a great deal of responsibility, he or she also has a great deal of guidance and support."

"Days are anything but typical when you represent the indigent accused of crimes. Some days are very client intensive, where I spend all of my time meeting with clients, reviewing the evidence with them, explaining the law to them, and learning from them what happened and how they want to resolve the case. Some days involve negotiating with the prosecution about a particular case and negotiating with the client about what sort of resolution is both acceptable and realistic. Some days are reading and writing days. One of the best things about our work is that it is not 'seat of the pants.' We do not just pick up a file the morning of trial and review it. Instead, we have time to investigate a case and file creative motions. Some days are active courtroom days with hearings and sentencings and the like. What makes the job great, though, is that most days are a bit of all of these things."

The American Civil Liberties Union

125 Broad Street, 18th Floor • New York, NY 10004-2400
Phone: 212-549-2500 • Web site: www.aclu.org

WHAT DO THEY DO?

The American Civil Liberties Union (known to most of us as the "ACLU") is the nation's foremost advocate of individual rights—litigating, legislating, and educating the public on a broad array of issues affecting individual freedom in the United States. Founded by Roger Baldwin in 1920, the ACLU has routinely been involved in more Supreme Court cases than any other private organization. Headline-making cases— from the Scopes Case, to school desegregation, abortion to creationism and many, many others—the ACLU has long been at the center of controversies that rivet the attention of the country.

The ACLU is frequently asked, "Why did you defend that person or that group—Nazis in Skokie, Illinois, the Ku Klux Klan, the Black Panthers?" The answer is that the ACLU defends the *right* of people to express their views, not the views that they express. And historically, the people whose opinions are the most controversial or extreme are those whose rights are most often threatened. Believing that once the government is empowered to violate one person's rights it can use that power against everyone, the ACLU works to stop the erosion of civil liberties before it's too late.

STRUCTURE . . .

The ACLU is a 50-state network of staffed affiliate offices in most major cities more than 300 chapters in smaller towns, and regional offices in Denver and Atlanta. (The ACLU's web site provides complete contact information for all offices.) Work is coordinated by a national office in New York, aided by a legislative office in Washington that lobbies Congress. The ACLU has more than a dozen national projects devoted to specific civil liberties issues: AIDS, arts censorship, capital punishment, children's rights, education reform, lesbian and gay rights, immigrants' rights, national security, privacy and technology, prisoners' rights, reproductive freedom, voting rights, women's rights and workplace rights.

The ACLU is governed by an 84-member board of directors which has one representative from each state affiliate and 30 at-large members elected by the affiliate and national boards. The affiliate boards, in turn, are elected by all ACLU members within the state. On a day-to-day basis, each affiliate is autonomous and makes its own decisions about which cases to take and which issues to emphasize. They collaborate with the national office in pursuit of common goals.

NUTS AND BOLTS

Executive Director: Ira Glasser
Legal Director: Steven Shapiro
How many attorneys work there: More than 60 in offices all over the country, as well as more than 2,000 volunteer attorneys. (Most of the offices are very small, with very few attorneys, and often only one.)

FULL FULL-TIME POSITIONS . . .

They hire as needed, on an office-by-office basis. Check the web site (or your phone directory) for your closest office.

SUMMER INTERNSHIPS . . .

Offices vary, but all accept law student and attorney volunteers, and many take self-funded summer interns.

TRADE UNIONS

United Mine Workers of America

900 Fifteenth Street, N.W. • Washington, D.C. 20005
Phone: 202-842-7330 • Fax: 202-842-7342 • Web site: www.umwa.org

THE UNITED MINE WORKERS OF AMERICA IN A NUTSHELL . . .

The United Mine Workers of America ("UMWA") was founded in Columbus, Ohio in 1890 by the merger of the Knights of Labor Trade Assembly No. 135 and the National Progressive Union of Miners and Mine Laborers. Throughout its history, the UMWA has provided leadership to the American labor movement. John L. Lewis led the Union for much of this century; Cecil Roberts, a third generation coal miner, has been president since 1996.

The UMWA was an early pioneer of health and retirement benefits. In 1946, in a contract between the UMWA and the federal government, a multi-employer UMWA Welfare and Retirement Fund was created. The UMWA Fund would change permanently the way health care was delivered in the coalfields of the nation.

The UMWA has also been a leader in the field of worker health and safety. In 1969, the UMWA convinced Congress to enact the landmark Federal Coal Mine Health and Safety Act. That law changed a number of mining practices to protect miners' safety and provided compensation for miners suffering from black lung disease. The UMWA also has taken an active international role by working to end apartheid in South Africa and by helping workers in the former Soviet Union and developing nations form democratic labor unions.

Today the UMWA continues its primary role of speaking out on behalf of American coal miners. The Union also represents workers in a number of other industries, including manufacturing, health care, and the public sector.

NUTS AND BOLTS

President: Cecil E. Roberts
Vice President: Jerry D. Jones
Secretary-Treasurer: Carlo Tarley
General Counsel: Grant Crandall (J.D., UCLA)
Personnel Director: Judy Medley, phone: 202-842-7220

In-House Counsel's Office . . .

Number of attorneys: 7. Some of the attorneys work part-time.

How to get into the in-house counsel's office: The in-house counsel's office periodically has job openings and they typically go to new law school graduates (or with less than five years' experience). They look for good writing skills and past experience in union or related work.

The starting salary is $$ ($35-50,000).

SUMMER INTERNSHIPS AND PART-TIME WORK DURING THE SCHOOL YEAR . . .

These are both regularly available at the UMWA's Washington headquarters. Summer interns and law students working part-time during the school year perform legal research on all of the subjects the UMWA handles, and get client contact as well. They receive $12 to 16 per hour.

WHAT LAWYERS SAY ABOUT WORKING FOR THE UMWA . . .

"The UMWA is not the kind of place you come to work if you want posh digs, fringe benefits, and lots of perks—I think thus far I've scored a tote bag, a baseball cap, and a T-shirt! It *is* a place you want to be, however, if you have a demonstrated interest in labor law, progressive views on worker's rights, and a commitment to public interest law.

"The work is very challenging, and a new attorney, even one fresh out of law school like me, is assigned cases just like the other attorneys in the office. Within the first few weeks on the job I was actively involved in negotiating a contract with a major corporation, was co-counseling complex federal civil litigation, and was filing charges before the National Labor Relations Board.

"Because the UMWA is such a progressive and pro-active union, there are unique demands on the Legal Department. We are expected to aggressively protect our membership's legal rights, and are encouraged to explore creative and sophisticated legal strategies in the cases we handle. Even though we are in-house counsel, we do some of our own litigation, which provides a great balance between advising the Union on matters and getting into the courtroom.

"Consistent with its mandate to protect workers, the UMWA provides a very livable work environment! The workload is quite manageable, especially by D.C. standards. Most of my friends from law school are attorneys at large firms, and I am by far the only one who could regularly get home in time to fix dinner during the week.

"For a small office, there is a lot of support for a new attorney. My co-workers are very helpful when I come across problems, and we have some great outside counsel who have made themselves available to call up, at no charge, whenever I have legal questions. I've also made some good friends here, both in the Legal Department and in the organization at large.

"Lots of my friends who are attorneys think I'm lucky, and I feel lucky. I don't think many of them, other than perhaps some who are clerking for federal judges, have the intellectual stimulation that I have on a day-to-day basis, and I doubt any of them working at large firms have the degree of autonomy I have in handling cases."

"This Union is a very special place to work because of the dedication, solidarity, and respect for tradition that union coal miners have for each other and for the union as a whole—as well as the camaraderie among the attorneys in the office and our outside counsel. I feel nothing like a drone; my cases and my clients are part of a progressive movement and have some lasting significance beyond the billable hours they may generate or the salary we take home. In addition, the office is very family-friendly and has great benefits . . . I was pregnant when they hired me and have had a second child since, and they have been very supportive throughout. I guess that makes sense; unions are known for their rhetoric about supporting working families, a/k/a working mothers, but this one really does so!"

"After I was hired but before I actually started working here, my boss-to-be told me that his philosophy is that everyone who works for the United Mine Workers of America is first and foremost a labor activist. He said that in the Legal Department, we primarily contribute our skills as lawyers because that is our particular area of expertise, but our calling is to advance the UMWA and the labor movement as a whole and we do whatever the Union needs us to do to accomplish this. This was music to my ears, and now that I've been here for awhile, I can honestly say that this is truly how the Legal Department operates.

"When I interviewed for this job, my boss-to-be asked me what part of labor law I enjoyed the most. I told him that my prior experience practicing Union-side labor law had shown me that I find organizing the most interesting and fulfilling. After I was hired, my boss remembered what I'd said and did everything in his power to get me involved in organizing activities. For example, within four months of starting with the UMWA, I had a chance to teach part of an advanced training for organizers and I was sent to Alabama to work on an organizing drive.

"Although NLRB and federal district court litigation are a definite component of this job, I also enjoy the variety of the thousand other projects that come across my desk. Working directly for the Union, you never know what you'll be called on to handle next. For example, I've helped set up a grant for undergraduate labor studies, I've written a position letter to our pension trustees regarding the interpretation of a particular section of the members' pension plan, I've helped a former UMWA employee get long term disability, and I've advised the president's office regarding a request from a movie studio that wanted to use the UMWA logo in a movie. This kind of diversity helps keep the job interesting and fresh!

"Another great aspect of this job is that you aren't continuously chained to your desk hundreds of miles from where the UMWA members actually live and work. For instance, within six weeks of starting here, I had the chance to tour a coal mine. I spent hours underground talking to miners and getting a small taste of what they have to face daily. I still can't say I understand what it is to work in those conditions every day, but I have a much better understanding than I did before. I also regularly get opportunities to travel to our members' hometowns, to talk with them, take their statements, and try to help them with their problems. Being able to do this every so often keeps me motivated during the periods when I work in the office. It helps me remember why I am doing this and who I am doing it for."

Writers Guild of America, west

7000 West Third Street • Los Angeles, CA 90048-4329
Phone: 213-951-4000 • Fax: 213-782-4801 • Web site: www.wga.org

WRITERS GUILD OF AMERICA, WEST IN A NUTSHELL . . .

The Writer's Guild of America is the union that represents "America's Storytellers"—writers in motion picture, broadcast, cable, and news media, covering approximately 90% of all U.S. film and television production in entertainment and news. It has over 8,000 members.

It was founded in 1933, when the Screen Writers Guild was established in 1933 when 10 writers met at the Hollywood Roosevelt Hotel. A month later 100 writers reconvened at the Roosevelt and founded the guild. It received its status as a union in 1937. It merged with several other television and radio unions to become the Writers Guild of America, east and west in 1953. The two unions negotiate together where joint jurisdictions exist.

WORD ON THE STREET . . .

"It's a phenomenal job. People *love* working there."

NUTS AND BOLTS

President: Daniel C. Petrie, Jr.
Executive Director: Brian Walton (who is an attorney)

General Counsel: Doreen Braverman (J.D., Wayne State University)
Personnel Director: Melinda Roberts

HIRING . . .

The Guild provides an excellent opportunity for law school graduates, because in their own words, "The Guild employs lawyers in a wide variety of departments. The executive director, assistant executive director, general counsel, director of legal services, associate counsel, business representative, law clerk, director of credits, director of contracts administration, contracts administrator, executive administrator for employment diversity, director of industry alliances, and director of residuals are all law school graduates.

"Because the Guild affords a stimulating and challenging work environment which is enjoyed by many, there is a relatively low turnover rate.

"Those departments that either expand or replace employees, or want to hire an attorney, more often than not hire lawyers with experience. Occasionally, departments other than the Legal Department do hire new law school graduates. In fact, the Legal Department prefers to hire laterals so that we can concentrate on educating new employees about the Guild, the work it does and the intricacies of its 400+ page collective bargaining agreement, rather than teaching them how to be a lawyer!

"When hiring for our Legal Department, we look for laterals with 3 to 10 years of experience. Other departments in the Guild have hired new admittees or lawyers with only a couple of years of experience, but by and large those attorneys are not engaged in the practice of law in the strict sense; that is, they are not handling litigation or arbitrations. The laterals we have hired generally have either a background in labor or employment law, or have prior work experience in the entertainment industry that gives them insight into the particular types of issues faced by the Guild and the writers. Examples would be lawyers hired to work in the Guild's residuals or credits departments, some of whom came to the Guild with experience in the residuals or credits departments of studios or production companies."

Where new attorneys come from: "Other than doing the occasional on-campus interviews for law clerks, we don't do on-campus interviews. Although we get a steady stream of unsolicited resumes, we usually recruit from ads in the *Los Angeles Daily Journal* or the entertainment industry trade papers."

BUCKS . . .

It varies greatly depending on the department and the level of experience and knowledge the candidate brings to the job. Salaries are generally in the $35,000 to 65,000 range. Because the WGA is a nonprofit labor union, "We can't and don't compete with law firm salaries. By the same token, we don't expect people to forego a personal life as some law firms do."

WHAT THEY LOOK FOR IN NEW HIRES . . .

"We rarely, if ever, ask a candidate for a copy of his/her law school transcript. We tend to feel that a candidate's accomplishments as a lawyer are more important than what grade they got in civil procedure. We do look at the school from which the candidate graduated, but that isn't in and of itself determinative of whether someone gets an interview. We often look for a commitment to labor unions or plaintiff-side employment law when recruiting for our Legal Department as well as for experience handling arbitrations and/or trials. Other Guild Departments look for knowledge and prior experience applicable to the particular issues likely to be encountered."

SUMMER INTERNSHIPS . . .

The WGA occasionally hires law students for summer jobs to assist the lawyers in the Legal Department. They do research, interview witnesses from time to time, draft court documents, analyze court cases, and perform other, similar duties. Summer clerks receive approximately $12 to $15 per hour and work 35 hours per week. While 1Ls have "occasionally" been hired for the summer program, summer interns tend to be 2Ls.

The WGA also employs law students part-time during the school year in return for school credit.

WHAT LAW SCHOOL GRADUATES SAY ABOUT WORKING FOR THE WGA . . .

"There are so many attorneys at the Guild working in different capacities. Only about half of the lawyers actually work in the Legal Department. It is rewarding to know that many of the skills you learn in law school are transferable to different areas. The Guild is a warm, friendly, almost family environment with fairly regular, humane hours."

"The Guild offers a bright and friendly physical environment—lots of light, space and air, great views, beautiful floral arrangements all around, and great food left over from board and committee meetings!"

"This is a place where innovative thinking and intelligent risk-taking are encouraged and rewarded. I attempt to negotiate access programs with employers at the studios, networks and production companies to help increase opportunities in film and television for protected class writers."

"We are facing an increasingly anti-affirmative action political climate. So when Reverend Jesse Jackson asked to meet with the guilds and affected communities in 1996, the WGA responded and hosted a series of meetings to provide information and suggestions relative to employment practices in the industry. This led, in turn, to the announcement of the "Hollywood Rainbow Covenant," by WGA's executive director, calling on Hollywood to "tell ALL of America's stories written by ALL of America's storytellers. This was done in the face of much criticism from industry employers and even some guild members. It is this 'courage under fire' displayed over and over again by WGA leadership that makes this an exciting, fulfilling, and challenging work environment."

"Among other benefits we have is that there are no billable hours. This translates into a number of different things that make this a great place to work. At a firm, the emphasis is as much on how much you work as it is on the quality of the work because the more you work, the more money the firm makes. You, the lawyer, are the commodity and they want to sell as much of you as they can. As a result, the tendency is to expect a young lawyer to ignore a personal life. Here, the main emphasis is on the quality of your work. The atmosphere allows, even encourages, the employees to have a personal, family life."

"Another thing that shows what makes the WGA great is the retention factor. Look how many employees have been here for years! I think it's because they are treated well, with respect and dignity, that you don't find at law firms."

PUBLIC INTEREST ORGANIZATIONS IN ONE (OR JUST A FEW) CITIES:

American Judicature Society

180 N. Michigan Avenue, Suite 600 • Chicago, IL 60601
Phone: 312-558-6900 • Fax: 312-558-9175 • Web site: www.ajs.org

WHAT DO THEY DO?

The focus of the American Judicature Society is promoting the effective administration of justice. Their primary areas of specialty are judicial selection, judicial conduct and ethics, judicial independence, jury studies, and alternative dispute resolution ("ADR").

WORD ON THE STREET . . .

"They hire lawyers all the time. They do fabulous work!"

NUTS AND BOLTS

Director: Sandra Ratcliff Daffron
How many people work there: 4 (all women, 1 minority)

Hours: Typically a 9 a.m. to 5 p.m. workday, for a total of 35 to 40 hours a week, although they spend more hours at the office as needed for special projects.

FULL-TIME POSITIONS . . .

They hire full-time attorneys "periodically" for various projects. They seek law school graduates with a special interest in the judicial system and social silence (primarily political science and sociology).

To find out about openings: Ask at your Career Services Office, or check Chicago newspapers, or send a letter and a resume.

Starting pay: $ (Under $35,000)

PART-TIME POSITIONS DURING LAW SCHOOL . . .

They have one or two students working at American Judicature Society during the school year. For more information on internship opportunities, check out their web site.

The Arms Control Association

11 DuPont Circle • Washington, D.C. 20036
Phone: 202-463-8270 • Fax: 202-463-8273
E-mail: aca@armscontrol.org • Web site: www.armscontrol.org

WHAT DO THEY DO?

As the name suggests, the Arms Control Association ("ACA") is a national nonpartisan membership organization dedicated to arms control issues. Issues the ACA is currently focusing on include strategic nuclear force reductions, ballistic missile defense, nuclear non-proliferation issues, conventional arms control, chemical and biological weapons, and ballistic missiles. Through its public education and media programs and its magazine, *Arms Control Today,* ACA provides policymakers, the press, and the interested public with authoritative information, analysis, and commentary on arms control proposals, negotiations and agreements, and related national security issues. In addition to regular press briefings that ACA holds on major arms control developments, the Association's staff provides commentary and analysis on a broad spectrum of issues for journalists and scholars both in the U.S. and abroad.

INTERNSHIP POSITIONS . . .

The ACA hires interns for "stipended" positions on a regular basis. As an intern, you are involved in all facets of the ACA's work, including researching and writing about national security, defense and arms control; assisting in preparing and editing ACA's monthly journal *Arms Control Today;* communicating with the press, the government and other arms control groups; monitoring activity on Capitol Hill; and supporting senior analysts in a variety of administrative tasks.

Hours: Ideally, 30 to 40 per week, but the program is also available part-time (as few as 16 hours per week). Fall internships run from the end of August through December (applications should be in by the first week of August); winter internships go from January through May (with applications in by the middle of December); and summer internships last from May or June through August, and (applications should be in by the first Friday in May). Missing a deadline is not fatal.

Applications: Include a cover letter, resume (with relevant coursework), and a 3 to 5 page writing sample.

Pay: You are compensated for commuting expenses and receive a $5 per day stipend.

Center for International Environmental Law

1367 Connecticut Avenue, N.W., Suite 300 • Washington, D.C. 20036
Phone: 202-785-8700 • Fax: 202-785-8701 • Web site: www.econet.apc.org/ciel

WHAT DO THEY DO?

The Center for International Environmental Law ("CIEL") is a public interest, not-for-profit environmental law firm founded in 1989. It's goals are fourfold: first, to solve environmental problems and promote sustainable societies through the use of law; second, to incorporate fundamental principles of ecology and democracy into international law; third, to strengthen national environmental law systems and support public interest movements around the world; and fourth, to educate and train public-interest-minded environmental lawyers.

CIEL provides a full range of environmental legal services in both international and comparative national law, including: policy research and publication, advice and advocacy, education and training, and institution building.

To achieve its goals, CIEL works throughout the world with non-governmental organizations, international institutions, and states, especially developing nations, and those with economies in transition.

CIEL's program areas include global commons, biodiversity and wildlife, trade and environment, international financial institutions, and policy analysis and capacity building. CIEL's work covers more than 60 countries on six continents, with an emphasis on the Western Hemisphere, Central and Eastern Europe and the Newly Independent States, and Asia.

NUTS AND BOLTS

President: Durwood J. Zaelke
How many attorneys work there: 15, and 5 "of counsel."

FULL-TIME POSITIONS . . .

CIEL hires as needed. Check its web site for openings.

INTERNSHIPS OR EXTERNSHIPS . . .

CIEL's intern/extern program gives law students an excellent opportunity to learn about international environmental law. You work full-or part-time during the school year, usually receiving class credit. Summer interns typically work full-time through the summer. Virtually all internships and externships are volunteer.

To apply: Send a letter, resume, and writing sample to: Dana Clark, at the address listed at the start of this entry.

FELLOWSHIPS . . .

CIEL offers a few year-long fellowships to recent law school graduates with a demonstrated commitment to pursuing a career in public interest international environmental law. The CIEL program is designed to give promising new lawyers the experience and expertise necessary for a successful international environmental law career.

To apply: Send a letter, resume, and writing sample to: Durwood Zaelke, at the address from the top of this listing.

Consumers Union

101 Truman Avenue • Yonkers, NY 10703
914-378-2000 • Web site: www.consunion.org

WHAT DO THEY DO?

You know Consumers Union best through its very popular magazine, *Consumer Reports*. A "Best Buy" ranking from *Consumer Reports* is a company's dream, and a "Not Acceptable"—well, remember the Suzuki Samurai? Sales of that car dropped out of sight when *Consumer Reports* revealed its tendency to roll over. You heard all about that. But what you may *not* know is that on top of putting out the magazine, Consumers Union engages in all kinds of consumer advocacy, investigative reporting, and the like, through offices in three locations: Washington, D.C.; Austin, Texas; and San Francisco, California.

The Consumer Policy Institute at Consumers Union's headquarters in Yonkers, New York, promotes the consumer interest through research and education projects—conferences, policy papers, and comment on legislative and regulatory initiatives.

WHAT DO ATTORNEYS DO THERE?

Attorneys at Consumers Union work as consumer advocates, tackling consumer issues that are regional, national, and even international in scope. They testify before federal and state legislative and regulatory bodies, petition government agencies, and file lawsuits on behalf of the consumer interest.

To apply: Contact them by mail, or through their web site (address above).

DNA—People's Legal Services, Inc.

P.O. Box 306 • Window Rock, AZ 86515
Phone: 520-871-4151

WHAT DO THEY DO?

Ignore what you're thinking about the letters "DNA"—*this* DNA doesn't have anything to do with the human genome project, or bringing back dinosaurs based on amber-trapped mosquitoes. Instead, *this* DNA provides free civil legal services to low-income members of the Navajo Nation and Hopi, Jicarillo Apache, Hualapai, Navasupai, Kaibab Painte, and San Juan Southern Painte tribes Reservation. DNA works in the areas of domestic relations and government benefits, and it also handles cases involving environmental, discrimination, and Native American jurisdictional issues. Different projects focus on discreet legal problems, including disability, housing, consumer, and youth issues.

DNA works out of nine offices throughout the Southwest, including three other offices in Arizona: Chinle, Keams Canyon, and Tuba City.

NUTS AND BOLTS

Director: Asa Begaye
How many attorneys work there: Approximately 40.

FULL-TIME POSITIONS . . .

They hire as needed.

SUMMER INTERNSHIPS . . .

DNA has 12 to 15 interns at any given time.

What you get to do: Interview clients, draft research memos and pleadings, investigate facts, and with supervision you get to represent clients at administrative hearings. Law students report that the internships offer the opportunity to do a whole variety of different kinds of projects, from juvenile court cases to arranging plea agreements to counseling clients.

Weekly pay: You need to seek a Public Interest Fellowship and work study funding. You do get free housing.

To apply: Send a letter, resume, references, and a writing sample by February 1.

Earthjustice Legal Defense Fund (formerly the Sierra Club)

180 Montgomery Street, Suite 1400 • San Francisco, CA 94104-4209
Phone: 415-627-6700 • Web site: www.earthjustice.org

WHAT DO THEY DO?

Earthjustice was established as the Sierra Club Legal Defense Fund in 1971, as an independent, nonprofit law firm to serve the growing environmental movement. Earthjustice lawyers and staff have pioneered the use of environmental laws to protect people and our natural world. Over the last quarter century, the Legal Defense Fund has been involved in the most important environmental protection lawsuits in the country. Representing more than 800 clients, the Legal Defense Fund has been at the center of major battles to protect the air we breathe, the water we drink, the communities we live and work in, and the special places we enjoy.

Its current cases include challenging timber sales in a grizzly bear habitat in Montana, stopping excessive sewage discharges into San Francisco Bay, preventing draining of High Sierra lakes by the El Dorado County water agency in California, challenging Utah counties' bulldozing roads, preventing siting of a hazardous waste facility in Colorado, and many, many more.

Earthjustice currently has nine offices across the country, including: Bozeman, MT; Denver, CO; Honolulu, HI; Juneau, AK; New Orleans, LA; San Francisco, CA; Seattle WA; Tallahassee, FL; and Washington, D.C.

WORD ON THE STREET . . .

"They require experience, but it's the best place for environmental defense work, bar none."

NUTS AND BOLTS

Acting president: Buck Parker

How many attorneys work there: Earthjustice employs about 30 attorneys in its nine offices.

FULL-TIME POSITIONS . . .

Earthjustice hires a few new attorneys every year, at various offices. Check the web site for current job listings.

Starting pay: $$ ($35-50,000) They also offer benefits including disability, maternity, paternity, as well as life, disability, health, and dental insurance.

To apply: Send a resume, recent writing sample (less than 10 pages), and a list of three references.

SUMMER INTERNSHIPS . . .

Earthjustice hires both 1Ls and 2Ls as summer interns. The weekly salary is around $400, although Earthjustice encourages applicants to apply for outside funding (check your law school Career Services Office for availability).

To apply: Send a resume, a recent under-10-page writing sample, and a list of three references. Check the web site for contact names at each office.

PART-TIME WORK DURING THE SCHOOL YEAR . . .

Earthjustice hires law students part-time during the semester as externs. To apply, send a resume, a recent under-10-page writing sample, and a list of three references. Check the web site for contact names at each office. Earthjustice encourages externs to apply for outside funding (check your law school Career Services Office for availability).

Employment Law Center

The Legal Aid Society of San Francisco
1663 Mission Street, Suite 400 • San Francisco, CA 94103
Phone: 415-864-8848

WHAT DO THEY DO?

The Employment Law Center ("ELC") handles class action and law reform suits on behalf of low-income workers. Cases cover all kinds of employment discrimination people experience in the workplace, including race and sex discrimination, sexual harassment, language rights, sexual orientation harassment, and wrongful use of the title 'independent contractor.' The ELC files cases with both the California and federal court systems.

NUTS AND BOLTS

How many attorneys work there: About 5.

FULL-TIME POSITIONS . . .

They hire as needed.

INTERNSHIPS . . .

They hire approximately 10 interns.

What you get to do: Student interns do legal research and writing for ELC cases, participate in strategy sessions, interviewing clients, conducting discovery, deposing witnesses, and weekly litigation meetings. Interns also act as employment counselors to working people with questions or problems concerning employment, through ELC's direct service project— the Worker's Rights Clinic. You are trained for this Clinic and you provide advice to callers under the supervision of ELC staff attorneys.

Weekly pay: Work/study, grants for which ELC pays required stipends, or volunteer positions.

What they look for: Strong interest and ideally experience in public interest, either in the form of a paid or volunteer position, as well as excellent legal research and writing skills.

How to apply: Send resume, cover letter, legal writing sample, and three references (including one for legal research and writing experience).

Florida Public Service Commission

Capital Circle Office Center • 2540 Shumard Oak Boulevard
Tallahassee, FL 32399-0854
Phone: 850-413-6044 • Fax: 850-413-6250 • Web site: www2.scri.net/psc/

WHAT DO THEY DO?

The Florida Public Service Commission is regarded as being on the leading edge of utility regulation nationwide. The work the FPSC does is a balancing act. Under Florida law, the Commission regulates every investor-owned electric and gas utility, every telecommunications utility in the state, and those investor-owned water and wastewater utilities in those counties which have opted to transfer such jurisdiction to the Commission. The Commission also regulates the rate structure of electric and gas service provided by municipalities and rural electric authority (REA) cooperatives. The Commission's mandate is to set fair, just, and reasonable rates so that adequate utility service is provided to consumers.

NUTS AND BOLTS

Chairman: Julia L. Johnson
General Counsel: Robert Vandiver

Hiring people:

Noreen S. Davis, Director, Division of Legal Services,
phone: 850-413-6199, e-mail: ndavis@PSC.State.FL.US
David E. Smith, Director, Division of Appeals,
phone: 850-413-6245, e-mail: dsmith@PSC.State.FL.US
How many attorneys work there: 27 (15 women, 5 minorities, 1 disabled)

FULL-TIME POSITIONS . . .

They hire as needed.

To find out about openings: Contact either the Florida Job Services Offices; other State of Florida agency personnel offices; county offices throughout Florida; law schools throughout Florida; and the FPSC web site (www.scri.net/psc).

What they look for: Class rank isn't very important. They look for bright, eager, self-starters who enjoy a challenge, and can work in a team setting.

HOURS AND BUCKS . . .

Hours: They work a 2,080 hour annual minimum, but they stay until the "job is done." Flex-time schedules are permitted, and the FPSC has a reputation for being understanding when it comes to family issues and juggling schedules to accommodate family obligations.

Starting pay: $ (Under $35,000); Florida has an attractive benefits package.

SUMMER INTERNSHIPS . . .

The FPSC hires summer clerks sporadically, as well as part-time clerks during the school year. When they do have intern positions, they are unpaid; instead, interns receive class credit.

WHAT IT'S LIKE TO WORK THERE . . .

The FPSC is managed by five commissioners (who are appointed by the governor), general counsel, division directors, and bureau chiefs, and it has 380 employees and an annual budget of $23 million. The Commission has quasi-legislative and quasi-judicial, as well as executive powers and duties. In its quasi-legislative capacity, the PSC makes rules governing utility operations. In a quasi-judicial manner, the PSC hears and decides complaints, issues written orders similar to court orders, and may have its decisions appealed to the First District Court of Appeals and to the Florida Supreme Court. As an executive agency, the PSC enforces state laws affecting the utility industries.

The FPSC is divided into several different divisions. Attorneys who work for the PSC are concentrated in the divisions headed by the General Counsel, Robert D. Vandiver: the Division of Appeals and the Division of Legal Services, which itself has three bureaus: electric and gas, communications, and water and wastewater. Staff attorneys in each of these bureaus handle a variety of responsibilities, including hearings and making oral presentations to the Commissioners.

Attorneys with the FPSC rave about the level of advice and mentoring they get from more senior people, the cooperation and teamwork they enjoy, and their flexibility with hours—such that FPSC lawyers with small children don't miss school functions!

G.L.A.D. (Gay & Lesbian Advocates & Defenders)

P.O. Box • Boston, MA 02112
Phone: 617-426-1350 • Web site: www.glad.org

WHAT DO THEY DO?

G.L.A.D. is the leading New England legal rights organization for lesbians, gay men, bisexuals, and people with HIV. Its mission is to achieve full equality and justice for all people in these groups through impact litigation and education.

G.L.A.D. attorneys handle lawsuits involving sexual orientation discrimination as well as cases involving HIV or AIDS discrimination or invasion of privacy and confidentiality.

G.L.A.D. also has a public education program that hosts educational forums on the law pertaining to lesbians, gay men, bisexuals, and people with HIV and AIDS. In addition, G.L.A.D. operates a toll-free telephone information hotline with a lawyer referral service serving Massachusetts, Maine, New Hampshire, Vermont, Rhode Island, and Connecticut; the attorneys are experienced in representing gays, lesbians, bisexuals, transgenders, and people with HIV/AIDS.

NUTS AND BOLTS

Director: Gary Buseck
How many attorneys work there: About 9

FULL-TIME POSITIONS . . .

They hire as needed.

INTERNSHIPS . . .

G.L.A.D. typically has two interns.
Weekly pay: Work study, as funds permit.
What you get to do: You get involved with all facets of civil rights litigation. Your primary responsibilities include researching and writing legal

memoranda. You also get to write pleadings, and take part in client interviews, depositions, and other litigation work.

How to apply: Send cover letter, resume, and writing sample by March 1.

Human Rights Watch

350 Fifth Avenue 34th Floor • New York, NY 10118-3299
Phone: 212-290-4700 • Web site: www.hrw.org

WHAT DO THEY DO?

Human Rights Watch ("HRW") exposes and works to stop human rights abuses in over 70 countries around the world. HRW's disclosures have made it an essential source of information for anyone concerned with human rights. Its experienced staff of over 100 regional experts, lawyers, journalists, and linguists helps foster understanding of why abuses break out and, most important, what must be done to curtail them. Through exposure in the press and tough advocacy campaigns, HRW seeks to make governments pay a heavy price in reputation and legitimacy if they violate the rights of their people.

Some of HRW's activities in the last few years include:

Germany: HRW documented the brutal physical assaults and murders of foreigners at the hands of right-wing and neo-Nazi movements. Its widely-publicized reports helped to generate pressure on the German government to safeguard its non-German population and to provide the moral leadership needed to promote racial tolerance.

Haiti: HRW successfully worked to avoid an amnesty that would have allowed the military permanently to evade accountability for the mass murder, rape, torture, and arbitrary detention it committed before the restoration of the Aristide government.

United States: HRW disclosed abhorrent conditions in 'super-maximum' prisons, rape of women prisoners, unjustified killings by Border Patrol agents, and racial discrimination in capital and drug cases.

NUTS AND BOLTS

Executive Director: Ken Roth
How many attorneys work there: Approximately 12.
Other than New York, HRW has offices in Brussels, Dushanbe, Hong Kong, London, Los Angeles, Moscow, Rio de Janeiro, and Washington.

POSITIONS . . .

Full-time: HRW periodically hires new attorneys; last year, it hired 5.

Starting pay: $$ ($35-50,000), along with benefits including disability, maternity, paternity, as well as life, disability, health, and dental insurance.

They list job openings on their web site.

HRW also has both summer interns and volunteers.

International Human Rights Law Group

1200 18th Street N.W., Suite 602 • Washington, D.C. 20036
Phone: 202-822-4600 • Fax: 202-822-4606 • E-mail: ihrlg@aol.com

WHAT DO THEY DO?

The International Human Rights Law Group ("Law Group") is a non-profit organization engaged in human rights advocacy, litigation, and training around the world. Current projects include a comprehensive roundtable discussion on trafficking in women organized by WRAP (the Group's Women's Rights Advocacy Program) and the Group's Women's Law Fellow, attended by experts around the country; trainings and monitoring for upcoming elections in the Atlantic Coast region of Nicaragua; and preparing a baseline survey of the justice system in the Democratic Republic of Congo.

As these suggest, Law Group projects seek to build the capacity of human rights advocates in countries around the world to transform their societies from within, strengthen legal systems in developing countries to better enforce human rights, promote the human rights of women through legal and political initiatives, and expand the scope of human rights protections at the national and international levels. Since its founding in 1978 by Richard B. Lillich, the Group has worked in more than 80 countries and on 5 continents. It currently has projects in Bosnia, Cambodia, Congo, and Nicaragua.

The Law Group is funded by grants from private foundations, donations from individuals and law firms, and USAID for the Group's project in Cambodia.

NUTS AND BOLTS

Executive Director: Gay J. McDougall

Hiring Person: Ria P. Burghardt, Executive Officer
How many attorneys work there: 45 (17 women, 27 minorities)
Of these attorneys, 9 work in Washington, D.C. (7 women, 2 minorities).
The rest work in the field.

FULL-TIME POSITIONS . . .

They hire as needed.

To find out about openings: Job openings are posted in trade publications like International Career Opportunities and the International Jobs Gazette. They also accept resumes.

What they look for: Grades and Law Review are not the most important credentials—although they certainly don't hurt! What is more important is a demonstrated interest in the field of human rights, such as work overseas, independent projects, and previous experience in the field of human rights. Public interest work in general is important as well. For field officers or program coordinators, work in the field and advanced studies in either the region (*i.e.*, Latin America, Africa, Asia) or human rights are essential. Generally, recent graduates are not considered for positions other than program assistants unless they have previous, *relevant* work experience prior to attending law school. There is also a short list of "Don'ts": Arrogance isn't appreciated in this highly-qualified but very laid-back staff; flashy clothes generally are a bad idea; and, perhaps most importantly, coming unprepared—for instance, not knowing what type of work the Law Group does—is an immediate reason not to hire.

Note that the Law Group hires both attorneys and non-attorneys, often for the same position. Its regional program coordinators, based in Washington, D.C., are hired based on their knowledge of the area where the field office is located. Currently, they have projects in Bosnia, Cambodia, Congo, and Nicaragua. Field officers are hired (lawyers and non-lawyers) based on their knowledge of the region or specific field of interest depending on the need. If someone is not an attorney (s)he always has a post-graduate degree in the area where the Law Group has a program or in human rights and international advocacy. Most of the Law Group's field officers are attorneys with field experience.

Also, administrative positions at the Law Group are filled by attorneys and non-attorneys. For example, the executive director, Gay McDougall, is an attorney, but the Group's development officers are not.

HOURS AND BUCKS . . .

The hours vary by program; for instance, the three staff members who work on the Group's Women's Rights Advocacy Program tend to work very late nights and weekends, as well as travel regularly. However, the office generally gets going at 9 a.m., and closes around 7 p.m. or later. They allow attorneys to work part-time on an as-needed basis, but this doesn't happen often.

Starting pay: $ (Under $35,000)

SUMMER POSITIONS . . .

They have a volunteer summer intern program, which typically has 6 to 10 interns. Last year, they had 13 summer interns. They only hire 2Ls for interns, not 1Ls.

PART-TIME POSITIONS DURING LAW SCHOOL . . .

They have interns year-round—2 to 3 during the spring and fall semester—but they do not regularly hire for pay.

WHAT IT'S LIKE TO WORK THERE . . .

"Our days span an extremely broad spectrum of experiences. For instance, a field member in Cambodia would start the day early to maximize the time of day that is relatively cool. Later in the afternoon (after a break mid-day), you'd expect to visit the courts, evaluate trainings with new defenders, and coordinate activities with the new Women's Litigation Unit and Resource Centre. In Washington, the project coordinator for Africa can be found behind her desk and stacks of paper, mostly correspondence from the field, requests for information, and research on funders . . . later in the day she might attend a meeting with representatives from other nongovernmental organizations, such as the National Endowment for Democracy ("NED") or USAID . . . perhaps a press release is being sent to Members of Congress regarding a governmental crackdown in Kinshasa, Congo that effects the human rights community. In Nicaragua, our field officer rides on horseback to reach the capital of Managua to meet with delegation members for election training. In Bosnia, a meeting with the Office of the Ombudsperson reveals a difficulty in moving forward litigating a particular case. In Chile, our representative is presenting the closing arguments before the Inter-American Court in the case of someone who has "disappeared" during the former dictatorship in Guatemala. Obviously, due to the large geographical distances and cultural contexts, a 'typical' day is hard to define here! The common link is that we are very dedicated and believe in the world we're doing. That is true no matter where in the world you find us."

"One year, one of the program associates for WRAP who is from Pakistan invited staff members to her house to celebrate a traditional Muslim holiday. We all cooked different dishes together, henna-dyed our hands, and dressed up in her saris."

"Our program director (who happens to be male and British) had an official 'Law Group field trip' to the movie theater to see 'Spice World.' Despite the fact he is technically the deputy director of the organization, he signed the memo discussing the field trip 'Spice Director.'"

"Every year in May, the Law Group holds its major fundraising event, the Human Rights Awards Dinner. It is a formal event which more than 400 people attend, including Members of Congress and representatives of the legal profession, the diplomatic community, and many non-governmental organizations that work on human rights and related issues. Afterwards, however, it is a tradition with the staff to have a rollicking party that generally spills over into area nightclubs into the early hours of the morning. It is something we look forward to every year after all the work preparing for the event."

"It's not the place to work if you expect a big support staff. If you need something done, you do it yourself."

"We work longer hours for less pay than most people in law firms, but our work is very interesting and rewarding. For instance, our special projects officer (who mainly works with our office in Bosnia and Herzegovina) is directly involved in advocating human rights protections that were instituted as part of the Dayton Agreement. A recent successful campaign carried out by our office highlighted the misinterpretation of the Dayton Agreement in terms of public education for children. The Minister of Education began segregating children of different backgrounds, and our field staff worked to change this policy and bring media attention to the issue. Since then, the practice has been stopped. It's easy to put the hours and pay in perspective when your work is inherently rewarding."

"The Law Group is a truly flexible and supportive place to work. Everyone is very tolerant of different lifestyles and is patient with those who may not share the same knowledge. We all learn from each other and it is a warm, supportive place to be. As staff members come from different parts of the world and have different backgrounds (for example, our office manager is German and has a background in anthropology, and our accountant is a Cambodian citizen of France) there is an understanding that every person has something valuable to share."

★　　★　　★　　★　　★

Legal Assistance
Foundation of Chicago

111 W. Jackson Blvd., 3rd Floor • Chicago, IL 60604
Phone: 312-341-1070 • Fax: 312-341-1041

WHAT DO THEY DO?

"For the most vulnerable people in Chicago, laws mean nothing unless they are enforced, and it is our job to enforce the laws the legislatures have passed to protect the poor"—Legal Assistance Foundation of Chicago, Executive Director Sheldon H. Roodman.

As that quote suggests, the Legal Assistance Foundation of Chicago ("LAFC") makes the promise of "equal justice under the law" a reality. Over the last 30-plus years, the LAFC has helped hundreds of thousands of Chicago's poorest and most vulnerable men, women, and children; each year, it helps approximately 40,000 men, women, and children.

There is no "typical" LAFC client. Clients include homeowners facing foreclosure, families who need government benefits to survive, tenants facing eviction, women being abused in body and spirit, migrant farmworkers, disabled people, and homeless people. Some have been poor all their lives; others were formerly middle-class, facing, for the first time, the prospect of no job, no home, no future. They have one thing in common: they are all very poor and they all need legal assistance to keep their lives together. LAFC provides an enormously cost-effective way to help thousands of Chicago's most vulnerable residents help themselves.

The LAFC is primarily funded by Congress, but because federal funding has been reduced in recent years to *all* organizations providing civil legal services for the poor, the LAFC also raises funds privately. It boasts an exceptionally low rate of administrative/fundraising expenses: under 6%. Virtually all of every dollar donated goes directly to program services for the poor.

NUTS AND BOLTS

Executive Director: Sheldon H. Roodman
Hiring Person: Alan A. Alop, phone: 312-341-1070
How many attorneys work there: 62 (34 women, 11 minorities)
Attorneys work out of four offices. Central (33—19 women, 4 minorities), Northwest (8), South Side (10), West Side (8).

FOR FULL-TIME POSITIONS:

The LAFC hires approximately 6 to 10 full-time attorneys every year. While the LAFC occasionally interviews on campus at law schools, interested applicants are more likely to hear about job openings from bar associations, their law school Career Services Office, job fairs, public interest-oriented web sites, the National Clearinghouse for Legal Services, the Public Interest Clearinghouse, and similar publications. They welcome letters and resumes.

What they look for: "LAFC looks for new attorneys who have demonstrated a commitment to providing legal services for the poor during law school, and the summers between law schools years, either by working at legal services programs or public interest law programs, or other examples of demonstrated interest in providing legal services to the poor. LAFC is also interested in individuals who have demonstrated creativity, initiative, and tenacity in their lives and law school experiences."

HOURS AND BUCKS . . .

The hours worked tend to hover around 2,000 per year. The office hours tend to be from 9 a.m. to 5:30 or 6 p.m., and while the hours may vary, depending on each lawyer's responsibilities, the hours don't vary greatly.

While LAFC does not offer part-time work at entry level, it has generous parental leave and part-time policies for ongoing employees. Many attorneys with young families choose to work for LAFC, often after a stint in private practice, as a way of striking a reasonable balance between personal commitments and professional satisfaction.

Starting salary: $ (Under $35,000).

SUMMER INTERNSHIP/PART-TIME LAW STUDENT POSITIONS . . .

The LAFC's summer intern program employed 20 interns last summer (of whom one or two will return full-time after graduation).

Summer salary: $350 to 400 per week.

Both 1Ls and 2Ls are hired for the summer program.

The deadline for summer applications is January 15th.

For part-time law student positions, the LAFC typically employs six students during the school year on a part-time basis. The positions are both paid and work-study.

WHAT LAWYERS SAY ABOUT WORKING FOR THE LAFC . . .

"Anything can happen on a typical day at LAFC: making court appearances, attending strategy meetings, editing briefs, networking with other public interest groups, drafting agency policy, or writing grant proposals. Nobody has ever had to do a six-month document review in a strip mall in Detroit."

"Working at LAFC is very different from being a junior associate in a private firm. The pay is less, but more than you might guess, and commensurate with many government and teaching jobs. The work is hard, but people go home at the end of the day. There are no 'billable hours requirements.' Autonomy comes from learning a particular area of the law thoroughly, not from having a large book of business. There are plenty of poor clients with legal problems to go around."

"A substantial part of LAFC's funding comes from the Legal Services Corporation, a federal entity. We value creativity in finding alternative ways to deliver effective legal services to poor people."

Minnesota Advocates for Human Rights

310 Fourth Avenue South, Suite 1000 • Minneapolis, MN 55415-1012
Phone: 612-341-3302

WHAT DO THEY DO?

Minnesota Advocates for Human Rights is a volunteer-based, nonprofit organization of more than 1,200 advocates dedicated to promoting and protecting human rights worldwide. They work impartially and independently on projects supporting the protection of internationally-recognized human rights. They work to prevent human rights violations, including torture, executions, genocide, and wrongful detention. They also work to protect the human rights of refugees, torture victims, political dissidents, women, children, oppressed ethnic groups, indigenous peoples, and others who are vulnerable.

In pursuit of these goals, Minnesota Advocates investigates and exposes human rights violations, promotes the universal acceptance of international standards, and trains and assists groups that protect human rights. The Minnesota Advocates administers the following projects: the building immigrant awareness and support project; the child mortality project; the death penalty project; the Mexico project; the partners in human rights education project; the refugee and asylum project; the women's human rights project; and the conflict prevention project.

NUTS AND BOLTS

Executive Director: Jack Rendler
How many attorneys work there: Approximately 8
What the attorneys do: The practice areas include Criminal Law, Education, International Human Rights, Immigration Law, and Women's Issues.
For full-time positions: Minnesota Advocates hires periodically; they hired two new attorneys last year.
Starting pay: $ (Under $35,000)

Minnesota Advocates also has summer interns and volunteers; send inquiries.

NAACP Legal Defense & Education Fund

99 Hudson Street, 16th Floor • New York, NY 10013
Phone: 212-219-1900 • Web site: www.ldfla.org
(this is actually for the Los Angeles office, but it offers information
on the NAACP Legal Defense & Education Fund in general)

WHAT DO THEY DO?

The right to a quality education . . . the right to adequate health care . . . the right to meaningful job opportunities . . . the right to live in the community you choose . . . the right to a fair trial by a jury of your peers . . . the right to freely choose your elected representatives.

All are part and parcel of our nation's historic commitment to justice and equality. Many of the freedoms cherished by all Americans—black and white, rich and poor—have the force of law thanks to the work of the NAACP Legal Defense and Educational Fund, Inc. ("LDF"). For more than half a century, LDF has used the law as a powerful tool to pry open doors of opportunity long closed to African Americans, other people of color, women, and the poor.

LDF was founded in 1940 under the leadership of the late Thurgood Marshall, who later became the first black United States Supreme Court Justice. As LDF's first Director-Counsel, Marshall led the successful campaign to eradicate the "separate but equal" doctrine that formed the basis for segregation. One of LDF's most significant early victories was the landmark 1954 Supreme Court ruling *in Brown v. Board of Education*. LDF defended the late Rev. Dr. Martin Luther King, Jr., and other civil rights activists who put their lives on the line for freedom, and helped translate the civil rights laws of the 1960s into instruments of real change.

Today, LDF is committed to staying on the cutting edge of the movement for racial justice. LDF fights for equality and empowerment for African-Americans and other disenfranchised groups in the areas of education, employment, criminal justice, voting rights, housing, health care, and environmental justice. Headquartered in New York City, LDF enhances its effectiveness through the office in Washington, D.C., and the Western Regional Office in Los Angeles.

Litigation, the foundation of LDF's strength, remains the central element of its efforts. LDF attorneys are vigorously pursuing a docket of hundreds of cases. LDF has participated in more cases before the U.S. Supreme Court than any institution other than the Solicitor General's office—and it has won an extraordinary number of those cases.

LDF is *not* part of the National Association for the Advancement of Colored People ("NAACP"), although LDF was founded by the NAACP and shares its commitment to equal rights. Instead, LDF has had, since 1957, a separate Board, program, staff, office, and budget.

NUTS AND BOLTS

Executive Director: Elaine R. Jones
How many attorneys work there: 25 in the three offices (New York, Washington, and Los Angeles).
For Full-Time Positions: They hire as needed.

The Nature Conservancy

International Headquarters • 1815 North Lynn Street • Arlington, VA 22209
Phone: 703-841-5300 • Web site: www.tnc.org

WHAT DO THEY DO?

"Nature's real estate agent." That's The Nature Conservancy. Among environmental organizations, The Nature Conservancy fills a unique niche: preserving habitats and species by buying the lands and waters they need to survive.

The Nature Conservancy operates the largest private system of nature sanctuaries in the world—more than 1,500 preserves in the United States alone, covering more than 9 million acres of ecologically significant land. Some preserves are postage-stamp size, others cover thousands of acres— *all* of them safeguard imperiled species of plants and animals.

The Nature Conservancy has 828,000 members and 1,385 corporate associates.

WHO'S WHO . . .

Chief Operating Officer: Douglas K. Hall

JOB OPPORTUNITIES . . .

Lawyers work in many of The Nature Conservancy's regional and field offices, all over the country. To find out about job openings, check the web site, or call The Conservancy's job hot line at 703-247-3721. (The web site will also give you a complete list of the addresses of The Conservancy's many offices.)

Public Counsel Law Center

601 Ardmore Avenue • Los Angeles, CA 90005
Phone: 213-385-2977 • Web site: www.publiccounsel.org

WHAT DO THEY DO?

Public Counsel is the public interest law firm of the Los Angeles County and Beverly Hills Bar Associations, as well as the Southern California affiliate of the Lawyers' Committee for Civil Rights Law. Public Counsel's activities are varied and impact a wide spectrum of people living at or below the poverty level.

Attorneys for Public Counsel specialize in children's issues, consumer law, community economic development, AIDS/HIV, homeless and housing law, immigration law, and public benefits. Apart from providing free counsel to people in need and to nonprofit organizations, Public Counsel co-counsels with private bar volunteers on a number of major litigations. Recent major cases include challenging local 'anti-loitering' ordinances which discriminate on the basis of race; halting the spread of liquor stores in South Central and South East Los Angeles, on behalf of a number of neighborhood groups; winning a $2.3 million judgment against a notorious South Central mortgage loan broker; bringing a class action suit against the INS concerning the failure to secure competent interpreters in immigration court; and a challenge to the fraudulent practices of offshore insurance companies.

WORD ON THE STREET . . .

"It's the largest pro bono law firm in the country. The starting pay is around $30,000. They do all pro bono work. It is a *fantastic* organization. They do children's rights, immigration, homeless issues, low income housing, family law, bankruptcy, those kinds of things."

NUTS AND BOLTS

CEO and General Counsel: Dan Brunfeld

How many attorneys are there: 12 attorneys, 20 summer interns, and over 9,000 volunteer attorneys from the Los Angeles area.

FULL-TIME POSITIONS . . .

They hire periodically.

Starting salary: $ (Under $35,000) They offer a benefits package including disability, maternity, paternity, as well as life, disability, health, and dental insurance.

SUMMER INTERNSHIPS . . .

They typically have between 10 and 20 summer interns.

If you summer intern for Public Counsel, you have to fund your own internship (*e.g.*, through a fellowship). The amount of work/study is $400 per week, but that figure must include outside funding that you arrange.

What they look for: A demonstrated commitment to public interest work, strong oral and writing skills, and high motivation, reflected by work experience, volunteer activities, and academic achievement.

Public Counsel also welcomes law student and attorney volunteers.

Women's Advocacy Project

P.O. Box 833 • Austin, TX 78767
Phone: 512-476-5377 • Fax: 512-476-5773 • E-mail: wapathena@earthlink.net

WHAT DO THEY DO?

The Women's Advocacy Project is a nonprofit organization founded in 1982. The Project's mission is to provide legal advice, expand legal education, and promote access to justice for Texas women in need. Because over 85% of poverty-stricken people are women and girls, the Project's target population is poverty-level women and their children. The Project accomplishes its mission primarily through the operation of two toll-free, statewide hotlines: the General Legal Hotline (800-777-FAIR or 512-476-1866) and Family Violence Legal Hotline (800-374-HOPE or 512-476-5770). Last year the Project's staff and volunteer attorneys provided legal advice to 13,694 Texans and helped 6,928 victims of domestic violence on the Family Violence Legal Line.

NUTS AND BOLTS

Executive Director: Shelia Enid Cheaney

How many attorneys work there: 8 (all women). Some work part-time. Of these attorneys, 7 work in the Women's Advocacy Project office, and the other works for the Family Violence Protection Team, also in Austin.

FULL-TIME AND PART-TIME POSITIONS . . .

The Women's Advocacy Project hires as vacancies occur, or new grants are received. It hires both full-time and part-time people.

To find out about openings: Call them, or stop by the office!

New attorneys normally come to the Women's Advocacy Project as volunteers, and then become paid employees.

What they look for: Apart from membership in the Texas bar, they seek people who demonstrate an interest in women's issues.

HOURS AND BUCKS . . .

The hours are flexible; a full-time workload is a 40-hour week, and part-time is 20 hours.

Starting pay: $ (Under $35,000) for full-time; $16,500 for part-time.

SUMMER INTERNSHIPS . . .

Women's Advocacy Project has summer interns every summer. Last year, they had six summer interns.

To be paid for the internship, you have to secure your own funding through your school or through fellowships.

PART-TIME WORK DURING THE SCHOOL YEAR . . .

The Women's Advocacy Project employs 1 to 2 law students on a part-time basis during the school year. The positions are fellowships funded by other sources, and sometimes law students volunteer.

WHAT LAWYERS SAY ABOUT WORKING THERE . . .

"At the Women's Advocacy Project, if you have an idea about women's legal advocacy, you can bring it to fruition. While you have to be a self-starter to make it happen, everyone here has many areas of interest and expertise to help you make your idea a reality. There's grant-writing support, a wealth of legal knowledge, an understanding of Texas and the Austin community, and an outspoken support of cutting-edge advocacy. Plus, we're very strongly supported by the local legal community, which makes people very willing to talk to us about all sorts of things."

"As a hotline attorney, you deal with clients every day, all day. This job isn't about pleasing the big corporate client—this job is about empowering people to realize how many different ways they can take charge of really awful situations in their lives. Another big difference here is that, as a hotline attorney, you get to learn constantly about new areas of the law. Callers' questions will teach you more than specializing in one particular area of law ever will."

"There really is no such thing as a typical day at the Women's Advocacy Project. Our attorneys answer calls from the general public, and there's no telling what will be 'in the air' on any particular day. Some callers need to know how to get a divorce, some need to know how to get the mechanic to fix their car, while still others need to know how to fire an attorney who isn't representing them to their satisfaction. The only thing typical is the support you get from the other attorneys who work here."

"The people who work at the Women's Advocacy Project are committed, caring people. They care not only about the clients we serve but also about all of the lawyers and volunteers who work here. I learned everything I know so far about being a lawyer—a *good* lawyer—from them. Without them, my three years in law school would have been a wash."

CHAPTER 10

Great Government Jobs

Federal, State, and Local

Federal Agencies

If you're like me, you're pretty surprised to see so many federal employers in this book. But the fact is, I heard tons of great things about many different departments, and the ones who received the most rave reviews are the ones I've included in this chapter. (Of course, the one that received *the* most huzzahs was the Department of Justice, and it's got its own chapter—Chapter 4.)

For the federal government in general, *other* than the DOJ, here's what you ought to know:

1. No billable hours. No rainmaking. No joke. With the federal government, you've got the latitude to bat issues around with your colleagues and generally get up to speed on any issue you're confronting without having to worry about how a client will react to the bill. And you don't have the pressure of drumming up business. For many people, those are *huge* benefits.

2. Contrary to popular belief, not *all* federal jobs are advertised. Federal government attorneys are hired through the "excepted service process," allowing agencies to set their own hiring policies. They don't *have* to advertise, although many do. In fact, many federal agencies advertise openings on the Office of Personnel Management's web site, at www.usajobs.opm.gov. Check that out on a regular basis to find job openings as they arise.

3. The starting pay isn't great, *but don't read too much into that*. Most entry-level positions for lawyers start at pay grade GS-11, which is approaching $40,000 (it varies somewhat around the country, to take into account different costs of living in different places. You can find a chart of government pay grades at www.usajobs.opm.gov/b5a.htm). You do get fairly quick raises, however, once you pass the bar you jump a few grand, and within a couple of years you're making out a lot better. So don't let the starting pay totally dissuade you from taking a government job. On top of that, federal benefits are all first-rate—medical, retirement, vacations, and savings plans.

4. Even if you don't intend to be a "lifer," the federal government is an excellent jumping-off point for a whole slew of private employers. I talked to many corporations, for instance, who consider government experience a real plus.

5. The hours *tend* to be less demanding than starting out in private practice, but that *isn't always necessarily the case.* For instance, SEC lawyers sometimes find themselves working very late. And jobs that require frequent travel—like working for the Federal Mediation and Conciliation Service—can be a grind if you don't like to be away from home frequently. On the other hand, Army Judge Advocates tend to work very livable hours. The point here is only that it's a mistake to assume that working for the government necessarily means a light work schedule—and it's very much a mistake to suggest in a job interview that the reason you want the job is that you're looking for 9-to-5 hours.

6. A few of the larger federal agencies do on-campus interviews at law schools. Since this varies from year to year, check with your Career Services Office at the beginning of the fall semester to see if an agency you're interested in going to will be interviewing at your school. More commonly, large agencies send letters to law schools soliciting applications. A few agencies conduct initial interviews by phone, or at regional offices. Note that if interviews require travel, it's at your own expense.

7. Do not underestimate the value of the dreaded "n" word—networking—when you're looking for a federal job. Many people think that because of the standardized application process for federal jobs, there's no point in getting to know people on the inside. Not true! It *never* hurts to have an advocate on the inside pulling for you, if for no other reason than to put in a good word for you to the person who does the hiring. I understand that even at the CIA—which you'd figure would be absolutely immune to networking—it helps to talk to anyone you can who might help grease the wheels for you. While I go into the whole process of getting to know people in my *Guerrilla Tactics For Getting The Legal Job Of Your Dreams* book, a simple step would be to check with career services and/or alumni relations at your law school to see which alums work in government agencies of interest to you. Drop them a note (or an e-mail) and ask for a few minutes to bend their ear, and then ingratiate yourself by showing your honest enthusiasm for the work you want to do. Having people who do what you want to do, pulling for you, *never* hurts!

8. *Call before you leap.* I've provided some deadlines for applications in the profiles in this section, but deadlines are always subject to change from year to year. As a rule of thumb, the earlier in the fall that you

apply for summer clerkships, Honors Programs or other entry-level positions, the better off you are. Before you apply for any federal agency position, either call the number given for the agency, check the agency's web site, or check with your Career Services Office for application deadlines.

9. The application process can be a pain in the butt. For any job in which you're interested, contact the address, phone, or web site given for specific deadlines and requirements. For Honors Programs, you'll find a very relaxed application requirement—no extensive forms to fill out as a general rule. However, for most government employment, you're going to wind up providing a resume, law school transcript, and either an OF-612, SF-171, "Expanded Resume," or a similar form. These are the credential equivalent of a body cavity search, with details about every job you've ever had, and even for lawyer positions, answers to questions concerning what kinds of machinery you can operate. These aren't *difficult* forms to fill out, but they're cumbersome, and you should be prepared for them. (You can find information about federal job applications at www.jobweb.org/search/jobs/fjapply.htm, which tells you about the information you should compile. And you can find examples of the OF-612 form at the Office of Personnel Management's web site, at www.usajobs.opm.gov/einfo/of612.txt).

10. As a general rule, it's easier to get into the federal government with a couple years' experience under your belt than to zip right in after graduating from law school. For departments and agencies that accept new law school graduates, you usually enter through what's called the "Honors Program," and as the name suggests, it's an honor to get in— the competition is fierce. If you start working for the federal government right out of law school, you typically have 14 months to pass a bar exam (in any state or D.C.); and before you pass, you're typically called a "law clerk," even though you're entering as a law school graduate. Don't worry about the title—these are great, highly-in-demand jobs, in spite of their lowly moniker!

If you have less-than-stellar paper credentials and you're bound and determined to work for the federal government immediately after graduation, consider doing an internship—paid or unpaid—in one of your law school summers, or even during the school year (if there's a field office of a particular government agency near your school that *has* a work-study or volunteer program). This will help you make the contacts and get the paper credentials, to ease your way into the job you want. And these internships may give you the chance to find back-door ways to accomplish your goal—for instance, people have been known to get their foot in the door at the Department of the Interior by taking a quasi-legal job with the National Park Service.

Note that law student positions fill up *very quickly.* Most 2L positions are filled in the fall, and 1L positions, early in the spring. Don't dawdle!

11. Most government agencies have first-rate web pages, with tons of information about the agency and all kinds of interesting related stuff. I got a lot of the information you'll find in this chapter from those web pages! I've listed the web pages at the beginning of each agency's profile. For a handy list of all federal agency web sites, visit http://winslo.ohio.gov/fdgvind.html.

12. Most attorney positions with the federal government aren't political. It's Schedule C political appointments where you find that political stripes count, but that *doesn't* include most attorney positions.

13. You might not have to be a U.S. citizen to get the federal government job you want. It's up to individual agencies to set citizenship requirements for attorney positions, so if you aren't a U.S. Citizen, check with the agency that interests you before you eliminate yourself from contention because of your citizenship. (Most federal agencies state on their web pages whether U.S. Citizenship is a requirement.)

A SALACIOUS LITTLE TIDBIT ABOUT GOVERNMENT WEB PAGES . . .

Here's a naughty little goodie for you, courtesy of a government lawyer who'd prefer to remain nameless.

When the Internet first started to become popular, some porn industry types figured a good way to snag unsuspecting visitors was to set up all of the federal agencies and add the word "com." As it turns out, if you put in the common abbreviations for a lot of government agencies and add "com" instead of "gov" at the end, you'll wind up looking at—well, stuff you probably didn't expect if you were surfing for information on the federal government, if you catch my drift.

THE AGENCIES RECEIVING RAVE REVIEWS:

Central Intelligence Agency

Office of the General Council • Washington, D.C. 20505
Phone: 703-874-3171 • Fax: 703-874-3208 • Web site: www.odci.gov/cia/

WHAT IS IT?

This tape will self-destruct in five seconds.

The name is Bond. James Bond.

If the theme music from *Mission Impossible* runs through your head, or you get the urge to order a martini shaken, not stirred, at the mention of the letters "CIA," then visiting the CIA's web page won't disappoint. The "Employment" section features a stylized human eye against a stark black background, with the words "Innovation & Intrigue" silhouetted alone on the page. Oh, boy!

As you probably know without having to be told, the CIA's mission centers around intelligence activities. It gathers and analyzes information on foreign adversaries, conducts counterintelligence operations abroad to frustrate foreign espionage, and undertakes covert action abroad at the direction of the President.

Lawyers at the CIA work in the Office of General Counsel ("OGC"). So put aside your Captain Crunch secret decoder ring for the moment, while we talk about working for the OGC. It's a highly coveted—and terrific—job.

NUTS AND BOLTS

How many attorneys work there: Approximately 100 (36 women, 7 minorities)

WHAT DO OFFICE OF GENERAL COUNSEL LAWYERS DO?

The OGC handles a wide variety of legal issues, including, among other things, both civil and criminal litigation, foreign intelligence and counterintelligence activities, counterterrorism, counternarcotics, nonproliferation and arms control, covert action, personnel and security matters, contracting, finance and budget matters, tax, immigration, international financial transactions, corporate law, copyright, intellectual property, foreign and international law, and legislation. The OGC's practice gives lawyers the opportunity to interact with a wide variety of U.S. government agencies, the Congress, federal and state courts, and the private sector. OGC lawyers have regular contact with the White House, National Security Counsel, Defense, State, Justice, Treasury, Commerce, and other Intelligence Community agencies.

The OGC is divided into five divisions: The Administrative Law and Ethics Division, Litigation Division, Intelligence Division, Logistics and Procurement Law Division, and Operations Division.

Many OGC attorneys get the opportunity to rotate frequently throughout the different divisions. However, some attorneys specialize in esoteric specialties that require considerable experience and, in some instances, advanced degrees.

WHO GETS HIRED?

The OGC hires experienced attorneys and new law school graduates (between 2 and 4 each year), and law students as summer clerks (they have between 5 and 8 of those every year).

Experienced attorneys: The CIA posts job openings on its web site (www.odci.gov/cia/), and also advertises them in newspapers.

New law school graduates: The direct route to the CIA is through the CIA Legal Honors Program (or through the summer program, which results in a lot of permanent hires—you'll find information about the summer program directly below). The Honors Program, as is true for every federal Honors Program, takes law students with exceptional paper credentials. It's a plum job and it's *very* competitive. The Program lasts for two years and gives you broad exposure to the practice of national security law. In the Honors Program you can spend both years at the OGC, assigned to one or more Divisions, depending on the needs of the Office. Alternatively, the OGC might arrange for you to spend your second year at another agency in the D.C. area with national security responsibilities, such as the Department of Justice or the National Security Agency.

HOURS AND BUCKS . . .

Hours: CIA attorneys typically work 40 to 60 hours per week. You get to travel all over the world as your caseload requires, but as an attorney you're not posted overseas.

Starting salary: $$ ($35-50,000)

HOW TO APPLY . . .

You can apply to the CIA directly, or interview on campus if they come to your school. The CIA interviews on campus at UVA, Michigan, Georgetown, Howard, Harvard, William & Mary, Yale, and Duke. The Agency also hires from law schools where it doesn't interview on campus. Send a resume, transcript, and writing sample (the writing sample is very important) to the OGC at the following address: Office of General Counsel, Central Intelligence Agency, Washington, D.C. 20505.

Ideally it is not going to surprise you that working at the CIA requires you to get a Top Secret security clearance. You also have to be a U.S. citizen. You have to successfully complete the CIA's personnel screening process (which includes medical and polygraph exams, and a background investigation). You have to graduate from an ABA-accredited law school, and you have to pass the bar in any state, the District of Columbia, Puerto Rico, or the U.S. Virgin Islands within 14 months of joining the agency (until you pass, you are called a 'law clerk,' which is common to pretty much all federal agencies). The whole personnel screening process takes between six and nine months.

SUMMER CLERKS . . .

Every year the OGC aims to hire 5 to 8 summer clerks (all 2Ls; they don't allow 1Ls into the program, not because they don't *want* to, but because, as a practical matter, 1Ls can't apply before the spring semester and the CIA screening process can take up to nine months). The weekly salary for summer clerks is around $700, and you have to be able to work for at least 10 weeks. The clerkship gives you a broad exposure to the practice of intelligence law.

While the summer clerkship doesn't guarantee you'll get an offer for permanent employment with the CIA, it's a great way to get your foot in the door, and historically a good number of summer clerks *have* received permanent offers; last year, out of six summer clerks, four were invited back.

Even as a summer clerk, you need to have a Top Secret security clearance to work at the CIA and you need to be a U.S. citizen. Because the personnel screening process (which includes a medical and polygraph exam, and a background investigation) generally takes between six and nine months to complete, you should apply for the program by the end of September.

To apply, send your resume, a law school transcript, legal writing sample, and legal references to:

Summer Legal Clerkship Program
Office of General Counsel
Central Intelligence Agency
Washington, D.C. 20505

WHAT THEY LOOK FOR IN BOTH SUMMER AND PERMANENT HIRES . . .

While it's impossible not to be attracted by the mystique of the CIA, they're looking for serious lawyers. Don't get too carried away with the shoe-phone and lapel-camera stuff!

While great grades and Law Review don't hurt you, they aren't mandatory. The CIA likes to see great paper credentials, but they stress that they hire the "whole person." As CIA lawyers point out, "Many law students have done other stuff before law school, and an interesting background helps. And that can mean all kinds of things. A summer or two with the Department of Justice or the Department of Defense doing comparable work is a plus. Having worked as a judicial clerk, or having been a summer or permanent associate in a big corporate practice doesn't hurt. Many people from the military apply to the CIA, and that background helps, as well, as does any experience living overseas. But none of those things are requirements. The thing we really like to see is interesting and productive work of any kind."

WHAT IT'S LIKE TO WORK AT THE CIA, FROM LAWYERS IN THE OGC . . .

"It's a *very* exciting practice, starting right away. We don't have the luxury of putting you in the library for a year when you start. Even very junior lawyers get out and do the work, dealing with senior government officials in all agencies, members of Congress at all levels, and foreign government leaders as well. The interesting work is definitely not reserved for senior people. We have a saying at OGC that the younger you are, the more fun you have!

"There are a few things that stand out about what we do. Most importantly is the variety of the work. We get to do some very enjoyable stuff. As is true of every law job, the work ranges from the mundane to the sublime, but a lot of what we do is very cutting-edge, in a whole range of specialties.

"For instance, take our First Amendment work. We have obligations to do prepublication reviews of things written by current or former CIA employees. Exactly what can they publish? We've been a major player in developing the law of national security vs. the First Amendment.

"Or the Fourth Amendment, search and seizure issues. When CIA personnel operate oversees and Americans come across our screen, they've got constitutional rights we've got to think about. We're often confronted with issues that you just don't find anywhere else. For instance, when you have Americans spying against the United States—what rights do they have? They still *do* have rights, but how do you determine what they are? Or electronic surveillance, there are obvious Fourth Amendment issues involved with it. In areas like that, we're helping to create the law and that's a real rush.

"Even everyday specialties have fascinating aspects here. For instance, let's say a CIA employee is going through a messy divorce. In discovery, typically you'll have the spouse asking salary questions, like where do you work? How long have you worked there? Well, if you're working undercover for the CIA, you can't answer those questions. So we have to come up with ways to handle those questions and protect secrets at the same time. In fact, in a whole range of areas we work very closely with the Department of Justice to allow intelligence to be used while protecting secrets.

"We also deal with international law issues because obviously we operate internationally in support of foreign policy pursuits, and that means we have to abide by treaties.

"There are separation of powers issues as well, because of the congressional oversight elements that we have to deal with. When Congress wants something from us they get it, but sometimes there's a test due to national secrets or executive privilege. At OGC we're the ones who decide how that gets handled. In fact, with Congress, we deal with legislative issues all the time. We have to be on the alert in looking at legislative matters to make sure that the CIA's interests aren't hurt. Not that it's done intentionally— many times there will be congresspeople proposing legislation that hurts us, but they don't realize it. We've got to alert them to those issues, and that means we've got to be aware of what's going on legislatively all the time.

"We have to do nitty-gritty, roll-up-your-sleeves corporate stuff as well. A lot of people don't realize that the CIA supports operations that involve setting up businesses and corporate practices. Remember Air America? The CIA created that business and it creates others, all in support of collecting intelligence, or counterterrorism, or counternarcotics. But when you're setting up a business, no matter what it's for, you've got to be aware of corporate issues, and we handle that.

"There are many, many others. We have an aggressive EEO practice. We have lawyers who handle copyright issues. We also do a bit of patent work, since we have CIA people who invent things. I guess you could say that if you can name it, we probably do it.

"What's especially nice about the variety you get at OGC is that almost everybody gets to be a generalist. We like to say that over the course of your career at the CIA, you can change jobs without quitting your job. You can move around every two to three years if you want. You can do things outside the office in the CIA, in non-lawyer jobs. You can go outside the CIA altogether to do lawyer jobs elsewhere in the federal government. For instance, over the years the CIA has sent lawyers to other agencies for a year or two—the White House, the DOJ, the FBI, places like that. It broadens your experience and that's always fun.

"The other aspect that makes working at the CIA very enjoyable is that we feel we're working for a worthy cause, without being zealots. The fact of the matter is that we aren't hired guns. We provide a service to our clients—the taxpayers—and that makes us feel good. We aren't here for the money. It's a combination of the variety, and the importance, of the work that keeps people here.

"And of course the very idea of working at the CIA is pretty exciting. You can move into being James-Bondish. You travel discreetly. You don't identify who you are. So there's some excitement with the travel. But the legal practice itself is very interesting, very exciting.

MISCONCEPTIONS ABOUT WORKING FOR THE CIA . . .

"There are many, many misconceptions people have about working for the CIA. Actually people are surprised when they hear that the CIA has a General Counsel's Office *at all!*

"And people are also surprised to hear that when you work for OGC, you're never coerced to come out a certain way on issues. I've never had any pressure to come up with an answer that is what I thought they wanted me to say. They appreciate, and respect, straight shooters.

"Another misconception is that the CIA is extraordinarily conservative. That's totally not the case. I'd say that most people here would consider themselves very liberal.

"One thing that used to be true, but isn't any more, is the problem with leaving the CIA. Twenty years ago there was a stigma that made it more difficult to go from the OGC into some other kind of work. That's not an issue any more. We have people leave to work in the U.S. Attorney's office, as corporate counsel, to the Hill as legal counsel, it runs the gamut. The fact is, we're usually generalists, and that translates well into a lot of other jobs.

"Another big misconception has to do with who gets into the CIA. There's a totally wrong-headed picture in people's minds that if you've ever smoked a joint, you can't get into the CIA. That's not true. Maybe you'd say, 'Oh, when I was a freshman in college, I'd light up a doobie, I drank a lot, but when I got to law school I grew up and I don't do that anymore.' That's not going to remove you from consideration. Obviously the CIA isn't going to hire a dopehead or an abuser. And if you're a tax cheat, forget it. Serious things *will* kick you out of the process. But casual drug use that took place years ago and is over now, that won't remove anybody from consideration by itself. What is a source of surprise to us is that there are a lot of people who self-select out, thinking that because of some old, casual drug use they won't get in. That's a shame. And on the other end of the spectrum you have people who've done really bad things, who keep applying and applying and applying, and they're just never going to get in and they should know better!

"Maybe the biggest misconception about the CIA is the idea that it's a no-holds-barred kind of place, that we feel as though there's a different set of rules that applies to the CIA. That's not true. The Constitution applies to us. We have huge concerns for the rights of Americans. There are a strong set of controls that we support concerning Americans.

"I think people are surprised to find that the CIA has evolved over the years. It's a lot more open than it used to be. When I tell people what I do, they'll say, 'Gee, that's neat.' And I've got to say—yes, it is!"

Comptroller of the Currency

250 E Street, S.W. • Washington, D.C. 20219
Phone: 202-874-5200 • Fax: 202-874-5374
E-mail: paul.chism@occ.treas.gov • Web site: www.occ.treas.gov

WHAT IS IT?

The Comptroller of the Currency ("OCC") is part of the Treasury Department. It charters, regulates, and supervises national banks. The OCC is in the forefront of efforts to modernize U.S. financial services systems, revise and reinvigorate antiquated banking laws, and streamline the regulatory process. In the last several years, Julie L. Williams, OCC Chief Counsel, has had four unanimous Supreme Court decisions affirming agency interpretations of banking law.

WHAT DO LAWYERS AT OCC DO?

Attorneys at OCC work in what's regarded as one of the most exciting and expansive areas of law: financial services. Specifically, OCC attorneys get to:

- Develop innovative, precedential opinions on contemporary issues (like derivatives, new bank products like bank sales of mutual funds and annuities, expanding bank markets, interstate banking, fair lending, community reinvestment and other consumer issues, and expanding bank powers);

- Enforce compliance with banking requirements by national banks through administrative actions;

- Develop banking regulations and legislation to modernize banking law;

- Investigate federal securities law violations and enforce applicable securities laws;

- Handle international banking issues and negotiate international agreements; and

- Represent the Controller in litigation involving any of OCC's operations.

STRUCTURE:

The OCC's Law Department, which is managed centrally by the Chief Counsel's office, consists of eight legal practice areas located in the Washington headquarters office, and six general practice offices in each of the six district office locations. The eight are the:

1. *Administrative and Internal Law Division ("AIL")*, which is responsible for matters relating to the OCC's operation as a federal agency: personnel matters, ethics program, assessments, delegations, financial management matters, FOIA appeals, and procurement. The Division is also responsible for some Law Department internal operations, including annual meetings and management meetings, training, legal precedent file system, law school recruiting and hiring.

2. *Bank Activities and Structure Division ("BAS")*, which handles corporate issues relating to banking organization and structures, including national banking associations, operating subsidiaries, and holding companies; branching issues, including interstate branching, and main office relocations; and mergers and related activities, including

bank combinations and antitrust issues. This division also handles bank lending and related activities, including lending limit requirements, and interest rate requirements; bank officer and director issues, including loans to executive officers, director responsibilities and liabilities; affiliate and insider transactions; bank real estate activities and related issues; bank resolution functions, including bank closings, conservatorship and receivership.

3. *Community and Consumer Law Division ("CCL")*, which provides legal interpretation and advice on consumer protection, fair lending, and community reinvestment issues. The Division is also responsible for legal issues related to bank community development powers and activities, including activities conducted within the bank, investments in community development corporations and projects, and participation in community development financial institutions.

4. *Counselor for International Activities ("IA")*, which is the focal point for legal issues relating to foreign banks' operations in the United States, U.S. banks' operations abroad, and legal issues arising in the multilateral and bilateral supervisory contexts. The Counselor coordinates efforts and provides legal advice on internationally related issues, provides legal advice on issues relating to cooperation with bank supervisors of other countries and U.S. treaties affecting financial services and works with other government agencies and international organizations.

5. *Enforcement and Compliance ("E&C")*, which is responsible for handling all non-delegated enforcement actions, including large civil money penalties; suspensions and removals; temporary cease and desist orders; and other administrative enforcement actions to assure compliance with federal banking laws by national banks and bank-related individuals. The Division also acts as a liaison with the Justice Department on significant referrals for criminal acts involving bank officials and works closely with Justice and the other bank regulatory agencies in coordinating law enforcement efforts involving insured financial institutions.

6. *Legislative and Regulatory Activities ("LRA")*, which is responsible for providing legal advice on a wide variety of legislative and regulatory issues. The Division prepares and reviews proposed banking legislation and regulations and advises on legal issues arising from those processes. The Division handles the Law Department's interagency coordination relating to these matters.

7. *Litigation ("LIT")*, which is primarily responsible, hand-in-hand with the Justice Department, for representing the Comptroller and OCC employees in federal and, where necessary, state court proceedings. The Division litigates administrative hearings in areas of personnel,

EEO, and procurement. In addition, the Division advises OCC management regarding litigation risks posed by proposed actions and decisions, and handling requests for OCC documents and/or testimony that arise during the course of litigation with the OCC and between private parties. The Division serves as counsel to the Comptroller in preparing agency decisions in administrative proceedings conducted pursuant to the Office's rules of practice.

8. *Securities and Corporate Practices ("SCP")*, which administers and enforces the federal securities and national banking laws that affect the securities and corporate activities of national banks. The Division provides advice and interpretations relating to securities, insurance, annuities, derivatives, corporate governance, shareholder rights, and fiduciary activities of national banks. The division also handles securities enforcement actions and serves as liaison with the Securities and Exchange Commission and the Commodities Futures Trading Commission.

And Districts—each of the Law Department's offices in the six OCC district locations is managed by a District Counsel. The District legal staff is the primary source of legal advice and counsel for the field examiners and District management, providing general interpretive advice on the full range of banking and securities law issues. The district legal staff also is responsible for handling a wide range of delegated enforcement actions including civil money penalties and non-contested cease and desist orders.

WHO RUNS IT?

Comptroller of the Currency: Julie Williams
Contact for attorney recruiting is Executive Assistant in the Law Department: Paul Chism, phone: 202-874-5200,
e-mail: paul.chism@occ.treas.gov

NUTS AND BOLTS

Number of attorneys in OCC: 129
Main office (Washington, D.C.): 97, field offices: 32
Total women attorneys: 58 (45 in D.C., 13 in the field)
Total minority attorneys: 22 (17 in D.C., 5 in the field)
Total disabled attorneys: 7 (all in D.C.)
Other offices: New York City (7), Chicago (5), Atlanta (5), Kansas City (5), Dallas (4), San Francisco (6).

WHO GETS HIRED?

Entry level: Approximately 4 to 6 new law school graduates (or attorneys with up to two years' work experience, including judicial clerks) are hired every year.

What they look for: "High academic achievement is preferred (but it's not mandatory that you be in the top 10% of the class!); extra-curricular activities like law review, clinical programs, and moot court are desirable; it's helpful to have taken relevant classes, like financial institutions law, securities law, and commercial law; financial institutions-related work experience, or a judicial clerkship, is desirable but not mandatory; good communication skills as demonstrated by a writing sample, correspondence, and interview(s)." On top of all of that, you have to be a U.S. citizen, and before you are hired, you're subject to a character investigation, and if you are being considered for a "critical/sensitive" position, you may have to undergo a background investigation.

HOURS AND BUCKS FOR ENTRY LEVEL ATTORNEYS:

Hours: First-year attorneys work an average of 2,080 hours. Part-time work is not available to entry-level attorneys, but it is available within a year of joining OCC. Flex-time is also permitted: You can work 80 hours in 9 days, with the 10TH day off, which provides for 3-day weeks (the day off can be Monday or Friday).

The starting pay is $$ ($35-50,000) in most of the field offices; there is a geographic pay differential which pushes the more expensive cities, like Washington, D.C., into the $$$ range ($50-65,000).

While the starting pay is somewhat lower than some private practice positions, OCC finds that there are many offsetting benefits (other than the quality of the work itself, private offices and a computer on every desk). For instance, "There's the contributory retirement plan, 13 to 26 days annual leave, 13 days sick leave, flex-time and part-time work schedules, medical/dental/vision insurance, and the best Thrift Savings Plan ("TSP") in the world (it's like a 401K plan)."

Laterals: OCC also hires laterals—Approximately 8 per year. For these openings, check out the OCC's web site, at occ.treas.gov, or call 202-874-5200.

SUMMER PROGRAM . . .

The OCC's summer program typically hires about eight 2Ls per summer. The pay is $640 per week in Washington, D.C. Field offices also have a summer intern—typically there is one summer intern in each of the New York, Chicago, and San Francisco offices.

HOW TO APPLY:

There are two choices: on-campus interviews or a direct application to OCC.

On-campus interviews: OCC interviews on campus at the following law schools: Boalt Hall, Boston College, Boston University, Chicago-Kent, Columbia, Emory, Fordham, George Washington, Georgetown, Harvard, Miami, North Carolina, Pennsylvania, Virginia, William & Mary, and Yale.

Direct applications: The application includes your resume, a cover letter (stating which office you're interested in), a brief (less than 10 page) writing sample, and if you have less than three years of legal experience, a copy of your law school transcript with your class rank (if your school has class ranks. (If your school has an unusual grading system, include an explanation of your law school's system.)

For permanent positions there is no strict deadline, although you should have your application in by mid-September in order to be considered for the first round of job offers in December. The hiring process takes approximately four months. Once your application is reviewed, you may be invited for an interview. The interviews take place in Washington, D.C., and sometimes at the district offices (New York, Atlanta, Chicago, Dallas, Kansas City, and San Francisco). Traveling expenses are reimbursed (within reasonable limits, which they tell you about when you get the invitation).

WHAT IT'S LIKE TO WORK THERE . . .

Practicing law in the OCC is very different from most federal agencies. Many agencies focus on one subject area or one activity. When you practice at the OCC, however, you get involved in all aspects of national bank organization and operations. OCC legal practice reflects the revolution occurring in the financial services industry today, and is characterized by breadth of subject matter, globalization of financial services, sophistication of clientele, diversity of population affected by OCC regulation, scope of individual responsibility, and the constant opportunity to hone legal skills and gain substantive knowledge in new areas.

When you join the OCC, you join one of the eight practice groups. Each group has multiple responsibilities. You're encouraged to rotate between the eight practice groups and also between the six district offices elsewhere in the country, and those kinds of rotations and transfers are common. Even as a new attorney, you get to deal directly with agency policymakers, national banks and their counsel, other regulators, and the public on a day-to-day basis. People who work at OCC rave about the "supportive, cooperative, and productive atmosphere" there, the fact that they get "exposure to various attorneys," and that "we deal with a huge variety of issues." One new OCC attorney I talked with said that she had come to OCC as part of the Treasury Honors program, which calls for a six-month rotation through all of the different divisions of Treasury, but when she got to OCC she liked it so much that she stayed there!

For *tons* more information about OCC, visit their web site at www.occ.treas.gov.

Equal Employment Opportunity Commission

Headquarters: Employment Division
1801 L Street, N.W., Room 3050 • Washington, D.C. 20507
Phone: 800-669-4000 • For attorney hiring: 212-748-8500
(push "5" and ask for personnel) • Web site: www.eeoc.gov

WHAT IS IT?

The Equal Employment Opportunity Commission ("EEOC") enforces federal laws prohibiting employment discrimination, including Title VII, the Age Discrimination in Employment Act, and the Equal Pay Act. It receives and investigates employment discrimination charges and complaints, and if it finds reasonable cause to believe that illegal discrimination has occurred, it tries to conciliate the charge or complaint. If conciliation doesn't work, the EEOC may file lawsuits in federal court against employers, labor organizations, and employment agencies.

WORD ON THE STREET . . .

"You get to be one of the 'good guys'—you're on the right side of legal issues. Also, you have regular hours, a job with security, and great federal benefits."

WHAT DO LAWYERS AT THE EEOC DO?

EEOC lawyers conduct all of the EEOC's civil litigation with the exception of Title VII cases against state and local government and Supreme Court cases, which are litigated by the U.S. Solicitor General.

About 400 of the EEOC's 3,200 employees are attorneys or law clerks, and of those, almost 300 work outside of Washington, D.C. at the EEOC's field offices. Most EEOC lawyers work in three offices: the Office of General Counsel (which handles litigation under Title VII of the Civil Rights Act, the Age Discrimination in Employment Act, and the Equal Pay Act); the Office of Review and Appeals (which handles final decision appeals of EEO complaints filed involving jobs with the federal government); and the Office of Legal Counsel (which is principal advisor to the EEOC on nonenforcement litigation matters, and represents the EEOC and its staff in defensive litigation, and in administrative hearings).

WHO GETS HIRED?

Law Students . . .

1. *Legal Intern Program.* If you've completed your first year of law school, you're eligible for these are paid internships. Each EEOC office hires independently (see the address list below).

2. *Summer Legal Intern Program.* For your first or second summer in law school this may fit the bill. You work from mid-May to the end of September; and if you do well, you may be invited back for a permanent position. You have to apply by mid-March; contact EEOC headquarters (address above) for details.

Entry Level Attorneys . . .

The EEOC hires new law school graduates. You apply either to the headquarters address (above) or to any of the field offices that interest you (addresses below).

WHERE TO APPLY . . .

The EEOC headquarters office is listed above. The district offices hire independently, and here are their addresses and phone numbers:

Albuquerque District Office
505 Marquette, N.W.
Suite 900
Albuquerque, NM 87102-2189
505-766-2061

Atlanta District Office
75 Piedmont Avenue, NE
Suite 1100
Atlanta, GA 30335
404-331-6093

Baltimore District Office
10 S. Howard Street, 3RD Floor
Baltimore, MD 21201
410-962-3932

Birmingham District Office
1900 3RD Avenue North
Suite 101
Birmingham, AL 35203-2397
205-731-1359

Charlotte District Office
5500 Central Avenue
Charlotte, NC 28212-2708
704-567-7100

Chicago District Office
500 W. Madison St.
Suite 2800
Chicago, IL 60661
312-353-2713

Cleveland District Office
1660 W. Second Street, Suite 850
Cleveland, OH 44113-1454
216-522-2001

Dallas District Office
207 S. Houston Street, 3RD Floor
Dallas, TX 75202-4726
214-655-3355

Denver District Office
303 E. 17TH th Avenue
Suite 510
Denver, CO 80203
303-866-1300

Detroit District Office
477 Michigan Avenue
Room 1540
Detroit, MI 48226
313-226-7636

Houston District Office
1919 Smith Street, 7TH Floor
Houston, TX 77002
713-653-3377

Indianapolis District Office
101 W. Ohio St., Suite 1900
Indianapolis, IN 46204
317-226-7212

Los Angeles District Office
255 E. Temple St., 4TH Floor
Los Angeles, CA 90012
213-894-1000

Memphis District Office
1407 Union Avenue
Suite 621
Memphis, TN 38104
901-722-2617

Miami District Office
1 Biscayne Tower
Suite 2700
Miami, FL 33131
305-536-4491

Milwaukee District Office
310 W. Wisconsin Avenue,
Suite 800
Milwaukee, WI 53203
414-297-1111

New Orleans District Office
701 Loyola Avenue, Suite 600
New Orleans, LA 70113
504-589-2329

New York District Office
7 World Trade Center, 18TH Floor
New York, NY 10048-0948
212-748-8500

Philadelphia District Office
1421 Cherry Street, 10TH Floor
Philadelphia, PA 19102
215-656-7020

Phoenix District Office
4520 N. Central Avenue, Suite 300
Phoenix, AZ 85012-1848
602-640-5000

St. Louis District Office
625 N. Euclid Street, 5TH Floor
St. Louis, MO 63108
314-425-6585

San Antonio District Office
5410 Fredericksburg Rd., Suite 200
San Antonio, TX 78229
210-229-4810

San Francisco District Office
901 Market Street
Room 500
San Francisco, CA 94103
415-356-5100

Seattle District Office
909 First Avenue
Suite 400
Seattle, WA 98104-1061
206-220-6883

Environmental Protection Agency

401 M Street, S.W. • Washington, D.C. 20460
Phone: 202-260-2090 • Web site: www.epa.gov

WHAT IS IT?

The Environmental Protection Agency ("EPA") protects the air, land, and water from pollution, by regulating the manufacture, use, and disposal of toxic substances. The EPA also supervises the cleanup of polluted sites, and it supports research and anti-pollution activities.

In any given year the EPA creates hundreds of regulations and defends hundreds of major lawsuits, primarily in federal circuit courts. It also handles hundreds of enforcement actions in Federal District Courts all over the country.

STRUCTURE . . .

As a lawyer at the EPA, you can work either at the Washington, D.C. headquarters or in one of the regional offices. The three elements of the EPA that hire the most lawyers are the Office of General Counsel, the Office of Enforcement, and the 10 regional offices.

The Office of General Counsel in Washington, D.C. has about 100 lawyers and basically handles regulation writing. The office is divided into seven divisions: air and radiation; grants, contracts, and general law; inspector general; international; pesticides and toxic substances; solid waste and emergency response; and water. Most of those are self-explanatory, with the exception of the Inspector General Division, which handles fraud, waste, and mismanagement issues within the EPA.

As a law school graduate you can also work in the Office of Enforcement in Washington, which does pollution policy enforcement work. There are about 100 lawyers who work for the Office of Enforcement.

The lawyers at the EPA's 10 regional offices (over 200 in total) act as counsel to the Regional Administrators and regional program staffs, offering advice on how national regulations apply to particular sources of pollution in each region. They also work on enforcement matters, and work with the Justice Department and with U.S. Attorneys on enforcement cases. The 10 regional offices are in Boston, New York, Philadelphia, Atlanta, Chicago, Dallas, Kansas City, Denver, San Francisco, and Seattle. As an entry-level attorney at the regional offices, you primarily handle client counseling, administrative hearings, settlement conferences, and second-chairing active litigation.

WHAT IT'S LIKE TO WORK THERE . . .

Apart from the obvious benefit of being on the side of the "good guys," the EPA has a serious dedication to quality of worklife issues. Among the benefits it offers are flexible work hours (including 'Flexiplace,' a new program giving employees a chance to work off-site during part of the work week), a fitness center, and a childcare center at a growing number of EPA facilities around the country.

WHO GETS HIRED?

The EPA hires entry-level and experienced attorneys, as well as summer clerks and law school interns during the school year, paid or work study. (Note that while working for an agency while you're still a student is a good way to get your foot in the door; at the EPA it's no guarantee that you'll get a permanent, entry level position—competition for those jobs is *fierce*). For attorney positions, it's helpful to have environmental experience, and the EPA likes to see public interest and a scientific or technical background as well. You have to be a U.S. citizen to be hired by the EPA.

HOW TO APPLY:

Contact the "Recruitment and Employment Program" at the 401 M Street address listed at the start of this entry for opportunities in Washington, D.C.

Here are the addresses for the regional offices. If you want to work for one of them, contact them directly:

Region 1 (Boston):
Environmental Protection Agency
One Congress Street
John F. Kennedy Building
Boston, MA 02203-0001
617-565-3420

Region II (New York):
Environmental Protection Agency
290 Broadway
New York, NY 10007-1866
212-637-3000

Region III (Philadelphia):
Environmental Protection Agency
841 Chestnut Building
Philadelphia, PA 19107
800-438-2474

Region 4 (Atlanta):
Environmental Protection Agency
100 Alabama Street, S.W.
Atlanta, GA 30303
800-421-1754

Region 5 (Chicago):
Environmental Protection Agency
77 W. Jackson Blvd.
Chicago, IL 60604-3507
312-353-2000

Region 6 (Dallas):
Environmental Protection Agency
Fountain Place 12TH Floor, Suite 1200
1445 Ross Avenue
Dallas, TX 75202-2733
800-887-6063

Region 7 (Kansas City):
Environmental Protection Agency
726 Minnesota Avenue
Kansas City, KS 66101
800-848-4568

Region 9 (San Francisco):
Environmental Protection Agency
75 Hawthorne Street
San Francisco, CA 94105
415-744-1305

Region 8 (Denver):
Environmental Protection Agency
999 18TH Street, Suite 500
Denver, CO 80202-2466
800-227-8917

Region 10 (Seattle):
Environmental Protection Agency
1200 Sixth Avenue
Seattle, WA 98101
800-424-4372

Federal Bureau of Investigation

935 Pennsylvania Avenue N.W., Room PA-750 • Washington, D.C. 20535-0001
Phone: 202-324-4991 • Fax: 202-324-8255 • Web site: www.fbi.gov

WHAT IS IT?

The "Ten Most Wanted" List. John Dillinger and Al Capone and Joseph Valachi. The crime lab. Efrem Zimbalist Jr. The FBI is etched in all of our minds by its headline-making work and, of course, the old TV show.

As you might imagine, it's a *very* interesting place to work—and lucky for you, they hire *lots* of law school graduates!

The FBI is part of the Department of Justice (which is such a wonderful employer it gets its own chapter in this book—Chapter 4). The mission of the FBI is to investigate violations of a variety of federal laws. In fact, the FBI's jurisdiction covers over 270 different federal laws in the areas of criminal and civil law and government intelligence.

The FBI was founded in 1908. Since then, it has grown to become the most powerful law enforcement agency in the country. Significant dates in the FBI's history include 1924, when its Identification Division opened. That serves as the country's repository for fingerprint records and it contains millions of fingerprint records. (You may have heard the story about John Dillinger trying to destroy his fingerprints by cutting off the ends of his fingers. Ouch! It didn't work; his fingertips grew back with the exact same prints. You probably *haven't* heard the story of a man who *was* successful in removing his fingerprints—guy named Roscoe Pitts, in the 1940s. A small-time American bandit, he removed his fingerprints through surgery, but it didn't help him in his criminal pursuits very much. The police actually found it easier to identify him because of the blank nature of his fingerprints—especially because he didn't have his prints removed below the first joint of each finger or his palm, and those prints are just as distinctive as the 'fingertip' prints.)

So much for the fascinating history of fingerprints. Back to the FBI. Another important year in FBI history is 1932, when it opened its scientific laboratory. That lab is a very interesting place. It is one of the largest and most comprehensive crime labs in the world, and it's the only full-service federal forensic laboratory in the United States. Among other groundbreaking advances, the FBI lab pioneered the use of DNA technology to enable genetic crime-scene evidence to positively identify—or rule out—suspects by comparing their particular DNA patterns.

Since its earliest days, the FBI has been a headline-maker. From investigating the mob, the KKK, the John Walker spy ring, white collar crime, to the World Trade Center bombing and the Archer Daniels Midland international price-fixing conspiracy—the FBI does the work that makes the news.

(For a more complete run-down on the FBI's history, you'll find a fascinating "short history of the Federal Bureau of Investigation" at its web site, www.fbi.gov).

STRUCTURE . . .

The FBI is a field-oriented organization in which nine divisions and four offices at FBI Headquarters in Washington, D.C. provide program direction and support services to 56 field offices, approximately 400 satellite offices known as resident agencies, four specialized field installations, and 23 foreign liaison posts (which are located in U.S. embassies). The foreign liaison offices, each of which is headed by a Legal Attache or Legal Liaison Officer, work abroad with American and local authorities on criminal matters within FBI jurisdiction.

WHAT LAW SCHOOL GRADUATES DO AT THE FBI:

Most attorneys enter on duty as Special Agents. The FBI likes to hire law school graduates because, since their mission is investigating crime, it helps to be familiar with criminal law and the Federal Rules of Criminal Procedure (which of course you memorized in school-right?).

As a Special Agent, you work at one of the 56 field divisions, investigating federal crimes. You might be assigned to investigate any kind of case regardless of its nature, or if you have specialized skills in some particular field, that's taken into account in your assignments.

Every case the FBI investigates involves a violation of federal laws. These include everything from espionage, mail fraud, sabotage, bank robbery, extortion, kidnapping, and fraud and theft against the federal government—a whole plethora of crimes. Special Agents also investigate any subversive act that might threaten the security of the United States. When cases are done, special agents submit full reports to FBI headquarters.

Special Agents accomplish their tasks in a variety of ways—they might interview people to gather information, search different types of records, and observe people, particularly those who are suspected of criminal intentions or acts. Special agents also take part in arrests and sometimes participate in or lead various raids. Sometimes they testify in court regarding their work and what they found out, focusing exclusively on the facts they found. Depending on the case they're investigating, agents might need to travel for periods of time or live in different cities. Needless to say, everything a Special Agent does is confidential—it can't even be shared with family or close friends.

NUTS AND BOLTS

FBI Director: Louis Freeh
Personnel Director: Roger Wheeler, phone: 202-324-3000

How many law school graduates work there: 1,081

FBI headquarters (Washington, D.C.): 116; Field offices: 938
Total women: 133, total minorities: 74, total disabled: 9

GETTING INTO THE FBI . . .

Permanent Positions . . .

The FBI routinely hires special agents and intends to go on doing so, so that means there are ongoing job openings for law school graduates.
Starting salary: $$ ($35-50,000)
The FBI does its hiring through its 56 field offices (note that unlike many federal agencies, it does *not* hire through the Office of Personnel Management). For locations near you, check your law school Career Services Office for brochures and applications, call the FBI's office of personnel (at 202-324-4991), or visit its web site at www.fbi.gov or the directory of FBI field offices at the Department of Justice's home page, at www.usdoj.gov/careers/oapm/lab/fbifield.html. (While you can choose your initial location, keep in mind that at some point during your career with the FBI you might be required to relocate.)
Note that some of the FBI field offices do on-campus interviews. Again, check with the field office where you'd like to work to see if they'll be visiting your law school.

The FBI application process is rigorous, as you might imagine. For instance, if you've smoked pot in the last three years, you might still be eligible for an Olympic medal but you're disqualified from joining the FBI. You have to complete a written test as well as an interview, and then there's a very thorough background investigation (which includes checking credit and arrest records, interviewing associates, contacting personal and business references, interviewing past employers and neighbors, verifying educational achievements, drug testing, a polygraph exam, and sometimes a physical exam as well).

Once you get into the FBI, you go to the FBI Academy in Quantico, Virginia, for a 16-week stint. You take classes on various academic and investigative subjects, and you also are trained in various skills including using firearms. In order to graduate from the Academy, you have to pass several exams (you can't fail more than two), you have to demonstrate proficiency in defensive tactics, firearms use and handling, and you have to pass simulated arrest exercises. Also, of course, you can't violate any of the FBI's rules and regulations for conduct.

Once you get out of Quantico, you are assigned to a field office for a one-year probation, and after that you become a permanent special agent. You learn the ropes during the first few months from veteran special agents. Throughout your career with the FBI you are continually educated and trained on new techniques and methods of criminal investigation, either through on-the-job training, advanced study courses, in-service training, or special conferences.

SUMMER INTERNS . . .

The FBI has a summer intern program called the "Honors Internship Program," and as with all federal honor programs, it's very competitive. (Of course that doesn't mean you shouldn't try for it!)

Last year there were 97 summer interns. While interns are typically college students, the FBI takes law school students, as well, and you're paid at the GS-7 level. You apply to individual field offices (check the FBI home page for locations) or with FBI Headquarters in Washington, but note that all of the summer internships take place in Washington no matter where you apply. The internships start at the beginning of June and end around the third Friday in August.

Deadline for summer internship applications: mid-December. Note that you have to complete the same background check as a permanent agent if you want to get into the summer program.

Check with the FBI home page (www.fbi.gov) for field offices where you'd like to work, and contact them directly for more information.

Federal Communications Commission

1919 M Street, N.W. • Washington, D.C. 20554
Phone: 202-418-0130 (Personnel), 202-418-0101 (Vacancies)
Web site: www.fcc.gov

WHAT IS IT?

From the V-Chip and parental guidelines for rating television programs, to determining standards for digital TV, to efforts to overcome the Year 2000 ("Y2K") problem in the telecommunications and broadcasting industries, you're looking at the fantastic variety of issues that face the FCC. It is an independent government agency that develops and implements policy concerning interstate and international communications by radio, television, wire, satellite, and cable.

STRUCTURE . . .

The FCC as a whole is divided into seven major regulatory Bureaus or Offices. They are:

1. The Common Carrier Bureau (which regulates telephone and telegraph);

2. The Mass Media Bureau (which regulates television and radio broadcasts);

3. The Wireless Bureau (which regulates private radio, cellular telephone, pagers and the like);

4. The Cable Services Bureau (which regulates cable TV and other services);

5. The International Bureau (which regulates international and satellite communications);

6. The Compliance & Information Bureau (which investigates violations and answers questions); and

7. The Office of Engineering & Technology (which evaluates technologies and equipment).

The FCC's approximately 250 lawyers work mostly in the Office of General Counsel, and for three of the bureaus: Common Carrier, Mass Media, and Private Radio (although there are other lawyers who work in other sections of the FCC).

WHAT IT'S LIKE TO WORK THERE . . .

As the explosive growth of the communications industry would suggest, FCC attorneys get to take part in a fantastic variety of projects: from drafting regulations, decisions, and opinions, to preparing comments on proposed legislation, to helping to negotiate and interpret international treaties, to reviewing applications for radio licenses, to representing the agency in administrative proceedings, to handling appeals and enforcement proceedings in Federal courts, to coordinating with other government agencies on national defense matters, and responding to public and congressional inquiries.

WHO GETS HIRED?

The FCC hires new law school graduates, experienced attorneys, and law students both during the summer and part-time during the school year. For law school graduates, the FCC has an Honors Program, which requires—as do all federal agency Honors Programs—excellent paper credentials. Contact the FCC for Honors Programs application information and deadlines. For the Summer Law Intern Program, you need to apply by November 1. And for the part-time work-study program, you aren't paid, but you do get course credit.

HOW TO APPLY . . .

Write to the address above, sending a resume, a transcript, and a recent writing sample reflecting your own writing (*i.e.,* not something that's been edited or revised by anyone else). (Experienced attorneys don't have to send a transcript if you graduated from law school more than four years ago.) For experienced attorneys, the FCC will hang onto applications for six months, and if you want them to consider you for an additional six months, you have to notify the Office of General Counsel in writing that you are still available for consideration. After one year you have to supplement your original application or it will be destroyed.

Federal Mediation & Conciliation Service

2100 K Street, N.W. • Washington, D.C. 20427
Phone: 202-606-5460 (human resources) • Web site: www.fmcs.gov

WHAT IS IT?

The Federal Mediation & Conciliation Service is an independent agency whose mission is to promote sound and stable labor-management relations. It accomplishes this by providing mediation help to labor and management in both preventing and settling collective bargaining disputes. The agency's services are offered free of charge to private and public-sector parties.

Per the FMCS's website, the services it offers include dispute mediation—mediating disputes in contract negotiations between employers and unions representing employees in the private, public and federal sectors; preventive mediation—providing services and training in cooperative processes to help labor and management break down traditional barriers and build better working relationships; alternative dispute resolution—providing services and training in a variety of joint problem-solving approaches which can be used in lieu of courtroom litigation, agency adjudication or traditional rulemaking by federal, state and local governments; and arbitration services—maintaining a computerized roster of qualified, private-sector arbitrators, retrievable by geographic, professional affiliation, occupation, industry experience or other specified criteria.

WHAT DO YOU DO THERE?

You come into the FMCS as a "Federal Mediator Trainee." In this role, you try to influence bargainers to adjust their differences. You conduct meetings where you encourage discussion and try to alleviate tension. You confer with labor and management representatives, analyze the issues over which they disagree, and try to determine the extent to which they will be willing to compromise. You develop suggestions for alternative solutions and create arrangements to cut crisis negotiations to a minimum.

WHO GETS HIRED?

The *typical* FMCS new hire has years of collective bargaining negotiation experience. However, the FMCS does hire a few Mediator Trainees without that experience and they do hire law school graduates for these positions. The FMCS also hires volunteer interns.

WHAT YOU NEED TO KNOW ABOUT THE FMCS . . .

There's a big caveat with the FMCS, and it's this: you have to be willing to go anywhere. The Service can assign you to any part of the country, and on top of that you can expect to travel and attend meetings with very little notice. If this lifestyle isn't attractive (or do-able) to you, don't consider it!

To Apply, Contact . . .

Bill Carlisle, Director of Personnel
Personnel Office
Federal Mediation & Conciliation Service
2100 K Street, N.W.
Washington, D.C. 20427
202-606-5460

Federal Trade Commission

600 Pennsylvania Avenue, N.W. • Washington, D.C. 20580
Phone: 202-326-2020 • Web site: www.ftc.gov

WHAT IS IT?

From monitoring mega-mergers to protecting consumers' on-line privacy, the FTC enforces the entire expanse of federal antitrust and consumer protection laws. The Commission seeks to ensure that the nation's markets function competitively and are vigorous, efficient, and free of any undue restrictions. The Commission also works to enhance the smooth operation of the marketplace by eliminating acts or practices that are unfair or deceptive. In general, the Commission's efforts are directed toward stopping actions that threaten consumers' opportunities to exercise informed choice. Finally, the Commission undertakes economic analysis to support its law enforcement efforts and to contribute to the policy deliberations of the Congress, the Executive Branch, other independent agencies, and state and local governments when requested. The FTC also engages in non-enforcement activities like consumer education.

STRUCTURE . . .

The FTC is divided into various bureaus. One of the major ones is the Bureau of Consumer Protection, which helps ensure a free marketplace by suppressing unfair, deceptive, and fraudulent practices. Its activities include investigations, litigation, rulemaking, and education. Then there's the Bureau of Competition, which regulates business practices that restrain competition. And finally, there is the Bureau of Economics, which advises on the economic merits of antitrust actions and helps formulate plans to improve competition.

WHAT DO FTC LAWYERS DO?

Lawyers at the FTC help in every aspect of the FTC's consumer protection, antitrust, and competition missions. Most FTC lawyers work in the agency's Bureau of Consumer Protection, Bureau of Competition, the General Counsel's Office, and the regional offices.

Lawyers in the Bureau of Consumer Protection (there are over 100 of them) handle unfair, deceptive, and fraudulent practices. The Bureau enforces federal consumer protection laws and the FTC's own trade regulation rules. The Bureau's employees investigate both individual companies and entire industries, handle both federal court and administrative litigation, taking part in rulemaking proceedings, and educating both consumers and businesses.

Lawyers in the Bureau of Competition (there are more than 150 of them) handle antitrust issues. This Bureau prevents actions in restraint of competition in two basic ways. One is to investigate restraints and recommend that the FTC take enforcement action (which can include injunctions, litigation before the FTC's Administrative Law Judges, consent agreements, or compliance investigations to see if FTC orders are being followed). The other chief role of the Bureau is to advocate for a free marketplace by filing briefs with courts and advising other government agencies.

Lawyers in the General Counsel's Office (there are over 30 of them) provide legal advice to everyone in the FTC, and supervise all of the Commission's litigation except for administrative cases. In this Office, you work with lawyers and economists from the Bureaus in Washington as well as with personnel from the Regional Offices to resolve any legal problems stemming from their work; you help ensure that the agency complies with FOIA-type statutes; and you advise the Commissioners on legal problems arising in antitrust, consumer protection, and administrative law. Once you get more experienced you can also help out on litigation in federal courts.

The 100+ lawyers in the Regional Offices do pretty much everything the FTC in Washington does, on a regional scale. They litigate before Administrative Law Judges and in the federal courts, educate local consumers and businesses, and coordinate activities with other local authorities. The regional offices are in Atlanta, Boston, Chicago, Cleveland, Dallas, Denver, Los Angeles, New York, San Francisco, and Seattle.

HOW TO APPLY . . .

You can find out about vacancies at the FTC in a couple of ways. The word on the street is that they haven't done as much hiring recently as they had in the past, but there are still positions available. You can find out about them on the FTC's vacancy hotline, at 202-326-2020, or at the

Office of Personnel Management's Internet site at www.usajobs.opm.gov. The FTC also posts vacancies in the Federal Career Opportunities Bulletin (you can find out about subscribing to that by calling 703-281-0200 or by visiting www.fedjobs.com).

You can get into the FTC as either an experienced attorney, new law school graduate, summer legal intern, part-time as a law student, or as a volunteer.

For experienced attorneys: Applications are accepted year-round. Submit a resume and a writing sample to the address listed at the start of this entry. Applications are kept on file for six months.

For new law school graduates: Third-year law students should submit a resume, writing sample, and law school transcript by September 30TH in order to be considered for positions available in October of the following year. The FTC typically looks for people with "superior credentials," meaning top third of your law school class, law review, special honors, those kinds of things. Offers are made by mid-November each year.

For summer legal interns: The FTC typically has a few paid summer internships for first- and second-year law students. 1L applicants should submit a resume, transcript, and writing sample by February 28TH for positions available that same summer. 2L applicants should submit a resume, transcript, and writing sample by September 30 for summer internships in the following calendar year.

For clerks and interns: Student clerk positions are non-legal, paid positions, doing mostly clerical support work during the year. It helps to be able to type (!) and computer proficiency is also helpful. Volunteer/unpaid interns are volunteer internships available to both law and economics students.

For information on any of these programs, contact Del C. Smith, Personnel Management Specialist, at 202-326-2357.

Department of the Interior

1849 C Street, N.W. • Washington, D.C. 20240
Phone: 202-208-3100 • Web site: www.doi.gov
Web site for the National Park Service: www.nps.gov
(this site includes cool virtual trips through national parks, like Bryce Canyon)

WHAT IS IT?

The Department of the Interior has a host of environment-oriented responsibilities. These include administering more than half a billion acres of federal land, and acting as trustee for 50 million more (mostly Indian reservations). The Department also handles conserving and developing fish and wildlife resources, coordinates federal and state recreation programs, preserves and administers scenic and historic areas, reclaims arid Western lands, operates and coordinates manpower and youth training programs, and manages hydroelectric power systems.

WHAT DO INTERIOR LAWYERS DO?

The Department is a magnet for lawyers with an interest in environmental law. Most of the work is public lands issues, and the most notable client agencies within the Interior Department are the Fish and Wildlife Service, the National Park Service, the Bureau of Mining, and the Bureau of Indian Affairs.

WORD ON THE STREET . . .

The two Interior jobs that get rave reviews are the National Park Service, and the Honors Program for new law school graduates, which is called the "Solicitor's Honors Program." The Honors Program is "very competitive," with only about 6 to 8 slots filled annually for the entire country.

We'll look at the National Park Service and the Honors Program separately.

The National Park Service

WHAT YOU NEED TO KNOW ABOUT GETTING INTO THE NATIONAL PARK SERVICE . . .

While the Honors Program is one way to start with Interior, many National Park Service ("NPS") offices hire attorneys in "quasi-legal" positions, and they do so on an independent basis—that is, not through the Honors Program. (I've provided contact information for each office below.) In these quasi-legal positions you get a tremendous variety of work on all kinds of issues. After all, part of the NPS's mission is resource management, planning, and administration of parks, all of which have property law aspects—and of course you spend a lot of time in gorgeous national park locations. Law school graduates who take these positions have been known to lateral into the Interior Department's Washington headquarters, so the NPS positions serve as a kind of "in-through-the-back-door" technique for getting into the Interior Department without going through the Honors Program.

Note that one method for getting into the NPS is by taking an exam through an Office of Personnel Management program called "Administrative Careers With America." For more information about both job openings and this particular exam visit this Web address: www.nps.gov/pub_aff/jobs.htm.

Here are the addresses for the National Park Service's headquarters and regional offices:

Washington Headquarters:
National Park Service
Interior Building
Room 3323
1849 C Street, N.W.
Washington, D.C. 20240
202-208-3100 (Information
   Locator)
202-619-7256 (Job Hotline)

National Capital Regional Office:
National Park Service
1100 Ohio Dr., S.W.
Washington, D.C. 20242
202-619-7111
202-619-7256 (Job Hotline)

Southeast Regional Office:
National Park Service
75 Spring Street, S.W., Suite 1130
Atlanta, GA 30303
404-331-5711

Midwest Regional Office:
National Park Service
1709 Jackson Street
Omaha, NE 68102
402-221-3456

Intermountain Regional Office:
National Park Service
12795 West Almeda Parkway
Denver, CO 80225
303-969-2020

Northeast Regional Office:
National Park Service
U.S. Customs House
200 Chestnut Street
Room 322
Philadelphia, PA 19106
215-597-4971

Pacific West Regional Office:
600 Harrison Street
Suite 600
San Francisco, CA 94101
415-744-3888

Alaska Regional Office:
2525 Gambell Street
Room 107
Anchorage, AK 99503
907-257-2574

The Solicitor's Office

The Solicitor is the principal legal adviser for the Secretary of the Interior. He is assisted by a Deputy Solicitor, five Associate Solicitors, eight Regional Solicitors, and a staff of almost 300 lawyers. The Solicitor's Office is divided into five substantive legal divisions in Washington and seven regions. The divisions in Washington (which is where about 130 Interior lawyers work) are the Divisions of Conservation and Wildlife,

General Law, Indian Affairs, Land and Water Resources, and Mineral Resources.

The seven regional offices are in Boston, Atlanta, Albuquerque, Denver, Sacramento, Portland, and Anchorage. Most of the regional offices have subordinate offices, called "field offices." About 160 lawyers work in the regional and field offices.

WHAT DO THE SUBSTANTIVE LEGAL DIVISIONS DO?

Each division is headed by an Associate Solicitor, and is subdivided into branches headed by Assistant Solicitors. Regional Offices are headed by Regional Solicitors. For all lawyers in the Office of the Solicitor, the client is the Secretary of the Interior, but each division has different responsibilities. They are:

1. *Conservation and Wildlife.* This division provides legal counsel and representation on program responsibilities and activities of the National Park Service, the Fish and Wildlife Service, and the biological research functions of the Geological Survey. Among other duties, the division also provides legal services revolving around acquiring and administering National Parks and wildlife refuges, the designation of wild and scenic rivers and wilderness areas, historic preservation, law enforcement, First Amendment activities, environmental protection, grants-in-aid, and endangered species protection.

2. *Land and Water Resources.* This division provides legal counsel and representation for the Bureau of Reclamation and the Bureau of Land Management (except for issues involving the minerals program). The division also handles legal issues for the Assistant Secretaries of Water and Science and Land and Materials Management. Legal services involve water resources development programs that manage natural resources on public lands, including logging and grazing activities.

3. *General Law.* This division provides legal counsel on such diverse matters as procurement and contracts, grants, patents, copyrights, trademarks, land titles, freedom of information, conflict of interest, the environment, personnel matters, equal employment and civil rights, labor management relations, tort claims, the territories administered by the U.S., departmental organization, and other administrative matters.

4. *Indian Affairs.* This division provides legal counsel to the Secretary of the Interior in his capacity as federal trustee to American Indian tribes and their members. This involves working directly with both the Bureau of Indian Affairs and Indian tribes and their attorneys in the protection of Indian-owned natural resources and tribal government

rights. The division also provides legal advice to the Bureau in connection with the administration of Indian service programs.

5. *Mineral Resources.* This division provides legal counsel and representation on issues relating to programs and activities of the Geological Survey (except for issues involving the Survey's biological research functions), the Minerals Management Service, and the Office of Surface Mining Reclamation and Enforcement, as well as matters involving the minerals program of the Bureau of Land Management. The Division also provides legal assistance and counsel to both the Assistant Secretary—Water and Science and the Assistant Secretary—Land and Minerals Management on matters relating to those bureaus. Legal services involve offshore minerals and international law; royalty management matters involving distributing revenues from leases on federal lands, the Outer Continental Shelf, and Indian lands; coal leasing and hard rock mineral patenting; and the environmental regulation of coal mining.

WHAT IT'S LIKE AT THE SOLICITOR'S HONORS PROGRAM . . .

For detailed information, visit this web address: www.doi.gov/sol/sohonpgm.html. Here, I'll give you a few basics. For the Honors Program, you report to the Solicitor's Office in Washington around the beginning of October. The program starts with an orientation to acquaint you with the role of the Solicitor's Office within the Department of the Interior and to make initial assignments.

During the first year or so with the department you rotate through five Divisions of the Office. You spend eight to 10 weeks in each division. During each eight-week rotation, you share an office with a program attorney from a prior year or some other junior attorney who can help you get familiar with the Department.

You report to the Honors Program Coordinator in the particular Division and you get assignments that are a cross-section of the work done in that office. At the end of each rotation you get evaluated by your immediate supervisor and by the Program Coordinator. You also are asked to evaluate your time in the division. Feedback from these evaluations is used to benefit the program attorneys and the division supervisors for future rotations. The evaluations are also incorporated into decision-making for permanent assignments at the end of the rotation and conversion of your trial status to permanent appointment under Civil Service procedures.

You have to pass a state bar exam, or the D.C. bar, within 14 months of when you start working for the Department of the Interior. After you've worked for one year, and assuming you've passed a bar exam and that your performance was satisfactory during your rotation through all of the departments, you get permanently assigned to a division, regional, or field office.

HOW TO APPLY TO THE SOLICITOR'S HONORS PROGRAM . . .

Deadlines are typically the end of September (for positions starting the following fall). Interviews are conducted in October and November and hiring decisions are made in December.
For Application Information, Contact . . .

The Office of the Solicitor
Department of the Interior
1849 C Street, N.W.
Washington, D.C. 20240

FOR EXPERIENCED ATTORNEY POSITIONS . . .

Job openings are posted at the general federal jobs page, www. usajobs.opm.gov, as well as at the Interior Department's own web page, at www.doi.gov/sol/soattyvac.html.

INTERNSHIPS . . .

The Department of the Interior also has a summer intern program. The deadline for second year students is the February of the year you'd like to summer intern for the Department. Contact the Office of the Solicitor for information (address immediately above).

★   ★   ★   ★   ★

United States Army Judge Advocate General's Corps

Judge Advocate Recruiting and Placement Service • Army Litigation Center
901 North Stuart Street, Suite 700 • Arlington, VA 22203-1837
Phone: (800) 336-3315 or (703) 696-2822 • Fax: (703) 696-2960
Web site: jagcnet.army.mil/jagcnet/jaraps.nsf

WHAT IS IT?

The Judge Advocate General's Office ("JAGC"), the legal branch of the Army, is "the Nation's oldest law firm." It was created by George Washington in 1775 while he was in command of the Continental Army.

Since that time, judge advocates have served the U.S. Army as soldier-attorneys. Judge advocates provide legal support to the more than one million men and women who serve in the Army, and their families, whenever and wherever needed throughout the world.

Here's an interesting historical tidbit for you: John Marshall, the famous Supreme Court Chief Justice, was a judge advocate in the Continental Army beforehand. Other famous judge advocate alumni include Henry L. Burnett, who was the Army prosecutor for the Lincoln conspiracy. Colonel William Winthrop, a noted legal scholar, wrote "Military Law and Precedents." Current alumni include Mr. Togo West, former Secretary of the Army and currently Secretary of Veteran's Affairs, and William Suter, Clerk of the U.S. Supreme Court.

NUTS AND BOLTS

Number of attorneys in the Army JAGC: 1,511
Women: 342; minorities: 197
Locations: Judge Advocates are in numerous office locations, including the continental U.S., Alaska, Hawaii, Puerto Rico, Germany, Italy, the Netherlands, Belgium, Korea and Japan.
Number of Judge Advocates in each location: It varies. A branch office might contain only one attorney, while a larger Office of the Staff Judge Advocate could contain between 20 and 35 attorneys. Several Army installations contain more than one legal office.

WORD ON THE STREET . . .

"It's just an excellent, excellent job." "People you think would never like the military just *adore* the JAG Corps." "You get to do *everything*, right away." "It's a great background for any civilian job you want later on. You get great skills." "They just love it. They get front-line responsibility and experience." "You never get bored with it."

WHAT DO JAGC LAWYERS DO?

When you *start* with the JAGC, you don't have to take basic training. You do have to attend a two-week military orientation course at Fort Lee, Virginia, The orientation course gives you time to establish personnel and finance records, purchase uniforms (you pay but you get a $300 reimbursement), and receive instruction in several basic areas of military life, including wearing military uniforms, military customs and courtesy, physical fitness training, and a 2-day overnight field training exercise. The field training exercise is not as grueling as regular basic training, but it's not a weenie-roast, either. You stay in barracks for two days, eat MRE's ("meals ready to eat") in the mess hall, learn how to shoot weapons, do a land navigation course (basically using a compass to find your way out of the woods), and sometimes you do experiments with gas masks.

After the two weeks of orientation you then complete a 10-week JAGC basic course at The Judge Advocate General's School in Charlottesville, Virginia, right next to the University of Virginia Law School. At the JAG school, you receive instruction on the organization, function, and mission of the JAGC, and an overview of the practice of law in the Army. The instruction focuses on areas of law that will be particularly important to a new military attorney, including military criminal law, evidence, government contract law, legal assistance, administrative law, tort claims, and international law. You also receive computer training and practical exercises in trial advocacy and attorney/client issues. (The school offers 44 CLE courses each year, covering all areas of JAGC practice; these CLE classes are approved for CLE credit by most states.)

After the 10 weeks, you proceed to your duty assignment (the Army picks up most of the expenses for the move). For your first tour of duty (three years), you probably won't have to move again—although if the Army needs you somewhere else, you go there.

One of the best things about being in the JAGC is that you get tremendous experience. You hit the ground running, and even if you only stay for one tour of duty—three years—you'll leave with excellent research, writing, interviewing, advising, negotiating, briefing, and litigating skills.

The primary practice areas include:

- *Legal assistance.* It is similar to general practice law. You see and counsel soldiers, retirees, and family members on issues like estate planning, landlord-tenant law, immigration and naturalization law, family law, and tax. If you serve overseas, you acquire hands-on experience in the laws of the country where you're working.

- *Military justice.* You might be called upon to prosecute or, after gaining some experience, you might be assigned to the Trial Defense Service, which gives you the chance to appear as a defense counsel in a courts-martial. With some experience at the trial level, you may serve as an appellate counsel. You get many opportunities as prosecutor or defense counsel to be an advocate in and out of the courtroom.

- *Tort claims.* During an average year JAGC lawyers represent the interests of the U.S. in a full range of tort claims totaling over $80 million. In addition, over $20 million is recovered from tortfeasors involving injuries to Army personnel and property.

- *Administrative law.* This is the government equivalent of corporate law. You advise commanders and staff officers on issues including personnel law, installation law, environmental law, the Privacy Act and the Freedom of Information Act.

- *Labor law.* As the largest employer of civilians in the country, the Army is involved in a considerable amount of labor litigation. JAGC attorneys advise on all aspects of labor management relations for both private and public-sector union matters. You may be called upon to represent the Army in federal court or in administrative hearings before the Merit Systems Protection Board, the Equal Opportunity Commission, or the Federal Labor Relations Authority.

- *International and operational law.* Because army personnel are stationed in many foreign nations around the world, it's inevitable that questions come up about the interpretation of international agreements as well as foreign laws. Judge advocates participate actively in negotiating and drafting international agreements such as base rights, status of forces, and personnel exchange agreements. JAGC officers observe and report on foreign trials of U.S. personnel and assist personnel confined in foreign prisons. They review military operations plans and provide advice on the laws of war, rules of engagement, domestic law relating to employment of forces and support of our allies, and the legal aspects of civil affairs.

- *Medical law.* This includes hospital administration and medical practice and research.

- *Contract law.* JAGC contract attorneys review most contracts for supplies, services, construction, and research and development; render legal opinions on procurement procedures, bid protests, contract terminations and contract appeal disputes; and serve as legal advisers to contracting officers and boards of award. Experienced judge advocates litigate contract disputes before the Armed Services Board of Contract Appeals and the U.S. Court of Claims.

- *General civil litigation* (in conjunction with the Department of Justice and U.S. Attorneys).

- *Teaching.* Some JAGC attorneys teach at The Judge Advocate General's School in Charlottesville, VA; The U.S. Military Academy at West Point; or other military schools throughout the country.

When you enter active duty with the JAGC, you usually have the chance to work in two or more practice areas during your initial three-year assignment. During a career with the JAGC, you can expect to practice law on a wide variety of legal topics. New attorneys are assigned based on the needs of the Army, but requests to work in a specific area of the law will be considered. Normally, officers are assigned geographically, then are assigned specific duties by supervisors. Most Army JAG officers assign Judge Advocates to a section of the office devoted to a particular area of the law, like a criminal law division, a legal assistance office, or an administrative law office. An experienced Judge Advocate or civilian attorney who is responsible for specific job assignments supervises each section. New Judge Advocates receive immediate responsibility and challenge with no apprenticeship period.

If there's a war, you'll find that JAGC officers are assigned to combat areas and perform legal duties there.

HOURS AND BUCKS . . .

Hours: A typical workday for Judge Advocates runs from 7:30 in the morning until 5:30 p.m. You get many opportunities to travel. Because the Army mission is international, there are assignment opportunities for Judge Advocates throughout the world. Also, you may travel to attend continuing education courses and in the performance of your duties.

On top of very livable hours, with the JAGC you get 30 days of paid vacation every year.

Starting salary: You enter the Judge Advocates General Corps as a first lieutenant, and you get promoted to captain six to nine months later. Military compensation is composed of three parts—and guess what! Here come the abbreviations! First, you get basic pay, which is taxable income; second, you get a basic allowance for housing ("BAH"); and third, you get a basic allowance for subsistence ("BAS"). Basic pay is based on rank and time in service. The housing allowance is based on rank and whether you have dependent family members—usually a spouse and/or children. If you choose to live in government-supplied housing, you don't receive the housing allowance but you do get housing, which includes utilities, at no charge. Both the housing allowance and the allowance for subsistence are tax-free.

How does this shake out? Typically, new Judge Advocates are paid between $31,000 and 40,000, with an increase when you get promoted to captain of $5,000 to 6,000. You get further pay raises after two, three, and four years of service. After four years, pay increases are biannual. You also typically receive an annual cost-of-living increase.

WHERE YOU GO FROM THE JAGC . . .

Initial assignments for new Judge Advocates are three years (four years for ROTC scholarship recipients). Some Judge Advocates leave active duty after one, or a few, tours of duty. Others remain with the JAGC for their entire careers. Some former Judge Advocates are now associates and partners in private law firms, judges, legislators and politicians, and law professors. Because of the wide variety of skills that Judge Advocates get very early on in their careers, they're well positioned for many civilian jobs.

WHO GETS HIRED?

The JAGC has both summer intern and active duty positions available.

ACTIVE DUTY POSITIONS . . .

The JAGC accepts applications from third year law students and licensed attorneys. If you're already a licensed attorney, you can apply any time. If you're applying for the JAGC as a 3L, this is how it works. You have to be at an ABA-accredited law school. There are two rounds of consideration so that you can apply by November 1 or March 1 (if you get turned down in November you can reapply by March 1). If the JAGC wants you, you get an offer contingent on passing a physical and any state (or D.C.'s) bar exam. You take the bar in July after you graduate, and since you're unlikely to hear the results until November or so, you typically enter the JAG School in the following January's class. In the meantime—between graduation and January—your time (other than studying for and taking the bar exam!) is your own. Some graduates stick with their law school jobs, others take a temporary job, and still others just chill out for a few months before they start!

SUMMER CLERKSHIPS . . .

The JAGC hires 100 law students (75 2Ls and 25 1Ls) every year for summer intern positions throughout the U.S. and overseas. These summer jobs don't create an obligation for military duty. While a good performance appraisal on a summer internship could give you an advantage in getting into the JAG Corps after graduation, it's not a bad job regardless of what your post-law-school plans are. You can go overseas if you want, so if you like to travel you'll love that (although you do have to pay your way to your destination, and provide your own housing). You state your geographic preferences and you'll usually get your first choice. Most offices will let you get your feet wet in all different areas, so you can help out with investigations, interview witnesses, help draft court-martial charges—all kinds of interesting things.

The summer internship program is open to first- and second- year students who are U.S. citizens. These summer internships are considered temporary civil service positions. You receive pay at the GS-7 level (about $510 a week) if you're a 2L, and at the GS-5 level (about $410 a week) if you're a 1L. The program lasts approximately 60 days. Application deadlines are March 1 for 1Ls and November 1 for 2Ls. Last year, of the 75 2L interns, 56 were given permanent offers.

HOW TO APPLY . . .

Contact the JAGC at 1-800-552-3978, at the JAGC web site (listed at the top of this entry), or by writing to:

The Judge Advocate General's School
Attn: JAGS-GRA
600 Massie Road
Charlottesville, VA 22903-1781

The application includes DA Form 3175, which is the preliminary application for the JAGC; transcripts of all undergraduate, graduate, and law school studies; a description of all full-time and part-time legal and non-legal experience (in other words, a resume); a 100 to 200 word statement of interests, objectives, and your motivation in applying for the JAGC; and if you've already passed the bar, a certificate or letter from the appropriate clerk of courts proving it. If you want, you can also include letters of recommendation and a writing sample, although they aren't required.

Once you complete an application, you are interviewed by an active duty JAGC Field Screening Officer. The application and interview report are considered by a Selection Board that meets twice a year in Washington, D.C. If you are selected by the Board, you have to meet the Army's medical and weight standards and be able to obtain a security clearance. You then let the JAGC know where you'd like to be assigned (and they do make an effort to send you where you want to go). Notification of proposed assignment to a Judge Advocate office in the U.S. or overseas occurs about two or three months before your active duty report date.

P.S.: I heard wonderful things about the Navy and Air Force JAG Corps, as well. Of course, they aren't *identical*—for instance, the Army has the largest JAG Corps and a somewhat larger pool of practice areas as a result, and it's the only one with a summer internship program, whereas the Air Force is reputed to have the nicest buildings (and when it comes to uniforms, you can make your own decision!). Nonetheless, from a JAG Corps perspective you'll find many of the same kinds of experience, benefits, and excellent skills development.

To contact them:

Navy JAGC:

Director of Attorney Recruiting
U.S. Navy, Office of the Judge Advocate General
200 Stovall Street
Alexandria, VA 22332-2400
Phone: 800-327-NAVY (800-432-1884 in Florida, 800-327-6289 in Puerto Rico, 907-272-9133 in Alaska, and 808-546-7540 in Hawaii)
Incidentally, the Navy JAGC has an *awesome* web page. You'll find it at finifter.com/jag/—it's got all kinds of information not just about the Navy JAG but also about TV shows concerning the JAG Corps and all sorts of other fun stuff. Also try out jag.navy.mil/.

Air Force JAGC:

Director of Attorney Recruiting
U.S. Air Force, Judge Advocate General's Department; HQ, USAF/JAX
1420 Air Force Pentagon
Washington, D.C. 20330
Phone: 800-JAGUSAF or 703-614-5941

The Air Force JAG also has a web page, where you'll find tons of information about not just the work but the application forms, history, you name it. You'll find the Air Force JAG page at ja.hq.af.mil/.

National Labor Relations Board

1099 14ᵀᴴ Street, N.W. • Washington, D.C. 20570-0001
Phone: 202-273-3900 • Web site: www.nlrb.gov

WHAT IS IT?

The NLRB is an independent federal agency, created in 1935 to administer the National Labor Relations Act. That's the basic law governing relations between labor unions and the employers whose operations affect interstate commerce.

The NLRA guarantees the right of employees to organize and to bargain collectively with their employers or to refrain from all such activity. It generally applies to all employers involved in interstate commerce, other than airlines, railroads, agriculture, and the government. It implements the national labor policy of assuring free choice and encouraging collective bargaining as a means of maintaining industrial peace.

STRUCTURE . . .

The NLRB has both judicial functions and prosecuting functions, and those functions are kept separate by law. On the judicial side, there is the five-member National Labor Relations Board, which acts in a quasi-judicial fashion in deciding cases. The Board has its own staff, with each Board member having a Chief Counsel, Deputy Counsel, three assistant Chief Counsel, a few senior Counsel, and a dozen or so Counsel, amounting to about 20 lawyers for each of the five Board members.

The Office of the General Counsel handles the prosecution function. It investigates and processes cases, and prosecutes cases in the courts. The General Counsel also supervises the Agency's field offices. There are over 100 lawyers in the General Counsel's office. The office has several different offices of its own, including the Division of Advice, the Contempt Litigation Branch, the Special Litigation Branch, the Supreme Court Branch, the Office of Appeals, and the Division of Enforcement Litigation.

There are many attorneys employed by the NLRB's field offices. There are approximately 50 field offices; for addresses, check out the NLRB's web page, at www.nlrb.gov/fieldoff.html. Field attorneys dig up the facts on cases, help in settlement efforts, draft complaints, and prepare and try cases before administrative law judges (the NLRB employs several dozen administrative law judges). Field attorneys also sometimes seek injunctive relief in federal court. Other possible responsibilities include acting as Hearing Officer in contested representation election cases, preparing drafts of decision for Regional Directors of the NLRB, and helping conduct representation elections. Working in the field offices involves frequent travel in the region where you work.

Overall, the NLRB employs over 700 attorneys, with about a third of them in Washington and the remaining two-thirds at offices around the country.

WHO GETS HIRED?

The NLRB hires both experienced attorneys and new law school graduates. When you're hired, the NLRB will ask you for a geographic preference, and you may be given a choice of several office locations.

Students are also hired for summer internships as the NLRB's budget permits; contact the NLRB in Washington for availability of internships in any given summer.

HOW TO APPLY . . .

Contact the NLRB in Washington, at:
Personnel Branch
National Labor Relations Board
1099 14TH St., N.W.
Washington, D.C. 20570-0001
202-273-3900

You may also apply to any NLRB branch office that interests you. You'll find those addresses on the NLRB's web page (the web site is given at the beginning of this entry).

★　　★　　★　　★　　★

Overseas Private Investment Corporation

1100 New York Avenue N.W. • Washington, D.C. 20527
Phone: 202-336-8413 • Web site: opic.gov/

WHAT IS IT?

Overseas Private Investment Corporation ("OPIC") is an interesting hybrid. It is wholly-owned by the U.S. Government, but at the same time it's organized like a private corporation. It was created by Congress in 1971 to encourage U.S. private direct foreign investment. Essentially, OPIC provides risk insurance, financing, and a variety of investor services to encourage U.S. private investment in more than 140 developing nations and emerging markets. More specifically, OPIC assists American investors through four principal activities designed to promote overseas investment and reduce the associated risks:

(i) Financing businesses through loans and loan guaranties;

(ii) Supporting private investment funds which provide equity for U.S. companies investing in projects overseas;

(iii) Insuring investments against a broad range of political risks; and

(iv) Engaging in outreach activities designed to inform the American business community of investment opportunities overseas.

Since its inception in 1971, OPIC has supported investments worth nearly $84 billion, generated $43 billion in U.S. exports, and helped create 200,000 American jobs.

STRUCTURE . . .

OPIC is divided into seven departments: insurance, finance, investment development, legal affairs, investment funds, management services, and financial management and statutory review. OPIC also has a Department of Legal Affairs, and predictably enough, that's where you'll find OPIC attorneys. There are just over 20 lawyers in the Department of Legal Affairs.

How many attorneys work there: Approximately 23 (including 12 women and 5 minorities).

HOURS AND BUCKS . . .

Attorneys with OPIC typically work from 9 a.m. to 6:30 p.m. or so. New attorneys start at pay level GS-14. (Note that OPIC hires exclusively experienced attorneys, typically with 5 to 15 years of experience).

WHAT IT'S LIKE TO WORK THERE . . .

Attorneys at OPIC perform legal work in project finance, political risk insurance, and investment funds. They provide advice and assistance to

OPIC officials, review pending or proposed actions, and participate as legal counsel in complex contracts, agreements, and claims settlements— including negotiating and preparing all necessary legal instruments. Attorneys also give legal opinions on issues of OPIC authority and operations.

On average, OPIC lawyers work from about 9 in the morning until 6:30 at night.

WHO GETS HIRED?

OPIC doesn't hire entry-level attorneys. Instead, you need at least four years of legal experience in general corporate and/or finance law, and they like to see international financial transactions experience, but it's not mandatory. Attorneys start at pay grade GS-14.

OPIC also has summer and academic semester internships for law students. They hire five summer law clerks and five during the academic year. The spring and fall semester internships are unpaid; the summer internship pay is "modest," at pay grade GS-5. As a student intern you help draft the various agreements and other documents necessary for project financings and political risk insurance contracts, participate in negotiations with investors and their counsel, and do some legal research. These internships are great if you want exposure to many aspects of international investment. You learn about everything from structuring project financings to assessing political risks in connection with issuing insurance contracts, to evaluating insurance claims.

For the internships, OPIC looks for a demonstrated interest in finance (*e.g.*, relevant classes or a work background in banking, accounting, or a related field), good grades and superior writing ability, and either an exposure to, or a demonstrated interest in, international affairs.

HOW TO APPLY . . .

For summer and semester-long internships, you need to send a resume, five- to 10-page writing sample, and, if you want, your law school transcript. The deadline for summer clerkship applications is mid November for 2Ls (call for specific dates), and January 1 for 1Ls.

For experienced attorneys, you'll find vacancy information either by calling OPIC's job line at 202-336-8682, or by calling the OPIC FaxLine at 202-336-8700. You can also find vacancy announcements on the "USA Jobs" web page, at www.usajobs.opm.gov.

For any kind of job with OPIC, you can contact:
Office of Human Resources Management
Overseas Private Investment Corporation
1100 New York Avenue, N.W.
Washington, D.C. 20527

Railroad Retirement Board

844 N. Rush Street • Chicago, IL 60611
Phone: 312-751-4500 • Fax: 312-751-7164 • Web site: rrb.gov
E-mail: ctkukla@attmail.com

WHAT IS IT?

Created in the mid 1930s, the Railroad Retirement Board ("RRB") administers the Railroad Retirement Act, which provides retirement and disability benefits for railroad workers and their families, and the Railroad Unemployment Insurance Act, which provides unemployment and sickness benefits for railroad workers.

The RRB employs a total of about 1,500 people in a variety of jobs, including auditors, claims examiners, claims specialists, contact representatives, criminal investigators, field office claims examiners, and railroad claims examiners. The Agency is divided into directors, which include the Office of Retirement and Survivor Programs, the Bureau of Unemployment and Sickness Insurance, and the Bureau of Field Service (encompassing the field offices, which are located in Atlanta, Cleveland, Kansas City (Missouri), Oakland, Philadelphia and Washington, D.C.).

NUTS AND BOLTS

Number of attorneys in RRB: 23 (22 at the Chicago headquarters, 1 in the Washington, D.C. field office).

Total women attorneys: 9 (all in Chicago); total minority attorneys: 2 (both in Chicago).

Where attorneys work: Office of General Counsel (1); Bureau of Law: (10); Bureau of Hearings and Appeals (6); Board Member offices (4); Office of Inspector General (2);Washington Field Office (1).

WHAT DO LAWYERS AT RRB DO?

There are 23 lawyers who work in the RRB in the Office of General Counsel. They handle any and all legal issues involving the wide range of services offered by the RRB and they get to handle cases before the U.S. courts of appeals and various administrative tribunals. They can be involved primarily in litigation, or can serve in an in-house counsel capacity, providing written and oral legal advice on any number of topics.

WHAT IT'S LIKE TO WORK THERE . . .

Attorneys at RRB like the "friendly and informal" atmosphere with "camaraderie among attorneys in the office and between attorneys and other officials and employees in the agency." They appreciate the fact that they "gain experience quickly" and that they are encouraged to assume responsibility for important work assignments early on. They get a "great variety of projects" and "whatever training they need, when they need it." RRB management "makes every effort to make the work experience worthwhile and satisfying."

DETAILS ON ENTRY-LEVEL POSITIONS . . .

First year attorneys typically spend approximately 2,000 hours at work. There is limited travel involved with training and litigation. Part-time work is available.

Most attorneys are hired directly out of law school (although the agency periodically hires experienced attorneys). The RRB likes to see high grades, Law Review or Moot Court, and legal writing experience.

Starting pay is $$ ($35,000-50,000).

Job openings are periodically posted at the Office of Personnel Management's home page, at usajobs.com.

HOW TO APPLY . . .

Contact the Railroad Retirement Board via the address, phone, and e-mail addresses at the beginning of this entry.

Securities & Exchange Commission

450 Fifth Street, N.W. • Washington, D.C. 20549
Phone: 202-942-4150 • Web site: www.sec.gov (this is a very extensive and informative home page!)

WHAT IS IT?

The Securities and Exchange Commission ("SEC") is an independent law enforcement and regulatory agency, charges with administering the federal securities laws. The laws that concern the SEC protect investors in securities markets and ensure that investors have access to—and disclosure of—all material information concerning publicly-traded securities. The Commission also regulates firms engaged in the purchase or sale of securities, people who provide investment advice, and investment companies. The SEC enforces six principal laws: The Securities Act of 1933, the Securities Exchange Act of 1934, the Investment Company Act of 1940, the Investment Adviser Act of 1940, the Public Utility Holding Company Act of 1935, and the Trust Indenture Act of 1939. (If you slept through your Securities class in law school—or avoided it entirely—the SEC's home page offers an *excellent* summary of what these laws are all about!)

STRUCTURE . . .

The SEC is headquartered in Washington, D.C., and it has regional or district offices in 11 cities (see addresses at the end of this entry). There are five SEC Commissioners, all appointed by the President, and five principal divisions. They are:

(1) *Division of Corporate Finance:* It has the overall responsibility of ensuring that disclosure requirements are met by publicly held companies registered with the Commission. Its work includes reviewing registration statements for publicly-traded corporate securities as well as documents concerning tender offers, proxy solicitations, mergers, and acquisitions.

(2) *Division of Market Regulation:* It is responsible for overseeing the securities markets, for registering and regulating brokerage firms, for overseeing the securities self-regulatory organizations (like the nation's stock exchanges), and for overseeing other market participants, such as transfer agents and clearing organizations. The Division also sets financial responsibility standards, and regulates trading and sales practices, policies affecting operation of the securities markets, and surveillance.

(3) *Division of Investment Management:* This Division is responsible for administering three statutes: the Investment Company Act of 1940, the Investment Advisers Act of 1940, and the Public Utility Holding Company Act of 1935. The division staff ensures compliance with regulations regarding the registration, financial responsibility, sales practices, and advertising of investment companies and of investment advisers. New products offered by these entities also are reviewed by staff in this division. The division reviews and processes investment company registration statements, proxy statements, and periodic reports under the Securities Act.

(4) *Division of Enforcement:* This is charged with enforcing federal securities laws. Enforcement responsibilities include investigating possible

violations of the federal securities laws and recommending appropriate remedies for consideration by the Commission.

(5) *Office of Compliance Inspections and Examinations:* This office is responsible for conducting and coordinating all compliance inspection programs of brokers, dealers, self-regulatory organizations, investment companies and advisers, clearing agencies, and transfer agents. The Office determines whether these entities are in compliance with the federal securities laws, with the goal of protecting investors.

NUTS AND BOLTS

Number of attorneys in the SEC: 1,000+ (women: 400+; minorities: 160+; disabled: 40+).

Other Offices: New York City, Boston, Philadelphia, Miami, Atlanta, Chicago, Denver, Fort Worth, Salt Lake City, Los Angeles, and San Francisco. Attorneys are employed in all SEC offices.

WHAT DO LAWYERS AT THE SEC DO?

There are over 1,000 attorneys at the SEC out of a total work force of more than 2,700 people. More attorneys work in the Enforcement Division than any other section of the SEC, but there are also substantial numbers of lawyers in the other divisions as well.

Enforcement Division lawyers have broad investigatory powers under the SEC's authority. They investigate things like insider trading, market manipulation, fraudulent accounting practices, and the sale of unregistered securities.

Corporate Finance Division attorneys primarily handle issues involving the financial information that publicly-held companies have to disclose. In this capacity the Division also deals with the issuance of new securities. Attorneys in the division must frequently offer legal interpretations concerning mergers and acquisitions, creative methods of raising capital, and issues arising from international securities offerings.

The Division of Market Regulation's attorneys address the regulation of securities markets and also the activities of investment bankers, stock brokers, and related professionals. Attorneys in this division often have to resolve difficult policy questions requiring a comprehensive understanding of securities trading and the operation of capital markets. (If you don't start out with this kind of knowledge, you quickly acquire it by working with the Division!)

The Division of Investment Management has attorneys who handle issues involving investment companies and investment advisers.

The Office of Compliance Inspections and Examinations has attorneys who handle issues of compliance with brokers, dealers, investment companies and advisers, and similar professionals.

"It's tremendous. It's like working at a top-notch firm that happens to be a governmental agency."

"You get lots of responsibility early on, for huge multi-million dollar matters. They're your own cases, although you handle them with supervision."

"It's very exciting! Even as a pretty new lawyer you can wind up bringing a case that has a huge impact."

"Your abilities are recognized and appreciated."

"There's tremendous camaraderie in the offices."

"While you're responsible for accounting for your time, you're not billing a client as you would in a private practice. So if you want to sit and bounce ideas off colleagues relating to a complex fraud scheme, you won't get beaten up for that."

"You have a strong sense of doing right. You feel like you do it for the public good. That motivates you."

"You handle incredible cases. Investment company frauds, violations of federal securities laws, fraudulent issuances of stock, Ponzi schemes, fraudulent filings, insider trading cases. They almost always have *very* interesting fact patterns. You might have some guy who purports to sell investments but he's really pocketing the income, for instance. The facts are complex and the laws are very interesting."

"It helps to be a self-starter. A number of people will wind up working long, hard hours, but because you feel you're doing the 'right thing,' you don't mind it."

"You have to be efficient and resourceful, and do what's necessary to get the job done. You'll do everything from taking testimony, to stamping in documents and typing your own letters."

"You have to be the kind of person who likes unraveling mysteries."

"You need to be detail-oriented. With insider trading, you have to sort through tons of documents and be on the ball constantly for evidence."

"You need to like both working alone and also as part of a team, on huge cases."

"You need to like to write. There's lots of intensive writing, formal memos to the commission, very long and detailed facts and applicable law."

"Depending on your role, you may not get into court, but you will take testimony and depositions."

"You have to have people skills, both in terms of dealing with questions from the public, and also in the context of dealing with all kinds of witnesses. Some of the people you deal with aren't happy. They might have lost their life savings in an investment scheme. You have to know when to be tough, and also to be able to work with people under tremendous stress due to their own situations."

"It's very intense. There's more work than there are people to do it."

WHO'S GETS HIRED?

Entry level: Approximately 20 to 30 new law school graduates are hired every year (see application details below).

Laterals: Approximately 100 experienced attorneys are hired every year. For laterals, you need at least two years of specialized experience directly involving complex securities or financial matters.

Summer interns: Approximately 25 are hired every year. This is a paid position. You provide legal research and other assistance to staff attorneys. (See application details below.)

Summer Honors Program: Open to 1Ls and 2Ls (as well as joint J.D./MBA students). This is an unpaid internship. (See application details below.)

Student Observer Program: Allows you to work at the SEC (or a regional or district office) during the semester. You receive law school credit for this program.

HOW TO APPLY . . .

Entry Level Positions: The SEC accepts applications from 3Ls only between August 1 and November 1 of any given year. Interviews may begin as early as October, but typically interviews and offers come about as late as January. The SEC conducts on-campus interviews at some law schools, and if you attend one of these schools, you don't have to go far out of your way to apply! The law schools with on-campus interviews are American, Baltimore, Catholic, Columbia, Duke, George Mason, George Washington, Georgetown, Harvard, Howard, Maryland, Temple, Virginia, and Yale.

If you are interested in working for one of the regional or district offices, you should apply directly to them (addresses are below). Until you pass the bar, you are called a "Law Clerk." (Remember—it's only temporary!) Law Clerk positions are paid at the GS-11 grade level. You are a Law Clerk for no more than 14 months, which gives you a chance to pass the bar exam in any state or the District of Columbia. Once you pass the bar, you are converted to an attorney, and if you don't pass the bar in 14 months—well, see ya.

To apply, send a resume, law school transcript, writing sample of no more than 10 pages, and the names of addresses of three references to the headquarters or whichever regional or district office you'd like to work for (addresses below).

FOR LATERALS:

Contact the SEC's headquarters or check for vacancies at the Office of Personnel Management's web site, usajobs.com.

FOR SUMMER LAW INTERNSHIPS:

2Ls enter at the GS-9 pay level, and 1Ls enter at a GS-7 level.

No applications are accepted before December 1st, and applications must be postmarked no later than the second Friday in February. Offers are made on a rolling basis starting as early as February.

Apply to the office where you want to work (either the headquarters in Washington, or any of the regional/district offices listed below). Send a resume, transcript, a writing sample of no more than 10 pages, and the names of three references.

FOR THE SUMMER HONORS PROGRAM:

This is an unpaid program. The Honors Program is run by the Division of Enforcement and the Office of the General Counsel. Positions are only available in Washington, D.C.

The Honors Program is open to 1Ls and 2Ls, as well as joint J.D./MBA students. You need "superior" undergraduate and law school credentials, as well as work experience related to the securities industry. (2Ls must have a B average, either Law Review or Moot Court membership, and/or a demonstrated interest in the securities field.)

Applications are usually not received before December 1, and must be postmarked no later than the second Friday in March. Offers for participation are made on a rolling basis starting the first week of February. The Program runs from late May through the end of July. You are expected to work full-time for the 10 weeks.

To apply, send a cover letter, law school transcript, writing sample of no more than 10 pages, and the names and addresses of three references to the SEC's Washington headquarters (Attn: Summer Honors Program Coordinator, Division of Enforcement, 450 5TH St., N.W., Washington, D.C. 20549).

STUDENT OBSERVER PROGRAM (A ONE-SEMESTER-DURING-THE-SCHOOL-YEAR OPPORTUNITY):

This program gives you the chance, with the approval of your law school, to volunteer up to 20 hours a week for a 12- to 14- week period during either the fall or spring semesters, in exchange for law school credit. The Program requires you to attend seminars one day each week.

You don't have to go to a Washington, D.C. law school to qualify. Students who *are* in or near D.C. apply to the Division of Enforcement at the Washington headquarters, but may be placed in other divisions based on your interests and the agency's needs. If you go to school near one of the SEC's regional/district offices, check with your Career Services Office for application deadlines for local offices. Note that the SEC has to receive your application at least six to eight weeks before the semester starts.

The Program is open to all law students, although first consideration is given to students with appropriate securities industry course work or comparable work experience. Alternatively, you can have great grades or a demonstrated interest in the securities industry.

To apply, send a cover letter, law school transcript, writing sample of no more than 10 pages, and the names and addresses of three references to either the regional/district office that interests you (addresses below), or for Washington D.C., write to: Student Volunteer Coordinator, Division of Enforcement, 450 5TH Street N.W., Washington, D.C. 20549.

REGIONAL AND DISTRICT OFFICES . . .

Other than its Washington, D.C. headquarters, the SEC has 11 offices around the country. You can reach them at:

Northeast Regional Office
7 World Trade Center
Suite 1300
New York, NY 10048
212-748-8000

Boston District Office
73 Tremont Street
Suite 600
Boston, MA 02108-3912
617-424-5900

Philadelphia District Office
The Curtis Center
Suite 1005 East
601 Walnut Street
Philadelphia, PA 19106-3322

Southeast Regional Office
1401 Brickell Avenue
Suite 200
Miami, FL 33131
305-536-4700

Atlanta District Office
3475 Lenox Road, N.E.
Suite 1000
Atlanta, GA 30326-1232
404-842-7600

Midwest Regional Office
Citicorp Center
500 W. Madison Street
Suite 1400
Chicago, IL 60661-2511
312-353-7390

Central Regional Office
1801 California Street
Suite 4800
Denver, CO 80202-2648

Fort Worth District Office
801 Cherry Street
Suite 1900
Fort Worth, TX 76102
817-978-3821

Salt Lake District Office
50 South Main Street
Suite 500
Salt Lake City, UT 84144-0402
801-524-5796

San Francisco District Office
44 Montgomery Street
Suite 1100
San Francisco, CA 94104
415-705-2500

Pacific Regional Office
5670 Wilshire Boulevard
Suite 1100
Los Angeles, CA 90036-3648
213-965-3998

Department of State—Office of the Legal Adviser

Employment Office
22ND and D Streets, N.W., Room 2819 • Washington, D.C. 20520
Job line: 202-647-7284 • Web site: www.state.gov/index.html
(this is a *very* extensive and useful web site)

WHAT IS IT?

The State Department is the lead U.S. foreign affairs agency. It advances U.S. objectives and interests in shaping a freer, more secure, and more prosperous world through formulating, representing, and implementing the President's foreign policies. It employs almost 25,000 people through-out the United States and the world in over 230 embassies and consulates in more than 140 countries.

STRUCTURE . . .

The State Department has both Civil Service and Foreign Service person-nel. We talked about the Foreign Service in Chapter Three. Here, the focus is on the State Department's Office of the Legal Adviser.

The State Department overall has a structure that you could best describe as byzantine. It is divided into all kinds of bureaus and offices, and is separated into both geographic bureaus (there are five of those) and functional bureaus (there are 14 of those). Rather than take you on a bazillion page tour of those bureaus, you'll find a thorough breakdown of what they do at the State Department's *extremely* thorough web page at www.state.gov/index.html. What we'll do here is to focus on the Office of the Legal Adviser, which employs about 100 attorneys.

WHAT DO ATTORNEYS IN THE OFFICE OF THE LEGAL ADVISER DO?

The State Department's slogan is: "The Most Interesting Work . . . In The World." The work the attorneys in the Legal Adviser's Office certainly fits that description. They work on a broad range of projects, mostly focusing on providing legal advice and services to policy officers in the State Department. Among many other things, they negotiate, draft, and interpret all kinds of international agreements, as well as domestic statutes and other regulations. They represent the U.S. in many international organizations, including the U.N. General Assembly and the Organization of American States. They participate in headline-making international negotiations and arms control discussions. They help the Justice Department prepare litigation involving State Department interests and assist state and federal prosecutors in extraditing fugitives from foreign countries. They represent the U.S. before international tribunals, like the International Court of Justice. It's no wonder that when you hear lawyers in the Office of the Legal Adviser talk about what they do they rave about how they love their job!

WHO GETS HIRED?

There aren't a lot of attorney openings at the State Department and the selection process is very competitive. But there are *some* jobs, and here they are:

Entry Level Attorney Positions: The Office of Legal Advisers hires a handful of 3Ls and judicial clerks every year to fill junior attorney positions. It helps to have some international legal training and to know a foreign language or two, but it's not mandatory. Because there are a lot of people applying for these positions, you typically need terrific paper credentials in order to get in. The deadline for applications is November 1.

Experienced Attorneys: The openings are few and far between, but they do exist. You'll find them posted on the State Department's web page, at www.state.gov/index.html (click on "Careers," and then "Civil Service Careers," and then click on "Fedworld" for current vacancies).

Internships: There are two types—paid and unpaid. There are over 600 internships available all together, and about 10% of them are paid. The internships are available both in Washington, D.C. and in some U.S.-based field offices. If you're willing to take an unpaid internship, you can also work abroad. While the prospect of no pay might seem daunting, these overseas internships get rave reviews—they are a great door-opener for the Foreign Service and the work itself is interesting.

For the paid internships: They are during the summer only, full-time, and you must be able to work for at least 10 weeks. As a 1L you can expect to make about $4,000 for a 10-week summer, and as a 2L about $5,000 (if you work longer you obviously make more!).

For the unpaid internships: These typically take place during the school year for a semester *or* during the summer for at least 10 weeks.

For information on vacancies call the 24-hour job line: 202-647-7284.

State Government

STATE ATTORNEY GENERAL OFFICES

"People give body parts to get jobs there."

"People who work there say it's the greatest thing they've ever done. What they give up in money they make up in fun."

"Morale is incredibly high. They feel there's meaning to their work. They're doing something that makes a **difference**."

These are just some of the raves I heard about state Attorney Generals' ("AG's") offices across the country. In fact, I heard so many good things that it's fair to say that working in *any* state AG's office is a great job!

Why? There are a *million* things to recommend these jobs. As the wonderful Mary Birmingham, Career Services Director at the University of Arizona School of Law, says, "Working for the state AG's office is the closest thing akin to the Department of Justice, but unlike most DOJ jobs, you *can* get into state AG's offices right out of school." She adds that, "When you work for the state AG, you're the state's law firm—you can be put into an area you like or think you'll like. Criminal litigation, civil litigation, environmental protection, you get the opportunity to be involved right away. And on top of that, you're involved politically with what's going on in your state. It's very exciting."

What do you need to know about AG's offices? For a start, you need to know that many AG's offices rival large law firms in size. In many states in fact, the AG's office will be the largest law firm in the state. Michigan's AG's office, for instance, has almost 300 lawyers. Washington State has more than 400 lawyers.

While all AG's offices are different, they are generally divided into numerous divisions, which are themselves divided into sections. The divisions and/or sections represent different state agencies. While there may be very few divisions in AG's offices in smaller states, in large states there will be a whole passel of them. When you join an AG's office, you typically go in as an "Assistant Attorney General" ("AAG") in a particular section or division.

WHAT PEOPLE LIKE ABOUT WORKING FOR ATTORNEY GENERALS' OFFICES...

1. You can get in straight out of school (although of course they hire experienced attorneys as well). All state AG's offices hire new law school graduates as Assistant Attorneys General, and some of them even have Honors Programs, mimicking federal agency honors programs. State AG's also hire lots and lots of law clerks, so you can get your feet wet while you're still in school.

2. Variety! No matter what it is that you want to do (or *think* you want to do) you'll find it at the AG's office. From different kinds of litigation, to environmental protection, to real estate, to excellent appellate practices—AG's offices are a regular smorgasbord of opportunities. For instance, in Michigan, specialties in the AG's office includes administrative, appellate, children/youth, civil rights/civil liberties, consumer law, criminal law, constitutional law, education, employment/employee benefits, environmental/energy, legislative, litigation, and tax. The Texas AG's office is divided into more than 40 different divisions covering everything from Medicaid fraud to juvenile crime intervention to litigation to bankruptcy and collections to citizen's assistance to natural resources.

3. Hours. AG's offices are well-known for offering particularly livable work hours. It's rare to work late, and weekend work is similarly scarce.

4. Flexibility when it comes to grade requirements. While no employer is going to admit to looking for *awful* grades, AG's are notoriously not grade-sensitive. Arizona's Attorney General, the charming and very funny Grant Woods, likes to say that he has the distinction of graduating with the highest GPA from Arizona State—"per hour studied." He freely admits that he's a bottom-of-the-class kind of guy. Instead, extracurriculars and prior work experience are significant plusses, as is any focus on a particular area. For instance, if you've taken part in a Child Advocacy Clinic, that will be a big help in getting your foot in the door at the child support section of an AG's office (every state has one of these), where they go after deadbeat parents.

5. While the starting salaries for AAG's don't rival big firms, they aren't terrible. Most AG's offices start you off at between $30,000 to $45,000, and you tend to get generous government benefits.

6. You're on the "right side." There's a strong "white hat" element to working in AG's offices, because much of the time you are either helping citizens of your state, safeguarding taxpayer funds, or rooting out wrongdoers. For instance, *everybody* complains about insurance

cheats. But if you work in the Insurance Fraud Division of a state AG's office, you get to *do* something about it!

7. Early and plentiful responsibility. When you start out as an Assistant Attorney General, you hit the ground running. As many AAG's point out, there's more work than there are people to do it. And rather than working on just one small part of a case, you handle most cases from their inception through all levels of state and federal appeals.

8. The opportunity to see your efforts translate into good government. By working as an advisor to state agencies, you can see the fruits of your advice translate, over the years, into tangible changes in the way things get done.

9. Excellent training and support. AG's offices not only offer training seminars and libraries of research materials, but they are known for offering plenty of advice from more senior lawyers. AAG's report quickly developing expertise in complex areas of the law.

10. No billable hours. You don't have to keep track of your time as you would in private practice, because your client—the state—doesn't receive a bill.

11. No need to generate business. States don't expect you to be a rain-maker!

12. AG's offices hire routinely and year-round. Getting into an AG's office isn't a matter of meeting a strict application deadline, as is true for so many employers.

WHERE ARE THE JOBS?

State capitols are obvious answers, but they're not the only ones. Most AG's offices have lawyers in every sizable city in the state, and some have offices in smaller cities and towns as well.

HOW MANY PEOPLE DO THEY HIRE?

It varies state-to-state, but it's safe to say that virtually every AG's office will hire new graduates every year.

SUMMER JOBS . . .

AG's offices all have paid summer internship programs, which typically pay $300 to $400 a week. In addition, AG's offices accept student volunteers (but you typically can't volunteer once you're a lawyer).

HOW ATTORNEY GENERALS' OFFICES ARE ORGANIZED: A LOOK AT ARIZONA

You can find out exactly how each state AG's office is organized by visiting any state's web page. Many states have web pages specifically for their AG's offices. I've given you the web sites for every state a little later in this section. But right now, for a representative snapshot of how AG's offices are set up, let's take a look at the Arizona AG's office.

It's divided into five divisions: administrative, civil, criminal, economic security, and civil rights.

The Administrative Section, as the name implies, provides the AG's office with overall policy direction and management supervision, and it's the focal point for agency emergency issues and extraordinary or highly-sensitive issues.

The Civil Division has over 130 lawyers, split into nine different sections. The nine sections are administrative law, consumer protection and advocacy, antitrust, insurance defense, land and natural resources, licensing and enforcement, solicitor general and opinions, tax, and transportation. The largest of these are the Administrative Law Section, the Insurance Defense Section, and the Consumer Protection and Advocacy Section. Here's what those three sections do: The Administrative Law Section focuses on specific legal areas, including employment, education, procurement, and health services. The section also provides day-to-day legal services to many of the State's departments, boards, agencies, and commissions. These services include counseling, written opinions, representation in lawsuits and administrative hearings, and drafting and reviewing legislation and other documents.

The Consumer Protection and Advocacy Section is responsible for civil enforcement of the Arizona Consumer Fraud Act, among other things. In its enforcement work, the section can seek restitution and damages for victims, civil penalties, and equitable remedies.

The Insurance Defense Section represents the state's departments and other entities, as well as State employees and agents, in lawsuits alleging that the state is liable for personal injuries, property damage, and constitutional law violations. It defends the state against allegations of civil rights violations and negligence brought by prisoners, as well as actions alleging wrongful discharge from state employment or employment discrimination.

So that's the Civil Division. The Civil Rights Division has just over 10 lawyers and it handles the kinds of issues that its name suggests: namely, discrimination in employment, fair housing, public accommodations, and voting rights. It investigates charges of discrimination and it also has an education function, developing seminars and presenting them throughout the state.

The Criminal Division is divided into seven sections and it has over 100 lawyers. The sections include the Criminal Appeals Section, the

Criminal Trials Section, the Drug Enforcement Section, the Environmental Enforcement Section, the Organized Crime and Fraud Section, the Special Investigations Section, and the Tucson Criminal Section. The largest section, the Criminal Appeals Section, represents the state in all criminal appeals filed by convicted felons, among other duties. The Criminal Trials Section, another large one, helps county attorneys with matters referred to the AG's office because of a conflict of interest or for other policy or economic reasons, including complex homicide cases that require substantial resources. It also handles white-collar crimes. Another section with more than 20 lawyers, the Environmental Enforcement Section, has as its principal client the Arizona Department of Environmental Quality. The section assists in developing rules and handles all civil and criminal environmental litigation, including administrative and judicial prosecution and defense. Among other duties, it also enforces state laws and appropriate federal environmental laws in cooperation with federal authorities. The Organized Crime and Fraud Section investigates and prosecutes, among other cases, those involving computer fraud, exploitation of the elderly, home improvement fraud, telemarketing fraud, illegal investment schemes, worker's compensation fraud, vehicle chop shops, fraud against the state, and trafficking in stolen property.

The Economic Security Division has two units: the Agency Counsel Unit (which acts as corporate counsel for the Department of Economic Security), and the Child Enforcement Unit (which prosecutes welfare fraud, unemployment insurance fraud and any other fraud committed against the Department of Economic Security).

WHERE TO LEARN MORE . . .

Visit the web sites or call for information on hiring deadlines and requirements (I've provided every state AG's web site, address, and phone number below). For more detailed information on contacts and individual departments in each state AG's office, check out the excellent *State Yellow Book,* published by Leadership Directories (it's in almost every library, as well as your Career Services Office at school).

Addresses, phone numbers, and web sites for state Attorney General's Offices:

Alabama:
Attorney General: Bill Pryor
Attorney General's Office
State House
Montgomery, AL 36130
Phone: 334-242-7300
Fax: 334-242-7458
General state executive branch
    web site: www.state.al.us

Alaska:
Attorney General: Bruce Botelho
Law Department
450 Dimond Courthouse
P.O. Box 110300
Juneau, AK 99811-0300
General Information: 907-465-3600
Fax: 907-465-2075
Attorney General's Office web site:
    www.law.state.ak.us/index.html

Arizona:
Attorney General: Grant Woods
Attorney General's Office
1275 W. Washington Street
Phoenix, AZ 85007
Phone: 602-542-5025
Fax: 602-542-1275
General state executive branch
  web site: www.state.az.us

Arkansas:
Attorney General: Winston Bryant
Attorney General's Office
200 Catlett-Prien Tower
323 Center Street
Little Rock, AR 72201-2610
Phone: 501-682-2007
Fax: 501-682-8084
General state executive branch
  web site: www.state.ar.us

California:
Attorney General: Daniel E.
  Lundgren
Justice Department
1300 I Street, Suite 1101
P.O. Box 944255
Sacramento, CA 94244-2550
Phone: 916-445-9555
Fax: 916-324-5205
Attorney General's Office web site:
  www.caag.state.ca.us

Colorado:
Attorney General: Gale A. Norton
Attorney General's Office
1525 Sherman Street, 5TH Floor
Denver, CO 80203
Phone: 303-866-3617
Fax: 303-866-5691
General state executive branch
  web site: www.state.co.us

Connecticut:
Attorney General: Richard
  Blumenthal
Attorney General's Office
55 Elm Street
Hartford, CT 06106
Phone: 860-808-5318
Fax: 860-808-5387
Attorney General's Office web site:
  www.cslnet.ctstateu.edu

Delaware:
Attorney General: M. Jane Brady
Attorney General's Office
Carvel Street Office Building
820 French Street
Wilmington, DE 19801
Civil Division Phone: 302-577-8400
Criminal Division Phone: 302-
  577-8500
Fax: 302-577-2610
General state executive branch
  web site: www.state.de.us

Florida:
Attorney General: Robert A
  Butterworth
Legal Affairs Department
The Capitol
Tallahassee, FL 32399-1050
Phone: 850-488-2526
Fax: 850-488-5106
Attorney General's Office web site:
  http://legal.firn.edu

Georgia:
Attorney General: Thurbert E.
  Baker
Attorney General's Office
40 Capitol Square S.W.
Atlanta, GA 30334-1300
Phone: 404-656-3300
Fax: 404-657-8733
General state executive branch
  web site: www.state.ga.us

Hawaii:
Attorney General: Margery S.
   Bronster
Attorney General's Office
425 Queen Street
Honolulu, HI 96813
Phone: 808-586-1500
Fax: 808-586-1239
General state executive branch
   web site: www.state.hi.us

Idaho:
Attorney General: Alan G. Lance
Attorney General's Office
210 Statehouse
Boise, ID 83720-1000
Phone: 208-334-2400
Fax: 208-334-2530
General state executive branch
   web site: www.state.id.us

Illinois:
Attorney General: Jim Ryan
Attorney General's Office
500 S. Second St.
Springfield, IL 62706
Phone: 217-782-9000
Fax: 217-782-7046
Attorney General's Office web site:
   www.acsp/uic.edu

Indiana:
Attorney General's Office
Indiana Government Center
   South
402 W. Washington St., 5TH Floor
Indianapolis, IN 46204-2770
Phone: 317-232-4866
Fax: 317-232-7979
General state executive branch
   web site: www.state.in.us

Iowa:
Attorney General: Tom Miller
Justice Department
Hoover Building, 2ND Floor
Des Moines, IA 50319
Phone: 515-281-5164
Fax: 515-281-4209
Attorney General's Office web site:
   www.state.ia.us/government/ag/

Kansas:
Attorney General: Carla Stovall
Attorney General's Office
Kansas Judicial Center, 2ND Floor
Topeka, KS 66612-1597
Phone: 785-296-2215
Fax: 785-296-6296
Attorney General's Office web site:
   http://lawlib.wuacc.edu/ag/ho
   mepage.html

Kentucky:
Attorney General: Ben Chandler
Attorney General's Office
118 State Capitol
700 Capitol Avenue
Frankfort, KY 40601
Phone: 502-696-5300
Fax: 502-564-2894
General state executive branch
   web site: www.state.ky.us

Louisiana:
Attorney General: Richard P.
   Ieyoub
Justice Department
P.O. Box 94005
Baton Rouge, LA 70804-9005
Phone: 504-342-7013
Fax: 504-342-7335
General state executive branch
   web site: www.state.la.us

Maine:
Attorney General: Andrew
 Ketterer
Attorney General's Office
6 State House Station
Augusta, ME 04333
Phone: 207-626-8800
Fax: 207-287-3145
Attorney General's Office web site:
 www.ptla.org

Maryland:
Attorney General: J. Joseph
 Curran, Jr.
Attorney General's Office
200 St. Paul Place
Baltimore, MD 21202-2021
Phone: 410-576-6300
Fax: 410-576-6404
Attorney General's Office web site:
 www.oag.state.md.us

Massachusetts:
Attorney General: Scott
 Harshbarger
Attorney General's Office
One Ashburton Place, Room 2010
Boston, MA 02108
Phone: 617-727-2200
Fax: 617-727-5768
Attorney General's Office web
 site:www.magnet.state.ma.us

Michigan:
Attorney General: Frank J. Kelley
Attorney General's Office
Law Building, P.O. Box 30212
Lansing, MI 48909
Phone: 517-373-1110
Fax: 517-241-1850
General state executive branch
 web site:
 www.migov.state.mi.us

Minnesota:
Attorney General: Hubert H.
 Humphrey III
Attorney General's Office
102 State Capitol
St. Paul, MN 55155
Phone: 612-296-6196
Fax: 612-297-4193
Attorney General's Office web site:
 www.ag.state.mn.us

Mississippi:
Attorney General: Mike Moore
Attorney General's Office
P.O. Box 220
Jackson, MS 39205
Phone: 601-359-3680
Fax: 601-359-3796
Attorney General's Office web site:
 www.mslawyer.com

Missouri:
Attorney General: Jeremiah W.
 (Jay) Nixon
Attorney General's Office
Supreme Court Building
P.O. Box 899
Jefferson City, MO 65102
Phone: 573-751-3321
Fax: 573-751-0774
General state executive branch
 web site: www.state.mo.us

Montana:
Attorney General: Joseph P.
 Mazurek
Attorney General's Office
Justice Building
215 N. Sanders
P.O. Box 201401
Helena, MT 59620-1401
Phone: 406-444-2026
Fax: 406-444-3549
General state executive branch
 web site: www.state.mt.gov

Nebraska:
Attorney General: Don Stenberg
Attorney General's office
2115 State Capitol
P.O. Box 98920
Lincoln, NE 68509-8920
Phone: 402-471-2682
Fax: 402-471-3297
General state executive branch
    web site: www.state.ne.us

Nevada:
Attorney General: Frankie Sue Del
    Papa
Attorney General's Office
State Capitol Complex
101 N. Carson St.
Carson City, NV 89710-4717
Phone: 702-687-4170
Fax: 702-687-5798
General state executive branch
    web site: www.state.nv.us

New Hampshire:
Attorney General: Philip T.
    McLaughlin
Attorney General's Office
33 Capitol Street
Concord, NH 03301-6397
Phone: 603-271-3658
Fax: 603-271-2110
General state executive branch
    web site: www.state.nh.us

New Jersey:
Attorney General: Peter Verniero
Law & Public Safety Department
Justice Complex
P.O. Box 080
Trenton, NJ 08625
Phone: 609-292-4925
Fax: 609-292-8268
General state executive branch
    web site: www.state.nj.us

New Mexico:
Attorney General: Tom Udall
Attorney General's Office
P.O. Drawer 1508
Santa Fe, NM 87504-1508
Phone: 505-827-6000
Fax: 505-827-5826
General state executive branch
    web site: www.state.nm.us

New York:
Attorney General: Dennis C.
    Vacco
Attorney General's Office
State Capitol
Albany, NY 12224-0341
Phone: 518-474-7124
Attorney General's Web Site:
    www.oag.state.ny.us

North Carolina:
Attorney General: Michael F.
    Easley
Justice Department
P.O. Box 629
Raleigh, NC 27602-0629
Phone: 919-716-6400
Fax: 919-716-6750
Attorney General's Office web site:
    www.jus.state.nc.us

North Dakota:
Attorney General: Heidi Heitkamp
Attorney General's Office
State Capitol
1ST Floor
600 East Blvd. Ave.
Bismarck, ND 58505-0040
Phone: 701-328-2210
Fax: 701-328-2226
General state executive branch
    web site: www.state.nd.us

Ohio:
Attorney General: Betty D. Montgomery
Attorney General's Office
30 E. Broad St.
17TH Floor
Columbus, OH 43215-3428
Phone: 614-466-4320
Fax: 614-466-5087
Attorney General's Office web site: www.ag.ohio.gov

Oklahoma:
Attorney General: W. A. Drew Edmondson
Attorney General's Office
112 State Capitol
Oklahoma City, OK 73105
Phone: 405-521-3921
Fax: 405-521-6246
General state executive branch web site: www.state.ok.us

Oregon:
Attorney General: Hardy Myers
Justice Department
Justice Building
1162 Court Street, N.E.
Salem, OR 97310
Phone: 503-378-4400
Fax: 503-378-3784
Attorney General's Office web site: www.dpo.org

Pennsylvania:
Attorney General: D. Michael Fisher
Attorney General's Office
Strawberry Square, 16TH Floor
Harrisburg, PA 17120
Phone: 717-787-3391
Fax: 717-787-8242
Attorney General's Office web site: www.attorneygeneral.gov (This is an outstanding web site—it has links to other AG's sites and a bunch of other interesting stuff)

Rhode Island:
Attorney General: Jeffrey B. Pine
Attorney General's Office
150 S. Main Street
Providence, RI 02903
Phone: 401-274-4400
Fax: 401-277-1331
Attorney General's Office web site: www.sec.state.ri.us

South Carolina:
Attorney General: Charlie Condon
Attorney General's office
P.O. Box 11549
Columbia, SC 29211
Phone: 803-734-3970
Fax: 803-253-6283
General state executive branch web site: www.state.sc.us

South Dakota:
Attorney General: Mark Barnett
Attorney General's Office
State Capitol
500 E. Capitol Ave.
Pierre, SD 57501-5070
Phone: 605-773-3215
Fax: 605-773-4106
General state executive branch web site: www.state.sd.us

Tennessee:
Attorney General: John Knox
    Walkup
Attorney General's Office
425 Fifth Avenue North
Nashville, TN 37243
Phone: 615-741-3491
Fax: 615-741-2009
General state executive branch
    web site: www.state.tn.us

Texas:
Attorney General: Dan Morales
Attorney General's Office
Price Daniel, Sr. Bldg.
P.O. Box 12548
Austin, TX 78711-2548
Phone: 512-463-2100
Fax: 512-463-2063
Attorney General's Office web site:
    www.oag.state.tx.us

Utah:
Attorney General: Jan Graham
Attorney General's Office
236 State Capitol
Salt Lake City, UT 84114
Phone: 801-366-0260
Fax: 801-538-1121
General state executive branch
    web site: www.state.ut.us

Vermont:
Attorney General: William H.
    Sorrell
Attorney General's Office
109 State Street
Montpelier, VT 05609-1001
Phone: 802-828-3171
Fax: 802-828-2154
General state executive branch
    web site: www.state.vt.us

Virginia:
Attorney General: Mark L. Earley
Attorney General's Office
900 E. Main Street
Richmond, VA 23219
Phone: 804-786-2071
Fax: 804-786-1991
General state executive branch
    web site: www.state.va.us

Washington:
Attorney General: Christine O.
    Gregoire
Attorney General's Office
1125 Washington Street, S.E.
P.O. Box 40100
Olympia, WA 98504-0100
Phone: 360-753-6200
Fax: 360-586-8474
General state executive branch
    web site: www.state.wa.gov

West Virginia:
Attorney General: Darrell V.
    McGraw, Jr.
Attorney General's Office
State Capitol
Room 26-E
Charleston, WV 25305-0220
Phone: 304-558-2021
Fax: 304-558-0140
General state executive branch
    web site: www.state.wv.us

Wisconsin:
Attorney General: James E. Doyle
Attorney General's Office
Justice Department
P.O. Box 7857
Madison, WI 53707-7857
Phone: 608-266-1221
Fax: 608-267-2779
General state executive branch
    web site: www.state.wi.us

Wyoming:
Attorney General: William U. Hill
Attorney General's Office
123 State Capitol
Cheyenne, WY 82002
Phone: 307-777-7841
Fax: 307-777-6869
General state executive branch
    web site: www.state.wy.us

WRITING LEGISLATION FOR STATES

You've probably heard the old saying about how it's not a good idea to see either laws or sausages being made. I don't know anything about sausages, but I *can* tell you that when it comes to making laws, *writing* them at the state level is a *great job*. It's exciting, you really feel like you're making a difference, the pay is good, and you can get these jobs coming right out of law school. *Yesssss!*

As with state Attorney General's Offices, every state is going to have its own set-up for writing legislation. What I'm going to give you here is a snapshot of one state, Connecticut. It will give you an idea of what the job is like and the general elements—like duties and hours—will be similar across the country. On top of that, we'll talk about how you break into the field, what the starting pay is like, and I'll give you a web site where you can learn about job openings all over the country.

My source for this profile is the wonderful Marcia Goodman, who is the Director of Legislative Legal Services and the Director of the Legislative Commissioner's Office for the Connecticut General Assembly. She's written laws for Connecticut for a few years now, and needless to say, she loves it. When you read what she's got to say, maybe you'll think about trying your hand at writing legislation as well!

An Insider's View of Writing Legislation, from Marcia Goodman:

"There is a lot to like about writing legislation. The legislature is a very exciting place to work. It's the center of where policy is made, and it's a hustle-bustle environment. I love having the sense of serving the public, I don't have to work against the clock—and I love to write!"

"What we do revolves around one activity: drafting bills. We get the raw material in a variety of forms, ranging from a couple of words to suggest a concept at one extreme, to a fully-drafted bill at the other. It's our job to take the material and put it into a form and in language that accomplishes what the legislator wants, precisely and unambiguously. The drafting process may involve collaboration with other drafters, particularly if the bill covers multi-disciplinary matters, but it is typically written by one person. So if you are working on a bill, it's typically your project and your project alone.

"We deal with a variety of constituencies. Naturally, we draft for legislators and legislative committees and maintain confidentiality with them until the bill or amendment is officially a public document. Therefore, technically, we deal with others only to the extent that legislators and legislative committees direct us to do so. But with regard to bills that the executive and judicial branches of state government propose, we have contact with them as needed to take care of their proposals. Also, legislative committees often want us to contact others as we prepare bills, which includes executive and judicial branch personnel, sometimes lobbyists, sometimes outside attorneys, sometimes constituents of the legislator—really all different kinds of people. We haven't historically had much contact with drafters from other states. Typically if a bill we're working on has been dealt with in another state, we'd look up that legislation and adapt it. But that's changing now, because there is a listserv for state legislative attorneys that is becoming increasingly active. I'm rather proud of that because I chair the subcommittee of an NCSL Committee that created it! Hopefully that will foster interstate relations among drafters.

"The hours we work are totally dependent on whether the legislature is in session or not. It's a Jekyll-and-Hyde kind of work schedule. Connecticut legislative sessions run from January to June during odd-numbered years, and February to May in even-numbered years. Regardless of whether the legislature is in session or not, our core hours are 40 hours. Attorneys have flexibility in when their days start and end. You can start anywhere between 7 and 9:45 a.m., and your day can end between 3 and 6 p.m. Any time worked before or after core hours are counted toward comp time (which I'll talk about in a minute).

"During legislative sessions, that 40-hour-week is out the window. Attorneys often work on weekends and evenings during the sessions. We work against successive deadlines that are contained in the legislative rules, and those deadlines drive each attorney's work. During the first part of the session, the hours depend on the committee you're assigned to, since deadlines are staggered among committees. Work weeks of 50 to 70 hours are not unusual. During the last month of the session, the number of hours increases and may reach 80 to 100 hours per week. This is when the House and Senate are in session more frequently and, finally, each day. It's during session that you rack up compensatory time, which works like this: you get an hour of comp time for every three hours you work beyond the normal workday, and one hour of comp time for every hour you work after midnight. The maximum comp time that can be earned is four weeks in a year. During odd-numbered years, when the legislature is in session from January to June, four or five attorneys in our office will typically reach the maximum comp time of four weeks off, and during even- numbered years, when the legislature meets from February to May, it's rare to reach that four-week maximum.

"When the legislature is in session, each attorney is assigned to a subject matter committee. During the first part of the session, the attorney works with the committee, drafting all the bills that the committee wants drafted, and advising the committee on matters like legal questions and committee procedures. This is a deadline-driven period. The rules of the legislature have deadlines for each step of the committee process, which drives the timetable of our attorneys.

"The most significant committee deadline is the deadline for acting on bills. Committees tend to save the bulk of their final decisions for the day of the deadline. They may vote out bills with changes, perhaps significant changes. After the committee's final action on bills, our office has a deadline—again, set by the legislature's rules—to get the bills finalized, reviewed and copyedited, and out of the office.

"After this 10-day period, the bills go to the House and Senate floors and our job turns mostly into drafting amendments. Sometimes, especially if the contents of a major bill are still in negotiation at the time the committee reports it out, the amendment may take the form of a rewritten bill. Other amendments may be new concepts that a member wants to add on to a bill on a similar topic. However, most amendments involve smaller changes that legislators would like.

"The amendment period is very busy and high-stress. People chip in and help each other, but that's not always possible, and sometimes you just have to keep many, many balls up in the air at once, not letting any of them drop!

"So that is our life while the legislature is in session. Out of session is a totally different story. Overtime hours are unusual between legislative sessions. The interim—that time between legislative sessions—is a time when attorneys in the office are encouraged to attend training programs to enhance their writing skills, learn more about the subject-matter of their committees, enhance their computer skills, and generally do some brushing-up. Also during the interim, everyone in the office develops his or her own projects, both individually and in teams. If people want to work in teams, they can include people from other offices, or join projects initiated elsewhere. The interim gives attorneys a wonderful opportunity to decide what they would like to improve and then go ahead and do it. Or if they want a procedure in the office changed, they can form a team to prepare a recommended plan to change. Some of the projects this past interim included revising parts of the general statutes that needed "cleaning up," and then presenting those proposals to committee chairs for introduction as bills during the next legislative session; designing and creating an intranet web site for the office; developing the groundwork for a training program for staff and legislators on Appropriations issues; developing the groundwork for including a tour of the central staff offices in the orientation program for new legislators; and creating a mentoring program in the general assembly for law students.

"Here's how our office is set up. There is a Director and several tiers of attorneys who report to the Director. You start out in our office as a 'Legislative Attorney.' You go to an in-house training program to show you the ropes, and the National Conference of State Legislatures also has a bill drafting workshop for less experienced attorneys.

"After a couple of years, if you're doing well, you'll typically become an Associate Attorney. After another four years, you're eligible for promotion to Senior Attorney. Then there's Chief Attorney (we have two of those), the Assistant Director, and the Director.

"One of the indications that this is a great place to work is that most attorneys in our office have been with us for more than 10 years, and seven have been here for more than 20 years! Of course, we have junior people as well—five have been with us for fewer than five years. When people *do* leave here, it's sometimes for jobs in the private sector and sometimes they go to the Executive Branch, although I know at least two people who have left here and then come back. And of course there are always personal reasons, like family matters and transferred spouses, that draw people away.

"Other states are different in their set-up, perhaps the most obvious difference being that some states have drafting done in partisan offices. That is, Senate Democrats, Senate Republicans, House Democrats, and House Republicans."

HOW TO GET IN . . .

"There are a few ways to get jobs writing legislation for states. One good source is the web site of job vacancies throughout the country, which is run by the National Conference of State Legislatures ("NCSL"). The URL is: http://www.ncsl.org/public/joblegis.htm

"In Connecticut, we advertise job openings in major newspapers. Also, we save resumes received during the year and notify those people when there is a vacancy. While all states are different, we typically have one or two vacancies every year."

STARTING SALARIES . . .

"For an attorney fresh out of law school, in Connecticut the starting salary is over $43,000. With two years of relevant experience, the attorney begins at just over $51,000."

THE SKILLS THEY LOOK FOR, IN BOTH NEW LAW SCHOOL GRADUATES AND LATERAL HIRES . . .

"Naturally, we want people with excellent writing and analysis skills, as well as professional interpersonal skills. Writing experience and the quality of the cover letter are especially important when we're selecting candidates for interview. And you must have been admitted to the Connecticut Bar."

"Many resumes by new law school graduates look the same, and we look for anything that distinguishes the applicant from other applicants in a positive way. Of course, Law Review and high class standing are positives!

"For laterals, again the quality of writing and analysis in the cover letter is primary, as is writing experience. Also helpful is experience in subjects that will be useful in drafting and government experience."

INTERNSHIPS FOR LAW STUDENTS . . .

"We sometimes have law students as interns on a volunteer basis during the legislative session. It's a challenge to have interns during the session because it's difficult to find supervision time, and supervision is critical to making it a worthwhile experience for both the law student and for us. But we do have them, and it is a great experience for students."

Local Government

CITY ATTORNEYS' OFFICES

If somebody told you about a job you could get right out of law school, where you could work livable hours, start at a decent salary, practice in virtually any specialty, and get immediate responsibility, you'd probably say, "Great! Which firm is it?" Well, it's not a firm at all—it's City Attorney's Offices. From San Diego to Chicago to New York to Miami, people *rave* about the work they get to do. It's a great job!

City Attorney's Offices generally have both civil and criminal divisions (like the San Diego office that's profiled below), while some only do civil work. Entry-level positions are typically only available in criminal divisions. You need a bit of experience (which you can get in the criminal divisions of the City Attorney's Office or elsewhere) in order to get the civil division jobs.

City Attorney's Offices typically have a variety of specialties unparalleled by any private firm, and they virtually all hire new law school graduates. Almost all of them have summer internship programs, many of them paid.

By the way, local government work doesn't have to mean working for a City Attorney's Office. There are also County Attorneys (I've heard raves about those jobs as well). County Attorney's Offices differ, but they are always the legal advisor for the county, handling all of the civil work for the county. Some County Attorney's Offices primarily prosecute people accused of crimes, and others also prosecute environmental and consumer fraud cases. Larger county offices will have units that specialize in a number of areas, including narcotics, juvenile prosecution, domestic violence, and appellate work. Some county attorney's offices don't do any criminal work at all—for instance, the Dade County Attorney's Office (and which by the way, gets *spectacular* reviews), which covers Miami, solely focuses on civil work, litigating at both state and federal levels and in a whole slew of practice areas. While some County Attorney's Offices hire entry-level people, many require a year or two's worth of experience first.

Incidentally, whether it's work with a city or a county law department that you're interested in pursuing—doing a summer internship, clinical externship, or volunteering with an office is a *huge* advantage in nailing down a permanent position after law school. In fact, you'll find that having one of these experiences on your resume is a big help even if you want to go "private" after law school, because the opportunity to polish your skills in these public positions is highly coveted by law firms.

What I'm going to do here is to profile the City Attorney's Office for San Diego. While of course cities will differ in the way they set up their law departments, I think you'll find that San Diego is pretty representative of what a good-sized city's attorney's office is like. (It just *coincidentally* happens to be in one of the most beautiful, livable cities in the country!)

Incidentally, everything about San Diego City Attorney's Office comes courtesy of David James, the Deputy City Attorney in the Civil Division. He's not only a terrific person but he happens to write a column you should check out: the "Jobs" column in the ABA's *Student Lawyer* magazine.

★   ★   ★   ★   ★

Office of the San Diego City Attorney

1200 Third Avenue, Suite 700 • San Diego, CA 92101-4199
Phone: 619-533-5500 • Fax: 619-533-5696
Web site: www.sannet.gov/city-attorney

Hiring Attorney: David C. James, phone: 619-533-5665,
e-mail: dxj@cityatty.sannet.gov

WHAT DO THEY DO?

The City Attorney's Office is San Diego's chief legal advisor and misdemeanor prosecutor. The excitement in the office comes from the very top; the City Attorney himself is the dynamic and highly-respected Casey Gwinn, recently recognized by *The American Lawyer* in "The Public Sector 45"—that is, 45 pioneering lawyers all under the age of 45, in the public sector. Among other breakthroughs, Gwinn pioneered the practice of prosecuting domestic violence cases, even without the victim's participation. The *American Lawyer* quoted Joan Zorza, publisher of the newsletter *Domestic Violence Report,* as saying that "He's incredibly influential. His model is probably the best model in the country."

The City Attorney's Office has a colorful history. The first City Attorney—for what was at that time the Pueblo de San Diego, under Mexican control—was Henry D. Fitch, an erstwhile sea captain who was also a storekeeper, surveyor, and trader. In fact, nobody has ever determined whether Fitch really was a lawyer!

From those auspicious beginnings, the City Attorney's office grew to the point where today, it employs 120 attorneys (including 64 women and 25 minority lawyers). (Note that City Attorney's offices often rival large firms in size—Chicago's Law Department, for instance, has more than 250 lawyers).

The Office is organized into two practice areas—a Criminal Division (with 63 attorneys) and a Civil Division (with 57 attorneys). Lawyers in the Criminal Division prosecute all kinds of misdemeanors committed in San Diego, including driving under the influence of alcohol or drugs, domestic violence and child abuse, theft offenses, sex crimes, gang and graffiti crimes, zoning and building code violations, consumer and environmental crimes, and many others. Each year the Criminal Division reviews more than 50,000 cases. The Division is divided into several different units, including:

- The Screening and Arraignment Unit which, as the name implies, reviews crime reports and files thousands of criminal complaints each year.

- The Trial Unit, which represents the People of the State of California in misdemeanor and non-jury trials. It handles all cases not prosecuted by specialized units.

- The Appellate Unit, which writes and argues pretrial motions, writs, and appeals on cases handled by the Screening and Arraignment,

Neighborhood Prosecution, and Trial Units. Each year this Unit prepares more than 600 motions and prevails on more than 90% of those heard in court.

- The Neighborhood Prosecution Unit, whose goal is to develop a partnership between San Diego's police, prosecutors, and communities to create a more responsive criminal justice system. The deputies in this Unit prosecute "Problem Oriented Policing" cases, which include quality of life crimes, including lewd acts in city parks, loitering for prostitution, and loitering for drug activity.

- The Consumer and Environmental Protection Unit, which investigates and prosecutes cases involving public health crimes, consumer fraud, environmental pollution, and governmental corruption.

- The Code Enforcement Unit, which works in partnership with City Council offices, code enforcement inspectors, police officers, and community groups to resolve code violations and abate public nuisances in San Diego's neighborhoods.

- The Child Abuse and Domestic Violence Unit, which prosecutes misdemeanor child abuse, domestic violence, elder abuse, and stalking cases.

The Civil Division is organized into four units: employment and safety services, public works, real property, and trial. The Employment and Safety Services Unit represents the mayor, the police and fire Departments, and other city personnel and agencies on a variety of issues relating to public safety, employment, labor relations, retirement, and worker's compensation. Public Works provides legal services to city organizations like Environmental Services and Transportation. The Real Property Unit advises the city on real property acquisition, management, use, redevelopment, and eminent domain and inverse condemnation cases. The Trial Unit represents the city, elected officials, and city employees in civil actions filed in both state and federal courts.

WHAT YOU DO WHEN YOU START TO WORK THERE . . .

New attorneys all begin in the Criminal Division. Spread out over the first four months in the office, they spend seven weeks in a comprehensive training program, which covers all of the various aspects of being a prosecutor. They rotate through certain units and they get a chance to settle down as openings occur in specialized units like Consumer and Environmental Protection or Domestic Violence, or in the Civil Division units (the Civil Division typically takes attorneys only after they've had intensive trial experience in the Criminal Division, which often takes about two years). To fill these openings, unit heads interview attorneys in the office who are interested in the reassignment.

As you rotate through departments, you receive assignments from supervisors in each unit. For instance, the Head Trial Deputy and his immediate subordinate supervisors assign trials to trial deputies. When the deputies aren't in trial, they review criminal cases and decide whether to file them. As "filing deputies," deputy city attorneys are assigned cases to review. When deputies rotate to the Appellate Unit, an appellate supervisor assigns motions and/or appeals for them to write.

HOW TO GET IN . . .

The City Attorney's Office interviews routinely at the following law schools: San Diego, Thomas Jefferson, and California Western. However, they routinely hire from other law schools, and like to encourage a diversity of law school representation among the Office's attorneys.

For new graduates, depending on the law school, the Office likes to see a class standing in the top 10% to the top one-third. Oral advocacy experience is a plus. The Office particularly likes applicants who have excelled in trial advocacy courses, have Moot Court honors, have taken part in mock trial competitions, and so forth. Besides a heavy dose of oral advocacy, the Office likes to see municipal law and civil litigation experience.

In addition to new law school graduates, the City Attorney's Office sometimes hires laterals as well. Typically laterals will have two or three years of experience (although even with experience laterals start with the Office at the entry-level as prosecutors in the Criminal Division). For its laterals, the Office likes to see experience in court, at least law and motion practice.

You can find out about job openings either by inquiring by letter, by phone, or by visiting the Office's web site (all particulars are in the heading of this profile).

HOURS AND BUCKS . . .

Average hours spent at the office on a yearly basis are between 2,250 and 2,500. There is limited travel associated with working in the City Attorney's Office—mostly you travel to seminars and conferences in California. Attorneys who transfer to the Civil Division, usually after at least a couple of years with the Criminal Division, may have opportunities to go to out-of-state depositions, but that's the exception to the rule.

Part-time work *is* available, but ideally attorneys would be with the Office for a year before going to a part-time schedule, to give them a chance to get beyond the training (formal training is spread out over the first three months). The Office doesn't allow part-time schedules during training, but even during training it *does* accommodate flexible schedules to the extent possible.

The starting salary is $$ ($35,000-50,000).

SUMMER INTERNSHIPS . . .

The City Attorney's Office routinely hires summer associates. Last year, they had 6 summer associates, 4 of whom received offers to return. Weekly pay for summer associateships is $861.68. The deadline for applying for the summer program is October 1.

1Ls are not eligible for paid summer associateships, although the office takes on a few 1Ls as volunteers every summer.

WHAT IT'S LIKE TO WORK AT THE SAN DIEGO CITY ATTORNEY'S OFFICE, IN THE WORDS OF LAWYERS WHO WORK THERE . . .

"Don't know if you want to prosecute or do plaintiff's work? Considering real property litigation or eminent domain? Civil or criminal work? Our office has all of that. Everyone starts out in criminal, prosecuting and getting court experience. Then, after you have the confidence to get in front of a judge, you can move on to other areas of the office. We have a civil litigation department that has positions in everything from defending the police department, to defending the City of San Diego in lawsuits involving the Stadium. Where else can you have this variety—and *not* worry about billable hours? I could stay here my entire career and never be bored!"

"There's a question that faces every female lawyer: Can I be an attorney and a mom too? I don't have kids yet, but certainly plan to. I also want to be a good mom and be involved with my kids' lives. I've noticed that our office is one of the best if you want to be a good attorney *and* a good mom. I've seen women in the office work with flexible schedules. One woman comes in at 6 a.m. and leaves at 2 p.m. so she can pick up her kids at school. Two women 'share' a contract, and each works 20 hours a week. Right now one of my friends/colleagues is working Monday through Wednesday in the office, and 'telecommuting' on Thursday and Friday. She has a six-month-old baby. Her schedule lets her contribute to the office *and* handle diaper changing! By the way, she was just promoted to a supervisor role. In our office it's do-able!"

"If you want a life, go government! At 11 p.m., after I have been home for four hours, eaten dinner, and gone to a movie with my husband, I call my friend Susan. Susan works in a private firm. She is still at the office. Hmm . . . sure my pay is less . . . but is it worth it? If you are worried about paying off your student loans if you work for the government, don't be. I have private student loans, too. So does my husband. But even though we both work in government jobs, we are doing fine. We just bought a home in our first year of marriage. We *are* able to make the loan payments with our government salaries—as well as take care of a mortgage. It's not as bad as you think. The loan companies love government workers, and they will work with you!"

"I thought I had to give up the idea of community service when I started a full-time job, but not here. One day I found myself speaking to a high school group about staying in school and career paths. Another day I was out 'painting out' graffiti. Another day I hung out with a high school student all day, showing her around the court house, and encouraging her to go to college. At Christmas I play 'Santa' and deliver all of the presents that our office donates to needy families. I get to do all of this during work hours, and as a part of my job! What a concept! In college and law school, I was always able to find the time to volunteer and serve the community. Now that I'm working full-time, our boss has made a public and personal commitment to community service, so my community involvement hasn't stopped. In fact, as part of our contracts here, we agree to be dedicated to that same mission."

"People care here. Last week, one of our support staff got off work and went home to a tragedy. Her 8-year-old son had just been killed—hit by a car while crossing the street. Almost instantly, memos and e-mails were distributed letting all of us know how and where to help. Our boss established a memorial scholarship fund on the little boy's behalf and made a press release encouraging all citizens in San Diego to help our fellow employee. A large group of people from the office went to the memorial services and are donating 'leave time' to the woman who needs our support now and in the weeks to come. This office cares."

"I was that law student who knew I had to be in the courtroom. The thought of sitting behind a desk, researching and writing all day long, made me squirm. But I wanted 'real' trial experience. Some of my friends work for the big 'litigation' firms, but have never even said 'Good morning Your Honor.' Not here. I am in court every day. Seriously. If I am not in a jury trial, I am in an evidentiary hearing, chambers conference, or handling a court calendar. It is a normal day around here when you need to be in three places at once, are expected to think on your feet when an issue takes you by surprise, or realize you are closing your case a day early. I love that stuff! Some people think we prosecutors are a bit crazy, but many of us know we have the best job in the world.

"Our office gives you hands-on court experience. I've been an attorney for only 18 months, and have already done 19 jury trials. Someone told me that you cannot really say you're a 'trial attorney' until you have 50 jury trials under your belt. Hey . . . at this rate, I'll be a *real* trial attorney in three years! Not bad for a 27-year-old, huh?

"I grew up playing team sports and have always been frustrated with people who are only out for themselves. Our office is built on the team concept. In fact, if you are not a team player, you will just not last as a prosecutor. One person issues the case, another may deal with it at arraignment, and still another person takes the case to trial. If the team breaks down, our taxpayers lose, and justice is not served. I remember once when I was in trial and the judge ordered me to turn in documents that would have taken me personally five days to prepare. One phone call back to my colleagues put the team in motion. One colleague did the research, another made the needed phone calls, and a third colleague got the proper support staff involved. By 3 o'clock that day, I was able to give the judge what she ordered. These colleagues dropped everything for me, and this case. It was a sweet victory to come back to the office and tell them that the defendant got convicted.

"We give 120% while we are at work. That's expected, and that's what we do. But our bosses know that we need to have a life too. The first year I worked here, the new attorneys formed the '5:01 Club.' Every Friday at 5:01 we went downstairs to the local pub and socialized. Our bosses were always invited and often joined us.

"After I had been here for about a year, my husband and I moved about 40 minutes away from the office. I was now a 'public transportation' groupie and the trolley/train system dictated my hours. I had to leave at 5:05 to catch the 5:20 trolley. I felt bad, at first, because sometimes our meetings at work ran past 5 p.m. I went into my boss's office, and let him know my situation. He assured me that it was no problem, and whenever I needed to leave early it was fine. We have an understanding around here. As long as the work is done with the excellence that our office demands we're fine."

"Six weeks after being hired, I picked up a trial at 4 p.m. the night before the case was to be tried. For six weeks, the eight other new deputies and I went through intensive training on the life span of a criminal case, from the responsible charging of crimes to the disposition of the case. We rode with police officers in search of drunk drivers and visited a crime lab. Finally, we were trained in the art of courtroom work, which culminated in a mock trial.

"Of course when I picked up my real trial, I had no idea how I would actually turn this manila file with a bunch of papers inside it into a cohesive presentation that would convince 12 citizens of the defendant's guilt. I went around the office looking for advice. Within 15 minutes I had collected 10 home phone numbers from senior deputies offering to talk about the trial at any time—including at night after my son went to bed.

"That night, I called the Head Trial Deputy, who patiently answered the variety of questions that I asked. The next morning several other deputies shared their thoughts about my trial. Incredibly, while I was in trial, the support continued. When issues came up, I could call back from court and get them answered. If the answer was not readily available, a deputy would research it and get back to me. Support staff located evidence or subpoenaed witnesses that were discovered at the last minute. Other deputies would help make charts or get jury instructions together.

"The support from everyone was unbelievable, and the level of support continued through every trial, and every other court appearance that I made."

"Our office takes part in community projects often, and we are encouraged to be involved. Recently, I was part of our 'Homeless Warrant Clearance' project. A public defender gave me a list of people who had been at a local shelter and wanted to take advantage of the project. These people had been working hard to get their lives back on track, through drug and alcohol treatment programs and life skills training. Many of them had warrants from cases out of our jurisdiction.

"Support staff at our office gathered all of the cases that were 'at warrant,' and I would make offers for disposition, taking into account the work that the people had done and were continuing to do to improve their lives.

"On the designated day, the public defender, the judge, bailiff, court clerks, and I all went down to the shelter and held court there. The defendants were able to take responsibility for their cases, and we got to contribute to a worthwhile community project."

"I went through law school as a single parent. Flexibility in a job was important to me. I had heard that working for the government had many benefits, but did not look into it immediately out of law school. I worked for a private firm and found the work to be draining, boring, and not a particularly supportive environment. The expectation was to be at the firm all the time—especially late at night—where you could be seen working. This expectation made it difficult to parent a young child.

"I was looking for another job and heard about an immediate opening at the City Attorney's Office. I applied and within a week I was hired. The move from private practice to public law was a blessing. I was no longer stuck in petty discovery wars that seemed to last for years.

"I now have the responsibility of upholding the criminal laws. I review police reports and issue appropriate criminal charges. I did rotations through the arraignment courts, trial setting, and presiding departments. I negotiate cases and work them up for trial. I was doing trials right out of training. The experience is unbeatable. If I get the desire to go back to the civil side, the City Attorney's Office has an entire division dedicated to a variety of civil work.

"The office gave me comprehensive training, from issuing criminal charges to taking the case to trial. They continue to provide training by sponsoring frequent 'brown-bags,' which provide updates on a variety of issues. The support system is endless. I have access to deputies at almost any time of day or evenings to discuss the stream of questions that come up. People are encouraging and want you to do your best. Management, including the City Attorney, has a very real open-door policy. You can always bring up issues or suggestions and management will take the time to talk.

"I no longer have billable hours. I still work an extraordinary amount of hours, but I do not have to keep track of every .6 hours of work that I do. More importantly, I can leave at 5 p.m. to pick up my son, without fearing that I will not be seen working at the office into the late hours. The office trusts that whatever work I have, I'll get it done. Because of the variety of work that I get, I can easily do some of my work at home."

CHAPTER 11

Prosecutors

(Federal and Local)

People just *love, love, love* being prosecutors. The sense of being one of the "good guys"—they sometimes semi-jokingly refer to "doing God's work"—the immediate courtroom experience, the lack of billable hour and business generation requirements—no wonder these are such popular jobs!

I've already touched on some prosecutorial jobs in earlier chapters. For instance, many City Attorney and County Attorney jobs involve prosecution, and so you shouldn't overlook those as possibilities if you're interested in prosecuting.

What I'm going to do in this chapter is to talk about the different possibilities for prosecutorial work at the federal and local level.

Federal Prosecutors—
The U.S. Attorney's Office

U.S. Attorneys make up the bulk of the lawyers who work for the Department of Justice (and we already know from Chapter 4 what a fabulous place *that* is). They prosecute all federal civil and criminal cases. U.S. Attorneys are spread out over 94 offices around the country. You'll find specifics on office locations in the DOJ's very useful "Legal Activities Book," which is at every career services office in the country, and you'll also find contacts, addresses, and phone numbers for them listed at www.usdoj.gov/careers/oapm/lab/usaoadd.html.

For information on working for U.S. Attorneys' Offices, I turned to wonderful Jim Castro-Blanco. Until recently, he was an Assistant U.S. Attorney in Brooklyn for the Eastern District of New York. Now he's with St. John's University School of Law (and more importantly, as we go to press, he's a new daddy to Kelly Anne Castro-Blanco).

Here are Jim's insights:

"I know it sounds corny, but being an Assistant U.S. Attorney is both exciting and daunting. You get *extraordinary* experience from day one. You make charging decisions that drive cases, and when you conduct cases you make all the decisions. Your work is reviewed by more senior attorneys, but you're the first chair. After a couple of trials where a senior attorney acts as consultant, you're doing it by yourself. And from the beginning, the decisions are yours. You determine pleas with cooperating witnesses. When it comes to investigations, *you* have oversight over FBI and DEA agents many years older than you.

"Different U.S. Attorneys' Offices are organized differently, primarily due to differences in size. Some offices cover entire states with only two attorneys. In the big cities, like New York, Los Angeles, and Miami, you'll have huge offices. In my office, the Eastern District of New York, we had 130 attorneys covering Brooklyn, Nassau, and Suffolk Counties.

"In the smaller offices, you'll be more of a generalist. With a dozen attorneys, everybody does everything. In bigger offices like mine, you will have different Civil and Criminal Divisions. You can apply to either side, and the offices will try to honor your choice. But as is true for every employer, need ultimately drives what you'll do.

"When you start, whether it's civil or criminal, you'll get the smaller cases. For instance, in Criminal, you'll do smaller transactional crimes like prosecuting drug runners, mules, credit card frauds, buy and bust narcotics operations, and tax cases. Generally, your cases will be smaller in dollars, complexity, and numbers of defendants. Sometimes early on you'll be second seat at trials of extraordinarily complex crimes.

"No matter what you do, you get *really* early trial experience. I was in court six weeks into my tenure at the Office, and that's not unusual. You're it. You try the case. You have more senior attorneys there for guidance, but you're making all the decisions. And you get seniority yourself very quickly.

"As you progress, in larger offices you'll go to a particular unit. We had Narcotics, Organized Crime, White Collar Crime, and Violent Crimes (which covers the newer gangs, like Vietnamese gangs). Again, at smaller offices you wouldn't have that kind of specialization.

"Making your choice between civil and criminal in offices that have that separation, depends on a few factors. On the civil side, you'll find a more manageable lifestyle. You'll get the level of complexity that you would at a large firm, but because the time frames are longer than for criminal cases, your time is more your own. As a result, civil-side people tend to stay with the Office longer.

"On the Criminal side, there's more excitement. You're wearing the white hat. You're prosecuting people charged with the most serious crimes. But the hours are longer and the time pressures are greater. For instance, complex wiretap cases are life-eaters, because of federal government requirements. You have to report to the judge every 10 days on each facility with a tap. You tap five phones, you compile five reports every 10 days. You'll be working on several other cases at the same time.

"That can be tough. What can make it tougher are the people you're sometimes prosecuting. It might be people who did something out of desperation. They risked their lives. Let's face it—you don't swallow bags of cocaine as a career choice if you feel you have other options. That doesn't bother some people, but really, you feel bad for them. You know that they're facing real time. There's no parole in federal crimes. With mandatory drug sentences, you're looking at 10 years minimum. You have a kid who is 20 years old, makes a mistake, runs crack—bingo. They're in jail until they're 30. But you have to accept that it's your job to prosecute them no matter what.

"Whether you do civil or criminal, there's *always* the risk that you'll let the job consume your life. The work is *so* seductive. It's the stuff that TV shows are made of. Relationships can fall apart because there's no time for them, you've got to make sure to make time for them. You've got to vigilantly guard against making your work your life!

"Despite the downsides, it is *tremendous* work. Apart from the experience itself, it sets you up to do so many things. Of course, there are a lot of DOJ lifers. But if you leave, you've got many, many options. For instance, in the area where I worked, in and around Brooklyn, *all* the judges are from U.S. Attorneys' Offices. Or you can go back into private practice, on a *very* short partnership track. Or you can teach.

"There are a number of ways to get into U.S. Attorneys' Offices First of all you have to remember that they don't hire new law school graduates. You need at least two years of experience after law school. And by the way, you don't apply to the Department of Justice for a job—you apply to particular offices.

Because so many people are clamoring for the jobs, you have to think *very* strategically about your campaign to get in. It helps to have superb law school credentials. Many people come to U.S. Attorneys Offices after spending a couple of years as associates at big firms. That's what I did. Another viable option would be to come in from judicial clerkships, since they count as work experience. Clerking for a federal judge, either district or appellate or a magistrate, would be good because you're dealing with federal law, just as you would at the U.S. Attorney's Office. State courts won't help you unless you're at the state's highest court. You can always follow a state court clerkship with a federal one, which would help.

"You have to marshal your forces, because there *are* politics involved with getting these jobs. You need very strong recommendations, people who can attest to your acumen. You need all the allies you can get.

"While you're still in school, there are many things you can do to lay the foundation for working in a U.S. Attorney's Office. Obviously getting the best possible grades is a huge benefit. But don't dismiss the idea of volunteering for a U.S. Attorney's Office. It is a *fantastic* way to get in. As an intern, you do substantive, real research. You draft briefs. You sit in on everything except grand juries. You learn a *ton*. In fact, in some states, including new York, there are student practice rules that even allow you to stand up and talk in court. You can argue cases while you're still in school! *(This is Kimm talking. Check with your career services office to see if your state has the "student certification" process, and what it's requirements are. Typically you have to have taken Evidence, which means you have to be a 2L.)*

"The more people who know you and are pulling for you, the better off you are. Volunteering at a U.S. Attorneys Office, talking to alums of your school who are at the offices, or making any other contact—it all helps.

"When you interview for the job, you'll go through several rounds of interviews. They'll *grill* you, because that's what they do for a living! My second interview was with the guy who put away John Gotti. He was *tough*. But the toughest question I got was in my final interview with the U.S. Attorney, Zack Carter. He asked me point blank: "Do you think drug interdiction works? Do you think what we're doing here works?" I responded that without cooperation from host countries as well as education, no I didn't think it worked. I thought it was part of the larger equation. I guess he must have liked that answer because I got the job—but let me tell you, I was sweating!

"Incidentally, when it comes to choosing which U.S. Attorney's Offices to apply to, it's a mistake to think that it's easier to get into rural offices than large, urban ones. Apart from the fact that they're much smaller and so will have correspondingly fewer job openings, people tend to stay with rural offices much longer. The reason for that is salaries. In rural areas, salaries for U.S. Attorney's Offices will often beat any private firm. If you're several years out of law school and you go to the U.S. Attorney's Office, you'll start out making $90,000. Leading firms in less populous states, like Vermont, won't pay at that level. So what ends up happening is that people in rural offices stay longer—10, 12, 15 years. So unlike many other kinds of jobs, competition can be just as fierce out in the country as it is in the big cities.

"No matter which office you go to, you'll do work you'll never forget. There's *nothing* more exciting. *Nothing.*"

District Attorney's and State's Attorney's Offices

District Attorneys ("DAs") and State's Attorneys ("SAs") do the same thing: they prosecute criminal violations which take place in their particular jurisdictions (typically counties). The only difference is that some states call their prosecutors District Attorneys, and other states call them State's Attorneys. Either way, these are *awesome* jobs—they give you an excellent opportunity to get tons of trial experience right at the start of your legal career.

First of all, let's talk about exactly what it is that DAs and SAs *do*. The District Attorney or State Attorney is the prosecutor for the county (there are more than 3,000 in the country). The DA/SA reviews police reports and talks to investigative officers, victims, witnesses and suspects, and then decides whether or not to issue a felony or misdemeanor complaint. If the complaint *is* issued, the DA/SA will recommend how much bail ought to be set, prepare the case for trial, and present the case in court, either alone or with Deputy or Assistant DAs/SAs.

Depending on how populous the county is, DA's/SA's offices can be *huge*. For instance, the New York County DA's office, which covers Manhattan, employs more than *500* lawyers and prosecutes more than 100,000 criminal cases every year. The Los Angeles DA's Office is also huge, and hires *five dozen* new attorneys every year. At the other end of the spectrum, DAs in rural counties are sometimes part-time officials with no staff. Many DA's and SA's offices hire only on an "as needed" basis—it's only the larger, urban DA's/SA's offices that will hire regularly and sponsor routine summer programs.

HOW TO BREAK IN TO A DA'S/SA'S OFFICE . . .

As is true of U.S. Attorney's offices, the best way to get into a DA's or SA's office is to get experience first as a summer clerk, intern, work-study student, as a volunteer, or via a clinical program. For some DA's offices—for instance, the prestigious Alameda County DA's office— the vast majority of permanent entry-level jobs go to people who clerked at the office as a summer clerk after their second year in law school.

If you can, try and get a summer job in the office where you would like to work permanently. This way you can start building a network of contacts that will help you nail down a permanent job.

Opportunities for law students in DA's and SA's offices are all over the board. Some offices have paid summer clerkships which have a salary exceeding $500 a week. Some don't pay at all, but do have volunteer and work-study positions available. Some have structured clerkship programs, while others hire a student now and then on an informal basis (the training you get tends to be better for structured clerkships than casual hires, by the way, but any experience is better than none at all).

As you already know, I'm not spending time in this book talking about interviewing, resumes, cover letters, and those kinds of things, because I cover them so exhaustively in my book *Guerrilla Tactics For Getting The Legal Job Of Your Dreams* (it's at your career services office). Everything that's true for every other kind of job is true for DA's and SA's office interviews—that is, research your quarry to the extent you can and bone up on the issues that are facing the office. Since DAs and SAs enforce the law, they are virtually always in the newspapers and researching them is relatively easy. The one thing I do want to mention here regarding interviews is that your interview with a prosecutor's office is likely to put you on the hot seat more than any other kind of interview. They will definitely test you to see if you can keep your cool under fire. When you're confronted with a tough hypothetical question, take a deep breath, smile, and if you need it, ask for a moment to organize your thoughts. Whatever you do: don't panic, and at the other end of the scale—don't be arrogant!

As a volunteer, work study student, or paid clerk, you'll get great experience, including researching and writing legal memoranda; writing briefs; attending trials and hearings; drafting subpoenas, motions and responses to motions; interviewing and prepping witnesses; investigating and recommending disposition of misdemeanor cases; and preparing evidence for trial. If you are "certified" (*i.e.,* your state allows certification, you're a 2L or 3L, you've taken Evidence and Civil Procedure, and you've taken a certification exam (typically 2 to 4 hours) before you work for the DA/SA—see your career services office for details), you'll get much more responsibility—you'll be able to conduct full jury trials—under the supervision of an attorney.

HOW DA/SA OFFICES ARE SET UP . . .

There will be one District Attorney or State's Attorney who runs each office. Every other attorney in the office is either a "deputy" or an "assistant" (the numbers of relative rank of deputies and assistants differs from office to office).

Let's take a look at one particular office for a typical set-up. In fact, why don't we take a peek at the New York County DA's office, which is more commonly referred to as the Manhattan DA's office. It's regarded as the most prestigious, sexiest DA's office in the country (followed closely by the Alameda County DA's office in California). The Manhattan DA's office is involved in cases that make the news all the time; DA Robert Morgenthau's name is in the papers on virtually a daily basis. If what you want is to have your finger on the pulse of what's going on in New York, the Manhattan DA's office is the place to be!

The Manhattan DA's office is divided into three broad areas: the Trial Division, the Investigation Division, and the Appeals Bureau.

The Trial Division prosecutes street crime. It consists of six trial bureaus, with approximately 50 Assistant DAs in each bureau. Felonies and the most serious misdemeanors are assigned to Assistants as soon as a suspect is arrested, and those Assistants prosecute the case all the way from filing the complaint through discovery to disposition via either a guilty plea or a jury verdict. (Note: this method for handling cases is called "vertical prosecution"—that is, the same attorney handles a case from beginning to end. In most DA's/SA's offices, this typically only happens in very complex or sensitive cases, and in specialized units like those handling family cases or homicides. Most other kinds of cases are filed by one attorney, another attorney handles the preliminary hearing, and a third will handle the trial.) Anyway—in the Manhattan DA's office, assistants of all levels of experience handle felonies and serious misdemeanors.

Experienced assistants from the trial bureaus handle special types of cases in smaller bureaus in the Trial Division, including the Career Criminal Bureau, the Sex Crimes Unit, the Homicide Investigations Unit, the Spanish Language Program, the Family Violence and Child Abuse Bureau, the Asian Gang Unit, and the Special Projects/Narcotics Eviction Program.

The Investigation Division has three bureaus, as well as several specialized units that handle complex long-term cases. The three bureaus are the Frauds Bureau (which handles complicated economic crimes like securities and bank frauds), the Rackets Bureau (which handles organized crime, public corruption and labor racketeering), and the Special Prosecution Bureau (where Assistants handle "white collar" crimes like tax fraud and crimes against consumers). The specialized units in the Investigation Division include the Asset Forfeiture Unit, the Official Corruption Unit, the Crimes Against Revenue Unit, and the Construction Industry Strike Force/Labor Racketeering Unit.

The Appeals Bureau does what its name suggests—that is, it handles appeals generated by other areas in the office. Assistants in this bureau make regular appearances before state appellate courts, in federal court, and sometimes even in the U.S. Supreme Court.

The Manhattan DA's office employs both experienced and entry-level attorneys, as well as summer clerks (the vast majority of permanent hires are entry-level attorneys; the office hires fewer than 10 experienced attorneys every year, while it hires upwards of five dozen entry-level attorneys in any given year).

Applications for permanent work have to be made in the fall (as is true of all DA's and SA's offices, it's a good idea to apply early—and to call for deadlines, as they all differ). Starting salaries are $$ ($35-50,000), which is typical of most Assistant DAs and SAs. If you want to work in the Manhattan DA's office as a permanent hire, as is true of all DA's and SA's offices, it pays to be an intern first—a substantial number of interns wind up as entry-level attorneys.

Being hired as a lateral requires admission to the New York Bar and at least two years of experience, with a proven dedication to public service, criminal litigation, and/or appellate work all being plusses.

Applications for summer clerkships have to be made in the early spring (again—it's a good idea to apply early in the spring, and call for deadlines). The Manhattan DA's office has approximately 50 summer clerks every year, with more 2Ls than 1Ls (although it hires both). The summer clerkships are paid in the range of a couple of hundred dollars a week. As I've mentioned before, these clerkships are a great springboard into DA's and SA's offices, and they play very well with private employers as well.

The Manhattan DA's office also offers internships during the semester—approximately 10 each semester. The semester internships are work-study.

HOW OTHER DA'S/SA'S OFFICES COMPARE TO NEW YORK . . .

Riverside County, California District Attorney's Office (covering Palm Springs): Just over 100 attorneys. New attorneys have a starting salary in the mid-$40s and summer clerks make more than $500 a week. The office typically hires a couple of entry-level attorneys and a couple of experienced attorneys every year. While they don't typically hire summer interns, they do have a few work-study opportunities in a typical year. As is true of every DA's/SA's office, you get excellent experience right away—both work-study students and new attorneys can expect to screen new cases, interview witnesses, prep for trials, research, negotiate, and work on trials.

Dade County, Florida (covering Miami) State's Attorney's Office: Almost 300 attorneys. New attorneys have a starting salary in the mid-$20s. The office typically hires about 30 entry-level Assistant State's Attorneys every year, as well as a few experienced attorneys. While they don't have paid summer clerkships, you can work for them during the summer or during the school year on a work-study or volunteer basis, or if you are self-funded (e.g., through a grant). The office prosecutes all criminal violations in Dade County. As an entry-level attorney you start with a two-month training program and then get assigned to a trial division. There is both general misdemeanor and felony trial work, as well as specialized divisions including Sexual Battery, Career Criminal/Robbery, Major Crimes/Homicide, Economic Crimes, Domestic Crimes, and Organized Crime/Public Corruption.

WHERE TO FIND OUT NAMES/ADDRESSES FOR DA'S/SA'S OFFICES . . .

The best resource for identifying DAs and SAs offices is available in every law school career services office: It's the National Directory of Prosecuting Attorneys.

WHAT IT'S LIKE TO BE AN ASSISTANT STATE'S ATTORNEY:

Rich Colangelo, ASA in Fairfield County, Connecticut.

Quick.

You're dealing with a 20-year-old guy convicted of selling drugs within 1,500 feet of a school. He also violated probation and has a robbery and a larceny on his rap sheet, and another larceny pending. The school drug selling conviction has an eight-year mandatory sentence. How many years should he serve for the whole ball of wax?

Another guy. Violates a protection order, goes to his girlfriend's house, wraps her head in cellophane and tries to kill her, then has a change of heart and lets her go. He's facing attempted murder, as well as a possession of marijuana charge. She wants to have him put away for four years so she can go to school, graduate, and move away and start a new life. What weight do you give to her wishes in deciding what kind of a plea bargain to offer him?

Bachelor Number Three. Road rage. He's driving on the freeway, gets mad, and shoots at another car. The other driver isn't hurt. The guy is a college grad wants to go to medical school. The victim doesn't care what happens. Do you charge the road-rager with a felony? Or just a misdemeanor?

Another upstanding citizen gives marijuana to a 13-year-old girl and has forceful sex with her. When the crime happens, the victim doesn't care about the punishment. Two years later, the case is going to trial and the victim now wants the guy to serve the mandatory sentence. What do you do?

Now, how about the parents of an uncontrollable 13-year-old who come to you, and say, "Our kid is nuts. We need help." What can you do— if anything?

Afraid of being bored at work? Consider being an Assistant State's Attorney. If you're in a typical office—like the State's Attorney's Office in Fairfield County, Connecticut—these are the kinds of issues you deal with all the time. From burglaries to bad checks to harassment to DWI to robberies to narcotics to carjacking to cruelty to animals—they see it all.

And they see a *lot* of it. Rich Colangelo, an ASA in the office, will typically have upwards of 200 open files—that is, cases that haven't settled pre-trial. In four years with the State's Attorney's Office, Rich has taken 10 trials to verdict and handled many, many more. In his office—which has four prosecutors who handle five southwestern Connecticut cities and towns—they handle 4,500 cases a year. Ninety-five percent of those cases go on a plea bargain, which in and of itself requires a whole variety of novel skills.

As Rich says, "You quickly learn things you could never have picked up at school. You don't, you *can't,* learn what a case is worth in law school, or what the appropriate disposition is. What's a drug case worth? A bag of cocaine versus a trunkful? Or a bag of pot? You look at the attitude of the criminal and you have to ask: is it worth it to send them to jail? Or should they go on probation? Is it a one-time thing, or are you looking at a habitual offender?"

And it's not as though criminals are the only people that Assistant State's Attorneys deal with. For a start, there are colleagues. Rich has three fellow prosecutors in his office, meaning there are always people around to look to for advice—and for cases the office hasn't handled before, they routinely call other State's Attorneys offices for pointers. The prosecutors in the office are all familiar with every case, because until there is a jury docket, cases aren't assigned to anyone. As Rich explains, "That means that everybody gets a chance to see every case, gets to handle it at some point." So if you wind up with a case and you want advice, your fellow prosecutors will all know who—and what—you're talking about.

Assistant State's Attorneys also have to learn quickly how to deal with judges. You have to be able to figure out whether the judge believes your case, and if (s)he doesn't, you have to come up with a Plan B for presenting the case.

Then there are defense attorneys. As Rich says, "You learn their style in a hurry." There may be people who will try and wear you down, filing motion after motion after motion. Or you might find out through the grapevine that there are defense attorneys who will never try a case and that everything they do pretrial is "smoke and mirrors."

And finally, of course, there are victims. While victims aren't really prosecutors' clients, prosecutors do pay attention to them. As Rich says, "The system is difficult for victims. If somebody is assaulted today, the case might come to court 18 months from now, and in the meantime, the person who assaulted them will be out on bond. And as a victim, you'll have to tell everything to strangers, and even if you do, the person still might be found not guilty." Rich says that "What victims really want is the answer to the question, 'Why?' You can't give them that because there's just no answer."

With serious ramifications hanging in the balance, Rich says that as a prosecutor, "You have to be careful not to get emotionally attached, not to take things personally. You have to remember your role." And things aren't *always* so serious. There are lighter moments. For instance, Rich talks about one guy who was picked up on a drug charge, "And while he's in jail, he writes his memoirs—'How to be a drug dealer.' Sometimes people make your job a whole lot easier!"

It's surprising to find out that with so much on their plates, prosecutors usually work very reasonable hours. A typical week in Rich's office goes like this. The mornings are busy because everybody who has been summoned to court, on everything from motor vehicle violations to attempted murder, is on the docket for 9 a.m. and the judge comes in at 10—and there may be between 100 and 400 cases to handle before noon! The prosecutors talk to everybody and discuss the cases either with the people themselves (if they're appearing pro se) or with their attorney, to see what their plea is going to be, and see if the cases can be disposed of quickly.

Tuesday is the day for court trials. Fifteen to 20% of the cases in the jury docket are up on any Tuesday. The prosecutors will work out some of them and reduce the charges or plea bargain.

Wednesdays are youthful offender days, with court trials for juveniles. Thursday is the day for handling hearings on probation violations and for drug programs. Friday is open, as are the afternoons the rest of the week. Of course, 'open' doesn't mean 'let's play golf'—it means handling all of the witnesses, victims, and the myriad of issues and duties that are on your plate when you've got a couple of hundred open files in your office. But with all of that, most days end by dinner time. While some prosecutors do the job and go home—and nobody frowns on that—many prosecutors get involved in the community. Some speak at schools. Rich, for instance, teaches Constitutional Law and Criminal Law at the local community college.

While states vary in the way they set up their systems, here's how Connecticut's system works. The state is divided into judicial districts, and in each district the State's Attorney's office is divided into a Part A and a Part B. As a rule of thumb, Part A handles any case where there's a body, and Part B handles everything else, up to attempted murder. When you start with the State's Attorney's office, you start as a Deputy Assistant State's Attorney in Part B. After three years, you become an Assistant State's Attorney in Part B. Then you become a supervisor in either Part A or Part B, and the move from there is the State's Attorney's role itself. The newly-appointed State's Attorney in Rich Colangelo's judicial district had spent 22 years working for the State's Attorney's office before he became State's Attorney.

ASAs who don't go on to become State's Attorneys sometimes become judges—a substantial proportion of judges are former prosecutors—and others go on to other government jobs or become defense attorneys. While prosecutors are paid well, have prestigious jobs doing work they believe in, and they are frequently in the limelight, there's certainly a bigger pot of gold in the private sector.

When you start with the State's Attorney's Office as a Deputy ASA, you're unassigned. Apart from your work at the office, you go to seminars where you learn about handling different kinds of cases and you're critiqued on your performance. The seminars also give you the chance to meet prosecutors from all over the place. The training and "elbow learning" with other prosecutors is important, because you're learning to do so many things that you never confronted in law school.

Because the skills you use as a prosecutor are unique, the background that's perfect for it is unique as well. Paper credentials are virtually meaningless, whereas experiences like school clinical programs are vitally important. Experience doing criminal work (not *as* a criminal, of course) is an important factor in getting a prosecutor's job—whether you've been a prosecutor elsewhere, or a defense attorney, or you've done an internship.

The internships vary from state to state, but in Connecticut an internship with the State's Attorney's office is worth 7 credits and it takes 20 hours a week (although it can be done in fewer hours, as well). You can do the internships anytime until you pass the bar exam. While some states pay their interns, in Connecticut the internship is strictly volunteer. The internships are key because you get to help out with, and sit in on, all kinds of pre-trial and trial activities.

Permanent job openings in Connecticut's State's Attorneys offices are posted in each district, as well as in the Connecticut Law Journal (and other states post job openings similarly).

What kind of person thrives as a prosecutor? The classic "people person." You have to deal with a huge gamut of people—from speeders to murderers to judges to defense attorneys to victims. You have to think quickly on your feet, since you never know what witnesses will throw your way. You have to know how to juggle many responsibilities, because although offices vary and some demand that you run things by superiors before you take action, there is a lot of autonomy that goes with the job. You have to know how to separate yourself emotionally from your work, because you're dealing with highly-charged situations every day. You have to maintain a professional stance and not let your compassion cloud your judgment.

With all of the criminals they deal with, do prosecutors become cynical? Rich Colangelo says that "To a certain extent you can't avoid it. You get an m.o. on everybody you deal with. Even with victims you quickly learn to tell if something is 'up', if there's something fishy. You know that not everybody is guilty, but you certainly look for every angle. Maybe cynical isn't the right word, but you definitely develop hyper-acute people skills on the job. People always surprise you. Sometimes people thank you when you send them to jail!" He laughs and reflects that, "This is the only job I wanted when I was in school. I didn't even consider anything else. It's turned out to be exactly what I hoped it would be."

Great Alternative Careers You Probably Haven't Thought About

When I was interviewing law school administrators for employers who ought to appear in this book, it quickly became obvious that there were certain kinds of employers who got raves not so much because of the particular employer, but because of the *nature* of the employer and the type of work. For instance, public defenders would fit that description. So would state's attorneys, district attorneys' offices, and state attorney generals' offices.

What I've done in this chapter is to pull out categories that don't appear elsewhere in the book and sort of lump them together. So what you'll find here is that I'm not telling you that it's great to work for specific employers. I'm not comparing law school administration jobs at the University of Nevada Law School to Fred's Law School in Marmoset, Indiana, or judicial clerkships with Circuit Courts as opposed to jobs with the U.S. Court of Claims Against People-Who-Insist-On-Driving-40-Miles-Per-Hour-In-The-Fast-Lane. What I'm going to do instead is describe to you categories of jobs that law school graduates find satisfying across the board.

Let's see what they are!

Judicial Clerkships and Related Court Jobs

If there had to be one job that I've recommended to more law students than any other, it's a judicial clerkship. As the Valparaiso Law School booklet on judicial clerkships says, "Working for a good judge is like getting to work every day with the best senior partner in a law firm."

You probably already know what judicial clerkships are, but in case you don't, they're one- or two-year assignments where you are essentially a research assistant either for a particular judge (an "elbow clerk") or for an entire court. Your duties will vary depending on the judge and the court, but by and large you're summarizing and analyzing cases, researching legal questions, and drafting opinions. (As we go into a little later on, your duties vary greatly depending on whether you're a trial or appellate clerk, so don't read too much into that basic description.) You can also get summer jobs and externships with judges as I discuss in the "Early Preparation" section a little later on.

What makes judicial clerkships so great? Here is the Spinal Tap *'But This List Goes To Eleven'* Set Of Great Reasons To Consider A Judicial Clerkship (if you don't get the reference, rent the movie *This Is Spinal Tap*. You'll love it). But about those reasons:

1. A judicial clerkship is an *excellent* credential, perhaps the best all-pur-pose credential you can get. Whether you want to go to a corporation, government agency, public interest organization, or become a law professor—no matter what you want to do next—judicial clerkships are the "universal solvent."

2. Judicial clerkships give you a chance to delay your permanent career decisions. I can't tell you how many students I've talked to who say, "I just don't know what I want to do yet." Well, if you're really in a deci-sion pickle, why rush yourself? A judicial clerkship gives you a year or two before you make that jump into something more permanent. On top of that, you may be in a situation where you can't—or should-n't—look for a permanent job. For instance, you've got a fiancé, spouse, or significant other in grad school, and they'll be graduating and moving to a different city in a year or two, and you'll go with them. It would be both career-ically unwise, and not terribly ethical, to interview for permanent positions knowing you're going to be hit-ting the trail in a year or two. It's *so* much better to take a job with a natural ending that coincides with your life plans.

3. The job is *very* intellectually stimulating—your judge will often look to you for creative ideas and use you as an intellectual sounding board. That's key, because intellectual stimulation has been deter-mined by ABA studies to be the single most important determinant of job satisfaction. (Free pizza was a close second.)

4. Judicial clerkships are frequently the great grade equalizer. One stu-dent at a small Midwestern law school, ranked very last in his class, struck out finding any kind of law firm job in his chosen city, Boston. He took a clerkship with a city court in the Northeast, did well at that, and got into one of Boston's 15 largest, most prestigious law firms immediately after his clerkship—the clerkship being his obvious key to entry. If you dropped the ball grades-wise in law school, you're going to have some talking to do to convince a judge you've got the writing and researching skills (s)he's looking for. But for lower-level, smaller courts, which are out of necessity less grade-sensitive, you've got a chance to get into the ultimate job you want via a clerkship.

5. Future buck-age potential. Many large firms pay a bounty for federal judicial clerks, and on top of that, they'll pay judicial clerks the salary of

a second or third-year associate (depending on whether you do a one- or two-year clerkship) when you start. In other words, while many large firm associates have been cutting their teeth in a library cubicle, you've been having the fun—and admittedly lower pay—of a judicial clerkship, and you're coming into the same firms just when things typically start to get interesting. (Great firms don't bore you to death your first couple of years, but many others, unfortunately, do exactly that.)

6. Clerkships are an outstanding opportunity to hone your research and writing skills. Virtually every legal employer values the ability to research and write, and everybody knows that judicial clerkships clean your clock on those basic skills.

7. You'll get an outrageously useful recommendation and contact. When it comes to looking for a job after your judicial clerkship, letters that begin with the words, "Judge Crater recommended that I contact you . . ." are letters that are going to get *read* and they'll *always* earn a response.

8. You have a real hand in determining justice. As a judge's right-hand person, you have input into every case the judge decides, and may have a significant impact on the lives and fortunes of people involved in the case. That kind of meaningfulness is a far cry from being a research drone who never gets to write a whole memo, let alone get anywhere near actual parties in a case. Couple that with the unique opportunity to peek behind the scenes of courts and you've got an unbeatable combination.

9. You'll get exposed to a wide range of cases and issues. This not only helps you make your long-term career choices, but it also makes you attractive to potential employers. You'll also get to *know* a bunch of potential employers and may, therefore, be able to avoid the whole sending-out-cover-letters-and-resumes grind entirely.

10. You'll typically work *much* more reasonable hours than first year associates in private practice. For instance, federal district court clerks work, on average, 40- to 60-hour weeks, and federal appellate clerks typically put in 40 to 50 hours a week. *All judges differ* of course, but that's the norm.

11. Not for nothing, lawyers who might otherwise sneer at a new lawyer will be kissing your butt just because of your connection to your judge. I realize this isn't the kind of thing most polite people would mention, but let's face it, when you've just spent three years in law school having strips of flesh torn from your back by the occasional sadistic professor, it's nice to think that there's a whole cadre of people who will feel compelled to treat you with respect!

Am I suggesting that judicial clerkships are for *everybody* and that they're *always* wonderful? No, of course not. There are a few downsides you should know about.

For a start, you may wind up with a judge who's a lunatic. There was recently a judge in the news (a woman) who was out driving and a state trooper following her car noticed that she was weaving. When he pulled her over and walked up to the window, she slurred, "Do you know who I am? I'm a (hiccup) goddamned judge!" When the trooper told her that didn't matter, she pulled out a gun, waved it at him, and warned him that if he gave her a ticket, she'd give him a .38-caliber vasectomy.

It's probable that a clerkship with this particular judge would be memorable, but for the wrong reasons. And while you can research judges to some extent up-front (we'll talk about that in a little while), you can't assure you'll always pick a winner. And even if you *do* get a judge who's usually a sterling character, everybody goes through tough times once in a while. If you catch a judge in the middle of, say, a nasty divorce, you're unlikely to find the most benevolent mentor.

And if you *do* have a bad experience, there's little you can do about it. As one former judicial clerk told me, it's not as though you can look to other people in the office for a job recommendation. You're uniquely at the mercy of one person, so you've got to bite the bullet and do whatever is necessary to make sure that recommendation is a good one, even if you're working under very difficult conditions. In these circumstances it's important to console yourself with the fact that judicial clerkships have a definite end, and when that time comes, your misery will be over.

There are other, more tangible downsides as well. For a start, there's the financial differential between judicial clerkships and some more lucrative kinds of private practice. Judicial clerks frequently make between $25,000 and $45,000 less than first year associates at large firms. You also typically have very little support staff or frills. Depending on the judge, you may work very long and hard hours. And if you just hate the idea of researching and writing, a judicial clerkship just isn't the route for you!

Having said this, do I think the disadvantages outweigh the benefits? Obviously not, or you wouldn't be reading about judicial clerkships right now. The vast majority of judicial clerks have an excellent experience and look back on their clerkships very fondly indeed!

What I'm going to do here is tell you everything you need to know about judicial clerkships. While I've culled the information here from a huge variety of sources, the person who contributed the most to this section is someone who must know more about judicial clerkships than anybody else in the country—Debra Strauss, the Director of Judicial Clerkship Counseling and Programs at Yale Law School. Not only did Debra attend Yale Law School herself, but she was also a judicial clerk. As the Judicial Clerkship maven at Yale, she generally shepherds about half of Yale's graduating class into judicial clerkships. What I'm saying is— you're getting the most expert of expert advice when you listen to Debra!

Here's what we'll do. First, we'll start out by talking about common misconceptions about judicial clerkships. I want to get this out of the way first, because I've got a strong suspicion that many, many law students who would *love* judicial clerkships self-select out without realizing a judicial clerkship *is* within their grasp. I don't want that to be you! Then we'll talk about early preparation—that is, how to use law school opportunities to set yourself up for a judicial clerkship.

Then we'll talk about the different kinds of clerkships that there are, and part of that is discussing the general framework of courts in this country. We'll then cover other court-related jobs (like staff attorneyships) and we'll follow that up with "a gold mine of frequently overlooked clerkship opportunities."

Then we'll look at what you can expect of different kinds of clerkships. We'll talk about how to nail down the clerkship you want. I'll start out there with a simple checklist to follow and we'll talk in detail about every item on it. We'll start with how you choose a court, and a judge. After that, we'll talk about the elements of applications for judicial clerkships— everything from cover letters and resumes to handling offers and going up to bat a second time if you don't get a nibble the first time around. Finally, we'll talk about research sources. Phew! Let's get started!

COMMON MISCONCEPTIONS ABOUT JUDICIAL CLERKSHIPS . . . LIKE 'MY GRADES AREN'T GOOD ENOUGH'

Misconception #1: You've got to have great grades to get a judicial clerkship.

This is not *universally* true. Yes, the United States Supreme Court is kind of fussy about the grades thing. As a rule of thumb, the more prestigious the court, the better the paper credentials you need. Judges almost always ask for "top 10%" credentials in published sources, but as many court insiders say, that's just done as a "scaring off" tactic. Judges rarely adhere to it in practice.

Of course, great grades and Law Review don't *hurt,* because judges want sharp people with excellent research and writing skills. But, the fact is that there are other ways to prove those skills beyond grades and journal experience, and beyond that, you never know what will ring a particular judge's chimes. One law student with awful grades got *100* clerkship interviews because he was an entrepreneur before law school and that piqued judges' interests. Some judges want long-haired tattooed musicians. Some judges may only want someone who's interesting in chambers. Maybe you'll go after a clerkship with a judge who doesn't care about grades overall, but *does* rely heavily on the opinion of a professor for whom you happened to excel, or for whom you were a stellar research assistant.

Of course, if you have fabulous paper credentials, it pays to be conservative and play your strong suit. But if you don't have sterling conventional credentials going for you, in your cover letters play up whatever you *do* have, be it a fascinating background or a sparkling personality. You never know what may spark a judge's interest!

Misconception #2: If you don't meet the strict deadlines for clerkships, you'll never get one.

Not true. The fact is, while judges traditionally fill their permanent clerkships *very* early (typically spring of your second year in law school, or thereabout), circumstances *do* change. New clerkships are authorized, new judges are confirmed, or clerks don't show up or don't work out or drop out for health or maternity reasons or they're abducted by aliens. The bottom line is that it pays to keep in touch with judges who've rejected you with a friendly card every couple of months, and/or to check late in the game to see if clerkships have opened up. I know one enterprising law student in St. Louis with strictly mediocre paper credentials who did federal district level clerkships during *both* of his law school summers. How did he get them? He just showed up at judges' chambers immediately after school ended, was *exceptionally* polite and ingratiating with everyone he talked to, and asked if they needed an extra pair of hands. Admittedly he had to knock on a lot of doors, and this is a *very* high risk strategy, but the point is that clerkships aren't static. Unscheduled openings *do* occur. (I talk more about freshly-minted judges below, under the section on "A Gold Mine Of Frequently Overlooked Clerkship Opportunities.")

Misconception #3: You've got to get a judicial clerkship, if at all, coming straight out of law school.

No! Judicial clerkships aren't the U.S. Olympic Gymnastics team—your opportunities aren't over at a painfully early age. Instead, as Yale's Debra Strauss advises, judges are increasingly hiring clerks with law firm experience. It's not a prerequisite by any means, but judges like it because "old" law school grads already have good work habits and won't be overwhelmed with a clerkship. This mirrors an ongoing trend for employers in general, who like to see maturity and a solid work ethic among their hires. So if you've got a bit of experience under your belt, take heart in knowing that you can still get a judicial clerkship if you want one.

EARLY PREPARATION—HOW TO USE LAW SCHOOL TO SET YOURSELF UP FOR A JUDICIAL CLERKSHIP INCLUDING SUMMER INTERNSHIPS AND EXTERNSHIPS.

If you think a judicial clerkship is the way you want to go, there are things you can do while you're in law school that will pave the way for you. Some of them—like getting great grades and taking part in writing contests—are things that would be excellent ideas no matter *what* you're going after. Others of them are unique to judicial clerkships. Let's see what they are:

1.   *Get great grades and do Law Review.*

Duh. Great paper credentials are the most obvious stepping stone to a judicial clerkship, and if the god of grades smiles upon you, nailing a clerkship will be *much* easier. But whether or not that happens, there are things to do to grease the wheels. Like . . .

2.   *Do a summer internship or school-year externship with a judge.*

If you read my *Job Goddess* column (and if you don't, you should), you know that the best all-purpose summer job you can get after your first year in law school is an internship with a judge. They're mostly volunteer positions, which means waitering on weekends if you need cash, but it's *worth* it.

You can also get part-time jobs during the school year with judges. And then there are judicial externships, which are available to 2Ls and 3Ls during the school year with federal district courts and various state courts. You typically get class credit for those.

While all judges differ, externs primarily research and write memos for the judge and clerks. They attend hearings, draft opinions, and help out administratively. In some cases what externs do very much mirrors law clerks' duties; other times, they get more menial tasks.

For information on judges and courts, check the "resources" at the end of this Judicial Clerkship section, and of course talk with your Career Services Director.

3.   *Consider taking a seminar course in the fall of your Second Year.*

Why? You'll have to write a paper, and seminar papers are good writing samples. Also, it gives you a pretty obvious recommendation source—the professor who teaches the course, and will thus be very familiar with your writing.

4.   *Take part in speaking contests and writing competitions where the judges are—well—judges.*

As you know, bulletin boards at school are choked with contest entries, and I'm not talking about the Publisher's Clearing House. You'd be amazed how few entries these writing contests get—sometimes as few as three! Not only do many of them come with cash prizes, some of them have real judges as judges. And if that's the case, entering and winning is a great way to become a blip on their radar screen (and I mean that in a positive way).

Speaking contests—be it client counseling competitions, Moot Court, or law fraternity oral advocacy tourneys—are other opportunities to exploit. These frequently feature local judges as judges. If you do well, introduce yourself to the judges, collect business cards, and follow up with a thanks-and-nice-to-meet-you note—which will help pave the way for a clerkship request later on.

By the way, if that's a little rumbling whine I hear in the distance, along the lines of 'I don't have *time* to do any more work Kimmbo blah blah blah . . . " I understand—I would have said the same thing in law school myself—but just go to school an hour, *one dinky hour,* early for a couple of weeks, and do your contest entry then. You won't miss the time and it could pay huge dividends.

5. *Take advantage of any opportunity to meet judges, whether at school-sponsored events or via personal contacts.*

Judges, like all employers, want to work with people they *like.* Because judges have such close daily contact with their clerks, it's even more important for them than it is for most employers. So if you meet them under *any* circumstances and they take to you, you'll be able to nail a clerkship a whole lot easier.

By way of hilarious example, I'll tell you about one law student's experience. (If you've seen my seminar, you've heard me tell this story. It's one of my favorites!) This student, a female student, wanted very badly to clerk for a particular judge—a female judge. The student tried everything she could to get through to this judge, but was rebuffed at every turn. Anyway, one day this student is having her hair cut and her hairdresser casually asks, "So how's law school going?" The student says "Ugh!" and responds, "I'm going nuts. I'm trying to get a job with Judge Blahdeblah, and I just can't get through to her." The hairdresser stops cutting and says, with interest, "Judge *Blahdeblah?*" The student nods her head, and the hairdresser waves over to a wall of manicurists and says, "No kidding! Trixie over there does her nails."

As soon as her haircut is done, the student gets up, walks over to the aforementioned Trixie, and says, "Is it true you do Judge Blahdeblah's nails?" Trixie nods, and the student goes on, "When does she come in?" Trixie responds, "She has a standing appointment every Friday at noon." The student turns to the manicurist in the chair next to Trixie, and says, "Are you available Fridays at noon?" The manicurist says she is, and the student thunders, "Sign me up!"

Sure enough, she shows up on Friday at noon, and guess who's sitting in the next chair—Judge Blahdeblah! Now if you're a man, I don't expect you to appreciate this whole manicure culture, but if you're a woman you probably know that when you're having your nails done there's not much to do but talk to the person next to you. So sure enough, Judge Blahdeblah innocently turns to this student, introduces herself, and says, "What do you do?" Intrepid student responds, "Oh, I'm in law school," and adds nonchalantly, "How about you?" The judge responds with "I'm a judge," and the student says, a surprised tone to her voice, "No kidding! What a coincidence!"

Over the period of the next few weeks, they chatted casually like this every Friday at lunch, until one day when the judge asked, "Hey, are you interested in a clerkship? Would you like to work for me?" I don't have to tell you the student's response!

The point here is pretty obvious. Take advantage of any opportunity you have to meet and get to know judges. It can't hurt you!

WHAT'S OUT THERE? THE TONS AND TONS OF COURTS THAT EMPLOY JUDICIAL CLERKS

There are three general types of courts for which you can clerk: Federal Courts, State Courts, and—well—"other" (including specialty courts like federal claims courts, and administrative law judges. I'll discuss those more offbeat opportunities in the section titled "A Gold Mine of Frequently Overlooked Clerkship Opportunities").

Federal Courts

Because the hierarchy of federal courts can be confusing, I've provided a diagram below (courtesy of Debra Strauss) to give you an idea of how the federal courts are set up. As you can see from the diagram, some federal courts are what we would characterize as specialty courts, including the Court of Federal Claims, the Court of Veteran Appeals, and the Court of International Trade. I discuss these in the "Gold Mine" section I mentioned a minute ago.

What you can't get from this diagram is the fact that there are *many* federal clerking opportunities. For instance, there are over 500 appellate clerkships *alone*—each judge has two or three clerks, and each court has a central staff that includes clerks. There are *several hundred* federal district court judges and each of *them* typically has two clerks.

State Court Systems

Let's take a look at state courts. The different states have different court structures, but as a general rule, you have a state supreme court (which in New York, as you may remember from civil procedure, is called the court of appeals, but it's *usually* called the supreme court), underneath that you have state intermediary appellate courts, and under that you have state trial courts of general jurisdiction. States also typically have specialty courts and courts of limited jurisdiction, including municipal courts, probate courts, and criminal courts.

Federal Court Structure

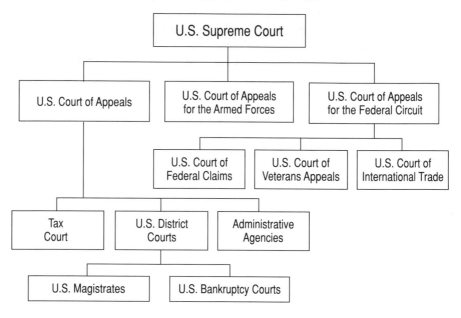

THE CLERKSHIP EXPERIENCE—THE NUTS AND BOLTS OF WHAT YOU DO AS A CLERK IN VARIOUS DIFFERENT KINDS OF COURTS

Of course, what *you* do as a clerk depends very much on exactly which judge you work for. Some judges might want you to maintain their library in chambers, draft speeches and lectures for conferences and bar functions, and some may even expect you to do administrative work. Others will expect you to run personal errands. But there *are* generalizations that can reasonably be made. As a rule of thumb, there is much more people contact at the trial level, and much more research in appellate courts. Trial courts, where you have to deal with parties (the litigant kind, not the beer-bong-and-vodka-slalom kind), witnesses, experts, and the rest of the cast of characters makes the setting lively, if not hectic. Appellate courts, by contrast, are more cerebral and some are downright monastic. Which you prefer depends on your personality.

By and large, here are the tasks you can expect in different kinds of clerkships:

Federal District Courts

You'll typically be involved in decision-making at every stage of the proceedings, including conferences, bench memos, pretrial motions, evidentiary hearings, and jury and non-jury trials in court. You can expect to prepare memos, attend oral arguments, attend or conduct settlement conferences, write draft versions of the judge's opinions and orders, prepare the judge's bench and organize exhibits, keep records and handle administrative tasks like scheduling, review motions and make recommendations on them, and prepare trial memoranda for the judge (including a summary of the issues presented in a case). You might also handle calls from attorneys and schedule court appearances or meetings for attorneys. You might check cites, and you may run personal errands for the judge.

Although you'll provide written opinions, you'll have less time for in-depth research than appellate clerks would. Instead, you'll frequently have to research issues on-the-spot at trials.

While judges vary, district court clerks typically work 40 to 60 hours per week.

Courts of Appeals

In some ways, you'll find that a court of appeals clerkship is like an extension of law school in that you can expect to research and write about issues presented on appeal. You'll handle fewer matters than trial-level clerks and you'll have more time, but the flipside of that is that there will be a higher level of expectation for the quality of your written opinions. You'll grow to appreciate compromise among a panel of judges, and you'll edit other clerks' draft opinions. While you'll have less contact with attorneys and factual documents than a trial-level clerk, you'll have more contact with other judges and staff.

Specifically, you can expect to help out with screening cases, drafting memoranda summarizing the parties' briefs, writing memos on key issues in rulings, helping prepare administratively for oral arguments, attending oral arguments, writing draft opinions including extensive research and analysis, and drafting dissents, concurrences, and rulings.

Although judges differ, appellate court clerks typically work between 40 and 50 hours a week.

State Courts

Right off the bat, remember that *most* legal disputes in this country are handled in state courts, which are the primary forums for contract disputes, torts, criminal prosecutions, divorce and custody matters, and probate of estates.

What you'll get to do depends very much on the court and the judge. For the highest state courts—which are typically called state supreme courts—you'll find that your tasks most resemble those of a Federal Appellate Court clerkship, except that you'll have a tremendous opportunity to influence state law since there's a virtual lack of higher court review. If you clerk for a "special" state court, like probate or family court, you'll clearly get a more specific background in a particular area of the law.

State court clerkships also give you the benefit of making local contacts for the future and gaining inside knowledge of procedural issues in state courts.

OTHER COURT-RELATED JOBS (INCLUDING STAFF ATTORNEYS)

Everything we've talked about until now has involved "elbow" clerks—that is, clerks for particular judges. There are many other kinds of clerk-related jobs at courts as well, and I've heard good things about all of these kinds of jobs.

For a start there are "staff attorneys" in some courts. As a staff attorney, you're part of the court's central staff. You typically review cases for the entire court, write memos, and work with the judges on things like motions, pro se petitions, and cases decided without oral arguments. These jobs differ from judicial clerkships in that they're not associated with a particular judge, they're permanent, and they *generally* require experience (although a few don't). For federal circuit courts staff attorney positions are sometimes for a fixed five-year term. Staff attorneyships are becoming increasingly popular; for instance, California appellate courts are gradually replacing judicial clerkships with staff attorneys.

Staff attorneys typically work a very reasonable 40- to 50-hour week, and some courts even allow staff attorneys to "split" positions. For instance, two people each work a 25-hour week (a real boon to people with young children).

Staff attorney jobs sometimes mutate into elbow clerkships at the request of judges, either temporarily or permanently.

At the federal district court level, courts also employ writ clerks or pro so clerks, who handle petitions from prisoners. (People who fill these positions may also be called staff attorneys.)

And then there are permanent law clerks. These *are* elbow clerks, but as the name suggests, the job is a permanent one rather than a temporary stint. These are hard to find right now, but they are becoming increasingly popular with judges. These positions are *highly* sought after. I talked with one woman who had been a judicial clerk, and then moved on to work at a large law firm as a litigator. She was in the middle of a trial when her judge called her to say that he'd been authorized to hire permanent clerks, and he wanted her to come back to work with him. She dropped everything—*everything!*—and went back to work for him.

A GOLD MINE OF FREQUENTLY-OVERLOOKED CLERKSHIP OPPORTUNITIES

When you think of clerkships, you probably think about just a few different kinds of clerkships. At least *I* do—federal district courts, circuit courts, and of course the U.S. Supreme Court. On the state side, trial level, appellate, and state supreme courts. But the fact is that those are only part of the story—there are *tons* of often-ignored clerkship opportunities, and what I'm going to do here is to talk a bit about some of those. First we'll look at courts and then we'll look at different types of judges.

COURTS AND FEDERAL AGENCIES

U.S. Bankruptcy Court

You can find this court on our federal court chart a little while back. As a clerk for the bankruptcy court, you primarily review and prepare the weekly calendar. Not many bankruptcy court opinions are written; instead, you focus on procedural and administrative matters. Every judicial district in the country has a bankruptcy court.

You'll find that this kind of clerkships is a good background for practicing either bankruptcy law (duh) or commercial law.

U.S. Court of Federal Claims

This is a federal court, whose decisions can be appealed to the Court of Appeals for the Federal Circuit. (It's also on the federal court chart a little ways back.)
This D.C.-based court handles cases where there are claims for monetary judgments from the United States. The claims it hears include, among others, government contract disputes, inverse condemnations, and Indian tribe claims. It doesn't handle criminal or tax cases.

Clerks for the Federal Claims court sometimes travel with judges to other cities to hear cases.

U.S. Court of International Trade

I'm starting to sound like a broken record, but this is also a court that appears on the federal court chart a few pages back. As the name implies, it handles civil claims involving tariff conflicts and it hears appeals from the U.S. International Trade Commission (which investigates and rules on unfair practices in the import trade).

U.S. Court of Appeals for the Federal Circuit

This court hears appeals from U.S. District Courts nationwide in cases involving patents and any disputes where the U.S. is a defendant. It also hears appeals (as our federal court chart shows) from the U.S. Court of Federal Claims, the U.S. Court of Veterans Appeals, and the U.S. Court of International Trade.

This is a *particularly* great clerkship to pursue if you're interested in a career in intellectual property or international trade law.

U.S. Tax Court

This D.C.-based federal court adjudicates appeals between the IRS and taxpayers, involving income, estate, and gift taxes. It is actually an independent judicial body within the legislative branch of the government. This is a particularly attractive choice if you want to practice tax law.

Court of Appeals for the Armed Forces

This court hears appeals from court martial convictions in all of the armed forces.

U.S. Court of Veterans Appeals

This court reviews decisions of regional Boards of Veterans Appeals on cases involving disputes over veterans' benefits.

U.S. Territorial Courts

If you want to perform a judicial clerkship *and* work on your tan, consider U.S. territorial courts in the U.S. Virgin Islands or Puerto Rico. There are also U.S. territorial courts in Guam and the Northern Mariana Islands and they all hire judicial clerks from U.S. law schools.

Federal Agencies

Members of agencies like the Commodities Future Trading Commission and the Benefits Review Board, among many other agencies, hire clerks. Check with your Career Services Office as well as agency web sites (there are plenty of these listed in Chapter 10 in the federal agencies section) for more information.

CATEGORIES OF JUDGES

Federal Senior Judges

These are judges who are semi-retired. They've lightened their caseloads but they haven't totally retired. The choicest senior judges to clerk for are former chief judges.

The benefits of working for these judges include the fact that they've spent a lot of time as lawyers and judges and can provide you with insights that a greenhorn judge may not have. Also, the competition for clerkships is often less fierce than it is for active judges—and the workload is lighter. Also, senior judges can typically pick and choose the cases they want to work on. They generally choose the most interesting cases, which means more interesting work for you as their clerk.

Administrative Law Judges

As we saw several times in Chapter 10 when we talked about jobs with federal agencies, there are many federal agencies that have administrative law judges. In all, there are over 1,000 administrative law judges in 28 different federal agencies. They hear cases pertinent to their particular agency. For information on these kinds of judges, check out the web sites mentioned in Chapter 10 (and for any other federal agency that appeals to you).

U.S. Magistrates

Magistrates are appointed by U.S. District Court Judges. They are judicial officers with limited statutory authority. Typically, they supervise pretrial (discovery) proceedings, conduct settlement negotiations, draft recommendations on motions, hold evidentiary hearings, and preside over civil trials. In criminal matters, they usually arraign defendants, hold detention hearings, and conduct misdemeanor trials. As an assistant to a U.S. Magistrate, your duties vary depending on your magistrate's responsibilities. However, because of their trial-court focus, they're an obvious choice if you want to become a litigator.

Judges in Small Towns and Lesser Populated States

Predictably enough, the most difficult clerkships to get are in the federal courts in Boston, Chicago, New York, and Washington, D.C. But there is tons of judicial talent outside the large metropolitan areas. These judges get fewer applications and, hence, clerkships with them are somewhat easier to get. Furthermore, for federal courts, federal law is the same everywhere. Clerkships in Midland, Texas can be just as valuable as geographically more sought-after postings, but they're *much* easier to get because there's less competition for them. If it's a clerkship you want, it doesn't pay to be a snob!

Newly-Appointed Judges

The attraction here is that these clerkships are typically easier to get since they get fewer applications than established judges. One of the reasons for this is that there is no fixed calendar for judicial appointments, so applying to them often means missing the usual clerkship "rush."

To find out about these opportunities, keep an eye on your local newspaper for judicial appointments and an ear to your Career Services Office. If you find someone who has been nominated for a federal judgeship but hasn't been confirmed yet, send an application and *acknowledge in your cover letter* that you know they haven't yet been confirmed, but you want to clerk for them when their nomination is confirmed. Request that they keep your application on file until they are actively considering clerks.

Unexpected Openings

As I've pointed out before, judicial clerks sometimes vaporize before their clerkships are over for a variety of reasons. As with newly-appointed judges, these openings can come up at any time. The best way to get these is to check frequently with the Career Services Office at school and to keep your eye on relevant web sites (you'll find them under "resources" at the end of the judicial clerkship section). Career Services is a particularly fertile source because judges faced with a sudden opening will often contact Career Services Offices for help.

HOW TO GET JUDICIAL CLERKSHIPS

According to the ABA Magazine *Student Lawyer,* most law students who successfully harpoon a judicial clerkship apply to at least 40 to 50 judges (although of course the ABA wouldn't use a word like 'harpoon' in this context). So be prepared for a bit of work. Getting a judicial clerkship is a job in itself!

When it comes to nailing down a clerkship, there are some technical procedures to follow and some smart things to keep in mind. What I'm going to do here is tell you what I'm going to *avoid* telling you about— that is deadlines for various different kinds of courts and specific procedures for individual judges. Egads! Isn't this book long enough *already*? You've got to do the footwork yourself. (I've given you a lot of research tools, below, and you can always, and *should* always, check with your Career Services Office.) Although I'm not going to discuss specific deadlines, you should know that decisions on permanent clerkships are typically made *very early*—for federal courts, the winter of your second year (yes, *second* year) in law school, and state supreme court clerkships a few months later.

What I'm going to focus on here instead are much more important things. Namely: the non-technical aspects of bagging a judicial clerkship—choosing a court, choosing a judge, and things you just have to know about cover letters, resumes, writing samples, transcripts, letters of recommendation, interviewing, how to handle offers and acceptances, and how to try again if at first you don't succeed!

Why don't we start off with a checklist for pursuing judicial clerkships?

JUDICIAL CLERKSHIP CHECKLIST

Here are the steps you need to follow, in order:

1. Choose the judges and courts you want to approach

2. Find references and ask for letters of recommendation

3. Update your resume

4. Write cover letters

5. Mail applications to judges

Choosing a Court and a Judge (Including Courts and Judges Who Are Known as United States Supreme Court Feeders)

There are a number of considerations to take into account when you're choosing judges and courts. For a start, if it's prestige that you want, as a rule of thumb federal court clerkships are considered more prestigious than state court clerkships, although *some* state supreme courts are on a par with federal circuit courts. (Typically the more populous the state, the more prestigious its clerkships, like New York and California.) And the higher the level of the court, the more prestigious the clerkship. So appellate courts are typically more prestigious than trial courts (although you may not enjoy them as much, as we'll discuss below). Obviously the grand poo-bah of courts is the U.S. Supreme Court, whose clerkships we discussed in Chapter 3 under "Ultimate Dream Jobs." Incidentally, a huge caveat to *all* of this talk of prestige is that certain individual judges, regardless of the level of their court, carry prestige. Check with your Career Services Office and favorite professors to see who they are locally.

Prestige is particularly important if you've got in mind that you're going to try for the brass ring later on—a United States Supreme Court clerkship. You can read about Supreme Court clerkships in Chapter 3 on "Ultimate Dream Jobs." I'm not going to rewrite that section here, except to point out that you need to do at least one lower-court clerkship first. And you've *got* to have major paper credential *cojones* to get a Supreme Court clerkship, so if your resume isn't suitable for engraving try for one of the hundreds of other great jobs in this book.

But if you *are* game, you should know that there are certain judges and certain courts that are known as "feeders" for the Supreme Court. The feeder courts tend to either be entire circuits, and/or individual judges. For instance, the 2nd (New York City), 9th (San Francisco), and D.C. Circuits are renowned Supreme Court feeders, largely because they're so big. A few judges who are known for being Supreme Court feeders include:

Judge Pierre N. Leval in the 2nd Circuit
Judges Alex Kozinski, William A. Norris, and Stephen Reinhardt in the 9th Circuit
Judge Laurence H. Silberman in the D.C. Circuit (who has the reputation of having sent more clerks to the Supreme Court than perhaps any other judge)
Judge J. Michael Luttig in the 4th Circuit (in Richmond)
The "Arnold Brothers" in the 8th Circuit (in Little Rock)—Chief Judge Richard S. Arnold, and Judge Morris S. Arnold

If you're going to go after a Supreme Court clerkship, consider giving these judges and courts a try (and any others that your Career Services Director can steer you toward).

No matter *which* court or *which* judge you want to clerk for, before we talk about the nuts and bolts of choosing judges and courts, a word of caution: don't *ever* apply to a court and/or a judge with whom you wouldn't want to clerk. For a start, you're paying the traveling expenses, so blanketing the country with applications can get pricey. More importantly, you're not collecting shrunken heads you know, you're dealing with *people*—very influential people at that. Don't even *think* of applying for judicial clerkships just to get the interviewing experience. What that all adds up to is that you've got to do your detective work up front to ensure to the greatest extent possible that the clerkships you go for are the one you want.

Now let's talk about choosing the courts to approach. I've already told you about the different kinds of courts. What you have to do is determine which kind of experience you want. If you prefer a more intellectual environment, you're going to prefer an appellate court clerkship. For more of an adrenaline rush, a more people-oriented experience, a trial court clerkship will make you happy. You also should take into account geography—in terms of developing contacts and paving the way for your future career, you're best off doing a clerkship in an area where you'd like to settle afterwards. But having said that, there are other factors that may influence which court you choose. For instance, you may want a specialty court because of your background. A technical background and an interest in Intellectual Property would suggest that you try for a clerkship in the Federal Circuit, which tries patent cases. And if you dream of being a litigator, a trial court (or magistrate) clerkship will serve you better than an appellate position.

When it comes to choosing specific judges to target, you've still got a number of factors to consider. Some of the elements that go into making a satisfying clerkship include the judge's ideology and background and the judge's personality especially vis-a-vis clerks (is it combative? Or relaxed?). Judges will also differ in the types of cases and the level and amount of work they give to clerks.

You also have to take into account the status of the judge. Your duties will be different if the judge is a Chief Judge, a Senior Judge, or a new appointee. Chief Judges will have more administrative responsibilities than other judges and some of that administrative work may trickle down to you. As I talked about in the "overlooked" clerkship opportunities section, working for Senior Judges—ones who are semi-retired—doesn't mean you'll have nothing to do. It depends on the judge. Some choose only cases in their areas of interest, or they prefer to travel around. Those appetites will obviously influence your work as a clerk. And finally, freshly-minted judges are actually an excellent choice, as I also mentioned in the "often overlooked" clerkship section. When you work for someone who hasn't been a judge before, you'll have an influence on setting up the chambers, and that's fun.

As I alluded to a few paragraphs back, remember that *you* pay your travel expenses for clerkship interviews. Don't apply to courts you couldn't afford to travel to!

To find out more about individual judges and courts, ask at career services for alums and profs who might know about particular judges, and speak with any lawyers or professors who have worked with or argued before particular judges. You should also check out the research materials—including web sites—that I've listed at the end of the judicial clerkship section.

Cover Letters, Resumes, Transcripts, Writing Samples, Letters of Recommendation, Interviewing, Following Up, Handling Offers and Acceptances, and How to Try Again if at First You Don't Succeed!

I've said at various points throughout this book that I wouldn't talk about cover letters, resumes, blah blah blah, because I covered them in such exhaustive detail in my last book, *Guerrilla Tactics For Getting The Legal Job Of Your Dreams.* Everything I said in that book would apply to every job in *this* book. *However,* pursuing judicial clerkships is a unique situation, and so I've violated my own prohibition about talking about these kinds of issues. That means that what you'll find here are tips specific to pursuing judicial clerkships.

COVER LETTERS

No matter what else your application includes, it will have to have a cover letter. While no source I've seen (or talked to) says what I'm about to tell you in so many words, it's pretty clear that the level of detail you should include depends to some extent on the paper credentials you're bringing to the table. For instance, a cover letter which states . . .

"I am writing to you to apply for the position of judicial clerk. I will be available any time after May 15ᵀᴴ the year after next. I am #1 in my class at the Harvard Law School and will be President of the Harvard Law Review beginning next fall. Thank you and good night."

. . . would undoubtedly do the trick nicely all by itself.

But most of us aren't three standard deviations above the mean on the old Poisson distribution of credentials. For the rest of us, as the Superior Court of Boston tells applicants, your cover letter gives you the chance to highlight your experience, interests, and individuality.

Here are tips for what you want to do with your cover letter:

- To the extent you can, personalize the letter to the judge and court. You'll find information on research in the "Choosing a court and a judge" and "Resources" sections.

- If you have a tie to the geographic area, particularly if you're applying to a state court, say what it is!

- On a related note, as a matter of practical reality, judges are less inclined to interview out-of-state candidates, knowing that you have to foot the travel bill. Stress *why* you want to be there in your letter.

- Be aware that your cover letter is the judge's first exposure to your writing style. Make it clear and lively, and brief—no more than a page. And as is true for every written thing any employer sees, *no typos*—double-check the spelling of the judge's name and have at least one other person read your letters.

- Keep in mind that a current clerk will likely read your letter first, so don't say anything arrogant like, "I'll be the best clerk you've ever had."

- Don't be cowed by the judge's stature and make your letter too pompous or too serious. Don't say, "I've always wanted to be a federal judge" or "I'm interested in taking part in the clash of superior minds."

- No gimmicks! Don't include a short story in the body of your letter or include a scrap book about yourself.

- In your first paragraph, include the date you will be available to start work.

- If you've got an unusual reason for wanting a clerkship and you have definite plans for what you want to do with your career after your clerkship, they're worth mentioning. Otherwise, don't bother with them. Judges know how desirable clerkships are, and stating the obvious won't help your campaign.

- Be enthusiastic but sincere. If you have an honest, particularized interest in working for this particular judge, if there's something that you truly think is great about them, something that motivates you to work for them, go ahead and say it. But if you send a form letter to 50 judges all saying "It's been my lifelong dream to work for you," it's going to smack of sleaze.

- Remember the old screenwriter's adage "Show me, don't tell me." Don't *say* that you're "hard working, a self-starter, with great research and writing skills." Instead, describe achievements that *show* what you've got. For instance, working 30 hours a week to finance your law school education shows hard work. A brief description of research for a journal or professor will show you like to research and write.

- Be sure that you accurately state the judge's title in your letter, whether it's Chief Judge or Judge or Justice. "Yo Babe" won't cut it. Always be formal. "Dear Chief Justice Amullmahay:" is appropriate. If you just aren't sure, check with career services or call the judge's chambers and ask.

- On the envelope and inside address, the judge's name is always preceded by "The Hon.," "The Honorable," or "Honorable."

- The preferred closing for letters to judges is "Respectfully." "Sincerely" is also common and acceptable, but certainly not "Hopefully," "With Fingers Crossed," or "Your Faithful Liege Man."

RESUMES

Yet again I feel compelled to say that if you want a thorough detailing job done on your resume, check out my book *Guerrilla Tactics For Getting The Legal Job Of Your Dreams.* It's at your Career Services Office and probably most libraries. All I'm going to do here is to address two unique elements that apply to judicial clerkships:

- Because you're typically applying for clerkships at least a year in advance, by the time the clerkship starts you will have experience that you don't have now. For instance, you'll want to say "Will work this summer for the American Judicature Society" or "Appointed Notes Editor for the Journal of Wood Tick Law, for the academic year XXXX-XX" or "Prospective judicial clerk for Federal Circuit Judge Crater." This is important because although whatever you're including is prospective experience *now*, it will be under your belt by the time you get to *this* judge.

- Include personal hobbies and interests. Because judges work so closely with their clerks, they want to see that you're personable and well-rounded (assuming, of course, that you *are*). It may be that your research reveals that you have a common interest with a particular judge—like tennis or fly-fishing. If you're lucky enough to find that out, include that hobby on the resume you send to that judge! (As I mentioned in Chapter 3, Chief Justice Rehnquist has a weekly tennis game with his clerks.)

TRANSCRIPTS

You wouldn't think I'd have anything to say about transcripts, would you? Well, I do. While these are obvious points, they're based on things students have actually done, and I don't want you to be tempted to follow suit.

Number one—don't white out any grades.

Number two—don't tell judges more than they want to know. One law student attended a school out West that allowed students to include on their transcripts comments explaining their performance. This particular student had bad grades Second Year and otherwise did very well. As he explained on his transcript—and I'm recounting this word for word: "My poor performance second year is attributable to the fact that I suffered from irritable bowel syndrome. However, it is all behind me now (no pun intended)."

WRITING SAMPLES

Because writing is such a significant part of judicial clerkships, judges really value writing samples. It's important to choose well! Your writing sample should be well-written and well-organized, demonstrating your legal research and analysis skill. Beyond that, there are two elements to address here—length and type.

For length, Debra Strauss says you want to stay below 20. Ten is fine. Five is too short. If your writing samples happen to be short then send two to fill out the page recommendation.

When it comes to type, take into account the *kind* of judicial clerkship you're applying for. If it's a trial level court like a federal district court, you're better off with something concrete like a brief. An often-overlooked source of excellent writing samples for trial level courts is unedited law school exam essays—they show better than anything else your ability to write under pressure.

For an appellate court, something theoretical like a law review note is more appropriate. No matter what you choose, if it's writing that you did for a law firm, *always* check with the firm first to ensure that it's all right to use the particular piece of work as a sample. Assuming that it *is,* be sure to mark on the sample that you've OK'd it with the firm. Black out any client names. Judges will appreciate your respect for confidentiality. It's a big, bad boo-boo to send a judge a writing sample that reveals something confidential!

No matter what kind of writing sample you choose, don't send something heavily edited by someone else—which covers just about every published Law Review note. Instead, send *your* draft of your Law Review or Journal note or a short excerpt of it.

Also, don't send a writing sample with a grade or a professor's comments on it, no matter how rapturous the praise.

LETTERS OF RECOMMENDATION

The purpose of recommendations is to verify your writing ability, so the references are going to have to be in a position to *know* that, be it a professor or employer or anyone else with that kind of skinny on you. I am reminded of the law student who insisted on putting Jerry Lewis—yes, *the* Jerry Lewis—on his resume as a reference, simply because he was a family friend and the student thought the recognizability of the name would be a plus. If you have a famous reference who also happens to know your work that's great, use it. Family friends don't count!

You're typically going to want two or three letters of recommendation, although different judges have different requirements so check first. (If you are lucky enough to have more people who can say concrete, great things about your abilities, great—there's no harm in sending too many letters. Some judges are impressed by an abundance of recommendations.)

Here are some other tips to keep in mind:

- It's a good idea to give your references a packet of information about you *before* they write your recommendation, so that the letter they write can encompass that information.

- Because a lukewarm or brief general recommendation can torpedo your chances, ask your "selectees" very frankly what they will say about you, and if you should choose someone else instead. In particular, state to your references any personal things about you that you do *not* want mentioned in the recommendation, like a pregnancy or a disability. You need to know that recommenders frequently *and totally innocently,* tank people's chances for clerkships by blabbing something inappropriate. For instance, if you've got a voice like Tweety Bird, a reference may mention that in your recommendation letter by way of ensuring that the judge isn't taken by surprise upon meeting you. A revelation like this may well have the effect of eliminating you from contention altogether. So be up-front about anything personal you don't want revealed, and if the reference insists on including it, then find other references.

- When it comes to choosing references, as a rule of thumb, judges view faculty references more highly than employer references (although you shouldn't overlook sterling employer references—use both!). If you *do* use an employer, be sure to use your supervising attorney. If you don't, judges will smell a rat. Also, it's better to use a professor with a familiarity with your work over one you perceive as having a "big name." The more specific the letter, the more credible it will be.

- You want recommendations that show that you stick out from the crowd. If need be, as a first-year or freshly-minted second-year student, look to an undergrad professor who knows your work well. Judges realize that first-year professors rarely get to know students well, so they don't expect raves from them.

- Keep in mind also that glowing letters from your first-year legal research and writing instructor aren't the *most* convincing, because the way you perform on rote, mechanical writing exercises common to those classes don't indicate creativity or true critical analysis.

A few words about technicalities. When you ask for a reference, provide an envelope with the judge's name and address and a "re: your name" line on the outside, in case the letter gets separated from the rest of your application. Offer to word process letters and return them to your references for review and signature.

Make sure that letters of recommendation are addressed to *particular* judges, *not* "To Whom It May Concern." Provide your references with complete, accurate lists of names and addresses of judges who are to receive letters.

Concerning delivery, there are really only two ways for judges to get your letters of recommendation: either from you or from your references. Having your references send letters directly to judges is a minefield, because if the letter gets to the judge either substantially before or after your application package, there's a serious risk of the recommendation being misplaced—and if you've got an incomplete application package in the form of missing recommendations, you won't be considered for the clerkship. Yikes!

How to avoid this? If you have any references who *insist* on sending their letter of recommendation directly to the judge, then be sure to needle them to send the recommendation at approximately the same time—ideally, the same day—as you send your application.

A far better alternative is to send the letters yourself, along with your application. No chance of misplacing them that way! The way to overcome any hint of funny business is to have your references seal their letters of recommendation and sign their name across the seal on the back flap. It's well worth trying to get your recommenders to go along with this plan. Letters arriving before or after your application packet reaches the judge's chambers are frequently lost.

INTERVIEWING

While I could write hundreds of pages about interviewing—and I just about *did* exactly that, in *Guerrilla Tactics For Getting The Legal Job Of Your Dreams*—here I'm going to pass along a few tidbits to you that are specific to interviewing with judges.

- For each clerkship, keep in mind that judges will interview typically between five and 25 candidates—so you need to stand out in a positive way!

- When it comes to scheduling interviews, you *may* be able to parlay your interview schedule into interviews with other judges that haven't contacted you yet. The way to do this is to call their offices to let them know that you'll be in their area interviewing and asking if they'd be interested in interviewing you while you're there. (Incidentally, don't talk with the judge directly about this—it's an etiquette boo-boo! The judge's secretary will handle this kind of scheduling.) Debra Strauss advises that this kind of leveraging may pull your application out of the pile and get you an interview. It's also important because judges won't reimburse you for your travel expenses, so you want to consolidate trips to the extent that you can.

- As with every interview, you need to research your prospective employer—in this case, the judge. You should find out if anybody from your law school has ever clerked for this particular judge—be it an alum or a professor—or for this particular court, and find out everything you can. Any other members of the legal community that you know would also be useful here. What kinds of nuggets might you be able to dig up? Well, here's an example. I talked with one judge who particularly looks for clerks with a lot of *chutzpah*—he only wants clerks who are willing to be open with him about their opinions. What he asks in interviews to get at this trait is this: "What would you do in this situation. I've given you an opinion to draft and I've told you how I want the case to come out. You strongly disagree with me. What do you do?" He said that most students who haven't researched him give him the answer they think he wants—"Hey, you're the judge, if you want to it come out that way, I'll write it that way"—*even if it's not truly what they feel*. What he *really* wants is the student who'll say, "If you hire me, you're hiring me for my mind, and if I disagree with you, I don't care if your mind is made up. I'm going to tell you what I think." He told me that any student who takes the simple measure of calling his chambers first to talk to any of his current clerks, would learn that about him. It often makes the difference between an offer and no offer. So you can see how important it is to research judges!

- Other kinds of research include doing a Lexis/Nexis or Westlaw search for the judge's recent opinions and articles (I've included information on doing exactly this in the "resources" section at the end of the judicial clerkship stuff). Pay particular attention to dissents and concurrences, which will tell you a lot about the judge's philosophy and writing style. Not only that, but judges aren't immune to flattery. Taking the time to study the judge's writing shows that your interest in the judge is sincere and personalized.

While this kind of research is always impressive, you don't want the judge to feel as though they've been cyber-stalked! I talked to one federal district court judge who told me about a woman who interviewed with him and brought with her to the interview a whole stack of his opinions, which she had not only read but had apparently memorized. As soon as she left the interview room he turned to one of his clerks—who'd also been present at the interview—and said, "Well, what did you think?" The clerk responded, "Judge, I think she'd eat you for lunch."

Over-aggressive enthusiasm aside, it *is* important to know the kinds of cases that the judge has decided recently—for this your cyber-search is helpful. For issues that are important to the judge, lean on any contact you have or can make. For instance, if you can talk to a former clerk of the judge, that would be *extremely* useful.

Once you're all prepped, what do you have to know about the actual interview itself? Here are a few things to keep in mind:

- For a start, you have to be conscious of what judges are looking for. They want a person whose judgment they can trust, whose abilities they can rely on, and perhaps most importantly, somebody they feel they will enjoy working with.

- In what you say and your whole demeanor, you have to show that you find the law very interesting. You don't have to be a bookish nerd, but on the other hand it's not a good idea to say that law school bores you to tears.

- Be aware that you may interview with a current clerk. You need to know that judges may view their clerks' opinions *very* seriously. As is true for interviewing with junior associates at law firms, don't be lulled into a false sense of security by the fact that the person who is interviewing you is very close to your age. They aren't your buddy. They are the judge's eyes and ears, so be eternally vigilant to what you say and do— no conspiratorial, "Hey, is it true that he's a heavy drinker?" or "Jeez, the secretary seems like a real hard-a**. Is she like that all the time?"

- Judges want to know your outside interests. Because they work so closely with their clerks, they'll want to get a sense of your three-dimensionality. One judge told me a particularly funny story about this. I asked him how he'd chosen his most recent clerk, and he said, "I'm somewhat embarrassed to admit it, because it wasn't as though his grades were the best—they weren't. And it wasn't as though his other experience was particularly stellar. What stood out during the interview was that he happened to mention that his hobby is Northern Italian cooking. For the rest of the interview, all I could envision was this guy preparing a meal for me and the other clerks. I'm quite sure he doesn't know what tipped the scales in his favor!"

There are a few unique aspects of clerkship interviews you need to know about. For a start, you have to be *very* conscious of an *exceptionally* important difference between interviews for judicial clerkships and any other kind of job interview: *judges frequently ask questions that would be a no-no anywhere else.* They'll ask you about your politics. They'll ask you about what your father does for a living. They're going to ask whatever they want to figure out what makes you tick. You might also find that the interview will be a hyper-technical discussion. At the risk of making you shudder, your interview may even include a writing assignment. Some judges are known to give prospective clerks an issue to research and then turn them loose in the library to come up with an answer. You might be asked about your Law Review topic, or how you'd approach a particular controversy in the news, or a theoretical problem or issue. You might be asked what issues concern you most, your favorite jurist, or least favorite U.S. Supreme Court holding. Also be prepared for questions not typical of permanent positions, namely, what you intend to do after the clerkship. And then of course there's the question that's very common to every employer: namely, why do you want *this* job? While your answers should be your own, common reasons include wanting to advance your legal education, your interest in learning about the judicial process, or your desire to get a great background for being a litigator (good for a trial level clerkship) or a law professor (for whom judicial clerkships are almost de rigeur).

You should also have questions to ask. Your questions, naturally, should show your interest in, and enthusiasm for, the job. Ask about the judge's opinions in cases you've read, how the judge resolved the issues, what a typical day is like for the judge's clerks, the judge's favorite case ever and what (s)he liked about it, ask about contact with clerks that the judge has, the judge's most difficult decision ever, what the judge looks for in clerks, timetables for making hiring decisions, and what the judge's clerks primary responsibilities are. You can ask about the judge's favorite clerk ever and what stood out about him/her. Tailor these questions to your own personality. For instance, with the "favorite clerk" question, if you've got a colorful imagination you would probably come up with something like, "If you were walking along and found a magic lantern, and a genie popped out and told you that you could have the perfect clerk, what would that clerk be like?"

If you know something more personal about the judge—as long as it's not *too* personal—bring it up. Hobbies, for instance, or civic involvement. Glancing around a judge's office may give you clues you didn't have before—bowling trophies, mounted fish or photos of the judge in waders. You might ask: "I see you're a fisherman. Are your clerks ever lucky enough to go with you?"

The moral here is this: while interview length and structure vary from judge to judge and staff to staff, from a casual chat to the intellectual equivalent of a body cavity search, your approach should be this: You've got to prepare yourself as best you can, dig up whatever information you can about the judge, then go in, take a deep breath, smile, and stay calm!

Incidentally, as is true in every interview—don't dis the help. Chambers are *notoriously* egalitarian. Even if the judge refers to his/her staff by first names, don't *you* do it unless expressly invited to do so by the person in question. Otherwise, it's Mr., or Mrs., or Miss, or Ms. And don't be arrogant! If you've high-hatted the judge's administrative assistant, it won't much matter that you consider yourself the second coming of John Marshall—you won't get an offer.

FOLLOW UP

Although I'm not overall a big fan of thank you letters (there's a column in my *Dear Job Goddess* book about exactly this issue), for judicial clerkship interviews the consensus is that it's a good idea to send a thank you right away.

After that, if you don't hear anything for three weeks, call the current clerk or secretary—whomever you feel the most comfortable with—and say you're still interested, and ask when a decision will be made. This phone call might also give you a chance for a casual chat, and if that comes up, take advantage of it! Judges tend to rely very heavily on the opinions of the people who work for them and any good word in your favor can only help your cause.

HOW TO HANDLE OFFERS AND ACCEPTANCES

You need to know that if a judge is going to make you an offer, it's likely to be speedy—perhaps even at your interview—and there won't be much flexibility in response time. Some judges will make "exploding offers"— that is, they'll expect an immediate response. Others will give you 24 hours.

This poses a real minefield for you, if you happen to get an offer from a judge who isn't your first choice. Why? Because judges talk. If you turn down one judge in a district or circuit, they'll pass that along and it will diminish your chances of getting offers from others.

What can you do about this? Not a whole bunch. Of course, you shouldn't apply for a clerkship with any judge you really wouldn't want to work for, but I've told you that already. Beyond that, you *may* try to say that you have to check with your spouse, or try another (valid) reason for delaying a day or so, but some judges will react badly to that, and there's no telling if the judge you're talking to is one of those. (It's also *not* one of those things you can really ask a current clerk—'hey, do you think he'll give me extra time to decide so I can see if I get a better offer?')

Incidentally, when the happy day comes when you accept the clerkship you really want, it's customary to withdraw all of your other applications immediately. It's not an Easter egg hunt you know—once you've got your clerkship, bow out of the game immediately!

HOW TO TRY AGAIN IF AT FIRST YOU DON'T SUCCEED!

So despite your best intentions, you didn't make it the first time out of the gate. You didn't get a clerkship. Don't give up! There are a few steps that Debra Strauss advises you to take:

1. Reevaluate your application and process. Sit down with your Career Services Director and review what you did—painful as that might be!—to see if there are any obvious glitches you can remedy. I spoke with one young woman who hadn't gotten a clerkship despite sterling paper credentials and she was totally flummoxed as to what had happened. Well, I immediately found that when she got nervous, her voice took on a tremulous quality that made it sound as though she was going to break down and cry. I was absolutely certain that she wasn't aware of this, but it was *very disconcerting*. With a bit more spadework, she found that this one thing was indeed what had eliminated her from contention with judges, and when she learned to control it she got the job she wanted.

2. Consider other options and courts. As you know from our discussion of courts and from the research items I've given you below, there's no excuse for limiting your search.

3. Research newly-confirmed judges. There are new judges all the time, and they all need clerks. They may prove to be fertile territory for you.

4. Remember that some clerking vacancies open up late because people change their minds, don't show up, or get struck by lightning—whatever. It's worth keeping an open mind, and making sure that your last contact with judges you really want to work for includes the line, "While of course I'm disappointed I'm not going to be working with you, if circumstances change I hope you'll consider me again." Do what you can, whether via anyone in the judge's chambers whom you've befriended or through professors or career services, to keep your ears open for late-breaking possibilities.

RESEARCH SOURCES

Hard Copy Sources

Almanac of the Federal Judiciary. Volume 1 is profiles of sitting judges of U.S. District Courts. Volume 2 is profiles of sitting judges of U.S. Courts of Appeals. These include judges' biographical information, publications, noteworthy rulings, and, for U.S.C.A. judges, lawyers' evaluations.

The American Bench: Judges of the Nation. Features short biographies of 17,500 federal and state judges, the judicial structure of each state, and judicial boundary maps.

BNA's Directory of State and Federal Courts, Judges, and Clerks. Listings of federal and state court structures, as well as names and addresses of judges at all levels.

BNA's Directory of State Courts, Judges and Clerks. Contains listings of each state court's structure and names and addresses of judges at all levels.

Judicial Staff Directory. Comprehensive directory of the federal justice system. Biographies and addresses of judges and staff are included, as are indexes of judges by appointing president and year of appointment.

Judicial Yellow Book. These yellow books pop up everywhere, don't they? This one includes biographical profiles of more than 3,200 federal and state judges, including education and previous experience, as well as staff information, including law clerks with law schools attended. It is updated semiannually.

NALP Federal & State Judicial Clerkship Directory. This includes information on hiring practices of over 500 judges, including application requirements, selection criteria, application acceptance and interview dates, information about past and present clerks, and bar exam requirements.

The Vermont Public Interest Action Project: The 1998 Guide to State Judicial Clerkship Procedures. Provides information on clerkship opportunities in all 50 states as well as the District of Columbia, Guam, and Puerto Rico.

Want's Federal-State Court Directory. Includes names, addresses, and telephone numbers of federal judges, highest state court judges, chief justices of major Canadian courts, and chief judges of selected supreme courts in other countries. Charts of each state court system and federal court statistics are also featured.

Want's Directory of State Court Clerks & County Courthouses. Names, addresses, and telephone numbers. Also includes state attorneys general.

Federal Judges and Justices: A Current Listing of Nominations, Confirmations, Elevations, Resignations, Retirements. Supplemented quarterly.

Weekly Compilation of Presidential Documents. Provides you with the names of people nominated to the federal judiciary.

U.S. Law Week. Take a look at the last page of the "News In Brief" subsection of "New Court Decisions" in the "General Law Binder." It lists judicial nominations by the President and confirmations by the U.S. Senate.

Lexis-Nexis and Westlaw

Both Lexis-Nexis and Westlaw provide a wealth of information on judges and clerkships. While this is not an exhaustive list—check with references librarians or your Lexis-Nexis or Westlaw rep at school for more files and databases—here are a few of the most helpful hunting grounds for information:

For Lexis-Nexis, check out the JCLERK file in the CAREER library. It contains listings of judicial clerkship openings with federal court judges and judges at the highest level of state courts. The information is gathered from questionnaires distributed to federal and state court judges who are asked to provide information on their interview and hiring processes, application deadlines, hiring criteria, the number of clerks they hire, judicial clerkship salaries, the names of past and present clerks, and the law schools their clerks attended.

In addition, while you're in the CAREER library check out the JUDDIR file (which contains biographical information on federal court judges) and the FCA file (which contains the text of the book *Federal Careers for Attorneys,* which features detailed descriptions of the legal work and application requirements for jobs in all three branches of the federal government). Also take a look at the OMNI file in the CAREER library, which will tell you which judges attended your undergraduate college and your law school. The CAREER library's ARCHV file will tell you which attorneys have clerked for a particular judge in the past, as well as courts which have hired clerks from your law school.

In the GENFED library in Lexis, check out the USLW file, which will give you the names of people recently appointed to the bench. The GENFED library is also a source for finding topical opinions written by any particular judge.

The ALLNEWS file in the LEGNEW library will retrieve recent news stories dealing with judicial clerkships. And the CURNWS file in the NEWS library will get you recent news stories on judges with whom you've scheduled interviews.

For Westlaw, check out the databases WLD-JUDGE, WLD-COURT, and WLD-CLERK to find valuable information on judges, courts, and judicial clerkship opportunities respectively. Westlaw's AFJ database features everything in the *Almanac of the Federal Judiciary,* which has biographies on all federal judges.

Web Sites

There are tons of useful web sites for finding out about courts, judges, and clerkships. Here are a few to get you started:

The U.S. Federal Courts home page: www.uscourts.gov

The National Center for State Courts home page:

www.ncsc.dni.us/ncsc.htm

Federal Circuit Courts: Check out the Emory Law School home page: www.law.emory.edu/2Circuit (or plug in the number for the circuit you want to find out about)

State Courts: You'll typically find information about state courts at each state's home page. For a 50-state listing of these, look at Chapter 10, in the section dealing with state attorney generals' offices.

For the DC Circuit: www.ll.georgetown.edu/Fed-Ct/cadc.html

For the 2nd Circuit: www.tourolaw.edu/2ndcircuit/ Also:

www.law.pace.edu/legal/us-legal/judiciary/second-circuit.html

For the 8th Circuit: www.wulaw.wustl.edu/8th.cir

For the 9th Circuit: www.law.vill.edu/Fed-Ct/ca09.html

The Internet

Ooh. The Internet. Talk about a buzz-word. In the movie "The Graduate," the magic word in careers was 'Plastics.' Now it's the Internet. As of this book's writing, adding ".com" to the name of any business you've dreamed up opens the Aladdin's chest of investment money.

But I'm not going to talk about *that,* not specifically anyway. What I'm going to do is give you a *very* brief overview of the kinds of jobs your law degree can help you get with Internet companies. It's a *tremendously* exciting industry with *lots* of opportunity, and if you're a real go-getter you can make a lot of headway very quickly.

As is true of so much of the rest of this book, the advice I'm going to give you isn't mine. It's from my friend, the incredible Adam Epstein. Although still a very young man Adam has done all kinds of fantastic things with his law degree. And no matter what he does, he knows how to make a big splash. One week he'll tell you he's interested in something new, and the next week you'll see him being interviewed on CNN as an expert about it. Really!

The reason his input is valuable here is that he's just taken on a job as Director of Corporate Affairs and General Counsel of a company called "Tickets.Com," which sells tickets to all kinds of events over the Internet. (Guess what their web site address is!). Here's Adam's advice about breaking into the Internet:

"From everything I've seen, law students and recent graduates have a tremendous advantage in seeking employment with Internet-based businesses. While many companies don't think they need in-house counsel, a savvy student/graduate can convince a prospective employer that they've got skills that the company needs.

"Remember, what you're looking at with Internet companies are by and large small start-ups. They don't think they need in-house counsel and they don't want to spend a lot of money. That means that you've got to emphasize all of the skills law school gives you and assure them that you can save them money.

"For instance, issue-spotting is important in start-up companies. They don't often known where the pitfalls are, and law school gives you three years of doing nothing but looking for the potential downsides in situations. Furthermore, many Internet companies cut hundreds of linking/partnering deals with other Internet companies. You can be of tremendous use to a fledgling company in keeping down costs by using business AND legal skills at the same time. Cost saving—not having to pay outside counsel every time a deal is made—is a very persuasive point for most Internet companies, since profits have to this point proven relatively elusive to many of them. Income generation is even more attractive.

Can you do marketing? Are you good at talking to potential second-stage investors?

"The trick is to emphasize the skills you have, negotiation, communication, and the like, as opposed to your 'lawyerliness.' You've got to convince them that you can 'facilitate' as opposed to 'prevent,' which is what so many people outside of the legal profession think that lawyers do. *(This is Kimm talking. To talk up your other skills check out Chapter 8 on Corporations, and specifically look at the section called 'Corporate Jobs Your Law Degree Can Help You Get, Outside of the Legal Department—And Getting a Grip on What You Bring to the Table!' That'll tell you the skills that your law degree implies.)*

"When you're looking for jobs, you should know that Internet companies are continuously barraged with employment requests. The squeakiest possible wheel will get the grease, so persistently press your promises of cost-savings and/or income generation.

"A word of caution: the Internet industry is not for everybody. You've got to be willing to rough it, empty your own trash, and sit at a makeshift desk. More importantly, you have to be willing to accept a high degree of risk. Many Internet companies are at various stages of 'startupdom,' and there are commensurate risks and rewards with that state of affairs.

"Internet companies, like all fledgling operations, require their people to wear many hats at first. Accordingly, do whatever you have to do to get in the door and then try and gravitate toward making your own career, carving out the responsibilities you want to undertake.

"You can find Internet companies through a variety of sources. Three employment web sites are particularly respected by techies. Those are headhunter.net, jobtrack.com, and monsterboard.com. They all have special sections for Internet-related employment.

"Visiting Internet company web sites is one of the best ways to get a job. Many of them will list openings. Conferences and seminars are also fertile territory. You can find conference and seminar listings in 'Wired' Magazine, as well as at the web site www.industrystandard.net. Many industry insiders utilize Internet World, which is at www.iw.com. You'll find an excellent section in that web site on careers in the Internet.

"Incidentally, when you interview with an Internet company, dress accordingly. As you probably know, the tech industry lives in jeans, flannel, you name it . . . double-breasted suits, and even ties, will scare the hell out of most Internet employers, especially if the person wearing that getup has a J.D.

"If you want to learn more about the Internet industry as a whole, you would be well served to look at the www.industrystandard.net web site, which is a first-rate resource.

"You will quickly find that the Internet presents a plethora of job possibilities, if you keep an open mind—and you're persistent!"

Trade Associations (In Both Lawyer and Nontraditional Roles)

I'll bet you'd *never* have thought of taking your law degree and working at a trade association. But guess what? Trade associations are *very* happy hunting grounds for great jobs, whether or not you want to be a lawyer. You get a broad perspective on an entire industry and there are a bunch of interesting things you can do—whether it's researching and developing an expertise on issues that face the whole industry, conducting seminars for association members (which typically involves a bit of travel), or lobbying. And working at a trade association is a great jumping off point for a lot of other terrific jobs. Interested? I'm not surprised!

To find out more about working for trade associations, I went to the delightful Suzanne Mitchell, Assistant Dean and Career Services Director at the University of Chicago School of Law. In a prior life, Suzanne worked for what was then called the American Hospital Association. She knows everything there is to know about working for trade associations, and as you'll see, she's a terrific font of information.

For a start, let's talk about what trade associations are and the kinds of activities they take part in. Trade associations are essentially advocates for an entire industry, and every single industry and profession you can think of, from skiing to biotechnology to the tiniest components of the media—they all have trade associations. The associations themselves range in size from hundreds and hundreds of employees to just one or two. And the kinds of things they do include lobbying, drafting legislation, researching issues, publishing newsletters, educating members and the public—just about everything that goes along with the idea of advocacy.

How do you find out who to work for? Well, as Suzanne Mitchell advises, you start out by thinking of an industry that interests you and then identify the constituents in that industry. We'll use the health care industry as an example, since Suzanne was involved in it. You'd have doctors, nurses, hospitals, hospices, respiratory therapists—literally dozens and dozens of components. Every single one of those components will have a trade association, and that gives you a *lot* of job possibilities.

After you've identified an industry that catches your fancy, you need to find out who the trade associations are in that industry. For that, Suzanne Mitchell suggests you try three excellent resources. One is the Yellow Book series, published by Leadership Directories. They've got a book of associations that you can find at virtually any library or Career Services Office. Then there's the "National Trade and Professional Associations of the United States," which is published annually by Columbia Books (Phone toll-free 888-265-0600 or check out their web site at www.d-net.com/columbia/). The third book is also published by Columbia Books and it's called "State and Regional Associations of the United States."

These kinds of directories will typically give you a wealth of information, including a listing of organizations by geography and by topic, an index by executive names, size of budget, subject, acronym, and even the management firm that represents the specific trade associations.

What will this research do for you? A couple of things. You can either use them to prospect for jobs or to take a longer-term view toward breaking into an industry—which is particularly useful if you're still in law school or you're a new law school graduate (since trade associations typically don't hire new law school graduates unless you've got some credibility in the industry already, for instance as a result of working in it before law school. More on this in a little while.).

Let's say that you're in law school or you have an eye toward going to a trade association in the next year or two. What do you do? Well, if you're still in school, Suzanne recommends that you do the kind of sleuthing we just talked about in terms of identifying relevant trade associations, and then join them as a student member. For a health lawyer, for instance, you'd join the American Academy of Health Lawyers, which is the association of hospital attorneys. What does that do for you? You'll get their mailings, you'll find out about their educational conferences, and most importantly, you'll get their membership directory. Armed with that information, get involved! Attend their conferences, or if you want to get in more cheaply (and develop a resume item at the same time), volunteer to help out. You can also help out by reading association publications, and offering to write articles for them. (Reading these publications will also give you insights into other people to talk to and an excellent opening for letters: 'I just read about you in the *Phlegm Reclamation Journal* and couldn't help being fascinated by your work . . .') If you've already graduated from law school you obviously can't join as a student member, but nothing stops you from requesting to be put on their mailing lists and doing all of the reading, writing, attending and volunteering as a means to get your foot in the door.

Whether as a student or a graduate, you can also do more detective work by visiting the association's headquarters, if that's convenient (there are lots of them in Chicago and Washington, D.C., for instance). As Suzanne points out, many of them have their own libraries—if you're in the area, pay them a visit. If you're going to school in a city that happens to be home to a trade association that interests you, consider volunteering there. Some trade associations even offer work/study for law students; Loyola/Chicago has a health care focus with externships for trade associations, for instance.

You can also trade associations' annual reports no matter *where* you are. Just call and request one. And since trade associations also have public relations people, it doesn't hurt to call them, be *very* nice, and get the information from them that you can, explaining that working for the association is something you'd like to explore and you'd love to spend a few minutes picking their brain about it.

It's also a good idea to go to relevant CLEs, which helps to show that you are truly interested in the field and will give you a chance to get in touch with people. Any law school Career Services Office or local bar association will have CLE information and schedules. Speaking of bar associations, join the relevant section—for instance, for hospitals it would be the health law section—to hear issues and meet people. You might also consider getting on a relevant committee at the local bar association and volunteering to be a speaker, or write for the newsletter. Any of these activities will endear you to the trade association.

Why is this so important? Because jobs with trade associations aren't often published. It's a matter of "who you know," or more importantly— as I point out all the time in *Guerrilla Tactics For Getting The Legal Job Of Your Dreams*—who you *get* to know. Taking part in industry functions, going to CLEs, volunteering—these are all great ideas not just for getting you in touch with people who could potentially hire you, but also because you'll be getting familiar with issues facing the industry and dealing with people in the industry, which are *exactly* the things you'd be doing if you already *had* a job at the trade association! It's kind of a "dress rehearsal."

Suzanne's own job came about in just this way. She joined every health law related organization that she could, and one of the people she met gave her the phone number for the guy who was general counsel at the AHA. She called him and talked with him about health lawyering in general. He was very gracious, but Suzanne thought the end of the conversation was the last she'd hear from him. Ha! A year later, he called her out of the blue, and offered her a job. She says that she doesn't know whether he'd heard her name as a result in her involvement in industry functions or whether he'd just remembered her from their conversation—either way, she got a wonderful job, and it was one that hadn't been advertised *anywhere.*

When it comes to seriously prospecting for jobs, what you'll want to do is look at the names of the different departments in the trade associations you've identified to figure out if there are any that are even remotely likely to need somebody with your skills. You might say "How am I supposed to know what my skills are?" Aaah. Easy. You've got two choices. Either look at what you did before law school (if you worked before law school), what you've done since law school (if you've graduated already), any clinics, seminars or work experience you had *during* law school, and see if any of that gives you credentials jack. The reason this is important is that it's unlikely you'll get a trade association job straight out of law school unless you have prior experience in the industry. Now don't write too much into this, because it doesn't take a lot to get the kind of experience that trade associations look for. Suzanne Mitchell herself had worked one summer at a firm in Washington, D.C. doing health law stuff, she'd had a health law seminar at school, and health law was her favorite class. Other than that, she points out that she didn't have any health law experience—she started her career doing litigation at a big firm in areas unrelated to health law, but she was good at talking up her summer clerkship and law school experience (and she also had joined relevant organizations and volunteered a lot—we'll talk about that a little later). She says that *any* related experience would do, including working in a related field in a state Attorney General's office (see Chapter 10 for those jobs—they're pretty easy to get and there's no grade sensitivity), or in a firm doing industry-related work. Prior industry experience is a big plus, obviously. For instance, as Suzanne Mitchell points out, if you were a nurse before law school and you worked in a substance abuse unit, you'd be a natural to work in a substance abuse-oriented division at a trade association.

The other option is to look at the skills that law school itself gives you. Obviously, if you took part in Law Review or any other journal or did research for a professor, you've got research and writing skills. Or perhaps you did moot court, so you can make speeches. Or you took part in clinical programs. These kinds of things are pretty easy to skill-shoot. But law school as a general matter gives you a whole raft of skills to offer, and if you find it hard to verbalize exactly what they are—I've already done it for you. You'll find the law school skill set at the front of the "Corporations" chapter, Chapter 8, under the heading "Corporate jobs your law degree can help you get, outside of the legal department—and getting a grip on what you bring to the table!"

It goes without saying that if you've done your spadework and volunteered for trade associations, relevant bar associations, conferences, or written articles for trade association publications, those are going to be a *huge* asset when it comes time to talk about jobs!

Once you know what kinds of skills you've got to offer, it's time to look at those components of trade associations that will find you attractive. Obviously, the General Counsel's office at any trade association is a target, because that will be exclusively law-related. Even as a lawyer for a trade association, however, you may have much broader opportunities than are otherwise obvious. Of course, trade associations always have lawyers who are traditional corporate lawyers, tax lawyers, real estate lawyers, and as Suzanne Mitchell points out, "They could have been at IBM or at the AHA—it didn't matter that what we did was health care related." However, as a lawyer herself for the AHA, Suzanne says that she spent very little time doing actual lawyering. The closest she came to "real lawyering" was when the association was sued by chiropractors who claimed that trade associations, including the AHA, had conspired to exclude them. She went to all kinds of strategy meetings about dealing with those claims. But otherwise, she spent a lot of time handling questions from constituents and traveling around, making presentations to industry groups. She says that hospitals would call all the time and say, "We're facing this issue," and she and the other lawyers at the AHA would talk with them generally (not specifically, of course) about the issue. She became an expert on a particular issue—the legal consequences of early discharge of patients—and she spoke to industry groups around the country about it.

So even as a lawyer for a trade association, you have the chance to do many non-lawyerly things. But you don't have to be a lawyer at all; you've got *many* more opportunities than that, if you want to look at nontraditional opportunities. Suzanne Mitchell says that when she was at the American Hospitals Association there were 12 lawyers, but *hundreds* of other people as well. She advises that you look for any sections whose names smack even remotely of law-related duties, like "legislative" or "regulatory" or "advocacy" or "lobbying" or "policy." By way of illustration Suzanne describes the Office of Public Policy Analysis at the American Hospital Association. She says that "In reality, they handled all basic policy development done for health care and 90% of policy had legal issues on the fringes. That kind of department is one where a law degree would be especially valuable, because there were always legal issues that would come up, and while nobody wanted to formally run everything by the Legal Department, a person *in* the department with a law degree could give them the informal background they needed to address those issues as they came up."

Another option is to look for departments whose names suggest topics of interest to you. For instance, if mental health (as a professional interest!) is an area you'd like to pursue with a trade association, clearly a department called "Office of Mental Health Issues" is one to target.

If you *can*, it's a definite help to get your hands on internal phone books for associations. Why? Those will give you the names and phone numbers of *exactly* the people you want to contact, and many times those phone books will clue you in to departments that you might not otherwise have been able to root out. They're hard to come by, but it doesn't hurt to ask *anybody* who might be able to help you—Career Services, any contacts in the industry, or a friendly voice on the other end of the phone at the association itself.

When it comes to positioning yourself to get a nontraditional job at a trade association, remember that the last thing you want to do is to lead with your law degree. As Suzanne Mitchell advises, "If you go in and say, 'Hi, I'm a lawyer,' their attitude will be 'Who cares?' Lead with the skill you know that they need," whether it's research or making presentations or lobbying or *whatever*. For instance, to go back to the substance abuse unit example, as a nurse/J.D. you wouldn't play up your J.D. You'd lead with, "I spent 10 years as a substance abuse nurse."

Let's look down the road a little bit and talk about things that you can do *after* you've worked for a trade association. There are a whole bundle of opportunities for you! For instance, you can go to a constituent of the trade association. Suzanne Mitchell did that—while she was working at the AHA she realized that she was developing an interest in the specific kinds of issues that faced hospitals, beyond the broad issues facing the industry. With her position as a lawyer for the trade association, it was *very* easy to make the jump into working as a lawyer for a hospital. Other possibilities would be government agencies, whether state or federal, related to the industry. Or a law firm with clients in the industry. Another possibility would be nonprofit management (what do you know, *another* category in this chapter!), if you've worked your way to a relatively senior position in the trade association.

All in all, what do you have? Interesting work, lots of nontraditional possibilities, travel, and the opportunity to take a broad view of an industry that tickles your fancy. You just can't *beat* it!

Law School and College Administration Jobs

Some people can't get out of law school fast enough. And others, it seems, *never* want to leave. As a matter of fact, hard as it may be to believe while you're still actually *attending* school, people as a rule really enjoy working in law school administration jobs (and their counterparts in colleges). And if you think that's not true, well, it's probably because the law school personnel to whom you're most often exposed are law professors, and let's face it—maybe some of them are pretty content, but I wouldn't have described *my* law school faculty as a collective Mr. Happy.

But the fact is, there are a lot of *other* law school administrators who on the whole enjoy their work. If you like an academic setting, you'll want to think about pursuing these kinds of careers. (Heck, you might even be happy as a law professor. But we're not going to talk about that here.)

What I'm going to do is to describe some of those other school administration jobs that you probably don't know much about. Actually, *I'm* not going to do it—my friend, the incomparable Susan Gainen of the University of Minnesota Law School, is going to do it. A law school graduate herself, she not only is a wonderful cook and has a personality that will knock your socks off, she also happens to know everything there is to know about, well, about *tons* of useful things—including, fortunately for all of us, higher education administration jobs. (Incidentally, before I started 'Job Goddessing' and got to know law school administrators, the only university administrator *I* ever knew was a guy I went to college with. He had a very button-down kind of personality, and after graduation he went straight to work for the university, in a pretty conservative job. A few years later they found him, dressed in women's clothing, lying on a set of train tracks. Pretty bizarre stuff. I gather most higher education administrators are both much happier—and *much* more normal—than he was.) Anyway! Here's what Sue Gainen has to say about all different kinds of higher education administration jobs you might enjoy, and trust me on this one, when Sue Gainen talks, it's worth listening:

With the exception of a dean or two, the registrar, and the director of career services, for most students academic administration is nearly invisible. That's too bad, because there are many really interesting jobs for lawyers on college campuses.

What kinds of jobs for lawyers are there in colleges and law schools?

While arguably most things that need to be done could be done by lawyers, some of the most common jobs for lawyers in colleges and law schools are in college/university attorneys' offices, as dean of students, director of international programs, director of judicial affairs, director of public interest programs and public interest counselors, athletic department compliance officers, director of alumni relations, and director of student legal services. You will find a greater number of these positions in larger colleges and universities, and you are likely to find lawyers in other positions, as well.

Who should work at a college, university or law school?

You've probably heard the line, "Other than that, Mrs. Lincoln, how did you enjoy the play?" Well, by the same token, if you don't like students— primarily young people with young peoples' perspectives and young people's problems—you won't like working in a school. If you have no interest in the institutions' missions—teaching, learning, and research— you're going to feel like a fish out of water. If you don't like lawyers and law students, don't even think about working at a law school. If, on the other hand, you are excited and challenged by young people as well as students of any age who are embarking on a new career, a job in higher education administration may just be your dream.

COLLEGE AND UNIVERSITY ATTORNEYS

A university's attorney is in-house counsel to a major corporation whose business happens to be education and research. At large universities with tens of thousands of students and thousands of employees, the university is very much like a small city or very large town, and the university attorney's office functions like a city attorney's office. Counsel to a college or junior college would have many of the same responsibilities but little or no research focus.

What do they do?

On the highest conceptual level, university lawyers advise the board of regents and the senior officers (presidents and deans) of the colleges. On a day-to-day basis, they perform much the same work as all in-house lawyers: conduct or manage litigation; draft contracts; and/or deal with environmental, employment or intellectual property issues. While there is no typical day, a university attorney's staff can handle employment (union and non-union), construction and environmental, real estate, health care (especially if the school has a hospital or medical school), patent and other intellectual property, contracts (domestic and international), immigration, criminal issues, as well as issues specific to college governance. Employment and discrimination issues are among the fastest growing sets of problems that cross these lawyers' desks.

Lawyers for a large university are really lawyers for small cities which have their own customs, rules, and administrative procedures. Whether in a large university or a small college, the general counsel functions in many ways like a general practitioner in a small town. Unlike a corporation's general counsel, whose work and policy are nearly always generated from the top down, the flat hierarchical system in a university requires the lawyers to work with many constituents: deans; department chairs; and heads of the school's administrative offices, including facilities management, housing, food service, judicial affairs, and financial aid.

Who should do this job?

A university's attorney "must love academia, and value education and pure learning," according to Tracy Smith, Associate General Counsel at the University of Minnesota. "You need to respect academics and intellectual pursuits," she added.

As you would as counsel to a small corporation, at a small college with a single lawyer, you would serve as a generalist. In a university with a large legal department, some lawyers work in substantive specialties (*i.e.,* real estate, intellectual property, health care), but the majority manage people and issues to avoid litigation, manage or conduct litigation, or manage outside counsel. According to Smith, in any specialty, a good university lawyer will focus on analyzing and managing legal risk.

In public schools attorneys regularly deal with constitutional issues, which sometimes surprises lawyers coming into the general counsel's office from the private sector. "In a public institution, you must like and remember Constitutional Law," said Smith. "In addition, a lawyer for a public university must be committed to public service."

The downside.

If you are doing litigation, you will find that you work the same number of hours that you would in the private sector but for less money.

What's fun?

Smith cited three elements of her job that she particularly enjoys: working in a non-competitive environment where everyone wants everyone else to do well; working with intellectuals who are excited about and committed to their work, like a person who is writing the next big book on cancer; and working in a place where the institution's leadership is committed to shaping the next generation of students. "And," she added, "dressing down on Fridays is a nice bonus!"

How do you get one of these jobs?

These positions are advertised in the *Chronicle of Higher Education*, in local newspapers, and on college and university web sites. These are not positions for new law school graduates. New hires come from public law and private practice, and university attorneys' offices recruit for specific specialties, *i.e.*, litigation, contracts, intellectual property, real estate, and/or business. Large universities may have 10 or more lawyers on staff; small colleges may have a single general counsel.

Another way to do the work.

Some state university's lawyers are Assistant Attorneys General ("AAGs"). According to Maryland Assistant Attorney General Rachel Zelkind, whose tasks include all of the University system's bond work, AAGs in Maryland work on litigation and constitutional problems like diversity, Equal Opportunity and sexual harassment, and issues concerning faculty as a special class of employee. Serving the university's corporate interests, other AAGs specialize in bonds and unrelated business tax. Still others work on the cutting edge corporate and securities matters such as issues raised by privatization and entrepreneurial activities which lead to new areas of state law raising the unfair competition questions necessary to determine whether a newly-created business entity is a state agency for limited purposes. They also deal with real property, intellectual property, and licensing, especially in high tech and patent work. "Every day is different," she said.

What do they earn?

Depending on the school, university attorneys earn upwards of $70,000.

DIRECTOR OF CAREER SERVICES

This is a job where you wear at least six hats: *counselor, teacher, lawyer, Mother or Father, nag, and cheerleader.* Those roles require multiple skills: active listening, understanding adult learning styles, superb juggling, creative team building, clever delegation, and the creativity to figure out how to do more with less. But the fact is that when you have a student who nails the job of their dreams and credits you for helping them get it, it's an incomparable rush.

Who should do this job?

According to Stephanie Rever Chu, Executive Director of Career Services at Chicago-Kent College of Law, the person who's going to do well in this job is someone who thrives on a fast pace and incredible variety, and who wants to see concrete results of his or her efforts, as well as someone who has the flexibility to deal with many tasks and interruptions. "If you need to stick to a schedule or if you feel unsuccessful if you don't complete everything on everything on today's to do list," career services might be a bad fit. Many days, she says, are "Hair On Fire Days," with what seems to be a million things to do at once. If this doesn't give you an adrenaline rush, consider another line of work!

Lawyers who become Career Services Directors as a means of escaping the business development responsibilities of private practice can well find that they've moved from a frying pan to *another* frying pan, because of deans' increasing emphasis on marketing the school and its students to prospective employers. Sales, marketing, and client development experience are increasingly considered as strong assets for career services professionals.

Counseling is an important aspect of the position as well. "Not only are you a coach for career development," Chu says, "you are also a de facto counselor. When you're asked a question, you have to have the interest and the persistence to get to the question behind the question that you were actually asked."

What do they do?

There's a common misconception among law students that Career Services Directors primarily run fall on-campus interviewing programs. In fact, that's pretty far from the truth. In service to their four constituencies—students and alumni, employers, alumni and development, and administration and faculty—every year Career Services Offices not only run on-campus interview programs, but also present dozens of career-related programs, train students and grads to write resumes and improve their interview skills, publish student and alumni jobs bulletins, counsel hundreds of students and alums individually and in groups, produce dozens of career-related pamphlets and brochures, collect graduate employment statistics, encourage hundreds (or thousands) of employers to consider recruiting their students, and, increasingly, they do all of these things both on paper and on their school's web sites. Creating alliances with other parts of the law school community, including student groups, Alumni and Development offices, and the Law Library staff, allows Career

Services Offices to guide and to co-sponsor additional career-related events and training programs.

Depending on the size of the law school and the budget the dean is willing or able to devote to career services, the office can be as small as a single professional with no clerical assistance to as large as eight or more professionals with considerable clerical and student assistance.

Caveats

It would be disingenuous to fail to note the pressures on career services caused by the statistics reported by *U.S. News & World Report,* which annually ranks law schools by many factors including "placement." A number of Career Services Directors have lost their jobs during the past five years, in part because of deans' responses to the figures reported.

Also, career services is a people-intensive job that is a flash point between the rising cost of tuition and a fluctuating market. Chu pointed out that career services staff must be sensitive to market-driven issues outside of the office and outside the law school. She also noted that in this fast-paced, year 'round job, that the biggest challenge is finding time to do strategic planning. "There are," she said, "perhaps two weeks a year when it quiets down—during exams."

What does it pay?

According to the National Association of Law Placement's most recent *Law School Career Services Survey,* the median compensation for the primary career services person was $47,848, and it topped out in the mid-90's. Median compensation for the secondary career services people was $35,000.

DEAN OF STUDENTS

In general, the dean of students enforces academic rules and assists students with getting through law school while maintaining personal and family lives. (S)he will talk with students all of the time, listening carefully to the stories they tell and the problems they present. Challenged to serve as both a support system and an enforcer, the dean deals often with students facing personal problems like disability, divorce, depression, miscarriage, birth, and bankruptcy. Because these issues impact a student's ability to go to class, take exams, and turn in assignments on time, often the dean's most important tools are a well-developed *Student Policy Handbook* and the ability to apply it evenhandedly—as well as a well-developed sense of humor.

Who should do this job?

A dean of students must like people and be able to live with unpredictability. The best have superb administrative skills, the ability to ask hard questions, and a lot of energy to apply to solving the problems that arise each day. In addition, the ability to rise quickly to challenges and the common sense to remember that you serve as a lawyer and not a therapist are crucial to success in the position. If you like students, this is a terrific job, because, according to Meredith McQuaid, Assistant Dean of Students and Director of International Programs at the University of Minnesota Law School, "This is an interesting population with bright, motivated people who are creative and experienced."

She draws on her real-world experiences often. "It helps to be a lawyer in this job because it gives you practical credibility," she says, because students appreciate the advice that reflects experience from law practice.

The downside.

According to McQuaid, deans of students may see 20% of the people 80% of the time. Unless the job is structured to include responsibility for programs that bring deans into contact with happy, stable students, the job can be very wearing. McQuaid is responsible for both study abroad and international LL.M. programs, which balance her activities and widen her day-to-day contact with students.

How do you get one of these jobs?

Positions are advertised in the *Chronicle of Higher Education.* Two to five years of law practice is often a requirement, and entry into the field often comes because candidates show that they like people and can work well with them. Demonstrating an interest in students by offering to tutor or mentor, and showing that you are willing and able to give good advice, are also good resume builders, and graduate work in higher education doesn't hurt.

What does it pay?

In a law school, a Dean of Students may earn anywhere from $33,000 to $90,000. An Assistant to a Dean of Students might earn between $28,000 and $40,000.

DIRECTOR OF INTERNATIONAL PROGRAMS

A law school may have two types of international programs: one which grants the LL.M. degree to graduates of foreign law schools, and the other which allows current law students to study abroad for a summer or for a semester. The director of international programs may report to a law school dean or to a dean of students, or the function may be part of a dean of student's responsibilities. At some schools the work is performed by a tenured faculty member.

What does this person do?

Working either alone or with an admissions committee, a director of international programs will admit LL.M. students, make visa arrangements, review files and process all immigration paperwork, teach one or more courses for foreign students, and give advice and counsel to the students during their year in the program. "We want them to have a good experience," said Meredith McQuaid, Assistant Dean of Students and Director of International Programs at the University of Minnesota Law School.

The director will maintain contacts with the foreign law schools with which the law school has exchange programs, select J.D. students who will study abroad, and ensure that they receive the appropriate academic credit for their work.

The director also works closely with the faculty committees that set standards for the LL.M. and study abroad programs to make certain that they meet ABA and AALS accreditation standards. (S)he will also be called on to serve on a variety of other law school and university-wide committees.

Who should do this job?

While speaking multiple languages would be a plus, a Director of International Programs must have the patience and the technical skills to deal with the complexity of immigration laws, and the special interest in and ability to work with graduates of foreign law schools who have come to America for a short time to study law.

DIRECTOR OF JUDICIAL AFFAIRS

It's not as racy as it sounds, because we're not talking about *those kinds* of affairs. Instead, at many colleges and universities, a Director of Judicial Affairs administers the code of conduct for students. The director administers policy, helps create and revise policies, and helps settle disputes about student conduct.

Depending the campus' philosophy of student affairs, the position can be considered an educational endeavor on the one hand, or punitive and corrections-oriented on the other. At the University of Minnesota, with graduate and undergraduates campuses with a population exceeding 50,000 students, the philosophy is to treat students as adults and as humanely as possible, and to give strong protection to students' rights According to Betty Hackett, Minnesota's Director of Student Judicial Affairs, because of the seriousness of depriving someone of a public education—the thrust is to do what is reasonable to keep students in school. The kinds of behavior that would require action include a pattern of disruptive behavior that persists after being repeatedly addressed, as well as assault, cheating, thefts, and bringing disorder or harm to others.

Who does this job?

While many of the people in this position have come from undergraduate dean of students positions with backgrounds in student services, financial aid, and housing, an increasing number of attorneys with experience in higher education law as a specialty are coming into the field. Because the fastest-growing sets of issues are sexual harassment and sexual assault, many Judicial Affairs offices are becoming increasingly adversarial, and a J.D. is becoming an important asset, if not yet a requirement.

Who should do this job?

According to Hackett, a candidate must have a real fondness and high regard for students and must never tire of the frailties of human kind. "You should be a student rights defender as well as a strong supporter of the academic mission, which is to get students and faculty able to do their real jobs, which are to learn and to teach."

How do you get one of these jobs?

Positions are generally advertised in the *Chronicle of Higher Education.* The professional organization for Judicial Affairs personnel is the International Association of Campus Law Enforcement Administrators, which meets annually.

DIRECTOR OF PUBLIC INTEREST PROGRAMS IN (OR NEAR) A LAW SCHOOL

With the increasing interest in and commitment to public interest practice in law schools around the country, a small but growing number of law schools have in-house public interest programs or counseling offices. There are at least two programs run as section 501(c)(3) nonprofits which are not directly connected to law schools, but which provide similar services.

Who should do this job?

"Lawyers with creativity, passion, vision, and commitment to connecting students to public service are the only people who should apply," according to Theresa Murray Hughes, Executive Director of the Minnesota Justice Foundation. They must also enjoy fundraising and development, and be interested in running what is essentially a small business.

Who should avoid this job?

The visionary who abhors detail, who requires large amounts of administrative support, who wants to continue to practice law, and who wants to focus on a single, specific legal problem will be profoundly unhappy as a public interest program director.

What the job is like.

The job will differ according to whether the program is connected with a law school or not.

If the program is connected to a law school: Depending on the size of the staff, the director will have some or all of the responsibility for developing programs, conducting training and workshops for students, as well as for counseling students and graduates. The director may do some grant writing, but will have little financial accounting responsibility. Other than the financial issues facing the law school as a whole, (s)he will have few worries about infrastructure (computers, paper clips, and the like). As part of a law school, the director may report to the dean or to a faculty committee and will serve at the pleasure of the dean.

If the program is *not* connected to a law school (that is, it's a free-standing nonprofit): At Minnesota Justice Foundation ("MJF"), Theresa Murray Hughes serves the three Twin Cities law schools. She reports to a Board of Directors which nominally assists her in her primary responsibility, conducting the fundraising to support between 20 and 25 summer clerkships. She also works with each law school's local board, each of which does fundraising for its own school's additional clerkships. MJF is also a founding partner in a Public Interest Law Consortium that participates in a clinical program at each law school. Both the MJF Program Coordinator and MJR Pro Bono Coordinator report to the Director. The Program Coordinator develops and presents training required of all MJF volunteers and counsels students on all issues related to public interest job searches, including summer and permanent positions. The Pro Bono Coordinator receives requests and makes all referrals for the nearly 6,000 hours of pro bono work that law students from the three schools do each year.

How do you get one of these jobs?

These positions are listed in the *NALP Bulletin*, in alumni job bulletins, and in local newspapers.

PUBLIC INTEREST COUNSELOR

Many law schools have full- or part-time public interest counselors as part of the Career Services Office or in a separate public interest advising office. The vision and commitment to public service required of those who work in the public interest programs are a base-line requirement.

NYU's Public Interest Law Center is a separate office in the Office of Career Counseling and Placement. As a separate public interest office, it has an executive director, a coordinator, associate coordinator, a coordinator for Pro Bono Students America, three to four support staff and work study students. Abel Montez, Coordinator of the Public Interest Law Center, is responsible for organizing an annual symposium which features public interest and public service representatives from more than 100 organizations which interview students or provide information about public service careers. This symposium is more than 20 years old, and students from more than 20 law schools participate. In addition, Montez spends about four hours a day counseling students who make appointments or who drop in to the office, as well as by phone and e-mail.

Who should do this work?

Montez, who began his legal career in government, said that his public sector experience was a great fit for a job that "allows me to talk to hundreds of public interest lawyers and employers and to encourage students who are thinking about public service."

He also believes that litigators are well-suited to this work. "Things come up all the time that we all must deal with immediately. Students from all over the country and around the world with multifaceted experiences and vastly different short- and long-term goals come to the office and we always have to be ready to respond." Because of the range of questions that his students ask, "A generalist with a little bit of information about everything will really enjoy the job. Someone with a scholarly nature who wants to know and impart absolutely everything about a subject would be frustrated," he added.

Montez also stressed the high level of autonomy in the position. Unlike his prior work as a government staff attorney where there were multiple layers of authority, he notes that in his job search "I was looking for an office where I could come in and own a piece of the project, feeling that it was *my* project. I wanted my decisions and my judgment to count."

He added that his job is made all the more challenging by the fact that recruiting for public interest and public service positions isn't on a fixed schedule, and there are no ready-made jobs for students. He pointed to the constant creativity involved in encouraging students to explore their interests, to learn to network, and to learn to seek out the time frames for hiring, noting with delight that "we really are able to help students seeking public service."

Who would hate this job?

"Anyone who can't be flexible would hate this job," Montez said. He believes that if you find satisfaction in the structure, for instance, of court-imposed deadlines, you would never be satisfied in a job with this much creativity.

How do you get one of these jobs?

These positions are listed in the *Chronicle of Higher Education,* the *NALP Bulletin,* the *National and Federal Legal Employment Report,* and on university personnel web sites.

ATHLETIC DEPARTMENT COMPLIANCE OFFICES

Because the National Collegiate Athletic Association ("NCAA") seems to promulgate rules at the same rate that rabbits procreate, there are an increasing number of jobs for compliance officers in Division I and Division II schools' athletic departments. And keep in mind that if your dream is to ultimately work for the NCAA itself, starting out as a compliance officer is a good jumping-off point for that.

What do they do?

According to Frank Kara, Deputy Assistant Director at the University of Minnesota Athletic Department Compliance Office, "Working with Big 10 and NCAA rules is not conceptually different from working with compliance in the securities industry. We have to make sure that our athletes, our athletic departments, and our fans comply with the rules."

Compliance officers monitor the NCAA and other conference rules, educate athletic department staff, student athletes, parents, and fans about those rules. Counseling students about the NCAA rules and the rules relating to turning professional include discussion of how the rules apply and what a student athlete's different options might be in the process of considering a professional career.

In addition, compliance officers work with parents, Booster Clubs, and fans, keeping them up-to-date on the limitations and consequences of everyone's generosity. For example, during a road trip, fans can't buy a quarterback's dinner. Anything and everything that players might get from fans is strictly regulated and mostly prohibited. These rules extend to their parents, who can't get free rides from the athletic department while they *can* ride on the Booster Club's bus. Compliance officers also train the athletic department's secretarial staff on issues as arcane as the correct color of stationery to use and the correct use and placement of the team and conference logos.

While the work cycle follows the academic year, summer is a time to finish reports and complete required audits. Although December may be slow, should a school's football team attend a bowl game, the compliance officers are hard at work. They are responsible for the documents certifying that each has signed and had notarized indicating that no agreements have been made with any agents for any money.

Who should do this job?

Because part of the job is going to games—*lots* of games—a compliance officer must love sports. But the fact that you're glued to your easy chair, a beer in one hand and a bowl of pretzels in the other, from opening kickoff to the end of the Super Bowl doesn't, in and of itself, qualify you for a job as a compliance officer (unfortunately!). To succeed, you also have to love people and be willing to work with athletes and their families, among others. A compliance officer must be sensitive to people's concerns yet tough enough to deliver unwelcome news and to enforce the rules. Communications skills, oral *and* written, are crucial. Patience and keen attention to detail are vital because the keys to managing an athletic program are in the fine print in hundreds of pages of NCAA and conference rules. When solving problems, as a compliance officer you may have to spend hours poring over those rules and regulations and you must then write your findings in clear and precisely worded letters to athletic directors, deans, and to NCAA and conference officials.

Who would be unhappy?

You don't do this job for the "big bucks," because this isn't the job where you'll make a percentage of Quinn Quadricep's $100 million dollar contract—this is academic athletics, not Jerry McGuire.

Entry level compliance officers earn between $20,000 and $25,000. Directors earn between $40,000 and $80,000, depending on how the job is structured. The highest salaries go to those titled Assistant or Associate Athletic Director.

Where are these jobs?

In 1994, Division I schools had a single compliance officer in each school. In 1998, every Division I program has at least two and some have more than three compliance officers. In an increasing number of Division II schools there is one person whose job is 75% to 80% compliance.

How do you get one of these jobs?

There are two common routes into compliance work. Former collegiate athletes who have played their sports under NCAA rules, and in an ideal world are thus presumed to know something about those rules, are often considered good candidates. For non-players, Minnesota's Kara recommends internships (paid or unpaid) during undergraduate or law school. Kara noted that an increasing number of compliance officers are lawyers, and that position descriptions for the Director positions often require a J.D. or Master's degree. Jobs are posted on the NCAA News web site (www.ncaa.org/news).

DIRECTOR OF ADMISSIONS

A law school's director of admissions must find, market to, evaluate, admit, and enroll students who will make a positive, significant impact on society. Because law schools are largely tuition-driven, (s)he must also fill the class.

What do they do?

The admissions office is the point of first contact for prospective students, and its staff (director, often one or more assistant or associate directors, and some amount of permanent and seasonal clerical support), talk to and write to thousands of prospective students each year. They are responsible for delivering the school's message in person, by phone, by mail via the school's admissions bulletin, and on the web.

According to Collins Byrd, Director of Admissions at the University of Minnesota Law School, a director must understand three things: marketing, logistics, and politics. "You must understand the tactical and strategic aspects of marketing, as well as understanding market research. There is a story in the numbers, and a school must make strategic marketing decisions based on those numbers."

As to logistics, Byrd notes that during each admissions year, the office must identify the group(s) of people to contact that will get a number of applicants that will generate a number of admitted students by a particular date, and that a number of those must be persuaded to commit and then enroll. All of this leads to an amount of tuition revenue which is calculated at the end of the second week of school.

Finally, he noted that admissions directors may have to deal with volatile political situations. "In a school with 100 open spots and 50 applicants, there are no politics," due to the low 2-to-1 ratio of applicants to admittees. However, where there are many more applicants than spaces in the class, admissions directors may encounter some difficulties. Byrd notes, however, that at many schools Deans have appointed Faculty Admissions Committees which have comprehensive review processes for all applications. Because a Committee's decision isn't subject to influence by "big donors" or others cashing in on political favors, what might have been a difficult conversation becomes relatively easy: "It was the Committee's decision, not mine or the Dean's."

Financial aid is another function that might fall to either the Dean of Admissions or the Dean of Students. Susan Palmer, Assistant Dean at Washington & Lee University School of Law ("W&L"), is responsible for admissions and financial aid. Although she does not perform the needs analysis, she administers and awards all scholarships. Her school has a very lean administrative staff, and all deans have considerable counseling responsibilities as well.

Who should do this job?

According to Eric Eden, Assistant Director of Admissions at Western New England College of Law, admissions is a terrific job for people who aren't interested in practicing but who enjoy talking to lots of people and have an aptitude for sales.

"You get to talk to really interesting people and you get to be an advisor. People are looking for more than information about our law school. It's a nice way to connect your own experience and share it with others in a way that will be useful. There is lots of satisfaction from that."

W&L's Susan Palmer says that being a lawyer gives her credibility with students. She can talk about the process of legal education, and reflect on the Socratic method and on exams. Because prospective students are interested in more than basic admissions information, often seeking guidance about an ultimate direction for their legal careers, her own experiences, including work at a large firm, in a prosecutor's office, and at a judicial clerkship are helpful. "It gives me a base of information to address student concerns," she said.

Who would hate this job?

If you don't like students, if you are frustrated by delivering the same message over and over again and then repeating yourself, and if you have difficulty saying and accepting "no" for an answer, you would hate this job. While it's clear that admissions offices decline to admit hundreds of thousands of applicants each year, Byrd pointed out that thousands of applicants say "no" to admissions offices each year by either declining to apply or turning down an offer of admission. "You have to have a thick skin that allows you to take rejection," he said.

Caveat

Admissions officers are on the road for a large portion of the fall. There are major events (called "forums") in Boston, Houston, Washington, D.C. and Atlanta, and there are trips to schools that are either historic feeders or schools that the admissions staff has targeted as a likely or desirable feeder. The forum events are scheduled for weekends; other trips are during the workweek. If you have responsibilities that require your presence at home year-round, this is not the job for you.

How do you get one of these jobs?

Admissions positions are published in the *Chronicle of Higher Education,* the *AALS Bulletin,* in local newspapers and on college and university web sites. Byrd noted that currently about 40% of admissions directors are lawyers, and that number is increasing. Palmer suggested that while it may help to be a graduate of the school to which you are applying, the relatively plentiful undergraduate associate director positions are good points of entry. She also noted that the entry level position in a law school is not likely to be the director's spot, and that someone committed to law school admissions would probably have to begin work at a regional law school.

Byrd suggests that undergraduate admissions experience is excellent training because in those offices you have to deal within parents, guidance counselors, family friends, and VIPs. In the end though, he said that the "maturity to understand someone's long-term career goals, some marketing experience, and enough comfort with numbers to understand and manipulate them to tell a strategic story" are the qualities that make a good candidate for admissions director. Finally, he added that "Admissions is a 'people place.' We always have to be human."

What do they earn?

Depending on the school, law school assistant directors of admissions earn between $32,000 and $50,000. Directors earn from the high $50s to the high $80s.

ALUMNI RELATIONS

Although tangentially related to fundraising, the primary function of alumni relations people is making sure that there is good communications between the school and its alumni. "We try to make it a two-way conversation," said Terri Mische, Director of Alumni Relations and Communication at the University of Minnesota Law School.

What do they do?

Most law schools publish alumni magazines at least twice a year, maintain alumni records, schedule reunions, homecoming events, and, depending on the state, continuing legal education seminars for alums. They may also schedule dean's visits with other cities and communicate with other departments in the university and the law school. The director may also be the school's point person for media contacts and serve as liaison from the law school to university communications committees and alumni committees. Many undergraduate schools have large alumni relations departments; law school staffing in this department can range from a single person with responsibility for development and alumni relations to an office of significant size with clerical and student support.

The alumni director may also handle complaints, requests for contacts with classmates, and requests for shared mailing lists. (S)he will also work with other parts of the school to connect students with alumni and professors.

While the University of Minnesota Law School has a separate director of development, Mische is responsible for the "Annual Fund," which requires developing and coordinating written solicitations for gifts of less than $1,000.

Who should do this work?

"Someone who likes people, who is comfortable with cold calls, and who likes detail will do well. You also need to really enjoy listening to stories and reminiscences," according to Mische. She also stresses the importance of being able to get satisfaction from the success of the event rather than having broad public acknowledgement of your work. "You need to be self-sufficient and to be able to recognize your own success," she says.

What's fun?

"Ninety-nine percent of the time, when I pick up the phone to call a graduate I get a very warm welcome," Mische said. "This is a real 'feel good' job. I get to plan events where people will probably enjoy themselves. Every day is different, and it is very, very hard to get bored."

Who would hate this job?

Because connecting the alumni and the school is the focus of the job, "you would hate this work if you need to be the center of attention," Mische says. "This is a job where you spread your ego around." Also, because the publications responsibilities require attention to detail, a person who couldn't see the 'big picture' at the same time would be frustrated.

Who does this work?

Approximately 40% of the alumni directors in law schools are lawyers and most work at their own alma maters. Alumni relations is an increasingly popular nontraditional career for lawyers, some of whom have chosen to work at their undergraduate schools.

What does it pay?

Starting salaries range from $30,000 to $60,000, depending on experience and on the school's budget.

How do you get this job?

These positions are posted in the *Chronicle of Higher Education*, the *Chronicle of Philanthropy* (which you probably already subscribe to, right?), in local newspapers, and through local colleges.

DIRECTOR OF STUDENT LEGAL SERVICES

Student legal services offices basically function as a kind of 'legal aid' office for students, making presentations and providing legal advice on a variety of issues ("How loud can my party be?" or "How do I handle a deadbeat roommate?"). More than 300 schools have these offices, which provide both direct client service and education about the law (as opposed to 'legal education,' which you already know about). Student legal services offices usually have between one and five lawyers and support staff that can include paralegals, administrative assistants, and one or more law clerks.

What do they do?

The legal aid analogy is appropriate, since most of the legal work that student legal services offices do is non-fee generating civil work and minor criminal work. The bulk of most caseloads is consumer counseling, tenant's rights, and family law. As legal educators, student legal services attorneys and their staff members provide written materials—usually a series of pamphlets—and educational programs on a wide variety of problems relating to student life, including: parties (how to have a party without getting into trouble with the law); noise ordinances; roommate problems; alcohol (the legal issues, as opposed to medical or addiction issues); tenants rights; debt management (how to handle your debt load and manage consumer debt); debtor's rights; family law including custody and child visitation issues; and how to go to court (where the courts are located, how to dress, why you shouldn't swear at the judge, and like issues).

In addition to presentations to the general student body, as students begin to plan for summers off-campus student legal services officers will present tenants' rights programs in dorms, fraternities, and sororities. Those programs can cover issues including what to look for in a lease, how to get your security deposit back, and how to work through a landlord's checklist. In the fall, legal services attorneys often do presentations on the legal problems resulting from alcohol use and abuse.

Who should do this work?

"You have to be an extrovert and a juggler, and you have to be able to handle a fast-paced calendar without ever feeling that you've finished your work, and above all, you have to respect working for students," says Linda Aaker, Director of Student Legal Services at the University of Minnesota. "I can't imagine a job where you get a chance to work with a greater concentration of diversity of students." In addition to working as a lawyer and teacher, the director of a legal services program has to work closely with university administration and with whatever entity represents the program's funding source. While some programs may be funded from university funds, many receive funding from student services fees, a process which requires presenting and defending an annual budget request, and from user fees.

How do you get one of these jobs?

These positions are posted in local newspapers, law school alumni bulletins, on college and university employment web sites and in the *Chronicle of Higher Education.*

What do these people earn?

Directing or managing attorney compensation ranges from $34,500 to $74,075. Staff attorneys earn from $29,500 to $50,400.

Law Librarianships

Ewwww! You're thinking. A *law librarian? Me?* I know you're reacting this way because that's how *I* reacted when I first started hearing about law librarianships. But I heard about them a lot, and so all I can say is, don't wrinkle your nose at the thought of it. The hours are *great*—classic 9 a.m.-to-5 p.m.—there's work for every personality from the most gregarious extrovert to the shyest introvert—it's a great back-door way to break into teaching, and the pay can be anywhere from pretty good to *awesome.*

If you're skeptical, at least keep an open mind until you read this *Job Goddess* column and everything else here about being a law librarian. (Incidentally, the *Job Goddess* column doesn't start out sounding as though it's going o talk about law librarianships, but trust me, it *does.*)

Dear Job Goddess,

I am a third year law student. Law will be my second career. Before law school, I was heavily involved in microcomputers. I started a $3 million business, consulted, and am now somewhat of an internet guru. My question is this: What kind of position should I be seeking where the employer will say, "Wow, we really need this guy, let's give him lots of money." Unfortunately, since I'm still in school, I don't have much legal experience.

Thank you in advance oh goddess of jobs.
TD, USA

Dear TD,

The Job Goddess applauds bluntness like yours, TD. No nattering on about job satisfaction, just a simple, heartfelt plea: "Show me the money!" In fact, as Orson Welles pointed out in the film Citizen Kane, it's not difficult to make a lot of money, if money is all you want. Let's see how you, TD, can turn a bit of computer knowledge and a law degree into a shower of doubloons and pieces of eight.

As Deidre Washington, Assistant Dean and Director of Career Services at St. Thomas University Law School, points out, "You're in a better position than most law students, with a strong background in computers." A career she recommends to you is director of automation for a law library. Why? "All law libraries are anxious about entering the 21st century, and so they are looking for people who can help them make the leap to computerization." Obviously this isn't the job for everyone—you do need a strong computer background. But on the plus side, you don't need a technical undergrad degree, and—here's the key—these kinds of positions can have a starting salary around a hundred thousand smackers.

You've got other options as well, of course. One that Deidre Washington recommends is keeping up with a publication called "Intellectual Property Today," which is published by LawWorks in Palatine, Illinois. As she says, "It covers all kinds of internet issues, and has a lot of classifieds," with jobs right up your alley. Another is to go back to all of those people you worked with while climbing your ranks to the position of grand poobah in your pre-law school career, letting them know that you've now added a law degree to your credential quiver and seeing what develops.

Now because the Job Goddess is ultimately concerned with your welfare, she can't leave you like this, TD. Even though you sloughed off any mention of career satisfaction, the Job Goddess encourages you to think at least a little bit about exactly what kind of work-related activities will make you happy. After all, if you can't get past the stereotype of nerds and wizened old yoda-like librarians hissing "sshhh!" a library position of any kind may not be your cup of tea, regardless of how much it pays (and how far your perception may be from the truth). So before you leap at any high-paying job, talk to people who've already taken the plunge into it and see if what they do with their time is something you'd enjoy. Then, TD, you've got the best of all possible worlds—a job you look forward to performing and a platinum American Express card.

Eternally eager to please,
The Job Goddess

Well! Isn't *that* a pleasant surprise! I'll bet you that you don't have any classmates who say, "I'm going after the big bucks. I'm going to the *library!*" It just goes to show that the best jobs are often in the most unexpected places.

Of course, being Director of Automation isn't the only law librarian job in the world. There are plenty of others, and for those I'm turning again to my wonderful friend Susan Gainen. Here's what she's got to say:

Some of the friendliest and most helpful people that first-year law students meet are law librarians. Most law students can't conceive of the fact that in all likelihood, many of them are lawyers as well as librarians, and that they believe they have some of the best jobs in the law business!

Who becomes a law librarian?

People seem to come to law librarianship through three routes: First, while they're in law school they figure out that law librarians have a higher rate of job satisfaction—and lower blood pressure level—than most people in traditional law practices, and they go straight from law school to library school, or if they are lucky, manage to get a joint J.D./M.L.S. (Master's in Library Science). Second, they go to library school after a few years of practice. Or third, having earned a library degree and worked in a law library, they discover that adding a J.D. would be the ticket to advancement in both salary and responsibility.

What do they do?

Librarians, including law librarians, are committed to collecting, preserving, managing, and managing access to all manner of information sources. According to Suzanne Thorpe, Associate Director of the University of Minnesota Law School Library, in broad, general terms, librarians try to find pertinent information, determine what structure is imposed on the information, and then try to make it accessible. "We are dealing with new subjects all the time, as well as new places to find the information," she added. Thorpe points out that information may be wholly or in part on-line, in microform, in print, as well as in video and audio formats. "The challenge is to preserve the knowledge, to manage technology, and to manage access to that knowledge through technology."

Once you go looking for what may seem to be the secret world of law librarianship, you find a category of job for almost every personality type. Public service librarians, in reference and circulation, are generally extroverted (although not necessarily extroverts!), and they delight in working with people and solving puzzles and problems. "Much of their job satisfaction comes from the thrill of the chase," according to Emily Greenberg, Director of the Law Library at the University of Baltimore School of Law, "the more complex the problem, the more challenging and satisfying the solution."

Thirty-eight percent of law school librarians teach in their schools, and many teach some portion or all of the first-year legal research and writing course. They can also teach advanced legal research. Law Librarian/Professor George Jackson teaches a highly-regarded advanced legal research course at the University of Minnesota Law School, for example. In some law schools, librarians may teach or co-teach in their substantive research specialties. If you are looking for another door into law school teaching, it may be comforting to know that 78% of academic law library directors are on tenure track, as are 28% of other academic law library professionals.

Because of their expertise and their willingness to work at or over the cutting edge of technology, they are also called on as expert teachers and support for the rapidly expanding uses of electronic and web-based research sources and methods.

Constantly busy but hidden from view are technical service librarians. Until books and other materials learn to transport themselves from the publisher's warehouse to the shelves, the people in library technical services will have work to do. In broadest outline, their job is to make sure that every book, pamphlet, magazine, journal, video, CD-ROM, or other information source is accessible to their patrons in a logical, organized way.

Where else do law librarians work?

In addition to law school libraries, law librarians work in law firms, public law libraries, bar libraries, and corporate and government law libraries, including the Law Library section of the Library of Congress. Many state courts and state attorneys general have separate law libraries, and many legislatures have separate legislative libraries. There is a growing subcategory of law librarians who contract with small- to medium-sized law firms to provide library management services as well.

How do you get one of these jobs?

During the past decade, it has become clear that the best ticket into a law school library is to hold both a J.D. and an M.L.S. These jobs are posted in the AALL (American Association of Law Libraries) web site (www.aall-net.org), as well as in local AALL chapter bulletins, in the *Chronicle of Higher Education,* and in the Special Libraries Association publications.

What is the library degree?

Depending on the school, it can be called a "Masters of Library Science," or a "Masters of Library and Information Science," or some combination of the two. After law school, Library Science school is a snap. Unlike law school, the study is eminently practical, with courses in all areas of technology, reference, technical services, and management. Because of its emphasis on management, some have characterized it as an MBA without the quantitative analysis.

What does it pay?

In the AALL Biennial Salary Findings, the average salary of a Director/Chief Librarian with no outside responsibilities was $57,315. Those with outside responsibilities averaged $63,405. In a one-person library, the librarian with no outside responsibilities averaged $39,681, and with outside responsibilities, the average jumped to $46,171. Directors of large, well-funded academic law libraries are paid comparably or nearly comparably to senior faculty (which is a *phat* salary).

Handling Debt

*How To Take On Your Dream Job
When Your Student Loans Make You
Think You Can't Afford It.*

Horrifying as this seems, it's not uncommon to get out of law school $60,000, $70,000, or $80,000 in debt. That is a sizeable chunk of change—but what you're going to find out in this chapter is that big loans don't mean you have to sell your soul to the Devil when you get out of school. There are ways to take the job you want, no matter how large your loans are, and we'll figure out exactly what's right for you.

That's not to say that law school debt isn't a hot-button issue. It *is*. I know for a fact that it's a source of great controversy among law school career counselors. In private some of them lament what they see as the inevitable creation of a professional "underclass"—lawyers who, in spite of an attractive salary, are forced to live on a modest scale by monthly $900 student loan payments. I've known others who *actually left their jobs* with private law schools, saying that they could not bring themselves to stay with schools where a substantial number of students will be unable to earn salaries commensurate with the debt they're running up pursuing their law degree. The figures bear out their concern. About a year and a half ago the National Association for Law Placement put together figures showing that a bare majority of new law school graduates would face a starting salary between $25,000 and $40,000. While private law firms are the highest-paying employer category, over a third of new graduates with law firms earn less than $40,000 a year to start. Almost 31% of new graduates working in public interest jobs, typically for nonprofit organizations, started at less than $25,000. So the concerns about law school debt are very clearly *real*.

Still other law school administrators point an accusatory finger at law students who live beyond their means in law school—"what happened to living like a student when you're a student?"—only to be burdened with huge debt when they leave law school. This is sometimes called the "$40 pizza problem"—that is, if you buy a pizza on student loan money, with interest that pizza will wind up costing you 40 bucks.

What I'm going to do here is to share with you all kinds of information about handling law school debt. I'll talk about general Do's and Don'ts, student loan vocabulary words you need to know, helpful web sites, loan consolidation and loan repayment assistance programs (which we're going to learn about through an eye-opening case study), and ways to avoid law school debt in the first place, as well as ways to economize once you're out of school. The bottom line is that you shouldn't have to turn down any job that you want just because you've got a lot of loans to pay back.

"DO'S" AND "DON'TS" WHEN IT COMES TO LAW SCHOOL DEBT

DON'T make assumptions about pay based on broad job market categories. It's a common practice to assume that law firms pay the most and public interest and government jobs pay the least. The reason I don't want you to do this is that you'll find yourself eliminating entire careers from consideration—*careers that might have made you very happy*—on the basis of what you think you'll make. There are plenty of public interest jobs that pay comparatively well—the Federal Defender Program, for instance. And when it comes to government jobs, I'll bet you didn't know that Assistant State's Attorneys—the entry-level rung for State's Attorney's offices—can start you at over $50,000 (at least in some states, like my home state, Connecticut). And for federal government jobs in general, which start you at a very reasonable $40,000, don't ignore the fact that your salary tends to jump dramatically in the first couple of years, as I explained in Chapter 10. On top of that, if you jump at a law firm job assuming you'll haul in the most shekels, you might not. Some firms, especially small firms, pay a starting salary comparable to many of the lower-paying public interest jobs. When it comes to the high end—you'll make more as a management consultant or investment banker than you will at a law firm. My sole point here is that it's a mistake to make salary assumptions based on employer categories. Don't do it!

DON'T get into debt blindly. Law school administrators report that many law students have *no idea* what their loan payments will be as they're piling up debt (yours truly was one of those, sad to admit). It's too easy to pop your signature onto documents bringing you thousands of dollars without thinking about the payout at the other end. *Whenever* you contemplate signing up for more debt, recalculate what your loan payments will be. (It's easy to do this on the Internet at www.salliemae.com:80/calculators/repayment). There are a million things you can do. You can tutor. If you've got computer savvy, you can pull in $100 an hour freelancing as a database or web page designer. Then there's the old standby: I realize that the words "waiting tables" are anathema to anybody in professional school, but if you're willing to give up two evenings a week waiting tables—even during the summers—you'll open up your post-law-school possibilities dramatically. I know. I did it. And I never would have been able to fund a fledgling career as a 'starving writer' if I hadn't.

DO structure your repayment options in a way that's most palatable to you. If you want to spread out your payments over many years, that will dramatically lower your initial payments and enable you to take a much lower-paying job than you'd have been able to pursue otherwise. But the flip side of that is that while other people are buying houses and pursuing their post-student-loan financial lives, you'll be soldiering on with loan payments. It all depends what's most important to you.

DO realize that student loans aren't a permanent problem. They loom large when you first get out of school mostly because that's when you're likely to make less money than you ever will. As your career progresses, your loan payments will diminish in significance, and before you know it, they'll be gone. There *is* light at the end of the tunnel!

DO be honest about your threshold of pain. You don't *need* anything. You don't need a new car, you don't need to live in a certain neighborhood, you don't need expensive clothes, you don't need to eat out. You may *want* them very badly, and you may *feel you deserve them* (and maybe you do). But be aware that every lifestyle choice you make will impact the salary you can start with, and trust me on this one—a job that makes you happy is one of the greatest gifts you can give yourself.

DON'T assume that if you close your eyes and wish really hard, your student loans will just go away. They won't. The newspapers report all the time about the huge student loan default rate in this country. Your loans won't go away, but what *will* happen is that your credit will be destroyed, making it very difficult to do things like buy cars and houses later on. The thing to remember is that loan companies *want* you to pay them back. They don't *want* to go after you for the money. If you think you can't make your payments, you need to lower them or put them off or spread them out—*call your loan company and talk to people there.* You'll be surprised how helpful they'll be.

Three Common Programs For Lowering (Or Temporarily Eliminating) Your Student Loan Payments

For more information on these programs, talk to your financial aid director.

1. Consolidation: When you consolidate your loans, you trade in your rag-tag government loans (*e.g.,* Stafford, SLS, Perkins, PLUS) for one big 'consolidation' loan with a longer repayment term and a lower interest rate. This doesn't reduce your debt, but it *does* reduce your monthly payments.

2. Forbearance: This is where your loan company lets you ride for a few months without making any payments at all, due to economic hardship. This is very helpful when you get out of law school without a job, or your new job has a low starting income but things will pick up soon. You ask for forbearance from them, and they'll let you go for at least six months or so (companies vary).

3. Deferment: This is a temporary reprieve from making student loan payments. You may qualify if for instance you're unemployed, you return to school full-time, you volunteer full-time for an eligible tax-exempt organization (like the Peace Corps), and a number of other ways as well. With a deferment, you can postpone your loan payments for up to three years.

HELPFUL WEB SITES

Here are some web sites that will help you deal with debt management, loan repayment, and loan options for financing your law school education. Check them out!

USA Group Web Sites:
    www.uysagroup.com:80/getready/roadrpy/consolid.htm
    www.usagroup.com:80/getready/roadrpy/level.htm
    www.usagroup.com:80/getready/roadpry/incsens.htm
    www.usagroup.com:80/loancons/calc/specinst.htm
    www.usagroup.com:80/loancons/menu.htm

Repayment Estimator Web Site:
    www.salliemae.com:80/calculators/repayment
    Predicting what you may need to live in any given geographic location:
    Salary comparisons: ww.homefair.com/homefair/cmr/salcalc.html
    State income tax rates: www.homefair.com/homefair/cmr/ ataxes.html
    A bunch of helpful stuff about handling debt:

The National Association for Public Interest Law home page:
    www.napil.org

And some useful phone numbers:

The U.S. Department of Education direct loan-consolidation program: 800-455-5889

The Student Loan Marketing Association (which offers debt-consolidation plans): 800-643-0040

The National Association of Twentysomethings (offers discounts on a number of services) 800-941-4711

"IDEALISM AND DREAMS OF SAVING THE WORLD WILL GET YOU SO FAR, BUT REALISTICALLY, YOU MUST ALSO EAT WHILE SAVING THE WORLD!"

Repayment Options: The Experiences of Chris Raistrick, Who Took a $25,000 Public Interest Job With $90,000 in Law School Debt—and Made it Work!

If you wonder if you can possibly take the job of your dreams because of law school debt, you've got to meet Chris Raistrick, because he did *exactly* that. He graduated a year and a half ago from Loyola University Law School in Chicago. With a technical background and a lot of law school debt, he believed he was going to have to take a job in intellectual property—and while a lot of people like IP, it wasn't where Chris's heart was. He wanted to help those who needed help the most, and that meant public interest work. With a lot of guidance and help from his Career Services Office, he figured out how to pursue his dream—and the way he did it is particularly instructive, because there's no reason you can't follow in his footsteps. Here's Chris's story:

"I plowed through law school at Loyola University Chicago like any public interest trooper. I was involved in the public interest law organizations. I volunteered at a legal aid clinic in the community. I took the legal clinic course through the Community Law Center—twice. I held two part-time jobs. I was involved in everything at Loyola that related to public interest law, and was sure that public interest law was the career for me.

"I also had $90,000 in student loans when I graduated!!! Don't panic! What is it all about?—Getting started!!"

"Idealism and dreams of saving the world will get you so far, but realistically, you must also eat while saving the world. So, how do you pay your loans, meet a modest budget, and do it all on a public interest starting salary? With a lot of hard work and planning, you can find a way."

Chris's Facts:

STUDENT LOANS:

Undergraduate	$ 17,000
Subsidized Stafford	25,500
Unsubsidized Stafford	20,000
Perkins	10,000
SLS	9,000
Alumni Loans	2,300
Bar Exam Loan	5,000
Total Student Loan Debt:	**$90,000 and change**

INCOME:

Employer: Chicago Legal Clinic	
Starting Salary:	$ 25,000
Part-time job (10 hours/week):	$ 4,500
Total Income:	$ 29,500
Total monthly income after taxes:	
from the Clinic	$ 1,600
from the part-time job	300
Monthly take-home pay:	**$1,900**

MONTHLY BUDGET:

Rent	$	500
Utilities		200
Food/Household		240
Loan Payments		400
Car Payment		100
Car Insurance		100
Credit Card		50
Other	$	300
Total Expenses per Month:	**$**	**1,890**

What loan payback options did Chris look into?

"I began researching loan payback programs in the beginning of my third year. First, a word about consolidation of loans. If you have a large student loan debt, you will have to consolidate your loans. Without consolidation, my loan payments would be at least $1,000 per month."

A *consolidation loan* combines all of your non-private loans into one big loan with a lower interest rate and a longer repayment term. Eligible loans usually include Stafford, SLS, Perkins, PLUS, and others issued through the government. Most consolidation companies will not consolidate your private loans, such as alumni loans or loans through banks. However, typically the majority of your student loan debt will be eligible for consolidation. Once the loans are consolidated, you make only one monthly payment for those consolidated loans.

The following are examples of loan consolidation programs:

Federal Direct Consolidation Loan(phone: 800-848-0982)

Features:

   a. Interest rate is variable, based on adjusted Treasury Bill rates. The interest rate will never go higher than 8.25%.

   b. No charge to consolidate.

   c. Repayment options:

       1. *Level Repayment Plan:* You pay a flat amount every month for the duration of the loan. Each payment includes interest and principal.

       2. *Graduated Repayment Plan:* Payments begin lower at first and then increase every two years over a period ranging from 12 to 30 years.

       3. *Income Contingent Repayment Plan:* Monthly payments are based on your annual income and loan amount. *After 25 years, any remaining balance on the Direct Consolidation Loan will be forgiven,* although you have to pay tax on the amount forgiven. The loan company determines your monthly payment.

Sallie Mae Smart Loan for Lawyers (800-524-9100)

Features:

a. Interest rate is based on a weighted average of your loans. By including some loans, such as Perkins, which have a 5% interest rate, you can drop your interest as low as 7%.

b. No charge to consolidate.

c. Repayment Options:

1. *Level Payment Plan.* You pay a flat amount every month for the duration of the loan. Each payment includes interest and principal.

2. *Max-2.* Low, interest-only payments for 2 years. One step-up in year 3 to fixed payments for the rest of your term.

3. *Max-4.* Low, interest-only payments for 4 years. Graduated step-ups in years 5, 6, and 7. Fixed payments begin in year 7 and continue for the remainder of your term.

4. *Income Sensitive Repayment.* Monthly payments are based on your monthly income and loan amount. *You determine your monthly payment.* You choose a percentage of your gross monthly income, between 4% and 25%.

d. Payment incentives:

1. After a year of on-time payments, you receive a credit on prior loan servicing fees.

2. After three years of on-time payments, your interest rate drops 1%.

e. When you buy a home, you can include your consolidation loan with your mortgage and lower your interest payments even more.

Other Consolidation Programs: There are other consolidation loan programs, such as Law Access, Citibank, Graduate Loan Center, and ones offered by other companies. Such programs offer variations on the Sallie Mae program. Your law school's financial aid director will have more information about other consolidation programs.

What did Chris decide?

"I chose the Sallie Mae Smart Loan for Lawyers. Among the alternatives, I didn't feel there was a better program than Sallie Mae, for my needs."

Chris' Sallie Mae Smart Loan for Lawyers

Consolidation Amount:	$	83,000
Weighted Interest Rate:		8%
Interest-Only Payments:	$	558 per month

Income Sensitive Payments	$	**312 per month**

(Chris chose to pay 15% of gross monthly income)

Loans not consolidated

Alumni Loans:	$	2,300, paid off
Undergraduate Perkins:	$	4,000 at 5%,
	$	**40 per month**
Bar Exam Loan:	$	5,000 at 8.4%,
	$	**50 per month**
Total Loan Payments:	$	**400 per month**

A final comment from Chris:

"I did a lot of research to deal with my own situation, and am continuing to live out my decisions. I'm working hard but making it, and still love my career choice, which is the most important thing. Maybe something I've learned can help you."

Christopher Raistrick, J.D. 1996
Chicago Legal Clinic

This is Kimm talking again: Something Chris didn't mention here, incidentally, is that his life recently took an even greater turn for the better: He got married this fall.

OTHER REPAYMENT OPTIONS THAT WEREN'T A PART OF CHRIS RAISTRICK'S STORY:

Loan Repayment Assistance Programs

These programs—called LRAPs—are relatively new developments. They are designed to help law school graduates with low starting salaries, *especially* people who are going to do public service work. These programs are available not just from law schools themselves but also from some individual public service employers, fellowship funders, and even some state governments. AmeriCorps/VISTA, the national service program, is one employer which offers loan reduction assistance with its full-time positions, as well as the NAPIL/VISTA Summer Legal Corps. The Peace Corps does the same thing.

How to keep up with these programs? Visit the NAPIL home page, at www.napil.org—they've got all kinds of helpful stuff along these lines.

Forbearance

You might find it difficult to begin making loan payments as soon as you begin your new job. Or you might be in the process of a job search when your loans start to come due. If you face this kind of economic hardship, you can obtain an Economic Hardship Forbearance from your loan company. A forbearance is easy to obtain because you decide whether you need it or not. All you have to do is send a form to your loan company. A typical forbearance will last for at least six months.

Income Contingent Repayment

(This information comes courtesy of NAPIL, the National Association for Public Interest Law. Visit their home page at www.napil.org)
Income contingent repayment ("ICR"), in a nutshell, is a federal program that can help you reduce your monthly student loan payments significantly, *and* it might provide for forgiveness of any debt you have left after 25 years of repayment.

Here's how it works. If you have one or more of 21 types of government or government-guaranteed loans, you may consolidate these loans into a "federal direct consolidation loan." In consolidating, you may select one of four repayment options (or you can negotiate with the Department of Education for an "alternative repayment" plan uniquely suited to your situation). The four standard repayment choices are standard repayment, extended repayment, graduated repayment, and ICR.

Under ICR, the amount you pay is based on your income. Your monthly payment amount is the lesser of the following:

- 20% of your monthly discretionary income. Discretionary income is your federal Adjusted Gross Income ("AGI") minus the poverty level for your family size. If you are married both your AGI and your spouse's AGI will be used to calculate your monthly repayment amount.

OR

- The amount you would pay if you repaid your loans in 12 years, multiplied by an income percentage factor (ranging from approximately 55% to 200%) that varies with your annual income.

Your repayment amount is adjusted annually. In addition, under this plan it's possible that you will not make payments large enough to pay off your loans in 25 years. If that happens (excluding periods in deferment, forbearance, the graduated and/or 15 to 30 year extended plans) any unpaid amount will be forgiven. However, be aware that any amount forgiven is considered taxable income.

A few other important facts about ICR:

1. **Job eligibility.** There is no restriction for participation in ICR based on occupation.

2. **Year of graduation isn't relevant.** You are eligible to participate in ICR even if you have already graduated from law school.

3. **Switching between repayment plans.** Generally speaking, you can switch between ICR and the other repayment plans (standard, graduated, extended).

Needless to say, ICR is a complicated program. Repaying loans this way has its advantages and disadvantages, so look before you leap! You can obtain more information, as well as application forms, by calling 1-800-557-7392.

WAYS TO AVOID STUDENT LOAN DEBT IN THE FIRST PLACE

Everybody I talked to in researching this book said that the best way to avoid problems with law school debt is not to get into debt in the first place. *Yeah, right!* You're saying. *How am I supposed to cover a $20,000 tuition bill with a summer job?* Well, you're probably *not* going to do that (unless you summer intern for McKinsey & Company or win the lottery). But what you *can* do is to minimize your debt load in the first place. It's just too damned easy in school to think "I'm already $50,000 in debt, what's another few bucks here and there?" The problem with this—as I alluded to at the beginning of this chapter—is that things you buy *now* with student loan money will wind up costing you *four times as much* when it's payback time, taking the interest into account. So those little money-saving habits you get into as a student—and carry over to your first couple of years out of school—will set you up for a much more attractive lifestyle in a very short time.
Here are a few ideas:

1. *Don't overlook **any** scholarship possibilities.* You may think that your grades don't qualify you for scholarships, or you may only be familiar with a few of the ones you *can* get. Don't cheat yourself! Bar associations, special interest groups, and civil groups all have scholarships, as do many, many more organizations. I had a law school classmate with *strictly* mediocre grades who got a lot of his schooling paid for a by a scholarship available to law students of Ukrainian descent. His Ukrainian-ness had never been very obvious to me, but he laughed when he told me that to qualify you only had to be one-eighth Ukrainian, and he was *that.* The point here: Talk to your financial aid director to find out about sources for obscure scholarships.

2. *Take part in writing contests with cash prizes.* This is not *only* a tremendous resume-builder—which you probably already know—

but what you probably *don't* know is that many writing competitions *only get a handful of entries—sometimes as few as three.* Your odds of winning are obviously much greater than they seem at first glance.

"Well, geez, Kimmbo, I don't have time to do any writing contests. I already have too much to do." I know, I know, I hear you. Here's how to squeeze in any project you want to accomplish while you're in school. Don't think that you have to spend *whole days* working on it. Just take half an hour a day—get to the school library a half hour early or stay half an hour after your friends leave—and you'll be *amazed* what you can accomplish. The prolific 19th century novelist Anthony Trolloppe wrote *dozens* of books, while holding down a full-time job at the British Post Office and supporting a passel of kids. How did he do it? He woke up early in the morning, before the kids were up and before he went to work, and did his writing them. He wound up with a huge body of work over the years. I'm only asking *you* to wring another half hour from your day. When you consider that some of these writing contest prizes run into the thousands of dollars, trust me, it's *worth it.*

3. Here's a quote I've heard a million times: "Live like a lawyer while you're still a student, and you'll live like a student when you're a lawyer." The point here is, if you're living on student loans, you don't really have any business driving a new car, having a wardrobe full of new clothes, enjoying lavish vacations, and eating out a lot. If that sounds painful, well, the truth hurts.

   But *actually,* with a little creativity you can have a lot of fun on very little money. As one lawyer I talked to told me, "Law school is the last time poverty is fashionable." With that in mind, consider:

   a. Attending every law school function that serves free food. When I go around the country visiting law schools and doing my *Guerrilla Tactics* seminar, I notice that the attendance is just about double when there's free food as opposed to when there isn't. I guess I could be insulted, but I don't insult too easily—and anyway, I'm *telling* you to take advantage of free food opportunities, so I could hardly castigate you for doing it!

   b. Sharing an apartment with roommates. You might think you *need* your privacy, but in fact you might find living with roomies very congenial. You can live in a much nicer place for much less money.

   c. Don't partake in "gratuitous shopping" (that's my boyfriend Henry's term). If you tell yourself you're just "going to the mall to look around," you're begging to be tempted into buying something you can't afford. Don't torture yourself that way!

  d. Don't get credit cards, and if you *do* get them, pretend you don't have them *except for emergencies*—and a new outfit you've just got to have *is not an emergency.* Credit card debt is the worst. I carried credit card debt for years, at 19% interest, until I realized that I had never paid off my credit cards down to zero. That meant that a $60 dress I'd bought with the credit card 10 years ago, while I was in school—it was my very first purchase with the credit card— wound up costing me *almost $400.* It's *frightening* how quickly those tiny minimum payments add up to horrific amounts.

  e. Go to consignment stores for your clothes. Almost every law school has a tony neighborhood somewhere nearby, and that's where you want to go. Wealthy people will consign things you'd be thrilled to have new, and my attitude is that once I've worn it once, it's used—so that once might as well happen before I buy it. The fact is, you don't need a multi-hundred dollar suit for your interviews. You can get away with a consignment outfit and nobody will be the wiser.

  f. *Cook cheap stuff.* If you don't think it's possible to eat cheap and eat well, I'm going to give you a simple recipe that will change your mind. It's pretty much the only thing I ate as a third-year law student, and I'll tell you, it's delicious. I was constantly having people beg me for the recipe but pride stopped me from telling them how I made it. As you'll see, it's very cheap and easy to make, even if you buy all of the ingredients, but at the end of the recipe I'll tell you my secret for making it *even cheaper.*

Phenomenal "Mystery Ingredient" Barbecued Chicken

A package of chicken parts (with the bones in)
Garlic salt
Paprika
Ketchup
Water

  Here's what you do. Take the chicken parts out of the package, wash and pat them dry, and either put them on foil or on a baking pan, sprinkle them on both sides with the garlic salt and paprika, and put them, bone side down, in a 350 degree oven for about 45 minutes. In the meantime, mix equal parts of ketchup and water in a bowl. When the 45 minutes are up, open the oven door and pour the ketchup-water onto the chicken pieces. Cook for another 15 minutes until the ketchup has turned into a glaze and no longer looks like ketchup. (You have to look at it every few minutes, because with its high sugar content, ketchup can have a tendency to burn. You don't want to *torch* it, you want to *caramelize* it to that nice, barbecue-y maroon color.)

  Now—that secret for making it cheaper. What I would do is every once in a while, when my friends and I would splurge on McDonald's or Burger

King (they were all broke, like me), I would grab a few extra ketchup packets, and keep them. When I had a couple of dozen ketchup packets saved up, *that's when I would make the barbecued chicken. I never actually bought ketchup for this recipe!* Pathetic as that sounds now, at the time it was actually *fun* trying to figure out ways to cut costs.

At least—it sure beats paying $400 for a $60 dress!

HOW TO SAVE MONEY ONCE YOU'RE OUT OF SCHOOL

Everybody who's ever graduated from law school—including me—experiences the same sensation: *Now it's time to cut loose!* After years of likely economizing and a bunch of hard work, you feel like it's time to relax a bit and ease up on the financial shackles you've been dragging around.

Well, guess what—if you've got a bunch of debt, that's a dangerous attitude. What's far healthier is to view your first couple of years in practice as a residency, just the way doctors do. I'm not talking about the phenomenal work hours (not *here*, anyway), but rather the idea of living on not much money. An apprenticeship, if you will. If you can continue to bite the bullet for a couple of years—forego the new car for now, and the expensive digs, and the fabulous restaurant meals—you can chew up a lot of law school debt. In fact, a strategy some law students use (or at least *try* to use) is to take on a high-paying job they think they're going to hate, with the idea in mind that they'll pay off their law student loans and then take the job they *really* wanted—something more meaningful to them that pays a lot less. (The risk here is "velvet handcuffs"—that is, you get used to a lavish lifestyle, high rent, a big mortgage, an expensive car, and you just can't bring yourself to give it up—you're 'handcuffed' to the high salary that comes with a job you dislike.)

What am I suggesting here? Don't view law school graduation as the watershed point, the difference between roommates, consignment clothes, homemade meals, and a lavish life. If you've got law school debt hanging over you, you really *can't* afford it yet even though you've graduated and technically speaking you're a "grown up."

I could go into *enormous* detail here about coming up with budgets, getting good deals on rent and cars, and that kind of thing, but what I'm going to do instead is to put you on to a couple of really good books on the topic. They'll give you everything I would have told you—and more!

Welcome to the Real World, by Stacy Kravetz (published by W. W. Norton & Company)

How to Survive Without Your Parents' Money, by Geoff Martz (published by The Princeton Review, Random House)

Great thanks for help on this chapter goes to Sara Joan Bales, the Director for the Center for Public Service Law at Loyola University Chicago School of Law.

CHAPTER 14

"Hair on Fire" Days

*How to Make the Most of Any Job,
No Matter Where It Is.*

Landing a job is one thing. *Doing* a good job is another

You've heard all of the stock advice. Be mature. Take the initiative. Be a team player. Don't gossip. What does any of that *mean,* anyway? And is it *good* advice? What *really* distinguishes people who are quickly deemed stars at work, and those who are consigned to the metaphorical slag heap?

And finally—would I ask you any of these questions if I didn't have the answers for you? You know me better than that. What we're going to do in this chapter is talk about *exactly* how you take that job offer and turn it into a brilliant success. We'll go over *all* of the "Do's and Don'ts" you need to know to make the most of your job. We'll discuss how to handle summer clerkships, what you should do before you start your job, handling every day from "Day One" onward, and how to handle all kinds of special situations—difficult personalities, evaluations, you name it. And we'll talk about how—and when—to negotiate for more money. You could probably summarize everything in this chapter in two principles: (i) Grow up, and (ii) Suck it up. But we'll be *much* more specific, *much* more "hands on" than that.

I think you're going to be *very* pleasantly surprised by what you read in this chapter. I'm convinced that what you read here may well be the difference between success and failure at work. It's not because I'm so confident of my own advice. As you'll see at various points in this chapter, my own work history is an almost unblemished list of what *not* to do to impress your employer! Instead, your "job tutors" are a bunch of very smart people all over the country. As I was gathering information from employers for all of the *other* chapters in this book, I asked them questions like: What makes people stand out when they come to work for you? What mistakes do they make that tank their careers? If you could give them *any* advice, what would it be? I asked the same of law school administrators, most of whom are either former lawyers or law firm recruiting coordinators. I wasn't at all sure there'd be any rhyme or reason to the advice I got, or anything I could weave into any semblance of a useful chapter. In fact, I got reams and reams of wonderful advice. Great, very specific insider tips, for all kinds of jobs—summer clerkships, jobs with large, medium and small firms, public interest jobs, you name it. And it's that information that you'll find in this chapter.

Incidentally, before we get started, you'll notice that the focus here would seem to be on law firms. That's because it's the job setting where a majority of law students wind up. Nonetheless, much of what you'll read here—communicating with superiors, peers and support staff, creating quality work product, handling social situations, displaying the right kind of attitude—those apply to *every* job, even if the specific examples I use mention "partners" and "associates." So if you're doing something off the beaten path, this chapter is worth reading anyway—you'll easily be able to customize what you read to your own, unique situation.

Here's what we'll do here. We'll start out by talking about how to handle summer clerkships. Then we'll talk about permanent jobs. And finally, we'll talk about negotiating for better scratch. Let's get going!

THE 1,640-HOUR INTERVIEW: THE 26 SECRETS EVERY SUMMER CLERK SHOULD KNOW

"Is it such a big deal," she asked, "to use the word 'masturbate' in front of a partner?"

Well—yes. And that question, from an attendee (who'd clearly had an unfortunate summer clerkship experience) at one of my *Guerrilla Tactics* law school job search seminars, proves that handling summer clerkships appropriately is a skill that must be *acquired*. What we're going to do in this section is to make sure that *you* don't do anything that tanks your chances with your summer clerkship employer, no matter *who* it is.

In some ways, you should approach summer clerkships very much the way you'd approach a "permanent" job after law school. Turning in the best possible work product, acting and dressing professionally, not getting crocked at employer social events—that's good advice whether you're there for 10 weeks, or 10 years. And because of those similarities, you'd be *very* well advised to read the "64 Do's and Don'ts" for permanent jobs, just below this section, before you start *any* job.

Having said that, there *are* differences between summer clerkships and permanent jobs that merit your attention. So what I'm going to do in this section is to share with you advice from employers about handling the issues that are specific to summer jobs.

#1: Be aware of what employers are looking for: the "Top Eight Hit List."

a. Excellent "output"—whether it be written assignments or oral advocacy or dealing with clients. For written projects, show your ability not just to write but also to research and give strong legal analyses. For oral advocacy projects (typically for prosecutors), show your ability to think quickly on your feet and handle pressure.

b. Good judgment—the ability to act and dress appropriately and deal sensibly and maturely with situations as they arise. One lawyer told me about a firm where a summer clerk house-sat for a senior partner while the partner was away on vacation, and the partner came back early to find that the associate had adorned statues in the garden with the partner's underclothes. I'm not suggesting that you need to be Solomon-like, but don't be an *idiot!*

c. Enthusiasm for the projects you do and for the employer itself. When faced with choosing between summer clerks for permanent offers, employers will take the clerk who shows the most interest in *them.*

d. Flexibility—the willingness to accommodate different work styles, personalities, and tasks.

e. Appreciation of the opportunity to work with the employer.

f. The ability to get along with support staff and colleagues—to "fit in."

g. An understanding of what the organization's goals are—whether it's a business (like a law firm) or any other kind of service provider (like a government agency or public interest employer), and respect the fact that even if your employer is a charity, it's not a charity for *you*— you've got a role to play in helping the organization reach its goals.

h. Realistic expectations of what work is, and what you can expect from it. Show that you don't expect the employer to fulfill all of your expectations.

#2: Anticipate that your first day will be a "Hair on Fire" Day.

When you enter *any* new situation, *expect* to feel chaotic. *Expect* to feel overwhelmed. That's normal. For many of us, our law school summer clerkships are the first time we've had a job that rises above the "you-want-fries-with-that" level. It's important to remember a couple of things that will make you feel better. First of all, *every single person* you meet, every person you work with, was once in your shoes. They *know* what it feels like to be you, and so on some very basic level they can empathize with you. And secondly, *don't* put pressure on yourself to dazzle everyone you meet with your wit and intelligence from moment one. As one employer explained it to me, "Your most important first assignment is to *listen carefully.*" In the section on handling permanent jobs, I talk about the importance of observing and learning on the job. Take a deep breath, smile, greet people in a friendly way, absorb what's told to you, and don't expect any more of yourself at the outset than that!

#3: Relax, and rely on the fact that if the employer hired you for a summer clerkship, they already believe you can do the work.

Many employers pointed out to me that summer clerks often overestimate what's expected of them. No one expects you, as a summer clerk, to be Perry Mason. They expect you to have the raw materials to be successful, and to work hard to learn what you need to learn. As one employer stated, "Take for granted that you belong here. Your credentials are OK. Relax! Don't be nervous. People who do spend too many hours, take too much time to do stuff, will feel insecure in their judgments. Remember that interactions with nervous people don't inspire confidence." Another adds that "Disasters at work are rarer than summer clerks seem to think. Sexually harassing a peer, failing to turn in an assignment—*those* are disasters. Take it easy, do your work, and talk to people. See who they work with, what they do, how they like it, how you can, and should, fit in. *Assume* that you'll be fine, and you undoubtedly will be."

#4: Make your job your first priority.

Nobody expects your work to be your life. But when you are on a 1,600-hour interview, your work has got to take priority over your other interests and commitments. If you have a family or a boyfriend/girlfriend, explain that it's very important to your career to make an excellent impression, and that may mean changed or cancelled personal plans. I realize this might make you cringe, and no decent employer will expect you to live your work, but they *will* expect a serious commitment from you for the summer. Arrange your private life so that you can show your employer, by your actions, that you value the opportunity to work with them.

#5: If you are clerking out-of-town, consider rooming with a lawyer from the office.

This isn't advice for everyone. It may be that you aren't the roommate type. But if you *are,* consider contacting the recruiting coordinator or hiring person at your summer employer, to find out if there are any people at the organization who take in summer clerks. Many large firms offer this option to their summer associates.

If you *do* think this sounds attractive, be sure that when you make your initial inquiry to the appropriate person, you accentuate your desire for a positive role model. When you stay with a person it's hard not to be identified with them in the eyes of other people at the employer, and the last thing you want is to be associated with a "bad egg."

#6: Get to know as many people as possible.

This is another piece of advice from virtually every employer. There are *many* good reasons for this. For one thing, you're evaluating the employer just as you're being evaluated. You don't want to make career decisions based on one or two people. You want to cut as broad a swath as possible so that you can get a feel for the flavor of the organization in general, good *and* bad.

Another reason to spread yourself out is to minimize the effect of any one sub-par experience. Despite your best efforts, it may be that one summer project doesn't work out for you, or you rub somebody the wrong way. You want to have as many champions as possible to negate the effect of anyone who'd want to blackball you.

#7: Stay in close contact with your supervisor and/or recruiting administrator.

Even if you are working on a monster project, be sure to poke your head in your supervisor and/or recruiting administrator's office at least once a week, to say "hello" and let them know what you're up to. It's a mistake to assume that they're keeping up with your progress without any prodding from you. This not only gives you a chance to express your enthusiasm for what you're doing (and make a good impression in so doing), but also gives you the chance to nip any potential problems in the bud.

#8: Leave your sense of what you think you deserve at the door as you walk in.

High on the list of behavior that infuriates employers is a sense of entitlement. If you've done well in law school, if you're on Law Review or you're #1 in your class or you go to a distinguished school, I applaud you. But don't expect your employer to scatter rose petals before your feet because of your academic accomplishments. One employer—one of the largest firms in the country—told me about a summer associate who demanded that staff personnel address him as "Mister." As this firm commented, "That's an unforgivable mistake."

It's *very* important that you show appreciation for what you get, *whatever* you get, and bite your lip before you complain. As one large firm advises, "Accept sharing an office, sharing equipment, rotating assignments or locations. In other words—go with the flow." The quality of the furniture you get, the art on the walls—these things are none of your concern, and not an appropriate source of verbal disdain.

One firm shared a story about a summer clerk who constantly whined about the fact that his office was small and had no view. In exasperation, the recruiting coordinator finally moved him into the office of an associate who was away on medical leave. As the recruiting coordinator told it, "I expressly warned this clerk *not* to use the computer in this associate's office; if he needed to use a computer, he had to go back to his original office and use *that* computer. The associate whose office he was using was resting at home during chemotherapy treatment, but he wanted to keep up with his work via modem. So we had wired his home computer so that he could access anything he needed at the office, through a modem connection with his office computer—the one on the desk where this summer clerk was now sitting. I stressed to the summer clerk how much we were concerned about the associate, and how we wanted him to feel part of 'the loop' even from home. The summer clerk agreed not to use the computer. Sure enough, a couple of days later I got a distressed phone call from the associate, saying he couldn't get through on his computer. And when I went down to the office, there was the summer clerk—using his computer, despite my direct request not to!"

The watchword here? Remove the phrase "I deserve" from your summer vocabulary. *Nobody* wants to hear it. Be humble, be appreciative, and the perks you feel you deserve will come to you soon enough.

#9: If you play sports—tennis, softball, golf—play with your colleagues.

Many law firms participate in local softball leagues and/or charity golf tournaments. Employers recommend that you get involved in as many of these activities "as you have the energy for." Why? "Besides the schmooze value, you'll have fun and get to know the people you work with in a non-pressurized atmosphere. You'll be happier and you'll do better work."

#10: Be flexible with your hours.

This is part of the idea of putting your employer first, during your summer clerkship. The reason I mention it is that if you read enough about summer clerkships, you get the impression that employers are scrupulously careful not to have summer clerks work past five o'clock, even if new lawyers work much longer hours. Well, that's not *always* the case. There *are* employers who take a different tack, and believe that summer clerks should have a realistic work experience. In most cases, "realistic" is a code word for "long hours." If your employer happens to be one of those, accept it without whining. If you have obligations that simply *must* take precedence, then explain the conflict to your employer, and offer to (i) go away to take care of your personal situation and then return to the office, or (ii) offer to take work home with you, or (iii) ask for suggestions on how you might compensate for not being there when they need you.

The point here is—don't let them see you being resentful of working when you didn't expect to. You'll be branded with a "selfish" and "not a team player" badge very quickly.

#11: Treat other summer clerks as your colleagues, not your competitors.

One of the biggest baddest boners you can commit is to adopt a "take no prisoners" attitude toward your summer colleagues. Employers *despise* seeing this kind of competition. As one employer explained it, "Don't be too tightly-wound or too paranoid. Most places don't hire 50 people for 20 spots." A Midwestern firm stated that "Some summer clerks come here, they want to work 12 to 14 hours a day, they get very competitive. They're making a huge mistake thinking that they're being judged exclusively by their work product. Sometimes you *do* need to put in the hours but *never* overlook the importance of personality. It's *all* personality. Being too competitive can *kill* your chances! We had a summer associate last summer who actually told the managing partner that there was too much pressure to socialize. This was an immediate black mark on his record—that kind of competitiveness is a real turn-off."

#12: Don't mistake secretaries for miracle workers.

As a summer clerk, it may well be that you've never before in your life had any kind of support staff (no, your mom doesn't count). While you should follow all of the advice we discuss for permanent clerks in terms of showing respect for support staff, what you need to know as a summer clerk is the importance of keeping your secretary informed of your schedule, to provide reasonable lead times, and to remember that the quality and accuracy of your work is *your* responsibility, not *theirs*. Always schedule in time to review the work any secretary performs for you, so that you have time to correct any mistakes before your deadline.

#13: Let your employer see only loyalty to them—*no matter what other opportunities you're contemplating.*

Something that drives employers *crazy* is to see summer clerks "wheeling and dealing" offers. One large firm told me that "It's so important to focus on the organization as the place you intend to make a long-term commitment. When an employer can make offers to only 80% of their summer class, they tend to focus on people who have shown the most sincere interest in them. Don't make the common mistake of 'wheeling and dealing' alternative offers during your current clerkship!"

#14: Don't sit on your hands when there is downtime between (or during) assignments.

No matter how well-organized a summer program you enter, there will be times when you're "at liberty." Maybe it will be between assignments, or maybe it will be when you're waiting for a document to be word-processed. No matter why it occurs, don't sit in your office waiting for your next assignment. Walk around, introduce yourself to people you don't know, see if there are any small ways to make yourself useful. This not only shows initiative and enthusiasm—two highly-prized traits—but also gives you more of a chance to get to know the employer, and determine whether *this* is where you want to start your career after law school.

#15: Detach your lips from your employer's butt.

Employers consider obvious brown-nosing laughable. There's a difference between honest flattery and patent toady-ism. As one Southern firm explained it, "Obvious sucking-up will alienate more people than you realize. We had one summer clerk who actually made a point of saying to important partners, 'I only want to work for you, not for associates.' You can imagine what a great impression that made on our associates, who had a prominent say on which summer clerks got offers."

#16: Recognize that your behavior at social events is just as scrutinized as what you do at the office.

The fact that you're not in the office doesn't mean that you can let your hair down. *Many* employers stress the importance of recognizing that social events give your employer a chance to assess your people skills. An associate at one firm told me about his experience as a summer clerk. He and the other clerks were invited to a partner's house for dinner. After dinner, they played Charades with lawyers from the firm. When the game was over, one of the lawyers pulled this summer clerk aside, and said, "Congratulations—you passed the creativity test." I'm not suggesting that every employer is quite this Truman Show-esque, but the point is that you shouldn't let your guard down entirely whenever you are around people from work.

What should you do? There are a few pointers to keep in mind about employer social events. As one employer advises, "Show you can enjoy yourself, but don't go overboard." One firm talked about a summer clerk who socialized every night, and drank too much. Not a good idea! The watchword is "moderation"—whether it's in jokes, alcohol, you name it. Your summer clerkship is not the time to wake up at a truck stop, unaware of how you got there and exactly how much you drank. You should *never* let your image or reputation be compromised.

If you are clerking with a law firm, Vanderbilt's Pam Malone advises that you "be mindful that social events are always a test of client development skills." They're looking to see how well you interact with people, with an eye toward how you'll represent the firm in the community. So make sure you talk with a number of people, brush up on what's going on in the news so that you have neutral topics of conversation, and remember that lawyers *always* like to talk about their own experiences. Ask lawyers you work with how they got their start, what their own summer clerkships were like, their favorite war story.

#17: Beware of high-risk humor.

The risqué jokes that the senior partners may get away with are no indication of the humor they expect from *you*. While every employer professes a desire to hire people with a sense of humor, don't explore the outer boundaries of what's appropriate during your summer clerkship. One firm told me about a female permanent associate who casually invited a male summer associate—we'll call him "Matt"—to her house for a barbecue. Another summer associate sent her flowers, signing Matt's name, saying "I can't wait for our evening together. Love, Matt." When the female associate got the flowers, she called Matt into her office and dressed him down for his unprofessional behavior. When they both figured out what had happened, she unfortunately didn't take the joke as it was intended— she was embarrassed and furious. Between you and me, I think it was *very* funny. But until you are absolutely sure of yourself around any particular colleague, don't risk offending—and alienating—them.

And don't *ever, ever, ever, ever, ever* tell racist or sexist jokes— even if all of your colleagues are telling them over a few beers at happy hour. Instead, stock up on your supply of "neutral" humor. If every joke you hear is inappropriate for a general audience, look for sources that *do* provide all-purpose jokes. Reader's Digest runs funny, non-offensive jokes every month. Bookstores are full of books of "clean" jokes (and they're not *all* corny). Here are a couple of riddles to keep in your back pocket for such situations.

> Q: What do you get when you cross an agnostic, a dyslexic, and an insomniac?
> A: Someone who stays awake all night wondering if there really is a dog.
> Q: What did the Zen Buddhist say to the hot dog vendor?
> A: Make me one with everything.

#18: Realize that indiscreet romantic involvement with colleagues will make your employer seriously question your professional judgment.

I'm not telling you how to run your personal life. But I *am* telling you that it's important for you to "keep it in your pants!" as far as your employer is concerned, as Kentucky's Drusilla Bakert puts it. As she says, "Summer events often involve alcohol, and when you couple that with the fact that many of your colleagues may be physically attractive you've got a recipe for disaster." One law firm told of a camp retreat, where there was one cabin for the female summer clerks and one cabin for the males. Two of the associates—one from each cabin, needless to say—took a tent, and slept in it between the cabins. *Yikes!* Other firms told of summer clerks making amorous use of the firm facilities—libraries, supply rooms, and the like. If you feel an unquenchable attraction to a co-worker, enjoy the feeling of the rush but *don't* make it obvious at any employer-related event, and *don't* confide in anyone else you work with. Remember—these are your first professional colleagues. You wouldn't think much of a colleague who flaunted their romantic life at work, so don't make that mistake yourself!

#19: Don't view the first couple of weeks as an acid test of your desire to be an attorney.

It's very easy to get impatient with your summer, and figure that if the first week goes badly, you weren't meant to be a lawyer. Even an entire *summer* isn't long enough to come to that conclusion, let alone an awful start. It could be that you're working with the one person in the organization with whom you'd just *never* be able to get along. Maybe you got a rotten or boring assignment. No matter what it is, don't ring down the curtain on your career before it's even started.

One law firm advised that "You have to expect a 'mood slump' toward the beginning of your summer. That is more likely related to the fact that it's summertime, you'd rather be outside, you haven't had a 'real job' in maybe two years, you're used to a flexible student lifestyle and not working 10-hour days in a suit, or nylons, or uncomfortable shoes. Give yourself the whole summer to draw conclusions."

Another firm added that "Most people spend much of the summer battling overwhelming feelings of stupidity and incompetence. Remember that you aren't incompetent *or* stupid. Be patient with yourself! Law is a difficult profession and you have a lot to learn."

#20: If you are volunteering, behave as though you were being paid.

It's easy to take volunteer opportunities lightly. Because you aren't being paid, you might be tempted not to be as prompt, to dress more casually, and take your assignments less seriously. *Don't do it!* As one employer told me, "Regardless of whether you're paid or not, always act as though you are a professional employee of the organization." This means behaving as though it's your career, not just an unpaid clerkship. Be prompt, meet deadlines, cultivate your colleagues, treat support staff and clients with respect, and dress like a professional, not a student. The point of volunteering is to expand your professional possibilities, and the only way to do that is to create the image in the mind of your employer that you *are* a professional.

#21: If you're doing a summer clerkship that is unlikely to result in a permanent offer, recognize the things that you should get out of it.

It may be that you're going to clerk for an organization that for whatever reason won't be hiring you back immediately after graduation. Maybe it's a firm that's not going to expand, and this is made clear to you before you start. Maybe you're clerking for the U.S. Attorney's Office, which doesn't hire anyone fresh out of school. There are myriad other situations where this might arise. The key here is to focus on what it is you can accomplish *aside* from getting a permanent offer. You should make it your goal to leave at the end of the summer with three assets:

a. Skills that you can transfer to other organizations or jobs, whether they be writing skills, handling certain kinds of transactions or clients, making presentations, or anything else.

b. Contacts that will be valuable to your job search. Remember that every single person you work with, from the most senior manager to the mail room clerk, knows other people—people who may make wonderful employers for you. Cultivating the people you come in contact with during your summer not only makes your summer more interesting and fun, but it's a very wise career move. Remember that lawyers tend to be closely-knit with other people who do the same thing, and word travels fast. Take advantage of this!

c. An enthusiastic reference from your employer. Drawing a rave from your summer employer, even without the possibility of a permanent offer, will pave the way for a much easier transition to your career after law school.

#22: Recognize that if you hate what you're doing, you only have to make the best of it for a few weeks.

Despite your best efforts in finding a great employer, you may in fact find that you've hitched your wagon to a slug, not a star. What should you do? Use it as a learning experience, and get what you can from it. And remember that the people you work with aren't fixtures. They could well go on to work at places you *would* enjoy, so if you make an effort not to alienate them no matter *how* bad a time you're having, you may find yourself open to opportunities down the road that you can't anticipate right now.

Comfort yourself with the thought that summers do end, so your agony is temporary. John F. Kennedy used to say that he could tolerate any pain if he knew it would come to an end. And in Alcoholics Anonymous, people are advised to "look past the drink"—look at the long-term benefits of restraint now. So if you're miserable at work, focus on a time when you *will* be happy, when the bad experience *will* be over. It's so much easier, and more productive, than wallowing in misery.

#23: Accept that a bad clerkship doesn't mean you won't be a good—or even great—lawyer.

As one law firm advises, "Accept the fact that some clerkships just don't work out. It doesn't mean you won't be a success. Just take what you can from the experience and look for a better place for *you*."

My clerkship, with a large law firm after my second year in law school, was an unmitigated disaster. I was no more suited to working there than I would be to playing in the N.B.A. (I'm five-foot-one.) Had the experience been even mediocre, I would have faced enormous pressure from both my family and myself to return after graduation. Instead, the fact that it went so badly forced me to take a step back and re-evaluate what I wanted to do with my career. If your clerkship goes even half as badly as mine did, you might be tempted to think you're doomed to failure. You aren't. As the old saying goes, "There are no obstacles, only opportunities." Look at the experience as a chance to determine what you *really* want to do with your life, and be grateful that you had the incredible good fortune to have your eyes opened so early in your career!

#24: For summer clerkships in prosecutor's offices (like District Attorneys or State's Attorneys), be aware that your enthusiasm and ability to think on your feet is more important than your writing skills.

When you summer clerk for a prosecutor, you will be judged on how well you react to pressure and how quickly you can think on your feet.

As one DA's office noted, "We want to see people who are prepared and eager. The real stars in our summer program are people who actively go after the attorneys to ask if there are any motions or trials they can handle."

The flipside of this is that no prosecutor's office expects you to be a "polished attorney. We want desire, potential, and the personality that, win or lose, can hardly wait for the next trial."

#25: In public interest clerkships, show compassion for constituents.

Public interest employers are particularly shocked when summer clerks seem unfeeling toward clients. When you work in public interest, you're not in law school anymore—these aren't hypothetical situations with names on a page. These are *real* people with *real* problems. While you don't want to appear an emotional wreck, take a compassionate and concerned tone. It's important to be sensitive to the suffering and situation of the people you serve. As the Los Angeles Public Defender's Office says, "Many times clerks conducting intake interviews do so with a cold detached manner that is somewhat chilling to observe."

#26: If you summer clerk for a public interest employer, don't assume that casual dress is the norm.

Before your clerkship starts, take the opportunity—if your interview didn't present you with one—to observe the way your colleagues dress. As one public interest employer advises, "It's not unusual for public interest employers to expect jackets and ties. Pay attention to grooming! We expect you to dress appropriately, and to observe, or ask questions, to find out what the norm is."

After You Graduate: The 130 "Do's" and "Don'ts" That Distinguish New Lawyers Headed for the Top.

If you ask employers to list the qualities they look for in new lawyers, you'll hear things like "common sense" and "maturity" and "good judgment" and "people skills" and "team player." Those are all well and good, but virtually *useless* in knowing how to *behave* at work. Employers can't "see" judgment—but they *can* see when you blow off the deadline on an assignment because you were afraid to ask questions and look stupid. They can't "see" common sense—but they'll certainly notice if you make a smart comment about the artwork in the lobby when you're being shown around the office your first day, not realizing that the paintings were created by the managing partner's spouse or donated by an important client. They can't quantify people skills—but they'll sit up and pay attention if you tell a client an off-color joke. "Maturity" isn't a function of age—you are *proving* your immaturity, regardless of how old you are, when you bridle at criticism, clinging to the childish belief that your work is perfect.

What we're going to do here is to take those intangibles and make them *real*. We'll talk *specifics* about writing assignments, billables, handling colleagues and clients—you name it. Everything we'll talk about here are things you can *do*, attitudes you can *adopt*. I am confident that there is *nothing* here, absolutely *nothing*, that is beyond you! The fact is, having talked with employers all over the country, I can tell you that there's no question that there are certain well-defined skills that workplace "stars" exhibit. The good news is that many of these skills—in fact, almost all of the most important ones—aren't inborn. They're *learned*. If you read this carefully and you are extremely vigilant, you can stop yourself from making any major career errors. You can shine at the office and open yourself up to great opportunities.

A word of caution before we go. Don't expect that you're going to be able to carry out this list perfectly. No one ever has, and no one ever will. So don't beat yourself up or make yourself crazy. Just be *mindful* of what it takes to succeed, and shape these traits to your personality and your particular situation.

DO'S AND DON'TS #1 THROUGH 4: PREP WORK— WHAT TO DO BEFORE YOU START

If you want to put your best foot forward, start shining your shoes before you appear at the office. There are a couple of things you've got to get out of the way first!

#1: Call up your employer, and ask to go out to lunch with some of the younger lawyers.

As Chicago's Suzanne Mitchell advises, "Go into any job with the broadest knowledge base that you can get! Disappointed expectations make people the angriest about their jobs—they feel blind-sided. Go in with your eyes *wide open*." Hamline's Joyce Laher agrees, adding that "Being realistic about what your job requires is 90% of success."

Ideally, you learned a lot about your upcoming employer during the interview process. And it may be that you summer clerked or worked part-time for the employer, and that's even better. But before you start to work, it's a good idea to get together with some new-ish lawyers. Ask whoever hired you to recommend a couple of people, and explain that you want to talk to them to make sure you get off on the right foot.

What do you want to know? In general, as per Boston University's Betsy Armour, "You want to ask questions about what life is like there, their advice for getting out of the starting gate quickly."

Of course, it's not politic to come right out and say, "Who's a jerk?" and "Who should I avoid?" Instead, ask questions that will give you those answers and many more, without making you seem boorish. Admit straight out that you don't know anything right now, and tell them that they were recommended to you as good sources. Ask them what they wish they'd known before they started. Ask whether people routinely eat lunch together, or work out together, or play sports together, or socialize.

If you can, meet them at the office, and as you walk through the offices, make a note of what people wear. If your contacts are the same gender as you, ask about what's appropriate to wear, and where they shop.

When it comes to work, ask them about the kinds of projects they've done, who they've worked with. You will find that if you project sincere enthusiasm and appreciation, your companions are likely to be very forthcoming with all kinds of advice. Lawyers *love* to be asked for their opinions!

#2: If you're thinking far enough ahead—learn a sport (and I don't mean curling).

Obviously, if you know that your employer has a softball team that everybody is expected to play for, brush up your softball skills. Call a local college or YMCA to see about classes or a coach who might help you. Similarly, if everybody at the office is a fly-fisherman, it would pay to visit a tackle shop and at least get familiar with the sport. Or it may be that everybody at the office is a tennis nut. Here's your chance to fit in, get great exercise and work on your tan as well!

Of course, the classic lawyer's sport is golf. I can't tell you how many lawyers have told me that they wish they'd learned how to play while they were still in school! In fact, a recent *New York Times* article cited the correlation between above-average golf skills and being a Fortune 500 CEO. Some law firms in this book recognize the business generation and networking aspects of golf so clearly that they pay for their new associates' golf lessons. So if you *can*, learn to play before you go.

One law student told me his very funny experience with golf. He received a call at home one night from the hiring partner at a local firm, who introduced himself and said, "I got your resume from a mutual acquaintance, and we'd like to bring you in for an interview." The student was thrilled, and the partner went on, "I see from your resume that you play golf. I do, too. Instead of sitting around the office, why don't we hit a few holes at my club? Pick me up at nine a.m. tomorrow, at the office." The student said "Great. See you at nine." Immediately after he got off the phone, he shook awake his roommate, and said, "Buddy, you gotta show me how to play golf!" It turns out that when he put "golf" on his resume, he meant that he liked to watch it on TV—*not that he knew how to play it. He didn't.* The roommate took him through a few basics, and the following day, the student showed up at the partner's office, and drove him to the club. To put it mildly, the very first hole was proof that the student had no idea what he was doing—he shot about 150, with bits of sod flying everywhere. The partner was *livid,* questioning his integrity in very colorful terms. To make it even worse, on the way back to the office, the student's car got a flat tire—and he didn't know how to change it. The beet-red partner had to get out of the car, in his golf clothes, and change the tire!

Think how different the outcome would have been if this student had known what you know now—play golf before you go! (And, of course, don't lie—or mislead!—on your resume.)

#3: *Get your personal life in order.*

Many employers suggest that if you're married, you should let your spouse know that you may be working as hard as, or harder, as a new lawyer than you did as a law student. And make sure that you have a good, reliable dry cleaner, barber or hairdresser, and mechanic lined up. If you have children, make sure that you have not just day care but contingency plans in place for when your primary source breaks down—as it inevitably will. *No* employer expects your personal life to run like clockwork, but when you start, you don't want to give your employer the idea that you can't control your personal life, if there's any possible way to avoid it.

#4: *Recognize that the* pace *of your life is going to change dramatically.*

Your reaction to the change of pace from school to work depends *very* much on whether you've ever worked full-time before, and what kind of job you take. If you've worked during the day and gone to school at night—jeez, *anything* would seem like a vacation after that! And if you go to an employer with regular hours—state's attorneys offices, state attorney generals' offices, some government agencies, and some law firms, for instance—you may actually find yourself with—dare I say it?—time on your hands. You'll have evenings and weekends free, without the burden of reading assignments. Missouri's Gerald Beecham says that "law school can consume everything! Your job may leave you with more free time. Some people take advantage of the time to get involved in the community. Others party. Some people work all the time not because they *have* to, but because they're so used to being busy."

So you may be pleasantly surprised, but the word I heard from most employers is that new law school graduates find that the demands on their time are much greater at work than it was in school—even though the *perception* of most of us, when we're in law school full-time, is that we just couldn't be more busy. However, even as a full-time student it's rare to have more than four or so classes in a day, taking up no more than about five hours of your time. That leaves breaks, and even though you've got reading assignments and presumably extracurriculars, you still have a *lot* of control over your own time. At work, you don't. It's a straight-through day. Most people find that that takes a lot more stamina than they're used to from law school.

DO'S AND DON'TS #5 THROUGH 24: HOW TO HANDLE DAY ONE . . . AND THE SEVERAL WEEKS AFTER THAT!

When you're facing your first day, there are a few things you need to do. But the first thing you need to do is to accept the fact that you're going to be nervous. Maybe very nervous. And why not? A new job is a big responsibility. You want to make the best possible impression. What do you do about the knots tying and re-tying themselves in your stomach? Accept them. As Boston University's Betsy Armour says, "It's so difficult to start! Embrace your nervousness and channel it appropriately. Look at the bright side of nervousness—it makes you alert and energetic, and those are two excellent qualities."

#5: Take a deep breath, smile—and make an excellent first impression.

Experts differ about how long it takes us to make a decision about people. Some claim it's four minutes. Others argue it's more like 30 seconds. No matter how long it is—it isn't weeks or even hours. As St. Louis' Wendy Werner says, "You don't get a second chance to make a first impression. You get a lot of breaks from a lot of people if you're perceived as nice from the start."

Be aware that you're being judged from the get-go. As Boston University's Betsy Armour advises, "When you're the fledgling, you need to have your guard up a little bit. Be *aware* of the image you're creating. You don't want to be a noodge or a nerd. Be polite, be friendly. Smile!"

#6: Be wary of people who are overfriendly.

Whether at school or at work, you've probably run into people that the English call "mixers." Instigators. Malcontents. People who are only happy when they're roiling the waters. Why am I mentioning this to you in the context of your first day at work? It's because these kinds of bad seeds tend to latch onto newcomers immediately. As Northern Illinois' Mary Obrzut says, "When you're new you need to keep your antenna up!

Margaret Mead used to say that when she went into a new environment, she didn't pay attention to the first people out to meet the boat. The ones with power were the ones standing on the shore, watching." She adds that "People who reach out to you first may not have power. On the way from the 'boat' to the 'shore,' be *very* kind to the people who meet you—the recruiting coordinator, first supervisor, secretary, librarian—but reserve your judgments on who to associate with until you've had more time to observe."

#7: Introduce yourself to everyone. Don't closet yourself!

When you start a new job, there's a point where the basic 'here's-the-office' tour is over, and you're in your office. *Don't* be tempted to waste 'down time.' Instead, roam the halls introducing yourself to every lawyer and staff person in sight. This kind of initiative is particularly welcomed.

#8: Figure out the food chain. Find out who can give you work, who to go to with overloads, and who will be evaluating you.

Maybe this is all the same person. Maybe not. When it comes to finding out who can give you work, what you're doing is to "stop the problem of an out-of-control workload" before it starts, says Quinnipiac's Susan Spalter. Lawyers who overload you with assignments frequently don't realize what else you've got to do. A point person to contact when that happens helps you handle the situation before it gets too crazy.

And for evaluations—while you want to do your best on every assignment, you'd be crazy not to be sure you make the right impression on your evaluators. What many new lawyers are surprised to find out is that it's not just partners who evaluate them, but senior associates as well.

#9: Follow the SHAW Principle when you start a new job: "Shut Up and Watch." Things to observe . . .

Some people would call this "culture." No matter what you call it, it's *extremely* important. As St. Louis' Wendy Werner says, "Hard work and being a team player aren't guarantees of success—you're crazy to think so. Keep one and a half eyes on your work, and one ear to the ground, all the time."

What's the general tone of the office? Is it prim and proper, with nobody saying good morning *ever?* Or is it jovial, with people bounding in and slapping each other on the back?

Is the organization big on community events, or does it focus on the bottom dollar?

Does the organization put a premium on playing pranks on each other, or does it abhor silliness? Some places have newsletters where they obtain and publish silly childhood photos of people who work there. Many offices feature lawyers' children's artwork. These kinds of things indicate a light-heartedness, where an austere setting and dark wood paneling don't.

Does everybody work late? If they do, you should, too. If you don't, you may miss what they're doing together.

Do people eat lunch at their desks, or do they go out together?

What do people do together outside of work? Do they work out together? Play softball? Golf?

As Minnesota's Sue Gainen advises, "Figure out what's going on by carefully looking around you. Don't isolate yourself and don't hang out exclusively in the company of support staff or your age peers."

#10: DO ask the business equivalent of "Mommy, where do babies come from?" Understand what's expected of you regarding business development (on the private side) or grant writing/fundraising (on the public side).

There are many jobs in this book that don't require either business development or grant writing—government jobs, judicial clerkships, corporate jobs—and that's generally considered a benefit of those jobs. But if you're in private practice or a public interest job that requires that you write grants or otherwise raise funds, Minnesota's Sue Gainen recommends that you get a handle on what's expected of you from the get-go. You can *never* express too early an interest in the way your organization's funds come in. St. Louis' Wendy Werner adds that "If you're in the private sector, you've got to think about the business aspect of practice. Ask where clients come from, how long they've been there, what business comes from them. You're responsible for your own career development!"

#11: DON'T be too visible, for the wrong reasons.

The desire to stand out at work can lead some of us to behavior that isn't advisable. Especially if you work for a large employers, you might be struck by a need to be noticed, and let that lure you into inadvisable behavior—being the loudest or the class clown or being the most outrageous at firm events. It's not a good idea, at least not at first. You'll likely alienate more people than you'll attract. The Kentucky firm Waller Lansden advises new associates to "Avoid being the funniest or the most clever or too visible early on." Be quietly efficient and get yourself noticed through excellent work product, enthusiasm for what you do and taking the initiative on projects. You want to be recognized as a future leader—not a potential member of the 'Beer Bong Hall of Fame.'

#12: DO conform your hours to what's regarded as acceptable.

It's hard to know without actually working in a place what kinds of hours are suitable. It's not necessary to be there when your boss gets in and stay later than (s)he does, but as one firm's recruiting coordinator told me, "You *should* know what's acceptable, what's expected." The way to do this is to ask colleagues flat out what's appropriate. It may be that you're expected to stay well past dinner every night. And it may be that "face time" on weekends is the norm. One lawyer told me that his firm expected associates to work 12-hour days, from eight in the morning until about eight at night. One associate worked from 4 a.m. to 4 p.m. so she could go home and ride her horses. She was dinged on her evaluations for not being there four hours a day!

The moral: pattern yourself after what everybody else does when you start. Setting your own hours is not an area where you want to stand out.

#13: DO figure out who really has power, and cultivate relationships with them.

You may think that the person at the top of the work pyramid is the one who has the power. That's not necessarily true! St. Louis' Wendy Werner advises that you "pay attention to signals, overt and covert. Who's on the management committee? Who are the predominant business-getters? What department generates the most revenue? Who loses the most and least associates? What are opportunities and risks depending on who you're doing work for? Who's getting clients—and who's losing them?" Connecticut's Diane Ballou advises that you "See which partners do things together, see who's in whose office. Ask secretaries. Normally, power is in the protégé of a senior partner. Keep your ears open!"

#14: DO quickly figure out what kinds of activities 'count'—the kinds of activities that get junior lawyers noticed in a positive way.

As I talked with law firms, I was struck by how different they can be, in the sense that when I asked "What makes a junior lawyer a star?" I got *very* different answers. Of course, excellent work product is always the baseline requirement. But the way you poke your head above the crowd otherwise depends on what your particular employer values. Some places put an emphasis on bar involvement and community leadership. Others like to see associates giving seminars to potential clients. Still others put an emphasis on charity and pro bono work. For instance, one firm raved about an associate who spent time updating the firm's practice manual. Another talked about associates who stand out by putting on various in-house seminars. Another pointed to an associate who had started a recycling drive, bringing the firm a lot of positive local media coverage in the process. Yet another talked about an associate who took it upon herself to summarize all key state court decisions and e-mail them to the entire firm. At yet another firm, an associate positioned himself as a key member of the recruiting team; he volunteers for all recruiting events and makes a special effort every day to ensure that the summer associates get to depositions, closings, and the like.

What's the pattern here? There isn't one. What all of these associates have done is to identify areas where they can distinguish themselves at work. What you might want to do is to take these kinds of ideas to a more senior colleague, someone whose opinion you trust, or even a long-time secretary, and ask their advice on the kinds of things they think the firm would appreciate. They'll be flattered by your question—and you'll get valuable insights into how to make yourself stand out.

#15: DO dress appropriately to the organization. As a new lawyer, your attire should fit in, not stand out.

As Minnesota's Susan Gainen advises, "*Look* at what people wear. Is Armani in or out? Do women wear slacks? Know as *much* as you can before you buy. Do *not,* in your first year, wear *anything* that will make people talk about you."

Be aware that every organization is different in terms of its "uniform." As Northern Illinois' Mary Obrzut says, "You can't dress like a Junior Leaguer if you're a public defender." And when it comes to casual day, "Different employers have different concepts of 'casual.' It's unlikely to be swimsuits, cut-offs and flip-flops."

It could be that you, like me, are "wardrobe challenged." I often tell people that I find it very easy to dress because I am not hampered by good taste. That works for a writer, but not for a lawyer. "You can't wear brown shoes with blue suits!" says Tulane's Kristin Flierl. Instead, if you're really at a loss, solicit the help of someone at work, who dresses well. Ask them to go shopping with you, and ask for their stylistic help. They'll be flattered—and you'll look great!

#16: DON'T adopt a 'monkey-see-monkey-do' work style—make an effort to understand why things are done the way they're done.

Law isn't practiced in a vacuum. It's a service business set up to most expeditiously meet the needs of clients. Every client is different, every problem is different, and whether you're a public or private lawyer, attorneys you deal with on the other side will require different approaches, because everybody's got different buttons to push. That's why it's unwise to adopt an approach by rote, without understanding *why* things are done a certain way. As Seattle firm Hillis Clark advises, "Avoid the temptation to adopt a 'monkey-see-monkey-do' practice style. Figure out the reasons *why* things are done a certain way, so that you can make appropriate adjustments given the facts and circumstances of the case or transaction. Many new associates just parrot what they see other lawyers doing, without regard for whether or not it makes sense, or is the most efficient course. Develop your *own* style, based on your *own* strengths."

#17: If you summer clerked for your new employer, DO recognize that, like Dorothy, you aren't in Kansas anymore. DON'T assume that your permanent job will be just like your summer clerkship.

Summer clerking for an employer, *any* employer, is a great idea. It makes it much easier to get the inside skinny on getting your career there off to a great start, and you've had an extensive opportunity to get an idea of office politics, expectations, power structure, and the like.

However, as Boston University's Betsy Armour cautions you, "Even if you're a former summer associate, you're starting your professional career *now*. It's *very* different! There are different stakes. Your status is different. As a summer associate, they want to impress and wine and dine you to lure you back. It's a honeymoon. As a full-time associate, you do have an advantage—you know how things work. But you're at a different level. You have to view *this* as the beginning of your professional life."

Added: I've pointed out before that summer clerking gives you a serious leg-up when you start. Ideally you know who's who and what's what. But you have to be careful to realize that permanent work is *much* different than a summer clerkship. As Kathy Biehl writes in the *ABA Journal,* "The transition from summer clerk to first year associate can be jolting. You aren't courted anymore. Everybody has work to do." And Mark Chouteau in the *Texas Bar Journal* says that "The summer clerk is left with the impression that the firm works eight-hour days, pays for lunch every day, and that time deadlines are easily forgiven, as well as a profound belief that a good time is always had by all." I'm not sure if *that's* universally true, but it *is* true that when you are a "permanent" employee, the honeymoon is over. You're soon to be the person who assigns the work to summer associates and makes sure they have a great experience. You're the "parent." So if you developed any summer-suitable habits—overlooking deadlines, leaving earlier than the permanent lawyers—get over them *now*. You're the work equivalent of a grown-up.

#18: DO recognize that what you do as a lawyer is *very different from law school,* in terms if consequences of your decisions.

In the vast majority of law jobs, "You've got responsibility for other people's lives!" as Oregon's Jane Steckbeck points out. "The *seriousness* of it startles a lot of people. If you make a mistake, you could destroy somebody's hope. That creates very real pressure." Employers point out that new law school graduates will often experience "an overwhelming sense of 'Oh my God,' this is *real*! Look at what I'm *doing*!"

While there will be a safety net for you (unless you become a sole practitioner), for many employers you'll be on the front lines very quickly. In many prosecutor's jobs, government employers, and public interest agencies, you'll have your own case load from Day One. That's a tremendous change from law school, where no matter *how* you argued, no one lost money and no one went to jail. Real life entails real—and sometimes serious—consequences.

#19: DON'T assume that because law school is over, it's time to relax, because the hard part is over.

Man oh man—this *should* be true, shouldn't it? After the three-year grind of law school (or four years, if you went evenings), you *want* a break. You *deserve* one. But if you go straight to work, you're not going to *get* one. As one employer described it, "When you're done with law school, you've only run the first leg of the marathon!"

As I described in the "prep" section, it *may* be that your job entails less time than law school did—but that's very unlikely. Instead, the pace, the structure, the pressures of your professional days will likely be more demanding than law school was. One law firm told me that "Too many law students come to law firms in general with an inflated sense of entitlement, an unrealistic idea of how hard they will have to work and the extent to which they'll have to take responsibility for their own professional development. As one associate said, 'Work and life at a law firm will take up a significantly larger portion of your life than law school did.'"

#20: DO recognize that if you're a new lawyer, you've got a lot to learn. There's no place for arrogance.

Did you see "Men in Black?" If so, you may remember the scene where Will Smith joins the MiB, and as he and Tommy Lee Jones are in the elevator going to MiB headquarters, Smith says, "There's a couple of things I want you to understand. First off, *you* chose *me*. So you recognize the skills." Tommy Lee Jones calmly replies, "Whatever you say, Slick. But I need to tell you something about all of those skills. As of right now, they mean precisely *dick*."

To some extent, that summarizes the difference between being a law school graduate and being a successful lawyer. As Chicago's Suzanne Mitchell says, "Success doesn't depend on what you were good at in school! People interact differently." Hamline's Joyce Laher adds that "A lot of your first or second year is whistling in the dark, and you've got to face that."

Arrogance is a cardinal sin for new lawyers. As one large firm associate sighed, "When you get out of school, you don't know jack." An in-house lawyer added that "You aren't as smart as you think you are! In law school we are taught that we are privy to a highly specialized body of knowledge—that we are special and brilliant people. The truth is that you have a *lot* to learn from people and experiences. Be humble! You'll learn more, be respected more, and have more friends!" And a public defender bluntly stated that "When you come to work, drop the egotistical b.s.! From the day we were accepted at law school we all thought we were just a little bit better than the average person. Wrong!"

You've got a difficult balancing act at work. You've got to be confident but humble. I'm not pretending that's easy, but it's a tightrope you *have* to walk. The fact that you're there *at all* suggests the employer thinks you have the skills to succeed. You don't have to hit people over the head with your status or your credentials. It can *actively* hurt you. As one large firm put it, "Once that 'arrogance' label has been placed on you, it's hard to succeed. Don't let it happen!"

#21: DON'T believe that the person who works the longest hours looks the best.

Not true! It *is* important to do what's *expected* of you. Some offices require "face time" on weekends, and associates show up to sort their mail, if nothing else. Different offices, different departments, all have their own norms. I've told you elsewhere the importance of fitting in with those norms. The point here is not to kill yourself racking up hours if you learn from older associates that that doesn't impress. The time you spend at the office may be better spent getting visibility in other activities—community involvement, for instance. Don't kill yourself if you don't have to!

#22: DO take copious notes. Put everything possible on paper, except complaints about other people.

Northern Illinois' Mary Obrzut advises you to "cover your ass and paper the world!" From keeping a case log to maintaining a slavish devotion to your calendar, it can help you in myriad ways to document your professional life. You'll prove to future employers the *precise* skills you have by quantifying what you've done, you'll protect your billable hours from unscrupulous superiors who may want to "appropriate" them, and you'll guard yourself against malpractice claims.

You should *not*, however, put complaints about people in writing. Whether it's placing blame or complaining about a difficult colleague, these are things that should be handled orally. You do *not* want a paper trail of complaints to follow you!

#23: DO recognize that when you start a new job, you'll feel overwhelmed at first, because law has a very steep learning curve.

What you've got with a law degree is the equivalent of playing the game *Pole Position* and then going out and getting into a real car. You've got the right instincts, but you've got a lot to learn. Don't worry about it! Every single person you work with, everyone you meet, was in your shoes once. They might seem comfortable now, but they were *you*. Brooklyn's Joan King recounts that "The first week of practice, I was doing a closing. I was asked to affix a corporate seal to a document. Someone handed me a corporate seal, and I sat there looking at it, dumbfounded. I didn't know how to put it together!" She adds that "Even if you summer clerked, there's going to be a *lot* that's new to you." As Loyola/New Orleans' Pam Occhipinti says, "Consider yourself an intern. You're there to learn—and you will!" She adds that "The first year or two, everything seems to take longer than you think it should, and you don't feel like you know what you're doing sometimes. That feeling goes away. It takes time." The recruiting coordinator at a large firm added that "You'll never know as much as you wish you did, but with time, it all gets easier and less nerve-wracking."

#24: DO accept the likelihood that you'll face a "sophomore slump" after six months or so on the job. It doesn't mean you hate your work.

Boston University's Betsy Armour recounts that as recruiting director at a large firm, she remembers that "new associates were pretty ebullient for the first six months. It was around February, after six months, that the reality would sink in. The first three to six month mark—it suddenly hits you, the profound nature of your career commitment." She attributes this to the fact that "It's hard to break out of that 'nine month' mode from school. There are no new semesters, no summer vacation. 'Depression' might be too strong a word, but it's a sinking feeling. It *can,* and *does,* happen. Don't worry about it—it will pass."

DO'S AND DON'TS #25 THROUGH 30: HOW TO MAKE YOUR LIFE IMMENSELY EASIER BY FOLLOWING SIMPLE ORGANIZATIONAL TIPS!

It's important to be perceived as handling your time well, and keeping a handle on everything you have to do. Any job will have its own unique set of organizational requirements. As a prosecutor, you'll have to have a method for keeping hundreds of files straight. As an associate, you'll have to juggle projects and keep track of your time. Missed deadlines, and a perception that you can't put your hands on information or that your work life is generally chaos is an obvious no-no.

#25: DO recognize that if you want a life outside of work, you need to be organized at work.

Time that you spend looking for files can't be billed. To minimize your time at work, you need to be able to find what you're looking for, *stat.*

There are all kinds of books written about how to organize your work life. Some of the pointers in the next few "Do's" and "Don'ts" offer you some tips specific to being a new lawyer. But to some extent, your system will be uniquely your own. My personal system consists of laying every piece of paper I have on every available surface in my house. On a book like this, you can imagine how my house looks—I have to *jump* from the doorway to my desk. In fact, I had friends over to dinner during the latter stages of working on this book. One of them calmly surveyed the living room, looked at me, and said: "Auntie Em! Auntie Em! It looks like a *cyclone* went through here!" OK, OK, it doesn't look very professional, and in an office with other people I probably wouldn't get away with it. But it *works,* and you've got to find the system that works for *you.*

#26: DO pay attention *at orientation, no matter how boring and unimportant it seems.*

Boston University's Betsy Armour encourages you to "take advantage of every orientation opportunity. They may seem tedious, or overwhelming, but they *will* afford you some training, like navigating the office, billing time, those crucial variables. Ask questions. Find out from layers of stuff what's most important, since it may not be immediately obvious." She adds that "Learning to manage and record time is *crucial* early on."

#27: DO begin a lifelong commitment to your calendar. Keep a detailed date book.

Keep track of the dates assignments are made and due. Note dates and times of meetings to attend. Obviously, record any court dates and client meetings. And include appointments and commitments from your personal life, to ensure there are no accidental conflicts or overlaps that might make you bow out of anything at the last minute.

Refer to the calendar *every* day. Your image as a reliable person depends *heavily* on keeping track of every time commitment you have.

And incidentally, if you rely on an electronic organizer—not only are they handy but they come with excellent solitaire games, by the way—be sure to download the information in it to your computer on a frequent basis, or keep a parallel hard-copy of everything in it. That way, if the internal battery on your organizer runs down, you'll lose all of the information in it, and *that* could be a disaster.

#28: DO keep a detailed "case log" for every case and project you do, as you do it.

There are at least three good reasons to keep a "case log." First of all, life happens. Projects and cases you start may be interrupted for a million reasons. If your work is organized so that another attorney can easily step in and take the reins, you'll be applauded for making everyone's life easier.

Second, senior associates have been known to "steal" billable hours. It ain't pretty, and it ain't common, but it happens. You can't prove what work was yours without a case log.

And third—and an even *less* attractive thought!—is this. If you're sued for malpractice, your standard of care is at issue. A "case log" showing exactly what you did will help establish your conduct in the case, and ideally get you off the hook.

How should you organize your case log? Loyola/New Orleans' Pam Occhipinti suggests one means of logging cases: "In a notebook, on the right hand side of each page, list documents involved with the case—motions, memos, briefs, pleadings, letters, everything. On the left hand side, write a detailed log of everything you do on a case: what you were told, who you talked to—summarize comments."

#29: DO keep a file of every single thing you do, to quantify your work experience.

When you go to look for *another* job in the future, keeping close track of the projects you're doing now will enable you to aim higher than your strict chronological experience suggests. Keep track of what kinds of issues you've researched, the motions you've argued, the cases you've handled and the issues they raised. You want to compile a quantifiable list of skills you will bring to the table in the future.

#30: DO create a "form file" of your own.

Loyola/New Orleans' Pam Occhipinti recommends that you establish your own form file, and you should include in it any forms that you have used. For one thing, this gives you easy, and instant, access to forms you've used before. And for another, "Because it's *yours,* you can take it with you when you change jobs. if you rely solely on your employer's form file, it stays when you leave."

DO'S AND DON'TS #31 THROUGH 35: GETTING A HANDLE ON BILLABLE HOURS—INCLUDING SQUEEZING OUT MORE BILLABLES WITHOUT SPENDING AN EXTRA MINUTE WORKING.

#31: DO recognize the difference between what time is billable and what time is not billable.

As Thomas Cooley's Bernice Davenport says, "Most new associates don't understand billable hours." When you start to work with a firm, *ask* precisely what their concept of billable hours includes—different firms treat billables differently. For instance, some firms consider pro bono hours "billable" for the purpose of reaching minimum billable hours goals, while of course these hours aren't going to be charged to a client. As a rule of thumb:

a. If you are doing "firm administration" work like writing the newsletter, working on a committee, interviewing students or doing marketing, although that time is not billable, you *should* record it.

b. Use your time wisely. Don't bill 12 hours on a general denial that your secretary is trained to prepare.

c. When in doubt, bill your time. Tell your assigning lawyer exactly what you worked on if you have any concerns, so (s)he can edit the bill for the client. Don't put pressure on yourself as a junior associate to make billing decisions.

#32: DON'T think you'll impress your superiors by padding your billable hours.

It's easy to slip into a mindset that says that the more time you consider "billable," the more your firm will earn from you, and the better you'll look. That's just not true. As one large firm advises, "Don't view billable hours as your chief purpose in life. The ultimate goal is to add value to the firm's client services. Stacking up billables in the wrong case is a negative, not a positive."

#33: DON'T delude yourself into thinking that every hour at the office can—or will—be billable.

There's just no way to bill every moment you spend at the office. One of the rudest surprises new lawyers get is to realize that billing 40 hours a week doesn't mean working 9-to-5. Instead, recognize that there are going to be hours spent that just aren't billable. Whether it's due to recruiting or lunch or bar functions or firm activities or just casual conversation—exercising the people skills that are so important to your advancement!—there's going to be time no client will pay for. Typically, a good ratio of total time to billable hours is 10 to eight. That is, for every 10 hours you spend at the office, expect to spend eight on billable time. Barring special circumstances—like working on firm administration or pro bono work—you're just not going to look good if you have 160 hours in a month, 60 of which are billable and 100 of which are not.

#34: DO recognize how to increase your billables without working one minute more.

Here's the key: record activities precisely and promptly. Before you start on something, mark down the time you're starting, and when you're done, record the time you finished. *Don't* wait until the end of the day to jot down what you did. The fact is, keeping track of time as you go gives you higher and more accurate numbers than waiting until the end of the day. Why? You'll forget some activities and underestimate the time you spent. It's the same thing that happens to overweight people who are asked what they eat in an average day. They forget about the broken cookies they "cleaned up" standing in front of the pantry. But when they keep a food diary of every bite that goes into their mouths, the truth comes out. You'll find the same thing with billable hours— you're cheating yourself out of billables if you delay recording your time.

#35: If your firm has a minimum billable hours requirement, DON'T shoot for the bare minimum.

I'm not telling you to double the minimum billable requirement. But it's a mistake to aim only for the bare minimum, because something unexpected might come up that drags you away from billable work, personally or professionally. It is true that in your first couple of years at most firms, your billable hours aren't taken as seriously as they are later on. But your particular employer may take them *very* seriously, and may be very put out if you don't meet the minimum requirement. Aim a little higher, so that you have a "cushion" for anything unexpected.

The reason it's important to meet minimum billables doesn't solely focus on how you'll be perceived. Rather, many firms calculate their minimum billables by looking at how much it takes to pay salaries, support staff, rent, other overheads, and allowing a 15 to 20% margin for uncollectables. They divide that by hourly rates, and come up with a break-even point. That's often what the minimum billables requirement represents. While a large firm isn't going to rise and sink on your particular hours, for a smaller firm, if you want it to survive, meet your minimum billables!

DO'S AND DON'TS #36 THROUGH 64: HOW TO CRUSH WRITING ASSIGNMENTS AND RESEARCH PROJECTS— AND GIVE THEM WHAT THEY REALLY WANT, BUT WILL HARDLY EVER TELL YOU.

Virtually every law firm in America values "writing well" as it's #1 requirement. That's also true for judicial clerkships, and for in-house corporate jobs. If you have a heavily people-oriented job—like being an assistant state's attorney, or a public defender—you'll probably do a lot less writing. But the fact is, for the majority of law-related jobs, your writing ability will be noticed, and it will have a strong impact on your success.

Let's talk about *exactly* how to handle every writing assignment and research project that you get, so that you ensure that it shows you off to the best possible advantage.

#36: DO make sure you aren't trying to "shovel smoke." Determine exactly what's being asked of you, in terms of basic facts, form, deadlines, on-line research parameters, and time estimates.

You can't possibly perform well if you enter projects blindly. To lay the foundation for excellent work on every writing assignment, you need to keep the following in mind:

#37: DO bring a pad and pen every time a more senior attorney asks to see you.

The best way to ensure you get all the information you need on any assignment is to *write it down.* This serves three purposes:

a. It impresses the assigning attorney with your foresight.

b. It minimizes the questions you will need to ask later on; you can refer back to your notes rather than rushing back to the assigning attorney for a recap.

c. It gives you a document to refer back to should there be a dispute later on over what you were told or asked to do.

#38: DO make sure you get all of the basic facts—and recognize that you may not get them all the first time around!

Florida's Ann Skalaski points out that if a client were telling you about a problem, you wouldn't hesitate to ask questions to flesh out the facts. But when it's a more senior attorney who's outlining a problem, you're likely to assume that they're giving you all of the relevant facts. That may not be true! Treat the assigning attorney as you would a client—ask questions to give yourself a complete picture of the problem you're being asked to handle. If you ask for something that's not relevant, no harm done; and if you aren't sure, you can always preface your question with, "In advance of researching this I'm not sure this is relevant, but does it matter whether . . . ?" It will show you're *thinking,* and that's always a positive.

#39: DO ask the context of the case, so you can propose other solutions.

As I discuss a little later on, under #54, the way to establish yourself as a star on the rise is to look beyond your assignments to solutions. If you don't know the context of the case, what it is the client is trying to accomplish, you won't be able to propose alternatives. So *ask* about the ultimate goal of your research, in case the specific route the assigning attorney has put you on doesn't pan out.

#40: DO ask the purpose of the writing, if the assigning attorney doesn't tell you.

Is the purpose of your research to explain? Or is it supposed to persuade? The way you present your work will differ depending on what it's *point* is, so make sure you ask.

#41: DO ask what form *your finished work product should take.*

Does your assigning attorney want a treatise? A brief memo? A casual oral report? Boston University's Betsy Armour says that "Lawyers often complain that law school graduates tend to overwork assignments. *Ask* what they're looking for. You may find its a bulleted three-page memo, not a phone book-length exhaustive survey of the field." Brooklyn's Joan King adds that "It's important not to let your nerves overcome you, no matter *how* senior they are. Listen for clues! For instance, if a lawyer thinks 'I don't know if this approach will work,' they just want a quick-and-dirty answer, not a thoughtful, analyzed paper." Brooklyn's Laurie Beck adds that "Stories are legion about associates who get pilloried for doing too much— 'I didn't want a 10-page memo, I wanted you to *tell* me the answer!'"

#42: DO ask how long *the assignor expects the project to take you.*

This will give you an accurate estimate of how much detail your assigning attorney expects. Brooklyn's Joan King recounts her experience as a new associate, when "I got a complicated matrimonial appeal. I took it seriously, and put in a lot of time on it. The senior partner got annoyed, because he couldn't bill my time for all of those hours."

Oregon's Merv Loya agrees, recommending that "Even if you get an informal assignment, get a sense of how much time they want you to put in. If you put in 50 hours on a 20-hour project, or 20 on a 10-hour project, the attorney handling the billing will hit the roof. I've seen it happen!"

One caveat: the time schedule they give you may be unrealistic, and as I suggest in just a moment, it's always good to give periodic "progress reports" to your assigning attorney. Many senior associates say that projects take anywhere from three to five times as long as assigning attorneys think. So if you seem to be taking longer than the time estimate, don't panic, and don't come down on yourself. The original estimate may have been highly unrealistic!

#43: DO ask your assigning attorney if there are any sources they think you should start with.

It may be that the assigning attorney has a specific source, or case, in mind, and that by asking what it is you can save yourself hours of effort. Or there may be a form file or memo file you can reference to avoid reinventing the wheel. As Georgetown's Marilyn Tucker advises, "Some people won't like it when you ask. Different supervisors will give different levels of detail willingly."

#44: When you do a project for an assigning attorney for the first time, DO ask for samples of prior work that they like.

Georgetown's Marilyn Tucker advises that when you do a maiden assignment for an assigning attorney, you say to them, "I'd appreciate it if you could share with me projects you've written, or things other people have written for you, that are acceptable to you." As she says, "This shows a willingness to get things done right!"

#45: DO ask how much—and if—you can rely on on-line research.

Brooklyn's Laurie Beck advises that "In an era of Lexis and Westlaw, *ask* before you use it. When you're in law school you get used to it, because it's free," but as Boston University's Betsy Armour points out, "In a law firm, the clock is running!" Laurie Beck says that "People in your firm may not think to warn you *against* using it—even though it's easy to run up a $2,000 bill! Remember that in a firm, *everything* you do is charged to a client. So *ask*: Can I use on-line research, and if so, for how long?"

#46: At the end of receiving an assignment, DO reiterate the basic parameters to ensure you've got them right.

Brooklyn's Laurie Beck says that when the assigning attorney is finished giving you the assignment, you should say, "You want ABC, by X date, in Y form (*e.g.*, a memo)?" She says that "By repeating it back you get assignments and expectations straight, in terms of form *and* time. Remember that lawyers are busy and not always clear!"

#47: DO tactfully admit it if you find yourself lost in the middle of receiving an assignment.

Brooklyn's Joan King has advice for the extreme situation when you're getting an assignment, and halfway through you realize that you have *no clue* what's going on. "No matter what, you've got to leave the room knowing what to do, where to start," she says. "You need to tactfully convey that you're lost. Ask something like, 'Would you mind going over this aspect again?'" She adds that "You won't get any brownie points for it, but it's better to avert disaster *now*."

#48: DON'T believe the old saw that "there's no such thing as a stupid question." As long as you have all the basic elements of the assignment in hand, do a little research, prepare a list of questions and get them answered all at once, rather than return chock-a-block for one question at a time.

It's true that every good employer stresses the importance of asking questions, and one of the hallmarks of great employers is that they have an 'open door' policy that *encourages* questions. But be that as it may, we all remember the scene in the movie *Animal House,* where Pinto and Flounder go to the Delta house during fraternity rush week, and Flounder walks over to a table where a group of guys are playing poker, and asks: "You guys playing cards?" Duh. We all intuitively know that the saying "there's no such thing as a stupid question" is pure dung.

So where do you draw the line? It *is* important to ask questions. I've just been telling you about questions you *have* to ask—basic facts, form, deadlines, those kinds of things are things you *have* to know. Lawyers also love to talk about strategy, insights on opposing lawyers and on judges—there are a whole *slew* of questions that are appropriate to ask. But there's a limit. Boston University's Betsy Armour acknowledges the "slippery slope" with questions. "You don't want to seem to lack confidence," she says. Kentucky's Drusilla Bakert adds that "There's a fine line between checking with people, and bugging them. You can't be in their office every two minutes. You're not showing your eagerness. You're annoying them."

So what *should* you do? Drusilla Bakert recommends that you "Read through your notes, make a list of questions, and *then* ask, 'I have a couple of questions. When would be a good time to talk about it?" Suffolk's Jim Whitters adds that "You don't want the reputation, 'He's always asking questions.' Some people *do* see you as dumb for asking. Ask around to see who will welcome questions, and who will be your worst critic." For people who *don't* welcome questions, try alternatives like seeking advice from other people who've worked with them before, and/or turning to their secretary for pointers.

#49: DO try alternative strategies for handling unclear assigning attorneys.

When you're faced with an assigning attorney who is simply incapable of giving a clear assignment—it happens!—Georgetown's Marilyn Tucker suggests that you try one of two approaches:

a. Say something like, "I need some time to sort through this assignment, and I don't want to waste your time. Would you mind if I put the issue, as I see it, on paper and ask you to take a minute to review it before I begin my research?" This question gives you the permission you need to return to the assigning attorney's office for clarification.

b. You can devote a limited number of hours to the project as you understand it and then leave a draft clearly marked as such on the assigning attorney's desk, with a note saying, "This is where I am with this issue after spending 5 hours on it. Would you like me to continue in this direction? If so, here are my questions . . . "

#50: No matter how perfectly you believe you interpreted the assignment, DO give a "mini report" early in your research to ensure that you're on track.

As you firm up your approach, check *briefly* with the assigning attorney to make sure you're going the right way. Many employers point out that charging off in the wrong direction is a big mistake that many new associates make. One firm pointed out that "New associates miss the connection that their time is money and the client doesn't appreciate paying for—or the partner doesn't appreciate writing off!—hours of unnecessary research, when a short meeting or quick phone call could have clarified the issue."

#51: DON'T "rush to judgment." Assume that assigning attorneys won't give you projects for which the answer is obvious.

When you practice law, you aren't taking the Multistate Bar Exam. There isn't a right answer you can fathom in 40 seconds. Many employers lament occasions where associates assume issues are easier than they really are. This is the flipside of overworking issues. As one law firm advises, "Often a partner will ask a new associate to research an issue which the associate thinks has an obvious answer." As a rule of thumb, "When an attorney with experience requests research, the answer is usually not so obvious."

#52: DO interpret cases and statutes carefully.

Employers lament that new associates often "fail to appreciate that a lot may be riding on a casual interpretation of a case or statute." Be *precise* in your analysis. Read carefully. If a case cites another case as standing for a given proposition, *read* that other case *before* you cite it—cases have been known to mis-cite others!

As a summer clerk, I had a research assignment that involved exactly this problem. My assigning attorney asked me to find case support for the proposition that a school teacher who fails to perform hall duty has gone on strike. He swore up and down that there was a case that stood for this proposition. I searched every possible avenue, including slip opinions, and couldn't unearth any case that made this particular point. The assigning attorney couldn't tell me the name of the case, and so I eventually took him xeroxed copies of every case on point, so he could glance through the names for one that might jog his memory. Halfway through the pile, he pointed to a case and said, "*That's* it!"

As it turns out, the case he pointed to had a line which said something along the lines of, "The case L v. L stands for the proposition that a teacher refusing to do hall duty is on strike." I had gone back and looked up L v. L, and in fact it didn't stand for that idea at all—it said just the opposite! I realize this is Research Skills 101, but had I been in a hurry, it would have been easy to take the Cliffs Notes-ish approach and rely on the first case's summary of the L v. L opinion. I would have looked like an *idiot* had that mistake appeared in a brief. There are plenty of chances to look like an idiot—I discovered most of them in my summer clerkship—but don't let sloppy research be *your* route to failure!

#53: DON'T fall victim to the "Marbury v. Madison" Syndrome— clients don't pay for history lessons!

If you're a judicial clerk, sure, history is important. If you're an academic, history is important. But if you're in any other work context—a government lawyer, a public interest lawyer, a corporate lawyer, or you're in private practice—it's *not*. Georgetown's Marilyn Tucker says that "When you're given an assignment, it's for a *client*. To answer an issue for a *client*. It's not a Law Review article. It's not a treatise. They don't want history. They want answers to questions like, 'Am I going to have to pay this fine or not?' 'Am I liable?' 'Can I win?'" She calls the tendency to fall in love with your research the "Marbury v. Madison" Syndrome, because people don't need to know what happened all the way back to the original recognition of judicial review. Wake Forest's Bill Barrett adds, "Remember the *business* side of what you're doing. Clients aren't paying you for Law Review articles. Learn what you can, and can't, bill for." Robert Major and Martha Fay Africa in *Legal Economics* recommend that you rely on your "common sense. Clients aren't going to want overresearch on peripheral issues, or reinventing the wheel."

#54: DO recognize that if you want to be seen as a "star," go beyond your assignments to address the client's problem.

Many, many employers stress the importance of thinking "outside the box." What this means is that you view assignments as having Chinese Walls around them. Look at the *whole* picture, and how your project fits in. As Oklahoma City's Gina Rowsam advises, "It doesn't matter if they tell you, 'Go out and find the law that will support this position.' If you go and look and it's just not there, come back with *alternatives* that will accomplish the same thing."

Kentucky's Drusilla Bakert advises that "You have to figure out how your piece fits in. If you're asked, 'Look this up and see if I can file this motion,' don't go back and say, 'No.' Go beyond it and say, 'No, but you can accomplish the same goal this other way.' If they ask, 'Can you do a 10b5 motion on this?' they don't want to the history of the Rules of Civil Procedure. They want a *solution*." As one law firm said, "Be open to other solutions! A partner may ask, 'But what about . . . ?' and they like to see that you've *thought* about other options. To the extent it's possible in any given situation, think creatively." Another firm adds that top associates "have the mental flexibility to recognize that there might be more than one way to approach an issue." As the old saying goes, there's more than one way to skin a cat!

How do you do this? Not skinning a cat, I mean, but coming up with other alternatives? Brooklyn's Joan King recommends that you "always be positive in your assignments, from the viewpoint that 'We *can* do *something* for this client.'" It doesn't mean distorting your research, because if case law and/or statutes don't support a position, they just don't. "But if a corporate client wants to do X, it's your job to find out *how,* not *whether* they can. This opens up your horizons." One law firm recommends that you "Look at problems as though you were the attorney in charge. Talk to your attorney about the steps that come next. Look for practical solutions. Make your supervisor's life easier."

A perfect example of what we're talking about here can be found in the Jim Carrey movie *Liar Liar.* (If you haven't seen it, rent it. It's spit-milk-through-your-nose funny.) In the movie, Carrey plays a lawyer representing Jennifer Tilley in a nasty divorce. He's convinced that the only way to prevail is to argue that she had not been cheating on her husband even though it is hilariously obvious that she was *terribly* promiscuous. As it turns out, his *better*—and honest—argument focuses on the fact that when Tilley signed her prenuptial agreement, she was under age. By obsessing on one avenue of attack, he'd ignored something much more fruitful.

Georgetown's Marilyn Tucker suggests that you add a section to research memos "noting new issues raised by your research which were not assigned in the original problem. Doing so alerts the assigning attorney to problems (s)he may not have realized existed." One law firm echoes this by advising that you "make suggestions for the next level of investigation and possible next steps. Even if you're off-base, your attempts to think through cases will impress your superiors."

#55: DO ignore the words "first draft" when you get assignments. Make sure what you hand in is "client ready" regardless of whether the assigning attorney asked for a "draft."

Many, *many* attorneys will tell you that there is no such thing as a first draft. Why? Law firms offer a couple of explanations for this. First of all, assigning attorneys are more used to seeing memos written by experienced associates who are more adept at putting together a good first draft. What you perceive as a first draft when you're a fourth-year attorney versus a greenhorn is *very* different. Secondly, soon after the assignment is made, the assigning attorney is likely to forget that you were instructed to produce a first draft. In that instance, a "rough cut" is likely to come as a rude surprise.

One law firm advises that "Many associates assume that their supervisor won't mind a few 'rough edges' in the work they submit. They *do* mind, and they *will* remember."

#56: DO recognize that typos and grammar mistakes diminish confidence in your ability.

Never, ever, *ever* mistake a casual work atmosphere for a casual attitude toward work quality. Employers often point out that when "associates fail to attend to details like organization, grammar, and typos, it suggests that they also failed to attend to the substantive points." At Akin Gump's Washington, D.C. office, new associates during orientation are told that they should never hand in a "rough draft" with grammatical or spelling mistakes to a partner or senior associate to edit. "This will not only make your supervisors doubt your ability, but it also wastes client money to have senior associates do your editing."

Chicago-Kent's Stephanie Rever Chu echoes that "It's *more* than spell-checking. Hand-count pages. Hand-count appendices or exhibits, if you have them. Make sure your blue book form is perfect. It is *so* hard to over-come the perception that you make mistakes!"

#57: DO remember that when it comes to your work, the buck stops with you.

I've told you elsewhere that an experienced secretary is an unbeatable asset. But when it comes to your written work, the ultimate responsibility for hav-ing it in the right format—the pages in order, the right number of copies, the perfect blue book form—lies with you. As Chicago-Kent's Stephanie Rever Chu warns, "Don't count on your secretary to know technicalities! You need to know the blue book, and it's obvious if you don't."

#58: DON'T forget to Shepardize!

We all know the feeling. You've been slaving away on a research project, you've looked at a bunch of sources, and now that you're done with the substantive work, the *last thing you* want to do is the "housekeeping" chore of shepardizing. But the fact is, one of the worst things you can do is to neglect to shepardize your work. Loyola/New Orleans' Pam Occhipinti tells you to "check volume dates on books and pocket parts. Make *sure* you're up-to-date. If your boss turns your work in to some-one else and it's out of date, your work is no good, and it will *never* be forgotten."

#59: DON'T hand in incomplete work.

Lawyers are very frustrated when they get work from new associates that has uncrossed t's and undotted i's. By way of example, one law firm advises its new associates that "drafting a pleading and submitting it without a signature line gives the impression that you aren't confident the pleading is yet worthy of a signature. Either rework it until it *is*, or you'll give the impression that you don't appreciate the partner's time, such that the partner can prepare a signature line. Incomplete work product is inexcusable!"

#60: DON'T miss deadlines (and helpful hints for making sure that you don't).

It's hard to imagine a tenet lawyers take more seriously than this: *meet the deadlines you promise.* There is *no* more serious mistake you can make than blowing off a deadline. One lawyer told me about a summer clerk at his firm who didn't even talk to the assigning attorney about what the assignment *was* until after the deadline had passed! Gee, I wonder whether he got an offer to return?

It's just never necessary to pull the move that will anger assigning attorneys more than anything else. Let's look at the reasons you might be tempted to miss a deadline, and address each one.

One is poor planning. Georgetown's Marilyn Tucker advises that you "set interim deadlines when you receive an assignment. Work backwards. If your firm has a word processing department, plan to get your draft in early so you have time to edit it. You don't want to leave editing for the last minute. If you can, set it aside so you can look at it with fresh eyes, check-ing for style, grammar, typos, and any holes in analysis. You want it to make sense and flow well. And if you *can,* give it to a colleague for a quick read." So good planning can help you avoid a missed deadline.

Another possibility for missing deadlines is that you hit a brick wall in your research. Despite your best efforts, you just can't find the answer that your assigning attorney wants; it's not there to be found. In this case, Boston University's Betsy Armour advises that "You shouldn't create the image that you're chugging along to a Friday memo if on Tuesday you know it won't happen." The key here is to go to your assigning attorney and explain the problem, explaining also what you've done so that it won't look like your problem is a result of laziness. The *worst* thing you can do is spring a last-minute surprise, and an early warning to your assigning attorney prevents this. You'll find they'll understand. *Everybody's* been in the same situation, and they'll appreciate your forthrightness.

Another possibility is that you've found much *more* than your assign-ing attorney—or you—anticipated. Brooklyn's Joan King says that "You may be behind schedule because you've found tons of alternatives. Go to the assigning attorney and tell them. Explaining what you've found. Give a progress report."

The key here is—don't suffer in silence. It is *much* better to keep the assigning attorney apprised of your progress, so that they can help you determine what to do. As I've explained elsewhere, *nobody* expects a new attorney to be perfect. Not every assignment will run like clockwork. Trying to mask difficulties is much worse than explaining problems as they arise.

#61: DON'T let projects without specific deadlines drag on and on and on . . .

It may be that you get an assignment for which there is no deadline. The assigning attorney might say, "Do it when you have time," or "Whenever you can get to it is fine." In spite of these casual statements, if you *do* get waylaid by more pressing assignments, check back periodically to make sure that you aren't disappointing the assigning attorney's expectations. The last thing you want is to make any senior attorney believe you've blown off their work.

#62: DO actively seek feedback on every project you do.

As St. Louis' Wendy Werner says, "Remember that your supervisors won't be good at feedback. No one gets training in feedback! They won't be honest with you, but not because they're deceitful. You've got to draw them out."

Oklahoma City's Gina Rowsam agrees, adding that "If you don't ask for feedback, you won't get it more often than every six to 12 months. You may find you've made the same mistakes over and over. Ask straight out, 'Is this what you were looking for?'"

Of course, the reason most of us *don't* seek feedback is that we fear the worst: we don't want to be criticized. This idea of handling criticism is addressed under #71, below.

#63: DO find out if "the butler did it"—that is, follow up subsequently to find out how projects you've worked on wound up being resolved.

Georgetown's Marilyn Tucker recommends that you "follow up to find out the resolution of matters you've worked on. What did the client decide? How was the case resolved? How did the IRS respond? Was the result expected, or was it a surprise?" She points out that if you're too shy or insecure to follow up, "You're making a tactical mistake." Why? For one thing, "Understanding case resolutions is an important element of developing professional judgment." And for another, "It shows you're buying into the interests of the firm. You're *concerned* about the firm."

#64: DO be a "legal chameleon"—recognize and adapt to different people's varying styles.

Georgetown's Marilyn Tucker advises you to modify your style to your particular audience on any given project.

"Be aware that when you go to this person, they want it written *this* way. When you go to another person, they want it written *another* way." Remember that as a new lawyer, your clients are your assigning attorneys, and you have to present them the answers they seek in a style that's pleasing to them. This will mean shifting gears for different people—so don't let your work get stuck in a rut.

DO'S AND DON'TS #65 THROUGH 69: JUGGLING MULTIPLE PROJECTS AND HANDLING OVERLOADS, INCLUDING TURNING DOWN WORK WITHOUT SAYING 'NO.'

#65: DO recognize that you are not helping your image when you agree to do work you are too busy to handle.

Missouri's Gerald Beechum characterizes this problem with the saying "Keep loading the wagon, don't worry about the mule." As Georgetown's Marilyn Tucker warns, 'No one will remember that you declined the initial assignment, but not one will *forget* it if you take it on and then do a poor job. Written work lives on!"

The fact is, *nobody* wants to turn down work. You *want* to be seen as super-competent, and you figure if they're giving you work, they must think you have time for it. But the fact is, it's better to have one great review and one slightly disappointed lawyer who *doesn't* fill out a review form, than two bad reviews! UCLA's Amy Berenson echoes this, saying "You get evaluated on what you *complete,* not on what you *don't* do."

#66: DO ask for advice if you honestly can't estimate if you have the time to handle a new assignment.

As Brooklyn's Joan King says, "it's hard at first to judge how much time projects take." If an attorney approaches you with new work and you just don't have the experience to tell you how much time it will take you to complete what's already on your plate, *tell* them what you're doing. Say, "Yes, I'd love to do the work for you. Right now I have these four assignments with these deadlines. Can I fit it in?" They'll probably decide for you.

#67: DON'T assume that assigning attorneys know what else you're working on, so that in assigning you work they expect you to handle it.

It's true that some law firms, corporations and government employers have people who control the flow of assignments to new lawyers. Even in *those* situations, lawyers will often skirt the system and assign work to associates, particularly ones they like. No matter whether your employer has a formal assignment system or not, remember that "partners usually don't know what other partners have given you," says UCLA's Amy Berenson. They're typically very busy and won't know without hearing it from you that you're overloaded. So don't feel incompetent because you're loaded to the gills when new work is offered to you. It's not a statement on your ability—it's a misunderstanding!

#68: DON'T prioritize your own assignments. Defer to people who assign you work.

As the hiring partner at one law firm advises, "There will always be many demands on your time from lots of different people, all of whom think their project is the most important." Whatever you do, *don't* take it on yourself to decide whose work takes priority. As one lawyer told me, "There are likely to be politics you don't know about. If *you* go to the partner whose work you're doing and say, 'X just asked me to do this project for him right now. Can I switch?' You might hear, 'What do you *mean?* You're doing *my* work!' You're dealing with busy lawyers. It's dangerous to throw them off schedule. Let *others* prioritize your work."

#69: DO learn how to turn down work without saying no. (Here's everything you need to know.)

Here's the thing: you can't take on assignments you're too busy to handle. But at the same time, you don't want to develop a reputation for turning down work. How do you negotiate between the Scylla and Charybdis? It has everything to do with *what you say* to the attorney who's trying to assign you work. Here are some successful strategies to try:

a. Come to bury Caesar, not to praise him. That is, profess a willingness to do the work, and follow that up with a description of your current tasks, which suggests you can't handle it right now. For instance: "I'm happy to take your assignment, but I have assignments for X, Y and Z, and I don't know if I can make your deadline." You may find that the attorney will talk to X, Y and Z to rearrange your schedule, and that by itself gets you off the hook.

b. Suggest that the assigning attorney talk directly with the person you're doing work for now. For instance, say, "I'd love to help you, but I'm working on this project for X. If you need me to help out, perhaps you could talk to X and see if they'd be willing to switch."

c. Defer briefly, and state your enthusiasm for working with the assigning attorney imminently. Chicago-Kent's Stephanie Rever Chu advises that "If you have to turn down work, say 'I'm sorry, I'm really swamped, but I'd really like the chance to work with you. I'm hoping that by next week I'll be free, and I'll come back to you." And follow up—as soon as you're free, go visit to see if they have projects for you. Brooklyn's Joan King agrees, suggesting language that "declines work without saying 'no.' Explain why you're busy. Tell the partner you are working on a memo for John Doe which is due in a week, and that you'd be pleased to work on the new project then." Another way to accomplish this is with a reference to the client's needs, saying, "I can get my current work out of the way by Friday, and do this for you. Would that meet the client's needs."

I think you get the point here. Never say a flat, "No, I can't." One lawyer told me that the best possible response to the question "Are you busy?" is "Yes, but what I can do for you?" If you can't honestly say that, at worst, you can say, "Yes I can—but not right now."

DO'S AND DON'TS #70 THROUGH 73: DEALING WITH THE FACT YOU AREN'T PERFECT—EVERYTHING YOU NEED TO TURN CRITICISMS, EVALUATIONS, AND MISTAKES INTO POSITIVES.

#70: DO exploit your resources and compensate for—or overcome—your shortcomings.

When you think of the actress Vivien Leigh—the one who played Scarlett O'Hara in *Gone With The Wind*—you probably get a picture of a hopelessly beautiful woman. She *was*. What you probably don't know is that she had really hideous hands—huge paws. As a young stage actress, she developed a personal style that minimized her hands' largeness. Even when you see her in posed photographs with her hands clearly visible, you don't notice how large they are. She studiously masked that one flaw.

Then there's Richard Nixon. Nixon realized early on that he wasn't the brightest star in the galaxy. But while he was at college, at Whittier, he resolved to work harder than his innately smarter colleagues. He *knew* that even though they started out with an advantage, he could outdistance them if he worked harder.

Similarly, at work, you don't have a perfect set of skills. *Nobody* does. In fact, we're somewhat engineered to have mutually-exclusive strong suits. For instance, people who are very outgoing—great "people people"—tend not to have great concentration. Those who are introverted may not be the life of the party, but they will tend to be able to stay focused on projects much longer than their more outgoing brethren.

Your success depends on making the most of what you've got, and either correcting or hiding what you don't. As Oklahoma City's Gina Rowsam says, "Show up for your life! Do a few little things here and there. Overcome personality quirks you identify." And Emory's Carolyn Bregman adds, "If your skills aren't as strong, if you're willing to work hard and progress, you'll go the extra mile, you'll stand out more and be more appreciated than the person who has more talent and does less."

#71: DO recognize that your work is not perfect, and taking criticism well is a crucial skill.

Nobody likes criticism. In fact, many of us don't seek feedback at all for fear of hearing negative comments. One of the *big* changes you have to accept in going from work to school is that in school, you *always* knew where you stood, with grades and class rank. At work, sometimes you won't get *any* feedback unless something needs to be changed—and something *always* needs to be changed! What makes it even worse is what you might have thought was "A" work may need changes, or your assigning attorney may *want* changes, for no reason. That can be hard to swallow!

There's a story that I tell in the *Guerrilla Tactics* seminar about criticism that always makes people cringe, but it highlights a very important point about criticism. I've written about a dozen feature film scripts, and it's my dream to win an Oscar for Best Original Screenplay. Of course, if you've ever watched the Academy Awards, you know that in order to win that particular Oscar, it helps to have a movie studio actually make a *movie* out of one of your scripts. And that's proven a bit more difficult for me to accomplish than actually *writing* these scripts. Anyway, the first time I ever sent out a script was about seven years ago. I sent this script to an agent in Los Angeles, agents being the gatekeepers to Hollywood. Mind you, I was *absolutely convinced* that this particular script was perfect. I could see it on the silver screen, I could imagine myself at the Academy Awards in some slinky gown, thanking the Academy—I had it all figured out. Well, I got that script back about a week later, along with a note that read as follows:

> *Dear Miss Walton,*
> *Enclosed, please find your script. I was not sufficiently enthralled to read past page ten.*
> (Ugh.)
> *However, I encourage you to send your script to other agents. I'm confident that you will find somebody whose standards are considerably lower than mine.*

Arrgghhhh!

I wanted to *die.* I couldn't even *look* at the script for a month after that. But then—more for my own curiosity than anything else—I picked up that script, and tore off the first 10 pages. I read them, pretending I didn't know what came next. And you know what? I came to the dreadful realization that if I had been that agent, *I wouldn't have read past page10 either.* My story didn't get going until page 30—before that, it was all background. And I *also* realized that there were probably a lot of people who felt the way this particular agent did—that if a story didn't grab them right away, they had no reason to read any further. That note— that *awful* note—wasn't really a comment on whether I had any value as a screenwriter, or whether I could think up good or salable stories. It said: you didn't grab my attention. And when I brought myself to accept *that,* my scripts got *much, much* better. And some time later, I did something I *never* at the time thought I would do: I sent that agent a note, thanking her for her insights.

I'm not telling you this story to make you think I'm made of stone. I'm *not*. But when it comes to criticism, you've *got* to accept it if you *ever* intend to become a better lawyer. There's no way to be a better *anything* without being told the flaws in what you're doing now. In a roundabout way, a person who takes the time to tell you what you're doing wrong is actually helping you become a better professional. And furthermore, if you accept criticism without getting defensive or whiny, you make it *much* easier for assigning attorneys to give you new responsibilities and continue to mentor you.

This isn't to say that you're ever going to *enjoy* criticism, no matter how constructive it is. Unless you're some kind of masochist, you won't. But there are several ways to make it easier on yourself. First of all, as New York attorney Alan Rosenberg says, remember that it is *always* easier to criticize and improve on a creditable first draft than it is to create the initial product from the empty drawing board. It's always easier to come second. The ideas that can be brought to bear on almost *any* legal issue are virtually infinite, so somebody reviewing your work can *always* come up with suggestions.

Another way to make criticism easier to bear comes from Georgetown's Marilyn Tucker: "You don't have to understand or agree with all the changes made to your work product. Some reviewers have an insatiable need to red pencil, to change each 'but' to a 'however,' and all kinds of stylistic changes. Take changes as a reflection of each lawyer's style, not an attack on yours." And UCLA's Amy Berenson adds "Don't take it personally! Look at it as learning from someone with more experience than you. Be open and learn from it!" And no matter how reasonable or accurate criticism is, what it *does* reflect is the opinion of the assigning attorney, and you *need* to know the assigning attorney's perception, whether you agree with it or not.

So when you get criticized, *don't* get defensive. *Assume* criticism is being given constructively, even if it really isn't. Don't argue. Don't have a bad, petulant attitude when you receive negative comments. Don't go into decline over the situation. Eliminate the word "but" from your immediate vocabulary. Don't let the look on your face, or your words themselves, convey the attitude, "Your editing is simply a matter of style, and mine is better," or "I know you've been practicing 15 years, but I'm smarter and my draft is better," or any other expression that shouts resentment. Instead, take a deep breath. *Force* yourself to smile. Use words like "I understand," and "I see what you mean," and "I'll have to work on that." when you defend yourself, be *respectful*. And when the criticism is over, say, "Thanks for taking the time to share this with me"—ideally not through clenched teeth. Make it *easy* for people to coach you— because that's what criticism really is. Your critic will leave with a much higher opinion of you if you take criticism gracefully than if you whine and mope—and isn't respect what you ultimately want?

#72: DO handle mistakes—and you are going to make them—the best possible way. (Here's how.)

New York attorney Alan Rosenberg recounts his impressions when he became a lawyer:

"The three most striking first impressions I had when starting as a junior associate in a large firm:

a. Partners never made mistakes.

b. Other associates rarely made mistakes, and when they did, the mistakes invariably related to inconsequential matters.

c. I made major errors on numerous occasions involving matters of cosmic significance."

He adds that "I came to the conclusion that the practice of law is an intellectually humbling experience."

It *is*. You *will* make mistakes—*everybody* does. But the good news is that much of how you will be judged depends on how you *handle* mistakes. Here are the tips to remember:

a. Don't try and cover up. As Arizona's Mary Birmingham advises, "Cover ups will kill you. Look at the stories in the news the last few years—the Berings Bank collapse, the Orange County bankruptcy. What happened? Things started to go wrong, they tried to cover up, and things snowballed." Emory's Carolyn Bregman adds that "People try and cover up for fear of looking stupid. But the truth is that your supervisor will have *more* respect for you if you own up."

b. Accept the blame when you make mistakes. Don't try and blame others.

c. *Immediately* do damage control, advises Indiana's Kelly Townes. "The worst thing you can ever do is to say 'I filed something I knew was wrong.'" Emory's Carolyn Bregman adds that "Your supervisor may be talking with clients or incorporating it into something they'll rely on—they'll put it in a letter."

d. Take your lumps in person. Acknowledging a mistake is not something you do via e-mail, a note, or a voice mail message.

e. If the mistake involves something that has not yet left the office, rewrite the memo or brief or whatever you turned in, and hand it to the person with a complete explanation of what it was that is wrong.

f. If the mistake involves something that has gotten out of the office, take responsibility for correcting the mistake yourself. For instance, if the mistake has been transmitted to the client, draft a letter to the client, from your supervising attorney, correcting the mistake and blaming you. If you made a mistake that was incorporated into a motion, redraft the motion and filing papers, and refile the motion.

g. *Don't* make the same mistake again! Nobody expects you to be perfect. But they *do* expect you to learn from your mistakes.

I talked to one junior associate who, four months into his law firm job, was given the task of drafting a motion. After he'd handed in the motion, he double-checked his shepardizing and research he'd relied on, and realized—to his horror—that the case he'd pinned his argument on had just been overturned. *Yikes!* He updated his research, redid the motion and filing papers, and went immediately to the partner explaining his mistake with the corrected papers in hand.

Most importantly, when you make mistakes, take heart. As one law firm advises its new associates, "You aren't judged on the basis of one mistake. A lawyer's career and professional development must be measured over time." Handling mistakes like a grown-up will earn you the respect you want.

#73: DO intelligently handle evaluations.

Ideally, whatever is said at your periodic evaluations will not be a surprise. You *can* take advantage of them to help propel your career forward. As Chicago-Kent's Stephanie Rever Chu says, "Evaluations are something to use wisely! They're not just an opportunity to be reviewed. Take initiative. *Ask* for advice on how you can improve, what projects to take on, how you can prove you can do this."

During my first evaluation at the large firm I summer clerked for, a project came up that was a particularly bad experience. The partner had asked me to cite a case for a proposition it just didn't represent. Rather than handling the situation like an intelligent grown-up—and at the very least talking to someone else about how to handle it—I ignored it. The partner gave me a stinging evaluation, and this was shared with me during the review. I was so upset I could have cried. In fact, I *did* cry. What a mistake! These people weren't my parents. They didn't have a vested interest in my success. What *they* saw was a woman who was supposed to be a professional, blubbering away over a stupid evaluation. Keep it in perspective. Evaluations are opinions, and opinions can be handled.

DO'S AND DON'TS #74 THROUGH 97: ULTIMATE PEOPLE SKILLS—WHAT IT REALLY TAKES TO GET ALONG—AND GET AHEAD!

#74: DO recognize that it doesn't matter how you feel. It matters what you project.

Getting along in the working world requires *all* of us to occasionally act at odds with the way we really feel. When you're feeling PMS-y or you're just in a bad mood the last thing you feel is compassion for a client's problems. If you work with a real jerk the last thing you want to do is be pleasant. You probably want to slap the idiot. And even now, when I present the *Guerrilla Tactics* seminar sometimes a 150 times a year—I'm not always a ball of fire. I've had to present Friday night on the East Coast, take a red-eye with two connections to the West Coast, and speak again at 9 a.m. to some bleary-eyed, very dedicated students. If you're at that Saturday morning seminar, I may be *looking* at you, but I'm imagining that your head is a fluffy pillow, just the way Elmer Fudd hallucinated that Daffy Duck was a roasted chicken when they were stuck in a lifeboat.

The point here is that it just doesn't matter how you really feel. Being a grown-up at work depends entirely on what you project. Nobody at work has x-ray vision—they can't see into your soul. They can only see the way you *behave*. And if that means sucking it up when you're in a bad mood, then that's what it means. As Chicago-Kent's Stephanie Rever Chu says, "Students are surprised at the kinds of things they're reviewed on! Even if you're not in court, you're still evaluated on oral skills. You're evaluated on your judgments. You're also rated on relationships with attorneys and staff."

#75: DO appear confident—and learn how to get all the questions you want answered without appearing clueless.

The key word here is "appear." It's unlikely that early in your career you're going to *feel* very confident (unless you're arrogant, in which case you've got a misplaced sense of confidence). Law is a difficult career with a steep learning curve. But you've got to put on a confident face. As Hamline's Joyce Laher advises, "Employers *want* to feel they've hired the best of the bunch. Self-effacing or self-deprecating or disclaimer statements have no place at work. 'I'm not really good at this,' 'I don't know much about X,' 'I only did that once before'—replace those with, 'Thanks for the opportunity. I'll do my best and if I have questions, I'll ask.'

Appearing confident is made even more difficult by the fact that it flies in the face of advice that you *always* get—namely, "Ask lots of questions." "How," you might be wondering, "Can I ask lots of questions and still look confident?" The answer is in the manual that the wonderful firm Strasburger & Price gives to its new associates. As the manual states, "Out of law school, you have a highly-inflated view of yourself, which quickly comes crashing down around your ears. Suddenly, you realize you don't know anything. There are 18 trillion practical things you don't know. The key? Alternate your questions between 4 and 5 people. Several good things will result:

   a. You'll get your answers;

b. Four or five people will be flattered you consider them knowledgeable enough to answer your questions;

c. No one person will feel pestered by your questions; and

d. Since you are alternating between four to five people, no one person will know how truly stupid you are."

You may also find yourself cowed by the brilliant credentials of your co-workers. Maybe you were on Law Review at Harvard, so you've got the 600-pound-gorilla resume. But maybe you don't—and maybe everybody you work with has gilded credentials that you feel you don't have. You *still* have to act confidently. In fact, the best way to deal with people with much better credentials is to *calmly acknowledge it, up front. Give* them that, and they won't have any reason to seek recognition from you after that. I can identify with this personally, since my own law school career was, well, lackluster. I went to a pretty good law school—Case Western Reserve—but when I clerked at a large firm, I was plunged into a pool of Harvards and Yales and Stanfords. When I would meet a fellow clerk from a distinguished school, I'd lead off with words something along the lines of, "I know you went to X, and I'm really impressed with that. You must have worked really hard to get in there. It's something to be proud of." That was it. Those words took any one-upmanship issues off the table. They didn't have anything to prove, because I'd already acknowledged that they were better-credentialed than me.

So don't let the credentials of your peers cow you. If anything, use that as a spur to do your best. As Suffolk's Jim Whitters says, "I went to Boston College, and I worked with guys from Harvard. I made the decision to out-work people from better schools. No task was too big. I decided to do more."

#76: DON'T think that top-notch work product means you can ignore everything else.

The actress Ethel Barrymore once said that "For an actress to be a success she must have the face of Venus, the brains of Minerva, the grace of Terpsichore, the memory of Macaulay, the figure of Juno, and the hide of a rhinoceros." Similarly, if you're going to be a great lawyer, you can't be a one-trick pony. It doesn't matter how great your work is if people can't stand you.

A lot of people start their careers thinking that if you do a bang-up job on the work assigned to you, your work will speak for itself. As the managing partner at one large firm said, "You can't be arrogant, smart, and lack people skills, and expect to get ahead."

The fact is that law is a service business. When you start out, unless you're a sole practitioner, your clients are your superiors. As your career progresses, you weave in skills like business generation (if you're in private practice) or grant writing or fund raising (in public interest) or faculty politics (if you teach), but in every single situation your success depends on *much more* than your actual work product. In fact, your value as a leader and/or business generator has much more to do with the way you deal with people than it does with your legal intellect. As one senior partner told me, "Standing out isn't always a matter of objective legal skill. How well do you work with others? If you are enthusiastic, you show a sincere desire to do well and work hard, you show a commitment to the law that shows that it's more than just a job, you always seem to welcome working with people, and as a bottom line you're simply fun to work with—you're going to stand out and attract good work."

So *don't* think you can closet yourself in the library and ignore everything else. People will resent you—and you won't succeed.

#77: DON'T kid yourself that you can 'rise above' office politics.

Employers are amused when people say they want nothing to do with office politics, as though there's some kind of *choice* in the matter. When people eschew office politics what they're really doing is saying that they want to deal in "tangibles," that they want to be judged by their work product and nothing else. It won't happen. Anytime an organization has more than two people, there are politics. As Emory's Carolyn Bregman says, "Anyone who reads Dilbert knows that there are always office politics *whenever* you work with other people." As one lawyer told me, "Politics are *everywhere.* Clients don't hire the objective 'best' lawyer—they hire people they trust, people they like. Creating that image is *political.*"

So if you cringe at the words "office politics" and despise "schmoozers," recognize that people's perception of you plays a large part in determining your professional development, your opportunities, your success. Of course you shouldn't be a phony—but recognize the fact that the messy, imperfect science of dealing with people is *unavoidable.*

#78: If you are arrogant, stand-offish, you don't bathe or you otherwise alienate people, for gosh sakes DON'T "just be yourself." People skills count!

Ironically, if you don't have great paper credentials, you probably *got* your job because of your facility with people. On the flipside, if you've got great paper credentials, and you start noticing that you're not getting invited to things that other new colleagues are taking part in, ask someone you trust for advice.

The simple fact is that nobody works in a vacuum. In any job, you're going to deal with a variety of constituencies—superiors, peers, support staff, clients. It is *crucial* that you be viewed, *from day one,* as not being arrogant nor too shy nor a turn-off to clients. As Robert Major and Martha Fay Africa wrote in *Legal Economics,* "Social skills count! Associate evaluations are *subjective.* They can be influenced by non-performance-related things like tastelessness, poor table manners, rudeness to support staff, and indiscretion, especially about client matters."

#79: DON'T treat the support staff like office furniture. They can make or break you. Nurture good feelings with them!

The *number one stupidest thing* you can do at the office is to alienate the support staff, both at the office and at the courthouse. Yes, you may have seven years' more education than they do. You may be a lot smarter. You've got a lot more earning potential and you dress a lot better. *Get over it.*

Minnesota's Susan Gainen gets this across with her "Five Stages Of Relations With Support Staff."

> STAGE ONE: On your first day of work, people are predisposed to think well of you. They are prepared to like you, to help you, and to invest in your success.

> STAGE TWO: You acted like a jerk. Whether you were rude to a support staff person or to a colleague, you can almost always repair the damage if you are sincere in your apologies, and never, ever repeat the behavior.

> STAGE THREE: You really *are* a jerk. Whether it's rudeness, incompetence, laziness or a tendency to make mistakes and blame others, you are riding for a fall. The support staff which can smooth the wrinkles in your appearance, cover for your small mistakes and chuckle at your eccentricities, will now take three steps back and watch you fall on your face. Real-life example: After an Associate General Counsel at a bank had been working for more than six months, staff began asking themselves questions like "Just how long should the learning curve be for remembering that each foreclosure needs a $75 filing fee check attached to it, and that the lead time for a request is 24 hours?" and "When will he stop blaming us for his mistakes?"

> STAGE FOUR: Singly and in groups they begin to approach their boss and your boss, saying 'I can't believe that he/she did/didn't do (whatever)." This becomes a chorus, and everything that you've ever done that you weren't supposed to do—or that you've never done that you *were* supposed to—becomes sheet music for this group.

> STAGE FIVE—THE PIRANHA STAGE: Not a pretty sight. Singly and in groups, they approach your boss and their boss and say "It's him/her or us." Now is the time to pack up your desk and sneak away into the night, or stand on your desk and disembowel yourself with the

Waterford letter opener you got as a graduation present. When weighing the value of a new *summa cum laude* graduate who quickly demonstrates an unerring ability to antagonize large numbers of valued employees against a group of irreplaceable experienced legal secretaries and paralegals, there is no choice. You're out.

As the "Five Stages" illustrate, mistreating the staff can be detrimental to your professional health. For instance:

a. Your work suddenly and mysteriously doesn't get done on time. Your documents for word processing get bumped—or misplaced all together. The clerk at the courthouse doesn't make a minor and simple correction in your documents, so that you miss a crucial deadline.

b. As the "Five Stages" make plain, if you get into an "It's-her-or-me" position with a valued secretary, you'll lose. As Indiana's Kelly Townes says, "Secretaries are there when you get there. And they'll be there when you leave." The hiring partner at one firm told me about a junior associate who locked horns with the managing partner's long-time, trusted secretary. When the associate confronted the partner, seeking support, the managing partner sputtered, "If I've got to choose between her or you, it's **her**." The recruiting coordinator at another large firm told me that "What most new associates don't understand is that it's a lot easier to find good attorneys than it is to find good secretaries."

c. You will lose a valuable source of mentoring. When you start out as a new lawyer, an experienced legal secretary understands more about the practice of law than you do. They *know* how many copies a court will require of a document. They *know* partners' styles and idiosyncrasies. They know a million valuable practical tips that you *won't* hear if you treat them disrespectfully.

d. You will develop a reputation as difficult to work with. You'll get bounced from secretary to secretary, and you'll look bad in the eyes of your superiors—the very people you're trying to impress.

Let's take a look at the flipside of that, and see how being kind and respectful to staffers can make your life a whole lot easier. For one thing, they'll go out of their way to help you when you're in a bind—as you inevitably *will* be. Brooklyn's Joan King recounts that as a young lawyer, "I went to word processing at 1 a.m., and got my stuff pushed through. Support staff may not even *deliberately* intend to help you, but it's human nature to deal better with people who are nice to you." Chicago-Kent's Stephanie Rever Chu recounts that when her lawyer husband is working late, "If he misses the FedEx deadline, the mail room people have actually driven him to the airport and taken him to the secret entrance for the *true* 10 p.m. deadline." If you nurture the support staff you will also have a valuable source of inside skinny. One lawyer told me about a new associate at a huge New York firm, who got to know the entire staff in the first two weeks he was there. The other associates laughed at him, but through this network he found out that the firm was thinking of adding an associate at its London office. He also found out who was doing the hiring, went to them, and said, "Take me." No other associate had even *heard* about the plum assignment. It paid off. He got the job.

As I discuss more fully when I talk about office gossip, under #97, the support staff can be an *incredible* source of "unofficial" information.

With all of this in mind, what should you do?

a. Overall, take the attitude that support staff works *with* you, not *for* you. Don't pull a power trip! One recruiting coordinator told me about a new associate who was being shown around the office by the office manager, when he touched her shoulder and said, "Shouldn't a *lawyer* be showing me around?" As this recruiting coordinator commented, "He should have packed his bags and left right then, because he was *dead meat.*"

b. Lewis & Clark's Lisa Lesage warns you not to pay attention to "how the senior partner treats support staff. It's *your* job to win them over, *regardless* of how senior management behaves toward them." One recruiting coordinator told me about a new associate who made a point of bringing in muffins once in a while for the support staff. Even a simple gesture like that made him stand out.

c. Pay attention to small kindnesses. Lisa Lesage advises that "with birthdays, a death in the family, any major occasion, send a card. If they look like they're having a bad day, say a kind word." Pay honest compliments. Remember Secretaries' Day. It's *important.*

d. Take a deep breath before you yell at a support staffer. As Denver's Anne Stark Walker advises, "Support staff wield more power and influence than most entry-level associates realize. A few instances of brow-beating a secretary, or berating an office messenger, can do permanent damage to your reputation at the office."

e. Ask staff members' advice. You cannot pay a person a more heartfelt compliment than to suggest that you have something to learn from them.

f. Be considerate with time deadlines. It's *your* job to prioritize your work; don't constantly be counting on support staff to pull a rabbit out of a hat at the last minute.

g. Learn and use your office's standard proofreading symbols.

h. If you use dictation, speak clearly and at an even pace. Spell out unusual or uncommon words, case names, and personal names.

i. When you have a rush project, call the word processing supervisor (or whoever is going to help you) and explain the deadline. Offer an explanation of why you're late—this will help ensure your work gets done. Be *apologetic,* and say "thanks"!

Having said all of this, it *is* important to know where to draw the line. If your secretary is having a bad day, you want to be compassionate without stepping into the role of therapist. Connecticut's Diane Ballou, herself a former recruiting coordinator at a large firm, says "Be nice to support staff, but don't be friends with them. Your job is to be with lawyers and clients." So the moral here? Be nice, be respectful, be caring, and be professional.

#80: DO recognize what people mean when they say "be yourself." They're saying: don't suck up! Be respectful but not phony,

You hear this more often as the advice "Be yourself." I *hate* that saying. What if the "real me" likes to sleep until noon and drink too much? Should I "be myself"? Of course not.

After a lot of probing on this particular subject—basically, saying to employers, how do you know when people *aren't* being themselves? It comes down to this: Don't kiss up. People recognize when someone is a hopeless brown-noser. One employer told me that "It's amazing how quickly it gets around to other associates when you're a phony. One guy who worked here was a *huge* phony. He was shocked to find that everybody knew it, attorneys, support staff, everybody."

It's important to be enthusiastic, but find *honest,* positive things you can say about what you're doing. (If you *can't,* you're probably doing the wrong work.) If you aren't the world's best writer or speaker or softball player or golfer, that's all right. Pull out the best of what you *do* bring to the table, and what's brought to the table *for* you. That's all "being yourself" means.

#81: DO exhibit an appropriate sense of humor.

"Sense of humor" is a loaded phrase. Every employer claims to want it, while at the same time demanding mature people who take their work seriously. What employers really mean when they say they want you to have a sense of humor has two aspects to it: First, they want you to have *their* sense of humor, both in terms of *when* it's appropriate to joke around and *what* it's appropriate to joke *about.* There is no question that a well-timed quip can save the day in a tense situation, and *every* employer appreciates that kind of quick-wittedness.

Second, they don't want you to take yourself seriously. Be able to poke fun at yourself. An associate at a large firm told me a story that perfectly illustrates this. A law student came in for an interview, and the associate noticed that on the student's resume he listed two jobs: He had been a bouncer at the Playboy Mansion, and he had been a land title abstractor, which in this associate's words is "the most boring job in the world." About halfway through the interview, the associate said, "I saw your resume, and I couldn't help noticing your work experience. I know everybody must ask you the same question, but I can't resist. What's it like to be a land title abstractor?" The associate told me that "The guy didn't bat an eyelash. Didn't even crack a smile. I sat there cackling like an idiot, and— nothing."

You *know* that as you proceed through your career, people will tease you about things. Take it in good humor!

#82: DO cultivate your peers. Don't appear competitive!

It's easy to look at your colleagues as competitors for promotions and great work. It's easy—but it's a mistake. If you cultivate your peers, you not only make your current work environment easier and more harmonious, but you're laying the groundwork for your future. As Denver's Anne Stark Walker advises, "Your first job is likely to be a stepping stone in a long line of career-building experiences. Remember that your fellow associates may be your partners some day, voting on your compensation and other partner perks. They may also move on to in-house positions and be in a position to provide you with client work. Make friends with people who may be your references or future sources of client and job referrals."

Almost *all* of the more experienced attorneys I interviewed for this book got their wonderful jobs *not* through jobs ads or headhunters, but because somebody who liked them tapped them on the shoulder and offered them their job. One who comes to mind immediately is Valerie Cohen, who works as in-house counsel at Walt Disney. We met Valerie way back in Chapter 3. She got that *terrific* job when one of her colleagues at a New York firm was offered the job of general counsel at Disney, and invited her along. The moral here: *Don't* alienate your colleagues, in a twisted sense of it's-me-or-them. It *isn't*. As George Washington's Laura Rowe Lane succinctly puts it, "Be nice to everybody else in the sandbox!"

#83: DO keep your personal life personal.

Part of the deal you make with your employer is that the time you sell them is *theirs*. We've already covered that. Part of that deal means that you will keep your personal life to yourself. That has a couple of important aspects. The first is that you should minimize personal calls at work. As Connecticut's Diane Ballou says, "Receptionists recognize voices. People walking by your office will casually notice when you're yukking it up on the phone with friends instead of working. You don't want your secretary complaining that you are doing your personal networking at work."

Everybody has crises come up that interfere with their work. But those crises don't come up five times a day, and they don't require your attention on a constant basis. If there *is* something that you have to take care of that requires more phonage than is appropriate at your work place, you have a couple of options. One is to go to a pay phone outside the office to take care of it. The other is to have a cell phone at work, so that your calls don't go through a secretary or receptionist and they aren't recorded. You should *still* keep them to a minimum, but the appearance of that is even more important.

The other aspect of keeping your personal life personal is not to act out your own personal "Melrose Place" at work. Don't make your personal life a matter of office gossip. Remember that even though some colleagues may turn out to be friends, and your office may have a family-like atmosphere, you are *still* a professional. The people you work with are always subconsciously judging your professional worth. Most of the things you'd share—plays or movies you've seen, sports activities, cute things your kid said—those are safe. But keep in mind that every time you share anything about yourself, you should act judiciously. As Diane Ballou recommends, "The less people know about you, the better. Don't talk about your dates. Listen more than you talk. Then less can be said about you!"

#84: DO align yourself with people you respect

Unfortunately, the most interesting people at work are often the malcontents. They're the most fun for the same reason that bad movie reviews are more fun to read than laudatory ones: there's something about complaining that draws us in. As Shirley MacLaine said in the movie *Steel Magnolias,* "If you don't have anything good to say—come sit next to me."

While it's a good idea to stay on the good side of the office gossip (I discuss this in more detail below, under the section "handling gossip"), don't become a member of the 'clique.' When people at work think of you, they should associate you in their minds with people who are respected, who share your values.

#85: DO keep open communication with supervisors—consider a weekly memo outlining what you're doing.

The way to make sure that you are meeting expectations is to keep your supervisor apprised of what you're up to. It's a mistake to think that anybody who supervises you has your workload in the front of their minds. Lawyers are *busy* and frequently overlook things that may be *very* important to you.

Georgetown's Marilyn Tucker has a great way to avoid problems with supervisors. She suggests that you "write a weekly memo to your group head, assigning partner or supervisor, listing all of the projects you've been assigned, their status, any deadlines and your availability for the next week." As she says, "This tells your supervisor exactly where your workload stands—and you won't miss deadlines!"

#86: If you are a woman, DO have a tolerance of older colleagues, making a special effort not to take offense where none exists.

I know that I'm treading on very thin ice here, because the point I'm going to make is likely to make a lot of people angry. But I heard this from an awful lot of employers—an awful lot of *younger* employers—so many that I think there's a lot to it. And it's this: If you're a woman and an elderly partner calls you "Honey" or "Dear," *don't* assume that they have no respect for your work. As Oprah Winfrey says, there is no discrimination against excellence.

People talk about the good old days, but if you look at America in the 1920s and 1930s, there were an awful lot of social mores that are totally unacceptable by our standards. The elderly lawyers you work with *grew up* in that environment. You may have heard about the story about the woman who graduated number three in her class at Stanford Law School in the 1950s. Despite her excellent academic credentials, the only job she could get at a law firm was as a secretary. Number *three* in her class! At *Stanford!* (Of course, the story has a happy ending. She somehow got over that disappointment, and went on to a legal career most people would consider a success. It's United States Supreme Court Justice Sandra Day O'Connor.)

My point here is this. From what I heard from young female associates, the vast majority of older lawyers make a real effort to adapt to enlightened attitudes about women. If elderly lawyers use a term of endearment with you that you would resent coming from a contemporary, remember for a moment who it is who's doing the talking. Hamline's Joyce Laher, a former lawyer herself, warns that "Too many women go into the work place overly concerned about political correctness. People in the workplace may be two generations older than you, and you need to be tolerant. When the grandfatherly type says 'Dear,' don't ruffle your feathers!"

#87: DO appreciate the loaded value of casual contact with senior management.

When you run into senior management in the hallways at work—people you don't work with on a routine basis—remember that what you say to them, the way you appear, may be their only exposure to you. Don't blow it!

One employer told me a very enlightening story about this. They had a summer clerk who was walking down the hall one day, and the managing partner came around a corner. The partner said to the summer clerk, "How are you doing?" The summer clerk answered flatly, "OK, I guess." The clerk wasn't unhappy, he was just answering honestly. But his flat response made the partner believe that something was wrong. He contacted the recruiting coordinator, and said, "What's going on with X? He doesn't seem to like it here." The whole thing spiraled from there, all because of a deflated "OK, I guess."

The point? Don't underestimate the value of casual comments. If you can honestly answer that you're doing "Great!" that's the best response. Nobody really wants to hear about that boil that needs lancing. If you can't honestly answer that you're doing well, you can always say something like, "I'm learning tons every day." It may be that you're learning you *hate* it, but you're *learning.* Don't let simple comments create the wrong impression in people's minds!

#88: DON'T yell and scream. Remember that everything you do professionally reflects on your employer.

We've all read the books, we've seen the TV shows, and we know how lawyers behave in fiction—and, unfortunately, sometimes, in real life. They yell. They scream. They berate opposing counsel. Don't *you* be deluded into behaving in the same way. As Loyola/New Orleans' Pam Occhipinti advises, "Always conduct yourself professionally! It's a profession, not a job. You're not a waiter! Everything you say and do represents your employer—including fights on the phone."

#89: DO follow the party line on office romances—which usually means avoiding even the appearance of romantic involvement with anybody at work.

We all know the temptations. *New York* Magazine recently published a study in which 19% of respondents had met the last person they dated at work, and 39% admitted to having had sex with a co-worker. And quite frankly, if you're single and you're working long hours, exactly who *are* you going to meet, *outside* of work? Your dry cleaner? The security guard? The janitor? Maybe—but it's more likely you'll develop a "thing" for a colleague—or they for you. In fact, one of the firms in this book has at least three married couples, all lawyers who met at the office.

Here's the problem. *Most* employers frown on inter-office romance. If you do develop a crush on a co-worker, you have a couple of options. One is just to enjoy the crush and not do anything about it. Remember, like you did when you were sixteen.

Option two is to pursue your mutual feelings. But if you decide to take this route, you're living very dangerously. Since there are only two possible endings to a relationship—you break up or you get married—there is a strong possibility that you will break up and one of you will likely have to leave the office. That's a very high price to pay for what may turn out to be a fling.

If you do decide ignore all the advice about not mixing business and pleasure, and you proceed, behave professionally and discreetly. But be aware that it's *very* hard to disguise attraction. The actor Charles Laughton used to say of the censors that, "They can't censor the twinkle in my eye."

Even if you have no intention of getting romantically involved with a colleague, realize the importance of appearances. One recruiting coordinator told me about a young associate who went to lunch with a female associate, and helped her on with her coat. "Next thing you knew, everyone had them sleeping together."

Finally—and it's a shame that this even has to be said—don't ever, ever, ever have an affair with a married colleague. As one recruiting coordinator advises, "That's one story that *cannot* have a happy ending."

#90: DO remember everything your mamma taught you when it comes to employer social events.

I'm not telling you that you have to attend every firm function. It would be wise if you did, especially at first, but you don't have to. What you *do* have to do is to remember everything your mamma taught you about good manners. When you get invited to anything at the firm, RSVP promptly. To firm dinners, meetings, everything. Here's why: If you don't respond, why should they trust you with a client? Or more responsibility? So respond quickly and politely.

Your mother would be so proud.

#91: DO avoid the "Monica Lewinsky" Syndrome—that is, don't pick a workplace confidant too hastily, and don't confide in people until they've earned your trust.

Having someone you can confide in at work can be very comforting. They already know the personalities, and can therefore appreciate everything you say. However, as Monica Lewinsky's unfortunate choice of Linda Tripp as a confidant showed, you need to be careful who you confide in. As Case Western's Barbara Weinzierl advises, "Wait until people *earn* your trust. Don't confide too soon!" Barbara tells a story about when she was an associate at a large firm. She confided in a junior associate that "I hated the project I was working on. This associate had a meeting after that with a senior partner, and mentioned what I'd said. The senior partner immediately confronted me with it," and Barbara was, of course, *mortified* that the junior associate had repeated her comment.

So don't spill your guts too readily to anyone at work. One of the reasons it's important to maintain a support network *outside* the office is to make sure these kinds of slip-ups don't happen!

#92: DON'T whine, complain, beef, or bitch. About anything. And for chrissakes never air your dirty laundry to the media.

A recent *Wall Street Journal* article, detailing the grueling life of new associates at some law firms, including the following passage (I've changed the name of the firm and the associate named in the article):

"For most young lawyers, working at a law firm is still a grind. Bart Simpson, a first-year associate at Onnest & Fortrue, says he recently spent a

week looking through boxes of papers in a 'dark, dank, dirty warehouse in Vernon, California.' When he isn't sifting through dusty crates, he can usually be found in his office . . . where he typically works from 8 a.m. to 8 p.m. Weekends? Still working. Mr. Simpson says he clocks in from noon to 6 p.m. two or three Saturdays a month, although he adds that he believes his work is valued, and 'it could be a lot worse.'"

I ask you—how are this guy's partners going to respond to *this?* In the *Wall Street Journal?* He did acquit himself a bit there right at the end, but for *chrissakes,* if you're going to *complain,* complain to your mom! Or friends! Or a trusted teddy bear! I couldn't think of a more *patent* example of how absolutely foolish it is to complain about work when there is *any* possibility of a colleague or superior finding out. *Just don't do it.*

It drives employers *crazy* to hear new lawyers complain. You wouldn't *believe* how much I heard about this. But everything I heard can be summarized in this statement: When it comes to the workplace, don't complain anywhere you wouldn't pick your nose. In other words—don't complain in front of *anybody.*

And that means about *anything.* Don't complain about the resources. Your secretary is useless. The library isn't big enough. Your parking space isn't close enough. You're working way too late. Northern Illinois' Mary Obrzut says that, amazingly enough, "Interns at Kraft had free housing—and complained that they didn't get maid service!"

Don't complain about the work. Employers *know* what's boring. They want to see you handle *every* project with aplomb, tedious or exciting. It's *never* a good idea to say or imply thoughts like, 'This case is really boring,' 'I really can't be bothered,' 'Okay, if I really have to.' As Mary Obrzut advises, "If you've got to, buy a punching bag for your house—and use it! Don't bitch or whine at work—it doesn't increase your standing in *anybody's* eyes!"

Don't complain about colleagues. If you have a beef with *anyone,* talk to *that person,* in *private,* and that's *it.* Talking about it with other people will only escalate the hostilities between you, and having gone public, it will be difficult to back down.

You may want to adopt a strategy Abraham Lincoln used. Whenever he wanted to blast *anybody,* he would sit down and write them a *nasty, stinging* letter. A real barn-burner. Then he would put those letters in a drawer, and he never sent them. *Never.* You get the point: get your whining out of your system some other way!

#93: DON'T let down your guard when you socialize with colleagues.

I'm not suggesting that you show up at a colleague's picnic wearing a suit. But remember that as long as you work with them, the people at the office are colleagues first, and friends second. They've got to be able to feel that you're reliable and that you can be trusted as a professional. For all of the socializing I heard at all of the employers I talked to across the country, people at great employers definitely enjoy each others' company. They have a lot of fun, and in some places they enjoy playing practical jokes on each other. But as a junior lawyer, follow the lead of more senior people (even if they're only a year ahead of you). Don't be the wildest partier at the office—it's a reputation you don't need.

#94: If you take on a nontraditional job, DON'T hit people over the head with your J.D.

If you decide to be a "not-lawyer," then that's what you are—not a lawyer. You happen to have a graduate degree that involved the study of law. That's all.

If you decide not to practice law, you've made a compromise. It's a compromise many people enjoy, but you've made a trade. You've taken on work you thought you'd enjoy more than practicing law—and you gave up the prestige associated with being a lawyer. You can't have it both ways. Last year a law student approached me and said he was pretty sure that what he wanted to do was to design software, but he said: "Aren't they going to resent working with a lawyer?" I responded, "They won't be working with a lawyer. They'll be working with a software designer."

I can identify with this, because as a writer, *I'm* not a lawyer. My law degree has the utility of a place mat. It's true that I've had the occasional argument with insurance companies and vendors during which I'd love to be able to say, "Don't mess with me. I'm a *lawyer*." But I'm *not*. And if you don't decide to practice law, you aren't, either, and if you throw around your J.D., you're likely to alienate all of the people you work with. As Chicago's Suzanne Mitchell says, "If you're going to thrive in a nontraditional job, you *can't* be hung up on legal issues, or being a lawyer!"

#95: DON'T fall into the trap of taking yourself seriously because your work is serious.

There's no question that law is a serious business. Whether it's money or liberty that's at stake, it's all about solving problems, and often very *big* problems. Especially if you are a government lawyer or you work as a prosecutor, you'll feel as though the world is on your shoulders. And that can lead you to drown in your work and lose your identity to it. The fact is, you *could* spend 24 hours a day making yourself a better lawyer. But you *shouldn't*. As one law firm suggested, "Your work is important and you should take it seriously, but don't take *yourself* too seriously. You can drive yourself and your colleagues *crazy* if you don't learn to relax and enjoy yourself." And one junior government lawyer said, "The law was here before us, and it'll be here after we leave. We aren't *that* important. You've got to keep it in perspective."

#96: DO learn how to handle difficult people—without taking it personally!

Jerks. Idiots. Tyrants. You are unlikely to get all the way through your professional life without working for someone you don't totally see eye-to-eye with, any more than you've gotten along perfectly with every person in your life until this moment. The problem is, when it's *work* we're talking about, and the difficult person in question is a superior, it can be a very thorny problem. It may be that every employer looks for people who are "leaders," but studies show that most of us spend 80% of our time being *followers*—and when someone you're following *drives you nuts*, what do you do? It depends on the circumstances. Let's look at the possibilities:

a. No matter where you work or what the problem is, the very first thing you have to do is to eliminate the possibility that the problem is with *you*. Of course, this is very easy, isn't it? "It's not *me*. It's *him!*" Well, give it a little bit more thought than that. Part of your professional development is learning how to get along with superiors. Maybe the person in question is angry that every time you aren't assigned a particular project, you sit in your office reading magazines. From your perspective, you may think there's nothing wrong with that—if they're not giving you work to do, your time is your own. There's an argument to be made for what you say, but employers won't like it— and if you act that way, you'll be getting an angry reaction without understanding that you're the source of the problem. Another possibility is that you just hate authority. You've got a real issue with taking orders from *anybody*. Again—it's going to be difficult for you to get along as anything other than a sole practitioner if you feel that way. My point here is, make sure that the "difficult person" label belongs on the other person, and not *you*. If you find people at work avoiding you, confide in someone you trust and ask honestly for information on how you're perceived. Remember, when you're starting out, there's a pecking order that you *have* to learn to deal with. Don't mistake other people for "difficult" too hastily.

b. Accept the fact that sometimes people go through stressful times, and the stress comes out at work. It may be that the person in question isn't a jerk at all, but is going through a difficulty you know nothing about. Don't *assume* that the person is a jerk, and put into motion the alternatives I discuss below—transferring to another supervisor or department or, in the extreme, leaving the organization. If you *can*, keep an ear to the office grapevine to find out if the person is facing a crisis of some sort, and just needs a bit of forbearance. You may find that today's chaotic supervisor is tomorrow's sweetheart. Or as Katharine Hepburn put it in the movie *The Philadelphia Story:* "The time to make up your mind about people is—never."

c. *Subtlety* ask around, to figure out whether what's going on is a personality conflict between the two of you, or, in the words of Minnesota's
Susan Gainen, "the person is an equal opportunity jackass." If you ask
other associates, "Have you ever worked with X?" or "I'm working
with X. Got any tips?" you'll quickly figure out whether the person is
viewed as a saint—or a sinner.

Let's look at the possibility that the person in question doesn't have
a generally hideous personality, and that instead, what's going on here
is a simple, age-old 'personality conflict.' Face it. Some personalities
just don't mesh, with no fault on either person's part. Some people like
brash, ballsy in-your-face types. They find it refreshing. Others eschew
that kind of bluntness. Some communicate most comfortably on
paper, and are shy and tongue-tied in person. Others prefer to talk
things out. If you and your boss don't have compatible communication styles, "It doesn't mean your boss hates you!" reassures Chicago's
Suzanne Mitchell. "You need to acknowledge different skills. There's
nothing wrong with you or the other person."

What can you do? First, try to adapt to that person's style when
you're dealing with them. If you don't do well face-to-face, try communicating via e-mail for routine questions and updates. When you
do deal with the person, no matter how angry or frustrated they
make you, take a deep breath and remain calm.

Consider trying to compliment them on things—*anything*—that
you *truly* respect about them. (If you're fake about it, they'll smoke
you out right away). Maybe they've got a particularly noteworthy
accomplishment or they've come up with an excellent strategy for
something. Don't always be focusing on their (obvious) flaws. Many
times you'll find that if you can *honestly* praise something in a person
you can't stand, they'll soften up. You may even find a lot to like, if
you look hard enough!

If you continue to have difficulties, consider addressing the issue
with that person, in their or your office, *alone.* Don't be defensive
and don't lay blame. Instead, take an approach that says you recognize that communications aren't as smooth as they might be, and
you'd like to know if there's anything you can do to make it better.
It may be that the other person will be grateful and relieved that
you brought it up, and you can talk out your differences. It may be
that they won't know what you're talking about. If things continue
on a rocky basis, consider *tactfully* telling someone in authority,
someone you trust, about the problem. As UCLA's Amy Berenson
says, "If a personality conflict affects your work, you need to *tell*
somebody. Your reputation is more on the line than theirs. In a
large organization, your best bet is to tactfully try to be reassigned,"
although Minnesota's Susan Gainen warns that "This may be
fraught with peril if your boss is perceived as a sweetheart." If it's a

small organization, your options are more limited, and you may have to move on.

If the person is a well-known jerk, things are a bit different. Recognize that everybody knows what you're up against, and they'll sympathize with you. As one hiring partner told me, "Don't take it personally if you don't get along with a partner! Realize that partners' personality flaws are basically their problem. If a partner is an unreasonable tyrant, you won't be the first to discover it. The world is *full* of unreasonable tyrants, however, and law firms aren't exempt." Maybe they don't have good coping skills. Maybe they don't deal with stress well. Whatever it is—it's *their* problem, not yours!

If you do have to deal with someone *nobody* can stand, recognize first of all that you will be applauded for being able to tolerate Torquemada at all. Of course, that doesn't mean you should willingly spend your career with Mr. Happy. Instead, angle as best you can to do work with another supervisor or department. But in the meantime—or if the tyrant does work you really want to do, and you're willing to bite the bullet to get the work—try these tactics:

1. If you *can,* smile to yourself, vow *never* to be like that, and do your job as best you can. If you think you're going to look back years from now and laugh at what you had to put up with when you started your career, you might as well get a head-start and start laughing *now.*

2. Consider confronting the person, calmly. As Minnesota's Susan Gainen advises, "Tailor your approach to the personality you're dealing with. If the person is a screamer, use the techniques your parents used with you when you had a tantrum. Calmly say, 'Why don't I come back when you've had a chance to calm down?' and leave the room. Or ask, 'Can I get you a glass of water?' to cut the tension."

3. *Whatever* you do, don't engage! As Thomas Cooley's Bernice Davenport says, 'if you have to, close your office door and cry. But don't yell back!"

4. *Tactfully* let others know what is going on. You don't want to whine or beef, but you *do* want to inform. You need to make sure that at least one other person in a position of authority knows what you're enduring. There's a very practical reason for this. As DePaul's Neal Fillmore says, "If you wind up having to leave the employer because of this person, you don't want to have to tell a new employer that it was a 'personality conflict' that made you leave. They'll assume the problem was with *you.* If you informed someone *at the time* about what was going on, you'll have credible back-up when you need it."

5. The person is impossible to work for, but is not your immediate supervisor. Instead, it's someone who *can* assign work to you.

The key here? Be an "Artful Dodger." Oregon's Jane Steckbeck says that "When I started out as a lawyer, there was a man in my firm who was *impossible*. His life was chaos. He'd wait until the last minute, grabbing every associate, keeping them all night, and if he made any mistakes, he'd find a scapegoat." Handling such a person requires keeping an ear to the grapevine to find out when trouble is brewing. Jane Steckbeck says that "When he was on the warpath, I'd walk to the other side of the offices to avoid him." As she recommends, "Be nice politically—but physically unavailable."

For more—*much* more—on dealing with people in general, I *implore* you to buy the excellent book, *Work Would Be Great If It Weren't For The People*, by Ronna Lichtenberg. It's excellent, and funny, too, and it gives you every strategy you'd *ever* need for dealing with everybody at work.

#97: DON'T believe the myth about avoiding gossip—gossip can be good *for you!*

Virtually everybody will tell you to avoid gossip at work. It's well-meaning advice, and to the extent it refers to saying personally hurtful things about people—yes, it's a *very* bad idea to do that. But as a general precept, avoiding gossip is wrong-headed.

Why is that? Because the way people get ahead in *any* organization has a *lot* to do with the skillful use of the office "grapevine." That was obvious for every employer I researched for this book. The firm brochure isn't going to tell you which specialties are growing and which are fading, which senior associates are viewed as future leaders, who to align yourself with and who to avoid. Press releases aren't going to let you know which non-law department functions in a company are open to hiring lawyers in nontraditional positions. Orientation materials won't tell you "unspoken codes of behavior, personality quirks of partners, clients and support staff, whether weekend 'face time' is required or frowned upon," as Georgetown's Marilyn Tucker points out. If you cultivate the right sources, you'll hear about major ground shifts at work before they're official—who's getting which clients, where new offices are opening, how the business is doing, who's on the way up and who's on the way out. You'll learn what really counts—who it's really important to impress. Who wields power. Stated another way—where *else* are you going to find out this kind of information, *other* than the gossip tree?

Even more importantly, gossip can tell you what people think of *you*, what *your* image is like—and what you need to work on.

And apart from all of those practical reasons to heed gossip, telling yourself to cover your ears anytime someone whispers "Hey—guess what *I* just heard!" is unrealistic. We are fascinated by intrigue—it's how we're wired. So it goes against human nature to make your motto "Just say no to gossip."

Having said that, there *are* intelligent ways to hire gossips, and mistakes you can make. They include:

a. *Listen* to opinions, but draw your own conclusions about people. Marilyn Tucker advises you "not to base your behavior toward *anybody* on someone else's view. Take their opinion under advisement. That's all."

b. Keep other people's opinions to yourself. If they want to tell anybody what they think of them, they can do it directly.

c. Pass along "good" gossip. If you have a colleague who is looking for a transfer to a particular city or for a particular kind of work and you hear about an opportunity, or you hear a compliment about somebody, pass *that* along. Be a bearer of good tidings!

d. Don't be suckered into offering negative opinions. Artfully dodge without offending the gossiper. For instance, if someone rants about another colleague, and winds up with, "X is such a son of a bitch, don't you think?" Be evasive! Say something like, "I really haven't had enough to do with X to say," or "It's hard to say, but it sounds like you're having a hard time." Don't huffily say, "*I* don't gossip," because you can then be sure that you'll be gossiped *about*. As the columnist Miss Manners advises, it is possible to avoid giving offense in virtually any situation. (My favorite example from her column is the situation where someone proudly shows you their baby, and it's *particularly* ugly. She advises that instead of compromising your integrity, you say something that they will *interpret* as a compliment, like: "Now, *that's* a baby!")

e. In a group, beware of chiming in when someone backhands someone else in the organization. As one lawyer told me, "If you're sitting with a group at lunch and you're tempted to jump on the bandwagon, watch out! You don't know who everybody else in the room knows— or if they agree."

f. Don't cross office gossips. People who are good gossips are relentlessly curious, about everyone including you. Remember that people who are talking *to* you about someone else today will be talking *about* you tomorrow. Don't give them a reason to talk about you!

g. Don't hang with gossips. Keep a respectful distance. While gossip is important, you don't want your own image to be the office gossip. It may be fun, it may be interesting, and it may be *very* good for your career, but it's bad for your image.

h. Don't be tempted to pass along gossip for lack of anything else to say. Keep up with what's going on in the news. Take the time to go and see new movies. Even if you're busy, make a point of listening to the National Public Radio news—it's on every morning and every evening, and it's very thought-provoking. That way, you'll never be stuck for a conversational topic, and be tempted to say, "Hey, have I got a tidbit for *you!*"

As I suggested for dealing with difficult people, an excellent resource for learning more about handling gossip is Ronna Lichtenberg's book, *Work Would Be Great If It Weren't For The People*. Check it out!

DO'S AND DON'TS #98 THROUGH 118: EVERYTHING ELSE THAT CAN MAKE YOU OR BREAK YOU AT WORK, FROM GETTING WHAT THEY MEAN WHEN THEY SAY "TEAM PLAYER" AND "MATURITY," TO THE SIMPLE SECRETS OF GETTING GREAT WORK AND THE ART OF DEALING WITH CLIENTS.

#98: DO recognize that a rapid route to stardom is to determine a niche for yourself, in terms of business development or expertise.

What do people at the top of any organization do? They look *outwards* to figure out how to bring in business. Depending on the size of the organization you join, that may or may not be possible; as a new associate at a huge firm you're not likely to be able to solicit a Fortune 500 client. But you *can* take steps that prove your business savvy, and you *will* get noticed for it. The two likeliest avenues are to establish an expertise niche for yourself, something no one else in the firm does, or to target a particular kind of client.

How do you do this? Keep up with what's going on in the news. Think organically about what your organization does, and what areas are logical expansions *of* that. If you practice real estate law, it may be that no one in your firm is familiar with the Fair Debt Collection Practices Act, and that's a niche *you* can fill.

Look at your *own* talents, contacts and background to see if those suggest business opportunities for your employer. For instance, one law student I talked to had been an architect for 20 years before law school, and in that capacity he had developed working relationships with *many* contractors. There's a fertile business development opportunity for him. Another law student, a Korean-American woman, lamented the fact that many Korean business owners who attended church with her family weren't happy with their non-Korean speaking lawyers. There's *her* niche. The West Coast firm Davis Wright Tremaine told me about a First Year Associate who "targeted

Oregon wine growers as clients. He began by convincing a partner in the Hospitality Practice Group that it was a good idea, and then finding out what resources he had in the firm." Needless to say, the firm holds up this associate as a "success." One corporate associate at a huge New York City firm distinguished himself by targeting Internet-based businesses as clients. He began attending Internet trade shows, determined the bars where Internet entrepreneurs hang out and started frequenting them himself (now *there's* a tough assignment), and in general talked the talk and walked the walk. He's made substantial headway in luring them as clients.

Use these examples to fire your own imagination for the niche *you* can fill!

#99: DO recognize that getting great work isn't a matter of luck—it's a function of taking the right kind of initiative.

When something good happens to somebody, you'll often hear it attributed to "being in the right place at the right time." When it comes to getting great work, *you* can take active steps to make *sure* you're the one in that enviable position. It's *not* entirely a matter of luck. The fact is, if you want the best assignments, go to the people doing the work you want and *ask* to help out. That kind of enthusiasm is always appreciated. One firm advises new lawyers to "actively seek out specific types of work you want to do." Another talks of "Taking control of your career. Go after the work you want and the partners you want to work with." Another stated that "Partners love it when associates show they really want to work on a particular project, when they show genuine enthusiasm and not just a deadpan 'I can do it.'" One partner at this particular firm said that "I really like to see associates volunteer to take work in a particular area or for a particular client. I like it when an associate comes to me and says something like, 'I've never handled an IPO before, and I've heard you're starting one. Can I help?' Partners enjoy including associates on client teams who appear to be genuinely interested in their work."

#100: DO view your work as a career, not a job.

If you look at what you do as part of a ribbon stretching into your future, you'll behave differently than if you just consider this particular job a "one-night-stand." The people you meet at *this* job are your professional colleagues, *forever*. Your supervisors are potential recommendations. The support staff may go on to work at other places, and a favorable impression on them could come back to help you later on. No matter how new you are, you have begun your career and you need always to remember that! While no one expects you to work as quickly or have the judgment that you will later on, you're still a professional. As one lawyer put it, "A first year associate has just as much responsibility to protect his client's interests as does a senior partner."

#101: DO recognize that exuding enthusiasm is the ticket to great opportunities.

If you want great work, showing enthusiasm for what you're given, *everything* you're given, is the way to get it. "I appreciate . . . ," "Thank you for the opportunity . . . ," "I'm really excited about . . . ," and "I'm really looking forward to . . . " are phrases that should appear often in your work vocabulary. Ask for work. Take on responsibility. Appear eager to learn. A large firm partner described to me the experience of "giving an assignment to an associate and then having to 'get out of the way' because she could charge through and take the initiative to see the project through to the next level."

Now notice that I *didn't* tell you to *be* enthusiastic. I'm not so sure it's possible to *create* enthusiasm in yourself. Regardless, all I'm talking about is what you *convey to other people.* You certainly *know* the indicia of enthusiasm, and that's what you want superiors at work to see.

#102. DO recognize that employers aren't interested in changing diapers and wiping noses. You need to be perceived as "mature"—and understand that that means that you understand, and accept, the deal you've made—including a loss of autonomy.

'Maturity' is a word that comes up a lot when you ask employers what they look for in people they hire.

What do employers *mean* when they use the word 'maturity'? After talking with hundreds of them, I've come to the conclusion that maturity has many facets. One aspect of it has to do with accepting the grown-up nature of what you're doing. You don't want the demeanor of an undertaker—employers *like* people with a sense of humor—but you can't be "juvenile or sophomoric," as one employer put it. "You can't be caught playing garbage can basketball or reading comics in the workplace."

But a more important aspect of maturity has to do with accepting the deal you've made when you take on a job. You have to understand the compromises you make when you decide to work *anywhere*—or in fact when you decide to be a member of society, period. As soon as you conclude that you're not going to be Mowgli the Jungle Boy, you're surrendering some of your freedom. *Every* choice you make involves compromise and sacrifice. By taking a job and accepting benefits in return you are inherently turning down *other* benefits that *other* jobs entail. If you don't accept and make that bargain your own, you'll never be happy—or successful—doing *anything.*

Coincidentally, an unwillingness to take direction is an interview-killer. One employer actually told me about an interview he conducted on campus, where in response to the question "What's your greatest flaw?" the student said, "I don't take direction well." *See ya!*

Most significantly, you are giving up a sizable chunk of your autonomy when you agree to work for someone else. If you were to put your bargain with your employer into basic terms, you'd have this: "In return for salary X, I am selling you my time." As Northern Illinois' Mary Obrzut puts it bluntly: "If you sell someone your time, they own it." Oregon's Jane Steckbeck adds that "You've got to come to grips with someone else owning ten hours of your day. Work means a loss of autonomy." It means a loss of the flexibility you had as a student. There will no longer be a long Christmas break, a spring vacation, and summer off (unless you become a teacher, of course). Admittedly, different kinds of jobs entail different degrees of loss of autonomy. You might be micro-managed, or you might be handed a stack of files your first day and be told to "deal with them." In a corporation's in-house counsel's office, Chicago's Suzanne Mitchell warns that "An institution's lawyer *never* runs the institution—you're there for support. If you're a prima donna, don't go in-house!"

No matter what level of autonomy you get when you start out, *accept* it. As UCLA's Amy Berenson says, "You have to take the attitude during your first years that 'I'm starting out. I don't have the judgment to make these decisions on my own yet.'"

This can be very difficult to accept, and the longer the hours are, the more difficult it can be. But maturity means that you're entering the job with your eyes wide open, and that for what you give up—your time— you're receiving not just money but skills, and if you do *whatever* you do the best you can, you're expanding your future opportunities.

#103. DO learn what it means to be a "team player," and be sure to exhibit a team player sensibility.

I have to admit that the phrase "team player" has always had a somewhat sinister aspect for me. For some reason I imagine some sleazy supervisor requesting illegal or unethical behavior, and leering, "So . . . are you a *team player,* or not?"

In the real world, people don't have my vision in mind when they talk about team players (at least, I sure hope not). When employers talk about being a team player they're talking about a whole panoply of behaviors, from the way you treat your colleagues to your place in the community.

Vis-a-vis your colleagues, being a team player means that you don't exhibit an attitude of protectiveness over your time. You help out colleagues in a crunch. You give up your time knowing that the same will be done for you, when you need it. Sometimes it means working late into the night or on a weekend to help prepare a comprehensive opinion letter a prospective client wants as a precondition to hiring your firm. Or you conduct crash research and prepare an emergency petition because of a last-minute change of direction by a client. Or a colleague has a family emergency and you have to jump in and help out with their work.

Teamwork means not making outwardly competitive statements. Comments like 'I worked *this* many hours,' or 'I'm more senior than so-and-so,' or 'It should be my turn for the big office' will do nothing but discredit you.

Being a team player in a larger sense means taking part in the local community, taking part in recruiting and marketing if you're at a law firm, and considering client's objectives (or victims if you're a prosecutor) in delivering legal services.

If you're concerned that you won't get ahead if you're not a prima donna, relax. The way to be a star has nothing to do with bragging and jealously guarding your time. It has to do with showing enthusiasm for your work, doing excellent quality work product, and looking beyond what you're asked to do (as I outlined in #54, above). Don't alienate people by acting as though you're not part of the "team."

#104: DO prioritize work and family.

If your home life is miserable, that can't help bleed into and affect your work. It's a balance that successful lawyers learn to strike. One law firm advises its new associates to "find your own balance between your work life and your life outside the office. This balance is different for different people at different times, and sometimes involves devoting more time and energy to work and at other times devoting time and energy to other interests. Others will mentor you, but nobody else can find that balance for you." And Mark D. Chouteau writes in the *Texas Bar Journal*, "Don't forget that what you have with your law firm is a job, and what you have at home is your family. Nothing affects the quality of your work more than problems at home. Manage your time at work and take advantage of lax times to give priority to your family—they'll be more forgiving, then, when you're busy."

Minnesota's Sue Gainen offers the practical advice to "Exercise and eat right. Find the best Chinese takeout or delivery. Commit to meeting with four to six pals for breakfast once a month, and make sure they aren't people you work with. Join organizations that are meaningful to you. Keep connected with your friends from law school and before." Colorado's Tony Bastone adds, "Call your mom once a week!"

#105: DON'T do anything to compromise your reputation or integrity

There's a fine line between being an advocate and being a jerk. And you may be faced with many situations where it would be *much easier* to act immorally or unethically, to tell the client what they want to hear even if it's wrong, to mis-cite cases, to do *anything* you know in your heart is wrong. But no matter how easy it is, it's a mistake. When you start your career you have both a good name and a good reputation. As Loyola/New Orleans' Pam Occhipinti shares, "My father used to say, 'You can always make all the money in the world, but you can't make your name back.' Don't compromise your reputation. All attorneys know who the sleaze-bags are—and they don't forget!"

If you feel that you are in a situation where a supervisor is pressuring you to do the *wrong* thing, look past the specific request to the goal they are trying to reach, and see if there isn't an ethical way to accomplish that goal. Inevitably there's a client who's insisting on a particular answer, and your supervisor is feeling that pressure. If you are still pressured to do something unethical, speak to a mentor or another supervisor, in private, as discreetly as possible to get advice on resolving the situation. Loyola/New Orleans' Pam Occhipinti advises you that "If your boss forces you to do something unethical—leave. One associate I know worked for three partners in a plaintiff's personal injury firm. One day all three part-ners were arrested for stealing from clients. Realize that if your boss is dis-barred, you'll be investigated too." The bottom line? *Don't give in.*

#106: DO respect the importance of confidentiality *in your work. Don't sacrifice it for the sake of a "good story."*

Confidentiality is something that is *very* hard to live with. As I was con-ducting interviews for this book, people routinely told me things I'm *sure* they didn't want to say, and shouldn't have said.

The fact is, as a lawyer almost everything you do is covered by attor-ney-client privilege. Even the *fact* that someone is your client shouldn't be disclosed without permission from them. And when you're working for the government—at the Department of Justice, or the FBI or CIA—confi-dentiality is obviously a very large part of your existence. What does that mean? It means that when you're out swapping war stories with friends from school, you're going to have to be very careful about what you offer. And at family picnics, when your Mom says, "Oh, tell Uncle Frank about all the great things you're doing," you're going to have to be circumspect.

Also keep in mind that if you talk about another client's case with your client, they'll assume that you are, in turn, blabbing *their* case to others. If you must discuss analogies, use fact patterns sweeping enough that they aren't traceable to a particular client.

#107: DON'T let the existence of a supply room and a large office phone bill delude you into thinking it's OK to swipe office supplies and services.

When you go to work, you're getting paid a fine wage. At least—you're getting paid what you knew you'd get when you started. Look at that as *all* you get. Don't do petty things like abuse phone or mail privileges or clean out the office supplies. People *notice* small indiscretions. One recruiting coordinator recounted that a summer clerk wasn't invited back largely because he was caught using the office copy machine to copy invitations to a pool party at the house he was renting. It's just not good judgment. If you want to copy your personal stuff, do it where you copied outlines during law school. You know. *Kinko's.*

I'm laughing as I'm telling you this, because the worst example of pilfering that I know about is what I and my fellow summer clerks did at our firm. The firm had a policy of giving summer clerks as many field level tickets to major league baseball games as we wanted. We found this *very* hard to believe when they first offered it to us. We started out gingerly requesting two or four tickets, and they gave them to us, no questions asked. Then we got bolder, and started asking for 10 or 15. Now if we were actually using those tickets to treat permanent associates to games and getting to know them, I'd be holding myself up as a shining example of savvy summer clerk behavior. But we didn't. I am terribly ashamed to tell you that we were going to the games early and *scalping* all of those extra tickets. *Yikes!* This firm was paying us unbelievably handsomely, and we greedy little buggers were using their generosity as an opportunity for pulling in a little extra beer money.

So when I tell you not to swipe stuff from the office, I realize there's a strong element of 'do-as-I-say-not-as-I-do' going on here. But you get the point. Don't trash your professional reputation over a few stinking dollars' worth of stuff. It's too valuable for that.

#108: DO understand the art of e-mail.

I personally think that e-mail is the greatest invention since-well, I don't know. What was popular *last* year? But anyway, as efficient as e-mail is, don't overuse it at the office. The reason is this: there's a lot more to face-to-face communication than just words. For instance, if you say to me "You *idiot!*" snarling and with a fist under my chin, I'll get the impression you're really angry with me. But if you lovingly say "You *idiot!*" when I've just dribbled Kool-Aid on my shirt, it's almost a term of endearment. Same words, totally different meanings.

At the office, a lot of communication you have—especially with superiors—requires that you understand clearly and completely what they're getting across to you. It's *very* easy to misinterpret tone and intent with e-mail. So *unless you are working with a difficult person*—and I cover this in the section on "Dealing With Difficult Personalities"—make sure that your important conversations, *especially* your assignments, come about face-to-face.

#109: DON'T believe that if people have work for you, they'll come to your office and give it to you, so that you can sit there and wait for them.

If you think that getting plum assignments and increasing responsibility is a matter of luck, you're flying in the face of *everything* I heard from all different kinds of employers. Don't *ever* be seen sitting on your hands at work. If you are lucky enough to finish what's assigned to you ahead of

schedule, take the opportunity to poke your head in people's offices looking for ways you can help out. It's a golden opportunity to broaden your
skills and take on different kinds of projects. Associates at firms with
glamorous specialties like sports and entertainment tell me that the way to
break into those kinds of specialties is to work very efficiently on everything else you do, and then let the appropriate partners know that you'd
like to take on extra work for them.

Apart from getting great work, taking the initiative is a favor to your
supervisor. It's a mistake to think that lawyers are always on top of what
they've given you to do. They're not; they're busy. It's *your* career and *your*
professional development, and they're *your* responsibility. Take advantage
of any "down time" to prove your enthusiasm.

#110: DO recognize that every job entails a certain amount of drudgery.

Every job has a certain amount of "chimp work." You will never talk to
anyone, in *any* profession, who loves every moment of what they do (at
least, when they're not talking in sound bites). *Especially* when you start,
you've got to expect some tedium. As St. Louis' Wendy Werner says,
"People have expectations that a law degree is a ticket to exciting and
interesting work. At the beginning, when you're the equivalent of an
apprentice, it might not be. Don't burden your career with inflated expectations, not at the very beginning, anyway." The hiring partner at one huge
firm said that "The practice of law, at least in the early years, is 10% pure
exhilaration, 5% depression, and 80% tedium. As you progress the tedium
ratio lessens significantly."

#111: DO recognize how to handle bad projects and boring work so that you aren't branded as selfish and whiny—and so that you aren't permanently relegated to it!

When you get out of school, you feel as though you're finally ready for
excitement. It's time to realize your dreams! And it may be that the job
you take involves immediate excitement. As a prosecutor or public
defender, you're unlikely to be bored. But then there are jobs where
tedium plays a big role. As the recruiting coordinator at one large firm
told me, "Students want large firms for sophisticated, cutting edge work.
Ironically, as a new associate you get the most repetitive, boring assignments. You are often a small piece of a big puzzle."

But no matter where you work, you won't like *every* job you work on.
And depending on your specialty and your employer, you may get a *lot* of
boring work. If you work on complex litigation or in antitrust, you're not
going to get a lot of responsibility coming right out of the box. St. Louis'
Wendy Werner points out that the transition from law school to work is
tough because "In school, you study important, precedent-setting cases.
When you go to work, those *aren't* the cases you work on!" I heard about

one associate at a large East Coast firm who spent nine months in Nebraska locked in a warehouse doing document reviews. As a colleague of his said, "Exactly how long can you spend in Big Moose before you go crazy?" As a summer clerk I once had to research whether or not a city was responsible for the mosquitoes that bred in the stagnant water in discarded toilets at the city dump. Do you think I *cared* about that? Do you imagine that it was *interesting?* When I went out after work with friends, do you suppose they waited with baited breath to hear me talk about *my* day? *Oh, puh-leeze!*

Let's talk about ways to handle boring work. First, let's look at what you should do with a boring assignment. Oregon's Jane Steckbeck summarizes the approach well when she says "Do your best, look for opportunities to do projects you want, and keep your bitching to a minimum!"

a. Job one: Reality check! If you have joined a large organization, ask yourself this question: Exactly who *should* be doing the "grunt" or "chimp" work that requires a law degree. Senior partners? Or *you,* who just walked in the door? Face it—when you've been around a few years, *you* won't want to do document reviews. You're part of a pecking order. If you're working at a firm (or any other organization, for that matter) that takes on huge, complex cases and/or deals, the detail work will trickle down to you, as a beginner. It's true that great employers try to minimize the mentally constipating work, but when it comes in, it's going to fall in *your* lap—at least for now.

b. Adopt the attitude that this is what "paying your dues" *means.* Every successful person has done menial work, you just rarely *hear* about it. Hollywood is rife with stories of what stars did early in their careers. Brad Pitt delivered refrigerators. Mariah Carey was a hat checker. Quentin Tarantino was an usher at a porno movie theater. Tommy Hilfiger sold clothes from the trunk of a car. Uma Thurman was a dishwasher. Kelsey Grammer waited tables. Robin Williams scooped ice cream. Jack Nicholson sorted mail. The moral? Don't feel sorry for yourself. This too shall pass.

c. Recognize that in some situations, the reason you're not getting the most exciting work has to do with client perceptions of your lack of experience. As St. Louis' Wendy Werner points out, "If you were up for a capital offense, would you *want* a lawyer who's been out of school six months? Or what if you were defending a $2 million medical malpractice case?"

d. Recognize the importance of handling boring jobs with aplomb. It's easy to do well when you're doing what you *love.* Many, many people make the mistake of thinking that if they mope and drag their feet with work they hate, their supervisors will take this as a cue to give them more interesting stuff. *Not true!* If you slip into shoddy work habits and a bad attitude when you're doing bad work, you'll never get the responsibility of doing good work. As one law firm advises, "produce excellent work product *every* time, not just on projects that interest you. Supervisors really notice that." Another adds that "Supervisors look for new attorneys to jump into a project, whether it's mundane or sexy, give it their best effort, and go the extra mile to see the project through to completion. The fact is, you have to work hard and throw yourself into an assignment to really learn the ropes." Hamline's Joyce Laher points out that "Work study students who *staple* well have been known to get responsibility on a par with law clerks. Don't handle menial jobs in a menial way!"

But what if you're not just getting *one* bad assignment. What if the bad work keeps on coming? What if you get tedious work for months and months at a time? Your strategies are going to be somewhat different:

a. Don't *immediately* decide to leave the organization. Florida's Ann Skalaski, formerly a recruiting coordinator at a large firm, says that, "Law firms recognize the difference between being a malcontent and having an honest problem. If you're not enjoying yourself consistently, *say* something. Don't just look for another job and leave. My firm would have been *happy* to reassign unhappy associates to other departments. But too often they'd suffer in silence and leave, without giving us a chance to do something about it." Georgetown's Marilyn Tucker agrees, saying, "Tell the firm that you're committed to being a great lawyer and are concerned you aren't progressing at an acceptable rate." Boston University's Betsy Armour suggests "A direct—but political!—approach. No employer will fault you for saying, 'I've had a taste for this kind of assignment, and would love something new.'" She adds that, "It's important to look at your own professional development. View yourself as self-employed. Think of the skills you're getting, so that you're equipped with transferable skills when you move. You don't *want* to get backwater assignments—you need diversity! You need to vie for variety." Send out feelers to people in the organization doing work you *want* to do, soliciting future work from *them*. Don't bad mouth what you're doing now, but as we talked about in #109 on taking initiative, this kind of action is the best way to get good work.

b. Consider taking on pro bono work that is meaningful to you. Pittsburgh's Chris Miller says that, "People often find a way to enhance their professional life by doing pro bono work. It can be difficult to fit it in, but if your work doesn't feed your value system, pro bono *can*."

How do you know when to leave? When you've exhausted in-house possibilities for doing work that challenges you, and the prospects for getting good work in the next several months doesn't look promising, it may be time to pack your bags. An associate at one large firm told me about a big case that came up, which would require heavy staffing for two years and lots of travel, doing document reviews all over the country. *Awful* stuff. The firm brought together the second and third year associates, and the partner in charge of the case asked for volunteers. No one volunteered. The partner chastised them, "If you're single and don't have family obligations, we expect you to volunteer first." A woman raised her hand and said, "How will we ever *not* be single if we take this assignment?" The fact is, sometimes your best option *is* to leave. Colorado's Tony Bastone says that "As a rule of thumb, try to stay with your first job a couple of years. After a year and a half, head hunters will start coming after you." And don't wring your hands, figuring that you'll never be happy. A change of environment can make a huge difference. As Emory's Carolyn Bregman says, "Firms are different than each other. And firms in general are different from DA's offices or government agencies or corporations. A slight change can make a big difference in your life."

#112: DO take action if you find you aren't getting assignments at all.

Work tends to ebb and flow. You'll find that there will be times when you'll have a steady stream of "Hair on Fire" days, and others when you've got time on your hands. In fact, lawyers often find it difficult to talk about the length of their "average" work day for just this reason.

Nonetheless, if you start to perceive that you aren't getting as much work assigned to you as you *should* be getting, it's worth investigating. As Florida's Ann Skalaski says, "It could be perfectly innocent. Maybe people just think you're busy. Or it could be more serious. Maybe you dropped the ball on a project, and word got out." What to do? "Go to a person involved in the hiring process and talk to them about it. They've got a vested interest in solving the problem." Brooklyn's Joan King adds, "*Always* volunteer. Go door to door looking for assignments. Be proactive! They may not realize you don't have enough work!"

#113: DO recognize that despite your best-laid plans, you'll have "Hair on Fire" days.

That's what Stephanie Rever Chu calls them—days that are out of control. *Everybody* has them sometime, in *every* job. You're overwhelmed by work, you get a sudden and unexpected deadline, you (or somebody else) dropped the ball in a heinous way. As the hiring partner at one law firm told me, "Practicing law isn't just a job. Typically clients aren't willing to pay lawyers until the problem has become severe, and then they expect their lawyers' undivided immediate attention. Most lawyers are surprised by how demanding the profession can be. Successful lawyers take it in stride, without excuses or complaints."

So when the sky is falling, take a deep breath, marshal the help you need, and handle the situation with outward calm. You can cry, scream, or curse in the bathroom—but the way you deal with crises is just as important as the way you deal with your day-to-day responsibilities.

#114: DO work with a variety of people, if you can.

There are a number of great reasons for this. For one thing, it gives you a greater opportunity to identify the precise work you want to do. I talked with *many* junior lawyers who would never have been able to identify their specialty when they first started, and lucked into it by taking on a variety of projects. Another benefit is that working with a variety of people minimizes the effect of any one person not getting along with you. As St. Louis' Wendy Werner says, "You need to find champions. In a meeting where they're trying to decide whether you stay or go, you need people who would stand up for you and be listened to. The more opinions there are of you, the better off you are."

And finally, you've got the career-enhancing fallout of knowing more people. I've mentioned many times that this job isn't likely to be your only one. The larger a net you cast now, the more people who know and like you, the more likely you are to hear about great opportunities down the road.

#115: DO recognize how to use mentors—and why you can't choose one yourself!

Everybody talks about the importance of mentors—a more senior person who takes a maternal/paternal interest in your career, a source of inspiration and a sounding board when you need to discuss problems. While a mentor is a great asset, here's the problem. You can't go after one yourself. You can't ask people, "Will you be my mentor?" As New York Attorney Alan Rosenberg says, "Generally your mentor picks *you,* not the other way around." Your employer may assign you a mentor, but don't put too much faith in that. Mentoring is organic, and studies show that assigned mentors typically don't work out.

So how *do* you get a mentor? How do you make sure you aren't sitting on the sidelines at the dance? Alan Rosenberg advises that you "remain open to personal overtures of friendship and respond when the opportunity arises." Working with, and meeting, as many colleagues as possible greatly increases your chances of finding a suitable mentor. And of course, a mentor doesn't have to come about through your own workplace—taking part in industry-oriented functions, like bar association meetings if you're a lawyer and trade association activities if you're in business—are happy hunting grounds as well.

Connecticut's Diane Ballou cautions that if you are a woman, be careful about male mentors. Not that they can't be great mentors—of course they can. But you don't want to attract a harasser instead of a mentor. If you start getting the sense that there are sexual overtones to your putative mentor's offer of help, politely and discreetly turn it down and keep your eyes open for a mentor who is interested in you in a more appropriate way.

#116: DO learn the art of dealing with clients. (Here's how.)

It may be that your employer gives you client contact very early on. If you are at a private firm, clients are customers. Their business is what makes *your* paycheck possible. With that in mind, it's very important for you to know how to handle them, from the get-go. New York attorney Alan Rosenberg says that successfully practicing law is 99% good service, and 1% genius. Handling clients is an area that is *crucial* to your long-term success! Here's what you need to know:

a. As one firm advises its new associates, "Watch how partners deal with clients. *Observe.* But remember, you can't treat clients with the same degree of familiarity as the partner does. Behave with respect and responsiveness and professionalism."

b. Be friendly but remember: you're still the lawyer. As one law firm says, "It's a mistake not to know where to draw the line with 'kidding' with friendly clients."

c. Understand the client's point of view. They seek your assistance to deal with issues of significance to them. To serve them best, when you listen to a problem, try to get to the root cause of the client's difficulty and his or her ultimate objectives, which frequently don't fit any textbook analysis.

d. *Always, always, always* return client calls promptly. As Georgetown's Marilyn Tucker says, "One of the major malpractice claims brought by clients relates to unanswered phone calls and the resulting feeling of abandonment." If you can, return phone calls within the hour, or if that's not possible, by the end of the day. Lewis & Clark's Lisa Lesage adds that "You don't need to answer the phone constantly. Instead, put in blocks of time during your day when you'll return calls. Let your secretary know when that is so that (s)he can tell clients. One good plan is to answer calls in two blocks—the first right before lunch, and the second just before the end of the business day."

e. If a client you're working for calls your superior, and your superior is out of town or otherwise tied up, make your superior look good by returning their call to the client. As Marilyn Tucker says, "Hearing from you is better than no communication at all. Leave a note to the supervising attorney and for the file recording the client contact and letting him/her know the substance of the call, to avoid embarrassment or confusion or misunderstanding." Similarly, if you are working on a client project with peers who are ill or in court or out of town when the client calls them, return *their* calls to make them look good. Marilyn Tucker says that "Clients don't expect their calls to go unanswered"—and in making your peers look good, you'll be treating them as you'd want them to treat you when *you're* in the same situation.

f. When you meet with a client, Lewis & Clark's Lisa Lesage advises you to "give them your full attention. Don't let phone calls or visits interrupt." Whatever the client is talking about with you is *very* important to them, and you should treat that concern with respect.

g. Don't take a position on behalf of a client or the firm without checking with superiors first. As one law firm advises, "Show initiative and independence, but don't be a 'cowboy.'"

h. Remember that e-mail "opens up ethical problems with clients, whether you're e-mailing them or they're e-mailing you" says Lisa Lesage. "Either don't e-mail clients or check with the firm first. The problem is twofold: first, there's a confidentiality issue, and second, you're creating a record. Ask Monica Lewinsky! If it's not privileged, it's subject to discovery. That's not true of a phone call with a client, which is privileged."

i. In the same vein, remember that there is no reasonable expectation of privacy on a non-hard phone line (*i.e.*, cell phones). If you need an image that will stay with you, remember when a cell phone conversation was recorded and made public a few years ago, purporting to reveal Britain's Prince Charles telling Camilla Parker Bowles that he'd like to be reincarnated as one of her—well—sanitary products. Presumably you will not have conversations like that with your clients. But no matter what you're talking about on a non-hard phone line, you have no expectation of privacy with regard to it.

j. For corporate clients, view each one in its entirety. Don't just focus on the particular legal problem at hand. As one law firm says, "Law isn't practiced in a vacuum. In order to serve clients, you have to understand their business and their business goals." Another advises that you "make an effort to understand the ins and outs of your client's business, not just its legal needs. New associates who really stand out are the ones who develop a relationship with the client which shows they are interested in the client's business and well-being, not just the narrow legal task."

k. Finally, in the words of Joseph Cammarata, former lead attorney for Paula Jones: "If a client comes to you and says, 'It's not about money, it's about principle,' remember this: Principle gets expensive."

#117: DO keep an eye to your ongoing career development, no matter how busy you are right at this moment.

It's very easy to figure that once you have a "permanent" job, your career planning is over. Not so! As St. Louis' Wendy Werner advises, "Your career planning doesn't end when you start work! You still need to devote a couple of hours a week to it. What's your long-term goal, and how do you get there? What skills are you learning? And are you developing skills that you can use later on? As a legal services lawyer, be on the board of a not-for-profit. As a trial lawyer, take seminars. Assume that no job is permanent, but skills *are*. You can take those *anywhere*."

In addition, make sure you aren't getting office "tunnel vision." Keep a hand in the community. Pittsburgh's Chris Miller advises you to "interact with other attorneys outside of your own work environment, like the young lawyer's section for the county bar association." In addition, Northern Illinois' Mary Obrzut encourages you to "Keep cards on everyone you meet, marking down when you talked, important details about them." She adds that when you see someone mentioned in the newspaper, if you know them "Clip the article and send it to them. Keep in touch!" As she advises, "The best way to your next great job is a 'live' network that you maintain in *this* one."

#118: DO acknowledge that some days you're the windshield, and some days your the bug: your career does *involve an element of luck.*

As New York attorney Alan Rosenberg advises, every legal career is studded with both unexpected and undeserved legal achievements and equally unexpected and undeserved legal defeats. Don't blame yourself—or pat yourself on the back—for *everything* that happens to you.

DO'S AND DON'TS #119 AND 120: ADVICE SPECIFIC TO NEW ASSOCIATES AT LARGE FIRMS.

Virtually everything you read in these 'DO's and DON'Ts'—writing assignments, dealing with people, getting organized, everything—applies to you. In addition, remember:

#119: If you go to work for a large law firm, DO recognize that the partners are your client base for your first few years. To get ahead, put yourself in their shoes and think about how you would want to be treated and the quality level of work you would want to see. That should give you a helpful frame of reference for relating to partners from the very beginning.

#120: DO recognize that the huge paycheck and the American Express Platinum Card, comes at a price: hours.

If you go to work for a large law firm, it is *exceptionally* likely that you will be putting in long hours. If everybody else is there late, *you'll* be expected to stay late, as well. You *cannot* be the only person to leave before dinner if everybody else is burning the midnight oil.

I'm not going to tell you working long hours doesn't stink. But I *will* tell you that in talking to all of the large firm associates I interviewed for this book, I noticed a very interesting phenomenon: the successful ones, the junior associates who'd been singled out as stars at their firms, *uniformly* were not resentful of the hours they work. The best analogy I can think of comes from the movie *Annie Hall*, where there's a split screen showing Woody Allen and his girlfriend at their respective therapists. The therapists each ask, "How often do you have sex?" Woody responds, "Almost never—twice a week," and his girlfriend tells *her* therapist, "All the time—twice a week." When I've talked with associates and asked them if they work long hours, some will respond, "Oh no, I'm out by seven or eight," while others say, "Yes. I usually have to stay until six."

If everybody in your office works late, resolve yourself to that reality before you start. Put your personal life on automatic while you undertake this crucial early part of your career. Have in mind the *reason* you're putting in all these hours—perhaps to get a great credential on your resume for your *next* job, or to pay off student loans, or to pave the way to partnership at *this* firm. Whatever it is, resolve yourself to the deal you've struck. And recognize that the long hours won't last *forever*.

DO'S AND DON'TS #121 THROUGH 125: ADVICE SPECIFIC TO LITIGATORS.

#121: DO understand when you're being an advocate, and when you're being a jerk.

Remember that you may get a much better deal for your client if you treat the other lawyer with courtesy and respect. Not only that, the other lawyer—and the other lawyer's client—may prove valuable to your career in the future. Public Defender Sarah Madden, who started her career at a small firm, recounts that "I worked on a case when I started out, and when it was over, the woman on the other side said to me, 'I wish I'd found you before *my* lawyer. You treated me with respect. Next time I need someone, I'll come to you.'"

#122: DO immediately make friends with secretaries and clerks at the courthouse.

Wake Forest's Bill Barrett warns that you should "*Never* offend court personnel. Clerks at the courthouse can make your life a living hell. They won't do what you want just because you're a lawyer."

As Sarah Madden, a public defender in Kentucky, advises, "If you treat court staff like dirt, that document you needed to file Thursday—it got dropped. It got filed Friday and you missed your statute of limitations. I once got stuck in traffic, and I wanted a motion heard the following week, and it had to be filed *that day*. I missed the deadline, but the clerk took care of it for me anyway. The same applies to sheriffs. If you want your summonses served on time, be nice to them! At a job I had a few years ago, I had a boss who once said to me, 'Why do you put up with that sheriff calling you 'Sweetie?' I answered, 'He may have tobacco dripping from his chin and he may call me 'Sugar,' but my summonses get delivered on time.' It's like the old saying goes—you catch more flies with honey than with vinegar."

#123: DO get to know the assigned judge before you get too far into a new case.

The Nevada firm Jones Vargas advises new lawyers that "Knowing the judge's likes and dislikes, his or her requirements, pet peeves, and the like, is so much more critical than you could imagine just coming out of law school. Knowing the judge will help you avoid the many pitfalls involved in learning the ropes of practice before the courts."

#124: DON'T rely on a "silver tongue" to win the day in court.

As Loyola/New Orleans' Pam Occhipinti says, "Remember that when you go to court, preparation beats skill nine out of 10 times."

#125: DO acknowledge that the quickest way to earn respect is to reread the Rules of Civil Procedure (if you do civil litigation).

By the same token, the quickest way to embarrass yourself is *not* to read the Rules of Civil Procedure.

DO'S AND DON'TS #126 THROUGH 130: ADVICE SPECIFIC TO NEW ASSOCIATES AT SMALL FIRMS.

#126: DO recognize the activities that will get you off to a quick start in client development.

Chicago-Kent's Stephanie Rever Chu observes that "Many new associates are aware of the importance of client development, and they'll say things like, 'I'll be active in the bar association.' The problem is that unless your business involves a lot of referrals from *other* lawyers, that will be of limited use. It will help you keep up with new issues, but it won't generate new business." Instead, "Depending on the clients you want to attract, look at community activities that will get you in touch with those constituencies. If you do estate planning and tax work, look at doing presentations at senior community groups and nursing homes. If you have a family law practice, talk to brokers with high net worth clients who may get divorced, and go to lunch with them periodically." Think *strategically* when it comes to getting to know people who could potentially become clients. Lewis & Clark's Lisa Lesage asks "Are you fluent in sign language? One new lawyer I know gets business from the deaf community because *he* is."

Wake Forest's Bill Barrett suggests being visible in the community by "volunteering with organizations to help them with articles and bylaws and other formalities. Look for places that aren't deluged with lawyers. As a new lawyer I talked about legal issues to the local AARP (American Association of Retired Persons) chapter, and got lots of estate planning work that way. You have to view being a lawyer with a small firm as building a practice, which is a business—not just having a job."

Sarah Madden points out that community involvement "Isn't just something that's good on your resume, and it's not just a good networking tool. If you move to another city, in another state, and they ask you what you're bringing to the table—it's got to be more than education and personality. 'I'm active with the JayCees, the Red Cross, I can bring those people to you.' You can do community work for the best reasons or the most selfish reasons."

#127: DO rely on other lawyers, in your office and elsewhere, for advice on things you've never done before (including the magic words that get you the help you need).

If you work for a small firm, you won't have the "safety net" that large firms have—there won't be layers of people between you and clients. That's both exciting and terrifying. Oregon's Jane Steckbeck recounts that as a new lawyer at a small firm, she was told "You've got to do expert witness depositions in two days." She says that "I'd *never* done it, and had no idea *how* to do it. I asked other lawyers in the office. One of them gave me the red 'Depositions Handbook.' There was a chapter in there on it. The fact is, maybe you haven't done it, but someone else *has*. You'll *always* be asked to do a bunch of things you've never done before. Don't show them tentativeness! Don't get a forlorn look on your face and say 'But I've never done this before.' Show humility, but be enthusiastic. Approach whoever gave you the project—and others!—for examples and advice. It's like that saying says: 'Face the fear and do it anyway.'"

Lewis & Clark's Lisa Lesage agrees. She recommends that you contact other lawyers in the community, through the local bar association or informally, when you need help. She points out that "Lawyers love to talk about (a) themselves, (b) what they know, and (c) advice about your case. Even with lawyers at other firms, the magic words are 'I've got this case—can I take you out to lunch and learn about criminal defense?' You'll be amazed. They'll have all kinds of advice, they'll send pleadings. There's help out there for you, even outside of your office."

#128: DO take every case and every client seriously, even if there is very little at stake.

As Public Defender Sarah Madden says, "Everybody's case is the most important thing in *their* life. Their divorce, their dog bite, it's all they can think about. They've paid you and they deserve you to take it seriously."

She adds that "Even when you can't help them out—the Statute of Limitations ran out, or they just don't have a claim—make an effort to make them feel better when they walk out than when they came in. Not only does kindness make you feel good, but you never know when they'll come back with a *big* case—or send someone else to you."

#129: DO have an intake form so you can get all pertinent information from clients during the first interview.

Lewis & Clark's Lisa Lesage says that if you take information in a systematic way, "You won't have to annoy clients with phone calls to follow up." She advises that you use "check off sheets—you'll find them in CLE books, and how to books, or an experienced attorney or law librarian or the young lawyer's section of the local bar can help you with them. If you can't find ready-made forms on something, think about the law—for instance, the fair housing law—and think of the facts you need." She adds that "These questions make you look like you know what you're doing—a valuable asset."

#130: DO copy clients on correspondence and pleadings you send out for them.

I've mentioned before the importance of keeping in steady contact with clients, and returning their phone calls promptly. Copying them on correspondence and pleadings is another valuable—and easy—way of keeping them involved.

Lewis & Clark's Lisa Lesage also advises that "If a case drags on for months, contact clients by letter once a month, just a couple of lines to say the status hasn't changed, you're waiting for X, and you'll keep them posted."

STICKS AND STONES MAY BREAK YOUR BONES AND WORDS AT WORK CAN KILL YOU

This chapter is about traits you should exhibit, actions you should take, attitudes you should adopt. I've provided this section to take care of something *very* specific—that is, *I want to make sure that there are words that never cross your lips.* You can't *imagine* how quickly an untoward comment can tank your career, if it's said to the wrong person. Don't *ever, ever, ever* use these words.

- *Self-effacing and self-deprecating comments.*

    There's a difference between humility and lack of confidence. As Hamline's Joyce Laher says, employers want to believe they've hired the best person when they hire you. Don't make them feel they've made a mistake! So don't *ever* say things like:
    "I'm not really good at this."
    "I don't know much about X."
    "I only did that once before."
    "I don't want to do that."
    "Okay, if I really <u>have</u> to."

- *Personally harmful comments.*

    "God, X is getting fat!"
    "Guess who's sleeping with . . . "

- *Complaints. I keep saying this and I keep meaning it. Don't say things like . . .*

    "I expected a better library."
    "I want a bigger office."
    "My secretary is useless."
    "This case is boring."
    "I really can't be bothered."

- *Anything to a colleague suggesting that you think they aren't important.*

    "I'm not too busy to work with Partner Important, but I'm too busy to work with you."

- *Anything competitive.*

    "I worked this many hours."
    "I'm more senior than so-and-so, make *him* do it."
    "It should be my turn for the big office."

    If you are tempted to say these things—and all of us occasionally *are*—I am going to give you a mental image that will zip your lips. It's this. Think of people you know who already *do* say these things. When they say them, do you consider them more competent? Do these statements inspire confidence? If you were their superior, would you promote them, recommend them, or vote them into your partnership? I didn't think so. Don't let *other* people form a negative opinion about *your* potential because of words you can easily avoid!

UPPING THE ANTE: HOW TO MAKE THOUSANDS MORE THAN YOU THOUGHT YOU WOULD

Don't tell me. Let me guess. You're going to work for a medium-to-small firm—maybe even a sole practitioner—and you're not happy with the money you've been offered. Or else you've heard about small firm salaries, and even though you think that's the direction you're going, the money issue makes your blood turn cold. What should you do? What *can* you do? What I'm going to do in the next few pages is to give you the basic strategies that could well line your pockets with more scratch than you expected.

From the outset, you need to know that money is a tricky issue. There aren't any guarantees that you can get more than you were offered. But you *might* be able to. And if what I'm telling you here doesn't help, you should spend a few bucks to learn more. That is, go out and get Kathy Brady's book, "What Lawyers Earn, and How To Negotiate For More." Kathy Brady is a genius and her book gives you all kinds of facts and statistics and pointers to help you make more money. A *lot* more money.

OK. So what do you need to do to make more money? I've got a simple, three-point plan for you.

STEP ONE: *Knowledge is power.*

You need to know as much as you can about what the market will bear. Kathy Brady's book gives you salary ranges for all kinds of lawyer-type jobs all over the country. The National Association for Law Placement puts out very comprehensive statistics (you'll find them at your Career Services Office) that tell you how much different kinds of law firms pay, in different geographic areas, not just as starting pay but several years out into the future, as well.

Why is this important? Two reasons. For one thing, if you find that the range for a small firm in the area where you're going to live is $30,000 to $35,000, and you want $65,000, unless you've got some very clear, very incriminating Polaroids, you're probably not going to get it. On the other hand, you might learn that the employer you're considering is at the low end of the scale. If so, you know—and you can assume that *they* know—that there's wiggle room. You've got negotiating power before you ever enter the room.

STEP TWO: *Recognize that in the absence of other considerations (which we're going to talk about in a minute), you have limited negotiating power as a new lawyer.*

When you are talking about a small-ish firm looking at *you,* as an untested lawyer, here's what they're seeing. "When you start, it will take you four hours to do a memo that years down the road you'll be able to knock out in twenty minutes. Much of your early time is written down or written off," says Emory's Carolyn Bregman. Connecticut's Diane Ballou adds that "When you start, you don't know anything. They can't send you out alone, you have to tag along, and they can't charge for you. And if you're going to work for just one person, bringing you on is a quantum leap no matter *how* much you get."

So don't get hung up on what you're coming to the table with, just because of your J.D. If you want more, you've got to *offer* more. Which leads me to . . .

STEP THREE: Answer the question "What's in it for me?"—or encourage them to overlook that question entirely.

Let's say that a small firm, Smith & Jones, offers you $35,000 a year as a new associate. And let's say that this is bang in the middle of the range for your geographic area. You want more. How do you go after it? You have three choices. You can bring more to the table, you can ask for "non-dollar-figure" compensation, or you can negotiate up-front for down-the-road increases.

Before we discuss what these are, remember that asking for more money is not without risk. They may be open to your ideas, with the idea in mind that they want you to be happy working for them. Or they might be resentful that you brought it up at all. Make your approach *gentle* and watch for signals telling you to negotiate further—or retreat. And *always, always, always* stress to them that you are *grateful for the opportunity* to work with them, the money issue aside!

So, let's talk about options for squeezing out more pay:

a. What else can you offer them? There are many possibilities, including:

- Consider negotiating for a cut of business you bring in. This is a particularly easy sell, because if you don't bring in more business, you don't make more money. It's a no-lose proposition for the employer.

- Offer to write a firm newsletter, as a means of gaining publicity, clients, and keeping their presence visible.

- Offer to give seminars to a key audience for them—be it the elderly (for estate planning work), investment clubs (for tax work), and the like.

- Offer to set up and maintain a firm home page, if you've got that kind of skill.

Any one of these would be viable options for earning more money. What you want to be careful about is any work you decide to do on the side. One lawyer told me about a woman who was doing contract work (it's basically freelance lawyering) for several small firms. One of them made her an offer to join them as an associate. She wasn't thrilled with the offer, but took it anyway—and maintained some of her contract work. The firm found out, and the managing partner went nuts and fired her. So be aware that if you'd rather do extra work elsewhere than negotiate for more money from your employer, you should do it openly. Obviously you can do things like tutoring law students and bar examinees, and there are other kinds of freelance work—like web page design, database management—that are unlikely to offend any law firm employer. In fact, it might shame them into paying you more, out of guilt that you've got to moonlight to pay your bills.

b. "Non-dollar-figure" compensation

This is a bit of a misnomer, because what you're really asking for here *does* have a monetary value. But since you're not saying, "I want another $3,000," it doesn't *seem* the same. It's somewhat the same psychological trick that's going on when you go to a casino, and instead of betting with money, you're betting with chips. It doesn't seem like money that way. Well, you're using that same principle when you negotiate for non-dollar-figure compensation. You can ask for things like:

- Paid parking.
- Reimbursement for car expenses, if you're expected to travel in your own car.
- Paid lunches.
- A 401K plan.
- Insurance (or alternatively, if they're offering you insurance and your spouse's policy covers you, ask for the money they'd have spent on it to cover you).
- If you haven't taken the bar yet, a bar review course.
- Professional fees.

You get the idea here—you're asking for small things in a non-monetary way to soften the blow.

c. Negotiating now for down-the-road increases.

If the prospects for getting a higher salary look dim—or you try and strike out—consider negotiating for fixed-period increases in the future. Connecticut's Diane Ballou suggests that "If you take a job at $28,000 now, you can ask for a reevaluation at three months, six months, nine months, with a chance to make more money then." As she points out, "This gives them a chance to get to know you and like you and need you, and your chances will be better as a result."

Actually, your chances of getting a big raise are *much* better if you can bite the bullet and negotiate after you've worked with them for at least a few months. Especially with a small organization, they may quickly find that they can't remember how they functioned without you, and that gives you leverage you didn't have at the outset. You'll also be able to say that you progressed with your work product, your writing skills, and perhaps your business development ability.

STEP FOUR: *What to do if your bid for more money fails.*

Trying to negotiate for more money at the outset is *fraught* with risk. You may alienate an employer who was otherwise willing to welcome you with open arms, but now feels that you are selfish and ungrateful. And you may be resentful that they don't value your time more than your paltry salary suggests. What do you do? *Fuhgedduhbadit. Pretend you never asked in the first place.* You've got to approach your job with enthusiasm, an air of appreciation and an obvious desire to learn, no matter *how* much money you make. Rest assured that you'll have *plenty* of opportunities to ask for more money once they've had a chance to actually discover for themselves how valuable an addition to the firm you prove to be—and you'll be able to look back on your early, lean years as the learning experience that they are!

Other Books to Read.

Who's kidding whom? This is a long book, but it's not the universal solvent. There are other great books on jobs and job search, and fortunately for you, I actually know about a few of them—and would like to recommend them to you.

First and foremost—knowing where it's great to work does you no good if you don't know how to get those jobs. The best source for that is one I'd be stupid not to recommend—*Guerrilla Tactics For Getting The Legal Job Of Your Dreams*. Duh! I wrote it. It's published by Harcourt Brace, and you can find it just about everywhere.

Perhaps the greatest compliment you can pay another writer is to say that they wrote a book you wish *you'd* written. I can say that about my new favorite book, the wonderful *Work Would Be Great If It Weren't For The People*, by Ronna Lichtenberg. It is funny and bang-on when it comes to handling all kinds of office relationships. It's published by Hyperion, and I beg you to run out and get it. You'll laugh, you'll cry—and you'll be a *much* better lawyer.

Two great sources for public interest jobs and internships: *The NAPIL Directory of Public Interest Legal Internships*, which is put out by the National Association for Public Interest Law. Your career services office probably has it, but you can call NAPIL directly at 202-466-3686 if you want a copy of your own.

The other public interest resource is the fantastic *Public Service Employer Directory*. It's put together by the University of Chicago Law School and the University of Michigan Law School. Again, this is probably at your law school career service library, but you can order your own copy from Legal Support Systems, Inc., at 617-864-6600.

My favorite book on internships is *America's Top Internships*, which is published by The Princeton Review. It is not only a great resource but also a fun read.

A few of the profiles in Chapter 3 on "Dream Jobs" came from another book I really like—*Alternative Careers for Lawyers*, by my friend Hillary Mantis. It's published by The Princeton Review. If you're interested in being a "not-lawyer," this is a great resource.

If you're looking at large firms in big cities, you definitely want to take a look at *The Insider's Guide To Law Firms*, by the Mobius Press. It's a very popular book, and justifiably so—it's a very interesting read.

If money's on your mind—and who's mind *isn't* it on?—check out my friend Kathleen Brady's *What Lawyers Earn, and How to Negotiate for more.* You'll get all kinds of information on money issues, and can make a bunch more money if you follow Kathy's advice.

The National Association of Law Placement's Directory of Legal Employers. This is an enormous, phone-book-sized reference to over a thousand of the country's largest legal employers, with all kinds of information on each employer.

If the Internet is your bag, then the person you've got to know is Bill Barrett. He's the Career Services Director at Wake Forest, but more importantly for our purposes here, he knows everything there is to know about finding jobs via the Internet. Fortunately for you, he publishes books on that very topic. One you'd like would be *The Lawyer's Guide to Job Surfing On The Internet.* To get a copy of it, write to Career Education Institutes, at P.O. Box 11171, Winston-Salem, NC 27116-1171. He also has a website; it's www.internships-ysa.com.

If you're interested in getting a job in sports, I can steer you to a couple of helpful books. One is *Career Opportunities in the Sports Industry.* By Shelly Field, published by Facts on File, 1991. The other is *How to Get a Job in Sports,* by Dale Ratermann & Mike Mullen, published by Masters Press, 1995.

Leadership Directories—those big yellow books, that are called, ironically enough, Yellow Books. They're very comprehensive resources. You'll find them for Corporate, Law Firms, Federal Government, States, a whole variety of topics.

Hoover's Handbook of American Business, published by The Reference Press. If you want to find out basics about companies, Hoover's is the place to look.

How to Get Your Two Cents Into the Next Edition of This Book.

You already know my sources for this book—law school administrators all over the place. I continued to hear about great employers even after I'd passed my cutoff for including them in this book, and those will appear in the second edition. You see this kind of book is like one of those giant underground funguses that keep on growing and growing, although perhaps that's not the most savory analogy I could have used. Employers who'll be in the second edition include the law firms Miller Cassidy (in Washington, D.C.) and Powell Goldstein (in Atlanta), and the legal department at Nabisco. There's a little preview for you.

But that's not very important right now. What *is* important is that for the next edition of this book, on top of catching up with the people I interviewed for this edition and *hopefully* talking to many more on my list—I'd love *your* input! Whether it's particular employers you think ought to be included, stories about employers in *this* book, whole categories of jobs you'd like to hear more about—let me know!

If you'd like to nominate an employer for inclusion in the next edition, here's what I'd like to know from you:

How do you know the employer is an excellent one? For instance, do you work there (if so, in what capacity)? Did you work there? Do you have friends there who love what they do? If you don't tell me how you know what you know, even I—the least skeptical person on Earth—will be a bit suspicious of what you've got to say!

Do you know about a whole category of jobs that ought to be included, like law school administration or law librarian jobs? For instance, I didn't hear anything one way or another about law-related journalism, even though my hunch is that it must be a great job. And Fellowships. I didn't hear about fellowships at all, and I'm hunching that they can be pretty terrific.

Anecdotes! It's one thing to tell me *that* an employer is great. It's so much more interesting to hear *why* (that's what the 'Word on the Street' sections in this book were all about). Do tell!

I'd tell you I'd send you an "America's Greatest Places" T-shirt or something like that, but hey—sorry. If you say something amusing enough I will e-mail you back, though. And if what you say is added to the second edition, I'll put you in the acknowledgements. You may *think* that's not such a big thing, but I gather, purely as rumor you understand, that many people in the acknowledgements of my books have gone on to win Academy Awards, serve on Supreme Courts, and score the Powerball Lottery.

A general note on the content of your message: being of British background, I am culturally conditioned to respond to politeness. If you disagree with anything in this book, I don't have a problem with that —I'd love to hear your opinion. But if your missive to me has a "Hey Butthead!" tone to it, I won't respond. I realize that the study and practice of law can lull people into a mode of, well, brusqueness in their communication styles. Kimmbo don't go there. It's my own personal mission to wipe out rude conduct by refusing to respond to it.

Having said that, you can get me—hmm, maybe *get* isn't the word I want—you can *reach* me two ways:

Snail mail:

Kimm Alayne Walton
Post Office Box 1018
Greens Farms, Connecticut 06436

(On the off-chance you're interested in this kind of trivia, my post office is about half a mile from Martha Stewart's house.)

E-mail:

My e-mail address for correspondence on this book is: kimmboi@aol.com.

I look forward to hearing from you! In the meantime, I hope your life is *everything* you want it to be.

Cheers,
Kimmbo

All of the Web Sites Mentioned in This Book

Note: Unless stated otherwise, all of these web sites are preceded by the following: http://

CHAPTER 2

The National Law Journal:
www.ljx.com

CHAPTER 3

The Arizona Cardinals:
www.azcardinals.com/

The Atlanta Falcons:
www.atlantafalcons.com/

The Baltimore Ravens:
www.nfl.com/ravens/

The Buffalo Bills:
www.buffalobills.com

The Carolina Panthers:
www.nfl.com/panthers

The Chicago Bears:
www.nfl.com/bears

The Cincinnati Bengals:
www.nfl.com/bengals

The Cleveland Browns:
www.clevelandbrowns.com/

The Dallas Cowboys:
www.dallascowboys.com/

The Denver Broncos:
www.denverbroncos.com/

The Detroit Lions:
    http://detriotlions.com/

The Green Bay Packers:
    www.packers.com

The Indianapolis Colts:
    www.colts.com

The Jacksonville Jaguars:
    www.jaguarsnfl.com/

The Kansas City Chiefs:
    www.kcchiefs.com/

The Miami Dolphins:
    http://dolphinsendzone.com/

The Minnesota Vikings:
    www.nfl.com/vikings/com

The New England Patriots:
    www.patriots.com/

The New Orleans Saints:
    www.nfl.com/saints/

The New York Giants:
    www.nfl.com/giants

The New York Jets:
    www.nfl.com/jets

The Oakland Raiders:
    www.raiders.com/

The Philadelphia Eagles:
    www.eaglesnet.com

The Pittsburgh Steelers:
    http://pittsburghsteelers.com/

The St. Louis Rams:
    www.stlouisrams.com/montage.html

The San Diego Chargers
    www.nfl.com/chargers/

The San Francisco 49ers:
    www.sf49ers.com/

The Seattle Seahawks:
    www.seahawks.com/

The Tampa Bay Buccaneers:
www.nfl.com/buccaneers/

The Tennessee Oilers:
www.nfl.com/oilers/

The Washington Redskins:
www.nfl.com/redskins

The Atlanta Hawks:
www.nba.com/hawks/

The Boston Celtics:
www.nba.com/celtics/

The Charlotte Hornets:
www.nba.com/hornets/

The Chicago Bulls:
www.nba.com/bulls/

The Cleveland Cavaliers:
www.nba.com/cavs/

The Dallas Mavericks:
www.nba.com/mavericks/

The Denver Nuggets:
www.nba.com/nuggets/

The Detroit Pistons:
www.nba.com/pistons/

The Golden State Warriors:
www.nba.com/warriors/

The Houston Rockets:
www.nba.com/rockets/

The Indiana Pacers:
ww.nba.com/pacers/

The Los Angeles Clippers:
www.nba.com/clippers/

The Los Angeles Lakers:
www.nba.com/lakers/

The Miami Heat:
www.nba.com/heat/

The Milwaukee Bucks:
www.nba.com/bucks/

The Minnesota Timberwolves:
www.nba.com/timberwolves/

The New Jersey Nets:
www.nba.com/nets/

The New York Knicks:
www.nba.com/knicks/

The Orlando Magic:
www.nba.com/magic/

The Philadelphia 76ers:
www.nba.com/sixers/

The Phoenix Suns:
www.nba.com/suns

The Portland Trail Blazers:
www.nba.com/blazers/

The Sacramento Kings:
www.nba.com/kings/

San Antonio Spurs
www.nba.com/spurs/

The Seattle Supersonics:
www.nba.com/sonics

The Toronto Raptors:
www.nba.com/raptors/

The Utah Jazz:
www.nba.com/jazz/

The Vancouver Grizzlies:
www.nba.com/grizzlies/

The Washington Wizards:
www.nba.com/wizards

The Mighty Ducks of Anaheim:
www.mightyducks.com

The Atlanta Thrashers:
www.atlantathrashers.com

The Boston Bruins:
www.bostonbruins.com

The Buffalo Sabres:
www.sabres.com

The Calgary Flames:
www.calgaryflames.com

The Carolina Hurricanes:
www.caneshockey.com

The Chicago Blackhawks:
www.chicagoblackhawks.com

The Colorado Avalanche:
www.coloradoavalanche.com/

The Columbus Blue Jackets:
www.columbusbluejackets.com

The Dallas Stars:
www.dallasstars.com

The Detroit Red Wings:
www.detriotredwings.com

The Edmonton Oilers:
www.edmontonoilers.com/

The Florida Panthers:
www.flpanthers.com/

The Los Angeles Kings:
www.lakings.com

The Minnesota Wild:
www.wild.com/

The Montreal Canadiens:
www.canadiens.com/francais.index.cgm (in french);
www.canadiens.com/english (in english)

The Nashville Predators:
www.nash-nhl.com/

The New Jersey Devils:
www.newjerseydevils.com

The New York Islanders:
www.xice.com/

The New York Rangers:
www.newyorkrangers.com/

The Ottawa Senators:
www.ottawasenators.com/

The Philadelphia Flyers:
www.nhl.com/teams/phi/index.htm

The Phoenix Coyotes:
www.nhlcoyotes.com

The Pittsburgh Penguins:
www.pittsburghpenguins.com/

The St. Louis Blues:
www.stlouisblues.com/

The San Jose Sharks:
www.sj-sharks.com

The Tampa Bay Lightning:
www.tampabaylightning.com

The Toronto Maple Leafs:
www.torontomapleleafs.com

The Vancouver Canucks:
www.orcabay.com/canucks

The Washington Capitals:
www.washingtoncaps.com

Major League Baseball:
www.majorleaguebaseball.com

The Anaheim Angels:
www.angelsbaseball.com

The Arizona Diamondbacks:
www.azdiamondbacks.com

The Atlanta Braves:
www.atlantabraves.com

The Baltimore Orioles:
www.theorioles.com

The Boston Red Sox:
www.redsox.com

The Chicago Cubs:
www.cubs.com

The Chicago White Sox:
www.chisox.com

The Cincinnati Reds:
www.cincinnatireds.com

The Cleveland Indians:
www.indians.com

The Colorado Rockies:
www.coloradorockies.com

The Detroit Tigers:
www.detroittigers.com

The Florida Marlins:
www.flamarlins.com

The Houston Astros:
www.astros.com

The Kansas City Royals:
www.kcroyals.com

The Los Angeles Dodgers:
www.dodgers.com

The Milwaukee Brewers:
www.milwaukeebrewers.com

The Minnesota Twins:
www.wcco.com/sports/twins

The Montreal Expos:
www.montrealexpos.com

The New York Mets:
www.nymets.com

The New York Yankees:
www.yankees.com

The Oakland Athletics:
www.oaklandathletics.com

The Philadelphia Phillies:
www.phillies.com

The Pittsburgh Pirates:
www.pirateball.com

The St. Louis Cardinals:
www.stlcardinals.com

The San Diego Padres:
www.padres.org

The San Francisco Giants:
www.sfgiants.com

The Seattle Mariners:
www.mariners.org

The Tampa Bay Devil Rays:
www.devilray.com

The Texas Rangers:
www.texasrangers.com

The Toronto Blue Jays:
www.bluejays.ca

The American Bar Association Forum on the Entertainment and Sports
Industries:
www.abanet.org/forums/entsports/home.html

The Institute for Sports Advancement:
www.ejkrause.com/sports/

The Sports Lawyers Association:
www.sportslaw.org/sla/

The National Football League:
www.NFL.com

The National Basketball Association:
www.nba.com

The NCAA:
www.ncaa.org

HBO:
www.hbo.com

MTV:
www.mtv.com

Universal Pictures:
www.universalstudios.com

MGM-United Artists:
www.mgmua.com

Paramount Pictures:
www.paramount.com

United States Foreign Service:
www.state.gov/index.html

The American Bar Association Central & East European Law Initiative:
www.abanet.org/ceeli

NASA:
www.NASA.gov

CHAPTER 4

The Department of Justice:
www.usdoj.gov

CHAPTER 5

Akin, Gump, Strauss, Hauer & Feld, L.L.P.:
www.akingump.com

Alston & Bird:
www.alston.com

Arent Fox Kintner Plotkin & Kahn:
www.arentfox.com

Baker & Botts, L.L.P.:
www.bakerbotts.com

Baker & Daniels:
www.bakerdaniels.com

Balch & Bingham, L.L.P.:
www.balch.com

Barnes & Thornburg:
www.btlaw.com

Best, Best & Krieger L.L.P.:
www.bbklaw.com

Brown, Todd & Heyburn PLLC:
www.bth-pllc.com

Burns, Doane, Swecker & Mathis, LLP:
www.burnsdoane.com

Burns, White & Hickton:
www.bwhllc.com

Carlton, Fields, Ward, Emmanuel, Smith & Cutler, P.A.:
www.carltonfields.com

Carrington, Coleman, Sloman & Blumenthal, L.L.P.:
www.CCSB.com

Cooley Godward L.L.P.:
www.cooley.com

Fish & Richardson P.C.:
www.fr.com

Frost & Jacobs LLP:
www.frojac.com

Gardner, Carton & Douglas:
www.gcd.com

Gibson, Dunn & Crutcher, L.L.P.:
www.gdclaw.com

Gray Cary Ware & Freidenrich:
www.gcwf.com

Gray, Plant, Mooty, Mooty & Bennett, P. A:
www.gpmlaw.com

Heller, Ehrman, White & McAuliffe:
www.hewm.com

Hillis Clark Martin & Peterson, P.S.:
www.hcmp.com

Jackson & Kelly:
www.jacksonkelly.com

Latham & Watkins:
www.lw.com

Long Aldridge & Norman L.L.P.:
www.lanlaw.com

McAndrews, Held & Malloy, Ltd.:
www.mhmhome.com

Mette, Evans & Woodside P.C.:
www.mette.com

Morrison & Foerster L.L.P.:
www.mofo.com

Nelson Mullins Riley & Scarborough, L.L.P.:
www.nmrs.com

Perkins Coie L.L.P.:
www.perkinscoie.com

Proskauer Rose L.L.P.:
www.proskauer.com

Rendigs, Fry, Kiely & Dennis:
www.rendigs.com

Robinson, Bradshaw & Hinson, P.A.:
www.rbh.com

Sachnoff & Weaver:
www.sachnoff.com

Sidley & Austin:
www.sidley.com

Snell & Wilmer L.L.P.:
www.swlaw.com

Steel Hector & Davis, L.L.P.:
www.steelhector.com

Steptoe & Johnson:
www.steptoelaw.com

Stradley, Ronon, Stevens & Young, L.L.P.:
www.stradley.com

Strasburger & Price, L.L.P.:
www.strasburger.com

Sutherland, Asbill & Brennan, L.L.P.:
www.sablaw.com

Vinson & Elkins L.L.P.:
www.vinson-elkins.com

Vogel, Kelly, Knutson, Weir, Bye & Hunke, Ltd.:
www.vogellaw.com

Warner Norcross & Judd, L.L.P.:
www.wnj.com

Winston & Strawn:
www.winston.com

Wyatt, Tarrant & Combs:
www.wyattfirm.com

CHAPTER 6

Martindale-Hubbell Lawyer Listings:
http://lawyers.martindale.com/marhub

The West Legal Directory:
www.wld.com/

The law firm Brett & Daugert, L.L.P.:
www.brettlaw.com

CHAPTER 7

McKinsey & Company:
www.mckinsey.com

Deloitte & Touche Consulting:
www.dttus.com

CHAPTER 8

American Airlines:
www.americanair.com

Bar/Bri:
www.barbri.com

The Coca-Cola Company:
www.coca-cola.com

Columbia/HCA Healthcare Corporation:
www.columbia.net/columbia/index.html

Federal Express:
www.fedex.com/us

Ford Motor Company
www.ford.com/us
(for job openings) www.ford.com/careercenter

Honeywell, Inc.:
www.honeywell.com

Host Marriott Corporation:
www.marriott.com

Kraft Foods:
www.kraftfoods.com

Lexis-Nexis:
www.lexis-nexis.com

Lincoln National Corporation:
www.lnc.com

Microsoft Corporation:
www.microsoft.com

Motorola, Inc.:
www.mot.com

Norfolk Southern Corporation:
www.nscorp.com

Partners HealthCare System, Inc.:
www.partners.org

Procter & Gamble:
www.pg.com

Qualcomm:
www.qualcomm.com

Shell Oil Company:
www.shell.com

Tyco International Limited:
www.tycoint.com

United Airlines:
www.ual.com

United Parcel Service:
www.ups.com

The Williams Companies:
www.twc.com

CHAPTER 9

National Association of Public Interest Law:
www.napil.org

National Legal Aid & Defender Association:
ww.nlada.org

Nonprofit Organization Listings:
www.essential.org

Positions with Minnesota public interest agencies and governmental positions:
www.des.state.mn.us

Nonprofit job listings:
www.nonprofitjobs.org

Pro Bono Students America:
www.pbsa.org

Public Interest jobs:
www.law.umich.edu/academic/opsp

Florida Public Defender Association:
www.nettally.com/fpda

Colorado Public Defender's Office:
http://governor.state.co.us/gov_dir/pdef_dir/pd.htm

Maryland Office of the Public Defender:
www.opd.state.md.us/

Delaware Office of the Public Defender:
www.state.de.us/govern/agencies/pubdefen/indexpd.htm

Michigan State Appellate Defender Office:
www.sado.org

Kentucky Department of Public Advocacy:
http://advocate.pa.state.ky.us/index.htm

Capital Post-Conviction Unit with the Kentucky Department of Public Advocacy:
http://advocate.pa.state.ky.us/kpcdo.html

Ohio's Public Defenders Office:
www.webtest.state.oh/us.scripts/phonelagency/pub.asp

American Civil Liberties Union:
ww.aclu.org

United Mine Workers of America:
www.umwa.org

Writers Guild of America, west:
www.wga.org

American Judicature Society:
www.ajs.org

The Arms Control Association:
www.armscontrol.org

Center for International Environmental Law:
www.econet.apc.org/ciel

Consumers Union:
www.consunion.org

Earthjustice Legal Defense Fund:
www.earthjustice.org

Florida Public Service Commission:
www2.scrinet/psc/

Gay & Lesbian Advocates & Defenders ("GLAD"):
www.glad.org

Human Rights Watch:
www.hrw.org

NAACP Legal Defense & Education Fund:
www.ldfla.org

The Nature Conservancy:
www.tnc.org

Public Counsel Law Center:
www.publiccounsel.org

CHAPTER 10

Federal Government General Interest Web Sites:

Chart of governmental pay grades:
www.usajobs.opm.gov/b5a.htm

Information on Federal Job Applications:
www.jobweb.org/search/jobs/fjapply.htm

Example of Federal Job Application Form OF-612:
www.usajobs.opm.gov/einfo/of612.txt

Listing of all federal agency web sites:
http://winslo.ohio.gov/fdgvind.html

Individual Federal Agencies:

Central Intelligence Agency:
www.odci.gov/cia/

Comptroller of the Currency:
www.occ.treas.gov

Equal Employment Opportunity Commission:
www.eeoc.gov

Environmental Protection Agency:
www.epa.gov

Federal Bureau of Investigation:
www.fbi.gov

Federal Communications Commission:
www.fcc.gov

Federal Mediation & Conciliation Service:
www.fmcs.gov

Federal Trade Commission:
www.ftc.gov

Department of the Interior:
www.doi.gov

National Park Service:
www.nps.gov

U.S. Army Judge Advocate General's Corps:
www.jagcnet.army.mil/jagcnet/jaraps.nsf

U.S. Navy JAGC:
www.finifter.com/jag/, and jag.navy.mil/

U.S. Air Force JAGC:
www.ja.hq.af.mil/

National Labor Relations Board:
www.nlrb.gov

Overseas Private Investment Corporation:
www.opic.gov/

Railroad Retirement Board:
www.rrb.gov

Securities & Exchange Commission:
www.sec.gov

State Department:
www.state.gov/index.html

State Attorney Generals' Offices:

Alabama: General state executive branch web site:
www.state.al.us

Alaska: Attorney General's Office web site:
www.law.state.ak.us/index.html

Arizona: General state executive branch web site:
www.state.az.us

Arkansas: General state executive branch web site:
www.state.ar.us

California: Attorney General's Office web site:
www.caag.state.ca.us

Colorado: General state executive branch web site:
www.state.co.us

Connecticut: Attorney General's Office web site:
www.cslnet.ctstateu.edu

Delaware: General state executive branch web site:
www.state.de.us

Florida: Attorney General's Office web site:
http://legal.firn.edu

Georgia: General state executive branch web site:
www.state.ga.us

Hawaii: General state executive branch web site:
www.state.hi.us

Idaho: General state executive branch web site:
www.state.id.us

Illinois: Attorney General's Office web site:
www.acsp/uic.edu

Indiana: General state executive branch web site:
www.state.in.us

Iowa: Attorney General's Office web site:
www.state.ia.us/government/ag/

Kansas:
http://lawlib.wuacc.edu/ag/homepage.html

Kentucky: General state executive branch web site:
www.state.ky.us

Louisiana: General state executive branch web site:
www.state.la.us

Maine: Attorney General's Office web site:
www.ptla.org

Maryland: Attorney General's Office web site:
www.oag.state.md.us

Massachusetts: Attorney General's Office web site:
www.magnet.state.ma.us

Michigan: General state executive branch web site:
www.migov.state.mi.us

Minnesota: Attorney General's Office web site:
www.ag.state.mn.us

Mississippi: Attorney General's Office web site:
www.mslawyer.com

Missouri: General state executive branch web site:
www.state.mo.us

Montana: General state executive branch web site:
www.state.mt.gov

Nebraska: General state executive branch web site:
www.state.ne.us

Nevada: General state executive branch web site:
www.state.nv.us

New Hampshire: General state executive branch web site:
www.state.nh.us

New Jersey: General state executive branch web site:
www.state.nj.us

New Mexico: General state executive branch web site:
www.state.nm.us

New York: Attorney General's Web Site:
www.oag.state.ny.us

North Carolina: Attorney General's Office web site:
www.jus.state.nc.us

North Dakota: General state executive branch web site:
www.state.nd.us

Ohio: Attorney General's Office web site:
www.ag.ohio.gov

Oklahoma: General state executive branch web site:
www.state.ok.us

Oregon: Attorney General's Office web site:
www.dpo.org

Pennsylvania: Attorney General's Office web site:
www.attorneygeneral.gov

Rhode Island: Attorney General's Office web site:
www.sec.state.ri.us

South Carolina: General state executive branch web site:
www.state.sc.us

South Dakota: General state executive branch web site:
www.state.sd.us

Tennessee: General state executive branch web site:
www.state.tn.us

Texas: Attorney General's Office web site:
www.oag.state.tx.us

Utah: General state executive branch web site:
www.state.ut.us

Vermont: General state executive branch web site:
www.state.vt.us

Virginia: General state executive branch web site:
www.state.va.us

Washington: General state executive branch web site:
www.state.wa.gov

West Virginia: General state executive branch web site:
www.state.wv.us

Wisconsin: General state executive branch web site:
www.state.wi.us

Wyoming: General state executive branch web site:
www.state.wy.us

Job vacancies writing legislation for states, listed by the National
Conference of State Legislatures:
www.ncsl.org/public/joblegis.htm

San Diego City Attorney's Office:
www.sannet.gov/city-attorney

CHAPTER 11

Listing of U.S. Attorney's Offices Nationwide:
www.usdoj.gov/careers/oapm/lab.usaoadd.html

CHAPTER 12

Judicial Clerkships:

U.S. Federal Courts:
www.uscourts.gov

National Center for State Courts:
www.ncsc.dni.us/ncsc.htm

Federal Circuit Courts (at the Emory Law School home page):
www.law.emory.edu/2circuit
(plug in the number for the circuit you want to find out about)

The D.C. Circuit:
www.ll.georgetown.edu/Fed-Ct/cadc.html

2nd Circuit:
www.tourolaw.edu/2ndcircuit/
www.law.pace.edu/legal/us-legeal/judiciary/second-circuit.html

8th Circuit:
www.wulaw.wustl.edu/8th.cir

9th Circuit:
www.law.vill.edu/Fed-Ct/ca09.html

The Internet:

Employment web sites:
www.headhunter.net
www.jobtrack.com
www.monsterboard.com

Internet conference & seminar listings at *Wired Magazine*:
www.industrystandard.net

Internet World:
www.iw.com

Trade Associations:

Information on the book *National Trade & Professional Associations of the United States*:
www.d-net.com/columbia/

CHAPTER 13

Web sites dealing with debt management, loan repayment, and loan options:
www.usagroup.com:80/getready/roadrpy/consolid.htm
www.usagroup.com:80/getready/roadrpy/level.htm
www.usagroup.com:80/getready/roadrpy/incsens.htm
www.usagroup.com:80/loancons/calc/specinst.htm
www.usagroup.com:80/loancons/menu.htm

Repayment estimator:
www.salliemae.com:80/calculators/repayment

Salary comparisons for different geographic locations:
www.homefair.com/homefair/cmr/salcalc.html

State income tax rates:
www.homefair.com/homefair/cmr/ataxes.html

Geographic Index of Law Firms, Public Interest Employers, and Corporations, By State.

Explanation of symbols and listings:

Here's what I did. For corporations and public interest employers, the symbol * indicates that the office in question is the main office—and it's the one that's described in this book (Chapter 8 for Corporations, and Chapter 9 for Public Interest Employers). For corporations, I only listed the cities where the companies disclosed that a fair number of law school graduates were employed as lawyers. It doesn't tell you every city where law school graduates work in any capacity.

Law firms require a little more explanation. The "+" sign indicates that the office in question is the one described in Chapter 5, on law firms (or for the law firm Brett & Daugert, Chapter 6 on small firms). The city appearing within the parentheses is the firm's main office. By way of example:

1. *Under the heading "Moreland Hills, Ohio" you see the listing:*

   Scylla & Charybdis (main office+)

   > This means that Scylla & Charybdis has more than one office, and that its main office is in Moreland Hills, Ohio.

2. *Under the heading "Moreland Hills, Ohio" you see the listing:*

   Scylla & Charybdis+

   > This means that Scylla & Charybdis has only one office, and gee, guess where it is—Moreland Hills, Ohio.

3. *Under the heading "Moreland Hills, Ohio" you see the listing:*

   Scylla & Charybdis (Chagrin Falls, OH+)

   > This means that Scylla & Charybdis has a main office in Chagrin Falls and another office in Moreland Hills, and since

the plus sign is next to Chagrin Falls, it's the Chagrin Falls office that's described in Chapter 5. By reading about the main office, you'll learn about the firm in general.

4. *Under the heading "Moreland Hills, Ohio" you see the listing:*

Scylla & Charybdis+ (Chagrin Falls, OH)

> This means that Scylla & Charybdis has a main office in Chagrin Falls and another office in Moreland Hills, and that the Moreland Hills office is described but the main office is not. (As I explained in Chapter 1, this means that I heard raves about the branch office and either heard nothing, or not such good stuff, about the main office). You *can't* assume that working at the main office would be the Bataan Death March. You can't draw any conclusions about the firm in general from a branch-only listing—only the office described.

5. *Under the heading "Moreland Hills, Ohio" you see the listing:*

Scylla & Charybdis+ (Chagrin Falls, OH+)

> You probably know by now, without me having to tell you, that this means that both the Moreland Hills and Chagrin Falls offices are described in Chapter 5.

I think that's about it, except for this: You need to know that some law firms are very sensitive about the idea of a "home office" or "main office" and a bunch of satellites or branch offices, the idea seeming to be that they don't want attorneys at the non-main-offices to feel like second class citizens. However, in every law firm there is an office that's considered the equivalent of a corporation's headquarter—typically the firm's largest office—and so even if a firm itself doesn't recognize a main office, I'm using the "main office" terminology.

You also should know that I used abbreviations for law firm names as follows: If the firm has three or fewer names, I used the entire firm name here. For firms with more than three names, I used the first two as an abbreviation. You would have figured that out without me telling you, but I thought I'd mention it anyway.

Listings By State

ALABAMA

Birmingham:
Law Firms
    Balch & Bingham (main office+) 588
    Dominick, Fletcher+ 611

Huntsville:
Law Firms
    Balch & Bingham (Birmingham, AL+) 588

Montgomery:
Law Firms
    Balch & Bingham (Birmingham, AL+) 588

ALASKA

Anchorage:
Law Firms
    Heller Ehrman (San Francisco, CA+) 623
    Perkins Coie (Seattle, WA+) 451

ARKANSAS

Little Rock:
Law Firms
    Armstrong Allen (Memphis, TN+) 585

ARIZONA

Nogales:
Law Firms
    O'Connor, Cavanagh (main office+) 643

Phoenix:
Corporations
    Honeywell Incorporated (Minneapolis, MN*) 731

Law Firms

    O'Connor, Cavanagh (main office+) 643

    Snell & Wilmer (main office+) 501

Sun City:

Law Firms

    O'Connor, Cavanagh (Phoenix, AZ+) 643

Tempe:

Corporations

    Bar/Bri Bar Review (Chicago, IL*) 723

Tucson:

Law Firms

    O'Connor, Cavanagh (Phoenix, AZ+) 643

    Snell & Wilmer (Phoenix, AZ+) 501

Window Rock:

Public Interest Employers

    DNA-People's Legal Services, Inc.* 795

CALIFORNIA

Burbank:

Corporations

    The Walt Disney Company* 70

Costa Mesa:

Law Firms

    Dorsey & Whitney (Minneapolis, MN+) 612

Cupertino:

Corporations

    Honeywell Incorporated (Minneapolis, MN*) 731

El Segundo:

Corporations

    Mattel* 95

Irvine:

Law Firms

    Morrison & Foerster+ (San Francisco, CA+) 430

    Snell & Wilmer (Phoenix, AZ+) 501

La Jolla:

Law Firms

Fish & Richardson (Boston, MA+) 253

Los Angeles:

Corporations

Bar/Bri Bar Review (Chicago, IL*) 723

Public Interest Employers:

NAACP Legal Defense & Education Fund (New York, NY*) 810
Public Counsel Law Center* 812
Writers Guild of America, west* 788

Law Firms

Akin Gump (Washington, D.C.+) 153
Arnold & Porter (Washington, D.C.+) 162
Folger Levin & Kahn (main office+) 259
Heller Ehrman (San Francisco, CA+) 623
Hogan & Hartson (Washington, D.C.+) 628
Jenkens & Gilchrist (Dallas, TX+) 322
Kirkland & Ellis (Chicago, IL+) 632
Klinedinst, Fliehman & McKillop (main office+) 353
Latham & Watkins (main office+) 360
Lord, Bissell & Brook (Chicago, IL+) 395
Morrison & Foerster+ (San Francisco, CA+) 433
Perkins Coie (Seattle, WA+) 457
Proskauer Rose (New York, NY+) 470
Sidley & Austin (Chicago, IL+) 491

Menlo Park:

Law Firms

Burns, Doane (Alexandria, VA+) 601
Cooley Godward (Palo Alto+) 232
Fish & Richardson (Boston, MA+) 253

Newport Beach:

Law Firms

Hogan & Hartson (Washington, D.C.+) 628

Ontario:

Law Firms

Best, Best & Krieger (Riverside, CA+) 594

Orange County:

Law Firms

Klinedinst, Fliehman & McKillop (main office+) 353
Latham & Watkins (Los Angeles, CA+) 360

Palo Alto:

Law Firms

Cooley Godward (main office+) 232
Gray Cary (San Diego+) 621
Heller Ehrman (San Francisco+) 623
Morrison & Foerster+ (San Francisco+) 442

Rancho Mirage:

Law Firms

Best, Best & Krieger (Riverside, CA+) 594

Riverside:

Law Firms

Best, Best & Krieger (main office+) 594

San Diego:

Corporations

Bar/Bri Bar Review (Chicago, IL*) 723
Qualcomm* 753

Law Firms

Best, Best & Krieger (main office+) 594
Cooley Godward (Palo Alto, CA+) 232
Klinedinst, Fliehman & McKillop (main office+) 353
Latham & Watkins+ (Los Angeles, CA+) 367

San Francisco:

Corporations

Bar/Bri Bar Review (Chicago, IL*) 723

Public Interest Employers

Earthjustice Legal Defense Fund (formerly the Sierra Club)* 796
Employment Law Center* 798

Law Firms

Burns, White & Hickton (Pittsburgh, PA+) 208
Cooley Godward (Palo Alto, CA+) 232
Fliesler Dubb (main office+) 614
Folger Levin & Kahn (main office+) 259
Gray Cary (San Diego, CA+) 621
Heller Ehrman (main office+) 623
Latham & Watkins+ (Los Angeles, CA+) 374
Morrison & Foerster (main office+) 427

Santa Clara:
Law Firms
Fliesler Dubb (San Francisco, CA+) 614

Silicon Valley:
Law Firms
Latham & Watkins (Los Angeles, CA+) 360

Victorville:
Law Firms
Best, Best & Krieger (Riverside, CA+) 594

Walnut Creek:
Law Firms
Morrison & Foerster (San Francisco, CA+) 427

COLORADO

Boulder:
Law Firms
Cooley Godward (Palo Alto, CA+) 232

Colorado Springs:
Law Firms
Hogan & Hartson (Washington, D.C.+) 628

Denver:
Law Firms:
Arnold & Porter (Washington, D.C.+) 162
Dorsey & Whitney (Minneapolis, MN+) 612
Hogan & Hartson (Washington, D.C.+) 628
Jackson & Kelly (Charleston, WV+) 315
Morrison & Foerster (San Francisco, CA+) 427
Perkins Coie (Seattle, WA+) 451

CONNECTICUT

Hartford:
Corporations
Lincoln National Corporation (Fort Wayne, IN*) 737
Law Firms
Wiggin & Dana (New Haven, CT+) 672

New Haven:
Law Firms
Wiggin & Dana (main office+) 672

Stamford:
Law Firms
Wiggin & Dana (main office+) 672

DELAWARE

Wilmington:
Law Firms
Stradley, Ronon (Philadelphia, PA+) 655

FLORIDA

Boca Raton:
Law Firms
Hodgson, Russ (Buffalo, NY+) 625
Proskauer Rose (New York, NY+) 470

Clearwater:
Corporations
Honeywell, Inc. (Minneapolis, MN+) 731
Fowler, White (Tampa, FL+) 264

Fort Myers:
Law Firms
Fowler, White (Tampa, FL) 264

Key West:
Law Firms
Steel Hector & Davis (Miami, FL+) 652

Lakeland:
Corporations
Host Marriott Corporation (Bethesda, MD*) 733

Miami:
Law Firms
Carlton, Fields (Tampa, FL+) 214
Steel Hector & Davis (main office+) 652

Orlando:
Law Firms
Carlton, Fields (Tampa, FL+) 214

Palm Beach:
Law Firms
Hodgson, Russ (Buffalo, NY+) 625

Pensacola:
Law Firms
Carlton, Fields (Tampa, FL+) 214

St. Petersburg:
Law Firms
Carlton, Fields (Tampa, FL+) 214
Fowler, White (Tampa, FL+) 264

Tallahassee:
Corporations
Bar/Bri Bar Review (Chicago, IL*) 723
Public Interest Employers
Florida Public Service Commission* 799
Law Firms
Carlton, Fields (Tampa, FL+) 214
Fowler, White (Tampa, FL+) 264
Parker, Hudson (Atlanta, GA+) 445
Steel Hector & Davis (Miami, FL+) 652

Tampa:
Law Firms
Carlton, Fields (main office+) 214
Fowler, White (main office+) 264
Hill, Ward & Henderson+ 302
Shumaker, Loop & Kendrick (Toledo, OH+) 486

West Palm Beach:
Law Firms
Carlton, Fields (Tampa, FL+) 214
Steel Hector & Davis (Miami, FL+) 652

GEORGIA

Atlanta:
Corporations
Bar/Bri Bar Review (Chicago, IL*) 723
Coca-Cola* 726
United Parcel Service* 756

Law Firms
Alston & Bird (main office+) 581
Long Aldridge & Norman (main office+) 388
Lord, Bissell & Brook (Chicago, IL+) 395
Nelson Mullins (Columbia, SC+) 640
Parker, Hudson (main office+) 445
Sutherland, Asbill & Brennan (main office+) 658
Troutman Sanders (main office+) 662
Webb, Carlock+ 669

Marietta:
Law Firms
Moore Ingram+ 421

ILLINOIS

Chicago:
Corporations
Bar/Bri Bar Review 723
McDonald's Corporation 738
United Airlines* 756

Public Interest Employers:
American Judicature Society* 791
Legal Assistance Foundation of Chicago* 806

Law Firms
Barnes & Thornburg (Indianapolis, IN+) 191
Gardner, Carton & Douglas (main office+) 276
Jenkens & Gilchrist (Houston, TX+) 322
Jenner & Block (main office+) 630
Kirkland & Ellis (main office+) 632
Latham & Watkins (Los Angeles, CA+) 360
Lord, Bissell & Brook (main office+) 395
Masuda, Funai (main office+) 637
McAndrews, Held & Malloy+ 406
Pretzel & Stouffer+ 647
Sachnoff & Weaver+ 651
Sidley & Austin (main office+) 491

Freeport:
Corporations
   Honeywell, Incorporated (Minneapolis, MN*) 731

Lake Forest:
Law Firms
   Jenner & Block (Chicago, IL+) 630

Northfield:
Corporations
   Kraft Foods* 734

Rockford:
Law Firms
   Lord, Bissell & Brook (Chicago, IL+) 395

Rolling Meadows:
Law Firms
   Masuda, Funai (Chicago, IL+) 637

Schaumburg:
Corporations
   Motorola, Inc.* 741

INDIANA

Bloomington:
Law Firms
   Bingham, Summers (Indianapolis, IN+) 598

Elkhart:
Law Firms
   Baker & Daniels (Indianapolis, IN+) 178
   Barnes & Thornburg (Indianapolis, IN+) 191

Evansville:
Law Firms
   Bamberger, Foreman+ 590

Fort Wayne:
Corporations
   Lincoln National Corporation* 737

Law Firms
    Baker & Daniels (Indianapolis, IN+) 178
    Barnes & Thornburg (Indianapolis, IN+) 191
    Beckman, Lawson (main office+) 593

Indianapolis:
Corporations
    Bar/Bri Bar Review (Chicago, IL*) 723
Law Firms
    Baker & Daniels (main office+) 178
    Barnes & Thornburg (main office+) 191
    Bingham, Summers (main office+) 598
    Stewart & Irwin+ 654

Jeffersonville:
Law Firms
    Stites & Harbison (Louisville, KY+) 518

Merrillville:
Law Firms
    Hoeppner, Wagner & Evans (Valparaiso, IN+) 627

New Albany:
Law Firms
    Brown, Todd & Heyburn (Louisville, KY+) 199
    Wyatt, Tarrant & Combs (Louisville, KY+) 560

South Bend:
Law Firms
    Baker & Daniels (Indianapolis, IN+) 178
    Barnes & Thornburg (Indianapolis, IN+) 191

Syracuse:
Law Firms
    Beckman, Lawson (Fort Wayne, IN+) 593

Valparaiso:
Law Firms
    Hoeppner, Wagner & Evans (main office+) 627

I O W A

Des Moines:
Law Firms
    Dorsey & Whitney (Minneapolis, MN+) 612

KANSAS

Overland Park:
Law Firms
Shook, Hardy & Bacon (Kansas City, MO+) 478

KENTUCKY

Covington:
Law Firms
Brown, Todd & Heyburn (Louisville, KY+) 199
Dinsmore & Shohl (Cincinnati, OH+) 609

Fort Wright:
Law Firms
Cors & Bassett (Cincinnati, OH+) 604

Frankfort:
Law Firms
Stites & Harbison (Louisville, KY+) 518
Wyatt, Tarrant & Combs (Louisville, KY+) 560

Hyden:
Law Firms
Stites & Harbison (Louisville, KY+) 518

Lexington:
Law Firms
Brown, Todd & Heyburn (Louisville, KY+) 199
Disnmore & Shohl (Cincinnati, OH+) 609
Frost & Jacobs (Cincinnati, OH+) 271
Jackson & Kelly (Charleston, WV+) 315
Stites & Harbison (Louisville, KY+) 518
Wyatt, Tarrant & Combs (Louisville, KY+) 560

Louisville:
Law Firms
Brown, Todd & Heyburn (main office+) 199
Dinsmore & Shohl (Cincinnati, OH+) 609
Wyatt, Tarrant & Combs (main office+) 560

MARYLAND

Baltimore:
Law Firms
Hogan & Hartson (Washington, D.C.+) 628
Wilmer, Cutler & Pickering (Washington, D.C.+) 674

Bethesda:
Corporations
Host Marriott Corporation* 733
Law Firms
Hogan & Hartson (Washington, D.C.+) 628

MASSACHUSETTS

Boston:
Corporations
Bar/Bri Bar Review (Chicago, IL*) 723
Partners HealthCare System, Inc.* 745
Public Interest Employers
Gay & Lesbian Advocates & Defenders* 801
Law Firms
Fish & Richardson (main office+) 253
Goulston & Storrs+ 284
Sugarman, Rogers+ 657

MICHIGAN

Dearborn:
Corporations
Ford Motor Company* 729

Detroit:
Corporations
General Motors* 729

Farmington Hills:
Law Firms
Foster, Swift (Lansing, MI+) 616

Grand Rapids:
Law Firms
Warner Norcross & Judd (main office+) 667

Holland:
Law Firms
Warner Norcross & Judd (Grand Rapids, MI+) 667

Lansing:
Law Firms
Foster, Swift (main office+) 616

Muskegon:
Law Firms
Warner Norcross & Judd (Grand Rapids, MI+) 667

Southfield:
Law Firms
Warner Norcross & Judd (Grand Rapids, MI+) 667

MINNESOTA

Minneapolis:
Corporations
Honeywell Inc.* 731
Public Interest Employers
Minnesota Advocates for Human Rights* 809
Law Firms
Dorsey & Whitney (main office+) 612
Fish & Richardson (Boston, MA+) 253
Gray, Plant+ 292

Rochester:
Law Firms
Dorsey & Whitney (Minneapolis, MN+) 612

MISSISSIPPI

Jackson:
Law Firms
Armstrong Allen (Memphis, TN+) 585
Baker Donelson (Memphis, TN+) 586
Watkins & Eager+ 548

MISSOURI

Kansas City:
Law Firms
Shook, Hardy & Bacon (main office+) 478

St. Louis:
Corporations
Anheuser-Busch Companies (main office*) 98
Bar/Bri Bar Review (Chicago, IL*) 723

MONTANA

Billings:
Law Firms
Crowley, Houghey (main office+) 607
Dorsey & Whitney (Minneapolis, MN+) 612

Helena:
Law Firms
Crowley, Houghey (Billings, MT+) 607

Kalispell:
Law Firms
Crowley, Houghey (Billings, MT+) 607

Missoula:
Law Firms
Dorsey & Whitney (Minneapolis, MN+) 612

NEVADA

Boulder City:
Law Firms
Jolley, Urga (Las Vegas, NV+) 327

Las Vegas:
Law Firms
Jolly, Urga (main office+) 327
Jones Vargas (main office+) 341

Reno:
Law Firms
    Jones Vargas (Las Vegas, NV+) 341

NEW HAMPSHIRE

Exeter:
Corporations
    Tyco International Ltd.* 755

NEW JERSEY

Cherry Hill:
Law Firms
    Stradley, Ronon (Philadelphia, PA+) 655

Clifton:
Law Firms
    Proskauer Rose (New York, NY+) 470

Mount Laurel:
Corporations
    Mattel (El Segundo, CA*) 95

Newark:
Law Firms
    Latham & Watkins (Los Angeles, CA+) 360

NEW MEXICO

Albuquerque:
Corporations
    Honeywell, Inc. (Minneapolis, MN*) 731

NEW YORK

Albany:
Law Firms
    Hodgson, Russ (Buffalo, NY+) 625

Buffalo:

Law Firms

Hodgson, Russ (main office+) 625

East Aurora:

Corporations

Mattel (El Segundo, CA*) 95

Gloversville:

Law Firms

Hodgson, Russ (Buffalo, NY+) 625

Great Falls:

Law Firms

Dorsey & Whitney (Minneapolis, MN+) 612

New York City:

Corporations

Bar/Bri Bar Review (Chicago, IL*) 723
General Motors (Detroit, MI*) 729

Public Interest Employers

American Civil Liberties Union* 783
Human Rights Watch* 802
NAACP Legal Defense & Education Fund* 810

Law Firms

Akin Gump (Washington, D.C.+) 153
Arent Fox (Washington, D.C.+) 583
Arnold & Porter (Washington, D.C.+) 162
Cohen, Weiss & Simon+ 603
Davis Polk (main office+) 243
Dorsey & Whitney (Minneapolis, MN+) 612
Fish & Richardson (Boston, MA+) 253
Gibson, Dunn & Crutcher (Los Angeles, CA+) 619
Hodgson, Russ (Buffalo, NY+) 625
Kirkland & Ellis (Chicago, IL+) 632
Latham & Watkins (Los Angeles, CA+) 360
Lord, Bissell & Brook (Chicago, IL+) 395
Morrison & Foerster+ (San Francisco, CA+) 427
O'Melveny & Myers+ (Los Angeles, CA) 645
Proskauer Rose (main office+) 470
Sidley & Austin (Chicago, IL+) 491
Sutherland, Asbill & Brennan (Atlanta, GA+) 658

Rochester:
  Law Firms
    Hodgson, Russ (Buffalo, NY+) 625

Yonkers:
  Public Interest Employers:
    Consumers Union* 794

NORTH CAROLINA

Chapel Hill/Durham:
  Corporations
    Bar/Bri Bar Review (Chicago, IL*) 723

Charlotte:
  Law Firms
    Alston & Bird (Atlanta, GA+) 581
    Nelson Mullins (Columbia, SC+) 640
    Robinson, Bradhaw & Hinson (main office+) 649
    Shumaker, Loop & Kendrick (Toledo, OH+) 486

Greenville:
  Law Firms
    Ward & Smith (New Bern, NC+) 541

New Bern:
  Law Firms
    Ward & Smith (main office+) 541

Raleigh:
  Law Firms
    Alston & Bird (Atlanta, GA+) 581
    Ward & Smith (New Bern, NC+) 541

Research Triangle Park:
  Law Firms
    Burns Doane (Alexandria, VA+) 601

Wilmington:
  Law Firms
    Ward & Smith (New Bern, NC+) 541

NORTH DAKOTA

Fargo:

Law Firms

Dorsey & Whitney (Minneapolis, MN+) 612
Nilles, Hansen & Davies (main office+) 642
Vogel, Kelly+ 666

Williston:

Law Firms

Crowley, Haughey (Billings, MT+) 607
Nilles, Hansen & Davies (Fargo, ND+) 642

OHIO

Canton:

Law Firms

Millisor & Nobil (Cleveland, OH+) 418

Cincinnati:

Corporations

Procter & Gamble* 747

Law Firms

Cors & Bassett (main office+) 604
Dinsmore & Shohl (main office+) 609
Frost & Jacobs (main office+) 271
Masuda, Funai (Chicago, IL+) 637
Rendigs, Fry+ 648

Cleveland:

Corporations

Bar/Bri Bar Review (Chicago, IL*) 723

Law Firms

McDonald, Hopkins+ 412
Millisor & Nobil (main office+) 418

Columbus:

Law Firms

Baker & Hostetler (main office+) 185
Dinsmore & Shohl (Cincinnati, OH+) 609
Frost & Jacobs (Cincinnati, OH+) 271
Millisor & Nobil (Cleveland, OH+) 418
Shumaker, Loup & Kendrick (Toledo, OH) 486

Dayton:
Law Firms
    Dinsmore & Shohl (Cincinnati, OH+) 609

Hamilton:
Law Firms
    Dinsmore & Shohl (Cincinnati, OH+) 609

Miamisburg:
Corporations
    Lexis-Nexis* 735

Middletown:
Law Firms
    Frost & Jacobs (Cincinnati, OH+) 271

Toledo:
Law Firms
    Shumaker, Loop & Kendrick (main office+) 486

OKLAHOMA

Tulsa:
Corporations
    The Williams Companies* 758

OREGON

Portland:
Law Firms
    Davis Wright Tremaine+ 246
    Heller Ehrman (San Francisco, CA+) 623
    Markowitz, Herbold+ 401
    Perkins Coie+ (Seattle, WA+) 457
    Tonkon, Torp+ 660

PENNSYLVANIA

Harrisburg:
Law Firms
    Kirkpatrick & Lockhart+ (Pittsburgh, PA) 346
    Mette, Evans+ 638

Malvern:
Law Firms
    Stradley, Ronon (Philadelphia, PA+) 655

Philadelphia:
Corporations
    Bar/Bri Bar Review (Chicago, IL*) 723
Law Firms
    Akin Gump (Washington, D.C.+) 153
    Stradley, Ronon (main office+) 655

Pittsburgh:
Corporations
    Bar/Bri Bar Review (Chicago, IL*) 723
Law Firms
    Burns, White & Hickton (main office+) 208

SOUTH CAROLINA

Charleston:
Law Firms
    Nelson Mullins (Columbia, SC+) 640

Columbia:
Law Firms
    Nelson Mullins (main office+) 640

Florence:
Law Firms
    Nelson Mullins (Columbia, SC+) 640

Greenville:
Law Firms
    Nelson Mullins (Columbia, SC+) 640

Myrtle Beach:
Law Firms
    Nelson Mullins (Columbia, SC+) 640

Rock Hill:
Law Firms
    Robinson, Bradshaw & Hinson (Charlotte, NC+) 649

TENNESSEE

Chattanooga:
Law Firms
Baker Donelson (Memphis, TN+) 586

Columbia:
Law Firms
Waller Lansden (Nashville, TN+) 533

Hendersonville:
Law Firms
Wyatt, Tarrant & Combs (Louisville, KY+) 560

Huntsville:
Law Firms
Baker Donelson (Memphis, TN+) 586

Johnson City:
Law Firms
Baker Donelson (Memphis, TN+) 586

Kingsport:
Law Firms
Wyatt, Tarrant & Combs (Louisville, KY+) 560

Knoxville:
Law Firms
Baker Donelson (Memphis, TN+) 586
Bass, Berry & Sims (Nashville, TN+) 591

Memphis:
Corporations
Federal Express* 728
Law Firms
Armstrong Allen (main office+) 585
Baker Donelson (main office+) 586
Wyatt, Tarrant & Combs+ (Louisville, KY+) 574

Nashville:
Corporations
Bar/Bri Bar Review (Chicago, IL*) 723
Columbia/HCA Healthcare Corporation* 727

Law Firms

Bass, Berry & Sims (main office+) 591
Boult, Cummings+ 599
Brown, Todd & Heyburn (Louisville, KY+) 199
Waller Lansden (main office+) 533
(downtown) Wyatt, Tarrant & Combs+ (Louisville, KY+) 569
(Music Row) Wyatt, Tarrant & Combs (Louisville, KY+) 569

TEXAS

Austin:

Public Interest Employers

Women's Advocacy Project* 813

Law Firms

Akin Gump (Washington, D.C.+) 153
Bickerstaff, Heath+ 596
Gray Cary (San Diego, CA+) 621
Jenkens & Gilchrist (Dallas, TX+) 322
Strasburger & Price (Dallas, TX+) 655
Sutherland, Asbill & Brennan (Atlanta, GA+) 658
Vinson & Elkins (Houston, TX+) 664

Dallas:

Corporations

American Airlines* 722
Bar/Bri Bar Review (Chicago, IL*) 723

Law Firms

Akin Gump (Washington, D.C.+) 153
Baker & Botts+ (Houston, TX) 170
Carrington, Coleman+ 224
Cowles & Thompson (main office+) 236
Jenkens & Gilchrist (main office+) 322
Jones, Day+ (Cleveland, OH) 332
Sidley & Austin (Chicago, IL+) 491
Strasburger & Price (main office+) 527
Vinson & Elkins (Houston, TX+) 664

Houston:

Corporations

Bar/Bri Bar Review (Chicago, IL*) 723
Shell Oil Company* 754

Law Firms
 Akin Gump (Washington, D.C.+) 153
 Jenkens & Gilchrist (Dallas, TX+) 322
 Shook, Hardy & Bacon (Kansas City, MO+) 478
 Strasburger & Price (Dallas, TX+) 527
 Vinson & Elkins (main office+) 664
 Weil, Gotshal & Manges+ (New York, NY) 670

McKinney:
Law Firms
 Cowles & Thompson (Dallas, TX+) 236

San Antonio:
Corporations
 United Services Automobile Association* 757
Law Firms
 Akin Gump+ (Washington, D.C.+) 147
 Clemens & Spencer+ 602
 Cox & Smith+ 605
 Jenkens & Gilchrist (Dallas, TX+) 322

Tyler:
Law Firms
 Cowles & Thompson (Dallas, TX+) 236

UTAH
───

Salt Lake City:
Law Firms
 Dorsey & Whitney (Minneapolis, MN+) 612
 Snell & Wilmer (Phoenix, AZ+) 501
 Workman, Nydegger & Seeley+ 676

VIRGINIA
───

Alexandria:
Law Firms
 Burns, Doane (main office+) 601

Arlington:
  Public Interest Employers
    The Nature Conservancy* 811

Harrisonburg:
  Law Firms
    Wharton, Aldhizer & Weaver+ 553

Henrico:
  Law Firms
    LeClair Ryan (Richmond, VA+) 634

McLean:
  Law Firms
    Hogan & Hartson (Washington, D.C.+) 628

Norfolk:
  Corporations
    Norfolk Southern Corporation* 744

Richmond:
  Law Firms
    LeClair Ryan (main office+) 634

Roanoke:
  Law Firms
    Gentry, Locke+ 618

WASHINGTON, D.C.

  Corporations
    Bar/Bri Bar Review (Chicago, IL*) 723
    General Motors (Detroit, MI*) 729
  Public Interest Employers
    Arms Control Association* 792
    Center for International Environmental Law* 793
    International Human Rights Law Group* 803
    NAACP Legal Defense & Education Fund (New York, NY*) 810
    United Mine Workers of America* 785
  Law Firms
    Akin Gump (main office+) 153
    Alston & Bird (Atlanta, GA+) 581
    Arent Fox (main office+) 583
    Arnold & Porter (main office+) 162

Baker & Daniels (Indianapolis, IN+) 178
Baker Donelson (Memphis, TN+) 586
Balch & Bingham (Birmingham, AL+) 588
Barnes & Thornburg (Indianapolis, IN+) 191
Davis Polk (New York, NY+) 243
Dorsey & Whitney (Minneapolis, MN+) 612
Fish & Richardson (Boston, MA+) 253
Gardner, Carton & Douglas (Chicago, IL+) .276
Heller, Ehrman (San Francisco, CA+) 623
Hogan & Hartson (main office+) 628
Jackson & Kelly (Charleston, WV+) 315
Jenkens & Gilchrist (Dallas, TX+) 322
Jenner & Block (Chicago, IL+) 630
Kirkland & Ellis (Chicago, IL+) 632
Latham & Watkins+ (Los Angeles, CA+) 360
Long Aldridge & Norman (Atlanta, GA+) 388
Morrison & Foerster+ (San Francisco, CA+) .427
Perkins Coie+ (Seattle, WA+) 451
Proskauer Rose (New York, NY+) 470
Shook, Hardy & Bacon (Kansas City, MO+) .478
Sidley & Austin (Chicago, IL+) 491
Stites & Harbison (Louisville, KY+) 518
Sutherland, Asbill & Brennan (Atlanta, GA+) 658
Troutman Sanders (Atlanta, GA+) 662
Vinson & Elkins (Houston, TX+) 664
Wilmer, Cutler & Pickering (main office+) 674
Winston & Strawn+ (Chicago, IL+) 557

WASHINGTON STATE

Bellevue:
Law Firms

Perkins Coie (Seattle, WA+) 451

Bellingham:
Law Firms

Brett & Daugert+ 692

Olympia:
Law Firms

Perkins Coie (Seattle, WA+) 451

Redmond:
Corporations
Microsoft Corporation* 740

Seattle:
Corporations
Bar/Bri Bar Review (Chicago, IL*) 723
Law Firms
Dorsey & Whitney (Minneapolis, MN+) 612
Heller, Ehrman (San Francisco, CA+) 623
Hillis Clark+ 309
Perkins Coie (main office+) 451

Spokane:
Law Firms
Perkins Coie (Seattle, WA+) 451

WEST VIRGINIA

Charleston:
Law Firms
Jackson & Kelly (main office+) 315
Steptoe & Johnson (Clarksburg, WV+) 510

Clarksburg:
Law Firms
Steptoe & Johnson (main office+) 510

Fairmont:
Law Firms
Jackson & Kelly (Charleston, WV+) 315

Martinsburg:
Law Firms
Jackson & Kelly (Charleston, WV+) 315
Steptoe & Johnson (Clarksburg, WV+) 510

Morgantown:
Law Firms
Jackson & Kelly (Charleston, WV+) 315
Steptoe & Johnson (Clarksburg, WV+) 510

New Martinsville:

Law Firms

    Jackson & Kelly (Charleston, WV+) 315

Parkersburg:

Law Firms

    Jackson & Kelly (Charleston, WV+) 315
    Steptoe & Johnson (Clarksburg, WV+) 510

Wheeling:

Law Firms

    Burns, White & Hickton (Pittsburgh, PA+) 208
    Jackson & Kelly (Charleston, WV+) 315
    Steptoe & Johnson (Clarksburg, WV+) 510

Listing of All Employers by Type (e.g., Law Firms, Government, etc.)

All Employers Alphabetically xvii
All Employers By State 1111

Clerkships

Courts and Federal Agencies 927
    Court of Appeals for the Armed Forces 928
    Federal Agencies 928
    U.S. Bankruptcy Court 927
    U.S. Court of Appeals for the Federal Circuit 927
    U.S. Court of Federal Claims 927
    U.S. Court of International Trade 927
    U.S. Court of Veterans Appeals 928
    U.S. Tax Court 928
    U.S. Territorial Courts 928
Courts of Appeals 925
Federal District Courts 924
State Courts 923
Supreme Court of Hawaii 100
United States Supreme Court 109

College Administration

See Law School and College Administration Jobs 953

Consulting

Deloitte & Touche Consulting 706
McKinsey & Company 702

Corporations and In-House Jobs

American Airlines (AMR Corporation) 722
Anheuser-Busch Companies, Inc. 98
Bar/Bri Bar Review 723

The Coca-Cola Company 726
Columbia/HCA Healthcare Corporation 727
Federal Express (a subsidiary of FDX Corporation) 728
Ford Motor Company 729
General Motors Corporation 729
Honeywell, Inc. 731
Host Marriott Corporation 733
Kraft Foods (a subsidiary of Phillip Morris) 734
Lexis-Nexis 735
Lincoln National Corporation 737
Mattel, Inc. 95
Microsoft Corporation 740
Motorola 741
Norfolk Southern Corporation 744
Partners HealthCare System, Inc. 745
Procter & Gamble 747
Qualcomm 753
Shell Oil Company 754
Tyco International Limited 755
United Airlines 756
United Parcel Services 756
United Services Automobile Association 757
The Williams Companies 758

Entertainment

The Academy of Motion Picture Arts & Sciences 83
HBO 85
MCA/Universal 83
MGM-United Artists 85
MTV 85
National Public Radio 84
Paramount Pictures 85
Walt Disney Company 70

Government

Central Intelligence Agency (CIA) 822
Comptroller of the Currency 828
Department of the Interior 872
Department of State-Office of the Legal Advisor 848
Environmental Protection Agency (EPA) 837
Equal Employment Opportunity Commission (EEOC) 834

Federal Bureau of Investigation (FBI) 839

Federal Communications Commission (FCC) 843

Federal Mediation & Conciliation Service 844

Federal Trade Commission (FTC) 846

National Aeronautics & Space Administration (NASA) 106

National Labor Relations Board (NLRB) 860

National Park Service (part of the Department of the Interior) 849

Office of the San Diego City Attorney 890

Overseas Private Investment Corporation (OPIC) 861

Railroad Retirement Board (RRB) 864

Securities & Exchange Commission (SEC) 865

The Solicitor's Office (part of the Department of the Interior) 850

State Attorney General's Offices, listed by state 874

United States Air Force Judge Advocate General's Corps 859

United States Army Judge Advocate General's Corps 853

United States Department of Justice 123

United States Navy Judge Advocate General's Corps 859

In-House Counsel

See Corporate and In-House Jobs 715

International

CEELI (American Bar Association Central and
Eastern European Law Initiative) 90

United States Foreign Service 87

Law Firms, list of

Akin, Gump, Strauss, Hauer & Feld, L.L.P.—San Antonio 147

Akin, Gump, Strauss, Hauer & Feld, L.L.P.—Washington 153

Alston & Bird—Atlanta, GA 581

Arent Fox Kinter Plotkin & Kahn 583

Armstrong Allen Prewitt Gentry Johnston & Holmes, P.L.L.C. 585

Arnold & Porter 162

Baker & Botts, L.L.P. 170

Baker & Daniels 178

Baker Donelson Bearman & Caldwell, P.C. 586

Baker & Hostetler LLP 185

Balch & Bingham, LLP 588

Bamberger, Foreman, Oswald & Hahn 590

Barnes & Thornburg 191

Bass, Berry & Sims, PLC 591

Beckman, Lawson, Sandler, Snyder & Federoff 593
Best, Best & Krieger L.L.P. 594
Bickerstaff, Heath, Smiley, Pollan, Kever & McDaniel 596
Bingham, Summers, Welsh & Spilman 598
Boult, Cummings, Conners & Berry 599
Brett & Daugert, L.L.P. 692
Brown, Todd & Heyburn PLLC 199
Burns, Doane, Swecker & Mathis, LLP 601
Burns, White & Hickton 208
Carlton, Fields, Ward, Emmanuel, Smith & Cutler, P.A. 214
Carrington, Coleman, Sloman & Blumenthal, L.L.P. 224
Clemens & Spencer 602
Cohen, Weiss and Simon 603
Cooley Godward L.L.P. 232
Cors & Bassett 604
Cowles & Thompson 236
Cox & Smith, Inc. 605
Crowley, Haughey, Hanson, Toole & Dietrich, PLLP 607
Davis, Polk & Wardwell 243
Davis Wright Tremaine L.L.P. 246
Dinsmore & Shohl, L.L.P. 609
Dominick, Fletcher, Yielding, Wood & Lloyd 611
Dorsey & Whitney, L.L.P. 612
Fish & Richardson P.C. 253
Fliesler Dubb Meyer & Lovejoy 614
Folger Levin & Kahn LLP 259
Foster, Swift, Collins & Smith, P.C. 616
Fowler, White, Gillen, Boggs, Villareal and Banker, P.A. xxx
Frost & Jacobs LLP 271
Gardner, Carton & Douglas 276
Gentry, Locke, Rakes & Moore 618
Gibson, Dunn & Crutcher, L.L.P. 619
Goulston & Storrs, P.C. 284
Gray Cary Ware & Freidenrich 621
Gray, Plant, Mooty, Mooty & Bennett, P.A. 292
Heller, Ehrman, White & McAuliffe 623
Hill, Ward & Henderson, P.A. 302
Hillis Clark Martin & Peterson, P.S. 309
Hodgson, Russ, Andrews, Woods & Goodyear, L.L.P. 625
Hoeppner, Wagner & Evans 627
Hogan & Hartson 628

Jackson & Kelly 315
Jenkens & Gilchrist, P.C. 322
Jenner & Block 630
Jolley, Urga, Wirth & Woodbury 327
Jones, Day, Reavis & Pogue 332
Jones Vargas 341
Kirkland & Ellis 632
Kirkpatrick & Lockhart L.L.P. 346
Klinedinst, Fliehman & McKillop 353
Latham & Watkins—Los Angeles 360
Latham & Watkins—San Diego 367
Latham & Watkins—San Francisco 374
Latham & Watkins—Washington, D.C. 382
LeClair Ryan, P.C. 634
Long Aldridge & Norman L.L.P. 388
Loomis, Ewert, Parsley, Davis & Gotting, P.C. 635
Lord, Bissell & Brook 395
Manier, Herod, Hollanbaugh & Smith, P.C. 636
Markowitz, Herbold, Glade & Mehlhaf, PC 401
Masuda, Funai, Eifert & Mitchell 637
McAndrews, Held & Malloy, Ltd. 406
McDonald, Hopkins, Burke & Haber Co., L.P.A. 412
Mette, Evans & Woodside P.C. 638
Millisor & Nobil Co., LPA 418
Moore Ingram Johnson & Steele, L.L.P. 421
Morrison & Foerster L.L.P.—Irvine 430
Morrison & Foerster L.L.P.—Los Angeles 433
Morrison & Foerster L.L.P.—New York 436
Morrison & Foerster L.L.P.—Palo Alto 442
Morrison & Foerster L.L.P.—San Francisco 427
Morrison & Foerster L.L.P.—Washington, D.C. 439
Nelson Mullins Riley & Scarborough, L.L.P. 640
Nilles, Hansen & Davies, Ltd. 642
O'Connor, Cavanagh, Anderson, Killingworth & Beshears 643
O'Melveny & Myers 645
Parker, Hudson, Rainer & Dobbs LLP 445
Perkins Coie L.L.P.—Los Angeles 467
Perkins Coie L.L.P.—Portland 457
Perkins Coie L.L.P.—Seattle 451
Perkins Coie L.L.P.—Washington, D.C. 462
Pretzel & Stouffer 647

Proskauer Rose LLP 470
Rendigs, Fry, Kiely & Dennis 648
Robinson, Bradshaw & Hinson, P.A. 649
Sachnoff & Weaver 651
Shook, Hardy & Bacon L.L.P. 478
Shumaker, Loop & Kendrick, LLP 486
Sidley & Austin 491
Snell & Wilmer L.L.P. 501
Steel Hector & Davis, L.L.P. 652
Steptoe & Johnson 510
Stewart & Irwin, P.C. 654
Stites & Harbison 518
Stradley, Ronon, Stevens & Young, L.L.P. 655
Strasburger & Price, L.L.P. 527
Sugarman, Rogers, Barshak & Cohen, P.C. 657
Sutherland, Asbill & Brennan, L.L.P. 658
Tonkon, Torp L.L.P. 660
Troutman Sanders 662
Vinson & Elkins L.L.P. 664
Vogel, Kelly, Knutson, Weir, Bye & Hunke, Ltd. 666
Waller Lansden Dortch & Davis, P.L.L.C. 533
Ward & Smith, P.A. 541
Warner Norcross & Judd, L.L.P. 667
Watkins & Eager P.L.L.C. 548
Webb, Carlock, Copeland, Semler & Stair, L.L.P. 669
Weil, Gotshal & Manges, L.L.P. 670
Wharton, Aldhizer & Weaver, P.L.C. 553
Wiggin & Dana 672
Wilmer, Cutler & Pickering 674
Winston & Strawn 557
Workman, Nydegger & Selley, P.C. 676
Wyatt, Tarrant & Combs—Louisville 560
Wyatt, Tarrant & Combs—Memphis 574
Wyatt, Tarrant & Combs—Nashville (downtown) 569

Law School and College

Administration 953
    Alumni relations 968
    Athletic department compliance offices 964
    College and university attorneys 954
    Dean of students 958

Director of admissions 966
Director of career services 956
Director of international programs 959
Director of judicial affairs 960
Director of public interest programs in (or near)
    a law school 961
Director of student legal services 969
Law librarianships 971
Public interest counselor 962
Visiting professorship at Pepperdine Law School 103

Public Interest

American Civil Liberties Union (ACLU) 783
American Judicature Society 791
Arms Control Association 792
Center for International Environmental Law (CIEL) 793
Consumers Union 794
DNA-Legal Services 795
Earthjustice Legal Defense Fund (formerly the Sierra Club) 796
Employment Law Center 798
Federal Defender Program (Chicago) 777
Florida Public Service Commission 799
G.L.A.D. (Gay & Lesbian Advocates & Defenders) 801
Human Rights Watch 802
International Human Rights Law Group 803
Legal Assistance Foundation of Chicago (LAFC) 806
Minnesota Advocates for Human Rights 809
NAACP Legal Defense and Education Fund 810
The Nature Conservancy 811
Public Counsel Law Center 812
United Mine Workers of America (UMWA) 785
Women's Advocacy Project 813
Writers Guild of America, west 788

Sports

Advantage International (Agents) 63
ESPN (In-House Counsel and Broadcast Headquarters) 63
Jobs aligned with particular teams 42
    Team general manager 42
    Business manager for a professional sports team 43
    Marketing director for a professional sports team 43

Sports agenting/marketing and director of a sports
   complex/stadium operations/sports event coordinating 43
Traveling secretary for a professional sports team 43
Major League Baseball (MLB) 63
National Basketball Association (NBA) 52
National Collegiate Athletic Association (NCAA) 63
National Football League (NFL) 64
National Hockey League (NHL) 54
United States Olympic Committee (USOC) 49

Other Titles Available from Harcourt

Author: Kimm Alayne Walton, J.D.
ISBN: 0-15-900453-5
Price: $19.95
(598 Pages, 6" x 9")

What Law School Doesn't Teach You... But You Really Need To Know

Expert Advice for Making Your Legal Career a HUGE Success

"Be yourself." "Avoid gossip." "There's no such thing as a stupid question." If you believe statements like these, you could jeopardize your job. Why? Because the new lawyers who stand out follow a much more subtle set of rules. Rules that you can use to transfer your job, whether you work for a law firm, government entity, public interest organization, or any other legal employer!

In this book, you'll learn the trade secrets that make top lawyers say, "I wish I'd known that when I started out!" You'll discover hundreds of tips and strategies, including:

- How to turn down work you're swamped without saying the dreaded "no"
- How to negotiate for more money
- How to use gossip to your advantage
- How to make an outstanding first impression
- How to take criticism and make yourself shine

Author Kimm Alayne Walton talked to lawyers and law school administrators all over the country, asking them for their best advice for new lawyers. Whether you're going for a summer clerkship, your first permanent job, or you've already started your career, you'll find a wealth of invaluable insider tips you can use right now. With *What Law School Doesn't Teach You...But You Really Need To Know,* you'll feel as though you have hundreds of top-notch mentors at your fingertips!

Author: Kimm Alayne Walton, J.D.
ISBN: 0-15-900317-2
Price: $24.95
(572 Pages, 6" x 9")

Guerrilla Tactics For Getting The Legal Job Of Your Dreams
Regardless of Your Grades, Your School, or Your Work Experience!

Whether you're looking for a summer clerkship or your first permanent job after law school, this national best-seller is the key to getting the legal job of your dreams.

Guerrilla Tactics for Getting the Legal Job of Your Dreams leads you step-by-step through everything you need to do to nail down that perfect job! You'll learn hundreds of simple-to-use strategies that will get you exactly where you want to go.

Guerrilla Tactics features the best strategies from some of the country's most innovative career advisors. The strategies in *Guerrilla Tactics* are so powerful that it even comes with a guarantee: Follow the advice in the book, and within one year of graduation you'll have the job of your dreams...or your money back!

Pick up a copy of *Guerrilla Tactics* today...and you'll be on your way to the job of your dreams!

Author: Kimm Alayne Walton, J.D.
ISBN: 0-15-900393-8
Price: $14.95
(191 Pages, 4-1/4" x 9")

The Best Of The Job Goddess
Phenomenal Job Search Advice From The Country's Most Popular Legal Job Search Columnist

"Should I wear my wedding ring to Interviews? How can I get a job in another city? I was a Hooters girl before law school — should I put it on my resume?" Questions like these are answered weekly by the popular Job Goddess columnist, Kimm Alayne Walton. The column is syndicated in more than 100 publications nationwide.

The Best Of The Job Goddess is a collection of the Job Goddesses favorite columns — wise and witty columns that solve every kind of legal job search question! If you're contemplating law school, you're a law student now, or you're a lawyer considering a career change — you'll enjoy turning to the Job Goddess for divine guidance! From what to say — to what to wear — to where to look — the Job Goddess has all the answers to your legal job-search questions.

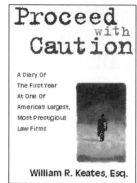

A Diary Of
The First Year
At One Of
America's Largest,
Most Prestigious
Law Firms

William R. Keates, Esq.

Author: William R. Keates
ISBN: 0-15-900181-1
Price: $17.95
(172 Pages, 6" x 9" hardcover)

Proceed With Caution
A Diary Of The First Year At One Of
America's Largest, Most Prestigious
Law Firms

Prestige. Famous clients. High-profile cases. Not to mention a starting salary approaching six figures.

It's not hard to figure out why so many law students dream of getting jobs at huge law firms. But when you strip away the glamour, what is it like to live that "dream"?

In *Proceed With Caution*, the author takes you behind the scenes, to show you what it's really like to be a junior associate at a huge law firm. After graduating from an Ivy League law school, he took a job as an associate with one of New York's blue-chip law firms.

He also did something not many people do. He kept a diary, where he spilled out his day-to-day life at the firm in graphic detail.

Proceed With Caution excerpts the diary, from his first day at the firm to the day he quit.

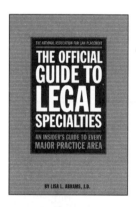

Author: The National Association
for Law Placement (NALP)
ISBN: 0-15-900391-1
Price: $19.95
(496 Pages, 6" x 9")

Includes the following specialties:

The Official Guide To Legal Specialties

With *The Official Guide To Legal Specialties* you'll get a behind the scenes glimpse at dozens of legal specialties. Not just lists of what to expect, real life stories from top practitioners in each field. You'll learn exactly what it's like to be in some of America's most desirable professions. You'll get expert advice on what it takes to get a job in each field. How much you'll earn and what the day-to-day life is really like, the challenges you'll face, and the benefits you'll enjoy. With *The Official Guide To Legal Specialties* you'll have a wealth of information at your fingertips!

Admiralty	Environmental/Energy	Legislation
Antitrust	Government Practice	Product Liability
Appellate	Health Care	Public Finance
Bankruptcy	Immigration	Public Service
Communications	Insurance	Real Estate/Zoning
Corporate	Intellectual Property	Securities
Criminal	International	Sports
Domestic/Family	JAG	Tax
Entertainment	Labor/Employment	Trusts & Estates

Author: The National Association
for Law Placement (NALP)
ISBN: 0-15-900182-X
Price: $17.95
(192 Pages, 6" x 9")

Beyond L.A. Law:
*Stories Of People Who've Done
Fascinating Things With A Law Degree*

Anyone who watches television knows that being a lawyer means working your way up through a law firm — right?

Wrong!

Beyond L.A. Law gives you a fascinating glimpse into the lives of people who've broken the "lawyer" mold. They come from a variety of backgrounds — some had prior careers, others went straight through college and law school, and yet others have overcome poverty and physical handicaps. They got their degrees from all different kinds of law schools, all over the country. But they have one thing in common: they've all pursued their own, unique vision.

As you read their stories, you'll see how they beat the odds to succeed. You'll learn career tips and strategies that work, from people who've put them to the test!

Author: The National Association
for Law Placement (NALP)
ISBN: 0-15-900454-3
Price: $39.95
(1,573 Pages, 8-1/2" x 11")

The National Directory Of Legal Employers
*38,000 Great Job Openings For Law Students
And Law School Graduates*

The National Directory Of Legal Employers includes a universe of vital information about one thousand of the nation's top legal employers — in one convenient volume!

The National Directory Of Legal Employers includes the name of the hiring partner. The starting salary. How many people the firm intends to hire over the next year, and the criteria they'll use to choose successful candidates. The *Directory* also includes the specialties each firm practices, how the firms view their working environments, their achievements, their major clients, and their plans for the future.